THE ALL COLOUR GUIDE TO

FIRST
AID

&

FAMILY HEALTH

THE ALL COLOUR GUIDE TO

FIRST AID

& ——

FAMILY HEALTH

CONSULTANT EDITOR
DR TREVOR WESTON MD, MRCGP

Marshall Cavendish

Note: While every reasonable precaution has been taken to ensure
that the information presented here accords with current medical
knowledge, personal circumstances vary so enormously that it is
not possible to be sure that all advice given is right for every
individual. So if you have any health problem, you must discuss it
with your doctor.

Contents

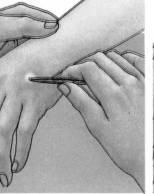
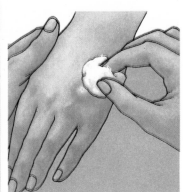
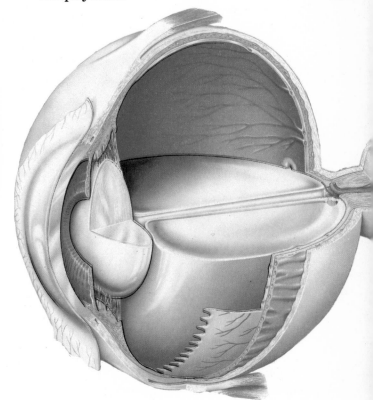

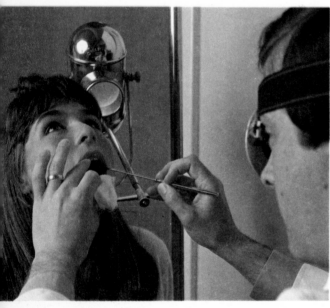

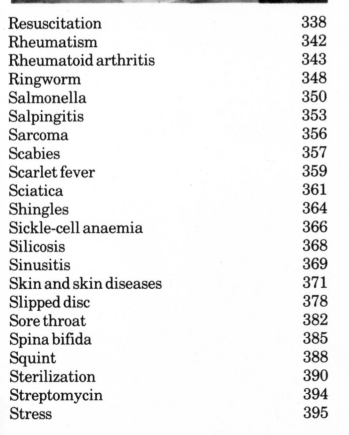

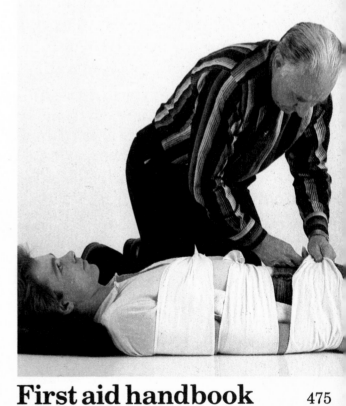

Introduction

For most of us, the possibility of living to a ripe old age in the best of health is not a matter of chance or luck. It is something over which we have a great deal of control. Unfortunately, many people still tend to take good health for granted, believing that the mind and body will continue to function as well in the future as they have in the past. Nothing could be further from the truth. All of us can and should be responsible for our own well-being, by taking steps to ensure that our body is working at optimum efficiency, and that we lead a life as free from stress as possible. And, finally, by making sure that we have at hand a source of reliable information and advice about health and disease — which is precisely the need that this book has been designed to fill.

Preventive Medicine

It is now accepted that emotional and social factors, as well as the physical condition of the body, influence the vital balance between health and disease. In addition recent advances in medical science mean that many conditions that were once incurable can now be successfully treated. Public health measures, such as safe sewage systems and pure water supplies, have virtually eliminated many of the serious illnesses of the past. What we need to be particularly concerned with now, are those many common killing illnesses that can be avoided, or prevented from reaching a critical stage, by common sense and personal care. For the most part they result from bad habits, unhealthy life-styles and incorrect attitudes and include such conditions as injuries, hypertension, heart disease, strokes and many respiratory diseases including cancer.

Preventing ill-health involves health education. We need to know where the dangers lie before we can do anything about them. So this book has been planned with that in mind as well — to be dipped into and learned from on a regular basis as well as when you need a particular piece of information.

Looking at your health

Even if you and your family seem to be in good health at the moment, you should look at your present situation to see if there is anything that could cause problems in the future. These are some of the questions you should ask yourself. Are you or anyone in your family overweight? Do you get enough exercise? Do you smoke, or drink too much alcohol or depend on drugs such as sleeping tablets or tranquillizers? Are there any potentially dangerous areas in your home — medicines that children could get at, loose carpets, electric plugs or wires in need of repair, and so on? Have you and your children had up-to-date immunization against such diseases as whooping cough, German measles and tetanus? Is any member of the family showing signs of stress, or have they been putting off seeing the doctor about a symptom — either emotional or physical — that needs attention?

If you are dissatisfied with any of your answers, do something about it now. You may decide that what is needed is some adjustment to your diet, or a little more exercise, or that a visit to your doctor is indicated. Remember that for you to get the most from your doctor there needs to be a partnership between you based on mutual trust and respect. And that he can't help you at all if you don't let him know when you are unwell or keep worries about your health to yourself!

Even in the best run households, however, things sometimes go wrong and accidents happen. In these situations prompt, effective First Aid is vitally important. It is for this reason that we have made it a major part of this book and provide detailed advice about dealing with the emergencies that you may meet.

For more than ever before in our history, what becomes of each one of us in terms of good health or ill is in our own hands rather than in those of any doctor. More illnesses can be cured than ever before, but only if we understand the importance of our symptoms and get medical advice early. More vital still, most of the common killing diseases can be avoided or prevented, but only if we are prepared to learn how. This book contains all that you need to know to achieve both these things.

Trevor Weston, MD, MRCGP

Abrasions and cuts

Q Is it better to cover wounds or let them heal in the open air?

A As a general rule, all wet, weepy wounds need covering. Most fresh wounds are best protected if you are working in dirty conditions, but dry wounds should be left uncovered in clean conditions.

Q Do old people heal as quickly as the young?

A Generally, older bodies heal just as quickly as young ones, but there are a few exceptions. Sometimes arterial disease diminishes the blood flow and makes healing a slow process. Infection is more likely and ulcers may develop, especially on the shins and ankles, where circulation is often bad. Cuts on an elderly person's leg need prompt, daily attention if ulcers are to be avoided.

Q If a limb is bleeding severely, should I try to make a tourniquet?

A Tourniquets—strips of cloth or other material wrapped tightly around a limb—stop bleeding by cutting off the blood supply. They were once widely used but are now thought to be dangerous because a low blood and oxygen level in any limb can cause permanent damage and make infection more likely. Tourniquets should only be used by a qualified person.

Q Do I need a tetanus injection every time I get cut?

A Like most people you will probably have been immunized against tetanus as a child. Immunization involves having a series of three injections within a year. To maintain protection you should have a booster every ten years. If you have not had one in the last ten years (five years if the wound is very serious) you will need to have a small booster injection if you are cut. An injection is particularly important if you were cut while gardening or in the countryside, as the bacteria which cause tetanus live in soil and animal manure. If you are uncertain whether you have been immunized seek medical advice. Tetanus germs cause lockjaw, a very serious condition that is often fatal.

The skin protects vulnerable internal organs from injury, but as the body's front line of defense it often gets damaged itself. Fast, effective first aid can help speed the healing process and prevent infection.

Scratches, abrasions, cuts, lacerations and punctures are all abnormal breaks through the skin and are generally referred to as wounds. The body itself has very efficient mechanisms for staunching bleeding, healing wounds and fighting infection, but it often needs help. Whenever the skin is broken blood vessels may be torn and germs can enter the body, so all wounds need to be cleaned and many need to be dressed.

How the body copes

Blood contains special proteins that form a protective mesh of strands and cells when tissue is damaged. Called a blood clot, it seals off the broken blood vessels and stops bleeding. At the same time the muscles in the walls of the damaged blood vessels contract to slow down the flow of blood. If bleeding is severe the blood pressure is lowered throughout the body.

Also, as soon as skin is broken, special white blood cells called phagocytes gather at the site of injury. They remove any microscopic particles like bacteria and so are the body's first line of defense against infection. As expected, the larger the damaged area the more likely it will be contaminated with bacteria and the greater the chance of infection.

When bleeding has stopped and the wound is clear of infection, a fibrous scab begins to form. The scab shrinks over the next few days and forms an extremely strong bond between the cut surfaces.

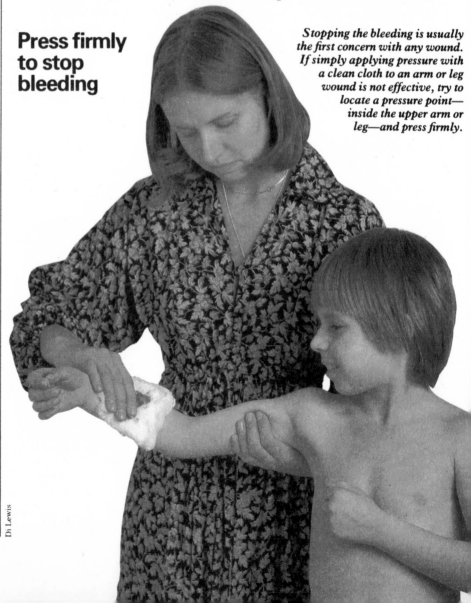

Press firmly to stop bleeding

Stopping the bleeding is usually the first concern with any wound. If simply applying pressure with a clean cloth to an arm or leg wound is not effective, try to locate a pressure point— inside the upper arm or leg—and press firmly.

Di Lewis

First aid for minor injuries

Stop the bleeding

Sometimes it is better to allow a wound to bleed for a while because the flow of blood can help to wash dirt and bacteria away. This is particularly important with a puncture wound, as these are very difficult to clean properly. However if bleeding is profuse, it should be stopped.

Unless you suspect a broken limb, in which case the limb should not be moved, raise the limb so that the blood pressure is reduced slightly.

Then, using a clean bandage, apply firm pressure to the wound. The pressure needs to be constant for at least five minutes to be effective. If blood seeps through the bandage, don't change it, just add more on top: dabbing a wound or changing a bandage removes any blood clot.

If blood is flowing with a pumping, squirting movement, an artery has been damaged. In this case medical help should be sought immediately,

but in the meantime continue to apply firm pressure. If you locate the local artery and press on it, this will be effective, but not for longer than 15 minutes at a time.

One exception: although scalp wounds bleed profusely, do not apply direct pressure if you suspect a skull fracture. Instead build up a dressing in the shape of a ring so that the pressure is applied around the wound, but not directly on it.

Clean the wound

Before you prepare to clean the wound, cover it with a clean cloth so that no more germs can enter it. Then wash your hands thoroughly, taking special care to scrub under the nails.

Wounds can be cleaned with a variety of liquids, from mild antiseptics to soap and water or mild detergents and water. Tap water is quite sterile, so it is not essential to boil water.

If you use any antiseptic other than hydrogen peroxide BP, which is safe to use straight from the bottle, be sure to dilute it as instructed on the bottle. Using too strong a solution may damage the tissues and make the wound worse.

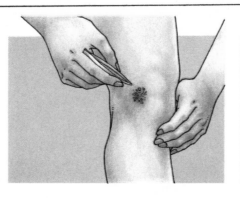

If there is any grit in the wound, a quick scrub with a clean brush under running water is an effective though painful way of removing it. Large pieces of grit and splinters should be removed individually with a pair of tweezers. If a large splinter will not lift out easily, it should be left until further medical care is given.

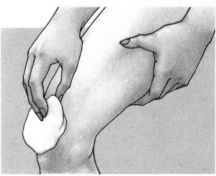

Brush any last bits of dirt from the surface of the wound with small swabs of gauze or absorbent cotton soaked in antiseptic. Then, working away from the wound, clean around it using fresh antiseptic swabs. Finally, clean the wound itself using separate swabs for every stroke. Work from the centre out.

Apply a dressing

A small, clean cut can be covered with 'butterfly' plasters. These are specially prepared, thin strips of adhesive material used to hold the wound closed. The strips should be placed diagonally across each other, pulling the edges of the wound together.

A non-stick dressing is the best protection for a small wound as it can be removed without harming the scab. Never use cotton wool or the woolly side of lint as this sticks to the wound. Large wounds should be covered with sterile gauze dressings that take in the skin surrounding the wound as well.

Nigel Osborne

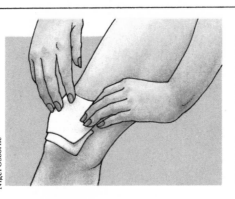

Then pad the dressing with cotton wool or additional layers of gauze: these will absorb any discharge and act as a protecting buffer. When the dressing is changed the layers should be peeled off individually.

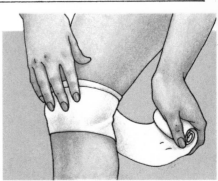

Wrap the whole area firmly with a cotton or crepe bandage. Crêpe is stretchy so it fits around awkward shapes easily. Dressings should be changed regularly. If the dressing has stuck to the wound, soak it off in a mild antiseptic solution. Never pull it off quickly as this will damage the scab.

Types of wound

There are five different types of wound: scratches, abrasions, cuts, lacerations and punctures. A scratch is a superficial tear through the outer layer of the skin called the epidermis. The edges of the skin are not separated and the small amount of bleeding comes from the tiny blood vessels within the skin itself. A scratch stops bleeding quickly but it is still a site for potential infection, especially if the skin is scratched by something dirty.

Abrasions

An abrasion is an area of skin that has been torn away by force. Light scuffing of the skin is called a graze, but sometimes a large, deep area of skin is affected and the abrasion is more like a severe burn. Occasionally an abrasion is so severe that a skin graft is needed some time later. Abrasions can be much more painful than cuts as millions of tiny nerve endings are exposed. They are nearly always full of dirt or grit, so the main problem is infection. After thoroughly cleaning the abrasion to remove dirt and grit, cover it with dry gauze until a scab forms.

Cuts

Any clean division through the layers of the skin is called a cut. Cuts are usually caused by sharp edges such as glass, razors, kitchen knives or even paper. They often bleed quite freely, especially if a deep cut damages large blood vessels underneath the skin, but this can usually be controlled.

Many cuts tend to gape slightly, so to aid the healing process keep the edges together with a butterfly plaster or porous synthetic surgical tape placed across the cut. This is especially advisable for cuts on the elbows or knees, which are constantly being bent, and on the fingers, which always seem to catch on something and so never stay closed long enough to heal.

If the cut gapes so badly that it cannot be held together with tape, or if it is deep enough to expose the layer of fat or muscle beneath the skin, it will need to be stitched. All cuts on the face, however minor, are best stitched to prevent scars.

Lacerations

A laceration is a tear in the skin and is usually caused by a hard blow or a serious injury. The skin edges are usually jagged, there is often considerable bruising around the wound, and infection is a particular hazard unless the wound is thoroughly cleaned.

Wounds of this sort will usually have to be seen by a doctor. They often bleed heavily and may be made worse by the

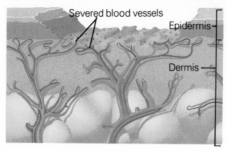

Abrasions are usually not as serious as they appear, though they may be very painful and leave scars afterwards. They must be thoroughly cleaned.

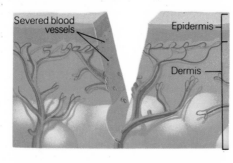

Cuts sometimes bleed profusely. They must be kept closed to heal properly and may need to be stitched, especially when they occur on the face.

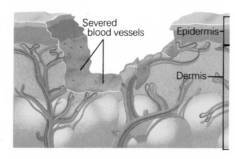

Lacerations are often serious wounds and take the longest time to heal. They should usually be seen by a doctor and kept covered meanwhile.

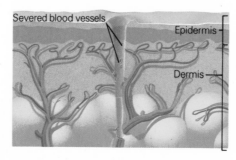

Puncture wounds are always more serious than they look, especially if to the abdomen or chest. Unless trivial, seek medical help as soon as possible.

presence of foreign objects like bullets or large splinters embedded in them. Never attempt to pull these out. They have already done all the damage they are going to do and trying to remove them may start off massive bleeding. You can stop them from working deeper into the wound by building up a thick 'ring' dressing around them, but leave anything more to the doctor. Bandage all lacerations with a large dressing until a doctor can treat the wound.

Puncture wounds

Finally, a puncture or stab wound is a small, deep wound of unknown depth caused, for example, when the prong of a garden fork is run through the foot.

It is most important that you do not try to stop the bleeding—this is the only way the wound can clean itself. Once the bleeding has stopped on its own, wash the wound and apply a clean, dry dressing.

Except for those made by something small and clean like a thumb tack, all puncture wounds require medical attention as there is danger of internal bleeding, damage to tendons and nerves and increased chance of infection and tetanus, as tetanus germs thrive in deep closed wounds, where there is no oxygen. A good rule of thumb is that a puncture or stab wound is always worse than it looks, so be sure to seek help for anything more than the most negligible wounds.

What the doctor will do

Although usually minor wounds will not need any medical attention, especially if first aid is applied quickly, major wounds or very dirty ones will need to be looked at by a doctor.

The doctor will clean the wound thoroughly and explore it to ensure that there are no remaining foreign bodies. If there is any risk that splinters of glass or bits of metal are still in the wound, an X-ray may be taken. The doctor will then check that the nerves and tendons are functioning normally and will decide whether a tetanus injection is necessary and whether the wound needs stitching (suturing).

Stitches are used to pull the edges of a gaping wound together. This closes the wound to further contamination, makes it easier for the edges to join together and decreases the chances of an unsightly scar. However, stitches will not be used if the wound can be held closed without them as they can injure the surrounding tissue slightly and may leave additional scars. To get the best result, stitching if it is needed should be done as soon as possible. A local anaesthetic will usually be given to deaden the area surrounding the wound.

Aside from the specific wounds that require a doctor's attention, there are a few obvious signs that indicate that medical attention is needed urgently. Ideally one person should apply first aid while a second calls for help. If you are alone you will have to assess each situation individually and decide what immediate first aid is necessary before calling for help. All the instances below require medical attention, but this may only become apparent after initial first aid has been applied. Lose no time in seeking help when needed—never feel you should try to cope alone.

Symptoms	Possible causes	Action
Bleeding persists	An artery may have been severed, in which case the blood will spurt out with each heart beat. Or there may be a deep puncture	Apply pressure in the normal way for at least ten minutes. If an artery is severed try to locate a 'pressure point', a place where a main artery can be pressed against a bone. Pressure can be applied at these points to stop arterial blood loss, but it should not be applied for any longer than 15 minutes without a break
Patient shows signs of shock. Usually all the following symptoms will be present: pale face and lips, cold and clammy skin, faint or dizzy feeling and weak and rapid pulse	Caused by a combination of low blood pressure, constriction of blood vessels and blood loss. The body diverts remaining blood to essential organs, such as kidney, heart and brain. If shock is combined with no visible sign of blood loss, there may be internal bleeding	Place patient comfortably on side and cover with blankets or clothing. If possible, raise the feet so that blood is concentrated in the area of vital organs. Loosen any tight clothing. It is important to reassure someone in shock, so stay by the person if possible. Never give the patient any liquids
Patient experiences loss of movement or tingling sensations in the wounded area	A tendon or nerve may be severed (tendons attach muscles to the bone at joints, such as the knee)	Apart from general first aid, there is no immediate treatment for this. Try not to move the patient while awaiting medical help

Healing

Healing begins very soon after injury. The white blood cells that rush to the site of the wound to clear infection also remove any cells that have died as a result of the injury, as well as the small quantities of blood that have collected around the wound.

Once the injury is clean, the healing process can begin under the protective covering of the scab. The remaining live skin cells divide rapidly and begin to produce fibrous scar tissue, which contains blood vessels and nerve fibres. The scar tissue grows up from the base of the wound, gradually filling the hole. When this process has finished, the scab will fall off.

The more quickly the surfaces of a wound are brought together, either by stitching or bandaging, the less fibrous tissue is produced to bind them. Healing is therefore quicker and the wound leaves a fainter scar.

Wounds that have been stitched become waterproof within 24 hours and generally heal within five days, when the stitches can be removed. Over the next few months, all the reddish scar tissue becomes white as it gets denser and loses blood vessels. As the scar tissue becomes denser it contracts, and this causes the puckering that is sometimes seen around large scars. If a scar is unsightly it can be improved by a skin graft. Scar tissue never grows hairs, doesn't have sweat glands and will not turn brown in the sun, but it is strong and protects the body just as well as the original skin.

TAKE CARE

Wounds that require a doctor's attention

- wounds that will not stop bleeding
- any very large, deep, gaping or jagged wounds
- any wounds where dirt or grit are embedded beneath the skin
- puncture wounds caused by anything dirty or rusty
- any cut on the face
- any wound that shows signs of infection.

Even when the greatest care is taken with a wound, there is always a danger of infection developing. Local infection in a wound is quite common and will produce discharge of pus. If the wound is relatively minor, the infection will probably be dealt with by the body's natural defense mechanisms, but if the area around the wound becomes very red and irritated, or the patient develops a fever, a doctor should be consulted as antibiotics may be needed.

Any pus that is formed should be allowed to drain off. If the infected wound has been stitched, it may be necessary to release some of the stitches. Infected abrasions should be bathed and freshly dressed each day.

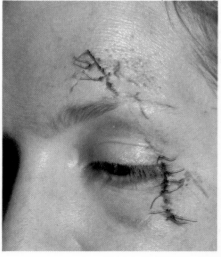

Ken Moreman

Abscess

Q If I have an abscess on a tooth, must I have the tooth out?

A Not necessarily. The abscess can be drained through the tooth, or more rarely, through the gum. Antibiotics may be given to prevent the infection spreading. Further treatment usually cures the abscess, though occasionally the tooth must be removed altogether.

Q Is a gumboil less serious?

A No. A gumboil is just the surface sign of a tooth abscess—often shown by swelling of the face and severe toothache. A gum abscess, however, occurs when infection gets between the tooth and the gum and is fairly harmless since it bursts easily. But although you may be able to soothe the pain of a gum abscess with a mouth wash of warm, salty water, you must still visit the dentist.

Q How does all that pus get into an abscess?

A It doesn't actually 'get into' the abscess but builds up as part of the body's natural reaction to infection. Blood automatically rushes to the site of any injury, and when there is an infection the white blood cells, the body's infection-fighting team, move out of the damaged area into the infected tissue to kill the bacteria. In the struggle, the white blood cells often die themselves, and it is these dead cells, together with the dead bacteria, that form the well-known patch of yellow pus. At the same time, reserve forces of white blood cells build a wall that encloses the abscess's dangerous bacteria to keep the surrounding tissue intact and free from infection.

Q Why is an abscess in the ear so painful?

A Abscesses always involve considerable swelling. In the skin, this does not cause much discomfort, but in an area surrounded by bone, such as the ear, there is not enough space for this to happen without stretching the tissues around it, giving rise to great pain. For the same reason, severe discomfort accompanies any abscess in bone itself.

An abscess is the body's way of fighting localized infection. Minor abscesses often clear up with simple treatment, but larger or internal ones invariably need medical attention.

Abscesses can occur anywhere in, or on, the body. They range from simple styes, pimples and boils, which are abscesses in the skin's hair follicles, to serious tooth abscesses or other internal abscesses like an appendicitis.

Causes

A skin abscess may result from an injury, such as a splinter, and is more likely to occur if damaged skin is dirty, or if the injury is in a moist area, such as the armpit, or if the person is run down.

Internal abscesses are usually secondary to some other problem—a 'grumbling appendix' may be caused by an internal abscess formed because an intestinal blockage has irritated the appendix—although, as with an abscess caused by tuberculosis, the disease-causing bacteria may be breathed in or ingested via contaminated food.

Symptoms

The earliest sign of a skin abscess is a red, hot, painful swelling, which becomes filled with pus. If white blood cells are able to cope with the bacteria, the abscess clears up without any discharge, becoming a hard, painless lump which may disappear after some months.

Other symptoms, particularly of internal abscesses, are a fever, feeling generally unwell and having swelling of the glands under the arms and elsewhere.

The great risk with an abscess is that on bursting it may release pus and dangerous live bacteria into the bloodstream causing a serious type of blood-poisoning called septicaemia, or as in the case of an appendix abscess, into the abdominal cavity producing peritonitis (inflammation of the abdominal lining).

Treatment

Providing that a skin abscess is treated at an early stage and the pus is drained safely away, it will cause little more than discomfort. A small superficial abscess will often discharge pus of its own accord —or if obstinate, it can be 'lanced' with a sterile needle heated to red-hot and then allowed to cool. A touch of iodine or phenol will both sterilize and weaken the overlying skin, and applying a poultice available from the local pharmacy will help to draw out any remaining pus after the abscess has burst.

Large, deep abscesses need medical attention as the pus can only be safely drained by making an incision. Antiseptics and antibiotics will ensure that there is no danger of bacteria multiplying and spreading to healthy tissue.

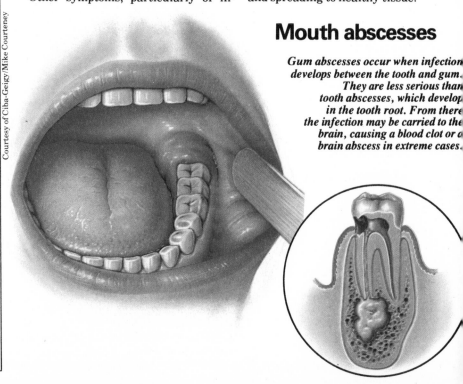

Courtesy of Ciba-Geigy/Mike Courteney

Mouth abscesses

Gum abscesses occur when infection develops between the tooth and gum. They are less serious than tooth abscesses, which develop in the tooth root. From there the infection may be carried to the brain, causing a blood clot or a brain abscess in extreme cases.

Accident prevention

Q What can I do to help make sure that my children won't get injured at home?

A First make a safe house—then get into the right safety habits. Here are some of the most important points to keep in mind. Make sure that you NEVER . . .

● assume that visiting children have the same safety awareness as your own.

● allow children to play with sharp objects or run holding knives or scissors.

● permit games such as chasing on stairs or pushing wheeled toys into the kitchen.

● allow children to play with matches, lighters or cigarettes. Cigarette butts can poison a child.

● leave little ones in the bath alone.

● allow children to move electrical appliances alone, and never take any into the bathroom.

● leave baby alone with a bottle or young children with their meal. They could easily choke.

● allow young children to help with do-it-yourself jobs around the house.

● leave children alone with a hot iron while you go out of the room.

● keep medicines in your handbag. Never take them in front of the children or describe them as sweets.

● keep nursery goods such as gripe water in the same place as household goods like surgical spirit so that the two could get confused.

● leave plastic bags or wrappers where the children can reach them and suffocate themselves.

● leave your child alone in the house even for five minutes.

Q Are there any particular times when my children are more likely to have accidents?

A Illness, tiredness, lack of supervision and general family stress may all make your child more prone to accidents. Weekends, when more is going on in the home, are a particularly hazardous time. Many injuries to children occur when their parents are either out of the house or asleep. Drugs can also contribute, so if, for example, your child is taking antihistamines for an allergy be especially watchful, as these medicines cause drowsiness.

Every year a large number of children have accidents in the home. Sadly, many die of their injuries. But most home accidents could easily be prevented if parents were more aware of the hazards—and made sure their home was safe for children.

Di Lewis

Safety in the home is of the greatest importance for the well-being of children and parents alike. Recognizing the risks in the first place, and then taking adequate measures to ensure that your children are not in any danger is a vital part of responsible parenthood and will relieve you of much anxiety.

It is sensible to start making your home safe *before* you have a family so that when your children are born they start life in the best possible situation.

Preparing a safe home

If you are expecting a baby, start by drawing up a checklist of home safety measures you can carry out immediately. This should include making (or buying) safety gates for stairs, kitchen and outside doors; fixing loose rugs firmly to floors to prevent them causing falls; installing dummy plugs in used electric wall sockets, keeping dangerous household equipment out of children's reach like knives, can openers, cleaning powders; investing in safe heaters and

fireguards; and ensuring that the home is well lit.

Next, learn safety habits yourself so that you automatically follow them by the time you have children.

Lock away all medicines, including contraceptive pills and creams, indigestion tablets and iron and vitamin pills. Start running cold water before hot into the bath to avoid any danger of scalding at bathtime. Test your furniture to discover which tables and chairs might be liable to topple over.

Take great care with fire and be especially careful in the kitchen, which is second only to the living/dining room as the most dangerous area in the house. If you do have a fire and cannot put it out easily, call the fire brigade. Make sure older children can do this and keep your doctor's number by the telephone.

Smooth areas of flooring in kitchens and bathrooms need non-slip surfaces like cork tiles, and liquid spills, especially of soap, cooking oil or other grease should be wiped up at once.

Day-to-day safety care

One of the commonest causes of death among the under-4s is suffocation—normally by choking on food—and the major cause of all hospital admissions for children under 14 is poisoning, either by medicines or by household substances. Among the 5s to 14s many deaths are from burns, while little ones aged one to two are vulnerable to all home accidents.

With a demanding baby, a safe daily routine will help when you are tired and preoccupied. Always put the things you use back in a safe place and do not use too much of anything—even talcum powder can cause choking. Be very watchful at bathtime. Do not be tempted to overfeed a baby, but if a baby does choke, keep calm and slap it between the shoulder blades to clear the air passages. After feeding always take the baby's bib off. Buy a cat net for the crib as cats are fond of seeking warmth from babies' blankets.

At the toddler stage—when children need particularly careful supervision—try to hear anything you cannot actually see, and beware of silence!

Clearly it is essential to supervise all meals. Spend time teaching your children how to climb stairs—they cause more accidents in the home than any other household objects—and show them how to balance and jump correctly from them. Help little ones to understand about hot and cold food and water, and show them how to carry breakable objects safely.

The only common pets that are potentially dangerous are dogs. They should be obedience trained and never left alone with any child.

Finally, to keep yourself alert, try to take some time off and hand the children over to someone you trust while staying on call should you be needed.

Children need careful supervision but it is also important to allow them the freedom to learn to deal independently and safely with their environment.

Safe for children

Equipment bought especially for children is high on the danger list, but properly chosen, used and maintained it can be safe.

Prams should not tie up easily and should have an attachment for a safety harness. The brake should not be within the baby's reach and should work well even if the pram is tipped forward.

Pushchairs should have two sets of locking devices and so should the handle if this folds separately. Neither prams nor folding pushchairs can work properly if they are overloaded with other children or shopping.

Carry cots and stands should be sturdy and not easily tipped, and the handles should ensure a safe ride when carried by two people. If the cot is collapsible, it must not be likely to collapse accidentally. Ensure that the cot and stand are made of harmless rustproof material.

High chairs must be without sharp ends, open tubes where small limbs might get caught, or mechanisms that could pinch. The chair should not move on castors. Buy one that is at a convenient height, is sturdy, and has attachment points for a safety harness.

Night clothes must be flame-resistant, as should other clothes or the fabric you make them from.

Babies' clothes should be free from cords or other ties, which can interfere with circulation or could even hang or choke a baby.

Toddlers' clothes should allow freedom of movement and growth. They should be in at least part-natural fabric to allow the skin to breathe.

Toys are subject to government safety regulations in terms of materials used, instructions provided and the design and stability of larger items like baby walkers and tricycles. If a toy is secondhand, check it very carefully; some old toys were painted in a highly toxic lead paint. In general, wooden and plastic toys are safest. Never give a baby any toy that has removable buttons or bits that might be swallowed. All toys should be easy to clean.

Keep a safe home

Child's room

Keep area around beds clear in case of falls

Fit safety locks and/or bars (removable in case of fire) to all windows so that children cannot open them more than 5 cm (2 in)

Use a toy basket that will not squeeze fingers if the lid slams shut

Make sure bars of bed or cot are not more than 5 cm (2 in) apart.

Garage

Keep DIY materials in locked tool boxes, on safe shelves, or hanging out of reach

When out of use, keep large toys where children cannot trip over them

Padlock old kitchen appliances or remove door so that children cannot lock themselves inside

Child's room

Beds and cots should be solid and smooth with no sharp projections inside and no horizontal bars, which could help a child climb out. Any dropside mechanism should fasten automatically so that the child cannot loosen it

A convertor heater is the safest way to heat a child's room.

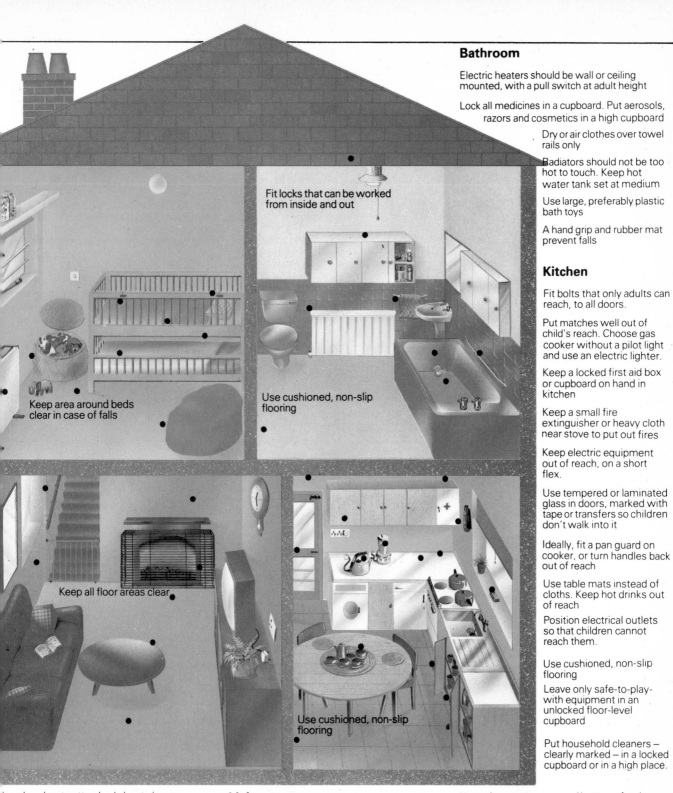

Bathroom

Electric heaters should be wall or ceiling mounted, with a pull switch at adult height

Lock all medicines in a cupboard. Put aerosols, razors and cosmetics in a high cupboard

Dry or air clothes over towel rails only

Radiators should not be too hot to touch. Keep hot water tank set at medium

Use large, preferably plastic bath toys

A hand grip and rubber mat prevent falls

Kitchen

Fit bolts that only adults can reach, to all doors.

Put matches well out of child's reach. Choose gas cooker without a pilot light and use an electric lighter.

Keep a locked first aid box or cupboard on hand in kitchen

Keep a small fire extinguisher or heavy cloth near stove to put out fires

Keep electric equipment out of reach, on a short flex.

Use tempered or laminated glass in doors, marked with tape or transfers so children don't walk into it

Ideally, fit a pan guard on cooker, or turn handles back out of reach

Use table mats instead of cloths. Keep hot drinks out of reach

Position electrical outlets so that children cannot reach them.

Use cushioned, non-slip flooring

Leave only safe-to-play-with equipment in an unlocked floor-level cupboard

Put household cleaners – clearly marked – in a locked cupboard or in a high place.

Fit locks that can be worked from inside and out

Keep area around beds clear in case of falls

Use cushioned, non-slip flooring

Keep all floor areas clear

Use cushioned, non-slip flooring

Use absorbent cotton bed sheets (never plastic). Sheets should be fitted or lightly tucked in

Children's furniture should be soft, low and free from sharp edges, and positioned so that they cannot climb onto shelves or window sills

To prevent suffocation, use a porous type pillow, or none at all for babies under 1 year. Pillow cases should be cotton and well fitted

Living room

Fit a hand rail. Keep stairs well lit and free from ill-fitting carpets or jumble

An open fire must be fitted, by law, with a fixed guard. Position an extra one far enough away so that it will not get hot and burn a child's fingers.

Keep area over fireplace clear to avoid attracting a child's attention

Use safety gates, at top and bottom of stairs, at kitchen doors and other potentially dangerous places

Make sure all furniture is secure and will support a child's weight

Ideally, fit a hard-wearing carpet except in kitchen and bath. Or fix any loose rugs to prevent slips. Do not lay rugs on polished floors. Keep all floor areas clear

Acne

Q Does acne always leave scars on the skin?

A No, but the chances of scarring are increased if you pick and squeeze the spots. However, even if the blackheads are not squeezed, scars may still form. If they are severe they can be partially removed by a minor surgical operation called dermabrasion, in which the top layers of skin are rubbed away, leaving the skin relatively smooth.

Q My daughter has very bad acne. Should I take her to the doctor?

A Yes. The doctor can prescribe antibiotics over a period of several months to reduce secondary infection of the spots by bacteria, or may put her on the birth control Pill, which contains hormones that help correct the hormone imbalance that causes acne. And the reassurance and advice about hygiene the doctor gives may well be easier for your daughter to accept as it comes from someone outside the family circle.

Q Is it true that chocolate causes acne?

A Acne has several causes that are not necessarily connected with diet. It is was once thought that cutting out chocolate would help it clear up more quickly and stop new spots forming. There is no certainty, however, that chocolate is the culprit but if you have acne, it may be worth dropping it from your diet for a while to see whether it makes any difference. There are several other foods which sometimes affect acne, and your doctor may suggest that you try avoiding them too. On the positive side, he may suggest you eat lots of fresh fruit and vegetables and drink plenty of water.

Q I get the occasional spot. Is this acne?

A No, acne is a whole mass of blackheads and pimples. The odd spot can also be caused by a hormone imbalance, as before a period, but it is just as likely that an unhealthy diet, poor hygiene or being run down is to blame.

The pimpled face of adolescence is so common that it could almost be thought of as normal. Four out of five teenagers suffer from acne to some degree, but the majority grow out of it. In the meantime, there are preventive measures and treatments which can ease the problem.

The mixture of blackheads, whiteheads and pink or reddish spots caused by *Acne vulgaris* occurs mostly on the face, the back of the neck, the upper back and chest, but can sometimes be found in the armpits and on the buttocks, too.

Causes

Acne affects young people of both sexes but tends to be more common in boys. It starts in adolescence because this is when there are great increases in the production of hormones from the sex organs and from the adrenal glands. These hormones are chemical messengers carried by the blood and transform a child into a sexually mature adult.

Under their influence, and particularly that of the androgens, or 'masculinizing' hormones, the oil-releasing sebaceous glands in the skin, which normally produce just enough oil or sebum to keep the skin healthily supple, become overactive. They release too much sebum, causing a condition called *seborrhoea*.

The female hormones, particularly oestrogen, have the reverse effect, which explains—at least in part—why girls are generally less prone to acne than boys.

Symptoms

Blackheads, accompanied by the pink or reddish inflammation which they cause, are the hallmark of acne. It was once thought that the bacteria that naturally thrive on sebum, particularly two called *Staphylococcus albus* and *Bacillus acnus*, were the underlying cause of the acne,

How to fight your acne

AVOID
- greasy hair oils or cosmetics.
- leaving makeup on overnight—or leave it off completely
- applying creams to dirty skin so that bacteria are pushed into the pores
- eating any foods that seem to cause spots

TRY TO
- wash affected areas several times a day with soap and hot water
- wash hair often, wear it off the face and reasonably short
- keep combs, brushes and face flannels clean and grease-free
- get as much sunshine as you possibly can

Di Lewis

but they are now known to be the cause of the inflammation, not the acne itself.

In response to the presence of bacteria, which multiply in the blackhead, the blood vessels expand to bring more infection-fighting cells to the site—this is the inflammatory reaction. As a secondary effect of acne, the bacterial infection may lead to the development of pimples, which are spots filled with dead white cells and bacteria, or pus.

This infection usually only becomes severe, involving the formation of larger boils or abscesses, if the deeper skin tissues become bruised and damaged as a result of squeezing the blackheads to release the 'core' of sebum plugged in the pore. Left undisturbed, each spot or blackhead usually clears up within about a week, but if secondary infection sets in it may take a month or more.

Dangers

Secondary infection is one of the chief physical dangers of acne, as it can lead to severe permanent scars and crater-like pits or pock-marks in the complexion. Even more severe is the psychological danger, for acne can turn a happy extrovert into a morose introvert. So anyone suffering from acne needs all the reassurance possible to prevent a temporary physical problem from becoming one that is psychologically permanent.

Try to take a practical approach to treatment and dispel any fears engendered by old wives' tales—for example, that acne is caused by masturbation or sexual intercourse.

Treatment

On a day-to-day basis, the most important treatment is washing. This is most effective if it is as vigorous as possible,

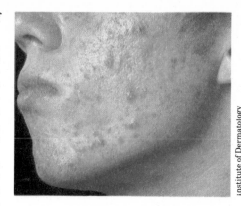
Institute of Dermatology

and a soft nailbrush or loofah—kept scrupulously clean to avoid reinfection—will help to remove grease and encourage the top layer of skin to peel away, taking with it some, if not all, of the plug of sebum. Drying, equally vigorously, with a rough, clean towel will have the same effect. An astringent cleansing lotion applied with clean cotton wool after thorough washing will help to remove any remaining oil.

It is possible to remove the blackheads with an instrument called a comedone extractor. However, this must be used with great care, preferably only on the recommendation of a doctor, and with meticulous attention to hygiene, to prevent the possibility of secondary infection.

A clean face will be of little help to the acne problem if it is then surrounded by lank, greasy hair. Unfortunately the overactivity of the sebaceous glands is not confined to the face but also affects the scalp, and the hair tends to become excessively greasy with the usual associated development of scurf or dandruff. The grease from the hair aggravates the acne, so hair should be washed regularly and kept reasonably short.

Creams and lotions can be useful to treat acne, as much for their camouflage effect as for medical reasons. The best preparations are those that contain substances such as calamine, zinc sulphate, sulphur, resorcinol or benzoyl peroxide, which tend to dry the skin and cause peeling of the top layer. Boys may regard such creams as an insult to their masculinity, but many modern ones are very natural-looking and may prove a very useful psychological prop.

A well balanced diet containing plenty of fresh fruit and vegetables is always good for the skin, and the acne sufferer is advised to drink a lot of water to keep the circulation well flushed of the toxins that are likely to aggravate the condition.

Many acne sufferers find that spots clear up more quckly in summer. This is because the ultra-violet light in sunshine helps dry up grease on the skin and aids peeling of the top layer. For the same reason, ultra-violet ray lamps are often advised for acne sufferers, but these should be used with care to prevent the skin burning.

It is always sensible for a teenager with very bad acne to see a doctor, who may be able to prescribe treatment not available over the chemist's counter.

Outlook

The best that can be said for acne is that it does not last forever. Usually there is only one really bad year, and acne is rare after the mid-twenties. Difficult though it may be to follow, the best advice is to resist with a will of iron the temptation to pick and squeeze blackheads.

Finally, keep a look-out for new treatments, such as preparations containing retinoic acid, which have shown encouraging results in clinical trials.

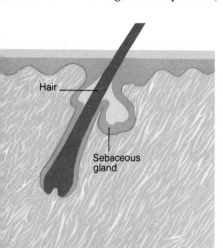

In acne, extra sebum (oil) first clogs up the pores through which sebum is released to the skin surface.

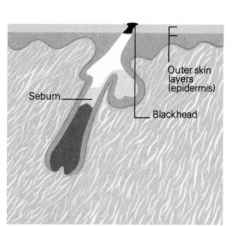

The sebum is trapped and forms a plug with a raised top which, when exposed to air, becomes a blackhead.

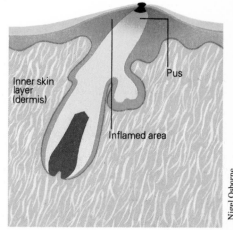
Nigel Osborne

The surrounding skin then becomes inflamed and infected, resulting in pimples filled with pus.

Adenoids

Q My child breathes through his mouth a lot. Does this mean he has adenoid trouble?

A Not necessarily. But if he also has nasal discharge and a night-time cough, adenoids are probably the cause. Otherwise it may be a habit, and is best cured by regular noseblowing. You should check his ability to breathe through each nostril in turn to make sure that something lodged in the nose is not the cause. A few children are born with bone abnormalities which prevent normal nose-breathing.

Q Can adenoids be diagnosed just by looking at a child's face?

A No. So-called 'adenoidal faces' have been found to occur in many other conditions. The description refers to a snub nose, high arched palate and protruberant upper teeth, which give the child a rather dopey look.

Q If my child has had his adenoids operated on can they regrow?

A Yes. They can regrow because it is surgically impossible to remove the whole of the glands. They are merely cut off as low as possible. This leaves a small stump which can enlarge again. However, as the stimulus to grow disappears around the age of six, regrowth does not usually cause problems.

Q How long is it safe to use decongestant nosedrops?

A Any runny nose will be dried up by decongestant drops. The problem is that if the cause has not been dealt with, stopping the drops will cause the discharge to return. In the case of adenoids, the problem for which they are needed will probably have improved after a week or so, and they should be stopped then. A slight discharge may return for a day or two, which will have to be tolerated without restarting the drops. If the drops are used for more than three weeks continually, there is a definite risk that the nose will counterbalance their effect by running all the time. And prolonged use can cause serious damage.

The adenoids have been called 'the watchdogs of the throat'. Like the tonsils, they guard against respiratory infection in the young child, but like the tonsils they sometimes become infected and swollen themselves.

Adenoids are lymph glands situated at the back of the nose just where the air passages join those of the back of the mouth or pharynx. The lymph system is the body's defense against infection and the lymph glands, such as the adenoids, are full of infection-fighting cells, the white blood cells. The adenoids are so placed that any infection breathed in through the nose is filtered by them and—hopefully—killed. Sometimes, however, things can go wrong.

Causes

Adenoids are present from birth, but on the whole they disappear before puberty. They are most obvious from the age of one to four. This is because between these ages the child is continually exposed to new types of infection.

Not a great deal is known about how the adenoids become infected, but any respiratory germ can affect them. Once they become damaged, chronic infection may set in. If the adenoids are recurrently inflamed, they tend to swell and this can give rise to ill-effects.

Symptoms

If the glands become swollen due to infection, they interfere with the flow of air through the nose so that the child has to breathe through the mouth. This may cause heavy snoring at night. The closed mouth also causes a nasal tone of speech. The child finds that his 'm' comes out as 'b' and 'n' sounds like 'd'. This is because when he closes his mouth to pronounce 'm' and 'n' through the nose, he cannot do so since his nose is blocked. Breathing

Location of the adenoids

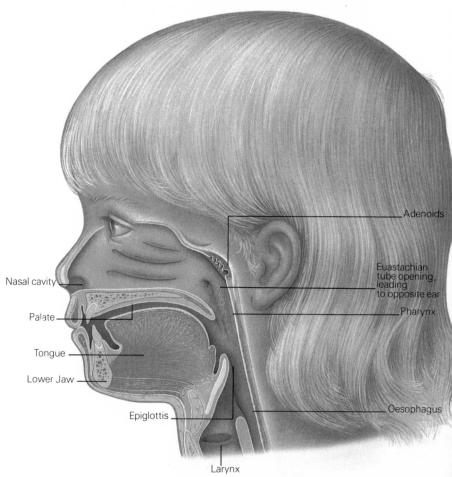

Nasal cavity

Palate

Tongue

Lower Jaw

Epiglottis

Larynx

Adenoids

Euastachian tube opening, leading to opposite ear

Pharynx

Oesophagus

Q Are sneezing and a runny nose due to adenoids?

A Usually not. These symptoms are more suggestive of an allergic nose problem. As research continues, many childhood illnesses are being found to be due to allergies. Often these are caused by dusts and pollens, and sneezing or a runny nose is their most obvious symptom. The medical treatment with decongestants and antihistamines is the same, but adenoidectomy would make no difference.

Q Is there a link between adenoids and mental deficiency?

A Certainly not! Though children with an adenoid problem may look dull and be slow to respond, careful studies have failed to show any such link. However, if left completely untreated, the complication of deafness can certainly prevent a child from realizing his true potential.

Q My child snores heavily. Could he have adenoids?

A Snoring can certainly be due to enlarged adenoids, but by itself this symptom does not need treating. Otherwise, snoring could be caused by an abnormality of the facial structure which the child probably had since birth. Many children breathe noisily at night, which is not true snoring but just a result of a catarrhal complaint such as the common cold.

Q Can antihistamines and antibiotics do anything to help treat adenoids?

A Antihistamines reduce the swelling of the adenoids when this had been caused by an allergic reaction as opposed to infection, and they will also tend to reduce the discharge as well. A further benefit is that antihistamines usually cause drowsiness and combat nausea so a bedtime dose will reduce coughing and the morning vomiting.

Antibiotics are of benefit for enlarged adenoids only when there is also a bacterial infection and must be prescribed by your doctor. The adenoidal symptoms may remain but painful complications such as ear infections can be prevented.

through the mouth also makes it very dry and the child may continually ask for something to drink.

As the adenoids fight infection, white blood cells—both dead and alive—are released in the form of pus. This pus will be seen as a discharge from the nose— quite different from the clear, watery discharge of a runny cold. The child sniffs to try to clear it but it then runs down the back of his throat and makes him cough. The cough is particularly obvious at night and is a typical sign of infected adenoids. In the morning, the swallowed pus may cause vomiting.

Dangers

Swollen adenoids can block the eustachian tubes, which are a pair of tunnels running through the skull bones from inside each eardrum to the pharynx. Their function is to equalize the pressure in the middle ears with that outside— they give rise to the familiar 'pop' you hear on swallowing. If the tube is blocked by the enlarged adenoids the pressure cannot be balanced.

But the main hazard is that natural secretions in the ear cannot drain from inside. This gives rise to a 'glue ear' in which the hearing apparatus is stuck up by secretions and hearing is impaired.

And the secretions themselves may become infected causing a condition called *otitis media*. This is painful and can affect the hearing permanently. If untreated, the eardrums will usually burst to release the infection.

Treatment

Gargling is useless, but three types of medicines are helpful in treating adenoids. Decongestants and antihistamines are generally available, but consult your doctor before using them. Antibiotics are available only on prescription.

As a last resort, when other methods have failed, the adenoids may be removed by an operation called an adenoidectomy. The operation is fairly simple and is carried out under a general anaesthetic in hospital. The tonsils are often removed in the same operation.

Outlook

Providing none of the serious complications occur, time, the decline of infectious diseases and improvements in treatment all mean that adenoids are not the problem they were twenty years ago. Often symptoms go away of their own accord when the child is six or so, and modern medicines usually save small children from an operation.

Some common symptoms of swollen adenoids

- hearing difficulties
- dry gums, which result in tooth decay, and halitosis
- loss of smell, taste and appetite
- listless expression, because breathing is such hard work

Alcoholism

Q I have heard that women are more at risk when they drink than men. Is there any truth in this?

A Drinking among women is on the increase. Not only is it now accepted that they can go into bars on their own, but they can also buy alcohol from the supermarket. Generally speaking, however, women still drink less than men—and so they come to less harm. But if a woman becomes an alcoholic she is more vulnerable to the effects than a man; her liver is likely to be affected earlier than a man's, and treatment is often not as satisfactory. Then there is the problem of the alcoholic expectant mother—she risks causing mental retardation in her baby, and it may also be born with congenital deformities such as dislocation of the hips or a cleft palate.

Q My brother-in-law drinks an awful lot, and in the last year I have noticed a marked change in his personality. He used to be pleasant and outgoing—now he is surly and introverted. Could his drinking be the cause of this?

A Almost certainly. Very heavy drinkers can become moody, violent and jealous, or think they are being persecuted. Even worse, they can have trouble in remembering things, they may hear imaginery voices, see visions and become unable to cope with life. All this can result in *delirium tremens,* the symptoms of which are trembling, sweating and a feeling of panic. If you recognize any of these danger signs in your brother-in-law, he should be encouraged to seek help as soon as possible.

Q Where can I go to get help for alcoholism?

A Go to your doctor for advice on physical aspects of alcohol addiction—he or she will refer you to a clinic if necessary. For family problems—and any others you may have—see a social worker. There are also self-help groups such as Alcoholics Anonymous, who can provide long-term help and support for anyone who wants to kick the habit.

Most people drink moderately, enjoy it, and come to no harm. But there are those who become so dependent on alcohol that they are unable to lead a normal life. This makes it vital to recognize the danger signals and to know when to stop.

When people talk about alcohol, they are usually referring to drinks which contain varying amounts of pure alcohol. Alcoholic drinks have a restricted food value in the form of sugar (as in sweet wines, for example) and carbohydrate (in spirits and beers made from grain), but basically alcohol is a drug—that is, a substance which affects the workings of the mind and body in a variety of different ways.

Taken in moderation, alcohol can encourage the appetite and produce a feeling of well-being. This is because the alcohol stimulates the blood flow to the skin which has the effect of making the drinker feel pleasantly warm. When it reaches the brain anxiety is reduced and self-confidence increases. Shyness seems to disappear, and the world becomes a happier, more friendly place.

Dependency

Heavy drinking, however, is quite another matter. If it is repeated over any period of time, subtle changes can occur in the personality—it is thought that these have a chemical basis—and this can lead to the need to carry on the drinking pattern. When this feeling becomes so persistent that every time a drink is delayed there is an urgent desire to have another, a state known as 'dependency' has been reached.

In the early stages of heavy drinking this dependency tends to be psychological rather than physical. After all, it is anxiety and stress that usually lead people into drinking in the first place, but then they come to rely on the alcohol as a prop to keep them at their ease.

Unfortunately, if the drinking becomes

Victor Yuan

22

much heavier, so does the psychological need. In the transitional period this may not be noticeable, but as physical dependence grows, withdrawal will become more and more difficult and uncomfortable. Eventually, deprivation for any length of time will result in trembling, sweating and acute stress. The first drink will always relieve these feelings—until the next time, and there is always a 'next time'.

Alcohol and personality changes
Alcohol tends to affect different people in different ways. The same amount can turn one person into the 'life and soul' of the party, bring out violent aggression in another, and merely send a third quietly to sleep.

Although it reduces tension, alcohol is not a stimulant, but a depressant. As soon as it enters the bloodstream, it begins to impair judgment, self-control and skill. Research has shown that workers with blood alcohol levels of between 0.03% (30mg, or the equivalent of one pint of beer) and 0.1% (100mg) have considerably more accidents than those with less than 30mg.

With driving, the likelihood of having an accident increases when the blood alcohol level reaches 30mg; at 80mg, it is four times greater; and at 150mg it is 25 times greater. This is because the co-ordination between hand and eye and the ability to judge distances deteriorates progressively.

The problems of alcoholism
Once an excessive drinker is unable to stop drinking without outside help, he or she can be classified as an alcoholic. And it is in this situation that the social, economic and medical problems—often already self-evident in the heavy drinker—can worsen, bringing despair and confusion to the life of the alcoholic—and everyone else with whom he or she has contact.

Alcohol breaks up marriages, sets children against parents, and vice-versa, and costs individuals their jobs and their reputation in the community. Ultimately, of course, it can also kill.

When most people think of alcoholics, they visualize meths drinkers and down-and-out inebriates, but it is not just the deprived and inadequate members of our

society that resort to the bottle as a means of escape—there are children too inebriated to take in their school lessons after lunch, businessmen incapable of working in the afternoons, and housewives barely able to prepare a meal at the end of the day.

Alcoholism can strike irrespective of age, class, creed, colour or sex, and once afflicted, alcoholics will mix only with like-minded friends, neglect their families, break promises, lie and steal, and live only to drink.

Reasons for heavy drinking
Drinking is an accepted and approved cultural activity. As such, it would appear that some people are more exposed to the risk of becoming alcoholics than others simply because of social pressures and conditioning. For example,

Drinking with friends is a relaxing way to unwind. But drinking for its own sake or showing a marked reluctance to stop, no matter how much has been drunk, are danger signals. Any one of the people (below) is potentially a 'problem' drinker, not just the 'obvious' one.

studies of national groups reveal that the Irish have a high rate of alcoholism; in contrast, the Jews' rate is very low. Certain professions seem to encourage alcoholism—travelling salesmen, barpeople and company directors, among others, are particularly at risk. Presumably, extensive socializing and the availability of drink are responsible in these cases.

The housewife is increasingly a victim of this form of addiction. Often isolated, either with small children or with too little to do once a family has grown up and left home, drinking can provide her with a welcome escape from an apparently humdrum existence. And the fact that most supermarkets today stock alcohol makes it only too easy for her to buy it as part of her routine shopping.

In most cases, drinking starts at an early age, with children, not surprisingly, copying the habits of their parents. It is statistically proven that the children of alcoholic parents have a higher than average risk of developing the problem themselves. Teenagers also tend to be strongly influenced by their friends' behavior, and the largest population of problem drinkers in the country is among single urban males under 25.

Today, so much socializing is built around the consumption of alcohol that it is hard to avoid it. You may easily find yourself mixing with others who drink, going to the same place regularly for this purpose, becoming accustomed to the sights, sounds and smells. In addition, advertising suggests that men are not men unless they drink, and drunkenness is a sign of masculinity. Finally, a refusal to drink is usually considered to be abnormal and often seen as a deliberately anti-social action. All these factors can combine to make it difficult to maintain a responsible attitude to alcohol.

Danger signals

The body develops a tolerance to alcohol, and the danger lies in the fact that more drinks are soon needed to reproduce the original feeling of relaxation and wellbeing. The higher the daily intake becomes, the more difficult it is to give it up. If an individual drinks to relieve worries, this can lead to an escalation in drinking: more worries mean more alcohol, and fewer worries become the reason for a round of celebratory drinks.

It can take between 10 and 15 years for someone to develop an addiction to the point where they can be classified as an alcoholic. But symptoms to watch for are an obvious obsession with alcohol and the inability to give it up or even restrict drinking to a reasonable level, moral and physical deterioration, and obvious work, money and family problems. The typical alcoholic will probably need a drink early in the morning and may need continual boosters to keep going during the day.

Safe drinking

In a situation where an individual wants to drink, but not to excess, alcohol should be consumed as slowly as possible and some food should always be eaten beforehand so that the alcohol will be absorbed more slowly into the bloodstream. Consumption can also be kept down by interspersing alcoholic drinks with nonalcoholic ones. It is better not to drink alone, as it is all too easy to consume more than usual just in order to combat

Regular drinkers can easily progress from one drinking stage to the next. Normal social drinking can slip almost unnoticed into dependency and from there to alcoholism, which is harmful physically and psychologically. Everyone should be aware of his own capacity.

Steve Campbell

24

Q What is the best cure for a hangover? I get a terrible headache and everyone has different ideas on what I should do about it.

A The only real cure for a hangover is rest. Paracetamol may be used to treat a bad headache, but aspirin should be left well alone. It will only cause further disturbance to an already irritated stomach. The 'hair of the dog' remedy (having another drink) is not recommended: it will simply lead to spending the rest of the day in bed in a drunken haze. As you say, everyone has their own pet cure—orange juice, vitamin pills, egg in milk, but the rule to follow is that prevention is better than cure. Drink as much water as possible before going to sleep after a drinking session. Dehydration is the main cause of a hangover and water will help reduce this effect of alcohol. But (to pursue the subject to its obvious conclusion) it is still best to try not to drink too much and to avoid having hangovers altogether.

Q Are some people more vulnerable to alcohol than others? I seem to get drunk on one glass of wine.

A It used to be thought that people who found themselves in trouble over drinking were different in their physical and psychological make-up to others, but this is now thought to be untrue. Anyone can become an alcoholic and if you find you do not respond too well to alcohol, try to avoid it. If everyone knew their limits and stuck to them firmly, the problem of alcoholism with all its risks would be greatly reduced.

Q My sister says her husband a drinking problem, but denies that he is an alcoholic. Is this possible?

A No. They are one and the same thing. Someone whose drinking over a period of time has made him dependent on drink and who may do harm to himself and others is an alcoholic—though he and his family may not wish to see the real nature of the condition. But sooner or later—and the sooner the better—they are going to have to face it for what it is.

The effects of alcoholism

Physical	Emotional and social
• Cirrhosis of the liver—there is no cure for this most common disease associated with alcoholism	• Alcoholics suffer increasingly from anxiety, depression, remorse and phobic fears
• Other diseases—alcoholics commonly develop kidney trouble, heart disease and ulcers, which fail to respond to normal treatment	• Obsession with drink overrides all else of importance in life and the need for drink increases as tolerance grows
• Frequent appearance of bruises and cuts resulting from falls and bumping into things	• Disruption or breakdown of family life and persistent marital problems
• Persistent vague physical complaints with no apparent cause, like headaches and stomach upsets	• Loss of friends and interests—alcoholic seek the company of others like themselves
• Coarse inexplicable trembling of the hands; sweating	• Frequent absenteeism from work and repeated job changes, with a loss of efficiency and reliability that can lead to job loss
• Loss of appetite and insomnia	• Lack of concentration and loss of memory
• Pins and needles in hands and feet	• Behaviour and social adjustment lower than previously experienced
• Delirium tremens—sometimes accompanied by frightening hallucinations	• Shabby appearance, poor hygiene
	• Surreptitious drinking, gulping of drinks
	• Arrests for drunken driving

Victor Yuan

feelings of loneliness.

If you do not want to drink, you should not feel shy about saying so. And if you know how much you can drink before going over the top, simply set a limit to the number of drinks you accept and stick to it.

Finally, the combination of drinking and driving—or handling any type of machinery—is extremely dangerous. In fact, 16 per cent of individuals involved in accidents at work, 22 per cent of those in home accidents and 30 per cent of those in highway accidents have elevated blood alcohol levels.

People who know they will be drinking should leave the car at home or take a non-drinker along to drive. Or they should leave the car behind and take a taxi or get a ride. There should not be any halfway measures; the rule is clear and simple: *never drink and drive*.

Allergies

Q I have been suffering from a food allergy for years and sometimes it really gets on top of me. What I want to know is can there be a lasting cure?

A There are several ways of relieving the symptoms of allergies, but they are not cures. Whatever treatment you receive, it is not going to change your basic sensitivity to the particular food in question.

Q My daughter's best friend has just developed an allergy to penicillin, and has terrified my daughter by claiming that she will die at the onset of the first disease she catches, as she won't be able to take penicillin to fight the infection. Surely there must be some alternative drugs to penicillin?

A There is really no need to worry. Although a penicillin allergy does reduce the number of antibiotics which a doctor might consider prescribing, there is still a range of antibiotics available for those people with this type of allergy.

Q My son of four is allergic to cats and touching them brings him out in a nasty rash. Will he grow out of this problem or will it remain with him for life?

A Possibly. Children who suffer from either allergic rashes or eczema often do grow out of those problems though they may suffer from other forms of allergy (asthma for example) when they are older because they have a basic tendency to be allergic.

Q I suffer terribly from hay fever and, as I am now pregnant, I am anxious to know whether my child could possibly inherit this condition from me?

A Unfortunately, this could happen, although it is by no means a certainty. Research shows that children of allergic parents are more likely to suffer from an allergy than other children. But there are still not enough facts available for us to fully understand why this should be so.

Allergy sufferers sometimes have to bear considerable discomfort and inconvenience, but although there are at present no cures for allergies, medical research is making encouraging progress in discovering the many causes and alleviating the symptoms.

An allergy is a sensitivity to a substance which does not normally cause people any discomfort or harm. Hay fever, which is caused by a sensitivity to pollen, is a well-known example. Asthma, eczema, rashes and a variety of other complaints can be caused partly or entirely by an allergy. In fact, allergies can affect almost any part of the body and be caused by a vast range of natural and artificial substances.

They are seldom life-threatening though they can be dangerous, and are often very uncomfortable for the sufferer. They are also a great puzzle to medical science, because although many allergic conditions can be relieved by medical treatment, we still have very little idea of their basic cause.

Allergies are a reaction to allergens, a name given to those substances (such as

Allergies are a common complaint. Distressing though the symptoms are, quite a lot can be done to improve the situation. Running eyes and sneezing are typical of hay fever.

Common allergies

Allergy	Allergen	Symptoms	Treatment	Prevention
Asthma	House dust Animal hair Pollen Some foods and food additives	Difficulty in breathing; wheezing	Prick test for diagnosis Bronchodilator if breathing problem severe. Series of shots	Keep house dust-free Avoid pollen; keep clear of allergic foods
Contact dermatitis	Contact with allergen, i.e. jewelry, chemicals in washing powder, poison ivy	Itchy, blistery inflammation	Steroid creams given on doctor's prescription	Avoid contact with allergen
Eczema	Some foods, especially cow's milk, flour, eggs; possibly some seafoods	Rash on hands, face, neck, arms and legs; looks like scaly skin.	Antihistamine tablets and creams given for skin condition	Take diet precautions to avoid allergen
Food allergy	Could be caused by almost any food—more commonly milk, flour, eggs; also strawberries, shellfish, nuts; some food additives	Upset stomach and general nausea, acute reaction produces swollen tongue and lips, as well as diarrhoea. If food is absorbed into bloodstream, it can produce skin rashes like eczema	Prick test. Elimination test. Provocation test for diagnosis of the allergen	Keep to diet; avoid allergenic foods
Hay fever	Pollen; may react to just one pollen or to several different types	Sore, itchy eyes, runny or stuffy nose, prolonged sneezing	Prick test to confirm allergy, Series of shots and antihistamine tablets to relieve symptoms.	Series of shots before season begins. Listen to pollen count on weather report. Avoid open air. Wear dark glasses
Migraine	Usually caused by cheese, red wine, yeast extract, but not only caused by an allergy	Blinding headache	Elimination diet test if complaint due to food allergy	Avoid allergen foods
Nettle rash	Foods Handling certain plants Hot and cold water	Red, irritating swelling with small white point in centre	Skin condition treated with antihistamine cream, if necessary	Avoid the allergens

pollen) that spark off symptoms of an allergy in someone who is sensitive to it. Common allergens are foods, pollen, spores, insect bites and stings, animal fluff, chemicals and certain metals.

A common allergen at home is dust, which settles on bedcovers and curtains and in carpets, and usually makes its victims sneeze. Some people are allergic to heat and cold and find that their hands swell when plunged into hot and cold water.

Symptoms
Allergy symptoms usually show up in those parts of the body which are exposed to the allergen. So an airborne allergen, like pollen, makes its severest impact in the nose, eyes and air passages. Food allergies reveal themselves through swollen lips, upset stomachs or diarrhoea.

An allergy to a metal or rubber would affect the skin, causing a rash on the part of your body which has come into contact with the allergen.

However, if an allergen, especially food, gets into the bloodstream, it can cause reactions anywhere, so food can cause a variety of reactions, including eczema, urticaria, asthma and even mental disorders.

Three basic forms of allergies affect the skin. The most common, especially among children, is eczema, which appears as a rash or scaly skin on the hands, face, neck, in the creases of the forearms and behind the knees.

Contact dermatitis, often caused by metal jewellery or by cleaning chemicals, is a blistery, itchy inflammation of the skin which has come into contact with the allergen. Urticaria (nettlerash) is a red irritating swelling which often has a small white point in the middle.

Eye allergies usually show up as irritation and redness in the white of the eye. Severe swellings can occur, but generally the symptoms are watering and soreness. When the ears are affected, fluid will build up inside the ear and may tem-

porarily affect hearing.

Hay fever can affect the eyes and ears, though its principal target is the nose, which becomes stuffy, runny or sneezy. Unlike the common cold which should clear up after four or five days, hay fever will last as long as the victim is exposed to his pollen allergen.

The most obvious symptoms of an acute food allergy are an upset stomach followed by nausea, vomiting or diarrhoea. Acutely sensitive people may also get a swollen tongue and lips, and some victims get two kinds of symptoms. Skin rashes may appear hours or even days after eating the food, but most symptoms appear right after eating.

Asthma can also be an allergic reaction to food and pollen, characterized by wheezing and breathing difficulty.

Doctors now believe that other physical and mental symptoms, such as depression, anxiety, headaches, schizophrenia, hyperactivity in children, bedwetting, cystitis and even convulsions, can be

Even dust from a well-aged bottle of wine or fur from a tiny kitten can be allergens.

Steve Campbell

How allergy-producing histamine is released

A defect in the body's immune system makes the body's defence mechanisms react to harmless substances (allergens) as if they were dangerous infectious organisms.

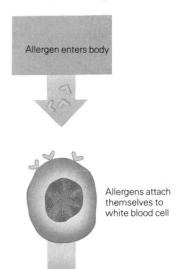

Allergen enters body

Allergens attach themselves to white blood cell

Allergens stimulate white blood cell to change into plasma cell

Plasma cell makes antibodies

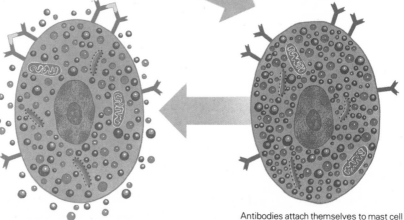

Allergens enter body for second time

Allergens and antibodies combine and histamine is released

Antibodies attach themselves to mast cell

caused by food allergies, though the cause can be difficult to identify.

Migraine can be caused by foods like yoghurt, chocolate, cheese, meat or yeast extracts and some red wines, which contain a substance called tyramine. Tyramine is not itself an allergen or poison, but some migraine sufferers seem to lack a vital enzyme that breaks tyramine down. When they eat these foods, tyramine builds up in their blood and sets off a chemical chain that eventually results in a migraine headache.

Coeliac disease, a digestive disorder, is another complaint that is not strictly an allergy but is caused by a food intolerance. Symptoms are wind and pain in the stomach after eating. Soft, smelly faeces full of undigested fat and weight loss result from an inability to absorb food properly. The disease is an intolerance of gluten, a protein found in wheat, so sufferers must avoid foods which contain it.

The most severe, though rare, allergy

Q I am worried that I may become addicted to the drugs I am using to treat an allergy. Could this happen?

A No. Nor do these drugs lose their effects if you have to keep taking them. However, they may have side-effects (antihistamines, for instance, can make you drowsy) and, like all drugs, should be treated with respect and caution.

Q Whenever my father is near my mother her eyes run and she can't stop sneezing. Can you be allergic to people, places or animals?

A No, you can't be allergic to a person, but there have been cases of wives who were allergic to their husbands' sperm. Some people who are acutely allergic to fish can get swollen lips from kissing someone who has just been eating fish. Allergy to animals is common, though it is the fine pieces of hair or fluff from the animal or bird which are to blame. You can only be allergic to a place if you are allergic to something found in that place—e.g. pollen.

Q I sit next to a girl in the office who has eczema and sometimes the rash is really bad. I can't help wondering if it is infectious.

A The simple answer is that allergies are not infectious. You cannot catch an allergy from another person, nor can you pick up a symptom—in this case eczema—of that allergy.

Q My husband and I have both suffered badly over the years from food allergies. Our two children have shown no signs of developing allergies, but we wonder whether they can be prevented.

A Some specialists say there is little that can be done, while others believe that some allergies can be prevented. The risk of becoming allergic to milk, for instance may be reduced by breastfeeding rather than weaning on to cow's milk at an early age. Some specialists believe that you can reduce the risk of other food allergies by eating a more varied diet.

symptom is anaphylaxis, in which the patient's air passages swell and close and blood pressure falls abruptly. This rare, but acute and life-threatening condition can be reversed quickly by a shot of adrenalin.

Causes

No one knows why some people have allergies and some do not. Allergies tend to run in families, due perhaps to an inherited characteristic in the cells of the immune system, the body's defence against disease. Most allergies are certainly the result of an error in the immune system. The body's defence forces react to the allergen as if it were a dangerous infectious organism.

White blood cells called lymphocytes are constantly on the lookout for foreign substances such as bacteria, viruses and proteins which are different from the body's own proteins and which may present a threat. When these white blood cells come across a potentially dangerous foreign protein, they form a substance called antibody, which combines with the foreign protein and neutralizes it.

A slightly different antibody is created to deal with each foreign protein, but once it has formed, the body is able to produce it again to deal with any future 'attack' by that protein, so we usually get infectious diseases like measles only once. After the first attack, the body has supplies of antibody to deal with the virus if it appears again.

By some highly complicated process not yet understood by scientists, the immune system of a normal, healthy person knows how to tell the difference between a dangerous foreign protein like a virus and a harmless one like a food protein. But the immune system of an allergic person reacts to a harmless protein as if it were dangerous and forms an antibody, which attaches itself to mast cells. These mast cells contain a number of important chemicals, the most significant of which is histamine.

If the body is exposed to the protein again, the antibody attached to the mast cells combines with the foreign proteins and tries to neutralize them. In doing so, it upsets the structure of the mast cells, which fall apart and release histamine. The surge of histamine produces an effect like the inflammation which follows a wound: tiny blood vessels dilate, their walls leak and the fluid from the blood escapes into the surrounding tissues. The dilation of the blood vessels causes redness and itching, and the escaping fluid makes the surrounding tissues swell. In hay fever, the mucous glands in the nose and sinuses are also stimulated to produce fluid, which causes stuffiness and a runny nose.

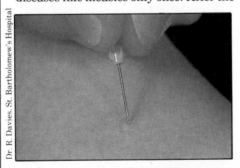

Dr. R. Davies, St. Bartholomew's Hospital

In the prick test, the skin of the arm is pricked several times and a drop of solution (left) containing a possible allergen is dropped on to test for a reaction. This allergy sufferer (below) has undergone the process and found that the cause of her allergy is cat fur. The large welt at the bottom is proof of a positive reaction to her allergen, while the marks above represent negative results to the test and show no adverse reactions.

Ken Moreman

Diagnosis

The diagnosis of pollen and food allergies is made with help of a prick test. The doctor or nurse gently pricks the arm with a needle and drops a watery solution containing a tiny amount of one single allergen on the spot.

Up to 40 prick tests can be performed in one session without much discomfort for an adult. If you are allergic to one of the allergens, a round red welt will appear in about 15 minutes.

An elimination diet is sometimes used to identify the cause of a food allergy. If the symptoms abate after several days on this diet, it is likely that at least one of the foods which have been eliminated is the cause of the allergy. You may be asked to try each food again in turn to see if the symptoms recur.

Provocation tests, in which a weak solution of various food is either injected under the skin or dropped under the tongue to see if they will provoke symptoms, are sometimes used to test for allergies to some foods or to chemicals usually found at home or used as colouring, flavouring or preservatives.

Treatment

If you have an acute allergy that makes you sick when you eat strawberries or shellfish, you hardly need a doctor to diagnose your complaint. The cause and effect are obvious, and the easiest way to prevent the allergy is to avoid the allergen.

Having discovered what you are allergic to, the doctor may prescribe a series of shots which contain small amounts of the allergen. Their aim is to desensitize you by encouraging your immune system to produce a harmless 'blocking antibody'. This antibody intercepts the allergen before it sets off symptoms by alighting on the mast cell antibodies.

Shots can be given during the pollen season, but are less reliable than those taken before the pollen season begins. They do not work for everyone, but can give about 70 percent of victims protection throughout the summer.

Several drugs are prescribed to deal with allergy symptoms. Antihistamines combat the inflammatory effects of histamine and are available as tablets, liquid and nose or eye drops, and there are shots that can be used for serious attacks. All these drugs will make most people feel drowsy.

Another drug, disodium cromoglycate, better known by its brand name Cromolyn, works by preventing the mast cells from exploding. It must be taken before symptoms occur, but can do nothing to counteract histamine that has already been released.

Corticosteroid drugs like cortisone, which are very powerful and anti-inflammatory, are sometimes prescribed for skin allergies or, via an inhaler to combat asthma, which can also be controlled by a group of drugs known as bronchodilators that dilate (open up) the bronchi, or air passages around the lungs.

None of these drugs are cures: they simply relieve symptoms. And they are not without problems. Corticosteroids must be used sparingly and for short periods, and it is possible to develop an allergy to antihistamine! Always let your doctor know if you have unpleasant side-effects from a medicine. He should be able to prescribe another of the many anti-allergic drugs which will suit you better.

Some food allergies can be relieved by drugs, but diets that eliminate all foods to which you are allergic are the preferable treatment.

Self-help

Sufferers can do a lot to help themselves. If you suffer from a food or chemical allergy, you should make every effort to

A soothing cream can often relieve the symptoms of a skin allergy such as eczema. This should always be prescribed by a doctor.

avoid your allergens. Read labels on food carefully to see if the products contains even small amounts of the substance causing your allergy.

Hay fever victims should be careful about going out in the open air during the pollen season, especially in mid-afternoon when the pollen count is highest. Dark glasses can protect your eyes against pollen or spores. Air conditioning in your home, office and car extracts pollen from the air. If you are going on vacation in late spring or early summer, remember that there is usually less pollen in the air at the beach than in the countryside.

Dust is difficult to eliminate altogether, but regular vacuuming of carpets and washing of bedcovers and curtains will reduce the amount. Artificial fibres in pillows and quilts are less likely than feathers to cause allergy.

Appendicitis

Q I am a model for a swimwear company and have to have my appendix out. Will I have an ugly scar afterwards?

A This rarely happens today. Various ways of sealing wounds have been devised which improve the cosmetic appearance of an operation scar. In any case, the scar from your appendix operation will be below the 'bikini line' so your job should not be affected.

Q Do people always pass wind after an appendix operation? I would be so embarrassed if this happened to me.

A Far from being an embarrassment, wind is a sign that the bowels are returning to life. After any abdominal operation, the bowels stop working for a while. In fact, food and drink cannot be taken until 'bowel sounds' return. The bowels are full of wind anyway, and as they gain strength, this is the first thing to be expelled.

Q My brother, who is a sailor, has a grumbling appendix. What would happen if it suddenly worsened while he was at sea?

A Obviously, if away from medical help, some treatment has to be tried, whether at sea or on a mountain top. Painkillers are essential and antibiotics may help. A large vessel may have a ship's doctor who is well qualified to deal with such an emergency. Otherwise, modern communications are so rapid that air-sea rescue services can be called in to cope with any crisis that may occur.

Q I am planning a world trip and will undoubtedly visit places with no medical facilities. Since I have had attacks of appendicitis in the past, is it possible to have my appendix removed as a preventative measure?

A This is sometimes done, but not as a general rule. In the 'developed world' the dangers of an unnecessary operation may outweigh the risks of sudden appendicitis. But in your case it may be a sensible precaution. Your doctor will be able to advise you.

The appendix is a small organ that was useful to our ancestors but is now virtually redundant. However, it can still cause trouble and sometimes has to be removed, but with modern surgical techniques an appendectomy is both speedy and safe.

The appendix is a narrow, tube-like piece of gut resembling a tail, located at the end of the large intestine. The tip of the tube is closed; the other end joins the large intestine. It can be up to 10 cm (4 in) long and about 1 cm (5/8 in) in diameter.

It is found only in humans, certain apes and wombats. Other animals have an organ in the same position that acts as an extra stomach where cellulose, the fibrous part of plants, is digested by bacteria. As we evolved and began to eat less cellulose and more meat, a special organ was no longer needed for the digestion of fibrous food. The appendix could therefore be described as a relic of evolution.

Appendicitis

Facts about the appendix seem to contradict each other. Nature appears to have adapted it to act as a watchdog for infection at the lower end of the gut. Like the tonsils and adenoids, it contains numerous lymph glands for the purpose, but if it becomes inflamed, appendicitis results and the organ may have to be removed. On the other hand, the appendix does not seem essential to health. It can be eliminated at an early age and has shrivelled up almost completely by the age of about 40.

Appendicitis can occur at any time, but it is rare under the age of two, more common among teenagers and increasingly rare again over the age of 30. Why it reaches a peak in youth is a mystery.

Causes

The entire history and incidence of the condition is baffling. It was relatively unknown until the late 1800s and still is in Asia, Africa and Polynesia. But in North America, Europe and Australia, appendicitis is now very common.

The reason is probably related directly to changes in our eating habits. The modern western diet has become so refined that it now lacks sufficient fibre, or roughage. This deficiency causes the food to slow down in the intestines. This sluggishness can lead to blockages which may be a cause of appendicitis. Food residues occasionally collect in the appendix and form an obstruction.

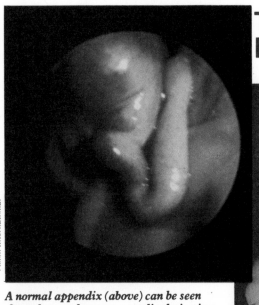

Vision International

Two views of a healthy appendix

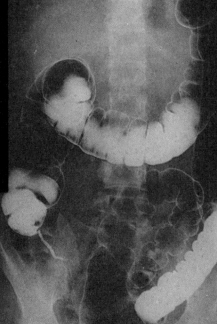

A normal appendix (above) can be seen through an endoscope, a medical viewing instrument which is inserted in the abdomen and which can be used to take photographs of organs inside the body. A healthy appendix appears as a long, thin tail in an X-ray (right).

Q A great-aunt of mine died of appendicitis. Could this happen nowadays?

A This is most unlikely. In the past, any operation was fraught with dangers. As a result, an appendix operation was often delayed until perforation occurred and the patient would then become rapidly ill and even die.

Q Several members of my family have had to have their appendix out. Is this just a coincidence or can a tendency to appendicitis be inherited?

A Yes, it is possible that you have an inherited tendency. It may be that you have all inherited a similarly shaped appendix. One that is long and thin will block more easily than one that is short and stubby, and so cause appendicitis.

Q I am 45 and have heard that it is highly unlikely that I will ever have appendicitis at my age. Is this true?

A Yes, it is. If you have reached middle life without having had appendicitis, the chances are that you are unlikely to get it now because the appendix shrivels as you get older and is completely shrivelled by the age of 45—so it is not likely to become irritated and inflamed. This is why appendicitis tends to be a complaint of young people.

Q I have heard that swallowing cherry stones can lead to appendicitis. As they are my favourite fruit, I am worried that I may get this problem. Is there any truth in this?

A When appendectomies were first performed years ago, surgeons thought that the small hard lumps they found in the appendix were cherry stones because they looked like them, but in fact they were fecoliths—that is, small lumps of faeces which had become trapped in the appendix because it leads nowhere. So you can continue eating your favourite fruit because swallowing fruit stones usually results in their being excreted from the body in the normal way and only very rarely will they cause any irritation to the appendix.

Parasitic worms, the result of eating contaminated food, may lodge there and eventually cause a blockage. Whatever their origin, any kind of a blockage can lead to the onset of appendicitis.

The 'grumbling appendix'
Recurrent attacks of appendicitis lasting a day or two can occur. As the appendix becomes inflamed, the intestines close to it form a wall around it to keep out infection. If the inflammation clears up, the intestines may still be stuck around the appendix. The adhesions can restrain the normal movement of food around the system and cramping pains may be felt in the area of the appendix during normal digestion. They can cause a 'grumbling' appendix, which will clear up provided it does not become further inflamed.

Serious symptoms
The early symptoms of appendicitis are not easy to distinguish from any other upset stomach. Pain, which comes and goes, is felt around the umbilicus (navel) as the appendix muscles contract while

After an appendectomy the wound is carefully stitched (right) so that only the smallest scar will remain. After a few months, a reddish mark will be only slightly visible (below), and over a few years most scars will become scarcely noticeable as a thin white line.

trying to drive out any obstruction. Otherwise, there will just be a constant ache.

After six to 12 hours, the symptoms will change, as inflammation builds up around the appendix, usually in the lower right abdomen. However, the site of the maximum pain is variable.

Diagnosis
Often the patient has to press his or her own stomach to establish where it hurts most. The most common site is two-thirds of the way along a line joining the top of the umbilicus to the top of the pelvic bone and is called McBurney's point, after the surgeon who first noted it. But the pain can move down into the pelvis or into the upper abdomen. In a woman, the symptoms can be particularly confusing as they can be mimicked by gynaecological pains from the ovaries or womb. A rectal examination may be needed to determine if the pain is in fact caused by appendicitis.

An inflamed appendix often lies on the right leg muscle where it joins the back

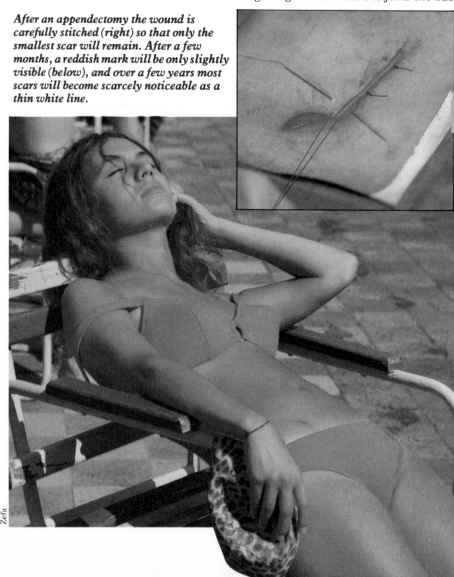

Zefa

32

The leg is stiff, so the patient bends it up to gain relief. Stretching it down again causes pain. The muscles in the front wall of the abdomen also go into spasm to protect the appendix from painful movements the patient may try to make.

The physician may have difficulty in diagnosing appendicitis in children. A child can have a respiratory infection with symptoms that imitate appendicitis which disappear as the infection improves. So if a child has obvious signs of chest trouble, be sure to tell the physician if he or she also has an upset stomach.

When to see the doctor

If the pain has continued for a whole day or night and has become increasingly severe, and if the patient is vomiting and unable to get up, seek immediate medical help. Home treatments such as pain-killers or soothing drinks should not be tried at this stage. An operation may be needed urgently, and the stomach must be empty of food and drink before anesthetic can be administered.

Dangers of appendicitis

If appendicitis is neglected, the tip of the appendix can become gangrenous, causing perforation. If pus spreads into the abdominal cavity, the result can be a serious inflammation called peritonitis, which can happen within hours. It can be localized in adults, but in children under 10, it can turn into general peritonitis. When the appendix is removed, a plastic drain has to be inserted to allow any infected matter to drain away. Infusions and antibiotics will also be given to combat infection and speed recovery.

Appendectomy

Because the risks of neglecting appendicitis are greater then the risks of an unnecessary operation, most surgeons will operate. But if the symptoms are inconclusive, the patient may be put to bed and kept under observation. If the condition does not improve, an operation will be performed.

The operation is quite simple and only takes half an hour under general anaesthetic. Modern drugs and antibiotics have greatly reduced the risk of complications. When the appendix is gone, the patient feels much better and is ready to leave the hospital a few days later. The stitches at the site of the operation are removed after about a week.

The scar still has to heal but the patient can soon lead a reasonably active and normal life again, although active sports like football, boxing, hard running or vigorous sexual activity, are out of the question for several weeks.

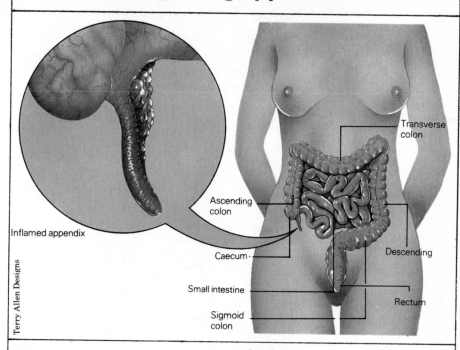

Recognizing appendicitis

Inflamed appendix

Terry Allen Designs

Transverse colon

Ascending colon

Caecum

Small intestine

Sigmoid colon

Descending

Rectum

Early symptoms	Action
Colicky (griping) pain is stomach that comes and goes	Give mild painkiller like paracetamol.
Loss of appetite	Try a soothing drink: warm milk or weak tea
Constipation	Give a hot water bottle. Do NOT give a laxative—this will be harmful, causing painful contractions of the appendix and increasing the risk of perforation

In children, symptoms imitating appendicitis may be caused by respiratory infection. These could, however, be genuine. TELL THE DOCTOR about tummy symptoms in a child.

Later symptoms
(Give no more home remedies. Get medical help at once)

More pain in the appendix area (right side of lower abdomen)	Slight increase in pulse rate
Pain may move up or down from umbilicus (navel)	Nausea. Vomiting. Foul-smelling breath.
	Diarrhoea; but constipation more common.
Slight rise in temperature, even to a mere 37.5°C (99.5°).	Patient lies with right leg flexed up; stretching leg producing pain

After-effects

Occasional twinges of pain will be felt during healing, but will disappear within a month or so. However, because the abdomen has been opened during surgery, air can enter the intestine, and the patient may develop severe wind a short time after the operation.

Also, after any abdominal operation, the bowels stop working, so breaking wind shows that the digestive system is resuming its normal function. This means that the patient can eat and drink again. If patients feel embarrassment, the best reassurance that friends and family can provide is that breaking wind is a sign that their bodies are getting back to normal and they are well on the way to a successful recovery.

Arteries and artery disease

Q I have been told that smoking causes artery disease. Is this true?

A Yes. Hardening of the arteries (arteriosclerosis) is aggravated by smoking, although exactly how this happens is unclear. But there is no doubt that nicotine in the bloodstream does cause arteries to narrow. After a while, they become permanently rigid and less able to carry blood to all parts of the body, particularly the heart—resulting in heart attacks—and the extremities (hands and feet). If blood cannot reach the extremities, tissues degenerate, gangrene sets in and a limb may have to be amputated.

 However, if smoking is given up in time, damage can be avoided.

Q I jog regularly. Will this reduce the chance of my having a heart attack?

A There is a reasonable amount of evidence to suggest that regular exercise does have a protective effect against heart attacks, but this is by no means conclusive. A recent study in England comparing the chances of heart attacks among bus drivers and bus conductors showed a small difference in favor of the conductors, whose job is more active than the drivers'. So it seems reasonable to assume that exercise is a preventive measure and jogging a good idea.

Q Three of my male relatives, including my father, have died of heart attacks. Are men more prone to arteriosclerosis than women?

A This does appear to be so, for several reasons. First, female hormones seem to protect women from atheroma (the build-up of fatty deposits in the arteries, which can cause blockages); after menopause, with its fall in the level of hormone production, atheroma increases. Secondly, until recently, more men smoked than women, but now the pattern is altering and, as a result, the number of women suffering from atheroma before and after menopause is rising. The conclusion is obvious: give up smoking.

The arteries carry blood containing nourishment and oxygen to all parts of the body. Artery disease is therefore very dangerous, so preventive measures are essential and early treatment vital.

The arteries are one of the two sorts of large blood vessels in the body. The arteries are like pipes, carrying blood outwards from the heart to the tissues while the veins carry the blood on the return journey. The entire body depends on blood for its supply of oxygen and other vital substances without which life could not go on.

The artery network

The heart is a pump which propels blood around the body through the arteries. The main pumping chamber on the left side of the heart, which is called the left ventricle, ejects blood into the main artery of the body—the aorta, a tube about 2.5 cm (1 in) across on the inside.

 The first of its branches arises from the aorta as soon as it leaves the heart. These branches are the coronary arteries which supply blood to the heart itself. The coronary arteries are the arteries most likely to be affected by disease. A blocked coronary artery—or coronary thrombosis—causes a heart attack.

 After giving rise to the coronary arteries, the aorta passes upward before doubling back on itself in an arch. Originating from this arch are the two main arteries to the head, the left and right carotid arteries, and one artery to each arm. The aorta descends down the chest and into the abdomen.

 In the abdomen there are three main arteries to the intestines and the liver, and one to each kidney before the aorta divides into the left and right iliac arteries which supply blood to the pelvis and the legs.

 After passing through the capillaries—a network of tiny blood vessels linking the smallest arteries and veins—from which oxygen and nourishment enter the tissues, the blood returns toward the heart in the veins. In general, the artery and vein supplying an area tend to run side-by-side. The veins empty into the right side of the heart, from where blood is pumped to the lungs and recharged with oxygen. From the lungs, oxygen-rich blood is drained by the pulmonary veins into the left side of the heart.

Blood is circulated through the body by muscles in the veins pushing it to the heart and then being squeezed back through the body along arteries. Running, or any regular exercise, keeps you healthy by forcing the heart to pump more blood.

The development of arterial disease

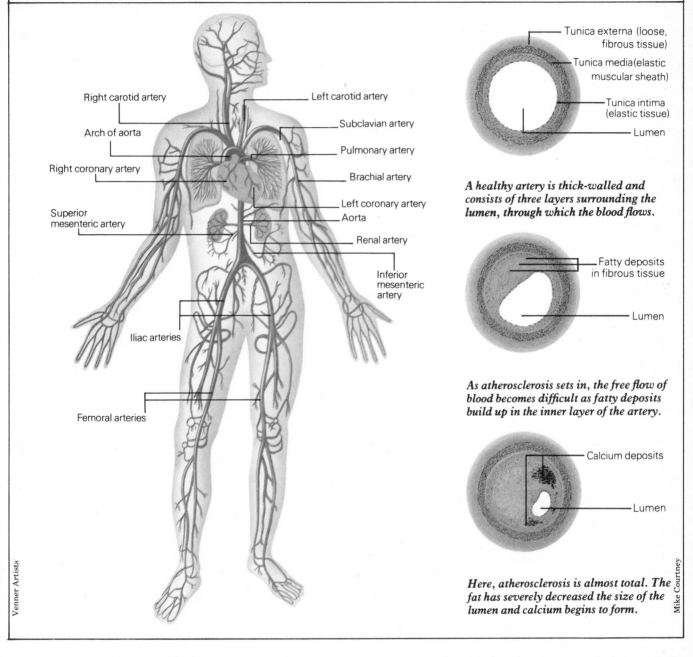

Tunica externa (loose, fibrous tissue)

Tunica media (elastic muscular sheath)

Tunica intima (elastic tissue)

Lumen

A healthy artery is thick-walled and consists of three layers surrounding the lumen, through which the blood flows.

Fatty deposits in fibrous tissue

Lumen

As atherosclerosis sets in, the free flow of blood becomes difficult as fatty deposits build up in the inner layer of the artery.

Calcium deposits

Lumen

Here, atherosclerosis is almost total. The fat has severely decreased the size of the lumen and calcium begins to form.

Right carotid artery

Arch of aorta

Right coronary artery

Superior mesenteric artery

Iliac arteries

Femoral arteries

Left carotid artery

Subclavian artery

Pulmonary artery

Brachial artery

Left coronary artery

Aorta

Renal artery

Inferior mesenteric artery

Venner Artists

Mike Courtney

Here, it starts off around the body again by being pumped into the aorta by the left ventricle of the heart. The left ventricle generates a considerable pressure to force the blood through the arterial network. The inflatable band which is wrapped around your arm during blood pressure tests reaches the same tightness as the maximum squeeze in the left ventricle with each heartbeat.

The structure of arteries

Since the arteries are subjected to this force with each heartbeat, they have to be thick-walled to cope with the pressure. The outer wall of an artery is a loose, fibrous tissue sheath. Inside this there is a thick elastic and muscular sheath which gives the artery its strength. There are also rings of muscle fibres encircling the artery in among the elastic tissue (the 'endothelium'). The inner layer of the artery is made of a smooth layer of cells which allows the blood to flow freely.

The thick elastic walls are most important to the way in which the system works. Much of the force of each heartbeat is taken up in the elastic walls of the big arteries. They continue to push the blood forward in the pause between each heartbeat.

Arterial disease

Arterial disease in any part of the body is dangerous because if an artery is blocked or narrowed it is possible that the part it supplies will die from oxygen starvation. There are two basic ways in which a blockage can happen.

Hardening of the arteries is the most common serious illness in the Western world. Age is the most important cause,

35

but many other factors affect the rate at which arterial disease progresses.

The changes in the walls of arteries which lead to hardening are called arteriosclerosis ('sclerosis' means hardening). These changes are caused by the development of an excessive amount of fibrous tissue. This can happen as a result of a straining of the artery walls caused by raised blood pressure.

The other type of disease is atheroma, which is the name given to fatty deposits which attach themselves to the arterial walls increasingly with advancing age. These fatty deposits look like porridge and 'atheroma' is Greek for porridge.

Changes in the arterial network resulting from atheroma, as opposed to arteriosclerosis, are usually referred to as atherosclerosis—a word your doctor is more likely to use than arteriosclerosis. Arterio- and atherosclerosis are words which can be used interchangeably.

Cholesterol

The atheromatous process first starts with a deposit of cholesterol—a normal constituent of the blood and one of the building blocks of normal cells—in the wall of the artery. However, it seems that cholesterol leaks into the inner surface (intima) of the artery and a 'fatty streak' forms within the arterial wall.

As the fatty streak grows in size and

The X-ray (left) shows healthy leg arteries, while a blockage has developed (right) where the arteries have narrowed.

depth two other things happen. First, the surface of the streak may break down and expose the middle portions of the arterial wall to the blood. When this happens it triggers the mechanism for clotting the blood. A clot normally forms as a plug of fibrous tissue to stop bleeding from a wound. When the process occurs around a fatty streak, a mixture of fibrous and fatty tissue is formed in the arterial wall and this is called an atheromatous plaque. As the plaque grows it starts to encroach upon the central blood-filled space—that is, the lumen of the artery through which the blood travels.

Finally, the development of the plaque involves changes occurring deep in the arterial wall. Fibrous tissue forms on the inner surface of the original fatty streak, but there is also a growth of fibrous tissue on the wall side of the plaque, growing from the outside of the artery towards its center. The end result is a mixture of fibrous and fatty tissue blocking a proportion of the arterial lumen. The disease extends to a considerable depth in the wall of the vessel and encroaches on a large proportion of its circumference making the flow of blood very difficult.

Once a large atheromatous plaque has formed it may have a number of consequences. It may steadily enlarge to block the artery. Because the artery is partially blocked, the flow of blood past the obstruction is reduced. This may activate the clotting system at the site of narrowing. The clot may well produce a complete obstruction known as a thrombosis.

Atheromatous plaques which are partly blocking an artery may become displaced and swing across the lumen of the artery, like a lock gate, to block it completely. Parts of an atheromatous plaque may break off and travel towards a smaller artery which will then become blocked. This is a phenomenon known as embolism.

Atheroma can affect any artery down to a diameter of about 2 millimetres. However, the process is most likely to occur in areas of arterial wall which are subjected to movement and most stress. For this reason, atheroma is commonest at sites where arteries branch into smaller arteries. There is a greater stretching of the lining of the arteries at these points allowing more cholesterol to get into the wall.

The results of blockage

Since arteries are necessary to supply oxygen to every part of the body, there is no organ which is completely immune to the effects of arterial disease. If an organ or a limb has its blood supply cut off by atheroma then it must eventually die. An area of tissue which has lost its oxygen supply is called an area of infarction. When this process occurs in an arm or a leg it is more usual to use the term gangrene.

There are obviously some areas where the effects of atheroma cause especially severe problems. The most important are the heart, the brain, the legs and, finally, the aorta itself.

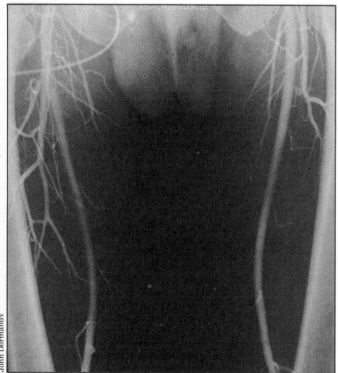
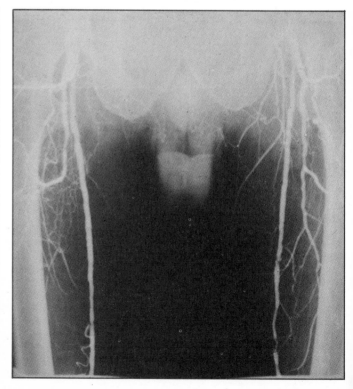

Heart attacks

Atheroma particularly affects the heart because the two coronary arteries, the arteries that supply blood to the heart, are under more mechanical stress than practically any other arteries in the body. The heart is continuously contracting and relaxing with each heartbeat and, in so doing, the coronary arteries, which lie on the outer surface of the heart, are alternately stretched and relaxed. This seems to give ideal conditions for atheromatous plaques to be formed. When a coronary artery becomes blocked as a result of atheroma, then a heart attack results. Such an event may also be known as a coronary thrombosis, or a myocardial infarction (the 'myocardium' is the heart muscle and infarction is the formation of a dead area of the muscle when it is deprived of blood).

But heart attacks are not the only problem which atheroma causes in the heart. Where there is a fixed obstruction which is not totally blocking the artery, the supply of blood to the heart may only be sufficient to meet the needs of the body when at rest. Exercise increases the need for blood in the heart and it becomes starved of oxygen. This causes pain arising in the heart which is known as angina pectoris, or simply angina. The two problems of angina and myocardial infarction are often lumped together under the title of ischaemic heart disease, ischaemia being a word which implies a lack of oxygen without total deprivation or infarction.

Strokes

In the brain atherosclerosis may result in a stroke. These may vary from the minor to the fatal and may occur as a result of an artery becoming blocked through atheroma or embolism, or through an artery leaking blood into the brain as a result of a weakened wall.

When the legs are severely affected by atheroma they become painful and this pain is worse during exercise, just like angina. If the disease is severe, then gangrene results and the affected leg may have to be amputated.

Finally, the aorta itself is a very important area of atheromatous disease. Two different things can happen. The wall of the aorta may start to balloon out as a result of the weakening effect of the disease. This produces sack-like swelling called an aneurism instead of the regular tubular structure of the normal aorta. Aneurisms are usually found in the abdomen but may occur in the chest. An aneurism may continue to expand and eventually start to leak, with disastrous results. Surgical treatment is the only hope and it is necessary to strengthen the aorta with a woven fabric tube. The re-

sults of this sort of surgery when carried out as an emergency are often good, although there are failures.

Another form of aneurism which tends to occur in the chest rather than the abdomen, is called dissection of the aorta. This means that the layers of the aortic wall become split by escaping blood, the end result being much the same. Occasionally, patients survive dissection without surgery but, again, surgery is usually necessary.

Those affected

There is now a well-established list of risk factors which indicate people who are more likely to suffer from 'accelerated' or 'early' atheroma. For instance, some diseases put people at greater risk. The two most important are high blood pressure and diabetes.

People from a family in which atherosclerosis has occurred are at greater risk of developing problems themselves. And, finally, there is the cholesterol level in the blood. Although this is a definite risk factor, the value of cholesterol measurements in individuals has perhaps been overemphasized as most cholesterol is manufactured by the body's own chem-

ical processes. However, it does seem sensible to reduce the amount of meat and dairy products in a high protein diet.

Remember, too, that every sensible diet should include plenty of unrefined carbohydrates, or foods containing dietary fibre such as wholemeal bread, pulses and bran.

Prevention

What can we do to prevent or postpone the development of atheromatous disease? Obviously both diabetes and high blood pressure must be treated. If there are no predisposing illnesses, then the most potent risk factor is family history, over which there is no control. However, there is one controllable factor left—smoking. The most effective way to prevent atheroma is to stop smoking, for it can counteract the benefits of other measures. In addition to significantly reducing the chances of your developing heart disease, giving up cigarettes will generally improve your health.

These thermographs, or heat-sensitive pictures, show the effect of smoking on the flow of the blood in the arm. Note the decreased circulation in the fingertips.

BEFORE SMOKING

Deleterious Effects of Smoking on Peripheral Vascular Circulation

The upper extremities of a 35-year-old man are illustrated in these color thermograms. The subject is a healthy individual with no history of smoking-related disease. He has smoked one package of cigarettes daily for 20 years. The test was performed at a room temperature of 74°F. The subject smoked one-half the length of a standard, non-filter cigarette. The upper thermogram was obtained before smoking. Maximal thermal changes occurred in the first 25 minutes, but significant abnormalities were still present 59 minutes after smoking, as noted in the lower thermogram.

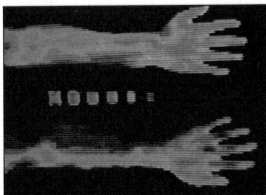

Smoking produced a drop in temperature of 3°C measured in the hands of this individual. The red color represents warmth, where as blue, green or violet are 'cool' colors. Ten color stages are reproduced and each color difference indicates a change of 0.3°C. Patients with peripheral vascular disease manifest greater decreases in temperature after smoking. (Illustration through the courtesy of Travis Winsor, M.D., University of Southern California, Los Angeles.

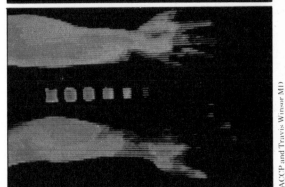

59 MINUTES AFTER SMOKING

ACCP and Travis Winsor MD

SMOKING AND ARTERIAL DISEASE

Arthritis

Q An old countryman once told me that he avoided arthritis by keeping a piece of cut potato in his pocket. Is there anything in this?

A You might as well as believe that the moon is made of green cheese! Although many herbs have proven medicinal properties, the potato is not one of them. Your friend was just lucky enough not to have developed arthritis

Q Is it safe to take a lot of aspirin to ease pain caused by arthritis?

A Yes and no. Because aspirin reduces inflammation and temperature and eases pain, it is often used as a first-line treatment for arthritis. Unfortunately, there are two side-effects that can happen when aspirin is taken for a long time. Bleeding can start from tiny gastric ulcers or an existing ulcer can flare up. If you start vomiting blood, or something that looks like coffee grounds, or pass black, tar-like bowel motions stop taking the asprin and seek medical help. The risk of stomach upsets is greatly reduced if you always use soluble aspirin. Another side-effect is ringing in the ears—if this happens, reduce the amount of aspirin.

Q Are some occupations more likely to cause arthritis than others?

A Regrettably, yes. Doctors are familiar with various 'wear and tear' effects, such as 'baker's cyst'—which is fluid at the back of the knee produced by excessive bending (when getting bread in and out of the oven), 'porter's neck'—which is osteoarthritis of the neck joints, caused by tilting the neck (when carrying objects over the shoulder), and even 'ballet dancer's toe'—which looks like a bunion.

Q Will it do any good to rub some oil on a painful, inflamed knee joint?

A Very little, but you may find it soothing. Painful joints are often helped by a good massage.

Many people are affected by some form of arthritis, which can range from temporary discomfort to a more serious disability, but medical help and physiotherapy can do much to relieve the condition.

Colorific!

Betty Ford, wife of former U.S. President Gerald Ford, is one of millions of sufferers afflicted by arthritis.

Arthritis is an inflammation of the joints and its causes are as varied and mysterious as the condition itself. It affects people of all ages and is a common complaint in temperate climates; it can be mild or severe, affecting one joint or several; and the different types include rheumatoid arthritis, osteoarthritis, rigid spine disease *(ankylosing spondylitis)* and arthritis that has been brought on by an injury or other infection. Although its study is a well-established speciality, called rheumatology, medical research cannot yet tell us all the answers.

Rheumatoid arthritis in adults

Although it is common, the cause of rheumatoid arthritis is unknown. It is thought that it may be due to an 'auto-immune' phenomenon—that is, some event, perhaps a severe illness or a shock, triggering a chain of chemical reactions within the body, eventually producing chemicals which react against the body's own tissues—in this case, against the lining tissue of the joints—the synovium. Inflammation and arthritis will follow.

Rheumatoid arthritis usually affects adults between the ages of 20 and 55, and women are three times more liable to it than men. Inflammation of the knuckles of both hands is the usual symptom, and the joints of the toes are affected in a similar way. At the same time, the sufferer may lose weight, feel generally unwell and become unusually lethargic. The symptoms may be either acute, starting with a fever or rash, or happen gradually over several weeks.

The joints most often affected are the knees, hips, shoulders, wrists, elbows, ankles and the bones of the neck. The stiffness is usually at its worst in the morning, and in acute cases the sufferer may be confined to bed or have great difficulty moving.

In about one quarter of cases, attacks will last about six months, but only happen every few years. Some cases are persistent, varying in severity, but tending to 'burn out' after many years.

In children

Rheumatoid arthritis can occur in children—a condition called Still's disease—

Types of arthritis and their treatment

Type	Symptoms	Treatment
Rheumatoid arthritis Affects adults between 20 & 55; also children (Still's disease)	Lethargy, high*temperature, rash (occasionally), pain, swelling, redness, stiffness and loss of function in joints of fingers or toes	Anti-inflammatory and pain-killing drugs, gold injections or steroids. Drawing off (aspirating) fluid, physiotherapy, exercise, splinting, joint replacement
Osteoarthritis Wear and tear due to aging	Pain, followed by stiffness, swelling, change of shape due to degeneration of cartilage over joint	Basic principles as above
Ankylosing spondylitis Possibly hereditary, more common in males between 15 & 30	Stiff lower back in mornings, pain on bending spine. Due to calcium deposited in joint ligaments	Anti-inflammatory drugs, exercise
Traumatic Injury, such as falling heavily	Joint becomes inflamed, painful and swollen a few hours after injury	Rest, bandaging, painkilling drugs, then physiotherapy, X-ray in case of fracture, possible aspiration of fluid

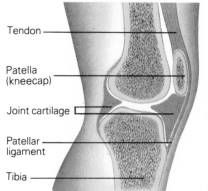

Tendon

Patella (kneecap)

Joint cartilage

Patellar ligament

Tibia

Normal knee

This knee functions without pain or stiffness because of healthy cartilages protecting the joint.

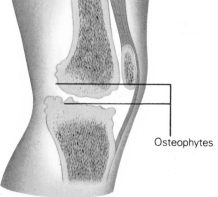

Osteophytes

Osteoarthritic knee

The ageing process has worn away the cartilages and bone causing pain and swelling.

Mike Courtney

but it is fortunately rare. Two main age groups are affected—between one and three and 10 and 15. The inflammation starts gradually, and in about one third of cases occurs in one joint only, commonly the knee. It can also affect the hands, wrists, feet and ankles.

This disease is slowly progressive, but burns itself out in late adolescence. The chances of a cure depend on the severity of the case, how early it is diagnosed and how quickly treatment is begun. Therapy should be started as soon as possible to prevent permanent stiffening and joint deformity.

Osteoarthritis

Osteoarthritis occurs as part of the ageing process. It happens mainly to weight-bearing joints: hips, knees and spine. In women the hands are also often affected, particularly the top joints of the fingers and the base of the thumb.

This condition is caused by degeneration of the cartilage, a tough, elastic tissue which protects the surface of the joint. This is normally glistening and smooth, but osteoarthritis causes it to roughen and the cartilage becomes 'dry'. This change has two effects: it compresses the underlying bone surface that the

cartilage should protect and inflames the synovium (the lining) lying over it.

The first symptoms are pain and loss of use; stiffness and swelling follow, and the joint eventually changes shape. There may be only one joint involved, such as the right hip in the right-handed person (because right-handedness means that the right side of the body is more active and bears more weight than the left), or, in many cases, the knees, spine, shoulders, hands and neck are affected. This condition is also slowly progressive, but disability rarely happens unless the arthritis in a weight-bearing joint is severe. Unfortunately, any injury will cause the condition to flare up.

Rigid spine disease

Ankylosing spondylitis is a form of arthritis which affects the pelvic joints and spine. This, too, is thought to be an auto-immune illness, like rheumatoid arthritis, but there is a definite tendency for it to run in families. It is more common in men, usually starting between the ages of 15 and 30.

The inflammation causes calcium to be deposited in the ligaments (fibrous bands which connects joints). This results in stiffness which can lead to the spinal bones (the vertebrae) being fused together if the inflammation is not alleviated by both medical treatment and exercise—hence its colloquial name 'poker back'. The illness progresses slowly for a few years, often spreading to the whole spine and involving the hip joints, before gradually petering out.

Other causes of arthritis

An injury can also trigger arthritis—this is called 'traumatic' arthritis. The injury can either be direct, for example from a blow to a joint, or indirect, as when you hurt your knee by falling heavily on it. Traumatic arthritis usually happens to men, although no one is completely immune.

The knee, ankle or wrist are the joints most commonly affected. A few hours after the injury, the joint becomes inflamed, painful and swollen. An X-ray is needed, in case a fracture has occurred, but rest, bandaging and painkillers may be all that is necessary.

Physiotherapy can also help restore mobility and muscle power to the affected limb. Occasionally the injury causes bleeding into the joint which becomes very tense and painful; this may have to be aspirated (drawn out with a needle) under a local anaesthetic.

Germs can also cause conditions like septic arthritis, which is brought on by a germ in the joint fluid. This happens either because of an injury or because it is transmitted from the blood. Half of such cases involve the knee, but it can occur in any large joint. Both children and the elderly can be affected, but it is fortunately rare.

Another rare form of arthritis can result from an attack of German measles (rubella). This can happen to adults, who may experience swelling of their finger joints, knees and ankles which subsides after few weeks.

Arthritis of the lower spine and hip, resulting from tuberculosis, is now also rare in developed countries. Other infections such as rheumatic fever, gonorrhoea and the skin disease psoriasis, can also give rise to arthritis.

Diagnosis and treatment

If you suspect that you have some form of arthritis, the worst thing you can do is to 'just put up with it.' Do not try to make the diagnosis yourself, but go and see your doctor. Any delay might mean the risk of permanent deformity, especially in the case of a child with Still's disease, a condition which needs hospital care and early physiotherapy.

Your doctor will ask for a history of your illness and give you an examination.

He may prescribe drugs such as aspirin, indomethacin and ibuprofen, which combat inflammation and ease pain, and painkillers such as paracetamol or 'distalgesic' tablets, which are stronger.

Gold injections may be given in the affected joints, but these can have unpleasant side effects and are used only when absolutely necessary.

You may have to rest the affected joints or wear an individually-made splint to keep them in the best position and prevent deformities from occurring. Swelling in joints can be treated by drawing off excess fluid under a local anaesthetic, or injecting an anti-inflammatory drug into the joint.

You may be feeling generally unwell and be advised to cut down some of your everyday activities and rest as much as possible. Steroid drugs (such as cortisone) may be prescribed to suppress the inflammation in the joints, but because they have side-effects they will only be used

when all other forms of treatment have been tried unsuccessfully. Doses must always be kept at the lowest possible level at which they will control symptoms, and progress must be carefully monitored by a doctor.

An acute attack of arthritis with fever, swollen joints and a general feeling of being unwell may need immediate hospital treatment, including splinting of limbs and rest on a special 'ripple' bed, in which an electric current 'ripples' through a plastic mattress, giving a cushioning effect.

Blood tests are made to establish the type of arthritis involved, to see if you are anemic, to check the amount of inflammation in the body at regular intervals and to assess the progress of the disease. Other tests will show whether the condition is caused by septic arthritis, gonococcal (VD) arthritis, or by bleeding into the joint.

Another technique, called arthroscopy, involves a telescope-type instrument

Any kitchen can be altered to make it easier for the victim of arthritis to use. The emphasis should be on things that give maximum efficiency when the sufferer is using his or her hands or bending. Adapted utensils and an eye-level oven, as well as easy-to-open cupboard doors and knee space under the sink are essential.

Easy-grip handle

Double-handled saucepan

Wall socket

Wall-mounted tin opener

Hand grip for cup or mug

Non-slip mat

Lever operated taps

Vegetable holder

Large-handled peeler

Long-handled dustpan

Stool with back and foot support

Brian Watson

Q My doctor says I have a 'frozen shoulder'. Is that a form of arthritis?

A No. It is simply a condition that mimics it. Others in this category include 'tennis elbow' and nerve-pain in the wrist, which is called carpal tunnel syndrome. What these conditions have in common is inflammation of the tissues around a joint—but in each case, other evidence confirming arthritis is absent.

Q My daughter is severely affected by arthritis but she is planning to get married in the very near future. What are her chances of enjoying any sex life or starting a family?

A When either partner has arthritis, they will want answers to many questions before they start a family. An important point is whether their children will be especially prone to this condition. Only one type of arthritis, caused by haemophilia, is clearly inherited. With many other forms the chances of an affected parent handing on the disease are rare. In an acute phase of the disease, it would be painful to attempt sex, but otherwise it is quite safe to attempt intercourse.

Q I've been told that heat is good for arthritis and am wondering if I could use an infra-red lamp to ease the pain?

A Heat is soothing and infra-red is a penetrating heat. Place it about two feet away from the joint and use it for about 20 minutes—up to three times daily. There is no long-term benefit, but it can be useful if done just before you begin an exercise routine.

Q My grandmother always wears a bandage on her arthritic knee. Is this really helpful?

A Bandaging or supporting an inflamed joint can stop any jarring movement and therefore ease pain. When a joint is swollen, the tissues feel stretched, and a support give the wearer a sense of stability. Wearing a bandage also serves as a notice to others that a jolt would *not* be appreciated.

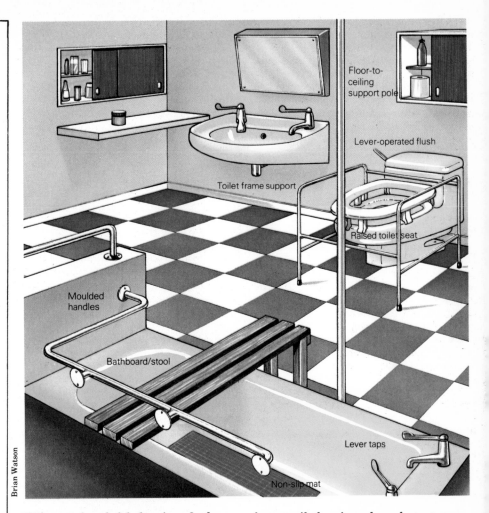

Brian Watson

Floor-to-ceiling support pole

Lever-operated flush

Toilet frame support

Raised toilet seat

Moulded handles

Bathboard/stool

Lever taps

Non-slip mat

With some thoughtful planning a bathroom can easily be remodeled for the arthritic user. If the sufferer is in a wheelchair don't forget to tilt the mirror, leave knee space under the sink and shelf and be sure to install a safe, non-slip floor covering.

which is used to look inside the knee joint under local anaesthetic. Both the cartilage and lining tissue can be examined by this method, and small pieces of tissue can be removed for further microscopic examination to help establish the cause of the condition.

Exercise and physiotherapy

Physiotherapy plays an important part in the treatment of all forms of arthritis. For affected joints that are in a 'quiescent' phase—that is, free of inflammation, exercise is essential to prevent stiffness and loss of mobility and restore muscles around the joint that may have wasted. There is no evidence that exercising an arthritic joint in the quiescent phase causes it to flare up.

A physiotherapist can teach you exercises which can be performed at home. Heat can be used to ease painful joints. These treatments can include short-wave diathermy, when a heating pad is placed near the affected joint, or hydrotherapy, which consists of exercis-

ing in a small, very warm swimming pool. The effect of the heat is to relax tense muscles and, because the water supports the body, movement is increased and made easier.

If your doctor or physiotherapist advises it, an infra-red lamp can be used at home. Paraffin wax baths for hands and feet is another treatment that can be used easily at home once the technique is learned. Some therapists favor ice packs as a form of pain-relieving therapy.

The benefits of surgery

Great advances have been made in the replacement of badly-damaged joints with artificial ones. In the first place, the decision that an arthritic joint needs surgery will be made by a specialist in the field, an orthopedic surgeon who has been consulted either by the patient's doctor or a rheumatologist. The results of such an operation can be a dramatic relief of pain, correction of deformity and increased movement. The benefits to the patient may include restoring enjoyment of sexual intercourse which may have previously been very difficult.

Surgery can also relieve pressure around a joint, free gummed-up ligaments or remove the inflamed lining tissue of a joint (synovectomy) if it is excessively inflamed. An excruciatingly painful and useless joint, such as may occur with osteoarthritis of the cervical spine (neck) or an arthritic knee, is sometimes surgically fused (arthrodesis) to give relief, though this does involve loss of movement.

Help available

An active person who has become seriously disabled must first come to terms with the feelings of dependence and helplessness that this brings. It is certainly not necessary to feel 'trapped' by the disease. Although there is no cure yet for every disability caused by arthritis, better general care and physical aids can make life more tolerable in many ways.

Aids such as splints, surgical collars, walking sticks and frames, elbow crutches, wheelchairs and some of the more complicated electrical hoisting aids can all be matched to individual needs by physiotherapists.

Advice can also be obtained from rehabilitation units about specialized aids to mobility, such as electric wheelchairs or hydraulic lifting devices that can be fitted to stairs.

Replacing one kind of lifestyle with another is always possible, although not always easy. Adjusting your employment must obviously take priority. You may need to change shifts, use especially adapted equipment or generally take on lighter duties. Your doctor can help by writing to your employer about your specific problems.

Structural changes in the home may be necessary and there are many helpful adaptations that can be made. Living in a bungalow is obviously more practical than living in a conventional two-storey house, but if it is not possible to move, the problems caused by steps can be overcome by using special equipment. Kitchens and bathrooms particularly may need to be altered to make them more suitable to the needs of the arthritis victim.

The effects of arthritis can spread into many areas of life. Hobbies and pastimes as varied as playing cards, gardening and needlecrafts need not be affected, how-

Many exercises have been devised to help arthritics retain the use of their muscles.

ever. Occupational therapists can advise about the many ingenious devices and techniques that have been developed to enable arthritics to continue enjoying their pleasures. One particularly useful gadget is a remote control unit for the television which means that arthritics do not need to move or use painful joints to change channels.

Coping with arthritis at home

- Build ramp to replace outdoor steps.

- Make door openings wide enough to take wheelchair, if necessary.

- Fix handrail on both sides of stairs.

- Replace worn carpets; keep floor space clear for walking aids.

- Raise electric sockets about three feet above ground.

- Replace light switches with pull cords.

- Raise heights of chairs with blocks fixed to end of chair legs; raise height of seat with firm cushions.

- To increase leverage on refrigerator handle, slip loop of leather or strong string over handle.

- Pad handles of kitchen utensils and brush and broom handles with foam rubber.

- Use basket on wheels to carry things from one room to another.

- Fix handrails to bathtub and around toilet; use raised toilet seat.

- Attach iron and ironing board to a convenient wall to avoid carrying.

- Electric 'ripple' bed: a current ripples through plastic mattress to give cushioning effect.

- Use long-handled garden tools.

- Use an adjustable seat in bathtub.

- Use a lightweight carpet sweeper.

- Extend toilet seat for wheelchair users.

- Install appliances and fit kitchen surfaces at convenient heights.

Asthma

Q Is there anything I can do if I forget my inhaler and then suffer an attack?

A There is very little you can do and this situation only emphasizes how important it is to carry your medication with you always. If you suffer a severe attack, you must go to a doctor or a hospital emergency room as soon as possible. In the meantime it is most important that you sit still and save your breath.

Q My father had asthma when he was a boy and my son and I have it. Can asthma run in families?

A Unfortunately, asthma does have a tendency to run in families, especially those asthmas which are strong in reponse to an allergy. The inherited link is not yet fully understood.

Q I use an inhaler for my asthma about five or six times a day. But I've heard that the inhaler is dangerous for the heart. Is this true?

A No. Bronchodilator inhalers had a bad reputation some years ago because they over-stimulated the heart. Modern inhalers affect the heart much less and so are far safer.

Q My two young children are both asthmatic, but they are also full of energy. Should they be allowed to play sports?

A Definitely yes. Any asthmatic should be vigorously encouraged to participate in sport. Some sports may be more likely to cause asthma than others, and in this case the child should make sure that he has his inhaler handy. Of all sports, swimming is the least likely to bring on an attack.

Q Why does my son always seem to get an asthmatic attack when we have guests?

A There is often a connection between emotional stress and asthma attacks. Try to make your son feel more relaxed. Involve him in the preparations, and avoid pushing him into the limelight.

Asthma is a very common respiratory complaint—so it is essential to know the symptoms, the treatments available, and the ways of preventing an attack.

Asthma involves a severe narrowing of the bronchial tubes. These lead from the windpipe—called the trachea—into the lungs and they carry the oxygen we breathe in to all parts of the lungs and provide a path for the carbon dioxide (a waste product of the body) to escape up the trachea when we breathe out.

The narrowing of the bronchial tubes—or bronchi—results from the contraction of the muscle lining them and causes difficulty in breathing that is most marked when breathing out. For this reason, asthmatics tend to breathe in with short gasps and breathe out with a long wheeze—a result of the effort required to breathe against the obstruction.

The body's defences

Two chemicals are responsible for causing the bronchial muscles to contract: histamin, which is released from mast cells that store histamin and other chemicals as part of an allergic reaction, and acetylcholine which is a chemical released from the nerve endings which control the bronchial muscle.

These nerves are branches of the important vagus nerve which originates in the brain. The vagus keeps the bronchi in a constant state of contraction all the time and, as such, can be regarded as the main control over bronchial contraction, with additional control being provided by histamine.

To keep the balance between contraction and expansion (dilation), there are other substances that cause the bronchi to relax, thus working against the histamine and acetylcholine. These substances are called bronchodilators and a number of them are manufactured in the adrenal glands situated above each kidney.

The most important bronchodilator is adrenalin, which acts as a stimulant during periods of stress and excitement; when we need more oxygen to provide energy during a dangerous situation, the adrenalin helps to open up the bronchi to allow more air through to the lungs during rapid breathing.

In addition to this, the bronchial muscles also contain enzymes—substances which are responsible for maintaining certain bodily functions on which life depends, among them respiration (breathing). The enzymes help to protect

The use of an inhaler containing a drug such as isoproterenol gives almost immediate relief from an asthmatic attack.

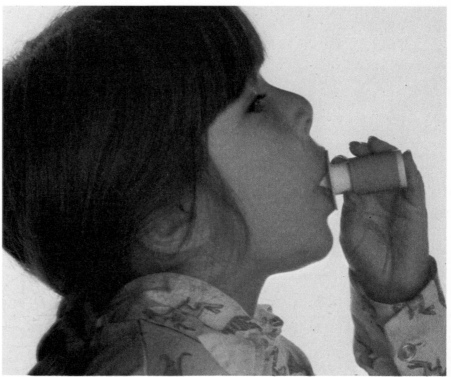

Fison's

How asthma is caused

Trachea

Bronchus

Lung

Bronchiole

Alveolar duct

Alveoli

Rib cage

Diaphragm

Tissue swollen and inflamed by edema

Terminal bronchiole

Mucus plug formed

Alveolar sac

Increased mucus production

Asthma is caused by excessive fluids in the tissue increasing mucus and plugging the bronchiole (top), or the smooth muscle contracting because of agitation or extra histamine.

Smooth muscle nerve

Terminal bronchiole

Alveolar sac

Mucus

Smooth muscle contraction

Histamine in excessive release from mast cells

Venner Artists

the lung tissues from the action of histamine and acetylcholine.

Causes

Asthma is brought on by a number of different causes, ranging from breathing polluted air to emotional upset, which makes it a rather complex problem to treat. However, since all the causes of asthma trigger the release of either histamine or acetylcholine, it is important to understand these two chemical reactions in order to see why people are asthmatic.

Histamin release is one of the most common causes of asthma, and the process which brings it about is rather remarkable considering that the substances which trigger it—dust, fur, pollen, fungal spores and others—are so varied.

Some people develop an excessive amount of antibody (a protein made by the body as part of its defence system) to some substances breathed in—these substances (some of which are listed above) are known as allergens and they cause allergic reactions. It is this malfunction of the body's defences which starts the reaction leading to asthma.

The antibody which is known as immunoglobulin E, or IgE, attaches itself to the mast cells where the histamine is stored. The next time the allergen is inhaled, each molecule (particles which make up the whole antibody) of IgE pairs up with a neighbouring molecule and, as a result of this mating, the mast cell releases its store of histamine. The bronchi then begins to contract, making it increasingly difficult to breathe: this is the condition that we call asthma.

Acetylcholine released from the nerve endings in the bronchial tubes can be caused by a number of substances which irritate both the bronchial tubes and the nerve endings. These nerve endings then send messages to the vagus with the information that they have been irritated. In response, the vagus nerve then contracts the bronchial muscles and so starts asthmatic breathing difficulties. The same sort of irritation is caused by viral or bacterial infections of the throat, which explains why asthma tends to get worse with chest infections and colds.

We also know that emotional upsets or anxiety may occasionally worsen an asthmatic condition, though how this happens is not clear.

Unknown causes

Unfortunately, there are a number of causes of asthma which are not fully understood. For certain people, asthma frequently occurs after vigorous exercise, especially running. It is probable that both histamine and the vagus nerve are involved, though, generally speaking, the more vigorous the running and the cooler the air which is breathed, the worse the asthma becomes.

Certain drinks, foods and preservatives can also produce an asthmatic response. Rather than being a straightforward allergic response, it is often the result of the body's sensitivity to certain substances. Again, the mechanism involved is still not fully understood.

Symptoms

The typical asthma attack is characterized by a sudden shortness of breath and wheezing, which is sometimes accompanied by coughing. The bringing up

How to counter asthma

Although asthmatic conditions must always be treated with drugs and according to a doctor's advice, there are some preventive measures

Infections: common cold, sinusitis, bronchitis, some viral infections
Measures: avoid people with colds; stick to balanced diet, have adequate sleep, take moderate exercise

Irritants breathed in: fumes, like tobacco smoke, paint fumes, air pollutants, cold air
Measures: avoid fumes where possible, stop smoking, keep out of cold air

Food allergens: may include milk, eggs, strawberries, fish, tomatoes
Measures: identify allergen through prick test, then avoid it

Psychological changes: stress, emotional disturbance
Measures: reduce or eliminate causes of stress; avoid emotional disturbance

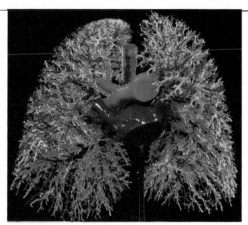

A clinical model, or cast, of the lungs.

Allergens breathed in: pollens, house dust, feathers, fungal spores, animal hair
Measures: keep house as dust-free as possible. Use foam pillows; avoid animals; use air conditioner

Trigger mechanisms: physical exertion; sudden changes in temperature
Measures: Avoid sudden physical exertion; approach exercise in relaxed manner; avoid constant temperature changes.

Drugs: can include penicillin, vaccines, anesthetics
Measures: Identify drugs that cause allergic reaction and avoid them. There are alternatives available

of phlegm is not a prominent part of the attack and if it happens, it suggests that the patient may also have bronchitis. Generally speaking, asthmatics are more prone to chest infections, and this is caused by failure to clear the lungs fully. Many patients often develop a hunched look which is brought about by the constant effort of breathing.

In many cases, the onset of asthma follows a seasonal pattern as the pollen count rises. This pattern is often accompanied by irritations to the nose and sneezing, which we usually refer to as hay fever.

Of course, allergies to house pets and dust will occur all through the year as the allergen is constantly in the air. Food allergies will likewise appear if the victim eats a food to which he or she is allergic.

Treatment
The treatment given for asthma largely depends on the type of asthma and the severity of the attacks, but it is broadly divided into two: emergency treatment for severe attacks, requiring an emergency house call by your physician or admission to the hospital, and everyday self-medication to prevent an attack from occurring, which is known as prophylactic, or preventive, treatment and can be carried out at home.

The aim of emergency treatment is to bring relief as rapidly as possible and so one of the three drugs is given by injection: adrenalin, aminophylline and hydro-cortisone, and these have an almost instantaneous effect. The first two act directly on the bronchial muscles, raising the enzyme level and so relaxing the muscles. The third is a steroid, and although it acts quickly to relieve the attack, how it works is not known. In very severe cases, oxygen may also be given to the patient.

Most asthmatics take some form of daily treatment, usually in the form of tablets or inhalers. the doctor will decide which type of drug is the most suitable after first diagnosing the cause of the asthma. To do this the prick test is used. This determines whether the asthma is a result of an allergic reaction and what the body is allergic to. A number of possible allergens are introduced into the body through the skin. If the body reacts to any of these and produces a red welt, then the person is allergic to that particular allergen. A doctor may also measure the patient's breathing rate and capacity using a flow meter. This indicates just how much he or she is affected by the allergen.

Once the doctor has identified the most likely cause of the asthma he will prescribe the appropriate treatment. Wherever possible the allergen should be avoided. Drugs like cromolyn—taken by inhalation—may be prescribed to decrease the release of histamine. Or a bronchodilator, such as isoproterenol, taken either as tablets or inhaled, will give rapid relief from the effects of a sudden asthma attack, though not all people will react to the drug with the same speed.

For those who suffer from a more persistent and severe form of asthma, doctors may prescribe steroid drugs. Because of the side effects of this type of drug, patients will be asked to stick rigidly to the doctor's recommended dosage, and to make sure that they always have the drug with them in case of an attack. The treatment should always be continued, as failure to keep up with the treatment could very easily encourage a further attack.

Prevention and outlook
Most asthmatics will have their condition worsened or even triggered off by everyday substances, and once the cause is identified, the only course is to avoid it by, for instance, keeping the house as clear of dust as possible, avoiding gasoline fumes and tobacco smoke, and also sudden exertion and emotional stress. There are, of course, many other irritants, but these are some of the more common ones that can make an asthmatic condition much worse.

However, it is difficult to be specific as what affects one asthmatic may actually have a beneficial effect on another. But it is accepted that regular, controlled exercise rather than sudden exertion does have a beneficial effect, and all asthmatics should be encouraged to take as much regular—but strictly controlled—exercise as they can manage at any one time.

Although there is no absolute cure—50 percent of child sufferers tend to grow out of the complaint during adolescence—asthmatics should be encouraged by the news that current research is producing positive results.

Athlete's foot

Q I have suffered from athlete's foot for some time now, and have just discovered a similar sort of irritation on my hands. Is it possible for athlete's foot to spread to other parts of the body?

A The athlete's foot fungus belongs to a group of fungi known as Trichophytons and these can live on various parts of the body. But they are not very contagious and so are unlikely to spread. However, there is a condition similar to athlete's foot that can affect the hands, and this should be diagnosed and treated by the doctor.

Q My daughter has athlete's foot. Can this spread to the rest of the family?

A Not if precautions are taken, the most important being hygiene; everyone should carefully wash and dry his or her own feet—with a personal towel—and use an antifungal powder on feet and shoes.

Q I have a severe form of athlete's foot that keeps recurring. Is there any chance that the condition will leave my feet scarred or deformed?

A Thankfully, the fungus causing athlete's foot lives only on the superficial layers of the skin, eating dead skin cells. For this reason, there will be no scarring, but in chronic cases the nails may become affected and need specialist treatment with drugs. With correct treatment of skin and nails, the foot should return to normal.

Q I have grown weary of trying to get rid of athlete's foot. But every time I think it is has gone for good, it makes a comeback. Is there a reason for this?

A The most common reason for re-infection is that the fungus has never been properly eradicated in the first place. For this reason it is important to dust your shoes and socks as well as your feet with antifungal powder as they can carry the fungus. It is also important to keep up the medical treatment for a considerable time after the symptoms have disappeared.

Athlete's foot is annoying and unpleasant, but usually responds well to treatment—and can be prevented.

Athlete's foot is a troublesome fungal infection and probably the most common foot complaint that doctors treat. It can affect almost everyone, though small children do appear to be immune. And you do not need to be athletic to catch it, in spite of its name.

Causes
The only real cause of athlete's foot is a failure to observe the necessary personal hygiene, along with carelessness in drying the feet after a bath. Those people who suffer from sweaty feet are particularly prone to this complaint and the situation can be aggravated by wearing airless synthetic leather shoes which prevent the feet from breathing.

It is the moist, sweaty areas between the toes that provide the soggy skin on which the fungus likes to settle. The fungus then lives on the skin, digesting the dead skin that the body sheds each day. Once the fungus starts eating the dead skin, it may then cause inflammation and damage to the living skin.

There is a small risk of picking up athlete's foot in bathrooms and in public dressing rooms.

Symptoms and treatment
The first sign of athlete's foot is irritation and itching between the toes followed by the skin beginning to peel. The infected areas, which can appear on the heels, soles and sides of the feet as well, are pinkish with silver-white scaly patches.

It can eventually cause cracking, blistering and bleeding of the skin and can be accompanied by bad foot odor.

In worse cases, painful red cracks known as fissures, appear between the toes, and in the odd severe case, the toe nails become either soft or more brittle as the fungus invades the nail substance. It may be possible to see the nail thickening beneath its outer shell. In extreme cases the foot swells and blisters—requiring prompt attention from the doctor.

The itching is usually much worse in hot weather, or if the sufferer is wearing shoes and socks that fit badly. If the blisters are scratched and opened, secondary infection can develop.

Modern antifungal creams and powders are successful in the treatment of athlete's foot. Substances such as clotrimazole and tolnafate are extremely effective as creams or ointments, and need to be applied daily while the condition lasts, and for two or three weeks after the symptoms have disappeared to prevent its recurrence.

If the infection is severe and the nails have been affected, a drug known as griseofulvin may be prescribed by the doctor to be taken orally. It is effective within a few weeks. It is then necessary to dust the feet, socks and shoes with antifungal powder to prevent re-infection.

Athlete's foot can be treated at home but if the problem begins to spread or refuses to respond to treatment, consult your physician.

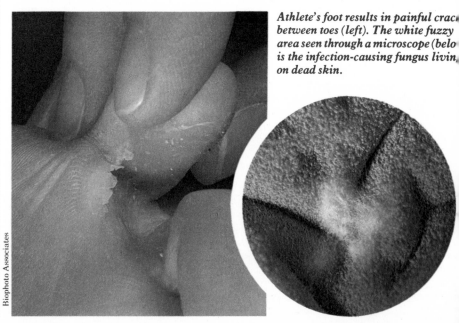

Athlete's foot results in painful cracks between toes (left). The white fuzzy area seen through a microscope (below) is the infection-causing fungus living on dead skin.

Biophoto Associates

Back and backache

Q I want to buy a bicycle to reduce my fares to and from work. Will cycling be bad for my back?

A No, because your body weight will be supported and balanced by two bone girdles that keep you square, straight and trim—the shoulders and the hips. In fact, cycling is very good for the back because the continual movement keeps the back supple and well exercised. However, it is very important that you adjust the handlebars and saddle to suit your height and the proportion of your limbs for comfort and to reduce the possibility of strain on the back. If you intend to buy a sports bike, you should perhaps lower the handlebars slightly for long journeys.

Q I am towards the end of my first pregnancy and am getting terrible backache. Why is this and what can I do to reduce the pain?

A Backache is a problem in late pregnancy and is caused by the weight of the foetus pulling the lumbar region forward, so causing the natural curve of the spine in to the waist to become exaggerated. This puts a strain on the sacrum bones in the back which causes the pain you feel. Ease it by being more conscious of your posture and rest every afternoon in bed.

Back pain in early pregnancy is usually due to the womb being tipped back and it should stop at around three months. If it persists after the first post-natal visit at six weeks, check with your doctor.

Q My daughter of 14 insists on wearing stiletto shoes. I am trying to dissuade her by warning her that they may hurt her feet. But will they also be bad for her back?

A Yes, they will. Stilettos—or any high heels—will alter your daughter's body balance and change her weight-bearing axis. It will tilt the lower spine, carrying her weight forwards. This will cause excess pressure on the lower part of the lumbar region, causing pain and accelerated ageing especially of the knee joints.

Most of us suffer from backache or back pain at some time in our lives. Exercise and treatment can help, but prevention is always better than cure.

However distressing back pain may be, it will usually get better on its own. In fact, 90 per cent of sufferers recover within a month of any attack.

The back

Ever since human beings stood upright they have been having trouble with their backs. This is why people gain such relief from getting down on all fours—we were just not designed to stand on two feet with our backs straight.

The natural position exaggerates the curvature of the spine at the waist, and this reduces pressure on the back. Standing, especially for long periods of time, provides little relief, and when combined with poor posture and uncoordinated or erratic movements, a considerable strain can be imposed on the back area, and the main structure that supports it, the spine.

Automatically, the back is the area of the trunk that runs from the base of the neck to the base of the spine—a column of bones known collectively as the 'vertebrae'.

Apart from the neck, the spine is made up of 12 thoracic vertebrae at the back of the chest, five much larger bones in the lumbar region (in and below the curvature of the waist) · and five fused vertebrae, called the sacrum, that form a triangular bone at the back of the pelvis. At the very base of the spine is the coccyx, five small vertebrae that are all that remains of the tail, a hangover from our evolutionary past.

At each end of our spinal column is a ring or girdle of bones that provides support for the limbs. At the top, the pectoral girdle, to which our arms are attached, consists of the collar bone and

Bones in the back

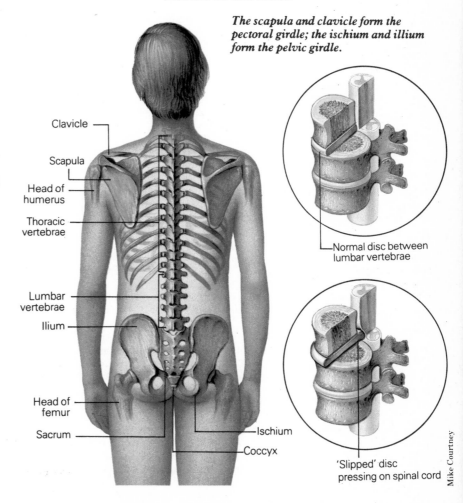

The scapula and clavicle form the pectoral girdle; the ischium and illium form the pelvic girdle.

Clavicle

Scapula

Head of humerus

Thoracic vertebrae

Lumbar vertebrae

Ilium

Head of femur

Sacrum

Ischium

Coccyx

Normal disc between lumbar vertebrae

'Slipped' disc pressing on spinal cord

Mike Courtney

Types of back pain and their causes

Condition	Causes
Related to the spine	
Lumbago—strained muscles or ligaments	Repetitive bending and lifting; bad posture—standing or sitting; twisting of spine while lifting or moving; moving; obesity; fatigue; lack of fitness; history of injury
Slipped disc (or discs)	Same as above; accidents (car, falling, etc.); excessive physical activity
Degenerative disc disease	Ageing; childbearing; housework; heavy physical work over a long period of time
Ankylosing spondylitis (form of arthritis)	Hereditary; sometimes unknown
Osteoporosis (bone diease)	Loss of minerals in bones—calcium, phosphates etc; inadequate supply of minerals in diet
Fracture	Accident
Bone cancer	Abnormal cell division
Relating to condition in another part of the body	
Kidneys (pain in)	Injury; stones
Gall stones	Blocking of tubes that empty gall bladder
Shingles	Virus infection that travels along nerves
Muscle abscess	Tuberculosis of spine
Gynaecological disorders —low back pain —burning sensation during menstruation	Prolapse of womb (protrudes into vagina) Retroverted uterus (tilted blackwards)
Psychosomatic illness	Imaginary; no physical cause; due to stress, strain, anxiety

shoulder blades, together with their various muscular attachments to the spine. At the base of the vertebrae is the pelvic girdle – the pubic bones, the iliac bones (that protect the small intestine) and the sacrum (part of the spinal column).

The vertebrae that take the greatest strain of physical activity are those in the lumbar region; the thoracic vertebrae can also suffer.

Causes
Backache and back pain can be due to any number of reasons, relating either to a physical defect in the spinal column, or indirectly as the result of another disease or condition in some other part of the body. It can even be psychological.

The most common form of backache is lumbago, it can occur quite suddenly or develop over hours—even days, and is caused by lifting or twisting, following injury or over-use, or it can happen for no apparent reason. The result is a tearing of the ligaments, inflammation of the joints between the vertebrae or a combination of all three.

Slipped disc
Backache is a complaint that most people can live with; a slipped disc is not. Each of the thoracic and lumbar vertebrae are cushioned against friction by a disc—a tough outer layer that contains a soft jelly-like centre. They allow for easy, comfortable movement, the discs expanding and contracting as the spine moves. If the ligaments are in a relaxed position when the vertebrae to which they are attached suffers a sudden jolt, one or more of the discs can be forced out of place.

This places pressure on the ligaments and the nerves, and pain results. Contact with the covering of the spinal column can also cause acute discomfort, aggravated further by coughing, sneezing or straining. An entire disc can slip out of place, but in being partly displaced, it can get pinched between the vertebrae on either side and rupture.

Wear and tear
These discs are also subject to a degenerative disease in later years. They can quite literally wear away, leading to great pain and disability. It rarely happens to anyone under 50, and is usually due to the general ageing process. Women tend to be the main sufferers, and the problem is caused by childbearing and housework, but men in physically arduous jobs are also potential victims.

The discs become progressively thinner, with those in the lumbar region being affected first. The condition places an increasing strain on the vertebrae and their supporting ligaments which often develop bony growths called osteophytes. These can cause a great deal of pain, and when the patient undergoes manipulation, he or she will often hear sharp cracking sounds as they break up.

Problems with bones can also cause backache and back pain. The most common of these is a condition called osteoporosis, in which the bones suffer demineralization. This means they lose calcium, phosphates and other important minerals, becoming increasingly weak and brittle. This usually occurs to a lesser extent as part of the ageing process, but it can suddenly 'take off' and accelerate. This leads to continual backache, the spine becomes increasingly bent and very occasionally the vertebrae can even crumble. A bad fall, compression of the spine in an accident and bone tumours will therefore cause bones affected by osteoporosis to fracture more easily.

Disease
Cancer of the vertebrae is rare, but it can spread to bones from other sites in the body. The disease makes a patient feel unwell, tired and run down and is confirmed by an X-ray or bone scan. Tumours usually respond well to radiotherapy which will relieve the pain and arrest further growth.

Tuberculosis of the spine, which creates abscesses on the muscles, is also a rare complaint, which can be quickly diagnosed by X-ray.

The pain from a gallstone can lead to intense pain in the back. These cause no trouble until they block the tubes that intermittently empty the gall bladder. Each time this happens, the patient will suffer pain that can last from two to three hours to several days.

Shingles can give rise to a type of pain in the back that is often confused with a slipped disc.

Q **I have a lot of back trouble and my doctor says I should wear a corset. I am afraid my mates at work will give me a terrible ribbing if they find out. Do I have to do this?**

A You don't *have* to, but if the pain is *that* bad, surely you would be willing to put up with some initial banter should your friends find out rather than continuing to suffer? They will soon forget, and anyway they should be pleased you are getting some relief at last.

Such a corset (correctly measured and fitted by a qualified practioner) will provide support for the spine while holding it in the correct position. This will immobilize it and prevent you from bending. You will find it very useful to relieve nagging pain after having rested because of acute pain.

A corset is also used to support a spine suffering from a degenerative disc disease, where the spine has developed curvatures. In both cases, however, it is vital that the spine, though immobilized, does not lose its muscular strength. Extension exercises will prevent the muscles weakening and wasting away.

Q **My granny is always moaning that her back trouble is due to her weak spine. She supposes that this is hereditary. Could this be true and could she have avoided the problem getting worse as she became older?**

A No, back pain is not usually hereditary. There are one or two disorders of the spine from birth which run in families but these are very rare. Most of them are obvious deformities or can be quickly diagnosed using X-rays.

There is no way of avoiding the chemical process of ageing during which the cartilage of the discs becomes brittle and dry. However, your granny could have damaged her spine and made it worse by lifting badly, poor posture and so on. Has she seen a doctor?

Q **Can a chill cause backache?**

A Yes. Cold may cause muscles to stiffen and become inflamed especially after exercise has made you sweat. Take a hot bath and get a good night's sleep.

Other causes

One form of back pain common to women is caused by prolapse of the womb, which usually occurs during the last three months of pregnancy. If it happens earlier, this could mean that the womb is 'lying back' (in a retroverted position), but 20 per cent of women have a retroverted uterus which rarely gives trouble or ever requires treatment.

Psychosomatic back pain means that no physical cause can be found. It is usually due to a patient being in a state of stress, due either to problems at home or at work. It may be short term or more persistent, depending on the underlying causes and the treatment given.

Symptoms

Lumbago is often difficult to pin down physically. Usually pain is located in the lumbar region but it can spread to the buttocks and thighs. Sometimes there is a history of injury (car crash victims, for example), or excessive use (labourers and gardeners) preceding the pain, which is made worse by bending, straightening or any side-to-side movement. It can also prove difficult to 'stand tall' without acute discomfort.

A slipped disc differs in that the onset of pain is usually the result of a particularly awkward movement. A patient may tell a doctor that he or she 'felt their back go', with a localized pain that may extend down one of the legs as far as the foot. This can be aggravated by bending forwards, and coughing or sneezing may send a sharp pain shooting through the back. Where a slipped disc slips straight back onto the spinal column (which is rare), pressure on the lower nerve roots may cause weakness in the legs and the inability to pass urine.

An osteopath is qualified to relieve certain types of back pain by spinal manipulation. Treatment can be obtained by referral from your own doctor.

Identifying the problem

The backache of worn discs and wear-and-tear arthritis can mimic the symptoms of a slipped disc, with characteristic intermittent bouts occuring every one or two weeks over several months.

The bone disease, osteoporosis, gives rise to various local symptoms which can be confirmed by X-ray or a bone scan, it causes a backache that leaves the patient feeling tender and sore. The bones are sensitive to pressure, there is constant pain and this can be made worse by any movement. Night pain is common and resting makes very little difference. Morning stiffness is also a symptom, just as it is of ankylosing spondylitis, a form of arthritis in which the vertebrae fuse to form a 'poker back'. The arthritic pain starts lower down, on both sides, with the spine becoming increasingly rigid as the condition worsens.

Any fracture of the vertebrae will result in a localized, unremitting pain that is intensified by movement. Bone cancer, which is fortunately very rare, is accompanied by a feeling of being generally unwell, tired and run down.

A burning sensation during menstruation usually indicates that a woman's womb is retroverted, and this can lead to pain early in the pregnancy. A low backache in the last three months is fairly normal, with the weight of the foetus increasingly placing a strain on the lumbar region.

The pain associated with gallstones is usually felt just below the right ribs at the front. It can also be felt in the back with secondary symptoms of nausea and a dislike of fatty foods. Only patience will enable a doctor to distinguish between a slipped disc and shingles. After a few days, a blistering rash will appear to confirm shingles.

Treatment

The main form of treatment for all types of moderate to severe back pain is bed rest

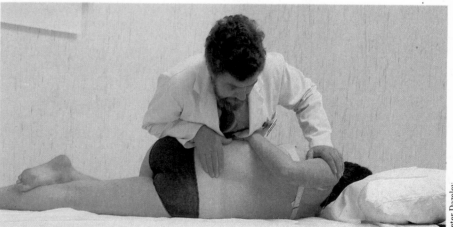

Peter Dazeley

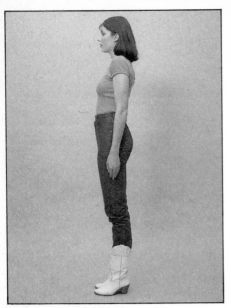

Correct standing position.

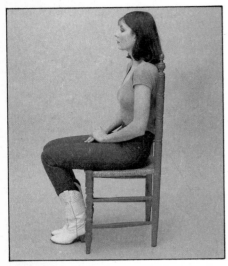

The right way to sit.

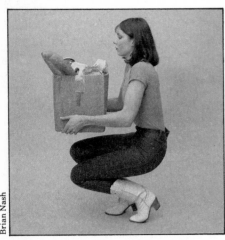

How to avoid backstrain when lifting heavy objects.

Brian Nash

in combination with painkilling drugs. Most cases will settle on their own if bed rest is adhered to. The patient should not get up for meals or to go to the toilet: the use of a bottle and bed pan will avoid this.

If the patient is not immobilized, the natural healing process will be slowed; what the back needs at this stage is total relief, with a consequent easing of strain on torn muscles and strained ligaments or discs, as the case may be.

The sufferer should lie and sleep on as firm a surface as possible. A board can be placed over a mattress; an alternative is to take to the floor. In some cases, such as lumbago, relief can be gained by bending the knees or lying on the side, with a cushion in the small of the back. Make the body comfortable and then keep still.

Persistent pain

If pain persists, take paracetamol, or something stronger if this does not work. Occasionally a muscle will go into spasm, resulting in a hot throbbing pain. This can be helped by administering a muscle relaxant, available by prescription only.

A doctor diagnoses the causes of back pain by a process of elimination. Strained muscles will improve within one or two days; torn muscles and ligaments take up to a week and a slipped disc at least two to get better. The only exception is the mild to intermittent pain of degenerative disease. In this case, shorter periods of rest are most helpful, with activity helping to maintain muscle tone and keep bones healthy.

Most people will seek advice on the onset of backpain, especially if it persists after a couple of days. If there is no improvement after two weeks, a doctor's help must be sought. Hospitalization will be advised so that tests can be run and bed rest monitored. The back may be manipulated, as in the case of osteoporosis, or the spine may be immobilized completely with traction. Alternatively, in the case of a fracture, a surgical corset or plaster cast is worn by the patient once he or she is back on their feet after two to six weeks.

For severe pain radiating to the leg, a spinal injection may be given to relieve pain and reduce swollen tissues. If this fails to help, a myleogram will be performed. A dye is injected into the spinal column under a local anaesthetic and then the back is X-rayed to reveal the damage and decide whether surgery is necessary.

Prevention

The likelihood of a slipped disc recurring will increase each time it happens, and the very fact that it has happened once should signal a warning to the patient that his or her lifestyle or habits should be altered to avoid any recurrence. For example, a teenager who has slipped a disc playing a sport or dancing too energetically should curtail those activities in the future: in the same way, a gardener with lumbago should hand over the job to someone else and find a more sedentary pursuit. The trouble is that people have short memories, and once they have recovered they choose to forget and resume the bad habits that bought about the problem in the first place.

Backache can be avoided by following some simple preventative measures. If you have to bend repeatedly, make sure you bend your knees to reduce strain on the spine. Then 'think tall'. Avoid slouching; ensure that all working surfaces are at a comfortable height; and only sit on chairs that have a good supporting back. A firm bed will be best for the spine at night.

If you have to twist while lifting—even if it is your own body weight—make each movement in two separate stages. If you have to shovel sand, lift some onto the spade, then turn and deposit it elsewhere; and in getting out of a low car, first twist your body and place your feet on the curb, then stand up.

Keep your weight down; this will reduce strain on the back and aid posture. Finally, do not get overtired or unfit as this can also lead to bad posture.

If, despite all these measures, you still suffer back pain, take care once you have recovered. Always eat at a table, never slouch in a chair in front of the fire or TV. Climb all stairs with a straight back and avoid lifting or bending. Only drive short distances, at least to begin with.

It is not a good idea to embark on a heavy keep-fit programme; follow a series of exercises recommended by your doctor to help you recover your strength. Walking will do you good, so will swimming. And use the opportunity *not* to walk the dog, carry heavy shopping or push a pram.

Outlook

Research work and planning is well under way on furniture design. The field of 'wear-and-tear' arthritis is also yielding evidence for possible treatment of back pain in the future.

In the meantime, medical rehabilitation centres are available at the request of a specialist to maximize recovery and fitness and assess whether the patient can return to work or needs retraining.

There are no miracle cures for backache or back pain. Consult experienced manipulators, osteopaths and trained physiotherapists only on the advice and under the control of your own doctor.

Daily exercises to avoid backache

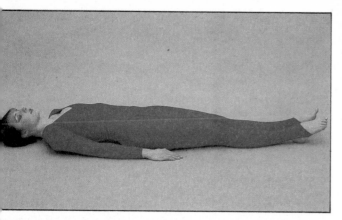

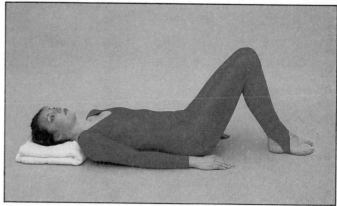

Lie flat on your back, legs straight, arms at sides. Slowly raise one knee at a time towards chest. Repeat 10 times.

Lie with head supported on folded towel, knees bent, feet flat on ground. Gently raise and lower your bottom. Repeat 10 times.

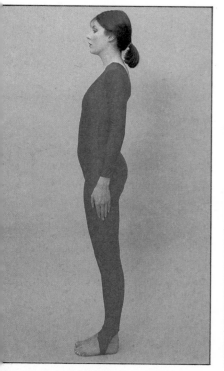

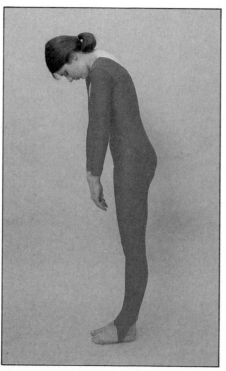

Stand upright with arms loosely by your sides and shoulders back.

Bend slightly from waist, letting head and arms fall forwards.

Continue movement by reaching gently towards your toes 10 times.

Bandages

Q Will it matter if I get my bandage wet?

A A bandage covering a recent wound or one where there is discharge from the skin should not be allowed to get wet, as germs could be washed through to the inner dressing. In most other circumstances, it does not matter. The bandage will be uncomfortable to wear and may become loose as it dries, however, so wet bandages are best replaced with dry ones.

Q Can bandages be washed and re-used? If so, how should they be washed?

A Heavily stained or infected bandages should be burnt, but most others can be washed either by hand or by using a medium wash in the machine.

Crêpe and other elasticated bandages can be washed four or five times before they lose their grip, although if they are in constant use they rarely last for much longer than one month.

The calico triangular bandages used by people trained in first aid will also need a light ironing, and these bandages may be laundered almost indefinitely.

Q Is it possible for bandages ever to irritate the skin or cause allergies?

A Allergy to cloth bandages is extremely rare. If a bandage appears to cause irritation or a rash, it is probably caused by the detergent in which it has been washed. The heavy elasticated bandages often used to treat severe leg ulcers do contain rubber, however, and could possibly be a source of allergy.

Q I'm afraid that in a real emergency I might completely forget how to do a bandage properly. Do you have any tips?

A The main thing is not to panic. It doesn't matter if you don't get the bandage exactly right, for it can always be redone properly later. What is important in most cases is to stop the bleeding—by bandaging firmly or at least pressing on the wound.

Bandaging is that vital part of first aid that is required in so many emergencies. But there are several different kinds of bandage, and it is essential to know which kind to choose and exactly how to use it for a particular purpose.

Each type of bandage can be used in a number of ways. Some of the uses a bandage might be put to include:
● holding a dressing in position over a wound and adding to the protection provided by the dressing
● preventing movement to restrain use of an injured part
● providing direct pressure to stop or control bleeding
● providing additional support to strengthen a weakened joint, for example a knee joint after it has been injured.

● applying pressure to reduce swelling
● holding a splint in position
● assisting in the carrying of an injured person.

Types of bandage
Bandages can be made from any cloth-like substance, including calico, linen, cotton, muslin, crêpe, flannel and even paper. They are available in a variety of sizes and shapes and designed to be employed for a wide range of uses.

The triangular bandage is made by cutting a square of linen or calico into two triangles with sides at least a metre (39 in) long. Although using it requires

A sling is a hanging bandage used to provide support for an injured limb. In an emergency improvise one from a scarf.

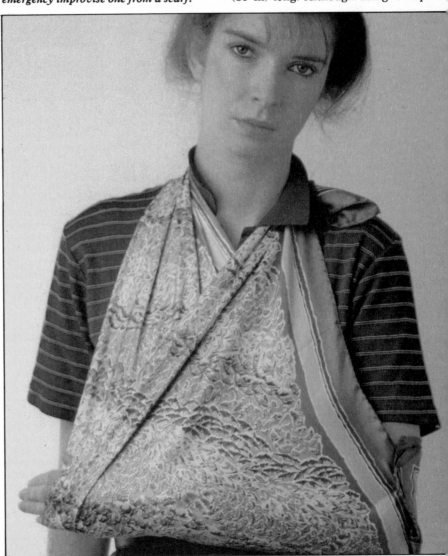

skill and it can sometimes be difficult to knot safely, the triangular bandage is ideal for the first-aider because it can be used in so many ways. As a whole cloth, it can hold on a large dressing or be made into a sling. It can also be folded to make either a broad or a narrow bandage. And, when it is folded into a ring pad, it forms an excellent pressure pad which is useful for either controlling bleeding or protecting the painful area around the site of a broken or fractured bone from being accidentally knocked.

The roller bandage is a roll of rigid, open-weave cloth such as cotton, muslin, crêpe, flannel or special paper. It is inexpensive and comes in various widths for different parts of the body. The roller bandage is non-elastic and is therefore safe to apply since it can only rarely be fixed too tightly. This type of bandage can be difficult to apply, however, because it does not mould firmly to the contours of the body in the same way as elasticated bandages do. More skill is required in applying it well.

The basic technique of applying it is to use the left hand firmly but gently to support and guide the injured part of the body while the right hand holds the bandage, letting it out to cover the limb It should be applied securely, with each turn covering about two-thirds of the previous turn.

The crêpe bandage is probably the most popular bandage of all. Woven to have elastic strength, it clings firmly to uneven body surfaces and provides a measure of firm support. It can be used in almost every circumstance, and very little skill is required to apply it correctly. If this kind of bandage is fixed too tightly, however, it could potentially be very dangerous, because it has enough strength to cut off the blood supply in the limb.

The tubular bandage is a long tube of gauze that is applied in layers to a finger or a limb using a special applicator. The size of the applicator will vary according to the particular part of the body for which it is designed to be used.

How to secure them

Bandages must be applied firmly to be effective. But any bandage that is applied too tightly may cut off the blood circulation and thereby lead to permanent damage of an area or possibly encourage the development of gangrene if the tightness is maintained.

A simple test for good circulation in a bandaged limb is to press on any nail, which immediately blanches. When released, the blood should return within two seconds, making the nail appear

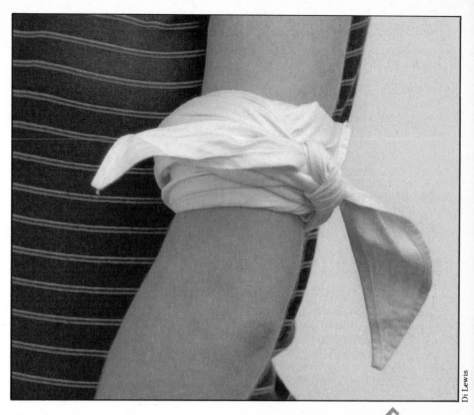

A bandage that is too tight cuts off circulation producing swelling and pain. The limb loses its pulse, becomes numb or tingling and shows a whitish tinge.

naturally pink again.

Bandages can be fixed in a variety of ways. If you secure them by tying a knot, it is best for you to use a reef knot. Since this is flat, it will not rub the injured part of the body which is under the bandage, which would only cause irritation, a sense of bulkiness and even more pain for the patient.

Small safety pins are ideal for fixing elasticated bandages and should be passed through the two outermost layers of the fabric.

Adhesive tape is often sufficient to hold bandages that won't be subject to a lot of wear and scuffing. If a bandage is likely to be rubbed so much that it could work loose, a small elastic bandage clip can be used.

When not to bandage

Never use a bandage to completely cover an area that requires regular observation.

When a limb is broken or a person is seriously injured and an ambulance has been called, it is best to leave the job of bandaging the victim to the ambulance staff or a doctor. Concentrate all your efforts on comforting the patient and seeing that he or she is settled as easily as they can be in spite of their injuries.

FIRST AID

Using a tubular gauze bandage

Applying to the finger

1 Cut off sufficient length of tubular bandage from the pack and load it on to the applicator. Slip the applicator over the injured finger then slip off the starting end of the bandage, holding it at the base of the finger if needed.
2 Withdraw the applicator, letting the bandage slip off the end. When clear of the finger, twist the applicator one half turn.
3 Push another layer of bandage down in the same fashion and repeat the process, providing as many layers as desired. Finally fix the bandage at the base of the finger with a ring of adhesive tape.

Using a triangular bandage

Making a broad or narrow bandage
1 Lay the triangular bandage on a flat surface with the point away from you.
2 To form a BROAD bandage, bring the point down to meet the middle of the base then fold again one more time. To make a NARROW bandage, fold the broad bandage once again. Smooth down any creases and fold lengthwise for easy storage.

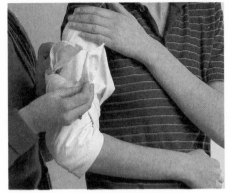

Making an elbow bandage
1 With the elbow bent, place the point of the bandage on the outer part of the upper arm with the base across the underside of the forearm. Cross the ends in front of the elbow, bring them back around the arm and tie above the joint. Finally, bring the flap formed by the point back over the knot and fasten with a safety pin.

Making a hand bandage
1 Place the flat of the hand down on the bandage and bring the point of the bandage over toward the base.
2 Take the ends of the bandage and cross them around the wrist. Tie a reef knot over the point lying on the back of the wrist.

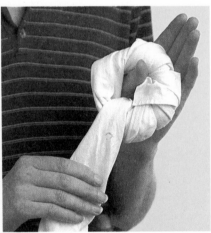

Making a ring pad
1 First make a narrow bandage and pass it loosely around the fingers of the left hand. Hold the circle which you have formed and slip the bandage end through the loop.
2 Keep wrapping the loose end through the loop until it is all used and a tight ring has been made.

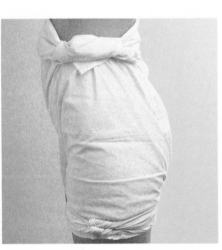

Making a hip bandage
1 Use the two triangular bandages for this. First make a narrow bandage and place it around the waist like a belt, tying the reef knot on the injured side. Now place the point of the second triangular bandage under the knot and fold a hem along the base of the second bandage.
2 Holding the two ends of the hemmed base, take them around the thigh and buttock to the outer side, tying with a reef knot. Finally bring the point of the bandage down and secure the bandage with a safety pin.

Making a shoulder bandage
1 First fold a one inch hem along the base of a triangular bandage. Position it on the arm so that the point of the bandage reaches the level of the ear.
2 Take the hem around the arm and cross the ends over. Bring them back to the outside and tie with a reef knot. Finally, apply an arm sling, securing the point of the bandage to the sling with a safety pin.

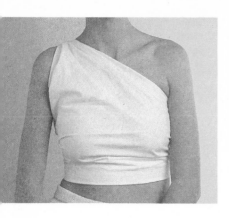

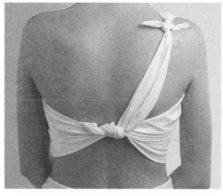

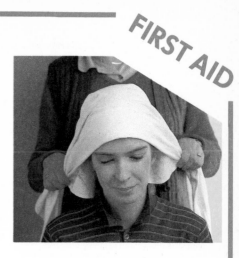

Making a chest bandage

1 Place the bandage over the front of the chest so that the point passes over one shoulder and the base lies across the chest.

2 Bring the two ends of the base around to the back and tie together. Now bring the long end up to meet the point and secure it by tying a reef knot at the shoulder.

Making a head bandage

1 Holding both ends of the triangular bandage, fold a one inch hem along that side. Place this hem on the forehead just above the eyebrows, letting the point drop over the back of the head.
2 Bring the ends around behind the head, crossing them firmly at the nape of the neck. Bring the ends forward again and tie with a reef knot over the forehead. Finally bring the point up over the crossed ends and pin to the bandage on the top of the head.

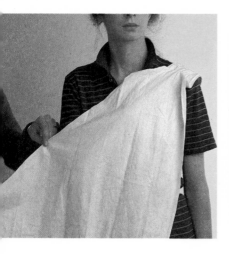

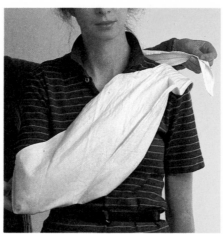

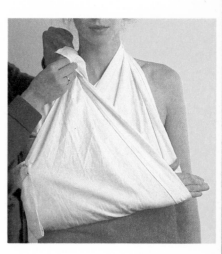

Making a triangular sling

1 The triangular sling is ideal for supporting an injured hand or forearm comfortably in a well-raised position. Place the injured arm or hand across the chest at the level of the opposite shoulder and support it gently. Then place the open triangular bandage over the injured arm with the point about 6 to 9 inches higher than the uninjured shoulder.

2 Gently ease the base area of the bandage underneath the injured arm, bringing the other end around the back and up in front of the uninjured shoulder.
3 Tie a reef knot in the hollow under the collar-bone and tuck the end of the bandage neatly in between the loose folds at the elbow. Secure the bandage with a safety pin.

Making a simple arm sling

1 The arm sling carries the weight of an injured arm and is the simplest sling to make. Place the injured arm at a level where the hand is just higher than the elbow. Pass an open triangular bandage between the chest and the arm, taking the point over the shoulder on the un-injured side.
2 Bring the lower end of the bandage up over the forearm to meet the point, and tie a knot over the natural hollow just above the collar-bone. Pin the loose end of the bandage at the elbow.

Q Is there any rule about how long you can leave a bandage on before you have to change it for a fresh one?

A Bandages need changing when they become stained with discharge, dirty from general use or loose from wear and movement. Elasticated bandages compressing the limb beneath stretch quickly and need to be changed and re-applied daily. Roller bandages covering a dressing need only be changed when the dressing itself has to be replaced. But this will vary according to the instructions of the doctor or nurse, and in some cases patients are asked to leave bandages completely alone, no matter how soiled or dirty-looking they may become.

Q How will I be able to tell if a bandage has become too tight as the result of swelling in the area over which it's been placed?

A Most injuries cause some degree of swelling as part of the healing process, and for this reason elasticated bandages are the safest ones to use.

If a bandage feels too tight, there is swelling above and below it and the area below it is painful, numb, blue or white, then the bandage could well be blocking off the circulation and doing more harm than good to the patient.

Loosening the bandage will produce an immediate relief of symptoms, but if you are at all in doubt, ask a doctor's advice immediately.

Q What can be used to make improvised bandages in an emergency?

A Almost any material can be cut or torn to make a bandage. Cotton from skirts and dresses is ideal. Even ties, scarves and belts can make good bandages, and tights or stockings have sufficient stretch in them to act as elasticated bandages and provide extra compression. Remember that the bandage is only there to hold the dressing firmly in place, so providing the dressing covering the injured area is clean, the bandage itself need not be completely sterile.

Using a roller bandage

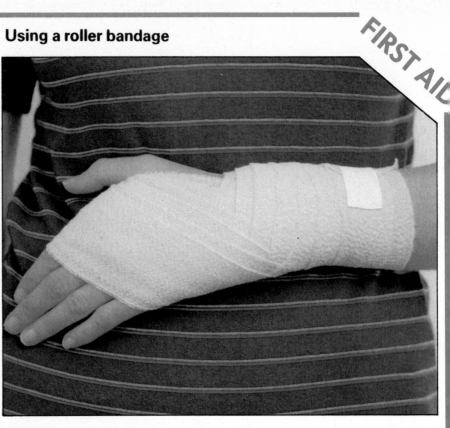

Applying to the hand
Using a 5 cm (2 in) wide bandage and starting from the wrist, make one turn, securing the starting end underneath. Pass the bandage over the back of the hand, round the little finger and across the palm, leaving the thumb free. Finally, bring the roll back to the wrist to finish off with a straight turn.

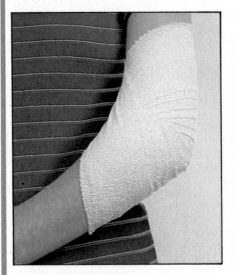

Applying to the elbow
1 With the elbow in a comfortable position, place the loose end of the bandage over the elbow crease and take the first turn right around the joint itself.
2 Make further turns above and below the original turns in a figure-of-eight until the bandage covers sufficient area of the elbow.

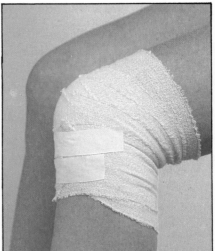

Applying to the knee
The technique is similar to bandaging the elbow. Make sure the knee is in a comfortable position. Starting at the back, take one straight turn over the joint, then bandage in a figure-of-eight above and below, finishing above the knee.

Bites and stings

Q Is it all right if I take an aspirin for pain relief after being stung by a wasp?

A Aspirin won't do any harm but local remedies such as a soothing ointment would probably relieve the pain better. The pain should soon subside.

Q How can I tell the difference between a bee and a wasp sting?

A The best method is to find the insect itself, which is quite likely to have died after stinging in self-defence. If this is impossible, remember that a wound with a sting remaining inside it is more likely to be a bee sting. If you have no idea whether the insect was a bee, a wasp, or indeed anything else, it is a good idea to apply a cold compress followed by antihistamine cream. If you are in real discomfort see your doctor.

Q My son was bitten by a dog. Should I take him to a doctor?

A In the UK and other countries without rabies, animal bites should be seen by a doctor if the skin is broken. The doctor may give a tetanus injection. With a severe cut stitches may be needed. However, if the skin is unbroken after a bite, cleaning the skin and applying soothing ointment are all that is necessary so long as no swelling or other symptoms of infection develop. In countries where rabies exists, medical help for animal bites should be sought immediately.

Q When I was on holiday last year, a mosquito bite on my arm swelled into a big lump. Does this mean that I am allergic to mosquitos?

A It may mean that the bite you had became infected and healed by itself, or it may mean that a mild allergy reaction occurred. If you use an antihistamine cream it will help to counteract such a reaction. Where a swelling becomes larger than expected following a bite or sting, it is a good idea to see your doctor. Infections can be dangerous, and allergies can get worse as time passes, and may require special care.

Basic first aid is usually all that is necessary to treat most bites and stings, but you must be able to recognize the occasions when medical help is urgently needed.

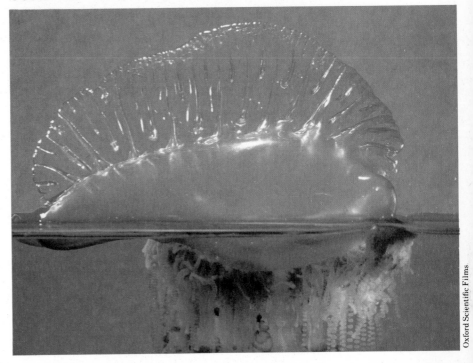

Oxford Scientific Films

The Portuguese Man of War jellyfish gives a serious sting. Get medical help.

Many insects, some plants and some marine creatures can sting. Many animals, some reptiles and insects can bite. In some countries poisonous insects are dangerous.

Deaths from such bites or stings are rare, but prompt action is important. The sufferer should be taken immediately to the nearest hospital or poison control centre along with the dead insect if possible, or at least a good description of it as this will help the doctor.

If you go abroad you should obtain information about harmful pests before setting out. You must not neglect innoculations and other precautions.

Keeping pests away

The greatest risk of being bitten or stung comes from insects such as bees or hornets, parasites such as mosquitos or fleas, and creatures you may meet on holiday, such as venom-secreting snails and jellyfish. Keep unwanted insect visitors out, both by general cleanliness and by killing them on sight.

During hot, damp weather, when insects breed most rapidly, a hanging insecticide will kill winged insects for several months.

In the garden, a stagnant pond will attract mosquitos—so site your pond at the furthest end of the garden. When picnicking or sitting on the grass, always put down a groundsheet, and avoid eating sweet, sticky foods which attract wasps. On holiday learn to recognize stinging jellyfish and poisonous snails.

Don't sit too close to flower beds where bees gather. Never approach a swarm of bees, wasps or hornets—call in an expert if a swarm approaches your house.

A common source of stings are insects living in gardening clothes or shoes normally kept outside. Shake gardening clothes and boots before putting them on in case there is anything there.

Domestic pets

Dogs kept as pets should be obedience trained to reduce the risk of their biting people. Don't touch other people's pets until they have had a chance to get to know you, and you them.

Teach your children to treat all animals with caution, respect and kindness, and don't let them use household pets like toys. Mauled kittens, puppies and even hampsters can turn into potentially dangerous biters through misuse.

Take special care when dealing with dogs bred for guarding purposes, such as alsations (German shepherds), Dobermann pinschers and bull terriers. Your children should be told not to go near.

Common bites and stings

Take care

Any bite or sting can lead to infection, so you must always clean the wound thoroughly. Warm water and soap is the best cleanser. If possible the soap should not contain a detergent, perfume or similar irritants.

After cleaning, the wound should be rinsed in clear water. If you have an antiseptic, it can then be applied.

Remember to check the bottle for the correct dilutions of TCP, Dettol or similar substances.

Cover the clean wound with a dry, sterile dressing or a laundered handkerchief. If there is increased pain and inflammation over the next day or two this shows that infection has set in, and you must see your doctor.

First aid essentials

- Pair of fine tweezers
- Tube of antihistamine cream (such as Anthisan)
- Insect-repellent cream or spray
- Antiseptic cream (such as Savlon)
- Antiseptic liquid (such as TCP)
- Packet of assorted-size needles to remove stings (sterilize in boiling water before use)
- Anti-flea powder (safe for use with pets or children)
- Antiseptic wet wipes for cleansing in the absence of soap and water
- Small packet of bicarbonate of soda (or baking soda)
- Small bottle of vinegar (or a plastic lemon)
- Large gauze dressing
- Roll of bandage
- Assorted non-waterproof plasters
- Calamine lotion
- Aspirin
- Freshly laundered white handkerchief

Source	Prevention	First aid	Later treatment
Jelly fish	Do not bathe in waters known to be frequented by jelly fish.	Get victim to shore and pick off pieces of jelly fish with sandy hands. Cleanse the area stung, and apply antihistamine cream.	Seek medical help, especially for the sting of Portuguese Man of War.
Nettles	Teach children to recognize and avoid nettles.	The sting is acid, so bicarbonate of soda paste or weak ammonia will ease the pain. If unavailable, use water or cool leaves.	Soothe residual soreness with calamine lotion.
Dog bites	Avoid strange dogs especially abroad, and train your own not to snap in play.	Wash and dress the wound and see your doctor if the skin is broken.	Stitches or anti-tetanus injection may be given in the UK. Serum treatment elsewhere.
Lice	Keep clean and do not lend or borrow combs or hats.	For head lice, crop hair short, use recommended emulsion followed by shampoo. For body lice, boil linen and take daily hot baths followed by clean clothes treated with recommended powder.	Continue treatment until all lice and nits (eggs) have vanished.
Mosquitos	Wrap up after dark. Avoid stagnant water. Burn a mosquito coil by the bed. Apply insect repellent.	Apply antihistamine cream, or surgical spirit; cologne or cold water will do if these are not available. Repeat as necessary.	Avoid scratching. Take antihistamine tablets if swelling is severe.
Ants	Do not sit on uncovered grass or disturb ants' nests. Wear an insect-repellent.	Treat them with bicarbonate of soda paste or dilute ammonia.	None is usually necessary.
Ticks	Do not sit on grass used normally by sheep or cattle. Keep dogs and cats free of ticks.	If the tick is embedded in the skin use petroleum jelly, oil, alcohol or petrol to loosen its grip and remove it with tweezers. Kill harvest mite ticks first with weak ammonia.	Soothe tick bites with calamine lotion.
Fleas	Keep dogs and cats free of fleas and keep them home.	Treat bites with calamine or antihistamine cream. Badly affected children should see a doctor.	Use a suitable powder on animals, clothes, bedding and cushions.

Problem bites and stings

Bee sting

If you are stung by a bee you will notice that the puncture area is surrounded by a blanched area of skin and then a reddish area which is usually swollen into a bump. You can often see the black sting embedded in the centre. You should scrape this away or gently ease it out with tweezers, taking care not to squeeze the poison sac.

A bee sting has acid venom. Once you have removed the sting and cleaned the wound you can treat the area with a paste of bicarbonate of soda or dilute ammonia. If you haven't got these, use surgical spirit or a cold compress.

Bee stings can cause severe pain and are among the most dangerous of stings likely in temperate climates. Young children, old people or those who are allergy-prone are particularly vulnerable to unpleasant results from them.

The sufferer should rest during treatment and you should be on the lookout for signs of shock. If there are multiple bee stings, call your doctor immediately. Stings in the mouth may prevent proper breathing. Give the patient a mouthwash of one teaspoon bicarbonate of soda to a tumbler of water, followed by ice to suck. Then take him (or her) to hospital. Take the dead bee along if you can find it.

Wasp stings

If you are stung by a wasp, the puncture may or may not contain a black sting. If the sting can be seen it should be carefully taken out with tweezers, a sterilized needle or clean fingernails. Don't squeeze as this might push the venom further into the skin. The surrounding area will be bleached, then reddened and probably swollen as in a bee sting.

Wasp stings contain alkali venom. After cleansing, you should dress the wound with vinegar or lemon juice, as the acid content neutralizes the venom. Avoid rubbing the skin.

If you have no vinegar or lemon juice, an antihistamine cream can be used until you can get some. Then the wound can be washed and dressed again. If the swelling is severe add a cold compress.

If there are multiple wasp stings and the person is shocked, you must call your doctor or get the patient to hospital. Put him on his side and give ice to suck in the meantime.

With a single wasp sting, the sufferer should feel better after an hour or so.

Snake bites

The adder, which is common in Europe, is a species of viper, and may be grey, yellow or reddish brown, about 30 inches long. It has a broad head and black zig-zag markings on its back. Its bite is rarely fatal. Following the bite the wounded part is painful and swollen and may appear inflamed or bruised.

If you get bitten keep calm and try to rest. Take a painkiller such as aspirin and do not move around. Treat the bitten limb as if fractured. Wash it with soap and water and remove any venom you can see. Cover the wound with a clean dressing and get your doctor's help.

Snake bites are so much feared that reassurance is vital. Adder victims should be assured that many people recover from the bites of much more dangerous snakes.

It is no longer considered advisable to suck venom from a snake bite or to make a tourniquet. Although rare, there may be reactions such as sweating, vomiting and diarrhoea.

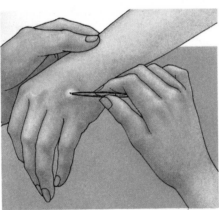

Top: scrape away a bee sting or ease it out very gently using tweezers. Bottom: dab the area with a bicarbonate of soda paste or dilute ammonia.

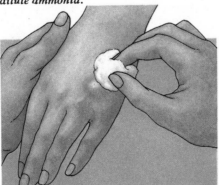

You should not be allowed to walk to hospital. If in rare cases breathing starts to fail artificial respiration will be given.

Snake bites received from unfamiliar snakes, especially when you are on holiday abroad, should receive immediate medical attention. Try to remember what the snake looked like

Sea urchin sting

Sea urchins are found in the coastal waters of Spain and other warm countries and are considered tasty to eat. However, their spikes can break off into human skin, causing intense pain and the risk of infection, so it is wise to avoid bathing where they are.

If you do step on one try to remove the spine from your skin. But don't do this without gloves. The wound should be covered with a dry dressing and a doctor seen as soon as possible.

If you fall, step on, or touch a sea urchin you will feel an acute burning pain and a numbness of the area where the spine goes in.

A doctor is necessary because of the high risk of infection from the sea urchin. The sufferer should be kept quiet and still during the journey to hospital, and measures taken for signs of shock. You need put on only a dry dressing, such as a clean handkerchief.

Shock

Shock can result from a bite or sting where there is also severe allergy, extreme pain, or deep emotional stress, such as fear. In most cases, shock victims recover well within an hour or so. But because shock can be dangerous it is important to recognize it, and to treat it correctly while waiting for the doctor.

The symptoms of shock are a pale skin, restlessness, confusion, anxiety, quickened pulse and rapid breathing. The victim may complain of thirst and may vomit, or even lose consciousness.

The treatment is to lay the victim on his (or her) side and staunch any bleeding for bleeding makes shock worse. You should loosen clothing and put a light blanket over the sick person. Do not offer any drinks and do not attempt to warm the victim, as warmth can make shock worse. Get a doctor as soon as possible to check the seriousness of the condition.

Blisters

Q I have a huge blister on my heel. Should I pop it?

A Generally it is best to leave blisters as long as possible before popping them because of the risk of infecting the underlying skin.

Some blisters less than 1.5 cm (¾ in) across will be a little more comfortable if the fluid is drained with a sterile pin or needle, but unless these blisters are uncomfortable, they should be left protected by a small plaster

All large blisters need medical attention.

Q My son is about to start a job on a construction site. How can he avoid blistering his hands?

A In the two weeks before he starts work, the skin can be hardened by an application of weak rubbing alcohol.

Once at work, the only protection is wearing gloves that fit well. When he handles tools, the secret is to grip the implement firmly. A loose grip allows more 'play' between skin and handle, producing more heat and friction causing a blister.

Q My father, who is 60, keeps developing large blisters on his arms and wherever he scratches himself. Why?

A These blisters are definitely not ordinary friction blisters, but are more likely due to a skin condition called pemphigoid. It is not serious, but will require quick attention with steroid drugs to prevent it from spreading.

The same symptom in a younger person could herald the beginning of the serious skin disease pemphigus, for which immediate medical attention should be given.

Q My teenage daughter always buys shoes that blister her feet. Can she prevent this?

A Often the cause of blistered feet is shoes which are either badly fitted or badly designed. Sometimes, however, the shoes merely need to be 'broken in'. Tell your daughter that she should be sure the shoes fit before she leaves the store: it is possible to buy reasonably priced shoes that look good and fit well.

Blisters can be extremely painful, but if they are left alone, most will heal by themselves. Should one become infected, or be the symptom of another illness, medical treatment of the blister is needed.

The skin has two layers. The outer one, called the epidermis, consists of layers of dead skin cells and contains no nerve cells or blood vessels. The deeper one, the dermis, contains both vessels and nerves. When fluid collects between the two layers, a blister is formed. A small, well defined build-up of fluid is called a vesicle; larger ones, often up to 7.5 cm (3 in) across, are known as bullae.

Causes

Blisters can be caused in a variety of ways. The most common blister is caused by friction and heat, and in response to the heat, a blister is formed. New shoes can rub areas of tender skin, and walking long distances will often raise blisters. A person not used to manual work who suddenly has to shovel snow can get blisters within thirty minutes of beginning work, while someone accustomed to manual labor who has thickened skin can work for many hours without any trouble.

All types of burns, including severe sunburn, can raise blisters. The heat and damage to the deep layer of the skin causes an almost immediate outflow of fluid from the capillaries, which forms blisters under the skin. Sunburn blisters tend to be small and numerous; the skin will peel a few days later.

In response to acute inflammation, tiny blisters may sometimes form around the site of an insect bite or a jellyfish sting. In more severe cases, large blisters may form, or they may become infected.

Another common cause of blisters is the inflammation produced by viruses. Chickenpox in children, and shingles in adults, are caused by the same virus. Shingle blisters are usually confined to one area of the body and may be painful. Medical attention should be sought.

Chickenpox blisters are far more widespread, covering the trunk and back and, in severe cases, the scalp, the inside of the mouth, ears and genitals, and may cause intense itching. During healing, both types of blisters burst: scabs are then formed which eventually fall off.

This child's chicken pox blisters will eventually burst and form scabs.

Richard and Sally Greenhill

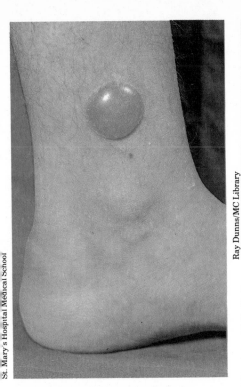

Scratching an itching blister like this insect bite can cause infection.

The virus which causes smallpox, another blister-producing condition, is no longer active in any part of the world.

The herpes simplex virus, which in some people lives within the deep layer of skin, produces a blister that is known as a cold sore. These appear on the lips or side of the mouth after a cold. If the cold is severe, or the skin is exposed to excess sunlight, the virus will multiply and crops of blisters will form.

Bacterial infections can also produce blisters. In impetigo, the bacteria breed quickly in the deep layer of the skin. Small blisters will form, usually on the hands, legs or face: these soon burst and form crusty yellow-brown scabs.

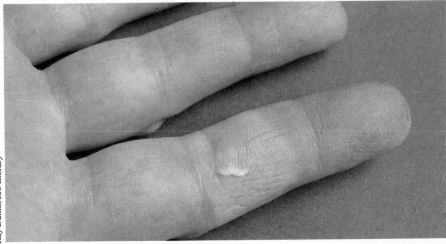

Blisters which result from skin conditions such as allergic eczema or chemical irritation will appear without any rubbing or burning. Medical treatment should be sought.

Two other conditions produce blisters. Pemphigoid causes blistering on the forearms of elderly people. They are rarely harmful, but do need treatment.

Pemphigus occurs in younger people. It arises because the layers of the skin lose the ability to stay together: the cause of this breakdown of adherence is unknown. Blisters can spread over the whole body, causing severe fluid loss and illness and the condition requires urgent treatment.

Symptoms

The common friction blister causes feelings of heat and pain, and by the time these symptoms have been noticed a blister will have formed. If a blister arises from a direct burn, the blister appears a few minutes after the accident.

Blisters from stings and bites arise more slowly, and cause itching and a swelling of the surrounding skin. Chickenpox begins as small dark red pimples, which within a few hours turn

This blister is beginning to heal after being covered with a protective bandage.

into blisters which look like droplets of water. Where there are multiple blisters with no symptoms, the cause is more likely to be eczema; with large blisters, pemphigoid or pemphigus may be the cause, particularly if the blisters arise painlessly and with little or no itching.

Treatment

Never burst a blister unless it is really painful or very large. Small blisters are usually reabsorbed but large blisters usually burst.

To treat a friction blister on, for example, the heel, cool and clean the area. If the blister is small, cover it with a plaster. If a blister has been caused by new shoes, pad the area with cotton wool.

If the blister is exposed to further friction, release some fluid with a sterile needle. Cover the blister and pad the area.

Medical treatment is taken by mouth for blisters caused by skin inflammations or other illness. Anti-viral lotions may be of help in virus infections such as shingles.

How to treat a blister

FIRST AID

First sterilize a needle to reduce the risk of infection.

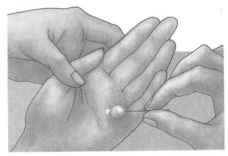

Holding the affected part of the body still, prick the blister.

Once the fluid has drained away, cover the blister with a clean dressing.

Blood poisoning

Q My husband works as a postman and while he was making deliveries very recently he was bitten by a dog. He is behaving as if it was nothing, but I am concerned that it might become worse. Is he likely to get blood poisoning from this?

A Yes, he could well do. Bites are notorious for causing infected wounds. They can introduce bacteria causing cellulitis, tetanus causing toxaemia, or an abscess that may break down to cause septicaemia. Blood poisoning is therefore a possibility, even though very unlikely. Check that your husband's immunization is up-to-date, and if the site of the wound forms an abscess or becomes red and painful, he must consult his doctor immediately.

Q Two days ago I cut my finger. But now I am becoming worried because it is discharging pus and quite painful. There is also a red swelling which seems to be spreading up my arm. What can I do about it?

A See your doctor who will probably give you a prescription for penicillin. This sounds like a clear case of a spreading infection which requires treatment with antibiotics as soon as possible.

Q The symptoms usually given for both blood poisoning and general viral infections like flu, for instance, seem to me to be very similar. How will I be able to tell the difference between them if I need to?

A It is true that it is hard to differentiate between septicaemia or toxaemia and a viral infection because the symptoms— fever, sweating, lethargy, feeling unwell and loss of appetite—are so similar. But virally-caused infections are usually less severe than those caused by bacteria. There will also be signs of the original source of the infection (skin wound, pneumonia, diarrhoea etc). A definite diagnosis is made by special tests which culture the offending bacteria from the blood, in order to identify the culprit causing the infection. The correct form of treatment can then be prescribed by the doctor.

Blood poisoning is a bacterial infection that can occur in any part of the body. How should it be treated?

Blood poisoning can occur in several ways: through a dirty wound in the skin or muscle becoming infected, the breaking down of an abscess so that bacteria are released into the bloodstream, an infection in the throat (e.g. diphtheria), the lungs (e.g. pneumonia), the gut (e.g. typhoid), or in the urinary system.

Types
There are two main types of blood poisoning, the most common of which is called septicaemia. It is not a localized infection and will spread throughout the body if not controlled. The bacteria that cause septicaemia can enter the blood in a number of ways, such as via a tooth extraction or an open wound, or internal bruising can become infected.

Normally, the white blood cells will cope by mopping up the bacteria, but if they increase to such a number that the body's natural defences are overwhelmed, septicaemia may result. This can occur in a person who is run down or debilitated by another disease, or even in a perfectly healthy individual if the disease is caused by a particularly virulent organism.

The symptoms of septicaemia include fever, shock and prostration together with a sudden lowering of blood pressure. A patient will feel extremely unwell, may lapse into coma and death can follow.

Sometimes the body may successfully confine an infection but this will not stop the bacteria releasing chemical poisons, called toxins, into the bloodstream. These cause a condition which is medically known as toxaemia.

There are two types of toxins. One is made by the bacteria and then excreted to cause separate side-effects to those of the original infection. These toxins produce specific symptoms such as the paralysis of tetanus. Secondly, toxins may be formed naturally inside the bacterial cells, which are then released into the blood stream after the destruction of the bacteria by either white cells or antibiotics.

A patient with toxaemia will feel unwell and feverish. He or she will often complain about unpleasant after effects of taking antibiotics, but these are caused by the release of the toxins, rather than the drugs themselves.

Some bacteria can break down the tissues beneath the skin, enabling bacteria to spread under the surface. This is called cellulitis and appears as a painful spreading red halo around an infected wound or abscess.

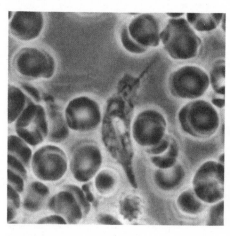

White cells (lymphocytes) defend the body by engulfing invading bacteria.

Treatment
The mainstay of all treatment for bacterial infections are antibiotics. These are usually effective in quelling infection.

If septicaemia is suspected, a specimen of blood will be cultured in a laboratory and sensitivity to antibiotics noted.

Toxaemia is more difficult to treat. Bacteria can be killed by antibiotics, but their toxins need to be neutralized with specific anti-toxins. These are available for tetanus, diphtheria and snake bites (another toxaemia). But because there can be serious reaction, they must be used with great care.

Instead, preventive medicine is practised wherever possible, and immunization is offered to every infant in its first few years against tetanus and diphtheria. Boosters against tetanus are then repeated at intervals as necessary.

Cellulitis responds well to antibiotics, with penicillin proving effective.

Dangers and outlook
Septicaemia can place a great load on the body's defences, and some people are more vulnerable to its effect than others. Diabetics, alcoholics, drug addicts, cancer victims (particularly those taking drugs), and patients taking steroid drugs, are all easy prey to bacterial infection. So too are the elderly and the undernourished.

Toxaemia can cause specific damage, such as in diphtheria where the heart can be affected. But providing adequate medical support is available, a previously healthy person can usually be helped through the danger period. In only a few unfortunate cases is tetanus still a killer.

Blood pressure

Blood pressure problems affect many people and are a major cause of ill health. But regular check-ups can detect warning signs and treatment does not usually interfere with a person's normal life.

When blood pressure is raised, a person is said to have 'high blood pressure', or hypertension, and if this is not treated, the chances of disease—or even death—are increased. In fact, the major causes of death in the Western world today are diseases of the heart and blood vessels. Blood pressure is therefore not just a sympton but an urgent early warning signal.

Causes

The trouble starts within the arteries themselves, the thick-walled vessels that carry blood from the heart to the tissues of the body. The blood is driven by the main pumping chamber of the heart, the left ventricle, and a great deal of force is required to send the blood out of the heart and into the arteries, through the tissues, and then back into the heart again to be re-delivered to the arteries. Therefore, even under ideal conditions, the walls of the arteries are continually under considerable stress.

The level of arterial pressure is of great importance. If the pressure within the system is raised for any reason—a con-

dition called hypertension—this stress is increased and paves the way for the development of arteriosclerosis, a narrowing of the arteries, due to the degeneration of the middle coat of the artery walls. The heart and the arteries can be severely strained and damaged by the blood pounding through with a quite unnatural force.

On the other hand, seriously low blood pressure, or hypotension, is not a common problem and is usually the result of shock from a heart attack, acute infection, or blood loss following an accident. Very occasionally it may occur in people suffering from Addison's disease—a failure of the adrenal glands—which is extremely rare and can be corrected by drug treatment.

Because the maintenance of an adequate blood pressure is so important, very sophisticated mechanisms have evolved in the body to stabilize it. In the West, the level of general stress has, however, led to many people developing a level of

Blood pressure can be tested quickly and easily at your doctor's.

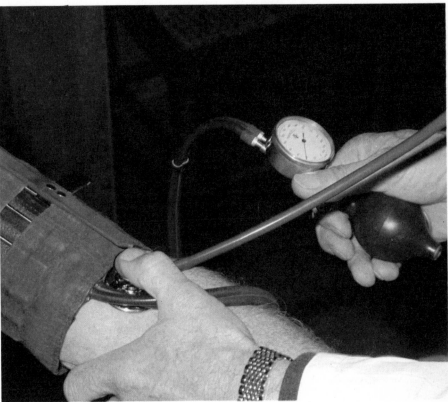

John Watney

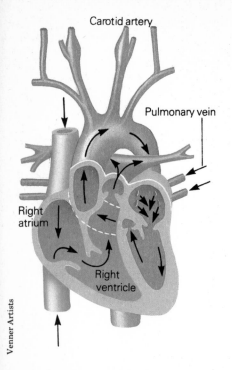

Venner Artists

The minimum (diastolic) pressure is taken when the heart has filled with blood from the head, arms, lungs and body and is fully distended.

blood pressure that is far too high for the continuing good health of the arterial system. When this is not the result of disease elsewhere this is called essential hypertension. The major long-term effect of high blood presure is on the arteries of the brain, the heart and the kidneys with the eventual likelihood of strokes or heart attacks.

What is normal?

The maximum pressure of each heartbeat, or systole, is called the systolic pressure, and the minimum pressure is called the diastolic pressure. It is these two pressures which are measured in order to determine a person's level of blood pressure. Obviously, some figure has to be adopted as 'normal'. For young and middle-aged adults, a pressure of 120 (systolic) over 80 (diastolic)—written as 120/80—is considered normal, 140/90 is cause for concern, while one of 160/95 is definitely high and requires treatment.

The difficulty of accurately measuring blood pressure is increased by the fact that it rises with age. This is not the case in primitive communities that are untouched by the industrial way of life. Such people enjoy stable blood pressure throughout their lives; in fact, in some cases it even tends to go down with increasing age.

Blood pressure starts to rise when people adopt a more 'developed' way of life. But why does the behaviour of blood

pressure change in this way? Currently, the popular answer to this question is that it is caused by stress, and there is considerable evidence that it is involved. The comparison between the degree of stress suffered by air traffic controllers compared with pilots, is a well-known example of this. The 'stressed' controllers had a significantly higher average pressure than the less stressed pilots.

The influence of diet

There is a significant difference in the

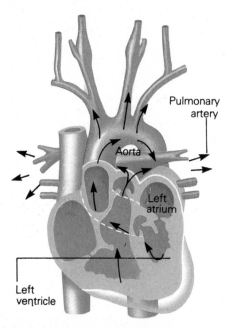

The maximum (systolic) pressure is measured when the heart is pushing the blood out into the body and lungs via the pulmonary artery and the aorta, and they are fully distended.

type of food that is eaten by developed communities as compared to primitive people. The amount of salt consumed is particularly important, since it has been found that salt tends to increase the volume of blood in the circulation and put blood pressure up. But although the average level of blood pressure in various groups has been found to tally with their average salt intake, it has been impossible to prove conclusively that a higher salt intake necessarily means a higher blood pressure. However, it is accepted that both salt intake and stress are among the factors that combine to produce essential hypertension.

Control of hypertension

Whatever the causes may be, the tendency to essential hypertension is definitely connected with some kind of overactivity of the normal control

mechanisms of the body.

There is an area in the lower part of the brain, called the vasomotor centre, which controls blood circulation and hence the blood pressure. The blood vessels which are responsible for controlling the situation are called arterioles and lie between the small arteries and the capillaries in the blood circuit. The vasomotor centre receives information about the level of your blood pressure from pressure-sensitive nerves in the aorta (the main artery of the body) and the carotid arteries (to the head), and then sends out instructions to the arterioles through the sympathetic nervous system.

In addition to this fast-acting nervous control, there is also a slower-acting control operating from the kidneys, which are very sensitive to blood flow. When this fails, they release a hormone called renin, which in turn produces a substance called angiotensin. This has two effects: firstly, it constricts the arterioles and raises the blood pressure; secondly, it causes the adrenal gland to release a hormone called aldosterone, which makes the kidneys retain salt and causes the blood pressure to rise.

This interaction of the pressure and salt-control systems is an important clue to the cause of essential hypertension, particularly since fluid-excreting tablets, called diuretics (known as 'water tablets') are widely used as part of the treatment of high blood pressure.

Diagnosis

Raised blood pressure may be the result of a number of conditions apart from essential hypertension. Many kidney diseases cause high blood pressure. Therefore, when a person is suspected of having this problem, their kidneys are usually checked. This is easily done in most cases with a single blood and urine test. Only occasionally is it necessary for the person to have a kidney X-ray. Much information can also be gained from the patient as well.

The blood test measures the urea in the blood—this is likely to be raised if there are kidney defects. The blood level of various salts (sodium, potassium and bicarbonate) gives clues to other secondary causes of blood pressure. The urine is screened for the presence of protein, which also occurs in chronic kidney infection or disease.

Many doctors will also perform a cardiogram and chest X-ray, to see if the raised blood pressure has affected the heart in any way.

If the kidneys are found to be functioning abnormally, it is possible that the raised blood pressure could be the result of renal (kidney) disease. On the other

How the kidneys control blood pressure

Kidneys secrete renin which produces angiotensin when pressure is low, constricting arteries and raising pressure. Simul- *taneously, adrenal glands produce aldosterone, causing salt retention which also raises pressure and stops renin production.*

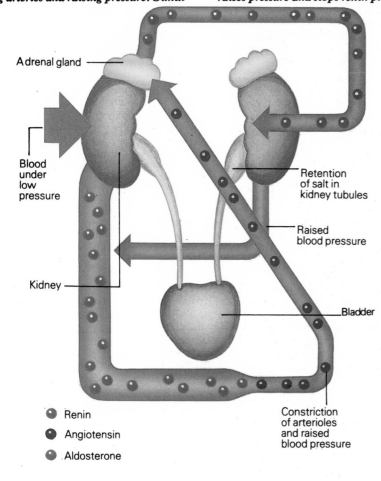

Adrenal gland

Blood
under
low
pressure

Kidney

Retention
of salt in
kidney tubules

Raised
blood pressure

Bladder

● Renin

● Angiotensin

● Aldosterone

Constriction
of arterioles
and raised
blood pressure

Apart from cases of malignant hypertension, symptoms of high blood pressure are not always definite. People may complain of headaches, but this does not necessarily mean you have hypertension. Dizziness and nose bleeds are also common. But the best guide to the state of your blood pressure is to have it checked regularly, every year or two.

Treatment

It has been shown that treatment dramatically improves the prospects of survivial for both young and middle-aged people, suffering from hypertension. But since no drug is without side-effects, doctors must consider very carefully at what point their use is justified. This is particularly difficult with the elderly patient who is much more prone to suffer from the side-effects of drugs.

There are three main types of drugs which are used to treat high blood pressure: diuretics—which cause salt-loss from the kidneys; 'beta-blockers', which lower blood pressure and get their name from their effect of blocking the action of adrenalin; and vaso dilators, which dilate the blood vessels.

Many other 'second-line' drugs are used for people, such as asthmatics or the elderly, who cannot tolerate the 'beta-blockers'.

Outlook

If high blood pressure is treated, the chances of a stroke are very greatly reduced and the risks of having a heart attack are also lowered. This is why it is so important for people to take the drugs they have been prescribed—even when feeling perfectly fit.

hand, the raised blood pressure can itself cause deterioration in the kidneys. This happens because continuing high blood pressure particularly affects the arterioles, causing their walls to thicken. This obstructs the flow of blood and has an adverse effect on kidney function. Sometimes it may be impossible for the doctor to distinguish between cause and effect. A vicious circle may be set up that maintains and even accelerates a raised blood pressure.

Essential hypertension accounts for 90 per cent or more of people with high blood pressure. Most of the remainder have kidney disease, leaving a few with abnormalities of hormone secretion such as an over production of cortisone or adrenalin. Another condition that may cause high blood pressure is excessive secretion of aldosterone by the adrenal gland. Fortunately, all these forms of high blood pressure will respond to treatment.

Symptoms

Sometimes, by the time that people feel it is necessary to see their doctor, their blood pressure is already very high indeed. They may already have blackouts, a minor stroke, and symptoms such as swollen ankles, or shortness of breath. This situation is particularly likely in malignant or accelerated hypertension and is fatal if left untreated.

The brain disturbances here are due to an increase in the pressures operating inside the skull and pressing on the brain. This can be detected by examining the eye with a strong light and if there is undue pressure, the central nerve at the back of the eye will look inflamed. Examination of the eye will also provide the doctor with other useful information. For example, small arteries at the back of the eye, which are the only ones which can be seen without an operation, will also show definite signs of hypertension.

Self-help with high blood pressure

● try and reduce the amount of stress in your life. Much of this is due to worry, frustration and disappointment. It may not be easy, but if you can deal with the problems that are causing stress, you can lower your blood pressure

● cut out smoking—the nicotine in cigarettes is rapidly absorbed into the bloodstream and is known to increase blood pressure

● keep your weight down—if you are overweight you are making a lot of extra work for your circulatory system—blood pressure can fall within weeks of excess weight being shed.

● take some kind of regular exercise. Jogging or yoga is excellent, both for reducing stress and at the same time being good for your body whatever sport you fancy

Breasts

Q My daughter is only ten but her breasts are already quite well developed. Isn't this unusual at her age?

A No, perfectly normal—your daughter has just begun her sexual development rather earlier than average. It is important that you don't let her become embarrassed about her body at this time when it is undergoing so many changes. It may help her self-confidence to take her out to choose some pretty light support bras. Remember, too, that girls now mature a lot earlier than they did 40 years ago. Your daughter's friends will soon be catching her up, if they haven't done so already.

Q I'm very embarrassed because my breasts are so large. Is there anything that can be done about them?

A This is just something you will have to put up with, for doctors are reluctant to recommend surgery to remove breast tissue unless the problem of breast size is causing a severe psychological disturbance. If you are above average weight, try going on a diet which may help you to lose some of the excess fat in your breasts. In the meantime it might help to choose clothes that flatter your figure rather than overemphasizing your shape, and wear a well-fitting bra.

Q My son is 15 and seems to be developing small breasts. He's very slim so it's certainly not just fat. Is this serious? What can I do about it?

A Some boys do develop breast-like swellings during puberty which are not the result of overweight, but are due to the increased levels of sex hormones in their blood. The swellings, which may feel very tender and are a cause for extreme embarrassment in any boy, usually disappear quite naturally in 12 to 18 months. However, it might be wise to take him to see your doctor; this problem deserves medical attention in case it is a symptom of a more serious abnormality, or needs surgical treatment.

Every woman should understand her body in order to stay healthy—the breasts are very important and regular self-examination is essential to ensure that all is well.

Most people think of the budding of the breasts, which begins before the start of the menstrual periods, as the first sign that a girl is on the road from childhood into womanhood. In fact, the breasts appear in rudimentary form in both boys and girls long before birth, and within a few days a baby of either sex may produce a few drops of colostrum, a clear but nutritious fluid that used to be called 'witch milk', from the nipples as a result of the action of the mother's hormones.

Development
At the start of sexual development, and stimulated by the pituitary gland at the base of the brain, a girl's ovaries begin to release large amounts of the hormone oestrogen. This hormone travels in the bloodstream to the breast area and triggers the enlargement of the nipples. It also encourages the growth of the channels or lactiferous ducts through which milk can be released, and the depositing of fat between and around them.

The completion of breast development, which takes about 18 months from the first appearance of small swellings on the chest, depends on another sex hormone, progesterone; this is produced monthly during the menstrual cycle. Under the influence of progesterone the ends of the ducts swell out into lobes, each composed of many smaller lobes (called lobules) containing glands that lactate; this means they can produce milk. Meanwhile the continued release of oestrogen by the ovaries results in more fat developing between the lobules.

The mature breast is roughly hemispherical in shape with a tail-like extension towards the armpit. The slightly upward-pointing nipple contains 15 to 20 minute openings from the ducts. These are too small to be seen with the naked eye and are surrounded by a ring of rosy-coloured tissue, called the areola.

Apart from the tissues directly involved in the production and release of milk, each breast contains nerves and fibrous supporting tissue that gives it its firmness and shape. The nipple is particularly well supplied with nerves. These are important in breast feeding because it is their stimulation that causes the nipple to become erect.

What happens in pregnancy
Whether the breasts are large or small, they increase in size when a woman is

Structure of the breast

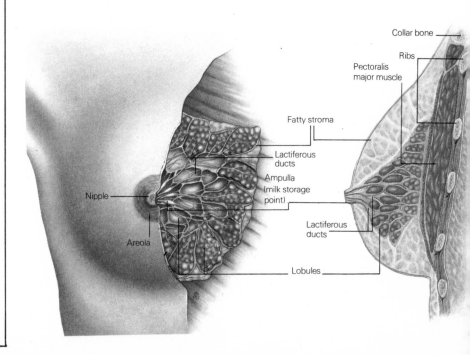

Collar bone
Ribs
Pectoralis major muscle
Fatty stroma
Lactiferous ducts
Ampulla (milk storage point)
Lactiferous ducts
Nipple
Areola
Lobules

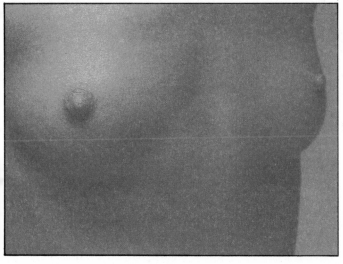
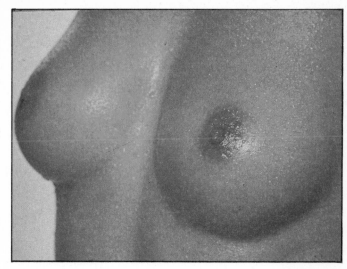

pregnant and may feel more tender than normal. During the course of pregnancy, the placenta makes enormous amounts of oestrogen which, together with other hormones from the placenta and secretions from the thyroid and other glands, causes the ducts to grow in size and form more branches. At the same time, the hormone progesterone, which is secreted by the placenta, stimulates the glandular tissue to enlarge. Sacs or alveoli lined with true milk-producing cells are formed, these produce the colostrum which flows into the ducts and out through the nipples even before birth.

At puberty large amounts of the hormone oestrogen are released which change the adolescent breast (left) to that of the mature woman. This also promotes growth of milk ducts and deposits of fat which give the breast its shape.

Large amounts of fat are also deposited in the breasts during pregnancy so that the total breast weight increases by about 1 kg (2 lb). Through the effects of hormones the areola round the nipple takes on a brownish hue.

Although they stimulate breast enlargement during pregnancy, the hormones oestrogen and progesterone, created by the placenta, are thought to suppress the secretion of milk until after the baby is born. But immediately following birth—and the loss of the placenta and its hormones—the pituitary gland in the brain begins to make the hormone prolactin which stimulates the milk-producing cells. For the first two or three days, the cells prior to releasing true milk, secrete colostrum—the thin, milky fluid that contains the protein, minerals and nutrients necessary for the baby.

Breast care

Because the breasts contain no muscle they are naturally liable to sag with age. The fibrous tissue within them becomes less elastic, and the heavier the breasts, the more likely this is to happen. This does not mean that it is essential to wear a bra, particularly if the breasts are naturally small, but many women find it more comfortable to have their breasts supported, if only lightly.

Another much more important part of the routine breast care for all women over the age of 20 is to get into the habit of making a thorough examination of each breast. This examination should be done immediately after the menstrual period when the breasts are smallest or, for women past the menopause, at monthly intervals. What you must look for are any abnormal lumps or swellings which may need medical investigation.

Changes in the breasts

Just as the breasts enlarge in pregnancy, so they become bigger and also feel tender just before a period. This is nothing to worry about; simply the body's natural reaction to the high levels of the hormone progesterone, present in the bloodstream at this point in the menstrual cycle. In fact it is a healthy sign that the sexual cycle is working normally. Because it

Breast problems

Symptoms	Possible causes	Action
Fullness and discomfort	Pre-menstrual changes, effects of the Pill, breast development at puberty	Try taking extra vitamin B but if symptoms persist see your doctor
Pain in one or both breasts, which may feel lumpy	Abnormal growth of fibrous tissue (fibroadenosis), presence of cyst or tumour	See your doctor as soon as possible
Discharge from nipple, may be yellow, greenish, blackish or bloodstained	As above or the release of pus from an abscess. Clear discharge normal in pregnancy	See your doctor as soon as possible
One or more lumps in breast	Fibroadenosis, cyst or tumour.	See your doctor at once
Inversion or puckering of nipple	May be normal, but can be a symptom of cancer	See your doctor at once
Breast very small	Probably normal but may be due to failure of hormone activity in puberty causing under-development	See your doctor. In cases of hormone abnormality, treatment with hormones is possible for women aged 20-30
One breast bigger than the other	Abnormal development during puberty	Hormone treatment not possible. Plastic surgery possible in severe cases. Wear padding in one bra cup

How to examine your breasts

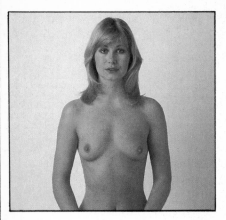

Undress to the waist and sit facing a mirror. Look for any changes in breast texture and or size.

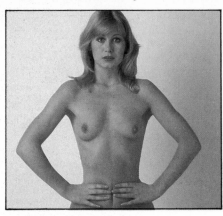

Hands on hips, shoulders back, see if nipples move up evenly or if there is a change in breast shape.

Lie down and relax. Place hand, with fingers together, gently but firmly just under the arm.

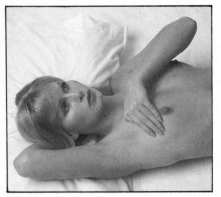

Gradually slide hand around and over breast area, moving towards the centre of the chest.

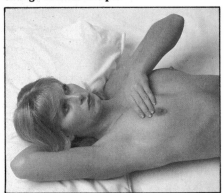

Carry on the action, passing the hand completely around the breast, feeling for any sign of lumps or abnormality.

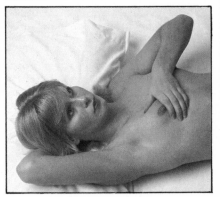

Working inward in decreasing circles, now check the nipple itself by pressing gently, again feeling for any lumps.

contains a synthetic form of progesterone, the contraceptive pill can also cause a similar type of breast enlargement.

Other changes in the breasts are a source of great anxiety to women because there is always a possibility that a lump discovered in the breast may turn out to be cancerous. For this reason alone it is always wise to report any such changes in the breasts to a doctor as soon as possible after their appearance.

The most usual sorts of lumps, however, are those due to a condition called fibroadenosis or sclerosing adenosis but still sometimes known by its old-fashioned name of chronic mastitis.

The lumps that are due to this condition can occur in women of any age from puberty onwards, but are most common towards the onset of the menopause.

What happens is that the hormones cause a thickening and growth of the fibrous tissue in the breast. Often the lumps disappear after menstruation but

they should nonetheless receive medical attention. This is because although this condition is not serious in itself and does not cause cancer, it may precede it.

As well as any thickening and growth of fibrous tissue, the hormonal ups and downs of the menstrual cycle may result in the formation of abnormal collections of fluid in the breasts. This can result in the development of rounded lumps, called cysts. Particularly common after the age of 40, they can cause pain and discomfort and sometimes there is a blood-stained discharge from the nipple.

As with other lumps, cysts need medical attention to distinguish them from cancer and may need to be surgically removed. Some cysts wax and wane with menstruation and may disappear spontaneously after a month or two.

Breast tumours
Tumours of the breast are of two kinds—benign and malignant (cancerous)—and

like other breast problems are most likely to occur after the age of 40. All tumours are the result of cells multiplying abnormally, but while benign tumours are confined in a fibrous capsule, malignant ones are free to 'wander' into other parts of the breast. And as their names suggest, benign tumours are not harmful, and certainly not potential killers, while malignant ones are.

The typical symptoms of breast cancer are a lump in the breast which is not painful and does not change in size or consistency with the menstrual cycle, a discharge from the nipple, involution (pointing inwards) of the nipple itself and dimpling of the skin on the remainder of the breast, so that it comes to resemble orange peel.

The appearance of any one of these symptoms may have a totally trivial cause, but because cancer can kill it is not worth taking even the slightest risk, so see a doctor immediately.

Bronchitis

Q I have recently developed a very chesty cough. Could it be bronchitis?

A No. To have bronchitis you must actually bring up sputum, which is then either spat out or swallowed. Chronic bronchitis is defined as a cough productive of sputum on most days of the week, for three months of the year, for more than two years.

Q I always feel a little better after coughing in the morning. As I smoke, does that mean that I am in the early stages of bronchitis?

A Heavy smokers will always tell you that they need a cigarette to 'cut the phlegm' in the morning. This is complete nonsense, and generally serves as an excuse to continue the smoking habit. Thus it is not in itself a sign of bronchitis, but smoking does contribute to the disease.

Q My uncle has difficulty in walking very far—even to the bottom of the garden. He blames this on his bronchitis. Is he right?

A Yes. Generally speaking, the worse the bronchitis, the less exercise the person can tolerate. Doctors tend to divide bronchitis into four stages: 1, a slight cough in the morning but no other trouble; 2, breathless on exertion; 3, so breathless that the patient is unable to leave the bounds of the house; 4, so breathless that the patient is unable to conduct a normal conversation.

Q Does bronchitis cause cancer?

A No. But the smoking which causes chronic bronchitis is a potent cause of cancer. If you smoke more than 20 cigarettes a day, you increase your chances of developing lung cancer 20 times, and your chances of getting chronic bronchitis 50 times.

Q If I give up smoking tomorrow, will my chronic bronchitis get better?

A The course of the disease is slowed and in some cases actually arrested by giving up smoking, but it is never reversed.

Bronchitis is a serious infection of the lungs and bronchial tubes which can become chronic. Breathing polluted air and smoking are mainly responsible.

Bronchitis is an inflammation of the main bronchial tubes—the bronchi—caused by a bacterial or viral infection. It may develop suddenly, following a head cold (acute bronchitis), or it may persist or return regularly for many years, causing progressive degeneration of the bronchi and lungs (chronic bronchitis).

Certain people are more susceptible than others; men are more so than women, outnumbering them ten to one—the reasons why are unclear. Smokers are 50 times more likely to get chronic bronchitis than non-smokers.

Causes
Generally, bronchitis occurs with greater frequency in winter, in damp, cold climates, and in heavily polluted environments. Chilling, overcrowding, fatigue and excessive smoking are contributory factors.

Most cases of acute bronchitis arise from a viral infection, which spreads to the chest. Chronic bronchitis causes irritation and coughing, which leads to the lining of the bronchi being damaged and narrowed by scarring. The lungs lose their elasticity, and the exchange of vital oxygen, which is breathed in, and waste carbon dioxide which is breathed out, is impaired. The bronchial tubes become permanently inflamed, and this results in an increased production of mucus from specialized cells in the walls of the bronchi, called goblet cells. The mucus coughed up is called sputum (phlegm).

Because it is difficult to look at the bronchi directly, doctors rely on the chief symptom, sputum production, in order to make a diagnosis. The colour of the sputum shows how serious the form of chronic bronchitis is.

Symptoms
In acute bronchitis, the initial symptoms are a head cold, running nose, fever and chills, aching muscles and possibly back pain. This is soon followed by the most obvious feature: a persistent cough. At first it is dry and racking, but later it becomes phlegmy. It is worse at night, and when the person breathes in smoke and fumes.

The main characteristic of chronic bronchitis is, again, a cough, with sputum, often occurring in paroxysms. Other symptoms depend on how much, or how little, emphysema is present. This disorder causes the lungs to become overstretched, making breathing out more difficult.

The chronic bronchitic with no emphysema tends to be overweight and have a bluish tinge to his lips due to cyanosis (a bluish colour in the blood caused by lack of oxygen). Shortness of breath only occurs during exercise. The bronchitic with a great deal of emphysema, who has lost a lot of his or her oxygen-exchanging ability, due to the condition, is short of breath at all times. Bronchitics with

How bronchitic mucus affects the respiratory system

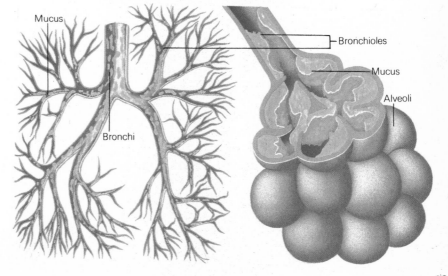

Mucus

Bronchi

Bronchioles

Mucus

Alveoli

Venner Artists

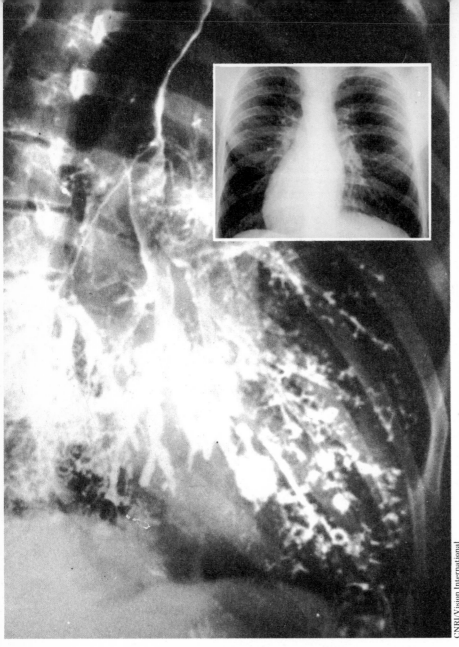

Note the grossly swollen alveoli in this lung of a chronic bronchitic. A normal, clear lung is inset (right).

emphysema tend to be underweight and, as the disease worsens, develop a barrel chest. The chronic bronchitic also wheezes because of the obstruction.

Treatment

The best treatment for acute bronchitis is bed rest in a warm room. Aspirin will reduce the fever, and cough medicines will relieve the cough. Antibiotics may be needed if the cause is bacterial.

Treatment of chronic bronchitis is more difficult. The patient's lungs are already damaged, and the obstruction of the airways is not easily reversible.

Bronchial dilator drugs may be given to relieve any such obstruction, while physiotherapy will help the patient get rid of any sputum. Postural drainage can also be tried: the patient lies on a bed, a large cushion raising the groin, and smaller pillows supporting the chest. Tapping the chest in this position causes the patient to cough up sputum. Yoga, and breathing exercises generally, may assist shortness of breath. In severe cases, urgent hospital treatment may be required. Oxygen might have to be given through the course of the illness.

However, the best form of relief is to try to remove as many bronchial irritants as possible. The patient should stop smoking immediately: although chronic bronchitis cannot be reversed, it can be arrested. Chronic bronchitics should try to avoid environments where there are irritants as these can bring on attacks.

Outlook

With acute bronchitis, the fever may last as long as five days, and the coughing for weeks afterwards, but if the patient receives treatment and takes sensible precautions the illness will simply run its course and outlook is good.

Chronic bronchitis is far more serious. It is a degenerative disease, particularly when combined with emphysema, and can result in death due to respiratory failure when there is insufficient oxygen in the blood.

One of the most important complications due to this problem is carbon dioxide narcosis (stupor), together with increasing breathlessness, ankle swelling, and even heart failure.

Treatment must therefore commence as soon as possible, beginning with giving up smoking. Frequent acute attacks only worsen chronic bronchitis, and make it harder to deal with. For these reasons, preventive steps must also be taken to stem the progress of chronic bronchitis.

Types of bronchitis

	Symptoms	Treatment
Acute bronchitis		
Bacteria or virus infection, often following a cold Smoking	Head cold, running nose, fever and chills, aching muscles Persistent cough: initially dry and racking, later loose and producing sputum	Bed rest in warm atmosphere; aspirin; cough medicine; fluids; antibiotics Stop smoking
Chronic bronchitis		
Persistent irritation of the bronchial tubes; bacterial infection; irritation to damaged bronchial tubes and lungs. Smoking; wet, cold climates; pollution, low resistance and fatigue	Sputum, cough; wheezing Bronchitis with emphysema: shortness of breath, weight loss, barrel chest Bronchitis without emphysema: shortness of breath, when exercising; weight gain; bluish tinge to lips	Stop smoking. Bronchial dilator drugs; physiotherapy of chest; postural drainage; yoga and breathing exercises; antibiotics. Severe cases may require hospitalization. Avoid bronchial irritants

Burns

Q My mother always believed in putting butter or olive oil on to a burn she got whilst cooking. Are these any good as burn dressings?

A No, in fact she was doing more harm than good. Both oil and butter act as 'food' for bacteria, which can develop and so increase the risk of infecting the burn. For the same reason, you should never apply ointments in first aid for burns; use clean dry dressings on their own instead.

Q How do I know when a burn is serious enough to call a doctor or to need hospital attention?

A If in any doubt, seek medical help immediately. This is especially vital for any of the following burns: on the face or genitals or over a joint; in the mouth or throat; if larger than 20 sq cm (3 sq in) or wet and oozing; if caused by electricity or if pain continues in spite of first aid; if on someone very young or old.

Q I read recently that it is not a good idea to drive a burn victim to hospital yourself. Wouldn't this save time?

A Not if you were stopped by the police on the way—remember, you do not have the same traffic priority as an ambulance. Besides your patient may need to be lying down and could vomit or collapse as you drive, when you couldn't do anything to help.

Q I am going on holiday soon. If I get sunburnt, should I see a doctor?

A If it is severe, or combined with sunstroke, then the answer is 'yes'. You should take special care to get acclimatized gradually if you are fair-skinned and unused to strong sunlight. By the way, you don't say whether you are going to a hot climate, or somewhere cold, so remember that you can even get sunburned in ice and snow on a mountain top, caused by the reflected ultra violet radiation from the sun. So take care in all situations in which you are exposed to strong sunlight.

The best way to deal with burns is to prevent them. But if an accident does happen, knowing what to do could mean the difference between life and death.

Countless people die or are severely injured every day through burns. Though it is generally assumed that the main cause is fire, burns can also result through touching hot objects, or be caused by scalding, harsh friction, electric shock or accidental contact with corrosive chemicals. The tragedy is even greater if you consider the ages of the victims. Understandably, the very old have the poorest chance of recovery from severe burns, but the young are also vulnerable, especially toddlers who do not understand the dangers involved in playing with fire.

Lesser burns

A burn is classified medically according to the depth that it reaches in the skin. There are three types: these are usually referred to as 'first', 'second' or 'third' degree burns. In the first group, also termed superficial partial-thickness burns, the epidermis (outer layer) of the skin is destroyed and the dermis (thicker underlying tissues) may also be affected. But the hair follicles, sweat glands and basic structure remain to form a basis for the growth of healthy new skin. The slighter burns that happen in the kitchen or from sunburn all fall into this category. The pain will stop within a couple of days and the skin will soon recover. Sometimes a blister is formed; this protects the underlying wound from infection and should not be pricked. All the affected part needs is to be covered with a clean dry dressing and allowed to heal.

More serious burns

In the second group of deep, partial thickness burns, all but the deepest cells, hair follicles and glands is destroyed. With this type of burn, healing is a slow process and the new skin that is produced is

Skin depths of 1st, 2nd and 3rd degree burns

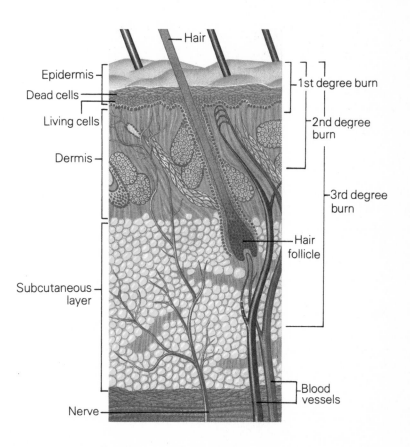

Epidermis
Dead cells
Living cells
Dermis
Subcutaneous layer
Nerve

Hair
1st degree burn
2nd degree burn
3rd degree burn
Hair follicle
Blood vessels

Venner Artists

Treating burns

The first treatment for every burn is to cool it off. For scalds, remove any clothing that has become hot from boiling fluid, fat or steam. If the clothing has already cooled, however, do not remove it.

A chemical burn can be nasty, so quickly remove any soaked clothing without touching the chemical yourself. Immediately wash away the chemical by flooding with water for ten minutes.

An electrical burn requires quick action. Do not touch the victim until you have switched off the current. If this is impossible, break the contact by standing on something dry and pushing the victim away with a wooden chair.

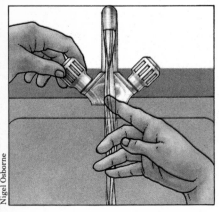

Always begin by cooling the burn. Major damage can be done by the heat from a burn penetrating deep into the body, and the application of cold water will help reduce this effect. A small part, like a fingertip or wrist, can be held under a running tap; a larger area should be plunged into a bucket or sink full of cold water.

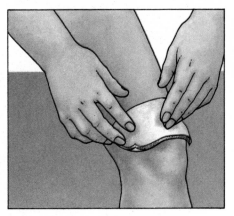

Areas like the face or chest that cannot be kept under water should be covered by a thick cloth, soaked in cold water. If the cloth gets warm and dry, renew cold water and re-apply. Continue cooling the burn for at least ten minutes. This quickly relieves pain and reduces the formation of blisters. If much pain persists, repeat the procedure.

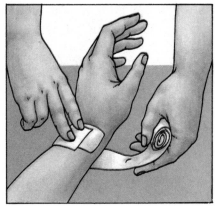

A large burn or a burn on the face should be covered with a non-fluffy dry dressing after cooling. Do not apply a lotion or ointment, and avoid touching the burn itself. Use the inside of a sterile surgical dressing or a clean handkerchief, handling it as little as possible. Cover with more folded padding and loosely bandage.

likely to be rough and not as elastic as before.

The most serious type of all is that classified as a third degree burn. Here the whole thickness burns, completely destroying the cellular structure of the skin; there is nothing from which new skin can re-form, unless it is at the very edges of the burn. In this event, healing is extremely slow and uncertain. The whole area is more or less free of pain however, because the nerve endings have been destroyed. But pain cannot be entirely absent, for at the edges of the burn there are likely to be some areas where nerve endings remain.

The loss of plasma (the colourless liquid part of the blood) is one of the major problems with severe burns. What happens is that burns can form blisters which are filled with plasma that oozes out from the damaged blood vessels in the surrounding area. The blood cells are left behind. From this point of view, the area covered by a burn is more significant than the depth. Plasma, although colourless and minus its cells, is still blood fluid, and a dramatic drop in its volume contributes to the condition known as shock. To make matters worse, the remaining blood in the body is now 'thicker', since its cells are concentrated in a smaller amount of plasma—this increases the difficulties of the heart, which may already be under stress.

Another problem is that a surface coating of plasma on the wound makes infection by bacteria more likely. A great deal of protein is also lost, together with the plasma.

Hospital treatment
This is needed for all the deeper and more extensive burns. Relief of pain is, of course, important, but the primary concern is to combat shock.

The percentage of skin area to receive a burn is also an important factor in deciding the treatment to be given—for example, the back or front of the trunk represents 18 per cent of the whole surface of the body, while a hand represents one per cent. A transfusion is likely to be needed when the burnt area represents more than 15 per cent of the total skin surface in an adult or more than ten per cent in a child. The fluid is generally plasma, but sometimes whole blood is included to replace red blood cells which have been destroyed.

Besides the transfusion, the patient's general condition must be closely watched, as the burnt area will have lost much of its natural defence against bacteria. Not only does infection delay healing; it also increases the risk of disfigurement from scarring, and these scars may contract and interfere with the movement of any joint they overlie. Antibiotics will be prescribed to combat infection and so help in the healing process.

Young children are fascinated by fire and do not understand the dangers. Matches and other potential hazards should be kept well out of their way.

A partial thickness burn is generally allowed to heal spontaneously, either by being left exposed or being covered by a dressing. Healing may take two or three months.

A full thickness burn will not mend in this way, since the regenerating tissue has been destroyed. The dead material eventually separates off as dark, hard slough, leaving a raw area below. Frequently it has to be helped off gently by the doctors and nurses and a skin graft will be necessary to close up the wound.

When a skin graft is performed, small pieces of skin are removed from another part of the patient's body (usually from a place that is ordinarily covered by clothing). This healthy skin is implanted into the burnt area and gradually grows to re-form a new skin surface. This process demands several months of skilful care, it being especially important to ensure that there are no disabling contractions of the grafted skin.

Victims of severe burns may also need a high calorie diet, containing extra iron and vitamins and also rich in protein to replace what has been lost in the plasma. Other organs, far from the original injury may also have been damaged: the liver, stomach, intestines, gall bladder and kidneys for example. This can happen because shock following the injury reduces the blood supply to vital organs, causing damage which will not show immediately, so these organs are kept under surveillance while the patient is in hospital. Physiotherapy will be given as soon as possible to maintain the fitness of undamaged limbs.

What to do in case of fire

If someone is trapped by a fire, cover your nose and mouth with a wet cloth. Reach the victim by crawling on the floor, where smoke is less dense. Guide or pull the victim out, and if he or she is choked by hot fumes, give artificial respiration.

Victims may panic, running around, beating at their clothes—actions which are likely to fan the flames. Try and stop this by getting the victim on the floor, with the burning area uppermost to allow the flames to rise away from the body.

To extinguish flames, use water if possible; if not, smother the flames with thick material such as a rug, heavy towel or coat. Throw this towards the victim's feet, so directing the flames away from the face. Press down gently to exclude air, but do not press any hot smouldering cloth against the skin. Pull this away, but do not try and tear away any material sticking to the skin. Never roll the victim round; this would only expose different areas to the flames.

Other forms of treatment

When a burn is extensive, the risk of shock is high. To treat for shock, keep the victim lying down and loosen any tight clothing. Cover lightly. In the case of a burn you can give a cupful of water, to be sipped every 15 minutes. Be reassuring and calm, but send for an ambulance immediately.

Leave any charred but cold material

which may be sticking to the skin. Remove anything such as a ring or bracelet that could constrict the burnt area which may swell. Do not prick a blister, nor apply anything other than cold water. If you have no surgical dressings handy, use a clean handkerchief or towel. To ensure maximum hygiene, handle the improvised dressing only by one corner, let it fall open to unfold and use the inside surface on the burn. Over this place padding of more folded material (another clean handkerchief or tea towel) and secure with an improvised bandage such as a necktie or tights.

If the face is burnt, cut holes in the dressing to let your patient see. However, badly swollen eyelids may keep the eyes closed. Move the victim as little as possible, but keep a burnt limb raised to reduce swelling—a large pillow or sling can be used.

Cancer

Q My brother-in-law has had a lot of X-rays recently. Surely these can cause cancer?

A Only if you have a very large number of X-rays, and even then the risk is quite small. Doctors today are aware of this risk and will only advise you to have an X-ray if they feel that it is absolutely necessary. In other words, the risk of not having the X-ray is greater than the risk of having it!

Q Can cancer cells become resistant to the effects of cytotoxic drugs which are meant to poison them?

A Unfortunately they can. The exact reasons for this are uncertain, but after a while a cancer cell will find ways of reproducing itself despite the presence of the cytotoxic drug, and the treatment must then be changed.

Q I have heard of a substance called latrile which is being used in the treatment of cancer. Does it work?

A There have been many reports that latrile, which is being purified in Mexico, has miraculous curative properties for cancer patients. As a result the substance has been studied by orthodox medical practitioners but found to be useless. There are still those, who usually have a vested interest, who are in favour of the drug, but it is not in use in the U.K.

Q My aunt, who lives with us, has cancer. Is it infectious?

A No. There is no risk of catching cancer from a relative or a friend with the disease, even if you are in very close contact with them.

Q I am very worried, having read somewhere that wounds can become cancerous. Does this happen?

A Almost never—only when ulcers have been present for a great many years can they possibly become cancerous, and that is very rare today. An ordinary household cut or graze never becomes cancerous.

Of all the medical conditions known, the one that creates the most fear in people today is cancer. But in many cases, early diagnosis and continually improving forms of treatment can mean a complete cure.

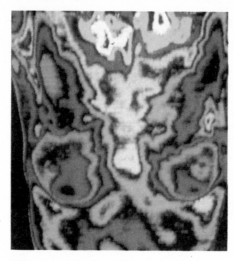

Thermography (heat X-ray) is used in cancer detection—this shows no cancer.

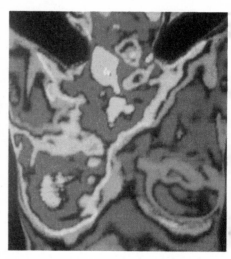

The red areas in the breast in this thermograph indicate the presence of cancer.

Cancer is the result of disordered and disorganized cell growth. This can only be fully understood by looking at what happens in normal cells.

The human body is made up of many different tissues—skin, lung, liver, etc, each of which is made up of millions of cells. These are all arranged in an orderly manner, each individual tissue having its own particular cellular structure. In addition, the appearance and shape of the cells of one organ differ from those of another. For example, a liver cell and a skin cell look completely different.

In all tissues cells are constantly being lost through general wear and tear, and these are replaced by a process of cell division. Occurring under strict control in normal tissues so that exactly the right number of cells are produced to replace those that are lost, a cell will divide in half to create two new cells, each identical to the original. If the body is injured, the rate of cell production speeds up automatically until the injury is healed and then slows down again.

The cells of a cancer, however, divide and grow at their own speed and in an uncontrolled manner—and they will continue to do so indefinitely unless treatment is given. In time, they increase in numbers until enough are present for the cancer to become visible as a growth.

In addition to growing too rapidly, cancer cells are unable to organize themselves properly, so that the mass of tissue that forms does not resemble normal tissue. A cancer obtains its nourishment parasitically from its bearer, and will serve no useful purpose for that person whatsoever.

Cancers are classified according to the cell from which they originated. Those that arise from cells in the surface membranes of the body, like the skin and the gut, are called carcinomas; those arising from structures deep inside the body, such as bone cartilage and muscle, are called sarcomas.

Carcinomas are much more common than sarcomas. This may be because the cells of the surface membranes need to divide more often in order to keep these membranes intact.

Benign and malignant tumours

Not all tumours are cancerous. Although tumour cells will grow at their own speed, tumours can be benign or malignant. Benign tumours tend to push aside normal tissues, but do not grow into them. Cells of a malignant tumour (a cancer), however, grow into the surrounding normal tissue, a process called invasion.

It is these claw-like processes of abnormal cells permeating the normal tissues, that are responsible for the name cancer—the crab, and its invasive properties. It is this that enables the cancer to spread, if unchecked, through the body and ultimately cause death.

The word 'malignant' means bad: this can be contrasted with 'benign' meaning harmless. Both accurately describe the outcome of the two types of tumour without treatment.

A benign tumour can look almost like normal tissue when examined under the microscope: it behaves accordingly by respecting its neighbours. It also grows more slowly, and although usually harmless, it can be serious if it arises in an important part of the body, such as the lung. Benign tumours should be removed and surgery is nearly always curative.

Origin of cancer cells

Cancer cells develop from the body's own normal cells, and a single cancer cell is enough to start the growth of a tumour. However, the change from normal cell to cancer cell is a gradual one, taking place in a number of stages over several years. With each stage the cell becomes slightly more abnormal in appearance, and slightly less responsive to the body's normal control mechanisms.

This process is usually unseen, until a cancer develops, but in a few situations pre-cancer can be recognized and treated. The best known of these is seen in the uterine cervix (neck of the womb) and this can be detected by a cervical smear.

How cancer spreads

It is the ability of cancer cells to spread inside the body that makes the disease so serious. Fortunately, the stages by which it does so tend to be orderly, with the cancer initially spreading into the immediately surrounding tissues. This produces local damage, which in time creates symptoms.

Next, cells begin to break off from the cancer and float in tissue fluid. In time, this fluid finds its way out of the tissues into a system of channels called lymphatics, which ultimately return the fluid (now called lymph) to the bloodstream. On its journey, the lymph passes through a number of glands called lymph nodes, which filter out dead cells and infection. Cancer cells are usually trapped in the lymph nodes nearest to the cancer where

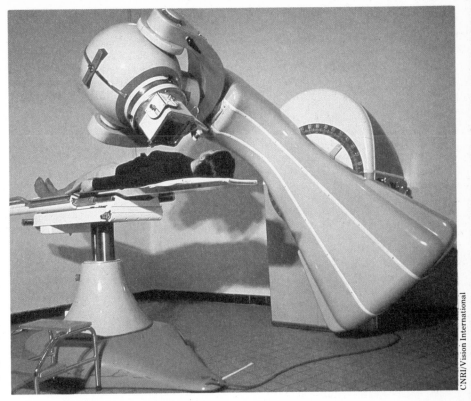

This patient is undergoing cobalt therapy, one of the newest methods used in the treatment of cancer. It acts by destroying the invading cancer cells.

most of them die. Sooner or later, however, one will survive and start to grow in the gland, forming a secondary growth.

Later, cancer cells are carried through the lymph nodes to reach the bloodstream; from here they are carried to the various organs of the body, such as the lung, liver, bone and brain. Most of these cells die but a few may survive to form secondary growths.

Causes

Cancer is commonest in late middle and old age. Thanks to sanitation and modern medicine people are living longer, and it is this rather than any defect in lifestyle, that is responsible for the increasing frequency of cancer in the Western world.

Of course, some cancers are associated with the Western way of life. Cancers due to smoking are still rare in the Third World, but are becoming commoner as industrial development takes place and more people start to smoke.

The commonest forms of the disease are lung, bowel, stomach, pancreas and breast cancer; and despite modern medicine cancer is still responsible for 20 per cent of all deaths in England and Wales each year.

The commonest cancers in children and young adults are leukaemias, sarcomas and kidney cancer. Fortunately, these cancers are rare, and their treatment has improved greatly in recent years. The cause of cancer is unknown, but two fundamental abnormalities are recog-

nized. Firstly, cancers are not subject to the normal influences that control cell growth; secondly, the body will tolerate the presence of the cancer without rejecting it as a foreign invader—the fate of parasites. This make them difficult to deal with.

Environmental factors, such as chemical pollution and exposure to radiation are thought to lead to cancer, but there are several other possibilities. The viral theory states that a cancer cell is infected by a virus (a tiny germ), and that it is this that causes the cell to grow.

The immunological theory considers that abnormal cells are constantly being produced by the body, but that these are destroyed by the body's defences. For some unknown reason, this defence system breaks down and an abnormal cell survives to form a cancer.

The chemical theory relies on the knowledge that certain chemicals—tar, for example—will cause cancer when painted on the skin of laboratory animals. These chemicals are irritants that may alter a cell's genetic structure and turn it into a cancer cell. Large numbers of experiments have identified chemicals that will cause cancer in animals; these are called carcinogens. A certain number have been identified, the

Steps you can take to avoid cancer

- Stop smoking
- Drink in moderation
- Examine your breasts once a month for lumps
- Have a cervical smear done at least once a year
- Eat a balanced diet
- Avoid repeated sunburn if you have a fair complexion
- See your doctor if you develop persistent pain, bleeding or a lump

best known being tobacco smoke. However, despite research, it has not yet been possible to identify carcinogens responsible for many of the common cancers.

Radiation is known to alter the genetic material of a cell—radiation from the atomic bomb dropped in Japan in 1945 is thought to be the cause of cancer, even years later.

As no single theory explains all the facts about cancer, it seems probable that it has many causes, some of which are still unknown.

Diagnosis

It is no longer true that cancer is invariably fatal. There has been a vast improvement in the treatment of cancer in recent years and many thousands of people are cured of the disease each year. However, a small cancer is much easier to cure than a large one, so early diagnosis is vital and is helped by the prompt re-

This woman suffered from cancer and had a mastectomy 22 years ago to remove her left breast. She now wears a prosthesis (artificial form of light synthetic material) under her bra.

porting of significant symptoms to the doctor. If he or she suspects cancer, this is usually followed by referral to the local out-patients department: from here the specialists will take over.

The diagnosis will first be confirmed. This may initially involve X-rays and scanning tests to show the presence of a lump inside the body. A part of the cancer will be then examined under the microscope. This can be done either by biopsy or by cytological examination.

A biopsy involves the removal, by a surgeon, of a small piece of the tumour

which is then sent for examination by a pathologist. This will determine whether the tissue is cancerous or not. Cytological examination is where body fluids, such as sputum or mucus from the uterine cervix, are studied specifically for cancer cells.

A thorough clinical examination is made, taking particular care to check the lymph nodes adjacent to the tumour. Simple blood tests are run to check liver and bone function and a chest X-ray looks for evidence of spread to these sites. If the doctor is suspicious of spread to a particular part of the body, this area may also be scanned. Various techniques are used. In isotope scanning a very small amount of radioactive substance is injected into the body and the blood carries it to the suspected organ or area of tissue. If it does contain a cancer this will take up a different amount of the isotope compared to the rest of the healthy tissue. The patient is then scanned with a special instrument which detects the radiation and the cancer can be seen. Many organs of the body can be examined in this way, bone and liver scans being the most commonly performed.

The doctor will now have a detailed knowledge of the type of cancer involved and the stage of its development and progress. Using this information the form of treatment that is most likely to be effective will be decided upon.

The aim of all cancer treatment is to kill or remove every cancer cell from the patient. With skilled use of the available treatments this is often possible.

Here it is impossible to detect that she is wearing a prosthesis. So it is easy to see that a mastectomy does not have to mean the end of an attractive appearance and a full and enjoyable life.

Smoking and cancer

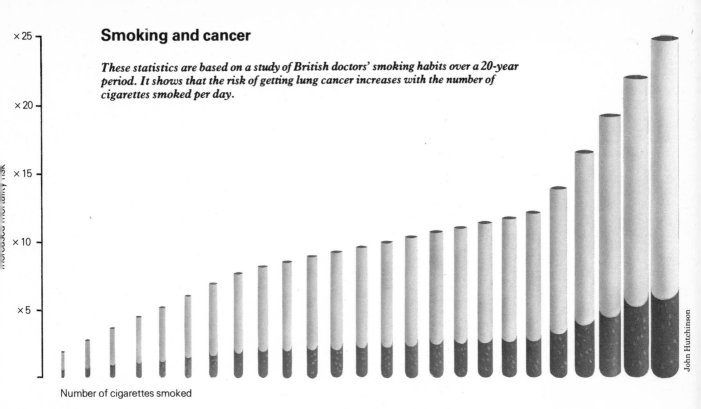

These statistics are based on a study of British doctors' smoking habits over a 20-year period. It shows that the risk of getting lung cancer increases with the number of cigarettes smoked per day.

Number of cigarettes smoked

John Hutchinson

Surgery

Effective cancer surgery aims at removing all of the cancer from the patient. It usually involves removing the visible growth with a wide margin of surrounding normal tissue, to make sure every cell has been removed. In addition, the surgeon will remove the draining lymph nodes. During the operation a thorough examination of any adjacent structures is made (e.g. the liver during an abdominal operation).

After removing the tumour, the surgeon will, where possible, reconstruct the patient's anatomy. In some circumstances this is not possible—following the removal of a cancer in the rectum, for example. Here the surgeon creates a new opening for the bowel on the abdominal wall, called a colostomy.

There are some circumstances in which surgery is carried out without investigating the patient first. Obviously when the patient is presented as an emergency, surgery is performed both to diagnose and treat the patient. There are also some situations when a biopsy and a cancer operation are carried out under the same anaesthetic. For example, it is common practice to biopsy a breast lump, examine the tissue and to then perform a mastectomy if the lump is found to be malignant. This has the advantage of speeding up treatment. Good cancer surgery has been practised for many years, and advances in other areas have improved treatment.

Symptoms of common cancers

Type	Symptoms
Breast cancer	breast lump, bleeding from the nipple, indrawing of the nipple, change in the shape of the breast
Lung cancer	persistent cough, spitting up blood, shortness of breath, chest pain, hoarseness
Cancer of the larynx	persistent hoarseness, spitting up blood
Cancer of the oesophagus (gullet)	increased difficulty in swallowing, vomiting, loss of weight
Cancer of the stomach	difficulty in swallowing, vomiting, bringing up blood, loss of weight, indigestion
Cancer of the bowel	blood in the motion or from the rectum, a change of bowel habit—either constipation or diarrhoea, or abdominal pain
Cancer of the bladder	blood in the urine
Cancer of the prostrate	increased difficulty in passing urine, recurring urinary infections and back pain
Cancer of the uterus or cervix	if menstruating, bleeding in between periods; if post-menopausal, vaginal bleeding. Offensive vaginal discharge, lower abdominal pain
Cancer of the mouth and throat	sore ulcer refuses to heal; pain in ear or ears; difficulty in chewing, swallowing; dentures increasingly do not fit
Leukaemia	tiredness, pallor, repeated infections, sore throat, bleeding from gums and nose, bruising
Skin cancer	sore throat that will not heal and continually bleeds

Radiotherapy

The aim of radiotherapy is to destroy the cancer with irradiation. Radiation damages the genetic material of cancer cells, so that they are unable to divide. Unfortunately it also damages normal cells, but thanks to the body's remarkable ability to repair itself, quite large doses of radiation can be safely given—provided that it is given slowly enough.

Radiotherapy is given in special rooms with thick floors, walls, ceilings and windows. Radiation leaks are thus prevented and the safety of the hospital staff ensured. The patient lies on a special couch beneath the machine and the machine is aimed at the tumour.

Before the treatment, the radiotherapist will have taken careful measurements of the position of the tumour to work out the best angle, or combination of angles, at which to set the machine. The staff then leave the room before the machine is switched on. It is essential that the patient is in exactly the same position for every treatment. The treatment only lasts a few minutes, is painless, and is usually given daily for five to six weeks as an out-patient.

Radiotherapy is not without side-effects, but these can be kept to a minimum by careful medical supervision. Soreness of the skin is less of a

There are trained counsellors to explain all the options to cancer sufferers and their families.

problem today and is avoided by not washing or rubbing the treatment area. Soothing creams are also given to the patient. Sickness and diarrhoea are only problems when the abdomen is treated and can usually be controlled with drugs.

Loss of hair may occur if the head is treated but hair usually regrows within six months, although the colour and texture of the hair sometimes changes. Damage to other parts of the body is now rare as the dose that sensitive organs such as the kidney and the lung will tolerate is well known, and this dose is not exceeded. The actual treatment itself is painless, and can be given to an out-patient.

Radiotherapy is used for localized tumours as is surgery. Some cancers can be cured by radiotherapy without the need for surgery (some cancers of the head and neck). In other situations, radiotherapy can be given either before or after an operation to increase the chances of successful cure (breast cancer).

Radiotherapy is also very good at relieving the symptoms of cancer, particularly pain, when cure is not possible. In some circumstances, it is possible to implant radioactive substances actually into the cancer. These give a very large dose to the cancer itself with only a small dose to the surrounding normal tissue. This form of treatment is ideal as the damage to normal tissues is kept to a minimum. Unfortunately it is only possible in accessible tumours such as small

cancers of the tongue and mouth and some that are gynaecological in nature.

Cytotoxic chemotherapy

If a cancer is too widespread or secondaries are present, it may not be possible to irradiate it completely or effectively. In this situation drug treatment is now available. These drugs used combine with and damage the genetic material of cells so that they cannot divide properly. They were originally developed from mustard gas, when soldiers recovering from this form of poisoning were noticed to have low blood counts. It was quickly realized that the gas was interfering with the division of cells in the bone marrow, where blood is made.

Nitrogen mustard (the active drug in mustard gas) was therefore tried in cancer patients in a attempt to poison the cancer cells and this proved successful. Treatment has now been greatly refined; many new and safer drugs have been discovered and effective combinations of drugs developed. Unfortunately, these drugs poison *all* dividing cells, hence the term cyto-toxic (cell poison).

The best way to minimize the damage to normal cells is to give larger doses of these drugs in single doses all together. There is then a gap of a few weeks (usually three) before the next course of treatment which allows time for normal cells to recover.

The cells in the body that divide the fastest are the cells of the skin, gut, and bone marrow. It follows that the side-effects of cytotoxic drugs are hair loss, nausea and lowering of the blood count.

Hair loss occurs with a few of the cytotoxic drugs but the hair regrows when treatment stops. The patient will be warned if hair loss is likely to be serious and a wig may be provided.

Nausea sometimes follows the injection of some cytotoxic drugs, but usually lasts only a few hours. Drugs that combat nausea can be prescribed. Alternatively, when it is expected to be severe, the patient is admitted to hospital and the treatment given under sedation. However, this is rarely necessary.

The safe dose for the various cytotoxic drugs is now known and allowed for by the doctor, so serious depression of the blood count is now much rarer than it was. However, the blood must be regularly tested both before and during such treatment.

Chemotherapy is not solely used for extensive cancer. It is also used to treat blood cancers, such as leukaemia, as it has proved effective on bone marrow. Other cancers, like Hodgkins disease, may respond better to chemotherapy than to extensive radiotherapy.

Stationery courtesy of Ryman's

Brian Nash

These women are residents in a hospice, an institution set up to care for the terminally ill. The symptoms will be dealt with drugs to ease the pain so that, most important of all, the sufferer can die in peace and dignity.

In some cases where there is an inclination to relapse after surgery and/or radiotherapy, chemotherapy is given even when there is no sign of cancer present. This is called Adjuvant chemotherapy and is being tried in breast cancer and childhood cancer. Very encouraging results have been obtained, though it is still too early to advocate this kind of treatment for all cancer patients.

Hormone therapy

Hormones are chemical messengers that circulate in the blood to control the growth and metabolism of tissue. If a cancer cell arises in a hormone-sensitive organ such as the womb, it may continue to recognize and respond to hormonal messages. If the patient is then given an inhibitory hormone—one that tells the cells to stop dividing, the cancer will stop growing. This type of treatment is particularly useful in breast, uterine and prostate cancers. Its great advantage is its freedom from unpleasant side-effects.

Interferon

This is a protein produced by the body in response to viral infection, and it seems to work like an antibody. The suggestion that cancer was due to viral infection led to its development for use in treating cancer. Unfortunately it is very difficult to produce and so, recently, there has been a programme of investment in order to produce more. As large amounts of money are involved, there is currently a great deal of publicity implying that Interferon is a cure for cancer.

Sadly, although it has some activity in cancer, it is not as effective as many of the cytotoxic drugs; it is also rather toxic, a fact that has often been overlooked by the press. In time, it will no doubt find a use in cancer treatment, but it is certainly not the magic cure for cancer for which we have all been waiting.

Combined treatment

Where more than one treatment is effective in treating a cancer it is logical to consider combining them in a planned sequence of treatment. In some childhood tumours, surgery is followed by local radiotherapy and then one year of chemotherapy; the results are very encouraging. In head and neck cancer, chemotherapy is followed by local radiotherapy, and then any part of the tumour remaining is removed surgically. Much

Differences between benign and malignant tumours

Type of growth:	Benign	Malignant
	Pushes normal tissue aside	Invades normal tissues
Spread:	Slight	May form secondary growths
Structure:	Similar to normal growths	May be disorganized
Rate:	Slow	May be slow to rapid
Outcome:	Usually harmless	May be fatal if untreated
Treatment:	Surgery curative (see Treatment)	Surgery alone may not be curative

research is now being done to determine the best way of combining treatments in all the various cancers in order to make the best possible use of all of them.

Whole body irradiation and bone marrow transplantation

In recent years it has been possible to transplant bone marrow from one person to another. This very specialized procedure requires large doses of radiation to be given to the recipient of the graft beforehand—called whole body irradiation. At present, this treatment is only used in rare anaemias and leukaemia. In the future, however, it may be possible to treat other forms of cancer in this way.

Outlook

Many cancers are curable in the early stages, and it is for this reason that one must emphasize the importance of regular screening, early diagnosis and immediate treatment. Any persistent unexplained symptom must be reported to your doctor. Once treatment has been completed, the patient is carefully followed up in the out-patient department. A regular examination of the original site of the cancer is made and any new symptoms are carefully investigated. In most forms of cancer, if the patient is alive and well five years later, there is room for optimism, just as there is over the constant advances in treatment.

Cataracts

Q My doctor says I have to wait for my cataract to 'mature' before I can have it removed. What does this mean?

A The term 'mature' simply means the cataract developing to such a degree that surgery is necessary. It can be removed at any stage, but this will always depend upon the improvement in vision that is likely to be achieved after the operation. No doubt your doctor will recommend surgery when it is necessary, but at the moment your eyesight would not appear to have deteriorated sufficiently.

Q My uncle has just had cataracts removed. How can I avoid getting them?

A Don't worry, they are not hereditary or catching! The only precaution you can take is to avoid ultra-violet sunlight which makes it advisable to wear sunglasses on bright days. Otherwise, cataracts are likely to be merely the result of advancing age—and there is nothing that can be done about that!
If you have diabetes or some other hormone or vitamin deficiency, the treatment might arrest their development. Expectant mothers should have a rubella vaccination and steer clear of certain drugs. Their doctors will advise them.

Q I have had a cataract removed and the operation was described as successful. Why then is my vision still so poor?

A One of the chief reasons is that the centre of sight in the retina has been affected; once the cataract and the lens are removed, the ability to focus is lost. For this reason, vision has to be corrected with spectacles, contact lenses or implants. You should be advised which would best suit your case and requirements, and once you have been prescribed the right visual aid, your sight should return to normal.

Q How can I tell whether someone has a cataract?

A Their eye will look as if it has a milky film over the surface. It's quite distinctive.

Cataracts are a common condition of the lens of the eye which, if left untreated, can result in complete loss of sight, but modern surgical techniques are very effective in restoring good vision.

The lens is a minor, focusing part of the eye, situated immediately behind the pupil, the bulk of the work is done by the cornea which is itself a fixed-focus lens.

Cataracts—which take the form of an opaque film like a snowflake—can form on the lens, dimming vision until only light and dark can be seen. Eventually the cataract reaches a 'mature' state and, if not surgically treated, vision can be permanently lost.

Causes

The most common cause of cataracts is old age, in which case they mostly affect the centre of the lens first, and blindness is delayed for many years until eventually the whole lens is affected. Many patients therefore outlive their eye problem and do not require surgery.

Some cataracts are congenital—that is, people are born with them. Within the first few months of development of the human embryo, the cells of many organs, including the eye, can undergo injury from infections or drugs that are in the mother's blood system during pregnancy. Other less severe congenital cataracts consist only of a light filming of the eye that resembles powder throughout the substance of the lens. Such cataracts rarely require any treatment at all, and vision is likely to remain good.

Disorders such as diabetes mellitus and parathyroidism—two types of hormone deficiency—can lead to the formation of cataracts. Other disorders and vitamin deficiencies can also affect the eyes, leading to cataracts. Sudden increases in blood sugar levels in young people can result in rapid clouding of the lens, but this can be reversed by early treatment of the underlying cause.

Cataracts can form for other reasons too. A high concentration of drugs in the blood can have a toxic (poisonous) effect on the lens, while steroid drugs, taken either by mouth, in the eye (in the form of eye drops), or by injection, may induce cataracts if given over a long period. Exposure to electromagnetic, cosmic, microwave or infra-red radiation can have a similar effect.

Cataracts can be formed as a result of accidents, and industrial and play injuries. A blow to the eye will sometimes cause a cataract to develop several years

Cataracts can be removed by ultrasound. Very small incisions are made in the eye and the cataract is washed out—the water bath is shown below.

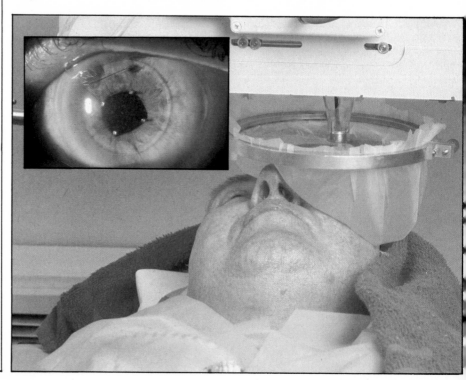

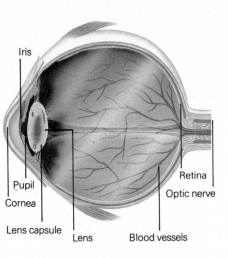

Iris
Pupil
Cornea
Lens capsule
Lens
Retina
Optic nerve
Blood vessels

Section of an eye with a cataract. When a cataract affects only the centre of the lens, dilation of the pupil with drops enables light to enter at the edges of the lens.

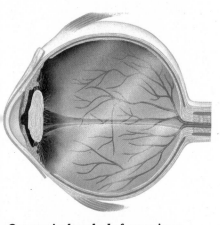

One surgical method of removing a cataract—extracapsular—involves removing the lens fibres of which the cataract is formed while leaving the lens capsule itself in place.

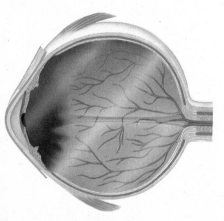

A third way of getting rid of a cataract surgically—the intracapsular method—is to remove the complete lens, including the lens capsule, with a forceps or a cryoprobe (a probe with a frozen tip).

later. A minute injury from a needle, thorn or metal foreign body, if it involves the capsule or lens of the eye, can lead to a similar problem long after the accident has occurred.

Symptoms
The most obvious symptom is a loss of distinct vision, and sometimes the inability to see in bright light. As the cataract matures, near vision is lost and finally only light and dark can be distinguished. Usually one eye is affected before the other, but nearly always both will show signs of developing cataracts, and if treatment is not given, blindness may occur.

Treatment
When cataracts affect only the centre (nucleus) of the lens, drops containing drugs which dilate the pupil are helpful; they enable light to enter the eye at the outer edges of the lens. However, the majority of cataracts affect the entire lens, and for this reason the only effective treatment is surgery.

There are three basic methods, depending upon a person's age and the type of cataract present.

The first method, which is mostly used for children and young people, consists of the removal of lens fibres of which the cataract is formed. If these lens fibres are soft and likely to be easily washed out by water solutions, then simple procedures are followed, and the cataract fibres are broken up by piercing the front capsule of the eye and the lens. Some that are left will slowly become absorbed and removed via the channels of the inner eyes.

The second method of removal is by ultrasound (Phako-emulsification). This advanced procedure combines the opening of the eye capsule and washing out the cataract, and can be used for any age group.

The advantage of this method is that only small incisions into the eye are necessary. The disadvantage is that a second operation is sometimes necessary at a later date to produce better vision.

The third type of operation, used in patients over the age of 20, is the removal of the complete lens. In this method the eye is opened and the lens removed by forceps or a cryoprobe (freezing tip of a probe). Often a substance is used to dissolve the ligaments that hold the lens in position. A return of good vision is usual and a second operation rarely needs to be performed.

Correction of vision
After the cataract has been removed, the vision must be corrected. Since the lens of the eye accounts for a third of its total

optical power, after successful surgery the sight can only be corrected by the use of strong optical lenses, either in the form of spectacles, or contact lenses. The only exception is when a cataract is removed from a very short-sighted person, and then the eye requires either no correction, as his or her normal spectacles will be adequate to give improved vision.

Spectacles can only be prescribed if both eyes have been operated on for cataracts or if one eye only has been treated and the other is not used. Unfortunately the lenses of spectacles tend to limit part of the field of vision and they also magnify objects. Sometimes resulting in difficulty in getting about.

Alternatively, contact lenses can be worn. If there is also astigmatism (a condition which causes distorted vision), and soft lenses are worn, additional spectacles will have to be prescribed. Hard contact lenses will correct all the vision.

Intra-ocular implants (plastic lenses) are the last option, and are useful for patients when one eye has undergone surgery. It is a complicated operation, with the implant being placed in the eye after the cataract has been removed. Contact lenses or spectacles might have to be worn once the eye has recovered.

Generally speaking, once a cataract has been operated upon and vision corrected, the patient will be able to see quite satisfactorily again.

Can cataracts be prevented?
There is some evidence that cataracts in the elderly can be prevented if ultraviolet light is avoided. Therefore, people should wear sunglasses on sunny days and when on holiday, or if they live at high altitudes or by the sea, to protect their eyes from sunlight.

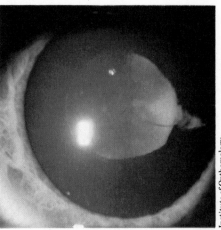

Institute of Opthamology

This close-up shows a congenital cataract; it is luckily an uncommon condition. It can be caused by an infection or drug in the mother's system during pregnancy.

Catarrh

Q I live in a damp house. Could this be the cause of catarrh? I seem to have it permanently.

A It is difficult to prove that damp fuggy air causes catarrh, but it does seem likely. Smog and fumes are also well known to predispose to bronchitis, and there is a connection between the two in that both conditions produce excess mucus.

Good advice for all catarrh sufferers is to take a last minute walk at night. The cool air clears the passages and helps induce sleep, which can sometimes be hindered by a blocked-up nose.

Talk to your doctor about the possible cause of your problem. Should this prove to be your damp home, try to do something about it.

Q Do all those pastilles I see on sale really help clear catarrh? Could they do harm?

A Most proprietary pastilles either contain old-established decongestants (unblocking agents) like menthol or eucalyptus, or an antihistamine drug. From this point of view they do help catarrh sufferers and are quite safe. They do not, however, give a permanent cure and many people find they quickly lose their effect.

Q A friend told me I should not give my children those nose sprays for catarrh because they can be harmful. Is it true?

A Yes. You should not use a spray or nose drops for more than a few days except on medical advice.

They often stop catarrh for a while, but this is frequently followed by worse catarrh than ever. They eventually act as irritants, damaging the lining of the nose and causing more catarrh.

Q Both my father and grandfather were catarrh sufferers. Does catarrh run in families?

A There is no evidence for this, but it does seem highly likely. One might explain it by saying that parents can pass on their allergies or sensitivities, which may easily be of the type that cause catarrh.

This common complaint should be regarded as no more than a temporary irritation which can be easily relieved by treatment at home. But if it lingers more than a few weeks, see your doctor.

Areas affected by catarrh

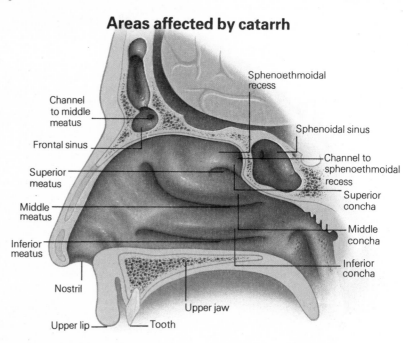

The sinuses and nasal cavity are lined by a mucus-producing membrane. During a common cold this membrane swells and produces excessive mucus (catarrh) which blocks the nasal passages.

Mucous membranes are the pliable, sheet-like connective tissues found throughout the body, lining, for example, the inside of the nose, the mouth, the throat, the windpipe, and air passages, they produce mucus to keep moist. Excess mucus, or catarrh, is so common in the nose that most people tend to think it only occurs there.

The cause of excess mucus is any irritation or inflammation, and without doubt the most common cause of catarrh is the common cold, whose virus irritates the lining membranes of the nose.

The resulting discharge trickles down the nostrils and the back of the throat. Should it then seep down to the chest, it is coughed back up as phlegm or sputum. This can also be produced in the lungs and bronchial tubes and coughed up in the same way.

Another cause of catarrh is hay fever; a chronic infection of the sinuses usually results in permanent cararrh.

Some small children may get catarrh because some object such as a pea or bead has been pushed up the nose, and remained in place, causing inflammation.

Adults sometimes suffer from persistent catarrh, known as vasomotor rhinitis. Its cause has not been discovered, although hormonal changes at adolescence, anxiety and the side-effects of some drugs may be involved.

The symptoms of catarrh

It is obvious to most people when they have catarrh. It causes a runny nose and, when it dries, blockage. As a result it may be necessary to breathe through the mouth rather than nose. Any bout that does not clear up within six weeks should be reported to your doctor.

Treating catarrh at home

● Regular nose-blowing temporarily clears the worst excess mucus and lessens chances of infection.
● Inhalations of one of the several preparations available (for example, menthol) soothes and temporarily clears the passages.
● Fresh air and exercise may give relief for an hour or two.
● If catarrh is permanent, see your doctor, but also try to stop or reduce smoking; reduce bedroom temperature and take a walk outside last thing at night and look for an allergic cause such as feather pillows, plants or cats.

Cervix and cervical smears

Q My doctor has told me I have a cervical erosion. Is this serious?

A No, and it is in no way associated with cancer of the cervix. In cervical erosion the cells from inside the cervix (the neck of the womb) begin growing on the outside, a very common condition, usually found during or after pregnancy. Erosions usually heal spontaneously, but if they persist, causing an excessive discharge, electrocautery (using heat) or cryotherapy (using cold) are possible forms of treatment.

Q Are cervical smears really necessary? I really don't like the idea at all.

A The purpose of the cervical smear, or 'pap' test, is to make an early detection of abnormal cells covering the surface of the cervix, which could, if left untreated, lead to the development of cancer, or less commonly, to the diagnosis of an already established cancer-in-situ. Try to overcome your fear and prejudice; it could save your life.

Q I have had one cervical smear taken. Do I need to have any more?

A Yes. It is advisable to have a cervical smear taken at regular intervals, starting in your twenties or earlier and having the test repeated at least every three years. With women who have had three or more children, or who have had abnormal cells discovered in a previous smear, more frequent testing is necessary.

Q Although my doctor said that the results of my cervical smear showed no serious changes, he wants another done in three months time, Why is this necessary?

A The changes found when the smear is examined under the microscope are described under various categories. You need not be unduly worried when the changes are only slight. The fact that your doctor wants you retested doesn't mean you have cancer; he may simply wish to repeat the test to assess the need for any further investigation.

The cervix is the neck of the womb, and consists of a ring of muscle that expands during childbirth. It is the site of some infections, and also of cancer, which can be detected by a cervical smear.

The cervix is the neck of the uterus (womb). It is shaped like a cylinder and its lower part projects into the vagina. The cervix is about 2.5 cm (1 in) long, and has a fine canal running through it which opens into the cavity of the uterus above, and the vagina below. If a finger is inserted into the vagina, the cervix can be felt as a small dimple.

In a woman who has not had children, this opening into the vagina is circular and quite small. During childbirth this stretches to allow the passage of the baby through it, and after childbirth it re-shapes into a crosswise slit. If it has been badly damaged, it pouts open to form what is called a cervical erosion. Dilation, or stretching, of the cervix that occurs during one of the methods employed for the termination of pregnancy, is another possible cause of this condition.

Sometimes, following damage or after a difficult childbirth, the cervix does not function properly. This leads to repeated miscarriages during the fourth to sixth months of pregnancy. When this condition is diagnosed early enough, however, a special stitch can be put into the cervix.

Problems
Sometimes during childbirth the cervix can become abnormally elongated—this can be felt if a finger is introduced into the vagina. An elongated cervix rarely causes any trouble, but, if necessary, it can be treated by a simple operation.

Occasionally the glands in and around the external opening of the cervix, which produce mucus, become enlarged to form follicles, or small cysts. These may cause a disturbance of the menstrual cycle, and perhaps abdominal swelling, though often there are no symptoms at all. Cysts seldom require treatment, as they often disappear by themselves; a few types may

Position of the cervix

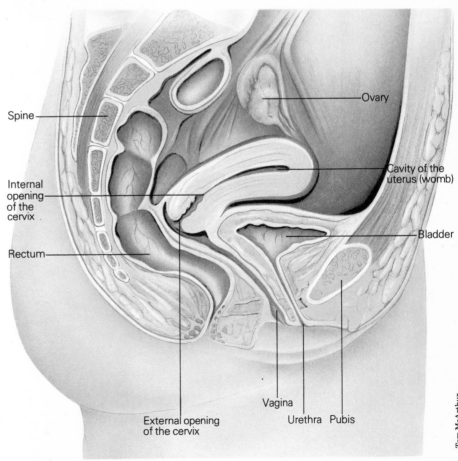

Spine

Internal opening of the cervix

Rectum

External opening of the cervix

Ovary

Cavity of the uterus (womb)

Bladder

Vagina

Urethra   Pubis

Tom McArthur

83

have to be removed.

A more important and probably more common problem is associated with the function of the mucus glands. These glands normally produce a thick and sticky mucus which forms a 'plug', filling the entrance to the cervical canal. At the time of ovulation, this mucus becomes clear and thin. This allows sperm to gain entrance into the uterus more easily and swim towards the egg, which has left the ovary and is travelling down the Fallopian tube. If this change in the mucus does not take place and it remains thick—a condition called cervical hostility—a woman may have difficulty conceiving.

Another possible cause for subfertility, (difficulty in getting pregnant) is the presence of antibodies in the mucus which interfere with the ability of the sperm to travel up to meet the egg.

Infections

A much more common condition affecting the cervix is that of infection (cervicitis). This may be due to one of the venereal diseases, such as gonorrhoea or syphilis, or to the less serious but more frequently seen non-specific genital infections, such as that due to a germ called Chlamydia, responsible for some cases of non-specific urethritis (NSU) in men.

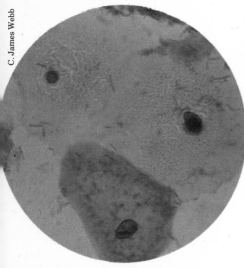

C. James Webb

These conditions may produce an unpleasant vaginal discharge, but it is most important to remember that in gonorrhoea—the commonest cause of cervicitis—there is often no discharge or, indeed, any other symptom at all. If gonorrhoea is a possibility, full examination by a doctor is an absolute necessity. Most vaginal discharges are, in fact, due to infection of the vagina rather than the cervix as for such conditions as thrush or trichomoniasis.

Syphilis does not cause discharge, but rather a sore or an ulcer on the lips of the vagina or on the cervix, where there is the additional problem that it cannot be seen.

Cervical erosions that have become infected may also give rise to discharge. They are treated by burning (cauterization)—either with some caustic chemical or electrically (diathermy)—or by being frozen (cryotherapy).

Syphilis or gonorrhoea of the cervix is treated with the appropriate antibiotic—most commonly penicillin—but both require very thorough follow-up to make quite sure that a permanent cure has been achieved.

Causes for concern

With cervical polyps, the vaginal discharge may be blood-stained, or actually consist of blood. Bleeding of this sort is due to a fleshy protuberance of the outer covering of the cervical canal, which is called a polyp. This might be 1 cm (0.4 in) in length and will continue to cause bleeding either spontaneously or during sexual intercourse until it is removed. Although it does not often happen, a polyp is capable of becoming malignant if left untreated. Sometimes the symptoms indicate cancer of the genital tract.

All of these conditions should be seen to without delay, and will require a careful

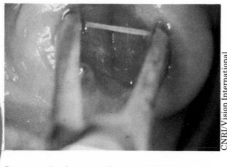

In a cervical smear the cervix is inspected through an instrument called a speculum. A few cells are scraped off then examined under a microscope, which shows up any abnormalities. Cells to left are normal.

CNRI/Vision International

examination by a specialist, who will examine the patient internally, and may study the cervix through an instrument called a vaginal speculum. Most doctors now also consider it necessary to take a cervical smear as a routine part of a full gynaecological examination, in addition to taking bacteriological swabs from inside the vagina and the cervix.

Cervical smears

The taking of a cervical smear, or a Papanicolaou ('Pap') test, is a very simple matter and not at all painful. Some women feel embarrassed about having any form of intimate examination carried out, but it is more important to consider the consequences if a serious condition is later diagnosed.

The procedure consists of the speculum being inserted into the vagina. Any discomfort that may arise is caused by the tightening of the muscles of the vagina during the examination, so it is important to relax. The cervix as well as the vaginal walls are inspected through the opened speculum with the aid of a bright light. The smear is then taken by lightly scraping off some of the cells of the outer lining of the cervix with a wooden spatula. The cells are treated with chemicals, which make it possible to see whether they are normal or show any changes that might indicate malignancy.

Out of every 1000 women in the UK who have cervical smears taken, about 20 will be found to have some abnormality, and 17 out of each 20 will have changes that could indicate a pre-cancerous state. For these, further smears will have to be taken every three to six months until it is decided whether the cells are benign and thus harmless, or if they have become malignant.

The remaining three women will be found to have a condition called cancer-in-situ, which is potentially malignant, and requires treatment of a relatively simple kind known as a cone biopsy. This entails the removal of the end of the cervix for further examination, and is carried on in hospital.

In the majority of cases, all the pre-malignant cells can be removed by this method. Occasionally, a cone biopsy shows the spread of these cells into the cervix, and the uterus must be removed.

Cancer-in-situ is about five times more common than invasive cancer (cancer of the cervix and/or uterus), so that the actual incidence of invasive cancer is less than one in every thousand of the women undergoing cervical smears. It has been estimated that cancer-in-situ is usually found only in women some seven to ten years after they have started to be sexually active. It is practically never seen in nuns, and the peak incidence is in women in their 30s.

Invasive cancer of the cervix is seen at its peak in women in their 40s, some ten years after the peak incidence of cancer-in-situ. If cancer-in-situ is detected early and treated surgically, the fatality rate is reduced considerably in cancer of the cervix.

Sexually active women should all have smear tests regularly, regardless of age, and so should those attending their first antenatal and postnatal examinations. But it is sexual activity rather than childbirth which seems most associated with the development of cancer-in-situ.

Chickenpox

Q What is the best way to prevent scars forming from chickenpox? Both my boys scratched their spots, and it would be a shame if my daughter were to scar her face when she gets it.

A Scarring takes place if the spots become infected or if the scabs are pulled off taking fresh tissue with them, so widening the area of damage.

Preventing itching with an antihistamine drug or calamine lotion is helpful, but it does take some will power not to scratch scabs.

All you can do is explain what will happen if she picks spots on her face and neck, and constantly encourage her to resist the temptation.

Q Could my baby get chickenpox, and if so is it more serious than in a child?

A Babies seem to have some immunity to chickenpox, even when the mother has no knowledge of ever having had chickenpox herself, and very few cases have ever been recorded. A baby could be seriously, but probably not fatally ill with chickenpox, and any child under the age of two with a rash should obviously be seen by a doctor.

Q My son appears to have chickenpox for the second time. Is this possible?

A This is highly unlikely and most doctors would try and persuade you that the first time the rash appeared the diagnosis must have been wrong. In general, chickenpox is a once-only infection. The first attack might have been scabies (severe itching and spots caused by a mite), or even a number of gnat bites occurring together. These may often look like chickenpox.

Q My daughter spent yesterday afternoon with a child who I've just found out had chickenpox, How soon can I expect her to come down with it?

A Your daughter may show the first symptoms—headache and a vague illness, followed by spots— within ten days or it could take up to three weeks before the illness develops.

Being so easily caught, chickenpox is almost a natural hazard of childhood. But it does not last long, it practically never has serious complications, and effective home nursing is a simple matter.

Chickenpox, whose medical name is varicella, is a highly infectious illness easily recognized by the rash that it causes, which occurs mainly in children.

It is a childhood illness because although babies are born with a natural ability to resist the infection (passed on by their mother), by the age of three or four this wears off, leaving the child likely to catch the infection from other children.

The virus

The virus (or germ) that causes chickenpox is the same as that which causes shingles (which has similar symptoms, including a rash) in adults. For this reason, an adult with shingles can start a chickenpox outbreak in a child, and similarly children who are infected can pass the virus on to cause shingles in an adult.

Although slightly similar in appearance to smallpox, chickenpox has no other similarity. Smallpox is a much more serious illness with a 40 per cent death rate and it is caused by a completely different virus.

The chickenpox and shingles virus is so highly infectious that many outbreaks occur in children mainly between the ages of two and six.

The outbreaks are strongest in the autumn and winter and appear to occur in three to four-year cycles as new groups of children lose their inborn resistance.

How it is caught

Although the virus is present, alive, in the spots which form on the child who catches chickenpox, it is chiefly transferred between people by droplet infection.

Someone who already has the virus spreads clusters of the virus in the tiny droplets of water which are exhaled as a matter of course with every breath.

When a child breathes in an infected droplet, the virus starts to multiply and another case of chickenpox begins. Outbreaks cannot begin on their own—there has to be a source and this is almost always another child.

First symptoms

Once the virus enters the body, it needs an incubation or breeding period of between ten days and three weeks in order to spread. The first a child will know of his or her illness will be a 24-hour period of vague headache, feeling unwell, occa-

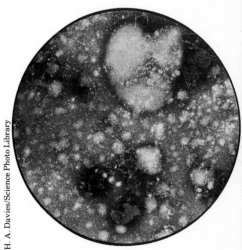

The chickenpox virus, enlarged about 8,000 times, is mainly transmitted through droplets of water in the breath.

H. A. Davies/Science Photo Library

sional slight fever and sometimes a blotchy red rash which quickly fades. A mother may note that her child is 'off colour' or 'sickening for something'.

The spots

Within 24 hours the first spots will appear and by the nature and position of these spots the diagnosis is made. In very mild cases it can be difficult to distinguish chickenpox from gnat bites, but in a full-blown case, with hundreds of spots, diagnosis is simple.

Spots first appear in the mouth and throat where they quickly burst, causing pain and soreness. They then appear on the trunk and face, only occasionally affecting the limbs.

The spot starts as a pink pimple which within five or six hours becomes raised to form a tiny blister, or vesicle, containing clear fluid which is full of viruses. These 'teardrop' spots gradually become milky in colour. Then they form a crust, and finally a scab. The time taken from the appearance of the teardrop to the formation of the crust is only about 24 hours. During this period the child may be fretful and run a temperature of 38°C (100 or 101°F).

Some children only have 30 or 50 spots while others may have several hundred.

Immediately the crust forms, the spots begin to itch and this may last until the scabs drop off, leaving normal skin, after one or two weeks.

Course of the infection

Chickenpox spots come out in crops, which means that new ones will appear every day for three or four days.

When examining the skin, an adult will notice that the spots will be at different stages even in the same area. This is typical of chickenpox and quite normal.

In the majority of cases the condition is very mild but in others the child is really quite unwell and needs attentive home nursing.

Dangers

The dangerous complications of chickenpox are extremely rare. Most children feel well enough to play during the illness.

Children who are taking steroid drugs or those suffering from leukaemia are the only ones likely to be seriously affected and in whom the condition may be fatal. In a very small number of cases a severe form of pneumonia is caused by the virus. Or there may be bleeding into the spots so that the patient becomes ill from loss of blood.

Children with chickenpox should, however, be isolated from old people in case they catch shingles.

Infection

The most common complications arise from infection of the skin at the spot, causing boils, or one or two other skin conditions. Similarly, spots near the eye may give rise to infective conjuctivitis, commonly called 'pink eye'. In such cases, treatment with antibiotics is needed.

Cases have been known of arthritis and even inflammation of the heart following chickenpox, but they are extremely rare. The only other serious danger is when the virus attacks the nervous system to cause encephalitis (inflammation of the brain), which it may do on the fourth or tenth day of the rash appearing. The patient becomes delirious and intensive hospital treatment is needed. The chances of complete recovery are high.

Treatment

Children with a high temperature who feel unwell may prefer to stay in bed or lie downstairs in front of the fire. Otherwise, there is no medical reason to enforce strict bed rest. The majority of children

Chickenpox spots begin to itch as soon as the crusts form, and calamine lotion is a soothing, cooling treatment.

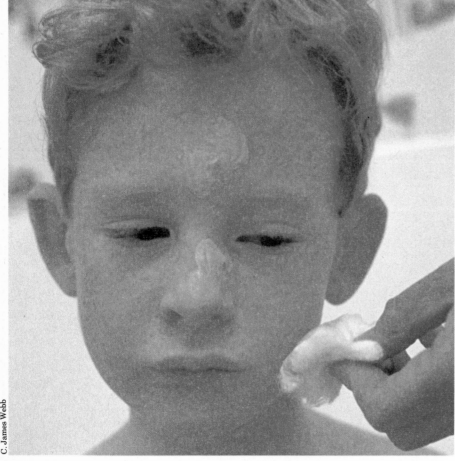

C. James Webb

require no treatment at all.

Any pain from sore throat or headache is best relieved with a painkiller such as paracetamol. As there is no medical cure for the virus, the condition is left to take its natural course.

Severe itching can be helped with application of calamine lotion, which has a cooling and an anti-itching effect. Alternatively, the itching can be reduced with an antihistamine drug.

Should any of the spots become infected they may take longer to heal, and antibiotics will be necessary.

Outlook

The majority of children with mild chickenpox start losing their scabs after about ten days and will then be completely clear of spots within two weeks.

Where scabs have been scratched, the process will take longer. The scabs themselves are not infectious and those which fall off on their own do not leave a scar. Scabs that have been prematurely picked or those that have become infected are more likely to scar, and for this reason it is important for children to avoid scratching their scabs.

Chickenpox infection produces life-long immunity to a widespread infection of chickenpox, but does not give immunity to shingles, which may occur later in life.

Because chickenpox is such a relatively harmless infection, a vaccine has never been developed.

Chilblains

Q My hands have suffered badly from chilblains and look swollen and awful. Will they ever recover completely?

A Providing none of your chilblains have ulcerated and therefore possibly caused scarring, there is every reason to hope that your hands will return to normal. You will probably need medical help and should certainly take rigorous precautions to avoid further chilblains.

Q At what point should I trouble a doctor with my children's chilblains?

A If you have tried all the precautions and home remedies and your children still have painful chilblains, it is well worth seeking medical advice. In many cases drug treatment over the two or three weeks in January or February is enough to keep chilblains at bay for the year. Ulcerated or blistering chilblains always need a medical opinion.

Q Are young people or the elderly more susceptible to chilblains?

A Children and young people get chilblains more than older people. Furthermore, most sufferers are female.

Young people tend to be out in cold weather and they are less likely to pay attention to the need for dry shoes or warm gloves; this makes them more susceptible. It used to be thought that women were more likely to develop chilblains because much of their work involved water and cold kitchens, but with modern home aids this is not true. There is possibly a hormonal reason which gives women a more sluggish circulation.

Q Ever since I had treatment for blood pressure I have had terrible chilblains. Is there a connection?

A One of the most effective groups of drugs used to treat high blood pressure are known as Beta-blockers, and in some people they do cause cold extremities, making chilblains more common.

Chilblains, as every sufferer knows, are irritating and painful. Due mainly to poor circulation, they can nevertheless usually be prevented altogether.

A chilblain is an area of soft tissue where the skin has become damaged by cold and damp so that it becomes red and swollen, and may itch and even ulcerate. Some people are predisposed to chilblains, especially young women, and those with sluggish circulation.

Chilblains most commonly occur on the toes or the outer side of the foot. The fingers can also be affected, particularly over the joints, as can the ear, nose and, in severe cases, the calves.

Causes
Chilblains are caused by a combination of the effects of cold and damp in an area where blood flow is reduced.

People with poor circulation, and thus permanently cold hands and feet, are susceptible, but chilblains can also be induced by certain drugs. Patients with muscle wasting due to polio, or those who take little or no exercise, are particularly prone to the condition.

Symptoms
Chilblains start as red or mauve coloured blotchy patches that itch and tingle. There is a tendency to want to scratch, which must be resisted.

With more severe chilblains, the swelling spreads over the whole area covered by the chilblains and tiny blisters containing clear yellow fluid may form. Very rarely the blisters break down to leave ulcer craters which are painful and sore.

Painful cracks may also appear on the joints: this is known as chapping. The chilblains do not cause the chapping, but cold and wet conditions will bring it on.

Severe chilblains require medical attention as they may easily become infected or become chronic.

Treatment
Once a chilblain has formed, then gentle massage and a very slow warming of the area will help. Painkillers may also prove useful. Where a blister has formed, it should be left and never burst on purpose.

Chilblain ulcers are uncommon, but will need medical attention. However, a dry dressing applied daily will help.

A course of ultra-violet light to affected areas during the autumn helps prevent chilblains in winter, and daily use of infra-red heat should be tried. Certain lotions and creams which increase the local blood flow are helpful, but these should not be applied when chilblains have actually formed. Various drug treatments are also of some use.

Outlook
Chilblains usually heal in five to 10 days. Severely ulcerated areas will take considerably longer to heal and may leave a scar. When joints such as the knuckle or toes are affected, healing of the skin may take longer, and painful cracks may continually re-open until the prime cause of the cold injury is removed.

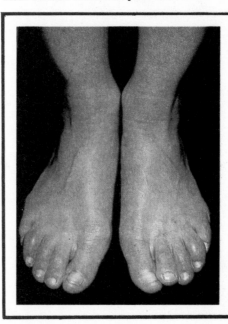

To prevent chilblains
DO
● Keep warm by wearing several layers of woolly clothing all over.
● Wear protection on hands and feet.
● Dry hands and feet carefully.
● Walk on rugs or carpets, not on bare floors. Always wear shoes or slippers.
● Massage likely chilblain areas daily.
● Eat plenty of hot nourishing food in cold weather.

DON'T
● Go out in freezing weather without a hat.
● Work in cold and damp surroundings.
● Sit in draughts.
● Wear wet shoes and socks.
● Warm cold hands or feet in front of a roaring fire or put in hot water.
● Wear tight garters or cuffs to gloves.

Circulation

88

Q My daughter sometimes complains of 'pins and needles'. Does this mean there is something wrong with her circulation?

A The pricking sensation of pins and needles is actually the irritation of a nerve caused when blood supply is restricted for some reason. Most usually, this comes about through lying in an awkward position, but it can also be a sign of circulatory disease which has damaged the blood vessels. So if the problem persists, take your daughter to the doctor.

Q I am considerably over-weight and my doctor has warned me that it is harmful to my circulation. Why is this?

A When you are overweight, you carry too much fat. This has to be stored somewhere and unfortunately a fatty build-up often occurs in, among other places, the heart and arteries. As a result, they cannot carry as large a blood supply as previously. And this causes further problems: to keep the blood flowing round the system, the heart has to work extra hard, which may strain it. A heavy body also requires extra effort when simply moving around and this too could be a strain on the heart. So it is worth trying to shed your extra pounds.

Q My teenage daughter keeps on fainting but she looks perfectly healthy. Do you think she might have problems with her circulation?

A The most usual cause of fainting is a temporary fall in the amount of oxygen reaching the brain and this is a common problem in adolescents, particularly girls. It often has a mental cause, for emotional disturbance can make the arteries widen, lowering the blood pressure and preventing blood from being pumped up to the brain.

This sort of fainting has been known to occur with remarkable frequency in groups of girls, but it is something they usually grow out of. If the fainting increases in frequency or is causing your daughter to worry, make sure that she sees her doctor promptly.

Blood pumped by the heart is constantly circulating around the body. This has several essential purposes, among them to supply the body's cells with food and oxygen, and to clear them of waste products.

The circulation is a closed network of blood vessels—in other words, tubes which carry blood around the body. At its centre is the heart, a muscular pump with the job of keeping the blood in constant motion.

Arteries and arterioles

Blood starts its journey round the circulation by leaving the left side of the heart through the large artery known as the aorta.

At this stage, blood is rich in oxygen, food broken down into the microscopically small components known as molecules, and other important substances such as hormones, the body's chemical 'messengers'. On the early part of its journey blood flows through relatively large tubes called arteries, and then it passes into smaller vessels known as arterioles. These lead to every organ and tissue in the body, including the heart itself.

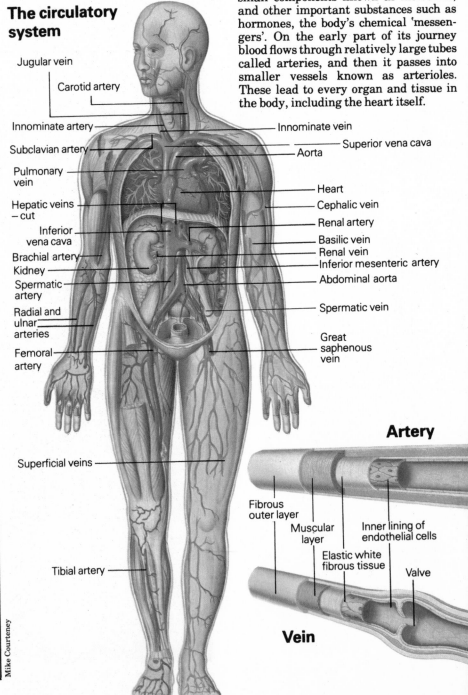

The circulatory system

Jugular vein
Carotid artery
Innominate artery
Subclavian artery
Pulmonary vein
Hepatic veins – cut
Inferior vena cava
Brachial artery
Kidney
Spermatic artery
Radial and ulnar arteries
Femoral artery
Superficial veins
Tibial artery

Innominate vein
Superior vena cava
Aorta
Heart
Cephalic vein
Renal artery
Basilic vein
Renal vein
Inferior mesenteric artery
Abdominal aorta
Spermatic vein
Great saphenous vein

Mike Courteney

Artery

Fibrous outer layer
Muscular layer
Elastic white fibrous tissue
Inner lining of endothelial cells
Valve

Vein

From the arterioles, the blood enters a vast network of minute vessels called the capillaries. It is here that oxygen and life-maintaining molecules are given up in return for the waste products of the body's activities.

The veins

Blood then leaves the capillaries and flows into the small veins, or venules, starting the journey back to the heart.

All the veins from the various parts of the body eventually merge into two large blood vessels, one called the superior, the other called the inferior *vena cava*. The first collects blood from the head, arms and neck and the second receives blood from the lower part of the body.

Both veins deliver blood to the right side of the heart and from here it is pumped into the pulmonary artery (the only artery to carry blood with no oxygen). This artery takes the blood to the lung where oxygen from the air we breathe is absorbed into it and the waste carbon dioxide given up and breathed out.

The final stage of the journey is for the now oxygen-rich blood to flow through the pulmonary vein (the only vein to carry oxygenated blood) into the left side of the heart, where it starts its circuit again.

Short cuts

In general, that is what is meant by circulation. However, there are certain refinements of the circulation which help supply the body's special needs.

On leaving the intestines, blood does not flow directly back to the heart but is taken to the liver by means of a special vessel called the hepatic portal vein. In the liver some substances are sifted out for immediate use, others are put into storage, and poisonous or toxic substances are broken down.

And if the body is put under physical stress, such as when suddenly breaking into a run, blood vessels in the leg muscles increase in size and those in the intestine shut down so that the blood is directed to the site at which it is most needed. When you are resting after a meal the reverse process occurs. This is assisted by a series or circulatory by-passes throughout the body called anastamoses.

Failsafe mechanism

In some parts of the body, such as the arms and legs, arteries and their branches are joined so that they can 'double up' on each other and form an alternative route for the blood if one is damaged: this is called a collative circulation.

And when there is damage to an artery, the branch of the adjoining artery which has taken over grows wider to give a greater degree of blood circulation.

As it grows to maturity, the body develops more and more of these failsafe back-ups in its network of arteries, but they cannot cope with an extreme emergency such as the formation of a clot.

The circulation of blood throughout our bodies is automatically regulated according to our activities, so that it is always in the places where it is most needed.

Distribution

The blood is not evenly spread throughout the system. At any given moment, about 12% is in the arteries and veins which carry it to and from the lungs. About 59% is in the veins, 15% is in the arteries, 5% in the capillaries and the remaining 9% in the heart.

Rate of flow

Nor does the blood flow at the same rate in all parts of the system.

It spurts from the heart and through the aorta at a brisk 33 cm (13 inches) per second, but by the time it has reached the capillaries it has slowed down to a gentle 0.3 cm (about a tenth of an inch) per second.

The flow back through the veins gradually increases in speed so that blood is delivered back to the heart at 20 cm (about eight inches) per second.

Pulse

One of the main guides a doctor has to the condition of a patient's circulation is his pulse, for it is a mirror of the heartbeat. Arteries have elastic walls which expand every time the heart pumps a wave of blood through them, and you can actually feel this happening if you can find an artery near the surface of the body and press it against a bone. One such place, of course, is the wrist.

The normal pulse rate is betwen 60 and 80 beats a minute but varies widely, so a doctor taking your pulse is not only counting the beats but feeling for changes in their strength and regularity.

Distribution of blood in the body

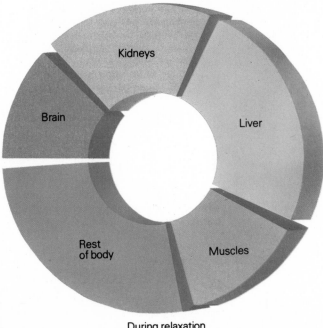

During relaxation

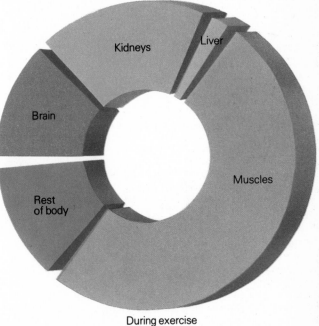

During exercise

Trevor Lawrence

Common diseases of the circulation

Disease	Symptoms	Action
Arteriosclerosis – hardening of the arteries	Raised blood pressure. Poor circulation to the part concerned. Can lead to heart attack or stroke.	Preventive measures the best. Stop smoking, reduce weight, eat less animal fat, take more exercise. A doctor will prescribe drugs to treat high pressure.
Atherosclerosis—build-up of fat in arteries.	Few symptoms, but blood pressure may be raised. Can lead to heart attack or stroke.	Preventive measures as for arteriosclerosis. Special diet may help by reducing fat and cholesterol levels.
Shock—collapse of circulation due to blood-loss, burns, heart failure or other causes	Fast, weak pulse. Skin clammy, breath short, blood pressure very low.	This is a medical emergency, and immediate treatment will be needed.
Peripheral vascular disease—severe narrowing and formation of clots in arteries and veins, usually of legs.	Cramps in legs during exercise; feet redden when lowered, turn white when raised; toes and fingers pale and cold.	See a doctor. Surgery may be needed to by-pass affected vessels. Take care to avoid foot infections. Stop smoking.
High blood pressure (hypertension).	Forceful pulse. There may also be dizziness, headaches, florid complexion, shortness of breath.	See a doctor. He will prescribe drugs to treat the condition and recommend preventive measures.
Stroke—clot of blood in a brain artery (cerebral thrombosis) or breaking of a blood vessel in the brain (cerebral haemorrhage).	Sudden paralysis, usually down one side of the body. May be preceded by headaches, vomiting and drowsiness.	A medical emergency. Hospital treatment followed by convalescence and rehabilitation.
Pulmonary embolism—clot in one of the arteries of a lung.	Pain in the legs and chest. Coughing, short breath, skin looks blue. Sputum may contain blood.	A medical emergency. Hospital care needed with the use of anti-coagulants and possibly surgery.
Phlebitis—inflammation in a vein, most commonly in a varicose vein of the leg. Often leads to the formation of a clot (thrombus).	Leg white, painful and swollen, feels heavy.	See your doctor. Rest in bed or drug treatment may be necessary. Give additional support to the area with a crêpe bandage.
Aneurysm—weakening of an artery causing it to balloon out.	There may be pain in the back, chest or abdomen depending on position of affected artery.	See a doctor. Surgery will be needed to remove or strengthen the diseased part to construct a by-pass.
Varicose veins	Swelling of veins, usually in legs. Legs ache.	If painful see a doctor. He will inject the veins or advise surgery. Support tights or stockings should only be used if these measures are not possible.

Measuring blood pressure

Blood pressure is different from the pulse, being a measurement of the force with which the heart pumps blood out into the arteries.

An artery in the arm is the usual site for a blood pressure measurement because by this stage the opening through which the blood passes is narrow enough to actually resist the flow. The instrument used to measure blood pressure consequently works on the idea that if you temporarily close the flow of blood through the artery (by inflating a special 'bandage' wound round the arm), the time taken for the flow to be re-established at full strength is a measurement of the force of the heartbeat.

High blood pressure

If the blood pressure is higher than normal, the heart is probably having to work harder to push the blood through the circulation, and this may indicate that there is some disease of the system.

There might, for example, be arteriosclerosis, or a narrowing of the arteries. Clearly, the smaller the opening in a blood vessel, the harder the heart has to work to pump the blood through. If the heart works too hard over a long period, its life may be shortened, and this is why doctors are on the look-out for high blood pressure.

Further controls

The width of the blood vessels is in fact a control on the circulation in its own right. Changes in the width of the blood vessels can be brought about by two means, the nerves and the hormones.

Overall direction of the behaviour of the arteries is provided by an area in the brain known as the vasomotor centre. It receives messages from nerve endings, and in response to their signals, the centre issues instructions to the muscles of the arteries. If the blood pressure is too high, the muscles are 'told' to relax, so allowing the arteries to widen. And if it is too low, the opposite occurs.

As well as this central control, there are certain other factors which can cause changes in the width of blood vessels. A build-up of carbon dioxide in the body tissues from increased activity makes the arteries widen so that the cells receive more blood.

If for some reason the blood pressure drops, the kidneys respond by producing a hormone called angiotensin, which makes the arteries grow narrow, raising the blood pressure back to normal.

Temperature is another local control. Heat makes the vessels expand so that more blood flows through them. As a result more blood is available to be cooled by the outside air, and the overall body temperature drops. Cold makes the vessels contract, with the opposite result.

The all-purpose system

Taken together, these controls make it possible for the body to undertake amazingly varied and demanding roles in life.

If we need to sit still, the blood supply is automatically distributed to maximum advantage for digestive and other processes, with 14% in the brain, 22% in the kidneys, 28% in the liver and 15% in the muscles.

But during hard exercise this changes again with no conscious effort on our part so that 14% is in the brain, 22% in the kidneys and more than 50% in the muscles where it is most needed.

Cirrhosis

Q How much alcohol can I drink before I develop cirrhosis of the liver?

A French experts estimate that the consumption of 40 g of pure alcohol a day for up to ten years will cause cirrhosis in most people. This is the equivalent of drinking five pints of beer, or ten whiskies, every day for that period of time. What matters is the total quantity of alcohol consumed: it makes little difference whether it is taken in the form of wine, whisky or beer.

Q I have been a heavy drinker for some time. How do I know whether I have damaged my liver?

A There are usually no symptoms in mild cirrhosis, and simple blood tests will not indicate how much permanent damage has been done to the liver cells. The only certain way of making a diagnosis is to have a small piece of the liver examined under the microscope, and in your case this may not be necessary. Talk to your doctor about your problem—and cut down your drinking. Better, stop altogether.

Q My father has been told that his heavy drinking has affected his liver. Is there any chance that it may recover?

A This very much depends on the severity of the damage. Liver cells do possess a tremendous capacity to repair damage, but it is unlikely that a cirrhotic liver will be able to replace all the lost tissue. Once the cirrhotic process takes hold, the disease is irreversible regardless of whether the original cause is removed.

Q I had cirrhosis over a year ago and am now quite better. Can I start to drink again?

A Certainly not, if the cause of your cirrhosis was alcoholism. However, if virus hepatitis or glandular fever caused the disease, you are now over the period when abstinence is advised. It is during this time that the patient's liver has greatest sensitivity to alcohol, increasing the chances of causing permanent liver damage. Take advice as soon as possible.

Although cirrhosis of the liver can develop after a bout of infectious hepatitis, it mostly affects heavy drinkers. If detected early enough, treatment can be effective.

Cirrhosis is a liver disease, characterized by a progressive destruction of liver cells (hepatocytes); these are then replaced with fibrous tissue, which gradually leads to hardening and less effectiveness of the organ. Clumps of small nodules give the cirrhotic liver a knobbly appearance.

Causes
The most common cause of cirrhosis is alcoholism. The quantity of alcohol necessary to damage the liver varies with each individual, but it is generally accepted that drinking for ten years at the rate of five pints a day or ten single whiskies can cause cirrhosis in susceptible patients.

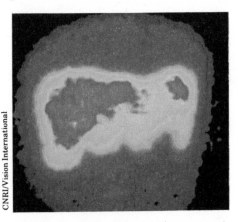

Viral hepatitis (there are two types, caused by two viruses, A and B) can also lead to cirrhosis. The virus responsible may be transmitted in blood from hypodermic needles or blood transfusions, and in drinking contaminated water.

Symptoms
In mild cirrhosis there are usually no symptoms. The onset of the disease is gradual, and many of the symptoms are the result of toxic chemicals accumulating in the body which are normally removed by the liver, and of internal bleeding, due to lack of clotting factors in the blood. Brain function is impaired, bile accumulates in the skin causing severe itching, followed by jaundice and the contraction of the liver. The abdomen swells, and fine red lines caused by smaller veins, appear on the skin. In men, the testicles may atrophy and breasts begin to grow as the liver is no longer able to cope with the small amounts of female hormone normally present in the body.

Dangers
In the worst cases of cirrhosis, death can result either from coma, or from bleeding, which is caused by the rupturing of the enlarged veins around the oesophagus (gullet). When bleeding is torrential, the patient will die within minutes of the rupture.

Microscopic picture (above) is of a section of tissue taken from a liver affected by cirrhosis. The picture (left) is taken with radioactive isotopes.

Treatment
When the cause of the disease is alcohol abuse, then the treatment is abstinence.

Protection against viral hepatitis can be given by an injection of gammaglobulin, blood rich in disease-fighting antibodies. Sufferers of virus hepatitis should be kept in quarantine, and abstain from alcohol for at least six to 12 months.

Once the cirrhotic process is established, there is no effective treatment, though diuretics (pills which remove fluid from the body) and steroid drug therapy to build tissues might be used to protect the liver.

Outlook
The liver cells possess a remarkable capacity to repair damage, but ultimately a point of no return is reached beyond which cell destruction outstrips cell replacement. Once the cirrhotic process is past this point, the disease progresses relentlessly, even if the original cause is removed, and death follows usually within ten years. However, in mild cases, if drinking stops and there are no further complications, life expectancy is normal.

Cold sores

Q Whenever I get anxious, I feel a prickling sensation in my lower lip—and a cold sore comes up. Is there any connection between cold sores and stress and anxiety?

A Possibly, but stress itself will not necessarily produce a cold sore, unless your body has somehow learned to use such situations as a trigger. Such a response is more likely to occur when you are run down, which could account for the feeling of not being able to cope which probably accompanies your anxiety.

Q I always seem to get a cold sore in time for a special occasion, just when I want to look my best. Is there any way I can stop this?

A Unfortunately not. Once the blisters have appeared, they have to run their course. The only thing you can try to do is to avoid catching a cold at such a time, which could either act as the initial trigger or simply aggravate the existing condition.

Q Do cold sores have a tendency to run in families?

A It has not been proved that this is so, though it is possible that the inability to develop a sufficient immunity to the virus that causes it is hereditary.

Q My mother suffers from cold sores and she will insist on kissing my baby whether she has them or not. Can they be passed on in this way?

A The cold sore virus can probably be passed on to very young children like this. So, when your mother has a cold sore, you should very tactfully persuade her not to kiss your baby until the sore is better.

However, most children will have come into contact with the virus by the time they are five and have developed their own immunity to it.

People over this age, therefore, are unlikely to catch a cold sore from anyone else through kissing. Neither will kissing trigger off a cold sore in anyone who periodically suffers from them.

A cold sore is an unsightly nuisance but not a serious health hazard. In fact, many people become naturally immune to them, and symptoms can be alleviated in those who are affected.

A cold sore is the term used to describe the blisters that form around the mouth and inside the nose; they most often appear towards the end of a cold—hence their name.

These sores can be irritating and unsightly, and cause a lot of local discomfort, but they are not dangerous. They are produced by a virus called herpes simplex, to which most people have been exposed by the time they are five years old; but the majority of us build up a natural immunity that is so effective that we never produce cold sores. Unfortunately, for the minority who suffer from them, they are a real nuisance.

The herpes simplex virus is related to the one that attacks the genital area. That virus, however, is a sexually transmitted disease and an immunity to the cold sore virus is not proof against genital herpes.

Causes
Once the herpes virus has infected the skin, it remains hidden there, lying dormant between attacks. The body produces a partial immunity that controls the virus for most of the time, until a certain 'trigger' causes it to flare up. This can be a cold, a bout of flu, a chest infection or a sore throat.

Exposure to sunlight or harsh winds can also act as triggers. Some women have a tendency to produce the sores during menstruation.

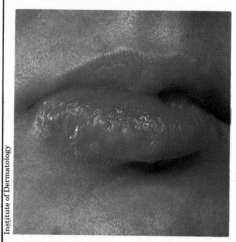

The typical cluster of tiny blisters forming a cold sore: these feel itchy and hot, then become painful. The healing process starts when they begin to dry up.

Institute of Dermatology

Symptoms
People who suffer recurring attacks of cold sores soon learn to tell when one is starting: there is a sudden itchy tingling in the skin in the affected area, which can begin up to two days before the cold sore erupts.

When this has happened, an inflamed cluster of tiny blisters develops; these fill with a yellowish-white fluid and feel itchy and hot, a sensation which is followed by tenderness and some pain.

Occasionally these inflamed blisters will burst within two to four days of appearing, but in all cases they start to heal by drying up. During this process, if the sore is left well alone, a crust forms which will eventually fall off.

Dangers
There is very little danger of scarring, except in severe cases. However, it is important to touch the sore as little as possible, or it will spread.

The crust should never be picked before the cold sore is fully healed and dried out, or it could become reinfected and the whole healing process would then be prolonged unnecessarily.

Treatment
Once the virus has infected the skin, there is no cure for it but patience. Some doctors have used smallpox vaccinations in an attempt to immunize sufferers against severe attacks, but the value of these is doubtful.

If a cold sore recurs constantly, your doctor might prescribe an antibiotic ointment.

In the early stages, before the sore has erupted, but the skin is itching and tingling, an anti-viral solution may be painted on, which can stop the sore from developing further.

Some people have found that applying ice cubes to the tingling area at this stage is also of some use.

Once the cold sore blisters have appeared there is no treatment that will stop it from running its course. There are preparations on the market, however, that will relieve the itchiness and pain, even though they will not shorten the healing period.

Outlook
Most cold sores will heal naturally within a fortnight or so—three weeks at most.

Colon and colitis

Q I have chronic colitis. Is there any chance my children will catch it?

A No. Although the cause of chronic colitis is uncertain—it may be a bacterial infection or a result of psychological disturbance—it is in no way contagious.

Q If I have chronic colitis, am I likely to get cancer of the bowel?

A It is highly unlikely. Modern drug treatment with salazopyrin is very effective and will usually control the symptoms. If the disease proves severe, the colon or a portion of it can be removed. Only five to ten per cent of those patients who have chronic colitis for ten years or more develop colonic cancer.

Q I sometimes have severe diarrhoea after I eat certain foods. How will I know if I have colitis?

A If you are certain that you are not merely suffering from a stomach upset, and that specific foods trigger off diarrhoea, then you may be allergic to them and possibly be suffering from acute colitis. If the diarrhoea is constant, possibly contains mucus, pus and blood and you are dehydrated and anaemic, then you should be examined by your doctor for chronic colitis. The lining of the colon is examined by a colonoscope: if you have chronic colitis, the appearance will resemble red velvet and bleed readily on contact.

Q My father gets attacks of acute colitis. How should they be treated?

A He should retire to bed with plenty of fruit juice to drink, and take kaolin and morphine mixture or codeine, to reduce the severity of the diarrhoea and pain. If his colitis is the result of an allergic reaction to foods, then simply avoid them in his diet.

Q Nothing helps my colitis. Do I need an operation?

A When normal treatment proves insufficient, your doctor may consider surgery as an alternative.

Colitis is unpleasant and debilitating. But while chronic colitis can become serious, and a long-term problem, acute colitis is usually easy to treat.

The function of the colon is to move solid material to the anus (the process of peristalsis) and to absorb salt and water delivered to it from the small intestine. Colitis is an inflammation of the colon's mucous membrane.

There are two kinds of colitis. Acute colitis is often a result of an infection or an allergy, and lasts only a short while. Chronic, or ulcerative, colitis is much more serious, can have serious complications and requires prolonged treatment. Chronic colitis is more prevalent in the 20-40 age group, but it occurs at any age.

Causes
Acute colitis is caused by such infections as amoebic and bacillary dysentery, typhoid, entero-viruses and, most commonly, allergies to certain foods.

The cause of chronic colitis is unknown, but there are a few possible theories. Bacterial infection and allergies to milk and milk products have been cited. It may be the result of emotional disturbance.

Symptoms and dangers
In both acute and chronic colitis, the symptoms are abdominal pain, followed by an explosion of watery diarrhoea.

How colitis affects the body

In chronic colitis, there may be as many as 15-20 bowel motions each day. Large quantities of mucus, pus and sometimes blood are passed with the motion. On occasion, there is rectal tenesmus (an urgent need to defaecate without results). In more severe cases, dehydration, anaemia, loss of appetite and weight, vomiting, and high fever may be present.

Treatment and outook
For acute colitis, bed-rest is advisable. Doses of kaolin and morphine mixture will stop the diarrhoea.

The mainstay of treatment for chronic colitis is a thrice daily dose of salazopyrin, a combination of antibiotic and aspirin-like drugs. A liquid preparation of hydrocortisone can be given as a suppository and this has a marked soothing effect. Diet should consist of bland, high protein food, with only a small amount of fruit and roughage. Psychotherapy, when the cause is psychological, might help.

With acute colitis, the outlook is excellent so long as the cause of the illness is removed. Some patients recover after a single attack of chronic colitis, but for a greater proportion it may become a fact of life, but one which can be controlled.

Colitis is inflammation of the colon. Here (inset) it is chronic and has caused ulcers in the mucous membrane.

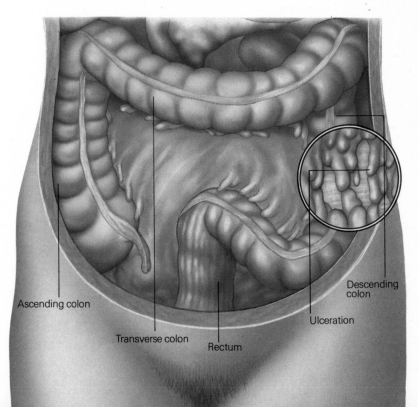

Ascending colon

Transverse colon

Rectum

Descending colon

Ulceration

Frank Kennard

Common cold

Q I've often been tempted to try cold cures that I see in advertisements. Do these work?

A There is no such thing as a cold cure, but some commercial products can relieve the symptoms of colds. These contain antihistamine drugs, which have the effect of helping you to sleep. But unfortunately, once you get a cold, it must run its course.

Q My husband always seems to have more colds in the summer than in the winter. Why is this?

A He may be suffering from hay fever, which has symptoms that can often mimic those caused by cold viruses. Such allergic reactions are usually seasonal, and this is an important clue. However, if someone becomes allergic to material that is present in the air all the year round, like house dust, it can be quite difficult, without tests, to distinguish between an allergy and the common cold.

Q Are there any special foods I can eat that would protect me from colds?

A Some people feel that taking large quantities of vitamin C, contained in citrus fruits, or in the form of ascorbic acid preparations, provides some protection. Hence the old belief in honey and lemon mixture. However, experiments have not proved whether this helps.

Q I've heard that standing in a draught can cause you to catch a cold. Is there anything in this?

A No. But it is possible that a period of exposure to wet and miserable weather may lower your resistance—making it easier for the cold virus to gain entry.

Q What is the difference between a cold and flu?

A The main difference is that flu is produced by a specific virus; colds are produced by many. As with colds, upper respiratory (breathing passage) symptoms are also part of flu—but this illness is more severe.

Even today a cure for the common cold has yet to be found, but there are ways of building resistance to it—and of making it a less unpleasant experience.

The common cold is not one disease, but many, which have similar symptoms, all of which are caused by viruses. These are transmitted to other people simply by sneezing.

Causes
There are at least 20 different types of virus which are known to produce the common cold. Antibiotics are of no use in treatment, nor are there yet any effective anti-viral drugs.

Not only is the body faced with a bewildering variety of different viruses, but in any one group of these there are many hundreds and possibly thousands of variations. A suitable protective vaccine would have to prime the cells of the body to recognize thousands of different types of viruses, and up to now no practical solution has been found to this very complex problem.

People at risk
The sick, the elderly or the undernourished are not as good at fighting infection as healthy people, and so they are more susceptible to the ravages of the common cold. Young children, whose immune system has not come in contact with so many viruses, can suffer 20 or more such infections each year—as is often seen with children starting school.

The common cold is caused by many viruses (inset), and its symptoms are aggravating for those who suffer from them.

Symptoms and dangers
These are unfortunately only too well known. The first sign is a feeling of being 'under the weather', which lasts a few hours. This is usually characterized by aching of the joints and a cold, shivery feeling. The body temperature is commonly subnormal at this stage, within the next few days—and sometimes hours—the body temperature goes up. You may have a sore throat and generally feel wretched. As the throat begins to clear, your eyes and nose begin to stream and there are bouts of repeated sneezing.

If you are a non-smoker, most of these symptoms will disappear within a week.

For most people, the common cold is a trivial illness, lasting only a few days. However, it is a serious matter for the person who suffers from bronchitis, especially if he is also a smoker.

Treatment
Unless complications like bronchitis develop, there is no need to call your family doctor. Your best plan is to make the two or three days of discomfort caused by a cold as pleasant as possible. Bed-rest, with a hot water bottle and plenty of soluble aspirin is ideal.

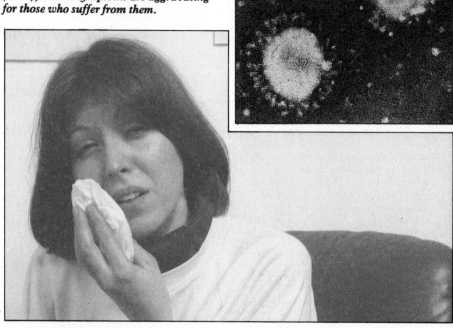

Conjunctivitis

Usually known as 'pink eye', conjunctivitis is a particularly common complaint among young children and babies who are constantly rubbing their eyes while playing. It usually responds quickly to treatment.

Q I want to buy contact lenses but have heard that they may give me conjunctivitis. Is this true, and does it apply to hard and soft lenses?

A When contact lenses are first placed in the eye they are like a foreign body, such as a speck of dust, and most people get an initial conjunctivitis. Usually it is not severe, but some people's eyes are particularly sensitive, and they find it is best to stick to spectacles.

The softer lenses seem to cause less trouble, but you need to weigh up all the advantages and disadvantages of hard and soft lenses.

Q I have just had conjunctivitis. How can I avoid catching it again?

A It depends on the type. Bacterial conjunctivitis will only come back if the source of the infection still exists, for example if there is a sore elsewhere on the body. So the answer is to try to eliminate this. A cure for allergic conjunctivitis depends on finding the cause of the allergy.

Q My seven year-old son has conjunctivitis and his eyes are sticky with pus when he wakes up in the morning. Will my other children catch it?

A The infection can be passed on if pus from the infected child gets on to the skin of another child. You must make sure that nobody else uses anything that touches his face, such as a towel or face flannel.

Q I know someone who has recently had Bell's palsy and now has to wear special glasses to prevent conjunctivitis. Why?

A Bell's palsy is paralysis of the nerves controlling the muscles of the face. The muscles which keep the eye tightly closed become weakened or paralyzed and the eye cannot shut properly even during sleep. It is thus easy for dust to blow into the unprotected eye and the chances of getting conjunctivitis are high. So to prevent this, special dust shields may be worn with spectacles.

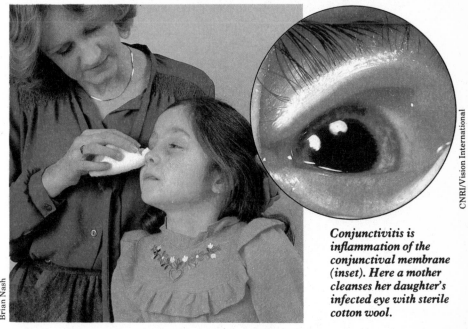

Brian Nash

CNRI/Vision International

Conjunctivitis is inflammation of the conjunctival membrane (inset). Here a mother cleanses her daughter's infected eye with sterile cotton wool.

The thin, delicate skin which covers the white of the eye and the underneath of the eyelids is known as the conjunctival membrane (or conjunctiva). Conjunctivitis is any inflammation of this membrane. The condition causes inflammation of underlying blood vessels, which become large and pink as a result.

The type of conjunctivitis common among children is not serious, but there are other more severe types, including one called trachoma—found mainly in the East—which can cause blindness. Conjunctivitis therefore needs to be seen by a doctor so that he can diagnose the type and whether it is infectious.

Causes

Usually, conjunctivitis is caused by a virus or a bacterial infection. Viruses are the smallest known type of 'germ'; bacteria are larger organisms. The viruses are spread by droplet infection in the air breathed out by an infected person, or by contact with some infected object, such as a towel. The bacterial infections are usually caused by bacteria settling in the eye—perhaps from another infected part.

Any irritation in the eye, caused for example by a speck of grit, could also cause conjunctivitis. Too much strong light can have the same effect. Wind, dust or smoke can all produce a temporary conjunctivitis.

Symptoms

The common signs of the complaint are painful red eyes, unusual irritation in strong light and either pus or a watery discharge which makes the eyes stick together first thing in the morning. Although the eye may itch, vision is quite normal. And in many cases the eyelids may swell up as well.

Treatment

Antibacterial creams or drops such as Chloramphenicol or Neomycin are frequently used to kill the bacteria or prevent damage from a virus. Antibiotics may be used for a recurring infection. Pus should be gently removed with salt water and clean cotton wool swabs. If it is infectious conjuctivitis, the person's face flannel and towel must be kept separate. If there is severe itching, the doctor may prescribe antihistamines. Dark glasses will give some relief from discomfort.

Outlook

The majority of cases clear up completely within a few days. With trachoma there may be damage to the eyelid and scarring of the cornea, and these have to be put right by surgery. With allergic conjunctivitis, the cure is more difficult. The cause has to be identified and, if possible, removed. For this you will need the help of your doctor, or possibly a specialist.

Constipation

Q Why am I always constipated when I go on holiday?

A Many people blame holiday constipation on a change in the water, but it is much more likely to be due to an alteration in your daily routine or the stress of travelling. Even using a strange lavatory can make you constipated, especially if it is a different height from the one you are used to, or has an odd smell which makes you reluctant to obey your body's signs telling you to defecate. Lack of exercise is also a cause of constipation, so next time you go on holiday, try to make sure you have a good walk every day as well as resting and relaxing.

Q Is it true that constipation can give you blood poisoning.?

A No. It is an old wives' tale that faeces are poisonous. They only become infected after they are exposed to the air and are attacked by bacteria. So constipation cannot cause blood poisoning; but it can make you feel drained of energy and generally 'off-colour'.

Q Why have I become so constipated since giving up smoking?

A The drug nicotine in tobacco smoke tends to speed up the movement of food through the digestive system and to stimulate defecation, so it is the withdrawal of the drug that has made you constipated. Don't be tempted to take up smoking again. Instead, follow the usual home treatment for constipation—high roughage diet, plenty of fluids and regular exercise.

Q A friend of mine goes on and on about how dangerous laxatives are and how you should always treat constipation 'naturally'. Is this right?

A Yes. This is not just 'crankiness'. Laxatives *can* harm your digestive system. The best remedies for constipation are bran, fresh fruit and vegetables which contain the type of substances, only occurring naturally, which encourage the bowels to move without harming them. And, of course, they are pleasanter to take.

Constipation is usually cured easily by a sensible diet and plenty of exercise. If it persists, never take laxatives—see your doctor for advice.

The sign of constipation is long, often irregular gaps of sometimes a week between bowel movements.

These are accompanied by an enlarged, uncomfortable abdomen and often by a furred tongue, flatulence (wind), bad breath, headaches and pain on defecation the passing of motions or stools during a bowel movement).

Everyone has their own particular pattern of bowel movements, and they vary widely from three times a day to once in every two or three days. So if you happen to be one of those who defecate at quite long intervals, do not automatically assume you are constipated. Worrying about constipation can actually cause it.

How it happens
Food is normally passed along the intestines—in other words, the passages from the stomach—by rhythmic waves of mus-

Fresh fruit, vegetables and bran, the natural cures for constipation.

cle action called peristalsis. Constipation is simply some interference with this process. Among the several causes of such interference probably the most common is food itself.

The digestive system can break up and extract the goodness from most substances we eat as food, but there is one it cannot cope with. This is plant cellulose, which in its common forms occurs in the outer husk of grains of corn (known as bran) and in fruit and vegetables.

The everyday names for plant cellulose are bulk or roughage, but they do not, by any means, imply that it is useless. The opposite, in fact, is true, for undigested cellulose in faeces stimulates peristalsis.

Some foods contain no roughage at all, and, as might be expected, if they are eaten alone, and in large quantities, they usually cause constipation. The most common such foods are eggs and cheese.

Simply a lack of food in the intestines is another cause of poor peristaltic movements, which is why some people on diets

Causes of constipation

Cause	Additional symptoms	Treatment
Persistent ignoring of signals telling the brain that the bowel is full	Headache, furred tongue, wind, halitosis, abdomen distended and may be painful	Try to set aside a regular time for defecation each day, increase roughage content of diet
Excess use of chemical laxatives	As above	Change to a diet with plenty of bran and other roughage. Drink more fluids and take more exercise
Muscle weakness in old age or after having a baby	As above; may be accompanied by abdominal pain	Change to a diet as above, but if problem persists, see a doctor
Reducing diet, anorexia nervosa, low food intake due to mental or physical illness	As above, plus symptoms of underlying cause of illness	If due to a reducing diet, take two tablespoons of bran daily (it contains no calories). Otherwise see a doctor for treatment of underlying cause
Obsession with bowel movements, anxiety or stress about constipation	May be accompanied by furred tongue, wind and the other symptoms of constipation	Try to ignore bowel movements and change to high roughage diet; take more fluids and exercise
Damage to anus, piles	Painful defecation, hard motions, possibly bleeding from anus, causing tendency to 'hold back'	See a doctor as drugs and possibly surgery may be needed to treat the problem
Intestinal obstruction due to twisting or constriction of intestine	Vomiting, acute pain in abdomen	A medical emergency. Get to a hospital as quickly as possible
Diverticulitis—formation and inflammation of small extensions from the colon	Pain in lower left abdomen, temperature may be raised	See a doctor as soon as possible. Long-term change to high roughage diet

become constipated.

For the same reason, people with illnesses that cause loss of appetite are also likely to suffer.

Two diseases of the stomach, colitis and diverticulitis, cause constipation. Pregnancy can cause it too, because the hormones produced at this time tend to interfere with the intestinal muscle movements, as does pressure exerted by the enlarged womb.

Weakness of the muscle in old age or after childbirth are also causes.

The psychological cause
Peristalsis, like breathing and heartbeat, is controlled by that part of the nervous system which works without our direct control.

However, we can, of course, control *when* we defecate. And this ability to hold back a bowel movement may cause trouble.

For if the brain can say when we shall defecate, it can also 'overlook', as if absent-minded, signals from the intestine that the bowel is full and a visit to the lavatory is due.

If constipation is accompanied by pain on defecation, it tends to create a spiral of worsening problems. The pain, which is commonly due to damaged veins in the anus (piles) or cracks (fissures) in the anus, causes reluctance to defecate.

Constipation can be caused by bad eating habits, or a wrongly-balanced diet.

This makes the faeces 'pile up' in the passage, which in turn causes water to be absorbed from them into the bloodstream. As a result they become even harder, and more painful than ever.

Treatment
Except when constipation is caused by a mental or physical illness, the best treatment is a common-sense one. Eat plenty of roughage. Drink plenty of fluids to soften the faeces. Take plenty of exercise to tone up the abdominal muscles, and give you relaxation from stress.

The worst thing to do is take laxatives. These work by irritating the nerves of the intestine, so speeding up peristalsis. They can cause griping pains, and the passing of semi-liquid faeces.

After the intestine has been cleared out in this way it tends to hold the next supply of food longer than normal, so causing what seems like yet more constipation. The sufferer is likely to take another dose of laxative at this stage, and possibly several more when the process is repeated. This creates a real danger that the intestinal nerves may become so conditioned to the artificial stimulation that they fail to work when it is withdrawn.

If a laxative is taken at all, it should be as a last resort. The best ones to choose are those such as bran tablets.

For children, or in cases of painful defecation, liquid paraffin may help.

If constipation occurs along with some obvious illness, such as appendicitis, consult your doctor—it could be dangerous to treat it yourself.

Should constipation remain after the commonsense treatments have been tried, also see your doctor. It might be a symptom of an underlying disease.

Contraception

Q If I have a coil fitted by my doctor how long will it take to start working?

A A coil is effective as soon as it is in place. But for the first three months you must check for the string once a week as this is the time it is most likely to be expelled, if it is going to happen, and then you would not be protected.

Q I am 21 and getting married soon. I would like to have a coil fitted but I have heard that it is not suitable for women who have not had children. Is this true.

A IUDs (coils) are not a first choice method of contraception for women who have not had children. The womb and cervix have not been stretched by having a baby and this makes it more difficult, and more painful, to insert a coil and there is more chance of the womb expelling it. There is also a higher chance of side-effects like painful periods, bleeding and pelvic inflammatory disease.

Your doctor may, however, agree to fit you for a coil in spite of all this if you have considered all other methods and are particularly keen to use this method of contraception.

Q I am pregnant and want to have a coil fitted after the baby is born. I plan to breast feed my baby: do I need to have it fitted during this time?

A Some doctors like to fit a coil soon after the baby is born while others prefer to wait six or eight weeks. Ask your doctor and if he wants to wait six weeks then you must use other contraceptive measures in the meantime. Just because you are breast feeding, does not mean that you will not get pregnant.

Q Can using a condom during intercourse really stop you from catching VD?

A A condom does give some protection to both the man and the woman but it cannot be relied upon to give total protection from venereal disease.

Some contraceptives which are available prevent pregnancy by creating a barrier between the sperm and egg; others either stop the fertilized egg from developing or persuade the woman's body that it is already pregnant. A couple must therefore give careful thought, and take advice, on what is best for them to do.

Over thousands of years all kinds of ideas have been tried to prevent women getting pregnant—ranging from crocodile dung put into the vagina to standing up after intercourse, sneezing, drinking something cold, and jumping backwards seven times.

Fortunately, nowadays the reproductive system is better understood and far more reliable methods are available. The Pill is one of the best known, but not every woman can use it, and here we will deal with the other very effective contraceptives available. Choosing which one to use can be totally confusing unless you know how they work and what they do to you. Only then can you decide which sort will best suit you and your partner.

Some methods are safer than others but may have side-effects while still other methods are more difficult to use and, therefore, have a higher failure rate because they are not used correctly. Some women are allergic to rubber so for them most forms of the cap and condom would cause too much irritation. Others have extremely heavy and painful periods so the coil would be unsuitable for them, as it can accentuate period pains and cause heavy bleeding.

If you go to a family planning clinic, tell them your medical history or ask your doctor which methods would be most suitable. Whichever type of contraceptive you choose, make sure you understand exactly how it works before you use it.

However, in certain countries the use of contraceptives is barred or discouraged for religious and moral reasons, the only method sanctioned being the Rhythm Method. This is a further reason why some couples must give careful consideration to all factors involved in contraception.

Spermicides

Spermicides create a barrier between the man's sperm and the woman's egg (the ovum). They contain chemicals which kill the sperm when they come into contact with them and they inhibit their movement up the vagina and through the cervical canal (the passage into the womb). They are not reliable just used on their own so they are generally used with either a condom or a cap. If then the sperm still somehow avoid contact with the spermicide there is yet another barrier which will prevent them from fertilizing the egg.

A woman should use a spermicide in the form of a cream, jelly or pessary when her partner uses a condom.

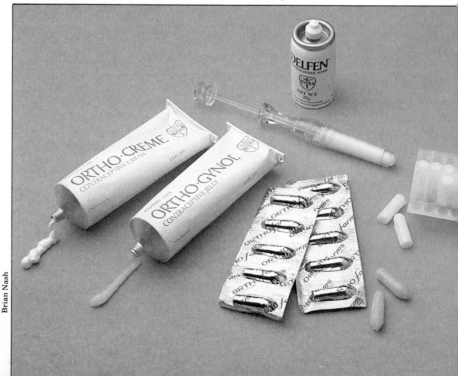

Brian Nash

They are readily available from chemists without a prescription and come in a variety of forms—aerosol foams (which are the most reliable), tubes of cream and jelly, pessaries and foaming tablets, which break up in the moist environment of the vagina and release the chemicals. Some have been found to be almost totally ineffective while others can cause rubber to deteriorate, so before you buy a spermicide consult your local family planning clinic to see which brands they recommend. The creams, foams and jellies come with a syringe-like applicator with a plunger. The woman fills the applicator with spermicide and puts it in her vagina with the applicator tip as close to the cervix (the neck of the womb) as possible to make sure that sperm which get this far will come into contact with the spermicide. The spermicide is released when the plunger is pushed.

When to apply

Used with a cap, it can be applied up to an hour before intercourse. If you do use spermicide on its own do not apply more than 15 minutes before full intercourse takes place. If you have intercourse a second time you will have to apply more spermicide as there is only enough in one application to deal with sperm from one ejaculation. Sperm can live for six to eight hours in the vagina so do not wash the spermicide away before that time.

Pessaries or tablets should only be put into place two to five minutes before intercourse takes place as they are not affective for long. Use your finger to place the pessaries as high up in the vagina as you possibly can.

Condoms

Known by a variety of names—including French letter, sheath, rubber, protective and prophylactic—a condom is a tube of fine rubber closed at one end. In its package it is rolled up so it looks like a flat circle with a thick rim. It unrolls as it is pulled over the erect penis. It can then catch all the semen that the penis ejaculates and stop it reaching the woman's womb.

The tip of the condom should be held between the forefinger and thumb of one hand when it is put on as this keeps the air out and allows some space for the ejaculatory fluid. It also reduces the risk of the condom bursting, and some condoms have a small teat on the tip for this purpose.

It should be put on not only before the penis enters the vagina but before it even touches the female genitals, because semen can leak out of the penis throughout loveplay. One of the common complaints against condoms is that the couple must stop their loveplay to put the condom on. However, many couples overcome this problem by making it part of their foreplay.

There are condoms available which have been lubricated to prevent them tearing when they enter the vagina. If this type is not being used it is a good idea to used spermicide as a lubricant (never use Vaseline as it destroys rubber). Spermicide should be used in any case as an extra precaution as there is always a chance of a condom being faulty.

Condoms come in varying thicknesses and are gradually unrolled over the full length of the erect penis.

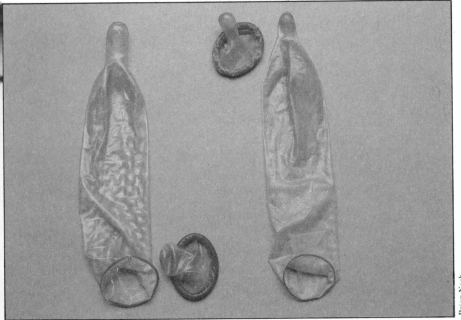

When the penis is withdrawn from the vagina either the man or his partner should hold the condom at the base of the penis so that the penis does not come out and allow sperm to escape. Condoms are available in some countries in a choice of textures, sizes and colours, without prescription, from chemists, slot machines and mail-order companies. They are the only method of contraception, apart from withdrawal and vasectomy (surgery which permanently prevents the presence of sperm in the ejaculation), in which the man takes the total responsibility. They are 96-97 per cent reliable if used properly with a spermicide.

Diaphragms and caps

These are round dome-shaped contraceptives made of rubber which are inserted into the vagina and cover the cervix, preventing any sperm from entering the womb. There are three different types but they all work on the same principle. Used correctly—with spermicide—they are 96-97 per cent reliable.

The Dutch cap or diaphragm is the largest varying from 5-10 cm (2-4 in). It has a strong spring and when it is in position the front rim rests on a little ledge on the pubic bone and the back in a small crevice behind the neck of the womb. They are the easiest to use, and for this reason the most popular. But they are not suitable for some women who, have poor pelvic tone, which means their muscles are not strong enough to hold it in place. In these cases one of the other types of cap can be used.

The cervical cap is much smaller than the Dutch cap and it looks like a thimble with a thickened rim. Some women find it is more difficult to handle and men can sometimes feel it during intercourse as it is not as flat as the Dutch cap.

The vault cap is a cross between the other two types and unlike the others can be made of plastic; so women who are allergic to rubber can use this type. Like the cervical cap, this can occasionally be felt by the man.

Using a cap

You cannot just go to the chemist and buy a cap. It must be fitted by a nurse or doctor to make sure it is the right size as every woman is slightly different inside. A properly fitted cap should stay in place during intercourse without causing discomfort to either you or your partner. If it is uncomfortable or it moves then either it has not been fitted correctly or it simply is not the right type of cap for you.

A spermicide should be used with a cap as a second line of defence just in case any sperm get past the cap. Squeeze out about a spoonful of spermicidal jelly or cream on

Brian Nash

How to insert a diaphragm

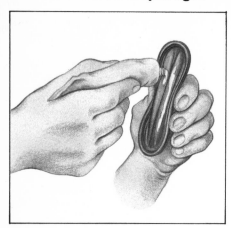
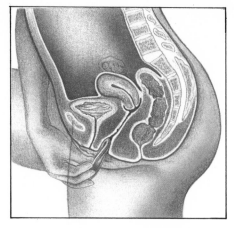
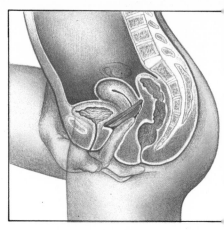

Place spermicide on both sides of the cap, with extra all around the rim. Squeeze into a cigar shape with fingers.

Squat or raise one leg and, after you have spread open the lips of the vagina, insert the cap.

Ensure that you can feel the cervix through the cap. Leave in place at least six hours after the last ejaculation.

to both sides of the cap or diaphragm (note that Dutch caps can be used either way up). Smear more jelly or cream all around the rim and then squeeze the cap into a cigar shape using your thumb and finger to make it easier to insert. You may find it easier to insert if you squat down as this shortens the length of the vagina. With your other hand spread the lips of the vagina and insert the cap.

Check that it is in place by making sure you can feel the cervix through the cap. Your doctor or clinic will show you how to do this when you are fitted for a cap. If you do not have intercourse until more than an hour after you have inserted the cap, apply more spermicide without removing the cap. Leave the cap in place for at least six hours after the last ejaculation since sperm can live this long. To remove a Dutch cap or vault cap, hook a finger over the rim and pull. Cervical caps have a string on which you pull in order to remove them.

Wash cap in warm water and check that there are no small holes or faults, especially around the rim. If there are any, see your doctor about replacing the cap and use additional contraceptive measures in the meantime. Dry the cap thoroughly and replace it in its box away from direct sunlight.

A cap should be checked by your doctor to make sure it still fits at least once a year especially if you have recently had a baby, gained or lost an excessive amount of weight or only just started having an active sex life.

All varieties of cap—cervical (top left), Dutch cap (right) and vault cap (bottom)— are used with spermicide, which can be re-applied with a special applicator when the cap is in place.

Benefits

The most important benefit of the cap is that is has virtually no side-effects. Occasionally it causes a slight vaginal irritation and some women find it causes an attack of cystitis (inflammation of the bladder). These conditions are however, quite minor and after a diagnosis by your doctor, they can be treated easily and effectively.

A few women find they cannot use any type of cap, either because their muscles are too relaxed for the cap to stay in place or some young women may have a vaginal opening that is quite small and they have difficulty inserting it, or some women just find it too distasteful. All contraceptives are not suitable for every woman. Doctors will help each one find one that is right for her.

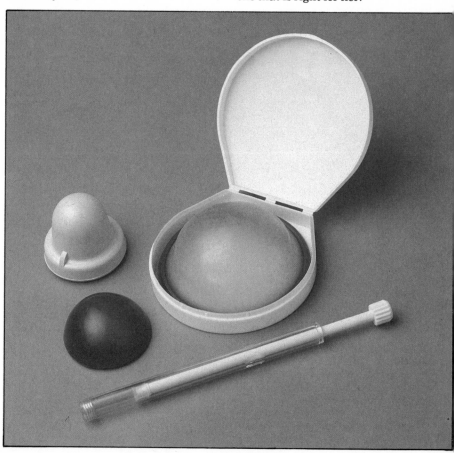

Q I have heard that there is a condom that only covers the tip of the penis. Would this kind increase sensation for the man during intercourse?

A This type of condom is often referred to as an American tip. However, it is not reliable as a means of contraception even if used with spermicide because it can easily become dislodged and slip off.

Q I like the idea of having a Dutch cap because, unlike other methods, it has no side-effects, but is it a very messy method to use all the time?

A It all depends on how squeamish you are—some women don't like to use tampons, for instance. A cap does involve using spermicide so it is more messy than a coil. It also takes a conscious effort to use it. On the other hand, the side-effects are less, so really it is a matter of weighing up all the advantages and disadvantages and deciding if it is worth it.

Q I have just been fitted with a Dutch cap but the doctor at the clinic said I must use a spermicide as well. I don't understand why this is necessary if the cap is a good fit. Can you tell me?

A Even though the cap is fitted for your size and has a strong spring to make sure it stays in place, sperms are very tiny and there is always the possibility that they could swim round the edge of the cap and into the womb. However, if spermicide is used around the rim of the cap and on the side nearest the womb it will kill any sperms that do manage to get past the cap.

Q Can I use a cap during my period?

A Yes. A cap can be used then. All that happens is that it will hold back the menstrual flow until it is removed. Keep the cap in for six hours after intercourse and then use a pad or tampon as usual. Intercourse during menstruation can be less messy and, therefore, more pleasant if you do use a cap.

Intra-uterine devices

Intra-uterine devices—commonly known as IUD's or coils—work in a different way from condoms and caps. They are inserted into the womb and, rather than forming a barrier between the sperm and the egg, they prevent a fertilized egg from implanting itself in the womb. Doctors are not sure why they work but they are known to prevent the lining of the womb from thickening so the right environment for an egg to develop is not created. They are the only form of contraception available—apart from the Pill—that do not require any pre-intercourse preparation.

Coils come in many shapes and sizes and must be inserted by a medically qualified person under sterile conditions. The most commonly used are the Lippes loop, Copper 7 or Copper T and the Saf-T-Coil. The Lippes loop is made out of plastic and looks like a double letter S placed one on top of the other. The Copper 7 is made of plastic in the shape of a figure 7 with copper wire wound around it, the Copper T is the same but T-shaped. The Saf-T-Coil is also made of plastic and looks like two coils coming from each side of a central stem. They have a slightly higher reliability rate at 98 per cent than caps and condoms.

Insertion

Most coils come in sterilized packs with a fine plastic tube about 2 mm in diameter used for insertion. A coil is usually implanted just after or during menstruation because the cervix is more relaxed then.

The depth of the womb is checked by passing a small probe through the neck of the cervix. This shows the doctor how deep to insert the coil and also which type is most suitable, as the size of womb varies a great deal. The coil is straightened out inside the tube and the tube is inserted through the cervix. When the correct depth is reached the tube is detached and the coil springs back into shape inside the womb. The whole process takes only a few minutes.

Side-effects

The insertion may be a little painful, for some women, especially if they are nervous and tighten all their muscles. If the pain, however slight, continues for more than a couple of days then you should see your doctor. Each woman will react differently to having a coil fitted but it is always a good idea to sit quietly for a while.

Some women may find they have heavier periods than usual for the first two or three months after having one fitted, sometimes there is a slight spotting between periods, backache or stomach cramp. These normally disap-

Lippes loop in uterus

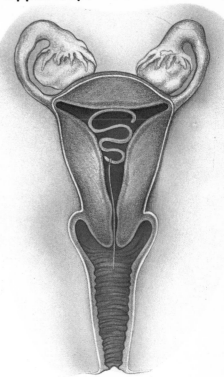

The IUD itself is in the uterus; the string protrudes down into the vagina.

pear within a couple of months but if you are in a lot of pain then see your doctor.

Checking

Occasionally a coil may be expelled from the body for no apparant reason other than a woman's internal anatomy being unsuitable. If this does happen it is usually within the first three months and may be during menstruation so it can pass unnoticed. They all have a fine nylon string attached which hangs down into the vagina and you should be able to feel this with your finger. If you cannot feel it or it seems longer than usual you should go back to your doctor. Use some other method of contraception in the meantime.

You should check for the string once a week for the first three months. After this check it once a month, preferably after menstruation as this is the time it is most likely to become dislodged.

Some men complain that they can feel the string during intercourse and if this bothers them it is possible for a doctor to shorten the string. Tampons rarely get caught up in the string but if you feel a sharp pain when you remove a tampon, check the string.

Staying in place

A coil can be left in place for years—ten years if you wish—but you should have a medical check-up at least once a year.

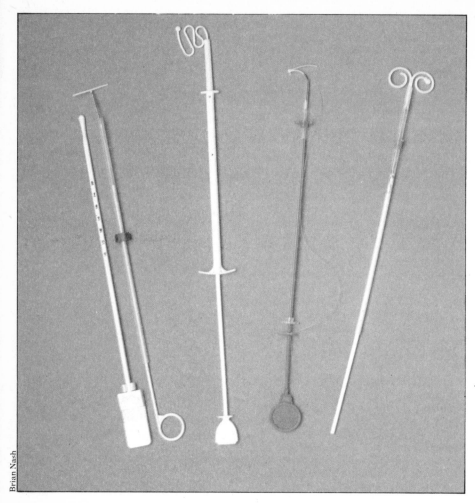

Shown here (left to right): an intrauterine sound, a probe used to measure the direction and depth of the uterus when inserting an IUD; Copper T, Lippes Loop, Copper 7 and Saf-T-Coil.

Hormone pellet insert

Another method that fools the body into thinking it is pregnant is a slow releasing hormone pellet the size of a grain of rice. It is implanted under the skin behind the neck and slowly dissolves, releasing hormones into the body. The device is removed by making a small incision and taking it out.

Progestasert IUD

This is a hormone-releasing IUD which was first thought to be more effective than the conventional IUD and less likely to cause bleeding. Unfortunately, there have been reports of an abnormally high rate of ectopic pregnancies (where the fertilized egg lodges in the Fallopian tube).

Collagen sponge

While this is still being researched, it does appear to be the most promising of the new developments. The Collagen sponge is prepared from the skin or Achilles tendons of cattle. It is impregnated with spermicide and moulded into the shape of a thick-walled diaphragm and is used in the same way. The sponge completely absorbs and traps ejaculated sperm. It must be left in for six hours, then taken out and washed. Each one can be used two or three times.

Nasal spray

This is a fine mist which is sprayed into the nose. It contains hormones which work on the gland which controls the release of hormones into the body.

The Copper 7 (and Copper T) has to be changed every two years. It discharges small quantities of copper which seems to form part of the contraceptive process.

You are unlikely to get pregnant with a coil in place but if you suspect you are, see your doctor immediately. It must be removed as it could cause a miscarriage.

Morning-after coil

If a woman has had intercourse at the midpoint of her cycle—her most fertile time—without using any contraceptives some doctors will fit a coil afterwards. It is usually the Copper 7 or the Copper T and it must be done within 72 hours of intercourse. It can be removed at the next menstruation and is considered more as a safety measure than a contraceptive.

Douching

It used to be thought that semen could be flushed out of the vagina with hot water or a mild solution hostile to sperm but this is not so. Not only is it totally unreliable, it can be dangerous. A syringe with a rubber bulb at one end is inserted into the vagina and the contents squeezed out. A dirty syringe can cause an infection.

New methods

There are other methods which are available only as clinical trials at the moment, but which nevertheless deserve some mention. Note that these methods of contraception are not at present in common use.

Depo-Provera jab

This is an injection of the female hormone progesterone given twice or four times a year. It is as reliable as the Pill (which is 99 per cent plus reliable) but as it does not contain oestrogen many of the dangers and side-effects of the Pill are absent. It is especially good for women who have difficulty in remembering to take the Pill.

Silastic ring

The Silastic ring is a flexible ring, impregnated with progesterone, which fits inside the vagina in the same way as a diaphragm. It releases the hormones into the body in the quantities normally present during pregnancy. The body is fooled into thinking it is pregnant and does not release any new eggs. The ring is worn for 21 days and then removed to allow menstruation. After seven days a new ring is fitted by the woman herself.

The Collagen sponge is still being tested. The loop aids removal.

Corns

Q Why do corns ache if they are just dead skin?

A Microscopic sections through corns show there is an area of mild inflammation in the skin below the corn. Corns will ache if pressed because the hard corn will be applying pressure to the soft tissue.

Q I have very soft skin. Is there anything I can do to prevent blisters and corns on a walking holiday?

A The best protection is to ensure you have a pair of very comfortable walking shoes and soft woollen socks. If these are new, be sure to walk several miles in them before going on a really long trek.

Sometimes soaking the skin with methylated spirit will help harden up areas that might otherwise blister, but if you are susceptible to corns this should not be done as it may encourage them.

Q The skin on my feet is very hard and thick. What can I do to prevent it from becoming painful?

A Aside from ensuring that your shoes fit properly, you should pare the hard skin on your feet down to a minimum as a hard area of corny skin will produce a blister beneath it if the rubbing or friction is severe enough.

Q Can corns ever turn malignant and become cancerous?

A This is so rare as to be virtually impossible. Although skin cell formation increases in corns, this is never malignant. A corn that bleeds, spreads unduly, or does not behave like other corns is probably not a corn and should be seen by a doctor.

Q I once picked a corn over my bunion and a plug came out. Should I have left it alone?

A In fairly rare cases a corn will become infected and a small abscess will develop. This only happens if the instruments used to pare away the dead skin are dirty. In your case you probably picked off an area of skin containing an old plug of an abscess.

Corns are so common that most people have them at some time in their lives. They can usually be treated at home or, if severe, by a chiropodist.

A corn is a localized area of hard, horny skin, which has formed as a result of repeated rubbing or pressure. Dead skin cells build up and create a thickening of the keratin (protein) in the skin. As this piles up, the deeper skin cells underneath become inflamed, causing pain and discomfort. There is basically only one type of corn, although those that are very large are usually called calluses.

Causes

Corns are likely to occur whenever there is excessive wear on the skin. Manual labourers and barefoot walkers develop pads of hard skin, which are quite normal, never painful and therefore not true corns. In other people, such as violinists, who are continually rubbing their chin against wood, or those wearing a new pair of tight shoes, pads of skin may form at the site of the rubbing, causing considerable pain. These are true corns.

Although ill-fitting shoes and high heels do cause corns, the most common sites are on the ball of the foot, the side of the toes between the joints, and sometimes, on the heel.

Corns frequently form over bunions, although there is no special association between the two. The reason is simply that the bunion, being a prominent bone, presses against the side of footwear, causing pressure. Corns invariably appear over the bony prominences where the hard skin protects delicate structures underneath. Some people are more susceptible to corns than others; this is particularly true of the elderly.

Calluses can also develop where arti-

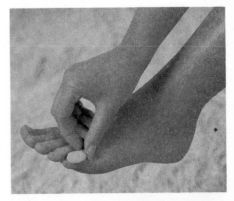
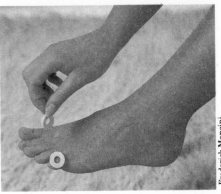

Frederick Mancini

Corn plasters (top) contain an acid that softens the hard skin so that it can be removed more easily. Corn pads (above) can be used to protect corns from rubbing.

ficial limbs or appliances rub on the skin, and as such are a normal response of the skin to excessive wear. In such cases they can be useful, taking the brunt of pressure and impact and thus protecting the skin; but occasionally they may become uncomfortable and need trimming.

Symptoms

A corn can be recognized as an area of hardened, thickened skin, which often looks yellow in comparison to the surrounding skin. It can be conical in shape. Corns between the toes can be soft.

Corns may first be noticed because they cause aching at the end of the day or because they feel tender under pressure. When chronic or severe, the surrounding area may be slightly red and the corn extremely painful, even when the patient is at rest.

Symptoms vary considerably, and it is sometimes difficult to tell a corn from a verruca (plantar wart). In general, verrucas are initially small and painful on

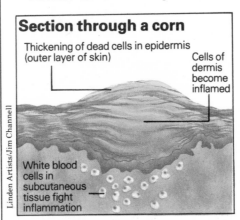

Linden Artists/Jim Channell

Section through a corn

Thickening of dead cells in epidermis (outer layer of skin)

Cells of dermis become inflamed

White blood cells in subcutaneous tissue fight inflammation

A corn is basically an area of hard, thick skin, underneath which the skin cells have become inflamed.

Causes and treatment of corns

Type of corn	Cause	Treatment
Simple corn (on ball of foot, side of toes between joints, on heel)	Excessive pressure on the skin. Occurs primarily through wearing tight shoes, but corns can also appear where there is a wearing away of the skin over a bone.	*Remedial action*: Wear soft, well-fitting shoes, with pads or arch supports to areas likely to rub. *Self-treatment* *Small corns*: Soak in warm water and rub pumice stone over corn. *Well-developed corns*: Gently pare off skin with a clean scraper or corn paring knife. Or apply corn plaster containing a chemical softener directly over corn. Leave for 24 hours. Lift off corn with pumice stone or corn paring knife. Or pad out corn with a ring of foam rubber surrounding the corn. *Treatment by a chiropodist* People suffering from persistent corns, or with arthritis, or who suffer from diabetes or other circulatory disorders, should consult a chiropodist.
Calluses	Same as above, only calluses are larger and can arise when artificial limbs or appliances rub on the skin.	Same as above. The best remedy for calluses is to alleviate the cause of the rubbing.
Corn on bunion	Bone of bunion pressing against the side of footwear.	Same as above. The best form of treatment is to have the bunion removed surgically.

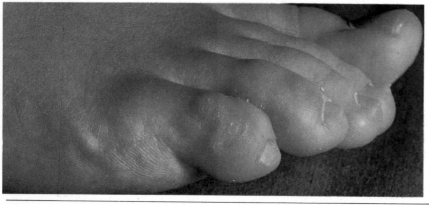

pressure. When the top skin is rubbed off, tiny black roots will appear as dots; the area may then be seen as a wart.

Dangers

Corns are uncomfortable and painful, but only rarely dangerous. There is a more serious condition known as hyperkeratosis, in which the skin of the palms and soles thickens for no known reason, and soon spreads. Medical attention should be sought immediately.

The chief danger of corns is that as the skin is pared off as part of treatment, infection will occur due to the use of unclean instruments. For this reason it is important to pare a corn very carefully indeed. This is especially necessary on the foot of a diabetic who is likely to have poor circulation, and in whom infection can so easily turn gangrenous. Treatment is best done by a chiropodist.

Treatment

As corns are merely hard skin, they can be treated by removing the excess skin.

After a good soaking in the bath, a pumice stone should be rubbed over the corn. This is enough to keep some people's corns at bay. For more well developed corns, scraping off the skin with a scraper or paring the corn with a safety knife is necessary. The tools used should be kept clean. The fine slivers of dead skin should be removed until soft pliable skin is felt beneath the corn. Care should be taken

not to pare away too much skin; this could cause bleeding or introduce infection. Also other tools may be used to remove corns, including a clean file or an emery board.

Corn plasters remove skin by softening it with chemicals: a 40 per cent salicylic acid is soaked on to a plaster. The plaster should be applied directly over the corn and left for 24 hours. The skin should

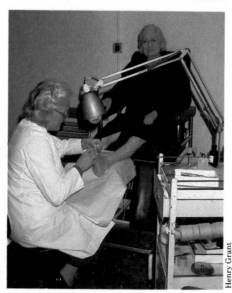

You should see a chiropodist if you have recurring corns over the bones of your feet or between your toes.

then be lifted off with a pumice stone or corn grater. If the corn persists, further applications of plaster may be used.

Some older people become so accustomed to tolerating their corns that they cease to attend to them, simply padding them so that they are not painful. A variety of products for this purpose is available, the simplest being a ring of foam rubber on a sticky base with a hole in the middle.

Calluses can also be treated by applying a solution containing salicylic acid on a plaster and then paring down the callus.

It is essential that diabetics and those suffering from circulatory disorders should have regular professional chiropody to minimize risk of infection.

Outlook

An isolated corn that has occurred because of a change of footwear or activity can usually be treated quite easily, and will not recur.

Calluses tend to need regular permanent attention and will only disappear if the cause is removed.

Recurrent corns over the bones of the foot or between the toes will require regular chiropody. Correct footwear will help, but such corns tend to be chronic.

Pain and aching should never be accepted as part of 'having corns': they can usually be treated and improved, although they do tend to recur.

Coronary arteries and thrombosis

Q Could I have had a minor heart attack without knowing it?

A Yes. It is fairly common to find clear evidence of a previous heart attack on the ECG (electrocardiograph) in patients who have never had any symptoms. These so-called 'silent' heart attacks are commonest in the elderly.

Q How old do I have to be before I'm at risk for a heart attack?

A Heart attacks are occurring in younger and younger patients. They are very occasionally seen in patients in their teens and twenties. By the late thirties and early forties they are really quite common.

Q Does jogging lessen the risk of having coronary disease?

A There is increasing evidence that exercise requiring stamina gives some protection against coronaries. So jogging, cycling, swimming or walking are likely to be good for you as well as simply making you feel good. Muscle- or body-building exercises on the other hand are unlikely to give any protection unless they are part of a specially controlled gymnastic programme. And if you have been sedentary all your life, do not suddenly start taking violent exercise; build up gradually.

Q Why is my angina much worse in cold weather?

A Cold weather commonly makes angina worse, and it may become worse still if you do physical activity in the cold. It is, however, quite all right to do as much exercise as usual once you are warmed up. The reason is connected with the fact that cold weather shuts down the circulation in the skin, increasing the resistance to the flow of blood, and the work the heart has to do.

Q I have angina, but my doctor says I shouldn't take the beta-blocker drugs as I am asthmatic. Why is this?

A These drugs are safe for most people but should not be used by those with asthma because they cause wheezing and breathlessness.

What actually happens when someone experiences a coronary thrombosis—in other words, a heart attack? And what are their chances of leading an active life again? Advances in medicine can do much to help sufferers, but prevention is always better than treatment.

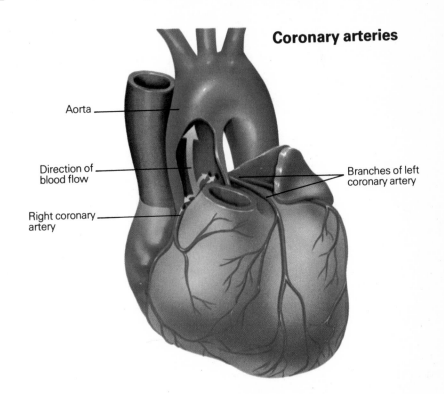

Coronary arteries

Aorta

Direction of blood flow

Right coronary artery

Branches of left coronary artery

Advertising Arts

The coronary arteries supply the heart muscle with the oxygen and nutrients it needs. There are essentially three main arteries—the two branches of the left coronary artery, and the right coronary artery.

The coronary arteries are the vessels which supply blood to the heart itself. They are particularly prone to partial or total obstruction by atheroma—the process of fatty build-up caused by many factors, but principally excessive stress, sedentary living, smoking and an unhealthy diet.

Obstructed coronary arteries are the cause of heart attacks; and disease of the coronary arteries is the commonest cause of death in Western countries.

The three arteries

The heart is a muscular bag which pumps blood round the body. Like any muscle, it must be supplied with oxygen and food to continue working. This supply is carried in the right and left coronary arteries, which are the first vessels to leave the aorta (the body's main artery) as it emerges from the heart.

Almost as soon as it branches off the aorta, the left coronary artery splits into two big branches. So there are, in effect, three coronary arteries: the right and the two branches of the left. They go on to completely encircle and penetrate the heart, supplying blood to every part of it.

Except in a tiny proportion of cases, the disease process is always the same. Fatty deposits build up on the wall of the artery, narrowing the whole artery and creating the risk of a total blockage.

The coronary arteries are particularly affected by the disease because, like the heart itself, they are always in motion and the resulting strain on their walls hastens the build-up of atheroma.

Heart attack

If a coronary artery becomes completely blocked, the blood supply to an area of heart muscle is shut off.

There is an intense, heavy pain, often lasting for hours or even days, and described by the patient as resembling a vice-like grip. There is also shortness of breath, cold sweat, palpitations of the heart, and the patient looks very pale. Eighty-five per cent of those who have a

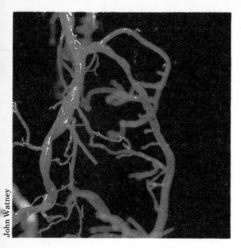

Heart attacks are caused by blocked coronary arteries like these.

heart attack recover, but in some patients there is a further attack, sometimes with disastrous results, in the first hour.

After the attack, the area of heart which was affected eventually heals into a scar known as a myocardial infarct. That part of the heart muscle will never work again. But with careful treatment, the patient will, in most cases, be able to lead a healthy, active life once more.

The blockage itself usually comes about as a result of what is known as a thrombosis (blood clot). The artery, narrowed by atheroma, restricts the flow of blood to such a slow pace that its natural

tendency to clot or thicken begins to operate. This clot makes the final obstruction. A heart attack, therefore, is often referred to as a coronary thrombosis or simply a coronary for short.

Angina
The other problem which coronary artery disease causes is angina. In this case, there is a partial block which allows the heart to function normally at rest but does not allow the extra blood flow necessary in response to exercise.

This relative lack of blood flow produces pain—the typical chest pain of angina which spreads to the arms, shoulders or neck. It is usually brought on by exertion or excitement and only lasts a few minutes. Patients who have angina may go on to develop a full-blown heart attack, and, conversely, patients who have had a heart attack may subsequently get attacks of angina.

Treatment
Angina may, however, be a crippling disease even when the patient has not suffered a heart attack. At its worst it may be impossible for the patient to move more than a few yards without pain.

Fortunately, modern treatment has made a considerable impact on angina, in terms of preventing the symptoms.

Since the early part of the century doctors have been using drugs that will widen the coronary arteries. Patients usually carry these pills about with them. When slipped under the tongue they quickly stop attacks. Unfortunately, they are not very good at preventing attacks, as their effect only lasts for a few minutes, and they are not a treatment in the true sense of curing or improving the condition.

There has, however, been a treatment for angina since the development of the beta blockers in the mid-1960's—a great medical advance. These drugs block some of the effects (the so-called beta effects) of adrenalin. In so doing they also reduce the amount of work the heart has to do and therefore its need for oxygen. Taken regularly, not just when there is a pain, they not only reduce the number of attacks of angina but probably have some effect in preventing heart attacks.

Surgery
As an alternative to medical treatment, the last 15 years has seen a considerable advance in surgery for the treatment of coronary artery disease.

The surgeon first removes a length of

Symptoms of heart attack and angina

	Heart attack	Angina
Type of pain	Dull or crushing or heavy pain. 'A tight band around the chest'. Patient often describes the pain by clenching a fist. A sure sign is that nitrate drugs will not relieve the pain, as they do the pain of angina	May be heavy or dull pain, or may be 'sharper'
How long the pain lasts	More than half an hour, often much longer	Minutes only
What brings it on?	May come on at rest or during sleep, but may be precipitated by exertion or excitement or a heavy meal	Almost always brought on by exertion or excitement, but also by sudden exposure to extreme cold
What stops it?	Usually nothing	Stopping the exertion; glyceryl trinitrate or trinitrin under the tongue
Sweating	Usual	Rare
Nausea or vomiting	Usual	Rare
Breathlessness	Common	Uncommon
What does the patient look like?	Often very ill and 'grey'	Most patients know they have angina and may not give any signs of pain or distress

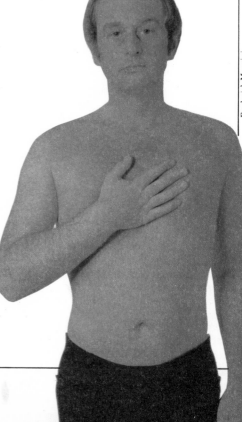

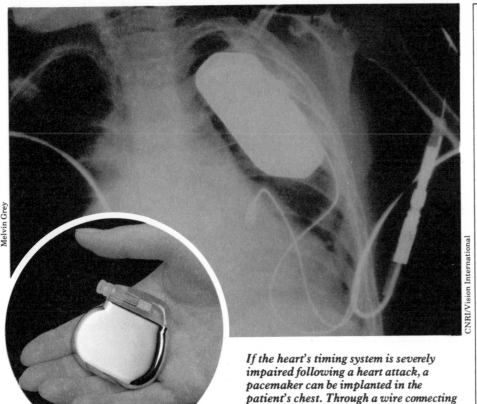
Melvin Grey

CNRI/Vision International

If the heart's timing system is severely impaired following a heart attack, a pacemaker can be implanted in the patient's chest. Through a wire connecting it to the heart, it gives out an electrical impulse which makes the heart beat at the correct pace.

vein from the leg, then uses this to connect the diseased blood vessel directly with the aorta so that blood is able to by-pass the obstruction.

Successful coronary by-pass grafting depends upon very sophisticated surgical techniques. The joins of the graft must be able to withstand high pressures, and the surgeon has to work, on blood vessels only a few millimetres wide.

Coronary artery surgery has only become widely practised in the last ten years. There is now no doubt that it can be very effective at relieving angina pains in those for whom they are a problem.

Treatment problems
The reason why blood flow in coronary arteries becomes obstructed is still being extensively investigated, but one fact seems clear: blockage nearly always occurs when there is atheroma.

Death from heart attacks occurs for two basic reasons. First, the death of an area of heart muscle caused by the blocked artery causes a major disturbance of heart rhythm which reduces the efficiency of the heart so severely that it may stop working.

Secondly, if too much heart muscle is destroyed, the heart is simply not powerful enough to pump an adequate amount of blood around the body.

In contrast, relatively minor disturbances of heart rhythm—arrhythmias—can usually be treated with drugs or by electrical shock. If the timing sequence becomes totally interrupted and the heart slows, or even stops—known as heart block—it may be necessary to use a pacing system.

A wire is passed into a vein and threaded in the direction of the blood flow, until it becomes lodged against the wall of the heart. The other end of the wire is connected to a pacemaker implanted in the chest. This gives out a regular, electric impulse which drives the heart at the correct speed.

Recovery
After one or two days in a coronary care unit, heart attack patients usually spend about ten days or two weeks in hospital, gradually regaining strength and resuming normal activities.

After leaving hospital most people can return to work within two or three months of a heart attack. Generally, patients are encouraged to resume an active and in every way normal life. There is no need to 'protect' the heart as though the patient is a permanent invalid, as lack of exercise was almost certainly a major cause of the heart attack in the first place.

Preventing coronary disease
● Exercise regularly, and properly. Swimming, walking or jogging is ideal, but don't suddenly start doing violent exercise if you have been sedentary for a long time. Build up gradually, and if in doubt, ask your doctor's advice. When you exercise, think about the exercise, not personal or work problems. If you are forced to sit at a desk all day, get up frequently, walk instead of drive, take the stairs, not the lift, and seek medical advice about programmed exercise which can be done by sedentary people without interrupting their routine.
● Eat a sensible diet. Work out a diet which cuts down intake of potentially harmful substances such as animal fats and carbohydrates. Information about this is freely available from health centres and books; but essentially you need to replace butter with certain types of margarine and use, say, sunflower oil for cooking, not animal fat. Cut down on sugar and starch and avoid large, heavy meals.
● Reduce mental stress. Stress is part of living, and your body is designed to put up with enormous amounts of it. However, it was never intended to tolerate *years* of *uninterrupted* pressure, such as is part of all too many people's business lives.

Coronary disease—are you at risk?
● Smoker?—Ten a day doubles your chances of a coronary because nicotine in the bloodstream causes the arteries to go into spasm, thus narrowing them, making thrombosis more likely.
● Overweight?—Anyone more than 20 or 30% above the proper body weight for their age, height and sex is two to three times more prone to heart disease than the normal person.
● Stress?—If you've been under work or family pressures for a long time, a coronary may well be just around the corner.
● Desk-bound?—People in desk jobs who do not take proper exercise are certainly more at risk than active people.
● High cholesterol level?—If you eat large amounts, especially of dairy foods or foods containing animal fat, you are at risk and ought to adjust your diet.
● Family history?—If heart disease runs in your family, don't be alarmed—you're not *bound* to have a coronary. But this should make you even more determined to avoid trouble by proper diet and exercise.

Coughs

Q A friend told me that cough medicines don't really work. Is this true?

A Cough medicines work in so far as they can either suppress or stimulate a cough, though there is much debate about whether they are necessary. Cough mixtures containing codeine will minimize an irritation to the airways, or inflammation caused by infection. Specially formulated mixtures (called expectorants) will help to dilute and loosen the mucus that has gathered in the mucous membranes of the respiratory system, making coughing easier. Home preparations of honey and lemon, or even a tot of whisky, will have a similarly soothing effect.

Q When I had a bad cold recently I began to cough up yellowish phlegm. What did this mean?

A Phlegm is normally white in colour and indicates that the secretions of the mucous membrane are normal. If the colour changes either to yellow or green, it implies that an infection has set in. Clearly, this is what happened to you, but since it cleared up by itself, it couldn't have been serious. For more serious infections, a visit to the doctor is necessary, who may prescribe a short course of antibiotics.

Q Does coughing spread infection?

A Yes. Although coughing and sneezing are reflex responses to outside stimuli, such as dust or gas, they can also transmit germs if a person has a cold or any other respiratory infection. This is why it is so important to cover your nose or mouth with a handkerchief and not cough or sneeze directly on to someone standing nearby.

Q Why is it that sometimes I cannot control my coughing?

A Coughing is the body's way of dealing with a foreign body in the upper airways or an inflammation in the trachea. It is a reflex action—which means that the messages to and from the brain are extremely rapid and are not under voluntary control.

Infection will cause one type of cough, smoking another—or a cough may simply be a nervous reaction. How can you tell the difference?

A cough is the result of an explosive current of air being driven forcibly from the chest. It forms part of a protective reflex to ensure that the air passages remain free of any obstruction. As soon as the obstruction has been cleared, coughing stops. Irritation of the upper airways by noxious gases, or inflammation by infections, causes coughing by a similar mechanism, but in this case the coughing is persistent.

Coughing is an essential protective mechanism designed to get rid of potentially harmful substances in the lungs and air passages. Trying to suppress it with medicines may do more harm than good.

Symptoms and treatment
Coughing, as such, is not a disease, though it may be indicative of some respiratory problem. The most important symptom is not the cough itself, but rather the material which is coughed up, the frequency of the coughing and whether there is any accompanying pain.

Coughs, particularly those due to colds, are not dangerous. However, persistent, exhausting coughs, accompanied by hoarseness of the voice, pains in the chest, breathlessness, fever, fatigue and weight loss should always be treated by a doctor.

In adults, a dry, persistent cough, without any phlegm, is an indication that the patient may be suffering from pneumonia or heart disease—though inflammation of the trachea (windpipe) or bronchi is the more likely cause. If the cough is productive—meaning it produces sputum (phlegm)—and the colour of this changes from white to yellow or green, this is a sign of infection, as in acute or chronic bronchitis. In asthma without infection the sputum is white and frothy. Blood-stained sputum may be an indication of lung cancer, pneumonia or tuberculosis. Coughing that becomes painful may indicate the development of pleurisy but is much more commonly due to strain of the chest muscles by persistent coughing.

In children, if a cough is initially dry and then produces mucus, and there is noisy, laboured breathing, then croup is likely. Coughs which are violent and sound more like crowing, with heavy phlegm, might indicate whooping cough.

Diagnosis is dependent on the colour of the phlegm and the other accompanying symptoms. Antibiotic drugs may be given to treat certain infections; broncho-dilators, which are inhaled, are usually used to relieve asthmatic attacks; and surgery may be recommended if cancer is suspected. Stethoscope examination of your chest, possibly followed by an X-ray, will enable the doctor to decide which of the many causes of a cough is occurring Minor coughs, however, will get better on their own.

Outlook
Coughing is a natural defence mechanism and should not be suppressed. Many of the diseases which have coughing as a symptom are treatable.

Simple cough remedies

Symptoms	Remedy
Post-nasal drip (mucus dropping down from back of nose) Inflammation of the back of the throat or larynx	Ephedrine or similar drops 3 or 4 times a day. Consult your doctor after 5 days. Inhalations of menthol or eucalyptus vapour several times a day.
Irritating, throaty cough	Cough lozenges
Dry cough, or cough interfering with sleep	Cough suppressant or linctus in doses of 2 teaspoonsfuls up to 3 times a day and at night.
Thick sticky sputum which won't come up easily	Expectorant such as ammonia and ipecacuanha mixture, in hot water 3 or 4 times a day.

Melvin Grey

Cystitis

Q I got cystitis for the first time a few days into our honeymoon and the doctor said this was 'honeymoon disease'. What is this?

A Those who are not used to sexual intercourse can often be over-enthusiastic and forceful, and thus the entrance to the vagina and around the entrance to the urethra becomes very bruised and swollen. Bacteria that normally 'sit' on the perineum causing no harm are thrust upwards into the bladder, where they begin to breed, thus causing an attack of cystitis. Hence the name 'honeymoon disease' or 'honeymoon cystitis'.

Q I am suffering from yet another bad bout of cystitis. But last time I went to the doctor the tests were negative. Is it worth troubling her again?

A Although about half of patients with cystitis have a negative test result, they still improve with a course of antibiotics, so it is worth seeing your doctor again.

Q My doctor told me I had urethral syndrome. Is this the same thing as cystitis?

A In some cases of recurrent pain on urination, the urethra, which is the passageway leading from the bladder down to the front of the vagina, becomes chronically inflamed. This is thought to be due to a deficiency in the female hormone oestrogen, and an oral supplement will usually cause the inflammation to subside. So urethral syndrome is not the same as cystitis.

Q My husband thinks he has cystitis. Is this possible?

A Certainly, but there may well be another reason for his discomfort. Cystitis in men tends to be less common simply because their anatomical make-up protects them to a great extent: the length of their urethra prevents bacteria entering the bladder and setting up an infection there. Your husband should see his doctor so that his problem can be properly diagnosed.

Cystitis affects many people, especially women, but until recently very little was known about it. Fortunately, much can now be done to relieve painful symptoms and prevent attacks recurring.

Cystitis is one of the most common conditions, but also one of the most distressing. An inflammation of the bladder, the organ responsible for urination it has three basic symptoms: pain when urinating, increased frequency of urination and sometimes blood loss in the urine. These symptoms vary in intensity.

Cystitis tends to affect women to a greater extent than men. A woman's first sign of cystitis is a pricking, sometimes knife-like pain when urinating. Gradually, this develops into a sharp lower abdominal pain and, as the inflammation spreads, she will get a dull backache, often a temperature and a feeling of general malaise.

The urinary system

The blood is the body's transport system, carrying all the body's needs, but also carrying the body's waste products. It is the kidney's function to select and remove the unwanted products, then expel them. As blood passes through the kidneys, they remove sugar, urea and many other waste substances from it.

The watery waste products removed by the kidneys pass down the ureters—tubes leading from the kidneys to the bladder. At the bottom of each ureter there is a valve which, allows the passage of the urine into the bladder. When the bladder is full, the nerves send a message to the brain telling it that the time has come to urinate. As the person relaxes, the valve (sphincter) and the exit from the bladder relaxes too, and opens allowing urine to pass into the urethra and out of the body. The bladder contracts and helps void all the urine.

Urination occurs normally four to five times a day (but not at all during the night), and obviously will be increased if

Some of the causes of cystitis

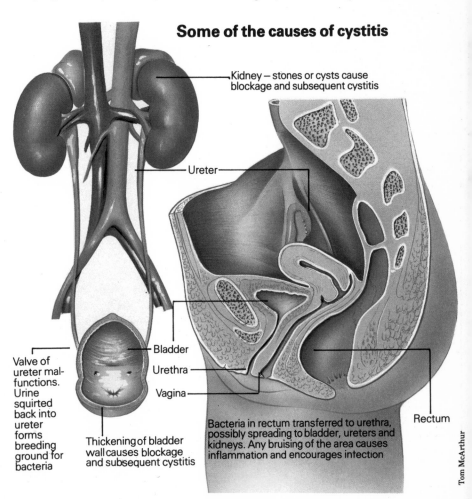

Kidney – stones or cysts cause blockage and subsequent cystitis

Ureter

Valve of ureter malfunctions. Urine squirted back into ureter forms breeding ground for bacteria

Thickening of bladder wall causes blockage and subsequent cystitis

Bladder

Urethra

Vagina

Bacteria in rectum transferred to urethra, possibly spreading to bladder, ureters and kidneys. Any bruising of the area causes inflammation and encourages infection

Rectum

Tom McArthur

a person has drunk large quantities of liquid.

Causes

Cystitis is most commonly caused by bacteria called E. coli (Escherichia coli). E. coli live in the bowel and, like other bacteria which live in the body, are not harmful in this area, and sometimes even useful. The problems arise when E. coli is transferred from the bowel and comes into contact with the urinary organs. E. coli flourishes in an acidic environment and thrives in the urinary passages

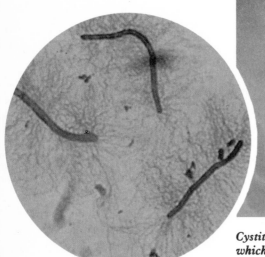

because of the urine's uric acid content.

The design of the female body makes this accidental transference of E. coli a particular problem—the woman's anal, vaginal and urethral orifices are so close that bacteria are very often transmitted from one to the other.

As E. coli multiplies, it causes an inflammation which, unless checked, can spread from the urethral opening and up into the bladder, ureters and finally the kidneys. If the infection reaches the kidneys, it is called pyelitis and, unless a cure is prompt, the infection can do lasting damage to the kidneys. The earlier the infection is checked the better.

Sex and cystitis

Cystitis is sometimes called 'honeymoon disease', and for good reason. Many women suffer their introduction to cystitis when they first make love, as having sex frequently can inflame the tissue around the vagina, including the urethral opening and also introduce bacteria and encourage infection.

If a woman makes love before she is adequately lubricated, the vaginal skin can be broken, presenting another good breeding ground for bacteria and infection. And some men inadvertently carry

Cystitis may occur when bacteria (left) which normally live in the bowel comes into contact with the urinary organs.

The bacteria flourish in this acidic environment, and can spread up into the bladder, ureters and kidneys (above).

C. James Webb

harmful bacteria under the foreskin of the penis.

Hormonal changes can also promote cystitis. During her life, a woman is subject to radical hormonal changes at times such as puberty, pregnancy, the menopause, or after a total hysterectomy. But the complex hormonal system can be affected by a variety of factors, including stress, and changes can also occur at almost any time in a woman's life.

Sometimes certain methods of contraception can bring on cystitis. Some spermicides, for instance, may irritate the sensitive urethral opening. The hormonal effects of the Pill can occasionally trigger cystitis, although it has also been known to diminish attacks.

Cystitis can also be related to blockage in the urinary system, such as kidney stones, cysts or a thickening of the bladder walls, but these problems are less common and are usually corrected by surgery.

Sometimes cystitis attacks children, often because their daytime liquid intake is inadequate. When only small amounts of liquid are drunk, the urine is more concentrated, sometimes resulting in a burning sensation during urination. This in itself does not constitute an attack of

cystitis but, if not remedied, can inflame the urethral tissues and result in cystitis.

Treatment

You should seek treatment for cystitis as early as possible because once it has a hold it may spread throughout the urinary system, and be more difficult to cure.

Cystitis tends to recur in some people. Many women get it three or four times a year and some have it once a month. This seems to be because the tissues situated in a previously infected area are weaker and more susceptible to re-infection, although some women seem especially prone to it.

An attack of cystitis can be cleared up in the early stages by following the self-help instructions given here, or with antibiotics if it is already well developed. One of the ways a woman can stop persistent cystitis is by determining the cause.

Your doctor can help you identify the cause and find a remedy. In a first case of cystitis, it is usual for the doctor to obtain a urine sample and to culture the offending organism. This will be tested for sensitivity to a variety of antibiotics and an appropriate one selected.

Another treatment is to alter the acidity of the urine to make it more alkaline. The bacteria which commonly infect urine dislike an alkaline solution and thrive more in acid surroundings; this means that the introduction of a substance which alkalinizes urine will alleviate the symptoms. Potassium citrate is most commonly used. In many cases this drug is prescribed as a preventative measure, to be taken daily.

Creams are seldom a help but those that contain oestrogen, may be used if there is a local deficiency of this particular hormone. The cream is applied to the vagina over a period of days: and makes it more difficult for infective organisms.

Where the diagnosis may be in doubt—in cases of recurrent cystitis, particularly in children—the doctor may order an IVP (intravenous pyelogram). This shows the outline and functioning of the renal system and reveals whether there is any physical cause of the problem.

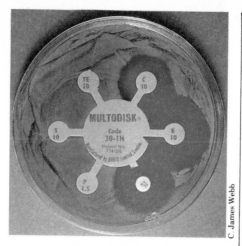

By culturing the bacteria from a urine sample, a doctor is able to identify which antibiotic will be most effective against the cystitis; the most effective is shown by the largest red area.

Self-help for cystitis

Even the most unrelenting cystitis can be self-induced, and unsuitable, self-taught routines can often aggravate the complaint. The following hints can help prevent cystitis occurring, as well as bring some relief.

● Bidets and bowls of water dilute bacteria rather than remove them, so after passing a stool, soap the anus only and pour warm water from a bottle down the perineum (the area between the vagina and the anus) from front to back. (If away from home, use moistened paper tissues.) Dry the area gently but thoroughly. Always wipe from front to back.

● Wash the vaginal area before and after making love. Pass water as soon as possible afterwards to flush out any travelling bacteria.

● Your contraceptive may also be causing cystitis. Ask your gynaecologist's advice.

● Drink three to five pints of water-based drinks each day.

● Wear cotton (never nylon) briefs which should be boiled in plain water away from the family wash. Avoid tights and tight jeans or trousers.

● Never use chemicals—either in toiletry form or as a medication—on the perineum as these may contain irritants.

● Avoid certain foods, like citrus fruits, soft fruits (strawberries etc), hot curries several times a week, or lots of black pepper seasoning on every meal—all of which can irritate the bladder. Try refusing foods with a high refined sugar or starch content.

If you still get an attack

Think back over the last 48 hours and try to pinpoint any unusual occurrence or change in routine. See your doctor for an accurate urine check from an early morning specimen.

In the meantime, you will get some immediate relief from the following:

● Drink a half-pint of bland liquid every 20 minutes for three hours. Cystitis and kidney patients should watch their alcohol intake as large quantities are an irritant.

● Take a level teaspoon of bicarbonate of soda in water each hour of the attack (unless you have heart trouble or kidney stones). Your doctor may prescribe potassium citrate for the same purpose.

● Place a hot-water bottle, wrapped in a towel, high up between the legs. This makes the skin around the urethral opening hotter than the urine and can bring relief when passing water.

Coping with cystitis

Times when you are most liable . . .

Various events or stages in a woman's life can trigger an attack. Here are some of the times when you will be most susceptible:

and ways of reducing the risk

The most effective way to deal with troublesome cystitis is to minimize the risk of developing the problem by following these simple rules:

Puberty

● Cystitis can often be linked to the commencement of menstruation and an unsettled hormone balance which can right itself in time.

● Wash the vaginal area daily with warm water. Always wipe from front to back. Wear pads rather than use tampons. Do not use talcum powder or a vaginal deodorant.

Sexual relations

● The cervix, vagina and urethra can be inflamed by frequent sex, incautious penetration or clumsy hand-stimulation.

● Use a lubricating jelly to cushion the vagina. Afterwards, wash the vaginal area with a good flow of cool, clean water from a bottle as you sit on the toilet, or from a hand shower.

Pregnancy

● An irritating discharge can develop during pregnancy, and urine retention can cause discomfort.

● Wash the vaginal area (as described above). Double-empty the bladder. Do this by stopping the flow of urine by consciously tightening all the muscles round the perineum (the area between the vagina and the anus), then bend over and release the muscles, pushing to help expel any residual urine.

Childbirth

● Inflammation can result from careless stitching, or catheterization with non-sterile tubes.

● Inform the midwife of any skin sensitivity. Take special care about washing of the perineum after delivery. Relieve sensitive, irritated skin with warm, salt baths.

Menopause/hysterectomy/old age

● Degrees of hormone imbalance often manifest themselves in women over 50, resulting in cystitis.

● Ask your doctor to refer you to an endocrinologist, or go to a local hospital's out-patient clinic for an examination and advice.

Depression

Q My son has just lost his girlfriend in an accident. I know he is broken-hearted about this, but won't let it show. Is it better to suppress grief or to let it out?

A The British 'stiff upper lip' has no place in grief, in either sex—in every case it is better to let it out. The suppression of grief, conventionally advocated as a means of showing emotional strength, can actually lead to psychological problems later. The real reason why people advise this is that they get upset by the sight of natural grief in others—their motives are, in fact, largely self-centred.

Q During family arguments, my teenage son has often said 'I'll just die and then you'll be happy'. Is there a real risk of him committing suicide because he is depressed?

A In this situation, the answer is 'No', because depressed people seldom have arguments. What he is actually asking, in a clumsy way, is for you to tell him that you will be unhappy if he dies because you love him, in spite of everything. If, on the other hand, he does have more than the average number of black moods that most adolescents suffer (and get over again), then you should take notice of the situation and keep your eyes open for other signs.

Q My friend had been prescribed drugs for her depression. Are these habit-forming?

A The amphetamine drugs can be habit-forming if taken in large quantities over a period of time. For this reason, they are now only prescribed under strict medical supervision, or avoided altogether. The other drugs that are used for this purpose are safe enough, and will not be habit-forming if the doctor's instructions are followed exactly.

Q Is there any specific age when people are most likely to be depressed?

A Not really. For serious depression, the peak is about 60 years old for men and 55 for women. For milder cases, the peak age is about 50 for men and 45 for women.

Depression can be conquered—but it sometimes needs skilled medical and psychological help as well as support and understanding from family and friends.

Many people feel 'down' from time to time, but these are usually passing phases. In wondering where such moods end and proper depression begins, it should be remembered that this is not a simple condition. It can show itself in various ways and have a number of causes. Neither does it respect sex or occupation, striking at any time from the teens to middle age, when it claims the greatest number of victims.

Early warning signals
If you suspect that someone you live with is suffering from depression, what are the signs of serious trouble? Perhaps the most significant fact is that the victim loses interest and enjoyment in every aspect of life. Such a change is quickly noticeable to other people.

It can apply to work, the home, the family, food and drink, hobbies, sports and the desire for sex, and may extend to personal appearance and hygiene. Then the complaints begin—about all kinds of physical problems—headaches, back pains, stomach troubles, 'tight' feelings

Going to your doctor to talk about your problems is not an easy thing to do when you are depressed, but he is trained to give sympathetic and practical help.

in the chest, giddiness, constipation or blurred vision. And the depressed are also so apathetic that they are often unable to ask for professional help—it is up to others to seek medical or psychiatric advice for them.

The many faces of depression
Not all the symptoms of depression are shown by every patient—two people behaving in markedly different ways can both be classed as depressed. What makes the picture even more complicated is that the condition can be accompanied by acute anxiety or by bouts of mania, a mood of almost forced gaiety, talkativeness and compulsive activity, giving rise to the term 'manic-depressive'.

In general depression, moods may vary from slight sadness to intense despair, and a feeling of utter worthlessness. Strangely, people with this condition seldom talk of these feelings to their doctor: instead they will grumble about aches and pains, tiredness or loss of weight. They may even find it difficult to speak at all; other people will seem to chatter constantly.

These variations in speech often occur as a result of thought difficulties. Patients often complain of not being able to think clearly, concentrate or make

decisions—they *know* that something is amiss. This ability to realize their own unhappy state, without being able to do anything about it, affects depressives in another way. They tend to be preoccupied with themselves, and seem completely unable to count their blessings. Instead, they magnify the mishaps of the past and tend to blow them up into major disasters, always regarding themselves as totally to blame for these misfortunes.

This habit of distorting events to their own detriment, affects their sleep, which may be already disturbed by the illness itself. On going to bed, they lie awake worrying about the past, their own state and the future. A vicious circle easily sets in, with worries about this inability to sleep added to all the others.

As if all this was not enough, the depression itself can cause early morning wakening. Small wonder, therefore, that for many such people the beginning of the day is the most wretched time of all.

When depression is accompanied by anxiety, the sufferer is nearly always restless and has a nervous way of talking; this is in marked contrast to the apathy of other depressives who tend to hide their worries from others.

Post-natal depression

A particular state that arises in some women soon after they have given birth to a baby is called post-natal depression. It was once thought of as little more than a 'mood', caused by the exhaustion of labour and the unaccustomed strain of looking after the new arrival. Nowadays,

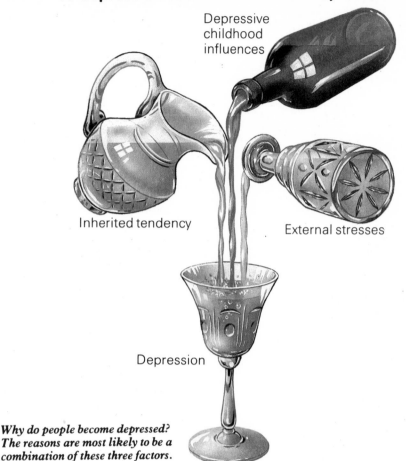

A 'depression cocktail' of contributory factors

Depressive childhood influences

Inherited tendency

External stresses

Depression

Why do people become depressed? The reasons are most likely to be a combination of these three factors.

Terry Allen Designs

Brian Nash

this is recognized as a definite illness. Its symptoms often include a surprising hostility towards the baby, with consequent feelings of guilt or indifference.

All this can cause quite serious neglect of the child and the home in general and a total feeling of being unable to cope with the situation. The result is often a worsening of both marital and family relationships. In serious cases it may even lead to suicide.

There is evidence now that the real cause of all these problems is a disturbance of the mother's hormonal systems, which is a side-effect of pregnancy and birth. Treatment must include the restoration of this hormone balance.

Heredity and environment

To some extent, depression is thought to run in families; but this influence is one of increased liability to the condition rather than actually producing it. In fact there is nearly always a definite stressful event or series of events that brings on the depressive state. Another way in which these symptoms can be 'transmitted' is that the parent who suffers from this condition invariably acts out their depression to others in the household. The children,

inevitably, in seeing this demonstration in terms of behavioural patterns and actions tend to copy it themselves in later

Post-natal depression How to help

● Ask the doctor's advice: treatment may be needed to restore the mother's hormonal balance. Psychotherapy might also be necessary, or even a period in hospital.
● Take over care, or help with the care of the baby, to allow the mother to rest and have undisturbed nights. The baby can be looked after by the husband, a close relative or even a professional helper if necessary.
● Help with, or take over, domestic chores like cooking, shopping, laundry and cleaning.
● Be tolerant, understanding and patient. Remember that the mother has very little control over her state and that the more the pressure is taken off her, together with medical or psychological treatment, the quicker will be her recovery.

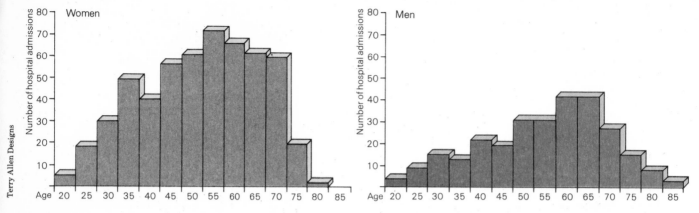

life, if they also feel depressed. This happens rather more easily than would be the case if they had no such model to copy.

When there is no family history of this condition, it is virtually always triggered off by powerful patterns of outside events which affect the victim deeply. In such cases, the chance of recovery from the depression is somewhat better.

The effects of grief
A temporary, but still very real depression can be caused by bereavement. When you experience the death of a loved one, it is normal to express grief: indeed, to attempt to suppress grief reactions because they are painful, because you feel this is silly or because the deceased person 'wouldn't want me to be sad' is never helpful; in fact it tends to prolong the period of grief.

Besides the usual reactions of distress, there are often feelings of guilt, irritability, lack of warmth towards others and sometimes an unnerving habit of taking on the personality traits or mannerisms of the dead person.

People in this state may also have problems with their relationships with other members of the family and with friends. They may show intense feelings of anger towards doctors, hospital authorities, or 'uncaring' relatives. Alternatively, there maybe a complete lack of apparent signs of grief, accompanied by periods of restlessness and virtually pointless activity, which are justified as 'keeping my mind busy', but which do no such thing. In any of these situations, the bereaved person should be encouraged to 'let out' their feelings and talk about their loss with friends, relatives or even with a doctor.

Treatment
Many people find it hard to appreciate the depths of despair which can affect the severely depressed person. In fact, about one in six cases of severe depression results in suicide. It is thought that this rate would be even higher were it not for the fact that the sufferer is often too apathetic to carry out a suicide attempt.

The use of drugs for the treatment of depression is less in favour than it used to be, possibly because psychological methods may better equip the patient for coping with the stresses or situations that contributed to their condition. However, drugs have their place, especially where inherited factors are concerned, because they are simpler to administer and do not involve extended visits to a specialist.

Stimulants, such as amphetamines may be prescribed if the depression is not severe. More often used are the so-called tricyclic antidepressants or MAOI (monoamine oxidase inhibitors) which do lift the mood quite well by altering the brain's chemistry. Tranquillizing drugs may also be used in order to relieve anxiety and tension.

Psychological methods, such as a course in thought-examination or self-assertion (which can be obtained at certain clinics and therapy centres) as well as behavioural therapy techniques can work well in many cases. Even making this examination has in itself a certain power to lift depression.

Living with depression
Psychological treatment can do much to help sufferers to change their way of thinking about themselves. But if you have to live with someone in this condition, do not expect too much too soon, however infuriatingly negative their behaviour may be. What is needed is your continual friendliness, interest and support—even if it does not seem to be having much effect. Often, a positive approach is appreciated by the depressed person, even if they cannot respond, and will be remembered with gratitude later.

Curiously, the technique of not doing too much at once also applies to relaxation. Often someone will advise the depressive to 'get away from it all and take a holiday'. But not only will they fail to benefit from this, they may even become more anxious at not being on familiar ground. Holidays should be reserved for the time when the patient is well on the way to recovery, when everyone concerned will benefit more.

Hospital treatment
In severe cases, home care may become impossible. Then the patient may have to spend some time in hospital for continuous care and therapy. Electroconvulsive therapy (ECT) may be given. For this, carefully controlled electric discharges are passed through certain parts of the brain while the patient is anaesthetized. The current induces a convulsion in the patient's brain and body. This is not felt, but often produces considerable improvement in the patient's condition—as few as two or three treatments may be enough to produce a complete recovery. Although some temporary forgetfulness of recent events may result, many depressives believe that this is a small price to pay for the dramatic relief that ECT can provide. However, it is a technique which some doctors and psychiatrists question, as its result in some cases may be only very short-term.

Outlook
In spite of the comparatively large number of people who are afflicted with depressive illness, and the severity of some of these cases, the outlook is reasonably good. It has been estimated that of all those with a clear-cut depressive illness, about 95 per cent will probably recover, and only four per cent will remain in a state of chronic illness. Of those that do recover, perhaps half may have another phase of depression—but for most the recovery rate is high.

Dermatitis

Q My best friend has dermatitis. I'm afraid that I will catch it from her and that it might leave me with scars. Is there anything I should do?

A Don't worry. Dermatitis does not cause scarring, and because it is not infectious, you will not catch it from your friend.

Q My neighbour's eczema was cleared up by the use of a hydrocortisone cream which was prescribed by the doctor. Would there be any harm in my using the cream she has left over to treat my eczema?

A It is a very bad idea to use any medicines which are passed on to you by someone else. Hydrocortisone and the other steroids are powerful medicines which do not suit everyone and have to be used sparingly. And if they have been stored in a hot, steamy kitchen or bathroom, they are likely to have gone bad anyway.

Q I have just bought a lovely ring, but it seems to bring me out in a rash. What would have caused this reaction?

A You may be allergic to the metal in your ring. Chrome and nickel commonly cause allergies, and they are quite often used in costume jewellery. Try not wearing the ring for two weeks and see if your skin gets any better.

Q I seem to know more women than men who have suffered from contact dermatitis. Does it affect women differently from men?

A Not really, though some contact allergies are commoner in one sex because members of that sex tend to be more exposed to the allergen. For example, one European woman in ten has an allergy or potential allergy to nickel, which can emerge as dermatitis. This seems to be due to the use of nickel in the clasps on women's underwear. On the other hand, chrome allergy dermatitis is commoner in men, largely because chrome is found in cement, which men handle more than women.

Most of us have dermatitis—skin inflammation—at some time or other. Discovering its cause is usually quite simple, and a wide range of remedies are available to treat the problem and reduce discomfort to a minimum.

Dermatitis is a red, itching inflammation of the skin. The term actually covers a variety of skin complaints, many of which result from the skin's becoming oversensitive to some normally harmless substance. But, while the symptoms of each type are similar, the causes are quite different.

The commonest form—eczema and contact dermatitis—are widespread, affecting people of all ages. But, though uncomfortable and unattractive, most types of dermatitis are temporary, not dangerous and not contagious.

Allergic reaction
Eczema, or atopic dermatitis, is largely caused by allergies, though it can be brought on or aggravated by other factors, especially stress or anxiety.

The main symptom is itchy skin, accompanied by a patchy rash, especially in the creases of the arms, legs and hands. The affected skin may be cracked and dry—or it can be wet and weeping, though this is often caused by scratching the skin.

Builders are in constant contact with cement, which can cause the form of dermatitis shown in close-up on this man's fingers.

Institute of Dermatology

Sally and Richard Greenhill

115

Di Lewis

Common causes
Closely related to hay fever and asthma, eczema is frequently caused by an allergic reaction to pollen or animal fluff. There are many different substances that can cause allergies—and almost any of them can bring on eczema.

In young children eczema is quite commonly caused by an allergy to milk, eggs or other protein-rich animal foods. Some allergens, or substances that trigger off an allergic reaction, can pass through a nursing mother's milk, so a baby's eczema can be caused by something the mother happened to eat. Babies often grow out of these allergies, though they may have other kinds of allergic complaint later in life.

Direct contact
The other common type of dermatitis is called contact dermatitis. Altogether its symptoms are similar to eczema—inflammation and irritation—the causes are rather different. This type of dermatitis is also an allergic complaint, but unlike eczema it is confined to those parts of the body that come into direct contact with the allergen.

Metals, especially nickel and chrome, are often to blame, though in fact the list of these contact allergens, as they are called, is almost endless.

Contact dermatitis most often affects the hands because they are so frequently exposed to contact allergens. But a rubber allergy would be most likely to show up on the parts of the body exposed to the rubber elastic in underwear. Similarly, a perfume allergy would be likely to show up as dermatitis on the parts of the body where the perfume was applied.

Although allergies do tend to run in families, contact dermatitis is believed to be due more to regular and prolonged exposure to the substance.

Contact dermatitis has, in fact, been called a 20th-century industrial disease, because modern industry—and its products—exposes workers, as well as consumers to so many potential allergens.

Dermatitis of the scalp
Another common type of dermatitis is seborrhoea, or seborrhoeic dermatitis. This is a condition that affects the hairy areas of the skin, particularly the scalp. It may be itchy and inflamed, with peeling of the skin and severe dandruff.

Seborrhoea is not caused by an allergy. It is thought that the condition is brought on by the over-activity of the skin's oil glands, or sebaceous glands.

Sensitivity to light
There is a type of dermatitis, called solar or photo-dermatitis, which is brought on by exposure to sunlight. In most cases the sun alone is not to blame, but sunlight can bring out some other allergy which has not been strong enough to produce symptoms by itself. Certain drugs, such as the antibiotic tetracycline, can increase the skin's sensitivity to light.

Treatment
Though there are no real cures for the various kinds of dermatitis, they can be relieved and controlled. The most important treatment is to keep the affected area clean and avoid scratching it. This allows the skin to heal naturally and reduces the risk of infections.

There is a wide range of ointments, creams, pastes and lotions which are prescribed by doctors or can be bought directly over the counter from a chemist.

Inflammations which are dry and flaking can be soothed and protected with oily preparations like lanolin or petroleum jelly, while wet, weepy inflammations are better treated with gum- or starch-based applications or with some form of astringent.

Some of the most potent medicines are steroids, such as hydrocortisone. They are anti-inflammatory, and are made into preparations for skin conditions, and are available only on prescription.

Though undeniably effective, these drugs have their drawbacks. If used for long periods on the same area of skin, they can damage its underlying layers. And if they are abruptly abandoned after being used for a long time, the dermatitis may suddenly recur.

Nor are they a cure. If the dermatitis is due to an allergy, steroids may suppress the symptoms, but will not stop them returning once you stop using the cream, which does not dispose of the cause.

The root of the problem
The only permanent cure for dermatitis is to remove the cause. If an allergy is at the root of the trouble, the allergen should be identified and then avoided. This may not be easy, for sometimes the dermatitis shows up only days after the exposure to the allergen.

People who are allergy-prone need to watch out for potential allergens from unsuspected sources—e.g. milk or eggs.

To help isolate the substance responsible, dermatology departments in hospitals keep stocks of all the major allergens, which can be tested on the patient.

Avoiding irritation
People with sensitive skin should use unperfumed, hypo-allergenic (i.e. non-allergenic) soaps and cosmetics, as ordinary types usually contain perfumes and other things that can cause contact dermatitis.

Barrier creams and sprays can protect the skin against irritating substances, and sun screens filter out some of the sun's ultraviolet rays which can cause solar dermatitis.

Contact with some industrial allergens can be reduced by wearing gloves, a face mask or other protective clothing.

Diabetes

Diabetes is no longer feared as it was before the treatment was discovered in the 1920s, and current research is constantly improving the outlook for diabetics.

Q Will eating too many sweets make my child more likely to develop diabetes—either now or later in life?

A No. If a child is going to get diabetes, it will be of the type caused by failure of insulin. This is a hormone (a chemical messenger which affects certain bodily functions) produced in the pancreas. Being overweight, or eating sweets has nothing to do with whether the insulin-producing cells in the pancreas are functioning properly or not.

Q Is there any age when diabetes is more likely to come on?

A It can start at any age, but it is unusual before a child reaches five years. If the disease does come on in early life, it is most likely to do so at the age of puberty or in the late teens or early twenties. After that, there is no particular age at which it is more or less likely.

Q My husband has been diagnosed as a diabetic, and I am afraid the illness may change his personality, for example by making him bad-tempered. Am I right to worry?

A Not really. Obviously, diabetes, like any illness, can put the patient under strain, but it does not cause personality changes. There is certainly nothing to suggest that diabetic children grow up having developed inadequate personalities.

Q Is it safe for a diabetic person to drive a car?

A Generally yes. The only danger is that the insulin-controlled diabetic might suffer sudden loss of consciousness as a direct result of a hypoglycaemic attack (blood sugar level falling too low as a result of the insulin dose getting out of balance). Diabetics have to declare that they suffer from the disease when applying for a licence to drive, and there is a regulation that no one may drive for a period of three years following a bout of unconsciousness.

Diabetes is a condition where there is an abnormally high level of sugar in the blood. The disease, and its symptoms, have been recognized for hundreds of years. Affected people pass abnormally large quantities of urine, as a result developing an abnormal thirst and losing a great deal of weight.

In the 17th century, when diabetes was known as 'the pissing evil', it was noticed that the urine of most sufferers was especially sweet. In a few cases, however, it was insipid—that is, it was not sweet.

The first type had *diabetes mellitus* (*mellitus* means 'like honey'), and is the disease we know today as plain diabetes. The second type, called *diabetes insipidus*, is extremely rare and results from a failure of the pituitary gland in the skull.

Widespread

Thousands of people in every country suffer from *diabetes mellitus*. In the UK, for example, about one per cent of the population have it in varying degrees of seriousness—which amounts to about 560,000 diabetics. In some peoples—for example the Pima Indians of Arizona in the USA—nearly half the population have the disease.

Diabetes results from a failure in the production of insulin, one of the body's hormones, or chemical 'messengers'. Its job is to keep the blood's sugar content in control by directing it into the cells, where it can be put to its proper use: 'fuel' to produce energy.

Without insulin, the body's cells become starved of sugar, despite the high level in the blood.

How diabetes starts

In most diabetes sufferers, the lack of insulin is due to a failure of the part of the body responsible for producing insulin. This is the pancreas, and the failure is caused by the destruction of its insulin-producing cells. No one knows exactly how the destruction occurs, but it is the subject of much research. It seems that some people are more likely to develop diabetes and that some event—possibly an infection—may trigger the onset.

The sort of diabetes which develops suddenly due to a complete or serious failure of insulin tends to afflict young people and children, and is often called juvenile diabetes. Luckily, it can be treated with injections of insulin made from the pancreases of cattle or pigs.

Because of dietary problems caused by diabetics' careful monitoring of sugar intake, there are many foods on the market prepared especially for them.

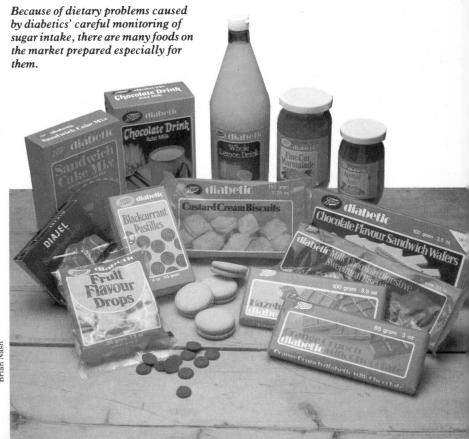

Brian Nash

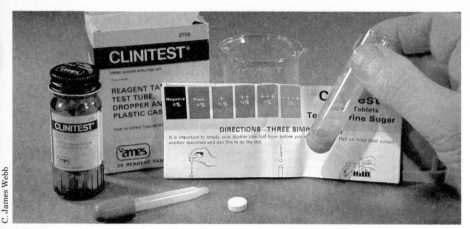

C. James Webb

Diabetics check the sugar level in their urine against a colour chart. If the level rises too high, insulin intake is likely to need adjusting.

I AM A DIABETIC

Ray Duns

Older diabetics

The majority of diabetics, however, suffer from what is called maturity onset diabetes. In this case, the pancreas does produce insulin, often in normal amounts, but the tissues of the body are sensitive to its action and it is this which produces the high blood sugar level.

The condition often goes hand in hand with being overweight, and the problem is treated by dieting so that the load of sugar is reduced. Usually there is a backup to the diet in the form of tablets which stimulate the pancreas so that it produces more insulin.

Unfortunately, this picture of two separate sorts of diabetes is too simple. In reality, the two types tend to merge into each other.

Some people and even children seem to have the maturity onset type, while some elderly patients may require insulin to keep their blood sugar level down.

How serious is diabetes?

The disease may be serious for two reasons. First, without insulin injections, the young diabetic simply continues to lose weight until he or she lapses into a coma and dies.

Secondly, diabetics can develop complications—in other words, additional complaints as a result of their condition. Generally speaking, the better the level of blood sugar is controlled, the less likely complications are to occur.

The most serious complications concern the eyes and kidneys and are caused by the disease's effect on the blood vessels. It is usually possible to see changes to the blood vessels in the back of the eye of any long-standing diabetic, and in a very few cases, this worsens to the extent that the patient eventually loses the sight of one or both eyes.

In addition, diabetics may also develop abnormalities in their nerves which,

among other problems, can lead to a loss of feeling in the hands and feet.

Finally, the diabetic has, unfortunately, a tendency to develop artery trouble, which in turn causes strokes and heart attacks. For this reason, diabetics are particularly encouraged not to smoke,

since this also increases the likelihood of arterial disease.

How insulin works

In general, it is the patient whose diabetes comes on early in life who needs insulin, although a fair proportion of

The role of insulin

- Insulin
- Glucose
- Acid

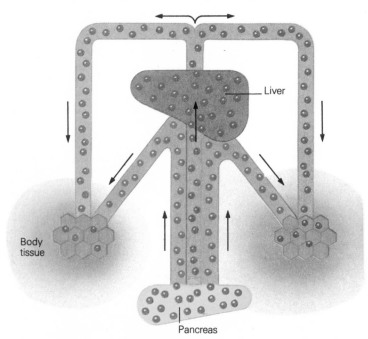

Insulin working normally

Liver

Body tissue

Pancreas

When insulin is being made by the pancreas, it enables glucose—which the body cells need to burn to produce energy—to be stored in the liver. When the body cells need more energy, and therefore more glucose, the glucose will be released and insulin enables it to be used by the cells.

those who start diabetes later in life will also eventually need it.

The hormone is given by injection, usually under the skin of the thigh. Diabetics learn to draw their own insulin up into a syringe and give themselves the injections. This usually has to be done twice-daily, and often different formulations of insulin are used to try and spread the total effect out during the course of the day.

Once a diabetic has taken insulin, his blood sugar level will start to fall, but this is not, however, the end of his problems. Sometimes the sugar level falls too far as a result of taking the insulin. Sugar is an essential food not only for the body's tissues in general, but particularly for the brain. If the sugar falls too low, the brain ceases to function properly and the patient becomes unconscious.

Luckily, diabetics can learn the early symptoms of a falling blood sugar level. These are shakiness, sweating, tingling around the mouth and often a feeling of being rather muddled. The treatment for these symptoms, known as hypogly-caemia (which means low blood sugar level) is to take some form of sugar by mouth immediately.

Balancing the insulin

Because of the risk of 'hypo' attacks, it is important for the diabetic to try and balance his food intake with his insulin injections so that the sugar level is kept somewhere near the normal range without too much soaring up and down.

This means regular meals containing similar amounts of carbohydrate (food that is broken down to sugar in the blood). All diabetics, whether insulin-treated or not, should avoid sugar itself or foods which contain sugar such as jam, sweets, cakes and fruit squash drinks. Their sugar content is absorbed rapidly in the stomach to produce brisk increases in the blood sugar level. But clearly, the use of sugar to halt a 'hypo' attack is an exception to this rule.

Measuring techniques

As well as carefully planned insulin injections and a regulated intake of carbo-hydrates, most diabetics use some form of measuring technique to keep a check on their blood sugar level.

The traditional way of doing this is to measure the amount of sugar in the urine, which gives an idea of the amount of sugar in the blood.

However, diabetics are making increasing use of special testing sticks to measure the blood sugar level directly. The sticks contain sugar-sensitive chemicals, and blood is taken from a small prick in the finger.

What causes a coma?

Diabetic coma is an unfortunate term, since it may refer to two completely different situations. One is hypoglycaemia (the 'hypo' attack) where a low blood sugar level causes loss of consciousness. The second is when the insulin-dependent diabetic starts to develop a high blood sugar level (hyperglycaemia).

Clearly, the two conditions are different, although some people may muddle them. A 'hypo' attack can develop in a matter of minutes, and is easily stopped by taking sugar.

A high blood sugar level, on the other hand, takes hours, or even days to develop, and may take hours to cure.

As the sugar level rises due to lack of insulin, the cells are starved of 'fuel'. They have to burn something to keep alive, and so they start getting through fat instead. Used-up fat produces waste products called ketones, and it is the presence of excess ketones which characterizes the sort of diabetes which requires treatment with insulin.

The future for diabetics

Apart from research into the basic cause of the disease, there have been, and will continue to be a number of helpful improvements in the treatment.

Insulin is becoming steadily more highly purified, and thanks to the technique of 'genetic engineering' we will soon have insulin which is identical to that produced by the human pancreas, rather than having to use animal insulin as at present.

Techniques for taking insulin are in addition becoming more refined. The twice-daily injections may be replaced, for some patients, by a constant delivery of insulin from a special pump. This is worn, possibly from a belt, and is only about 15 cm (6 in) in length. The insulin enters by a needle inserted in the skin of the abdomen.

And, finally, the treatment of eye problems caused by diabetes has advanced tremendously since the introduction of lasers to treat abnormalities at the back of the eye.

How lack of insulin causes a diabetic coma

Brain

Liver

Body tissue

Pancreas

Venner Artists

If there is no insulin, glucose cannot be stored or utilized. The result is a great deal of urine with a high glucose content. Instead, the cells produce energy by burning up fats, but these cannot be burnt properly without glucose and so produce high acid in the blood. If untreated, a diabetic coma will result.

Diarrhoea

Q I am breast feeding and I have been told not to eat grapes because they will give my baby diarrhoea. Is this true?

A Some foods can certainly affect the baby's bowels. These include fruit, onions and spicy foods. The wise thing to do is to have a rather bland diet when the baby is very tiny, and introduce foods you are fond of one by one so if anything does upset your baby, you can tell what it is.

Q I am on the Pill. The clinic has told me that I must take extra precautions if I get diarrhoea. Why is this?

A The Pill is taken every day and suppresses ovulation (egg production) so that you cannot get pregnant. If the hormones in the Pill are not absorbed, ovulation may occur. When you have diarrhoea, food and pills move very quickly through the intestines where absorption takes place so that the Pill may become ineffective.

Q My grandmother started to get diarrhoea but when the doctor came, he said the problem was really constipation. How could this be?

A This is a rather common symptom in the elderly called spurious diarrhoea. What happens is that the lower bowel gets clogged up with faeces. However, some liquid matter manages to get past the blockage and gives rise to diarrhoea, which may cause the old person to lose control of the bowels and become incontinent. It is very important to recognize this as it is easily treated.

Q I find that whenever I eat cheese, I get diarrhoea. Am I allergic to it?

A You might well be. Food allergy is probably more common than was previously realized. When you are allergic to certain foods, you frequently get problems such as rashes or wheezing in other areas besides the intestines. If you think you are allergic to a specific food, then exclude it from your diet and see if your symptoms disappear.

Everybody is likely to have attacks of diarrhoea during their life. The cause may be trivial or more serious, but in most cases treatment will alleviate the symptoms in a day or two.

Diarrhoea is a symptom, not a disease. Usually it is caused by an infection in the intestines, though in some cases it may arise from a more serious problem. Diarrhoea can be dangerous in children, particularly in babies, and therefore medical attention should be sought if there is an abnormal change in a baby's stools.

Causes

Diarrhoea occurs because the lining of the intestine becomes irritated, either due to an infection, the presence of a toxic (poisonous) substance or some other cause. As a result, food and water pass through the length of the intestine much quicker than usual and fluid is not absorbed by the large intestine; this means that the stool remains very watery.

Not only may the walls of the intestine fail to absorb water, but they may also actually lose fluid as a result of inflammation, and this adds to the water lost in the diarrhoea. In severe cases, dehydration may occur, which may be fatal.

Diarrhoea may be due to a variety of causes. Food is one of the culprits. In food poisoning, bacteria grow on fly-blown food, producing toxins or poisons that give rise to diarrhoea and stomach upsets. This type of food poisoning is caused by the staphylococci toxins in such diseases as botulism, which is very rare.

In other types of food poisoning, it might be the bacteria itself which causes the infection. One bacterium called salmonella is responsible for causing diarrhoea, in addition to pain and, sometimes, vomiting.

Diseases like typhoid and dysentery are spread by bacteria being eaten with food. Cholera is spread by drinking water that has been infected by faeces. The difference between food poisoning and dysentery is that in food poisoning, diarrhoea starts within a few hours of eating bad food, but dysentery may take up to 24 hours to produce diarrhoea, and will also last longer.

Much larger parasites can get into food

The best remedy for diarrhoea is a liquid diet. Fasting is recommended and once the diarrhoea abates, solid food should be introduced gradually. A mixture of bacteria (inset) cause diarrhoea.

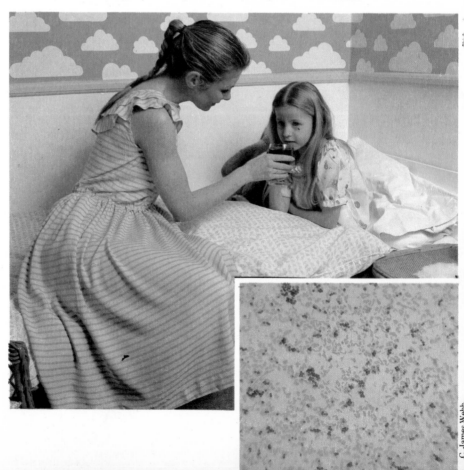

and water and, once ingested, cause diarrhoea. This includes an amoeba, a single cell parasite, which can cause amoebic dysentery, a disease common to the tropics, and which, with its vague symptoms of malaise and diarrhoea alternating with constipation, can go on for years.

Often diarrhoea is not due to bacteria or larger organisms, but to the smallest of germs, the viruses. In gastro-enteritis, a virus infection causes diarrhoea, vomiting and abdominal pains. It can go under a variety of names: gastric flu, summer diarrhoea and so on.

Traveller's diarrhoea occurs when new strains of bacteria replace the usual bacteria which live in the large bowel, and are usually beneficial. It is a common experience for people to have this form of diarrhoea when they go abroad, and it is not caused by a 'change in the water' as is commonly supposed.

Chronic problems

Chronic diarrhoea is not due to infections, but rather to other medical problems. One of the most common diseases is ulcerative colitis. The colon becomes inflamed and the bacteria invade the mucous membranes which have already been damaged. No one cause has been found to contribute to ulcerative colitis, and theories range from an allergic reaction to an emotional upset.

Diarrhoea occurs also when some other disease of the intestinal wall stops the proper absorption of foods. These malabsorption problems, which include coeliac disease, in which the pancreas cannot absorb gluten, not only cause diarrhoea, but also leave patients badly undernourished.

There are other causes of diarrhoea. If there is sustained nervousness, fear and anxiety, the intestine becomes overactive and diarrhoea occurs. Highly spiced foods can upset the bowels if a person is unused to eating them. Large quantities of fruit and shellfish can cause minor stomach upsets and loose bowels.

In children, diarrhoea can be caused by an infection which is completely unconnected with the bowels. Typically this happens in toddlers with ear and throat infections.

Gastro-enteritis is a common affliction in babies, but loose stools should be distinguished from diarrhoea. Newborn babies do not pass normal stools, but instead pass greenish-brown sticky motions called meconium. Breast-fed babies often have very loose motions, and they may pass several stools a day, whereas bottle-fed babies' stools are more like the consistency of adults' but the colour may vary greatly.

Controlling diarrhoea

● Drink as much fluid as possible, but no alcohol. Fluid consumption should be particularly high for infants, as they become dehydrated very easily.

● If possible, fast for a day. This will do you no harm. If you don't feel hungry, don't force yourself to eat. When the diarrhoea begins to lessen, resume eating with a very bland diet, with no spicy foods. Even if you feel ravenous, try not to over-eat. Small meals at intervals are preferable.

● To stop diarrhoea, a mixture of kaolin and morphine should be taken.

● Maintain scrupulous hygiene. Wash hands carefully after going to lavatory and before eating or preparing food.

● If a baby has diarrhoea, give him or her a half strength feed if you are bottle feeding. This consists of half as much powder or liquid for the normal amount of water. If the baby is vomiting, see your doctor. He or she may suggest that you stop all milk feeding and only give clear fluids. A weak salt solution may be prescribed to correct the salt lost in the diarrhoea.

● Traveller's diarrhoea can be prevented from recurring by drinking only boiled or purified water, wine, beer, well-cooked meats, bread and peelable fruits. Stay away from uncooked food or fruit and vegetables that cannot be peeled.

Thus, in spite of the appearance of the stool, the baby who is breast-fed is less likely to have gastro-enteritis as the breast milk protects the baby's intestines from any infection and breast-feeding does not depend upon sterilizing bottles and teats for their safety.

Symptoms

Diarrhoea is an uncomfortable symptom, particularly if it is accompanied by colicky pains in the abdomen. The stools are much more fluid and less well formed than usual. In severe diarrhoea, the stool may be very watery, and may be passed much more often than usual. In some cases, there may be a bit of vomiting.

Dangers

Diarrhoea is not serious if it lasts a day or two in adults or older children. However, in babies and young children, diarrhoea can be dangerous, particularly if there is also vomiting as the baby may not be able to take any fluid to replace the considerable amounts it is losing.

Persistent diarrhoea causes considerable loss of water and salt, which leads to dehydration. If untreated, it can be fatal. It takes much more to dehydrate an adult than a baby, but really serious infections, such as cholera, can cause death by dehydration.

Treatment

The treatment for diarrhoea is dependent in many instances on finding out what the cause is, but basically the treatment is very simple.

The first priority is to keep up the level of fluid intake by drinking plenty of liquids—this is essential. Eating is not necessary, and if the patient does not feel like it, food should not be forced, particularly if vomiting occurred initially.

Drugs may help by reducing the level of activity of the intestine and slowing up the passage of its contents. Kaolin and morphine is commonly used to bulk up the stools and slow down the working of the intestines.

In some forms of food poisoning, especially those caused by bacteria, or in dysentery, sulphonamides (drugs containing bacteria-fighting sulpha) or an antibiotic may be needed to combat infection. For cholera, sufficient fluids should be drunk to maintain those lost through diarrhoea. Antibiotics are of secondary importance. The patient should not eat or drink infected foods or liquids, and maintain scrupulous hygiene.

Colitis can only be treated by a change of diet to bland foods, a course of antibiotics or sulphonamides to combat infection and, if emotional disturbance is the cause, psychotherapy.

Diarrhoea in babies is serious, particularly if the stools are abnormally loose and watery. Immediately stop feeding the baby any solids, give extra clear fluids and a half-strength milk (half as much powder or liquid for the normal amount of water) if you are bottle feeding. If the baby appears well otherwise and takes fluid, then keep a careful watch for the next 24 hours. If the baby is ill, or is vomiting or the stools are tinged with blood, call your doctor. When the baby is seen, have a soiled nappy on hand for the doctor to examine.

The doctor may advise stopping all milk feeding and giving the baby clear fluids, and may also prescribe very weak salt solutions to correct the salt lost in the diarrhoea. It is very unusual to give medicine to 'dry up' diarrhoea in small babies; minor attacks get better quickly, and seriously ill babies should really be in hospital.

Outlook

In the majority of cases, diarrhoea should clear up within a few days, with no serious after-effects. If the diarrhoea has been caused by an infection, swift treatment should alleviate the symptoms.

Diet

Q I have always given my daughter a proper diet, but suddenly she has become very slim—almost skeletal. I am afraid she is anorexic and has begun hiding her food. How could this have happened?

Q Anorexia nervosa is commonly known as the 'slimmer's disease', but it is much more complex than this implies. It almost always strikes people between the ages of 11 and 30 (more girls than boys), and dramatic loss of weight is the most obvious sign that something is wrong. There may be other indications, such as constipation alternating with diarrhoea, hypersensitivity about appearance, or sudden personality changes such as withdrawal from friends.

The anorexic may secretly be tortured by a basic lack of confidence, self-esteem and a true idea of herself as a person. Under this lurks a fear of maturity which makes thinness seem desirable: keeping a childlike figure seems to postpone adult responsibilities.

If you suspect your daughter is anorexic, you must get her to see the doctor. The treatment depends on identifying and dealing with the underlying psychological causes.

Q My son often refuses to eat when he is unwell. Should I insist that he eats?

A No. It is not necessary for him to eat solid foods when ill, and may even be detrimental.

Make sure he has plenty of fluids to drink instead. A little sugar in weak tea or milk will give him energy, and with soups or broth will provide all he needs. When he is feeling better, he will ask for solid food again.

Q My daughter has suffered from eczema for five years. Is it true that allergies to certain foods can cause this?

A Yes. Recent research has shown that some skin disorders are allergic reactions to various foods. Finding out if this is the case with your daughter will involve tests to isolate possible reactions. There are some clinics which offer this service, or your doctor may be able to provide a plan for you to test it yourself.

The body is like an engine, and food is the fuel it needs to keep running. Just as petrol comes in different octanes, so foods have different energy-producing levels. How well your body works depends on what you eat.

The food we eat is converted into energy and used by the body for its different functions. These include not just obvious, physical activities such as walking or running, but the equally important, and constant process of growth and repair of the tissues in the body. Throughout life, body tissues are continuously broken down and replaced by new cells to keep us whole and in good working order.

We have to eat just enough food to supply energy for all these needs. Eat more than you need, and the excess will be stored in the body and lead to overweight.

Most foods have a different chemical structure to the body, so they have to be changed into a form that the body can absorb—and this is what the digestive process does.

Types of food
Food can be divided into three main types—carbohydrates, proteins and fats. Carbohydrates and fats are used to fuel all the body's processes and functions while protein is used as building material for the body's tissues. This means that insufficient carbohydrate or fat in the diet will result in lack of energy and a general feeling of lethargy and fatigue, while lack of protein will cause gradual wasting away of the tissues.

It is important to a healthy diet to eat as great as variety of food as possible so that you get all the nutrients, vitamins and minerals you need. Aim to eat carbohydrate, fat and protein at each meal.

Carbohydrates

Carbohydrates are commonly found in starch and sugar. Starch is present in all cereals and root vegetables, and sugar is found in its natural form in fruits or honey, or, in a refined state, in table sugar. Carbohydrates are found in greatest quantities in potatoes, breads, bananas, peas, corn, beans and lentils, parsnips, rice and yams.

Sugar-rich foods are jams, biscuits, chocolate, sweets and ice cream. These prepared products have high concentrations of refined sugar so they should be eaten in moderation.

Over half our dietary needs are provided by carbohydrates and they are especially important for people doing heavy physical work. They are converted to glucose (a form of sugar) in the body and this fuels the muscles and the brain. It is the sole form of energy for the brain which uses more than half of the daily supply.

Sugar levels

The amount of glucose in the blood is kept at constant levels under normal conditions. If too much carbohydrate is eaten, the excess is stored as glycogen in the liver and the muscles. When these have taken as much as they can hold, the excess is stored in the fat of the body.

If the level of sugar in the body becomes too high, insulin (a chemical manufactured by the pancreas) is released to make the liver absorb the excess from the blood. If the blood sugar level falls too low, the liver releases the stored glycogen and converts it back to glucose.

A diet that is high in refined sugar puts a strain on the pancreas by calling for more insulin than is normally required—so a sweet tooth indulged to excess is not only bad for the teeth, but for the whole body.

If there is not enough carbohydrate in the diet, it will lead to weakness and tiredness. To compensate, the body will change fats into energy instead, but the rapid burning of fats in this case creates toxic by-products which make the blood too acid.

Carbohydrates are additionally important because they act as protein sparers—they are burnt in preference to protein, leaving the proteins for body building.

Protein

Proteins are chemicals that form an essential part of every living cell. Muscles, for instance, consist largely of protein and water. Proteins also go into the making of chromosomes (the gene carriers), enzymes (substances which break down tissue), blood plasma (the liquid part of blood) and haemoglobin (the red colouring matter in blood).

In their turn, proteins are made up of smaller units called amino acids. There are various types of protein, made of different arrangements of 20 or so amino

Calories used in everyday activities

MC Library

Henry Grant

Colin Molyneux/Bruce Coleman

Sedentary occupations office workers, drivers, doctors, journalists.	**Calories needed over 24 hours** male 2,500—2,700 female 1,700—2,200	**Moderately active occupations** housewives, postmen, plumbers, bus conductors, light industry, waitresses.	**Calories needed over 24 hours** male 2,700—3,200 female 2,100—2,400	**Active occupations** coal-miners, dockers, builders, labourers, army recruits, athletes.	**Calories needed over 24 hours** male 3,300—4,400 female 2,400—2,800

● These figures are an average guide—they will vary according to age and weight.

acids. When protein is eaten, the digestive juices break it down into the amino acids. They are then carried in the bloodstream to various parts of the body and built up into new proteins as required.

Any surplus is burnt as fuel for energy. The body uses up 25-40 gm a day (0.88-1.41 oz) and this is the minimum amount which must be replaced to maintain the tissues. A good rule of thumb is to eat 1 gram (about 0.03 oz) of protein for each kilogram (2.21 lb) of body weight daily.

Children, however, need more protein than adults—a baby requires five times as much per unit of weight, young children two and a half times as much and adolescents one and a half times. Insufficient protein leads to stunted growth and weak body structure.

Sources of protein

Animal foods such as meat are very rich sources of protein, especially the organs such as the liver, kidneys and heart. Fish, eggs, cheese and milk are also good sources, as are soya beans, nuts and some pulses. Lentils and the seeds of pumpkin, squash, sunflower and sesame are also quite rich in protein. The average diet in the UK provides about 95 gm (3.35 oz) of protein daily, which is more than enough for any one under most circumstances.

Complete and partial proteins

Complete proteins are those which have the same mixtures of amino acids as the body's proteins, and can therefore be used 'whole'. They are found mostly in meat, fish, eggs and dairy products.

Partial proteins; typically found in vegetables and cereals; lack one or other amino acid and cannot be absorbed by the body without first being broken down. This means that a vegetarian, for example, will have to eat more protein foods to make up the required amount of protein. Unfortunately, different vegetable proteins have different missing amino acids and these can be combined to provide complete proteins.

In countries where animal foods are scarce or forbidden on religious grounds, many such combinations have been developed. Rice and dhal (lentils) are common in India. In England the traditional 'ploughman's lunch' uses the combination of bread and cheese in the same way.

Fats

Fats provide more than twice as much energy as other foods; which means we need considerably less of them. In the West, people get about 40 per cent of their energy from fats—a sign of prosperity.

Fats also add taste and flavour to other foods and make certain foods easier to cook. They are a source of vitamins (A, D, E and K) and a sufficient amount of fat in the diet is essential to provide these vitamins.

In the body, fat provides a layer of insulation beneath the skin and helps to maintain an even temperature, especially in cold weather. It also serves as a cushion against minor injuries by absorbing the impact of blows or falls.

Types of fat

Fats are classified as saturated or unsaturated fatty acids according to their chemical structure. Saturated fatty acids are found in the fat of animals, milk, butter and some vegetable oils. Mono-unsaturated fatty acids are found in olive oil, peanut oil and fish oils while the polyunsaturated fatty acids used in margarine and cooking oils come from soyabean, corn, sunflower, cotton seed and safflower plants.

Certain of the polyunsaturated group are known as 'essential fatty acids' because the body cannot manufacture them and they must be provided in the diet. A lack of them can impair normal growth, making the skin dry and scaly. The minimum intake of these fatty acids is between three and five grams a day.

However, too high a proportion of saturated fats in the diet may damage the arteries and lead to heart disease. Consequently, most nutritionists recommend using mainly unsaturated fatty acids, and this is easily done by eating only lean meat, using vegetable oils for cooking and not over-doing the dairy products.

Vitamins

Apart from carbohydrates, proteins and fats, the body must have vitamins and minerals. Vitamins are essential for normal growth and development and, as they cannot be manufactured in the body, they must be included in the diet or, in certain cases, as supplements to the diet.

Vitamins are divided into fat-soluble and water-soluble types. The fat-soluble ones are vitamin A,D,E,F and K and the water-soluble ones are vitamins B,C and P. The body cannot store large amounts of water-soluble varieties. They circulate in the blood and any excess is excreted in the urine.

In contrast, the fat-soluble vitamins are not excreted, and any excess is stored in the liver. Too much vitamin A and D, however, can be harmful, causing toxic symptoms.

If there is a shortage of the water-soluble vitamins, the deficiency will become apparent within a matter of weeks. Reserves in the body are sufficient to prevent deficiency for weeks or even months, unless there is some other irregularity in the body. There is little cause for worry about vitamin deficiency in most developed countries—a good mixed diet normally contains enough of them.

Minerals

Minerals are also essential for keeping the body healthy. They assist in many of the processes needed for normal nerve and muscle function and must be supplied frequently in the diet.

The minerals that the body requires are calcium, phosphorus, iron, iodine, potassium, magnesium, fluorine, zinc and copper. A balanced diet nearly always provides sufficient quantities of these and as excess minerals may be harmful, it is not a good idea to take vitamin pills or tonics except on your doctor's orders.

Roughage

Roughage or dietary fibre consists of the walls of plant cells which cannot be broken down by digestion and so pass through the stomach and intestines in solid form.

Their use is to stimulate the action of the intestine so that food passes through the digestive system. They also provide the bulk to make faeces solid.

The best-known example of roughage is bran, which many people take as a natural method of relieving constipation. All vegetables, nuts and cereals, however, also contain fibre. Some fibres carry increased quantities of bile acids down the colon and help reduce the level of potentially harmful fats in the body.

Diseases of the intestines and colon, appendicitis and haemorrhoids are rare in African tribesmen who eat a low-fat, high-fibre diet—all of which reinforces the belief that these are diseases of civilization.

Energy

The food we eat provides energy for the various activities of the body whether they are running, working in an office or repairing body tissue. The amount of energy we need (and, therefore, the amount of food) depends on how much we use up.

The energy from food is measured in calories—one calorie being defined as the amount of energy required to raise the temperature of one kilogram of water by 1°C.

Carbohydrates and proteins yield about the same amount of energy (four calories per gram) while fats yield more than twice as much (nine calories per gram). The average person living in industrialized Western countries gets about 15 per cent of their energy from protein, 40 per cent from fat and 45 per cent from carbohydrates. In the rest of the world, carbohydrates make up far more of the diet, with people in Asia and the Far East, where there is less animal food, getting about 85 per cent of their energy from carbohydrates.

Energy requirements

The amount of energy that anyone needs varies not only according to the type of activities performed but also with body size, sex, age, climate and health.

Figures are usually given for the needs of a person resting and this is known as the basal metabolic rate (BMR). It is lower for women than men, mostly because women have a better layer of insulation in the form of body fat.

For the average adult male this basic minimum requirement is about 1,700 calories per day to maintain vital functions. Digestion of a normal diet requires about 200 calories, while sitting in a chair all day would use another 200 or so. This means about 2,000 calories a day are needed to maintain normal function.

Calories used in everyday activities

Activity	Calories used per hour
Sleeping	65
Standing still	110
Fast typewriting	140
Walking slowly	200
Carpentry and painting	250
Swimming	500
Walking upstairs	1100

Calorie chart

Type of food	Energy provided: calories per 100g (3.5 oz)	Water content % of weight	Protein content % of weight	Fat content % of weight	Carbohydrate content % of weight
Whole wheat flour	340	15.0	13.5	2.5	69.0
White bread	243	38.2	7.8	1.3	52.7
Brown rice	360	11.7	6.2	1.0	86.5
Whole milk	65	87.0	3.4	3.7	4.8
Butter	790	13.9	0.4	85.1	a trace
Cheddar cheese	425	37.0	25.4	34.5	a trace
Beef steak	273	56.9	20.4	20.3	0
Fish (cod)	175	65.0	20.5	8.3	3.6
Potatoes	70	80.0	2.5	a trace	15.9
Cabbage (boiled)	9	95.7	1.3	a trace	1.1
Oranges	27	64.8	0.6	a trace	6.4
White sugar	395	a trace	a trace	0	99.9
Walnuts	702	5.0	15.0	64.4	15.6

Q My baby is fatter than my friend's baby, who is the same age. Is it just 'puppy fat' that will wear off, or should I put her on a diet?

A Babies who are overfed will become obese and this is not normal. Ask your doctor if your baby is overweight. If she is, he will probably suggest reducing the carbohydrate content of the diet and concentrating on protein foods. This means cutting out cereals, cakes and sugar, reducing the amounts of potatoes and bread, and limiting milk to half a litre (one pint) a day.

Q I want to become a vegetarian but my friends say I won't get enough protein if I don't eat meat. Is this true?

A It is perfectly possible to supply all the body's needs without eating meat, but to do so does mean making adjustments to the whole diet. It is not recommended to simply replace meat by eating, for example, more eggs and cheese. Some of your protein will have to be provided by nuts, pulses and cereals instead. It may also be necessary to take the supplementary vitamin B 12 as meat is by far the richest source of this.

Q My children will not eat green vegetables. Is there any way I can make sure they get enough of the right vitamins?

A Fortunately children who develop these dislikes usually grow out of them if they are not made into a big issue.

Also, your children will get much of what they need from other foods. But if you are worried, talk to your doctor about giving them a multi-vitamin and mineral supplement.

Q I want to lose weight but I'm confused by all the different diets and their claims. What should I do?

A The reducing diet prescribed by many doctors allows for a maximum of 1,200 calories a day. It should include sufficient bulk to prevent hunger pangs, about 50 gm of protein, 125 g of carbohydrate and adequate quantities of vitamins and minerals. Include very little fat and no alcohol.

Special diets

There are times when the diet has to be changed for one reason or another. A pregnant woman needs to increase her intake of calories by 300 per day and protein by 30g per day and to take supplementary vitamins to feed the growing child and maintain her reserves.

Patients suffering from kidney disease may be put on a temporary protein-free diet since the kidneys cannot remove waste products effectively.

People suffering from liver or gall bladder disease will be put on a low-fat diet since their ability to digest fats is impaired.

High blood-pressure, heart disease and liver disease all call for low-salt diets to reduce the volume of fluids in the body and take the strain off the affected organs.

Any drastic change in your diet should only be undertaken on the advice of your doctor, nutritionist or other qualified health care practitioner. Too sudden or severe changes in the amount you eat can be dangerous under certain circumstances. Even eating less in order to lose weight should be done gradually and under supervision.

Many of a child's favourite meals—such as fish fingers, peas and a jacket potato, with some fruit for dessert and a glass of milk—will provide a large part of the dietary requirements of a child for a full day, and will give him all the energy his rapidly growing body requires.

A balanced diet

A balanced diet is one which supplies all necessary nutrients in quantities that suit the particular individual. This includes the correct calorie intake and the right proportions of different foods.

The following example of a balanced diet for a normal person provides about 1,600 calories a day.

Dairy products (including milk, cheese, butter or margarine):

Children up to 12 years	3-4 cups
Teenagers	4
Adults	2
Pregnant women	4
Nursing mothers	6

Meat or fish: 1-2 servings (one serving = 75g (about 2.5 oz).

Eggs: instead of meat, to a maximum of six per week.

Nuts and pulses: as an alternative protein source instead of meat, fish or eggs (one serving = one cup, cooked).

Vegetables: four or more servings (one serving = half a cup). A dark green or deep yellow vegetable should be included at least every second day.

Fruit: a citrus fruit or one of another kind every day.

Bread and cereals: four or more servings (one slice = one serving or one cup = one serving).

Diphtheria

Q I am expecting a child in two months' time. Is it really necessary for the child to be vaccinated against diphtheria?

A Yes. Although the cases of death from diphtheria are few, this is mainly due to the programme of immunization that many countries now carry out. There are, however, always minor outbreaks of diphtheria even with this immunization, and an epidemic is always possible if large numbers of children are not vaccinated.

Q If my daughter comes into contact with another child who has diphtheria, can she catch it as well?

A Yes. Diphtheria is a highly contagious disease. If you even suspect that your daughter has been in contact with the infection, keep her away from other children and seek medical advice immediately, even if she has been immunized. She may have to have a Schick test, where a minute dose of diphtheria toxin is injected into the skin. This will show whether she needs to be re-immunized.

Q Can a person's immunity to diphtheria wear off?

A No. However, booster doses may be required if there is a possible epidemic. And although diphtheria is caused by one bacillus, there are different strains that cause differing degrees of infection. There is evidence to suggest that one strain has the ability to cause epidemic diptheria even in those populations that have extensive immunization programmes.

Q My baby had a terrible reaction to his first diphtheria injection. I am afraid of continuing with the course. What should I do?

A Some patients have an extreme reaction to the serum. Since your child reacted badly, seek your doctor's advice. As continuing with the course is essential, your doctor may suggest that your child receives a number of small injections, with the amounts of serum gradually increased. This would help to overcome the difficulty.

Diphtheria is a disease which occurs mainly in children under the age of ten. Today it is relatively rare, due to the routine immunization of young children, usually in the first year of life.

Diphtheria is an acute infection of the throat and nose which may prove fatal if untreated, or if treatment is delayed.

Causes

Diphtheria is caused by a bacillus, the corynebacterium diphtheriae. It produces powerful toxins, or poisons, which attack the mucous membranes of the throat and nose and, if no anti-toxin is administered, the heart, nervous system and kidneys. In the tropics it has been known to affect the skin.

Diphtheria is usually contracted by contact with an infected person who spreads the bacteria when coughing or sneezing. Diphtheria can also be transmitted by a carrier who has no symptoms of the disease and, sometimes, by infected milk.

Symptoms

After a brief incubation period ranging from two days to a week, the patient develops a mild sore throat and fever, feels weak and generally ill. A soft membrane that gradually thickens from the consistency of raw egg white to a crust, forms over the affected tissues. The throat becomes painful, especially in swallowing and breathing, and the lymph glands at the side of the neck swell considerably, sometimes giving rise to a condition known as 'bull neck'. The infection rarely spreads further, but in severe cases it can affect the larynx and bronchial tubes.

Danger

The growth of the membrane can impair breathing, and a tracheotomy, an operation which opens the airways, may have to be performed to allow the patient to breathe.

If the infection is not treated swiftly, it will begin to spread. The jaw becomes paralyzed, followed by the eyes, the pharynx and finally the limbs and trunk. A massive attack can kill within three days, but a slighter attack may take three weeks to cause heart failure.

Treatment

Hospital treatment in isolation is essential. Treatment consists of antibiotics to combat the bacterial infection in the throat, and anti-toxins to counteract the diphtheria toxins. Total bedrest is required, followed by a convalescent period and a very gradual return to normal routine. If diphtheria is treated in time, the patient should recover completely.

To combat diphtheria, all infants must be immunized. This will make the body capable of producing anti-toxin immediately infection occurs. An initial injection, followed by two more injections and then a booster shot a year later are usually sufficient, but a further booster can be given before the child enters school.

The Schick test, where a small amount of toxin is injected into the skin, will determine whether the child is naturally immune before vaccination.

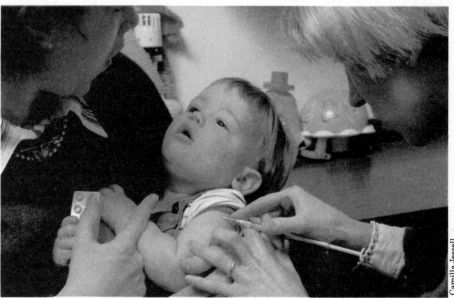

Camilla Jessell

Dyslexia

Q My son is dyslexic and left-handed. Is there a relation between the two?

A Yes. Left-handed people are more likely to be dyslexic, but the two do not necessarily go together. This combination may occur because the left half of the brain controls most of the speech processing mechanisms and the actions of the right hand. If there is some brain malfunction on the left half of the brain, the speech process may be affected, leading to dyslexia. At the same time, the right hand may lose its dominance, inducing left-handedness or ambi-dexterity (ability to use both hands).

Q My daughter has always had difficulty reading. Is she a bad reader, or is she dyslexic?

A Dyslexia *is* often being a bad reader, among other things. Do not jump to the conclusion that she is dyslexic. She may have faulty vision or hearing, so have these checked. Or she may be a late developer, or even a little lazy! She may have emotional problems which interfere with her concentration, or she may not have had enough exposure to reading and writing.

Once you have eliminated these possibilities then find out what type of reading mistakes she makes, and try to get an assessment of whether these mistakes are of the type associated with dyslexia. Ask whether she is receiving remedial reading at school and, if not, press for this to be arranged. If she is dyslexic, special tuition will help, but occasionally not all the ground can be made up and she may have to learn to live with a certain amount of deficiency.

Q My wife and I both always misread certain words. For example, we always read 'shopfitters' as 'shoplifters'. Is this a minor example of dyslexia?

A No. That's like asking if you are an alcoholic because you like a glass of sherry before Christmas dinner. This kind of slip is generally due to a chance original misreading which you found amusing, and your spotlighting the event locked the two words together in your memory.

One of the first real tasks children are faced with at school is learning to read and write. Most manage reasonably well, but some do not, and one possible reason for this is that they are dyslexic.

Helping dyslexic children as much as possible will ensure that they become more competent readers.

Dyslexia is extreme difficulty with reading and writing—word blindness is just one of the terms used to describe its many facets. It affects about one in ten children, is more prevalent among boys than girls and is caused by a small number of faulty cells in the brain, or by a delayed or incomplete development in one part of the brain.

Its consequences, if untreated, are serious as it will affect the child's progress in school, which in turn will create difficulties in adult life. For-tunately if it is recognized early, there is much that can be done to remedy the problem.

Causes

Dyslexia is caused by a localized brain lesion, an area of scar tissue which can arise due to a brain injury, or by incomplete brain development. However, dyslexics should not be thought of as brain damaged as this implies that the whole brain is seriously affected, which it is not.

Dyslexia may be inherited: in about half the cases it runs in families. It may strike both male and female members of the family, but it need not affect them all. It may produce different effects in different members of the same family, or affect them to very different degrees.

Yet whether the hereditary theory is valid or not, it is evident that in dyslexia something goes wrong in the perception of words or letters. There is nothing wrong with the dyslexic's hearing or vision. The information goes into the brain satisfactorily, but something goes awry at the recording or playback stage, or at the stage which converts marks on a paper to sound, or vice versa.

Symptoms

Being a symptom of a small and localized brain malfunction or incomplete development, dyslexia can take may forms. Sometimes it is confined to difficulty in reading and affects the person's ability to understand not only long or complex words but also words of one syllable. Often writing is affected, either because the child has difficulty in forming letter

---

lash Monday We wenïïg
the Zoo. We spenï much
Time in frunt of an eboh
ion Cag with hal Senner
mahgen they made hea
us¼ bulrfe wenl Wen
They uig puy ouT they
pours for nuts.

Last Monday we went to the Zoo. We spent much time in front of an iron cage which held seven monkeys. They made us laugh when they put out their paws for nuts.

This is a sample of a writing from dictation of an 11-year-old dyslexic. Note the variety of errors in spelling and use of words and punctuation.

The most common kinds of mistakes which are made by dyslexics.

Confusion of letters similar in shape: d and b, u and n.
Confusion of letters similar in sound: v, f and th.
Reversals: was and saw.
Transposals: left and felt, auction and caution.

Reading

Difficulty in keeping place on a line.
Difficulty in switching from end of line to start of next line.
Mispronunciation: rember for remember merains for remains.
No expression, or intonation in the wrong place.

Writing

Foreshortening: rember for remember.
Letter fusion: up for up, and for and.
Repetition of a word or words.
Capitals left out or in the wrong places.
Difficulty keeping on the line.

Remember:

Every child makes these sorts of mistakes when first learning to read. Do not label a child as dyslexic just because these mistakes occur.

---

shapes or because spelling is affected.

Sometimes an inability to do arithmetic is involved, though the difficulty may largely be to do with problems of writing down figures correctly. Some children with this form of dyslexia perform fairly well with verbal questions, but if asked to write down the answer, however, they reverse the correct order of the numbers or even include a completely irrelevant number. Alternatively, there may be difficulties in touch recognition, where the child fails to recognize the shape of an object that he or she handles, or cannot tell the identity of a letter or number traced with the fingers. However, a dyslexic may have only one or a combination of these difficulties.

Dangers

Although dyslexia affects one ability, albeit an important one, many people believe that other skills are affected too, which is untrue. Thus dyslexics may be labelled as lazy, wilfully disobedient or 'thick', and typecast as not being worth worrying or bothering about.

Consequently the child may be relegated to a slow learning group, and being often otherwise bright and intelligent, will become bored by school, come to dislike it and start playing truant. He or she will fail examinations, be left further behind, and if the dyslexia is untreated, the child will not be able to catch up.

Treatment

Once the problem is recognized, there are remedial programmes for both children and adults, some of which may have to be tailored to the individual. This special tuition will not only help with the general difficulties of reading and writing, but also they will teach the speedy recognition of road signs and essential words

---

such as 'danger', 'fire', 'no entry', 'caution' and so on.

Released from the pressure of achieving a 'normal' reading competence, the child may start to feel confident in other fields. Oral instruction, tape recorded notes, films, pictures or video tapes are other alternative learning methods the child can use to minimize any reading difficulties.

Outlook

Dyslexia sometimes improves and even disappears by itself. This is either because the brain has finished its delayed development, or it has found some alternative way of achieving the necessary processing—for example, through bypassing the brain lesions that originally caused the trouble.

In other cases, skilled help with reading and writing problems will minimize or even eliminate the deficiencies that the child would otherwise retain.

Helping the young dyslexic at home

DO

● Praise the child whenever possible: dyslexic children are ashamed of their difficulty and suffer from doubts and uncertainties about their other skills.
● Concentrate on what the child is good at: this will help build confidence.
● Help the child read longer words by dividing syllables with a pencil line.
● Teach the child to pronounce words correctly.
● Give the child plenty of time with any reading done with your help. Dyslexic children may not understand what they have read, or they may read something correctly one day, but then get it wrong the next.

DON'T

● Ridicule the child about lack of reading skill.
● Give the child lists of words to learn: one or two at a time is enough.
● Compare the child with other children, especially brothers and sisters.
● Overdo remedial work: dyslexics tire more easily than other children when trying to read.
● Try to make the child change his writing style for the sake of neatness.
● Think the child is dreaming if he looks away from something he is reading: there may be difficulty focusing on the page or finding the place he last stopped reading.

Eczema

Q My five-year-old son has had eczema for a year now. I'm told it may get better as he grows older. Is this true?

A Half the children who suffer from eczema when they are very young have grown out of it by the time they are six, and in most of the others it will have cleared up by their teens. However, eczema is notorious for disappearing and reappearing without obvious cause. It does sometimes return in adolescence or adulthood, especially at times of stress.

Q If I touch or sit near someone with eczema will I catch it?

A Definitely not. It is not an infectious disease and cannot be passed from person to person. Scratching inflamed skin may make the sufferer prone to infections, but this does not make eczema in any way a contagious disease.

Q I have heard that sunshine will do my eczema good, so should I sunbathe while on holiday?

A Generally, sunshine—or to be more exact, the ultraviolet rays in sunlight—is good for the skin and will improve eczema. Some sufferers, however, are very sensitive to sunlight and their eczema does get worse if it is exposed to strong sun. So if your eczema seems worse while you are on holiday, stop sunbathing immediately.

Q Is it safe for people with eczema to bathe in the sea or in public swimming pools?

A Eczema sufferers should take care over bathing, not so much because of any risk of infection to them or other people, but because it tends to make dry skin even dryer. Ointments and creams protect the skin against drying out, and sufferers who like swimming can use them.

Q Will breast feeding prevent my baby from developing eczema?

A It is possible, though this has not yet been proved conclusively.

Eczema is an irritating and unsightly skin condition, but a nuisance rather than a danger, and one which can be controlled by simple treatment.

Eczema is a skin complaint that affects about one person in 12 at some point in life. It is an unpredictable and rather puzzling disease, often caused by allergies but just as frequently brought on by emotional upsets or by no obvious cause. It can be distressing, not only because it is irritating and itchy but also because it affects the skin in visible parts of the body.

The most familiar form of eczema—whose scientific name is atopic dermatitis—is closely related to asthma and hay fever, and it is quite common for people who have it to have one or both of these other complaints too. Hay fever is clearly an allergic disease, usually brought on by exposure to pollen. Asthma and eczema also can be caused by an allergy to inhaled substances, such as pollen, or by an allergy to a particular food, notably eggs and cow's milk. However, this is not always the case: attacks often occur at times of stress.

Eczema usually makes its first appearance during infancy or early childhood, and tends to fade away as the child gets older. Sometimes, however, it appears in an adult who has not suffered from eczema as a child.

Most people who get it come from families with a history of eczema, asthma or hay fever, although it is common for one child in a family to be affected while the others escape it altogether. Babies may suffer from eczema because they are allergic to cow's milk, and recent research suggests that babies from 'at risk' families will have a better chance of avoiding eczema if they are breast fed.

Symptoms
The typical sign of eczema is an inflamed area of skin which becomes dry and cracked or covered with tiny red pimples or blisters. The most annoying symptom is an itch, and scratching the irritating area aggravates the condition, causing wet, bleeding sores and increasing the risk of infection spreading to other parts of the body. Eczema usually appears first on the face and scalp and then spreads to the hands and limbs, especially to places where the skin folds or is rubbed by clothing. Much of the discomfort is caused by scratching the patches of rash, rather than by the eczema itself.

Cotton mittens will prevent a young child from scratching the eczema itch to ease the irritation and making the affected patches of skin very sore.

Precautions

Eczema in itself is not dangerous or in any way a threat to life. The main problem for the parents of a child with eczema is to discourage him from making the condition worse by scratching the infected skin. Young babies with eczema often rub themselves on their bedclothes in a vain attempt to make the itch go away. Little children can be protected from hurting themselves if they wear cotton mittens (in bed as well as during the day), to prevent them from scratching.

It is essential that sufferers from eczema should not come into direct contact with anyone who has cold sores (herpes simplex) because eczematous skin is very vulnerable to the herpes virus and is liable to widespread infection if it is exposed to it. Obviously, no one with a cold sore should kiss anyone with eczema.

The other danger to people with eczema is smallpox vaccination, because they run the risk of getting vaccinia, an infection which resembles chickenpox but which can be fatal to a young child. Fortunately, smallpox now appears to be extinct, so there is no longer any need for vaccination.

People who suffer, or who have suffered from eczema are more sensitive than most to irritant chemicals, so it would be wise for them to avoid jobs which involve exposure to such substances. The risks are considerably reduced by taking such simple precautions as wearing gloves and a face mask, but young people with eczema should think twice before taking a job where it would be difficult to avoid well-known irritants such as cutting oils, resins and shampoos.

Treatment

If the eczema can be traced to an allergy, clearly the particular cause (the allergen) should be avoided. Breast feeding disposes of the problem of an allergy to cow's milk in young babies, but if the mother cannot breast feed, or if the child has to be weaned, there are alternatives: goat's milk does not cause allergic eczema as often as cow's milk, and there are also artificial milks based on soya which provide a nutritious diet for babies.

Dealing with an allergy is often only a part of the problem: other measures are necessary to relieve the eczema and prevent it from getting worse. First, materials such as wool, which can irritate sensitive areas, should be kept away from the skin. If it is dry and cracked it should not be washed too often as this will tend to dry it even more. Obviously it should be kept clean to discourage infection, but in place of soap, people with eczema should

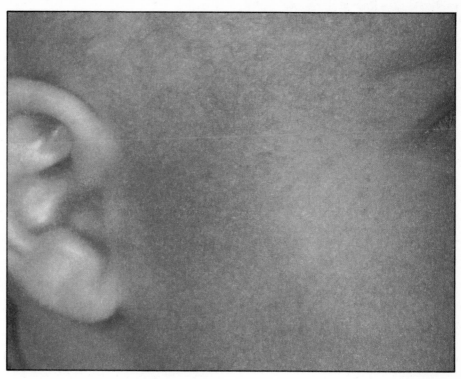

use aqueous cream or emulsifying ointment, both available from chemists. Alternatively, products containing liquid paraffin added to the bathwater prevent the skin from drying out—various proprietary brands can be bought from chemists or obtained on prescription.

There is a variety of medicines to control the inflammation and itching of the skin. Zinc paste and coal tar are old and tried remedies, sometimes applied in specially prepared bandages which are laid on the skin and covered with a protective layer of cotton. Creams containing small amounts of steroids such as hydrocortisone can reduce itching and inflammation very effectively. However, they should only be applied for limited periods and on a doctor's advice: their continual use could damage the skin.

Creams containing urea are sometimes prescribed to increase the water content of the skin to counteract the dryness of eczema, and an antihistamine drug can control the itching and burning sensations. A drug called sodium cromoglycate, also used in the treatment of asthma, has proved useful for controlling the effects of food allergies and can be prescribed in tablet form by a doctor.

As people with eczema have an often irresistible temptation to scratch their skin, they should keep their finger nails short, smooth and clean and, when possible, wear cotton gloves or, better still, mittens, because these prevent independent finger movements.

Eczema is generally not serious enough to need treatment in hospital. However,

Eczema usually appears first on the face and scalp. The skin is inflamed, dry and cracked, or covered with tiny red bumps.

in certain cases, children seem to benefit from getting away from their home environment, particularly when they are upset or deeply worried by some aspect of home life, even though the cause of their distress may not be obvious to the rest of their family or to outside observers.

Outlook

The chances are that children with eczema will 'grow out' of it after a time. Fifty per cent of them are, in fact, free of it by their sixth birthday, and only 10 per cent still have it by the time they reach their teens.

However, like most allergic complaints, eczema has a habit of vanishing, only to make an unwelcome return in adolescence or adulthood. Emotional stress seems to be the main cause of its reappearance: exams, job worries and moving house are typical 'triggers'.

Uncomfortable and unsightly as eczema can be, it is not something to be brooded over. Parents who worry about their child's skin will make the child worry too—and that is more likely to aggravate the condition than it is to improve it.

Although eczema cannot yet be cured, it can be relieved and controlled by medicines and ointments, and so it should be seen as a nuisance—and probably a passing one—rather than a cause for alarm.

Emphysema

Q My doctor says that my emphysema has been caused by smoking. Do you agree?

A Smokers are far more likely to get emphysema than non-smokers, but as only a minority of smokers actually develop severe emphysema, and as a few sufferers have never smoked at all, some additional factor must be involved. In smokers this is thought to be the lack of a substance in the blood called alpha$_1$antitrypsin, which helps protect the lungs from damage done by the accidental release of elastase, an enzyme which can destroy them.

Q When I run for a bus I often get breathless. Could I have emphysema?

A You are probably just out of condition! Take more exercise, cut down or cut out cigarettes, and see if your breathlessness improves. If it doesn't, or it gets worse, see your doctor.

Q Is emphysema dangerous for someone with a heart condition?

A Yes. It may also cause heart conditions too. The heart has to pump much harder to force blood through blood vessels in the lungs whose functional powers have been reduced, and over time this strains the heart. Also, as the lungs lose the ability to exchange oxygen for carbon dioxide in sufficient quantities, the body is deprived of oxygen and the heart has to pump more blood through the lungs. In the worst cases, the additional load on a malfunctioning heart may eventually lead to death.

Q My daughter who recently had whooping cough has been diagnosed as having emphysema. Why is this?

A Your daughter has interstitial emphysema, a less serious condition in which air bubbles appear in the chest. These result from the sharp intake of breath preceding each cough, which ruptured some of the alveoli in her lungs, causing a release of air. The air bubbles may cause discomfort, but she should make a full recovery.

Lung diseases are always distressing, particularly when, as with emphysema, the sufferer is perpetually short of breath. Since damage is permanent, the best approach is to try to avoid lung disease in the first place.

The different types of emphysema

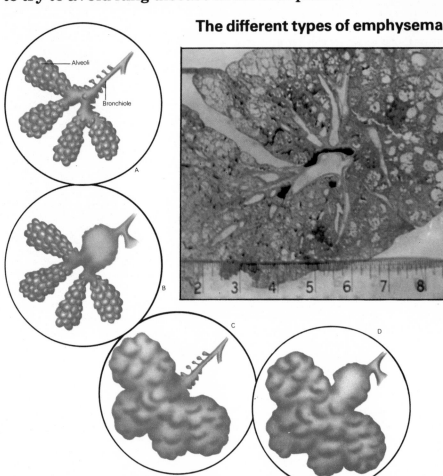

(A) shows normal bronchioles and alveoli In pulmonary emphysema, as suffered by coal miners, the bronchioles may be distended (B) & sometimes the air sacs (C).

Occasionally, as in alpha$_1$antitrypsin deficiency emphysema, both are swollen (D). This paper-thin section of lung (inset) shows emphysema and bronchitis.

Pulmonary emphysema is a serious and debilitating lung disease. The tiny air sacs in the lungs, called alveoli, and the narrow passages leading to the air sacs, called bronchioles, become permanently distended with air. The lung tissues lose their elasticity, and the number of blood vessels is reduced. As a result the lungs' ability to supply the blood with oxygen is progressively decreased, and the patient becomes breathless on the slightest exertion.

Pulmonary emphysema is less frequent in women: there may be a hormonal factor that protects them from the disease. It rarely appears before the age of 40, but if it occurs in middle age it causes disability and eventually death.

Smoking is one of the greatest contributory factors, but continuous exposure to dust or high levels of air pollution may bring on various forms of emphysema. Many people with chronic bronchitis also suffer from emphysema, which is also made worse by smoking.

Causes
Smoking is therefore a possible cause of emphysema, but not all smokers contract the disease, which may also occur among non-smokers. One theory is that a substance called elastase is produced by the white cells in the lungs. Smoke or dust particles may interfere with the cells, releasing elastase. Unless it is inactivated by a blood substance called

alpha₁ antitrypsin, it will attact the lung tissue. People who lack alpha₁antitrypsin are particularly susceptible to pulmonary emphysema; if they smoke they are likely to develop a severe form of the disease.

Chronic bronchitis may also be a contributory factor. The airways of the lungs are blocked by mucus produced as a response to irritation by smoke or other pollutants. To breathe in, a person must make a great deal of effort to overcome the resistance of the mucus, and the inspiration of air may result in the distension of the alveoli. Bacterial infection, which is common in chronic bronchitis, may contribute to the process by weakening the lung's elastic tissue.

In addition to pulmonary emphysema, there is focal dust emphysema, or coal worker's pneumoconiosis, which is caused by coal dust covering the walls of the air passages leading to the lungs air sacs, and interstitial emphysema, which results from whooping cough, or a broken rib which punctures the lungs.

Symptoms

The most obvious symptom is breathlessness, followed by coughing, which can be brought on by the slightest exertion such as talking or laughing.

Chewing and swallowing may also be difficult, because of the breathlessness, and there may be discomfort after a meal because the lungs have expanded, pushing the diaphragm into the stomach. Loss of appetite and weight loss might occur.

In severe forms of the disease, lung enlargement may cause the chest to expand into a barrel shape. Lack of oxygen in the blood may produce cyanosis, a blue coloration in the skin which is most noticeable on the lips and under the fingernails. As the disease is progressive, these symptoms will get worse with time.

Dangers

The loss of elasticity of the lungs and the presence of mucus in the the airways may result in carbon dioxide no longer being efficiently eliminated from the lungs and insufficient oxygen being breathed in. The patient may have to make strenuous efforts to breathe, and may rapidly become out of breath.

In some patients large holes may develop in the lung tissue and large air bubbles called bullae appear on the lung surface. Coughing may burst the bullae, causing the release of air into the chest. In severe cases, the lungs collapse, and an operation may be required to remove the air.

Emphysema can also affect the heart. The loss of blood capillaries and thickening in the alveolar walls greatly increases the resistance of the lungs to the flow of blood. The heart has to pump much harder to force blood through the lungs, and it also has to pump a greater volume of blood when the patient exercises to deliver the amount of oxygen required. In time, this can cause the heart to become strained and begin to 'fail'.

Treatment

Although pulmonary emphysema cannot be cured, its progress may be slowed. The most important thing to do is to stop smoking. Some patients, particularly those who also have chronic bronchitis, may benefit from using bronchodilator drugs which help clear the airways, and which may be either taken by mouth or administered by aerosol spray. Breathing pure oxygen from a cylinder will allow enough of the gas to enter the blood. Portable cylinders can be used for short trips outside the home.

Operations to cut out the bullae can be performed. Weight loss can be combatted by having small, frequent meals consisting of high energy foods. Moderate or heavy exercise may help maintain patients' muscle tone and prevent them from becoming house-bound.

Outlook

If smokers give up their habit, and treatment is given, then emphysema can be arrested. Unfortunately, there is no way of repairing damage which has done already to the lungs. This is why it is so important not to begin smoking.

How lung tissue of smokers may be damaged by emphysema

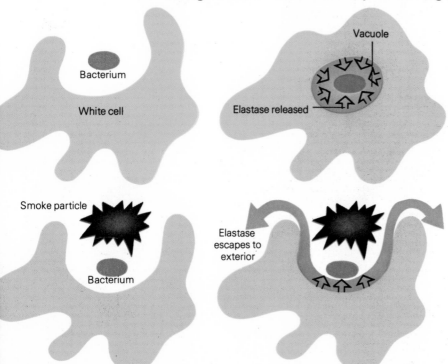

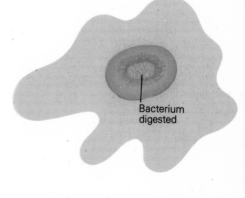

In non-smokers, white cells destroy bacteria by engulfing them in a vacuole, and then releasing an enzyme, elastase, which digests the bacteria (above). In smokers, smoke particles may interfere with vacuole formation. Elastase may then leak to the white cell's exterior, and unless it is made harmless by a substance in blood, alpha₁antitrypsin, which some people lack, it may damage the lung tissue (left).

Eyes and eyesight

Q I am extremely short-sighted. Does this condition gradually worsen until I go blind?

A Neither short-sightedness nor long-sightedness in themselves lead to blindness. Nor do they have to get worse, although it may become difficult to see well without glasses. Short-sighted people tend to become less short-sighted as they get older, whereas some long-sighted people actually become normally sighted over the years.

Q My child has had measles. I have heard it is dangerous to read during or soon after this disease. Is this true?

A No, there is no truth in it whatsoever—although the disease causes inflammation of the eyes and 'photophobia' (discomfort in strong light) there is no danger to the sight.

Doctors are generally quite puzzled about exactly why this particular old wives' tale should have arisen.

Q My aunt claims that her eyesight has gradually worsened since she started wearing glasses. Why should this happen?

A It is most unlikely that your aunt's eyesight will have worsened as a result of wearing glasses. What is much more likely is that your aunt hadn't realized just how bad her eyesight was—so that she now notices the enormous difference when she takes her glasses off.

Q What actually causes a black eye to happen?

A The tissues surrounding the orbit of the eyes—in other words the cavities in which the eyes are set—are very soft. Any injury to the face or scalp which causes bleeding beneath the skin tends to drain towards the orbits. Disrupted red blood cells in the skin look yellowish at first and then turn black after a while. So all you are seeing in a black eye is a collection of old blood beneath the skin.

A marvellously versatile, accurate, self-repairing moving 'camera', the eye will give a lifetime's service with the minimum of attention. And it is prone to relatively few diseases.

The eye is usually likened to a superbly designed camera when people want to explain how we can see. However, to understand fully how the outside world can be viewed inside the tiny chamber of the eye, one has to go back to basics.

Light

The fact that we can all see is, as most people instinctively realize, due to light.

The best way to think of light is as a transmitting medium. From whatever source, it 'bounces' off objects in countless directions, 'carrying' with it the possibility of the objects being seen.

The other important thing to understand about light is that although it usually travels in straight lines, it can be bent if it passes through certain substances, such as the specially shaped

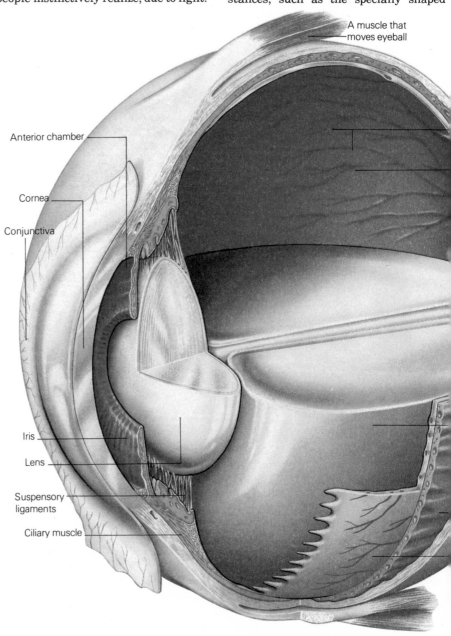

A muscle that moves eyeball

Anterior chamber

Cornea

Conjunctiva

Iris

Lens

Suspensory ligaments

Ciliary muscle

Frank Kennard

glass of a camera lens, or the lens made from tissues in a human eye.

Moreover, the degree of bending can be precisely controlled by the shape in which a lens is made. Light can, in fact, be bent inwards, or concentrated, to form tiny, but perfect images of much larger objects.

The cornea

When a ray of light strikes the eye, the first thing it encounters is a round, transparent 'window' called the cornea. It is the first of the eye's two lenses, is fixed in position, always the same shape, and does a major part of the light bending.

It is surrounded by the 'whites' of the eye, tough substances known as the sclera, which admit no light.

Structure of the eye

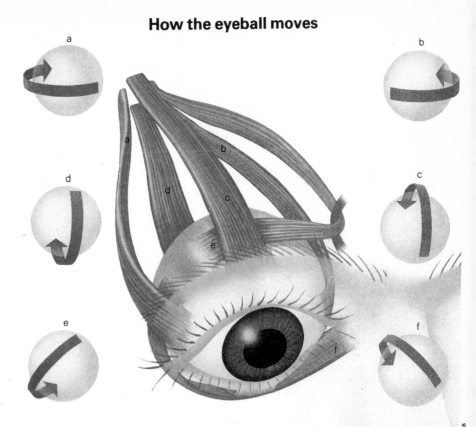

How the eyeball moves

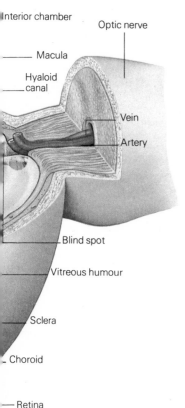

- Blood vessels on retina
- Interior chamber
- Optic nerve
- Macula
- Hyaloid canal
- Vein
- Artery
- Blind spot
- Vitreous humour
- Sclera
- Choroid
- Retina

Venner Artists

The aqueous humour

After passing through the cornea, a ray of light enters the outer of two chambers within the eye, properly called the anterior chamber.

This is filled with a watery fluid called the aqueous humour that is constantly drained away and replaced.

The iris

Forming the back of this first chamber are the iris, and just behind it, the lens.

The iris is a circular, muscular diaphragm—in other words, a disc with an adjustable hole in the centre.

In a human eye, this hole is called the pupil, and alteration of its size is done by two sets of muscles.

The iris is pigmented, or coloured and it is this which gives the eye its colour when viewed from outside (in fact, the word iris itself is derived from the Greek word meaning rainbow).

The purpose of the iris is to control the brightness of the image entering the eye. If too strong a light falls on it, the pupil grows smaller, without our having to make any conscious effort. In dim light, it grows larger. Excitement, fear and the use of certain drugs also make the pupil widen or contract.

Six main muscles move the eyeball. Muscle (a) swivels it away from the nose, (b) towards the nose; (c) rotates it upward, (d) downwards; (e) moves it down and outwards and (f) moves it upwards and outwards.

The lens

Just behind the iris is the soft, elastic (and transparent) lens. Its job is the fine focusing of light rays.

For this reason, the lens is adjustable. It is held round its edges by a muscle, the ciliary muscle, which can change the shape of the lens.

The vitreous humour

Behind the lens is the main, interior chamber of the eye.

This is filled with a substance called the vitreous humour which has a jelly-like texture, and makes the eye feel firm and rubbery. Running through its centre is the hyaloid canal, the remains of a channel which carried an artery during the eye's development in the foetus.

The retina

As has been explained, the eye is ball-shaped, and the curved inside of the ball is lined, all round the back chamber, with

Short sight

Long sight

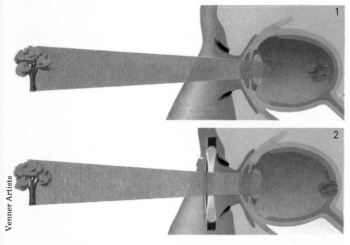

a light-sensitive 'coat', or layer, which is called the retina.

This is actually made up of two different types of light-sensitive cells, called rods and cones because of their shapes.

Rods are sensitive to light of low intensity and do not interpret colour, which is 'picked up' by the cones. These are also responsible for clarity and are most plentiful at the back of the eye in an area known as the macula. Here the lens also happens to focus its sharpest image, and this is where our vision is best.

Surrounding the macula, the retina still registers images with clarity, but out towards its edges is what is known as peripheral vision—all that area which we 'half see'.

Together, this 'central' and peripheral vision make up a wonderfully complete view of the outside world.

How we look at objects
We operate our eyes by scanning them rapidly, moving the eyeball around by means of a specially arranged set of muscles attached to it. Looking at someone's face, for example, we concentrate on the eyes, darting glances from one eye to the other and occasionally down to the mouth.

The optic nerve
All this information which comes in through the eyes—focused by the two lenses, adjusted to a manageable level of intensity by the iris, and 'recorded' by the light-sensitive 'film' of the retina—is then transmitted to an area of the brain called the visual cortex to be processed and understood.

The transmitting is done along one main cable from each eye called the optic nerve. All the nerve fibres which lead to the cable are cleverly crossed over in a

'doubling up' system designed to ensure that if the visual cortex suffers damage, say in a stroke, we do not go blind.

The blind spot
Where the optic nerve leads away from the back of the eye there is a small area where we are completely blind, although we are not actually aware of this because the eyes overlap their fields of vision.

However, you can prove the existence of this blind spot by the simple experiment on the opposite page.

Focusing

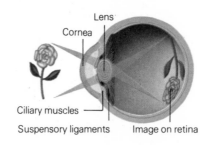

Light rays from a near object diverge and the surface of the lens becomes more curved (top) to focus them. From a distant object, light rays are almost parallel and the lens (above) has less focusing to do.

The most common cause of short sight (1) is an eyeball which is too 'long', so that light rays form an image in front of the retina. It is corrected (2) by a concave lens. In short sight (3), the eyeball is 'short', so the image cannot be formed within the eye. A convex lens (4) focuses the image on the retina. (The brain turns it the right way round.)

The arteries of the eye
Leading into the eye, alongside the optic nerve, is a large artery. From it, many smaller blood vessels branch out and spread over the retina like tributaries of a river.

Their vital job is to 'service' the nerve cells of the retina: feeding with nutrients and draining waste products. They also enable a doctor, by means of an ophthalmoscope, to examine some of the body's blood vessels without the hindrance of skin.

Common problems
Few eye disorders actually end in blindness. Starting at the front of the eye, one of the most common, minor problems, especially among babies and young children, is conjunctivitis.

This is an inflammation of the conjunctiva, the thin membrane covering the whites of the eyes. It is caused by bacteria, viruses or irritation. Treatment with antibacterial eye drops or creams usually clears it up quickly.

Also at the front of the eye, the cornea is subject to various types of inflammation. Pain in the eyeball, redness, blurred vision and clouding of the cornea are all typical symptoms and anyone experiencing these needs immediate medical attention.

Because the cornea contains no blood vessels, grafting a new one in its place is usually successful.

Q My son is colour-blind, but he says he doesn't see in black and white. So what is colour-blindness?

A There are three types of light-sensitive cells in the retina, specializing in seeing red, green or blue light. Colour blindness results from having too few of one of these types of cell. A person who is colour-blind does not actually see in black and white, but they will be unable to distinguish between colours of a certain shade, the most common being red and green.

Q Should I give my children vitamins for good eyesight?

A Eyesight is only affected by severe vitamin deficiency, which happens only when people are on the verge of starvation. In the days when sailors got scurvy from being without fresh vegetables for long periods, their eyesight also suffered—in fact they got 'night-blindness'—and this only improved when they returned to a normal, balanced diet.

We now recognize that night-blindness can result from severe vitamin A deficiency. Carrots are a rich source of this vitamin, but people who have a normal diet do not, as some believe, improve their night vision by eating large quantities of the vegetable.

Severe deficiency of vitamin A can also cause disease of the cornea, the outer, transparent 'window' of the eye, ultimately resulting in total blindness.

Lack of vitamin B may also cause blindness by interfering with the normal nutrition of the optic nerve. Eyesight is restored to normal if vitamin B is put back into the diet.

Q What do I do about grit in my eye?

A A foreign body in the eye is always worrying because it may scratch and damage the cornea.

A simple remedy is to rinse the eye out with a warm solution of salt in water. If this fails to remove the object, then it is wise to go and see the doctor. A penetrating injury to the eye such as happens to people who fail to wear protective glasses at work is a much more serious matter and requires hospital attention.

Some people have an imperfectly curved cornea, and this throws a cock-eyed image on to the retina: astigmatism, which is corrected by glasses.

Glaucoma
Sometimes the normal circulation of the aqueous humour in the chamber behind the cornea is interrupted, and this causes a rise in pressure, which is painful and may lead to blindness but if treated early, chances of complete recovery are good.

The lens
Going on into the eye, one reaches the iris. This rarely gives trouble, but the lens, immediately behind it, is different.

About half the adult population of most Western countries wears glasses because of defects of the eyeball or of the lens or the muscle which changes its shape.

If the eyeball is too long, or the lens lacks elasticity, it will be too round and fat, giving good close-up vision, but poor distant vision. This is short sight. If, by contrast, there is difficulty in increasing the thickness of the lens, poor near vision, but good distant vision results—which is long sight.

Cataracts
Cataracts are a clouding of the lens which, for the person affected, is rather like looking through a window that is slowly frosting up. Most commonly caused by advancing age or diabetes (an abnormally high level of blood sugar), they are painless and develop slowly.

To discover your blind spot, close your right eye and look at the cross (above). While you look, continue to move the page back and forth. There is a point where the dot will vanish—this is your blind spot.

These days, treatment is effective and safe—namely removing the lens. Special glasses or contact lenses are then worn to restore normal vision.

Diabetes may also affect the retina because the blood vessels in the back of the eye gradually degenerate. If not treated with insulin, the condition may eventually lead to blindness.

Squinting
Squinting is an inability to focus both eyes on the same spot at the same time. This is caused by 'laziness' of one of the muscles which move the eyeball, and can be corrected by a simple operation, or by wearing glasses.

Outlook
Short and long sight may be common complaints, but at least they are easily corrected. Blindness, of course, is a terrible affliction, but compared with some other serious human ailments, it is quite rare—and becomes more so with each passing year.

Sight testing a child below reading age: he looks first at letters displayed at a distance and then if he can see them he points to the same letters on the card held in front of him.

Eye Clinic, Dept of Optometry, The City University, London

Fainting

Q I am three months pregnant and have fainted several times recently. Is this harmful?

A No, there is no risk that your baby will be harmed by these fainting fits, although you could hurt yourself if the faint makes you fall over—such episodes can happen in the early months of pregnancy. If you do feel faint, lie down or sit with your head between your knees, to get the blood flowing back to your brain. If this fainting becomes more frequent it would be wise to mention it to your doctor at your next antenatal visit.

Q My grandmother always used to swear by smelling salts as the best treatment for fainting. Why does no one use them now?

A Smelling salts have gone out of fashion largely because it has been proved that they are no more effective in curing a faint than taking a few deep breaths. Smelling salts consist of a chemical, ammonium carbonate, that gives off strong-smelling ammonia gas. Its effect is to make you gasp several times as you breathe it in. This gasping helps to get more oxygen into the blood, which is then carried to the brain to relieve the oxygen lack which caused the faint in the first place.

Q My elderly mother has been prescribed drugs to treat her high blood pressure, and since she started taking them she has fainted several times. What should she do?

A She should go back to her doctor and tell him or her about the problem, so that the treatment can be changed if necessary. Sometimes, drugs given to treat high blood pressure can work too powerfully, so that the blood pressure becomes too low and this, in turn, causes a faint.

Q When someone faints, how can you tell it isn't a coma?

A Doctors make a clear distinction between faints and comas. The chief difference is that if someone suffering from a faint is laid flat, he or she quickly recovers full consciousness, while someone in a true coma does not.

People faint for a variety of reasons. If you understand why it happens and know what to do, you will be better prepared to help others and avoid fainting yourself.

Fainting, known medically as syncope, is a sudden loss of consciousness, usually preceded by a feeling of weakness and dizziness, and possibly nausea as well. You can usually tell when someone is about to faint, because their skin looks ashy white and feels clammy to the touch, and their breathing becomes quick and shallow. As the sufferer faints, he or she falls to the ground and, having done so, usually recovers full consciousness within a couple of minutes.

Causes
The most usual cause of fainting is a reduction in the blood supply to the brain; without this blood, which brings essential oxygen, the brain cannot work properly. Normally, the strength and regularity of the heartbeat, and the action of the blood act together to create enough pressure in the circulation to push the blood up to the brain against the force of gravity. But if this system fails for some reason and the blood pressure falls too low, the body reacts by fainting. This makes the person fall flat and so places the body in a position in which the blood can easily travel to the brain, so restoring things to normal.

The exact sequence of events within the body varies with the reason for fainting. For example, you could faint from the shock of seeing an unpleasant sight, on receiving bad news or if you experienced intense pain. When such things happen, the brain sends out messages to the vagus nerve that supplies branches to the heart, lungs and stomach. This acts to slow the heart and reduce the vigour of its beat, and at the same time widens the blood vessels in the centre of the body. As a result, blood becomes dammed up in the abdomen and too little reaches the brain, so producing a faint.

When fainting is likely
You could faint as a result of standing still for too long; blood gradually accumulates in your legs, and has the effect of making the heart and blood vessels work too hard to push blood upwards. If you must stand for an extended period, the best way to avoid fainting is to make small movements of your legs and feet which help to squeeze the blood upwards, in other words, against the pull of gravity.

Fainting often occurs when you stand up suddenly after lying or sitting down. In this case it is caused by a failure of the blood vessels to adjust quickly enough to

Fainting can result from standing too long in one position, as is the experience of this unfortunate guardsman on parade.

Rex Features

raise the blood pressure as the body changes position. Blood is trapped in the limbs and abdomen and cannot get to the brain sufficiently quickly to prevent a faint. This adjustment of blood pressure relative to alterations in the posture of the body is monitored by a small group, or plexus, of nerves in the neck known as the carotid sinus.

Lack of oxygen in the blood, due to anaemia, being in a hot stuffy room or from being at high altitude where the air is thin and low in this vital gas, can also cause fainting. This is not because the brain is getting insufficient blood, but because the blood is not bringing enough oxygen with it.

Many people feel faint, even if they do not actually collapse, if they leave home in a rush first thing in the morning, without having breakfast. In this case, fainting may be due to a combination of stress, which lowers the blood pressure, and the lack of nutrients in the blood. So it is sensible to eat a light breakfast.

Heart disease is rarely a cause of fainting but, in the elderly, fainting can be a sign that the blood vessels have become narrowed due to arteriosclerosis and are not allowing enough blood to get to the brain.

Fainting in pregnancy

Fainting is not uncommon in the early months of pregnancy. This is due to the fact that the hormones concerned, particularly progesterone, tend to make the muscles in the blood vessel walls more flabby. This dilates the vessels and lowers the blood pressure, which causes the blood to accumulate in the lower parts of the body.

Another cause for fainting in the early months of pregnancy is the sudden diversion of blood to the uterus, where it is needed to provide food and oxygen for the developing foetus, so leaving less available to be carried to the brain. But as pregnancy progresses, the volume of blood in the circulation increases, so providing a natural solution to the problem.

People prone to fainting

Those who have a very sensitive connection between the vagus nerve and the blood vessels are particularly apt to faint. Such people should always try to avoid any situation that they know from past experience will tend to cause them to faint.

Many mothers worry about fainting episodes in their teenage daughters. Such attacks are common at this age and are usually due to the emotional effects of growing up, combined with mild anaemia due to the onset of menstruation, plus a phase of rapid growth. Any mother concerned about this problem should make sure that her daughter eats a good diet containing plenty of protein and iron-rich foods, such as liver and spinach. If the fainting persists she should make sure that her child sees a doctor as she may need some form of treatment or help in sorting out some deep-seated psychological problem, since this may be the cause of the trouble.

Cases have been recorded of groups of adolescent girls suffering from epidemics of mass fainting. After much investigation of one such incident, doctors could find no traces of disease which might have caused this and concluded that the fainting could only have been the result of a kind of mass hysteria.

Tall people often faint more easily than short people when they stand for a long time simply because their blood has further to travel through the body from the legs to the brain.

Fainting in young children is unusual, but can occur in one rare hereditary condition called dysautonomia.

When people feel faint, the quickest way to put this right is to get them to lie down for five minutes, or to put their head between their knees. Going outside for air is never a good idea—a sudden faint could cause a nasty injury.

Fibroids

Q What is the difference between a fibroid and a polyp?

A Both fibroids and polyps are benign tumours in the reproductive organs. Fibroids appear on the uterus; polyps can either appear inside the uterus or along the cervical canal. Both may cause excessive bleeding during periods or bleeding mid-cycle, though in a few cases fibroids may prevent conception. If difficulties arise, the fibroids or polyps can be surgically removed.

Q I have recently had a fibroid removed. How long will I have to wait before I conceive again?

A It is probably sensible to wait until your scars have healed and you have had two normal periods. This should be a minimum time of eight weeks.

Q I have a blood-stained discharge between periods. As it may only be due to fibroids, need I see a doctor?

A Yes. There are many other reasons for such a discharge, and it may be necessary to have a D & C (dilation and curettage, where the lining of the uterus is scraped) to be certain of the cause. If a polyp, rather than a fibroid, is found, it can be removed during the D & C. Alternatively, some other surgical treatment may be necessary.

Q I have some small fibroids which give me heavy periods. As I am nearing the menopause, must I have a hysterectomy?

A It is important to be certain that the heavy periods are only due to fibroids: your doctor may arrange diagnostic tests to confirm this.

If fibroids are the cause, then hormone tablets are sometimes successful in controlling heavy periods. If the tablets do not work, then you will have to decide how inconvenient the periods are and whether you can wait for the menopause, or whether you would be happier with a hysterectomy (womb removal). Remember fibroids very often disappear after the menopause.

One in five women under 40 has fibroids—the most common tumour of the female reproductive organs.

Fibroids are solid, whitish tumours composed of muscle and fibrous tissue which grow on the uterus. They vary in size from that of a pea to that of a football.

Causes
Fibroids are more prevalent in women who have reached middle age without bearing children as the uterus is less able to cast off the accumulated tissue and lining shed during each menstrual cycle.

Growth of fibroids in women who already have these tumours may be stimulated by the hormone oestrogen, which is of a higher level in pregnant women and women on the Pill. After the menopause, when the level of oestrogen falls, the fibroids may shrink or disappear.

Symptoms
Fibroids can cause excessive menstrual bleeding or a blood-stained vaginal discharge, especially if they hang into the womb cavity by a fine stalk. Women with very large fibroids may experience discomfort from the pressure on the bowel or bladder. Very rarely fibroids may interfere with pregnancy if they block the tubes or, if the woman is already pregnant, the blood supply to the fibroids may be blocked up, in which case the fibroid will degenerate and cause some pain.

Dangers
There is a very tiny risk that a large fibroid can change into a cancerous tumour called a sarcoma, but this is a rare occurrence.

Treatment
Fibroids which cause no problems should be left alone. If difficulties occur, especially in women who wish to have more children, then the fibroids only may be surgically removed from the womb, which is left intact (myomectomy). In older women who do not wish to have any more children, a hysterectomy (womb removal) can be performed.

Outlook
In a tiny proportion of women who have had a myomectomy, the fibroids may recur within a few years.

Fibroids in the Uterus

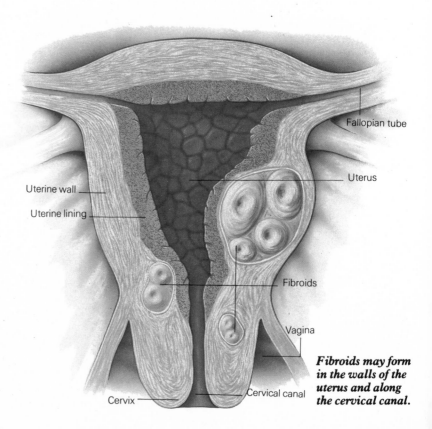

Fallopian tube

Uterus

Uterine wall

Uterine lining

Fibroids

Vagina

Cervical canal

Cervix

Fibroids may form in the walls of the uterus and along the cervical canal.

Frank Kennard

Fractures

Q **I am getting on in years and am terrified of being crippled by a fall. Is a fracture less likely to knit properly the older we get?**

A Age makes very little difference to the speed with which a fracture heals, provided the bone is healthy. Just take care there are no polished floors, or loose carpet or linoleum in your home that could possibly trip you up.

Q **Do fractures leave abnormalities of the limb after they have healed?**

A If the broken ends have been correctly aligned, the break usually heals so well that it may be difficult to find at a later date, even with X-rays. However, even if the bone ends are not correctly aligned, nature seems to straighten everything out in the fullness of time—a process known as remodelling.

Q **My son has his entire leg encased in plaster after a serious car accident. Is it possible for infection to set in because the leg cannot be cleaned whilst it is in the plaster?**

A The plaster does not contribute to infection in any way. The most important deciding factor as to whether or not a fracture becomes infected is the type of fracture involved. Compound fractures—where the bone has been driven through the skin—carry the greatest risk of infection.

Q **I have been told that fractures in babies are a sign of baby battering. Is this an unfair suspicion?**

A Accidents can occur in the home, of course, but a young baby with a fracture of the skull, or more than one fracture of a limb raises the suspicion that the injuries are not due to accidents. The parents may need professional help, as well as the child. If you really suspect a child is being ill-treated, you should inform your doctor or the NSPCC; any such information will be treated as strictly confidential.

Many people will break a bone at some time in their lives, but modern methods of treatment ensure complete recovery in most cases.

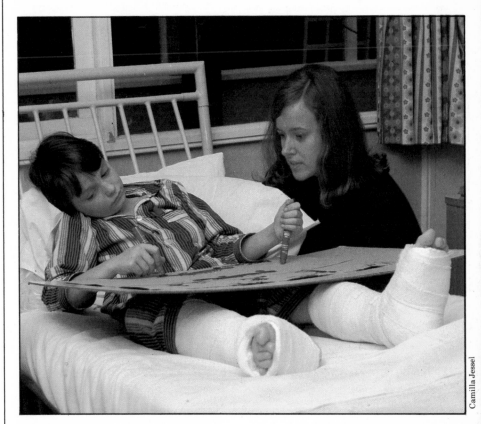

Camilla Jessel

Periods of hospital confinement with immobilized limbs can be trying—especially for active children. Every effort should be made to occupy them.

The word 'fracture', when it refers to a bone, means it is broken, but the severity of the injury can vary. The fracture may be a crack which runs only part-way across the bone, when it is called a greenstick fracture; if it is bad enough for the bone to be separated into several small pieces, it is known as a comminuted fracture; if part of the bone is driven through the skin, it is a compound fracture, as opposed to a simple fracture where the skin is not damaged; and if the break occurs as a result of disease of the bone, the fracture is described as pathological.

The greenstick fracture gets its name from the way in which a willow sapling breaks along its outer edge if it is bent too far. Only the very young and supple bones sustain this type of injury, which is why it is usually found in infants and children.

Compound fractures are always more serious than those in which the skin is not broken (simple fractures), because of the greatly increased risk of infection. But both simple (closed) and compound (open) fractures may be comminuted.

When bones are excessively weak due to a condition known as osteoporosis, found mainly in older people, or where there is a tumour of the bone, pathological fractures may occur without any force being applied. This type of fracture which happens spontaneously, or as a result of minimal force, is always due to disease of the bone.

Causes

A great deal of force is needed to break a healthy bone, but its susceptibility to fracture also depends upon other factors—its anatomical location in the body, its thickness and the circumstances in which force was applied. The limbs, for example, are more prone to damage than the pelvis, so a footballer is more likely to break his leg than a snooker player.

The long bones of the limbs are very resistant to force applied along their length, but are much more likely to break if the same force is applied across the length. These long bones are not of uniform thickness, and tend to break at

Q Recently I broke my femur and friends tell me I'll probably get arthritis years from now because of it. Is this really true?

A The great majority of fractures, providing they are speedily treated, do not give rise to any harmful after-effects. If there has been a delay or complication in treating a fracture, particularly if a joint has been involved, this may 'wear out' faster then normal and in such cases arthritis could develop in later life.

Q Is it possible to break a bone and not know it?

A Most bones are broken as a result of some definite accident and the resulting pain, swelling and change of shape in the part concerned make clear that something serious has happened. The smaller bones in the body, however, can be broken as a result of undue stress without the patient being aware of it. This sometimes happens with the small bones of the hands or feet. For instance, a fall on the outstretched hand that is not sufficient to break the arm can fracture one of the metacarpal bones in the hand without there being much to show for it. Similarly the so-called 'march' fracture of the foot sometimes occurs in soldiers following a long period of marching. Such fractures heal without treatment.

Q I've heard of bones being 'chipped', but not broken. Is it dangerous to have these chips floating around inside the body?

A A bone may become chipped or cracked when the force of the injury is not sufficient to completely break it and the damage usually only comes to light when the part is X-rayed. No special treatment is usually necessary and the chip or crack simply joins up. There is no danger of loose chips or bone moving freely around the body. Occasionally a chip may float near the break, but not join up. If the site is near a joint, pain may result on movement and the chip may have to be removed.

Common types of fracture

Comminuted fracture

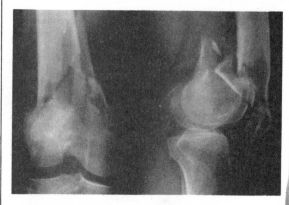

In a comminuted fracture (above and right), the bone shatters into small pieces. A femur (thigh bone) fractured above the knee is shown from the front (above left) and the side (above right). Treatment involves operating to remove fragments, joining the bone ends with a metal plate and immobilizing the limb in plaster.

Simple fracture

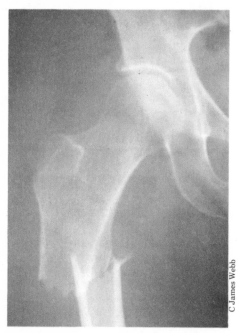

A simple fracture of the neck of the femur near the pelvic socket in a 60-year-old woman (above). To hold the two parts together and enable the bone to heal, a nail and screws were used to secure a metal plate to the bone.

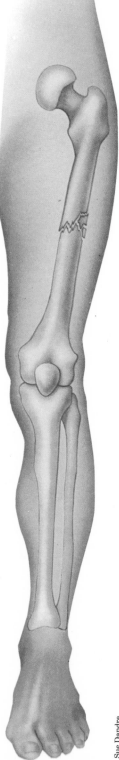

Greenstick fracture

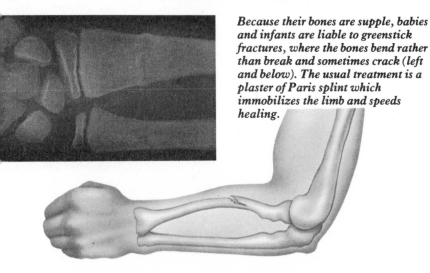

Because their bones are supple, babies and infants are liable to greenstick fractures, where the bones bend rather than break and sometimes crack (left and below). The usual treatment is a plaster of Paris splint which immobilizes the limb and speeds healing.

Compound fracture

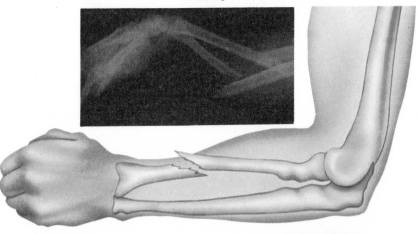

The broken bone pierces the skin in a compound fracture (top and above). The limb will be operated on to remove damaged tissue and bone fragments, the bone realigned and the limb set in plaster. In an upper arm or leg, the bone may also be secured by a metal plate.

Skull fracture

In treating a skull fracture (see arrow, right), the patient is first observed for signs of brain damage. If internal bleeding is causing pressure on the brain, an operation will be necessary. A steel or plastic plate may be used to replace shattered bone removed during the operation.

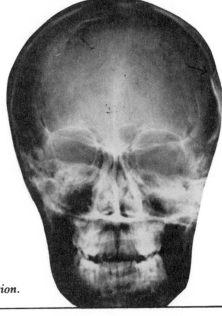

their narrowest point. This is known as the surgical neck. The three types of break that occur most frequently are fractures of the wrist, hip or ankle.

The commonest injury to the wrist is caused by a fall on an outstretched hand (which is used automatically to break the fall) and results in separation of the lower end of the large bone of the forearm (the radius). The broken lower end is displaced backwards, so that the forearm takes an upward bend before it reaches the hand. When viewed from the side, the resulting deformity looks like a dinner fork. This is known as Colles' fracture and can happen to people of all ages, but tends to be more common in the elderly.

Fractures of the hip occur almost exclusively in old people. The injury results from a sideways fall and the fracture takes place across the upper part of the thigh bone (femur) at its narrowest point, just behind the joint with the pelvis. This is a medical emergency, because the unfortunate victim is unable to walk. Any elderly person who has suffered a fall at home and is then unable to get up needs to be taken to hospital by ambulance for an immediate X-ray.

The injury caused by a twisting motion of the ankle, with the full weight of the body above, is a mixture of a fracture of the bones of the lower end of the leg, combined with tearing of the ligament of the ankle. This is called Potts' fracture, after the man who first described it, and can happen to girls wearing very high heels, if their ankle 'turns over'.

Symptoms

Whatever the cause of the fracture, the symptoms are similar: the victim is in pain, the limb may be in an unnatural position and cannot be used, there may be signs of shock (sweating and pallor) due to loss of blood from the broken ends of bone. If the bone is moved, the fractured ends may grind together (producing creaking called crepitus) which doctors feel by placing one hand over the fracture site. However, though pain is usually present, if the bones are not displaced at all, other signs may not be apparent. So an X-ray is necessary to check the diagnosis and exact position of the damage in the bone.

Fractures of weight-bearing bones, like those of the leg, are more obvious, because the victim finds it difficult to walk, but a fracture elsewhere—for example, of the ribs or hand—may pass unnoticed. Fractures in very young children are also harder to spot, simply because they cannot explain where it hurts. And the very old may break fragile bones without much force being applied and without suffering much pain.

Q Why do some people end up with one leg noticeably shorter than the other after a break has healed?

A In badly comminuted fractures, where the bone has fragmented, there may be a little shortening. But in most cases there is no change in bone length. However, if a child's bone is broken at the 'growing' end, the affected limb may not reach its full size.

Q My neighbour's little boy is always breaking his bones. She says he is accident-prone. Is this true?

A Active young children inevitably run a greater risk of injuring themselves, as any schoolteacher will tell you. But a person who breaks bones repeatedly may have an inherited bone disease, especially when these fractures occur when the child is very young, and your neighbour would be wise to seek her doctor's advice.

Q Is it possible for a bone to mend itself without any form of treatment?

A Bone possesses remarkable healing powers, and a fracture may mend without any outside help. The result may not be as strong or as straight as before, but full use of the limb does return—and so the failure to diagnose a fracture will not necessarily result in a complete disaster. But, obviously, the outlook is far better if a fracture receives prompt medical attention.

Q I am planning my first skiing holiday and am terrified of breaking my leg. As this seems to happen to so many people, I am wondering if there is any way in which it can be avoided.

A You can do a great deal to improve your chance of avoiding injury by ensuring that you are physically fit before you go. It is a good idea to start toning up your muscles for a few weeks before you leave, especially concentrating on the legs by jogging and doing bicycling exercises. Or better still, take a course of dry-ski lessons, which will certainly save you a few unnecessary falls.

Dangers

The chief danger from a fracture is shock, due to blood loss and pain. This can be a potentially life-threatening complication. Bone, like any other tissue of the body, is nourished by a rich blood supply and the bigger the bone that breaks, the greater the loss of blood. For example, a motor accident victim who suffered a fracture of the pelvis and two fractures of the leg, could lose up to 4 l (7 pt) of blood in a short space of time. This is why the immediate aim of medical treatment is to deal with shock and relieve pain before the fracture itself is repaired.

Fractures of certain bones must be treated very cautiously indeed because of the risk of damage to tissues underneath. Fractures of the skull, for instance, may be complicated by damage to the brain from increased pressure due to bleeding, and whenever a fractured skull is suspected the patient is admitted to hospital as a routine precaution and is kept under observation for at least 12 hours. The best-known warning sign of brain damage is an increase in drowsiness after the injury.

A fracture of the lower part of the rib on the right side could be complicated by rupture of the spleen and on the left side

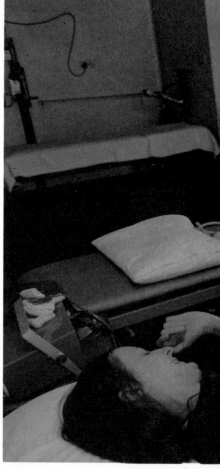

Fractures may occur, especially in the limbs, when an accident occurs during a dangerous sport.

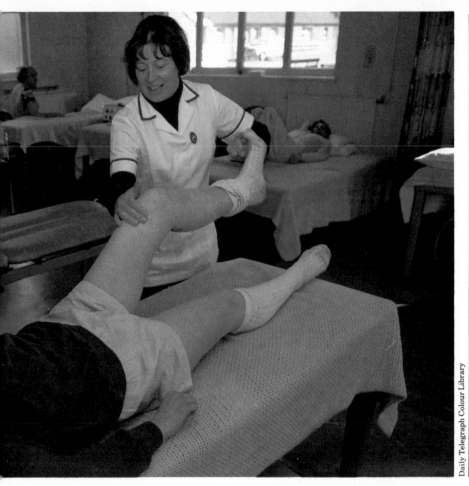

Physiotherapy (above) strengthens the muscles which have a tendency to waste away while the fracture is mending.

by rupture of the liver. In each case, shock develops due to loss of blood, which must be dealt with urgently.

Fractures of the pelvis can lead to damage to the bladder or urethra. Fractures of the spine need particularly skilled handling to avoid damage to the spinal cord and subsequent permanent paralysis.

Fractures of the limbs, although very painful, are not particularly dangerous, providing that loss of blood has been controlled. However, damage to blood supply to the bone sometimes occurs, with the result that the fracture does not heal. Examples of this are damage to one of the small bones of the hand or foot.

Young bone may stop growing if the line of the fracture runs across the 'growing' end. The result of this is that the affected limb does not reach the same size as the one on the other side. Obviously this problem will only affect children. The growing end of the bone is always close to the joint, so a fracture at the joint is more serious than a fracture through the shaft.

Treatment

Shock is corrected by giving the patient blood and pain is relieved with drugs. Then the fracture is repaired. In cases where there has been no displacement of bones, the fractured ends need not be realigned; but in other cases, especially fractures of the leg, muscle spasm pulls the bone ends past one another and a pull needs to be applied in the opposite direction to correct this—this procedure is called traction.

Badly comminuted fractures or spiral-shaped breaks may be impossible to bring together and in these cases, the bone is joined with a metal plate screwed along the side. A good example of this type of 'unstable' fracture is through the neck of the thigh bone, which is held steady by a metal nail secured to a plate screwed along the side of the femur.

After realignment, the bone ends must be held in the correct position while healing takes place. This is done by means of a plaster cast, which is worn for a variable period of time, depending on the type and position of the fracture. Because of having to bear the body's weight, a fractured leg usually has to be kept in plaster for at least 12 weeks. But non-weight-bearing injuries, such as

those of the arm, only need be immobilized for six weeks, or even less in children. Some fractures, for example fractures of the ribs, need no immobilization whatsoever.

The recovery period

The speed at which healing takes place depends upon the blood supply at the fracture site. Age does not matter. We heal just as fast at 80 as we do at eight. If a screw has been inserted, a simple supporting plaster is all that is needed and weight-bearing can begin again as soon as the pain and swelling have subsided.

People often forget that after not being used for a time, the muscles waste away a little. It is important that the surrounding muscles are strong and afford good support, so strengthening the area. For this reason, patients are encouraged to do active exercises from an early stage. This is painful at first, but gets easier with every day that passes. Isometric exercises (muscle contraction without movement) are especially useful. Here, physiotherapy is important in speeding patients on their road to recovery.

Bone possesses remarkable healing powers, and a fracture may mend completely without treatment.

145

Gall bladder & stones

Gallstones sometimes form in the gall bladder where bile, produced by the liver, is stored. They may well cause no trouble, but if they do, treatment is straightforward and effective.

Bile drains from the liver, where it is made into a channel called the common bile duct and from this passes, during digestion, into the intestine through an opening in the side of the duodenum (the first part of the small intestine). Here it plays an important part in the digestion of fatty foods before passing on to join the faeces (solid waste matter).

The gall bladder

Spouting from the side of the bile duct, however, is a channel leading to a bag called the gall bladder, where 0.14 l (¼ pt) of bile can be stored.

Gall bladder water is absorbed from the bile, so that it eventually becomes up to as much as ten times more concentrated than it was in its original form.

Exactly why our bodies store bile remains something of a mystery. If your gall bladder is removed by surgery, you can do perfectly well without it.

The gall bladder empties its bile into the intestine whenever fatty food arrives from the stomach. Bile, in fact, has the ability to break down or emulsify fat, much like detergent.

Formation of stones

Once again, doctors cannot agree exactly why, but we have quite a common tendency to form stones from the concentrated bile in our gall bladders.

These are exactly as they sound—hard, 'stoney' objects, varying in size from a pigeon's egg to a tiny bead.

About one in ten people over the age of 50 probably has a stone or stones in the gall bladder which may cause trouble.

Position of the gall bladder

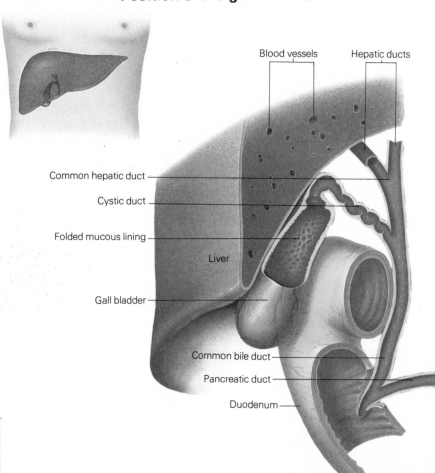

Mike Courteney

Blood vessels

Hepatic ducts

Common hepatic duct

Cystic duct

Folded mucous lining

Liver

Gall bladder

Common bile duct

Pancreatic duct

Duodenum

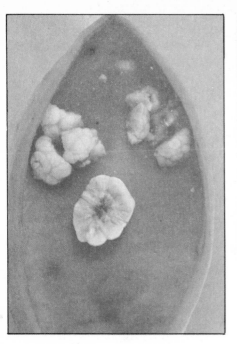

When opened, this gall bladder reveals the presence of cholesterol stones.

These dark stones are mainly composed of the green bile pigment.

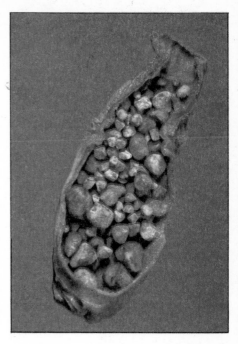

Mixed stones, a combination of cholesterol and bile, can occur in large numbers.

Types

There are three different kinds of gall-stones. The most common is known as mixed stones because these contain a mixture of the green pigment in bile and cholesterol, one of the chemicals produced in the body by the breakdown of fats. They develop in clutches, up to 12 at a time, and have facets so that they fit together in the gall bladder.

Cholesterol stones, as their name implies, are formed largely from cholesterol. They seldom occur in more than ones or twos, and can grow up to 1.25 cm (½ in) in diameter, which makes them large enough actually to block the common bile duct.

Pigment stones are made largely of the green bile pigment, occur in large numbers, and are usually small. They tend to form as a result of illnesses affecting the composition of the blood.

Gall bladder problems

The main problem with the gall bladder itself is that it can become inflamed, a condition known as cholecystitis. The inflammation, in itself caused by a bacteria, develops in many cases as a complication of gallstones already present in the gall bladder. Symptoms vary between individuals, but there is usually pain and vomiting.

Acute cholecystitis is quite sudden with agonizing pain in the upper right side of the abdomen accompanied by fever and vomiting. Chronic cholecystitis is a long-standing inflammation causing an ache, nausea and flatulence.

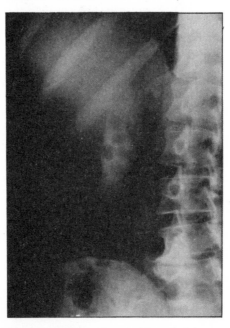

Dye, either injected or swallowed, shows up gallstones on an X-ray.

Biliary colic

Very occasionally, a large stone will find its way out of the gall bladder and become stuck in the common bile duct. The resulting complaint, called biliary colic, causes severe pain in the abdomen, high fever and sweating.

It also prevents bile from reaching the intestine, so that the faeces turn putty-coloured. This damming-up of bile also means that the pigment normally excreted in bile enters the bloodstream, and the patient turns a yellowish colour: in other words, gets jaundiced. At the same time, the body tries to compensate by getting rid of the excess pigment in the urine, which turns dark brown or orange.

Diagnosing gallstones

Anyone suffering from cholecystitis, biliary colic or jaundice is examined for gallstones in order that the root cause of the problem may be found.

There are various techniques for this. Not all gallstones show up on X-ray pictures, and so certain dyes may be introduced into the gall bladder or its adjoining areas to give a clearer indication. The fibre-optic tube, which transmits an image down its length, is also used and most recently a technique similar to echo-sounding, involving high frequency sound waves, has been effective.

Treatment

Whether to leave gallstones well alone if they are not causing problems, or to remove them, is another point of disagreement between doctors. Some prefer to wait until the stone or stones actually cause trouble.

A single attack of cholecystitis can be effectively settled by antibiotics, and it may be possible to dissolve stones over a period of months by means of a course of tablets.

Obstruction of the common bile duct does, however, require an operation because finding and removing the stone is the only way of relieving the blockage.

Gastric & duodenal ulcers

Q I have heard that aspirin can give you ulcers. Is this true?

A Aspirin can give you indigestion, and it can make ulcers that are already present worse, but there is no firm evidence that it actually causes ulcers. So aspirin is safe unless you suffer from indigestion.

Q My father had a gastric ulcer and it turned out to be malignant. Does this often happen?

A No. Only a small number of stomach ulcers are malignant. Fortunately they are fairly easy to distinguish from benign gastric ulcers as they tend to occur in different parts of the stomach. If there is any doubt about an ulcer, a small piece can be examined under a microscope. If malignant, it will then be removed by surgery.

Q I first had an ulcer 20 years ago, and on that occasion was taken into hospital for a rest. When the symptoms happened again recently, I was just given some pills. Why the change in treatment?

A Twenty years ago there was very little treatment for ulcers, other than rest, which was effective enough, but not as useful as the modern alternative of drug therapy.

Q My husband says my ulcer is due to worry. Is he right?

A It is difficult to say how far he is right. Worry *may* help start an ulcer, but this is one of those factors which are almost impossible to pin down. Even if it could be, doctors are not sure how useful the knowledge would be, because changing an anxious person into a calm one is easier said than done.

Q I have a gastric ulcer and am worried that it might burst. Is this likely?

A It would be far better to worry about maintaining a sensible diet, as advised by your doctor, and making the most of the treatment for the ulcer. Bursting, or perforating as it is properly called, is not common enough to be of everyday concern.

One in every five men and one in every ten women in the UK will suffer from a gastric or duodenal ulcer at some time in life. It is not known exactly why ulcers develop, but fortunately modern treatment is effective.

When food is being broken down during digestion, it churns round and round in acid produced by the stomach wall. So that the wall of the stomach is not digested as well, it is lined with a layer of tissue which is resistant to the acid. Any break in this layer of acid-resistant tissue is called an ulcer.

Such a break in the tissue allows the acid gastric juices to attack the tissues underneath and gradually eat them away until a hole may develop

Gastric or duodenal

Ulcers in the stomach itself are called gastric ulcers and those which occur in the duodenum (the part of the intestine which leads immediately off the stomach) are called duodenal ulcers. Gastric and duodenal ulcers are often grouped together and referred to under the general term peptic ulcer.

Duodenal ulcers are two or three times as common as gastric ulcers. In fact, gastric ulcers are becoming less common as time goes by, whereas at the end of the last century they were more common than duodenal ulcers. No one knows why this change is taking place, but it suggests that people's way of life may influence the development of ulcers.

It also appears that people with blood group 'O' have a higher chance of peptic ulcers than people with other blood groups. It is not known why this happens.

Causes and symptoms

It is not known why some people's stomach and duodenal linings are adversely affected by stomach acid. Diet and stress may well play a part, but there is no advice that can be given to people which will stop them having ulcers.

Smoking certainly makes ulcers worse,

Development of a duodenal ulcer

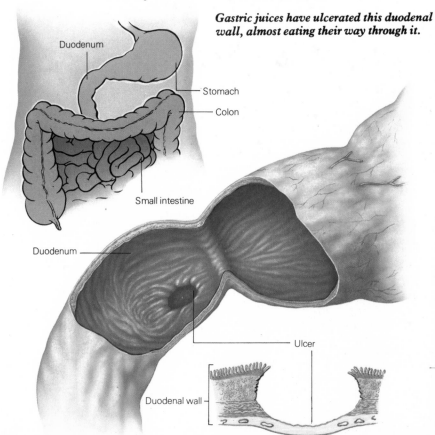

Gastric juices have ulcerated this duodenal wall, almost eating their way through it.

Duodenum

Stomach

Colon

Small intestine

Duodenum

Ulcer

Duodenal wall

Severe gastric ulceration led to this patient (right) having a partial gastrectomy—that is, having part of his stomach removed (light area within circle).

Anyone with ulcers, or a tendency to ulcers, should avoid eating highly spiced foods such as curries.

Ken Moreman

and it may play a part in causing them, but it is not a sole cause.

It is hard to tell the difference between gastric and duodenal ulcers. The symptom of both is a pain in the upper part of the abdomen. It is usually brought on by eating, but it may be only certain foods that do it. The pain tends to come in bouts of a few weeks or months and then it goes away again.

The pain is also similar to that caused by oesophagitis, which is an inflammation of the lower end of the gullet, caused by acid washing back into it from the stomach.

Ulcers can cause complications such as bleeding, when the patient may vomit blood or pass blood in the stools. This can cause serious blood loss.

Diagnosis and treatment

Diagnosis is carried out either by X-ray or fibre-optic tube. The X-ray diagnosis requires the patient to first eat a barium meal, a special preparation which makes the stomach show up on an X-ray. The fibre-optic tube is a flexible tube which can transmit images up its length, and is passed via the mouth into the stomach or duodenum so that the walls can be examined.

If an ulcer is diagnosed, the initial treatment is with drugs. There are several which promote the healing of peptic ulcers. They work by reducing the amount of acid secreted by the stomach.

Antacid mixtures and tablets help to bring relief by soaking up the acid, lessening the pain it causes in the stomach wall. But if drugs don't stop the pain, or if the ulcer causes additional problems, surgery may be necessary. But simply removing an ulcer by surgery does not necessarily cure the patient because another ulcer may well form somewhere else. So an ulcer operation usually aims to reduce the amount of acid the stomach produces by cutting away acid-producing cells. The ulcer will usually be removed at the same time.

Sometimes gastric or duodenal ulcers perforate: in other words, they wear right through the wall of the stomach or duodenum, whose contents are then released into the abdomen. This inflames the lining of the abdomen (the peritoneum), causing severe pain, a condition known as peritonitis. Surgery is then required to repair the gap in the stomach or duodenum wall.

Outlook

With modern drugs to promote healing—and with sensible eating and drinking habits—the outlook for ulcer sufferers is good, though some may need treatment over several years.

Gastro-enteritis

Q My husband had gastritis and now has enteritis. What is the difference between them?

A Gastritis is an inflammation of the stomach, whereas enteritis affects the lower bowel. The two may be part of an infection of the intestinal tract and the symptoms of gastric upset may be combined with diarrhoea. However, they usually have separate causes: gastritis is often due to eating or drinking something which irritates the stomach lining, whereas gastro-enteritis can result from food-poisoning, food allergies, and adverse reactions to certain drugs.

Q What do I do if I suspect that someone in the family has gastro-enteritis as a result of food poisoning?

A Pack them off to bed, keep them isolated and, if possible, put someone responsible in sole charge. This person must wash his or her hands thoroughly after any contact. Give the patient nothing by mouth except sips of water. Get in touch with your doctor, who will advise on how to proceed. Give no medicines except those which are prescribed by the doctor.

Do not throw away any suspect food that is left over: put it aside in a sealed plastic bag, in case the doctor wishes to have it tested. Say where it was obtained. It may also be necessary to examine specimens of the patient's faeces or vomit; keep these in closed containers.

Q My son is a trainee chef. How soon can he return to normal active life after an attack of gastro-enteritis? Can he continue working while he has treatment?

A If the work entails handling food in any way, he must not return to work until permitted by his doctor, as the bowel may continue to carry the offending bacteria after the actual symptoms have subsided. Tests on the faeces will show when he is free of infection.

If there were no question of handling food, a patient recovering from gastro-enteritis may be allowed back to work, provided he or she is meticulously careful about hygiene.

The inflammation of the stomach lining is called gastritis; that of the bowels, enteritis. When both are infected by a virus, the resulting condition is known as gastro-enteritis.

To avoid stomach infection, use great care in preparing feeding bottles.

An attack of gastritis is usually caused by eating or drinking something that irritates the lining of the stomach and causes inflammation, pain and sickness. Highly spiced foods or an excess of alcohol are most commonly responsible, though smoking can also be a culprit. Some drugs seem to have a similar effect: aspirin is particularly irritating.

The causes of gastro-enteritis are more complex. Microbes are by far the major source of the condition, especially those that cause food poisoning. Bacteria contaminate food in one of two ways. They either produce toxins (poisons) which interfere with the absorption of food and the normal digestive processes of the bowel and result in inflammation, or they work more directly by attacking the

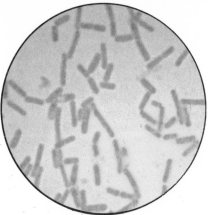

Close-up of the rod bacilli that attack directly if they are swallowed in food.

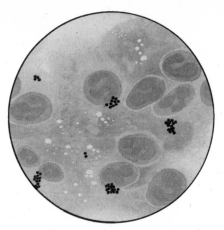

Staphylococci work indirectly by producing toxins in food, causing gastro-enteritis.

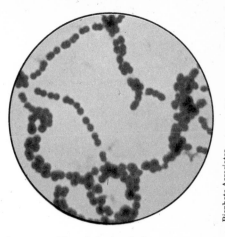

Streptococci work in much the same way as staphylococci.

lining of the stomach and the intestines. Here they cause minute ulcers, resulting in bleeding and loss of the fluids, salts and proteins that the body needs.

Poisonous mushrooms and berries can have serious ill-effects and large quantities of alcohol, aspirin, laxatives or over-spiced food are also possible causes. A few people are allergic to certain foods, and these, too, can cause an attack.

Symptoms

An early symptom of gastritis is loss of appetite. Nausea and vomiting may ensue, and there may also be a good deal of discomfort from 'heartburn', a burning sensation behind the breastbone. There may be profuse vomiting, including blood in severe cases. This can occur after a heavy drinking session.

If the patient suffers from diarrhoea and pain in the abdomen as well, the attack could be caused by infective gastro-enteritis. The stools (faeces) may be very liquid; sometimes they contain blood and slimy material called mucus; and these symptoms should be reported to a doctor.

Suspicion that harmful food has been responsible becomes stronger when there are a number of victims at the same time. Even so, to pinpoint the precise cause can be difficult. Symptoms may appear within a few hours of eating the food, but where there is infection by bacteria or viruses, this may take time to develop and the illness may not show itself until a day or two later.

Dangers

If an excessive intake of alcohol has produced an attack of gastritis, an especial danger lies in taking aspirin—because the two enhance each other's irritation of the stomach lining. The main danger, with acute alcoholic gastritis, is that the inflammation may progress to

cause several minute ulcers (erosions) into the stomach wall. These may perforate into a blood vessel and cause vomiting of blood, which will need treatment in hospital.

The diarrhoea and vomiting that occur in an attack of gastro-enteritis cause the rapid loss of a number of chemical elements such as sodium and potassium. This sudden deprivation can bring about serious biochemical changes in the body and may even lead to kidney or liver damage.

The effect may also be serious if the patient is already unwell, elderly or very young. Babies, in particular, can become seriously ill. The sick child is very thirsty, but can suck only feebly and then be unable to retain what has been taken in. The result is dehydration (loss of water), a situation that needs immediate medical help.

Treatment

In gastritis, a light diet for a couple of days, consisting mainly of fluids will allow the stomach to rest and is all that is needed in most cases. But where complications arise, such as vomiting of blood, the doctor may feel it necessary to send the patient to hospital.

In gastro-enteritis, too, the first aim of treatment is restoring fluids to the body. Vomiting may be overcome by taking tepid drinks in very slow sips. This can be followed by well-diluted meat or yeast extracts, weak sweetened tea or citrus fruit juices. If the attack has been caused by a bacterial organism, an antibiotic may be necessary.

Rest in bed is important, and an easily digested diet with plain foods like milk or strained broths, once the main symptoms have eased.

A seriously ill baby or small child, however, may need urgent hospital care to restore their fluid balance.

Prevention of gastro-enteritis

The majority of gastro-enteritis attacks are due to infection by bacteria or viruses entering the mouth and reaching the bowel. This is often due to inadequate care with food or poor hygiene in the lavatory.

Hygiene in the kitchen

● Follow manufacturers' recommendations about dates by which foods should be used. Many packed foods have date stamps to guide you.
● Wash hands and scrub fingernails before handling food.
● Keep work areas scrupulously clean.
● Do not allow pets near where food is being prepared. Prevent cats jumping on to tables.
● Keep food cool in summer. Use a refrigerator whenever possible.
● Avoid meats which have stood a day or more at room temperature after being cooked: recooking may not ensure safety.
● Eliminate flies.
● Keep all food covered.
● Dispose of food scraps, wrapped in plastic or paper. Keep waste bins covered and lined with a plastic bag. Do not allow children to play near waste bins.

In the lavatory

● Wash hands thoroughly and scrub fingernails after using the lavatory. Remember that microbes could be transferred from the flush handle and the seat of a lavatory previously used by an infected person. Clean these with household disinfectant if there is an infected person in the house.

Genitals

Q We have been attending a fertility clinic and my husband has been told that he has a low sperm count. Could this be caused by wearing nylon underwear?

A Unlike any other organ in the body, the testes—which produce sperm—cannot function properly at body temperature, which is why they are situated outside the body. Nylon underwear which does not absorb perspiration will therefore raise the temperature of the testes. It is unlikely, however, that hot underwear alone will cause infertility as most people do not wear their underwear for 24 hours at a time. But if your husband's sperm count is naturally low nylon underwear may affect his fertility.

Q My mother always used a douche for personal cleanliness. Is this necessary to keep my vagina clean?

A No. The vagina is well lubricated with secretions of its own and from the womb. The natural flushing of the vaginal canal keeps it clean and free from germs. In fact, by removing these secretions, douching can make the vagina more vulnerable to infection.

Q My teenage daughter is worried because her pubic hair is ginger, although she is dark-haired.

A Hair colour is a result of pigments in the hair cells. It is quite normal for people to have pubic hair a different colour from the hair on their head. Just tell your daughter that many men with dark hair may also have ginger beards.

Q When I was a schoolboy I remember that the school doctor would check to see if our testicles had dropped. What does this mean?

A During development of the foetus the testes lie in the abdomen and descend before birth into the scrotal sacs. Sometimes at birth they have not descended. This can be surgically corrected, but if it is not done before the onset of puberty, sterility may result.

Although people are far less embarrassed than they once were by this subject, there are still many who do not fully understand the structure and working of their own reproductive organs.

The word genital derives from generation, meaning 'bring into existence' and signifies the creation of life. The genital organs in men and women are those that nature designed for the purpose of sex and reproduction.

The male genitals

In men, the genitals consist of the testes and the penis, which are situated outside the body, and the prostate gland, seminal vesicles and various tubes linking the genital system, which are found inside the abdominal cavity.

The testes are enclosed in a pouch of loose skin called the scrotum that consists of two compartments called scrotal sacs, one for each testis. Two functions are performed by the testes—the production of sperm and of the male hormone testosterone. The latter is responsible for the development of the male genitals and has an important role in the secondary sexual changes of puberty in boys, such as the growth of body hair and the 'breaking'

and deepening of the voice.

The male genital system is designed to produce sperm and deposit them in the female. Sperm production is a continuous process, beginning in a mass of small tubes—the seminiferous tubules—where sperm are first formed. As new sperm cells are formed they push the older ones along until they reach a part on each testicle called the epididymis where they mature and gain the ability to move. The sperm are stored here until ejaculation (ejection), but if they are not emitted for several weeks they break down, turn into liquid and are then reabsorbed by the system.

Before ejaculation they travel up from the epididymis along a tube called the vas deferens until they reach the prostate gland. Here they are mixed with seminal fluid secreted by the seminal vesicles and the prostate itself, to form the semen, the fluid in which the sperm are suspended. From the prostate the semen passes into the urethra and into the penis for ejacu-

The female genital organs

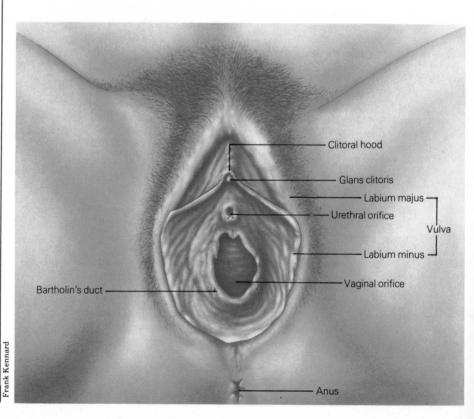

Clitoral hood

Glans clitoris

Labium majus

Urethral orifice

Vulva

Labium minus

Vaginal orifice

Bartholin's duct

Anus

Frank Kennard

lation. A single ejaculation contains more than three hundred million sperm. The urethra, however, is also the passageway for urine from the bladder, but during sexual excitement the tube is shut off from the bladder so that the two functions are kept quite separate from each other.

Sexual arousal

Besides providing an exit for urine, the main function of the penis is to deposit semen in the female vagina. Normally the penis is soft and therefore unable to penetrate, but when sexually aroused by either physical or mental stimulation it becomes longer, wider, stiffer and erect. It can achieve this because it consists of spongy erectile tissue that is well supplied with blood vessels and covered with loose skin that can adapt to the changes in size. At the end of the penis there is a bulge called the glans penis that is sensitive to physical stimulation and this is usually covered by a collar of skin called the foreskin. This is often removed for cultural or medical reasons by the minor operation called circumcision.

During sexual excitement there is an increased flow of blood into the penis. Muscles at the base of the penis tighten and blood is trapped so the penis enlarges. On average, the length of the penis before erection ranges from 2.5 cm to 13

cm (1 in to 5 in) increasing to between 15 cm to 19 cm (6 in to 7½ in). Length, however, bears no relationship to the amount of semen produced or the length of time for which intercourse can be prolonged.

Problems

Because the urethra serves the dual purpose of carrying semen and urine, pains in the penis may be caused by problems with the kidneys and bladder, such as kidney stones that lodge in the penis.

The testes are relatively free from infection but sometimes become inflamed as a complication of mumps when it affects adolescents or men. For reasons that are not yet clear, the prostate gland sometimes increases in size with age. This can cause pain on urinating as it presses on the neck of the bladder, and once an enlarged prostate is diagnosed it is best to have it surgically treated as soon as possible.

Common skin infections of the genitals, such as ringworm and herpes, can be treated simply but can usually be avoided by careful daily washing with soap and water.

However, the sexually transmitted venereal diseases, syphilis and gonorrhoea, can cause serious problems if left untreated.

The female genitals

The woman's reproductive system must not only receive the sperm but also must produce ova (eggs) for fertilization and eventually nurture one egg if it is fertilized, so that a baby can develop. However, it is only the parts of the female reproductive system below the cervix, or neck of the womb, that are usually understood to be included in the term genitals.

Below the cervix is a muscular canal 10 cm to 13 cm (4 in to 5 in) in length called the vagina that encases the penis during sexual intercourse, although normally the walls lie flat against each other. The vagina is usually moist, lubricated by secretions from its walls and the Bartholin's gland. These increase with sexual excitement and at different times during the menstrual cycle. The continual secretion passing down the vaginal canal keeps the vagina free from infection.

The entrance to the vagina is covered and protected by the external genitals known as the vulva. The vulva consists of two folds of flesh—the outer and inner labia (so-named after the Latin word for lips). The outer labia grow larger with age and from the onset of puberty become covered in pubic hair. Between them lie the smaller inner labia which are sensitive to touch and swell up during sexual excitement and change from pink to a darker colour.

The inner labia join together in front of the clitoris, a small fleshy organ that is covered by a flap of skin called the clitoral hood. The clitoris corresponds to the male penis and is made of erectile tissue that swells up during sexual excitement. It is extremely sensitive to touch and for most women is the centre of orgasm (climax of sexual excitement). Unlike the penis, however, the clitoris plays no actual part in reproduction or urination, as the urethra opens directly into vulva.

In virgins the entrance to the vagina is partly closed by a thin membrane called the hymen. Usually this is very thin and may be perforated, and can easily be ruptured by such things as vigorous exercise and the use of tampons. However, it may be stretched and torn by the first experience of sexual intercourse, causing temporary pain and bleeding. Sometimes the membrane is so thick that penetration is impossible and the hymen has to be surgically removed.

Medical problems associated with the female genital tract can be serious, such as cervical cancer and venereal diseases if left untreated, but generally they are fairly minor. Many are bacterial, fungal and viral infections that cause a burning sensation and itching of the vulva, but they can usually be cured simply by a course of antibiotics.

The male genital organs

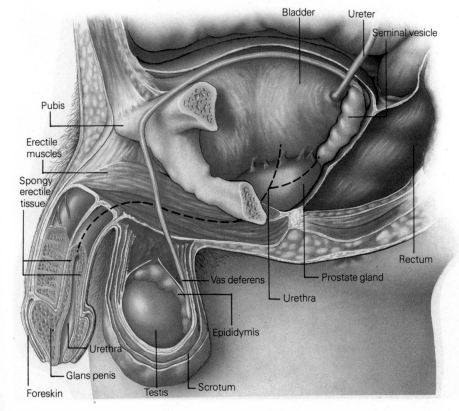

Bladder

Ureter

Seminal vesicle

Pubis

Erectile muscles

Spongy erectile tissue

Rectum

Vas deferens

Prostate gland

Urethra

Urethra

Epididymis

Glans penis

Testis

Scrotum

Foreskin

German measles

Q I missed my German measles vaccination when I was at school. I am now married and my doctor recently took a blood test and told me I needed immunization. He said I must not get pregnant for a while. Why did he advise a delay?

A The vaccine used for the immunization is not as harmful as the German measles virus itself because it is a strain that has been changed by laboratory conditions. Nonetheless, if you were to become pregnant after being vaccinated, you would be subjecting the baby to an unnecessary risk. It is best to be certain by avoiding pregnancy for at least two months, by which time the live vaccine will have disappeared.

Q I am six weeks pregnant and my son has caught German measles. What should I do?

A Go and see your doctor immediately. He will be able to tell from your medical records if you have been immunized.
If you are immune, you have nothing to worry about. If not, you may need treatment to prevent your getting the infection and tests to check your baby is normal.

Q My sister is six months pregnant and has just developed German measles. Will the baby be all right?

A By six months her baby will have developed all the essential organs and systems, so it is very unlikely that it will be affected. However, she should see her doctor as soon as possible so that he can reassure her.

Q When I was young we used to hold German measles parties so all the children could catch the illness and become immune. Why not do this today?

A German measles parties were fun. If you had a child with German measles, you invited all the neighbouring children round to catch it. The only trouble was it did not protect all young girls. Today we have a vaccine which gives 100 per cent protection to all who are given it. Not such fun, but safer.

German measles is a common virus infection, mild in children, but damaging to a developing baby if a pregnant woman catches it. Fortunately, vaccination is now available to give women life-long protection from German measles.

German measles, or rubella, is a common, mild virus infection which occurs mostly in children. Infection appears to be most likely in the spring or summer months and to run in four to six-year cycles of minor epidemics.

The virus itself causes virtually no serious illness in an adult or child. Once the diagnosis is confirmed the illness can usually be forgotten.

However, the virus can be extremely damaging to a foetus developing in the mother's womb (uterus), causing serious abnormalities if the mother catches it in the early months of pregnancy.

For this reason it is important to make sure that pregnant women do not catch German measles.

Cause

German measles is caused by a virus found in the nose and throat of the patient. Like most viruses living along the respiratory tract, it is passed from person to person by the tiny droplets in the air breathed out. It is transmitted from a mother to her developing baby through the bloodstream via the placenta.

The virus has an incubation period of about two to three weeks, during which it is getting established and the patient shows no symptoms.

The commonest symptoms of German measles are a rash of fine pink dots under the skin and swollen, tender lymph nodes.

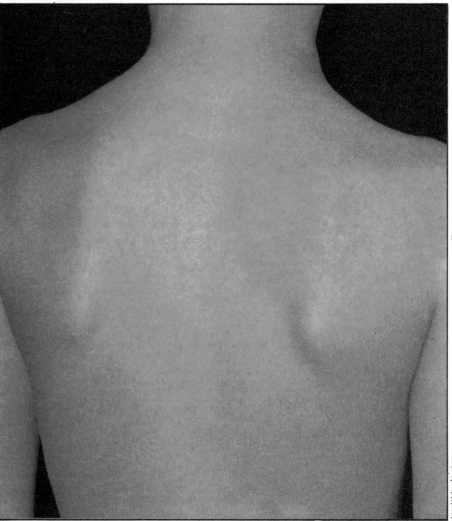

V—DIA—Verlag

Protection for Women

- Inform the school or place of work if you or your child has German measles. Mention the risk to any pregnant women.
- Be especially sure to avoid your doctor's surgery or ante-natal clinics if you have German measles.
- There is no need for strict isolation bu it is best to stay at home for four or five days and mention you have German measles to all new contacts, especially female ones.
- All girls aged between 11 and 13 should be vaccinated.
- Women who are not pregnant, but might be in the future, should check whether they need vaccination. This will mean having a blood test.
- If a pregnant woman develops German measles in the first three months of pregnancy, the doctor will confirm the diagnosis by taking one or more blood tests. The risk of abnormalities in the baby will be explained to her. She may be offered an amniocentensis, a test whereby a sample of developing cells from the womb is tested for abnormality.

There is no guarantee that abnormalities will show up on the test, and the mother may decide to take the risk. If the tests show abnormalities, she will be eligible for abortion on medical grounds.

- A pregnant woman who is in contact with German measles need not worry if she has been immunized or knows she is immune. A blood test can confirm this.

Injection of anti-German measles

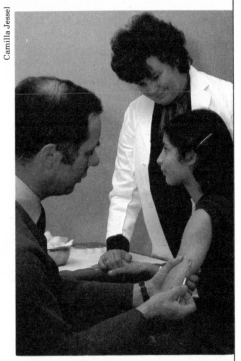

Camilla Jessel

antibody can be given to a woman who has not been immunized and is in the first three months of pregnancy. However, not all doctors will recommend this.

In general, just contact with German measles is not medical grounds for abortion. It is necessary to prove infection has taken place. If an abnormal baby is at all likely, the doctor will probably advise termination.

cent are affected, and between nine and 17 weeks, 12 per cent of babies are affected. Older foetuses are well enough developed for the virus not to harm them.

The defects the virus can cause include retarded growth, eye defects, heart defects, deafness, nerve defects (which can cause mental backwardness), encephalitis (inflammation of the brain), bone defects and enlarged spleen and liver. Often two or more of the defects occur together.

The reason developing babies are so susceptible is that while they are forming they have no defence against such viruses and the breeding virus disrupts the developing cells. The mother's antibodies cannot help because they do not all cross the placenta with the foetus's own bloodstream.

Vaccination
A vaccination is now available for girls which gives them life-long protection against German measles. A single dose is all that is necessary, and is given to girls between the age of 11 and 13. It has no side-effects.

Because German measles can be so mild that it goes unnoticed, it is important for girls to have the injection even if they think they have had German measles. The only people who should not have it are those on steroid drugs or with a serious illness. If in any doubt, your doctor will be able to advise you whether you run any risk.

Tests
Some women will not have caught German measles as a child, or may not be sure about it. If they are likely to get pregnant in the future, they should have a blood test to see if they have natural immunity and if not naturally immune, they will then be vaccinated.

Treatment and outlook
There is no treatment which will cure the disease and only the body's own defences—in other words its antibodies—will end infection. Although most patients hardly know they are ill (apart from the rash), some may get a sore throat. Aspirin gargles will help, as will painkilling drugs. For the average case there is no treatment other than to rest if the patient feels unwell.

A large proportion of adults will be able to continue work and most children will be able to attend school—depending on the school rules—and play normally throughout the illness.

The rash disappears after a few days, but the swollen glands may persist for up to a week. If there are complications, recovery may take as long as a month.

Symptoms
The illness takes its name from measles proper because in some cases the initial symptoms are similar—a runny nose and mild conjunctivitis followed by a rash. But whereas measles can be a serious illness, German measles is often so mild that an attack passes unnoticed.

In most cases there are only two symptoms. A rash appears on the face and neck, spreading to the trunk and limbs, and some of the lymph nodes or glands swell and become tender.

The rash looks like fine pink dots under the skin. It appears on the first or third day of the illness and disappears within four to five days with no staining or peeling of the skin.

The doctor will usually look at the rash and feel for enlarged nodes at the back of the neck to confirm the diagnosis. In older people, nodes may also swell in the armpit or groin. The nodes enlarge

because they are producing antibodies to destroy the virus.

Some patients develop a low fever, but this rarely rises above 37°C (100°F) and medical complications are rare. A joint may become inflamed and develop mild arthritis, but this goes after a period of rest. Very rarely, nerves may become affected by the virus, with accompanying weakness or numbness.

Cases are often difficult to diagnose because the symptoms are so mild. Similar symptoms can be produced by other viruses, but the German measles, or rubella virus is the only one known to damage developing babies.

Risks
The earlier in pregnancy the virus infects the foetus, the greater the risk of damage. If it is caught between conception and four weeks, 50 per cent of babies are affected, between five and eight weeks, 35 per

Glandular fever

Q My daughter has glandular fever and can't settle at anything and is most unhappy. Why is this?

A One of the side-effects of glandular fever is malaise and depression. This arises because many patients feel low and lack energy and drive, often for several weeks. It is important that you explain this to her and help her through her moods, while at the same time being sympathetic. Within a few weeks she will return to the person she was before.

Q Is glandular fever harmful in pregnancy?

A For some reason pregnant women virtually never get glandular fever as their immunity is enhanced due to their pregnancy. However, virus infections in pregnancy are dangerous, and so a pregnant mother who suspects she has the disease should see her doctor immediately for diagnosis, and to check that no harm has been done to the foetus. This can be done through an amniocentesis test on the foetal fluid.

Q Why should glandular fever make some people very ill and others hardly at all?

A There is no explanation for this. The response to a virus depends on the susceptibility of the patient. Some people have an inbuilt immunity, others only a partial immunity, and others have none at all, and the illness can drag on for many months.

Q Is there anything you can do to avoid catching glandular fever?

A No. There are no really effective preventive measures because the virus is carried long after the illness is over, and some people seem to carry the virus without any symptoms at all. The virus is only transmitted by close personal contact, so staying away from people who have glandular fever will not help. It is just one of those illnesses young people may or may not get, though older people usually become immune.

Glandular fever is a viral infection which mainly affects young people. Most cases are mild, but sometimes there are serious complications. However, in almost all cases, complete recovery is usual.

The cause of glandular fever is thought to be a virus known as the Epstein-Barr virus. The virus causes some of the white blood cells, known as lymphocytes, to multiply and enlarge, and the increased activity of the immune or lymphatic system causes the lymph glands to swell and become tender. For this reason, glandular fever is a generalized infection and not just a complaint of the glands or, the nodes, as they are more correctly called.

The virus lives in the mouths and noses of people who have the disease, and can remain there for several months after the illness is finished. The virus is passed from person to person by close contact, probably in the tiny droplets that are exhaled normally with each breath, but possibly also by kissing. However, not all people who come into intimate contact with people who have glandular fever will develop the illness, as susceptibility varies greatly from person to person.

Symptoms

After a symptomless incubation period of between four and seven weeks, the patient will begin to feel listless and fatigued. Headache and chills are followed by a high fever, an extremely sore throat, and swollen lymph glands in the neck and sometimes in the armpits and groin. The spleen may also become swollen.

Young people are those who are most affected by glandular fever, which is a virus infection that is transmitted by close or intimate contact.

Two sorts of rashes may appear, and it is the formation of the rash which helps the doctor make the diagnosis. In about 15 per cent of cases, a redness appears under the skin of the trunk and inner surface of the arms and legs. This may develop into fine pimples which do not contain fluid. In a much larger proportion of cases, a similar rash can be brought out by ampicillin, the antibiotic drug .

In many cases, the illness may be so mild as to be missed, or mistaken for another illness where the symptoms are a sore throat and swollen glands. In severe cases, the symptoms are more obvious, and there may be dangerous complications. The liver may become inflamed, producing jaundice. The spleen may become so enlarged while it is forming white blood cells to fight the infection that it becomes painful and tender. The virus may affect the nervous system, producing a form of meningitis, or it may affect the lungs or heart, causing pneumonia or an inflammation of the pericardium, the fibrous sheath sur-

red blood cells of sheep. In 90 per cent of infected cases, the sheep cells mass together and agglutinate. In non-infected cases they do not. This test is often used to confirm the disease.

Dangers

Glandular fever is not normally dangerous, but in rare cases some dramatic medical events may occur.

If pressed too hard or bumped in error, a very enlarged spleen may rupture. This condition would necessitate immediate blood transfusion and the surgical removal of the organ.

In very rare cases, meningitis may occur. This causes headache and photophobia (pain looking into bright light), but permanent damage is unlikely.

The danger of infecting other people is not great, but patients are barrier nursed in hospital to prevent sick people from contracting the disease. This means they are kept in total isolation from the other patients. In normal circumstances, no such isolation is necessary.

Treatment

There is no curative treatment for glandular fever, only treatment for each of the separate symptoms. Because the illness is caused by a virus, antibiotics have no effect, although in certain circumstances they are sometimes used, such as when the throat becomes ulcerated or the lungs become inflamed.

In mild cases, the patient should gargle frequently for the sore throat and take painkillers such as aspirin or paracetamol for headache. Bed rest is advisable, particularly in the early stages.

In severe cases, bed rest is absolutely necessary. The patient should have adequate fluids and a light diet, and take aspirin or paracetamol for fever and sore throat. A hot water bottle will help to relieve the swollen glands. In rare cases glandular fever is accompanied by thrombocytopenia (an abnormal decrease in blood platelets, the cells which clot blood), and hospitalization and giving steroid drugs will be necessary.

Those patients who have a mild form of the disease may not need to take time off from school or work, but most patients will require a few weeks of resting and home treatment. The convalescent period is longer than with the most infectious illnesses, and patients might not feel right in themselves for several months, even when the symptoms have gone.

Outlook

Glandular fever is usually mild and virtually never fatal. Most patients make a complete recovery over a period of about six to eight weeks. Others may take longer, even up to six months.

A small number of people get recurrent bouts of depression for as long as six months after the illness, which can be quite debilitating. These patients should be reassured that the illness will eventually clear itself.

A tiny proportion of patients suffer a relapse which causes a renewal of such symptoms as fever and swollen glands.

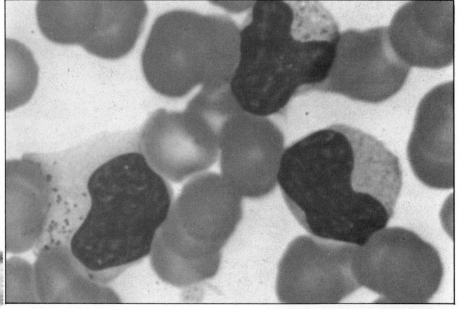

The glandular fever, or Epstein-Barr virus is thought to cause the disease. The white blood cells (above) (stained purple), are invaded by the virus (stained white), and once this occurs, the white cells multiply and enlarge to attack the infection (right).

rounding and enclosing the heart.

The two most helpful diagnostic tests are made from a blood sample. In one test the blood cells are analysed under a microscope to see if the enlarged, abnormal lymphocytes, the glandular fever cells, are present. In the second test, known as the Paul-Bunnel test, a sample of serum is taken and tested against the

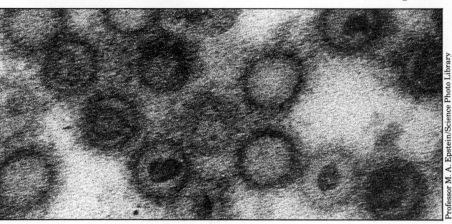

Glaucoma

Q My father has glaucoma and his eyesight has been deteriorating over the past year. Is there any hope of an improvement?

A Even when glaucoma is treated properly eyesight may not actually improve—usually what happens is that further deterioration in sight is prevented.

Q Several members of my family have suffered from glaucoma. Does this often happen or is it just a coincidence?

A Yes, glaucoma does often run in families. Some people are born with a liability to glaucoma due to abnormalities of drainage of the anterior chamber of the eye; but the condition does not become obvious until adult life.

Q My mother has had an operation for glaucoma. Does this mean that her eyesight will not get worse?

A This is impossible to say. Unfortunately, there are a few cases in which progressive loss of sight resulting from glaucoma, fails to respond to treatment.

Q I have heard that glaucoma has no symptoms, so how do I know whether I have the disease or not?

A It is most unusual for glaucoma to affect you before you are 40. But if you are worried, go and see an optician, who can examine your eyes and tell you whether there is any trouble or not.

Q I am nearly 40 and have heard that this is the age when you can get glaucoma. How can this be prevented?

A Because the early symptoms of glaucoma are often not noticeable, it is important that people over 40 should have their eyes checked regularly, to ensure that there is no change in their field of vision. This is even more vital if there is glaucoma in your family, because the condition can lead to blindness if it is not diagnosed and treated promptly.

In a condition like glaucoma, early detection can often prevent serious deterioration of sight.

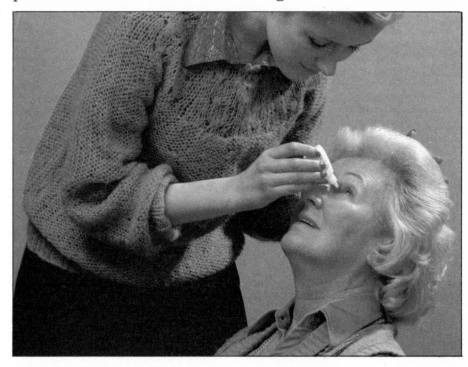

If glaucoma has been detected, further deterioration in vision can sometimes be prevented by the use of special eye drops.

Although it usually develops late in life, glaucoma is a common cause of blindness, affecting one in fifty people who are over the age of forty.

Causes

The eye is separated into front and rear portions (anterior and posterior chambers) by the lens, and the ciliary muscle supporting it. Just in front of the lens around the rim of the eyeball is a structure called the ciliary body which manufactures the fluid, called the aqueous humour, which fills the anterior chamber. Since this fluid is constantly being produced, it needs to be continually drained away, and this is where the problem arises.

In glaucoma there is an obstruction to the drainage of the fluid and as a result the pressure in the eyeball rises. No such trouble ever develops with the fluid in the posterior chamber, because it does not circulate.

Symptoms

In many cases there are none. Deterioration of vision develops so gradually that the patient seldom notices what is happening. A doctor may be able to spot the trouble early by looking into the eye with an instrument called an ophthalmoscope. What he or she sees is the retina and the optic nerve supplying it, at the back of the eyeball. Normally, the optic nerve has a pinkish colour and an edge which is continuous with the rest of the retina, but in glaucoma the nerve looks pale and is pressed back.

An optician may notice an area of blindness in that part of the retina not used for detailed vision, and the reason that people are not at first aware of the onset of blindness is probably because part of the eye used for detailed vision is not affected at first.

Occasionally, glaucoma may begin suddenly, with agonizing pain in the eye, as well as nausea and vomiting. Treatment in hospital is urgently required if the eyesight is to be saved.

Treatment

The aim is to improve the rate at which fluid is drained from the anterior chamber of the eye by means of drug treatment: special drops (usually pilocarpine) are placed in the eye three or four times a day. If this fails, surgery may be necessary; a piece of the iris is cut out to relieve pressure.

In some cases, glaucoma can lead to progressive blindness, in spite of treatment—and once sight has been lost it cannot be restored; so early diagnosis and treatment are absolutely essential.

Goitre

A goitre is a swelling in the neck caused by a disorder of the thyroid gland. It is a condition which responds well to treatment.

Q I noticed that my neck swelled when I was pregnant. Was this a goitre?

A Yes, probably. A small goitre is common in pregnancy and is not serious. The thyroid seems to be very sensitive to other hormonal changes and, of course, hormonal changes occur during pregnancy. The goitre almost always disappears when the pregnancy is over.

Q I had an overactive thyroid which caused a goitre. It is now better after two years on tablets. I noticed that when I started the tablets my goitre got bigger. Why was this?

A The tablets stop the release of thyroid hormone which leads to an accumulation in the thyroid gland. For this reason the goitre may get larger on starting treatment, although after a month or two it will begin to shrink.

Q My mother has a swelling in her neck which I think is a goitre. She won't go to the doctor because she is afraid it is cancer. Could she be right?

A It really is most unlikely to be cancer if this swelling is a goitre. Her doctor will probably be able to reassure her just by examination so she should certainly go to him. Even if the cause were thyroid cancer, it responds very well to treatment.

Q I have a goitre and whenever I go to my doctor he makes me drink a glass of water as he examines my neck. Why?

A The characteristic of the thyroid gland is that it moves up and down on swallowing. By observing this movement your doctor can be confident that the swelling is the thyroid rather than some other problem.

Q I have been advised to have surgery for my goitre. Won't it leave an ugly scar?

A No—usually not. The incision used normally follows a natural skin crease. Some thyroid operation scars can hardly be seen after a few months.

Goitre is a common condition and it is not usually serious. It is a swelling of the thyroid gland and may be accompanied by the overactivity or—less frequently—by the underactivity of the thyroid. Goitre and thyroid trouble in general is more common in women than in men; the reasons for this are unclear. Most goitres, however, are not associated with any other form of thyroid disease and are called simple goitres because their causes are not obvious.

Causes and symptoms

There are a number of causes of this condition and the commonest is called Grave's disease. The symptoms of thyrotoxicosis, or overactive thyroid, are weight loss, inability to tolerate heat, a fast heartbeat with palpitations, sweating and irritability. In addition, when the thyrotoxicosis is due to Grave's disease the eyes may become prominent giving the pop-eyed look that most people associate with thyroid trouble.

An underactive thyroid results from the thyroid being attacked by the body's own defence mechanism—the immune system. Why the thyroid should be so affected is unknown. A particular form of underactive thyroid is Hashimoto's disease and this is the sort of underactivity which may be associated with a goitre. The symptoms of underactivity of the thyroid gland, or myxoedema, are weight gain, thinning of the hair and inability to stand the cold.

The other causes of goitre are not at all common. Cancer of the thyroid does occur but is very rare. Finally, the thyroid can become infected with a virus causing a goitre. This is a condition known as thyroiditis, which can be relieved by drug treatment.

When the thyroid gland swells up it is visible below the level of the Adam's apple. The size of the goitre may range from barely perceptible to a huge swelling. Usually the symptoms of the goitre are very minor and the main reasons why people go to their doctors are either because they have the symptoms of over- or underactivity of the thyroid or because the goitre is unsightly.

Diagnosis and treatment

If you go to your doctor with a goitre he will not only feel the swelling but listen over the area to see if he can detect the sound which results from excessive blood flow to an overactive gland. He will then make blood tests to determine the level of thyroid hormone in the blood. If it is high this means thyrotoxicosis is present. If the pituitary gland is working overtime to stimulate the thyroid, then myxoedema is the cause.

If the appearance of a simple goitre is unpleasant, it can often be made to shrink by a course of thyroid hormone taken by mouth over eighteen months or more. Only if they become gross and uncomfortable or spread down into the chest and cause difficulty with swallowing will an operation be necessary.

Goitres due to an underactive thyroid are treated by giving thyroid hormones by mouth, a treatment which has to be continued for life.

Overactive thyroids can be treated by tablets which suppress the gland's activity. If the condition recurs most of the thyroid can be removed by surgery, a treatment which can be very effective. Otherwise, the overactive thyroid tissue can be destroyed by giving the patient a controlled measure of radioactive iodine to drink.

A typical goitre caused by thyrotoxicosis or overactive thyroid. It will respond to drugs which suppress thyroid activity.

Gout

Q My husband has just had an attack of gout. I have heard that gout is connected with rich food. Should he go on a diet?

A It is true that certain foods rich in the chemicals known as purines will, after digestion, produce uric acid, an excess of which can lead to gout if the body does not excrete it efficiently. High purine foods include sweetbreads, liver, kidney, brain, venison, heart, meat extracts, goose, duck, turkey, fish roe, whitebait, sardines, herring, bloater and sprats. These foods are best avoided in large amounts, but if eaten in moderation their contribution is relatively slight. Alcohol in moderation is all right, but an alcoholic 'binge' may temporarily decrease the power of the kidneys to pass out uric acid and so provoke an attack.

Q Does gout have anything to do with cancer?

A Only very indirectly. Gout certainly will not cause cancer but sometimes cancer can cause gout. In some cancerous growths the creating and degeneration of tissues increases and this can lead to an increased production of uric acid. Also, certain tumours which are treated with deep X-ray therapy or drugs may produce uric acid.

Q After my last attack of gout the doctor advised long-term treatment with drugs to reduce the formation of uric acid. But he would not let me start the treatment for over a month. Why was this?

A The drug used in this type of treatment must have its dose built up gradually. It is important to start this treatment when the body is well clear of an acute attack of gout, otherwise it might produce a counter-reaction which would mobilize uric acid in the body instead of decreasing it.

Q If someone suffers from gout does it help to lose weight?

A If the patient is grossly overweight and has gout then he or she should certainly lose weight, but it should be done gradually and under medical supervision.

Most people dismiss gout as just a painful inflammation of the big toe resulting from over-indulgence in food and drink. In fact, the causes are more complex and if left untreated gout can lead to serious bone and kidney damage. Fortunately, drugs can keep it well under control.

Gout is caused by an abnormally high amount of uric acid in the tissue fluids. Uric acid is always present in the body as it is a product of certain foods when they are broken down and also of naturally worn out tissue cells. Normally the gut and the kidneys excrete uric acid so that the level in the body remains constant. In patients suffering from gout either too much uric acid is formed or it is inadequately excreted.

Causes

There are various reasons for an increase in uric acid formation. In the past the blame was put on over-indulgence in rich food—such as sweetbreads and goose—and alcohol, which produce uric acid after being digested. However, it is now known that the part played by diet is relatively small and other causes are far more likely.

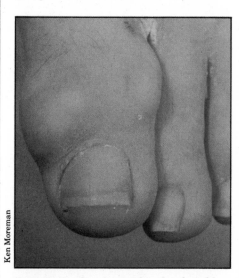

Long-term, chronic gout has developed in this big toe which may need treatment for the rest of the patient's life.

The most common cause is the filtering process of the kidneys becoming inefficient at getting rid of uric acid. This can happen in some kidney troubles such as chronic nephritis (inflammation of the kidneys) or be due to the effect of certain drugs, such as diuretics.

Sometimes gout is caused by diseases of the blood and tissues which involve an excessive breakdown of their cells. There are also certain congenital (existing from

birth) conditions in which the body chemistry creates more uric acid than is normal.

A person with a raised level of uric acid does not necessarily suffer from gout. However, in many cases the excess uric acid is deposited in the joints, skin or kidneys. When this happens the person may suffer either an acute (sudden) attack or a chronic (long-term) form.

Acute attacks

The first attack of gout is likely to be sudden and severe; it almost always involves the big toe. The condition used to be known as 'podagra' from the Greek words meaning a seizure of the foot.

The patient may be woken in the middle of the night by intense pain. The toe is extremely tender and will hardly bear the weight of the bedclothes. Its base is swollen and the skin is dry, hot, red and shiny. The veins on the top of the foot may be distended. Sometimes the patient is feverish.

Treatment

If an acute attack is not treated the patient will suffer considerable pain for three to 10 days and then the symptoms will subside.

However, treatment with anti-inflammatory drugs work successfully and quickly. The digestive systems of a

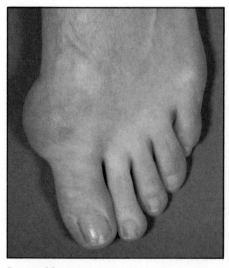

In a sudden, acute attack of gout the skin becomes red and shiny. The veins on the top of the foot may be distended.

few patients are sensitive to these drugs and they cause vomiting and diarrhoea. If this happens they may be given as suppositories or injections.

They should be taken as soon as possible as delay makes them less effective. Aspirin should be avoided as it tends to lessen the kidneys' filtering out of uric acid.

Once the pain has gone the patient may think that that is the end of the matter. But the condition may be latent within the patient, making them prone to further acute attacks at unpredictable intervals of weeks or months. Other joints may then be involved besides the big toe—usually extremities of limbs such as fingers or wrists. It is unusual for more central ones like hips or shoulders, or several joints at the same time to be affected.

The doctor will take blood tests and watch the patient's general condition to see whether further treatment is needed to try and prevent the gout developing into chronic gout. Patients who have had only a mild rise in their uric acid level, or have quite infrequent attacks, may not need further treatment.

Chronic gout
In chronic cases of gout, crystals of uric acid salts settle in joints, skin and kidneys causing permanent damage.

At the joints, crystals of salts are deposited in the cartilage of the bone

ends, roughening their smooth surfaces, causing swelling and stiffened movement similar to osteoarthritis.

The skin may develop bumps at various points. These are formed of collections of salts and are known as tophi. Often they appear as small knobs on the rims of the ears but they may also form quite large swellings on the hands or the back of the elbows. Generally, they are more disfiguring than harmful, but occasionally a tophus becomes so large and inconvenient that it needs to be removed surgically.

Severe gout can cause kidney damage in two ways. Either deposits of uric acid can block the delicate filtering mechanism of the kidneys, leading to progressive damage, or the highly concentrated uric acid may crystallize and form kidney stones. About one fifth of patients who are not treated for gout develop kidney stones.

Long-term treatment
Patients who suffer frequent acute attacks, joint changes, the appearance of tophi, kidney damage or consistently show a very high level of uric acid in blood tests, need long-term treatment.

Treatment may be with drugs to reduce the amount of uric acid in the body by encouraging the kidneys to excrete more of it. However, there is a danger that with so much extra uric acid passing into the urine it could crystallize and form kidney stones. This risk is reduced if the patient keeps the salts dissolved by drinking plenty of water and taking preparations which make the urine alkaline as the crystals are then very much more soluble. Alternatively, the patient may be treated

with a drug which prevents the formation of uric acid.

Patients who start on long-term treatment are likely to have to continue for the rest of their lives. Blood tests will be taken from time to time to show how they are getting on and whether the drugs or the dosage needs altering.

If the patient does not continue the treatment the uric acid level may rise again and there may be further attacks.

With long-term treatment the attacks are likely to stop completely. If there are any they will not be as severe or as frequent as they would be without treatment.

Those affected by gout
Men are more likely to be affected by gout than women and older people are affected more than young people.

For every 1,000 people in the 15-44 age group, 1.7 men will have gout in one form or another but only 0.1 women. In the age group 45-64, 11 men and one woman in every thousand people will be affected. In the age group 65 and over, 12 men and three women in every 1,000 will be affected.

Occasionally an abnormality in the body's chemistry produces gout in a young person but these cases are very rare.

About a quarter of gout sufferers have a family history of the disease, though gout seems to occur more among affluent people. The typical patient is described as an active man, a 'go-getter' of high intelligence, over the age of 50.

People who are grossly overweight are more at risk, but this only plays a small part in causing gout.

Collections of tophi, also known as chalk stones, may develop—usually on the hands or ears—in chronic cases of gout (above). The businessman (right), who also tends to live well, is particularly at risk from gout, especially if he is overweight.

Zefa

Haemorrhage

Q My husband has noticed blood in his urine but is reluctant to go to the doctor. What can I say to him to make him understand that he should have this checked?

A Anyone who notices blood in his urine should see his doctor as soon as possible, even if he feels perfectly well, simply because the blood may indicate the presence of serious disease of the kidneys, bladder or sex organs—particularly the prostate gland in men. If such problems are seen to as soon as they are noticed and receive prompt attention, they are nearly always curable. Tell your husband this right away.

Q Is a cerebral haemorrhage another way of saying someone has had a stroke?

A A stroke can have several causes, but one of the most common is bleeding or haemorrhage into the brain from a burst blood vessel. As a result, some of the brain cells are starved of blood and so cannot work properly, and this is what causes the characteristic loss of movement in various parts of the body. It also explains why a cerebral haemorrhage can be fatal—because death follows the total failure of the brain.

Q Why do some parts of the body, such as the scalp, seem to bleed profusely when they are damaged while other parts don't bleed nearly so much?

A The main reason is that the scalp, tongue and lips have a very rich supply of blood vessels which tend not to constrict as much as those in other parts of the body. Also, the skin of the scalp forms an attachment for muscles, unlike elsewhere in the body, and so tends to pull open when cut and takes longer to heal. Any haemorrhage from the area of the mouth may continue for a long time because the saliva in the mouth and the movements of the tongue tend to interfere with the natural clotting mechanism by dislodging the clots that form to dam broken blood vessels.

Haemorrhage—bleeding from any severed or damaged blood vessel—should always be treated seriously and immediately. A knowledge of first aid will help to minimize its effects.

Dealing with a nosebleed: sit up, bend the head forward very slightly, pinch the soft part of the nose for ten minutes.

Haemorrhage threatens life because it means that the body loses blood, the vital fluid that supplies the tissues with oxygen and food. Whether bleeding is external or internal, haemorrhage is always a cause for concern.

Medically, haemorrhage simply means bleeding from any severed or damaged blood vessel in the body. Caused by accidents and diseases, or as the result of surgery, haemorrhage is described as *external* if the blood from the vessels is lost to the outside of the body, and *internal* if the blood is retained unseen within it.

Types of haemorrhage
The blood lost in a haemorrhage may come from arteries, veins or capillaries, and each sort of bleeding has its own distinctive characteristics which are important to first aid and treatment.

If an artery has been severed, bright red blood, on its way from the heart to the body tissues and full of oxygen—which accounts for its colour—spurts and pumps out, often with great force. As the heart goes on pumping regardless of the damage, an enormous amount of blood can be lost in a very short time, so arterial haemorrhage is always a medical emergency demanding hospital treatment.

Veins are vessels carrying blood low in oxygen back to the heart from the body tissues. For this reason, the blood that issues from a vein haemorrhage is a dull, dark red, and wells out of a wound rather than gushing out. Although not as serious as arterial haemorrhage, bleeding from a cut in a large vein can endanger life because bubbles of air may be sucked into the vein and cause a fatal blockage in the circulation.

Blood lost from capillaries, the tiny vessels that link arteries and veins, is usually the normal dark red colour, but it is released very slowly so that it seems to ooze out of the body.

Treating haemorrhage from special areas

**Clotting of blood at the site of the wound is a protective reaction,
but it cannot take place while the blood is flowing.**

The tongue

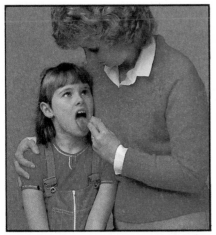

The tongue is often bitten in accidents and can bleed profusely. Unless the patient is unconscious, sit him up and grasp the tongue over the part that is bleeding, using a clean dressing or piece of material. If this is not possible—for example, if you are treating a struggling child, place ice on the tongue or give an ice cube to suck; this will contract the blood vessels.

If the patient is unconscious, lie him on one side.

The palm of the hand

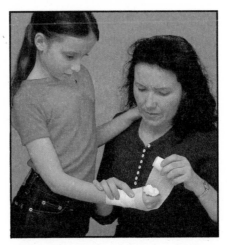

Roll a pad of some clean material into a sausage shape, and get the patient to grip it as tightly as possible for ten minutes. In treating a child, it may be better to bind the fist in this clenched position. Give additional help by lifting the patient's arm if he is unable to do this for himself. This will decrease blood flow to the hand.

For a serious wound, always follow up first aid by getting medical help. This should be done without delay.

The thigh

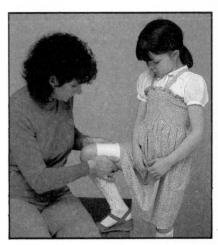

Raise the injured leg to reduce the flow of blood through it. Press firmly on the wound, after first covering it with a pad of gauze or other clean material. Keep up the pressure for at least five minutes. If blood oozes through the dressing, don't remove it, as this might disturb any clot that is forming: cover with a clean bandage. If the wound is serious, get medical help immediately: heavy blood loss can result in shock due to lowered blood pressure.

Causes

The most common cause of haemorrhage is accidental damage to the blood vessels, but many diseases also can lead to bleeding. Infections of the tissues, such as abscesses, can make the blood vessels rupture. Ulcers and tumours (both benign and malignant) can eat into vessel walls and make them burst. Scurvy, due to lack of vitamin C, can make the capillaries very fragile and liable to break. These sorts of diseases often damage capillaries over a wide area, and small arteries and veins may also be affected.

When arteries haemorrhage, the cause may be degeneration or infection, which makes them dilate and eventually burst as pressure builds up inside them. In atheroma, however, which is one of the most common causes of potentially fatal haemorrhage brought about by disease, the arteries are weakened by deposits of fatty material on their inner walls. If this form of artery trouble is linked with high blood pressure—which it often is—blood is forced through the arteries so hard that

External haemorrhage

General rules

- Place a clean pad of gauze or material over the site of the bleeding.
- Raise the part of the body that is bleeding.
- Press firmly on the site of the bleeding for at least five minutes.
- If an artery has been severed, press on the artery at the side nearest to the heart for 15 minutes at a time.
- Don't remove a blood-soaked pad. Bandage it in place and put a clean dressing over the top of it.
- SEEK MEDICAL HELP.

their walls rupture and haemorrhage results.

The body's protective reactions

Except when haemorrhage is severe, the body is normally able to put a whole series of protective reactions into effect,

first to dam the bleeding and then to repair damaged vessels. The damming reaction involves the clotting of blood round the site of the injury, but in some diseases, including haemophilia, certain types of jaundice and vitamin K deficiency, the clotting mechanism is impaired, making haemorrhage much more serious than in someone in sound health.

Effects

The effects of haemorrhage vary greatly, according to the amount of blood lost, where the haemorrhage occurs, how fast blood is lost, the health of the person involved and, in the case of an accident, any other injuries received.

As a general rule, very rapid blood loss is more serious than slow bleeding because it puts more stress on the heart, causes collapse of the general circulation and gives the body no chance to control the problem on its own. In a healthy adult or child, the amount of blood which can be lost without the need for emergency treatment (and blood transfusion to make up the loss) depends on the amount of blood in the system but not on the site of the haemorrhage: the effects are the same whether the patient is found lying in a pool of blood or has lost the same amount of blood into the alimentary canal from a burst ulcer. The safe figure for blood loss is usually taken as 15 per cent of the total blood in the system, but this total varies according to body weight. On average, everyone has one pint of blood for every 6.3 kg (14 lb) of body weight. This means that a child or a small woman is endangered by losing much less blood than a man of large build. For most adults, the rough figure for the upper limit of safety is usually rounded up to 1 litre (2 pints).

Slow haemorrhage over a period of several days, although it may not pose such an immediate threat to life as the sudden loss of a lot of blood, is still dangerous and can also be deceptive. In slow bleeding, fluid percolates back into the blood vessels from the tissues to make the blood up to the correct volume and keep the circulation going. However, the body's capacity for making new red blood cells to carry oxygen works much more slowly so that the result is potentially fatal anaemia. In anyone who is already anaemic, slight haemorrhage can quickly reduce the oxygen-transporting capacity of the blood to a dangerously low level.

Severe haemorrhage
The unfailing symptom of severe haemorrhage is shock—a term used to describe the failure of the blood circulation. When a lot of blood is lost, the immediate result is a fall in blood pressure. The blood vessels then constrict (narrow) and so increase the resistance to flow, to keep the blood pressure up. Despite this, and despite extra work by the heart, the flow of blood to tissues may fall. Life is then threatened because vital tissues—particularly the brain—cannot get enough oxygen to survive, although the body does its best to divert blood to where it is needed most: the brain, lungs and the heart itself.

Shock, which may be accompanied by raging thirst because the body has become deficient in fluid, is typified by an extremely pale skin, which feels cold and clammy to the touch, a weak, fast pulse, and panting or gasping for breath, often described as air hunger, as the person in shock tries to boost the oxygen in the blood by taking more air into the lungs.

Anyone who has lost more than the critical amount of blood is likely to go into shock, and needs an immediate transfusion.

Arteries can be weakened by deposits of fatty material on their inner walls, to such an extent that they rupture.

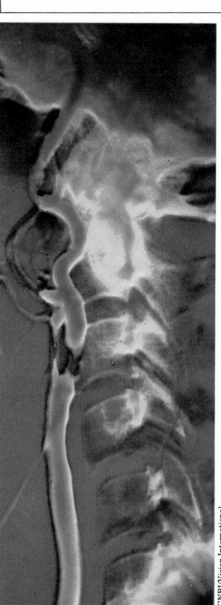

CNRI/Vision International

fusion to restore the blood volume to normal and save his or her life. This explains why someone suffering from haemorrhage must be taken at once to hospital, preferably by ambulance. Once there, a transfusion of blood is given as soon as the patient's blood group has been determined, so that there is no risk of adverse reaction to blood of an incompatible group.

In the case of haemorrhage which is not bad enough to result in shock, the body's natural systems are able to work unaided. The blood vessels are sealed off with clots, then gradually repair themselves over a period of weeks; at the same time, the blood gradually recovers its full oxygen-carrying potential through the addition of new blood cells which are formed in the bone marrow, a reaction which is automatically stimulated by the loss of any blood.

Haemorrhage after surgery
Anyone who has to go into hospital for surgery worries about the amount of blood that may be lost in the operation. However, he or she can be sure that surgeons and nurses are all intensely aware of the dangers of haemorrhage and will do their utmost to avert excess loss of blood, giving transfusions if necessary to make up the loss.

Hospital staff will also be on the watch for, and ready to treat, so-called secondary haemorrhage, the term used to describe bleeding that results from internal infection. Many of the usual symptoms of haemorrhage, such as blood in the faeces or urine, are secondary haemorrhages because they are caused by disease and not physical damage to the blood vessels: the latter causes what doctors call primary haemorrhage.

Hay fever

Q **I am a hay fever sufferer and so is my husband. Will our children inherit the trouble?**

A Allergies like hay fever tend to run in families. As both you and your husband are sufferers there is a chance that your children will also be affected.

Q **My daughter is severely affected by hay fever. She is coming up to her exams this summer. What can I do to prevent her having an attack while she is sitting them?**

A In instances like this when it is extremely important to avoid trouble for a short time and ordinary treatments are not sufficient to control the symptoms, some doctors think it is worthwhile giving a small dose of steroid by injection. Ask your doctor and see what he advises.

Q **My doctor gives me tablets for my hay fever, but they make me feel very sleepy. Is there something else I could take instead?**

A There are now very effective preparations which can be put directly into the nose. These usually have no side-effects.

Q **Why is the pollen count so important to hay fever sufferers?**

A If you are a pollen-sensitive patient then your symptoms will be worse if the pollen count is high. This is most likely to occur after a hot dry spell, especially if there is little wind. The pollen count is usually low shortly after a heavy shower of rain.

Q **My daughter is 12 and has suffered from hay fever for several years. Is she likely to grow out of it or will she always suffer from it?**

A This is difficult to say. It is very common for young people with allergies of all sorts to get better as they pass through their teens and early adult life. However, occasionally the symptoms may return later. The reason for this is not known.

Hay fever results from an allergy to inhaled dusts, the most common of which is grass pollen. About ten per cent of the population in the Western world is affected. But although there is no complete cure for this unpleasant affliction, the symptoms can be relieved.

The parts of the body that are affected by hay fever are those which are most commonly exposed to allergy-causing dusts—the eyes, the nose, the sinuses and the upper part of the throat.

There is a watery discharge from the nose and eyes, as well as irritation and sneezing.

Causes

While the most common cause is an allergy to grass or tree pollens, identical symptoms may result from inhaling other dusts such as fungal spores, animal hair and scurf, and house mites.

The symptoms are usually seasonal and the precise timing of their appearance depends upon the sort of dust to which the patient is allergic.

The first pollens to appear each year are tree pollens and, depending upon the severity of the winter, these can cause hay fever in the UK as early as mid-March. Pollen from plane trees and silver birch are powerful allergens (substances that cause allergic reactions) and frequently cause hay fever.

Later in the season, typically in mid-summer, grass pollens appear and have a short season, and are then followed by nettle pollen.

From mid-summer until late autumn, fungal spores are abundant in the air and are the most likely to cause trouble in autumn.

Other agents present in the air throughout the year may also cause trouble from time to time and may seem to result in seasonal symptoms.

How it develops

Hay fever develops because of an error in the body's inbuilt defence mechanism, the immune system. Normally the immune system can tell the difference between a harmless organism, such as pollen, and a dangerous, infectious organism but, in an allergic person, the immune system treats pollens and other allergens as if they were dangerous and the white blood cells, whose function it is to fight infection, start forming an antibody to neutralize the intruder.

Eye drops given three times a day help by preventing the release of histamine which causes watery eyes and running nose.

Pollens which cause hay fever throughout the year

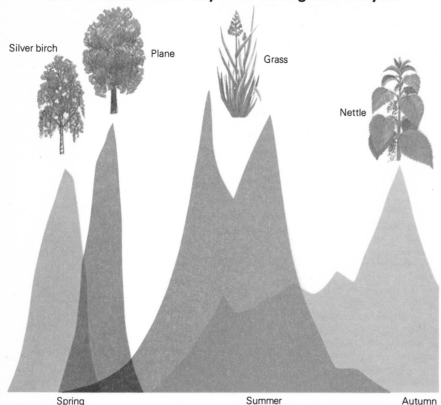

Silver birch

Plane

Grass

Nettle

John Hutchinson

Spring   Summer   Autumn

Sneezing is common first thing in the morning; the patient may sneeze repeatedly between rising and eating breakfast. If asthma is associated with hay fever, the patient usually suffers his worst symptoms at night.

Treatment
By far the best treatment is to avoid the cause of the allergy. So, if the cause is the family cat or the rabbit at the bottom of the garden this is a fairly simple matter.

However, there is no way of avoiding exposure to dusts like tree and grass and pollens, although if you take your holidays by the sea you are less likely to be affected—as there are no trees or grass on the beach, so if these are causing the hay fever there are three possible methods of treatment.

Local treatment
Local treatment is by medicines placed in the nose by means of a spray or puffer, or in the eyes by means of drops. A solution of sodium cromoglycate is made up to treat both the eyes and the nose. This prevents the mast cells from releasing histamine. It usually has to be administered three times a day throughout the hay fever season.

An alternative preparation, for use in the nose only, is a puffer containing a steroid which is given in very low doses three times a day.

Both these medicines stop the symptoms from developing but are of little relief once they have developed.

General treatment
Antihistamines may be of some help in hay fever, but many cause sleepiness which some people find intolerable.

Steroid injections bring dramatic relief, but because they have side-effects they are not used unless the symptoms are really incapacitating.

Desensitizing injections
The only really effective desensitization course of treatment is the one against grass pollen.

The vaccine which may be 'tailor-made' to fit the particular patient's allergy, is given as a course of injections, in the early part of each year.

If the vaccine gives good protection, then the course can be repeated year after year. However, it is not effective in all people and some get allergic reactions to the vaccine itself, which contains a minute dose of pollen. For this reason, the doctor is extremely careful how he gives the injection and may ask the patient to wait 15 or 20 minutes after receiving an injection to make sure that no allergic reaction is going to occur.

The antibody attaches itself to cells, called mast cells, which contain a number of chemicals, the most important of which is histamine. It then tries to neutralize the allergen and, in doing so, upsets the structure of the mast cell which falls apart and releases the histamine and other chemicals.

People who make a great deal of antibody to these common dusts tend to develop childhood eczema and asthma, and they are known as atopic individuals. The condition tends to run in families.

Symptoms
The release of the histamine and other chemicals from the mast cells causes the blood vessels to increase in diameter and the mucous cells in both the nose and the sinuses begin to generate more mucus (see page 29).

As a result of this, the eyes itch and stream, the nose and sinuses become blocked and cause feelings of stuffiness and heaviness in the head. The throat becomes sore and the patient feels generally unwell.

Some tree pollens—such as silver birch pollen—are powerful allergens and can cause hay fever early in the spring in certain people.

Harry Smith

166

Heart attack

Q Is there anything I can do to prevent a heart attack?

A There is one thing which will definitely reduce the risk, if you are a smoker, and that is to stop smoking. Smoking causes the arteries in the extremities (hands and feet) to contract and eventually become permanently rigid, making arterial blockage, which causes heart attacks, more likely. There is also strong evidence that you can lessen the risk of your coronary arteries becoming narrowed by cholesterol deposits if you eat less dairy produce, eggs and meat, all of which contain cholesterol. Exercise in the form of running, cycling and swimming may also be of value, but the evidence is not so conclusive that you should feel guilty if you don't go jogging every day.

Q I have recently had a heart attack. Will I be able to go back to the active and enjoyable sex life that I used to have before the attack?

A Yes, you will. However, you should not engage in very strenuous activity, such as sex, immediately. Your doctor or the hospital will have given you some advice about exertion when you left the hospital. It is usual to suggest to people that they should build up to their previous level of activity over about a month to six weeks.

Q My husband, who has always been very active, has just had a heart attack. Does this mean that he will have to slow down now?

A No, not necessarily, unless he has been told to avoid exertion by the hospital. He should aim to get back to normal but avoid sudden bursts of activity; he should build up to any exertion more gradually than he did before—like a sportsman increasing the amount of time taken to 'warm up' before exertion.

A time when he should be particularly careful is in very cold weather. Again, he should aim for normal activity, but with more emphasis on keeping warm and gradually 'warming up' for physical activity at his normal level.

A heart attack is the most common serious illness of the developed world today. Many patients make an excellent recovery, but leading a healthy life can prevent heart attacks from occurring in the first place.

The heart depends on its own blood supply to provide it with the oxygen that is essential for it to function properly. If the oxygen supply to an area of heart muscle is interrupted then that area of muscle cannot function. It will not contract with each heartbeat and so cannot contribute its share of work to the pumping of blood around the body.

Cause
Over a period of months or years, atheroma (fatty deposits) can attach themselves to the wall of a coronary artery (the two arteries which supply the heart with blood).

In time, this impedes the blood flow passing through that artery. A total blockage occurs when a blood clot forms in the middle of the artery at the point of maximum narrowing. It is not known exactly why this clot (thrombosis) should occur, but the fact that the wall of the artery is heavily coated with atheroma is obviously a contributing factor.

A heart attack is a continuous process. Interruption of the blood supply is the first stage. As the blood supply to the heart muscle (myocardial cells) is stopped the patient feels pain. The affected cells die and, if the blood supply remains obstructed, that area of muscle will die and be replaced over a period of weeks with fibrous tissue scar, which could weaken the heart if a very large area of muscle has been affected.

The people most at risk from a heart attack are smokers, people who eat a lot of fat, people under stress, diabetics and those with a family history of heart attacks. They are most likely to occur in middle-aged men. They are unusual in women before the menopause and in men under 35.

Warning signs
In some people the first coronary will be totally unexpected, but in many there is a warning sign—the development of angina.

Angina is a central chest pain which happens during exertion or excitement and lasts a few minutes. Often the pain spreads to the arms, shoulders and neck.

Anyone who develops angina, or has angina which is increasing in frequency or in the length of each attack, should see their doctor to have a check-up.

The patient convalescing after a heart attack can be nursed successfully at home. It is important that he rest completely and have meals that are low in cholesterol.

How arteries become blocked

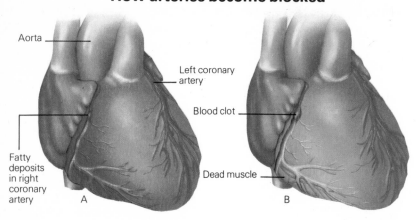

Aorta

Left coronary artery

Blood clot

Fatty deposits in right coronary artery

Dead muscle

A

B

Frank Kennard

Symptoms of an attack

The main symptom of a heart attack is a dull or heavy pain, usually in the centre of the chest. There may be sweating, nausea or vomiting, and breathlessness as well. The patient may look ill and grey. The severity of the symptoms varies from a severe pain to very trivial discomfort. It is even possible to suffer a heart attack without noticing any symptoms at all.

If you do suffer from an attack of pain which you think might be a heart attack you should see your doctor, but do not get too alarmed; there are other conditions with similar symptoms, such as indigestion, a chest infection, gall bladder problems or the washing back of the acid contents of the stomach into the gullet.

Diagnosis and treatment

The first priority for any doctor treating a patient with a heart attack is to relieve the pain. This is usually done with an injection of morphine or a similar drug.

Then it is important to confirm the diagnosis and this may be done with an electrocardiogram (ECG) which traces out the pattern of the heartbeats. Usually it will show characteristic abnormalities on the trace which confirm that the pain is due to a heart attack.

Having confirmed the diagnosis the next stage is to try and prevent any complications or to deal with them if they occur.

Coronary care units

Coronary care units in hospitals provide special care to both prevent and treat the disorders of heart rhythm which occur after heart attacks.

Modern treatment of rhythm disturbances, is with drugs and electric shock treatment where necessary.

However, this does not necessarily mean that patients will definitely need to go to hospital in order to be put in a coronary care unit.

A: fatty deposits have caused a partial blockage which restricts the blood flow. B: a blood clot (thrombosis) has now caused a total blockage in the already narrowed artery. Because the artery cannot supply some of the heart muscle with blood that area of muscle dies.

Home or hospital?

The major problems with heart attacks occur in the first two hours. Many patients are not able to reach hospital during this time and after the first hour or two it may well be decided that they are better off staying at home.

There is no evidence to support the view that people with heart attacks must go into hospital. In the elderly particularly, there is some evidence that care at home may even be better than hospital care. The decision about whether to send someone into hospital has, of course, to be made by the patient's doctor.

Rehabilitation

Patients who are admitted to a coronary unit will probably spend a day or two there receiving treatment and then be transferred to a general ward. They are not usually kept in bed for longer than a few days and if there are no complications they will be discharged in 10-14 days.

Patients should aim to build up to their normal level of activity gradually.

In a few cases, there may be severe damage to the heart muscle and these patients usually take a little longer to recover full physical activity.

Gentle exercise helps the patient build up to his normal level of activity.

Heart disease

Q My grandmother has a pacemaker which has so transformed her life that she no longer has dizzy spells. But what is going to happen when the batteries in the machine run out?

A The answer to that is simple. The pacing box is replaced during a small operation rather similar to the one your grandmother had when her pacemaker was put in.

Until a few years ago, pacing boxes had to be replaced every three to four years. Nowadays the batteries last much longer—they may even last as long as 10 years. Your grandmother will be attending a pacemaker clinic every so often and here they check the working of the machine and predict when the system will need replacing.

Q Can holes in the heart ever close up on their own?

A Yes, small holes in between the two ventricles (the lower pumping chambers) often close up on their own. However, holes in between the two atria (the upper pumping chambers) are less likely to.

Q My doctor says my three-year old son has a murmur. Will he need an operation?

A No. Murmurs in children are exceedingly common and one study found a murmur in up to 80 per cent of normal children. These murmurs are called innocent murmurs and no action is necessary. If your doctor had thought that the murmur was of some significance he would have asked a specialist to see your son, so don't worry.

Q I have got a problem with one of my heart valves and I am worried that I will need to have it replaced. Is it true that there is only a 50 per cent chance of surviving open heart surgery?

A If heart surgery was as dangerous as that it would have been given up years ago! It depends on which valve is concerned and how many other problems there are. But, in general, it would be fair to say that for uncomplicated replacements of a single valve the chances of surviving are virtually 100 per cent.

Heart disease is very common, but fortunately advances in the techniques of investigation, treatment and heart surgery have done a great deal to help sufferers.

Because the heart is vital to life and has to work continuously, it is very prone to disease. The majority of people with heart problems suffer from hardening of the arteries (see Arteries and artery disease, pp 34-37) but there are also other types of heart disease.

The heart depends on four valves to keep blood flowing in the right direction. Diseases of these valves used to be very common—often as a result of rheumatic fever in childhood. But valve disease has become much less common because of a general increase in the standards of nutrition and hygiene.

Most valve problems arise from abnormalities in structure which have been present since birth (congenital problems). The inlet and outlet valves (mitral and aortic valves) of the left ventricle, the main pumping chamber of the heart, cause the most trouble.

There are two things that may go wrong with a valve. It may become blocked and impede the forward flow of the blood—a condition called stenosis—or it may leak and allow backward flow—which is called regurgitation or incompetence. Stenosis and incompetence often occur together.

Usually people with minor abnormalities of the heart valves have no problems. However, there is a small risk of them suffering from infective endocarditis.

This happens when an infecting organism becomes lodged on the valves and starts to grow there. Because the heart valves are actually made of fibrous tissue with no blood supply of their own, the organism finds it easy to become established in them and because they have no blood supply to provide infection-fighting white blood cells, the body's defence system is less effective.

Comedian Eric Morcambe (left) underwent open heart surgery and led a normal, active life for several years after.

Rex Features

Treatment of heart diseases

Disease/problem	Causes	Symptoms	Treatment
Coronary artery disease	Results from hardening or blocking of the coronary arteries with atheroma (fatty deposits)	Angina pain. May cause a heart attack and heart failure	Treatment is with drugs or by surgery to improve the heart's blood supply and end the pain. Diuretics remove excess fluid from lungs and tissues
Heart failure	May result from almost any form of heart disease	Breathlessness on exertion due to fluid in the lungs. Swelling of the ankles	May be treated with diuretics or possibly surgery, in the case of valve disease for example
Valve disease	Sometimes caused by rheumatic fever. May be congenital (present from birth)	The symptoms of heart failure. Aortic valve problems often cause angina because heart wall thickens. Fainting can also occur with aortic stenosis (blocked outlet valve) where there is insufficient blood in the circulation. Mitral (inlet) valve problems usually cause palpitations	Treatment is surgical in cases where the symptoms are sufficiently bad. Otherwise drugs are used to control the symptoms. An operation is often necessary for marked aortic stenosis
Cardiomyopathy a) congestive	In most cases the cause is unknown; however, alcohol, metal poisoning and some hormonal conditions can cause it	Heart failure, problems with heart block (slow heartbeat) and possibly palpitations. Valves may become leaky	Symptoms are treated with drugs and sometimes a pacemaker is necessary
b) hypertrophic	Cause unknown, may run in families	Angina and occasionally fainting attacks due to obstruction of left ventricle's outflow	Drugs may relieve the obstruction. Occasionally an operation may be necessary
Endocarditis	Always happens as a result of pre-existing heart problem—usually an abnormal valve. Wall of the heart becomes infected	Temperature, heart failure and general ill health	Antibiotics. Badly damaged valves may need surgery
Palpitations	a) in normal hearts may be caused by anxiety and by overactivity of the thyroid gland b) there may be abnormalities in structure c) may occur after heart attacks	Sensation of rapid heartbeat with dizziness or fainting if insufficient blood reaches the brain	Drugs are used to suppress the abnormal heart rhythm
Heart block (very slow heartbeat)	a) a degenerative disease of the heart b) may be complication of heart attack	Dizziness and fainting	Pacemaker

Congenital heart disease

The reason the heart is so prone to abnormalities is that its development in the womb is very complicated. During the early weeks of pregnancy it evolves in the foetus from a single straight tube into a four-chambered pump with two separate circulation systems. This is a complex process which can occasionally go wrong.

Sometimes a baby is born with holes in the partition between the two atria or the two ventricles. These are called atrial and ventricular septal defects.

If the blood flow to the lungs is insufficient, the blood never becomes enriched with oxygen, and the result is a 'blue baby' (a condition known as cyanosis).

Modern heart surgery has advanced so much in recent years that it is now standard practice to operate on tiny babies.

Inadequate pumping

Sometimes there are problems if the force of the pumping is inadequate because the power of the muscular walls of the left ventricle starts to fail. The usual reason for this is coronary artery disease where there is insufficient blood supply to the heart itself.

Cardiomyopathy

Congestive cardiomyopathy is a heart muscle disease which makes the muscle become weak and flabby so that the heart

gets bigger and bigger as the muscle wall dilates under the strain. In most cases the cause is not known.

Occasionally the muscle thickens and obstructs the flow of blood out of the left ventricle. This condition is known as hypertrophic cardiomyopathy and is one of the very few heart diseases that runs in families.

Heart rhythm disorders

The electrical conducting system of the heart is responsible for making sure that each part contracts in its proper sequence. There are two disorders that can happen—either the heart beats too quickly or too slowly.

Either of these may cause dizziness and even loss of consciousness because of an inadequate supply of blood to the brain. With a slow heartbeat—known as a heart block—the heart beats so slowly that not much blood flows forwards. On the other hand, when the heart is going very fast it does not have time to fill properly between each beat with the result that again very little blood moves forward.

When the dizziness and fainting are due to fast rather than slow beating there are often palpitations—an uncomfortable sensation of the heart beating. Heart rhythm disorders can happen as a result of other heart diseases or they may occur on their own.

To diagnose the cause of symptoms, an ECG (electrocardiogram) will be done.

A great advance in this field is the 24-hour ECG recording using a small tape recorder which the patient wears for a whole day. The results are then analyzed on a machine which speeds up the recording by about 60 times.

Slow heart rates are treated with pacemakers (see page 107) and fast ones with drugs.

In a coronary angiogram (right) dye is injected into the bloodstream so that any narrowing of the arteries can be seen on a X-ray. The doctor (below) is listening to heart sounds to detect any murmurs.

Symptoms of heart disease

Despite the fact that there are so many causes, the symptoms of heart disease are remarkable few.

There is pain (angina) when the heart is starved of oxygen. However, other conditions, such as indigestion, can give angina-like pain.

The other main symptom of heart disease is heart (cardiac) failure. When the left ventricle is failing to pump blood adequately, fluid accumulates in the lungs causing breathlessness, particularly on exertion.

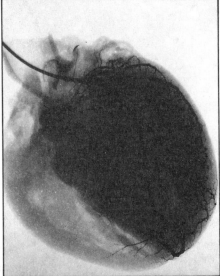

However, chronic (long-term) heart failure usually involves both ventricles in the end, so that in addition to fluid in the lungs, there is excess fluid in the tissues. This causes swelling (oedema) of the ankles. Treatment is by means of diuretics which will cause much excess fluid to be excreted through the kidneys with the result that the swelling is greatly reduced.

Diagnosis

The presence of heart failure is easy to discover. Fluid on the lungs can be heard through a stethoscope as 'crackling' with each breath and fluid around the ankles is quite obvious by the uncomfortable swelling it causes.

The key to diagnosis is examination of the heart itself. The doctor will feel the patient's pulse for irregularities and to measure its rate, and the chest wall where the heart can be felt. The heart becomes enlarged with heart failure and its beat becomes unduly forceful if the wall of the ventricle is thicker than normal and this can be felt through the chest wall.

The doctor also listens to the sounds of the valve closing during different phases of the heartbeat and listens for murmurs. Murmurs are sounds caused by the turbulent flow of blood through the heart. When a valve is obstructed or leaking it will cause a murmur.

Further examination

Having examined the heart, a doctor may decide that there should be further investigation. This may be with an ECG and a chest X-ray, or it may be with an echocardiogram. This test is very simple for the patient and completely painless. It uses sound waves, or ultrasound, to build up a complete picture of the heart valves and detect any problems.

Hospital tests

Further examination may also be done with a cardiac catheterization. This is an X-ray procedure where tubes (catheters) are passed into the heart through the arteries or veins. Patients will have to go into hospital for a few days to have this test done.

The tubes measure the pressure in the various chambers of the heart. Special X-ray dye may be injected into the tube to outline one of the heart's chambers and show up abnormalities. Catheterization is usually done on patients who are being examined before a heart operation because, while basic diagnosis is easy, more technical matters have to be investigated before heart surgery can be undertaken. This is only done after very careful consideration.

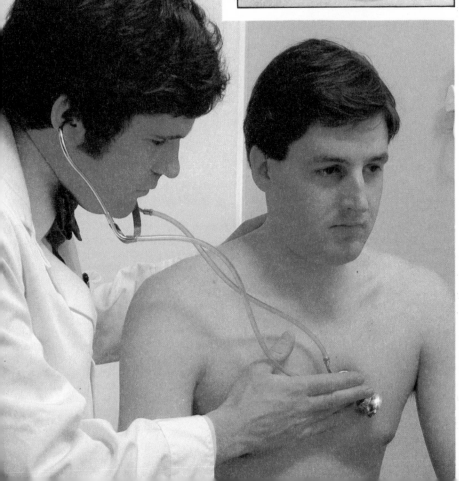

Hepatitis

Q My son has just gone to sea, and now he writes that he wants to be tattooed when he reaches the next port. Is there any risk involved?

A You are probably referring to the risk of contracting hepatitis, but this is purely a question of hygiene. Although there are many competent practising tattooists about, it is still possible to be infected with a hepatitis virus through the use of unsterile needles, which could introduce the infection into the recipient's body. Unfortunately, there is no central regulatory body for tattooists, nor is there a code of professional practice which would act to protect the public as well as reputable tattooists. Although there are moves afoot to get a professional body organized, at the moment people must simply use their common sense and not patronize unhygienic-looking tattooists' premises.

Q I would like to go on to the Pill, but have had hepatitis. People tell me that this means that it will not be allowed. Is there a special reason for this?

A Medical opinions vary on this point, but most doctors would agree that if you have had chronic (infectious) hepatitis you should never use this means of contraception. The reason is that the Pill contains powerful chemicals, which could cause further damage to your liver if they did not pass through it very quickly—the result could be complete liver failure. You should use other methods of contraception, rather than run the risk of this serious state of affairs.

Q I am five months pregnant and have just been told that I have caught hepatitis. Does this mean that my baby will catch it from me?

A Unfortunately your baby may also develop hepatitis and may have the virus in its blood when it is born. However, both of you can be treated with an injection of gamma-globulin, which is given shortly after the child is born to deal with the infection.

Hepatitis—inflammation of the liver—is an unpleasant illness, but many people recover completely. However, it is advisable to give up alcohol for at least six months as a preventive measure after an attack.

Tattooing must be done with sterile needles to avoid risk of infection.

Hepatitis is a highly infectious virus disease, involving inflammation of the liver. The virus is transmitted in blood, in faeces or saliva. It is a disease affecting people of all ages, but tends to occur more in the young or amongst those whose work entails handling contaminated material.

Causes
There are two viruses that are chiefly responsible, known as hepatitis A (formerly called infectious hepatitis) and hepatitis B (formerly called serum hepatitis).

Hepatitis A is usually transmitted by food or water that has been contaminated, although this virus can also be transmitted in infected blood. The disease is only infectious in the incubation stage, and it is not transmitted by carriers. Outbreaks happen from time to time in areas with overcrowded housing and poor sanitation. This is the type of illness that can be caught on a trip abroad, for example, after eating contaminated food. Epidemics can also break out in schools and other institutions if hygiene is poor.

Hepatitis B takes longer to incubate, probably many months. Although it may be transmitted in the same way as hepatitis A, the B virus is more often transmitted in infected blood, either from hypodermic needles or as a result of a transfusion of infected blood or plasma, though stringent precautions against these forms of transmission are taken in hospitals. It has also been known to result from the use of unsterile tattoo needles or razor blades. About 40 per cent of heroin addicts are carriers of the B virus.

This virus also has the ability to infect an unborn child, by crossing through the placenta and so getting into the foetal bloodstream. Another theory suggests that hepatitis B may be transmitted venereally, because so many male homosexuals have been found to be carriers.

A group of people especially at risk are hospital personnel, particularly those whose work involves handling blood regularly in operating theatres or renal dialysis units (where sick patients are treated on kidney machines). This virus can also be a problem for dentists, and some patients who are known to be carriers, may be refused treatment.

Symptoms

It is known that the majority of infections with either the A or B virus are mild and may even pass unnoticed, although both viruses leave chemical evidence in blood after an infection and signs of this can be found in blood tests.

When the disease is severe enough to cause sufficient inflammation of the liver to block the drainage of bile, the sufferer becomes jaundiced. When this happens, the skin and the whites of the eyes develop a yellowish tinge. This is caused by bile pigments made by the liver entering the circulation instead of being eliminated through the intestine.

Jaundice may occur fairly rapidly after an infection by hepatitis A, but is usually slower if the illness is due to hepatitis B.

Very often the victim feels unwell for some time beforehand, going off food and losing any desire to smoke. Pain is felt high in the abdomen, on the right side. There may also be arthritic-type pains in the joints as well as a rash. While the

jaundice is most marked, the patient feels sick and frequently vomits. The jaundice does not usually last for more than a fortnight and recovery takes place within six weeks or so.

Unfortunately, in a few cases, the infection does not clear up and chronic inflammation of the liver develops, ultimately resulting in cirrhosis. (The liver cells are progressively destroyed and replaced with fibrous tissue, which gradually makes the liver less effective).

Doctors have little difficulty in diagnosing hepatitis when typical symptoms are present, which can be confirmed by blood tests.

One diagnostic test that is used is to measure the coagulation (clotting) time of the blood, because one of the vitamins essential for blood clotting, vitamin K, is made by the liver. So people with severe liver disease tend to have blood that does not clot as it should. If the diagnosis is in doubt, a liver biopsy is performed, in which a tiny sample is taken from the liver for examination. This is neither risky nor painful and is performed under local anaesthetic.

Establishing whether the disease is caused by hepatitis A or hepatitis B is more of a problem and doctors are now finding an increasingly common group of patients who are infected with an unknown agent, transmitted in the blood, which is neither virus A nor B.

Dangers

Until the recent increase in liver disease produced by alcoholism, viral hepatitis was without question the most common cause of cirrhosis of the liver. Because the virus is still present in their blood, such patients then become sources of infection to others and cause problems if they have to be admitted to hospital for any reason at all. But not all hepatitis sufferers are carriers; for reasons that are still unknown, some patients recover from the disease completely.

Treatment

It is not necessary to admit all hepatitis sufferers to hospital—only those who become extremely unwell or who are at risk, for example expectant mothers, diabetics or the elderly.

While the liver is inflamed and also while it is recovering, its cells will be sensitive to all kinds of drugs and it is advisable not to take any medicines at this time. It is particularly important to avoid alcohol, which has a poisonous effect on the liver.

Whether the patient is being treated in hospital or at home, it is essential to try and reduce the chances of cross-infection by using separate cooking and eating

How hepatitis affects the liver

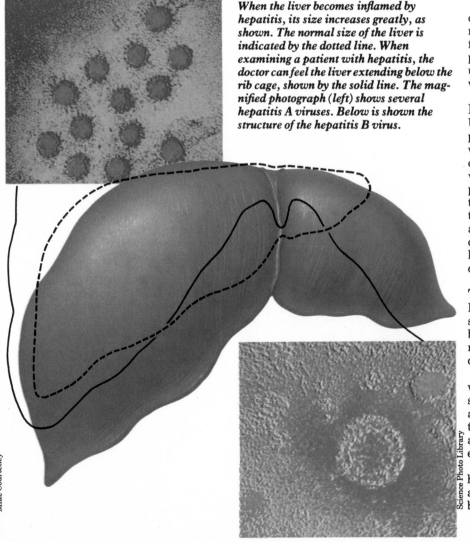

When the liver becomes inflamed by hepatitis, its size increases greatly, as shown. The normal size of the liver is indicated by the dotted line. When examining a patient with hepatitis, the doctor can feel the liver extending below the rib cage, shown by the solid line. The magnified photograph (left) shows several hepatitis A viruses. Below is shown the structure of the hepatitis B virus.

Mike Courtney

Science Photo Library

Q My boyfriend is a heavy drinker. Will he get hepatitis?

A People who drink heavily are known to suffer more from chronic hepatitis or from cirrhosis of the liver which could result in death from liver damage. The message is clear, persuade him to cut down.

Q My baby son had jaundice soon after he was born. Does this increase the danger that he might develop hepatitis?

A No, this is not significant. Young babies sometimes develop jaundice through the destruction of numbers of red blood cells that are no longer needed in their blood. The condition is rarely due to inflammation of the liver, as in hepatitis, but hospitals always watch out for symptoms of jaundice in newborn infants so that prompt treatment can be given if necessary.

Q My mother is ill with an attack of infectious hepatitis for which she is being treated at home. Must we keep away from her, or take special precautions?

A During the infectious stage, you should cook her food in separate utensils and use different crockery; you should also take extra care with personal hygiene. But your mother will stop being infectious soon after the jaundice begins to disappear.

Q I have read that you are not allowed to be a blood donor if you have had hepatitis. Is this true?

A Yes, this is true. The reason is that the organisms that cause this disease can go on living in your blood long after you have recovered. If this blood was given to someone else, they could contract the disease.

Q My teenage daughter has been suffering from glandular fever and has now developed jaundice. Isn't this rather odd?

A Not at all. It is not uncommon for people with glandular fever to develop jaundice due to hepatitis. This also happens in a number of other viral diseases because numerous viruses are potential causes of liver inflammation.

utensils for the patient and being careful about personal hygiene.

There has been a good deal of medical argument as to the importance of complete bed rest. But it is felt by some doctors that the later complications (cirrhosis or chronic hepatitis) could be avoided, provided the patient rested as much as possible while jaundiced.

There are no particular dietary restrictions, but care should be taken that the patient eats properly, despite feeling unwell. Food should be made as tempting as possible to encourage the appetite.

People who are exposed to infection by hepatitis, or who intend 'living rough' on walking or camping holidays in areas such as southern Europe, India or Africa can be protected by an injection of gamma-globulin. This is especially effective against hepatitis A, but not so good at preventing infection by hepatitis B.

Abstinence from alcohol is essential if you have had hepatitis. Orange juice can provide a healthy alternative.

Infants born to mothers with hepatitis can also be protected in the same way if they are injected within a week of birth.

Outlook

The majority of hepatitis attacks are mild, can be nursed at home and are followed by complete recovery.

Hepatitis can recur, but it is rarely caused by the same type of virus. It is, however, possible for patients who are carriers to suffer a relapse.

If you have recovered from an attack of hepatitis, the best advice is never to drink alcohol again; but if this is to hard to bear, and it is socially important to you, abstinence from all alcoholic drinks for at least six months is essential.

Hernia

Hernias are a common problem. Sometimes they cause no discomfort at all, and when they do need treatment, they can be cured with complete success.

A hernia is a protrusion through a weakness in the abdominal wall. It can either be external—i.e. it shows as a lump on the surface of the abdomen or in the groin—or it can be internal: for instance, a hiatus hernia, caused by a weakness in the diaphragm.

Types of hernia

The commonest types of hernia occur in the groin, and are called inguinal or femoral hernias, depending on the exact site of the weakness. They can also occur near the navel (umbilical hernia), in the upper part of the abdomen in the midline (epigastric), and through weakness in the posterior wall of the abdomen, when they are usually not visible as a lump. Hernias can also develop at the site of an operation, where the muscles have failed to heal strongly, and they are then called incisional hernias.

Common sites of hernias

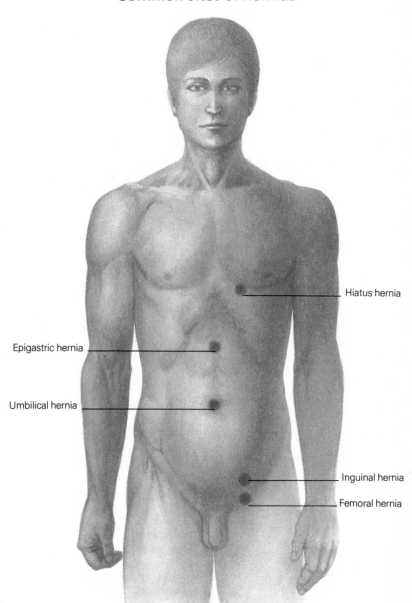

Hiatus hernia

Epigastric hernia

Umbilical hernia

Inguinal hernia

Femoral hernia

Marion Appleton

A hernia usually consists of a sac made of peritoneum, the thin membrane lining the abdominal cavity, which protrudes through the weakness in the muscular wall of the abdomen. If it is an external hernia, the sac will be covered with a layer of fat, over which will be the skin. The sac contains either part of an intra-abdominal organ, such as a loop of small intestine, or of the omentum, the fatty membrane which covers the intestines. In fact, the omentum often fills the sac completely, preventing any other structures from entering it and, as will be seen later, this helps to prevent the complications which may result from the presence of a hernia.

Causes

Hernias are very common and there are various causes for them. First of all, people may be born with a particular weakness which makes them prone to develop a hernia. This may mean that they develop a hernia in infancy, or later in life, due to, for instance, heavy lifting.

The commonest type of groin hernia, the inguinal hernia, occurs more often in men than women, and in men is related to a weakness caused by the structures connecting the testis to its blood supply passing through the muscular wall of the abdomen. Women are more prone to developing hiatus hernias (where the upper part of the stomach moves upwards into the chest through a weakness in the diaphragm), and this is probably related to the increase in intra-abdominal pressure during pregnancy.

Symptoms

An inguinal hernia caused by heavy lifting will often come about suddenly: the patient may describe a feeling of something giving way, accompanied by some pain. This usually lasts only for a short time, and the patient then notices a lump in the groin. This lump is usually soft, bulges when he coughs, and goes away completely when he lies down. If it gets very large it may extend down into the scrotum, but hernias can get surprisingly large before they cause a number of symptoms. Of course, if the patient's job involves a lot of heavy lifting, the hernia may become uncomfortable all the time and prevent him from doing his job satisfactorily.

Sometimes, a hernia develops so slowly that the first thing the patient notices is a lump in the groin.

A hiatus hernia, because it bulges through into the chest, is never seen or felt as a lump, but makes itself manifest by its effect on the junction between the oesophagus (the gullet) and the stomach. Normally, there is a valve at the lower end of the oesophagus, just where it joins the stomach, which allows swallowed food to pass into the stomach, but prevents it from going back up the oesophagus. When a hiatus hernia is present, the effect of the valve is lost, and so food (and acid) can pass freely out of the stomach, up into the oesophagus. Because the lining of the oesophagus is not designed to withstand acid, it becomes damaged and inflamed (the condition is known as oesophagitis).

The symptoms of this type of hernia are burning pain behind the sternum (breastbone), which is made worse by bending down or lying flat. If the oesophagus is severely damaged over a number of years, it may become narrowed and make swallowing difficult. Hiatus hernias are very common indeed, especially after middle age, and many people may have a small one of which they are unaware and which causes them no harm whatsoever.

Dangers

If strangulation occurs, a hernia becomes extremely serious and potentially lethal. Strangulation happens when the blood supply to the contents of the hernia is cut off by pressure on the blood vessels by the neck of the sac. First, the veins are obstructed, and this causes the contents to swell, causing further pressure on the arteries, eventually leading to gangrene of the contents. If the hernia contains

Types of hernia

Inguinal hernia (below), the commonest type, occurs more often in men than women. It is sited at the point where the inguinal canal meets the peritoneum. The soft lump which develops in the groin (inguinal means 'of the groin') bulges when the patient coughs and disappears completely when he lies down.

A strangulated hernia (below) is dangerous and could cause death. The blood supply to the contents of the hernia is cut off, they swell and may eventually become gangrenous. If this does happen, the gangrene may be followed by perforation and peritonitis.

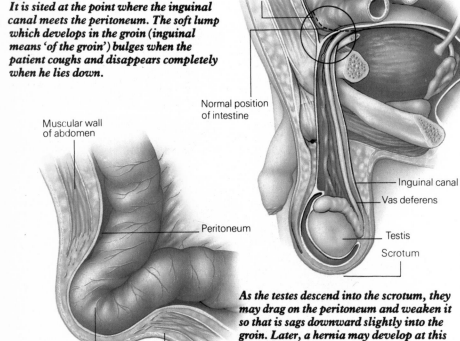

Peritoneum — Intestine
Normal position of intestine
Muscular wall of abdomen
Peritoneum
Intestine — Fat

Inguinal canal
Vas deferens
Testis
Scrotum

As the testes descend into the scrotum, they may drag on the peritoneum and weaken it so that is sags downward slightly into the groin. Later, a hernia may develop at this weak point.

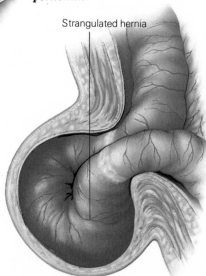

Strangulated hernia

intestine, gangrene of the latter may develop, followed by perforation and peritonitis.

The hernia, which had previously been soft, and perhaps only uncomfortable, becomes tense, tender and irreducible (i.e. it does not go away when the patient lies down). If the bowel is strangulated, the patient may develop symptoms of intestinal obstruction—vomiting, abdominal pain, distension and constipation. If this does happen, an emergency operation is needed to free the strangulated bowel and repair the hernia. If left more than a few hours, the bowel may become irreparably damaged, so that part of it will have to be removed and the two ends joined together again. Of course, if strangulation occurs in one of the rare internal hernias, there is no lump to feel and the patient becomes ill because of bowel obstruction.

The commonest hernia to strangulate is a femoral hernia, followed by inguinal and para-umbilical hernias. Hiatus hernias can strangulate, but rarely do.

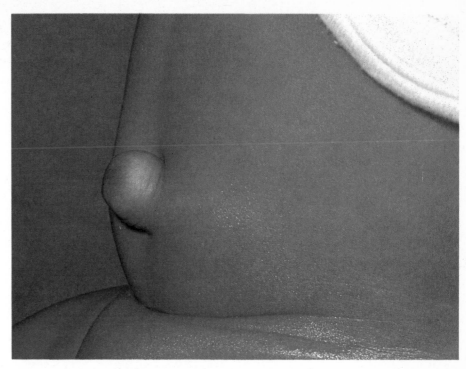

Treatment

If there is a recognizable cause for a hernia, such as obesity, constipation, a cough or difficulty in passing water, this should, if possible, be treated. Secondly,

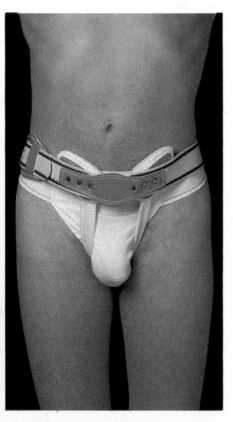

A truss for an inguinal hernia has a strap passing between the legs and a pad pressing on the area of the hernia.

most hiatus hernias can be treated without an operation. Weight loss is probably the most important measure, but in order to deal with the symptoms it is useful to avoid bending; use several pillows at night; avoid drinking just before bedtime; take regular antacids to neutralize the stomach acids.

Only after these measures have failed and if the symptoms are severe is surgery contemplated. An operation can be performed either through the upper part of the abdomen or through the chest wall, when the weakness in the diaphragm is repaired. Nowadays, however, it is quite rare to have to operate on a hiatus hernia.

Treatment for inguinal hernias involves either the wearing of a truss or surgical repair. A truss is a special belt, with an extra strap that passes between the legs to prevent it from riding up. It has a specially designed pad which presses on the area of the hernia, preventing it from bulging out. It may be uncomfortable to wear, and it can be dangerous in that it may allow the hernia, containing bowel, to bulge out, and then press on the neck of the sac, making strangulation more likely. This will usually happen if the hernia has not been fully pushed back before the truss is put on.

By far the best treatment for inguinal hernia is a surgical operation. This may be carried out to prevent strangulation in the future, or because the hernia is uncomfortable and is preventing the patient from working, or finally, because there is strangulation (as an emergency).

The operation is very simple, and can

Umbilical hernia, near the navel, is common in babies. The swelling, covered by skin, flattens easily. If it does not, consult a doctor.

be performed under a local anaesthetic if the patient is thin and the hernia is small, or if the patient is unfit for a general anaesthetic, although it is usually performed under the latter. The thin sac of peritoneum is carefully removed and tied off at the neck, after all its contents have been returned to the abdominal cavity. In a child, this is all that would be done, but in an adult the defect in the muscle wall of the abdomen is repaired. Usually, a strong, non-soluble stitch is used, such as nylon, and the defect is 'darned'. When the scar tissue has formed round the stitches (about three months after the operation), the area should be as strong as normal.

After an operation for a hernia, when the first soreness has worn off, there is a period when the muscle wall round the region of the hernia is becoming strong again. The length of time this takes varies, but it is probably in the region of three months. After this, there is no reason why a person who has had a hernia repair should not lead a completely normal life, including doing a job that entails heavy lifting.

A hernia operation does not guarantee that there will never be a recurrence of the hernia. However, the chances of this happening are very small indeed, and if it does, a second operation can always be done. If a hernia does return, consult your doctor for advice.

Hives

Q Is it possible to catch hives from someone?

A No, you can't catch hives. You could pick it up from contact with a plant or animal, but only if you were allergic to the animal's fluff or some chemical in the plant. And these are just two out of a whole range of allergens which can cause the reaction.

Q My little boy loves strawberries but he gets a nasty rash when he eats them. Could this be hives?

A It's possible. Quite a lot of people get hives from strawberries. This may be due to an allergy or to the fact that strawberries contain small amounts of histamine which cause the symptoms of hives. The only answer is for your son to avoid strawberries—though he might try eating one or two in a year's time just to see if his allergy is still as strong. But if his hives is severe, you should consult the doctor before he tries this.

Q Whenever I sunbathe I come out in hives. I am going on holiday soon, is there any medicine I can take with me to prevent this?

A Although the rash and itching from sunburn are caused by histamine being released into the tissues in and around the skin, it would not be very wise to use an antihistamine cream to deal with it. It might give temporary relief, but antihistamines are quite potent drugs and it is possible to develop an allergy to them. The best answer is not to expose yourself too quickly—however much you want to develop a good tan.

Q I suffer from hives and am worried that I may pass it on to my children. Does it run in families?

A Allergic complaints do tend to run in families, though there is no obvious rhyme or reason in the way they are passed on. However, hives is not a dangerous ailment (except in rare severe cases) so parents should not be unduly worried about a child developing it.

This skin complaint is one of the commonest allergy symptoms, but, fortunately, attacks of hives are usually temporary and fleeting, often clearing up without treatment.

Hives, also known as urticaria or nettle-rash, has several similarities to insect bites or stings—though it may vary from small spots to large, reddish, raised weals. The skin becomes red and often feels burning and itchy.

It may appear in patches on areas of the skin which have been exposed to a substance the sufferer is allergic to, but it can appear on almost any part of the body. It also has the odd habit of appearing in one place, disappearing for no apparent reason and re-appearing elsewhere.

Causes

Hives is almost always caused by an allergy. It may be an allergy to something which comes into direct contact with the skin—like wool or a hairy plant—or to a food or, occasionally, some chemical in the environment.

Among the food allergies, eggs, strawberries and shellfish are common culprits, but other allergens include animal fluff, house dust mites, silk, perfumes, pollens, primulas, cow parsley, aspirin, penicillin and red and yellow food dyes. Exposure to heat, cold, or pressure causes hives in some people. The heat rash many people get from a hot bath is a form of hives.

The arm (below) shows hives in their most common form, nettle-rash. The patient (right) has giant hives, a rare form.

Hives can also appear, with or without a simultaneous allergic cause, at times of emotional stress.

As with other allergies (such as hay fever, see pp 165-66) the body's defence mechanism, the immune system, reacts towards the allergen as if it was a dangerous organism and in trying to neutralize it, releases histamine which produces the allergy symptoms.

Treatment and outlook

The most important task is to identify the allergen and then try to avoid it—but this is not always easy.

Fortunately the attacks are usually temporary and fleeting, often clearing up without the need for treatment. Persistent hives is treated with antihistamine preparations.

Giant hives or angio-neurotic oedema is a particularly severe form of hives. Large swellings appear in such places as the lips, eyelids back and throat. This needs treatment with drugs.

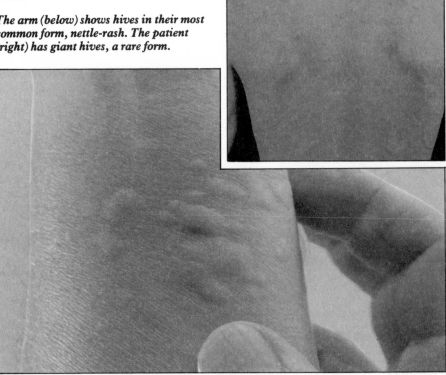

Hormones

Q My complexion is getting wrinkled. Can hormone creams really help before it goes too far?

A Although some beauticians claim they do, there is a risk of dangerous side-effects which outweighs any benefit. It is possible for the hormones to be absorbed by the blood vessels in the skin and carried in the bloodstream to other parts of the body. So, the best advice is to avoid such hormone preparations. You can, however, take good general care of your skin with other commercially available creams.

Q Is it true that morning sickness in pregnancy is caused by hormones?

A Morning sickness is one of the symptoms of early pregnancy which coincides with a big upsurge in the ovaries' production of the hormone progesterone. This hormone helps bring about physical changes in the uterus lining which prepare it for nourishing the foetus. The effects of progesterone may produce feelings of nausea and also tenderness of the breasts. These discomforts pass when the placenta takes over much of the hormone production. This will occur about 14 weeks after the beginning of the pregnancy.

Q Since having treatment for problems connected with her thyroid gland, my wife is much easier to live with. She is calmer and more even-tempered. What could have brought about this total change?

A The thyroid hormones, of which your wife was probably producing an excess, have many physical effects on the body, but also emotional ones. For many people, they produce a state of jumpiness or over-anxiety when too much is made, and this is not helped by the fact that the sufferers know they are not reacting normally. Once this problem has been dealt with, not only are the physical symptoms relieved, but also the emotional problems are quite often brought back into balance.

The correct balance of hormones is essential to physical health. So what are hormones and why are they so important to our well-being?

The body's chemical 'messengers'

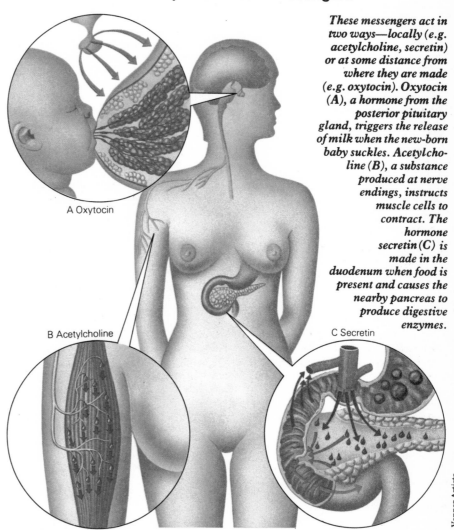

A Oxytocin

B Acetylcholine

C Secretin

These messengers act in two ways—locally (e.g. acetylcholine, secretin) or at some distance from where they are made (e.g. oxytocin). Oxytocin (A), a hormone from the posterior pituitary gland, triggers the release of milk when the new-born baby suckles. Acetylcholine (B), a substance produced at nerve endings, instructs muscle cells to contract. The hormone secretin (C) is made in the duodenum when food is present and causes the nearby pancreas to produce digestive enzymes.

Venner Artists

Hormones are the body's chemical messengers. Unlike nerve impulses, which carry information round the body in the form of electrical charges, hormones are made and released in one part of the body, and are circulated in the blood to other body cells—known as targets—where their effects are brought about. The organs largely responsible for making and releasing most of the body's hormones are the collection of ductless or endocrine glands, so-called because they discharge their products directly into the blood and not via a tube or duct.

How hormones work

Compared with nerves, hormones tend to act more slowly and also to spin out their activity over a much longer time. Not all hormones act so slowly, but many of those that do are involved in fundamental 'whole life' activities, such as growth and reproduction. In general, hormones tend to be concerned with controlling or influencing the chemistry of the target cells, for example, by determining the rate at which they use up food substances and release energy, or whether or not these cells should produce milk, hair or some other product of the body's metabolic processes.

Because they have the most widespread effects, the hormones made by the major endocrine glands are known as general hormones; these include insulin and the sex hormones. The body makes many other hormones which act much nearer to their point of production.

One example of such a local hormone is secretin, which is made in the duodenum in response to the presence of food. The hormone then travels a short distance in the blood to the nearby pancreas and stimulates it to release a flood of watery juice containing enzymes (chemical transformers) essential to digestion.

Other examples of local hormones, or transmitters, include the substance acetylcholine, which is made every time a nerve passes a message to a muscle cell, telling it to contract.

Proteins and steroids
All hormones are active in very small amounts. In some cases, less than a millionth of a gram is enough for a task to be carried out.

Chemically, hormones fall into two basic categories: those that are proteins or protein derivatives and those that have a ring, or steroid structure. The sex hormones and the hormones made by the outer part or cortex of the adrenal gland are all steroid hormones.

Insulin is a protein and the thyroid hormones are manufactured from a protein base and are protein derivatives.

When each hormone reaches its target, it can only go to work if it finds itself in a correctly-shaped site on the target cell membrane. Once it has become locked into this receptor site, the hormone does its work by stimulating the formation of a substance called cyclic AMP (adenosine monophosphate). The cyclic AMP is thought to work by activating a series of enzyme systems within the cell, so that particular reactions are stimulated and the required products are made.

The reaction of each target cell depends on its own chemistry. Thus, cyclic AMP produced by the presence of the hormone insulin, triggers cells to take up and use glucose, while the hormone glucagon, also made by the pancreas, causes glucose to be released by cells and build up in the blood to be 'burned off' as energy-giving fuel for physical activity.

After they have done their work, the hormones are rendered inactive by the target cells themselves, or are carried to the liver for deactivation, then broken down and either excreted or used to make new hormone molecules.

Controlling the system
The whole system of hormone production and use in the body is very complex and is often likened to an orchestra whose 'conductor' is the pituitary gland. Lying at the base of the brain and connected to it by a short stalk, the pituitary gland is divided into two parts. The front portion,

or anterior pituitary, secretes many hormones, which exert their influence by stimulating other endocrine glands to release their products. These are the trophic, or stimulating hormones, and include thyroid-stimulating hormone, which triggers the release of thyroid hormone, adrenocorticotrophic hormone, which stimulates the adrenal cortex to make cortisol, and sex hormone, follicle-stimulating hormone, which controls the release of hormones by the ovaries and luteinizing hormone, which triggers the output of testosterone in a man and progesterone in a woman.

Other hormones made by the anterior pituitary exert their influence directly and include growth hormone, which acts on cells throughout the body to promote both growth in cell size and replacement. Prolactin, also produced by the anterior

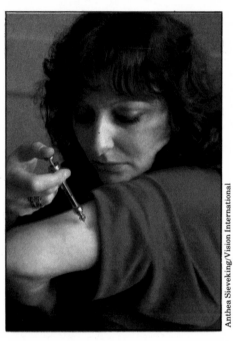

Injections of the hormone insulin are used to control diabetes.

pituitary, stimulates milk and inhibits menstruation while breast feeding.

The posterior part of the pituitary makes two important hormones—antidiuretic hormone which travels to the kidneys and helps to maintain a correct fluid balance within the body, and oxytocin, which triggers the 'let down' of milk from the breasts once a new-born baby starts to suckle. These posterior pituitary hormones are interesting in that their release is directly controlled by nerve impulses generated in the hypothalamus, the part of the brain to which the pituitary is attached.

The only other hormones directly controlled by nerve impulses are adrenalin

and noradrenalin, which are made and released by the inner medulla of the adrenal gland. It has been found, however, that there is an important, if less direct, link between the nerve cells of the hypothalamus and the secretions of the anterior part of the pituitary. What happens is that special nerve cells in the hypothalamus make so-called releasing factors, which must act on the cells of the anterior pituitary before they can send out their hormones.

Effects on emotions
The strong link between the brain and the pituitary goes a long way towards explaining why there is such a definite connection between the hormones and the emotions. Many women find, for example, that if they are anxious or upset, the timing of their periods may be altered. And the levels of the same hormones—oestrogen and progesterone—that control the periods can also have profound effects on a woman's moods.

The sudden fall of hormone levels that happens just before menstruation is thought to play an important part in creating the symptoms of what has become known as premenstrual tension, while the high hormone levels in midcycle are thought to give many women a sense of well-being. And it may not be an accident, that this is the time at which women are both most fertile and most responsive sexually. But hormone levels can also be altered by emotional factors.

During sexual foreplay, for example, it is thought that levels of oestrogen and progesterone rise, as a direct result of pleasurable impulses on the brain, while the very thought of having sexual intercourse with someone who is physically repulsive is, quite literally, a 'turn off', because it inhibits hormone production.

At the end of her reproductive life, i.e. the time of the menopause, a woman may experience great emotional ups and downs. This is partly because her ovaries stop responding to follicle-stimulating hormone, and so stop making oestrogen and progesterone. These changes of mood may also be due to psychological factors. But it is interesting to note that the sudden withdrawal of hormones from the system after a woman has given birth may have emotional effects similar to those of the menopause.

Hormones can be found in a huge range of preparations, from the contraceptive Pill to the ointments used to treat eczema. If your doctor recommends that these drugs can be useful to you, or a member of your family, it is important that he or she should point out the potential dangers to you; they must be used with care and, of course, exactly as prescribed.

Hormone-related disorders and their treatment

Hormone	Disorder	Symptoms	Treatment
Growth hormone	Too little	Failure of growth, often linked with failure of sexual maturity	Administration of growth hormone. (This is in very short supply.)
Growth hormone	Too much	Excessive growth in childhood leading to very long limbs (gigantism). In adults causes excess growth in skull, feet and hands, enlargement of larynx, deepening of voice, thickening of skin (acromegaly)	Treatment of gland by radiotherapy, or removal of part of gland (the other pituitary hormones may then need to be replaced)
Prolactin	Too much	Periods stop, breasts may produce milk and be tender; infertility	Tablet treatment to reduce production
Antidiuretic hormone	Too little (or kidneys fail to respond to hormone produced)	Production of large quantities of very dilute urine (diabetes insipidus)	Synthetically produced hormone usually given as a nasal spray. Hormone then absorbed into blood
Thyroxine	Too much	Weight loss, large appetite, excess body heat, periods may stop in women. One form, (Graves' disease) also causes 'popping' eyes	Anti-thyroid drugs; radioactive iodine by mouth to destroy cells that are overproducing; surgery to remove part of gland
Thyroxine	Too little	Loss of appetite, but overweight and general body swelling. Lassitude, constipation. In infants produces condition called cretinism, associated with failure of physical and mental development	Replacement of missing hormones at carefully-controlled doses needed for life. It is now a widespread practice in the UK to screen new-born infants for cretinism, so the problem can be dealt with as early as possible
Parathormone	Too much (usually due to tumour)	Passing a great deal of urine, indigestion, kidney stones, feeling of malaise	Removal of tumour
Parathormone	Too little	Muscular spasms, convulsions, lassitude, mental disturbance	Administration of vitamin D tablets mimics the action of the missing hormone
Hormones of adrenal cortex (e.g. aldosterone, cortisol)	Too much	Muscle wasting and weakness, leading to thin limbs but obese trunk. Fragile bones and blood vessels leading to purple stretch marks on skin. Diabetes, high blood pressure (Cushing's syndrome)	Drug treatment to block cortisone production. Where only one adrenal gland is involved, it is removed. Usually both are involved as a result of a tumour in the pituitary or elsewhere
Hormones of adrenal cortex	Too little	Faintness, nausea, vomiting, loss of weight, low blood sugar, increased pigmentation on skin (Addison's disease)	Cortisone tablets administration for life at carefully-controlled dosage
Adrenalin	Too much	Episodes of palpitation, fright, raised blood pressure, fast pulse, leading to permanently raised blood pressure, pale face or occasional flushing	Removal of adrenalin-secreting tumour (usually found in the adrenal medulla)
Insulin	Too little	High blood sugar which may lead to loss of weight, thirst and passing large quantities or urine (diabetes mellitus)	Diet is the cornerstone of treatment, with reduction in the amount of sugar. This may be supplemented by anti-diabetic tablets or insulin injections
Male sex hormones	Too little	Failure of growth and sexual development or, in adulthood, impotence and infertility	Replacement of missing hormones by monthly injections
Female sex hormones	Too little	Failure of growth and sexual development, menstrual periods do not start. Later in life, menopause (a normal event) due to reduced hormone levels	Replacement of hormones by tablets

Hysterectomy

Q Is it possible to conceive after a hysterectomy?

A This is very rare—so rare that when it does occur, it is reported in the press. What happens is that the foetus grows inside the abdominal cavity instead of the womb.

Q After a hysterectomy, what happens to the blood a woman normally loses every month? Does it still appear and build up inside her?

A When a woman has a period she loses the lining of the womb, together with some blood which has built up behind it. After a hysterectomy, since she no longer has a womb, she no longer produces this blood or lining and so there is nothing to be shed each month.

Q I have to have a hysterectomy. Will I get backache after it?

A There is no reason why the operation should cause backache unless you develop a urinary infection at the time of the operation, and if you do, this can be treated by antibiotics.

Q Do all women who have a hysterectomy gain weight?

A After the operation women are less active for a few weeks and so require fewer calories. Provided they are aware of this and do not eat to 'build up their strength', they should not gain weight.

Q If my ovaries have to be removed when I have a hysterectomy, shall I be given artificial hormones to replace my own natural ones?

A This must depend on whether you have any problems without these hormones and on your doctor's advice.

Q Will I still experience the same pleasure during sexual intercourse after I have had a hysterectomy?

A Yes! There is absolutely no need to worry about this.

Hysterectomy is the removal of a womb that is diseased, misplaced or malfunctioning. By improving a woman's general health, it can also increase her enjoyment of life.

The words hysteria and hysterectomy both come from the Greek word *hustera*, meaning the womb. In ancient Greece and for many centuries later, it was believed to be the source of many emotional or hysterical disturbances in women. Of course, this view is no longer favoured, but the reverse may sometimes be true: that nervous disorders may have an effect on the way the womb functions. Women with anorexia nervosa (compulsive self-starvation), for example, often cease to have periods.

Because of a lingering association between the womb and emotional instability, many women approach the idea of having a hysterectomy, an operation to remove the womb, including the neck (the cervix) and the body (the fundus) with greater anxiety than is truly necessary.

The operation may be very advisable because of a serious tumour in the womb or associated tissues, or it may be suggested as a treatment for symptoms which are not always due to serious disease, such as heavy periods. In these cases, only the woman concerned knows how incapacitated she is by her symptoms and so she must decide whether or not she wants a hysterectomy.

The operation is becoming less common in Britain because many of the conditions for which it used to be performed are being treated in other ways: for example, abnormal bleeding from an otherwise healthy womb can often be successfully treated with hormone tablets, and cancer of the cervix may be treated by radiotherapy.

Hysterectomy is, if possible, avoided in women who have not completed their family. Because of this and of the higher incidence of disease of the womb later in life, the operation is most commonly performed on women between 45 and 55.

During a woman's reproductive years the lining of the womb is shed at regular intervals and so she has a period. When she becomes pregnant the foetus grows in the womb, so removal of this organ will put a stop to periods or pregnancies.

Different types of hysterectomy

Abdominal hysterectomy involves the removal of the womb through an incision in the lower abdominal wall. In a vaginal hysterectomy, the womb may be removed through the front passage.

Abdominal hysterectomy is the more

In subtotal hysterectomy the cervix is not removed. In total hysterectomy the entire womb is removed (and sometimes the ovaries and Fallopian tubes). Dotted lines show usual extent of surgery. A prolapsed womb is one of the conditions which may necessitate a total hysterectomy through the vagina.

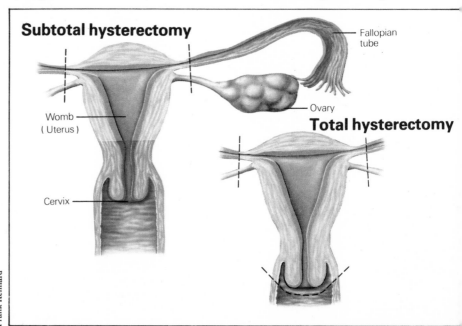

Subtotal hysterectomy

Fallopian tube

Womb (Uterus)

Ovary

Cervix

Total hysterectomy

Frank Kennard

removed, together with the ovaries and tubes. This procedure goes under the long name of total abdominal hysterectomy and bilateral salpingo-oophorectomy. When a woman reaches the change of life (menopause) it is in part because her ovaries no longer release their hormones; if a woman who has not reached the change has her ovaries removed she may experience the sudden onset of symptoms which occur during the change such as hot flushes.

Reasons for hysterectomy

The reasons for performing a hysterectomy fall into five main categories: removal of a normal womb which is giving the woman heavy or frequent periods (called dysfunctional uterine bleeding) when other, simpler treatment has been unsuccessful; removal of the womb because of a tumour in it or in a related structure, such as an ovary; for sterilization (but this is unusual unless the woman also has other problems related to her womb); because of pain related to a woman's genital tract, as in chronic pelvic infection, which has not improved through other measures such as antibiotics; and finally because the womb has prolapsed (slipped down) into the vagina though a hysterectomy is not always needed to put this right.

What is involved

A hysterectomy is a fairly large operation which is only undertaken after much thought and several investigations, often including a D & C (dilation and curettage, in order to determine that this is the best operation for the patient. She is admitted to hospital a day before the operation. This allows time for her to be examined to check that she is fit enough for an operation. It is often necessary to shave her pubic hair as the incision in the abdominal wall may go through this area. She is also given an enema or suppositories to ensure that her bowel is empty and that it will not get in the way during the operation.

The hysterectomy is performed under general anaesthetic. During the removal of the womb it is necessary to strip the bladder from the lower end of the womb, and this often bruises it. To allow the bruising to heal quickly it is sometimes necessary to rest the bladder for a day or two, by passing a catheter into the bladder and letting it empty continuously.

The bowel is also handled during the operation and may not function well for a few hours after it. Until it regains its capacity to work normally, the patient is not given food, but fluids are given through a drip: in any case, during this time she would not particularly want food

common operation in Britain. It gives the surgeon a view of all the pelvic organs and he can therefore check that they are healthy. The incision is larger than in vaginal hysterectomy, which makes it easier to remove an enlarged womb or one that is stuck in an abnormal way to other structures, such as the bowel. The disadvantage of the method is that it leaves

A hysterectomy does not affect a woman's enjoyment of life.

a scar on the lower abdomen.

The womb is normally supported in the abdominal cavity by a floor of muscle and ligaments which are attached to the region between the neck and body of the womb. These ligaments can become loose with age or child-bearing and the womb tends to fall into the front passage. This is called a prolapse. Sometimes this on its own causes discomfort and at other times it also affects the bowel and bladder, which are also pulled downwards. If this becomes a severe problem it may be treated by removing the womb through the vagina and putting tissue and stitches in place to support the bowel and bladder in their correct positions. One advantage of having a hysterectomy vaginally is that there are no visible scars afterwards.

Removal of the entire womb is called a total hysterectomy. Sometimes it is too difficult to remove the neck of the womb, which is attached to the bladder, and this area is left behind. This operation is a subtotal hysterectomy. When it is performed it is still possible for the woman to get very light periods and she should remember to have regular smear tests for cancer of the cervix.

Infrequently, the entire womb is

Prolapsed womb

Ovary

Fallopian tube

Womb

cles

Labia

Vagina

Tom Belshaw

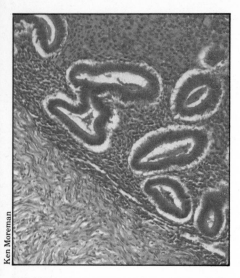

Ken Moreman

anyway. Within twenty-four hours of the operation most patients are out of bed and feeling much better.

Women who have had hysterectomy are encouraged to get up and walk about soon after the operation. During the first six weeks of their convalescence it is important that they avoid heavy lifting or housework to allow time for their tissues to heal without undergoing strain.

Many women find that they feel very tired during this time and some are slightly depressed. Both these problems pass as health is regained.

If womb lining (upper part of picture) is deposited, as here, on an ovary—a condition called endometriosis—a total hysterectomy may be needed.

Women can resume their normal sex life once they have been examined by their doctor to check the wound is well healed—usually six weeks after the operation. Many couples find sexual intercourse more enjoyable after the hysterectomy as they need have no anxiety about an unwanted pregnancy.

Most women who have had a hysterectomy are left with normally functioning ovaries and so those who are prone to pre-menstrual tension may still have the same signs and symptoms but without the accompanying period. At the appropriate age they may also experience some of the symptoms of the change of life.

Most women who have a hysterectomy derive great benefit from it and feel much healthier within a few weeks.

Possible reasons for a hysterectomy

Reason for hysterectomy	Type of hysterectomy usually performed	Purpose of operation	Outcome (in all cases no further periods or pregnancies)
The womb has dropped (prolapsed) from its intra-abdominal site into the front passage	Vaginal hysterectomy	During this operation it is possible to put stitches in the front wall of the passage to support the bladder and in the back wall to support the bowel. This may cure some bowel or bladder problems which the patient had	Cure
Early stages of cancer of the womb	Total abdominal hysterectomy and removal of the ovaries and tubes	To remove the growth and areas which a few malignant cells might have affected	Result will depend on many factors. Doctor's advice should be asked
Abnormal bleeding from an otherwise healthy womb (dysfunctional uterine bleeding) not cured by drugs	Abdominal hysterectomy, usually leaving the ovaries	To remove the organ from which the bleeding came	Cure
Large fibroids (benign growths), or fibroids causing symptoms such as heavy bleeding	As above	To remove the fibroids. Sometimes a larger abdominal incision is made to facilitate removal of very large fibroids	Cure
Rarely used form of sterilization.	Abdominal hysterectomy, leaving ovaries	Removes the organ in which the foetus would grow. Stops sperm from meeting the egg	One recently reported pregnancy following a hysterectomy but very, very rare
Cancer of Fallopian tubes—rare	Total abdominal hysterectomy with removal of the ovaries	Removes the growth	So rare that survival rates are uncertain
Cancer of the ovary (area which releases the eggs)	Total abdominal hysterectomy and removal of the ovaries and tubes	Remove growth and areas to which small parts of growth may have spread	If early—patient may be cured. If the woman has not already gone through the menopause, she will do so after the operation
Severe chronic pelvic infection which has not responded to antibiotics	Total abdominal hysterectomy; if possible, ovaries are left	Remove infected area which may have caused pain, especially during sexual intercourse	Usually curative
Tissue resembling the lining of the womb may be deposited at abnormal sites (endometriosis).	As above; may rarely also involve removal of the ovaries	To remove this tissue	Usually curative

Immunization

Q **Why should I be immunized against German measles before thinking about becoming pregnant?**

A Infection with German measles (rubella) during the first three months of pregnancy often results in an abnormal baby. This is because the German measles virus gets across the placenta and invades the baby's tissues. Apart from its damaging effect on the young baby, German measles virus causes very little trouble. Because of this it is felt reasonable to inoculate only the population at risk: that is, girls who have not already contracted German measles before childbearing age. Boys are left unvaccinated because the disease for them is trivial.

Q **Why are three tetanus injections needed, spaced out in the way that they are?**

A This is done in order to get the utmost antibody response: it is the level of IgG antibody which is so important. After the first injection at three months, very little change in antibody level occurs. However, after a second dose there is a very large rise and after the third dose an even bigger one. Throughout life subsequent injections of tetanus toxoid will result in these very large rises in antibody response so the injections are used as boosters.

Q **Can being immunized against a disease go wrong and result in actually giving you the illness it is supposed to protect you against?**

A Yes. This happens only when a live, as opposed to a dead, virus is used. For example, the first form of smallpox vaccination discovered in Turkey over 300 years ago could cause an extremely unpleasant disease called vaccinia. Later forms, however, were much safer. The measles virus used in vaccination may be associated with a type of inflammation of the brain which can result in permanent damage. However, these side-effects are extremely rare and the odds are very much in favour of having a vaccination.

Immunization increases our resistance to certain infectious diseases by adding to the body's natural supply of protective antibodies.

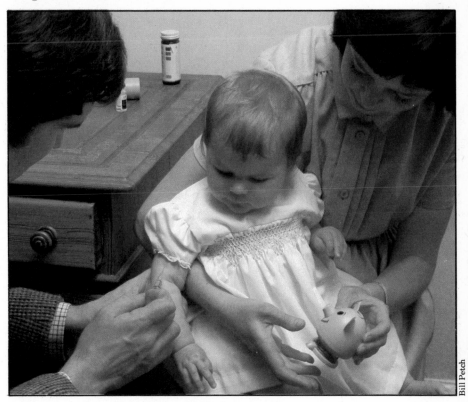

Bill Petch

Triple vaccine is given at three months, repeated twice in the first year, and again on entry and leaving school.

Immunization may be done either by injecting antibody which has been made outside the patient directly into him or her (passive immunization), or by injecting an inactive form of the germ into the patient, thereby provoking an antibody response against further infection (active immunization). After passive immunization, protection against infection is immediate and gradually diminishes over the next three to four weeks. After active immunization, complete immunity does not develop for a month or so but in some instances is lifelong.

Passive immunization

Passive immunization is used regularly only in the prevention of tetanus (lockjaw). The patient selected for treatment is one who is seriously exposed to the risk of developing the disease—for example, from a cut from a garden fork. The object of the treatment is to supply the patient with antibody which has been derived from another source. Horses have been used as reservoirs for this type of antibody since 1894, but more and more use is being made of human immunoglobulin (IgG). This has certain enormous advantages over horse globulin, the most important being that patients no longer have the allergic reaction to horse serum itself which was so common a few years ago. The disease caused by horse serum and known as serum sickness developed within 36 to 48 hours of an injection and was characterized by fever, aching joints, a rash and sometimes by the appearance of protein in the urine.

It is important to remember that passive immunization, although it provides protection immediately after the injection is given, does not last long and in no way protects the patient against the possibility of subsequent infection. For this reason the anti-tetanus serum (passive immunization) is followed by an injection of tetanus toxoid (active immunization), unless the last injection of toxoid was given less than ten years previously. (A toxoid is a harmful substance treated to destroy its harmful qualities, but able to make antibodies when it is used in injections.)

Q Why does the body not become immune to some diseases, such as venereal disease, for example?

A There may be a number of reasons for this, the most important being that the infecting germ is capable of changing its structure or that it may exist in many different forms. For example, polio virus exists in three forms, and natural infection with one does not lead to immunity against the other two. The common cold is caused by a variety of different viruses and to produce a vaccine against all of these is extremely difficult.

Q Are flu jabs any use against flu epidemics? If so, does the effect last until the next year's epidemic?

A There is a good deal of evidence to suggest that people who have been vaccinated against influenza are less likely to get it and that, if they do, their illness is less severe than in unvaccinated people. At present, influenza is still regarded as a fairly trivial disease for fit people but for the elderly or sick, especially those with severe bronchitis, it is wise to have a flu injection before the onset of winter.

Q When travelling abroad do I need to be vaccinated against smallpox?

A Smallpox was wiped out in 1975. There are now very few countries in the world which insist on a vaccination certificate. Ironically enough, the last two cases of smallpox have both been in England though they resulted from laboratory accidents.

Q Does my child have to have a tuberculosis vaccination?

A No. There is no compulsion to have this vaccination at all and it is questionable whether it is always necessary. It is probably wise for children in areas where there are large numbers of immigrants, or for people such as doctors, nurses and dentists who are very likely to be exposed to patients suffering from tuberculosis.

Active immunization

The very earliest forms of protection against disease by immunization were practised in Turkey over three centuries ago against *poxvirus variolae* which caused the dreaded smallpox. The process was known as variolation and was first introduced into England in 1721. Inoculation was effected by scratching the skin of the patient with pus from the ulcers on the skin or a sufferer, thereby transmitting the infection. The disease transmitted in this way was usually less severe and the patient survived infection to live on with permanent immunity to smallpox.

A much safer form of inoculation by injection of cowpox germs was introduced by a country doctor, Edward Jenner in the early 19th century. He noticed that farm labourers who suffered a mild disease known as cowpox—for it was from cows that the disease was contracted—developed a surprising resistance to smallpox. He reasoned that the cowpox germ was sufficiently similar in structure to the deadly smallpox germ for the antibody-producing system of the body to be fooled into making globulins which

When the polio vaccine is given to a tiny baby, it is made up into a syrup, which is put into a dropper and squeezed into the baby's throat.

would kill both smallpox and cowpox. Jenner's method was so successful that variolation was banned in England in 1840.

The widespread use of smallpox vaccination has led to one of the great success stories of medicine; the last time smallpox was seen as a natural infection was in 1975. Since then there have been only two cases, both in England and both

Polio vaccine is given orally. For school-age children, the vaccine is put on a sugar cube which the child then sucks.

When vaccination and immunization procedures are carried out

Age	Vaccine	Interval
During first year of life	Triple vaccine (diphtheria, whooping cough, tetanus)	Given together
	First oral polio vaccine (OPV) dose	3 months later
	Triple vaccine and second OPV dose	6—8 weeks after first OPV
	Triple vaccine and third OPV dose	Preferably 4—6 months after second OPV
During second year of life	Measles vaccine	Not less than 3 weeks following another live vaccine
At entry to nursery or primary school	Triple vaccine and OPV	Given together
Between 11 and 13 years	Rubella (German measles) vaccine and OPV	Given together
	BCG (tuberculosis)	There should be at least 3 weeks' gap between BCG and rubella (German measles) vaccination
On leaving school or before starting employment	Triple vaccine and OPV	Given together
Adult life	OPV	During polio outbreaks only

the result of accidents in laboratories keeping strains of smallpox virus for reference purposes. Since the disease has been wiped out there is no further need for vaccination and a certificate of vaccination is no longer necessary for travellers abroad.

The principles of immunization by vaccination are now widely applied to a variety of infectious diseases. The injected material used to raise the antibody response and provide protection may be living or dead. In certain instances, only a portion of it may be injected: for example, a protein derived from its cell wall. The live vaccines are made less vigorous by growing them in the laboratory for generations or by growing them in animals. The process by which the vigour of the vaccine is blunted is known as attentuation. Live attentuated vaccines cause mild illnesses in the patient to whom they are given and are infectious.

Considering vaccination

The decision to use vaccination rests upon balancing the risks of the side-effects of vaccination itself against the risks of suffering from the disease. Measles, for example, causes severe illness in one in every 15 patients while the vaccine which is live and attentuated offers good protection and causes only a mild illness, sometimes with a rash in ten per cent of patients. Mumps doesn't usually produce severe disease and although a vaccine is available it is not used.

Geographical location is also important. For example, it is not necessary to vaccinate against yellow fever or cholera in western European countries or Australasia, where both diseases are very rare.

Diseases prevented by vaccination

The diseases most commonly prevented by vaccination include:

Diphtheria, whooping cough, tetanus: Vaccines are prepared from dead bacteria and given mixed together as a single injection known as the triple vaccine. The first dose is given at the age of three months. After six to eight weeks, another dose is given in order to boost the antibody response and a third dose is given four to six weeks after that, so that all three injections are completed within the space of the first year of the child's life. The triple vaccine is repeated when the child enters nursery school, and ideally once again when he or she leaves school and starts work, although this is not done in all countries.

Polio: Polio vaccine is given by mouth and combines a mixture of three types of live attentuated virus giving good protection to the three types of naturally occurring polio virus. Since this virus is live, it may occasionally cause mild symptoms such as abdominal discomfort, fever and diarrhoea, but these are never a problem. The vaccine is given on a lump of sugar at about the same time as the triple vaccine, with a booster dose when the child goes to primary school. Outbreaks of polio still occur in most Western countries and it is wise during these outbreaks to revaccinate.

German measles (rubella): Infection with German measles in the first three months of pregnancy frequently results in the birth of an abnormal baby. Immunization should be given before childbearing age to all girls who have not already contracted the disease, which would give them lifelong immunity.

Tuberculosis: Seventy per cent protection against tuberculosis is given by injection of an extract from the cell wall of the tuberculosis germ itself. This is known as BCG (bacillus Calmette-Guerin) and it need be given only to people whose skin test for tuberculosis is negative, which means that they have never been exposed to the tuberculosis germ and so are susceptible to infection. Most cases of tuberculosis in Britain and Australasia are imported from Asia and Ireland. So vaccination with BCG is a sensible policy.

Before long it will be possible to vaccinate against such diseases as syphilis, malaria—and even the common cold.

Impetigo

Q Should children have their routine injections when they have impetigo?

A Doctors are very reluctant to give injections against diphtheria, tetanus and whooping cough and oral polio vaccine when a child has any other infection at all, as the immune system, which fights disease, is already under stress.

Q When I was a girl fifty years ago, there seemed to be more impetigo around than there is now. Is this true?

A Yes, for several reasons. Firstly, antibiotics are effective in curing the condition. Secondly, people are generally living in better housing, with less overcrowding, and they have a higher level of personal hygiene. Impetigo was also much more severe when there were more malnourished children.

Q All my children have had impetigo at one time or another. Can impetigo run in families?

A A tendency to impetigo is not inherited. However, if one member of the family has impetigo, the others are very susceptible to it by contact as it is highly infectious. Also, a tendency to eczema is inherited and eczematous skin is more likely to be infected than normal skin, thus providing a perfect breeding ground for impetigo.

Q My son recently had impetigo. Is it possible for the bacteria to stay in the house, for example in the bedclothes, and cause an infection in the future?

A The impetigo bacteria will not survive in dry, well-aired, frequently washed bedding. They survive best in people, and in moist materials such as face flannels and towels, and hence these are common carriers of impetigo. For this reason the face flannels and towels of a person with impetigo should be kept separate from the rest of the family, and boiled frequently.

One of the most common skin infections which affects children, and occasionally adults, is impetigo. With prompt treatment it can easily be cured.

Impetigo is a highly contagious skin infection which may arise in both apparently healthy skin, and in skin damaged by eczema, insect bites, scabies or cold sores.

Causes
Impetigo is caused by the staphylococcus bacteria which is found in the nose. It may be transmitted by breathing or sneezing on to damaged skin, where it spreads rapidly, causing inflammation and weeping blisters. Unless hygienic precautions are taken and treatment given, impetigo may spread quickly to other members of the household or school, either by direct contact or contact with towels or face flannels used by the patient.

Symptoms
Impetigo first appears on the face, scalp, hands or knees as little red spots. These soon become blisters which quickly break, exuding a pale yellow, sticky liquid. They then dry to form large, irregularly shaped, brownish-yellow crusts.

If only a small area of skin is affected, there are usually no other symptoms, but if large areas are involved, or if the surrounding skin is also infected with another bacteria, the patient will feel unwell, with a temperature and swollen lymph nodes. Adults are usually less severely affected than children, except in hot climates where the spread of infection may be extensive.

Dangers
Impetigo is a life-threatening illness for new-born babies, who have very little immunity, and therefore it is extremely important that no one with impetigo should be in contact with babies or their mothers.

Very rarely, untreated impetigo may cause abscesses elsewhere in the body, or nephritis (inflammation) of the kidneys.

Treatment
Treatment must commence immediately. If the area is small, then an antibiotic cream should be applied three or four times a day until the crusts have healed. Larger areas will require additional antibiotics by mouth or occasionally by injection. Thick crusts may have to be soaked off with liquid paraffin.

Most importantly, spread must be prevented, both to patients, who may re-infect themselves, and to others. Always keep patients' face flannels and towels separate and boil these, and also clothing and bed-linen after use. Children with impetigo should be told not to scratch the crusts, as scars may form. They should be kept off school until the infection has cleared, usually after five days. If there is an underlying skin condition, such as eczema, both this and impetigo should be treated together.

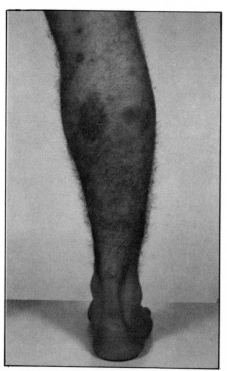

Impetigo initially looks like small red spots. These can turn to blisters (see eyebrow below). Once the blisters break and ooze pus, they dry and form oddly-shaped crusts, as on this leg.

Impotence

Impotence is rarely a long-term sexual difficulty, but if it is, a man can go to his doctor without embarrassment because nowadays lack of sexual performance is mostly regarded as the result of minor and temporary psychological problems.

Q I have been away on a business trip for a month and was very eager to make love to my wife when I returned, but when the time came, well—I couldn't perform. I've never been incapable before. Am I going to be impotent for good?

A Almost certainly not. You would be amazed at how many men come to doctors with the problem you describe.

Impotence is almost certainly temporary, and probably caused by being too keen, rather than anything like incapability. The simple answer is to adopt a lighthearted attitude and just carry on as normal. It's almost certain to come right next time, or the time after.

But if the problem persists, go to your doctor.

Q I don't have a particularly hairy chest and am worried that this means I am inclined to impotence. Could I be right?

A Absolutely not. You might be at a slightly greater risk of becoming impotent because you worry about it, but not because of your lack of body hair.

Q Am I bound to become impotent in old age?

A No. Sexual desire does lessen with age, but you just have to come to terms with making love less often, less energetically, and in gaining a different sort of pleasure from it. Surprising numbers of men have been sexually active in their eighties. Even more are happily making love in their seventies, and fathering children.

Q My first husband used to make love to me two or three times a night. My new husband can only do it once. Does this mean he is becoming impotent?

A No. Men vary enormously in this, not only between individuals, but at different times during their lives. So it would be unwise to suggest that this may be the case. Once you plant a seed of doubt, there is always a risk that it may become a reality.

Sexual failure in men comes down, physically, to three things: non-production of sperm in the testicles; not being able to have or keep an erection, and finally, not being able to ejaculate.

Strictly speaking, only the second factor is impotence. The first comes under the heading of infertility and the third is distinguished as a problem of its own.

Premature ejaculation, meaning the problem of reaching orgasm too quickly, is also different to impotence, although it has similar causes and responds to broadly similar treatments.

All types of men, in all walks of life, are more likely than not to experience impotence at some stage of their lives.

This is because impotence is most commonly caused by stress, partnership problems or lack of self-confidence.

Ageing is the other universal factor in impotence. Sexual functioning, just as other physical processes, naturally declines with age, so that once again, all men are susceptible, though impotence caused this way is by no means inevitable.

Sexual arousal

The purpose of sex is the penetration of the vagina by the penis so that fertilization (if contraception is not used) can take place. To do this the penis has to be stiff and erect, rather than limp or flaccid as it usually is. The stiffness is caused by blood flowing into three spongy cavities within the penis, and being kept there by a muscular contraction at the base of the penis.

For the blood to flow to the penis, there must be a sexual response—in other words, a reaction to something which is sexually exciting. In humans the 'trigger' for sexual excitement is mainly in the mind. Non-mental triggers for sex do exist, such as the cycle of hormone production, hormones being the body's chemical messengers. But unlike animals, we are not automatically 'turned on' sexually.

Once a man has an erection, physical stimulation does the rest. Friction of the walls of the vagina on the head of the penis, which is rich in nerve endings, stimulate various muscles until, at orgasm, they contract, pumping semen out through the penis.

It should be no surprise, therefore, that a system so dependent on mental and nervous triggers should occasionally fail for mental or nervous (that is, psychological) reasons. By far the most common psychological reason for failure is the fear of failure. Society puts men (and women) under great pressure to be sexually successful.

It can take something quite small to plant the seed of fear. Scornful words may do it—spoken, for instance, by a woman who, understandably enough, is disappointed when her partner is too tired to make love, perhaps because of overwork or stress.

Closely related to fear as a psychological reason for impotence is general lack of self-confidence. This is caused, typically, by redundancy, or failure to win promotion at work. Or there may be partnership problems—perhaps a lack of confidence in the relationship, or in the girl herself. But in all these cases, impotence is only a real problem if it persists.

Physical causes

In young, and not-so-young men, alcohol is the most common (and joked about) physical cause of impotence. Anyone who has had too much to drink knows how it makes them willing, but not able to make love. There may be an erection, but ejaculation either takes a long time, or does not happen at all.

Ageing is the physical cause of impotence to worry about least. At 60, a man is less able to perform sexually—in terms of frequency of erection, the length of time it can be 'held' and the time taken to reach orgasm. However, there is no set pattern, and some may find the rate of decline eases after 60.

As many elderly people know, this does not mean a deteriorating love life, just one with a different pace. Indeed, the length of time it takes a man to reach orgasm may mean greater pleasure for both partners, particularly the woman.

If you have a bout of 'flu, or even a cold, your sexual powers are likely to be weakened. Severe diabetes can cause impotence, as can a few other serious degenerative diseases, such as cancer of the colon or prostate—although they may not always do so.

Childhood events can make a man

impotent in later life. Unhappy dealings with females—perhaps in his family—may give him an in-built resentment of women. Or he could have a naive tendency to idealize them.

Some men fear the consequences of sexual intercourse, not wanting the responsibility of children, or they may have a fear of hereditary disease.

Treatment

Temporary psychological impotence is almost always treated, at first occurrence, by the doctor. He will try to identify the cause and offer reassurance.

If the problem does not go away, it is likely to need treatment by psychotherapy. Today, this offers great hope to couples who are prepared to co-operate with the therapist.

Sexual therapy entails a couple going to therapy sessions together to learn techniques which they then practise in their own home.

They begin with 'sensate focusing' exercises, which show that pleasure can be achieved simply through physical contact free of any demand to perform successfully.

Soon the man begins to forget his tendency to judge his sexual performance—simply because he is not being asked to perform—and begins to associate physical contact with simple pleasure. If all goes well, the couple are allowed to move on after two or three weeks to specifically sexual stimulation.

If they report that an erection occurs, no particular comment is made. If it goes soon afterwards, nothing is made of this either. The likelihood is that it will re-establish itself. Once the counsellor hears that erection can be easily achieved, the couple are allowed to move on to simple forms of intercourse. All the time, the counsellor insists that the activity is demand-free. If ejaculation happens, which it usually does, it is just accepted.

For the most common physical cause of

The loving encouragement of a partner in a relaxing situation is often the most effective means of regaining proper sexual functioning.

Excess alcohol, and persistent use of cannabis, are known physical causes of impotence, both occasional and long term.

impotence—excess drinking—pointing out the cause is usually treatment enough. The same may well apply to young people who complain of impotence as a result of heavy use of cannabis.

If impotence is caused by a short-term illness or over-tiredness, the treatment is equally simple—explanation, followed by reassurance that normal sexual functioning will return. More than 90 per cent of cases are psychological, and most respond to treatment.

When it is caused by disease, for example diabetes, patients can often look for improved sexual ability in step with the progress of their treatment.

Decline due to ageing is not a medical problem, but doctors, or sex therapists, may offer advice on love-making positions which are easy and comfortable.

Indigestion

Pain and discomfort after over-eating or eating the wrong food is a common complaint, but one which should never be ignored, as persistent and severe indigestion may have an underlying medical cause which requires treatment.

Q Whenever I get painful wind I take a little bicarbonate of soda in orange juice. Although it gives me more wind, it does relieve the pain. Why is this?

A In some types of indigestion, gas becomes trapped in the stomach, producing pressure and pain. Bicarbonate of soda causes more gas to be formed which is enough to break the wind and release the trapped gas, making you more comfortable. The antacid effect of the bicarbonate of soda neutralizes stomach acid and also aids digestion.

Q How can I prevent indigestion following a big meal?

A The commonest cause of such indigestion is eating late, eating spicy or rich food, eating too much and drinking alcohol as well. If you eat slowly and miss out one of the courses, you may reduce the indigestion. Whenever possible, go for a walk after eating. And, allow time for your food to be digested before going to bed.

Q I never had indigestion until recently. Could I have an ulcer?

A Your indigestion may be due to a change of life-style or foods. However, if the pain is severe and occurs in between meals, and is relieved by eating, it could be a sign of a duodenal ulcer—consult your doctor.

Q Our entire family suffers from indigestion. Does it run in families, and will my children suffer from it too?

A It is possible that indigestion runs in families, but it really depends on the exact nature of the symptoms and the situations in which they are experienced. Indigestion is so common that you could say that every family has sufferers because most people get indigestion at some time or other. Children rarely suffer from indigestion—they tend to be sick and solve the problem instantly!

Jerry Harper

Apart from the occasional rumble or belch, we do not usually notice the functioning of our digestive systems. For most of us, the term 'indigestion' covers a wide variety of digestive complaints, but most commonly it means pain after eating food, often accompanied by a bloated, sick feeling.

Types of indigestion

Mild indigestion occurring after a heavy meal, particularly if rich or spicy food has been eaten, is extremely common. It is a complaint that mainly affects adults.

Chronic indigestion is more persistent and severe, and is often a symptom of a medical condition which can usually be treated. In some people, the pattern of indigestion is indicative of a specific medical complaint, such as a peptic ulcer (see pp 18-49), a hiatus hernia (see pp 175-77) or migraine.

Take your time and chew your food properly, as hurried eating is one of the easiest ways to give yourself indigestion.

Causes

Indigestion is either a symptom of illness or, much more commonly, the result of eating unsuitable food. It may also result from the way food is eaten.

Depending on the individual, certain foods can cause indigestion. Cucumber and pickled onions are common culprits, as are spicy foods, such as curry or garlic, and rich foods loaded with cream or butter. Unripe fruit, uncooked meat and excesses of tea, alcohol or tobacco can also cause types of indigestion. It is not that these substances cannot be digested, it is only that the stomach takes longer to deal with them and is slow to pass them on into the remainder of the gut. The stomach contents and stomach acid lie in

191

the stomach without being passed into the duodenum. Acid is poured out which causes heartburn and belching.

For some people, indigestion is brought on simply by hurried eating and failing to chew food properly. Or the cause may be poor dental hygiene, because bad or septic teeth, leaking pus or blood around the gum margins, will taint food and produce chronic indigestion.

There may also be psychological reasons behind bouts of indigestion. The nerve supply to the stomach is through the vagus nerve which controls acid production and the rate at which food leaves the stomach. Both anxiety and depression affect this part of the nervous system. Excess acid and slow emptying both cause indigestion and can lead to the formation of ulcers.

Symptoms

The degree of indigestion produces an individual combination of symptoms, from pain and flatulence (wind) to severe discomfort and regurgitation of acid food.

Symptoms vary depending on the cause. There is usually pain which is either colicky or constant and situated in the pit of the stomach or upper chest.

Or there may be nausea, accompanied by a full and heavy sensation in the stomach; if the sufferer can be sick, the indigestion is relieved immediately.

Acid regurgitation from indigestion is also common. Acid comes up into the mouth to produce hoarseness of the voice and a pain in the chest, better known as heartburn. Sometimes a person with indigestion will experience a symptom known as waterbrash—where saliva flows like water—accompanied by excess belching, flatulence, or hiccups.

In chronic indigestion, the tongue is dry and is coated with a brown fur-like substance, and the breath is stale.

Dangers

Isolated bouts of indigestion following heavy meals or drinking sprees are not dangerous. However, where the indigestion is chronic, or when the pain does not pass or becomes extremely severe, it is important to see a doctor, as some serious conditions have pains and symptoms which often mimic indigestion.

Inflammation of the gall-bladder, for instance, produces wind, sickness and central abdominal pain. Some rare cases of appendicitis can produce the same symptoms. A heart attack or clot on the lung may also appear, at first, to be an acute bout of indigestion, but the pain remains fixed or worsens and is not relieved by taking an antacid. And where chronic indigestion is caused by a peptic ulcer, which is left undetected, the ulcer may perforate or bleed. Persistent

indigestion may also be the first indication of stomach cancer. Failure to diagnose any of these conditions is dangerous and could even be fatal.

Treatment and outlook

In the case of chronic indigestion where a medical condition, such as a hiatus hernia, cancer or an ulcer, is suspected, the sufferer will usually have a medical investigation, such as an X-ray or an endoscopy, to establish the cause.

If the cause is a hurried way of life, stress or poor diet, this must be corrected or, in the case of isolated bouts of indigestion, treated with antacids.

The outlook for people with a medical cause for their indigestion varies from case to case. Many people suffering from a hiatus hernia may have to control the condition by taking regular antacids and avoiding certain foods.

People with ulcers can normally be cured by medical or surgical means, although if stress was the original cause of the ulcer, another may form if the way of life is not altered.

For the great majority of indigestion sufferers, an occasional antacid allows them to eat freely as it relieves the indigestion quickly and effectively. Others with more severe symptoms need to modify their lives, in particular their eating habits.

A dose of antacid offers quick relief for the occasional bout of indigestion.

Avoiding indigestion

● Eat regularly and slowly, chewing food adequately so that it is swallowed easily.
● Do not eat when wet or cold, as the digestive mechanism of your body will be slowed down.
● Avoid heavy drinking or smoking.
● Take plenty of exercise.
● Eat plenty of fibre to avoid constipation.
● Visit your dentist for regular check-ups.
● If anxious or depressed, seek help from your doctor.

Home treatment for indigestion

● Take a dose of antacid. Bicarbonate of soda or magnesium trisilicate are both good but neither should be a substitute for better eating habits.
● Take sips of water and sit in the cool air. Sit up rather than lie down and it may help to walk around.
● If the indigestion persists or is more severe than usual, you should get medical advice.
● If you have never had indigestion before, be sure to tell your doctor to aid him in his diagnosis.

The natural way to aid digestion is to take plenty of exercise.

Infection and infectious diseases

Q Is there any difference between an infectious and a contagious disease?

A Strictly speaking, a contagious disease is one which is caught by touching an infectious person. However, many people use the word contagious just to mean infectious.

Q My neighbour told me that you can catch some forms of cancer. Is she right?

A No. It is true that viruses may be involved in producing the irregular division of cells that is the basic abnormality in cancer. A disease called Burkitt's lymphoma, which is a cancer affecting African children, is caused by a virus called the Ebstein-Barr virus. It is also suggested that viruses may be involved in producing cancer of the cervix. However, you cannot actually catch cancer from someone.

Q My husband has just had a very bad case of mumps. Are childhood diseases more severe when you are an adult?

A Although this does not apply to all the normal childhood illnesses, as a general rule, yes. It is particularly true of mumps which can cause severe inflammation of the testes in men. Chickenpox in adults may leave permanent lesions on the lungs which can be seen in a chest X-ray, but which are harmless.

Q Is it possible to have some diseases without knowing it?

A Yes. This is called a 'sub-clinical infection'. Some people may be exposed to an infection and gain immunity to it without developing the full-blown symptoms of the disease. This seems to occur in young children with mumps, and in quite a high proportion of the population with German measles.

Q Can people catch disease from animals?

A Yes. Birds, dogs and insects carry infections which can be transmitted to humans. But only those who work with animals are very likely to be affected.

Infectious diseases were once the commonest causes of death. Improved sanitation, housing and hygiene, immunization and antibiotics and other drugs have greatly reduced deaths from infection.

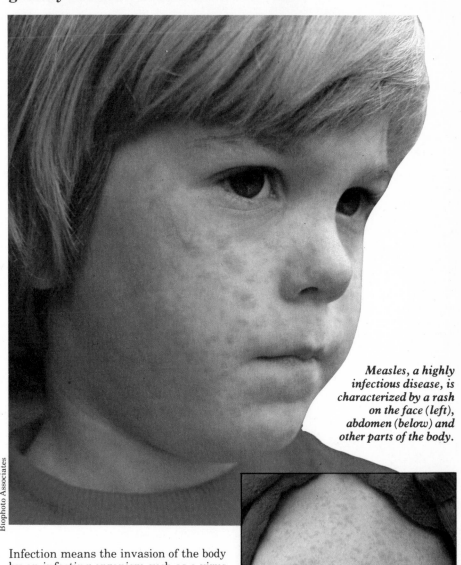

Biophoto Associates

Measles, a highly infectious disease, is characterized by a rash on the face (left), abdomen (below) and other parts of the body.

Infection means the invasion of the body by an infecting organism such as a virus or bacterium. Infections can range from minor ailments like colds and flu to invariably fatal illnesses like rabies. Infections may be localized, affecting only a small area (an abscess, for example), or one system (the way that pneumonia affects the lung), or they may be generalized, affecting a greater part of the body, as in septicaemia (blood poisoning).

Causes

Infections are caused by tiny organisms (living creatures) which are too small to be seen by the naked eye: they are therefore called micro-organisms. Two sorts of micro-organism, the virus and the bacterium, cause the vast majority of important infections.

Viruses are not really complete organisms on their own: they are unable to maintain a separate existence outside the cells of another living thing. Many viruses infect humans, but there are also viruses which infect other animals, plants and even bacteria.

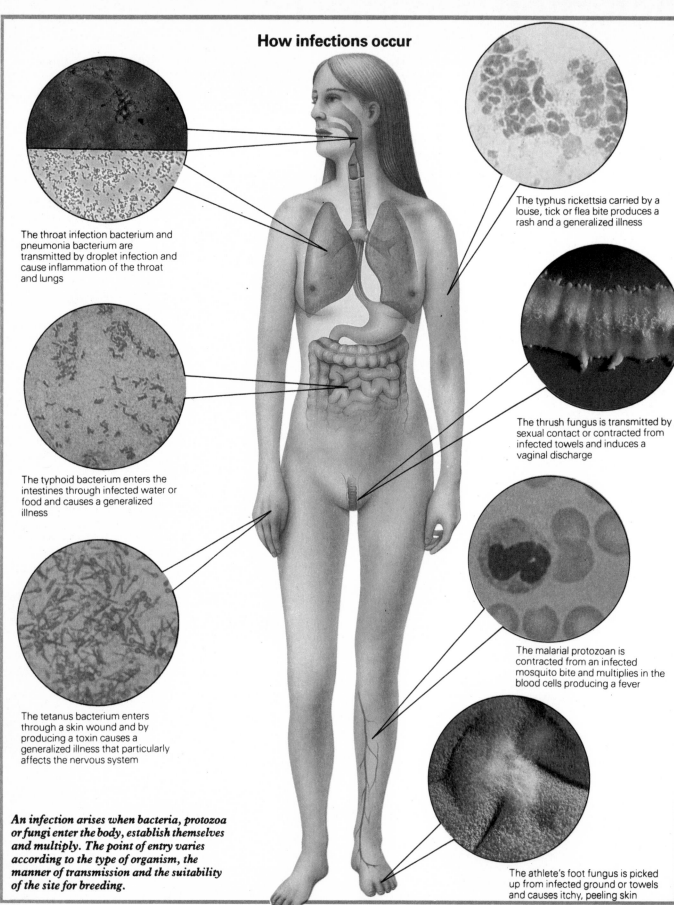

How infections occur

The throat infection bacterium and pneumonia bacterium are transmitted by droplet infection and cause inflammation of the throat and lungs

The typhus rickettsia carried by a louse, tick or flea bite produces a rash and a generalized illness

The thrush fungus is transmitted by sexual contact or contracted from infected towels and induces a vaginal discharge

The typhoid bacterium enters the intestines through infected water or food and causes a generalized illness

The malarial protozoan is contracted from an infected mosquito bite and multiplies in the blood cells producing a fever

The tetanus bacterium enters through a skin wound and by producing a toxin causes a generalized illness that particularly affects the nervous system

An infection arises when bacteria, protozoa or fungi enter the body, establish themselves and multiply. The point of entry varies according to the type of organism, the manner of transmission and the suitability of the site for breeding.

The athlete's foot fungus is picked up from infected ground or towels and causes itchy, peeling skin

A virus consists of an outer shell of protein which contains a particle of genetic material (DNA or RNA). When this infects a cell, it instructs it to make other viruses and this way it reproduces itself.

In contrast, bacteria are single-celled organisms which can and often do exist quite happily away from other living things. Many bacteria live in the soil and don't cause any infections. In man, some bacteria enter cells during the course of infections, while others remain outside the cells. There are many bacteria which are normal inhabitants of the colon (large bowel) where they do no harm and may be helpful in preventing the growth of other more dangerous bacteria. These are called commensal (living with) bacteria.

A third type of infective microorganism is the protozoa: larger single-celled organisms and fungi. Malaria, probably the most important infectious disease in worldwide terms, is caused by a protozoa called plasmodium.

How infections begin
Once a micro-organism has entered the body, its object is to reproduce itself using the tissues as a food substance. Viruses go one stage further by using the chemical building apparatus of the cells to build new viruses. In contrast the bacteria reproduce simply by means of each individual bacterium splitting into two.

Micro-organisms cause disease in a number of different ways. Often the organism produces some poisonous substance, called a toxin, which causes symptoms. Diphtheria is an example of such a disease. Organisms also cause disease by tissue destruction or by interfering with the normal functioning of an organ. Viral hepatitis, for example, causes jaundice by interfering with the function of liver cells, while pneumonia may make large areas of the lung ineffective.

How the body defends itself
The body deals with infection by a remarkable and complex defence system called the immune system.

Before an organism reaches the cells of the body, it must break through the skin: the skin acts as a primary barrier against infection. However, many infections enter the body through the respiratory tract or the alimentary (digestive) tract and so avoid having to cross the skin. Once inside the body the organism may be consumed by a phagocytic cell, a cell which swallows up and destroys viruses and bacteria. These are the white cells of the blood; there are similar cells in the tissues. In some cases, both the organism and the phagocyte will die and this leads to the production of pus, which is no more than a collection of dead organisms and phagocytes. The activity and effectiveness of phagocytes depends upon the immune system.

The immune system works through two major arms to combat invasion by foreign organisms. The first is the production of antibodies: these are protein molecules which travel in the bloodstream and among the tissues and bind on to the surface of specific micro-organisms. This makes it easier for the phagocytic cells to attack. Antibodies may also stop organisms from being effective: for example, they may stop viruses entering cells. Finally antibodies may trigger a system which actually leads to invading bacterial cells being broken down.

The other arm of the system is called cell-mediated immunity. The cells of this system, which are called lymphocytes because they come from the lymphatic system, may be specially primed to react with a particular organism and kill it. They may also produce substances which help phagocytes to attack infecting organisms.

The development of vaccines to protect against infection has been one of medical science's major contributions to health. These vaccines rely on the same basic idea, which is to find a substance that will cause the immune system to react to a specific disease without producing the disease itself. Most vaccines rely on the production of dead bacteria or viruses which have the same cell wall structure as the live organism and therefore cause antibody production.

Diseases and their symptoms
Most viruses enter the body and then spread to cells throughout it via the bloodstream. They enter the cells and more viruses are produced. The symptoms of the disease usually start as this second wave is released from the cells.

Many organisms show a particular tendency to infect only one organ. For

Viruses reproduce by instructing the cell's DNA to make new viruses which are directly or indirectly transferred to other cells.

How viruses reproduce in the body

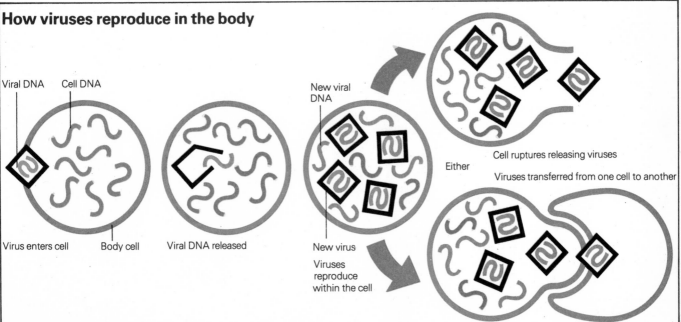

Viral DNA   Cell DNA

Virus enters cell   Body cell

Viral DNA released

New viral DNA

New virus

Viruses reproduce within the cell

Either

Cell ruptures releasing viruses

Viruses transferred from one cell to another

John Hutchinson

Q I seem to catch one infection after another. Is there something wrong with the way my body copes with infection?

A People vary in their ability to fight off infections, but it is equally true that having had one infection, your resistance is lowered and therefore you are more likely to catch another. Virus infections often leave the way open for further infection by a bacterium. This is why some people with diseases like chronic bronchitis take antibiotics at the first sign of any cold. Although the antibiotics will not help to treat the cold, they may stop it spreading to the chest in the form of a bacterial infection. So even if you do seem to have nasty runs of infections, you are probably quite normal in the way you respond to them.

Q Can you die from an infectious disease?

A Yes. Rabies (usually caught through a bite or scratch from an infected animal) is always fatal in people who have not been immunized, or who are not immunized immediately after exposure. Similarly, smallpox had a very high mortality rate in people who were not immunized against it. Fortunately this disease seems to have been eradicated by a combination of isolating infected patients and immunization.

Q Like everyone else, I can't stand having colds or flu. Why can't the scientists develop a vaccine against the common cold and flu?

A The trouble is that the common cold is caused by all sorts of different viruses. If a vaccine were to be successful against one sort of virus it would not protect against all the others. There is a further difficulty which limits the effectiveness of influenza vaccines: the influenza has the capacity to change the way it appears to the body's immune (defence) system, so if you have flu one year it does not necessarily mean that you will be immune to the disease the next. The makers of flu vaccine have to try to decide which strain is likely to be about in any one year and to produce a vaccine against that strain.

instance, the hepatitis virus lodges in the liver; the bacterium pneumococcus causes pneumonia in the lungs; and the pneumococcus' close relative the meningococcus which causes meningitis results in an inflammation of the membranes lining the brain. Why organisms show this preference is unknown.

Other organisms, like the staphylococcus, may produce disease in any system. Once this organism has entered the bloodstream it gets carried around the body and settles in organs far away from the point where it originally entered. Once settled, the staphylococcus can multiply and produce an abscess.

Finally, abscesses may produce toxic substances which poison particular areas of the body. Tetanus produces such a toxin which only affects the nervous system, while the cholera organism produces severe diarrhoea as a result of toxins.

However, in many cases much of the problem that a disease may cause results from the effect of interaction between the infecting organism and the body's defence mechanism. The production of large amounts of phlegm as a result of pneumonia is really a result of the immune response and this phlegm is often the leading symptom of the disease. Similarly, the lung destruction that may follow from tuberculosis is primarily caused by the immune response rather than the disease itself.

Treatment
Antibiotics have made a great difference to the treatment of infection. These are drugs which are toxic to bacteria but not to human cells. Many of them actually act by interfering with the bacterial cell wall which has a different sort of structure to human cell walls. Antibiotics are ineffective against virus infections, protozoa and worms: other drugs are used.

In crowds (above), try to avoid coughing or sneezing if you have a cold. To avoid spreading infection: wash all tea towels regularly in hot water; if dried outdoors, the sunshine kills bacteria.

Infectious diseases and their treatment

Disease	Caused by	Source of infection	Immunization available	Symptoms	Medical treatment
Chickenpox	Virus	Person to person	No	Rash	None
Common cold	Virus (many types)	Person to person	No	Runny nose	None
Diphtheria	Bacterium	Person to person	Yes	Obstructed throat, localized paralysis	Antibiotics
Gonorrhoea	Bacterium	Sexually transmitted	May become available	Discharge from genitals	Antibiotics
Hepatitis	Virus (at least three types)	May be via skin, via infected food or by sexual transmission	May become available	Jaundice	None
Influenza	Virus (many types give flu-like illness)	Person to person	Yes, but not 100 per cent effective	Cold, sore throat, muscle aches	None
Legionnaire's disease	Bacterium	Air conditioning or water systems	No	Pneumonia, general ill health	Antibiotics
Malaria -	Protozoa (three types)	Mosquito bite	No	Fever	Antimalarial drugs which are also given to prevent infection
Measles	Virus	Person to person	Yes	Runny nose and eyes, rash, ill health	None
Meningitis	Virus (many types) or meningococcal (bacterium)	Person to person	No	Neck pain, pain on looking at light, drowsiness	Nursing care for viral, antibiotics for bacterial
Mumps	Virus	Person to person	No	Swelling of salivary glands	None
Pneumonia	Bronchopneumonia (usually bacterial, may be virus)	Person to person	No	Cough	Antibiotics
	Lobar pneumonia (bacterial)	Person to person	Yes, for patients at risk	Cough and chest pain	Antibiotics
Ringworm	Fungus	Person to person (contact required)	No	Skin rash	Antifungal drugs applied to skin
Scarlet fever	Bacterium	Person to person	No	Skin rash and shedding of skin	Antibiotics (penicillin)
Syphilis	Bacterium	Sexual contact	No	Many symptoms, often years after infection	Penicillin
Tetanus	Bacterium (disease caused by poison)	Soil infection of wounds	Yes	Lockjaw and other spasms	Support on respirator if necessary
Tuberculosis	Bacterium	Person to person, usually by infected phlegm	Yes, but effectiveness varies worldwide	Usually affects lungs, causing cough with blood	Special antibiotics
Thrush	Fungus	Sexually transmitted or on infected towels	No	Irritating white vaginal discharge	Antifungal drugs
Typhoid	Bacterium	Infected food or water	Yes	Fever and headache, later diarrhoea	Antibiotics
Typhus	Rickettsial (different types)	By lice, tics or fleas	No	Fever, rash	Antibiotics and tetracycline

Infertility

Failure to produce a much-wanted child can cause great psychological stress in both the man and the woman. Fortunately, treatment of infertility is improving all the time as new advances are made.

Q My husband and I have been trying for a year to have a baby. A friend told me that she conceived when her doctor told her husband to wear loose underpants! Can this really work?

A Tight underpants or trousers can cause the temperature of the scrotal sac to be much higher than sperm can tolerate, thus killing them off. But this is only one of several possibilities. Go to your doctor to find what your problem is.

Q You often read of people who thought they were infertile adopting a child and almost immediately having a child of their own. Why should this be?

A A couple who are keen to have a child and then worry themselves into a state when they don't conceive may be infertile for this very reason. Once they have adopted a child the pressure is off and this may be all that is necessary to restore fertility.

Q My doctor has suggested I take a fertility drug, but I couldn't cope with a large number of children at once.

A Fertility drugs are associated with multiple births because those are the ones that get into the newspapers. There is a slightly increased chance of twins being conceived, but more babies than that is rare.

Q My doctor is recommending me for AID (artificial insemination by donor). My husband agrees that I should do this as he is infertile and we both long for a child. What does it involve and will it work?

A AID involves gently opening the vagina with a speculum (a gynaecological instrument) while a plastic tube carries the donor sperm from a syringe to the cervix (neck of the womb). It is usually done on three consecutive days around the time of ovulation, when the woman is fertile, and continued for six months to a year. The procedure takes place at a clinic. About two thirds of women who have AID conceive within three months.

It can come as a severe blow to a couple to find that they cannot have children. Many of the causes of infertility have no accompanying symptoms so it is only when the couple try to conceive that they realize they have a problem.

The indication of possible infertility is when a couple fail to achieve conception after a year or more of intercourse without contraception. Some doctors prefer the couple to have been trying for two years before they begin tests and treatment, but this will depend to some extend on the age of the woman.

Between 10 and 15 per cent of couples are infertile and the numbers seem to be rising gradually, possibly because of the increasing incidence of VD.

Sex becomes a strain, focused as it is on the fertile time of the month, and many couples experience a loss of desire when they feel that each time they are trying (and failing) to make a baby rather than making love.

It is important that both partners go to see their doctor as the problem is just as likely to affect the man as the woman.

If the reason for infertility is not immediately obvious then tests are carried out to find the cause.

Causes

There are many different causes of infertility and it is a subject constantly under review with new discoveries of causes and treatments being made all the time. Infertility is just as likely to be caused by a problem in the man as in the woman and in 30 per cent of cases it is combined factors.

The most common cause in women is failure to ovulate (release an egg from the ovary each month) due to a hormone failure. Sometimes hormone imbalance can produce hostile mucus in the vagina that actually repels the male sperm or stops the fertilized egg from attaching itself to the uterus (womb).

In some women the problem may be a physical one such as a hymen or vagina too tight for intercourse, or a malformation of the vulva (external genitalia), the vagina or any reproductive organ.

Other disorders that can lead to infertility may happen at any time—such as

Reasons for infertility

Problems	Possible causes	Symptoms and diagnosis	Treatment
IN MEN			
No sperm or low sperm production	Infection after puberty; certain drugs; exposure to X-ray; high temperature of scrotal sac, excessive alcohol	Semen analysis will show sperm count. Less than 20 million per cubic centimetre is below average	Male hormones may increase sperm count temporarily. Where the sperm count is low, women may be artificially inseminated
Inability of sperm to swim	Chronic prostatis (inflammation of the prostate gland) surgical removal of the prostate; hormonal imbalance	Semen analysis will show whether the sperm can swim actively	Steroid treatment may be prescribed
Inability to deposit sperm in vagina near the cervix	Impotence; premature ejaculation; obesity	Physical examination and case-history will diagnose the problem	Sexual therapy for impotence and premature ejaculation
Blockage of tubes carrying sperm	Untreated VD; variocele (varicose veins in scrotum)	As above	Drugs to treat VD. Surgery to tie off variocele
IN WOMEN			
Pelvic inflammatory disease such as parametritis which affects the uterus; salpingitis which affects Fallopian tubes or salpingoophoritis which affects the tubes and ovaries	Gonorrhoea; certain bacteria; viruses; irritation from IUD	Pelvic pain; pain with intercourse; pain with menstruation; irregular bleeding	Occasionally surgery is suggested to clean out scar tissue formed during long-term infection
Endometriosis (tissue which normally lines the uterus found in abnormal places)	Tissue forms in response to abnormal hormonal stimulation; cells from the uterus travel up Fallopian tubes and implant themselves elsewhere	Menstrual pain; pain on intercourse	Surgical removal at an early stage may halt the problem, accompanied by hormone treatment
Venereal disease (untreated)	Intercourse with an infected person	Routine tests will show gonorrhoea	Drug treatment of any infection; possible tubal surgery
Failure to ovulate (release eggs)	Malfunction of pituitary, thyroid or adrenal glands that influence the menstrual cycle	Endometrial biopsy (biopsy of uterus) may be performed; also hormone tests	Treatment with fertility drugs
Cervical problems	Cervical infection; mucus which repels sperm; polyps	General examination, possible scrape of cervix	Treatment with drugs or possibly surgery depending on cause
Inflammation or blocked Fallopian tubes	Could be caused by peritonitis, infection; tuberculosis	Rubin's and sterosalpingography tests and laparoscopy inspection	Treatment will depend on results of tests. May need surgery

infection from bacteria or viruses, venereal disease or the growth of fibroids, polyps or cysts.

Emotional stress is another common cause. Psychological factors can stop ovulation or cause spasms in the Fallopian tubes which inhibit the passage of the egg to the uterus.

Infertility in men can be due to no sperm or low sperm production, or sluggish sperm which do not swim as they should. High numbers of abnormally-shaped sperm can cause infertility.

A blockage of one of the tubes that carries the sperm is another cause of male infertility. This may be the result of varicocele (varicose veins inside the scrotum), a tuberculous infection of the prostate gland or untreated venereal disease. Alcohol can reduce fertility.

Impotence and premature ejaculation are other causes of male infertility and these may have a psychological basis.

Diagnosing the problem
An infertile couple will be referred by their doctor to their local hospital or infertility clinic and they should go together as it is just as likely for the man to be infertile as the woman, or for there to be a joint problem.

Diagnosing the trouble can be a lengthy affair. To start with, both partners will have a general physical examination and medical histories will be taken. The doctor will want to know when the woman's periods started, whether she has a regular menstrual cycle (that is, regular periods), as well as details about both partners' past and present health and of their sex life.

The man will have a semen count as there would be no point in carrying out tests on the woman if the man has a very low sperm count. He produces a sperm sample by masturbating into a clean, preferably sterile, glass or plastic container. The couple should not have had intercourse for at least two days before that because the number of sperm in the semen should be as high as possible.

It is generally believed that the man has no fertility problem if the count is no lower than 20 million sperm per cubic centimetre of semen, that at least 40 per cent of the sperm are active and 60 per cent are of normal shape.

If no abnormality is found then tests will continue on the woman. She will be shown how to prepare a basal temperature chart to show when she is ovulating. The basal body temperature (the temperature of the body at rest) rises when a woman ovulates but as it varies with many factors—such as the time of day—it should be taken at the same time each morning before getting out of bed or having anything to drink.

Ovulation is indicated by a rise of about 0.2°C (0.4°F) or more. Sperm can live for three-five days in a woman's Fallopian tubes, the egg only lives for about 12 hours after it is released from the ovary so the couple must make sure they have intercourse at that time.

Doctors will usually recommend keeping a basal chart for several months so that they can establish the woman's ovulation pattern.

But not all doctors consider this method of pinpointing ovulation reliable, so other tests may be used, among them the serum progesterone test. Using the woman's temperature chart as a guide or, alternatively, by giving her a blood test about six days before her next period, the rise in the level of the hormone progesterone—which happens immediately after ovulation—can be measured.

An endometrial biopsy is another test. By taking a sample of the endometrium

The ovulation pattern
The basal chart below shows the hormone and temperature changes during a woman's menstrual cycle.

On Day 1—the first day of the period—a low oestrogen level makes the pituitary gland produce FSH (follicle stimulating hormone). BBT (basal body temperature is normal.

On Day 4 FSH stimulates the egg follicles. Oestrogen is produced and stimulates growth of the uterus lining as pituitary produces LH (luteinizing hormone) instead of FSH. BBT normal. Period finishes. Increased oestrogen causes production of thick mucus:

Days 10-13 progesterone produced softening uterus lining for an egg.

On Day 14 LH causes egg follicle to burst—ovulation. Peak mucus occurs and progesterone raises BBT.

From Day 15 if no pregnancy, oestrogen and progesterone levels fall. BBT remains high.

On Day 28 low progesterone level causes shedding of uterus lining. BBT is back to normal.

(womb lining) and examining it under a microscope, the doctor can tell whether or not ovulation has occurred and approximately when. It is a reliable test and is usually done under general anaesthetic.

Post-coital test
An abnormality of the cervix or the mucus in the cervical canal can be diagnosed by a simple, painless test called the post-coital test. This involves taking some of the mucus from the cervix to see what is happening to sperm in the vagina after intercourse and whether the sperm are still active after several hours. The test is best carried out around the time of ovulation and the woman will be asked to have intercourse the night before or on the morning of the test. The mucus should be clear and still contain moving sperm.

Rubin's test
This is one of the tests that is done to see if the Fallopian tubes are blocked. Gas is passed through a special applicator into the uterus, sometimes under a general anaesthetic, and the doctor listens to the

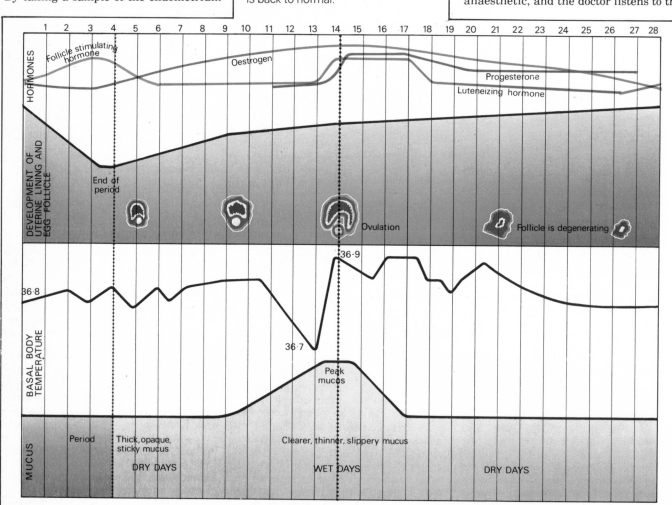

Trevor Lawrence

200

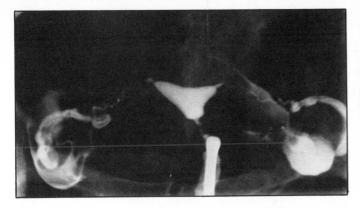
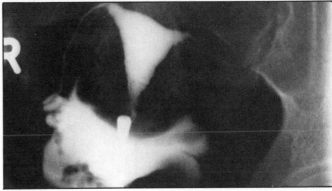

gas passing through each Fallopian tube with a stethoscope. The pressure of the gas is measured and if both tubes are blocked the pressure gauge will show a steep rise almost immediately.

Hysterosalpingography
This is a more accurate test which involves injecting dye through the cervix and up each Fallopian tube. Then X-rays are taken to reveal any blockage of the tubes, the shape of the womb and show whether the cervix is functioning properly. The test is usually carried out during the first ten days of the menstrual cycle. An anaesthetic is not usually necessary.

Laparoscopy
This is a relatively new test which allows a direct view of the uterus, Fallopian tubes and ovaries. It is done under a general anaesthetic as it involves piercing the abdominal wall with a slim needle through which gas is passed to distend the abdominal cavity. Then an optical instrument called a laparoscope is passed through a slightly larger incision just below the navel. The ovaries and uterus can then be biopsied if necessary. It is sometimes possible to carry out minor surgery through the laparoscope.

Treatment
In over 10 per cent of all infertile couples no reason for infertility is found but, taking all the cases, a five per cent spontaneous cure results before any treatment is started. The very fact of being in the hands of infertility specialists can cause an easing of tension when the problem is emotional.

Treatment varies according to the diagnosis. Failure to ovulate may be treated with fertility drugs with a very good success rate.

Surgery is sometimes necessary to clear blocked tubes, scrape the uterus,

Most women can cope quite happily with twins. Using a fertility drug can result in two babies but rarely more than that.

Left: dye has been injected through the cervix and can be seen flowing along the Fallopian tubes. Right: the dye cannot get through the blocked right-hand tube.

correct congenital (present from birth) abnormalities, and remove fibroids, polyps or cysts.

The man may be treated with hormones or steroids. If his sperm count is low, then his wife has more chance of conceiving if she is artificially inseminated with his sperm. This is known as AIH (artificial insemination by husband) and the technique is exactly the same as AID (artificial insemination by donor). It may be possible to clear blocked seminal tubes and tie off varicocele by surgery.

When there is no effective treatment artificial insemination by donor (AID) may be recommended.

Any infection which may affect the fertility of either partner will be treated with drugs.

In both men and women, psychotherapy may be more helpful than physical treatment when the problem seems to have an emotional or psychological basis.

Outlook
Some problems respond well to treatment. On the whole, male problems respond less well than female fertility problems.

Couples who have not found a treatment that works for them should not give up hope entirely. It is worth their while keeping in touch with their hospital or infertility clinic in case their problem is solved by research at some future date.

Influenza

Q The factory where I work offers free flu injections. Should I have one and will it have any harmful side-effects?

A An injection won't do you any harm at all, and the only side-effects—which don't often occur—are a sore arm and a raised temperature for 24 hours. The injection will offer you 60 per cent protection against flu in the winter of the year when you have it, and even if you do get flu, it may make it a much milder attack than you would otherwise have had.

Q My son of 12 has caught flu at school. He shares a room with his younger brother, aged six. Shall I move the younger boy to another room?

A People who are ill sleep badly, and may require attention during the night, so it would probably be better to move the younger boy.

As for preventing him from catching flu from his brother, it is probably too late to do that. Flu is infectious for one or two days before symptoms develop, and it is almost impossible to stop it from spreading round a family.

Q My mother of 70 has had flu recently. Her doctor says that she is better now, but she has lost a lot of weight, her appetite is poor and she doesn't eat. What can I do to help her recover completely?

A A small amount of alcohol stimulates the appetite and also contains calories which will increase your mother's weight. A glass of sherry or stout, or some other tonic, once or twice a day before meals, will help your mother to feel better.

Q What is the difference between mild flu and a bad cold?

A Colds and flu are both caused by a virus. The flu virus tends to make people more unwell and feverish and is totally different from the cold virus, which makes them sneeze and gives them a runny nose. However, the symptoms can overlap, even though the viruses causing the illness are different.

Influenza is one of the most common illnesses in the world, and one of the most infectious. What can be done to keep attacks to a minimum?

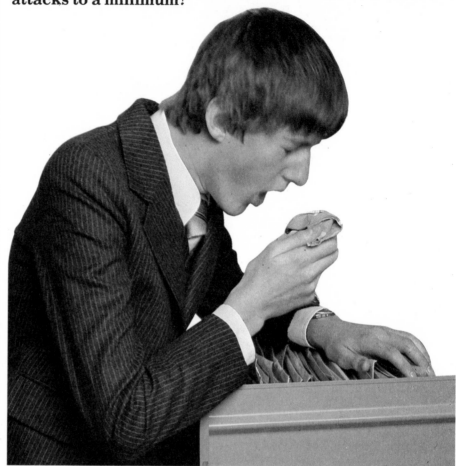

Influenza usually occurs in epidemics when lots of people catch the illness at once. This usually happens in the winter, but it is also present somewhere in the population at all times, which is why people can get flu at any time of the year.

The cause

The virus which causes influenza is special in that it is always changing its appearance to fool the body's defence mechanisms, called the immune system. Every year it changes by a process known as drift, resulting in outbreaks of flu. Every 30 to 40 years a bigger change takes place, known as shift, during which a very different virus appears and causes a worldwide epidemic—a pandemic. Occasionally the flu virus changes to a form which resembles a previous virus, and people who were infected by that first virus are immune to the second one.

Influenza is transmitted from person to person by coughing and sneezing. This

Once caught, the influenza virus spreads rapidly from person to person through coughing and sneezing.

causes droplets of secretions containing the virus from the infected person to be breathed in by someone who is not infected, who starts to have the symptoms from one to three days later.

The part of animals in the spread of influenza is not well known. Certainly domestic pets do not carry the disease. There is some evidence, however, that farm animals—for example, horses, hens and pigs—do get a similar illness. In the pig it is known that the virus is the same as the flu virus in human beings. In fact, the pig is thought to act as a potential carrier of swine influenza which caused a pandemic in 1918/19.

Symptoms

The symptoms come on suddenly, with shivering and generalized aching in the arms, legs and back. The patient may have a headache, aching eyes, a sore or dry throat and sometimes a cough and a runny nose. Occasionally there may also be the symptoms of a stomach upset, with vomiting and diarrhoea. If the temperature is taken at this point, it is above normal, usually over 38.5°C (101°F) and up to 39°C (102°F).

The symptoms and fever continue for two-five days and leave the patient feeling tired and weak. He or she may also feel depressed and washed out and should be reassured that a period of depression after flu is quite normal and may last a few weeks. The cough also may persist for one or two weeks after the other symptoms have gone.

If a patient with flu is examined by a doctor when he or she is ill, there is usually little to see, except a feverish person with an inflamed throat. These are the

To aid a quick recovery after the first flu symptoms appear, go straight to bed and drink plenty of energy-giving fluids.

In case of flu . . .
- Go to bed and keep warm
- Drink plenty of fluid: much more important than food if the appetite is poor for a few days. Drinks containing sugar provide some energy
- Take one or two aspirin tablets every four hours to relieve aches and bring the temperature down
- Be careful to cough and sneeze into a handkerchief to limit the spread of infection
- When the temperature returns to normal, get up but take things easily for a few days
- If symptoms persist or become worse, ask your doctor's advice

classic signs of flu. If a patient has some immunity he may often have a milder illness, with fewer symptoms and only a small rise in temperature.

The difference in immunity explains why some people get the disease worse than others, and why people who have been in very close contact with an infected person may not feel ill at all. People become immune once they have had influenza, because their body's defence mechanism recognizes the virus a second time and prevents it from multiplying and causing a real attack of flu. (This recognition does not happen if the flu virus has altered its appearance).

Complications and treatment
Influenza can strike all age groups, but the old are particularly prone to the complications of flu.

The most common complication is a chest infection. This can vary from a mild cough to pneumonia. Sometimes the virus itself causes this, but more commonly another germ enters the body which has been weakened by flu, and infects the chest. Old people and those who already have chest trouble are more likely to develop a chest infection after an attack of flu.

If the flu patient has a severe cough, is producing green or yellow sputum, has chest pains, or feels breathless, it is advisable to call the doctor. People who have other things wrong with them—for example, chest trouble, heart disease or kidney problems—should let their doctor know if they catch flu because he may want to give them an antibiotic to prevent them from having complications.

If an attack of flu seems prolonged and is not progressing normally, it is wise to call the doctor without delay.

Very, very rarely the flu virus itself can cause severe pneumonia, or the disease can be caused by another germ, a staphylococcus, which gets into the body already undermined by flu. In very severe cases the flu virus can also affect the heart or the brain, but fortunately this hardly ever happens.

Prevention
There is at present no cure for flu. The flu virus is always changing its appearance to fool the body's defences, and this explains why vaccination sometimes does not work.

In spite of this difficulty, it is very useful, especially in communities such as schools, factories and old people's homes. It is also useful in attempts to prevent flu in people who are likely, because of some other illness such as chest trouble, or because of old age, to develop more serious complications.

The flu injection is given in a single dose in the autumn. It usually has no side-effects, but occasionally makes the arm sore or causes a slight rise in temperature for 24 hours.

Kidneys and kidney diseases

Q I know that alcohol causes damage to the liver, but does drinking have any effect on the kidneys?

A Alcohol tends to have no detrimental effect on the kidneys, although constant heavy drinking can, of course, damage the liver. People with urinary infections are encouraged to drink large quantities of water, so that the infection is flushed out. The amount of fluid you need to drink each day depends on how much you lose, and thus, upon the amount of physical work you do, since this will increase the volume you lose in sweat. Even office workers should drink at least a litre (1.76 pt).

Q My mother has high blood pressure. Will this harm her kidneys?

A High blood pressure causes the small blood vessels to thicken. This, in turn, causes damage to the nephrons (filtering units) in the kidneys and, as these are lost, the ability of the kidneys to remove waste products is hampered, ultimately resulting in kidney failure, unless the condition is treated.

Q If one kidney fails, can the other one become larger and cope on its own?

A Yes. In fact, we have so many nephrons in each kidney that we can quite easily do without not one, but almost half of the other kidney as well. For this reason, it is perfectly reasonable to remove a kidney from a healthy person and donate it to someone else. The donor can live with one kidney for the rest of his or her life, provided that it remains healthy.

Q Do some forms of VD lead to kidney trouble?

A Venereal disease is a very rare cause of kidney disease, although occasionally gonorrhoea can lead to infection of the kidneys by spreading up the ureter from the bladder. A much more common cause of kidney trouble is infection caused by other organisms or because of urinary infections.

The main purpose of the kidneys is to extract impurities from the system. They are amazingly efficient and as there are two, it is possible to live perfectly normally if one fails.

The kidneys contain a complicated system of filters and tubes. Apart from their main function of filtering off impurities from the blood, they enable many essential nutrients to be absorbed back into the bloodstream from the tubes. It is here that another important function of the kidneys is performed. This is balancing the amount of salt and water that is retained.

We have two kidneys, lying on the back wall of the abdomen. From the inner side of each kidney a tube called the ureter runs down the back of the abdominal cavity and enters the bladder. The tube leading from the bladder is called the urethra. In women, its opening is in front of the vagina, and in men at the tip of the penis. The urethra in women is much shorter, and for this reason they are more prone to bladder infections than are men (see Cystitis pp 109-11).

Functions

The kidneys contain thousands of tiny filtering units, or nephrons. Each nephron can be divided into two important parts—the filtering part, or glomerulus, and the tubule, where water and essential nutrients are extracted from the blood.

The glomerulus consists of a knot of tiny blood capillaries which have very thin walls. Water and the waste dissolved within it can pass freely across these walls into the collecting system of tubules on the other side. So large is this network of blood capillaries that it may contain—at any one moment—almost a quarter of the circulating blood and filters about 130 ml (4.6 fl oz) from the blood each minute.

A baby needs fluid in order to keep his kidneys flushed. So give him drinks of cooled boiled water between feeds.

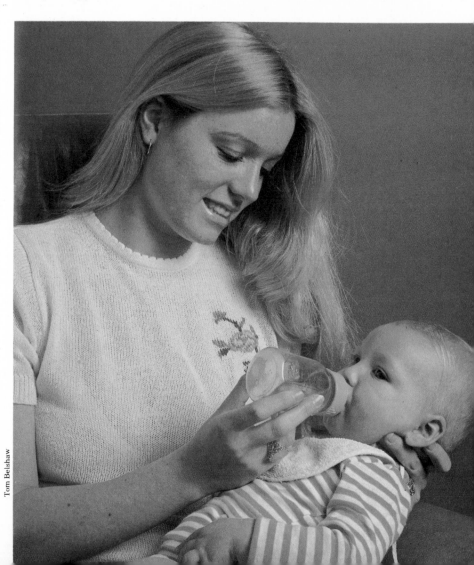

Tom Belshaw

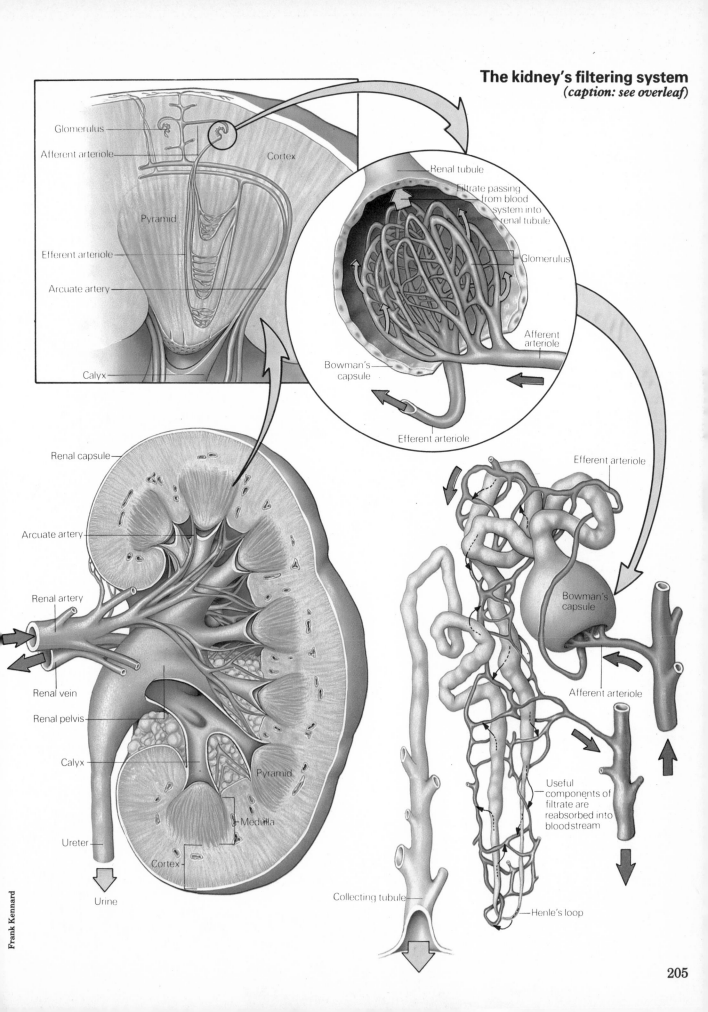

Glomerulus

Afferent arteriole

Cortex

Pyramid

Efferent arteriole

Arcuate artery

Calyx

Renal tubule

Filtrate passing from blood system into renal tubule

Glomerulus

Afferent arteriole

Bowman's capsule

Efferent arteriole

Renal capsule

Arcuate artery

Renal artery

Renal vein

Renal pelvis

Calyx

Pyramid

Medulla

Ureter

Cortex

Urine

Efferent arteriole

Bowman's capsule

Afferent arteriole

Useful components of filtrate are reabsorbed into bloodstream

Collecting tubule

Henle's loop

Frank Kennard

205

Overleaf: Magnified view of a kidney's different components and how they work. The renal artery carries blood to the kidney, splitting into arcuate arteries and finally into afferent arterioles. Each of these ends in a glomerulus (inset). As blood passes through the glomerulus, it is filtered through the glomerular wall and enters the renal tubule. The basic components of blood (plasma, protein, red and white corpuscles, and so on) are too large to cross the semi-permeable membrane of the glomerulus, but most of the other material e.g. water, salts and hormones, that the blood carries around the body can pass across it. The next stage is called selective reabsorption, which is seen in the detailed enlargement (below). Materials essential to the body are reabsorbed into the efferent arterioles, across the tubule wall. Once the blood has been thoroughly filtered and all the required materials have been reabsorbed, the blood leaves the kidney in the renal vein, while waste products are excreted in the urine via the urethra.

The holes in the capillary wall form a biological sieve, and are so small that molecules beyond a certain size cannot pass. When the kidneys become infected, the glomeruli inflame and the 'sieve' fails to be so selective, allowing larger molecules to escape into the urine. One of the smallest protein molecules to find its way into the urine is albumin. This is why your doctor tests your urine for protein to see whether the kidneys are functioning properly.

The tubules run between the glomeruli to a collecting system which ultimately drains into the bladder. Each glomerulus is surrounded by a Bowman's capsule, which is the beginning of its tubule. It is here that almost all the filtered water and salt is reabsorbed, so that the urine is concentrated. To reabsorb all this water, the body has a highly sophisticated system in which a hormone secreted into the blood from the pituitary gland in the brain changes the permeability of the tubule (its ability to reabsorb water).

While the hormone is in the blood, the tubule allows a great deal of water to be reabsorbed. When the hormone is 'turned off', however, the tubule becomes less permeable to water and more is lost in the urine—this is called diuresis and the hormone concerned is known as antidiuretic hormone (ADH). In certain conditions, such as diabetes insipidus (not to be confused with 'sugar diabetes' or diabetes mellitus), this hormone may be totally lacking. When this happens the patient cannot conserve water, and so loses large quantities in the urine, which have to be replaced by drinking.

Another hormone, aldosterone, secreted by the adrenal glands just above the kidneys, is responsible for exchanging sodium salt for potassium salt—so helping to control blood pressure and the balance of salt in the body. Para-thormone, another hormone made by four small glands buried behind the thyroid gland, regulates the reabsorption of the essential mineral calcium, from which our bones and teeth are made.

Kidney disorders

Once a nephron is destroyed, it seldom regrows. From birth onwards we gradually lose nephrons. Fortunately, we have so many that this seldom becomes a problem. Indeed there are many more than are needed in the kidneys; in fact, about a third of all our nephrons do very little. They are gradually brought into use as wear and tear takes its toll.

Doctors can get a good idea of the number of nephrons working by measuring the level at which certain waste substances are present in the blood and removed in the urine. One such waste product is called creatinine. Its level is kept very low in the blood and it rises when the blood becomes concentrated, as it does when we are thirsty, or when there are not enough nephrons to get rid of it. When doctors see a rise in the level of creatinine in the blood, it is a warning sign that the kidneys are failing. The rate at which creatinine can be removed from the blood is a better indication of renal (kidney) failure. If a patient's kidneys fail to clear more than 10 ml (0.35 fl oz) of blood of creatinine each minute, the assistance of a dialysis machine, or artificial kidney, will be needed before long.

Inflammation of the glomerulus leads quite suddenly to kidney failure. The early signs are the appearance of albumin protein in the urine and sometimes particles of red blood cells. If your urine changes to a pink or rust colour, you should go and see your doctor as soon as

People living in hot climates need to drink more to replace the volume lost in sweat.

Q Are there any drugs which are likely to cause damage to the kidneys?

A Yes. There is a dangerous form of kidney disease, which results in damage to the duct system, caused by certain drugs. Phenacetin has been particularly linked with this kind of kidney disease, but there is reason to believe that other anti-inflammatory drugs, like paracetamol and aspirin may also cause trouble if large amounts are taken regularly; so the people most at risk are those who take tablets of this kind habitually—especially if they live in hot climates, where the amount of the drug concentrated in the urine is likely to be high and so cause kidney problems.

Q My father's doctor has told him that he needs an IVP. What is this test and how is it carried out?

A IVP stands for intravenous pyelogram, which is a test done in hospital to check the kidney's function. A dye which concentrates in the kidneys is injected into the bloodstream. By taking an X-ray, soon after the injection, the kidneys can be seen outlined by this dye, so giving doctors a good idea of their size. Later on, when the dye is excreted, the position of the ureters and the bladder can be seen. Patients suffering from an enlarged prostate tend to be unable to empty their bladders completely, so any residual dye left in the bladder will show on the X-ray and confirm the diagnosis quite conclusively. This test is quite painless.

Q The doctor has told me that I have bacteria in my urine and have to take antibiotics. Why does this happen?

A The urine is normally sterile and this can be tested by pathologists. However, some people shed bacteria in their urine, and this is a sign of infection somewhere in the urinary tract. As long as the bacteria persist, you have the chance of developing acute inflammation of the kidney. Doctors may switch from one antibiotic to another over several weeks, until the most effective is found and the infection is completely cleared.

John Watney

possible. Excess water and salt cannot be excreted and so collects in parts of the body—which means either swollen ankles in patients who are up and about, or at the base of the spine in patients who are lying in bed.

In most cases, acute kidney inflammation settles down completely and full recovery is normal. Rarely, however, damage to the glomeruli is progressive, and the patient gradually develops renal failure. This is known as chronic glomerulonephritis. The most common cause of this condition is an allergy to the streptococcus bacteria. In the days before penicillin, streptococci caused epidemics of sore throat, followed by acute glomerulonephritis, and a high proportion of these victims developed chronic renal failure. However, this type of disease is seldom seen.

Inflammation of the kidneys, usually coming up the ureter from an infected bladder, is the most common cause of tubular disease. Repeated infections caused in this way can ultimately result in the destruction of sufficient nephrons to cause kidney failure. A tell-tale sign is the appearance of pus in the urine. In the early stages of disease, the patient's water may appear quite clear, and a microscopic examination is needed to spot the white cells which make up pus, but later the urine becomes cloudy. Of course, there are many other causes of cloudy urine, the most common being the first amount passed in the morning, which usually contains a deposit of undissolved salts which have collected overnight, go and see your doctor if worried.

Inflammation of the kidneys due to infection is called pyelonephritis, and this usually responds very well to treatment with antibiotics.

Various types of kidney stones, including the strange 'stag's horn' formation.

Called calculi, kidney stones are composed of the salts of calcium and phosphorus. The two main causes of kidney stones are infection and an excessive amount of calcium in the blood. Stones associated with infection are more common in women, and reach very large sizes so that they cannot pass down the ureter. They lie inside the kidney, and as they grow they take up the shape of the collecting duct system in which they lie. When an X-ray picture is taken, they show up as a branched lump of chalk, looking rather like the antlers of a stag. Smaller stones may be passed down the ureter, causing colic and severe pain.

High blood pressure
The kidneys regulate the amount of salt in the body and produce a hormone called renin. The level of renin depends upon the level of salt, which in turn is controlled by the action of the adrenal hormone, aldosterone, on the tubules. Renin activates another hormone, angiotensin. It is this which causes a rise in blood pressure.

How the kidney's control blood pressure is described on page 65.

See your doctor If
- urine is discoloured, particularly if it is red
- you have pain passing urine, lasting more than two days
- you pass urine frequently, for more than three or four days
- you have accompanying pain in the loin or abdomen
- your ankles are swollen

Lacerations

Lacerations are wounds where the skin is torn rather than cut. As it takes great force to tear the skin, lacerations are often serious; internal organs can suffer laceration, too. First aid and prompt medical treatment are essential.

Wounds are traditionally divided into five kinds—scratches, abrasions, cuts, lacerations and puncture wounds (see pp 10-13). The distinction between cuts and lacerations is often unclear but, in general, a cut is a neat incision through the skin, usually caused by a sharp object such as a knife or piece of broken glass, whereas a laceration is usually caused by a blunt instrument, leaving a ragged wound with crushing and bruising of the surrounding tissue. However, many doctors use the word laceration to describe all sorts of cuts.

The damage a laceration does depends on the area of the body involved. Lacerations of the hand, for instance, frequently involve damage to the tendons or nerves. On the arms and legs, the impact that causes a laceration may be enough to break a bone. This sort of injury needs immediate medical attention because if

bone is exposed to the air it can become infected, thereby making the injury worse.

Scalp lacerations bleed profusely because of the rich blood supply but this good blood supply also means they tend to heal more quickly. Lacerations involving the eyelids or lips need careful treatment in order not to spoil the person's looks.

Internal damage

The term laceration is also applied to the damage sustained by internal organs in major injuries—lacerations of the spleen and liver for instance.

Such lacerations may occur in two ways. A violent compression such as a kick in the abdomen can cause a ragged

The blood vessels near the surface of the skin are badly crushed so there is little bleeding from this laceration.

A skin laceration

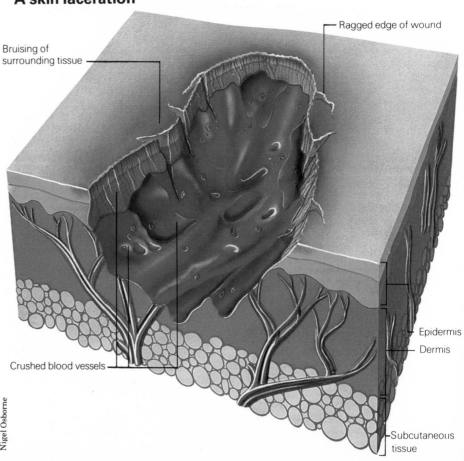

Bruising of surrounding tissue

Ragged edge of wound

Crushed blood vessels

Epidermis

Dermis

Subcutaneous tissue

Nigel Osborne

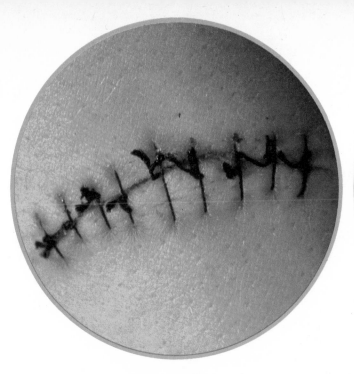
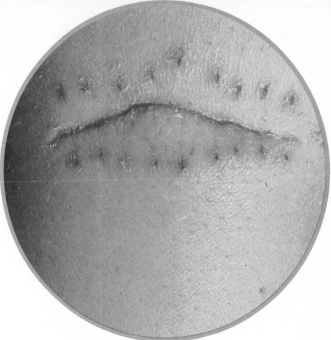

tear and profuse internal bleeding, or a sudden force as might occur in a car collision or a fall from a height might well produce a violent movement of major organs and cause a laceration.

Lacerations of the vagina can occur during a difficult birth—if the baby is face first for instance. If an episiotomy (a surgical cut across the muscle surrounding the opening of the vagina) is not done, the risk of laceration increases.

Lacerations usually have a ragged edge and the surrounding skin is bruised. They may bleed less than expected, however, because blood vessels are crushed.

Slanting blows may raise a flap of skin—this is particularly likely to happen on the scalp. Lacerations on the hands are likely to involve nerves or tendons and this will be indicated by a loss of some movement, such as bending of a finger, or an area in which feeling is lost or there is a pins and needles sensation. Prompt treatment is essential to restore function and avoid disability.

Liver and spleen lacerations are usually indicated by a severe and constant pain in the abdomen and in the case of a laceration to the spleen there may also be a pain in the shoulder. If the lacerations are severe there will be internal bleeding and the patient will be in a state of shock—the skin becoming cold and clammy and the pulse rapid and weak. Immediate treatment with blood transfusion is required.

Laceration of the vagina usually becomes evident immediately after delivery with bright red bleeding from the vagina. Vaginal tears are usually repaired immediately and there are few after-effects, but if the cervix is torn this only requires repair if bleeding persists.

This laceration needed stitches to close the edges. A neat scar was left when the stitches were removed 14 days later.

┌ TAKE CARE ┐

What to do

Minor lacerations, where there is no damage to nerves, muscles or tendons, can be cleaned at home with antiseptic.

With more serious lacerations, it is important not to do more damage than has already been done. If there is profuse bleeding, direct pressure over the wound with a gauze pad or some other clean cloth for at least ten minutes will usually control it.

A tourniquet should be avoided as it can do more harm than good in inexperienced hands. It should only be used when bleeding is life-threatening—when direct pressure on the wound makes no difference to the rate of blood loss.

Foreign bodies, such as grit or broken glass, are best left where they are until the patient can receive treatment.

If a fracture is suspected, the wound should be covered until help arrives and the limb left unmoved.

Where laceration of internal organs is suspected a doctor or ambulance should be called and the patient should not be given anything to eat or drink as he or she may need to have an anaesthetic. If the patient is suffering from shock he should be kept warm, with clothing loosened if necessary, and feet raised, injuries permitting, to maintain blood flow to vital organs.

Treatment

Minor lacerations, when no important structures have been damaged, can be treated at home. Thorough cleaning with an antiseptic solution, ensuring that any dirt is removed, is the most important step. A simple dry dressing is best as antiseptic ointments left on the wound may make it soggy, and delay healing.

If the laceration is more serious you should see your doctor or go to your local hospital's casualty department. There the wound will be examined to see if any underlying structures have been damaged. If they are not the wound is cleaned and foreign material removed. Stitches may be needed.

Where important areas have been damaged, the repair will be carried out in the operating theatre. Sometimes lacerations involve a considerable loss of skin and a skin graft may be needed to cover the defect at a later date.

If internal injuries are suspected an intravenous infusion, or drip, may be set up in case a blood transfusion is needed.

Sometimes an abdominal 'tap' will be performed. A special needle is inserted into the abdominal cavity to take a fluid sample. Liver or spleen lacerations usually produce a bloody tap.

Outlook

Most surface lacerations heal over within two weeks. Some scar tissue is inevitable but usually this tissue becomes as strong as intact skin, though it may take several months to do so.

The outlook for internal lacerations depends on the seriousness of the injury and how quickly it is treated. Blood transfusion and early surgery to stem the bleeding will prevent shock setting in.

Larynx and laryngitis

Q My husband keeps coughing and clearing his throat. He says it is a smoker's cough, but he is also hoarse. What should he do?

A It sounds as if your husband has chronic, meaning long-term, laryngitis from smoking. He will have to cut down on smoking considerably, preferably altogether, if there is to be any improvement. And because he has had the condition for some time, it is essential that he sees a doctor. There is a possibility that he might be developing cancer of the larynx, and to postpone treatment is to risk spread of a disease which is curable in its early stages.

Q I've just been hearing about someone who had his larynx removed. How can he still manage to speak?

A He is using what the experts call oesophageal speech. The oesophagus is the tube that takes food down to the stomach, and what this person does is to swallow air so that it passes down to the stomach, then belch it up, controlling the amount released, and the sounds produced, by means of the oesophagus.

With practice, people who have had their larynxes removed become skilful at this type of speech, and can express themselves perfectly clearly, although they do have a rather unusual voice.

Q Can my larynx become tired? My voice often seems to 'crack' after a lot of conversation.

A The larynx does become tired, like any other organ, especially if over-used. This means shouting, screaming or singing for too long, or talking for hours on end, especially in a dry or smoky atmosphere.

In fact, what you describe is a mild laryngitis, or irritation of the vocal cords within the larynx. The cure is to stop talking completely for a few hours. You could also try inhaling steam with a soothing aromatic preparation added. Boil the kettle, and pour the hot water into a jug or bowl. Don't try inhaling steam directly from a kettle—you could burn your mouth and throat.

The larynx is the body's 'voice box', so any disorders will affect speech. However, early treatment can usually cure even the most serious conditions involving it.

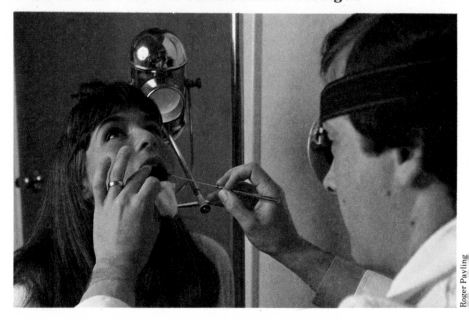

Roger Pavling

The larynx cannot be seen easily because of its position in the throat. Doctors use a special technique in order to view it.

The larynx is the body's 'voice box', containing the vocal cords, which vibrate to produce speech. As such, it is an extremely delicate instrument, but it also has a less complex function—a 'valve', guarding the entrance to the lungs.

When we eat or drink, it closes tightly, making food or liquids slide over it down into the oesophagus, which leads into the stomach. When we need to breathe in or out, it is, of course, open.

Position and structure
The larynx is placed at about the centre of the neck, at the top of the windpipe or trachea, out of sight round the 'corner' of the back of the throat.

The larynx is essentially a specialized section of the windpipe with an external sheath of cartilage. Positioned over it is the epiglottis, the flap-valve which comes down to cover the opening from the back of the throat into the larynx, known as the glottis.

The action of the epiglottis is automatically controlled by the brain, but sometimes it fails, and then liquids, or food particles go down the 'wrong way'. Unless a lump of food is so large that it sticks in one of the passages below the larynx, it will be coughed up.

The voice
Within the larynx are the vocal cords, mounted on specially shaped pieces of cartilage. Air breathed out over them makes them vibrate, which produces sound. The cartilages can move in such a way as to tighten or relax the cords, producing high- or low-pitched sound.

However, the quality of sound produced is also strongly influenced by the nature and action of the tongue, lips and jaw because the sound waves resonate or 'bounce around' the adjacent passages.

Injury to the larynx
If the larynx is damaged by injury, such as a blow, or a knife wound, it may become blocked; equally, scalding vapours, liquids or poisons can burn and irritate its lining, which may in turn cause swelling and blockage. The difficulty in breathing, and the pain of such injuries usually disable the patient severely.

Obviously the vital need is to restore the air flow to the lungs, and this is usually done in hospital. It may be possible for a tube to be passed down the trachea, creating a new, artificial passage; or it may be necessary to make a hole in the trachea below the larynx so that air can pass directly to the lungs. This is known as a tracheostomy.

Acute laryngitis
Acute laryngitis means inflammation of the larynx caused by an infection, such as

a cold or influenza, or by over-use of the voice (typically shouting or singing) or by irritation, usually through too much cigarette smoke.

The sufferer either has difficulty speaking, and has a hoarse and throaty voice, or else the voice disappears completely. There is pain in the larynx, and often tenderness is felt in the region of the larynx.

It is an irritating, but not a dangerous condition, and passes if the voice is given a complete rest—which means exactly that—i.e. not speaking for as long as it takes the condition to cure—normally a day or two. Inhaling hot, steamy air with a soothing additive can help; antibiotics help only rarely.

Chronic laryngitis
As opposed to acute, chronic means a condition occurring over a period of time. Its cause is always irritation, mostly of the sort caused by violent shouting. Tobacco, smoke and dust and over-use of the voice are again common causes.

Mild laryngitis can be relieved by inhaling a soothing preparation in boiling water, with the head covered.

Disorders of the larynx and their treatment

Disorder and cause	Symptoms	Treatment
Trauma—by any of the obvious causes, particularly burns from scalding liquids or inhaling hot steam	Sudden pain, difficulty in breathing, harsh, hoarse cough or croup	Urgent medical attention. Tracheostomy—an opening made in the windpipe may be needed to save life in severe cases
Acute laryngitis—meaning short-term hoarseness and soreness	Infection, either by a virus, or a bacteria—both of which are 'germs'	Strict voice-rest; steamy inhalations; possibly antibiotics
Chronic laryngitis—any hoarseness that lasts more than ten days—usually caused by too much smoking, dust or over-use of voice	Hoarseness, constant 'frog in the throat', occasionally tenderness in the larynx or adjacent areas	Specialist examination to exclude the possibility of cancer; strict voice-rest; removal of the irritant
Diphtheria—the severe, mainly childhood disease which has now been virtually eliminated by mass vaccination	Sore throat, fever, coughing, but the tell-tale sign is a 'web' over the larynx, caused by white blood cells and other substances produced in response to inflammation	If severe, a tracheostomy is required. Antibiotics. Immunization would have prevented the disease.
Laryngotracheo-bronchitis — caused by a virus or 'germ', occasionally by an allergy	The larynx suddenly becomes swollen. Severe cough or croup. Difficulty in breathing	Urgent hospital treatment; possibly antibiotics; steamy inhalations and moist atmosphere; tracheostomy in some cases
Benign tumour—meaning a lump or growth which will not spread. These are described as polyps or nodes, and their cause is abuse of the voice—too much singing, shouting or even loud talking, as for example in teaching	Hoarseness, which develops gradually	Removal of polyp or node. This provides a complete cure, but speech training may be required to prevent recurrence
Cancer of the larynx. The majority of cases are males aged between 50 and 69, and a high proportion of them are heavy smokers	Hoarseness becoming progressively worse over several weeks. Difficulty in breathing or swallowing. Coughing blood and often a sticky mucus which necessitates constant clearing of the throat. Pain in the throat, ears, and enlarged glands in the vicinity of the larynx usually occurs when the condition is established	Radiotherapy, or surgery if the case requires it. Recovery excellent; speech therapy, if the larynx is removed, will be needed to teach the patient to speak with the oesophagus—the tube leading down to the stomach, and to breathe through a permanent tracheostomy

Continued hoarseness may also be a symptom of cancer of the larynx. But, whatever the cause, chronic laryngitis should always be reported to a doctor.

Cancer of the larynx

This type of cancer is ten times more common in men than women, and most common in heavy smokers.

It arises in the cells of the larynx and its initial symptom is hoarseness lasting several weeks. This is followed by a dry cough and occasionally by coughing up flecks of blood, followed some weeks later by swallowing and breathing difficulties.

Untreated, it can end fatally. Detected soon enough, it is one of the cancers which can be completely cured by radiotherapy alone. More severe cases require removal of the larynx. The patient learns to speak using his oesophagus, and to breathe through a permanent tracheostomy.

Polyps and nodes

Polyps are tiny lumps attached to tissue by a stalk—like a berry. If they develop on the vocal cords as a result of a long-term vocal abuse, they cause hoarseness and a 'breathy' quality of the voice. Vocal cord nodes, (sometimes called singer's

Front and side views is of the larynx (right). The tracheotomy (below) is an emergency operation which restores breathing. An incision is made in the larynx and air pumped into the lungs.

Position and structure of the larynx

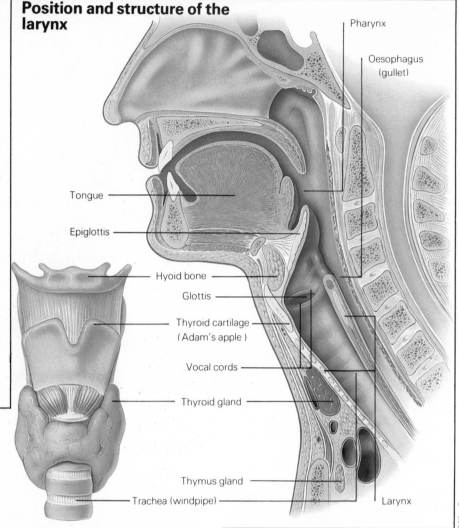

Mike Courteney

A tracheotomy

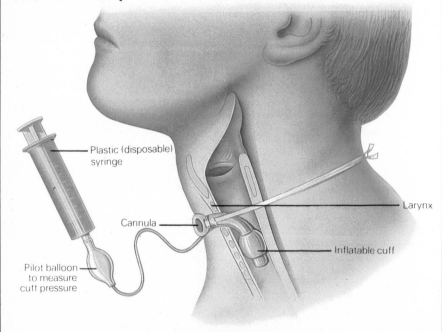

or teacher's nodes) are also lumps and develop from long-term abuse. They both need to be removed surgically.

Laryngeal diphtheria

Diphtheria used to be a feared disease, but today it has been almost eradicated by vaccination. It is still a danger, however, affecting children for the most part, but adults are not immune. It is extremely contagious.

If contracted, it tends to spread via the throat, which with the larynx becomes sore and inflamed. In response to the inflammation, a sticky, greyish, false membrane or 'skin' forms across the larynx and obstructs the airway.

Without an emergency tracheostomy, and appropriate antibiotics, given urgently, death can occur from obstruction to the airways.

Laryngotracheo-bronchitis

This is the technical name for croup, the dry, distinctive-sounding cough caused when inflammation narrows the larynx.

Q Is it true that cancer of the larynx can now be completely cured?

A Indeed it is. If cancer of the larynx is detected early enough, it can be cured with radiotherapy. This is a controlled dose of radioactive rays delivered to the area of the cancerous tumour. The malignant cells 'melt away' under their influence, and provided the cancer has not spread too far, this can completely cure the condition. In these cases there is no need to remove the whole larynx unless the condition is comparatively advanced.

Q My neighbour's three-year-old contracted croup the other day and was rushed to hospital because it was feared he would be unable to breathe. Why was this?

A Your neighbour's child was almost certainly rushed to hospital because he was so young. It is generally children under the age of five who have severe croup because the larynx is so small. If it becomes inflamed—which is what happens in croup—the airway narrows and there is a danger of suffocation. This is why emergency treatment was needed.

Q My husband's doctor has referred him to the hospital for a specialist examination of the larynx. Why should this be necessary when the doctor said that he had laryngitis?

A Your husband's doctor was behaving very properly. Laryngitis is not a serious condition, and it does clear up of its own accord if the voice is rested, but its initial symptom—hoarseness—is the same as that of cancer of the larynx. This, of course, is a serious disease, but it can be cured completely if diagnosed in its early stages.

This involves examining the larynx closely. As the organ is situated rather awkwardly, out of sight round the 'corner' of your throat, a special technique is required to view it, and a certain amount of specialist skill.

Sometimes, too, a person cannot tolerate anything near the back of the throat, in which case an anaesthetic may be required if the larynx is to be seen at all.

Richard E. Aaron/David Redfern

Such inflammation is frequently caused by a bacteria, but it may also be caused by a virus (a different sort of 'germ'). The larynx, trachea and bronchi (the airways leading to the lungs) become so inflamed and swollen and such a sticky, heavy mucus is formed that the air supply is in considerable danger of being cut off.

If the case is severe, a tracheostomy is once again necessary. Milder cases respond to oxygen, antibiotics and ensuring that the atmosphere around the patient is warm and humid—which soothes the inflamed areas.

The nerve which serves the vocal cords travels down into the chest before ascending to the larynx. So injury, or disease affecting the chest can paralyze the vocal cords or produce hoarseness.

For this reason, hoarseness is a symptom that may be difficult to interpret, and you should not be surprised, or unduly alarmed, if your doctor refers you to a hospital for simple tests.

The number of disorders involving the larynx is relatively high, but today they can all be cured if their main symptom—hoarseness—is recognized early enough. For this reason, any hoarseness lasting more than ten days should be reported to doctor without delay.

People who use their voices a great deal, like singers or teachers, are liable to get laryngitis or, in some cases, to develop polyps (tissue lumps or nodes) on their vocal cords.

Home treatment of laryngitis

If you are suffering from a short-lived hoarseness, loss of voice or from pain felt deep in the throat:

● Don't speak any more than is absolutely necessary. Seriously set about resting your voice—carry a notepad and pencil with you and write messages to other people, rather than talk to them.
● Avoid dusty or smoky atmospheres. If you smoke, give it up, if possible for good.
● Try inhaling steam from hot water in a jug or bowl. Don't inhale directly from a boiling kettle. An additive, such as lemon or honey, may make this more pleasant. A helpful dispensing chemist will advise on other preparations available.
● If you have been hoarse for more than ten days, report it to your doctor.

Lazy eye

Q I heard recently that my young cousin has a lazy eye. Is this painful?

A No. A lazy eye is totally painless because the brain is ignoring it. If pain were felt, it would be due to some other problem, such as infection or injury.

Q My daughter's hairstyle completely covers one eye. I am worried in case this causes her to develop a lazy eye. Could this happen?

A If your daughter's hair really is covering one eye all the time, then the brain will forget about that eye and it will become lazy. However, it is likely that she sweeps it out of the way most of the time, and so the eye will probably be all right. Even so, it might be worthwhile pointing out this possibility to her and she may decide to change the way she does her hair.

Q My father had a lazy eye as a child. Is this condition hereditary?

A The tendency to squint can be inherited, but provided you keep a vigilant watch for signs of the eyes deviating, and bring your child to the doctor if and when a squint does appear, then treatment can be started early and no harm will occur.

Q My son has a slight squint. Will it correct itself in time?

A No. Any sign of a squint, however slight, should be shown to a doctor before a lazy eye develops. A lazy eye is the end result of squinting and quickly becomes irreversible if left untreated.

Q Originally my son's left eye was lazy, but after treatment his right eye seemed the worse. Why was this?

A Obstructing the vision of the good eye can often lead to a temporary shift of brain effort away from that eye. Fortunately, once the patch covering the good eye has been removed—the length of treatment varies from person to person—normal vision will return.

Lazy eye is a common eye complaint among young children and is usually the result of a squint. Prompt treatment is simple and effective.

A lazy eye can still work, but the brain has chosen to ignore it. Initially, sight in the affected eye becomes poor, then, as the problem gets worse, the eye ceases to follow objects, and looks lazy because of its sluggishness and poor responses. Finally, the brain suppresses its signals altogether and the eye is effectively blind.

Causes
Amblyopia, or 'lazy eye', as it is known, usually comes on in childhood when the most common cause is a squint, brought on by a defect in the lens or muscles of the eye. For instance, a short-sighted child will strain his or her eyes to focus properly and so make the eye turn inwards.

Normally, the two eyes are moved by their muscles so that the images on the brain are identical. However, if one eye is not quite pointing at the same object as the other a squint results, producing a double image for the brain. And as the double vision is unpleasant for the brain, it chooses to ignore one image and concentrate on the other. A single image results, but at the expense of the sight of one eye, which then becomes 'lazy'.

Spectacles which have a frosted or covered lens over the good eye will make the lazy eye work and so correct the condition.

Any disease that only affects one eye will also lead to visual supremacy of the other eye and hence to a lazy eye.

Treatment and outlook
The aim of treatment, which must be carried out under the supervision of a qualified ophthalmic practitioner, is to encourage the brain to use the lazy eye and to correct the defect causing the problem. Spectacles which have a frosted or covered lens over the good eye will force the lazy eye to work. This will be adequate for most cases of lazy eye.

The only other common form of treatment is surgery, which may be used to correct a defect in the eye, such as a congenital cataract, or to correct a squint by adjusting the slack eye muscles.

Provided the underlying problem is sorted out before the age of seven, a lazy eye will usually respond fully to treatment. After this age, however, the damage is likely to be permanent as the brain has stopped laying down new nerve pathways, and if a source of information has been suppressed, nothing can be done to reverse it. For this reason, a squint in a child should be brought to the doctor's attention immediately—however slight the squint may be, the child will not grow out of it.

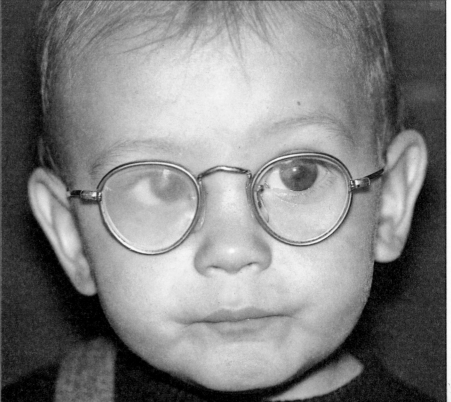

Leucorrhoea

Q Is it possible to get 'the whites' while pregnant? And, if so, is there any threat to the health of the baby before it is born?

A Vaginal thrush, which is the commonest cause of the discharge often called 'the whites', is particularly common during pregnancy. This is probably because the increased blood supply to the pelvic organs encourages the growth of the fungus that causes it. The condition does not affect the developing baby in any way. Some doctors prefer to leave it untreated until after the baby is born, because of the possibility that the pessaries that are used might irritate the womb and bring on a premature labour.

Q I have been told that I have leucorrhoea. Is it safe to go on using tampons, or is it better to use sanitary towels when I have a period?

A Tampons can be used quite safely, as long as care is taken to change them frequently. If left in for more than a few hours in this sort of situation, they will not only become offensive and unpleasant, but may also be a source of additional infection and make the condition worse.

Q My mother told me that the cotton underwear that they used to wear in the old days was much better for you than nylon, and women were not as likely to get 'the whites' as they do nowadays. Is this true?

A Nylon tights or panties do give rise to soreness and inflammation in some women, and this is often followed by the development of a vaginal discharge. Jeans or tight trousers may have a similar effect. The situation is sometimes due to an allergy to nylon, but more commonly the cause is the fact that fabrics of this kind do not allow the skin to 'breathe'. Cotton panties are more comfortable, especially in hot climates, and stockings are definitely preferable and can be worn if tights are causing the problem.

A heavy vaginal discharge, or leucorrhoea, is not a disease in itself, but a symptom—although a certain amount of discharge is perfectly normal. So what are the signs that mean you should visit your doctor?

Vaginal secretions are the body's natural way of cleansing, lubricating and guarding the vagina against infections. Like the mouth and anus, the mucous membrane of the vagina constantly sheds and replaces its cells, passing them out of the body in a mucus secretion.

It is still quite rare for young girls to be told that, as well as starting periods, they may begin to notice a transparent, slightly milky fluid, which comes from the vagina and leaves a whitish-yellowish patch on their underwear. If a young girl does not know this, she may think it is abnormal; at the same time, if she does have an abnormal discharge, she may not be able to identify it. Leucorrhoea, more commonly known as 'the whites' is not a disease in itself, but it can be a symptom.

Normal discharges

The normal secretions of the vagina are related to the menstrual cycle. They come from the cervix (neck of the womb), the walls of the vagina and the Bartholin's glands in the vaginal lips (labia majora). Vaginal and cervical secretions and mucus are present throughout the menstrual cycle in varying amounts.

Around the time of ovulation, these secretions become wetter and thinner, and about 24 hours before they ovulate many women notice that their vaginal mucus is clear and stringy. This change in the secretion makes it easier for sperm to survive in the vagina and also helps their upward movement towards the womb, increasing the chances of fertilization. Two or three days after ovulation the vaginal secretions usually become thicker and dryer, which make it more difficult for sperm to penetrate and fertilize the egg.

The slight, clear and slippery secretion from the Bartholin's gland, together with increased 'sweating' from the vaginal walls and secretions from the cervix, are signs of sexual arousal.

An increase in the level of female hormones during pregnancy produces an associated increase in vaginal secretions. Women taking the Pill may also notice an increase, because the synthetic hormones

Panties made of absorbent natural cotton fabric are more comfortable and hygienic than those made of synthetic materials.

Q I've developed a nasty discharge. How can I tell if it is VD or not?

A You can't. The only safe thing for you to do is to go to a Special Clinic for diagnosis and treatment.

Q How can you tell if a vaginal discharge is normal or not?

A It's the nature and quality of the discharge that is important, rather than the amount. But if the discharge is discoloured, smells offensive, or gives rise to soreness or irritation, the chances are that it is due to something that needs treating. You should go and see your doctor about it. If you feel embarrassed about this, you can go to a Special Clinic or Genito-Urinary Medicine Department in a hospital.

Q I have just gone on the Pill and seem to have developed thrush. Is there any connection?

A There could be. This does not always occur, but any of the contraceptive pills could make the vagina more susceptible to thrush (monilia). The condition is treatable, but if it persists, you may have to stop taking the Pill. Increased vaginal discharge can be due to the hormone oestrogen and does not necessarily indicate that you are suffering from an infection.

Q What happens at a Special Clinic?

A When you arrive, you will be given a card with your name and clinic number. You then see a doctor, who takes down your case history. This will mean being asked questions which may seem embarrassing to you, but are necessary to give the doctor some guidance before he or she can make a diagnosis. You will then be asked to undress from the waist down and lie on an examination couch. Several tests will be done: these include a cervical smear and vaginal swabs for examination under a microscope; blood and urine tests and a bi-manual pelvic examination. You may get the test result immediately, or you may have to wait and return to the clinic within the next few days. Either way, any necessary medication will then be prescribed for you.

of the Pill imitate the state of pregnancy. This kind of increased discharge production is harmless.

The quantity of discharge can vary widely from one woman to another, and is likely to increase in certain situations, particularly in those related to worry about sexual matters.

Abnormal discharges

Any discharge that is discoloured, causes soreness or irritation of the vagina or lips (vulva), or has an unpleasant smell is likely to be related to infection somewhere in the genital organs. A thin yellow discharge may be due to an infection by a parasite called trichomonas, a thick, white one may be due to thrush (moniliasis), caused by a yeast-like fungus, and brown discharges are really decomposed blood, and thus an indication of internal bleeding. This is most likely to be due to an erosion or ulceration of the neck of the womb or cervix, but it can also be caused by cancer of the womb, and must therefore always be thoroughly investigated, especially when it occurs in women between the ages of 40 and 60.

Vaginal lubrication decreases after the menopause and becomes more alkaline. Sometimes this causes irritation and there is a greater likelihood of getting infections like thrush. Hormone replacement therapy (see page 181) can also help minimize menopausal effects on vaginal secretions.

Gonorrhoea in women does not always give rise to vaginal discharge, or indeed to any other symptom, but there may be slight discharge and pain on urination.

When to see your doctor

Any heavy vaginal discharge that happens before puberty is likely to be abnormal and should be investigated.

Women should not let an unpleasant

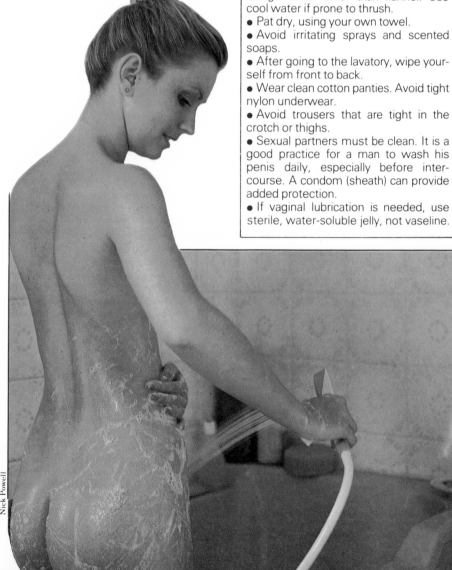

Nick Powell

Preventing abnormal discharges

- Wash your vulva and bottom regularly, using hands rather than flannel. Use cool water if prone to thrush.
- Pat dry, using your own towel.
- Avoid irritating sprays and scented soaps.
- After going to the lavatory, wipe yourself from front to back.
- Wear clean cotton panties. Avoid tight nylon underwear.
- Avoid trousers that are tight in the crotch or thighs.
- Sexual partners must be clean. It is a good practice for a man to wash his penis daily, especially before intercourse. A condom (sheath) can provide added protection.
- If vaginal lubrication is needed, use sterile, water-soluble jelly, not vaseline.

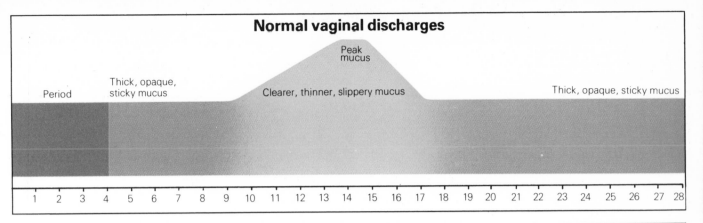

Normal vaginal discharges

Peak mucus

Period | Thick, opaque, sticky mucus | Clearer, thinner, slippery mucus | Thick, opaque, sticky mucus

1 2 3 4 5 6 7 8 9 10 11 12 13 14 15 16 17 18 19 20 21 22 23 24 25 26 27 28

Abnormal vaginal discharges

Disease or infection	Type of discharge	Symptoms	Causes
Thrush (monilia, candida albicans, yeast infection)	Thick, whitish-yellow, 'yeasty' smelling	Itchiness and soreness around vagina and vulva	Sexual intercourse with man carrying the infection. Contamination from the anus. Spontaneous occurrence as a result of chemical changes in the vagina
Trichomonas vaginalis	Thin, frothy, greenish-white or yellow, bad smelling	Irritation of vagina and vulva, making them red, itchy and inflamed. Uncomfortable sex	Sexual intercourse with man carrying the infection. Occasionally caught by sharing towels or flannels
Haemophilus vaginalis	Creamy-white or greyish, bad smelling, expecially after intercourse	Similar to trichomonas. Walls of vagina sometimes become swollen and exude pus	Sexual intercourse with man carrying the infection
Gonorrhoea	If any—slight in early stages, thin, transparent. In late stages, thick, yellowish-green	Often none. Possible irritation of genital area, frequent and burning urination	Sexual intercourse with a man who has gonorrhoea

discharge continue for more than a week before consulting a doctor about it. If you experience an unpleasant discharge you should see a doctor without delay if it is accompanied by fever or abdominal pain, if there is a possibility of venereal disease, if it is blood-stained or brown and you are not close to an expected period, or if it is accompanied by pain on passing urine, soreness, irritation or smells unpleasant.

Questions asked

The doctor will need to know about the type of discharge and recent sexual activity. An internal examination will probably be necessary (see page 84). He or she may take specimens from the vagina and the neck of the womb for laboratory analysis. It may be necessary to refer you to a specialist (venereologist or gynaecologist) for further investigation.

If the cause is straightforward the doctor will prescribe appropriate medication—tablets to take, pessaries to be inserted into the vagina or cream, these will quickly deal with the condition.

If the idea of talking to your family doctor about your sex life embarrasses you, it is not difficult nowadays to go to a Special Clinic (sometimes called a Genito-Urinary Medicine Department) where you will be treated in confidence.

Is douching necessary?

Women often wonder about the value and advisability of douching (spraying) to treat vaginal discharge. There is nothing positively in its favour, and there is a risk that any infection is as likely to be flushed upwards into the uterus as to be washed out—which is definitely undesirable. Chemical douches may cause inflammation and damage to the lining of the vagina. Similarly, it is also risky to apply antiseptic lotions and ointments to the genitalia. The best thing is to wash thoroughly, using cool water if you are prone to thrush and allowing the water to flow freely into the vagina.

Causes of trouble

Tampons sometimes give rise to soreness and discharge, particularly if they are left in for a long time. In a few women, the vagina reacts badly to them. If this applies to you, give up tampons except for special occasions and use sanitary towels instead.

Warm, sweaty, enclosed areas are the best breeding ground for bacteria and fungi and modern fashion often creates these conditions—nylon panties do not allow the skin to breathe and tight trousers or jeans increase sweating, cause chafing and increase the chances of infection and abnormal discharges.

Similarly, vaginal deodorants ('feminine hygiene sprays') and other toilet preparations may also damage the delicate skin of the vulva. They are at best unnecessary and, at worst, often harmful and so should be avoided.

Some infections, bacterial or viral, are very contagious and can be transferred through sexual contact. They can only be prevented by avoiding sex with someone who may be infected. Using condoms, spermicidal creams and pessaries can offer some protection, but they should not be depended upon.

Outlook

Vaginal discharges are not something to be ashamed of—almost every woman will have a problem of this kind some time in her life. So, if you are unsure that a discharge is abnormal, even if you think you know what the problem is, it is always worth a prompt visit to your doctor or clinic,—the sooner a discharge is treated, the easier the solution will be.

Liver and liver diseases

Q Is it only heavy consumption of alcohol that damages the liver, or is it just any amount of alcohol that causes damage?

A A regular intake of 40 gm of pure alcohol per day over a decade is a serious health hazard. In terms of drink, that is roughly equivalent to five pints of beer or 10 single measures of any spirit. However, recent evidence suggests that women are more susceptible than men, and the level at which women start suffering liver damage is probably about half this level of consumption.

Q For years I have avoided aspirin in the fear that it would damage my stomach. I now hear that the paracetamol I have been taking can damage the liver. Is this true?

A Yes. If taken in large quantities, paracetamol causes severe and sometimes irreversible damage to the liver. The usual dose of paracetamol taken for headaches—for example, two tablets four times a day, is perfectly safe.

However, death has resulted from destruction of the liver following overdose. The tragedy is that it takes several days for the damage to show itself, and by then it is generally too late to help the patient. Paracetamol is an extremely dangerous medicine to take in overdose and it is possible that some restriction to its prescription may be applied before much time passes.

Q Are there such things as liver transplants?

A Yes. Liver transplant operations have been conducted for at least 15 years.

However, it is fair to say that the success rate associated with kidney transplants has not been shared by patients receiving new livers. The survival rate in the first year is less than 25 per cent. However, in time and with improvement in the drugs used to damp down the body's tendency to reject the new organ, no doubt the operation will become more successful.

The liver has such amazing powers of regeneration that only the most persistent abuse, such as by alcohol or drugs, can really damage it. Otherwise there is comparatively little that can go wrong with this vital organ of the human body.

The liver has two vital roles: making (or processing) new chemicals, and neutralizing poisons and wastes.

The organ stands four-square in the way of every drop of blood coming away from our intestines—blood which carries all the nutrients absorbed from the food we eat. In other words, blood can only get back to the heart and lungs from the stomach by first passing through a system of veins into the liver, known as the portal system.

Location and appearance

The liver is the largest organ in the body, weighing between 1.36 and 1.81 kg (3 and 4 1b). It is tucked underneath the diaphragm, protected from damage by the lower ribs.

There are two projecting parts, or lobes, called the left and right lobes, the right being the largest, occupying the whole of the abdomen's right side. The left is smaller, reaching the mid-point of our left side. It is not usually possible to feel the liver, but when it enlarges—as a result of disease—it protrudes from behind the rib cage, and can then be felt if the abdomen is pushed in.

Functions

As in any other part of the body, it is cells that do the real work, at a microscopic level, of maintaining life's processes.

Medical science calls the 'creative' cells of the liver hepatocytes. They are specialized to handle the basic substances our bodies run on—proteins, carbohydrates and fats.

Protein processing: proteins are essential for renewal and creation of cells all over the body, for the formation of hormones, the body's chemical 'messengers', and for making enzymes, substances secreted by cells to bring about chemical change.

We eat protein in various forms, both vegetable and animal in origin, and from 'raw' proteins, the liver has to create proteins acceptable to the body by first breaking them down, and then actually re-building them.

Put simply, this process—you may hear it called synthesis—means raw proteins being 'taken' or absorbed from the blood flowing through the portal veins into the surrounding hepatocytes, being synthesized by the liver's enzymes, and then being 'handed back' in their new form. Waste, however, does not return to the bloodstream.

One of the simplest ways of detecting liver disease is by feeling the abdomen for signs of liver enlargement.

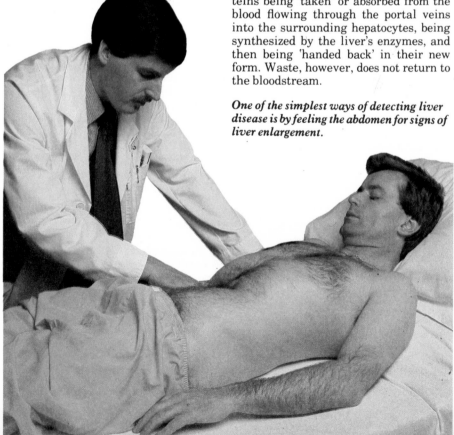

Kim Sayer

How the liver works

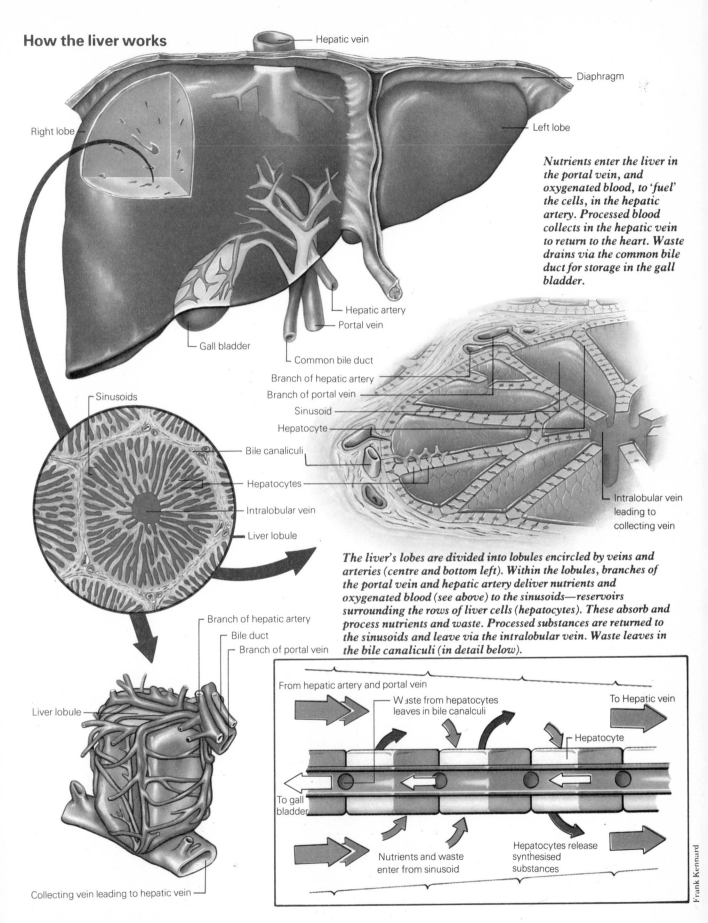

Hepatic vein

Diaphragm

Right lobe

Left lobe

Nutrients enter the liver in the portal vein, and oxygenated blood, to 'fuel' the cells, in the hepatic artery. Processed blood collects in the hepatic vein to return to the heart. Waste drains via the common bile duct for storage in the gall bladder.

Hepatic artery

Portal vein

Gall bladder

Common bile duct

Branch of hepatic artery

Branch of portal vein

Sinusoid

Hepatocyte

Hepatocytes

Intralobular vein leading to collecting vein

Sinusoids

Bile canaliculi

Hepatocytes

Intralobular vein

Liver lobule

The liver's lobes are divided into lobules encircled by veins and arteries (centre and bottom left). Within the lobules, branches of the portal vein and hepatic artery deliver nutrients and oxygenated blood (see above) to the sinusoids—reservoirs surrounding the rows of liver cells (hepatocytes). These absorb and process nutrients and waste. Processed substances are returned to the sinusoids and leave via the intralobular vein. Waste leaves in the bile canaliculi (in detail below).

Branch of hepatic artery

Bile duct

Branch of portal vein

Liver lobule

Collecting vein leading to hepatic vein

From hepatic artery and portal vein

Waste from hepatocytes leaves in bile canalculi

To Hepatic vein

Hepatocyte

To gall bladder

Nutrients and waste enter from sinusoid

Hepatocytes release synthesised substances

Frank Kennard

219

Q I heard that the liver has great powers of self-healing. Is this true?

A Yes. Liver cells are amongst the most rapidly dividing in the body, and it is well-known that if a portion of the liver is removed at an operation, then within a few weeks that piece is completely regenerated. The reason why certain cells in the body are capable of this rapid replacement and others, like nervous tissue and muscle, are not, simply isn't known.

Q I have been told that eating shellfish may cause hepatitis. Why is this?

A Shellfish such as oysters and mussels commonly grow near sewage outlets because of the rich supply of food they provide. Sewage commonly contains a virus which causes hepatitis and if this is absorbed by the shellfish, it may affect humans, especially if—like oysters—the shellfish are eaten raw.

If you go collecting mussels, check whether it is the right season. Also, leave them in fresh water for 12 hours before cooking. Mussels constantly pass fluid through their bodies, and the fresh water will help clean them.

Q I have a busy social life which involves entertaining a good deal. A few weeks ago I had hepatitis, with slight jaundice. How long must I refrain from alcohol?

A To be absolutely safe, it is wise to avoid any form of alcohol altogether for six months after the jaundice disappears. Some doctors recommend abstaining for six months after the liver tests have returned to normal. The danger of taking alcohol while the liver is inflamed is that acute liver failure may result.

Q Do health salts and bicarbonate of soda clean the liver? Should I take a spoonful of such sodas each morning?

A This will certainly do you no harm. On the other hand, it will not do you any good either. If you really want to do your liver a favour, you should avoid alcoholic excesses.

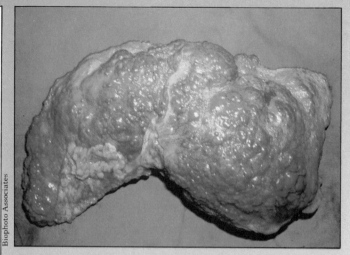

The main cause (below) and the deadly effect (left) of cirrhosis of the liver. The greater the consumption the greater the risk—and expert opinion suggests that a regular daily intake of five pints of beer, or the alcoholic equivalent, is highly dangerous.

Carbohydrate processing: these are the large class of chemical substances made of three atoms—basic building blocks of all physical matter: carbon, hydrogen and oxygen.

They occur most typically in sugary or starchy foods, and we need them for energy. Our muscles literally 'burn' sugar, or sugar-like substances whenever they work—a process assisted by oxygen. The liver plays a vital role in organizing this 'fuel' into forms which can be used.

This it does by turning carbohydrates into two forms, closely akin to pure sugar. One is 'instant energy', glucose. The other is storable energy, a substance similar to glucose and called glycogen. Sugar shortage rapidly causes brain damage, and so the level of sugar in the blood must be precisely maintained, hence the need to store sugar for times of need, such as sudden exertion, or starvation. Equally, if too much sugar is present in the blood, a hormone made by the liver can store the excess as glycogen.

Conversion of fats: fats are essential to the body, too. They are turned by the liver into forms which can actually be built into or renew existing fatty tissue, typically the subcutaneous layer beneath the skin which acts as insulation and shock absorber. Fat, in addition, is a means of storing energy.

Waste disposal: lining the veins of the liver are highly specialized cells, called Kuppfer cells after the man who identified them, which 'vacuum clean' the blood of impurities, such as bacteria. These cells also 'weed out' excess red blood cells manufactured (our bodies always over-produce these) and 'hand them across' to the hepatocytes for processing.

From all the sources mentioned—blood itself, proteins, fats but to a much lesser extent carbohydrates—by-products are produced during the rebuilding that goes on in the hepatocytes. Some, such as ammonia (produced during the breakdown

Liver diseases and their treatment

Disease and cause	Signs and symptoms	Treatment
Acute liver failure, brought on by hepatitis virus, alcohol, paracetamol poisoning	Coma and jaundice	Low protein diet, Vitamin K, blood transfusion, antibiotics, intravenous fructose
Hepatitis, caused by hepatitis virus A and B, glandular fever and other viruses	Abdominal pain, nausea, distaste for cigarettes, loss of appetite, jaundice	Bed rest. Abstinence from alcohol for at least 6 months after the jaundice has disappeared
Cirrhosis—alcohol and viral hepatitis are the best-known culprits, but there are several unknown causes	May be none until quite late in the disease when signs associated with hepatitis and finally liver coma develop	Stop drinking
Kernicterus, caused by jaundice in new-born babies	Yellowing of eyes and skin—if allowed to persist, brain damage may result	Jaundice is common in babies, but if severe should be treated by complete replacement of the blood, known as exchange transfusion

of protein), is poisonous, and the liver cells neutralize this, sending the harmless waste product urea, back into the main circulation. Fat and blood waste products pass out as bile.

The same applies to actual poisons we consume—like alcohol—and indeed medicines. If a drug is to be long-lasting in its effects, it needs either to be resistant to the liver's enzymes or to by-pass the liver completely.

What can go wrong
The liver has a marvellous capacity to renew itself—a whole lobe cut away in an operation can be replaced in a few weeks. However, on rare occasions, destruction of liver cells outstrips the rate of replacement, and this leads to acute—meaning immediate—liver failure.

The most common form is viral hepatitis, or infection by a particular type of germ. Paracetamol poisoning, due to deliberate overdosage, is also a common cause.

The results of liver failure are easy to imagine by considering the jobs the liver performs. Blood sugar falls, and without a proper level, brain damage can result. Failure of protein production, including manufacture of those which cause clotting in the blood, make the patient bleed easily; it also leads, for various technical reasons, to complications such as accumulation of fluid in the abdomen, called ascites. Failure to eliminate waste causes jaundice (the yellowish tinge given by too much bile pigment in the blood) and also coma.

Certain inborn defects can cause long-term liver problems, notably failure of the liver enzymes to remove excess bile. Known as kernicterus, the condition is most common in premature babies.

The enzymes which make and store glucose may also be deficient, causing rapid fall in the blood sugar level.

The liver sifts an enormous amount of blood, and this is why the liver is a common site for cancer to settle in after spreading from the primary site through the bloodstream. Primary liver tumours are relatively rare.

Poisons such as paracetamol and alcohol, or infections such as hepatitis can cause such rapid destruction of liver cells that repair is not possible. This then causes scarring, and if severe, cirrhosis may follow: hardening and shrinking of the liver, and failure to properly regenerate. It is eventually an irreversible condition, and the most common cause of liver failure and coma in the West.

Treatment
Liver tumours are treated either by surgery or radiotherapy. Hepatitis clears up after a few weeks if proper rest is taken. Cirrhosis, if caught early, can be slowed by a special diet and giving up alcohol.

But if liver disease has progressed to the stage where coma is likely, emergency action is required. Protein intake has to be restricted, and essential substances introduced intravenously. The blood may even have to be filtered.

Lung and lung diseases

Q **I get very short of breath when I run. Does this mean that there is something wrong with my lungs?**

A Almost certainly not. But it probably does indicate that you are not particularly fit. After you run for the first time, you may notice that you bring up a lot of phlegm. This is quite normal. If you continue to exercise, this will gradually get better and your performance will improve.

Q **Is it true that asthma can be caused by nerves?**

A No, but it is known that people who suffer from asthma tend to get worse when they become excited or upset. Although it is recognized that emotional problems are not the commonest cause of asthma, the reason why they make the condition worse is still not completely understood.

Q **My daughter has measles and a friend told me that this can also cause serious lung disease. Is she right?**

A Yes, but this also depends on other circumstances. Although the measles virus may infect the lungs, it also tends to reduce the patient's resistance to other infections and it is these that cause the trouble. If your child develops a persistent cough after the measles infection has run its course, take her to your doctor for a check-up.

Q **I have heard that having just one cigarette is sufficient to damage the delicate tissues of the lungs. Is there any truth in this?**

A It is doubtful if one cigarette is sufficient to cause any damage— it is when smoking becomes a compulsive habit that the danger arises.

Q **Does it hurt to have the inside of your lungs examined?**

A No. The instrument used is called a bronchoscope. It is a flexible string of glass fibres which can be passed down the trachea, enabling the deeper parts of the lung to be seen.

Our lungs are essential to life, yet they are frequently misused—subjected to smoking or industrial pollution. Stopping smoking, although not a cure for lung disease, is definitely a preventive measure.

The lungs have an essential purpose—it is here that a vital exchange of gases takes place, when life-maintaining oxygen is absorbed into the bloodstream from the air we breathe and waste carbon dioxide is removed from the body.

The lungs themselves form little more than a dense latticework of tubes—those containing blood mingling with another system of tubes containing air; the whole structure is suspended on a framework of elastic strands and fibres.

Of the two lungs, the right is larger as the heart takes more room on the left side. Each lung is divided into lobes, which are fed by divisions of the bronchus, leading from the trachea (windpipe). The right lung has three lobes, upper, middle and lower. The left has only two, upper and lower. The lobes are separate from one another and are marked by grooves on the surface, known as fissures. These give important information to doctors, as they can be seen on a chest X-ray. By looking carefully at their position and observing, for instance, whether they have moved up or down, they can tell whether you have suffered a collapse of part of your lung.

The entrance to the bronchus is guarded by a flap valve, the epiglottis. When we swallow, this shuts, preventing food from entering the lungs. Should this mechanism fail and food get into the trachea, violent coughing results.

How the lungs work

If the lungs were removed from the chest, they would shrink like deflated balloons. They are held open by surface tension, which is created by fluid produced by a thin lining around the lungs and the chest wall, the pleural membrane. To picture this, think of two sheets of glass. If dry and laid on top of one another, they can be easily separated, but if wet the surface tension of the water sticks the glass sheets together. The only way in which they can be separated is by sliding them apart. In the same way, as long as a thin layer of fluid separates the lungs from the chest wall, the lungs are held open. When the chest expands the lungs are pulled out and air is taken into the alveoli—millions of tiny air sacs in the lungs, each surrounded by fine capillaries (blood vessels) where the exchange of oxygen and carbon dioxide takes place.

When we exhale, the rib muscles relax gradually. If we were to relax completely, the lungs would spring back rapidly. If air gets into the space between the lungs and the chest wall, the surface tension is broken and the lung collapses.

If the lining membrane becomes inflamed or irritated it may produce an excess of fluid which accumulates in the space between the lungs and the chest. Commonly called 'fluid on the lungs', its medical description is a pleural effusion.

In the alveoli, the exchange of oxygen and carbon dioxide takes place in less than one-tenth of a second. Oxygen is taken up by haemoglobin in the blood and the red cells discharge their load of carbon dioxide back into the alveoli, to be exhaled by the lungs.

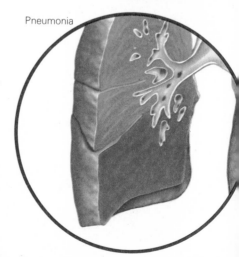

Emphysema

Pneumonia

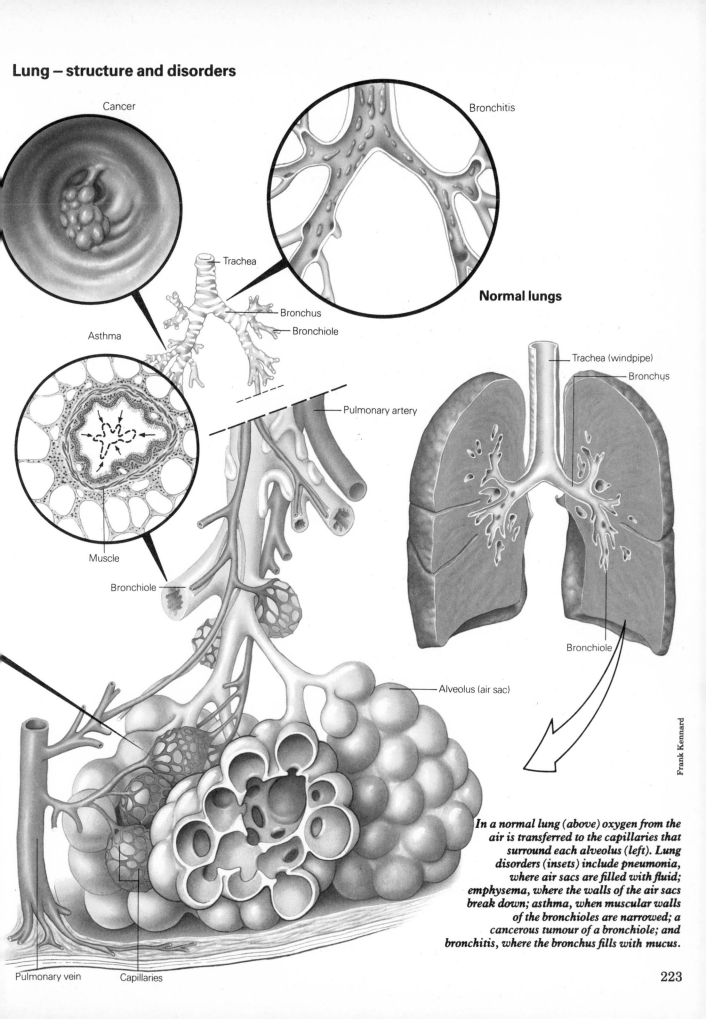

Lung – structure and disorders

Cancer

Bronchitis

Normal lungs

Trachea

Bronchus

Bronchiole

Asthma

Trachea (windpipe)

Bronchus

Pulmonary artery

Muscle

Bronchiole

Bronchiole

Alveolus (air sac)

Bronchiole

Frank Kennard

In a normal lung (above) oxygen from the air is transferred to the capillaries that surround each alveolus (left). Lung disorders (insets) include pneumonia, where air sacs are filled with fluid; emphysema, where the walls of the air sacs break down; asthma, when muscular walls of the bronchioles are narrowed; a cancerous tumour of a bronchiole; and bronchitis, where the bronchus fills with mucus.

Pulmonary vein

Capillaries

How the lungs start working

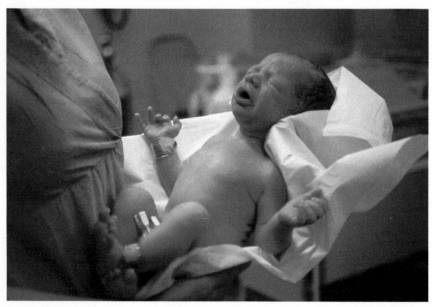

Before birth

Oxygenated blood
Deoxygenated blood
Mixed blood

After birth

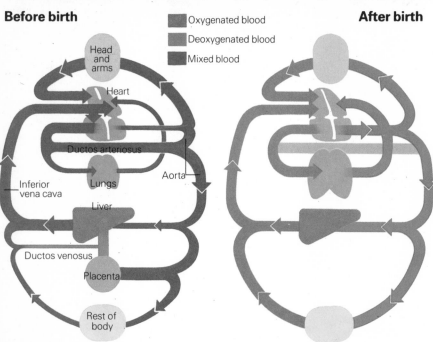

Head and arms

Heart

Ductos arteriosus

Lungs

Aorta

Inferior vena cava

Liver

Ductos venosus

Placenta

Rest of body

Breathing is started by the baby's first cry. before it is born, the foetus derives oxygen from the mother's blood via the placenta. Blood passing to the liver or the inferior vena cava via the ductus venosus is fully oxygenated, but blood in the rest of the body is mixed (being neither completely oxygenated nor deoxygenated). A large proportion of the blood reaching the atrium of the heart is shunted to the left atrium through an opening which closes after birth. Much of the blood that reaches the right ventricle goes via the ductus arteriosus. Before birth, very little blood passes through the lungs, which contain no air and are not yet functioning (left). After the child is born, its oxygen supply from the blood in the placenta is cut off, but its first cry expands the lungs so that they start to work (right). There is no more need for the ductus arteriosus, which closes naturally after a few days. If it does not, it can be corrected.

How babies begin breathing

The fact that a foetus spends the whole of its existence before the birth completely immersed in water, means that its lungs are not used. All the oxygen it needs is obtained through the mother's placenta. The lungs contain no air and all the little air sacs (alveoli) are flat, like deflated balloons. Very little blood is pumped around the lungs either and this causes a great deal of pressure on the main pump to the lungs—the right ventricle of the heart. In order to relieve this pressure, there is a connection between the pulmonary artery and the main artery of the body, the aorta. Blood is pumped from the right ventricle into the pulmonary artery and then through this special vessel, the ductus arteriosus, into the aorta.

At the moment of birth a startling transformation occurs—the placenta separates from the uterus and suddenly cuts off the previous oxygen supply. It is then that the baby takes its first breath. Breathing starts with little gasps, which are followed by a prolonged cry. Both the rapid breathing and the long cry that follows are designed by nature to expand the alveoli and hence the lungs. At first, only a few alveoli expand, but gradually more and more are brought into use, and after a few hours both lungs are fully expanded. The resistance to blood flow in the pulmonary artery falls sharply and now, instead of flowing into the aorta, blood goes through the baby's lungs.

For the first few days the ductus arteriosus is open and now blood comes back the other way from the aorta, where the pressure is high, into the pulmonary artery, where it is low. The vessel closes off naturally in the first week or so of the baby's life. However, sometimes the ductus remains open. When this happens an abnormal sound, called a murmur, is produced and can be heard with a stethoscope when the child is examined by a doctor. It is one of the congenital heart conditions loosely described as 'hole in the heart', but this can be corrected by a simple operation.

Lung diseases

In adults, bronchitis and emphysema are by far the commonest chest conditions in Western countries. Smoking is contributory to both and to some extent, pollution. In bronchitis (see pp 68-69), the bronchial tubes become chronically inflamed and produce an excess of mucus, resulting in a cough that produces phlegm.

If suffering from emphysema (see pp 132) the patient becomes breathless, but does not usually cough or bring up phlegm. Both conditions occur together.

Some impairment to breathing may also result due to obstruction in the

Lung disorders

Condition	Signs and symptoms	Causes	Treatment
Lung cancer	Weight loss, coughing blood, persistent cough, hoarseness of the voice	Smoking, exposure to asbestos dust, exposure to silica dusts (as in mining), industrial pollution	Surgical removal or radiotherapy and anti-cancer drugs. Painkillers
Chronic bronchitis	Persistent cough with phlegm for more than three months of year for two years in succession. Phlegm changes from white to yellow or green when infected	Smoking, industrial pollution, inheritance (the English have 20 times more chronic bronchitis than Scandinavians)	Stop smoking. Wear an approved face mask for dust protection in industry. Antibiotic protection may be needed in winter
Emphysema	Breathlessness. Enlargement of the chest	Smoking; long-standing chronic bronchitis, rarely may be inherited	Stop smoking, breathing exercises
Pneumonia	Cough with green or yellow phlegm, occasionally streaked with blood. Fever, sweating, loss of percussive resonance (sounds solid when tapped)	Bacteria (pneumococcus or haemophilus influenzae), viruses (whooping cough or measles). Smoking makes adults more liable	Antibiotics (ampicillin, tetracycline or co-trimoxazole). Stop smoking
Asthma	Breathlessness and wheezing	Allergies—commonly house mite or pollens, household pets, irritants. Some types aggravated by stress	Ask to be referred to a hospital unit specializing in the treatment of asthma

Smoking is known to increase man's liability to many potentially fatal or disabling lung disorders, including cancer, emphysema and bronchitis. Typically, after years of smoking, pink, healthy lungs turn black.

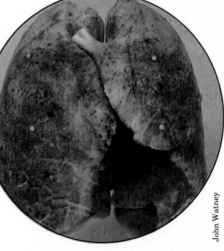

John Watney

bronchial tubes. This may be persistent and difficult to treat. Where the obstruction is easily reversed by medication or rapidly gets better by itself, the condition is called asthma.

Pneumonia is an infection of the deepest parts of the lungs, beyond the main bronchi and involves the alveoli, so that it can interfere with oxygen exchange. It caused many deaths in the days before antibiotics. The infection may be confined to only one lobe of the lung. This is called lobar pneumonia and is caused by the pneumococcus bacterium which, mercifully, is sensitive to penicillin.

Other bacteria may invade the whole lung, causing bronchopneumonia, when breathing may be severely affected. The organism responsible is the haemophilus influenzae, which is not related to the influenza virus. Unfortunately it is resistant to penicillin.

Viruses can also cause pneumonia; they also weaken the patient and make him or her more susceptible to bacterial infections. Serious bacterial pneumonia can complicate the viral diseases of childhood, such as measles, whooping cough, chickenpox and influenza. Pneumonia typically affects the weak, the sick, the very old or the very young. Adolescent or middle-aged people who develop pneumonia are often smokers.

There are several types of lung cancer, but in the last 40 years there has been an enormous increase in one type—known as a squamous carcinoma. This is certainly due to smoking, but may in part be caused by industrial pollution.

Malaise

Malaise is the enervated state that precedes some illnesses. It is the body's way of reacting to sickness and disappears when the underlying cause is cured.

Q When I am coming down with 'flu I feel terrible. Why does this happen?

A This is true malaise and it is caused by the virus spreading through the body and by the mobilization of the defence system of antibodies and white cells. The malaise makes you rest and is a natural way of helping you to help your body fight illness.

Q My small son becomes fretful and clinging before a cold. Is this normal?

A Yes, indeed. Children get a type of malaise before being ill in just the same way as adults. Comfort your sick child with lots of extra affection—he needs it even more than usual at this time.

Q Why do we have to suffer from malaise?

A Malaise is the natural reaction of the body to certain types of illness. It acts as a warning that you may be ill or about to develop a fever and it also enforces a certain amount of rest, as you feel unwilling and unable to do very much. Once the underlying illness has passed, interest and activity return.

Q My normally active teenage daughter has suddenly become very lazy and seems to be suffering from malaise. What should I do?

A Malaise which persists for more than a few days needs investigating. Your daughter should see her doctor in case she is suffering from glandular fever or even depression. You should always consult your doctor if malaise is persistent.

Q When my husband is coming down with 'flu, he ignores all the signs and simply pushes himself harder. Is he wise to act like this?

A No. Malaise is a warning sign that illness is going to occur and it is better to rest and cosset oneself than to try and beat it.

A child who is 'coming down with something' may be tired, bad-tempered and weepy for 24 to 48 hours before the actual symptoms appear. During this period of malaise, he needs extra rest and attention.

Roger Payling

Viral illnesses such as influenza are probably the most common malaise-producing conditions. There is that lack of energy, lack of interest, lack of drive which tells you that you are ill.

In children, the period before an illness when they are fretful and thought to be 'coming down with something' is a type of malaise.

Causes
When malaise occurs on its own, it nearly always heralds the onset of an acute viral or bacterial illness, such as a feverish cold or influenza. The time when the virus is spreading and reproducing throughout the body and before it actually gets to the target organs, such as the nose or throat, is the period during which the patient feels malaise.

In children malaise is caused by such illnesses as mumps, measles, German measles and chickenpox. The patient feels unwell for 24 or 48 hours before the main symptoms appear. The child knows he is sick but shows no symptoms at this stage. He may just be fretful.

Symptoms
Malaise often shows itself as a loss of appetite, sudden tiredness, a great desire to lie in bed longer than usual and then lassitude, lack of energy and drive when at work.

A child may be more clinging and weepy than usual or may sleep more. In the five-to-eight-year-old group there may be temper tantrums and general naughtiness.

These symptoms are most often followed by headache, nausea and bouts of shivering as the body temperature rises.

Treatment
Malaise is a symptom of illness, so its treatment depends entirely on the cause of the illness. For the first 24 hours there is little point in any action except keeping comfortable, taking painkillers for headache, drinking plenty of liquid and waiting. Once the condition causing the malaise has passed then the normal feeling of health and vigour returns. When malaise persists and no other symptoms occur, you should consult your doctor.

Mastectomy

Q I've always been very active and enjoy swimming and playing tennis with my family. I have just had a mastectomy; does this mean I must give up sport?

A You will have to take it easy in the first months after the operation. But when you are better, there will be nothing to stop you being as active as you were before the operation.

Some women worry that they will never be able to wear attractive swimwear again. But it is surprising how many swimsuits, and even well-cut bikinis, look fine on mastectomy patients. Instead of wearing your usual prosthesis, you may prefer to cut a sponge to shape and sew it into the cup of your swimsuit. This ensures that it stays in place while swimming. When emerging from the water, a good tip is to press your arm against the sponge so that it drains quickly.

Q I have been told that I must have chemotherapy as a follow-up to my mastectomy. I don't want to go through with it as I have heard that it makes people go totally bald. Should I refuse?

A If it is the idea of baldness that worries you, then you can put your mind at rest. Some people do lose their hair temporarily while undergoing chemotherapy, but it does grow back. In some countries, the Health Authority will provide a wig until regrowth is complete.

Q I have always loved wearing pretty underwear. Now that I have had a mastectomy, will I have to wear some horrible surgical-looking bra?

A Not at all. As long as your bras are well-fitting and do not ride up on you, your underwear can be as pretty as ever. You certainly do not have to wear a special mastectomy bra. Most good manufacturers have a wide range of good quality, pretty bras that are perfectly suitable for a prosthesis. If you are at all worried about the prosthesis slipping, you can sew ribbons diagonally across the back of the bra cup to form an X shape. The prosthesis can then be slipped in behind the ribbons.

The loss of a breast can be a distressing experience for a woman. But, given time and the support of family and friends, most women who have had mastectomies find that they can lead happy, active and fulfilling lives.

Cancer is a frightening disease wherever it strikes. Women, though, find the idea of breast cancer particularly distressing. This is partly because it is the most common kind of cancer to be suffered by women, and partly because they fear the treatment, which usually involves some form of mastectomy (breast removal).

A loving family will help a woman come to terms with life after a mastectomy.

Mastectomy is not the only option open to doctors who discover a women has breast cancer, but it is the most common solution currently used because it is felt that it provides the best chance of cure. The purpose is to stop the cancer spreading through the body by taking all the adjacent tissue from around the growth. Some doctors just remove the lump and then administer a course of radiation as a follow-up. However, this is

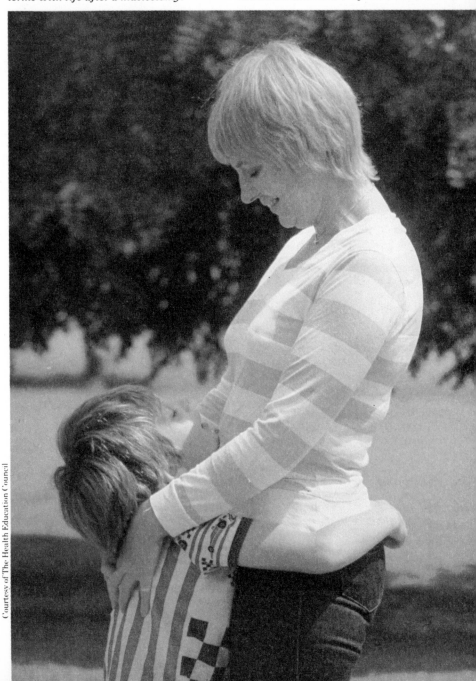

Courtesy of The Health Education Council

Q I'm healing up well after my mastectomy, but I've lost all my confidence. I am frightened of going into a shop to buy clothes in case there is a communal changing room and people see how I look. No one seems to understand. What can I do?

A Ask your doctor or the medical social worker at the hospital where you had your mastectomy to put you in touch with a mastectomy association. These groups are made up of volunteers—all of whom have had mastectomies—who are willing to give non-medical advice to others like themselves. They will put you in touch with someone near you who will come and talk to you and really understand what you are going through. She will also be able to recommend shops in your area where you will find helpful assistants and privacy in the changing rooms.

Q Is breast reconstruction possible after a mastectomy?

A It is possible, but not many doctors are prepared to do it at the moment. In some cases they remove the breast, leaving the skin and nipple intact, and insert a bag of silicone gel, as in breast augmentation. Other doctors do the breast reconstruction a year or more after the mastectomy, in which case skin has to be grafted to the area, including skin from the vagina to form a nipple. Some doctors are unhappy about the operation because it might not be as easy to detect further outbreaks of cancer.

Q I had a miserable time in hospital after my mastectomy. The false breast they offered me was the wrong shape and size, and was nothing like a real breast. They said it was all that was available on the health service. Is this true?

A No. You have been very unlucky. Unfortunately, though most are good, not all hospitals are helpful after the operation. The health service has a good range of prostheses. You could try insisting they offer you others. If this does not work, then you will have to buy one privately. It is worth spending the money to get a prosthesis you are really happy with.

After a mastectomy, a woman can still wear a low-cut dress or a swimsuit, and feel confident that she looks every bit as attractive as she did before.

of little value if the tumour has spread; doctors usually want to remove some tissue from around the breast to try to estimate the degree of spread.

Types of mastectomy
There are various kinds of mastectomy, depending on how far the disease has spread, and sometimes on the particular policy of the doctor or the hospital.

Simple mastectomy involves removal of the breast and nothing else. It is sometimes the choice of operation when the cancer seems to be confined to one lump and has not spread beyond the breast.

Modified radical mastectomy is used when the cancer has spread through the lymphatic system. In breast cancer the first glands or lymph nodes to be affected are those under the arm, and these are removed at the same time as the breast so that the spread may be checked.

Radical mastectomy is a much less common operation nowadays. It also includes removal of the pectoral muscles under the breast, which go to form the 'flap' above the armpit.

Super-radical mastectomy is the least common of all. As well as the breast, glands and pectoral muscles, the muscles of the chest wall and some chest nodes are also removed.

Simple mastectomy

When the cancer is confined to the breast, a simple mastectomy is performed.

Diagnosis

Every woman should examine her breasts regularly, and should see her doctor immediately if she notices anything different about one or both of them (see pp 66-67). Most women know that any lump found should be looked at by a doctor, but there are other changes that should also be reported, such as a blood stained discharge from a nipple, one nipple becoming inverted, puckering or dimpling of the skin, or a change in size or shape of the breast. Sometimes a doctor can be reassuring about the symptoms; at other times he will send the woman to be checked at a hospital or clinic.

If the woman has a lump on her breast, a needle biopsy may be performed. This often reveals the lump to be a fluid filled cyst, which is then drawn off through the needle. If the lump is solid, it still might be possible, with a local anaesthetic, to take out a core of the solid material and to test it to see whether there are any cancer cells. When this is not possible, it is usually decided to perform a surgical biopsy. For this, the patient is admitted to hospital and, under general anaesthetic, a small cut is made in the breast, some

tissue is removed and analyzed immediately. More than 85 per cent of lumps turn out to be benign. In the remainder of cases, it is usually decided to perform a mastectomy.

A common fear among women is that they will go in for a surgical biopsy and wake up minus a breast. Fortunately, however, this does not have to happen. Although many women do sign a consent form giving the doctor the right to proceed with the mastectomy in the event of cancerous cells being found, they are quite within their rights to ask the surgeon to wait and tell them the results of the test so that they can prepare for the operation, and adjust to the idea of having a breast removed.

The operation

Once consent has been given, the biopsy cut will be lengthened, and the surgeon will remove the breast and any associated tissue that is affected or may be affected. The cut is then stitched, and when it is healed, a single scar remains which gradually fades to a thin line. To promote healing a tube to drain liquid from the site of the operation is inserted and will

be there when the patient wakes up.

The patient is usually encouraged to be up and about the day after the operation, although she will be expected to stay in hospital for another ten days. In the majority of cases the wound is healed within six weeks, although it could take a good three months before the woman feels fully recovered.

Often there will be post-operative follow-up tests, and radiotherapy or chemotherapy may also be suggested. While most doctors try to explain what they must do and why, some are too busy or else do not realize that their patient might be worried or frightened. Some women have lots of questions they want to ask the doctor both before and after the operation, but forget them all when they are talking to him or her. It is worth writing down every single worrying question—no question is silly or unimportant—and going through them one by one with the doctor. Many women are in a state of shock when they are told that they must have a mastectomy, and also after the operation is performed. This can mean that they do not take in what the doctor tells them, or else they do not

Radical mastectomy

The wound is then stitched and the scar eventually fades to a thin line.

Where the disease has spread, a more extensive operation may be necessary.

This includes removal of the underarm lymph glands and some pectoral muscles.

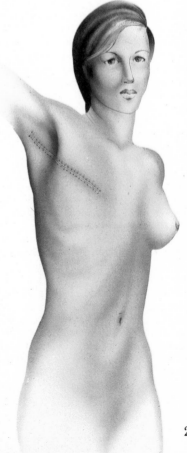

Aziz Khan

229

The range of prostheses (false breasts) available today has improved to such an extent that now a woman can be fitted with one that is exactly the same size, shape and weight as her own breast. The prosthesis can be easily slipped into the cup of a well-fitting bra and is totally undetectable under normal clothing.

remember it later. It is much better, therefore, if they can take someone with them so that afterwards they both can go over what the doctor said.

Psychological effects

The immediate response to the loss of a breast is one of grief. Coming to terms with a mastectomy has to include a period of mourning for the breast, and this cannot be hurried up by well-meaning people telling the patient to 'cheer up and look on the bright side'.

The grief often comes after the woman has been released from hospital. The shock of the brush with cancer has subsided, the ward routine is no longer there, and neither are the medical staff and the other patients who have been helping to cushion the final blow. And it is in her own home that the woman often feels most desolate. At this time, most women

need to talk about their feelings. They need to be reassured by husband, family and friends that they are loved and wanted more than ever before. Meeting and talking to other women who have had mastectomies performed and now lead full and happy lives is also a great help.

The problem worrying most women initially is how the operation will affect their sex lives. Husbands or lovers may also share the worry. The fact is that most people find it draws couples closer together. Some relationships do break up, but rarely good ones. If a couple has problems, the mastectomy may be used to end the relationship. However, many single women go on to marry or have lovers and most marriages do survive.

Learning to cope

A woman with a strongly supportive family is well on the way to learning to cope with her mastectomy. But there are also practical considerations which are very important.

After the operation, the woman is usually given a lightweight false breast of the same size and shape as her own. This is comfortable and easy to wear while the scar is healing, as it protects the incision. It is often a good idea to wear it

at night as well, inserted into a sleep-bra, to protect against accidental knocks in the first weeks after the operation, and to help the body adjust to the sudden loss of the breast.

When the scar is fully healed, the woman should think about getting a more permanent false breast. There are now many good types available. The most popular kind is made of silicone gel, similar to that used for breast implants, and looks and feels very much like a real breast. All of the false breasts, or prostheses as they are also called, come in all shapes and sizes so that a good match can be made with the woman's own breast. When dressed, it is impossible to tell that the woman has had a mastectomy.

There are special bras made for mastectomy patients, with pockets for the prostheses. Most women, however, find that a normal, expertly-fitted bra will do just as well.

All clothes can be as pretty and feminine as before, and it often does a woman's confidence good to go out and buy some new clothes after she has recovered from the operation, if she can afford to; she can prove to herself that she is as attractive as she was before.

Mastication

Q As a child, I was told to chew my food 32 times. Is this necessary?

A Not really. There is no magic in the number 32 except that it corresponds to the number of teeth present in the full adult set. No doubt the idea was that food should be chewed once for each tooth. However, it is important to chew your food well as this makes swallowing easier and helps the digestive enzymes in the alimentary canal work more efficiently.

Q Do babies have to learn to chew or do they do it instinctively?

A Babies are born with a sucking reflex as they are expected to take milk from their mother's breast. Teeth do not develop until later and as babies come on to solid food they may need to be told to chew it.

Q I have problems chewing my food as my mouth is very dry. What could cause this?

A Older people sometimes suffer from a dry mouth because the salivary glands become less efficient with age. Other causes may be blockage in one of the salivary glands, vitamin B deficiency, the effect of some drugs and smoking.

Q I have to have dentures. Will I be able to chew as efficiently as if I had my natural teeth?

A Today's dentures are so well fitting that you should be able to eat most things. You may find you are not able to eat very sticky foods like toffee but your basic diet should cause you no problem. If your dentures do slip, buy a dental fixative from your chemist.

Q My young son bolts his food. Should I try and persuade him to eat more slowly?

A Some children, eager to play, do gobble their food. In adults this would probably cause indigestion but children seem to get away with it. However, it might be wise to try and slow him down, if only to get him to appreciate what you've cooked.

Mastication, or chewing, is an everyday action we take for granted. But it involves a series of facial muscles working in conjunction with the teeth and salivary glands.

Mastication, the medical word for chewing, is the first stage in the long process of digestion. The purpose of chewing and biting is to reduce food to pieces that can be swallowed easily, and to create a large surface area on which enzymes can begin their work of chemically breaking down the substances that can be used by the body for its maintenance.

The teeth

The full complement of adult teeth numbers 32. The eight incisors are shaped like chisels to cut food into small pieces; the four canines are longer and are used for tearing; the eight pre-molars slice food by shearing the top ones against those in the lower jaw; the twelve molars have flattened surfaces and grind food into a pulp.

Biting is controlled by two muscles, the masseter and the temporalis, moving in conjunction. The masseter stretches from the cheek-bones to the base of the lower jaw and raises the lower jaw, while the temporalis on the side of the head clenches the teeth.

The chewing process

Chewing consists of three actions—positioning the food in the mouth (assisted by the tongue), side-to-side grinding movements and back-and-forth grinding movements. Contractions of muscles called the buccinators compress the cheeks and position the food in the mouth. The internal pterygoid muscles move the jaw sideways while the external pterygoids move it back and forth.

The salivary glands

As we chew, three pairs of salivary glands come into action and secrete saliva. It lubricates food so that it can be swallowed easily and it enables us to taste our food since our taste-buds will not work on dry substances. Saliva also contains the enzyme ptyalin which begins the digestion of starches in food by converting them into more simple sugars. We secrete about three pints of saliva a day.

Once food has been sufficiently chewed and lubricated it is pushed to the back of the mouth by the tongue and enters the oesophagus to begin its journey through the alimentary tract.

When we chew, teeth break down the food, facial muscles control the lower jaw and salivary glands secrete a digestive enzyme.

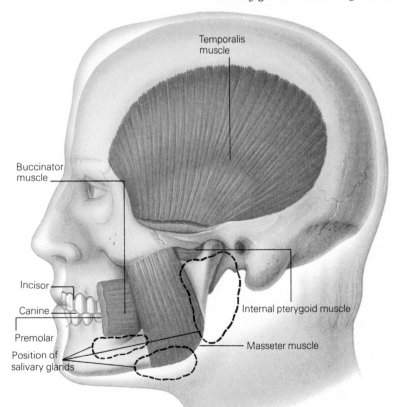

Temporalis muscle

Buccinator muscle

Incisor

Canine

Premolar

Position of salivary glands

Internal pterygoid muscle

Masseter muscle

Mike Courtney

Mastitis

Q If I get mastitis while still feeding my baby, can the milk become infected or go off?

A No. The breast that has become infected will probably be too tender for you to feed the baby from, but the milk itself is not likely to be harmful. It is best to avoid feeding from this breast as it will inflame it further but there is no reason why the baby should not continue to use the other side.

Q I got mastitis after having my last baby. The lady in the next bed told me I should bind myself up, but my sister told me that was the worst possible thing to do. Which was right?

A Neither was absolutely right. Giving your breasts firm support if you have mastitis, either by binding them up or with a bra which gives strong support, will prevent the inflamed tissues from being stretched and thus ease the discomfort. On the other hand, if they are too tightly bound up this will put too much pressure on the inflamed tissues and, as a result, increase the pain.

Q I have been worried for some time about the side-effects of taking the Pill. Will it make me more likely to get lumps in my breasts from mastitis or cancer?

A There is no evidence that taking the Pill causes either of these conditions. In fact, some people think that the hormones in the Pill reduce the chance of developing chronic mastitis.

Q I am having a baby in three months' time and naturally I want to do everything I can to prevent mastitis. Is there any particular type of bra I should wear that can help?

A Adequate support for your breasts, both during the late stages of pregnancy and while you are breast feeding, is what is important. So any bra that gives you that is going to help. However, avoid bras with waterproof linings as they trap any milk which leaks out and increase the chance of soreness.

At some point in their lives, many women suffer from mastitis or inflammation of the breast. If this should happen to you, your best plan is to go to your doctor at once. Prompt investigation and treatment are needed to relieve discomfort and resolve any fears.

This condition has several forms and it is probably so common because of the structure of the breast and the purpose it serves. The breast is a sponge-like structure made up of thousands of sac-like glands or alveoli which can manufacture milk. Each gland forms a small, totally enclosed pocket and if bacteria get in from outside, it forms an ideal breeding ground for bacteria which can feed off the milk the breast secretes.

There are two main types of mastitis, acute and chronic. Though both cause inflammation, pain and tenderness in the breast, they are totally different in cause, features and treatment.

Acute or infective mastitis
This occurs when bacteria get into the breast and multiply. The breast is protected from infection by the skin enclosing it but infection can enter through

How acute mastitis affects the breast

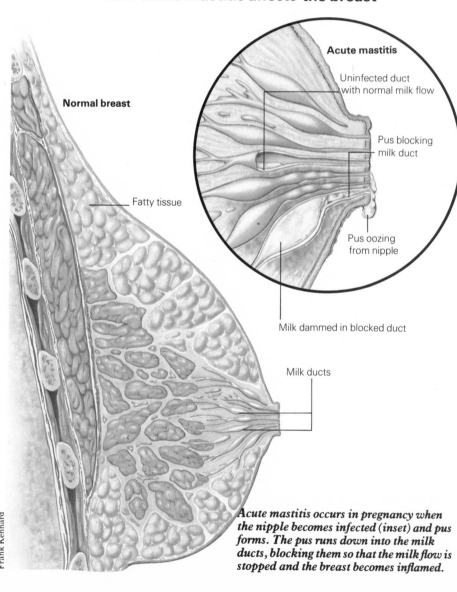

Normal breast

Fatty tissue

Acute mastitis

Uninfected duct with normal milk flow

Pus blocking milk duct

Pus oozing from nipple

Milk dammed in blocked duct

Milk ducts

Frank Kennard

Acute mastitis occurs in pregnancy when the nipple becomes infected (inset) and pus forms. The pus runs down into the milk ducts, blocking them so that the milk flow is stopped and the breast becomes inflamed.

Prevention of puerperal mastitis

During pregnancy

● In the later stages, wear a bra which gives you firm support, even if you do not normally wear one.

● In the last month, rub the nipples with a towel for one or two minutes after bathing. This hardens the skin so that it is ready for feeding.

● If nipples turn inwards (inverted), squeeze them out gently once or twice a day. If this has little effect, you should wear shells (small plastic or glass shields) inside your bra.

During breast feeding

● Wash the nipples thoroughly after each feed using water alone. Soap, spirit, antiseptic creams and ointments can all interfere with the skin's natural secretions.

● Avoid soreness by not allowing the baby to tug at the nipples and using each breast alternately.

● Wear a firm bra but avoid waterproof liners which trap milk leaks.

● Leave your bra off for some of the day as constant rubbing can irritate nipples and make them sore.

● Express (squeeze out) any excess milk either by hand or with a breast pump as engorged breasts and retained milk increase the risk of infection.

Susan Griggs

a break in the skin, usually a small wound or a crack or fissure in the area of the nipples.

This is particularly likely to occur during breast feeding. The baby can suck too hard, causing the skin of the nipple to become raw and open, or accidentally scratch the nipple when grasping the breast during feeding.

Sometimes infection develops during breast feeding without there being any wound or sore. This is because the openings of the milk ducts in the nipple are much wider and more exposed than normal. So it is relatively easy for any bacteria on the nipple to get into the ducts. They spread down the ducts and, as each collects milk from all the glands in a particular section of the breast, the whole segment may become infected.

When mastitis occurs while breast feeding, it is often called puerperal mastitis. Infection is first indicated by tenderness in the nipple and area behind it. Often it is too painful to have the baby sucking on it. Then the breast begins to ache and a hard, very tender red area develops. Pus may come out of the nipple, either on its own or mixed with the milk. Sometimes infection develops in a seg-

ment of the body of the breast rather than the nipple area. If treatment is delayed an abscess may develop in the breast tissue. It may be necessary to drain this by making an incision under anaesthetic. Any illness following childbirth should be avoided at all costs as the mother needs all her resources at this time. Antibiotics, usually penicillin, are used to kill off the infecting bacteria. Hot flannels around the breast will help ease discomfort but pain-killing drugs may be needed too.

It is usually possible to resume breast feeding once the mastitis has subsided and there are no permanent after-effects or an increased likelihood of cancer developing later.

Chronic mastitis

This is rather inappropriately named as the condition is not serious, although it is certainly a nuisance and can be extremely worrying as women may associate the symptoms with cancer.

It usually occurs in women in their thirties and forties and seems to be related to changes in the amount of hormones from the ovaries circulating in the blood. It is a mystery why some

women develop it and others do not and no connections have been established between chronic mastitis and breast feeding, contraceptive pills or breast stimulation during love-making.

The symptoms are either a dull aching pain, most marked before and during menstruation, or a lump. It is essential to see the doctor immediately to ensure these symptoms do not indicate something serious. A doctor should be able to make a positive diagnosis by examination alone but a patient cannot.

Any doubts can be resolved by mammography involving either X-rays or infrared rays. As a final resort, a small biopsy operation is performed to remove a sample of tissue for examination under a microscope. If the lump is caused by an underlying cyst, which occasionally results from mumps, this is usually removed as a precautionary measure by a minor surgical procedure which leaves only a very small scar.

There is no specific drug treatment for chronic mastitis. The condition tends to come and go of its own accord and may disappear altogether. However, a treatment involving making changes in the hormone level is under investigation.

Measles

Q My mother insists we put our child with measles in strict isolation, and his brother in quarantine. Is this necessary?

A It is neither necessary, nor even useful. In the past, before immunization and antibiotics, people were indeed put into isolation if they caught measles. But immunization gives excellent, if not complete protection (you can have mild measles, even after vaccination); and modern antibiotics have reduced the dangers of complications.

In any case, isolation and quarantine would have to be far more thorough than is possible in the home if it is to have any effect—the disease is extremely catching.

If a child has measles, the precautions are simply a question of staying away from school for at least 14 days after the rash appears.

A child who has been in contact—however brief—with a measles case should be kept away from school for at least 16 days. This represents the maximum time usually taken for the virus to become established in the body (the incubation period, plus an extra couple of days for safety).

Q How do you identify measles for sure when so many illnesses that children have produce a rash or spots?

A The only way is to look for what are known as Koplik's spots (named after the man who first identified them). These appear in the mouth (actually on the inner lining of the cheeks) on the third day after the initial symptoms (feverishness and runny nose) appear. They look like grains of salt surrounded by a rosy—slightly inflamed—area.

Q I can't remember whether or not I had measles as a child. As I'm hoping to have a baby soon, should I consider being immunized at this stage?

A Most doctors would not recommend immunization in your case, especially if there is a chance that you are already pregnant—the vaccine could harm the developing baby. In any case, measles is not nearly so harmful in pregnancy as German measles.

This most common of childhood illnesses may not always be harmless and routine. But measles and its possible complications can be avoided simply by being immunized against the disease.

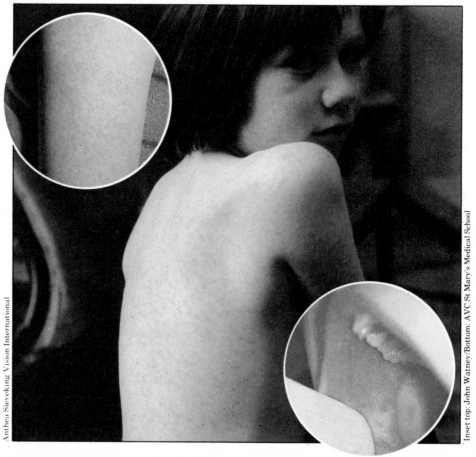

Anthea Sieveking Vision International

Inset top: John Watney/Bottom: AVC St Mary's Medical School

Most children catch measles—for it is a virus (a type of 'germ') which is passed about—between the ages of one and six. A baby has what is known as natural immunity, or inborn resistance, inherited from the mother, which gives protection for several months.

From the age of about one year, all children are at risk. Epidemics, or mass outbreaks tend to occur, for reasons not fully understood, during the spring every two or three years.

In older children and adults, measles is rare. Having the disease once provides immunity for life—you will not get it again—and it is highly infectious—easily caught—so that few escape it.

Measles in perspective

In most communities of the western world (where measles has been established for centuries), the condition is mild, and hardly ever dangerous. The only worry is its complications.

Measles spots can appear all over the body in severe cases. But the most common tell-tale spots are on the back, on the arms and those that appear inside the mouth, called Koplik's spots.

While the virus has a hold, the body is weak and particularly susceptible to a variety of infections in such sites as the ears, lungs and eyes.

These are what is known as bacterial—caused by germs which are different in nature from the measles virus. As such, they can be controlled with antibiotics—drugs which kill bacteria—but this may, in a few cases, require hospital admission. All such problems can be avoided if children are immunized.

Measles should not be confused with German measles, whose scientific name is *rubella*. Rubella is a milder infection, less catching. Adults are likely to be affected simply as a result of having escaped it as

Q **I know of a child who was immunized against measles, then caught it three years later. How can this occur?**

A It occurs because the measles vaccine currently in use does not give 100 per cent protection—indeed there are several vaccines of which the same is true. Its usefulness is that if an immunized child does have measles, the attack is extremely mild, and there is no danger of complications.

Q **Could a new strain of measles appear which might overcome the effectiveness of the usual vaccine?**

A It is highly unlikely, mainly because the measles virus has been living for centuries among humans without changing. In addition, the measles 'bug' or 'germ' is of a particular type known as a virus. Compared with bacteria, which cause infections such as pneumonia, viruses are simple organisms, which do not have the ability to change themselves in order to overcome immunization.

Q **I've heard that measles is becoming less and less severe. Why should we bother with immunization in this case?**

A In fact, measles is no less potent a virus than it ever was. The only thing that has changed is the severity of the attacks, and this is on account of widespread immunization.

Although the measles virus in itself is rarely dangerous, the complication it can cause may be. Long-term lung trouble, deafness, even blindness could arise if such complications it can cause may be untreated. Apart from saving a good deal of misery from the illness itself, immunization is therefore a worthwhile precaution.

Q **I've heard measles can lead to insanity. Is this true?**

A A rare, and dangerous complication of measles is encephalitis—inflammation of certain parts of the brain. A tiny proportion of these cases do, on recovery, suffer from changes of mood and personality, which could, indeed be regarded as insanity.

children, and in pregnancy it is a potential menace, capable of deforming the child. Measles, by contrast, is scarcely encountered in pregnancy and in any case is less harmful to expectant mothers.

First signs

The virus is passed from person to person, like many others, on the tiny droplets of moisture we constantly breathe out and in. Following contact with an infected person, there are no symptoms for generally between seven and 12 days, during which the virus is incubating or multiplying in the cells of the throat and passages leading down to the lungs.

Then follow the two stages of measles proper. The first is known as the catarrhal stage, because the virus is confined to the mucous membranes (the 'linings') of the eyes, nose and mouth. The patient develops what appears to be a heavy cold with a husky cough. The nose is runny with catarrh, and the eyes are red and watery. There may even be a fine, red rash which lasts a few hours, then disappears.

A mother usually notices the child is upset and 'off colour'. Most children have a temperature rising to 38°C (100.4°F). There is loss of appetite and possible sickness and diarrhoea.

If the inside of the mouth is examined at this stage, tiny, white spots are seen lining the cheeks. Known as Koplik's

A darkened room helps to ease the irritation of conjunctivitis that comes with measles.

spots (after the man who first identified them) these identifying spots are unique to measles.

In this initial period, some have no fever at all, and the other symptoms may be extremely mild.

The rash

On the third or fourth day, (occasionally in five to seven days), the temperature falls and the rash appears. This is typically a dusky, red colour, with slightly raised spots which group together in patches to give the blotchy appearance typical of measles.

It starts to form behind the ears, then spreads to the neck and forehead, eventually covering the face and trunk, and, in severe cases, the limbs. This usually happens over a period of about 24 hours. There is only slight itching, sometimes none at all. Over the next three days, the rash disappears in the order in which it appeared. A brownish staining of the skin remains, which usually disappears with peeling of the skin.

After the rash starts to appear—and on the same day—the temperature rises once more. It is the time when the patient feels most ill, and in severe cases absolutely wretched. The cough and inflammation of the eyes are at their worst, light is likely to be irritating to the eyes, and complications, if they are to occur, will begin to develop now.

After the rash has begun to fade, most patients recover speedily without any long-term side-effects.

Tom Belshaw

The dangers

In a tiny minority of cases, the patient just happens to have a low resistance to measles. In these, the temperature rises uncontrollably, and there is the danger of bleeding, either in the skin affected by the rash, or in certain organs. Known as haemorrhagic measles, it needs hospital treatment if the patient's life is to be saved. Tiny haemorrhages sometimes occur in the rash of mild measles, and these should cause no alarm. But if bleeding is widespread, a doctor should be called without delay.

Ear and lung infection

The measles virus temporarily destroys the lining of the passage leading to the lungs, and paves the way for bacterial infection of adjoining or connected areas such as the ears and lungs. Some cases develop infection of the middle ear (roughly halfway into the ear), with earache and a discharge of pus. Report this to a doctor without delay—antibiotics will prevent any spread of the infection and clear it up.

Measles-bronchitis

A chesty or wheezy cough developing in a measles patient is a sign of bronchitis, or chest infection. Some coughing is normal enough, but if it produces phlegm and is a wheezing one, rather than dry, hacking and unproductive, antibiotics are essential to prevent lung damage. Once again, do not delay in calling the doctor so

Courtesy of Glaxo

that proper treatment is given.

Severe, untreated cases sometimes develop chronic (long-term) lung infection known as bronchiectasis. Although the condition can be treated, prevention is doubly worthwhile as it

The vaccination trail starts here in the laboratory where measles viruses are cultured (inset). The viruses are then made into vaccine doses like the one being injected into this child's leg.

Home treatment of measles

- Mild painkillers—aspirin or paracetamol—can help the patient to deal with the fever.
- A regular mouthwash if the mouth is sore from infection.
- Plenty of fluids to drink during feverish periods.
- Calamine lotion is ideal to apply to the spots if they itch.
- An eyeshade, or the curtains drawn, for irritated eyes.
- A simple syrup for the cough—your chemist will advise.
- Persistent ear-ache, a chesty cough, widespread bleeding of the spots or unexpected drowsiness must be quickly reported to the doctor.
- A light diet during the recovery period, with plenty of glucose-filled drinks to give the patient energy.

The simple, old-fashioned remedy of calamine lotion dabbed on itchy spots with a cotton wool ball is the best way to soothe the irritation.

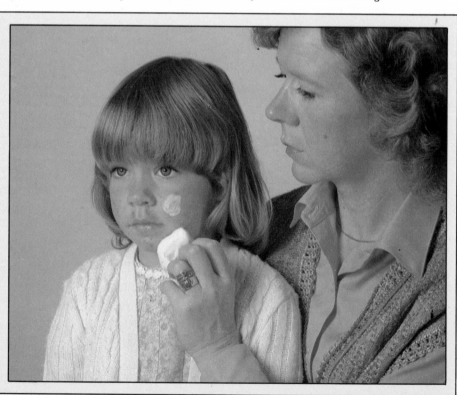

Tom Belshaw

236

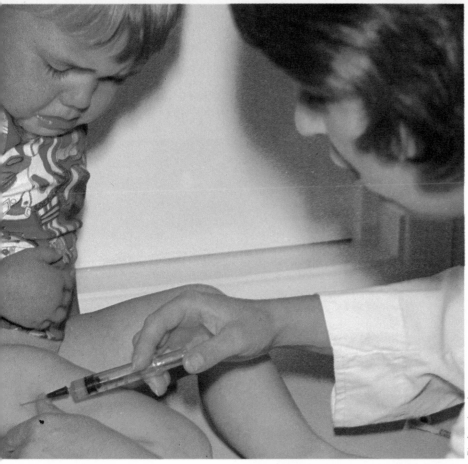

Treatment

Mild measles needs no treatment, other than appropriate home nursing. The patient will retire to bed when feeling too ill to stay up. This is quite normal and should not be cause for alarm.

Some doctors give antibiotics to all cases, others reserve them for the most severe, and for complications.

Severe cases need intensive home nursing and plenty of reassurance that they will come to no harm; but even these need only retire to bed if feeling too poorly for anything else.

Outlook

One attack of measles gives life-long immunity, and recovery is complete, with no after-effects, except when patients are unfortunate enough to suffer from one or two of the most severe complications.

In view of this, immunization makes overwhelming sense, especially if a child is ill or delicate. It involves a single injection, and about ten days later, the possibility of a slight rash and fever which is not nearly as bad as in normal measles. In measles epidemics, patients already ill can be protected with an injection of gamma globulin; one of the best defence weapons against infection.

Biophoto Associates

is one that can retard growth.

In young children, measles sometimes leads to bacterial infection of the larynx, the 'voice box' situated round the 'corner' of the throat. The passage of air is obstructed, and a 'croupy', or hoarse, croaking cough is produced. This is a serious complication: call the doctor without delay.

Mild conjunctivitis—irritation (producing pinkness) of the 'whites' of the eyes—is normal in measles. If there is bacterial infection as well, the discharge produced is thick and sticky—containing pus and other matter. Untreated, this can cause scarring of the conjunctiva and blindness. Again, call the doctor if this condition develops.

Encephalitis

This was the most dreaded complication of measles. It means inflammation of the brain and central nervous system as a response to the virus's presence; the symptoms are drowsiness, hallucination and delirium occurring about ten days into the illness. In these times of immunization it is rare—developing in one in 1000 cases—but it needs urgent hospital treatment if it does develop because the consequences are so severe.

The virus that causes measles (right) takes 12 days to incubate in the nose, mouth and eyes after contact has been made.

CNRI/Vision International

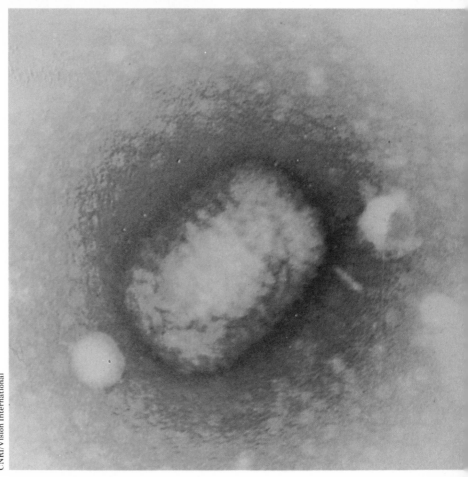

Megacolon

Q My son has not had a bowel movement for a couple of days. When should I worry that he might be retaining his faeces and be getting megacolon?

A It is quite normal for children and adults to open their bowels only every few days. The main way you can help your child is not to worry about bowel movements unless he complains of abdominal pain, pain at the anus, diarrhoea, or unless he is generally feeling unwell.

Q Does megacolon happen to older people?

A Occasionally, a very painful condition of the anus such as piles or a torn lining of the anus can prevent a person from passing a motion. The person is so afraid of the pain caused by opening the bowels that he 'holds on'. This retention of faeces builds up and the lower bowel expands. The method is to treat and relieve the pain of the original condition, and the chronic constipation will subside. Megacolon may also occur in severe forms of colitis (inflammation of the colon).

Q If I give my child plenty of roughage-rich foods will it prevent megacolon or will it do him any harm?

A Roughage helps to soften the stool by providing bulk with some absorbed water. It cannot do harm, although it may not appear to do much good at first, if the child already has accumulated large quantities of hard faeces in the colon from refusing to pass a motion. It is wise to have a diet with a large roughage content as this prevents constipation, which with complications could sometimes lead to megacolon.

Q Does a furred tongue and bad breath mean constipation and possibly megacolon?

A Although these symptoms might sometimes occur with constipation, you should never presume just because they are present that the person has constipation which might lead to megacolon.

Severe constipation in a young child can be extremely distressing, but with the help of understanding parents it can normally be easily resolved.

A mother should not try to force her child to pass a daily motion—she should let nature take its course.

Megacolon is a rare condition in which most of the large intestine (colon) becomes enlarged and full of faeces.

It can be very severe so that the abdomen becomes hugely swollen and the peristaltic or 'squeezing' movements of the bowel are clearly seen below the skin.

Severe constipation can also cause megacolon in an adult. This is when, for example, there is a tear in the lining of the anus or piles and severe pain prevents opening of the bowels.

Causes

There are two main causes. The first and most common cause of this distension of the bowel is when a child refuses to open his or her bowels and then retains the faeces in his lower bowel for several weeks. The basis for this chronic constipation is almost always a psychological problem—the most common one being a difficulty in the parent-child relationship. A mother cannot force her child 'to perform' and he or she enjoys refusing to do so.

The second cause is a rare congenital condition known as Hirschsprung's disease, which is brought about by abnormal peristalsis or movement waves of the bowel, caused by poor nerve stimulation in a part of the muscular wall of the bowel. The faeces are not carried efficiently towards the anus and therefore collect in the colon.

The condition varies from weight loss and vomiting in the infant, which can be severe, to chronic constipation with faecal soiling in the older child. The diagnosis is usually made by barium X-rays and by taking a biopsy or small piece of the inside of the lower bowel and examining it for particular nerve cells. Absence of these tend to suggest the presence of Hirschsprung's disease.

Treatment and outlook

Constipation which started some time after birth can only be treated effectively if all the pressures and anxieties about bowel action are removed. The condition will right itself if there is a relaxed atmosphere at home.

With Hirschsprung's disease surgical removal of the inefficient part of the large bowel often proves necessary.

Menstruation

Menstruation is the natural loss of blood and cellular debris from the womb. It usually occurs at monthly intervals throughout the reproductive life of a woman, and is commonly referred to as a 'period'.

Tom Belshaw

Q When my 16-year old has to take an exam she starts a period. What can she do?

A Your doctor can give her synthetic hormonal tablets such as prostogens or the Pill to stop her period coinciding with the exam. Consult your doctor a couple of months before to ensure there are no unpleasant side effects.

Q I become constipated just before my period starts. Why does this happen?

A At this time the high levels of progesterone in the blood tend to make the bowel less mobile and cause constipation. Make sure you eat fruit and have plenty of fluids; if this fails, taken an ordinary laxative.

Q Can I become pregnant during my period?

A This is the least fertile part of the cycle, but in rare cases pregnancy has occurred.

Q I have just had a baby. Is it possible to become pregnant again before I have a period?

A Yes. To become pregnant, an egg must be released from the ovary; 78 per cent of women do this before their first period after the birth of a baby.

Q Since taking oral contraceptives I have suffered pre-menstrual tension. Is it possible to cure this without stopping the Pill?

A Many women find these symptoms can be relieved by taking Vitamin B6 (Pyridoxine). Your doctor will advise you further.

Q I have just stopped taking the Pill as I wish to start a family, but I now get painful periods. Can this be cured without taking the Pill again?

A Painful periods can be caused by a substance produced by the lining of the womb called prostaglandin. Tablets which block its production may cure the pain, but won't prevent pregnancy.

The time from the first day of one period to the first day of the next is known as the menstrual cycle. During this cycle the reproductive organs undergo a series of changes which make it possible for an egg to be released from the ovary and travel to the womb. If this egg is fertilized by a sperm, it will be nourished by secretions from the cells lining the womb until it burrows its way into the lining of the womb and is nourished from the mother's blood supply.

If the egg is not fertilized, the lining of the womb is shed in the menstrual flow. This allows a new lining to grow, ready to nourish the next egg.

The menstrual cycle

This intricate cycle of activity is controlled by a centre in the brain called the hypothalamus, which acts as a menstrual clock. The clock operates through a small gland called the anterior pituitary gland, situated at the base of the brain. This gland releases several hormones, two of which are particularly important for reproduction. One stimulates the growth and maturation of several small eggs in the ovary, while the other stimulates the

There is no basis for old wives' tales about not bathing or washing hair during menstruation. Even swimming while using a tampon is perfectly all right.

release of these ripened eggs.

The eggs which mature during a menstrual cycle are surrounded by hormone-producing cells. The egg, together with these cells, is called the Graafian follicle. The main hormone produced by this follicle is oestrogen. During the cycle the surge in oestrogen production is responsible for stimulating the growth and formation of glands in the lining of the womb. It also changes the secretions at the neck of the womb, making it easier for sperm to swim into the womb and so meet the egg. Approximately 15 days before the next period is due, the pituitary gland releases a large amount of luteinizing hormone which stimulates the release of an egg from the ovary about 36 hours later. The egg then travels down a Fallopian tube into the womb. Fertilization usually takes place in the Fallopian tube.

The cells in the ovary which had formed the Graafian follicle now undergo

Q If I forget to take my contraceptive Pills, I start to have a period the next day. Is this because I have caused some damage or is it a false period?

A No damage has been done. This bleeding is similar to the false period you normally get when you stop taking the Pill for seven days between courses. If you have forgotten to take your pill for longer than the safe time recommended by the manufacturer, you must take additional contraceptive precautions until you have finished the packet of pills.

Q I always bleed from the vagina after intercourse. I have been told that I have an erosion on the neck of the womb which is harmless. Could this be causing the bleeding?

A Yes, this is the probable cause. However, there are many other possibilities such as a polyp or growth at the neck of the womb.

Q My 70-year-old mother tells me that she has started having periods again. Is this possible at her age?

A This bleeding cannot be due to a true period. The commonest cause of bleeding from the reproductive tissues at this age is a condition called atrophic vaginitis, which means that the vagina is sore and infected. This is easily treated by applying an oestrogen cream or a slightly acidic gel. In rare cases, this bleeding can be due to a growth in the womb. It is important for your mother to see her doctor as soon as possible.

Q I have had a D and C because my periods are heavy. This does not seem to have cured the problem. Can anything else be done for me?

A D and C is not usually performed to cure a menstrual problem, but it sometimes does work in this way. The main reason for this procedure is to exclude the possibility of any serious disease in the womb, before deciding on the best treatment. You should consult your gynaecologist again for further advice.

changes, which include taking up fat. They are now referred to as the corpus luteum. They still produce oestrogen, but now also produce a hormone called progesterone. Progesterone has two main functions in the menstrual cycle. The first is to alter the mucus at the neck of the womb, making it too thick for sperm to swim into the womb; the second is to make the glands lining the womb secrete a fluid which will nourish the newly fertilized egg.

If the egg is not fertilized, the corpus luteum degenerates. Small blood vessels in the area go into spasm so that cells lining the womb no longer receive oxygen and die. They are then shed together with some blood as menstruation, and the cycle is complete. All the hormones released during the cycle can influence the menstrual clock.

Duration
Women taking oral contraceptive pills do not undergo the cyclical changes in their reproductive capacity described above. However, when they stop taking their Pills, the lining of the womb is shed in the same way as it would be at menstruation. The length of the Pill cycle is 28 days. For those not taking the Pill, the cycle can vary from 21 days to three months in the normal woman. The menstrual clock can also be triggered by emotional problems such as stress; stringent dieting may stop periods entirely.

Menstrual flow
Average blood loss during menstruation is between 20 ml (0.7 fl oz) and 80 ml (2.8 fl oz) over a few days. Women taking the Pill tend to lose less blood. We do not really understand why some periods are heavier than others. Heavy periods can be caused by inflammation of the womb, the use of intra-uterine contraceptive devices, and certain endocrine diseases, such as an under-active thyroid gland. Occasionally, the surface area of the lining of the womb is increased by fibroids, also causing heavy periods.

Menstrual flow often has an unpleasant odour, largely due to the action of bacteria on the blood and cells which have been expelled from the womb. During menstruation it is important to pay particular care to personal hygiene. If a tampon is left in the vagina for too long or forgotten completely, it can give rise to a foul-smelling vaginal discharge. There is no truth in the old wives' tale that a woman should not bath or wash her hair during a period.

Not all blood loss from the vagina is necessarily due to menstruation. Blood loss can occur from the neck of the womb if the tissue is very weak; it can also occur

from a polyp in the womb, or from a cancer. Should you experience bleeding after intercourse or between periods it is always wise to consult your doctor about the problem.

Pre-menstrual tension
Women are subject to enormous hormonal changes during each menstrual cycle. Some experience unpleasant mood changes, a tendency to gain weight or a tenderness of the breasts between the time of ovulation and the start of menstruation. This is known as pre-menstrual tension and it coincides with the time when their production of progesterone is at its maximum. There is some evidence to suggest that women who suffer in this way do not produce adequate amounts of this hormone.

Probably one of the more successful treatments for severe pre-menstrual tension has been to raise the circulation level of progesterone by giving naturally-occurring progesterone, taken from a woman a few days before the anticipated onset of symptoms. Unfortunately this progesterone cannot be absorbed orally, and must be administered in the form of pessaries to the vagina or the rectum. Some women find the cure more unpleasant than the disorder.

Tranquillizers may occasionally be necessary, but probably a better way of alleviating tension is to identify and deal with the cause, and for sufferers to arrange to be less busy at this time of the month. Tablets can be taken to make a woman pass more urine, thus avoiding weight gain, but if her fluid intake is normal she will regain this weight.

Period pains
We are not sure of the exact cause of menstrual pains (dysmenorrhoea). Possibly the muscle of the womb goes into spasm; a substance released from the cells lining the womb called prostaglandin is another possible cause. Often a mild pain-killer like aspirin, or a warm hot-water bottle will help; more painful periods can sometimes be cured by taking the Pill.

Tablets which block the production of

The chart (right) shows the changes that take place on each day of a woman's menstrual cycle. Triggered by the pituitary gland's control of the ovaries with follicle-stimulating hormone (FSH) and luteinizing hormone (LH) an egg matures and is released. Hormone levels alter, secretions in the neck of the womb change and body temperature rises at the time of ovulation. If the egg is not fertilized, menstruation follows with the lining of the womb being shed around the 28th day.

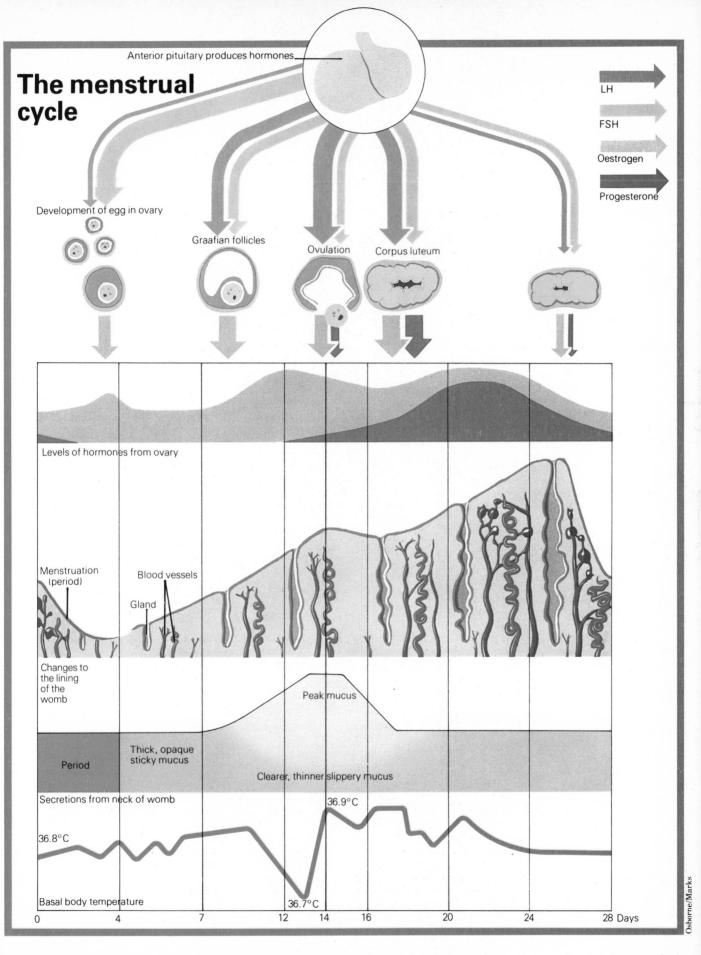

The menstrual cycle

Anterior pituitary produces hormones

LH

FSH

Oestrogen

Progesterone

Development of egg in ovary

Graafian follicles

Ovulation

Corpus luteum

Levels of hormones from ovary

Menstruation (period)

Blood vessels

Gland

Changes to the lining of the womb

Peak mucus

Period

Thick, opaque sticky mucus

Clearer, thinner slippery mucus

Secretions from neck of womb

36.9°C

36.8°C

Basal body temperature

36.7°C

0   4   7   12 14 16   20   24   28 Days

Osborne/Marks

prostaglandins are also available and may relieve the pain. In the past, many women had to undergo a D and C to cure the problem on the theory that the stretching of the neck of the womb will make expulsion of the menstrual blood easier. Unfortunately there is no real evidence to support this theory and painful periods could return a few months after having surgery.

If painful periods are caused by the uncommon condition called adenomyosis and endometriosis, surgery may be necessary, but this is very rare.

Dangers
Probably the most worrying problem occurs when a period is unusually heavy or painful. This can mean that the woman is having a miscarriage, especially if the period is a few days late. She should always seek her doctor's advice if this happens, as a D and C may be necessary to clean out the womb.

If a woman usually has very heavy periods she may gradually lose so much blood that she becomes anaemic. This can be diagnosed very simply by the doctor, and can usually be cured by taking iron tablets. However, it is more sensible to try to cure heavy periods by diagnosing the cause and giving appropriate treatment. A diagnostic D and C may be necessary for this.

Menstrual problems
Many menstrual problems will simply resolve themselves, but if they persist it is worthwhile for a woman to seek reassurance from her doctor.

A frequent worry is when periods do not occur (amenorrhoea). This takes two forms: primary amenorrhoea, when menstruation does not start at puberty and secondary amenorrhoea, when for some reason periods stop. If this happens the primary cause could be pregnancy, but if this is ruled out, emotional factors may be responsible for upsetting the normal cycle. This is often affected by stress—for example after leaving home, changing jobs or a broken love affair. A visit to the doctor for a simple test will establish whether or not a woman is pregnant, otherwise infrequent periods are generally of no concern. In an established menstrual cycle periods may be uneven in quantity, prolonged or occur at differing time intervals. This pattern of menstruation is described as metrorrhagia. Excessive periods are called menorrhagia.

In younger women serious disease of the reproductive system is uncommon and most problems such as heavy or painful periods can be treated with tablets once examination, which may

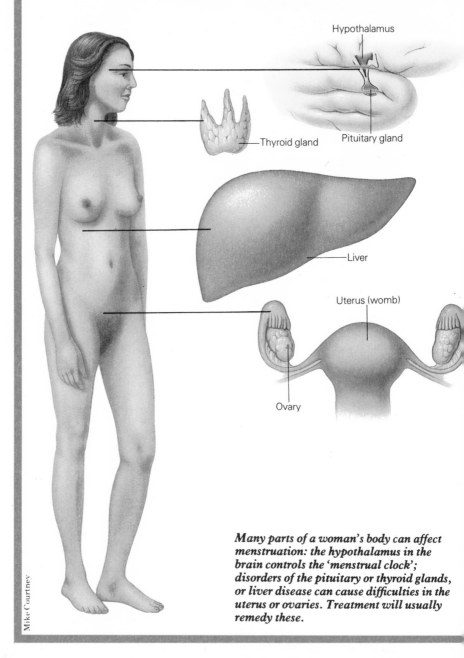

Menstrual disorders

Hypothalamus

Thyroid gland

Pituitary gland

Liver

Uterus (womb)

Ovary

Many parts of a woman's body can affect menstruation: the hypothalamus in the brain controls the 'menstrual clock'; disorders of the pituitary or thyroid glands, or liver disease can cause difficulties in the uterus or ovaries. Treatment will usually remedy these.

Mike Courtney

include a pelvic (vaginal) check, has conclusively established the cause.

Effects of contraceptives
During the reproductive years, some menstrual problems may be due to a woman's choice of contraceptive. The Pill may cause bleeding between periods, but this usually settles down within a month or two—if not, a different Pill containing a higher dose of a synthetic hormone called progestogen often cures this particular problem.

Women who use the coil (IUD or intra-

uterine device) may find their periods become a little heavier; many women are prepared to tolerate this for the sake of the convenience of this form of contraception. However, if the IUD causes severe discomfort it may have to be removed and a different contraceptive used. Your doctor or family planning clinic can advise you.

When to see your doctor
Four problems are of particular importance and would justify an early visit to the doctor. These are: very heavy pro-

Problem	Cause	Treatment
Menstruation does not start at puberty	Genetic abnormalities e.g. no uterus, hormonal problems	Specialist investigation
Menstruation stops	Emotional problems, excessive dieting (anorexia nervosa)	Usually returns spontaneously, but may need treatment with clomiphine (if periods infrequent for over six months, seek medical help)
Periods absent or irregular, in irregular amounts	Premature menopause. Disease in genital tract or hormone system. Liver disease (liver is unable to break down oestrogen)	None. May need specialist treatment. Difficult to treat
Infrequent, light periods	Over-active thyroid	Treat thyroid disease
Irregular periods	Failure of ovulation: commonest during puberty	No treatment strictly necessary, but hormonal treatment may be given
Irregular periods, often heavy	At the menopause	D and C to exclude serious disease, hormonal treatment, hysterectomy may be needed
Irregular periods, possibly excessive weight gain, anxiety	Malfunction of 'menstrual clock' caused by psychological factors. Rare ovarian tumours	Treat problem causing emotional upset, hormonal tablets to regulate periods. Removal of diseased ovary
Infrequent periods, secretion of milk from breasts, infertility, headaches, visual problems	Tumour of pituitary gland	Bromocryptine tablets or shrinkage or removal of tumour
Prolonged gaps between periods, brown or lightly bloodstained discharge before period	Abnormal hormone production by ovaries	Hormonal tablets
Bleeding between periods	Taking oral contraceptive pill incorrectly e.g. forgetting to take pill	Taking the pill regularly. (Take alternative contraceptive precautions if pill forgotten)
Bleeding from vagina between periods	Uterine polyp	Removal of polyp
Occasional heavy periods	Fibroids	No treatment if no problems caused; if bleeding severe, removal of fibroids from womb (myomectomy) or hysterectomy
Heavier periods and a little bleeding between periods	Insertion of intra-uterine contraceptive	Usually settles within one to two months. Consult your doctor if you continue to bleed between periods or get pain in abdomen
Bleeding after sexual intercourse, heavy prolonged periods, bleeding between periods	Could indicate cancer of womb	Radiotherapy or surgical removal of womb or combination of both treatments
Heavier periods and lower abdominal pain	Pelvic infection	Antibiotics
Heavy regular periods	Abnormalities of blood, stopping clotting. Under-active thyroid	Treatment of blood disease; hysterectomy. Treat thyroid disease

longed periods which occur at the usual time (menorrhagia); bleeding after intercourse; bleeding from the vagina between periods; bleeding from the vagina after the menopause. All of these symptoms, although usually caused by a minor problem, can occasionally be early symptoms of cancer of the womb, which can be cured if treated at an early stage.

As women become older, menstrual disorders are more often associated with disease of the reproductive organs. Diagnostic tests, such as a D and C are generally performed to exclude this possibility; otherwise the condition may be treated with synthetic sex hormones. At the time of the menopause periods become infrequent, before finally stopping. This is normal and needs no further treatment.

Menopausal problems
A frequent disorder at this time is menorrhagia (heavy periods). Doctors often try prescribing hormonal tablets to control their severity. Unfortunately, this treatment does not always work and a hysterectomy (removal of the womb) may be suggested as an alternative. This is a difficult decision for the patient to make. She has to decide whether her symptoms are severe enough to warrant a major operation or if she is prepared to tolerate her heavy periods.

The intricacies of the menstrual cycle are still not entirely understood, but by performing a pelvic examination and doing a smear test, your doctor will often be able to diagnose a menstrual problem. An obvious condition can be dealt with by surgery or the condition can be treated with synthetic hormones.

Migraine

Q I suffer from migraine. Would it help if I stopped smoking and drinking alcohol?

A Probably. Smoky air can trigger off a migraine and so can alcohol, especially if you drink when you are tired or on an empty stomach.

Q I have been told that my migraine will get worse if I take the Pill. Is this true?

A The hormones in the contraceptive Pill, especially the types with a low oestrogen dose, sometimes cause an increase in headaches. The Pill may also occasionally be associated with high blood pressure which can make migraine worse. If you are considering taking the Pill consult your doctor about which type would be best and if you suffer adverse effects tell your doctor immediately.

Q I have tried all the available drugs for migraine and none have helped. Are there any 'alternative' forms of treatment which I could try?

A Yes. You could try homeopathic medicine or acupuncture, where fine needles are inserted at different points in the body. Bioenergetic therapy treats physical symptoms such as migraine through exploring emotional tension and repressed feelings. Research is also currently under way into the effectiveness of a herb called feverfew which has been claimed to relieve migraine if three leaves a day are eaten over a period of months. You can obtain it from some of the more specialized health food shops.

Q I have suffered regular migraine for many years, and it upsets me that my child now seems to be suffering from them as well. Has she inherited this complaint from me?

A She may have, but she will not necessarily suffer as badly as you. Child sufferers generally have abdominal migraine with only a mild headache, and half grow out of them before adulthood.

Migraines—violent headaches accompanied by nausea, vomiting and disturbances of sight, hearing, feeling and speech—can affect anyone. What causes migraines and what can be done to prevent or alleviate them?

Tens of millions of people in Britain suffer from regular migraine attacks which can disrupt their work, home and social life. Women are far more often affected than men, and it is most likely to strike young or middle-aged adults. However, children or the elderly can also suffer and indeed anyone may suddenly find himself or herself victim of migraine, even if it only occurs once in a lifetime.

Causes and symptoms

Although the causes of migraine are not fully understood, it is thought to be the result of the blood vessels in the head narrowing down and then expanding. This affects the flow of blood to the brain and so triggers off the disturbances in perception and the painful headache.

Research has suggested that a migraine attack is triggered by changes in the body in 'vaso-active amines', which are amines affecting blood vessels. These amines are normally present in the body tissue but their level may be raised by a person consuming chocolate, alcohol or cheese, or released when sufferers are under stress and when their blood sugar level is low as a result of going too long between meals or eating too many sweet or fatty foods. A substance called serotonin is raised by the 'positive ions' which are found in the air of stuffy, smoky rooms and in hot, dry winds and this can trigger off a migraine.

Additionally it has been found that migraine sufferers are deficient in the 'mono-amine' enzymes which are responsible for breaking down the amines. This may explain why sufferers may be so badly affected by the hormone changes of the menstrual cycle and by the hormones in the Pill, resulting in worse migraines

Migraines are far more severe than any ordinary headache, are longer lasting and are often accompanied by other disturbances.

Charles Clarke

British Migraine Association

The two paintings (above) are by migraine sufferers and show how they visualize themselves and the world during an attack. Some sufferers see stars or blotches or lines; the photograph (right) portrays this.

at the time of their menstruation or while taking the Pill.

There are several other factors which contribute to causing migraine. People who already have a tendency to migraine may experience more frequent and severe attacks if they get high blood pressure, or if they are involved in an accident which results in an injury to their head or neck. When the salt and water content of body tissues is raised, attacks may be precipitated; this can occur in both sexes, but especially in women before and during their periods. For some sufferers, certain foods may also set off a migraine.

Symptoms vary considerably between individuals and from one attack to another. However there are certain characteristic features that separate migraine from ordinary headaches. These include a headache above or behind one eye or mostly on one side of the head, nausea and vomiting, and blurred vision, flashing lights or an extreme sensitivity to light and sound.

Sufferers may also shake and feel giddy, have difficulty in speaking and seeing normally and experience intense 'other worldly' sensations.

The classical migraine is usually preceded by a warning 'aura', with feelings of exaggerated well-being or visual disturbances. This symptom usually fades with the onset of a headache and is most common in adolescence or in early adulthood.

Dangers

Some symptoms, such as loss of vision and severe pain, may be frightening, but they are not permanently damaging or fatal. Sufferers should not drive or undertake any activity requiring accurate co-ordination of sight and movement during a migraine as the visual disturbances may cause blind spots and difficulties in calculating distance and direction.

People who have never previously had migraines and who suddenly experience recurrent, severe headaches should consult their doctor to see if the cause is a more serious disorder such as a tumour or a blood clot in the head.

Treatment

The best treatment for migraine is prevention. First isolate the factors which trigger migraine. This can be done by keeping a 'migraine diary': note everything you ate and any stressful factors in the 24 hours preceding the migraine. You may be able to identify foods which have an adverse effect either by eating them or omitting them from your diet for a month. If eye-strain seems to be causing problems, have your spectacle prescription checked: dark glasses or polaroid lenses may reduce general glare or dazzle. Overtiredness, crowds, stuffy places can be avoided if these contribute.

Generally, migraine sufferers need to accept that they may be more sensitive than other people: they need to rest adequately, eat regularly and well, and take life at a gentle pace. Stress at home, in personal relationships and at work can contribute to the severity of migraine and sufferers should learn not to 'drive' themselves and to avoid situations where they are under pressure. Many migraine sufferers tend to 'bottle up' their feelings, and talking about them may ease some of the tension. Regular gentle physical exercise such as swimming and yoga can help by relaxing the body and making it less likely to become tense. Regular meditation has also been found helpful.

As a preventive measure, some doctors prescribe sedatives to keep stress at bay and anti-depressants to relieve depression. Others prescribe drugs to control the nervous impulses controlling blood vessel diameter or to counter the

Q Can migraines be caused by a food allergy?

A They can be. You may be able to detect for yourself which foodstuffs are affecting you. Do this by making a sample meal and seeing if an attack follows. It is also possible to get hospital tests done to track down any substances to which you may be allergic. Consult your doctor about getting these done.

Q My friend says I suffer from migraine because I worry too much about looking after my family. Could she be right?

A Surveys suggest that migraine sufferers are sensitive people who may react more strongly to outside pressures and experience more anxiety and depression than other adults. They may also be over-conscientious and sacrifice their own health to looking after others. If you feel this is true for you, you could look for ways to share some of the responsibility and work load you carry, for example by getting your husband and children to help more with the housework. Don't set yourself impossibly high standards and remember that you need time and space to look after yourself as well as your family.

Q During my migraine attacks I often feel sad and want to cry. Is this a normal reaction?

A Emotional tension, especially holding in strong feelings, can be a factor in causing migraines. It is perfectly normal to cry if you wish to and you may find that this brings some relief. Symptoms can become worse while you are crying, but you may find that the attack passes more quickly than usual.

Q I recently had a terrible migraine attack for the first time in my life. Does this mean I will get them regularly from now on?

A Not necessarily. It is thought that each individual has a 'migraine threshold' and can have an attack if the circumstances are strong enough to provoke it. This may only occur once or twice in a lifetime.

potentially harmful effects of serotonin.

Simple pain-killers such as soluble aspirin, codeine or paracetamol are also suggested for pain relief when an attack occurs. However, as the stomach becomes inactive early in an attack, drugs may not be well absorbed and may be vomited back. For this reason anti-vomiting and nausea drugs may have to be taken first.

For most people, however, the headache is the most painful part of the attack and is often quite unaffected by simple painkillers; for this reason drugs derived from ergot, a substance which constricts the swollen blood vessels in the head, are often prescribed and taken early in an attack. These drugs need to be used with extreme care. They should never be taken during pregnancy and the recommended dosage should never be exceeded.

Because many of the prescribed drugs are unsatisfactory in treating attacks, have unpleasant side-effects and may cause long-term dependence, other methods of treatment should be tried. These methods are often most effective in the early stages of an attack.

Sufferers should lie flat on a bed, without a pillow, in a quiet, darkened room. At this stage gentle massage may help to loosen tension at the neck and base of the skull, on the back and shoulders and on the stomach. Finger pressure on the bridge of the nose, or on the pulse points at the temple and behind the ear may relieve the pain temporarily. Depression or emotional tension can be contributing factors, often as a result of 'bottling up' anxieties; being consoled, holding someone's hands, talking about any current problems may help to relieve tension and reduce the severity of the attack. Breathing fully into the stomach with a sensation of 'letting go' on the out breath may also aid relaxation and may be more productive than bracing yourself against the pain.

During a migraine the capillaries or small blood vessels in the arms and legs contract, sending less blood to the extremities of the body. To increase the blood circulation in the hands or legs and therefore ease the pressure of blood circulating in the painful swollen blood vessels of the head, relax the limbs, shake them and place them in hot or cold water. Ice bags or cold compresses can be placed on the head to relieve painful throbbing.

Outlook

Some people are more physically prone to suffer from migraine, often because of inherited tendencies. Such a tendency cannot be eradicated, but much can be done to alleviate attacks and to keep them down to an acceptable level.

Preventing migraine
● Start a migraine diary: note down foods eaten and stressful situations during the preceding 24 hours
● Have your eyes and spectacle prescription checked. To reduce glare, wear dark glasses or polaroid lenses
● Rest adequately, eat regular and well-balanced meals: avoid becoming over-tired and 'eating on the run'
● Avoid crowded and stuffy places
● Minimize stress by being gentle on yourself; consider your own feelings
● Take regular exercise and, to aid relaxation, try meditation
● Consult your doctor about drugs

Alleviating migraine
● Rest flat on a bed, without a pillow, in a quiet, darkened room
● Massage pressure points in the neck, back, skull, shoulders and stomach, or on the bridge of the nose, temples or behind the ear to relieve tenseness
● Talk about your worries and anxieties
● Try breathing exercises
● Increase circulation by shaking arms and legs, and placing them in either hot or cold water
● Use a cold compress or ice bag on your head or take a long shower

A migraine diary—noting skipped meals or greasy food, smoking cigarettes, drinking and tension at home or in the office—will alert sufferers to factors precipitating attacks.

Once the diary is complete, sufferers should be able to pinpoint precisely the causes of their migraines. Attacks can then be averted by a change of habits and learning to deal with stress.

Multiple sclerosis

Q I am 26 and have just been told that I have multiple sclerosis. Does this mean I shouldn't have a family?

A It is thought that the physical stress of a pregnancy does increase the likelihood of an exacerbation during the period of the pregnancy. But it is now thought unlikely that a pregnancy affects the long-term outlook of the illness, though no one is completely sure. Discuss it all fully with your doctor—but remember, in the end, the decision is up to you and your partner. Many women with multiple sclerosis have been able to cope perfectly well with children and are very glad they decided to become pregnant. Since multiple sclerosis is not hereditary you won't need to worry about passing it on.

Q Is multiple sclerosis catching?

A There is no evidence for this at all. It is true that the illness is more frequent in temporate climates, but no one can explain this enviromental factor. It is interesting that Northern Europeans born and brought up in the tropics are unlikely to get the disease. It is a strange and unexplained fact that the place with the highest incidence of multiple sclerosis is the Orkneys in Scotland.

Q I once had a tingling sensation in my fingers and ever since I have been frightened that I might have multiple sclerosis. Should I see a neurologist?

A Nearly everybody experiences the occasional odd sensation at some time in their lives. People who know about multiple sclerosis often interpret these feelings as the possible beginning of the disease, so it is understandable that you are fearful. There is almost certainly nothing wrong, though you may have had a minor neuritis (nerve inflammation). Tingling or pins and needles can result from sitting or sleeping in an uncomfortable position. If it happens again and you still feel worried, then see your doctor who may make a referral to a neurologist for further tests that will clear the matter up.

This mysterious illness affects the central nervous system—and while it incapacitates some individuals, others continue to live full, vigorous and normal lives.

Reg Wilson/EMI Ltd

Jacqueline du Pré, the celebrated cellist, has made a new career for herself as a teacher, passing on her skills to a new generation despite her illness.

Multiple sclerosis is an illness that affects the central nervous system. It is unpredictable and can result in only minor physical impairment as well as in severe disability. As yet no one fully understands its causes and how its progression can be arrested. It tends to strike between the teens and middle thirties. Women seem more likely to get multiple sclerosis than men—two out of every three sufferers are female. It appears to be a disease of temperate climates. No one understands the factors involved in this.

The first parts of the nervous system to be affected are those that control physical sensation, co-ordination and movement. This tissue in the nervous system is called the white matter and it carries sensory messages to the brain, as well as impulses from the brain to the muscles. The fibres are surrounded by the myelin sheath, which insulates and protects them. In multiple sclerosis the myelin sheath becomes inflamed, sometimes causing damage to the nerves themselves. The nerves may make faulty connections with each other or be so damaged that they will not work at all.

The grey matter of the nervous system which makes up a section of the brain—the part that is conscious and can think and remember—is not normally affected. Multiple sclerosis does not result in any kind of mental handicap or disorder.

Causes

There are a number of theories about what causes multiple sclerosis but none has yet been proved. It may be that some people have a deficient immune system in their bodies which could mean that they react abnormally to common viruses like

248

colds, influenza or measles. But why this should be is not understood.

What actually happens during the course of the disease is not really known either. It is clear that physical or emotional stress can trigger off an exacerbation (aggravation leading to an attack) in some people, but why a remission happens no one is sure.

Symptoms

The illness takes the form of repeated exacerbations. For no known reason, the exacerbation usually stops of its own accord and a period of remission follows when the disease is not active.

During a remission, the nervous system tries to heal itself and scar tissue forms around the affected areas. But the scar tissue cannot perform the functions of the destroyed myelin sheath and may cause more harm to the affected nerve, sometimes leaving permanent damage. Scar tissues are called scleroses and can occur in various parts of the nervous system: hence the name of the illness.

The severity of the illness varies enormously from person to person. The pattern of exacerbation followed by remission can mean that one person can

The illustrations, show how the spinal cord is affected at different times by multiple sclerosis. Damage is only marginal to the areas of the spinal cord shown right, but top right larger portions have been affected. The white areas show the demyelinating process of the illness.

Many mothers have happily gone ahead and and had families despite multiple sclerosis. The illness is not hereditary.

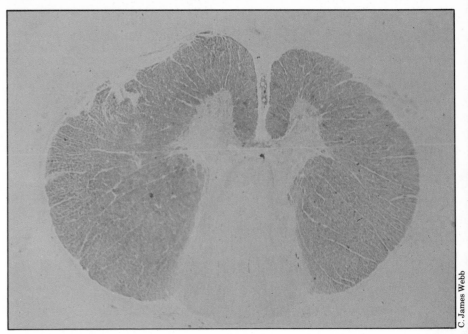

C. James Webb

Biophoto Associates

John Beckett

lead a completely able-bodied life while another may be unable to co-ordinate movement and be confined to a wheelchair. Many find that they are weak and easily tired for most of the time—indeed, this can be a major problem. Blurred or double vision may occur, particularly when the sufferer is fatigued. Some people find that their very first symptom is severe disturbance in one eye.

A common physical symptom is tingling in the hands, arms, feet, legs or trunk. The feeling is like 'pins and needles' and may produce a sensation of numbness. These feelings are not painful but can become uncomfortable. There is unlikely to be anything wrong with the nerves of the affected areas: the site of the damage may well be in the upper part of the spinal cord. This means that incorrect nerve messages are getting through to the brain—hot bath water may feel cold to the feet, for example.

Some sufferers from multiple sclerosis

Q I have recently been diagnosed as suffering from multiple sclerosis. So far, I am perfectly well apart from a few patches of numbness in my legs. I have a full-time job I enjoy—should I tell my employers?

A That is really up to you and will depend on how well you get on with your employers. Many people are very ignorant about multiple sclerosis and will think that you are likely to be immediately wheelchair-bound as a result. Unfortunately, this attitude could result in discrimination against you and you may not be able to re-educate your employers. If you feel it is important to tell them, you could wait a while so that they can have time to see that you are still as capable of doing your job as you ever were. Many people would feel it is not necessary to tell your employers unless the illness became incapacitating.

Q Does multiple sclerosis interfere with one's sex life?

A Multiple sclerosis is not thought to affect the sexual response of women, but it sometimes interferes with a man's ability to have an erection. Many men find that their power to have an erection is not impaired in any way but impotence can occur in the later stages of the illness. However, sexual desire remains and a man will still be able to enjoy making love in other ways although he may not be able to have intercourse. If either partner has some paralysis, the couple can find ways of making love in which the able-bodied partner is the more physically active.

Q Is it possible to recover from a bad relapse in multiple sclerosis, or will it always leave severe disability?

A Many people have had exacerbations (attacks) which have given them temporary paralysis or other major symptoms from which they later recover. It is impossible to predict what is going to happen after an exacerbation: sometimes there may be some residual disability but then again, the remission may be complete. Multiple sclerosis seldom affects two people in the same way.

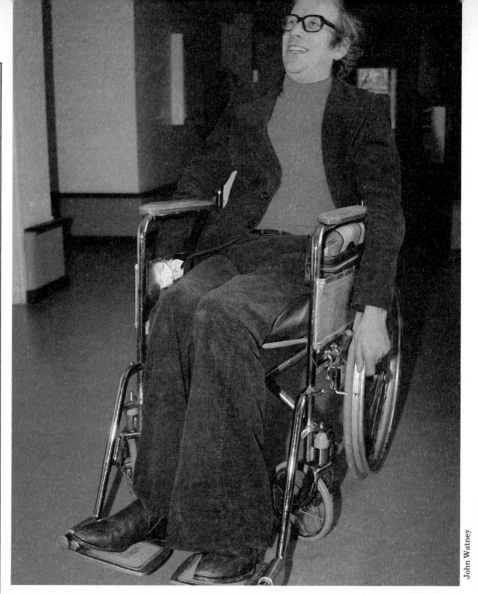

John Watney

find that they cannot move or co-ordinate a limb. One foot may drag, making walking difficult. Some lose control over their hands so that it becomes difficult to write or hold cups or cutlery. If any of these symptoms become severe, it may be difficult to walk or stand unaided and a wheelchair may be necessary. Nerves in other parts of the body, too, can become affected and cause problems with urinary control, giddiness and tremors.

It is possible for any number of these symptoms to occur during an exacerbation. During the subsequent remission individuals may find themselves as physically able as ever they were before the attack. But approximately five per cent of multiple sclerosis sufferers go into speedy physical decline without any kind of apparent remission.

Treatment and outlook
There is no cure at the moment for multiple sclerosis but doctors sometimes use the steroid drug ACTH. This accelerates the action of the healing mechanisms of the body.

Many people carry on an active life from a wheelchair. Some work, many take part in sports and most have taught themselves to be as mobile as possible.

Special diets seem to help some people. Sufferers seem to be deficient in a certain kind of fatty acid in the blood, which can be found in sunflower and safflower oil. These products can be bought from health food shops. Lowering the amount of animal fat in the diet may also help, as may a gluten-free diet. (Gluten is a constituent of wheat germ.) However, there is as yet no scientific proof that special diets are beneficial.

Many multiple sclerosis sufferers have turned to alternative medicine for relief and have taken to yoga, homeopathy and acupuncture. It is advisable to keep an open mind about these aids.

Research into multiple sclerosis is taking place all over the world and is thought to be progressing well. It may only be a decade or so before the disease is understood and a treatment found that can arrest progression for all sufferers.

Mumps

Q Should I keep away from children with mumps when I am pregnant? Could infection damage the baby?

A No, there is no evidence to prove that the mumps virus can harm the developing baby. However, as a general guide it is best to avoid any children with viral infections during the first three months of pregnancy.

Q My son has mumps but he does not want to stay in bed. Can he stay up and watch television?

A Yes, it is perfectly all right to let your son stay up and watch television if he wants to. He is obviously suffering from a mild case of mumps. If his swollen glands are painful, painkillers will help.

Q In severe mumps can the salivary glands be permanently damaged?

A No. The mumps virus causes a temporary inflammation of the salivary glands which completely clears up with no long-lasting effects. In some rare cases a bacterial inflammation follows the mumps infection and this can scar some of the saliva-producing cells. However, there are so many of these cells that it has little effect.

Q When my daughter had mumps she had terrible back pain. Was this a normal symptom?

A It is very likely that your daughter had mild pancreatitis as a complication of mumps. The pancreas lies on the posterior wall of the abdomen and when inflamed it can cause a lot of back pain. This will have been resolved without treatment and will have left her with no harmful effects.

Q I have heard that people can be made sterile as a result of mumps. Is this true?

A Sterility after mumps is extremely rare. The virus can cause inflammation in the testicles and the ovary, but damage so severe that it destroys all sperm and egg production is extremely unlikely.

Like many of the common childhood illnesses, mumps carries with it the guarantee of future immunity. In adults the condition can be more serious—but it is usually not as drastic as old wives' tales would make it.

Mumps is a very common acute viral infection which produces fever and swelling of the salivary glands. The illness is most common in children aged five to fourteen. Only a small percentage of adults contract it, but the symptoms can be severe and complications more common.

In men, mumps commonly causes a painful inflammation of the testicles. Other glands can also be affected but the only really serious complication that can ensue is inflammation of the nervous system, which can occasionally prove to be fatal. But this is extremely rare.

Mumps is also known as parotitis, because it is the parotid gland which most commonly becomes enlarged and tender.

The virus is not as highly infectious as chickenpox or measles. The mumps patient is infectious for about two days before the swelling appears and for about a week after it subsides.

Causes

Mumps is caused by a specific virus that is similar to the influenza virus. The virus spreads from person to person by contact with the moisture expelled in the

Mumps usually affects one salivary gland causing moderate swelling. But if other glands are involved, swelling spreads.

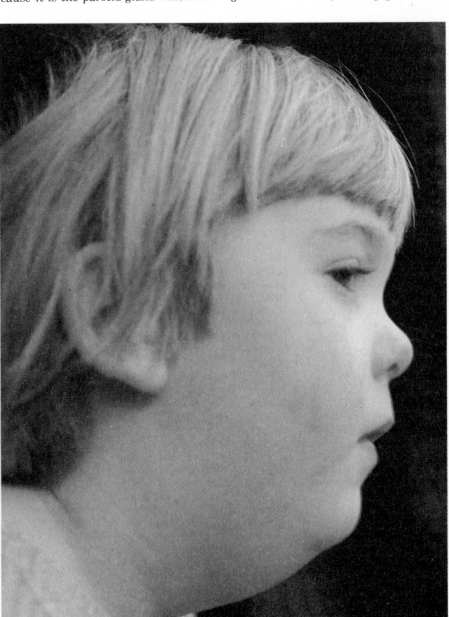

glands rarely become inflamed because of mumps. However, if affected, the patient complains of pain and swelling of one or both breasts. Pain-killing tablets and good breast support is all the treatment necessary. The condition quickly subsides and the swelling disappears.

Pancreatitis: the mumps virus can cause inflammation in this gland. It produces symptoms of pain in the upper part of the abdomen, fever and vomiting.

Severe cases can need hospitalization. The inflammation settles within three or four days and the outlook is excellent.

Meningitis: mild meningitis—inflammation of the membranes covering the brain—is found in less than one per cent of cases and occurs about 10 days after the initial symptoms of mumps. The patient complains of mild neck stiffness, headache and possibly vomiting. The symptoms subside within three or four days on recovery.

Mumps in an adult male can cause painful swelling of one or both testicles. Relief can be obtained by bed-rest and an ice pack.

A child with a mild case of mumps need not be confined to bed, and indeed may be happier playing or watching television.

coughs, sneezes and breath of the infected person. It enters the body through the mouth or respiratory tract—has a two to three week period of incubation—and then begins to affect the gland tissues and very rarely the nervous system.

Symptoms

The first symptoms noticed are slight fever, a sore throat and shivering, and these can often be mistaken for influenza. The gland which is first affected is generally the parotid, the large salivary gland between the upper and lower jaws. It becomes tender and swollen making opening the mouth wide and eating extremely painful. Fever increases and the temperature can rise to 39.4°C (103°F).

Often only one gland will be swollen, but the swelling can spread to the other salivary glands developing under the jaw or even under the tongue. Commonly both sides of the face become swollen at the same time but sometimes one side is not affected until the other is almost better. The swelling increases for two or three days and then gradually subsides. The temperature also begins to fall. The patient makes a complete recovery and returns to normal eating.

Dangers and complications

It is very rare for mumps to be dangerous but the virus can cause inflammation in other glands and the nervous system.

Orchitis: inflammation of one or both testicles occurs in about 20 per cent of male cases of mumps. A week after the virus has caused swelling of the salivary glands, there is a painful enlargement of the affected testicle. In rare cases this can even occur without fever or swelling of the salivary glands.

The testicle is swollen and painful so that the patient is obliged to lie still in bed. Providing support for the testicle, applying ice packs and in some cases steroid drugs, prescribed by a doctor, can give relief.

Most testicles return to normal size within a week and, even in the most severe cases where both testicles are involved and they shrink in size following the infection, sterility is rare and impotence virtually never occurs even with shrinkage of the testicles.

Oophoritis: this inflammation of the ovary is uncommon but can produce severe lower abdominal pain and bouts of vomiting. The complication subsides within two or three days and has no long-term effects.

Prostatitis: inflammation of the prostate gland is a relatively rare complication of mumps. The patient complains of high fever and of passing urine frequently a few days after the mumps fever has subsided. No treatment is necessary and the symptoms soon abate.

Mastitis (see pp 232-33): the mammary

Encephalitis: this is an extremely rare inflammation of the brain and is the only really serious danger from mumps. The patient develops severe headaches, high fever and vomiting. In most cases the trouble is short-lived and full recovery usually occurs. In a small proportion of cases there is permanent disability or even death.

Treatment

There is no curative or specific treatment for mumps. In mild and moderate cases simple painkillers are the best treatment and confinement to bed unnecessary.

In more severe cases the patient should stay in bed, keep warm and drink plenty of fluid during the feverish period. When gland swelling is severe and eating is painful, bland food and adequate fluid are recommended. Pain-killing tablets are needed to reduce the discomfort and frequent mouthwashes with weak salt water are needed to keep the mouth clean and prevent bacterial infection of the gums or salivary glands.

Parents of a child suffering from mumps should provide a great deal of reassurance as the child is often worried by the temporary size and distortion of his or her face caused by the swellings.

Precautions and prevention

One attack of mumps provides life-long immunity but as yet in Britain there is no compulsory immunization. Vaccine which gives unspecified immunity is available on prescription and can be given to children aged one year and over. Women in the early stages of pregnancy should avoid contact with people who have mumps, but if the virus is contracted it should not harm the growing baby in the womb.

Adults, particularly males, in whom the condition can be more serious, should avoid contact with contagious mumps patients if at all possible.

Few schools insist on quarantine of brothers or sisters who have been in contact with the mumps virus. Most allow a child back when the swelling has been absent for one week as at this stage infection is not likely.

Outlook

The outlook for cases of uncomplicated mumps is excellent. The patient feels better once the fever subsides and the swelling starts to go down. Even severe swelling rarely lasts more than three or four days and within a week there is complete recovery.

Q Can I have my children immunized against mumps?

A Children are not vaccinated against mumps as a matter of course in Britain. A safe vaccine is available through your doctor for children aged over a year. This vaccine is still relatively new and it is not known whether it gives immunity for life.

Q I was told mumps had only affected one of my salivary glands. Does this mean I could get the illness again?

A No. Mumps quite often only inflames one salivary gland and leaves the others unaffected. The fact that you have had the mumps virus means that you now have immunity for life.

Q My doctor says he was not positive that my children had mumps. How can the virus be detected?

A Only a blood test will positively identify the mumps virus. However, with a mild case of mumps it often happens that the swelling disappears before the doctor sees it, making it more difficult for him to make a diagnosis.

Q My young son has caught mumps. Should I keep his sister away from school during the infectious period?

A Check with your daughter's school as obviously regulations vary from school to school, but generally they do not now insist on a quarantine period.

Q My friend's daughter had meningitis as a complication of mumps. Is this a common occurrence?

A Mild meningitis can occur in about one per cent of cases of mumps. It follows about 10 days after the first symptoms of mumps are noticed. The patient experiences neck stiffness, headache and sometimes vomiting. These symptoms usually clear up within three or four days and complete recovery is usual.

Bill Petch

Muscular dystrophy

Like most inherited diseases, muscular dystrophy tends to strike early in life. The age at which the symptoms first appear is one way of distinguishing the many different types of this uncommon disease.

Q The little boy next door has muscular dystrophy, but there is no history of it in his family. How did this happen?

A Inherited diseases occur when there are abnormal genes in a person's make-up, and these are passed on to his or her child. Sometimes, however, an abnormal gene is formed when an egg or sperm is being produced—a process known as mutation. A number of people with one of the 'inherited diseases' suffer from them as a result of a new mutation passed on by their parent, and therefore do not have a family history of the disease.

Q My brother has muscular dystrophy. Could I possibly be a carrier?

A You will have to have a blood test. This will indicate the level of the enzyme called CPK (Creatinephosphokinase) which is released from muscle into the blood and is present at a raised level in people who carry the disease. As a sister of an affected person, there is a 50 per cent chance that you will be a carrier.

Q My little nephew has just been diagnosed as having muscular dystrophy. Is there any chance that the diagnosis is wrong and his weakness will get better?

A It is very unusual to find muscle weakness in children, and where it occurs, muscular dystrophy is a common cause. When this is taken into account with factors such as positive blood tests, it is highly unlikely that the diagnosis will be wrong. Unfortunately his weakness will not improve or simply go away.

Q My husband's brother had Duchenne's dystrophy. Will my children inherit it?

A You have no more need to worry than anyone who has no family history of the disease. This type of dystrophy is carried on the X-female chromosome, and your husband has only one of these. If this had been a carrier chromosome he would also have the disease.

The term muscular dystrophy describes a group of disorders that produce weakness in the muscles themselves, rather than a weakness resulting from disorders of the nerves that make the muscles work. The dystrophies make up only a small number of all the disorders that affect the muscles alone, and are characterized by two things: they do not appear to be a consequence of disease elsewhere in the body and they are always inherited.

Causes

Although the cause of the disorder is unknown, it is fairly certain that the problem arises in the muscle cell. When the muscles of people affected with the disease are examined under a microscope, the cells are seen to be in varying stages of destruction.

Just like any other cell in the body, a muscle cell has to convert food and oxygen into energy. In addition, it has to convert energy into physical power by contracting. An abnormality in any one of the many processes involved in this activity could result in muscular dystrophy. Also, it seems likely that the various types of the disease each result from a different abnormality.

Symptoms

These depend on the type of dystrophy which is present. Generally, symptoms appear earlier in the more severe types than the less severe ones.

There are approximately 20 different types of the disease, but only four of them occur at all commonly: Duchenne's, Becker's, Landouzy-Déjerine, and myotonic dystrophy.

Duchenne's dystrophy is the most severe form of the disease, and may occur in quite young children. About one in every 5000 male babies is affected. It is a sex-linked disease inherited on the X

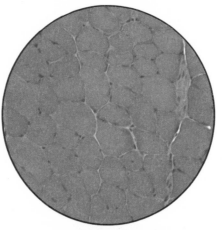

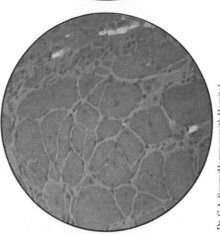

Muscle cells (left) of a healthy person (a) and a patient with muscular dystrophy (b); disintegration of the muscle cell may be a cause of the disease, which can affect children at a very early age (below).

Dr. C.A. Sewry/Hammersmith Hospital

John Beckett

chromosome, so that when only one X chromosome is present—as it is in boys—the disease becomes evident. Where two X chromosomes are present, as they are in girls, the disease is prevented by the other 'normal' chromosome. However, girls can carry the disease and pass it on to their sons.

The disease starts with weakness of the thighs and pelvic muscles, which causes difficulty in standing, walking and climbing. Weakness may be obvious at a very early stage, even before the boy can walk. However it is more usual for it to come to light between the ages of two and seven. Continuing progression affects the neck, shoulders and back so that loss of power may eventually lead to deformities of the spine and to difficulties in breathing. The heart, which is also a muscle, may become involved, and this combination of difficulties in breathing and heart function can lead to a very early death, often before 20 years of age.

A rather unusual characteristic of Duchenne's dystrophy in its early stages is that the muscles involved are not necessarily wasted and shrunken, but may be large and powerful-looking, even though in reality they are weak.

Common types of muscular dystrophy

Disease	Type of Inheritance●	Characteristics
Duchenne's	X—linked	Starts early in childhood, often before two. The calves may show hypertrophy (over-development). Survival beyond 20 is unusual.
Becker's	X—linked	Like Duchenne's, except that it starts later and sufferers may live into middle age.
Landouzy-Déjerine	Dominant	Very variable in the way it affects people, ranging from minor weakness of the face and cheeks to severe disability. Face, arms and shoulders affected.
Myotonic	Dominant	Weakness of the face muscles and an inability to relax muscles. Affected people often go bald. Children of affected mothers may be worse than those of affected fathers.

● The characteristics of X—linked inherited dystrophies is that only boys are affected but girls may be carriers, and of dominant, that 50 per cent of children of an affected person will have the disease.

Becker's pseudohypertrophic dystrophia is a similar type but comes on later, usually after the age of ten. People are much less severely affected and can live on into their thirties and forties.

The face, shoulders and upper arms are the areas that are worst affected in Landouzy-Déjerine dystrophy. It can occur in both males and females, and affected individuals will have at least one

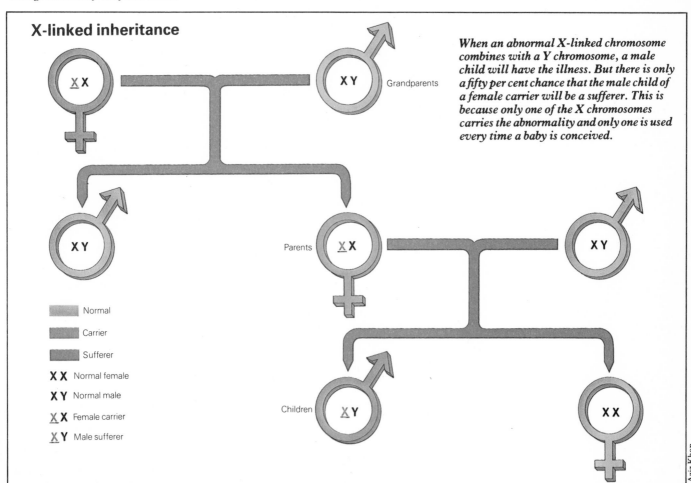

X-linked inheritance

When an abnormal X-linked chromosome combines with a Y chromosome, a male child will have the illness. But there is only a fifty per cent chance that the male child of a female carrier will be a sufferer. This is because only one of the X chromosomes carries the abnormality and only one is used every time a baby is conceived.

Grandparents

Parents

Children

Normal
Carrier
Sufferer
X X Normal female
X Y Normal male
X X Female carrier
X Y Male sufferer

Aziz Khan

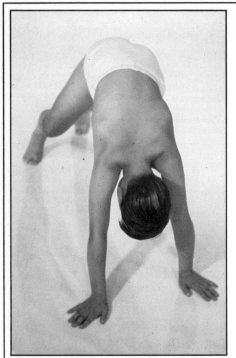

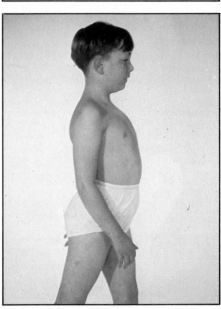

Although girls can be carriers of Duchenne's dystrophy, the disease normally only afflicts boys. Weak leg muscles, particularly those in the thighs, result in difficulties in walking and climbing when the disease is in its early stages. An inability to stand up after a fall is another sign. The patient shown here illustrates how children are taught to get themselves off the ground into a standing position. After raising himself up on all four limbs, he balances on his legs and places his hands on his knees. From there he helps himself into an erect position by 'walking' up his legs with his hands.

parent with the disease. Anyone with this type of dystrophy has a 50 per cent chance of passing it on to each of his or her children.

The face is affected first, with difficulty in puffing up the cheeks or blowing up a balloon being an early sign. Normally the symptoms appear in the teens, but it is possible to find signs of the disease in people in their fifties who did not know that they were ill. The heart is usually unaffected, although people with this condition can occasionally have all the problems that are associated with Duchenne-type dystrophy. As a rule, however, it does not diminish life expectancy and people can be quite old before they suffer a significant disability.

Myotonic dystrophy or dystrophica myotonica differs significantly from the dystrophies described above, and is the type people are most familiar with. Myotonia means an inability to relax a muscle after it has contracted. This is the earliest symptom that patients will experience and it may occur in the teens. The disease often affects the hands and an inability to relax a hand shake is one of the first signs. In later life the muscles of the face, neck and hands may become wasted and weak, and this may eventually spread to the legs. Unlike all other types of the disease, myotonic dystrophy may produce symptoms in other parts of the body. For example, baldness (in both male and female patients) and cataracts are common. It is also the most variable of the dystrophies, with symptoms ranging from a minor degree of failure in muscle relaxation in a person who lives out a normal life span, to severe weakness that comes on in early life.

Treatment and outlook

Unfortunately there is no treatment that will stop the progression of weakness in the dystrophies, although drugs such as quinine are used to aid relaxation in myotonia. However, patients are encouraged to take as much exercise as possible. This will keep those muscles which are in good condition functioning normally.

Because the outlook for muscular dystrophy is poor, it is important that would-be parents with a family history of the disease seek professional advice from a genetic counsellor before they decide to begin a family. Advice prevents reoccurrence.

Nephritis

Q I keep getting attacks of cystitis, and I have even had one attack of acute pyelonephritis. Is there a risk that I will develop chronic pyelonephritis?

A No. Cystitis can lead to acute pyelonephritis, and this has happened to you once already, but doctors think that most cases of the chronic condition become established in childhood. However, your doctor may want to have a kidney X-ray to check that there is no abnormality in the structure of your kidneys that might make you more at risk from attacks of pyelonephritis.

Q My litle grandson has the nephrotic syndrome. We are terribly worried that it will get worse and he will need to go on a kidney machine. Is something like this likely to happen?

A No. Most young children with the nephrotic syndrome have what is called minimal change disease. This means that when the kidney tissue is examined under a microscope, very little difference can be seen from normal tissue. Minimal change disease is so common in young children that doctors do not always perform a biopsy for this age group, whereas they do for all older patients. It is also most unusual for this type of glomerulonephritis to fail to get better on its own, so there is no need to worry about the need for a kidney machine. However, you may need to be prepared for a series of relapses before the condition finally gets better, and your grandson may need to have treatment with steroid drugs for a while to help him over the problem.

Q My face is very puffy in the mornings. Could this mean I am developing the nephrotic syndrome?

A It is most unlikely. It is not uncommon for a person's face to be a bit puffy in the morning. If, however, your urine is very frothy, your ankles are also swollen, or you feel generally off colour, it is worth seeing your doctor. It will only take him a few minutes to check your urine for protein.

Malfunction of the kidneys is rather unusual, but when it occurs, nephritis—inflammation of the kidney—is often the cause. Fortunately, knowledge and treatment of the disease has advanced considerably in recent years.

Inflammation of any organ often results from infection by bacteria, and the kidney is no exception. Nephritis which arises from bacterial infection is called pyelonephritis. However, nephritis may result from changes in the structure of the kidney tubules (tiny tubes), particularly the glomerulus—a part of the tubule that filters the blood and extracts the waste products that are then expelled as urine (see pp204–07). This second type of kidney inflammation is called glomerulonephritis.

Pyelonephritis

There are two forms of pyelonephritis: acute pyelonephritis, a feverish illness that usually results from an infection (normally cystitis) lower down in the urinary system, and chronic pyeloneph-

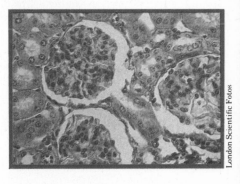

The healthy kidney (above) shows the tubes (glomerules) through which blood is filtered. Below is a renal biopsy. This kidney section is shown to be diseased with a glomerular dysfunction (inset).

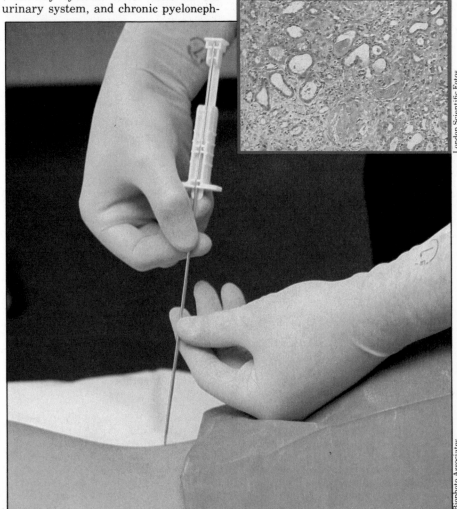

London Scientific Fotos

Biophoto Associates

ritis, which results from repeated infection of the kidney. Chronic pyelonephritis causes the affected kidney to become scarred with fibrous tissue. It has recently become clear that in the majority of cases the damage is done early in childhood. The kidneys do not necessarily deteriorate at this stage, but once the process of fibrosis and shrinking begins, it leads to a slow deterioration in the function of the kidneys which may not cause problems until adulthood.

Chronic pyelonephritis occurs in a very small proportion of children who have a deficiency at the end of the ureter where it empties into the bladder. This allows the urine to flow back up into the ureter and therefore to carry infection towards the bladder. This 'reflux' shows up on a special X-ray taken during the passing of urine. Any child with a history of repeated urinary infections should have this test (IVP X-ray) done. Chronic pyelonephritis and repeated attacks of acute pyelonephritis can also occur in people who have some abnormalities in the structure of their kidneys and ureter.

The symptoms of acute pyelonephritis are a feverish illness, pain over the kidney and in the loin, and both pain and burning on passing water. Chronic pyelonephritis does not cause pain. The first indication that it is present may be when the patient's kidneys stop excreting all the body's waste products. This leads to tiredness and general ill-health, and is known as chronic renal failure. Alternatively, the disease may cause high blood pressure. A characteristic feature of this disease is the presence of blood and protein in the urine.

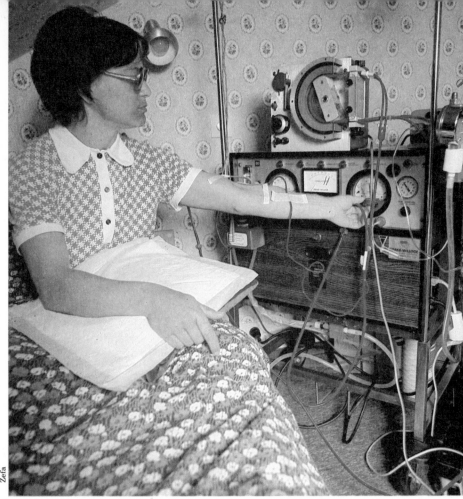

Glomerulonephritis

Glomerulonephritis is a group of disorders, all of which result from inflammation of the kidney material in general and the glomerulus in particular. It is only by examining kidney tissue under a microscope that the various forms of the disease can be differentiated.

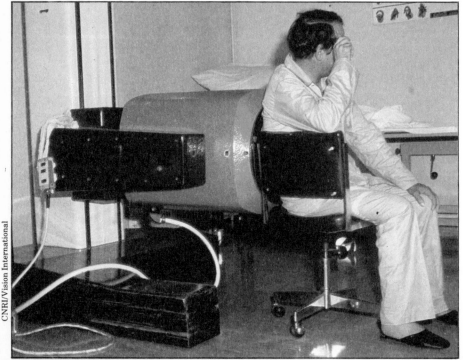

Patients can operate a kidney machine in their own home. The machine takes over the function of the kidney which it clears.

Glomerulonephritis can result from a wide range of different diseases, for example a sore throat caused by a streptococcal infection, or it may be associated with the rheumatic disorder, lupus erythematosus. More frequently, however, the disease has no obvious cause, in which case it is described as idiopathic.

The disorder comes to light as one of two syndromes (a group of symptoms that occur together and produce a characteristic picture). In the first, acute nephritis syndrome, there is some reduction in the amount of urine that is passed, together with some retention of fluid. This leads to swelling (oedema), often around the face and ankles, and even to pulmonary oedema, fluid in the lungs which results in breathlessness. Blood is always present in the urine and the blood pressure is often raised a little,. When waste products cleared by the kidneys are measured in the blood, some degree of deficiency in kidney function may be found through the tests.

To diagnose abnormalities in the kidneys, such as a narrowing of the renal artery, a renal scan will be performed.

Symptoms and treatment of nephritis

Type of disease	Symptoms	Treatment
Acute pyelonephritis	Fever; pain over the kidney and in the loin; pain and burning on passing water	Antibiotics and plenty of fluids; surgery in cases when the condition is caused by damage to the ureters
Chronic pyelonephritis	Tiredness and general ill-health; high blood pressure; presence of blood and protein in the urine	Control of blood pressure with drugs; dialysis or kidney transplant in cases of kidney failure
Glomerulonephritis	Fluid retention; blood and protein in the urine; high blood pressure	Varies according to the type of condition; includes use of steroids, dietary control, dialysis or kidney transplant in cases of kidney failure

The urinary system

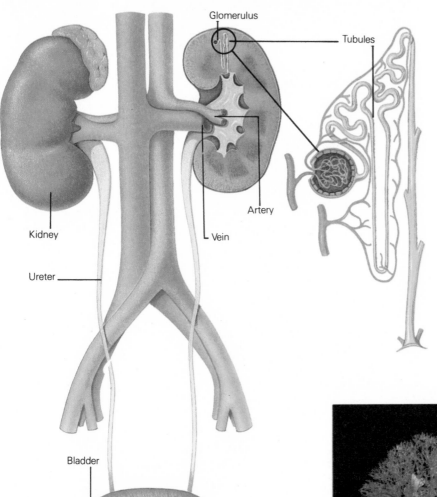

Glomerulus

Tubules

Artery

Vein

Kidney

Ureter

Bladder

The second disorder that glomerulonephritis may cause is called the nephrotic syndrome. It is quite common in children: about 30 children in a million have the condition compared with 8 adults in every million. Nephrotic syndrome differs from acute nephritis in the higher amount of protein that is lost in the urine. As in acute nephritis, swelling is the first symptom, and indicates a large accumulation of fluid in the tissues. It can appear on any part of the body, but is more common in loosely knit tissue such as the skin around the eyes and the male genitals. The legs and ankles may also swell. The syndrome usually occurs when 5 gm (about 1/6th oz) of protein are lost in the urine every day, although in severe cases five times this amount can pass out daily. The loss of protein permits fluid to leak out of the blood vessels into the body tissue.

The main diagram, left, shows how the kidneys and bladder link up. It also indicates the glomerulus. Glomerulonephritis is an inflammation of the glomerus—shown in detail in the diagram. Chronic pyelonephritis causes the kidney to become scarred. Below is a model of a pair of healthy kidneys.

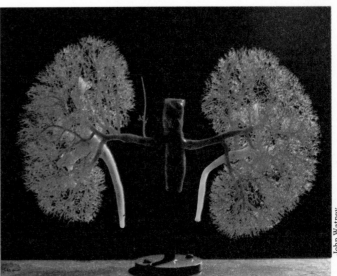

Q On each visit to the antenatal clinic, the nurse tests my urine. Is this because there is a risk of nephritis in pregnancy?

A Your urine is tested to detect any presence of sugar or protein. The nurses look for sugar because there is an increased risk of diabetes in pregnancy. The reason for looking for protein is to prevent the occurrence of the condition called toxaemia of pregnancy. The condition involves raised blood pressure, swelling of the legs, fits, and protein in the urine. As the kidneys are involved it is quite reasonable to call it a form of nephritis, although it is normally just referred to as toxaemia. Fortunately, it is possible to detect the early signs of this at the clinic, which is one of the main reasons for attending. Further complications can then be prevented by taking the expectant mother into hospital for a rest.

Q My brother has been told he has glomerulonephritis, and that he must go on a low protein diet. As he is losing protein in his urine, I would have thought he should increase his protein intake. Is this wrong?

A Controlling the amount of protein in the diet is one of the more important factors in treating people with kidney disease. A patient with the nephrotic syndrome loses a large amount of protein in his urine, so initially it is quite reasonable to increase his protein intake. However, the situation changes if the kidney begins to deteriorate. In such cases the kidney has to deal with a high level of urea—the main protein waste product—which makes the patient feel rather ill. By reducing the amount of protein in the diet the doctor can reduce the load on the kidney and so improve your brother's well-being.

Q I have been diagnosed as suffering from acute pyelonephritis. Will I need to be put on a kidney machine?

A No. Acute pyelonephritis can normally be treated with antibiotics and an increased intake of fluid. Don't worry: you won't need to be put on a kidney machine.

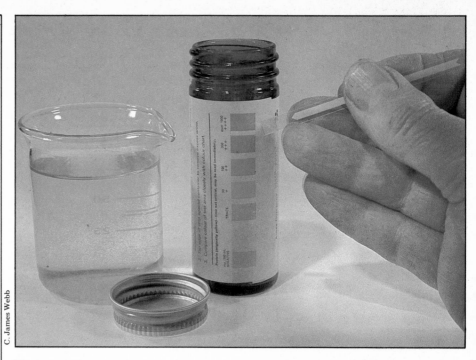

C. James Webb

Dangers

The main danger of any type of kidney disease is that it will develop into kidney failure. In such cases patients are unable to survive unless the kidneys are helped to clear waste products with the aid of a kidney machine, or he or she is given a kidney transplant.

Acute pyelonephritis is not likely to develop into kidney failure but chronic pyelonephritis and most types of glomerulonephritis may. Generally, the chances of kidney failure are increased with high blood pressure. Since high blood pressure alone can damage the kidneys, its effect on a diseased kidney is much greater. However, careful control of blood pressure with drugs can help to lessen the risk.

Treatment and outlook

Acute pyelonephritis can normally be treated with antibiotics and an increased intake of fluids. However, recurrent attacks of acute pyelonephritis, particularly in children, can indicate a reflux of urine back to the kidneys from the bladder. In this case it is possible to perform an operation to reimplant the ureters into the bladder and stop this happening. Investigations are being carried out to see if antibiotics can halt the scarring in chronic pyelonephritis when it is found in children.

In order for the correct treatment to be given for glomerulonephritis, the exact form of the disease must be known. Some forms of the disease get better without medical treatment; others are divided into those that respond to steroids and those that do not. Diuretic treatment in

To test for nephritis, a measurement is made of the level of protein in the blood. A dip stick is put in a urine sample and the colour is checked against a chart.

the form of water tablets helps reduce swelling, and diet is altered to limit the intake of salt, which contributes to the swelling. Protein intake sometimes needs to be restricted in order to lessen the work load of the malfunctioning kidneys. However, where cases lead to kidney failure, no form of treatment seems able to halt this progress, and the patient is put on a kidney machine or, alternatively, is given a kidney transplant.

The outlook in pyelonephritis is generally quite good and people often do not run into any trouble until later in life. They may then develop both a raised blood pressure and some degree of failure of the kidneys. As with all forms of kidney failure, a kidney machine or transplant may eventually become necessary. Usually, however, the treatment of blood pressure and reduction of protein in the diet keeps the kidneys functioning well.

In the minor form of glomerulonephritis—the commonest type in children—the outlook is good. The condition usually responds to steroid drugs.

The outlook in the other forms of glomerulonephritis depends on the microscopic appearance of the kidney: the patient may go on to develop high blood pressure and kidney failure.

One of the common forms of nephritis follows on from streptoccocal infection—and may be serious while it lasts—but once the patient has recovered there should be no long term problems.

Nettle sting

Q Does the sap from a dock leaf really relieve the irritation of a nettle sting?

A Many old herbals recommend freshly gathered, well-washed dock leaves as a healing agent for itches, sores and skin infections. Although many people experience relief when they rub a dock leaf on a nettle sting, doctors remain sceptical about its value. It may well be that the moisture in the crushed leaf cools an inflammation that has already begun to subside.

Q Does rubbing the rash from a nettle sting make the itching last longer?

A Yes. The blisters that form in nettle-rash contain the allergen. If you scratch and break them you will spread the allergen and therefore the rash. In addition, when it punctured your skin the nettle created a pathway into your body, so if you rub the area with a dirty hand you will increase the risk of infection.

Q When I was pregnant I read that itching can be relieved by bathing with a lotion made by steeping nettle leaves in hot water. If nettles sting, how can this remedy work?

A Heat destroys the stinging hairs in nettles, and infusions of their milky juice have been used for centuries to stop bleeding and to cure blocked sinuses. It is possible that the action of bathing itself relieves itching. Many modern treatments originated as folk remedies, and as this one has survived for so long perhaps it is due for scientific investigation.

Q My grandfather says nettle stings are good for you. Can he be right?

A Probably not, but his belief is understandable. Many people think that nettle stings can both prevent and cure rheumatism, and this belief has been current since Roman times. The Romans even introduced a nettle more virulent than the native British species in order to resuscitate limbs made stiff by harsh winters.

Stings from nettles can be quite painful, especially for children. But both the soreness and the rash are usually short-lived and easily treated.

Nettles belong to a class of allergens that cause a reaction after direct contact with the skin. The leaves and sometimes the stems, flowers and fruits of nettles are covered in minute stinging hairs which can puncture the skin and cause severe pain. Nettle stings are a cause of hivés (see page 178) and the rash of red and white weals looks the same after a nettle sting as in a case of hives.

The nettle's hairs are hollow and have a bulbous gland at the root which contains a stinging juice. At the end of the hair is a single, sharply pointed cell that penetrates the skin on contact and then breaks off.

Symptoms

The symptoms of a nettle rash begin with the sting. A sudden sharp pain is felt as the plant-hair pierces the skin. This is followed by a burning sensation as the stinging juice enters the wound. The body retaliates by surrounding the area under attack with special white blood cells which produce organisms that neutralize the poison. The blood cells also release histamine and it is this which causes the skin to itch.

Effects and treatment

If only a small area of skin is affected the pain will subside in a few minutes. But the itching reaction of the histamine is likely to linger for six hours or more. The mild effects of European nettles usually do not last more than 24 hours; but most nettles are tropical species and the effects can be quite pronounced.

Most nettle stings are adequately treated by soothing the itching with calamine lotion.

Nettles pose a real hazard for children, who may not recognize what they look like (left) and are therefore accidentally stung.

Bruce Coleman Ltd

Tony Stone Associates

Nits

Q If my children get nits, does it mean they are dirty?

A No, not at all. Of course, nits can thrive more easily in unkempt, uncombed hair which may or may not be dirty. But the idea that lice feed on dirt and therefore are only found on dirty people is a myth. Lice can survive long immersion in water, so your children could wash their hair every day and still have nits. See your doctor if your children get head lice. He or she will prescribe a preparation or shampoo that will kill the lice. It is not necessary to comb out every nit—this can be time-consuming and painful, especially for a young child. If the preparation has been used properly, the nits will be dead and will eventually disappear as the hair grows out.

Q Can I catch nits off a pillow or train seat?

A Nits are cemented so firmly to a single hair that it is extremely unlikely that they will be brushed off to lie in wait for another host. They need a constant temperature of not less than 22°C (72°F) to survive and hatch, so if they are shed—perhaps on a loose hair—it is more likely that they will die before you come along.

Q Could I catch head lice from second-hand clothing?

A No. Head lice do not live on clothes. They can only be caught by close contact with a person who has head lice, usually by sitting or lying close enough for heads—or at least hair—to touch, when the adult louse will walk across. It is also highly unlikely that you would catch body lice from old clothing. Adult lice need a certain temperature to survive, and a constant supply of human blood to live off. If you are still worried, wash old clothing and iron all seams carefully—this is where nits may lurk.

Q Can one get nits in pubic or chest hair?

A Yes—but not the nits of head lice. Body lice and pubic lice are different adaptions of the louse family and the three types are never found on each other's territory.

There is no shame attached to having nits, or head lice—they are no respecters of persons and will infest clean as well as dirty hair. They are easy to treat with a preparation prescribed by your doctor.

Nits are eggs of the head louse, pediculus humanus capitis, which are found stuck to the hairs on the head, quite close to the scalp. The adult head louse is passed on from person to person by close contact, can carry diseases and always causes irritation and discomfort. Head lice are an increasingly common problem but one that can be treated.

The life of the louse

The egg or nit is cemented on to a hair close to the scalp by the female louse. The nit is yellow-whitish in colour and transparent—the embryo louse can be seen quite clearly through the walls. After eight to nine days the louse hatches out. Since hair grows one third of a millimetre a day the egg is clear of the scalp, so the louse leaves the case behind and scrambles down the hair to the scalp.

The louse—or nymph as it is known at this stage—is wingless, flat and has claws adapted to clinging to hair. It lives exclusively on blood. On hatching, the nymph will need an immediate meal—its transparent body turns ruby red as it feeds. The nymph grows by moulting out of a smaller body—this occurs three times in six days, by which time it is fully grown. The adult louse is greyish in colour although it adapts to the colour of the hair in which it lives—the lice of blondes are paler than those living on brunettes.

Eight or nine days after it hatches, the female louse will start to lay her eggs. She is capable of lying eight to ten a night

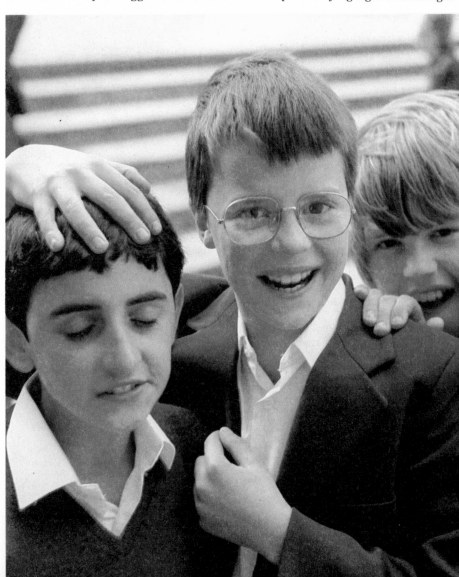

for the rest of her life, which in ideal conditions can be up to 28 days.

Head lice are quite large—two to three millimetres in length and the nits or eggs are not much smaller. Lice are therefore visible to the naked eye, so they have become very adept at hiding in our hair. Because the nit is often the most obvious sign that someone has head lice, we tend to talk about people having nits rather than lice. Lice need about 10 mm (⅓ in) of hair on which to cement the nits. So it is obvious that a skinhead haircut will prove impossible to them. To hatch out, the nits also need the temperature of their surroundings to be at least 22°C (72°F).

Lice are extremely vulnerable when in the nymph or adult phase and will die if they are even slightly damaged—if a

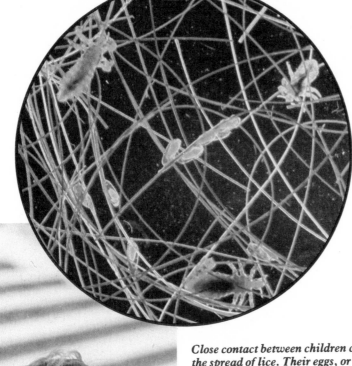

Close contact between children could mean the spread of lice. Their eggs, or nits, are shown above cemented fast to human hair.

comb severs a leg, for instance. So both long and short hair which is not adequately and frequently combed will harbour lice. The nits, or eggs, of the head louse, however, are very strong—the cement holding them to the hairs will withstand onslaught of all but a very fine-toothed comb.

Head lice will only leave a human head in one situation—when there is another head on offer!

Schools or playgrounds are obvious places to catch head lice. As children play or study, they often lean their heads together over a book or to chat and giggle. Lice can also be passed on if combs are shared, although lice caught in the comb's teeth are usually fatally injured. It is rare to catch lice from pets.

Illness
Lice used to carry typhus and relapsing fever, but these diseases no longer occur in Britain. However, the bite of a louse can make you feel quite ill. Each time a louse bites into your scalp to feed—on average, every three hours, although more frequently at night—it injects a little saliva containing a local anaesthetic (so you will not feel the bite and brush it off) and an anticoagulant, so the blood does not clot immediately and stop its meal. These chemicals will cause a local irritation in about nine hours. The severity of symptoms varies from individual to individual but in the second or third week of infestation the victim will have swelling and irritation around the bites, a mild fever, muscular aches especially in the calves of the legs and may have swelling and pain in the cervical glands (in the neck at the top of the spine).

For this reason many people believe that nits only live on dirty heads and only infest the poor and deprived. But the dirty, scabby head of a louse victim is more the result than the cause of the infestation. Lice cannot be drowned, either as nits or as adults, so ordinary shampoo and even frequent washing have absolutely no effect on them.

If the nits are not detected, or are left untreated, the infestation will expand and continue. Whole families can be infected, from one louse which has crawled onto the head of one member of that family.

Treatment
There are preparations for the treatment of lice which your doctor can prescribe for you. Consulting your doctor is better than buying a de-lousing lotion or shampoo which is commercially available.

┌─ **TAKE CARE** ─────────
How to prevent nits
● Encourage each child to have his or her own fine-toothed comb, to use it often, wash it frequently and *never* lend it to friends.
● Examine your children's hair—make it a game while shampooing them. You may miss the lice which will hide but nits are easily seen, firmly cemented to a hair. On girls, nits tend to be found in the area just behind or over the ears: in boys near the top of the head.
● Watch out for lice when combing your own or your children's hair. A louse you find will be dead or dying, but may have left nits. Dandruff and lice are easy to tell apart if you look carefully.
● With teenagers, encourage them to take pride in their appearance, even if you find their fashions bizarre.
● If you do find nits, tell your children's school so that other sufferers can be found and treated.

Oral contraceptives

Q Can the pill cause loss of interest in sex?

A Some women do find that their interest in sex is decreased when they go on the pill. However, this can often be put right by a change of pill, so it is well worth seeing your doctor about the difficulty and getting a prescription for a pill containing a different balance of hormones.

Q I have varicose veins and I have heard that the pill can make them worse. Is this true?

A If your varicose veins are minor, and you are not in a high risk category for any other reason (medical history, smoking and so forth), you will almost certainly be able to take the pill without extra risks, or greater problems with varicose veins. However, be sure to talk to your doctor about your medical conditions, including the varicose veins, before the pill is prescribed.

Q Should I regularly give the pill a rest to allow my body to get back into the menstrual cycle?

A There is no need to do this frequently, as used to be thought. Neither is there any indication that women who have irregular periods when they are off the pill need to have extra breaks from it. It is generally thought that, provided you are fit and healthy, the pill can be taken without a break for as long as ten years. At that point you might want to consider another form of contraception.

Q Should I tell any doctor I see that I'm on the pill, even if the consultation is about something entirely different?

A Yes, you should. A doctor knows what drugs might interfere with each other, and can avoid prescribing those that will reduce the effectiveness of the pill for you. He or she needs to be aware that you are taking it because this sometimes affects the results of laboratory tests. It is particularly important for a doctor to know what pill a woman is taking if she has to have an operation.

The oral contraceptive – 'the Pill' – is the most reliable reversible method of birth control that exists at present, and one of the most widely used.

Oral contraceptives are made of synthetic hormones similar to those that occur naturally in a woman's body. They prevent pregnancy, and are taken by mouth in pill form. Some oral contraceptives work by stopping ovulation, others by making it difficult for sperm to reach the egg, or for implantation of a fertilized egg in the uterus' wall to take place.

The combination pill is made up of oestrogen and progestogen, and is taken daily for 21 days, followed by seven—or in some cases six—pill-free days in which a withdrawal bleed takes place. The progestogen-only pill (also known as the mini-pill) is taken every day. The triphasic pill is a type of combination pill, but contains a different amount of the two synthetic hormones for different times in the month.

How oral contraceptives work

Different types of pill work in different ways. The combined pill has hormones that are very much like those produced by the body when a pregnancy has occurred. This means that the pituitary gland, which normally sends a message to the ovary to produce its monthly egg acts as if the body is already pregnant; it therefore does not send its egg-stimulating hormone and so no ovulation takes place.

The progestogen-only pill—the mini-pill—does not always stop ovulation from occurring. It makes fertilization by the sperm more difficult by thickening the mucus in the cervical channel leading from the vagina to the uterus (womb), and inhibits the formation of uterine lining which is necessary for the fertilized egg if it is to implant itself. As a result, implantation (and pregnancy) do not take place.

The different types of pill

There are a number of pharmaceutical companies making these pills, and although some of them have different brand names, they are made of identical chemical constituents. Combination pills have two constituents listed; progestogen-only have, of course, just one constituent.

Triphasic pills provide different amounts of the two hormones found in an ordinary pill packet for each week of the cycle, and are said to mimic the menstrual cycle more effectively.

The combination pill is taken for 21 days, with a seven-or six-day break every month. Some women prefer to have a pill every day, so there are some 21-day combination pills that include seven dummy tablets to be taken throughout the fourth week. If you think you will find these pills easier to remember, it is worth asking your doctor for them.

The progestogen-only pills must be taken every day, and can cause changes in periods while they are being taken. Some women don't have any bleeding for several months, others have frequent breakthrough bleeds during the month. Many women have no problems of this sort at all. Bleeding does not mean that the pill isn't working properly, but if you find irregular bleeding troublesome ask your doctor's advice. You are probably not pregnant, but if you are more than two weeks overdue, see your doctor. Which pill you take will be up to you and your doctor. The progestogen-only pill is thought to involve less change of circulatory problems, so is often a first-choice method for those who may be at risk from this kind of disease.

Effect on the body

There are many positive effects of the pill, not least the protection from unwanted pregnancy: 99 per cent or more reliability for the combined pill, 98 per cent for the progestogen-only pill. The pill can also actively protect a woman from certain kinds of disorders, such as the formation of benign breast lumps, can help to clear up acne, and reduce wax in the ears. Since the body is no longer going through the menstrual cycle many of the problems associated with periods—pre-menstrual tension, pain, or heavy bleeding—can be alleviated. Research also suggests that there may be some protection against thyroid and uterine disorders, but this has not yet been confirmed.

Troublesome side-effects may occur at the beginning of a course of pills. Some women find that when they first start taking the pill they feel slightly sick, or that their breasts become a little swollen and sore. Some women who suffer from migraines may find that their condition is made worse by the pill, although for others the opposite is the case. The pill can also affect the ability to wear contact lenses, since the amount of fluid on the surface of the eye may be reduced. It is also thought that the absorption of some

Facts about 'the Pill'

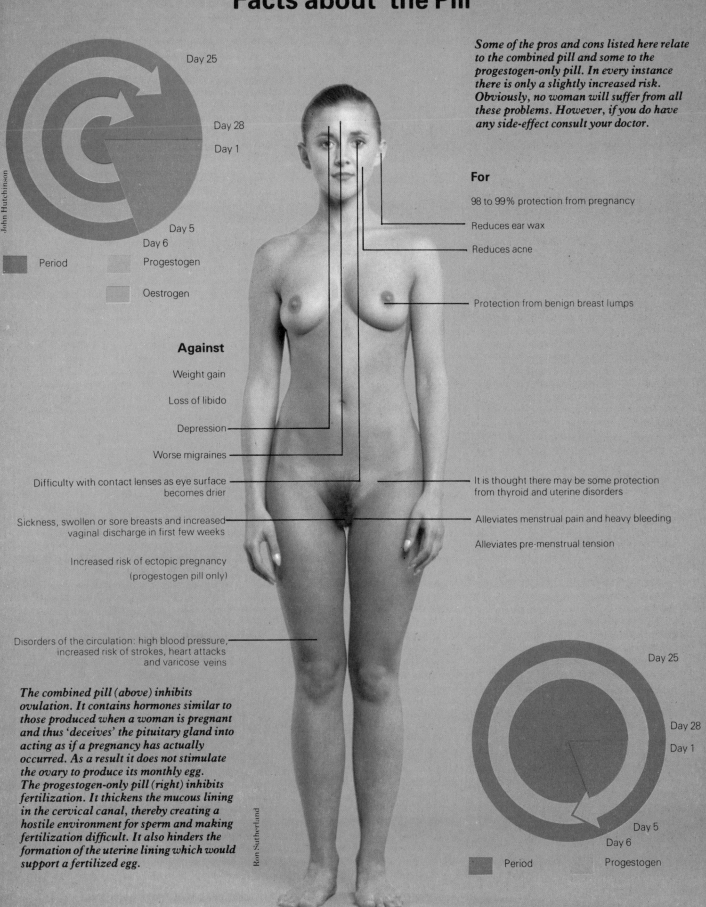

Day 25

Day 28

Day 1

Day 5

Day 6

John Hutchinson

Period   Progestogen

Oestrogen

Some of the pros and cons listed here relate to the combined pill and some to the progestogen-only pill. In every instance there is only a slightly increased risk. Obviously, no woman will suffer from all these problems. However, if you do have any side-effect consult your doctor.

For

98 to 99% protection from pregnancy

Reduces ear wax

Reduces acne

Protection from benign breast lumps

Against

Weight gain

Loss of libido

Depression

Worse migraines

Difficulty with contact lenses as eye surface becomes drier

Sickness, swollen or sore breasts and increased vaginal discharge in first few weeks

Increased risk of ectopic pregnancy (progestogen pill only)

It is thought there may be some protection from thyroid and uterine disorders

Alleviates menstrual pain and heavy bleeding

Alleviates pre-menstrual tension

Disorders of the circulation: high blood pressure, increased risk of strokes, heart attacks and varicose veins

*The combined pill (above) inhibits ovulation. It contains hormones similar to those produced when a woman is pregnant and thus 'deceives' the pituitary gland into acting as if a pregnancy has actually occurred. As a result it does not stimulate the ovary to produce its monthly egg.
The progestogen-only pill (right) inhibits fertilization. It thickens the mucous lining in the cervical canal, thereby creating a hostile environment for sperm and making fertilization difficult. It also hinders the formation of the uterine lining which would support a fertilized egg.*

Ron Sutherland

Day 25

Day 28

Day 1

Day 5

Day 6

Period   Progestogen

Q I've been on the pill for five years, and I now want to become pregnant. When should I go off the pill?

A It is worth going off the pill straight away to give your body time to get back into the menstrual cycle, and you may find that there is a delay before regular periods return. Use other contraceptive methods until you have had two periods, after which time you can try to become pregnant. The delay that sometimes happens between going off the pill and the hoped-for pregnancy may not be due to the pill at all, or it may be that the body needs a little more time before ovulation begins again. If you have tried for a year or more to become pregnant without success, a fertility clinic may be able to help you.

Q I got pregnant when I forgot two pills, but I went on taking them for a time, assuming that I wasn't pregnant. Will this have harmed the baby in any way?

A Taking the pill during the early weeks of pregnancy has not been shown to harm the developing foetus, but research into this is still going on. This is why doctors advise any woman who suspects that she may be pregnant to stop taking the pill and use another method until it has been confirmed whether she is pregnant or not.

Q How often should I have a medical check-up when I'm on the pill?

A You should see your doctor after the first three months on the pill, and thereafter have a check-up every six months. Your blood pressure should be checked, you should have a urine test, and you should be weighed. If your own doctor is not able to do this for you, if you are in Britain it is worth changing to a family planning clinic for advice on contraception, for check-ups—and for the pill itself.

Q Will I gain weight if I go on the pill?

A You may find that you put on a few pounds when you first start taking the pill, and that your weight returns to normal after that.

Taking 'the Pill'

● Taking the combination pill at bedtime, as part of a routine, makes it easier to remember.
● If you do forget one pill, but remember it *within 12 hours,* you will still be protected if you take the rest of the packet at the right time. If you are more than 12 hours late, you will need extra contraceptive precautions for the next 14 days of pill-taking.

● The progestogen-only pill is at its most effective four hours after it is taken, so the best time to do this is at a settled time in early evening.
● If you forget to take the progestogen only pill *for three hours,* you will be unprotected.
● Take the pill first on the first day of your period. Continue to take it *at the same time every day.*

vitamins may be slightly reduced, but this does not need to be a problem: the solution is a healthy diet providing more than enough vitamin intake.

Depression can also be caused by the pill, and in some cases so can loss of libido (sex drive). If you suffer from these symptoms when you are on the pill, discuss them with your doctor, so that an alternative to the combination pill can be considered.

The most dangerous side-effect of the combination pill is the increased likelihood of blood circulatory disorders, such as high blood pressure, thrombosis, heart attacks and strokes. These affect only a tiny minority of women on the pill, and the risk has been greatly reduced by the introduction of those pills containing a lower dose of hormones. However, because the pill does increase the likelihood of these disorders, prospective pill-

users must be carefully screened to see if they are particularly at risk. Your own medical history, and that of your family, will need to be studied. Smoking, being overweight, and being over 35 years of age all increase the risk of these disorders, so women who are in any of these categories are often advised not to use the combination pill. The progestogen-only pill does not seem to carry such risks, and is the one most often prescribed for older women.

The progestogen-only pill is not quite so effective in preventing pregnancy as the combined pill. There is a tiny risk that if an egg is fertilized it will implant itself outside the womb, since the uterine lining is not soft or spongy enough to receive it. This is called an ectopic pregnancy, and it can take place in one of the Fallopian tubes. The risk of it happening is very small indeed, but it is a dangerous condition, needing immediate treatment. Any pain in the lower abdomen should be reported to your doctor.

The return of the menstrual cycle may sometimes be delayed once a woman is off the pill, but it is now thought that it does not affect fertility in the long run.

The choice of which pill is best for you to start off with will be made by your doctor. Most women start with a low-dose combination pill, and are given three months' supply. Any immediate side-effects should be discussed with your doctor on your next visit, or sooner if you feel that they are serious.

Your doctor will advise you to start taking the combination pill on either day one or day five of your next period. If it is the latter, you will need to take additional contraceptive precautions (sheath or cap, both with spermicide) for 12 days after your first pill-taking day. After that time you are protected by the pill and do not need any extra protection. The combination pill should be taken at whatever time of day is most convenient for you. Many women find that taking it last thing at night becomes part of a routine which is easy to remember. If a pill is forgotten, but you are not more than 12 hours late in remembering to take it, you will still be protected as long as you continue to take the rest of the packet normally. If you are more than 12 hours late you will need to use additional contraceptive precautions for the next 14

Ron Sutherland

days of pill-taking, to make provision for the build-up of hormonal protection.

The progestogen-only pill will be taken first on day one of your period, and must be taken *at the same time every day*, since it is not quite so effective in protecting you against conception as the combination pill. You will need to take additional precautions for the first 14 days. Progestogen-only pills are at their

A woman taking the pill is able to lead a full and satisfying life, free of anxiety about unwanted pregnancy and of many of the discomforts that can accompany periods.

most effective four hours after they are taken, so it is best to do this at a regular time early in the evening. If you are three or more hours late in remembering to take the progestogen-only pill, you should consider yourself unprotected.

The effectiveness of both sorts of pill may be affected by a stomach upset (either vomiting or diarrhoea), as it could mean that the pill has not been absorbed. Other drugs, such as some antibiotics, drugs for epilepsy, sedatives and pain-killers, can also reduce the effect of the pill. Always check with your doctor if you are given any drug, to make sure that there is no risk of this happening.

Coming off the pill

How long a woman stays on the pill will depend on a number of factors, but doctors do recommend that the pill should not be used continuously for more than 10 years, since its very long-term effects are still not fully known.

Women who have to have any major surgery, or who are confined to bed for a time or have a leg in plaster, are advised to come off the pill until they are well again, since these conditions in themselves increase the risk of circulatory problems. Anyone who takes the combination pill would almost certainly have to come off it six weeks before an operation. A woman should, in fact, discuss this point with her doctor, whatever pill she is taking.

Common problems and solutions

Missed one combination pill but have remembered within 12 hours.	Take the missed pill immediately, take the next at its usual time, continue with the rest of the packet as normal.
Missed one combination pill but did *not* remember within 12 hours.	Take the missed pill immediately, the next at its usual time, and the rest of the packet as normal. Protection may have stopped so use additional contraceptive precautions.
Diarrhoea or vomiting	Continue to take pills as normal, but use additional precautions for the next 14 days.
No period in the pill-free week.	Check with your doctor whether you are pregnant and so whether to start the next packet of pills or not. Until you see him, use a cap or sheath (both with spermicide).
More than three hours late taking a progestogen-only pill.	You are no longer protected. Use another contraceptive for the next 14 days. Keep taking the pills at the regular time, starting with the one you forgot.

Orthodontics

Q I am 28 years old and have overlapping front teeth. Am I too old to have them fixed?

A No. Orthodontic treatment can be carried out on adults. It tends to take longer than when it is done in childhood; but provided you can accept the idea of wearing an appliance, it may be possible for your teeth to be corrected. Very severe discrepancies of tooth position are sometimes beyond the scope of orthodontics, even in childhood, and occasionally it may be necessary to give surgical treatment.

Q My daughter's teeth are very crooked and unsightly. Every time I speak to my dentist about this he tells me that he cannot consider giving orthodontic treatment until she improves her oral hygiene. I have great confidence in the dentist and have been his patient for many years, but I feel his attitude is rather unreasonable. What should I do?

A I'm afraid you will just have to nag her until she does clean her teeth properly. Your dentist is quite right in refusing treatment without satisfactory oral hygiene. Unless your daughter cleans her teeth and gums thoroughly she will probably lose her teeth when she is an adult. Also, wearing orthodontic appliances without cleaning the teeth properly can result in gum disease and tooth decay. This is because the presence of an appliance may make an existing oral hygiene problem worse.

Q Is there any danger that wearing an orthodontic appliance might damage my teeth?

A Provided you clean your teeth well to prevent plaque from accumulating, the presence of bands or wires on the teeth will not cause damage. If the appliance becomes a reservoir of bacterial plaque, however, tooth decay will result.

Q Is wearing an orthodontic appliance painful?

A No. There may be a slight discomfort initially, but within a few days this feeling disappears.

Uneven or protruding teeth need not be a cause of lifelong embarrassment. In most cases they can be fully corrected by orthodontic treatment.

Orthodontics is a branch of dentistry. It is concerned with correcting the position of teeth which are irregular and correcting any fault in the way upper and lower teeth come together, or bite. This form of treatment usually requires using appliances, such as braces, which move the teeth into their correct position. In cases where the teeth are too crowded together, some of them may have to be extracted to provide the necessary space for them to grow normally.

The normal position of teeth

Ideally, the upper and lower rows of teeth – the dental arches – should be symmetrical, with teeth in even positions. There should be no sign of overlapping (crowding) or spaces. The upper arch should be slightly larger than the lower one so that when the teeth bite, the upper teeth all fit just outside the lower ones.

This perfect arrangement of teeth is found only rarely. Just as people vary in

Normal bite

Normal bite: the upper and lower rows of teeth should be symmetrical, with teeth being in even positions, not overlapping or overcrowded. The upper teeth should fit just around the lower teeth, the upper arch being slightly larger than the lower. Such an ideal rarely exists. Incorrect bite: malocclusion occurs when the front teeth grossly overlap or protrude over the bottom row. Teeth may be spaced or overcrowded. Treatment for malocclusion is by a fixed appliance.

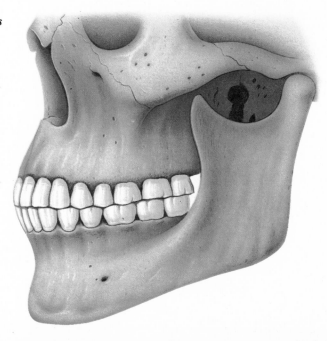

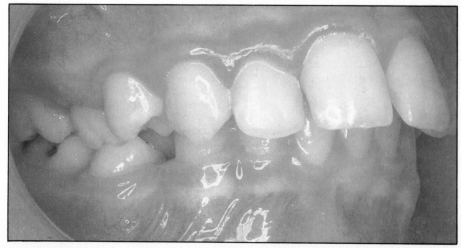

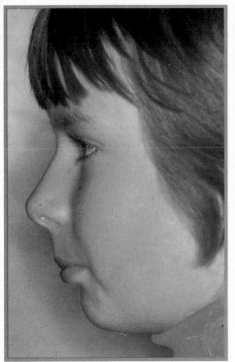
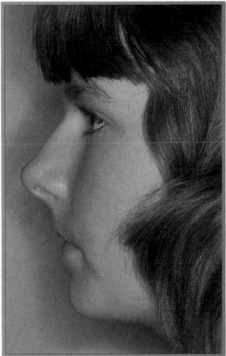

their height and in other physical characteristics, so they vary in the position of their teeth and structure of their jaws. Slight variations from the ideal pattern do not affect the health of the teeth or a person's appearance. In fact, many people would consider a minor degree of tooth irregularity attractive.

Orthodontic treatment is required when teeth are so uneven that they spoil the individual's appearance, or cause dental problems, or when they do not give a proper bite. The latter condition is known as malocclusion.

Causes of irregularities

Most of the factors that determine the size and position of the teeth, as well as the size of the jaw, are inherited. The characteristics inherited from both parents will therefore affect how the teeth will grow. For example, a child who has a father with large teeth and a mother with small jaws may have a combination of teeth and jaws which do not match, and may have overcrowded teeth.

In some cases, environmental factors will influence how teeth develop. Persistent finger- or thumb-sucking, for example, will change the position of the incisors (the four central teeth in both the upper and lower jaws). Tooth position may also be affected by diseases of the jaw, but this only occurs in a very small minority of cases.

Where significant irregularity is present, several problems may occur.

Teeth which are overlapping are more difficult to clean and this may result in gum disease and tooth decay. An incorrect bite, where the lower incisor teeth bite against the roof of the mouth instead of against the upper teeth, may give rise to inflammation of a part of the palate.

In some cases, when the teeth come together they bite on the wrong side of the teeth in the opposite jaw. This may have damaging effects on the jaw joints because the patient needs to bite to one side to avoid teeth which are in the way.

Incorrect bite: malocclusion

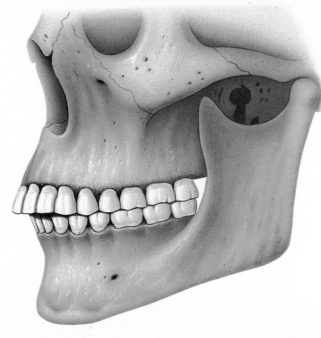

Mike Courtney

The photographs above show a child before and after orthodontic treatment. Note the striking changes in her profile. The photographs below show the same child's teeth in their original state and during and after treatment. The teeth were irregular, spaced, protruding and maloccluded. A fixed orthodontic appliance was used to correct these irregularities and was worn for three years. After that time, her bite became regular, with the teeth in correct position.

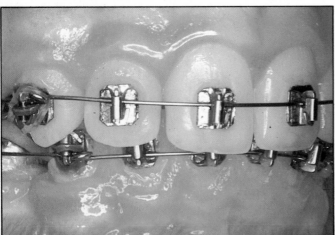

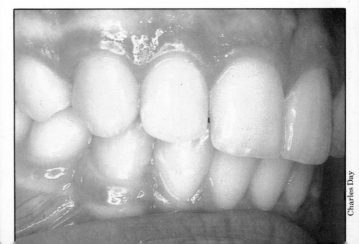

Charles Day

Grossly irregular or spaced teeth may cause problems with speech, although this is unusual. However, a person may feel embarrassment because of irregular teeth and treatment to correct the irregularly if frequently requested precisely for this reason.

Treatment

The time when treatment is given depends largely on the rate of development of the teeth. It is sometimes possible to start before all the milk teeth have fallen out but it is often necessary to wait for the premolars (the teeth in front of the molars) and permanent canine teeth (those next to the incisors) to come through – usually between 11 and 12.

When there appears to be a need for treatment, this is discussed with the patient and in the case of a child, with his parents. Impressions of teeth are taken from which plaster models are made. X-rays are taken to confirm the presence of and to locate any teeth which have not yet grown, and to assess the jaw's shape. The patient's face and teeth may be photographed. A treatment is then worked out.

Why extractions are necessary

Crowding of teeth usually occurs when the tooth size is so large that there is not enough space for all the teeth. Patients who have only a mild degree of overcrowding are often best advised to accept the situation. However, where it is more severe, treatment is indicated to help avoid the development of other problems, such as difficulty in cleaning the teeth adequately.

At one time it was thought that overcrowded teeth could be aligned simply by enlarging the dental arches. Although this treatment helps in the short term it has been shown that overcrowding will eventually recur. In most cases, the only long-term treatment is to extract some of the teeth already in place. This provides sufficient space for the rest of the teeth to come in and develop normally.

Careful consideration is given to choosing which teeth to extract. When all the teeth are in good condition, the first premolars are frequently removed. However, if certain teeth are very heavily filled or are badly positioned, these teeth

Children who persist in thumb-sucking once their permanent teeth come through may require orthodontic treatment (below).

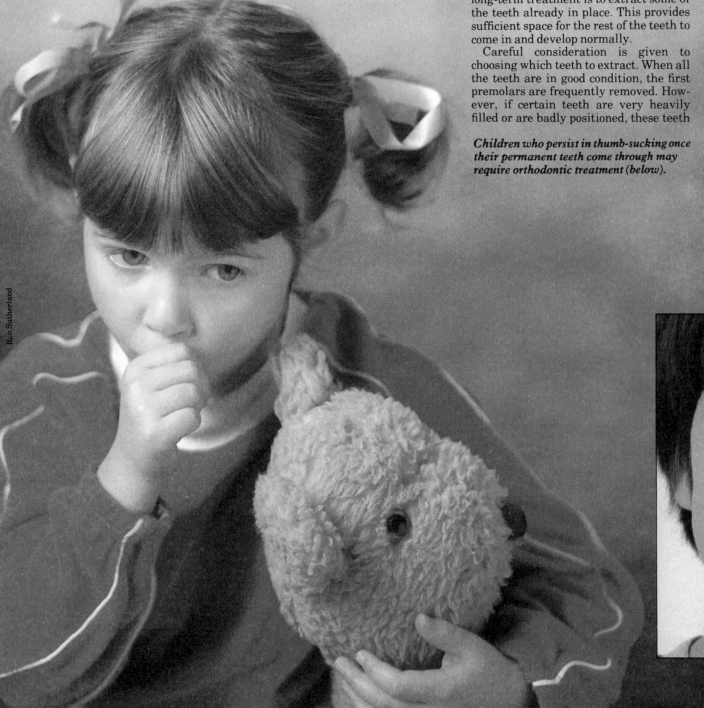

Ron Sutherland

Removable orthodontic appliances

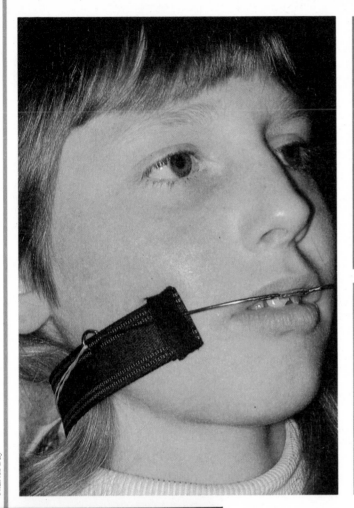

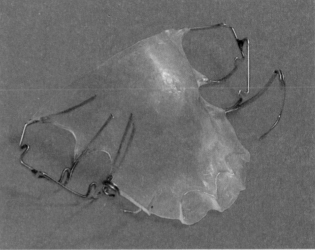

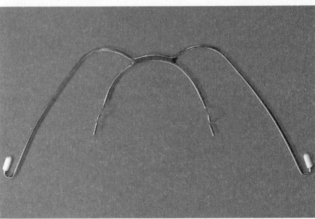

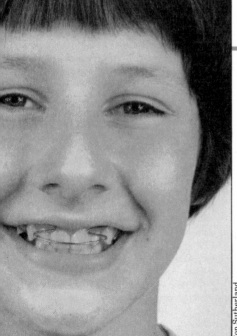

There are various types of removable orthodontic appliance, one of which is illustrated (top right). An extra-oral traction appliance (above) can be fitted in some cases. The two appliances are worn by the patient at night (above left).

will be extracted instead of the first premolars.

After the extractions have been carried out there is often a spontaneous improvement in the positions of adjacent teeth which tend to move into the space. However, such improvement is usually insufficient to correct the irregularity of the teeth fully, and an appliance will also be required.

Orthodontic appliances

There are two main types of orthodontic appliances: functional and mechanical. Both types move the teeth into the correct position and hold them there until they will maintain their place unaided. Functional appliances improve the way in which the upper and lower teeth meet, or bite. They move the entire dental arch as one unit, unlike fixed and removable appliances which move individual teeth. They are therefore only effective when a child is growing rapidly. For example, if all the upper teeth are too far forward, a functional appliance at the right age can mould the upper arch back as it grows, insuring a better contact with the lower arch when biting.

Mechanical appliances do not necessarily require growth in order to work, although their effect is more rapid during a phase of growing. The two main types of mechanical appliance are removable ones (which the patient can take out) and fixed appliances (those that are bonded to the teeth). Fixed appliances exert a greater degree of control on the teeth and produce movement in any direction. Removable appliances can only produce a tilting action on the teeth.

In general, fixed appliances are used in

271

Q What special precautions are required while wearing an orthodontic appliance?

A The most essential one is to maintain good oral hygiene. Removable appliances should be taken out at least twice a day, and teeth thoroughly cleaned with a brush and with dental floss. The appliance should also be scrubbed using a tooth-brush and tooth-paste. This should keep it free from any bacteria that may have accumulated.

Fixed appliances are more difficult to clean and therefore take longer to attend to. The use of a very small tooth-brush is the most effective way of cleaning around them. If the gum begins to bleed on contact with a tooth-brush, this suggests that some inflammation of the gums is present and even more thorough brushing is required. This may make the gum bleed at the time, but if thorough brushing is maintained, before long the gum will become firmer and then will no longer bleed on brushing.

If any problems with your gums occur, see your dentist.

Q I have heard that badly misplaced teeth can be transplanted. Is this true?

A It is possible to transplant completely buried teeth, but there must be adequate space for them. This method of treatment is used mainly in cases where upper canine teeth have failed to erupt. This occurs in about 2 per cent of people, and the teeth concerned remain below the surface—usually in the palate. Such a tooth can be removed surgically and then immediately inserted into a specially prepared socket in the right place.

After the transplant has been done it is necessary to hold the tooth in place with a splint while healing takes place (usually for three weeks). While most teeth that have been transplanted remain in good condition, a small number have to be removed subsequently either because of infection or because the root has been destroyed.

This technique is useful when teeth cannot be moved into the correct position by any other means, but it does not provide a substitute for routine orthodontic methods in cases where many teeth are incorrectly placed.

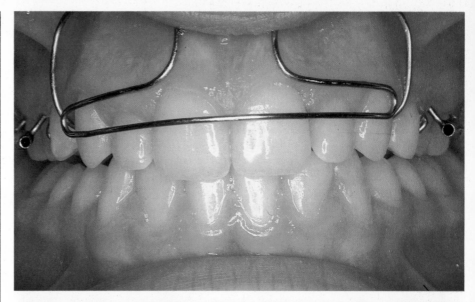

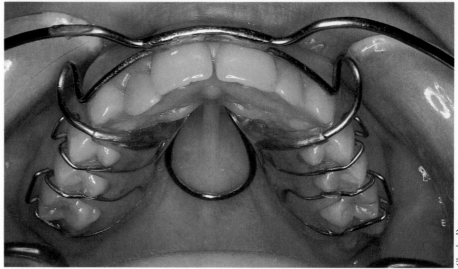

the more complex cases, where rotation or bodily movement of teeth is required. Removable appliances are utilized in cases where the teeth can simply be tilted back to their correct position.

Generally, removable appliances need to be worn day and night if they are to move the teeth effectively. The appliance is adjusted by the dentist, but there may be 'auxiliary' components such as elastic bands which the patient must change.

Extra oral traction (the application of force to the teeth from a source outside the mouth) is sometimes applied either to removable or fixed appliances. In these cases, additional force needs to be applied to move teeth back further.

Orthodontic appliances usually need adjustment at monthly intervals, and treatment generally takes between 18 months and two years. Although there is often some initial discomfort, after a few days the patient is usually perfectly comfortable wearing the appliance.

This shows the front view of a removable orthodontic appliance in place (top), and a view of the mouth when extra-oral traction is fixed permanently to it (bottom). The whole appliance is worn 14 hours a day.

Outlook

Treatment of malocclusion is possible because the bone which supports the teeth respond and adapts to light pressure and so teeth can be pushed into place. Irregular teeth can be made even and to a considerable extent the bite of the teeth can be corrected. It is doubtful however if the shape of the jaws themselves can be improved by orthodontic appliances, but nevertheless correction of tooth position can result in a great improvement in the facial profile.

Patients with very severe discrepancies of the jaw position generally require surgical treatment, although this is often facilitated by preliminary orthodontic realignment of the teeth.

Osteoarthritis

Many people regard aching and painful joints as an inevitable part of ageing. In fact the cause may be a disease called osteoarthritis. Drugs can relieve pain, and in severe cases surgery can effect dramatic improvement.

Q I have suffered from osteoarthritis for many years. Can my daughter inherit it?

A Osteoarthritis is not an inherited disease. However there is a tendency for people in the same family to develop osteoarthritis of the hands. This may reflect the fact that members of the same family often have the same sort of interests, and so subject their hands to the same sort of stresses, therefore increasing the likelihood of the disease.

Q I've read that professional footballers often suffer from osteoarthritis. This is worrying because I thought that exercise was good for you. Which is correct?

A Doctors are divided in their opinion about whether sportsmen like footballers really do have a higher rate of the disease. It may be that sportsmen, being active, are more likely to try and get help for minor degrees of osteoarthritis and so come to doctors' notice.

However the general view is that there is a small increase in the disease among professional sportsmen, particularly those who play contact sports like football. Indeed particular sports give rise to particular complaints: professional cyclists get knee problems, while professional footballers get a very unusual form of arthritis in the middle bones of the foot. This is probably due to the fact that these parts suffer from repeated small injuries.

Therefore, to put your mind at rest, we can say that exercise itself is not bad for you, but repeated injuries are, and may be a cause of osteoarthritis.

Q Is it true that damp weather makes osteoarthritis worse?

A This is such a common thing for patients to report that it seems almost bound to be true. However there is no obvious explanation of why it should occur. In fact there is nothing to suggest that a cold damp climate makes the disease progress or become more severe. It just seems that people are more aware of the pain that osteoarthritis causes when the weather is cold.

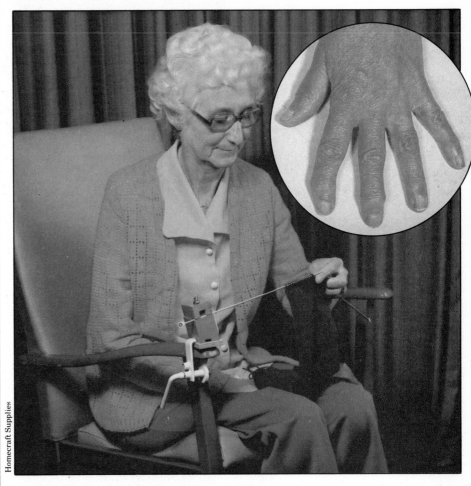

Homecraft Supplies

People whose osteoarthritic fingers have become deformed and stiff (inset) can keep up their hobbies by using ingenious aids.

Osteoarthritis is one of the commonest forms of arthritis. In fact half the population over the age of 50 have some signs of the disease, which can also affect some people in their thirties and forties. Although it is possible to get osteoarthritis, or OA, in almost any joint in the body, there are some joints where it is particularly likely to occur. These include the hips, the knees, the hands, the back and the neck.

Osteoarthritis is painful, and in some cases can be crippling since it reduces the amount of movement in severely affected joints. Treatment is with aspirin or other painkillers, but in severe cases surgery can be performed to replace some of the affected joints.

Causes

Although a great deal is known about how osteoarthritis develops once it actually occurs, the causes of the disease are obscure.

Joints between bones are lined with a membrane called the synovial membrane. This forms a kind of bag surrounding the joint which is filled with synovial fluid. The actual parts of the joint where the bones are in contact with each other are lined with cartilage, and it is the two cartilage surfaces coming into contact with each other that bear the load of the joint. Cartilage itself is made up of a hard network of fibres that contain cartilage producing cells and fluid, so that it provides an excellent lubricated surface for the moving parts of the joint. Osteoarthritis is a disease which results from the alteration in the structure of this cartilage.

In the first stage of osteoarthritis, a number of small clefts appear on the surface of the cartilage and there is an increase in the number of cartilage-producing cells. At this stage the patient may not notice any symptoms or only experience some very slight degree of pain and stiffness.

In the next stage, the cartilage caps to the bone ends begin to wear thin until finally there is no cartilage left and the bone ends bear directly onto one another. There may be considerable destruction of the bone as it is worn away by movements of the joint, and also a thickening of the capsule of the synovial membrane that surrounds the joints.

Unlike cartilage, though, bone is able to repair itself as it gets eaten away, but in osteoarthritis the way in which bone does this around an osteoarthritic joint is disorganized. This can sometimes lead to rough deposits, which do more harm than good to the joint.

It would appear that the cause of osteoarthritis is the continual stress on the joint – hence the name 'wear and tear' arthritis. But this theory does not explain the fact that joints which bear the same amount of weight are not equally affected: that is, the hip and knee are likely to be involved, whereas the ankle is not.

Some factors, however, may predispose a patient to osteoarthritis. For instance a background of repeated small injuries may be a causative factor: sportsmen –

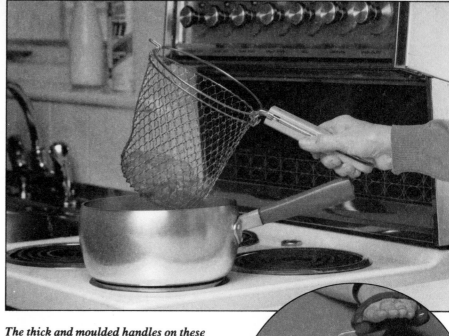

The thick and moulded handles on these cooking utensils enable osteoarthritis sufferers to deal with food more easily.

footballers for example – are said to get more osteoarthritis than normal, particularly in the feet.

Deformity of the limb or a joint may be another contributing factor, and this may lead to stresses on the joint that are so severe that they amount to repeated injury.

Another factor which makes osteoarthritis more likely is when the nerve supply to a particular joint is interrupted

Treating osteoarthritis

Site	Symptoms	Treatment
Hands	Usually affects the joints between the bones of the fingers, producing characteristic lumps on either side of the furthest joint (Heberden's nodes). The thumb is often involved. Joints are painful on movement	Aspirin and related drugs. Occasionally immobilizing the thumb in plaster may be helpful
Feet	Pain on walking, most commonly in the joint at the base of the big toe	Aspirin and related drugs. Occasionally surgical shoes, or surgery
Ankles	Very rare, unless there is some bone deformity	
Knees	Affects more women than men. Sometimes very little pain. Knock knees can result	Basic treatment is with drugs, but very painful or deformed joints can be treated surgically
Hips	Pain particularly on walking. Can lead to a limp or a 'waddle' if both hips are involved	Initial treatment is aspirin or a related drug. A walking stick may be helpful. Surgery, particularly joint replacement, in more severe cases
Spine	Commonest in the neck. Causes pain and limitation of movement. Neck involvement can lead to blackouts or weakness in arms and legs	Aspirin and other pain-relieving drugs. A neck collar worn at night may be helpful
Shoulder	Rare, unless there has been some injury. Immobility and stiffness are usually more of a problem than pain	Exercises combined with painkilling drugs may help to ease shoulder movement
Elbow	Rare. Pain is the main problem and it may occur at rest, but there may also be numbness in the arm and hand and loss of muscle power	Aspirin and related drugs for the pain. Trapped nerves may have to be freed by surgery

Q I have had both the cartilages removed from my left knee. Am I likely to get osteoarthritis as a result?

A There is no certainty that you will get the disease (though do remember that half the population over 50 have some symptoms). However, people who have had their cartilages removed do have more osteoarthritis of the knee than people who haven't. Moreover, the chances of this occurring are increased if you get a knee injury where a cartilage is torn. This may lead to abnormalities in knee function, which in turn may cause osteoarthritis.

In order that you can avoid risking a repeated injury to your knee, you may have to give up contact sports if you play them.

Q I have osteoarthritis and I find that if I sit down for an hour, my joints seize up. Is this a common thing to happen with the disease?

A Yes. People with arthritis do tend to feel stiff after they have not been moving their joints for a while. In one of the other common sorts of arthritis – rheumatoid arthritis – affected patients frequently feel stiff in the mornings, and this also happens in osteoarthritis. The stiffness only lasts about a quarter of an hour in osteoarthritis, whereas in patients with rheumatoid arthritis, this symptom may go on for a much longer period of time.

Q Who is more likely to get osteoarthritis – men or women and does it affect them differently?

A Osteoarthritis is a disease that particularly affects the elderly, and since women live to a greater age than men, it would appear that more women suffer from it. Among the younger age groups, men and women are almost equally affected, with men perhaps sometimes slightly more so.

In spite of this, the two sexes tend to get the disease in different joints. In men it is more common for the hips to be involved, while in women it is the hands, knees and the base of the thumb.

These X-rays of an osteoarthritic hip (left) and knee (below) show how the disease has affected the joints. Normally bones are lined with cartilage and joints are protected. Here the cartilage caps have worn away and because the bone ends bear directly on each other, they too are worn away by movement. Pain and stiffness result.

due to some problem in the nervous system. Since the sensation of pain is interrupted, the patient may injure a joint repeatedly and not be aware of it.

However the fact remains that there is no obvious cause in the majority of patients with the disease.

Symptoms

The main symptom of osteoarthritis is pain. This can vary in severity from a dull ache in an affected joint to an excruciating pain on movement which may make patients practically immobile. Usually the pain from an osteoarthritic joint is worse during movement. There may also be pain of a duller aching character when the joint is at rest. This pain is thought to result from the disorganization of the way that the veins drain blood from the joint: rest pain may well be due to the joint being congested with blood.

The pain tends to become steadily worse, although the severity of the joint's involvement is not always a good indication of the degree of pain. Further, the pain may not actually be felt in the joint involved: it is common for osteoarthritis of the hip to come to light as a result of pain in the knee on the same side, or in the back.

Osteoarthritis also causes stiffness. This is usually worse in the morning, but tends to get better within a few minutes. The affected joints may also swell in some cases.

As the disease progresses, there may be considerable deformity in the joints. Badly affected hips and knees creak;

doctors call this crepitus. The range of movement decreases as the arthritis progresses, and in some cases the joint may become almost fixed.

Osteoarthritis may affect one joint in the body or it may affect several. If only one joint is involved, it is likely to be a big joint such as the knee or hip. Occasionally the only joint involved is where the palm and wrist meet on the thumb side. Other common sites for multiple affected joints are the hand and the spine.

Dangers

Although very unpleasant, osteoarthritis is not often dangerous. However serious problems can arise when the disease affects the spine in the neck, causing pain and stiffness. This condition is known as cervical spondylosis. Three problems can arise from this; the first is pain and stiffness of the neck.

275

The second and third, which are serious but rare, arise from attempts of the bone to repair itself, leading to bone overgrowth. Pressure on the blood vessels to the lower part of the brain will cut off the blood supply, leading to blackouts and dizziness when looking upwards or round to the side. Pressure on the spinal cord or its nerves will lead to weakness in both the arms and legs.

Treatment
Painkilling drugs are the best treatment to stop pain and to reduce any inflammation. Aspirin is the most favoured, but other drugs can be taken where patients cannot tolerate it. Supportive measures include using a walking stick for cases of osteoarthritis of the knee and hip.

Joint replacement surgery is used in severely affected cases, resulting in a dramatic lessening of pain, and improvement of joint movement. The most successful operation is on the hip joint, although there has been some progress in knee joint replacement.

Apart from joint replacement, an operation called an osteotomy, where the bones on either side of a joint are remodelled, can be of great value as it improves the way the joint carries weight. This operation tends to be used in younger patients, since no one is certain how long replaced joints last, and there is always the option of replacing the joint at some later stage.

Finally the joint can be completely fused so that it cannot move and cannot cause pain. Although this sounds drastic, it can be extremely successful in some patients. It can bring tremendous pain relief, often without much loss of function in the affected limb, which probably was fairly stiff in the first place.

Outlook
Once osteoarthritis occurs, it will not disappear. However most people have very few symptoms from the disease. Where symptoms are a problem, they can be greatly relieved by drugs in the majority of cases.

Surgical treatment can also bring about tremendous relief of pain, especially in the hip, although in other joints this form of treatment should be regarded as a last resort.

Hip replacement

The head of the femur is removed, holes are drilled and plastic cement is pushed in.

A prosthetic ball and stem is inserted into the femur, and held in place by the cement.

Stem and head are rejoined and traction is applied to maintain the position of the leg.

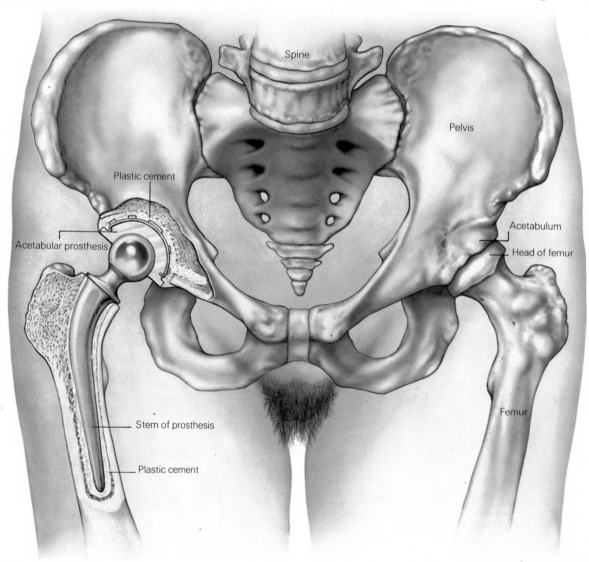

Spine

Pelvis

Plastic cement

Acetabular prosthesis

Acetabulum

Head of femur

Stem of prosthesis

Plastic cement

Femur

Frank Kennard

276

Osteomyelitis

At one time osteomyelitis – bone infection – could have had very serious consequences like amputation of an infected limb. But nowadays, antibiotics and modern medical care usually give a complete recovery.

Q My daughter has got osteomyelitis, is it possible that the infection can spread from the bone to the surrounding tissue?

A It is much more usual for infection to spread from the bone to the surrounding tissue than for it to happen the other way round. What usually occurs is that infection breaks through the fibrous coating of the bone into the surrounding muscle and then penetrates the skin forming a sinus which will not heal until the infection is completely eradicated. However, in rare instances tuberculosis may spread in the opposite way – in other words from the lung tissue into the bone.

Q Could osteomyelitis possibly lead to developing cancer of the bone?

A Yes, but it is an extremely rare complication. However, it is recognized that bone infection can lead to the development of osteosarcoma which is one type of bone cancer.

Q I have recently suffered from osteomyelitis of the leg, will I be able to return to my normal sporting activities?

A Yes. Modern antibiotics, in combination with surgical draining procedures, can now completely cure osteomyelitis. Provided that all the dead bone is removed, all the damage is repaired completely within the course of about six months and full sporting activities can then be resumed. It is important to remember that complete bed-rest is essential while the infection is in its most virulent stage.

Q My son has a boil on his leg, is it likely that he could develop osteomyelitis?

A No. Since the introduction of antibiotics a boil can be effectively treated in the early stages and it is extremely unlikely that the bacteria would spread through the bloodstream to infect other areas of his body.

Osteomyelitis is an infection of the bone by bacteria or fungus. The infection can be acute which is sudden and severe or chronic which is gradual. It is introduced into the bone through compound fractures, infected wounds or after surgery.

Children under the age of 12 are particularly at risk and before antibiotics the disease could cause bone deformation and lameness.

Causes
Bacteria can enter the bone during surgery when the skin has been cut or as a complication of compound fracture when bone breaks through the skin, or else infection is carried from inflammation elsewhere via the blood to lodge in the bones. This is known as hematogenous spread and accounts for about 90 per cent of the cases of osteomyelitis.

Structure of a long bone

Bacteria which have been introduced into the blood can get trapped in the end arteries of the growing ends of long bones and cause infection, pain and inflammation.

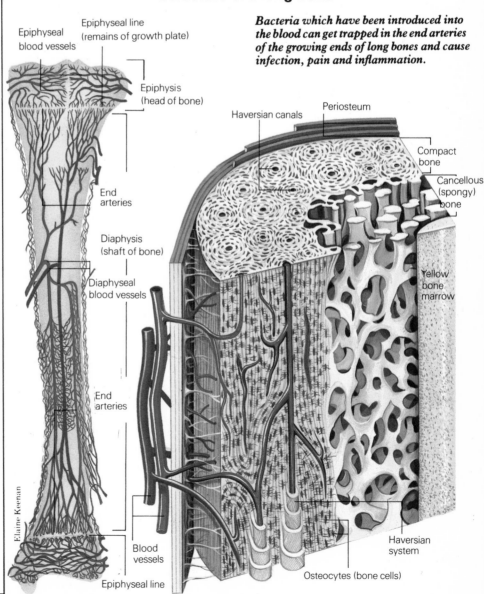

Epiphyseal blood vessels

Epiphyseal line (remains of growth plate)

Epiphysis (head of bone)

End arteries

Diaphysis (shaft of bone)

Diaphyseal blood vessels

End arteries

Blood vessels

Epiphyseal line

Elaine Keenan

Haversian canals

Periosteum

Compact bone

Cancellous (spongy) bone

Yellow bone marrow

Haversian system

Osteocytes (bone cells)

A large majority of cases of osteomyelitis are caused by the bacteria known as staphylococcus. This bacteria is often carried to the bone by the blood from skin infections such as carbuncles or boils. Rarer bacteria may affect people with poor resistance to infection, such as newborn babies and people with blood diseases like leukaemia.

Symptoms

The first symptoms are pain, inflammation and the formation of pus in the affected limb. However, because the bone is a rigid structure the swelling is contained. The production of pus causes a rapid rise in pressure in the bone causing severe pain which may develop quite dramatically; sometimes overnight. Vomiting is sometimes experienced and there is, in addition, always the symptom of an accompanying fever.

The infection particularly affects the growing ends of the long bones around the knee joint and around the elbow joint in the arms. The reason for this is that the blood vessels here do not run into veins—they are known as end arteries. This means that any bacteria finding their way to bone get filtered here and stick. Once the bone infection is established the pressure within the bone slows the circulation of the blood so that areas of bone may die. Eventually the pus may pass out of the bone through a skin opening—a sinus.

Dangers

Before antibiotics were introduced acute osteomyelitis proved fatal in 50 per cent of cases. This was because the infection spread in the blood to involve other organs like the lungs.

Now the main danger is that chronic osteomyelitis may develop. The problem is that inflammation continues with swelling and pus, the bone is weakened and the infection may become acute again.

Different types of osteomyelitis

The tuberculosis bacteria can also infect bone and when it does it attacks the back bones by direct spread from the lungs. The progression is slow but bone is eaten away, leaving behind normal discs which form the fibrous padding between the vertebrae. When sufficient bone has been destroyed the weight of the body is no longer supported and the spine then crumbles resulting in a bent back. This sharp angulation created at the centre of the back is known as kyphosis. Sufferers of this condition are commonly called hunchbacks.

Tuberculosis infections can normally be diagnosed by an accurate X-ray.

In the USA infection with a fungus called North American blastomycosis occurs. This does not respond to antibiotics and a special anti-fungal agent needs to be used. Another fungus called actinomycosis causes cases in Asia.

Treatment

Early treatment of acute osteomyelitis is essential, because once areas of dead bone have formed, chronic osteomyelitis is likely to follow.

Admission to hospital will be necessary. The doctors will take blood samples to try to identify which bacteria is causing the infection. Antiobiotics will be given intravenously at first, and later by mouth. Many people will need an operation consisting of drilling small holes in the bone. This relieves the pressure caused by the infection, and also allows the doctors to test the pus to make sure that the bacteria causing the infection will be killed by the antibiotics they are currently using in order to treat the patient's condition.

If there is chronic osteomyelitis, antibiotics alone cannot cure the infection. An operation will be necessary to remove all the infected and dead bone. If the chronic osteomyelitis is extensive, this may mean amputation of the affected limb.

Outlook

With early treatment there is now a good chance that a full recovery will be made from acute osteomyelitis.

The onset of osteomyelitis can be very sudden causing extreme pain in the affected joint. Prompt diagnosis and early treatment is essential.

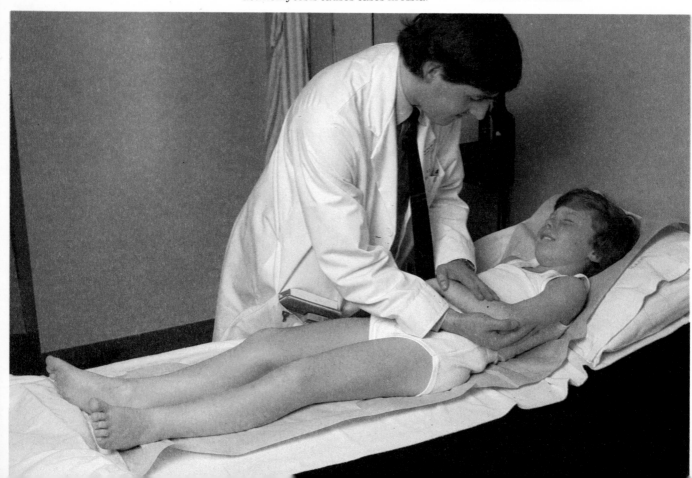

Otitis

Q My husband has had otitis but needs to travel by air. Is this dangerous?

A The air pressure in the cabin of an aeroplane is usually the same as that at about 1500 m (5000 ft) above sea level outside, and it varies only during take-off and landing. This may be uncomfortable for your husband if he cannot equalize the air pressure on either side of his eardrum by swallowing, but it is not dangerous.

Q My child loves swimming in the local baths, but one of his friends had to stop going because he was told it caused otitis. Is this true?

A Swimming and diving in the local baths are fine when you have healthy ears. The trouble starts when a keen swimmer ignores the first signs of otitis, which can arise from many causes, and would then be aggravated by swimming. Occasionally it is an adverse reaction to the swimming itself, so anyone who knows they have this tendency should protect themselves with a swimming cap.

Q What should I do if my child inadvertently puts something in his ear which cannot be removed easily?

A Any foreign material can and should be removed by a doctor or nurse, so you should seek medical help as soon as you suspect one of your child's ears is affected. Do-it-yourself exploration can damage the ear-drum, and you should not even use cotton wool buds in children's ears. Similarly, too much wax should be medically treated. It is easily softened with almond oil before being syringed out by a trained nurse or your doctor.

Q Is it true that otitis sometimes needs hospital treatment urgently?

A The ear lies very close to the brain, so if infection is not controlled there may be a risk of meningitis which must be treated by a specialist. This should not happen however if otitis is treated early.

Thanks to antibiotics, otitis – infection of the ears – should not be dangerous these days. However, it is still important to seek early treatment, especially as this will help prevent recurrence of ear problems.

Parts of the ear

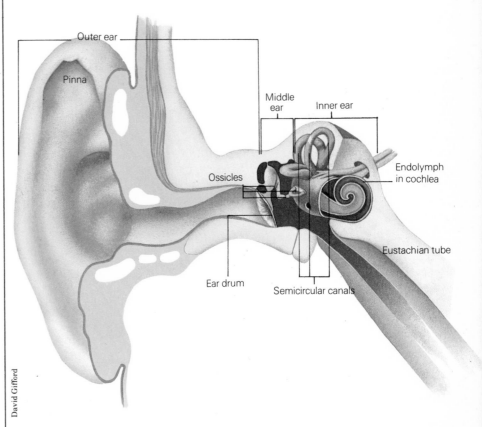

David Gifford

Each ear has three parts which combine to make it the organ of both hearing and balance. The outer ear, or visible part, receives sound waves which are transmitted via the ear-drum to the middle ear. Here they are amplified by a series of three bones called the ossicles, before passing through another membrane into the inner ear. In this compartment sound vibrations are converted into electrical impulses which reach the brain along a pair of nerves, to be interpreted, or perceived there, as sound.

There are membranes between the three parts of the ear which help to ward off infection, particularly from the inner ear which must always be protected. The process of transmitting information in the form of sound can be interrupted by infection. The three types of infection relate directly to the three parts of the ear, and are called respectively otitis externa, otitis media and otitis interna.

Otitis externa

Otitis externa is inflammation of the skin of the outer ear by bacteria or fungi. It usually arises when the ear is not dried after getting wet, or if the skin is very sensitive and prone to eczema. The canal leading towards the middle ear may also be affected if the wax in it becomes irritated, which may occur if the ear is explored with a sharp instrument, such as a matchstick or paper clip.

The ear may become red and itchy, sometimes with a watery discharge, although the condition itself may not be very painful. Drops and ointment are useful in clearing up mild cases of inflammation, but where infection is severe and painful, antibiotics taken by mouth are the best treatment, especially since it may not only be the outer ear which is affected. It is always important to remember that any unskilled treatment of ears is extremely unwise.

infection to the mastoid cells or the skull cavity, which in the past was a serious complication called mastoiditis. Where a virus is the cause of otitis media antibiotics are of course not given.

It is a very common condition of babies and toddlers who may not even complain of earache but simply feel unwell with perhaps a temperature. For this reason doctors always examine the ears of young children who have a fever.

Chronic otitis media

Occasionally the problem recurs when infection enters the middle ear through the discharging hole in the drum. Earache persists, and there may be a slight discharge of pus. Impaired or painful hearing may ensue as the ear-drum and ossicles become scarred, hence the need for prompt treatment to prevent this.

With careful cleansing the infection can often be controlled, but where the bone is affected surgery may be necessary. Serious defects in the drum may be repaired by grafting once the infection has completely cleared up.

Otitis interna

Otitis interna is now very rare, but may still arise if middle ear infection has been allowed to spread, resulting in deafness and giddiness. Treatment should therefore be sought early, before any permanent damage can be done.

Swimming is best avoided where there is any ear infection. A simple tuning-fork test (below) will reveal any reduction in hearing due to fluid in the middle ear.

Otitis media

Otitis media is most likely to result from a bacterial or viral infection of the nose and throat. This reaches the ear along the Eustachian tube, the passage leading from the back of the nose to the middle ear. Such complications are very common in children, and may follow an illness like measles, tonsillitis or common cold.

Acute otitis media can cause violent earache and fever, accompanied by muffled hearing. This is due to a build-up of fluid in the middle ear, which normally contains only air. Where bacterial not viral infection is suspected, antibiotics are given otherwise the earache persists until the ear-drum perforates to discharge the pus. Sometimes the ear-drum has to be drained surgically to drain off pus but once the infection has cleared up the drum heals and there should be no further trouble.

A doctor should be consulted at once in any suspected case of middle ear infection. Sulphonamides and other antibiotics nowadays prevent the spread of

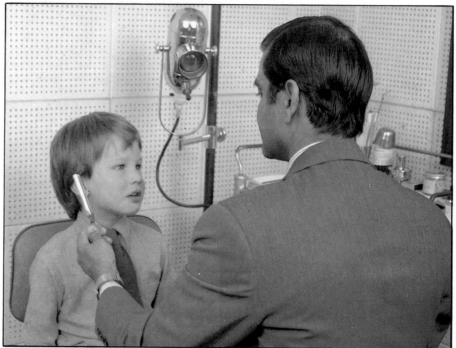

280

Parathyroid glands

The minute parathyroids are among the most important glands in the body. They produce a hormone called PTH which is vital for maintaining the delicately balanced quantities of calcium in the bloodstream.

Q I heard that years ago when the thyroid was removed in an operation the parathyroids were often accidentally removed as well. What happened in such cases?

A The results were disastrous. The patient would develop a very low level of calcium in the blood, and this led first to tetany – an uncontrolled muscular spasm particularly in the hands and feet – and eventually to the loss of respiration unless the trouble was corrected. Fortunately, once the condition was recognized it was relatively easy to treat by giving the patient vitamin D. These days the parathyroids may deliberately be removed in cases of cancer around the thyroid region, but this is done with a view to replacing the parathyroid activity with vitamin D which will serve the same purpose – namely, release calcium into the bloodstream.

Q My mother has an overactive thyroid gland. Is there any chance that her parathyroids will be affected?

A No. Although the thyroid and parathyroid glands are very close together the disease processes that affect each are quite separate, and her parathyroids should be fine. Incidentally, though, it is possible to develop a raised level of calcium in the blood simply as a result of a severely overactive thyroid gland.

Q My brother has kidney trouble but he had to have his parathyroids removed. Why did he have to have this done?

A When the kidneys stop working properly they may release large amounts of calcium into the urine. The parathyroid glands will make the normal response: they will put out more PTH in order to maintain a satisfactory level of calcium in the blood. Over a few months or years, however, they may be working so hard that they no longer respond properly and start to put the calcium level up too high. A small tumour might even develop; so it's necessary to remove some parathyroid tissue to bring calcium levels under control.

The parathyroids are four tiny glands situated behind the thyroid glands, which in turn is found just below the larynx. They play a major part in controlling the levels of calcium in the body. Calcium is a vital mineral: not only because it is the major structural element in the formation of bones and teeth, but also because it plays a central role in the workings of the muscles and nerve cells. The body's calcium levels have to be kept within pretty constant boundaries, otherwise the muscles stop working and fits may occur. This is where the parathyroid glands come in: they keep the calcium levels in balance.

The absorption of calcium into the bloodstream is controlled by vitamin D, which we get from sunlight and some foods, and an important hormone produced by the parathyroids called parathyroid hormone or PTH. If the level of calcium is too low, the parathyroids secrete an increased quantity of the hormone, which actually releases calcium from the bones to raise the level in the bloodstream. Conversely, if there is too much calcium, the parathyroids reduce or halt the production of PTH, thus bringing the level down.

The parathyroids are so small that they can be difficult to find. The upper two are

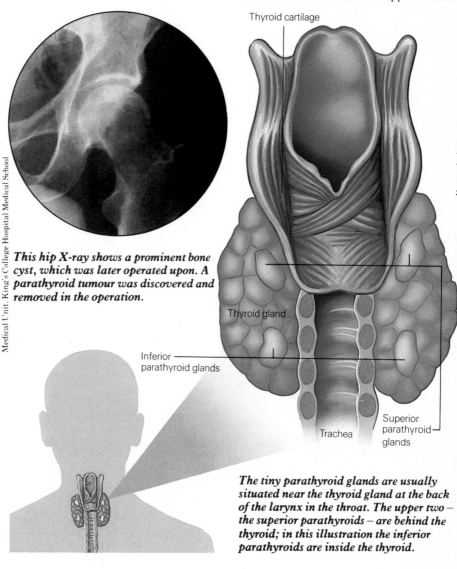

This hip X-ray shows a prominent bone cyst, which was later operated upon. A parathyroid tumour was discovered and removed in the operation.

Medical Unit, King's College Hospital Medical School

Venner Artists

Thyroid cartilage

Thyroid gland

Inferior parathyroid glands

Trachea

Superior parathyroid glands

The tiny parathyroid glands are usually situated near the thyroid gland at the back of the larynx in the throat. The upper two – the superior parathyroids – are behind the thyroid; in this illustration the inferior parathyroids are inside the thyroid.

Q How are the parathyroids affected if the diet is deficient in calcium?

A A low level of calcium in your diet will certainly tend to raise the output of parathyroid hormone from the parathyroids. In fact it is rather more common for the diet to be deficient in vitamin D than in calcium – but this, too, will result in a low blood calcium level, since vitamin D is essential for the absorption of calcium from the bones into the bloodstream.

Q My father had an operation on his parathyroids, and was injected with blue dye. Why was this done?

A The parathyroid glands are very small organs, and not surprisingly they are extremely difficult for a surgeon to find during an operation. Oddly enough they take up a dye called 'Evan's Blue' so that they can be seen more easily, and distinguished from the rest of the tissues. Many surgeons now use this technique to help with the operation.

Q If you start having muscular spasms does it necessarily mean that your parathyroids have failed?

A There are many different sorts of 'muscle spasm': anything from an epileptic fit to a touch of cramp may be responsible. However, if you have tetany, which is uncontrollable contraction of the muscles usually starting in the hands and feet, a lack of PTH may be responsible. In fact a more common cause of tetany is a disturbance of the blood's acid and alkaline balance.

Q Can PTH arise from anywhere except the parathyroid glands?

A Yes – it's a sobering thought that a number of different hormones can be manufactured by various cancers, and PTH is one of these. It can be manufactured by cancers of the lung and kidney. It's worth noting too, that PTH used to be injected to correct calcium levels, but that this has been discontinued because of its uncertain biological activity.

situated behind the thyroid gland; the lower two, however, may actually be *inside* the thyroid or occasionally right down inside the chest.

Like most endocrine (hormone) glands the parathyroids can cause two main problems. They can be overactive, and this leads to a high level of calcium in the bloodstream, or they can be underactive, allowing the level to get dangerously low.

Overactive parathyroids
Overactive parathyroids – hyperparathyroidism – are quite a common problem. It has now become usual practice to measure the level of calcium in the

Vitamin D – so essential for the absorption of calcium – occurs in fish oils and is synthesized from sunlight.

blood as a routine part of the biochemical screening test that is carried out on practically all hospital patients, and also on many patients by their own doctors. As a result rather more instances of unexpectedly high blood calcium levels have been found – in the past the level of calcium in the blood was measured only when an abnormality was suspected. It is now thought that as many as one person per thousand may have some degree of parathyroid overactivity.

The interaction between blood calcium and PTH

Vitamin D enables calcium to be absorbed into bloodstream — normal calcium level

Blood calcium level increased as a result of high PTH level

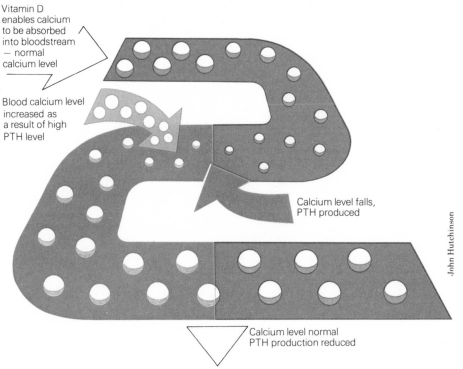

Calcium level falls, PTH produced

Calcium level normal PTH production reduced

John Hutchinson

This diagram shows how as the level of calcium in the blood drops the parathyroids increase production of PTH; once the blood calcium level is normal again production of PTH is reduced.

half. The remaining half gland provides enough PTH to keep the calcium level under control.

In the remainder of cases there is a tumour. Usually this affects only one gland, and only a tiny minority of patients will be found to have a tumour that is malignant (cancerous).

It is not certain what the best treatment might be for those people who are found to have a slightly higher blood calcium level without any symptoms. In general most younger patients are advised to have an operation, since the high level of calcium may eventually damage the kidneys. The outlook following treatment is usually very good.

Underactive parathyroids
In contrast, underactivity (hypoparathyroidism) is very rare – unless, of course, the parathyroids are removed during surgery on the thyroid. People suffering from this disease are often rather tired; they may start having fits and there may be signs of tetany – a muscular spasm which affects the hands.

There also may be marked mental problems. Many patients will have depression, but a surprising number show irrational overactivity – known as mania. As well as all the symptoms of low blood calcium people with hypoparathyroidism are susceptible to candida infection of the nails (thrush).

Fortunately this disease can be combated effectively by taking vitamin D by mouth. Although a careful eye has to be kept on the calcium level, the outlook · after treatment is very good.

Symptoms
A raised blood calcium level *may* be caused by hyperparathyroidism. It is important to realize that there could be other causes. For example, the other common cause of high levels of blood calcium is a cancer that gives rise to secondary deposits of cancer tissue in the bones. This causes the bones to be eaten away and a lot of calcium is released into the bloodstream. An excessive intake of vitamin D, too, can also cause a raised calcium level.

Generally speaking, the two main symptoms of a raised calcium level are thirst and passing a lot of water. There may also be feelings of tiredness and poor concentration. Loss of appetite and vomiting may also result. Where overactive parathyroids are the cause of the high blood calcium many patients develop kidney stones. In this disease the urine contains a lot of calcium and it tends to settle out in the kidneys to produce stones. People with overactive parathyroids also seem to suffer from indigestion. In about 10 per cent of cases the amount of calcium that is released from the bones as a result of the high levels of PTH is so great that the bones themselves begin to show signs of strain – there may be bone pain, some loss of height and even spontaneous fractures. X-rays will show a characteristic picture of cysts in the bones, particularly the

hands. The combination of the bone problems, kidney stones and indigestion has led to the old saying among doctors that the disease causes problems with 'bones, stones and abdominal groans'.

Treatment
The only really effective treatment for the disease is surgical removal of the overactive gland or glands. In most cases all the glands are found to be bigger than normal (hypertrophied) and standard surgical procedure is to identify all four glands and then to remove three-and-a-

What can go wrong?

Symptoms	Causes	Treatment
Overactive parathyroids (Hyperparathyroidism) Thirst, passing abnormal amounts of urine. Pain in the stomach, kidney stones, general feeling of ill health.	1. Benign tumour of one or more glands. 2. Hyperplasia (enlargement) of the glands, often due to kidney disease.	Surgical removal of the affected gland or glands. The outlook is good, but in kidney disease it depends on the kidney problem.
Underactive parathyroids (Hypoparathyroidism) Tetany, uncontrollable muscle spasms. Tiredness and often serious mental problems.	1. Idiopathic (this means cause unknown). There may be thrush infection of the nails. 2. Surgical removal of the glands.	Vitamin D by mouth is very effective, but the level of calcium in the blood has to be monitored carefully.

Parkinson's disease

A common illness of the elderly, Parkinson's disease causes the limbs to shake and makes simple movement difficult. But modern drugs have done much to prolong the active years and hold the disability at bay.

Q Is it true that Parkinson's disease can be caused by alcoholism?

A No. Although alcoholism does cause damage to other parts of the brain, it does not seem to attack the cells linked with this illness.

Q Is it correct that although Parkinson's disease does not affect the intellect, some mental illnesses have similar symptoms?

A It is true that the mind is not affected until the disease becomes very advanced, when slight mental deterioration is not uncommon. But no mental illness has symptoms like those of Parkinson's disease.

Q I am in my thirties, and sometimes my hand shakes almost uncontrollably when I reach for my coffee mug. Is this Parkinson's disease?

A No. The trembling of the hands, so characteristic of the disease, is at its worst when they are doing nothing. Reaching for a cup of coffee would end the shaking if you had Parkinson's disease.

Q My father was disabled by Parkinson's disease. Does this mean I will be too?

A There seems to be no clear-cut link with heredity, so just because your father had the condition does not mean you will be more at risk. Even in the unlikely event that you do contract the disease current treatment should ensure that you will not be as disabled as he was.

Q My mother is being treated for Parkinson's disease, and sometimes her hands do curious twisting movements. Is this part of the symptom pattern?

A No. It is probably a side-effect of L-Dopa, the drug your mother is most likely taking. Such hand movements do not indicate harmful effects, but if they trouble her they can be stopped by adjusting the treatment she is receiving.

Rex Features

The state of Chairman Mao's health was a subject of international speculation during the latter part of his life; many false rumours circulated but he did in fact suffer from Parkinson's disease.

The old names for Parkinson's disease – paralysis agitans or shaking palsy – help to describe one of its most common symptoms. A person who suffers from this disease – named after an 18th century English physician, James Parkinson – experiences a shaking or tremor of the limbs (especially the hands), stiff limbs and difficulty in carrying out certain types of movement. In advanced stages there are associated troubles with control of circulation and perspiration.

It is a disease of the middle-aged and elderly and is commonly encountered, but treatment can, to a great extent, postpone the onset of disability for years.

Causes

In most cases, Parkinson's disease is caused by premature ageing of deep-seated brain cells in what is known as the basal ganglia. These cells normally form a complex control system that co-ordinates the muscle activity which allows us to perform specific types of movement freely and unconsciously. This sort of muscle activity is involved in the swinging of our arms when we walk, in facial expression and in the positioning of limbs before we stand up or walk.

Difficulties occur when the brain cells that allow the body to perform these tasks die off prematurely.

Symptoms

The symptoms usually develop very slowly and are often assumed to be part of the normal process of ageing. At the beginning, they seem to occur on only one side of the body. Ultimately, however, both sides are usually affected.

Most noticeable is the trembling of the hands, which shake in a 'pill-rolling' tremor as if the person is rolling something between his fingers and thumb. It is most evident when the arm is inactive, for the shaking usually stops as soon as movement begins – when reaching for a cup, for example.

The muscles of people afflicted with the disease become unusually stiff. In the early stages it causes aching shoulders and discomfort first thing in the morning, after hours of rest. The face is also less mobile than usual, which gives the person a 'dead-pan' expression.

Walking is also very difficult. After a hesitant start, a person with Parkinson's disease moves forward quickly in a shuffling manner. He takes small steps and leans forward in a stoop. This difficulty in walking can sometimes lead to severe falls if the usual automatic reaction of using the hands to break the fall is also impaired – as is often the case.

Initially the intellect is not affected, but after some years the patient may gradually lose the ability to perform higher mental tasks. In this advanced stage of the disease every physical movement becomes increasingly difficult. Yet, curiously, many instances have been recorded of a person with Parkinson's disease being impelled to act very quickly – running away from a fire, for example.

The disease is accompanied by a drop in blood pressure when the patient stands up, which results in fainting, and by slurred and distorted speech, caused by damage to the relevant muscles.

Treatment and outlook
The usual treatment is the drug L-Dopa, which is given in tablet form. It replenishes the brain's supply of dopamine, the chemical 'transmitter' produced by cells in the basal ganglia, and alleviates many symptoms of the disease. Surgery is only rarely performed.

Although degeneration of the brain cells cannot be reversed, drug therapy, regular exercise and proper nourishment will allow the patient to lead a full life for at least 10 years from the onset of the disease. After this period it becomes more difficult to control the symptoms, but new dopamine-mimicking agents are now available which are able to extend even further the years of useful activity.

Progressive symptoms
● Limbs become stiff, causing aching joints
● Face becomes immobile
● Limbs stiffen further, starting movements difficult
● Gait becomes small-stepped and stooping
● Reduction in sweating or increased occurrence of greasy face, due to abnormal working of sweat glands
● Feelings of faintness accompany standing
● Walking now difficult because of stiffness
● Hands tremble almost constantly when inactive
● Fingers increasingly affected by slight tremor

Muscle-rigidity and akinesia – difficulty in carrying out automatic movements – produce the abnormal, stooping posture that is characteristic of Parkinsonism.

The position of the basal ganglia

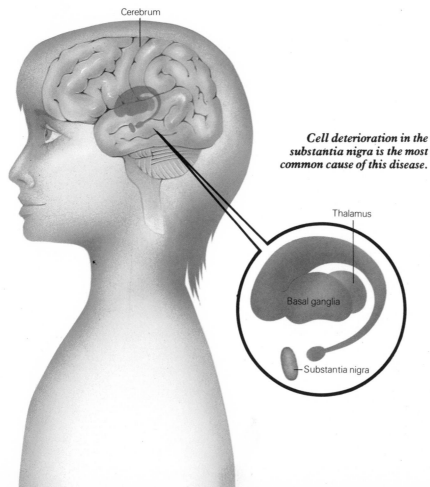

Cerebrum

Cell deterioration in the substantia nigra is the most common cause of this disease.

Thalamus

Basal ganglia

Substantia nigra

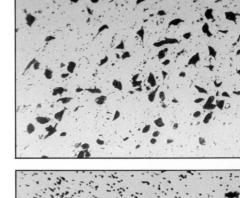

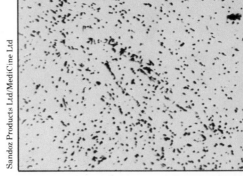

Sandoz Products Ltd/MediCine Ltd

Dopamine, produced by cells (top), in the basal ganglia is severely lacking in patients with Parkinson's disease (above).

Peptic ulcer

Q Can you have an ulcer without knowing it?

A Certainly. Many people accept a small amount of indigestion as being quite normal. A fair proportion of these people would be found to have an active ulcer, or the signs of an old ulcer if they had a gastroscopy. It doesn't matter if you're not getting any symptoms from your ulcer, and the complications are really quite rare.

Q I have an ulcer in my duodenum. How likely am I to suffer from bleeding or perforation?

A Very unlikely. A doctor working in the casualty department of a hospital might think that everybody gets these complications, since he sees so many of them. In fact, bleeding and perforated ulcers are really an uncommon complication of a very common disease so that the individual sufferer is unlikely to be affected. If you do get bleeding, however, a transfusion may be necessary and the bleeding will probably stop with a period of bed rest. A perforated ulcer is more serious: an urgent operation will usually be vital.

Q Does an operation for an ulcer leave a huge, ugly scar?

A The sort of scar that you will be left with will be about six inches long, running up and down at the top of your abdomen. Although this sounds very big, the scars often fade away so that they are no more than a thin line, so you shouldn't be too worried about it.

Q I've been told that I have to eat frequently because of my ulcer. Now I'm putting on a lot of weight. What can I do about this?

A The trick is to take frequent *small* meals. The idea is that frequent small meals do not allow the level of acid in the stomach to build up, since the acid is continually being neutralized by the food. Obviously you risk putting on weight, and you should aim to eat a normal amount of food – but split it into a greater number of smaller meals.

'Peptic ulcer' derives its name from the enzyme pepsin, and it describes gastric and duodenal ulcers, which occur in the stomach and duodenum respectively.

'Ulcer' simply means a break or lesion in the lining, mucous membrane or skin in any part of the body. It is possible to get an ulcer almost anywhere: in your mouth, on your leg or in any part of the lining of your gut. A peptic ulcer is any sort of ulcer that results from the action of stomach acid.

Peptic ulcers normally occur in the stomach itself – when they are called gastric ulcers, or in the duodenum—duodenal ulcers (see pp 148-49). However it is possible to get peptic ulcers in other places: for example, the effect of acid washing back from the stomach into the oesophagus may cause an ulcer. But the problem is mainly confined to the stomach and the duodenum.

Causes
No-one knows exactly why some people are prone to the condition while others remain unaffected. What *is* known is that stomach acid, aided perhaps by digestive enzymes such as pepsin (hence *peptic* ulcer) is at the root of all peptic ulcers. Various situations seem to make an ulcer more likely. For example heavy drinking and steady consumption of drugs like aspirin are two well-known causes. Smoking is another important factor: although it has not been proved that smoking causes ulcers, there is no doubt that it delays healing of existing ulcers.

Many ulcers are the result of an excess of acid production by the stomach, but not all. About 80 per cent of patients with

When perforated duodenal ulcers occur, a simple closure operation is performed. **1** *Sutures are passed through the wall of the duodenum.* **2** *A piece of the omentum (fat-filled flap of peritoneum) is pulled over the perforation.* **3** *Stitches are tied over the 'plug' of omentum.*

Perforated duodenal ulcer

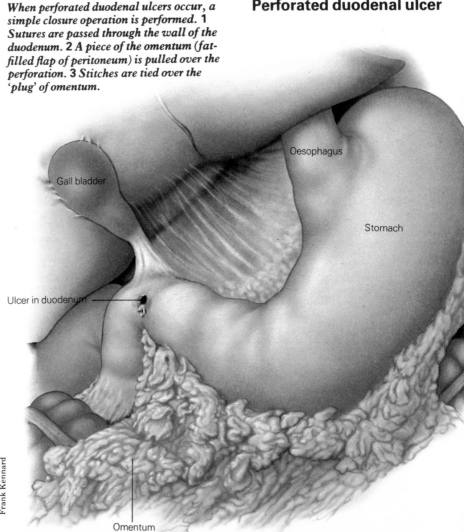

Oesophagus

Gall bladder

Stomach

Ulcer in duodenum

Omentum

Frank Kennard

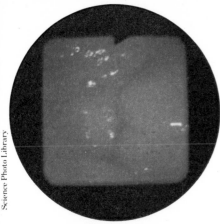

This photograph shows benign pyloric stenosis, an obstruction of the outlet of the stomach into the duodenum: a condition caused by a duodenal ulcer.

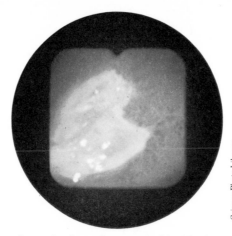

A gastric ulcer, photographed inside the stomach. Generally, for a precise diagnosis of its condition a biopsy should be performed on the patient.

duodenal ulcers suffer from an overproduction of acid, while with most gastric ulcers there is no evidence of the same level of overproduction.

Symptoms

Pain, usually in the upper part of the abdomen, is the main symptom of a peptic ulcer. This pain is called dyspepsia – which is also used to describe pain from inflammation of the lower oesophagus or gall bladder disease.

The pain tends to occur in bouts lasting a week or two. Food may both bring it on or make it better: only about half the ulcer sufferers notice any relationship between the pain and food at all. The pain may also occur at night.

One of the odder aspects of this pain is that it almost always seems to get better if a patient is admitted to hospital to rest. But unless more specific treatment is given the pain is sure to recur.

Dangers

Only a small percentage of people suffering from peptic ulcers are likely to need intensive medical attention. However, complications may occur which require hospital treatment.

The most important of the various complications is bleeding. Patients may start to vomit blood, which will come out as small, dark brown lumps called 'coffeeground' vomit, or they may feel faint and then pass the black, tarry motions that are associated with altered blood passing through the colon. A lot of blood can be lost by bleeding from an ulcer, and the doctor's first priority is usually to treat the shock associated with blood loss. The bleeding will often settle down if the patient rests in bed. If it does not settle, however, an operation may be necessary to stop the flow. In such operations it can be difficult to work out where the bleed-

People who suffer from ulcers must ensure that they eat several small, regular meals throughout the course of a day.

ing is coming from, and the surgeon's job is made easier with the help of a gastroscope, which looks down into the stomach and the duodenum.

Other complications may arise out of a peptic ulcer. The ulcer may perforate, causing inflammation – a condition called peritonitis. The signs of this complication are obvious, with collapse and severe abdominal pain. An operation at the earliest opportunity is usually vital as the consequences are serious.

The inflammation that surrounds a peptic ulcer may also cause problems by constricting part of the stomach that drains into the duodenum, resulting in a blockage. This can often be controlled with drugs.

Treatment and outlook

The discovery of drugs that stop the stomach from secreting acid, so allowing the ulcer to heal, has been a major recent advance in the treatment of peptic ulcers. Where the drugs fail, however, it may still be necessary to operate. Most peptic ulcer operations aim to reduce the amount of acid produced by the stomach rather than to 'cut out the ulcer'.

The outlook for the majority of ulcer sufferers is very good. Although dyspepsia may prove uncomfortable it is quite likely to get better, even if no treatment is given. Now that the new drugs are on the scene treatment with them will make most ulcers better, and operations will be needed in only a few of the more serious cases.

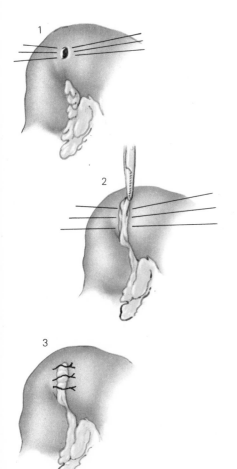

Pericarditis

Q **If you have pericarditis, do you have to have an operation to cut the pericardium away, and can you manage without it?**

A It is very unusual to need an operation for pericarditis. The only cases where the surgeons have to operate, is where the pericarditis results from TB and the pericardium has become very thick and rigid. This can cause heart restriction if it is not removed. Surgery may also be performed if there has been a large pericardial effusion and fluid in the pericardial sac keeps accumulating despite being drained through a needle.

No ill effects seem to result from operating on the pericardium or even removing it completely; in fact surgeons don't always close it up when they have operated on the heart for other problems.

Q **Does the heart get damaged as a result of pericarditis?**

A The common cause of pericarditis is viral infection, and this can often involve the outer layers of the heart as well as the pericardium. This doesn't seem to cause much harm though, except in the few cases where all the layers of the heart's muscular wall are involved, which can result in heart failure.

Q **My husband is only 35, but when he got a bad pain in the chest I thought it must be a heart attack – particularly since he's rather overweight. However, the doctors who treated him at the hospital told me a few days later that it was only pericarditis. How can they be sure?**

A The symptoms of a heart attack and pericarditis can be very similar and even with an ECG it can be difficult to diagnose. However, the way the ECG pattern changes over the next few days confirms whether it was a heart attack or pericarditis. Tests would also be done to check whether there was a rising level of antibodies in the blood – this would confirm that it was viral pericarditis.

Frank Kennard

Severe chest pains are often associated with heart attacks; but inflammation of the heart membrane – pericarditis – produces the same symptoms.

When people suddenly suffer from a bad pain in the middle of the chest, they often imagine that they are having a heart attack; this may in fact be the case, but in a small proportion of people, it is pericarditis that is causing the trouble. Pericarditis is inflammation of the fibrous membrane (pericardium) in which the heart sits. It may arise from a number of different causes but virus infection is particularly common.

The pericardium can also become full of fluid as a result of inflammation; this may give no symptoms although it can be picked up on a chest X-ray. In a small number of cases when there is fluid in the pericardial sac – pericardial effusion – there is a build up of pressure on the heart that stops it working properly. The only other way that a pericardium can give rise to trouble is when it becomes very much thickened following an infection like TB (tuberculosis); this too restricts the action of the heart and can lead to heart failure.

Causes
Pericarditis can suddenly attack perfectly fit people. When this happens it is usually the result of a virus infection. The

Tubercular pericarditis

Thickening of the pericardium – the fibrous membrane around the heart – can result from tuberculosis; left untreated this condition can lead to heart failure.

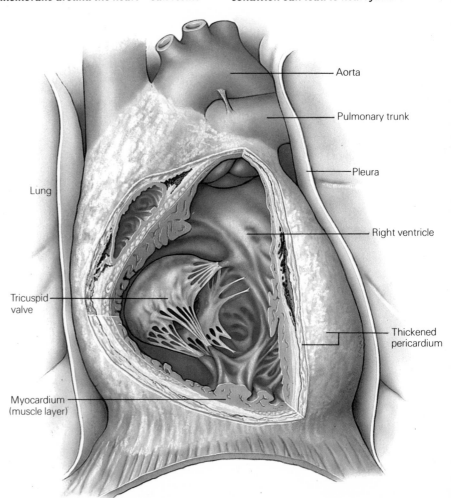

Aorta

Pulmonary trunk

Pleura

Lung

Right ventricle

Tricuspid valve

Thickened pericardium

Myocardium (muscle layer)

symptoms of sudden, acute pericarditis are very like those of a heart attack, and it can be rather difficult initially to tell them apart sometimes – even with an ECG (electrocardiogram). This situation is made more complicated by the fact that there are two different sorts of pericarditis that can come on *as a result* of a heart attack. The first is death of heart muscle which can give rise to inflammation around the heart as the body attempts to clear away the damaged tissue. The second, which is more rare, is known as Dressler's syndrome: this follows about a week after the heart attack when an abnormal response in the body's defence system leads to antibodies being formed against the heart.

Occasionally cancer can involve the pericardium; this does not usually arise from the pericardium itself, but spreads from elsewhere – particularly the lung. It may often give rise to a big pericardial effusion and this in turn may lead to restriction of the heart's movements and so to heart failure (cardiac tamponade). This can also occur when the pericardium is thickened as a result of tuberculosis.

Pericarditis also happens in severe kidney failure and in diseases like systemic lupus erythematosus where there is a generalized inflammation in various parts of the body because of a disturbance of the immune system.

Symptoms

Pericarditis usually causes pain in the middle of the chest and does not spread into the arms and shoulders to quite the same extent as the sort of pain that arises from angina or a heart attack. Sometimes

the pain is worse on moving position – sitting forward, for example – and on other occasions, movement of the lungs past the heart during breathing can cause pain.

The presence of pericarditis can be diagnosed from the ECG in many cases, and where there is an effusion the heart can appear larger on the chest X-ray. With echocardiography (using ultrasound to look at the heart) it can be quite easy to see whether there is any fluid present in the tissues.

An echocardiogram shows whether there is any fluid present in the pericardium. A normal pericardium (left) shows up as a thick, almost solid, black line along the bottom.

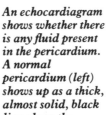

Chronic pericarditis as shown in the X-ray (above) can be caused by tuberculosis. The red rod-like organisms in the photomicrograph (inset) are TB bacilli.

Dangers

The heart failure that results from a collection of fluid in the pericardial sac – tamponade – is a serious condition, and the pressure on the heart has to be relieved. This can normally be done using a needle which is passed through the wall of the chest and into the pericardium. When the constriction of the heart is a result of a very thick pericardium – as it is in TB – an operation is necessary to remove the thick lining.

Treatment

Aspirin-like drugs, particularly one called indomethacin, are the best form of treatment and help relieve the pain. In Dressler's syndrome indomethacin may not be quite enough and steroid drugs can often be needed to reduce the inflammation. In diseases like systemic lupus erythematosus and kidney failure there can be inflammation but no pain, so no treatment is necessary.

Outlook

The outlook in viral pericarditis is really very good. The types of pericarditis that follow a heart attack do not really make the outlook any worse for the patient than the attack itself.

In TB the operation to strip all the thickened pericardium from the heart is a big undertaking, but it has very good results.

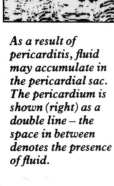

As a result of pericarditis, fluid may accumulate in the pericardial sac. The pericardium is shown (right) as a double line – the space in between denotes the presence of fluid.

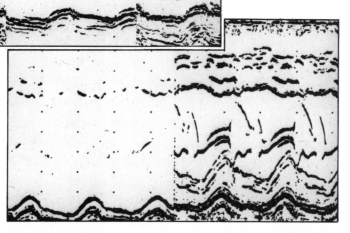

289

Pernicious anaemia

Q My mother is starting to look terribly pale. Could she have pernicious anaemia?

A Since all types of anaemia may make people look very pale, doctors examine the eyelid lining to gauge how much of the red oxygen-carrying pigment (haemoglobin) is present in the blood. However people with pernicious anaemia do display other characteristics, among them grey hair and a rather striking lemon-yellow skin colour. If the paleness persists, your mother should see her doctor.

Q Does pernicious anaemia run in families?

A Pernicious anaemia is one of a number of diseases where the body's immune (defence) system has turned on some normal part of the body. With pernicious anaemia, the stomach lining is attacked, preventing absorption of vitamin B_{12}. Immune system problems do run in families, but these may vary from family member to family member.

Q My aunt is receiving injections for pernicious anaemia. Will the condition right itself, or will she have to continue treatment?

A Pernicious anaemia can be totally cured by having injections of vitamin B_{12}. These can be given every month or every three months. With these injections, your aunt will be totally protected from the effects of the disease, which would eventually be fatal if left untreated. However, the vitamin deficiency will not go away, and she will always need injections.

Q I have been told I need a bone marrow examination for suspected pernicious anaemia. Will it hurt and is it necessary?

A The normal way of looking at the bone marrow is to extract some from the sternum (breastbone) through a short needle. This is done under a local anaesthetic, and although uncomfortable, it is not painful. Doctors can tell from the blood film if you have pernicious anaemia, but the bone marrow will confirm the diagnosis.

At one time pernicious anaemia – as its name implies – was a fatal disease of unknown origin. Now it can be controlled by life-long vitamin B_{12} injections.

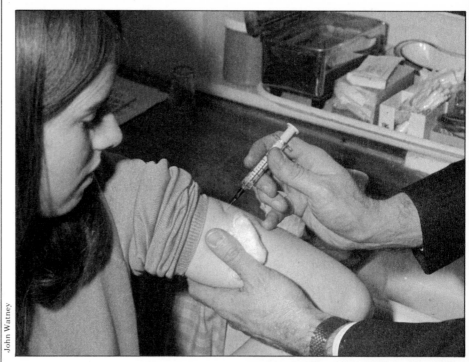

John Watney

Regular injections of vitamin B_{12} keep patients with pernicious anaemia healthy (above). Finns (inset) are particularly vulnerable to vitamin B_{12} deficiency because they are fond of raw fish which may contain a tapeworm that absorbs the body's supply.

Alan Dunns

It would be difficult to invent a disease that causes both severe anaemia and disorders in the nervous system simply by attacking the lining of the stomach. Nevertheless, pernicious anaemia is just such a disease.

Causes
Pernicious anaemia results from the formation of antibodies, by the body's own immune (defence) system, to the cells that make up the stomach's lining. As a result, no intrinsic factor (the substance vitamin B_{12} depends upon for its absorption) is produced, and because of this a vitamin B_{12} deficiency occurs. Vitamin B_{12} and folic acid are necessary for the bone marrow to make an adequate number of red blood cells; when the deficiency occurs, the number of red cells is reduced, and those that remain are larger and more irregular than normal (megaloblastic anaemia). Additionally a lack of vitamin B_{12} results in a reduction

in the amount of white (infection fighting) cells.

Although pernicious anaemia only refers to the disease when antibodies to the stomach wall are produced, there are other reasons why the body may run short of vitamin B_{12} and folic acid. The human body contains about 3mg of Vitamin B – an infinitesimal amount – and the average daily requirement is only one thousandth of this. B_{12} is only found in food of animal origin, so people who never eat anything of animal origin – strict vegetarians – may run short of the vitamin, but otherwise dietary deficiency is rare.

People can also become deficient in vitamin B_{12} if they have an operation to remove their stomachs; this may result in a shortage of intrinsic factor. Intestinal disease may also produce pernicious anaemia, particularly if the ileum (the last part of the small intestine where vitamin B_{12} is actually absorbed) is involved. An inflammation of the intestine known as Crohn's disease is the most common reason for this.

Folic acid deficiency can be due to a lack of fresh vegetables in the diet. Intestinal disease can cause folic acid deficiency much more commonly than vitamin B_{12} deficiency. Folic acid may also be lacking in pregnant women, so an additional amount is given.

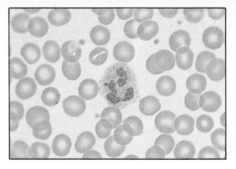

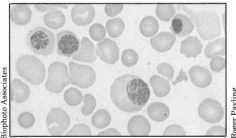

Biophoto Associates

Roger Payling

Symptoms and dangers

Symptoms include paleness, lethargy, tiredness and breathlessness. Nosebleeds may also occur and, in extremely severe cases, heart failure.

As well as the anaemia symptoms, patients exhibit a number of other characteristic features: prematurely grey hair and yellow skin.

Pernicious anaemia develops over a very long period: this means that the level of haemoglobin (the red oxygen-carrying pigment in the red blood cells) falls very slowly so the body is able to

In comparison with normal blood (top left), the red blood cells in pernicious anaemia are large and irregular and the neutrophil white blood cells are more segmented (above left). Typical sufferers have prematurely grey hair and pale or yellow skin (above).

adjust to its effects. Often the haemoglobin level has to get to a seriously low level before the condition comes to light.

Without treatment, anaemia due to any cause may be fatal. However death is very unusual since the condition is easy to recognize and can be treated promptly by giving a blood transfusion.

Since pernicious anaemia is associated with stomach antibodies, there is also a loss of the normal hydrochloric acid production by the stomach. Though this produces few symptoms, there may be a slightly increased risk of stomach cancer.

Perhaps the most serious complication of pernicious anaemia is its effect on the nervous system. A lack of vitamin B_{12} causes problems in the spinal cord, resulting in failure of those parts of the cord which carry sensation from the legs. There is a tingling in the legs, followed by a numbness, weakness and difficulty with balance. In later stages, the arms are affected. This complication, called subacute combined degeneration of the cord, responds well to treatment with vitamin B_{12} injections which are given to patients on a regular basis.

Treatment and outlook

With pernicious anaemia, the missing vitamin B_{12} has to be given on a regular basis (either monthly or every three months) by injection. And since the cause of the missing vitamin is the stomach's failure to secrete intrinsic factor – a disorder that will never improve – the treatment lasts for life. However, with the injections patients should remain completely well.

Geoslides

Pharynx

Q My son constantly complains of a sore throat. Does this mean that he needs to have his tonsils out?

A This is really a question that only your own doctor can answer after he has examined your son's tonsils. Very often, constant sore throats in childhood *are* caused by infections of the tonsils, and disappear once the tonsils have been removed, but this is by no means the only cause. If you are a smoker, it could be that inhaling cigarette smoke is the cause of your son's problem.

Q Why is it that so many illnesses seem to start off with a sore throat?

A The reason for this seems to be twofold. Firstly, some of the tissues found in the pharynx or 'throat' are directly involved in the body's defence against disease and these become swollen and inflamed as they attempt to fight off attack by bacteria and viruses. Secondly, if these defences fail, disease-causing organisms attack the tissues of the pharynx as part of an overall picture of a disease.

Q Is it a good idea to gargle with some kind of antiseptic mouthwash if you have a sore throat?

A Gargling in the way you describe may afford some temporary relief for a sore throat. But some doctors feel that gargling can cause more problems than it cures because it leads to a spread of the infection to other parts of the mouth and throat. Sucking lozenges is probably a better way of soothing the soreness rather than using a gargle.

Q My daughter's sore throat has developed into a middle ear infection. Why?

A This is quite a common complication of a sore throat as the infection travels easily along the Eustachian tube from the pharynx to the middle ear. But the condition is easily treated.

Apart from the odd sore throat, most of us do not give much thought to the pharynx – that vital link between the nose, mouth and voice-box which plays a central role in the essential jobs of breathing, eating and speaking.

The pharynx is the part of our body we commonly call our 'throat' – the area at the back of the mouth, extending a little way down inside the neck, that gets sore when we have a cold or tonsillitis. Deep-lined with muscles, it is shaped, very roughly, like an inverted cone, extending for about 12 cm (5 in) behind the arch at the back of the mouth to where it joins up with the gullet or oesophagus (see p. 420).

The upper and wider part of the pharynx is given rigidity by the bones of the skull, while at the lower and narrow end its muscles are joined to the elastic cartilages of the voice-box or larynx. The outermost tissue layer of the pharynx, continuous with the lining of the mouth, contains many mucus-producing glands which help to keep the mouth and throat well lubricated during eating and speaking.

The parts of the pharynx

Anatomically, the pharynx is divided into three sections according to their positions and the jobs each is designed to perform. The uppermost part, the naso-pharynx, gets its name from the fact that it lies above the level of the soft palate and forms the back of the nose. Below, the nasopharynx is bordered by the soft palate itself; upward movement of this

Using a small torch, a doctor can look at a patient's throat to determine the cause of inflammation. In children, the culprits are often the tonsils.

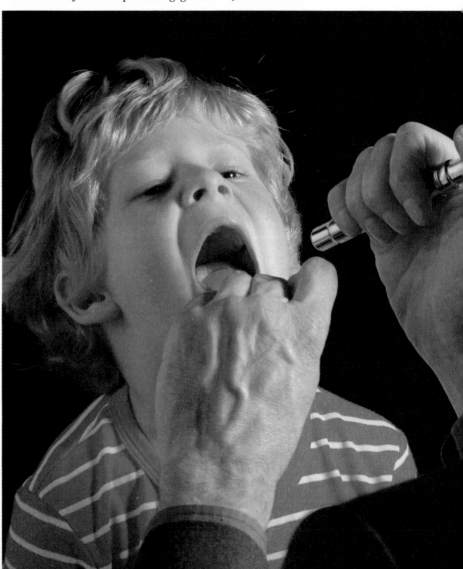

Roger Payling

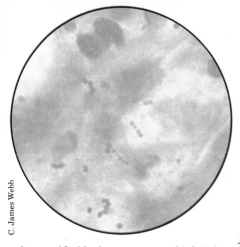

C. James Webb

A magnified look at streptococci (above) – the bacteria responsible for causing inflammation of the throat.

Steve Bielschowsky

Small fish bones and other similar objects get stuck in the throat very easily. When this happens the best course of action is to chew a couple of mouthfuls of bread and then have a drink of water. If this does not move the offending object, seek medical help rather than try to get it out yourself. One reason for this is that the bone may not actually be stuck at all — instead it may have grazed the pharynx and led to a sensation mimicking that of a stuck bone.

palate closes off the nasopharynx when you swallow to prevent food being forced up and out of the nose. The uncomfortable outcome of a failure in co-ordination of this mechanism can sometimes be experienced when you sneeze.

In the roof of the nasopharynx are two clumps of tissue particularly prominent in children, known as the adenoids. The nasopharynx, also contains, either side of the head, an entrance to the Eustachian tube, the passage between the middle ear and the throat. The problem, however, is that disease-causing micro-organisms of the mouth, nose and throat have easy access to the ears and commonly cause middle ear infections.

The part of the pharynx at the back of the mouth, the oropharynx, is part of the airway between mouth and lungs. Much more mobile than the nasopharynx, the squeezing actions of the muscles of the oropharynx help shape the sounds of speech as they come from the larynx. With the aid of the tongue, these muscles also help to push food down towards the entrance to the oesophagus. The most important organs of the oropharynx are the notorious tonsils, two mounds of tissue which are often implicated in the sore throats common in childhood. Like the adenoids, the tonsils are composed of lymphoid tissue characteristic of the body's self-defence system and which produces specialized white blood cells which engulf invading bacteria and viruses.

The lowermost or laryngeal section of the pharynx is involved entirely with swallowing. This section lies directly behind the larynx and its lining is joined to the thyroid and cricoid cartilages whose movements help to produce the sounds of speech. Again, squeezing actions of muscles help to propel mouthfuls of food through this part of the

pharynx on their digestive journey. Just above the laryngeal part of the pharynx is the epiglottis, a flap of tissue which closes down over the entrance to the airway as you swallow and so prevents food from getting into the lungs and choking you.

What can go wrong?

By far the most common problem of the pharynx is inflammation, known medically as pharyngitis and experienced as a sore throat. Pharyngitis can either come on suddenly (acute), or it can persist over several months or years (chronic).

The most usual cause of acute pharyngitis is the common cold – the sore throat is the tell-tale sign of an impending infection even before the first cough or sneeze. While the common cold is caused by a virus, there is also a bacterium called streptococcus, which can cause a form of pharyngitis known as 'strep throat'.

As well as direct infection, pharyngitis can be a subsidiary symptom of other diseases. Inflammation and infection of the parts of the body adjacent to or sited within the pharynx, including the larynx, mouth, sinuses and tonsils, can result in pharyngitis. Some other diseases that usually include pharyngitis as part of their spectrum of symptoms are glandular fever, measles and German measles. Scarlet fever, once a dreaded child-killer but now easily controlled with antibiotics, is an infection confined

to the nose and throat which is associated with severe pharyngitis.

The chief culprits in chronic pharyngitis are smoking and excessive drinking. Too much of either can certainly result in pharyngitis, and cutting down or, especially in the case of smoking, stopping altogether, is needed to effect a permanent cure. Another common cause of chronic pharyngitis is post-nasal drip – a constant drip of fluid from the back of the nose. This results from persistent mouth-breathing owing to a blocked nose. The causes of this are many and so need diagnosis by a doctor.

Treatment

Treatment of pharyngitis depends, of course, on its cause, but in general falls into two categories: first there is the treatment of those cases caused by viruses, such as the common cold virus, which do not respond to antibiotics; and secondly, the treatment of cases such as 'strep throat' which are caused by bacteria and so can be cleared up quickly with antibiotics.

Always use your common sense in deciding whether you or a member of your family needs medical attention. When an acute sore throat first comes on, soothe it by sucking proprietary lozenges. If the sore throat persists, or if you have a very high temperature, then you do need medical attention.

Phlegm

Q What is the difference between phlegm and catarrh?

A Catarrh is a term used to refer to the discharge – usually mucous in character – that results from inflammation of any of the body's lining tissues. It most commonly occurs in relation to the nasal, bronchial, urethral and vaginal passages. It is no longer regarded as a disease in itself, but as a symptom of some underlying condition. The excess mucus produced in bronchial and nasal catarrh would block vital airways if it were allowed to accumulate, and so it is got rid of by being coughed up as phlegm.

Q My mother has been bringing up phlegm persistently for the past month, but says it's only due to smoking and that there is no point in going to the doctor about it. Should I try to persuade her to do something about it?

A You certainly should. Phlegm that persists for more than a few days is almost always due to something – not necessarily serious – that requires investigation and treatment, both to stop it getting worse and to put a stop to the phlegm. As a smoker it is particularly important that your mother gets her cough checked by a doctor.

Q I always seem to cough up a little phlegm when I get up in the morning, but have none for the rest of the day. Why is this?

A It sounds as though you have a slight chronic inflammatory condition of some part of your respiratory tract — the sort of thing that used to be called catarrh — possibly due to a mild allergy. The amount of mucous secretion from this is not sufficient to make you cough during the day, but it collects during the night while you are asleep. Obviously if you are a smoker you need look no further for the cause. Smoking paralyzes the fine hairs that line the bronchial tubes (cilia) and move the phlegm along. When you are asleep you give the cilia a chance to work. Phlegm is moved along and collects in the large airways. This stimulates a cough when you get up.

A hacking, phlegm-producing cough is usually associated with heavy smokers, but this mucous substance can be produced in a wide variety of stituations and often results from something as minor as the common cold.

Phlegm or sputum, as it is called medically, is a term used to refer to any material which is produced as a result of coughing. It may contain mucus, saliva, pus, blood, particles of inhaled dust or fibre, shreds of tissue from diseased parts of the respiratory tract – or any combination of these things.

Where phlegm is formed
We tend to assume that the material in phlegm comes from the lungs, but this is not necessarily true. Whatever else is in it, phlegm usually consists largely of mucus which acts as a vehicle for trapping and then getting rid of unwanted and potentially dangerous substances. Most parts of the respiratory tract have mucus-secreting glands – the mucus being needed both as a general lubricant, to form a protective coating over the delicate lining, and as a sticky liquid in which dust, bacteria and so on will get stuck and can then be coughed out of the body either from the throat itself or from the lungs or bronchial tubes.

Phlegm can originate in the pharynx at the back of the throat or consist of material that has run down from the back of the nose in the form of nasal catarrh or post-nasal drip, as well as coming from further down in the respiratory tract from such areas as the lungs and bronchi.

Types of phlegm
The most common type of phlegm known as white or mucous sputum consists largely of mucus – it is clear white and often frothy. Its presence means that an excessive amount of mucus is being secreted and is an indication of inflammation somewhere in the respiratory passages; the extra mucus being secreted to soothe the raw, inflamed surfaces. White

Our phlegm can say a lot about our health and the air we breathe. Coalminers often have black phlegm due to the coal dust they inhale, and this can lead to a condition known as pneumoconiosis or coalminers lung: normal sputum (above right); a smear of pneumoconiosis (right).

Rex Features

Steve Bielschowsky/Dressing gown by Fenwicks

Biophoto Associates

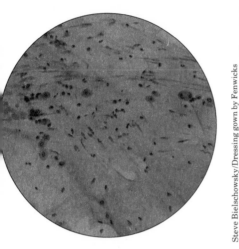

Depending on the type of cough mixture chosen, these preparations can either loosen up thick, sticky phelgm so that it can be coughed up more easily, or they can dry up excessive amounts of sputum.

sputum that originates in the lungs is commonly the result of asthma, smoking, chronic bronchitis or the early stages of ordinary bronchitis. It is sometimes referred to as bronchial catarrh. Mucous phlegm may also come from the nose, running down from the post-nasal space to the back of the throat. This can be caused by a common cold or hay fever where the tissue which lines the nose has become inflamed.

If the phlegm contains yellow or green pus-like matter it is called mucopurulent, and this indicates that an infection has developed in some part of the respiratory tract. Common causes are a fully developed bronchitis, a flare-up of chronic bronchitis, bronchopneumonia and sinus infection.

Other discoloration of the phlegm usually depends on changes in the air that is being breathed. Coalminers often have black phlegm due to particles of coal dust, and the sputum of town dwellers is usually similarly discoloured after a foggy night. People working in dusty atmospheres are very likely to cough up in their phlegm particles of the material concerned unless they wear proper protective masks.

The coughing up of bloody phlegm should never be ignored and should always be reported to your doctor. The commonest cause, giving rise to blood-streaked phlegm for only a day or two, is energetic coughing – the violence of which is sufficient to break some of the tiny blood vessels in the lining of some part of the respiratory tract, causing them to bleed a little. More heavily blood-stained phlegm, especially if it is persistent, or coughing up pure blood

may have more serious causes; although it is always possible that it has come down from the back of the nose, and is really a nosebleed in disguise. The more serious causes of coughing up blood include cancer, tuberculosis, bronchiectosis (inflammatory destruction of the bronchi) and some types of heart disease.

Diagnosis and treatment

Examination of a patient's phlegm can give a doctor a considerable amount of information about what is likely to be wrong with the patient. Just looking at the amount of sputum, its colour, consistency and smell can help considerably in making the diagnosis. Microscopic examination and laboratory tests will enable the doctor to look for special types of cells indicating cancer, asthma, asbestosis, silicosis and various other conditions; or to establish which germ is the cause of the trouble in cases involving infection.

As far as treatment is concerned, the most important thing is to find out why phlegm is being produced. It is most important that you do not let a cough producing phlegm continue for more than two weeks at the most without getting medical advice about it. As well as dealing with the cause of the phlegm, your doctor will be able, if necessary, to prescribe a suitable cough medicine depending on the precise nature of the cough and phlegm. For instance, if you have thick, sticky phlegm that is difficult to get up, you might be helped most by a medicine that makes it thinner and stimulates coughing; whereas if it is so copious that its sheer volume is causing a problem, cough mixtures are available that tend to dry it up.

Piles

While the conditions commonly referred to as 'piles' can sometimes cause extreme pain and much embarrassment to the patient, they are essentially minor medical problems that can be easily and often painlessly cured.

In a medical context, the word 'piles' refers to several different conditions of the anal canal, each of which has different symptoms. Most commonly, the word refers to haemorrhoids, or internal piles, but it is often used also to denote anal fissure, thrombosed external haemorrhoids and simple anal skin tags.

There is some confusion about the treatment of these conditions, probably because of the patient's difficulty in visualizing what the problem is. The result is that any condition of the anal canal that consists of bleeding, pain or the presence of a lump, is referred to as 'piles'. This situation is further aggravated by the patient's natural reluctance to seek medical help because of embarrassment or fear of painful remedies.

Only with a knowledge of the anal canal's structure can the various conditions and their related symptoms be fully understood.

Structure of the anal canal

The anal canal is a short tube, about 3.8 cm (1½ in) long, which connects the rectum (the last part of the large bowel) to the outside. Its upper (or innermost) half is lined with mucous membrane – the type of lining found throughout the gut. The lower half is lined with skin. This lower half is extremely sensitive to painful stimuli, whereas the upper or inner half is insensitive to pain.

The whole of the anal canal is surrounded by a ring of muscle, the anal sphincter, which can relax during the passage of a bowel motion, but which normally remains tightly contracted so that continence of faeces is maintained.

The discomfort and pain that sometimes result from piles can be relieved by sitting in a warm salt bath. This home treatment can be useful in all cases of haemorrhoids that induce swelling.

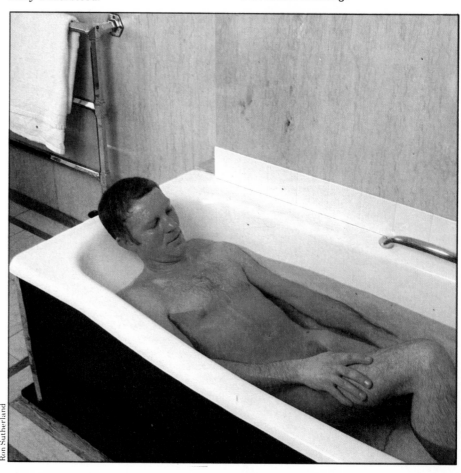

Ron Sutherland

Anatomy of the anal canal

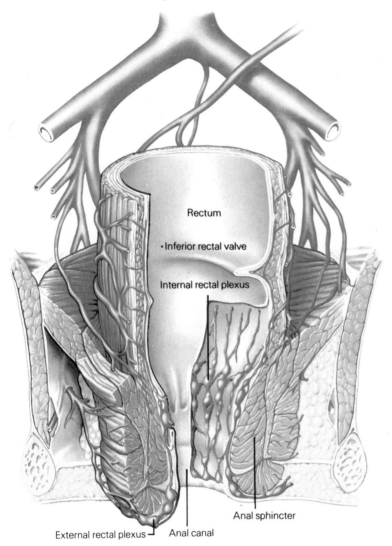

Rectum

· Inferior rectal valve

Internal rectal plexus

Anal sphincter

External rectal plexus — Anal canal

Conditions and their symptoms

Different conditions of the anal canal occur in different parts of it, and as such, produce different symptoms.

Internal haemorrhoids are swellings that arise from the upper part of the anal canal (the insensitive part) and gradually become larger over a period of years. They are probably caused by prolonged straining to pass small, hard faeces, but they are made worse by pregnancy. Internal haemorrhoids used to be thought of as varicose veins, but are now thought to be made of spongy tissue rich in small blood-vessels. They generally occur in threes and the first symptom is usually bleeding. The blood is bright red; the amount of bleeding is small, occurs at the end of defaecation and does not usually cause any pain.

Patients with small internal haemorrhoids have bouts of bleeding on and off over several years, and because of the length of time they have had the symptoms they are perfectly used to the fact that they have haemorrhoids. Also, they may never have more than minimal symptoms. If the haemorrhoids become larger, as well as bleeding during defaecation, they may come out of the anal canal and be visible as a lump. The lump may only be evident during defaecation, or, if the haemorrhoids are very large, may be present all the time. The essential thing about the lump is that it appears to emerge from inside the anal canal.

Occasionally, these kinds of haemorrhoids can become painful. When this happens the patient usually notices a large tender lump that becomes excruciatingly painful, and without specific treatment lasts for several days. This is probably what is known as an 'attack of

Frank Kennard

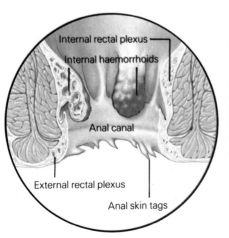

Internal rectal plexus —
Internal haemorrhoids

Anal canal

External rectal plexus

Anal skin tags

The diagram above illustrates how networks of veins (the plexuses) are concentrated in certain areas of the rectum. It is in these areas that piles may occur, either as external haemorrhoids (inset right) or internal haemorrhoids (inset left). Skin tags, (inset left) are not true haemorrhoids but are often diagnosed and treated as such, although they seldom cause any serious problem.

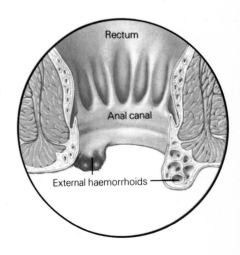

Rectum

Anal canal

External haemorrhoids

297

Q Is it it true that piles always cause pain?

A No. If by 'piles' you mean haemorrhoids, which are increased amounts of spongy tissue situated inside the anal canal, then the commonest symptom is bleeding, and you might not otherwise know that you have them. They can occasionally become painful when they strangulate, or get 'trapped' outside the anal canal. Anal fissure however, which is often referred to as piles, is nearly always painful.

Q What is the normal sort of bleeding to be expected from piles?

A Bleeding caused by piles is usually bright red and appears in small amounts. Often it is only evident as a few spots on toilet paper. Other conditions can cause bleeding, notably cancer of the rectum, and in this case the blood is likely to be more noticeable. It may also be mixed in with the motion. In addition there may be an associated change in the patient's bowel habits. For instance, a person who has been having his or her bowels open once daily for years may suddenly start to have a bowel action twice every day.

Q Is an operation to remove piles likely to be extremely painful?

A No. Most of the operation is internal, on the insensitive part of the anal canal. Also, the surgeon performing the operation should stretch the muscles of the anal canal. This makes it very easy for the patient to have a bowel action without straining, even before the wound has healed.

Q Why are pregnant women likely to suffer from haemorrhoids?

A Essentially, piles are the result of an interference in the return flow of blood from veins in the anal region. During late pregnancy in particular, the presence of the baby in the womb tends to obstruct the return flow of blood. This causes a swelling of the veins in the anal area.

Ron Sutherland

Whether or not a person develops piles is, to some extent, a matter of good or bad luck. However steps can be taken to help prevent the condition and to minimize the damage when it does occur.

Be sure to include some high-fibre foods in your diet every day – bran, fruit, raw vegetables, nuts and wholemeal bread – to prevent constipation.

If you do suffer from constipation which persists for several days, see your doctor. In any case of constipation however, never strain to pass faeces.

If you have a tendency to pass hard stools, the condition may be helped by using a glycerine suppository available from the chemist.

Should piles develop, pay particular attention to anal hygiene by bathing and wiping the area thoroughly.

piles'. It must be stressed, however, that haemorrhoids are not usually painful, and when they are it is because they have become strangulated, or squeezed by a tight anal canal.

Anal fissure bears no relation to internal haemorrhoids. It is due to a split in the skin of the anal canal in a longitudinal direction. This condition is probably caused by straining in a person who has constipation. Because the split is in the highly sensitive skin of the anal canal it is extremely painful. The usual story given by the patient with an anal fissure is that of extreme pain during defaecation, together with the passage of a small amount of blood, often only on the toilet-paper. The pain may be so severe that the patient is afraid to have a bowel action. A vicious circle of pain and constipation arises.

This condition, which is common after pregnancy, is often diagnosed as 'piles' and therefore treated inappropriately. If a careful case history is taken from the

patient there should be no doubt about the diagnosis. Anal fissures can sometimes heal up spontaneously and at other times can become severe and prolonged enough to warrant a small operation.

Some people develop tags of extra skin around the anal canal. These are not strictly speaking an abnormality, but they do cause problems with hygiene in some patients. They are, however, commonly diagnosed as haemorrhoids or piles, and treated as such, even though treatment is usually not necessary in many cases.

Thrombosed external piles is a condition in which a small blood-vessel bursts, just beneath the skin's surface at the edge of the anal canal. The patient experiences severe pain during defaecation and the pain persists after it is finished. Some time later a painful lump is noticed. This becomes red and inflamed. The condition is easy to treat but like anal fissure relies on the doctor taking a careful case history and examining the patient properly. A thrombosed external pile can be easily seen as a lump, often with some bruising on it, just near the opening of the anal canal.

The condition known as anal fistula is also occasionally diagnosed as piles, but really should never be confused with the above condition. The main symptom is a discharge of fluid, often like pus, and there is seldom much bleeding, a lump or pain. Anal fistula is usually the after-effect of a tiny abscess in the lining of the anal canal. There is an abnormal connection between the skin next to the anal canal and the inside of the canal. Secretions therefore leak out through this channel, leading to soiling of underclothes.

Treatment

Treatment of true internal haemorrhoids takes several different forms. Initially, the doctor will want to make sure that there is no other serious cause for the bleeding by examining the lower part of the rectum. If the haemorrhoids are small, there are a number of ways in which they can be treated.

The haemorrhoids can be injected with a special substance that makes them shrivel up. This may sound painful but if done properly should not hurt at all as the injection is put into the upper insensitive part of the anal canal. Other methods of treatment are to use a special freezing instrument called a cryoprobe which shrinks the haemorrhoids, or to put tiny rubber bands around them that cut off their blood supply.

None of these treatments is in any way painful and can be done in the out-patient department of a hospital. As well as these treatments, a high fibre diet is recommended. It is thought that lack of fibre, or roughage, in the diet is one of the main factors in the formation of haemorrhoids. Sometimes, adding fibre to the diet in the form of natural bran may be all that is needed to effect a cure.

Because anal fissure is so frequently confused with haemorrhoids, many patients soldier on with severe pain when they could easily have simple treatment.

The treatment of an anal fissure depends on whether or not it is a small, recent one, or a larger one of some months' duration. In the mild form the use of some local anaesthetic cream, together with the intake of increased amounts of dietary fibre, may allow the fissure to heal up. In the more severe cases, the pain on defaecation causes intense spasm of the ring of muscle around the anal canal, making it more difficult to pass a motion. This in turn aggravates the condition even further.

In these cases, there is so much pain that it is usually impossible to examine the patient properly. The best thing to do is give the patient a general anaesthetic before attempting an examination. If a fissure is found, than a 'canal stretch' is performed; the ring of muscle around the anal canal is stretched so that it is unable to contract strongly. This allows the patient to have an easy bowel action, and the fissure to heal up quickly. Most patients notice an immediate relief in the amount of pain after the anal stretch has been performed.

Thrombosed external piles can easily be treated under a local anaesthetic. After cutting through the skin the blood clot is removed, with instant pain relief.

Anal skin tags do not usually need any specific treatment. However they can be removed easily during a small operation, sometimes performed under a local anaesthetic.

The condition of anal fistula can also be easily treated, but again, it has to be correctly diagnosed first. Most cases can be treated by opening up the abnormal track onto the surface of the skin. Sometimes a longer operation is necessary but this is very rare nowadays.

Outlook

All the above conditions are minor in a medical sense although an anal fissure, and occasionally haemorrhoids, can be very painful. However there is no inherent danger in having any of these conditions. In an indirect way haemorrhoids can be dangerous, as they can mimic symptoms from a tumour of the rectum, making it more likely to be missed by the patient and the doctor. A careful doctor

Resting with legs raised can temporarily alleviate the condition of strangulated haemorrhoids, especially if it is combined with the application of an ice-pack to the anal region.

should always be aware of this pitfall and if there is any doubt, the rectum and colon should be examined by means of a special instrument or a special X-ray.

Home Care

If haemorrhoids prolapse (appear as lumps) then sitting in a warm bath with a handful of salt dissolved in it often helps a lot. Salt baths soothe the area and can reduce swelling; while taking an ordinary bath softens the skin, allowing water to pass through – and thus increasing swelling – salt water actually draws water out of the area.

Occasionally, when haemorrhoids become strangulated, a polythene bag full of crushed ice applied to the enlarged haemorrhoids may help as well.

When to seek medical help

If the bleeding is persistent or profuse.
If there is pain in the abdomen.
If there is a change in the normal bowel-habit, for example an increase or decrease in frequency persisting for more than two weeks.
If there is persistent pain in the anal region.
If symptoms attributable to 'piles' start in a person over the age of 50.
If the blood from the area is dark in colour.

Pimples

Q My mother is always telling me not to squeeze my pimples because it will only make them worse. Is this true?

A As a general rule it's better not to squeeze spots and pimples, if only because of the risk of increasing the inflammation by introducing harmful bacteria through a break in the skin surface. If, however, the pimple is small and very superficial, and you make sure that your hands and nails are scrupulously clean, there is probably no harm in squeezing a pimple gently with a tissue or piece of cotton wool. One sharp squeeze should be enough to release the pus.

Q I always seem to get pimples on one area of my back. Why should this be?

A The most likely reason for this is that the skin in this area has larger pores than normal, and so is more prone to infection. It could also be that this area of your back is inaccessible and gets missed when you wash, so providing an ideal breeding ground for bacteria. If you think this may be the reason ask someone to scrub your back for you when you have a bath or shower.

Q Is it true that you get pimples if you masturbate?

A No, this is certainly not true. There may, however, be some connection between stress and spots, so perhaps excessive worrying about masturbation could help cause pimples. Both pimples and masturbation are aspects of growing up and you should be ashamed of neither.

Q Why do I get pimples when I'm constipated?

A The answer to this probably lies in your diet. Many of the foods that help prevent constipation – particularly fresh fruit and vegetables – are the very ones that help keep the skin healthy and free of spots and pimples. Try eating more fresh foods, and you should notice an improvement in the condition of your skin – and your constipation may well disappear.

Unsightly spots are an inescapable fact of life for most adolescents. And it's important to ensure that they do not cause psychological – as well as physical – scars.

Ron Sutherland

Pimples are a common problem in the years from puberty to the early twenties – the years that witness the transformation of a boy or girl into a mature young man or woman. The time of life at which pimples are likely to occur gives a clue to one of their most powerful underlying causes: the upsurge in hormone production that takes place as a child becomes an adult.

What is a pimple?
'Pimple' or 'spot' is generally used to describe a pus-filled blemish on the skin. Usually the formation of a pimple is triggered off by the excess production of an oily substance called sebum from glands in the skin. Sebum normally lubricates the surface of the skin and the hairs that grow out of it. Excessive sebum output, however, causes the pore on the surface of the skin, through which sebum is released, to become blocked and the hair inside the pore dies. As a result the sebum becomes trapped within the pore, and the skin tissues beneath the surface become red and inflamed. Finally, the pore fills up with pus which is composed of white blood cells and bacteria.

It is not completely clear how pus is formed. The indications are that when the pore becomes clogged with sebum the environment created inside it is ideal for the growth of bacteria, particularly Staphylococcus albus and Bacillus acnes. In response to the presence of these invading micro-organisms, the body mobi-

Teenagers are particularly prone to pimples – almost certainly because of the great upsurge in hormone output that occurs during this time. But it is important not to worry too much about this problem.

lizes its defence forces: white blood cells. The white cells multiply in number, more blood is pumped into the infected area and the tissues become red and inflamed. As the white cells work at neutralizing and then engulfing the bacteria, they themselves die, accumulate and form pus. At the same time the dead 'bodies' of the bacteria also build up.

Normally, a pimple left undisturbed will burst of its own accord, releasing the pus. The damaged tissues will then repair themselves and the skin will return to normal. In more deep-seated, closely related infections of the skin such as boils or abscesses, the pus may build up and not be released. In these cases a doctor may have to cut into or lance the area.

Causes
Traditionally, all kinds of things, from chocolate to masturbation, have been blamed for the appearance of pimples in adolescence. Nothing has been conclusively proved to cause pimples: the only virtual certainty is that there is a relationship between pimples and the adolescent rise in hormone output. Spots, unfortunately, are all too frequently part of growing up.

The most influential hormones are the androgens, which are produced in both sexes, but in much greater quantities in boys than in girls. These hormones act on the sebaceous glands in the skin, stimulate them and lead to a great increase in sebum output, one symptom of which is the greasy, lanky hair typical of young people in their teens. As a result of excess sebum output, a pimple-producing environment is created, of which the common halfway house is the blackhead – a plug of sebum on which air acts so that it changes colour from white to black.

In girls, hormones seem to play a role in that pimples are most common just before the menstrual period, a time when the levels of the female hormones oestrogen and progesterone are at their lowest.

As far as other classic 'criminals' like chocolate or fatty foods are concerned, a degree of scepticism should be adopted, although circumstances will vary from individual to individual. Lack of fresh air, however, has been suggested as a contributory factor, and the ultraviolet rays in sunshine have been shown to be an effective cure.

Good personal hygiene is an effective cure and prevention all in one. Wash affected areas thoroughly with soap and water daily; dry vigorously with a clean towel.

Treatment
Apart from getting out into the fresh air, there are several ways in which pimples can be treated and prevented. The length of time a pimple lasts depends on its size and the severity of the inflammation. Often superficial pimples, in which the deepest layers of the skin are not affected, last only a few days. Acne pimples, how-

Q Are pimples contagious and can you catch them by kissing someone who has them?

A To the extent that the inflamed tissues in a pimple contain bacteria, and these bacteria do pass from one person to another, pimples are contagious: but it is highly unlikely that this will occur during kissing. The most common way the infection is spread is not by kissing, but by someone who has pimples picking at them and carrying the bacteria under his fingernails. Even then this most often results in infection spreading on the same person, not from one person to another.

Q I often get pimples at the corners of my mouth which turn into cold sores. Can I do anything about this?

A Unfortunately, cold sores are caused by a virus that does not die off when a cold sore clears but lies dormant in the skin. The virus starts into active growth again when you get a cold or become run down, and it first shows itself as a small, fluid-filled pimple. The only way to help cut down the number of attacks is to pay careful attention to your general health, both physical and mental.

Q Whenever I am very hot I get a rash of pimples all over my chest. What are these and do they need medical attention?

A These pimples are probably just the physical signs that the skin has become overheated. They result from the accumulation of fluid in tiny pockets or vesicles in the skin and are nothing to worry about. The best treatment is to wash well after taking exercise and to dust the affected area with talcum powder.

Q My daughter is extremely embarrassed by her pimples. What can I do to reassure her?

A Part of the treatment for pimples is understanding from parents and friends. Emphasize to your daughter that pimples are part of growing up and that she should not worry about them – they will clear up, and good personal hygiene will keep them at bay.

How a pimple develops

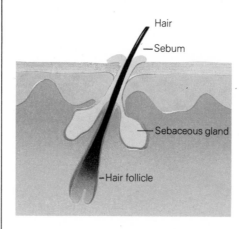

The formation of a pimple is triggered off by the excess production of an oily substance called sebum, whose function it is to lubricate the surface of the skin and the hairs which grow out of it.

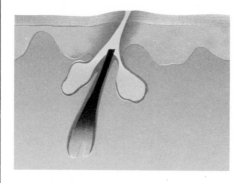

When sebum output is excessive, however, the pore of the surface of the skin, through which the sebum is released, becomes blocked. As a result, the hair inside the pore dies.

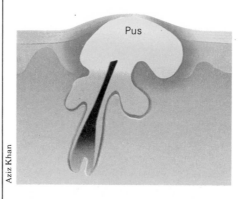

The sebum becomes trapped inside the pore and the skin tissues beneath the surface become red and inflamed. Eventually the pore fills up with pus, which is formed from bacteria and dead white blood cells.

ever, may last much longer – possibly two to three weeks.

So what advice should be given to the teenager suffering the physical and mental agonies of pimples? First and foremost, personal hygiene is important, for clean skin and hair is a good cure and prevention all in one. The face, and any other affected area should be washed thoroughly with soap and water every day and dried vigorously with a clean towel to help rub off the outer layers of dead skin cells. Washing or dabbing pimples with water as hot as the skin can stand can help bring pimples to a head so that they burst of their own accord more readily. Proprietary creams, which kill off the bacteria, are also effective and can be bought over the counter.

Some sufferers find that changing clothes is important because wearing wool next to the skin can sometimes trigger the appearance of new pimples and delay the healing of old ones. Diet may also be important in many cases: some teenagers manage to keep pimples at bay by eating a diet containing plenty of fresh fruit and vegetables and few sweets and puddings.

It has also been suggested that stress and pimples are related. For this reason one of the most essential treatments for pimples is understanding and sympathy from friends and parents, so that physical scars do not become transformed into psychological ones.

How to avoid pimples

DO . . .
- get plenty of fresh air and sunshine.
- observe good personal hygiene. Wash the affected area well and frequently with soap and water and dry vigorously with a clean towel.
- wash your hair.
- eat plenty of fresh fruit and vegetables: they keep the skin healthy.
- use a proprietary cream: these disguise the inflammation and kill off the bacteria which cause infection.
- consult your doctor if the pimples are persistent or widespread. No doctor worth his salt will laugh at a youngster with bad pimples, or fail to take the matter seriously.

DON'T . . .
- worry about them. Stress may actually cause pimples.
- squeeze them unless they are very small – in which case use a piece of cotton wool or a tissue – not your fingernails.
- stay indoors all the time.

Plaque

Q How can I tell whether I have plaque on my teeth?

A Some plaque deposits are too small to be visible, while larger deposits are apparent to the naked eye. Plaque shows up as a soft whitish-yellow material, either near to the gum's edge or on areas where teeth overlap. Bleeding gums are another tell-tale sign.

To find out whether your teeth have plaque in significant amounts, you should use a disclosing agent (coloured tablets which are chewed) which stains plaque pink, but does not affect the teeth's surface. Plaque deposits can then be removed by thorough brushing and dental floss.

Q I have bad breath. Could it be caused by plaque?

A Possibly. There are a number of causes of halitosis, but the most common culprit is poor teeth and gums. This may arise because of plaque deposits. Plaque itself can cause an unpleasant smelling breath, and so may gum breakdown, which is due to the effects of the bacteria in plaque. Good dental care may eliminate bad breath, but it would also be advisable to see your dentist.

Q Which is better for plaque removal: a soft or hard toothbrush?

A Neither! A soft brush is usually not effective enough to remove plaque, and an excessively hard brush may damage teeth and gums. A medium brush is the most suitable – choose one with a straight head.

Q Will eating certain foods prevent plaque formation?

A Plaque formation takes place all the time – there is no way to prevent it totally. However foods containing a fibrous material have a cleansing effect on teeth, and are preferable to soft foods which stick between teeth. The best way to prevent plaque from accumulating to any significant degree is to take good care of your teeth, and to restrict your intake of sugar. This will limit acid production in plaque and minimize tooth decay – though it will not stop plaque forming.

Look at your teeth in a mirror: notice any yellowish-white deposits? This is plaque – one of the primary causes of tooth decay and gum disease. With good dental care, its harmful effects can be prevented.

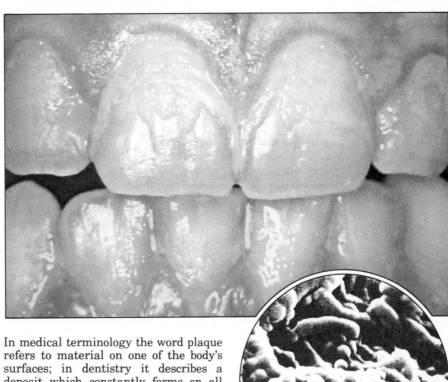

By kind permission of Gibbs the makers of SR toothpaste

In medical terminology the word plaque refers to material on one of the body's surfaces; in dentistry it describes a deposit which constantly forms on all surfaces in the mouth, in particular the teeth. A whitish-yellow sticky material, plaque is sometimes invisible to the naked eye, but very visible once it has accumulated. Because it spreads and clings to teeth, it can cause a great deal of damage to them and to gums. Correct and regular brushing and use of dental floss will prevent plaque and lessen the chances of tooth decay and gum disease.

Although these teeth look clean to the naked eye, they are covered in plaque deposits. When magnified thousands of times, plaque is revealed as a mesh of billions of bacteria of all shapes and sizes (inset).

What is plaque?

Plaque is composed of bacteria and their by-products, together with the constituents of saliva. The bacteria are of many types, and are classified according to their shape: spherical (cocci), rods (bacilli), filaments and spirals. Vast numbers are present, and it has been estimated that each gram weight of plaque contains some two billion bacteria. The bacteria are derived from those already present in the mouth – yeasts, viruses and others. These tiny organisms are enclosed in a sticky material composed of proteins derived from the saliva, together with polysaccharides and glycoproteins of the plaque bacteria themselves. Food debris is also present, but not in significant amounts.

Sometimes plaque may only exist as a thin, invisible film, but if it is allowed to build up, it may become a millimetre thick. Plaque that has accumulated over a long period may eventually calcify and it is then known as calculus or tartar which, unlike plaque which is soft, is a hard deposit.

How plaque is formed

The bacteria involved in plaque formation are present in the mouth from birth. Once teeth begin to emerge, they become coated with a glycoprotein layer which is derived from the saliva. This forms a thin

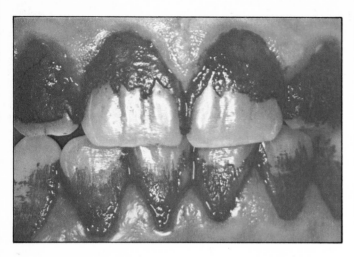

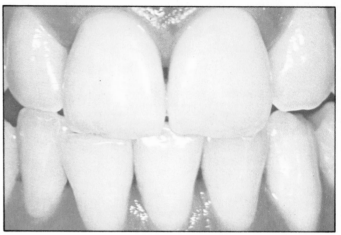

'skin' or pellicle over the teeth. Subsequently, bacteria from the saliva adhere to this skin and multiply, forming colonies. The first bacteria to do this are round and rod-shaped forms which derive oxygen from the saliva.

Later on organisms begin to multiply deep within the plaque which do not require oxygen – these are called anaerobes. As the plaque layer thickens, spiral and filamentous organisms also begin to multiply, and these constitute a significant part of the plaque flora. Over a period of time, the layer of plaque, which starts as an invisible film, thickens to the stage where it is clearly visible as a surface deposit on the teeth.

Effects of plaque

The bacteria of plaque are responsible for dental caries (tooth decay) and periodontal disease (disease of the gum and other structures which hold the teeth in position).

Dental caries is the progressive breakdown of the enamel and dentine of teeth, leading to the formation of a cavity within the tooth. Enamel and dentine are both hard tissues which are very strong mechanically, but they can be dissolved by chemicals like acid.

The bacteria within plaque will produce significant amounts of acid when provided with a source of sucrose, which in turn is produced from the breakdown of carbohydrates as well as being the main constituent of sugar.

Within only a few minutes of a person eating sugar-containing food, the level of acidity adjacent to the tooth surfaces rises to a critical level and the enamel then starts to dissolve. This process may continue for about half an hour, even without the person eating any further sugar or sugar-containing food.

Tooth decay therefore depends upon a number of factors: plaque, sugar in the diet and the amount of resistance of the tooth enamel to decay. In view of this, it

A disclosing agent (tablets which are chewed) will stain the teeth in places where plaque is present (above left). Once the deposits have been removed, the teeth will be truly clean (above right).

would appear that tooth decay could be prevented if plaque could somehow be eliminated.

Unfortunately, however, it is only possible to reduce, rather than completely remove, all traces of plaque. For this reason the most effective methods currently available for preventing tooth decay include controlling the amount of sugar you eat, protecting tooth enamel by the use of fluoride, and sealing the crevices within teeth's surfaces in which plaque would otherwise accumulate.

In chronic periodontal disease, the process whereby plaque damages the gum and other structures is, like tooth decay, caused by the products of bacterial metabolism. However with gum disease, the process is different in that the damaging factor is not acid, but rather the production of toxic organic chemicals by the plaque bacteria.

Chronic periodontal disease is present to some degree in most people. There is a slow, progressive destruction of the various tissues which hold the teeth in position, leading eventually to tooth loss.

Dental floss is useful for cleaning the spaces between teeth where plaque can become trapped. It should be used regularly, and gently, to prevent damage to gums.

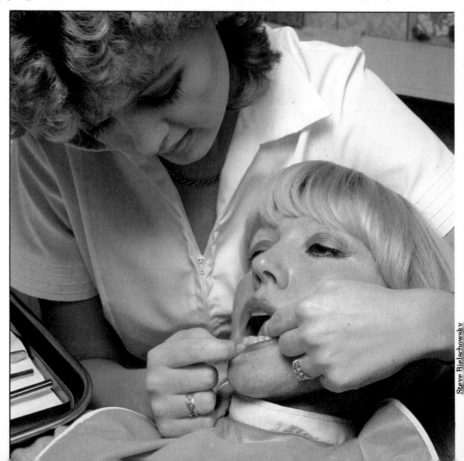

Steve Bielschowsky

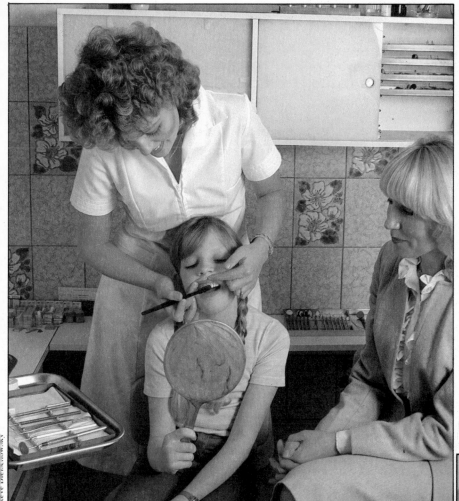

Therefore the measures to be taken revolve around preventive methods. Teeth should be brushed at least once a day, but thorough brushing is more important than the amount of times teeth are brushed. The type of brush that should be used is flat-headed, with medium bristles, and a short, straight handle as this can reach the awkward corners of the mouth. Teeth should be brushed for three minutes – from the gum downward or upward – since each area must be brushed several times in order to remove the plaque, which is very sticky. An electric toothbrush will make plaque removal less laborious, but water irrigation devices will not remove plaque fully since plaque clings too strongly to the teeth.

Areas not accessible to the toothbrush, such as regions between the teeth, should be cleaned by using dental floss. The waxed and unwaxed kinds are equally effective, but the waxed kind feels smoother.

In addition, restricting sugar in the diet will limit the amount of acid production in plaque and will minimize tooth decay. Taken together with other preventive measures against tooth decay, this can make it possible for the teeth to remain caries-free. Chronic periodontal disease can also be prevented this way.

The only way to prevent tooth decay and gum disease is by correct and regular brushing so that plaque is removed. While a dental hygienist will clean the teeth properly, her main task is to show the child — and parent — how it is done and ensure that the technique is mastered.

Chronic periodontal disease is so widespread that people accept tooth loss as inevitable with ageing. However tooth loss *can* be prevented, providing effective measures are taken to remove plaque.

How to avoid plaque
Unfortunately it is not, at present, possible to avoid plaque forming, as the bacteria involved are the normal inhabitants of the mouth. Immunization techniques and the long-term use of antibiotics have both been tried, but they are not effective as in the former there are too many types of bacteria to counteract, and in the latter there would eventually be a build up of resistance. Antiseptics have also been tried, but long-term use causes tooth discoloration and, over time, resistance may occur.

Pleurisy

Q Is it true that pleurisy is always painful?

A It is certainly usual for pleurisy to cause pain, and this pain will be made worse by deep breathing, since the two inflamed layers of the pleura rub against each other. If the two layers of the pleura are separated, as happens in a pleural effusion, the pain may well stop.

Q Can pleurisy cause permanent damage to the lungs or the pleura?

A Yes. This happens particularly in tuberculosis. In this disease pleural infection tends to leave thick scars on the surface of the pleura. Sometimes the scarring becomes even thicker as a result of infiltration by calcium, and in very rare cases this process can lead to the lung becoming encased in a hard, bony cage.

Q How soon after having pleurisy can a normal life be resumed?

A The time it takes to return to a normal, active life depends on the seriousness of the original cause of the pleurisy, and how fit you were to begin with. An attack of pleurisy due to a viral infection, which is quite a common problem, would take only a week or so to improve in a fit young person thanks to modern medicine – a far cry from the days when pleurisy was a killer, particularly of children.

Q Recently my father had to have some fluid taken out of his chest with a needle. Was this fluid anything to do with pleurisy?

A It sounds like your father had a pleural effusion: the fluid came from the pleural cavity, and was certainly lost from an inflamed surface of the pleura. Pleural effusions are just one type of pleurisy. As a matter of fact, doctors tend to make a distinction in terminology: they call the sort of illness that gives you pain on deep breathing pleurisy, and will refer to a pleural effusion – which often involves no chest pain – as just that.

This inflammation of the membrane that lines the lungs was once feared as a killing disease. Nowadays, however, it can be controlled by the use of antibiotics.

In the past the very mention of pleurisy frightened people. This was because it was invariably associated with yesterday's great killer of young children – lobar pneumonia.

Nowadays, however, lobar pneumonia is a rare disease and one which in any case can be controlled with antibiotics. In modern parlance pleurisy is a name given to problems involving inflammation of the pleura – the delicate lining membrane of the lungs. It can be associated with all sorts of diseases, from the serious to the very minor.

The pleura
Each lung is surrounded by a lining membrane, which is called the visceral pleura. It lines the whole lung on each side and even lines both sides of the fissures (cracks) that divide the lung up into its various lobes. As this sheet of visceral pleura leaves the lung surface at each hilium (the roof of the lung at the point

The pleura lining the lungs

Lungs are surrounded by two layers of pleura – visceral and parietal. Pleurisy *occurs when the pleura are inflamed or the space between the layers is filled with fluid.*

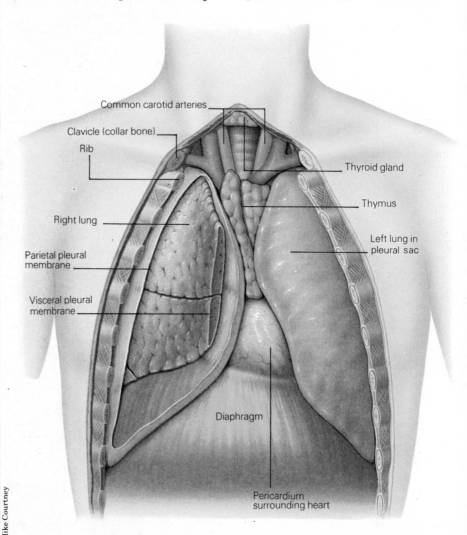

Common carotid arteries

Clavicle (collar bone)

Rib

Thyroid gland

Thymus

Right lung

Left lung in pleural sac

Parietal pleural membrane

Visceral pleural membrane

Diaphragm

Pericardium surrounding heart

Mike Courtney

where the windpipe joins it) it carries on to form another sheet – the parietal pleura – which spreads around the inside of the chest wall and the upper half of the diaphragm on one side of the chest.

In healthy people the visceral and parietal layers of pleura are always in contact with each other, and they slide over each other as the lung moves in the act of breathing. Of course, there is some space between the two layers. In healthy people this 'potential' space is minimal: just enough to accommodate tiny amounts of fluid that help to lubricate the two layers as they glide over each other. In one aspect of pleurisy, however, the space can fill up with large amounts of fluid: this is called a pleural effusion.

Unlike the lung, the pleura is equipped to feel pain, and it is this pain that is characteristic of pleurisy. Any sort of inflammation will make the surface of the pleura raw, and the pain will arise as the visceral and parietal pleura slide past each other in the process of breathing.

Who gets pleurisy?

Pleurisy can attack people of all ages, from children right through to the very elderly. When infection is the cause it is a disease which doctors tend to associate with young people. When the pleurisy is associated with pneumonia, though, it is generally considered to be a disease of older people.

When a pleural effusion occurs then a variety of different problems may be at the root of the trouble. This too, tends to affect older people.

Causes

Viruses are a common cause of pleurisy. They may cause the pleural membranes to become inflamed and sore in the same way as they affect the membranes of the nose when you have a cold. Like any other sort of viral infection, pleurisy can occur in small epidemics.

Painful chest muscles, together with pain on breathing are the hallmarks of the disease. It settles down without treatment, and without giving rise to complications.

Bacteria can also produce pleurisy, although they usually do this as a result of underlying pneumonia. As infection spreads through lung tissue it eventually leads to inflammation on the outer surface of the lung. This then leads to the symptoms of pleurisy.

Bacteria can also cause pleurisy in tuberculosis. This disease is really still quite common, particularly in people with an impoverished life-style. Here there is a big pleural effusion, although the painful breathing so typical of many sorts of pleurisy is not nearly as common

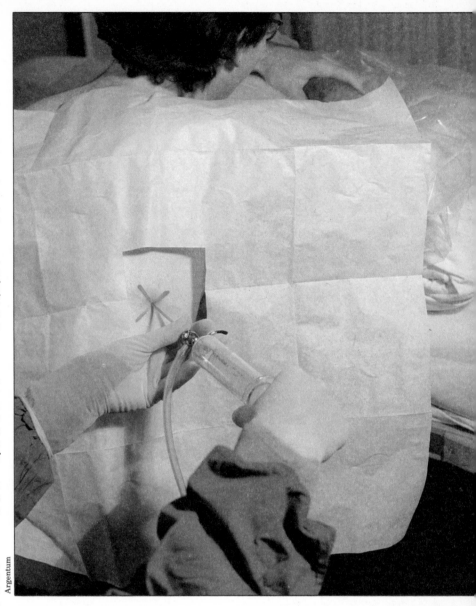

in cases related to tuberculosis.

Occasionally a pleural effusion turns out to be due to neither infection nor a tumour, but to some other disease. For example, diseases which set up a general level of inflammation in the body as a result of disturbances in the body's immune system can cause a pleural effusion. One such disease is called Systemic lupus erythematosus, which is often abbreviated to SLE.

There is also a very rare hereditary disease that really only occurs in Armenian and Sephardic Jewish families. It is called familial Mediterranean fever, and involves repeated attacks of inflammation in all the membranes of the lung as well as in the peritoneum and the pericardium.

Perhaps the most serious pleural problem is called pulmonary embolism. In this condition, a clot, which may have

When liquid is present between the pleura, as in a pleural effusion, it must be drained. A section of the chest is frozen with anaesthetic and a needle is passed into the pleural space to draw off the fluid.

formed in the leg, for example, breaks off and travels through the heart to get stuck in the lung. This causes typical pleural pain, since the affected area of the lung becomes inflamed and the inflammation spreads to the pleura. Pulmonary embolisms can be fatal and doctors are anxious to make a definite diagnosis, since treatment with blood-thinning pills can stop further clots forming.

Symptoms

The typical symptom of pleurisy is pain in the chest. This is made worse by breathing – particularly deep breathing – as the two inflamed pleural surfaces rub against

Q I had an attack of pleurisy about six months ago. I found it very unpleasant and am worried that it may have made me liable to repeated attacks. Is this likely?

A No, it is not likely. Pleurisy nowadays is usually the result of an acute chest infection such as bronchitis or pneumonia, which, once it has been treated, is completely cured and not likely to return; although it is, of course, possible for you to catch a further infection at a later date. However, should you get any further chest pain it would be wise to consult your doctor about it so he can re-examine your chest and possibly get it X-rayed in order to determine the cause of the trouble.

Q A few weeks ago I fell and struck my chest on the corner of a table. Ever since it hurts when I breathe. Have I got pleurisy as a result of the accident?

A No. It's much more likely that you injured your ribs when you fell, and since your ribs move to some extent when you breathe, this is probably why you experience pain similar to that of pleurisy.

Q A few weeks ago I had bad pain in my chest that was much worse when I coughed or took a deep breath. I was certain it was pleurisy, but my doctor insisted it wasn't. What could it have been?

A Understandably enough, people feel that any pain in the chest is likely to be due to pleurisy. There are, in fact, many possible causes, the majority of them a great deal more common than pleurisy. That which occurs most often is due to the kind of inflammation of the muscles in the chest wall that is often called fibrositis. Obviously, since the muscles are used every time you breathe the pain will be felt when you take a particularly deep breath or when you cough. When this is the cause of pain in the chest, a particular part of the chest wall is usually tender – a feature that does not normally occur with pleurisy.

Chest pain caused by pleurisy is more likely to be felt at the sides or back of the chest than in the centre.

George Roger/Magnum

each other. Variation in position may also make a difference.

When fluid begins to collect in the pleural space, inflamed layers of pleura are separated, and the pain may disappear. Thus with a large pleural effusion the main problem is likely to be breathlessness rather than pain.

Your doctor can diagnose pleurisy simply by listening to your description of the pain. He will also be helped in his diagnosis if he can hear what is called a pleural rub through his stethoscope. A pleural rub is exactly that: the sound of the two inflamed layers rubbing against each other. It sounds a bit like a foot crunching through packed snow with each breath. Chest X-rays are also helpful, particularly in cases of patients suffering from pleural effusions.

Treatment
The sort of treatment depends on the underlying condition. Pleuritic symptoms can be very painful, and will certainly require a painkiller – probably something on the principle of aspirin,

Sephardic Jews are among the principal sufferers from a rare hereditary disease called familial Mediterranean fever, which involves inflammation of the pleura.

where inflammation is damped down as well as pain relieved.

When a large amount of fluid is present, this has to be drained. This is a simple procedure: the doctor freezes a small section of the chest with local anaesthetic, and then passes a needle into the pleural space to draw off the fluid. In addition, by using a special needle, your doctor can remove a piece of the pleura for examination under a microscope – this will be useful if the diagnosis is not clear.

Outlook
The outlook in pleurisy again depends on the underlying condition. Pleurisy itself holds very few dangers, although when it is due, for example, to a fast-growing tumour it is obviously a serious condition. The outlook is excellent in a healthy person who gets an isolated attack of pleurisy as the result of a virus.

Pneumonia

(caption: see overleaf)

Q Is double pneumonia much worse than 'ordinary' pneumonia?

A In the past, one of the commonest forms of pneumonia was lobar pneumonia: where one complete lobe of one of the lungs became infected, usually with the pneumococcus bacterium. (There are three lobes on the right lung, two on the left). Double pneumonia simply meant that more than one lobe had become involved with lobar pneumonia: this was obviously more serious than when a single lobe was affected. Lobar pneumonia is not very common nowadays in Great Britain, but it is common in African countries and other less developed parts of the world.

Q My father had pneumonia, and when he was very ill, a physiotherapist came and she hit him on the chest. What good could this have done him?

A The physiotherapist has a vital role to play in the treatment of pneumonia, and that is to ensure that all the infected secretions of the inflamed mucous membranes are brought up from the depths of the lungs and coughed up. If this isn't done, these secretions harbour the infection and prevent the infected part of the lung becoming properly filled with air during breathing. Hitting the chest wall is one of the techniques that a physiotherapist will use to loosen the secretions, and many patients find that it brings a lot of relief from breathlessness.

Q Does pneumonia tend to be worse in people with asthma?

A The main problem that happens in people who suffer from asthma is that their bronchial tubes tend to become constricted (narrowed) very easily. Any infection in the chest will increase this problem, and there doesn't have to be full-blown pneumonia for someone to get a bad asthmatic attack. When an asthmatic does have pneumonia, on the other hand, it will definitely tend to constrict the bronchial tubes, making matters worse.

Pneumonia used to be one of the great killers – attacking the young and fit almost as readily as the old and infirm. Treatment with antibiotics has now made it possible to save countless lives.

Pneumonia means inflammation of the substance of the lungs. Although it most commonly occurs as a result of a bacterial infection, it may also arise from a viral or fungal infection, or from inhaling foreign matter. Treatment with antibiotics has meant a decline in fatalities, although the elderly, those with chronic lung disorders and those already weakened by other serious illness remain at risk.

Causes

To understand how pneumonia affects the lungs, it is necessary to look at their structure (see Lung and lung diseases, pp 222-25).

The main breathing tube that supplies air to the lungs is the windpipe (trachea). This splits into two branches (the bronchi), which in turn divide into three branches on the right and two main

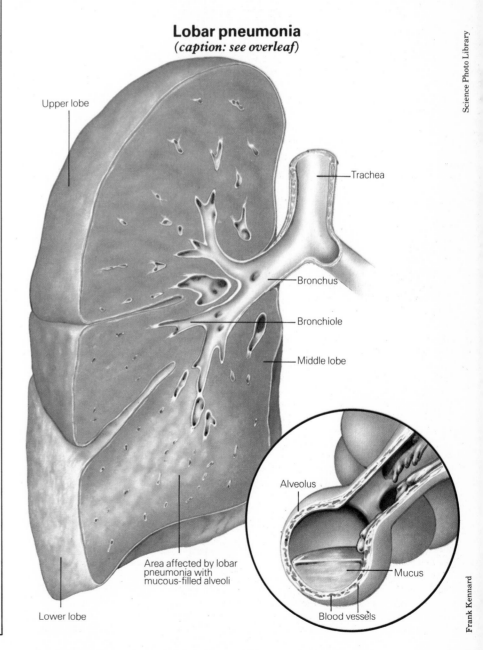

Lobar pneumonia
(caption: see overleaf)

Upper lobe

Trachea

Bronchus

Bronchiole

Middle lobe

Area affected by lobar pneumonia with mucous-filled alveoli

Lower lobe

Alveolus

Mucus

Blood vessels

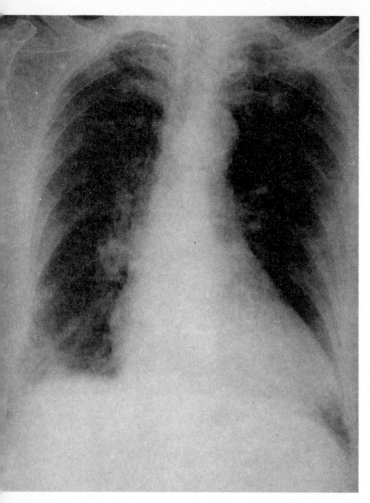

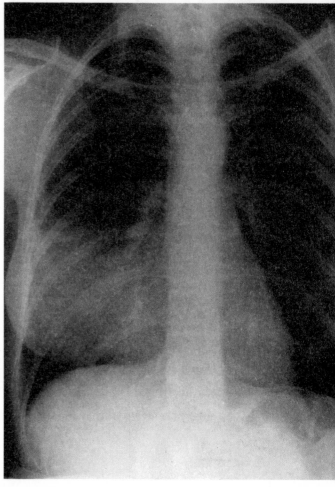

branches on the left. Each of these branches supplies one lobe of one of the lungs: there are three lobes on the right and two on the left, divided from each other by thin membranes of fibrous tissue.

Each of these main bronchi to one of the lobes then splits down into a series of finer branches which supply all the tiny air sacs or alveoli where oxygen finally crosses from the air inside the lungs into the blood.

When infection strikes the chest, the inflammation it causes may be confined to the bronchi. This inflammation, called bronchitis, results in a thickening of the bronchi's lining membrane and the production of large amounts of secretions from the bronchi's glands (see Bronchitis pp 69-70).

In pneumonia, the infection occurs in the smaller bronchi and the alveoli. These become solid with secretions, rather than filled with air. This is called consolidation and on a chest X-ray, the

Overleaf: In lobar pneumonia, the alveoli (air sacs) become filled with secretions. This restricts pulmonary function and causes shortness of breath and often pain on breathing.

A chest X-ray reveals the type of pneumonia. Bronchopneumonia (above left) is distinguished by white patches on the whole or part of a lung: note those on the left lung. Lobar pneumonia (above right) involves the whole lobe.

Here the pneumococcus bacterium has been found to be the cause of bronchopneumonia.

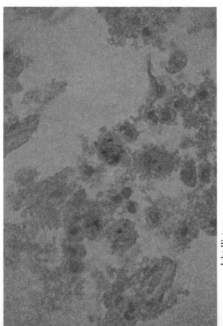

affected area shows up as a white patch, rather than a black area as in a normal lung. The congestion may severely affect breathing.

There are two main types of pneumonia: lobar pneumonia and bronchopneumonia.

Lobar pneumonia was, in the past, the commoner of the two. Although it has now become rather rare today in countries like Great Britain, it is still common in less developed countries. Lobar pneumonia is nearly always due to the pneumococcus bacterium. Only one lobe of the lung tends to be involved, and this lobe becomes consolidated while the rest of the lung remains relatively normal.

Bronchopneumonia can be caused by many different sorts of organism, although normally some sort of bacterium is responsible. Of these, the most common is the haemophilus influenzae bacterium. Other kinds of bacteria that can cause bronchopneumonia include the pneumococcus, and the staphylococci, which is the more serious. This kind of bronchopneumonia tends to appear after a dose of the flu and fatalities may occur in people who previously were well; but it is not very common nowadays.

In lobar pneumonia, a sputum sample looked at under a microscope will reveal the presence of pneumococcal bacteria.

Bronchopneumonia is characterized by little white patches of consolidation which appear all over the lungs, and though these patches may be concentrated in one lung, or even in one part of one lung, a whole lobe is not involved. Bronchopneumonia can occur at the same time as bronchitis, and often results from bronchitis spreading to involve the rest of the lung. This frequently happens to people who have had long-term (chronic) chest problems, but it is also common for people to get acute bronchopneumonia on top of chronic bronchitis.

Viruses can also cause pneumonia, although more often it is a virus infection in the upper part of the respiratory system (the throat and nose) that paves the way for a bacterium becoming established lower down in the chest.

Tiny organisms such as the chlamydia (which causes psittacosis, a disease caught from caged birds), rickettsia (which causes typhus and Q fever) and the mycoplasma (fungus) can also cause pneumonia.

Pneumonia may also arise as a result of a blockage of one of the main bronchial tubes – for instance from cancer of the bronchus. Similarly, chronic disorders of the bronchus, such as bronchiectasis (where the bronchi continually produce pus as a result of a chronic infection that also destroys the normal bronchial wall) can produce pneumonia by blocking the tubes and allowing pus to be sucked back into normal lung tissue.

Finally, pneumonia can result from inhaling things such as loose teeth or peanuts into the lungs. However the main kind of aspiration pneumonia occurs as a result of unconsciousness as at this time there is a failure in the coughing mechanism that prevents food and other foreign substances from going down the

wrong way. For this reason a careful watch is kept so that no such inhalations occur when an anaesthetic is given, or when emergency resuscitation is needed.

Symptoms

The main symptom of pneumonia is a cough, which varies according to the type of pneumonia. In bronchopneumonia with added acute bronchitis, there may be a lot of infected (yellow or green) sputum produced, while in a viral

Though beautiful to look at, the cockatoo may transmit the chlamydia virus which causes psittacosis, a type of pneumonia. Fortunately it is fairly uncommon.

pneumonia there could be a dry cough with no sputum at all.

In bronchopneumonia, there is usually a cough, though it is not the main symptom. Lobar pneumonia is a feverish illness and unless it is treated with antibiotics, very high temperatures will result. Since the whole lobe is involved, the inflammation may spread to the lining of the pleura, causing pleurisy, with the ensuing result that pain on coughing or taking a deep breath is often a common additional symptom.

In bronchopneumonia due to bacteria, symptoms tend to vary according to how much extra bronchitis there is. However there is nearly always more sputum produced in bronchopneumonia, while pleurisy is a less common occurrence. There is usually a temperature but it is not so high as in lobar pneumonia.

Bronchopneumonia is a disease that is more likely to affect the old and the ill or infirm. Often there are fewer symptoms in the elderly than in the young and fit, despite the fact that when the disease occurs in older people it may cause death after a long illness.

In the rarer forms of pneumonia due to organisms that are not bacteria, the symptoms vary but, by and large, feverish illnesses are common. Changes in the lungs are obvious in the X-rays, while the cough and sputum production is less than in bacterial pneumonia.

Dangers and complications
One of the commoner complications of all kinds of pneumonia is pleurisy. This may lead to a pleural effusion – a collection of fluid within the pleural cavity. This can become infected, leading to a large collection of pus forming in the pleural cavity (empyema).

Pockets of pus can also form within the infected lung, causing a lung abscess. This is especially likely to happen in staphylococcal pneumonia and in a rare form of lobar pneumonia called Klebsiella. Lung abscesses are a serious problem, and only occur as a result of severe lung infection.

In general, though, it is pneumonia which is a complication of other diseases, rather than pneumonia which gives rise to other complications. It is for this reason that pneumonia, usually severe bronchopneumonia, may be fatal, because it is so often the final event in the life of someone who is already very weak, ill or elderly.

Treatment
In fit people, treatment with antibiotics is generally all that is necessary. In older people, or people who already have a chronic chest disease or another illness, it is very important to make sure that the secretions in the lung produced by pneumonia are coughed up and not allowed to remain in the chest so that they cause further problems. The physiotherapist has a vital role to play in helping people with pneumonia to clear these secretions. Drugs that are inhaled through a vapour in an oxygen mask may help to widen the bronchi, which tend to narrow down in pneumonia.

Outlook
The outlook in pneumonia depends upon the age and the state of health of the patient. A young, fit person who gets lobar pneumonia should make a total and swift recovery, while an elderly, chronic bronchitic who has probably already had a number of attacks of bronchopneumonia is at some risk of dying with a further attack. Pneumonia in someone who is very weak as a result of disease can be fatal despite their having had treatment with antibiotics.

Causes and treatment of pneumonia

Type	Cause	Symptoms	Treatment
Pneumonias caused by a bacterium			
Lobar pneumonia	Pneumococcus bacterium	Cough, pain on breathing, high temperature. Rust-coloured sputum	Penicillin
Bronchopneumonia	Various organisms, particularly haemophilus influenzae	Cough is the main symptom, but there may also be fever. Green or yellow sputum	Antibiotics that are suitable for the organism concerned, expectorant cough medicine and physiotherapy where necessary
Pneumonia leading to abscess formation	Staphylococcus and Klebsiella bacterium	A severe feverish illness with a cough	Antibiotics, expectorant cough medicine and physiotherapy
Aspiration pneumonia	A number of organisms. Occurs as a result of inhalation, usually while patient is unconscious	Fever and cough	Antibiotics, expectorant cough medicine and physiotherapy
Pneumonias not caused by a bacterium			
Viral pneumonia	Chickenpox, influenza	Cough and fever without much sputum being produced	Antibiotics if the lungs then get infected by a bacterium
	Respiratory sincitial virus	Occurs in newborn babies. Causes breathlessness	Ventilation by machine may be required
Psittacosis	Chlamydia virus, caught from caged birds like parrots	Cough and temperature, not much sputum	Tetracycline or erythromycin
Q fever	Rickettsia virus	Cough and temperature, not much sputum	Tetracycline or erythromycin
Mycoplasma	Very small fungal organisms, similar to bacteria but with no thick cell wall	Cough and temperature, not much sputum	Tetracycline or erythromycin

Post-natal depression

Q I had post-natal depression with my first baby; will I get it again with my second – and will it be as severe as the first time?

A Not necessarily. There is a one in five chance that you will have post-natal depression, but that is a statistical chance. As for severity, what is important is that this time you have plenty of support and not too many other changes in your life. This is not the time, for example, to move house, or for your partner to change jobs. And remember that two children mean far more work than one, and accept all the help that's offered.

Q What should I do if I think that I have post-natal depression?

A Accept the fact without feeling guilty about it. It is no personal reflection on you: thousands of other women suffer in the same way. Seek help from family and close friends. If the symptoms are seriously affecting your life, consult your doctor.

Q Are the 'baby blues' and post-natal depression the same thing?

A No. 'Baby blues' start within a few days of birth and rarely last longer than two weeks. If it does last longer, the condition has probably turned into a more serious depression. Post-natal depression may develop from the blues, but it may start two or three months after the birth and is much more serious than the occasional bout of crying.

Q Can anything be done to prevent post-natal depression?

A Very little without major social changes. Mothers are too isolated and given too little help during the first months of their babies' lives. They are expected to cope 'naturally' with a very difficult and responsible job. If mothers were given less romantic publicity and more practical, realistic support, fewer of them would suffer from post-natal depression.

For a great many mothers a bout of 'baby blues' follows the major event of giving birth – and for some a severe depression sets in. This is when sensitivity and support from those around the mother are vital.

Depression after birth is a very common condition. It ranges from the temporary 'baby blues' to black despair. It can occur after the birth of any child, not just the first, and may last for a long time. The most worrying aspect of this condition is that mothers who are depressed often feel ashamed of their unhappiness and thus neither seek nor receive help.

Before birth
It is impossible to make predictions during pregnancy about who is likely to suffer from post-natal depression. It has been suggested that a great deal depends on how much emotional support the new mother receives and what she expects of

Post-natal depression can take many forms: one of the most striking is an overwhelming feeling of isolation – both social and, ironically, from the baby.

herself. There are indications, too, that women who don't have a close, loving relationship with anyone are very much at risk. A woman who lost her own mother when she was 11 or younger is known to be vulnerable; and there are suggestions that women who have easy pregnancies tend to suffer depression after birth.

'Baby blues'
'Baby blues' are experienced by 80 per cent of all new mothers. It usually occurs between three and four days after delivery, and it takes the form of a general feeling of vulnerability and a persistent weepiness. This feeling normally passes after one or two weeks. If it continues for longer it is a sign of more serious depression. Twenty per cent of mothers suffer from low-grade post-natal depression, serious enough to make life

Steve Bielschowsky

Q My mother had terrible depression with all her children. Might this also happen to me when I come to have children of my own?

A Post-natal depression is not an inherited condition. But if your relationship with your mother was difficult you may have problems seeing yourself realistically as a mother in your own right.

Q My friend has post-natal depression. What can I do to help her?

A Let her know that you care for her and still like and accept her despite her depression. Try to build up her self-confidence by giving her genuine praise for the things that she does well. Ask her if she needs practical help and, if possible, do the things that she asks you to. Don't attempt to solve her problems for her, because you can't. It is more important to listen and accept. Give as much support as you can without allowing it to affect your own life too much. Accept that it takes time to come through a depression but have faith in her – she will certainly recover in the end.

Q I understand that I can ask for progesterone hormone supplement and that this can help; is this true, and how does it help?

A The usefulness of progesterone therapy has not been medically proven. Some women, however, claim to have found it helpful. In its defence, you should appreciate that profound hormonal changes take place in a mother's body in the days after delivery, and progesterone, the pregnancy hormone, disappears suddenly after the birth. Because hormones have a strong influence on emotional states, progesterone can sometimes help in combating post-natal depression. An exciting possibility of progesterone therapy is that it may be used as a preventive treatment for women who have already suffered post-natal depression after a previous birth. This offers hope to women who would like to have children but fear another depression. Really, the best thing to do is to discuss the therapy with your own doctor.

seem rather grey, but not so severe that they are unable to cope. Very serious psychotic depression occurs in one in every 500 mothers, and usually requires hospital treatment.

Depression
Depression is not like measles: it doesn't have a set incubation period or follow the same course in all cases. 'Baby blues' are generally regarded as trivial since the condition clears up quickly, but this is not always the case. Anyone suffering from it should be watched over carefully.

The more serious forms of post-natal depression may not start for a long time after the birth. It is not always easy to say at what point a feeling of being low or tired or fed-up turns into a fully-fledged depression, but in general if the mood lasts longer than a few weeks or if the symptoms affect the sufferer's life, then she should seek help.

Causes
Post-natal depression is a response to an event that causes great change and stress in a woman's life. There is no single cause: just a combination of factors which may be difficult to cope with. There are six main areas of stress:
Birth: Giving birth is one of the most important experiences in a woman's life, and a bad birth experience can be damaging emotionally.

Motherhood: Mothers are both idealized and undervalued. They are told that they are important and yet may be treated as if they didn't exist. Coping realistically with such a situation can be very difficult.
Loss: All depression has an element of grieving about it. The birth of a baby may be an obvious gain, but it also involves a loss of identity for the mother.
Isolation: Social isolation is one of the worst problems any new mother has to cope with. Getting out of the house and talking over worries with other adults are very important.
Exhaustion: Broken nights and the lack of regular sleeping patterns can easily produce feelings of disorientation.
Hormonal changes: A woman's body goes through considerable change as a result of pregnancy and birth. This often makes women more vulnerable to stress.

Symptoms
The main symptom of depression is a lack of self-esteem. When you feel really low you blame yourself for virtually everything. Other emotional symptoms include tearfulness, feeling inadequate and unable to cope, especially with the baby, and feelings of guilt – for not loving the baby enough.

Physical symptoms include loss of appetite and reduced sexual interest. The mother may also have problems sleeping at night – even when the baby *isn't*

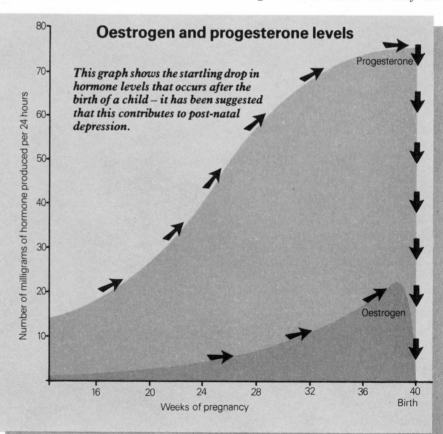

Oestrogen and progesterone levels

This graph shows the startling drop in hormone levels that occurs after the birth of a child – it has been suggested that this contributes to post-natal depression.

Progesterone

Oestrogen

Number of milligrams of hormone produced per 24 hours

Weeks of pregnancy

Birth

Mick Gillah

accept it. Once she has accepted the fact that she can't cope very well without help, it becomes much easier for her to ask for it, and to talk to other people about her feelings. She should try to get out of the house at least once a day and make time to do things that she enjoys, and which have nothing to do with the baby. If she finds it hard to talk about her feelings, she should write them down. And she should try to find ways to ensure that she sleeps and eats properly.

Support from the family is also important. Telling a depressed mother to 'snap out of it' is the worst thing to do. She needs to be cared for physically and emotionally. If practical help is offered, it should be done in the spirit of caring for her, not just taking over completely and making her feel even more incompetent.

Medical treatment, either with tranquillizers or anti-depressant drugs, can be useful in helping to remove the symptoms of depression, but on its own is rarely the answer. Emotional support is always needed.

It takes time for a depression to lift, but with the right attitude on the mother's part, and with adequate support and care from the people around her, it almost invariably clears up in the end, allowing the mother to relax in her new role.

A warm, friendly environment and consistent support from her family and friends are crucial to help a mother avoid depression. It will be a comfort, too, if she knows that there are other people who will help with the baby – her own mother, for example, delighted to baby-sit.

crying. Nightmares are quite common.

Sometimes anxiety is more marked than depression, and this can take different forms. Anxiety over health – the baby's, your husband's or your own – is common, as is the fear of leaving the house (agoraphobia).

Treatment

Most women try to fight depression by hiding it behind a smile and feeling guilty or ashamed about their problems. However, once a mother accepts that she needs help there are a number of things that can be done to give her the support and care that she needs.

The best course for a mother suffering from depression is never to fight it, but to

Pregnancy

Q How soon after becoming pregnant is it worth having a pregnancy test done?

A All pregnancy tests depend on the fact that the fertilized egg releases a hormone called Human Chorionic Gonadotrophin which is then passed in the mother's urine. This can first be detected from about 41 days after her last period and is in greater concentration in the first specimen of urine which she passes in the day.

Q I always suffer from indigestion during pregnancy. Is there anything I can do to prevent it?

A Yes. The hormones of pregnancy and later the womb pressing on the stomach tend to make the acid pass back from the stomach into the oesophagus where it causes a burning sensation. This acid can be mopped up by drinking milk, eating small frequent meals and taking medicines called antacids. Another tip to stop you getting heartburn at night is to raise the head of the bed.

Q Can you prevent stretch marks forming during pregnancy?

A Unfortunately some women, especially very fair women, seem more likely to get these marks, which form on the breasts, stomach and thighs. Once the baby is born they lose their reddish colour and fade but never completely disappear. Very little can be done to prevent them although some women believe that a little olive oil rubbed into the skin every day helps.

Q My husband is worried about making love to me now I am pregnant. Is he right to be?

A No. You may continue to make love as long as you feel comfortable enough to enjoy it. Occasionally we advise women who have had many miscarriages to avoid making love in the first three months although there is no absolute proof that this makes her less likely to miscarry.

In pregnancy, changes occur in the mother's body which are designed to meet the needs of the growing foetus. For most women it is an exciting and happy time; modern antenatal care has also made it safe.

Pregnancy is the remarkable and highly complex process between conception and labour and lasts on average 38 weeks. Because the date of conception is often not known exactly, it is easier to date the pregnancy from the first day of the last menstrual period, which is usually about a fortnight before conception, making a total of 40 weeks.

The first signs
The first sign of pregnancy is usually a missed period, although this can be caused by other conditions. However, if intercourse without contraception has taken place, pregnancy is the most likely cause. Other early symptoms include a sense of fullness and tingling in the breasts and a need to pass urine more frequently. Nausea, and even vomiting, is suffered by many women in early pregnancy. Popularly known as 'morning sickness', it can actually in fact come at any time of day and is often aggravated by preparing food. A cup of tea and a dry biscuit taken first thing in the morning can sometimes help, and it is sensible to take small amounts of food at fairly frequent intervals throughout the day rather than large infrequent meals.

If you think you are pregnant
It is important that you should go to see your doctor as soon as you suspect you might be pregnant – say, two weeks after your missed period. Take with you to your appointment a sample of the first urine you passed that morning. A pregnancy test can then be done to detect the presence or absence of a hormone called Human Chorionic Gonadotrophin which is produced by the developing egg and excreted in the mother's urine. Simple home pregnancy tests are available from chemists, and these work on exactly the same principle. If you carry out the test yourself you should still consult your doctor if the result is positive.

Once your pregnancy is confirmed, your family doctor will arrange for your care during pregnancy and labour. If the baby is to be born in hospital, he will arrange a booking examination at the hospital which usually takes place when you are 12 to 13 weeks pregnant. Visits to the antenatal clinic are then arranged on a monthly basis during the first 28 weeks of pregnancy, then fortnightly until 36

weeks and thereafter weekly until the baby is born. Obviously, these arrangements have to be flexible to allow for any unusual circumstances.

Antenatal check-ups may take place entirely at the hospital throughout the pregnancy; or the hospital may send you back to your own doctor after the initial 'booking' examination. You will then be examined regularly at his surgery until you are about 32 weeks pregnant, when you will return to the hospital for later appointments. Alternatively, you may choose to attend a local clinic where you will be looked after by midwives during your pregnancy.

Antenatal clinics not only check that the mother and baby are healthy, they also arrange classes on baby care and preparation for labour and childbirth. Most courses include at least one session for the prospective fathers to advise them on how best to help their partners during pregnancy and labour and after the birth.

Minor discomforts
During pregnancy a woman may suffer from several minor discomforts which, although trivial, can cause some anxiety.
Nausea The feelings of nausea noticed early in pregnancy usually continue until about 16 weeks. If it is so severe as to be incapacitating, your doctor may prescribe tablets which can help.
Vaginal discharge Women have an increased vaginal discharge in pregnancy. This is quite normal and, unless offensive or irritating, does not require medical attention.
Backache and cramp may present a problem as the pregnancy advances. A pregnant woman tends to throw her shoulders back in an attempt to counteract the weight of the growing uterus, and this can put undue strain on the back. Improved posture and comfortable, low-heeled shoes may relieve it. Leg cramps are common in late pregnancy and may be troublesome at night. They can sometimes be relieved by gently stretching the affected muscle.
Constipation and heartburn are commonly experienced during pregnancy. They are both the result of the effect of the hormone progesterone, which relaxes the smooth muscle fibres. Unfortunately. its action is not confined to the growing uterus, but affects the bowel, making it

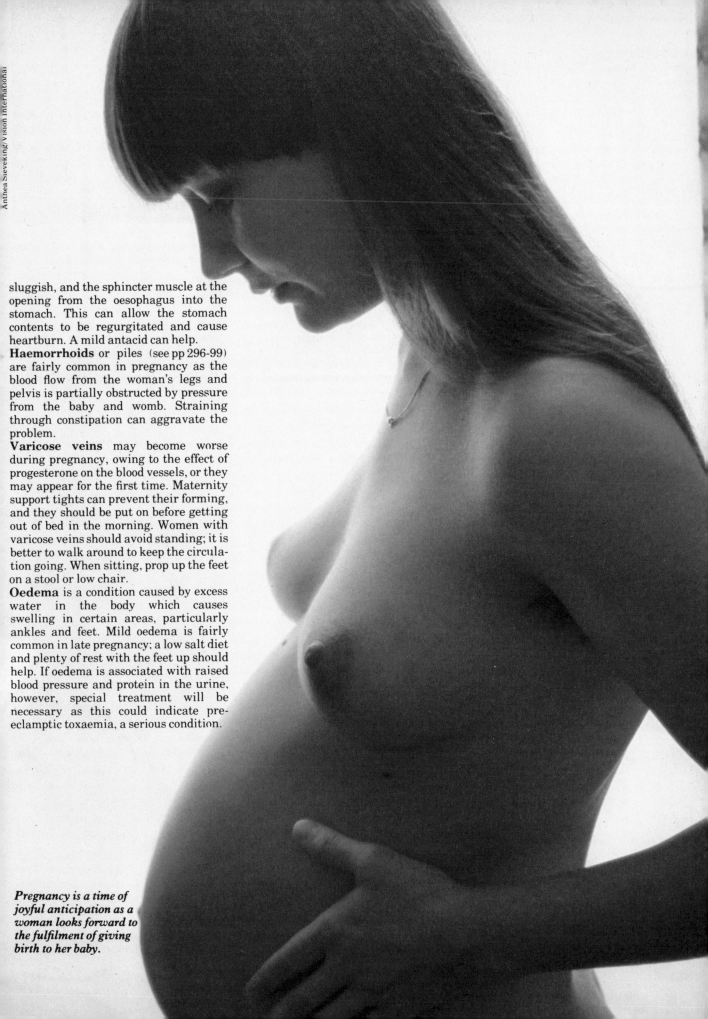

Anthea Sieveking/Vision International

sluggish, and the sphincter muscle at the opening from the oesophagus into the stomach. This can allow the stomach contents to be regurgitated and cause heartburn. A mild antacid can help.

Haemorrhoids or piles (see pp 296-99) are fairly common in pregnancy as the blood flow from the woman's legs and pelvis is partially obstructed by pressure from the baby and womb. Straining through constipation can aggravate the problem.

Varicose veins may become worse during pregnancy, owing to the effect of progesterone on the blood vessels, or they may appear for the first time. Maternity support tights can prevent their forming, and they should be put on before getting out of bed in the morning. Women with varicose veins should avoid standing; it is better to walk around to keep the circulation going. When sitting, prop up the feet on a stool or low chair.

Oedema is a condition caused by excess water in the body which causes swelling in certain areas, particularly ankles and feet. Mild oedema is fairly common in late pregnancy; a low salt diet and plenty of rest with the feet up should help. If oedema is associated with raised blood pressure and protein in the urine, however, special treatment will be necessary as this could indicate pre-eclamptic toxaemia, a serious condition.

Pregnancy is a time of joyful anticipation as a woman looks forward to the fulfilment of giving birth to her baby.

Skin changes As pregnancy proceeds, stretch marks may appear on the abdomen, thighs and breasts. Little can be done to prevent these, but they fade once the baby is born.

Changes in the uterus and breasts

Pregnancy is divided into three 'trimesters', each lasting about 13 weeks. In the first trimester the uterus is still contained within the pelvic cavity although it is growing rapidly. It is during the second trimester that a woman becomes obviously pregnant. By about 22 weeks the upper edge of the womb, or fundus, reaches the navel and at 36 weeks most of the abdominal cavity is taken up. The intestines are pushed upwards and sideways so that they press on the stomach and diaphragm. The pressure on the diaphragm means that the lungs cannot expand fully and many women find themselves short of breath.

Around 22 weeks in a first pregnancy and 18 weeks in a later one, the mother will feel her baby's movements. The foetal heartbeat is usually audible through a stethoscope by 24 weeks.

The main change a woman will notice in her breasts during pregnancy is that

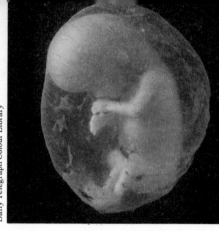

Daily Telegraph Colour Library

This 11-week-old foetus, although only 5 cm (2 in) long, is recognizably human.

6 weeks

At six weeks of pregnancy the embryo is still not recognizably human, and is only 1.3 cm (about ½ in) long. A pregnancy test now would prove positive and the mother may feel some symptoms such as breast sensitivity and nausea.

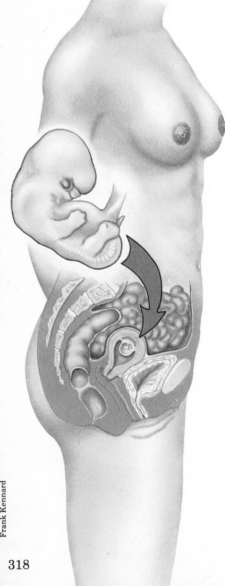

12 weeks

At 12 weeks the uterus can just be felt above the pelvis. By now all the major foetal organs are formed; nails are appearing on the fingers and toes. The foetus is about 7½ cm (3 in) long and weighs about 14 g (½ oz). The breasts begin to produce colostrum.

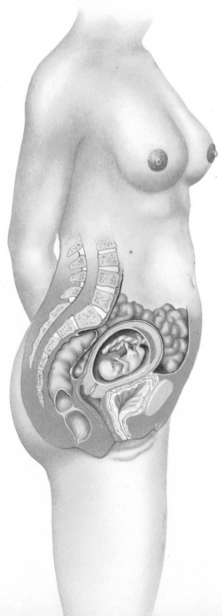

20 weeks

By 20 weeks of pregnancy the uterus has reached the level of the mother's navel, and she becomes aware of her baby's movements. The foetus now measures about 21 cm (8 in) and is covered in fine, downy hair called lanugo.

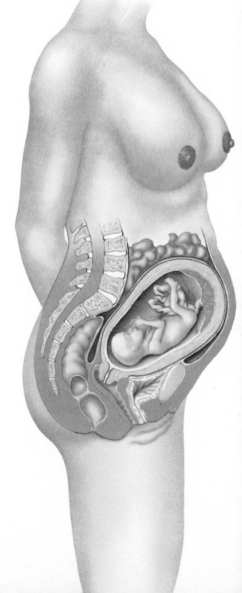

Frank Kennard

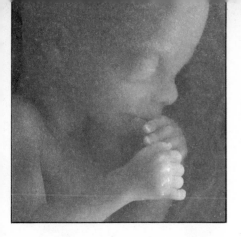

By four months, the foetus has developed eyebrows, but the eyelids are still fused.

they grow larger in preparation for feeding. The areola – the ring of darker skin around the nipple – gets larger and darker in colour and a secondary areola appears which helps to improve the strength of the skin. From about 12 weeks of pregnancy the breasts produce a protein-rich substance called colostrum and in the last few weeks this fluid may leak. Colostrum provides all the nutritional needs of the newborn baby until the milk appears on the third day after birth.

Antenatal care

At each visit to the antenatal clinic the pregnant mother will be weighed, her blood pressure taken and a urine sample checked. At some visits a blood sample will also be taken to establish her blood group and type, to check that she is not anaemic and to find out if there are German measles antibodies present. The blood sample can also reveal whether or not the placenta, through which the foetus is nourished in the womb, is working efficiently. Some foetal abnomalities, such as spina bifida, can also be shown up in tests on the mother's blood, although further tests would be needed to confirm the presence of this abnormality.

28 weeks

At 28 weeks the uterus reaches about halfway between the navel and the breastbone. Foetal movements are vigorous and the mother may feel rhythmic painless contractions. The foetus is now 'viable', meaning that if it was born at this stage it could survive. Its skin is covered by a protective coating called vernix and it can now open its eyes. It measures about 37 (15 in) cm.

40 weeks

At 40 weeks the pregnancy is at full term and the mother is often impatient to 'get on with' the delivery of her child. The upper edge of the uterus descends from its position high under the rib cage as the baby's head moves down into the mother's pelvis. This is called engagement. The mother's breathing and digestion become easier, although pressure on her bladder increases.

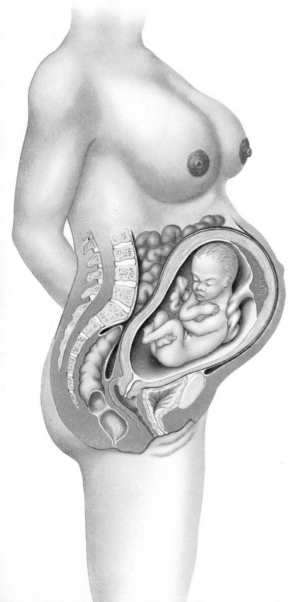

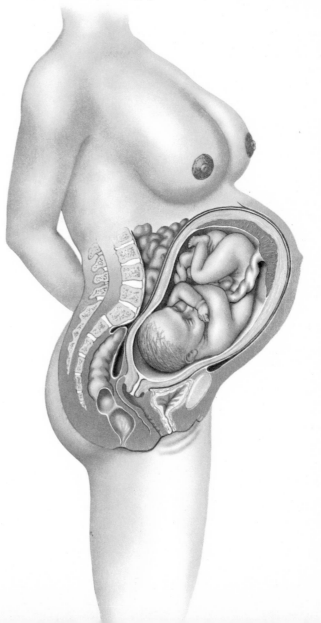

Q I often feel faint when I lie on my back. Why?

A This usually only happens in late pregnancy when the weight of the baby in the womb can press on a large blood vessel called the inferior vena cava and so decrease the blood supply back to your heart and brain. If you feel faint, turn over on to your side and the faintness will soon pass.

Q Since I have become pregnant I need to pass water more frequently. Does this mean I have cystitis?

A This is a possibility, and your urine will be tested at the antenatal clinic for any signs of infection. The more likely reason is that your womb and bladder are competing for space in the pelvis and so your bladder feels full sooner. In the middle part of pregnancy, when the womb has grown out of your pelvis, you will probably return to normal, but in the last weeks the baby's head often presses on the bladder and you will find again that you need to pass urine more frequently.

Q Is it true that a woman 'blooms' during pregnancy and, if so, why?

A Pregnancy seems to suit some women very well. This is because the hormones of pregnancy often improve her complexion and make her feel warmer, so that she has rosy cheeks. Even more important is the sense of well-being that some women feel at this time, which is also thought to be related to an increased production of hormones called steroids.

Q My mother tells me that now I am pregnant I must eat for two. I am worried about this as I don't want to starve my baby, but I don't want to be fat after the birth either.

A Your mother is wrong, as you burn up your food more efficiently and gradually use up less energy yourself as you become less active late in pregnancy. You simply need to eat a normal sensible diet with plenty of milk products, fish, meat and fruit. Your antenatal clinic will keep an eye on your weight gain.

Every antenatal check-up includes an examination of the mother-to-be's abdomen to establish the baby's size and position. Internal examinations are usually only carried out at the booking appointment and at the beginning of labour.

In addition to the routine checks, there are certain specialized tests which are carried out in certain cases.

Amniocentesis. A sample of the amniotic fluid which surrounds the baby in the womb may be tested if there is a risk that the baby is abnormal. For example, women over 40 who are pregnant for the first time are more likely to give birth to a baby with Down's syndrome (mongolism). Amniocentesis can detect this abnormality, and also spina bifida and rhesus disease. If for any reason the baby has to be delivered early, for example if it is not growing well, amniocentesis can reveal whether its lungs are mature enough.

Ultrasound. This form of examination, using sound waves too high to be heard, involves passing a scanner over the woman's abdomen. The womb and its contents can then be seen on a radar-like screen. In this way the size of the baby, the position of the placenta, or the presence of twins can all be established.

X-rays. These are only carried out in late pregnancy when it is safer for the baby. They can show whether the mother's pelvis is wide enough to allow the baby's head to pass through, or whether delivery by Caesarean section will be necessary.

While you are pregnant

It is important that a pregnant woman should eat a sensible, well-balanced diet with plenty of protein (meat, fish, cheese), milk, fresh fruit and vegetables. Too many cakes and biscuits should be avoided as they can lead to excessive weight gain which will be difficult to shed after the birth. The amount of weight gained should not be more than 12 kilos (26 lb) but crash slimming diets should never be undertaken in pregnancy, as you will under-nourish the baby. If your doctor has prescribed iron tablets, be sure to take them.

Moderate exercise is a good idea, although pregnancy is not the time to take up a new, strenuous sport. You will be taught exercises at the antenatal clinic to strengthen your back and muscles.

Smoking should be avoided if at all possible. Every time a pregnant mother smokes, the blood vessels in the placenta are constricted and the blood flow decreases. As a result the baby gets less nourishment and oxygen. Smoking even 10 cigarettes a day significantly reduces birthweight and increases the risk of

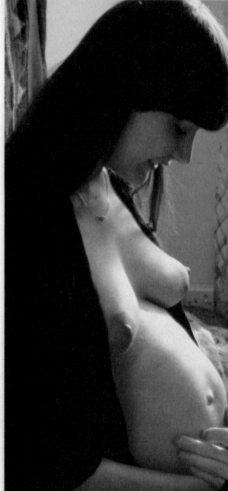

John Watney

Anthea Sieveking/Vision International

mental and physical damage to the foetus. In fact, no drugs (and nicotine is a drug) or tablets should be taken without your doctor's advice.

While the occasional alcoholic drink will do no harm, it is not wise to indulge in heavy drinking as this could damage the baby's brain and slow the baby's growth.

Apart from these sensible precautions, a mother-to-be should remember that pregnancy is a normal, healthy state for most women. With adequate rest, a good diet and moderate exercise the majority of women pass happily through pregnancy with no serious complications.

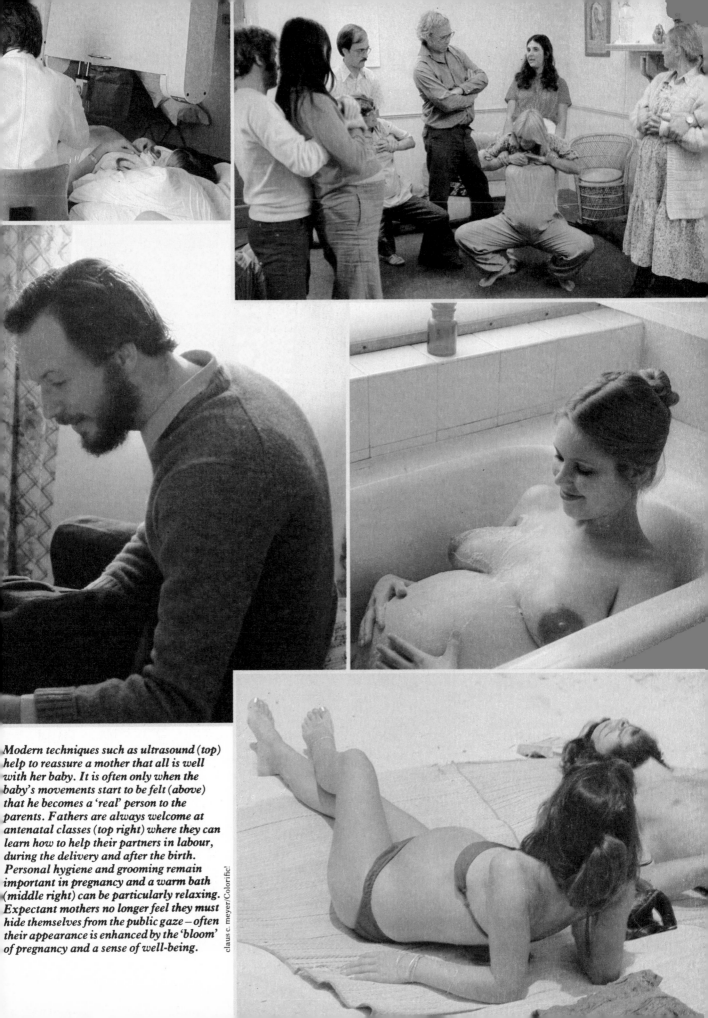

Modern techniques such as ultrasound (top) help to reassure a mother that all is well with her baby. It is often only when the baby's movements start to be felt (above) that he becomes a 'real' person to the parents. Fathers are always welcome at antenatal classes (top right) where they can learn how to help their partners in labour, during the delivery and after the birth. Personal hygiene and grooming remain important in pregnancy and a warm bath (middle right) can be particularly relaxing. Expectant mothers no longer feel they must hide themselves from the public gaze – often their appearance is enhanced by the 'bloom' of pregnancy and a sense of well-being.

claus c. meyer/Colorific!

Pre-menstrual tension

Q I have never suffered from PMT but my mother told me that I might have it after I have had a baby, since this is what happened to her. I am pregnant at the moment and am worried that PMT will start after the baby is born. If my mother is right is there anything I can do to make sure it doesn't happen?

A There are some women who find that PMT does not occur until after the birth of their first baby. It is difficult to tell whether this could happen to you, but it is important not to worry about it as you'll find yourself searching for symptoms. This in itself may make you feel tense and anxious.

Q My daughter is 15 years old and becomes impossible to live with immediately before her period. She's very grumpy and bad-tempered and as a result we're always arguing. What can I do to help her?

A You should start by discussing what you have noticed and see if she has noticed a pattern of negative feelings that coincide with her periods. If she has, you may find that your doctor can help. But it is also very important that you try to avoid getting into arguments with her which will result in both of you feeling annoyed and depressed. She may find it useful to read a book about pre-menstrual tension so that she can understand what is happening to her. This in itself may make it more easy for her to cope with the problem.

Q I went to see my doctor about my PMT but he said he couldn't help. He just told me to take more exercise and get extra sleep, but I've tried this and it hasn't helped. My friend told me that PMT can be treated, so what should I do now?

A Return to your doctor and tell him that his suggestions have not helped. He may then be able to refer you to a specialist or a clinic for investigation and treatment. If he refuses to help it might be worthwhile going to see another doctor.

Pre-menstrual tension, or PMT, can make a woman's life a misery prior to menstruation. Medical treatment can relieve some symptoms but self-help and understanding from friends can also alleviate much of the distress.

Not every woman going through the menstrual cycle has problems in the pre-menstrual phase. While some women experience changes in their body or moods they do not find these distressing enough to seek treatment; others even report that they feel particularly productive and fit during the pre-menstrual phase. It has been estimated however that over 50 per cent of women suffer from some type of noticeable pre-menstrual symptom and of these about 10 per cent need treatment.

The menstrual cycle

If you experience pre-menstrual tension, commonly called PMT, or suspect that you might, it is important to understand what happens during the menstrual cycle. The one described below is a 28-day cycle but this is only an average; the length varies from woman to woman and may be longer or shorter than this.

During menstruation the uterine lining is shed and the body gets ready to begin a new cycle. The period lasts for about five days and as soon as menstruation stops the pituitary gland in the brain sends a hormonal message to one of the two ovaries, instructing it to ripen an egg.

The hormone oestrogen is then produced from the Graafian follicle (made up of the egg and the cells surrounding it); one of the functions of oestrogen is to begin preparation of the lining of the uterus for any possible pregnancy. The amount of oestrogen that is produced continues to rise until it is time for ovulation.

On or near the 14th day of the cycle the egg is fully ripened. The pituitary gland then releases another hormone to stimu-

For some women, the feeling of being 'down in the dumps' is not just a result of normal mood changes; it is a symptom of pre-menstrual tension to be taken seriously.

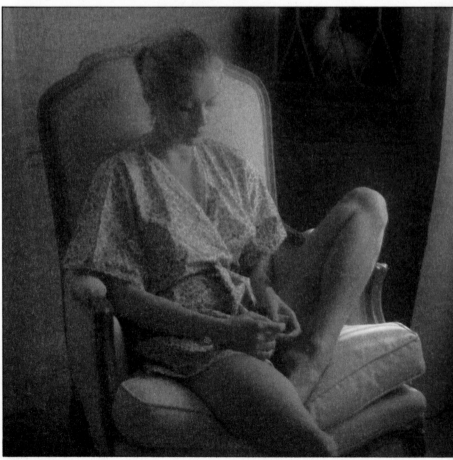

Daily Telegraph Colour Library

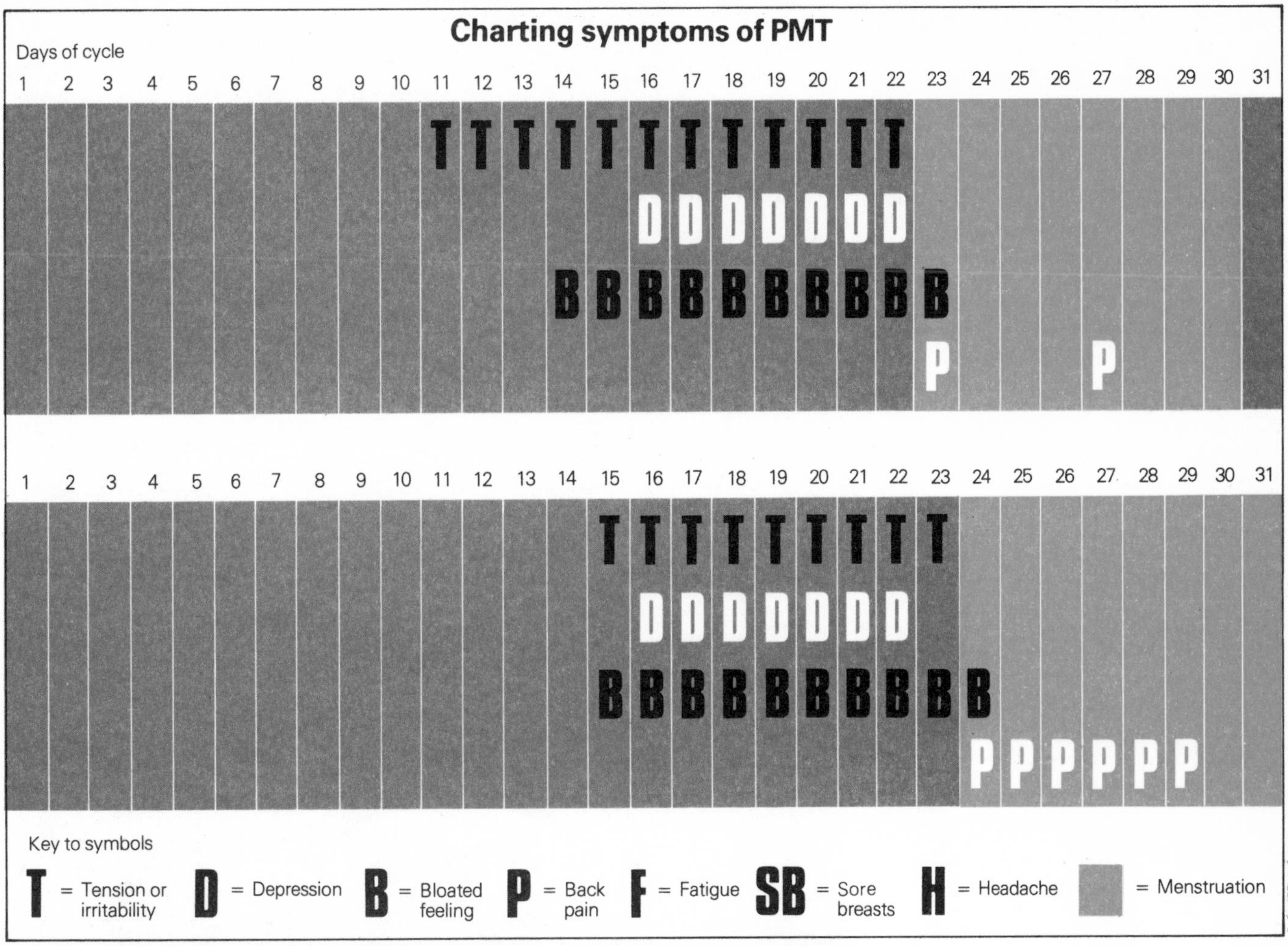
Charting symptoms of PMT
Days of cycle
1 2 3 4 5 6 7 8 9 10 11 12 13 14 15 16 17 18 19 20 21 22 23 24 25 26 27 28 29 30 31
Key to symbols
T = Tension or irritability
D = Depression
B = Bloated feeling
P = Back pain
F = Fatigue
SB = Sore breasts
H = Headache
= Menstruation

John Hutchinson

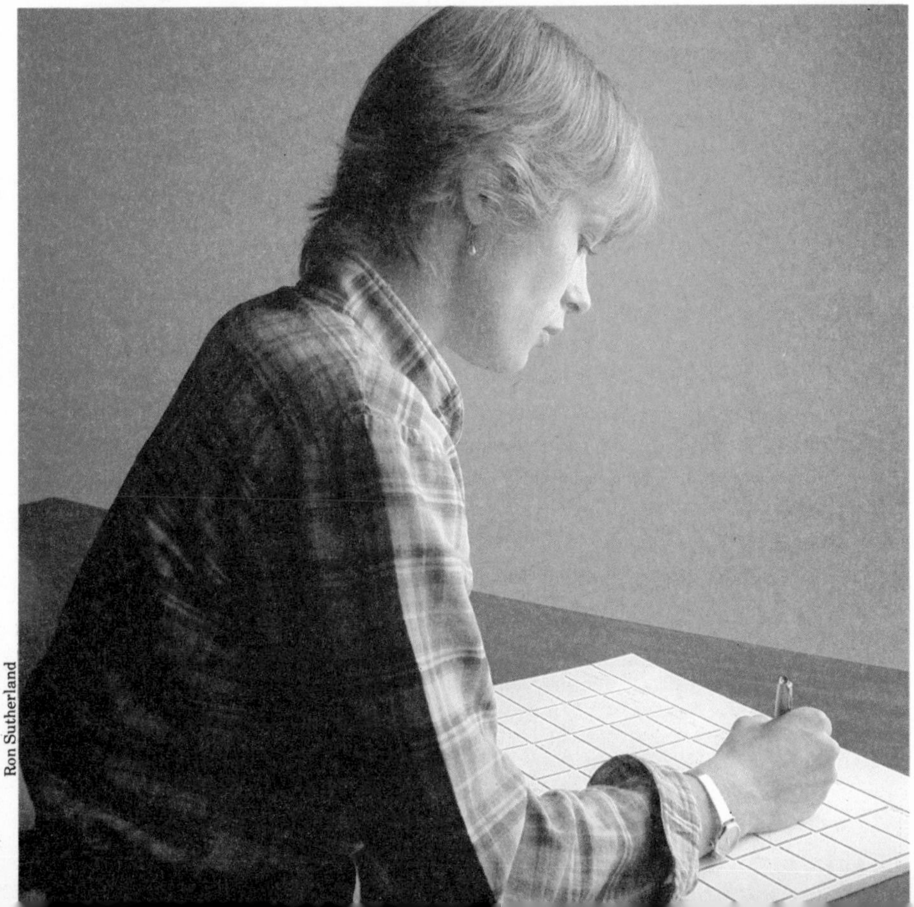

Ron Sutherland

If you suspect that you suffer from PMT, keep a calender of your symptoms – noting the incidence of things like headaches, back pain and tension. This will help your doctor and you plan a suitable treatment programme. In the above examples, Day 1 of the menstrual cycle is taken as the day after the end of menstruation: ovulation occurs on Day 9 or 10, not Day 14.

late the release of the egg which travels into the Fallopian tube adjacent to the ovary. The follicle left behind after ovulation now starts to produce oestrogen and progesterone. These hormones make the uterine lining thicker and more spongy, ready to nourish a fertilized egg. It is at this stage of the cycle that a pregnancy can occur but this will be possible for only a day or so.

If the egg is not fertilized it quickly begins to degenerate. The levels of oestrogen and progesterone begin to fall and as a result the uterine lining cannot be maintained. The lining is shed – menstruation – and the cycle begins again. It is during the second phase of the menstrual cycle that women who suffer from PMT may experience symptoms.

Symptoms and related problems

The physical symptoms of the pre-menstruum (the days immediately preceding menstruation) vary a great deal in type and severity from woman to woman. For example, one woman may experience slight tenderness and swelling of the breasts while another may experience swelling in most parts of her body, making her feel clumsy and awkward. Swelling and bloatedness are related to water retention: not all of the water that is taken into the body is passed in urine, but some of it accumulates in body cells and tissues. This results in weight gains and some women put on as much as 1.5-3 kg (3-6½ lb) just before menstruation begins.

Other physical symptoms associated with PMT are skin problems such as spots or blotchiness, an increase in the likelihood of cystitis and a general feeling of being 'under the weather'. In addition, women who suffer from conditions such as epilepsy, asthma, migraine and conjunctivitis may find that the condition worsens at this time. Women who wear contact lenses may find that their lenses become uncomfortable.

The reasons for some of these physical symptoms are not yet fully understood. What is known is that the symptoms are likely to improve dramatically once menstruation begins and return at the next pre-menstrual phase.

The psychological symptoms that are related to PMT are also likely to improve as soon as the period starts. A woman with PMT may feel depressed and anxious in the days before her period, suffer from lack of energy and a marked increase in irritability, be less interested in sex or find it difficult to concentrate. Because any one of these problems can exist independently of the pre-menstruum, this can make it difficult for a doctor to diagnose PMT.

In recent court cases, PMT has been used as a defence for women charged with violent and criminal behaviour, and some women have been acquitted on the grounds of diminished responsibility due to pre-menstrual tension. But the question of whether the pre-menstrual phase can produce such behaviour is still at issue.

A number of research studies have also suggested that women are more likely to commit crimes and acts of aggression during the pre-menstrual phase and that they are most likely to attempt suicide in the days before a period. Many of the studies are based on women who have been convicted of an offence so it is difficult to know whether PMT has brought about the offence itself or made it more likely for a woman to be caught.

Jacqueline Rathbone-Jones

PMT is also said to cause marital problems and in some cases to lead to divorce. It is still impossible to tell whether PMT increases the likelihood of marital problems or marital problems increase the likelihood of PMT. As yet, no reliable conclusions have been reached.

Causes

Although a number of explanations have been put forward, scientific debate is still going on about the causes of PMT. Some doctors believe that it is directly related to problems with the production and

Women who suffer from physical or emotional tension may benefit from taking up yoga or doing similar exercises that help relax both the body and the mind.

balance of progesterone and oestrogen in the body. Others have suggested that the brain may not be producing the correct amount of an important chemical called pyridoxine.

However, there may be other factors involved that are not strictly medical. It may be that many women are ashamed of their body's reproductive processes or

Q I'm sure that I get PMT but my husband says that it's just psychosomatic and that I'm making a fuss about nothing. Is it possible that he could be right and that I am just imagining it?

A It can be very upsetting to be told that there is nothing wrong with you when you are sure there is. If you have discovered a clear relationship between how you feel and your menstrual cycle then it is likely that you do get PMT. Your husband should try to accept this and be more supportive. His lack of sympathy may in fact make your tension worse, and you should make this clear to him if this is the case. If you can see your doctor and get his help, this might convince your husband that you do get PMT. No-one knows what role social and psychological factors have in causing pre-menstrual tension but it is clear that it is a real and severe problem for many women.

Q I am on a diet at the moment and get really disheartened when my weight goes up before a period. Does this mean I should restrict my eating even more during this time?

A No. The weight gain is almost certainly due to water retention, and this will disappear once your period has begun. You should eat sensibly throughout the pre-menstruum and cut your fluid intake to about four cups a day. You should also reduce the amount of salt in your diet as this increases water retention. Don't go without food for hours at a time as this may result in your feeling faint and dizzy. Experts on the pre-menstrual phase say that you should eat little but often during the days before a period.

Q Will I stop suffering from PMT once I have reached the menopause?

A The menopause (change of life) means that you are no longer going through the menstrual cycle, so once your periods have stopped you will no longer get PMT. Any mood swings, depression or anxiety may be due to other factors with which your doctor may be able to help.

Daily Telegraph Colour Library

Normally stressful situations such as sitting a typing exam can be made worse for those girls who are unlucky enough to have PMT and are feeling far from their best.

associate the menstrual cycle with something negative – for example some women still refer to their period as 'the curse'. But because it is difficult to measure the effect of such ideas on individual women it is also difficult to arrive at any proof for such theories.

Other scientists say that PMT may be caused by a mixture of medical and social factors; while there is no doubt that the body and its chemistry do change throughout the menstrual cycle this fact alone may not be an adequate explanation of the causes.

Diagnosing the problem

Any problems that particularly occur during the pre-menstruum may be a sign that you suffer from PMT. You may find that your mood swings and physical symptoms follow a pattern that coincides with the days before menstruation. One way to discover if this is the case is to record these changes in a diary, on a calendar or on a special chart. From this you may discover that you are especially clumsy, short-tempered or tired in the days before your period. Your record will be useful not only for yourself but for your

doctor if you decide to seek medical help.

Keep your record for at least three months; if you discover that there is a clear pattern of negative symptoms you may find that you are able to help yourself.

Self-help

Try to adjust your routine in the days before a period so that you do not put yourself under physical stress. This applies particularly to dieting, which may increase the likelihood of faintness or dizziness. Do not go on a very strict diet during the pre-menstrual phase and make certain that you eat regularly – little, but often – when pre-menstrual problems arise.

A leading expert who has worked for many years on pre-menstrual problems recommends that your liquid intake should be restricted to about four cups a day if you suffer from water retention. She also suggests a reduction in the amount of salt in the diet as salt increases water retention.

Exercise can also help a great deal and it will make you feel generally fitter. Relaxation exercises can help with tension, both physical and emotional.

If you find that your pre-menstrual problems affect your emotions – you feel irritable or depressed, for example – then it is important to explain to those who are close to you just what is happening. You may wish to tell them that your reactions to difficulties are likely to be more intense during this time and to ask for their understanding and support. It is impossible to avoid all sources of difficulty during this phase but forward planning may enable you to avoid particularly stressful occasions and obligations. However, there is no reason why PMT should prevent you from doing things you wish to do and of which you are normally perfectly capable.

Help from your doctor

PMT can be helped by various types of medication but it is clear that at present no one form of treatment is helpful to all.

Most doctors will prescribe one of two types of treatment: hormone tablets or Vitamin B_6. Progesterone therapy is based on the theory that PMT is caused by a lack of progesterone and that therefore it can be cured by improving the hormone balance. You will be given tablets, suppositories or an injection. The amount and frequency of treatment will depend on your symptoms, the type of progesterone used and how successful the therapy is in your case. The amount may be increased if your symptoms do not improve.

Some doctors prescribe oral contraceptives to help with PMT, but this may not be suitable for you and may not even work if it is suitable. The pill prevents a normal menstrual cycle from taking place but is unlikely to have any lasting effect once you stop taking it. Some women find that they have PMT just as severely on the pill as they do off it.

Vitamin B_6 can either be prescribed by your doctor or bought from a chemist. Tablets are taken starting three days before symptoms are expected until the period starts. At first the dose may be 20 mg twice a day, but this may be increased if no effect is noticed. No more than 200 mg a day should be taken and, if you do buy the vitamin over the counter, it is advisable to ask your doctor about the dosage and any alterations you should make to your diet while you are taking it.

The vitamin is intended to replace the brain chemical, pyridoxine. Beneficial effects may take some time – a month or two – to be noticed but many women report that Vitamin B_6 has put an end to monthly problems such as depression, anxiety and headaches.

Tranquillizers and anti-depressants may be prescribed if your doctor is unsure whether or not your problems are caused by PMT. A record of your symptoms will be useful if you are sure that they are related to the pre-menstrual phase. Many women say that tranquillizers and anti-depressants make them suffer even greater problems from such things as lethargy and lack of concentration and they are therefore of no use to them.

In the past, diuretics have been used a great deal to help with water retention during the pre-menstrual phase. They should not be bought over the counter at a chemist's and should only be taken if prescribed by your doctor. Taking too high a dose of diuretics can cause other problems and they should therefore be used with care. Cutting down fluid intake and salt may be a more useful way of helping to reduce water retention.

An affectionate hug and reassurance can take some of the misery out of PMT; conversely, the feeling that nobody cares can make the symptoms much worse.

Prolapse

Q When my doctor examined me to take a smear test she told me I had a small prolapse of the womb. I have not noticed any problems but am frightened that I may eventually need an operation.

A Many women, especially in their later years, have some degree of prolapse but provided it causes no problems there is no need to treat it.

Q My husband and I are in our fifties and still enjoy our sex life together. I am about to have an operation for a prolapse and am frightened that this will prevent our making love.

A You should discuss this beforehand with the doctor who is going to perform the operation. Pieces of loose tissue are usually removed from the vagina, as part of the operation, and this will inevitably make the vagina narrower. However, the vagina is left wide enough to allow you to continue to enjoy sex.

Q My nine-year-old nephew is suffering from a rectal prolapse. Will he have to have an operation?

A Prolapse of the rectum in children is not usually a serious condition and can nearly always be pushed back, or reduced, without too much discomfort.

Q My elderly mother had a prolapse of her womb which has been corrected with a ring pessary. She is supposed to attend the hospital every six months to have a new pessary but finds it difficult to get there. Would it matter if she did not have the pessary changed as she has no trouble with it?

A Most elderly ladies with ring pessaries dislike having them changed as they find the experience uncomfortable and embarrassing. Unfortunately, these pessaries can cause an unpleasant vaginal discharge, or ulcers in the vagina which bleed. For hygienic purposes it is necessary to have a clean one fitted. One bonus is that the doctor may find that your mother no longer needs a pessary.

Prolapse means literally to 'fall forward' and can be applied to any organ which has been displaced from its normal position through weakness in supporting tissues.

The fibrous and muscular sling which lies across the bones forming the pelvic girdle is called the pelvic floor. This has to support the weight of all the contents of the abdominal cavity such as the gut and the bladder; and in women the womb as well. Occasionally, if the support system becomes weakened, the womb may slide down into the vagina. This is called a uterine prolapse.

The vaginal wall is ounded by many important structur, which can also lose their support and bulge into the vagina. When the bowel bulges into the vagina it is called an enterocele or rectocele depending on which part of the bowel is involved. When the bladder prolapses into the vagina the condition is called a cystocele and when the urethra loses its supports it is described as a urethrocele. All these conditions are forms of prolapse, more than one of which usually exist in the same woman.

Causes
Anything which exerts too much weight or pressure on the pelvic floor, or weakens it, will make a woman more likely to develop a prolapse – for example, coughing, heavy lifting or regular straining to open the bowels. Frequent pregnancies, especially if the babies are large or the labour prolonged, will weaken the mother's pelvic floor. It is also weaker if the woman is overweight.

The supporting tissues seem to need a hormone called oestrogen to retain their strength. This is mainly released from a woman's ovaries. After the menopause the ovaries no longer secrete large amounts of oestrogen, the pelvic floor becomes weaker and as a result the woman is in greater danger of developing a prolapse at this time.

Symptoms of uterine prolapse
The symptoms which a prolapse produces depend on its severity and whether or not the bladder or bowel are involved. Many women have no symptoms; some simply experience a downward pressure in the vagina. Others feel a lump (the womb) in the vagina or something 'coming down' and in a few cases the entire womb protrudes from the vagina. Obviously this makes walking and sitting very uncomfortable but, fortunately, it is very uncommon. If the bowel is involved in the prolapse, the woman may find it difficult to pass a motion without pushing the womb back into the vagina.

If the bladder is part of the prolapse the woman may find she is unable to pass

Teaching a new mother exercises to strengthen her pelvic floor is an important part of post-natal care as it can prevent a prolapse of the womb in later life.

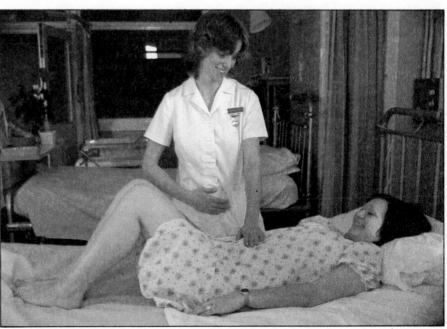

Camilla Jessel

Rectal prolapse

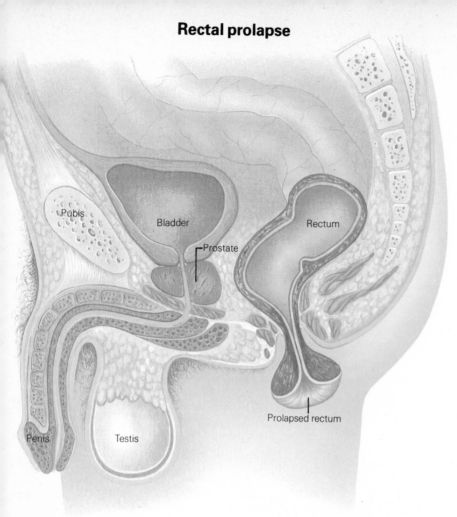

Pubis

Bladder

Rectum

Prostate

Prolapsed rectum

Penis

Testis

natal ward are taught these exercises. It is not always easy for a mother of a young baby to find the time to perform the exercises but it is important for her future that she should try to spare a few minutes each day. Oestrogen therapy after the menopause may also help some women to avoid a prolapse.

Treatment
If a woman's prolapse is very small it can sometimes be corrected if she loses weight and is prescribed a course of exercise treatment by a physiotherapist. Elderly or unfit women who wish to avoid an operation for more severe forms of prolapse can be treated by placing a plastic or rubber ring (a ring pessary) in the vagina which will hold the uterus in place. Fit women with severe symptoms are usually advised to have an operation. There are several different types of operation but they are almost all performed on or through the vagina so that the woman has no visible scar.

In rectal prolapse the rectum protrudes from the anus. While men and women may need an operation, in children the prolapse can be pushed back without much discomfort.

Prolapse of the bladder and urethra

A prolapse of the bladder and urethra into the vagina often leads to the leakage of urine when a woman runs, laughs or coughs (stress incontinence).

urine without replacing the womb in the vagina. However, a much more common problem is that the woman leaks urine if she runs, laughs or coughs. This is called stress incontinence.

A prolapse does not cause vaginal bleeding nor does it cause pain, but occasionally women may notice a dull backache at the end of the day which is relieved by lying down.

Fortunately, prolapses in women are becoming less common, partly because women have better nutrition, and tend to have smaller families, but largely due to better antenatal preparation.

Prevention of uterine prolapse
It is important to try to prevent prolapses occurring. The muscles of the pelvic floor can be strengthened by exercises: women both at antenatal classes and in the post-

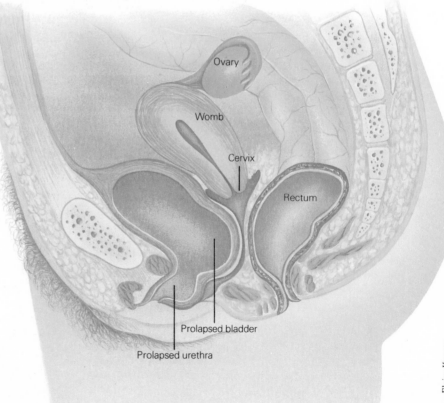

Ovary

Womb

Cervix

Rectum

Prolapsed bladder

Prolapsed urethra

Elaine Keenan

To avoid straining the pelvic floor it is important to lift heavy objects correctly. Bend at the knees and, keeping your back straight, use your arm muscles to lift the object. Then use your leg muscles to help you straighten up again.

Other forms of prolapse

Although it is customary to think of a prolapse as something that only affects the womb, there are in fact other structures which can prolapse: the word just means 'to fall forward'. One of the most dramatic but fortunately rare forms of prolapse is a prolapsed cord. This means that in the process of birth a baby's umbilical cord comes out of the birth canal before him and may be compressed against the bones of his mother's pelvis, thus interfering with the supply of blood to the baby. Special measures are necessary to deal with this situation and ensure that the baby survives without damage.

Doctors also talk about a prolapsed intervertebral disc. This is normally called 'a slipped disc' and means that one of the spongy middle sections of the tough discs that lie between the vertebrae has broken through the fibrous ring that surrounds it, and is now pressing on a nerve leaving the spinal cord.

After uterine prolapse, however, perhaps the most common sort of prolapse is that of the rectum. This condition means that the rectum is pushed down through the anal orifice. Since the rectum is a tube which is tethered to the anus, it can be pushed down through it rather like a sock being turned inside out. This tends to happen more frequently in women than in men, but it may also happen in children. When a child is involved the condition is not usually serious, and the prolapse can nearly always be reduced (pushed back) without much discomfort – it is very rare for an operation to be required in a child. In contrast, in adults there is often a need to operate and the prolapse cannot be reduced so easily. For a severe prolapse it is usually necessary to open the abdomen and repair the damage from inside.

It is not clear why rectal prolapse should occur. In children, constipation and excessive straining to open the bowels may be a cause. When adults are concerned, the condition is usually found in elderly women, although where a male is affected it can occur at any age. A certain laxity of the muscles of the floor of the pelvis may well be a part of the cause, just as in the case of uterine prolapse, although the rectum does not seem more likely to prolapse if women have had a lot of children. Fortunately, it is not a common condition.

Outlook

It is usually possible to cure a prolapse of the womb completely. Unfortunately, in a small percentage of women their symptoms return many years later so it is important for a woman who has been cured once to avoid putting too much strain on the pelvic floor.

329

Prostate gland

Ron Sutherland

Q What is the function of the prostate gland, and can it be removed without endangering health?

A The prostate gland produces a special fluid which makes up part of the seminal fluid. This fluid allows the sperm to remain motile and probably increases the chances of fertilization. It can be removed successfully without any adverse affect to health, although, of course, fertility (*not* sexual performance) will be affected. And as this operation is usually performed on elderly men, infertility may not be a problem.

Q My father has been told that he has cancer of the prostate, but they are not going to operate. Does this mean that the growth has spread too far?

A No. Surgery in cancer of the prostate is reserved for patients who have difficulty in passing urine because the growth is obstructing the outflow from the bladder. The obstruction would be removed – but not the entire gland – by means of a transurethral resection or 'closed' prostatectomy. However, most cancers of the prostate respond to treatment with hormone tablets, without the need for any surgery.

Q Do the hormones used in the treatment of cancer of the prostate have serious side-effects?

A They do have side-effects in some patients, but these effects are rarely serious enough to have to stop taking the drug. They consist of enlargement of breast tissue, loss of body hair, increased retention of fluid in the tissues and loss of libido.

Q I am going into hospital soon for a prostatectomy. Is there a chance that I will be incontinent of urine after I have my prostate gland removed?

A There is a very small chance of this in the first few months after the operation because the muscles of the bladder which prevent leakage may be damaged during the operation, but it usually gets better in time and incontinence stops.

The main function of the prostate gland is to aid male fertility. Fortunately, this gland remains relatively trouble-free until late in life, and if problems do occur they can usually be treated successfully.

The prostate gland is a walnut-shaped structure found only in males. It is situated at the base of the bladder and surrounds the urethra – the tube through which urine and seminal fluid pass out of the body.

This gland produces the fluid that mixes with semen to make up part of the seminal fluid. Although the exact function of the prostatic fluid is unknown, it is thought that one of its roles is to help keep the sperm active so that fertilization can occur more easily.

Owing to its position in the body, problems associated with this gland can often affect the normal functioning of the bladder – although this is more common among elderly men.

Prostate problems

There are various things that can go wrong with the prostate gland during a man's lifetime. The gland can become inflamed as a result of bacterial infection. This troublesome condition, known as acute prostatitis, causes flu-like symptoms and pain in the lower abdomen, groin and perineum (between the legs).

More rarely, there may be a discharge from the penis. Occasionally, this infection can lead to an abscess forming in the gland, or to chronic prostatitis where there is a persistent low-grade infection.

As a result of chronic prostatitis the gland may become calcified and gravel-like stones may be formed. Prostatitis is treated with antibiotics, although recurrent problems are common. Surgery may be required to treat the abscess.

Another problem to affect the prostate gland is the development of a tumour. The treatment of this condition varies depending on whether the tumour is benign or malignant.

Signs of a benign enlargement

The commonest tumour of the prostate gland is a benign increase in the size of the gland – a non-cancerous condition affecting a great many elderly men, although young men can suffer from it too.

Prostate problems can be troublesome and inconvenient – but as long as treatment is received promptly, a complete cure can usually be effected.

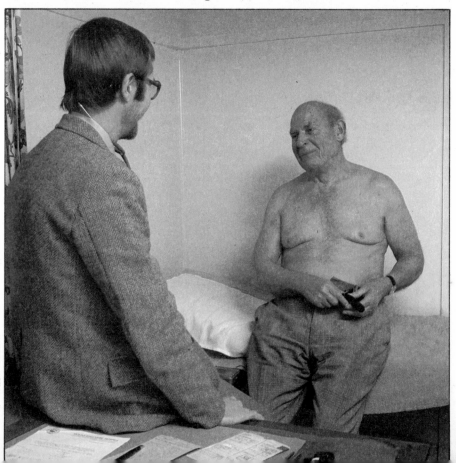

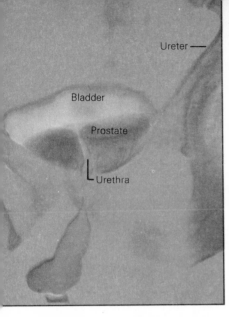

Ureter

Bladder

Prostate

Urethra

Biophoto Associates

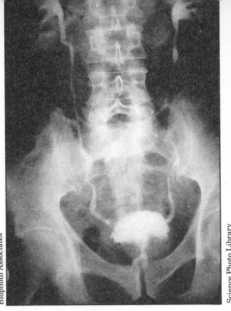

Science Photo Library

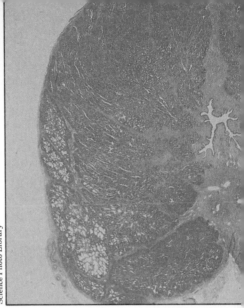

The state of the prostate gland – whether it is enlarged or not – can be determined by means of special X-ray techniques. A

normal-sized gland can be seen in the cystogram (above left) and an enlarged gland in the pyelogram (above).

As seen in this micrograph (above), the prostate is made up of glandular tissue and smooth muscle fibres.

Benign tumours of the prostate gland are so common that many doctors believe that every man over the age of 50 years or so has some degree of benign enlargement – it just has to be accepted as part of the ageing process.

Because the prostate gland surrounds the urethra, and because it is so close to the base of the bladder, enlargement of the gland can seriously impair the normal mechanism of urination.

A man with an enlarged prostate may notice the following symptoms: increased frequency of urination during the day;

getting up at night to urinate; the development of a poor urinary stream; a tendency to stop and start with the sensation that there is more to come; having to stand and wait several seconds before urine starts to flow; dribbling of urine after the stream; and, sometimes, a sudden urge to to pass urine.

All these symptoms are due to distortion of the normal anatomy at the base of the bladder. The enlargement of the gland squeezes the urethra, causing it to become narrow. Sometimes, the central part of the gland becomes elongated and

extends up into the bladder, where it can then block the entrance to the urethra and thereby inhibit the exit of urine.

If a man continues to have these symptoms without seeking medical help, two things can happen. There can be a sudden and total inability to pass urine (acute retention), which is extremely painful and requires immediate treatment. A catheter (tube) has to be passed into the bladder to drain off the excess urine. Alternatively, the bladder can become stretched so that every time the man passes urine he does not quite empty it. Because the bladder expands so gradually, there is no pain and the symptoms may go unnoticed for a while. Eventually, he passes urine in a dribble, and may even find that he is permanently wetting his underclothes and his bed. In the end, there is so much back-pressure on the kidneys that they start failing, and waste-products build up in the blood stream, with extremely serious consequences – a situation known as chronic retention of urine with renal failure.

Treatment

When a patient goes to his doctor complaining of difficulty in passing urine, or, perhaps, passing small quantities frequently, he will be sent for a series of special tests, including an X-ray of the kidneys and bladder, and blood tests. Special equipment may also be used to measure his urine flow.

If the tests show that the prostate gland is enlarged, surgery would be recom-

Urinary complications are the most common side-effect of an enlarged prostate, and can be very restrictive. After treatment, however, a man will be able to resume as active a life as he had before.

Zefa

331

mended as leaving the gland to enlarge further would complicate treatment later on. An operation would also be recommended for a patient who develops acute retention of urine as he would be unable to urinate if the catheter were removed. And, a permanent bladder catheter can be not only a social problem but a medical one, too, because of the increased risk of infection in the urine.

If the prostate gland is causing symptoms because it is enlarged, there are no drugs which can cause the gland to get smaller. Some drugs may help the symptoms to a certain extent, but they probably only help to postpone and operation which is inevitable.

The operation

The prostate gland is situated in an extremely inaccessible part of the body, and because of this, an operation to remove it can be difficult. Also, because it is near the opening of the bladder, the delicate muscles which prevent urine from leaking in between the acts of urination can be damaged if great care is not taken.

Nowadays there are two types of operation. The retropubic prostatectomy, also known as the 'open' method, and the transurethral prostatectomy or TUR.

The 'open' method is reserved for very large glands and also where an operation on the bladder has to be performed at the same time. It consist of making a cut across the lower abdomen and approaching the gland via the space between the back of the pubic bone and the bladder. The capsule of the prostate gland is opened and the gland is 'shelled out' from inside the capsule. Fluid is then passed via a tube into the bladder to prevent the formation of blood clots. This tube is usually left in the bladder for about five days after the operation, and is then removed if there is no residual bleeding. A patient having this operation is usually in hospital for seven to ten days.

The 'closed' method or TUR, is performed using a fine telescope-like instrument which is passed up the penis into the bladder. This instrument has a viewing-piece and a special cautery (searing) device which has a wire loop on the end. Using this method, the prostate gland is chipped away from inside the urethra, little pieces of tissue being cut away each time the wire loop, which is attached to an electric current, moves through the tissue.

The great advantage of the TUR method is that the patient is spared a surgical incision and there is less discomfort or pain after the operation. As with the 'open' method, a tube is left in the bladder but, here, the tube is often taken out after two or three days.

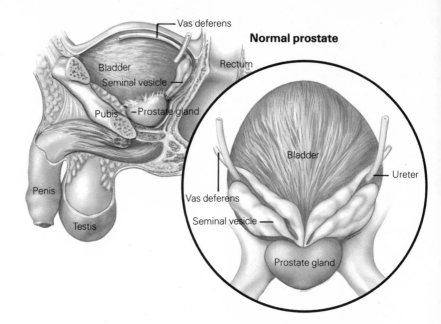

Normal prostate

Vas deferens · Rectum · Bladder · Seminal vesicle · Pubis · Prostate gland · Penis · Testis

Bladder · Ureter · Vas deferens · Seminal vesicle · Prostate gland

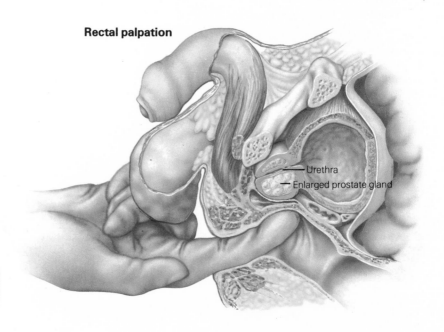

Rectal palpation

Urethra · Enlarged prostate gland

Frank Kennard

Patients make a much quicker recovery from this operation, because it is less traumatic to the body.

After a prostatectomy, the urinary stream is noticeably better, but there will be side-effects, Because of the anatomy of the prostate gland, patients who have had either type of prostatectomy are unable to ejaculate semen normally. In this condition, known as retrograde ejaculation, the semen goes back into the bladder instead of travelling down and out the penis, in effect making the man infertile.

This is because in removing the gland the muscle at the base of the bladder has to be cut. This muscle usually contracts during orgasm, preventing semen from going up into the bladder.

As this operation is usually performed on elderly men, infertility may not be a problem (sexual performance need not be affected). But a younger man suffering from an enlarged prostate may be worried by the prospect of retrograde ejaculation if he wants to have children. Sometimes the surgeon will be able to postpone

Treatment of prostate problems

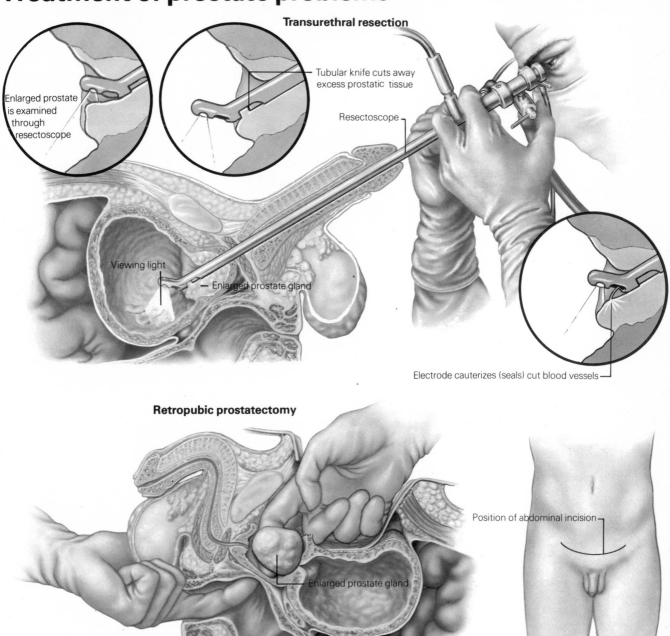

Transurethral resection

Enlarged prostate is examined through resectoscope

Tubular knife cuts away excess prostatic tissue

Resectoscope

Viewing light

Enlarged prostate gland

Electrode cauterizes (seals) cut blood vessels

Retropubic prostatectomy

Enlarged prostate gland

Position of abdominal incision

treatment until the man has fathered a child, but this is not always possible if the symptoms are very severe. Fortunately, it is sometimes possible for the man's partner to be artificially inseminated.

Cancer of the prostate

Cancer of the prostate is one of the most common cancers to occur in males. In fact, it has been found in routine post-mortem examination of the prostate gland that nearly all elderly men have a tiny focus of cancer in the prostate gland. Most of

these people would not have known that they had anything wrong.

However, when a malignant tumour does manifest itself during a man's life, it does so in a number of ways. Firstly, it may be found on a routine examination by a doctor who notices a lump in the gland (the gland can be felt through the anterior wall of the rectum). Secondly, the patient may have difficulty passing urine because the tumour is so close to the urethra. Thirdly, the patient may have no urinary symptoms, but develops symp-

The condition of the prostate gland can be diagnosed by a rectal examination. If it is enlarged, an operation – either a retropubic prostatectomy or a transurethral resection – will be recommended.

toms from the spread of the tumour outside the gland. One of the commonest sites for the secondary spread of the tumour is in the bones. The spread probably occurs as a result of tiny clumps of cells breaking off the main tumour and circulating in the bloodstream.

Q My husband is gradually developing difficulty in passing urine. He has to stand for ages before the urine starts to flow, and he seems to be getting up several times in the night. Does he need an operation on his prostate gland?

A Possibly. There are some other causes of the same symptoms, but he certainly should see a specialist and have some investigations carried out. These tests, which would include a blood test, a special X-ray, and a urine flow test, will reveal whether or not the prostate gland is the cause of the trouble. If it is, then an operation would be recommended.

Q Why does the prostate gland enlarge in older men?

A No-one really knows the answer to this. The finding of an enlarged prostate gland is so common that it is difficult to equate it with factors earlier in life, such as sexual activity.

Q Is removal of the prostate gland using an 'open' operation likely to be more 'permanent' in its effect than removal with an instrument through the penis?

A It can be, but doesn't have to be. Removal of the gland can be complete when done by the closed method – that is by a transurethral resection (TUR) where a fine tube complete with a viewing-piece and a cautery device is introduced into the penis and the prostate is actually 'chipped' away. However, using the TUR method, some surgeons might only remove part of the gland in a very old person, just so that he can pass urine easily.

Q Can anything be done for the pain in the bones that my father has, as a result of his prostatic cancer spreading?

A Yes. If hormone treatment has been tried and has not been successful, X-ray treatment to the painful area is often extremely effective in relieving the pain of secondary tumours in the bones.

Ron Sutherland

A prostatectomy relieves one of the most awkward symptoms of an enlarged prostate gland – that is, repeatedly having to get up at night to go to the toilet.

Treatment and outlook

The treatment of cancer of the prostate depends on many factors, but one of the most important is the extent of spread of the tumour. Therefore, a patient who is suspected of having a malignant tumour of the prostate will have several tests, including X-rays and radioactive scans of the bones, to determine the exact extent of the spread.

If the tumour has been found quite by accident, and consists of a small nodule confined to the gland itself, many surgeons would treat this simply by observation, with no specific drug or radiation treatment, and certainly no surgery. The majority of these patients will live for years with no problems.

If the tests show that the tumour has spread outside the prostate gland, then treatment in the form of hormone drugs will be given. Most cancers of the prostate have been found to be dependent on male hormones for their growth; so by counteracting their effect with female hormones, the cancer can be kept at bay. The drug is given in very small doses and often has quite dramatic effects on the primary and secondary tumours. Bones which have been riddled with secondary tumours become normal again, and the swelling in the gland becomes smaller.

The female hormone drug does have side-effects, however. It can promote the loss of hair, increase the growth of breast tissue and decrease libido. It can also cause the body tissues to retain more fluid than usual, leading to swelling of the ankles, and sometimes heart failure.

These side-effects are troublesome in only a few patients, however, and the benefits of the drug in controlling the tumour far outweigh the disadvantages. Some surgeons, to produce the same effect, remove the testes (the glands that produce the male hormone testosterone), as they find that there is the same response from the tumour without the possible side-effects of the drug.

Surgery in cancer of the prostate gland is usually reserved for those patients in whom the growth of the tumour has caused a narrowing of the urethra, so that urine cannot be passed easily. In these cases, the blockage is removed but no attempt is made to remove the whole tumour. Treatment with X-rays is sometimes given, but usually only when the secondary tumours in the bones are causing a lot of pain.

There are a small number of patients whose tumours do not respond to drug treatment. Luckily, though, they are only a very small proportion of the many patients with cancer of the prostate. The outlook for a lot of patients with prostatic cancer is very good indeed. Some men live for many years, taking a small dose of the hormone drug every day.

Rashes

Q My friend has a rash on her hands and arms. She says it's a form of dermatitis that isn't catching. Is this right?

A Yes, probably. Dermatitis simply means inflammation of the skin. A few types like impetigo, ringworm and scabies can be spread from person to person by direct contact, but usually the condition is due to a skin sensitivity to a substance, or to an emotional or nervous disorder, and is not at all contagious.

Q Why is it so important not to scratch chickenpox spots? And what happens if you do?

A There's no mystery about this! It has nothing to do with not spreading the condition, as many people think, but is simply a way of avoiding scars. If chickenpox spots are not scratched there is a good chance that they will heal without leaving scars. Scratching tends to infect the spots making them larger and deeper, and thus more likely to leave permanent marks on the skin.

Q What is the best thing to put on a measles rash?

A You should not put anything at all on a measles rash. The eruption is dry, does not form sores or ulcers, and will follow the natural course of the condition whatever is put on the skin. Since nothing will make any difference, either to the illness or the rash itself, it is best to leave well alone.

Q How can I tell the difference between a rash due to an infectious disease and one due to an allergy?

A The rashes of the common infectious diseases differ from each other in appearance, and rarely form weals or irritate so acutely. Also, a person with an infectious disease will probably have a fever and feel ill, while someone with an allergy usually feels quite well in himself. There is nothing specific about the rash due to an allergy except when it consists of raised areas or weals with white centres surrounded by a red area. These usually irritate considerably.

To most of us a rash means any redness of the skin or outbreak of spots – and in medical terms it indicates a skin eruption which may have a variety of causes.

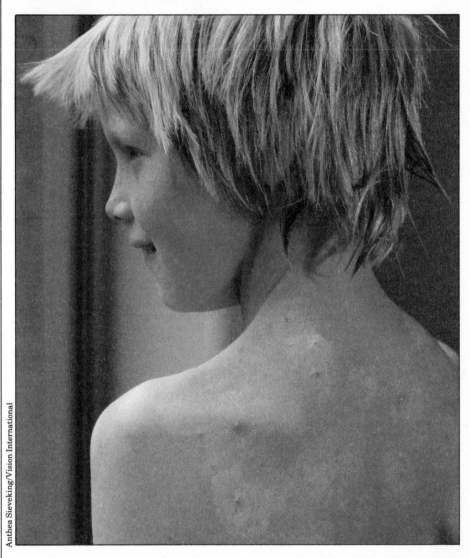

Anthea Sieveking/Vision International

A rash may be an outward sign of a condition affecting the body as a whole. Thus infectious fevers, emotional disorders and allergies all may have accompanying rashes.

They may equally, however, be an indication of a localized disorder in the skin – the kind of inflammation that is commonly called dermatitis. Included in this kind of local inflammation are nappy rash, prickly heat, eczema and fungal infections of the skin.

Rashes can take many different forms. The rash which is present at the beginning of an illness is called the primary rash. It may subsequently change in character and appearance during the natural course of the causative disease, or

A chickenpox rash always causes irritation and the best remedy is calamine lotion, applied liberally and often. This should minimize the need to scratch the spots.

as a result of complications or in response to treatment. New rashes or changes in the appearance of the original rash are called secondary eruptions, and each has its own set of characteristics.

Primary rashes
The commonest of the primary rashes are areas or spots of redness which doctors call macules. Any abnormal change in the colour of the skin over a limited area qualifies as a macular rash, the redness itself being given the name erythema.

Q The doctor gave my husband a very effective ointment for a rash he had last year. I now have a similar rash. Would it be a good idea for me to use some of this ointment that was left-over?

A No, it wouldn't. It is quite possible that you are right and that your rash has the same cause as your husband's, in which case the ointment would probably do it good, or at least not do it any harm. Even so it would be the wrong thing to do, and could even be dangerous for at least two reasons. Firstly, using a medicine of any sort – other than those you can buy over the counter – that has not been prescribed for you personally is very risky. People can, and do, injure themselves in this way. Secondly, the skin can develop a sensitivity to any medication, and skin disorders are anyway difficult to deal with in many cases. Never put anything stronger than calamine lotion or cream on your skin without first consulting your doctor. It is always wise to remember that the skin, although quite tough in some ways, is very individual – even temperamental – in its reactions. This is why great care is taken in the diagnosis and treatment of skin conditions.

Q Every few months I develop an irritating rash on my hands, which I find worrying. My doctor says it isn't anything serious, but what could be wrong with me?

A Since your rash occurs intermittently and your doctor has ruled out a serious disorder, it may be due to a condition like nervous tension, that comes and goes. Equally it could result from periodic exposure to something which triggers an allergic reaction in you. As the rash develops on your hands, this is likely to be a substance you touch or handle. Try to remember if you had any particular worries at the times the rash has occurred, or if it coincided with doing a job where you had to handle something unusual, perhaps while gardening or dyeing curtains. To pinpoint the precipitating factor you may need to keep a detailed diary of everything you do, including items you touch. The only cure is to track down the cause, so that you can avoid it in future.

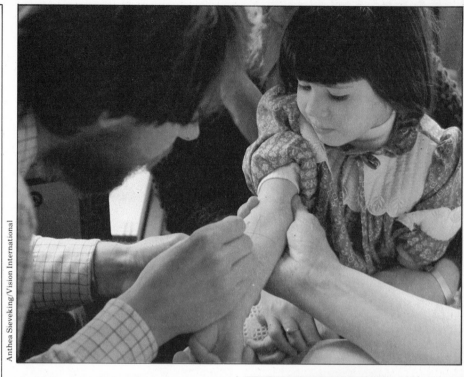

Anthea Sieveking/Vision International

A prick test can help to isolate the cause of an allergic response (above). Possible allergens are dropped onto the skin, and a positive reaction will appear as a weal.

Sometimes, as in the early stages of measles, the rash consists of hundreds of tiny red spots, each separate or 'discrete' from each other.

In other cases the spots enlarge until they run into each other, joining up to form blotchy patches. This is called a confluent rash. Usually if you press your thumb on a part of the rash it will not fade, but sometimes it will temporarily leave a white area. This is an important diagnostic feature and is characteristic of several conditions including typhoid fever in particular.

The second common type of rash consists of spots which are not necessarily red but project above the surface of the skin. They can be felt as small raised pimples if a fingertip is run over the skin, in contrast to a macular rash which is not raised. These little pimples are known as papules, and the rash as a papular rash. A maculo-papular rash is halfway between a macular and a papular one.

When the rash is made up of pimples containing a clear or milky fluid doctors refer to it as vesicular, with each pimple being a vesicle. Chickenpox and smallpox are typical examples.

A rash may also consist of raised areas of skin much larger than papules. These are known as weals, and they are usually white at the centre and pink or red at the outer edge. This type of skin eruption –

Tony Stone Associates

urticaria or hives as it is called – is usually highly irritant and indicates an allergic reaction which releases histamine into the skin to cause the inflammation.

Secondary rashes

In some cases the primary rash, whatever its type, simply fades away or 'resolves' as

Rashes associated with infectious diseases

Chicken pox	Small flat spots turning into pimples then small blisters. These become pustules which burst to form scabs. The rash starts on the trunk, itches and lasts about a week
German measles	Tiny red spots, often very faint, appearing first on the face and spreading down to the trunk
Measles	Tiny red spots first on the forehead and behind the ears, spreading down to the chest and abdomen. The rash is preceded by small white spots inside the mouth, takes two days to develop fully, and starts to fade after about a week
Scarlet fever	Flat red spots or small blotches, most marked at the armpits, and elbow and groin creases, leaving a clear area around the mouth
Smallpox	Similar to chickenpox in appearance, but by contrast spreading from the face, hands and feet towards the trunk
Syphilis	A faint copper-coloured rash appears in the secondary stage of the disease, most often on the trunk, palms of the hands, soles of the feet and the forehead. A blood test can confirm the diagnosis
Typhoid and paratyphoid	Successive crops of a dozen or so 'rose-spots', about 0.5 cm (¼ in) across, on the chest and abdomen, lasting two to three days

frequently become infected by bacteria from the atmosphere, especially in moist, heavily contaminated situations. This sometimes happens with nappy rash, cold sores or shingles.

Treatment
Rashes as such do not require or benefit from any particular treatment, except that needed for the underlying condition. If itching is a problem, calamine cream is as effective as any preparation that can be bought without a prescription, and has the advantage of cheapness. If this is not adequate to control the irritation, a doctor may prescribe a short course of antihistamine tablets or syrup.

Antihistamine cream should never be used to treat such irritation. It is now clear that this can give rise to an allergy to the antihistamine itself, making it dangerous to use on a future occasion which might be a real emergency. If the papules or pustules of a rash burst, or there are ulcers present, a mild antiseptic cream or lotion can be useful in preventing infection.

Many women find that jewellery containing nickel provokes an allergic rash – this is less true with gold and silver (left). Great care is needed in handling chemicals since they may cause skin damage which is further complicated by inflammation (right).

the condition improves, without going through any secondary stage and without leaving scars or any other after-effects. Secondary eruptions are common, however, and may take a variety of forms.

Often the area of skin covered by the rash peels away. This normally occurs if the original rash was a dry macular or papular one, or, as in some cases, a mixture of the two.

The type of rash usually seen in the later stages of chickenpox, by contrast, is pustular, which means that the spots have become infected pustules, containing pus. This type of moist lesion will dry out to form a crust or small scab. New skin will grow under the scabs which will eventually separate and drop off. If the deeper layers of skin have been affected – as when chickenpox spots are scratched – there may be scarring in the form of pock-marks, or tiny pits in the skin.

Other types of secondary rash include thickening of the area of skin concerned, giving it a leathery look and feel which is characteristic of long-term or chronic inflammation. Similarly, permanent discoloration or pigmentation may develop.

Finally, entire areas of skin may break down, exposing the underlying or subcutaneous tissue. Without the protective covering of skin, the ulcers so formed

Resuscitation

Q How long can your heart stop for without there being permanent damage?

A The standard answer to this is between three and four minutes. However, in reality there is tremendous variability; a child can survive much longer than an elderly person for example, and children can be without a pulse for five minutes or more without having brain damage.

Q Is it true that anyone can learn resuscitation? Isn't there a risk of it doing more harm than good?

A Yes, it certainly is true that anyone can learn the simple techniques of heart massage and the 'kiss of life' method of respiration. If more people were properly prepared to do this there might be many lives saved. As to whether it might do more harm than good, you have to remember that if you are the only person present when someone's heart stops and he stops breathing then either you are going to resuscitate him or he will die – it is always worth trying. To avoid the possibility of doing harm you simply have to make sure that there is no pulse, and that the person is not breathing – if this is the case then there is no chance of doing any harm whatsoever.

Q My father is 75 and has just gone into hospital after a heart attack. Will he be too old for them to try and resuscitate if he has a collapse?

A Absolutely not. If he gets into trouble, they will try just as hard to resuscitate him as they would a younger person. Of course it is true to say that many people die in hospital, and attempts at resuscitation are not made on all of them. Different hospitals have different ways of going about this, but it is obviously wrong to resuscitate people who are clearly dying of cancer when they will inevitably die a short time later; similarly there must come an age where death is allowed to occur peacefully and naturally.

The knowledge required to practise resuscitation need not only be the preserve of the skilled hospital emergency team. Anyone can learn the simple techniques that can save the life of a fellow human being.

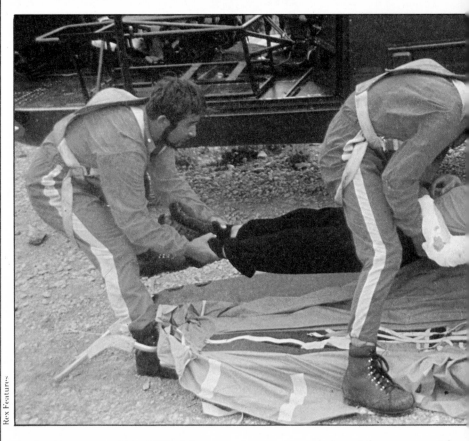

Rex Features

During the course of the 1960s it became commonplace in hospitals for people who had not only stopped breathing, but who also had lost their heartbeat to be saved from death; the basic techniques of cardio-pulmonary resuscitation (CPR) were born. Hospitals set up their own 'crash teams', or emergency squads who were on standby 24 hours a day, to rush to the bedside of anyone who had collapsed and was in imminent danger of death, in the hope of performing a 'miracle'. Nowhere was this more successful than for patients who had suffered a heart attack. Because so many of these patients' lives could be saved, they tended to be gathered together in a special ward equipped with all the facilities for immediate CPR. These wards became known as coronary care units – now found in many hospitals.

The crash team and its equipment
Hospitals vary in the way that they organize their crash teams, but there must be few hospitals in the developed world taking emergency cases that do not

have some sort of special arrangement for dealing with cardiac arrests – the term used to describe a collapse where the heart is assumed to have stopped. Normally there are at least two doctors – sometimes four or five – including an anaesthetist and a physician in the team. They often carry a radio-controlled bleeper which alerts them at once if there is an arrest to attend. There will also be some arrangement for the special equipment they need to be brought to the place concerned – ideally it would be present on all wards, but this is not always the case.

In fact, the equipment necessary is fairly simple. There must be the standard anaesthetist's equipment that he uses to pass a tube down into the patient's trachea (windpipe). This makes sure that oxygen can be supplied to the lungs.

The other essential is a machine called a defibrillator. This is a device that delivers a carefully measured charge of electricity, an electric shock, to the chest. The defibrillator has two flat metal plates with insulated handles, known as pad-

These days, many different types of emergency teams have the training and equipment for life-saving and resuscitation. The helicopter rescue crew (below) can keep someone alive until reaching hospital where he can be treated. Some ambulances (bottom) are equipped with both oxygen apparatus and heart defibrillators.

dles, which are applied to the front of the chest wall. The doctor can release an electric shock by pressing a button on one of the paddles. He has to make sure that none of the other members of the team are touching the patient or the bed he is lying on, otherwise they may get a shock as well. These shocks across the heart are the one thing that can correct disorganized electrical conditions within the heart muscle and bring it back to a normal pattern of beating.

In addition to the defibrillator another piece of equipment called a cardiac monitor is needed. This displays an electrocardiogram (ECG) on a screen. This is a trace of the heart's electrical activity and it gives a constant check on the heart rhythm. Often, modern machines are combined, so that the ECG can be recorded through the paddles of the defibrillator.

How resuscitation works

There are only three basic principles to successful resuscitation, and these are the same whether they are being applied by the highly skilled team in a hospital or by a member of the public in the street.

First, the patient's airway must be unobstructed. This means that the air passages in the upper part of the throat and the mouth must be clear so that air can get down into the lungs – such things as vomit or false teeth must be removed from the mouth without delay.

Second, air must be pumped into the lungs. The simple way of doing this is with the 'kiss of life' called Arti-

ficial respiration. The basic technique is easy: the mouth is placed firmly over the mouth of the patient and the patient's mouth is blown into about 10 times a minute. It is essential that the head of the patient is tipped backwards since this allows the airway to remain open.

Third, the oxygen that is being supplied to the lungs must be carried to the rest of the body via circulation of the blood. This is done by using the non-beating heart as a sort of pump by means of cardiac or heart massage. It was really the development of this technique that led to the widespread use of CPR.

Before today's techniques of external cardiac massage, people used to carry out an emergency operation to open the chest at the bedside and then squeeze the heart in their hands to circulate the blood. It was later realized that the same effect could be achieved without opening the chest at all. Pressure on the sternum (the breast bone), causes the heart to be emptied of blood that then flows to the rest of the body. When the pressure is removed, the heart fills up again with blood. So, regular applications of pressure produce an almost normal, regular pulse, sending blood to the vital organs.

The kiss of life with additional cardiac massage, if no pulse can be felt, can save lives without any other sort of additional help at all. In addition to this, these

On-the-spot resuscitation gives the patient a chance of arriving at a hospital where more sophisticated treatment further improves the chances of survival.

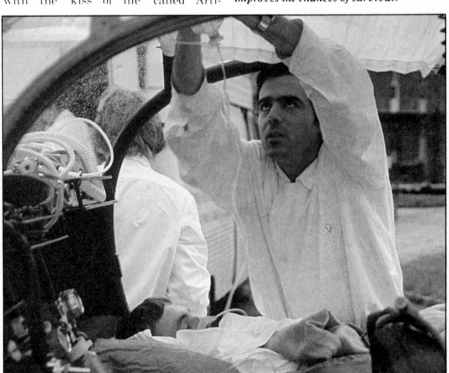

Resuscitation

The basic aim of resuscitation is to restore, as best as possible, the flow of oxygenated blood to all parts of the body, especially the brain. Normally, oxygen mixes with the blood in the lungs and the blood is then pumped round the body by the heart. If a person stops breathing or the heart stops beating, resuscitation must be started or the body will die – the brain takes only about four minutes – because it is denied the life-giving oxygenated blood.

Anyone can be faced with the situation where knowledge of resuscitation techniques can save life, whether it is at the scene of a road accident, in the street or even at home. By learning the steps outlined below, you might, in an emergency, be able to save a life by acting quickly. Only send for help if there is a spare person at the scene and keep going until professional help arrives.

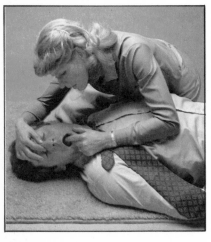

If someone is obviously not breathing, the first thing to do is to make sure that air can get to the lungs by clearing the airway. Tip the head to one side and remove anything that might be in the mouth like vomit or false teeth. Use your fingers to clear the mouth.

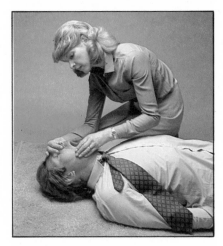

When you have made sure the mouth is clear, pinch the nostrils shut and tip the head back. With your other hand on the chin, hold the mouth open. Tipping the head back so the neck is arched makes certain that the tongue cannot flop back and block the passage of air.

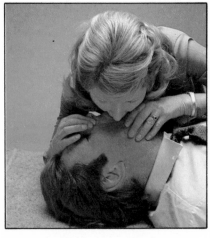

Now begin mouth-to-mouth resuscitation. Take a deep breath, seal your lips firmly around the mouth and then breath out. As you do this, the chest should rise. If it does not, check that the airway is clear. Between 10 and 12 breaths a minute are needed.

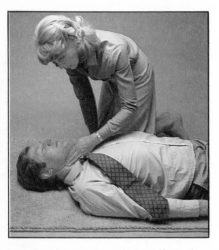

Now feel for a pulse. It is best if another person can do this while someone carries on with the kiss of life. But if alone, you must feel for a pulse by putting your fingers about an inch below the corner of the jaw. If you've never felt the pulse in the neck, try now—it's easy.

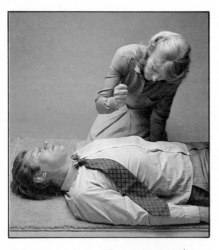

If there is no pulse, first try to get the heart going again by giving one hard thump to the centre of the chest with a clenched fist. Do not be afraid of hitting hard – this simple action often restores the near-normal rhythm of a heart disorganized by a heart attack.

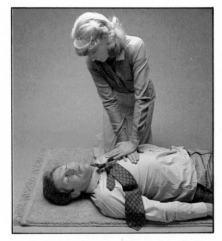

If you still can't feel a pulse, place the heel of one palm on the centre of the chest just below the line of the nipples. Put your other hand over the first and press down hard. Keeping your hands on the chest, give about 60 pressures a minute. Alternate with the kiss of life.

techniques can keep people alive long enough for them to be taken to hospital where more sophisticated equipment like defibrillators and mechanical ventilators (breathing machines) can be used.

Clearing airways
One of the problems associated with any sort of unconsciousness is that the normal swallowing mechanism is lost so that food, and particularly vomit can go down into the lungs instead of being directed into the gullet. In hospital this problem is avoided by placing a tube in the trachea (windpipe) which is then sealed with an inflatable cuff – this of course means that nothing can slip down into the lungs.

The trouble with tracheal tubes is that it is a very skilled job to put them in place. Although it is a basic skill for an anaesthetist it would not be easy for someone to perform in the street.

In order to get over this difficulty there is an exciting new development called an oesophageal obturator airway. This too is a tube with a balloon-like cuff at the end of it, but instead of being put into the trachea, it is put into the oesophagus (gullet) where the tube naturally tends to go. Unlike the tracheal tube it has a blind end so that vomit cannot get past it up into the mouth and then down into the lungs of the patient.

Once the oesophagus is blocked off, any air pumped into the mouth has to go down into the lungs, so that with the aid of this device air can be pumped into the mouth and then into the lungs using a bag instead of having to give the kiss of life. With this sort of airway, a semi-skilled person can have almost the same advantages as the hospital anaesthetist when it comes to resuscitation.

Resuscitation outside hospital
In light of the success of resuscitation in hospitals, people started to turn their attention to the possibility of bringing the techniques of CPR onto the streets in the hope of saving even more lives, again, particularly in those people who had just suffered, or were in the process of suffering a heart attack. Different ideas were tried in several cities around the world, and many of the schemes were and are very successful.

In the city of Seattle, Washington, a person has perhaps the best chance of being successfully resuscitated on collapsing in the street. Not only are there teams of specially trained resuscitation technicians on call throughout the city, but the general public has received the benefit of a massive public education campaign to recognize the simple signs of a cardiac arrest and to start basic CPR.

There are also cities in the UK where similar programmes have been started. In Brighton there are specially equipped ambulances, with trained ambulancemen, while in the City of London there is a special service based at St Bartholomew's Hospital which operates during working hours when the City is full of people. The thing that all these services bring to patients is the availability of a defibrillator, and this is what saves so many lives particularly in the first minutes or hours after a heart attack.

Nevertheless it is quite possible to save life by the simple and straightforward business of basic CPR (see First aid panel). If you find someone who is not breathing, clear his or her airway and start the kiss of life. If you cannot feel a pulse get someone else to give heart massage, and if you are on your own at least try giving the chest a good hard thump, since this sometimes has the same effect as an electric shock in starting the heart off again. Remember you can't do any harm – if someone's heart has stopped and he isn't breathing he is going to die anyway; but at least you can give him a chance of life. And don't hang back – time is often of the essence and every minute counts.

What the 'crash team' does in a hospital cardiac arrest

Nurses and anyone else present at the arrest start routine resuscitation with massage and the kiss of life until the team arrives. When they do, a tube is inserted into the trachea (windpipe) by the anaesthetist so that oxygen can be squeezed into the lungs with an oxygen bag connected to a cylinder. Meanwhile, cardiac massage continues. Then, the defibrillator is used to give a shock over the heart. This is done very early because most arrests result from abnormalities of heart rhythm which can be converted back to normal by a shock.

Next, electrocardiogram (ECG) electrodes are attached to the patient's chest so that the heart rhythm can be determined accurately on a heart monitor. Modern defibrillators actually show this on a screen as soon as they are put on the chest. Then an intravenous infusion line (drip) is put in, in order to give drugs quickly straight into the patient's bloodstream.

If a normal heart rhythm has not been started by this stage, drugs are given via the drip in the hope of either stimulating the heart, or suppressing the chaotic electrical activity that will stop the heart pumping. Also, more shocks may be necessary. Once there is oxygen going into the lungs, and there is massage to make sure that the circulation carries the oxygen around the body, then the immediate urgency has passed and there is time to see if recovery is possible. Sometimes the heart recovers, but breathing doesn't return immediately – the patient is then put onto a ventilator to await breathing recovery.

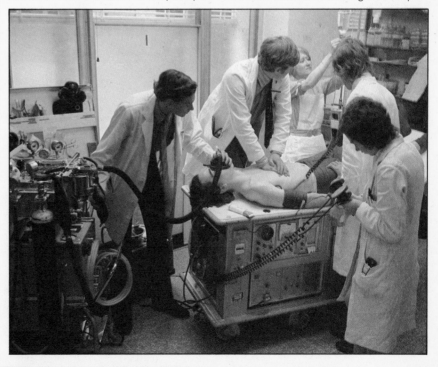

Rheumatism

Q My mother always claims that her rheumatism gets worse in cold, damp weather. Do weather conditions really affect rheumatism?

A Quite a number of people do claim that their aches and pains get worse in the cold wet weather, even that their bones can predict wet weather on the way! But scientific studies have failed to show any effect of weather on various rheumatic diseases. However, certain people are sensitive to changes in the weather, and this allied to the rather depressing effect of cold, wet weather may explain the 'rheumaticky' pains.

Q My father believes that the copper bracelet on his wrist protects him from rheumatism; is there any truth in his theory?

A There is no scientific evidence to suggest that the bracelet can help, but as with many remedies, if someone believes that it will help in some way or other, then his body may respond positively. It is most probably not the copper bracelet that is helping your father, but his state of mind – his faith in the bracelet.

Q When young, my son had two bouts of rheumatic fever. I am worried that he may develop rheumatism later on in life. Is this possible?

A No. Rheumatic fever and rheumatism are really quite different. Although rheumatic fever does cause joint pains at the time of the illness it will not cause joint problems in the future. Despite its name, it tends to damage the heart rather than the joints.

Q Does the fact that I am 'double-jointed' make me more likely to develop rheumatism?

A Those who have a greater range of movement in their joints (double-jointed) may be more prone to developing aches and pains in their joints later on in life and this is probably related to their over-use and the unusual stresses and strains to which they are subjected.

Rheumatism is one of those vague terms we attribute loosely to a range of aches and pains. It is not a disease in itself; rather it is a set of symptoms.

Rheumatism is a term used to describe aches and pains in joints and their surrounding structures such as muscles, tendons and ligaments. It is not a specific condition; more a collection of symptoms.

These symptoms – often referred to as 'rheumatics', rheumaticky pains – include swelling, pain or tenderness and stiffness in the affected part. They tell us little about the underlying disorder as they are symptoms which are common to a wide variety of different diseases that affect the joints and their surrounding structures. Doctors now prefer to give specific names to the cause of the pain.

There are two types of rheumatism; articular or non-articular, and it is the site of the problem that determines the difference. If the problem is within the joint itself, involving the synovial membrane or cartilage, then this is called articular rheumatism.

Non-articular rheumatism usually develops from inflammation of the structures surrounding the joint, such as tendons and muscles.

Causes
Rheumatism may occur during the course of many illnesses and these are collectively referred to as rheumatic diseases. The best known of these that give rise to the articular form of rheumatism are osteoarthritis, rheumatoid arthritis, juvenile arthritis and ankylosing spondylitis.

Conditions such as bursitis (tennis elbow and housemaid's knee) and fibrositis (inflammation of the fibrous tissue in the muscles) are examples of non-articular rheumatism.

Treatment
The treatment of rheumatism depends on the diagnosis of the underlying cause. The diagnosis may involve a physical examination and one or two blood tests.

Most cases of non-articular rheumatism get better on their own, or simply require rest. More prolonged cases are given heat treatment, exercises and cortisone injections.

As articular forms of rheumatism are more serious and longer lasting prolonged treatment and substantial rest may be necessary. Cortisone and pain-killing injections into the joint are sometimes used in combination with gentle physiotherapy. More specific treatment is dependent on the diagnosis.

There is no medical evidence to explain why, but sufferers complain that damp weather makes their rheumatism worse.

Rheumatoid arthritis

Q I suffer from rheumatoid arthritis but since I became pregnant the pains in my joints have completely disappeared and I feel much better. Will the joint pains return after the baby is born or does this mean that I am completely cured?

A It is not uncommon for people with rheumatoid arthritis to improve markedly during pregnancy. With some women this improvement may be lasting but others find that their symptoms return after the delivery of their child. The actual reason for the improvement is not known although it is thought that it is due to the body's production of an anti-inflammatory substance. Research is currently being carried out in an attempt to find out exactly what this unknown substance is.

Q I have heard that people with rheumatoid arthritis are treated with injections of gold. Is this really true or was my leg just being pulled?

A This is certainly true and in fact gold injections are one of the most effective treatments available at the moment for rheumatoid arthritis. The compound injected is actually a water soluble gold salt and it is given as an intramuscular injection. However preparations which can be taken by mouth are now becoming available. The reason why this treatment is so effective is not known.

Q My mother has rheumatoid arthritis and frequently has fluid removed from her knees. What is this and where does the fluid come from?

A When a joint becomes inflamed fluid leaks out of the synovial membrane that lines the joint space and this collects in the joint cavity. The fluid is called an effusion and it is this that causes the joint to swell. If the joint is large and a larger effusion is present then it is often possible to remove the fluid with a needle and syringe. This can give the patient considerable relief from pain and stiffness in that joint.

In the past, this disease almost inevitably led to crippling deformities of the joints. Now, with early diagnosis and treatment, such disablement can very often be avoided.

To most people rheumatoid arthritis conjures up horrific pictures of patients in wheelchairs, crippled by their disease and worst of all living out the remainder of their lives racked by pain. This concept is now out of date and while it is still true that people may be severely disabled by the disease this is certainly not so in the vast majority of cases.

This woman continues to carry out her normal activities despite the fact that she suffers from stiffening of the joints and other symptoms of rheumatoid arthritis.

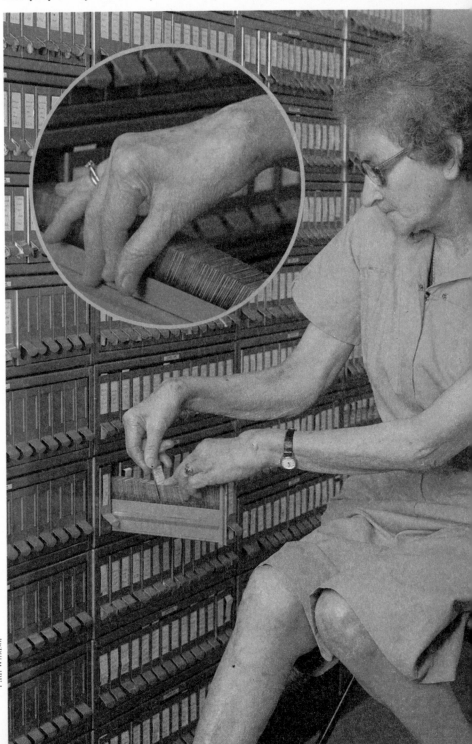

Paul Windsor

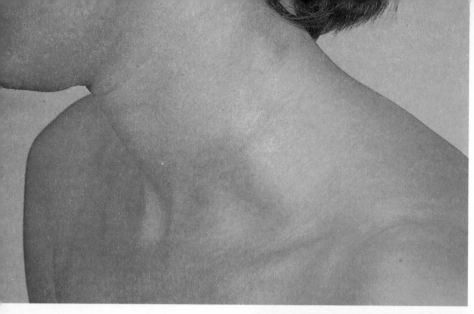

This immune response causes an accumulation of inflamed cells (known as lymphocytes and macrophages) within the synovial membrane that lines the joints and secretes lubricating fluid. Enzymes that are released from the inflamed cells lead to the breakdown of bone and cartilage within the joint, causing characteristic symptoms. Unless treatment is given the joint will eventually become deformed.

Two particularly interesting results of the inflammatory response are the production of the rheumatoid factor and the development of rheumatoid nodules. Rheumatoid factor is an antibody produced in large amounts in people with the disease and is most unusual in other

Injections of gold salts are given to some patients when anti-inflammatory drugs fail to work. However, a side-effect may be the production of a 'gold rash' (above).
The X-ray (right) shows an ankle joint that is affected by rheumatoid arthritis. Such deformities often involve contraction of the joint space, thus limiting movement.

Early diagnosis, improved methods of treatment and rehabilitation where appropriate make the life of a patient with rheumatoid arthritis easier in every respect. By controlling the progression of the disease, relieving pain and preventing the development of deformities the patient is able to lead a normal or as near normal a life as possible.

What is rheumatoid arthritis?

Rheumatoid arthritis is a disease which mainly affects the joints but may, in severe cases, affect many other organs such as the heart, lungs, nervous system and the eyes. It occurs in both men and women but is more common in women, generally occurring in a ratio of about three to one. The usual age of onset is from the middle to late twenties until late middle age. However it may also occur outside this age range in both younger and more elderly people.

Rheumatoid arthritis is a chronic condition which is frequently punctuated by periods when for no apparent reason the symptoms become worse, lessen or disappear. The disease itself may even disappear completely, in which case it is sometimes referred to as 'burnt out' rheumatoid arthritis.

Cause

Although the basic cause of rheumatoid arthritis has not been discovered it is known that the disease occurs when the body's defence mechanisms (the immune system) react to the presence of the initiating agent and try to eliminate it.

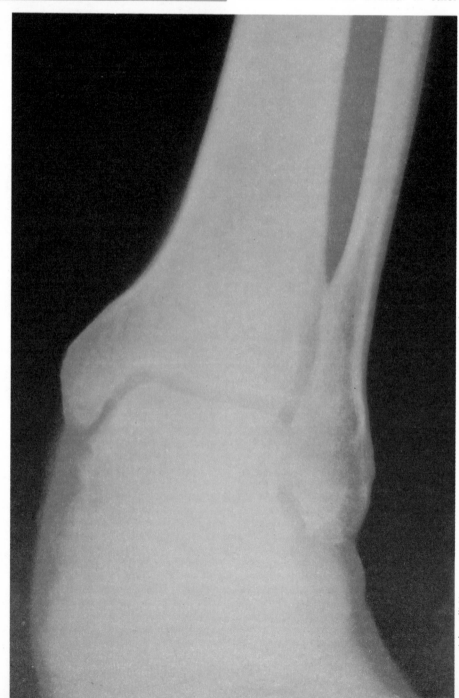

344

© James Webb

Wrist and hand section showing synovial joints

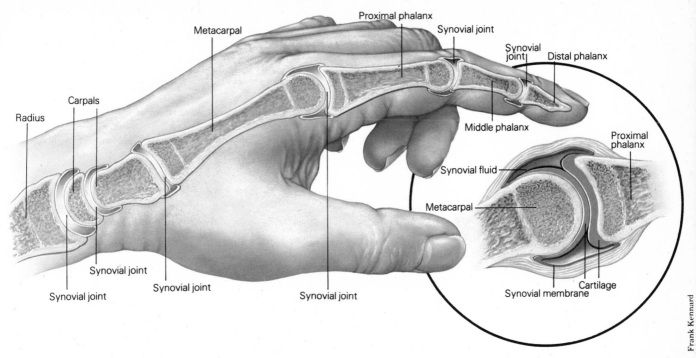

Frank Kennard

The hand contains numerous synovial joints; it is easy to see how, in severe cases of rheumatoid arthritis, deterioration of the affected joints can result in crippling deformities of the fingers and wrist.

forms of arthritis. By doing a blood test the amount of rheumatoid factor in the blood can be measured and this forms the basis for a simple test which can be performed to see if a patient has the disease.

Rheumatoid nodules are lumps which may occur over the elbows or on the backs of the hands and feet. They are composed of collections of inflamed cells similar to those seen within the joints and if present are a further aid to diagnosis.

Symptoms

Pain, swelling and stiffness of the affected joints are the main symptoms of rheumatoid arthritis. Characteristically the small joints of the hands and feet – for example the knuckle joints and the balls of the feet – are affected first, but other joints may become involved, particularly the wrists, knees, ankles, elbows, shoulders and eventually the hip joints. The number of joints affected depends on the severity of the disease which may vary enormously from one individual to another.

A characteristic feature that distinguishes this form of arthritis from others is the symmetry of the disease; that is, if a joint on one side of the body is affected then the same joint on the other side is usually involved. This is called a sym-metrical polyarthritis and is typical of rheumatoid arthritis particularly when the disease occurs in a young to middle-aged woman.

Usually the stiffness that occurs in the joints is most pronounced first thing in the morning on rising and it may last for varying lengths of time – from a few minutes to a few hours. This is often accompanied by a general feeling of malaise and tiredness which reflects the fact that the disease affects the whole body and is not confined to a particular area. The patient will experience difficulty in gripping things such as a cup or eating utensils because of the stiffness in their hands. Dressing, particularly doing up buttons, may also become a problem and in addition the patient begins to ex-perience pain in the affected joints.

As well as joint symptoms, patients may complain of symptoms which relate to other organ systems, although this is unusual. One of the commonest of these involves the eyes and the usual complaints are of soreness and redness resulting from inflammation in the various parts of the eye.

Symptoms will characteristically fluctuate so that they are much worse at certain times without there being any obvious reason for this.

Dangers and complications

The complications and dangers of the disorder relate largely to the joints; through incorrect use and positioning during acute stages, deformity may develop

---

Rheumatoid arthritis

Cause	Unknown	
Symptoms	Joint pain Joint swelling Early morning stiffness Generally unwell	Mainly involves the small joints of the hands and feet
Treatment	**Medical** Anti-inflammatory drugs (for example aspirin) Injections of gold salts Penicillamine	**Rehabilitation:** Physiotherapy Occupational therapy

Q I have rheumatoid arthritis and am worried that I may pass this on to my children. Is this likely to happen?

A Rheumatoid arthritis is not inherited directly and it is most unlikely that your children will get the disease, although it is possible. There is a slight tendency for members of the same family to develop rheumatoid arthritis, although it is not the disease itself that is inherited, but rather a susceptibility to develop the disease when exposed to the cause.

Q Are people with rheumatoid arthritis allowed to drive?

A Certainly! Even those who find it difficult because they are more severely disabled can usually learn to cope with a car that has been adapted for people with a disability.

Q Is there any chance that rheumatoid arthritis is an infectious disease?

A This is a debatable point. And many people believe that rheumatoid arthritis is caused by a bacterial or viral infection in a susceptible individual. While some bacteria and viruses certainly can cause arthritis none have been isolated as being the cause of rheumatoid arthritis. It is not a contagious disease however and there is no danger that you could catch it from someone else.

Q Why are splints sometimes provided for patients with rheumatoid arthritis?

A Splinting of a joint prevents excessive movement and enables a joint to be rested in the best position possible, thus preventing deformities which may arise if it is in the wrong position.

Such splints are usually used during acute phases of the disease when the joints are actively inflamed and need resting. Splints however can also be useful in preventing pain by inhibiting movement at a painful joint. Thus working splints which can be strapped on to the wrist are often very useful to people who would otherwise experience some discomfort when carrying out everyday chores.

leading to loss of use of the affected part. A patient may thus develop contractions of a joint resulting in limited movement and function. Alternatively the joint may become unstable owing to the destruction of the ligaments and this may result in its dislocation.

In addition to these specific joint complications, the involvement of other organs in the body may complicate the picture further. In particular patients with rheumatoid arthritis are more liable to infections generally, especially chest infections and bacterial infections of the joints. Other complications relating to the loss of function may also arise, so that the patient has difficulty carrying out normal physical movements.

Treatment

The treatment of rheumatoid arthritis requires making a close assessment of the problems of each individual patient and planning an appropriate programme of treatment to meet his or her needs. The usual approach involves prescribing a pain-killing drug such as aspirin or a closely related compound that has the same or a similar effect.

These compounds act by their anti-inflammatory action which reduces the inflammation present in the synovial membranes of the joints and leads to a reduction of pain and swelling because of the improvement in function. Many patients will find that these tablets alone are sufficient to enable them to overcome their pain and continue to lead a relatively normal life.

Anti-inflammatory drugs therefore form the 'first line' of treatment and may be combined with appropriate physiotherapy. If the disease begins to take a relentlessly progressing course (usually shown on X-rays as increasing destruction of bone) then it may well be necessary to begin 'second line' therapy. This usually involves using slightly more toxic drugs which have been shown to slow or halt the progress of the disease.

movement and also helps to prevent joint deformities. In addition patients may be trained by the therapists to perform everyday activities such as dressing, cooking and washing. The therapists will also provide aids where necessary. These enable patients to deal with many essential tasks much more easily.

Coping

As in any chronic or long-lasting disorder the patient often has to learn to accept and live with their disability to a certain extent. However with modern methods of treatment combined with physiotherapy and occupational therapy most problems should be surmountable, and advice should be sought from the family or hospital doctor if and when problems arise that the patient cannot cope with.

Patients should be practical wherever possible in order to make life easier for themselves. Thus they may have to choose larger and wider shoes than normal in order to be comfortable and they

The wide range of aids available for people with rheumatoid arthritis (above and left) make everyday tasks somewhat easier. They play an important part in allowing patients to retain their independence.

Microscopic slide (right) showing cells of the synovial membrane. The presence of inflamed cells, or lymphocytes, is a characteristic of rheumatoid arthritis.

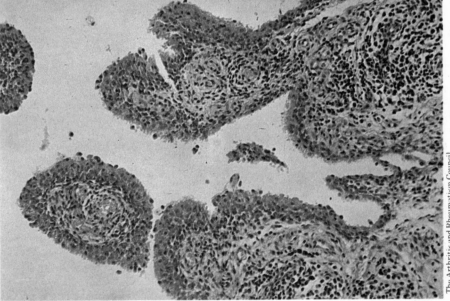

Such compounds include gold salts and penicillamine, the former usually given as weekly, fortnightly or monthly injections. Penicillamine is taken in tablet form. Both of these compounds seem to modify the disease and in some individuals may even stop it completely. However they can have serious side-effects which involve the kidneys and the blood and it is for this reason that most patients given these compounds have weekly blood and urine tests. In this way abnormalities induced by the drugs can be detected early before any serious damage is done and the drug can then be stopped.

In a few patients even these second line drugs are ineffective and so 'third line' drugs may be used. The most common of these is prednisolone, a steroid compound with anti-inflammatory effects. While these are often extremely effective in reducing the joint inflammation and associated symptoms they do have side-effects if taken over long periods and therefore are best avoided if possible.

In most cases of rheumatoid arthritis the disease can be controlled by one or a combination of these tablets and research continues in order to find more effective drugs with fewer side-effects.

Surgery can be useful as an addition to drug therapy. Occasionally the inflamed joint lining (the synovial membrane) is removed, although the effect of this operation, called synovectomy, is not permanent and the problem will recur.

Joint deformities may be improved by operations such as repair of the tendons and ligaments around the involved joints. The most important type of surgery now done is replacement of the diseased joints by artificial joints, particularly the hips, knees and knuckle joints.

Both physiotherapy and occupational therapy also play a major part in the treatment of rheumatoid arthritis. Exercise maintains muscle strength and joint

may have to forgo the pleasures of stylish footwear. Clothing may have to be loose to allow more freedom of movement; modifications may be necessary in the home to make life easier; and in some cases bungalow or ground floor flat accommodation may be more desirable than a house with stairs.

Outlook

The outlook for patients suffering from rheumatoid arthritis is now good in general, and with research continuing into the mechanisms of the disease and improved ways of treating it, the outlook for the future is not only promising, it is extremely encouraging.

347

Ringworm

Q I remember that when I was young children often had to be kept in isolation for months, and also had to have their heads shaved because of ringworm. Why is it that this never seems to happen nowadays?

A This type of suffering, which was once commonplace, has now been prevented because of an antibiotic called griseofulvin. This drug, which is taken by mouth, is effective in curing stubborn ringworm of the scalp which resists local treatment with creams. Despite this, however, children with ringworm should still be kept away from school while they are infected to avoid spreading the infection.

Q I have had recurring athlete's foot for years, but now I notice with alarm that one of my toe-nails has become very gnarled and odd-looking. Is there any connection and what can I do?

A The ringworm fungus that causes athlete's foot can also lodge itself and grow underneath the toe-nail, eventually leading to the kind of condition you describe. You should seek prompt medical attention for this problem before it spreads any further or you may lose the nail completely.

Q Why was it that when I had a ringworm infection my doctor told me I should lose weight?

A The reason for this is that overweight people have more folds in their skin, and it is in these folds that ringworm fungi can thrive. Being overweight is a health hazard for all sorts of reasons, and losing weight should help you in many ways apart from helping to prevent ringworm.

Q Why is it that wearing nylon underwear in summer always gives me an itchy infection in the vaginal area and in my groin?

A The combination of a warm, enclosed atmosphere and the retention of sweat, which has no chance to evaporate, add up to ideal conditions for the growth of the fungi that cause ringworm.

Ringworm is a contagious fungal infection which affects the feet, nails, scalp or groin. Fortunately, even severe cases of the condition respond well to treatment.

Paul Windsor

To prevent the ringworm infection known as athlete's foot, it is important to dry the feet thoroughly after washing, particularly between the toes.

Ringworm is a common skin disease whose name is somewhat misleading. This condition has nothing to do with worms and certainly does not always manifest itself in the shape of a ring. It is, in fact, caused by a contagious infection of the body with one of a variety of fungi. The areas of the body most likely to be affected are the feet, nails, scalp, armpits, genital areas and groin.

Wherever they become established, ringworm fungi work in the same sort of way. Feeding first on the dead tissues of the epidermis, the outermost layer of the skin, they then 'eat' their way into the living tissues beneath, producing a raised red ring or, alternatively, an extensive sloughing off of the skin which leads to a greying, scaly appearance. The exact symptoms of ringworm vary with the area of the body infected, but itching, which may be very intense, is a symptom common to all types.

Areas of infection

Ringworm of the scalp is the condition that helped give the disease its name. This is because the fungus usually grows outwards in a ring, and as the inner area begins to heal up, the red, itchy area spreads in a circle of ever-increasing diameter. As this spreading takes place, the hairs in the centre snap off and leave

a stubble overlying the scaly skin. As the skin heals in the centre of the ring, new hairs begin to grow, giving the scalp an even more mottled appearance. Ringworm of the scalp is usually due to an infection by the microsporum fungus. It is particularly common in childhood and spreads rapidly through schools.

The fungus that usually infects the feet is called trichophyton and causes the common condition known as athlete's foot (see page 46). The infection usually begins between the toes, starting as small blisters and spreading out to form large red areas. Sometimes the soles of the feet may be infected too, leading to scaly grey areas and flaking off of dead skin. Athlete's foot, which spreads rapidly through direct contact via the floors of bathrooms and changing rooms, can be irritatingly itchy and painful. And there is also a risk that infective bacteria may enter the skin and cause secondary infection if the skin surface becomes broken and living cells are exposed to the air.

Sometimes athlete's foot may spread to the toe-nails, causing them to become abnormally thickened and ridged. And

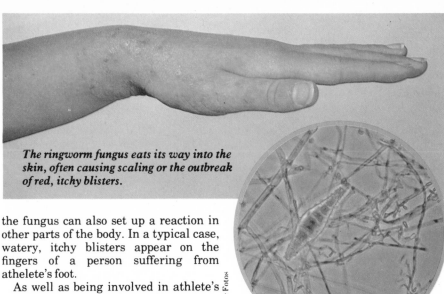

The ringworm fungus eats its way into the skin, often causing scaling or the outbreak of red, itchy blisters.

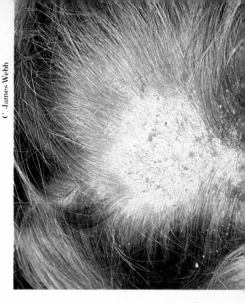

C. James Webb

the fungus can also set up a reaction in other parts of the body. In a typical case, watery, itchy blisters appear on the fingers of a person suffering from athelete's foot.

As well as being involved in athlete's foot infections, the nails are also prone to ringworm on their own account, either by the trichophyton fungus or by means of another closely related fungus called epidermophyton. The symptoms are similar to athlete's foot, but both toe- and finger-nails may be affected. In severe cases, the area of skin around the deformed nail may also be red and itchy.

The epidermophyton fungus also causes ringworm of the genital or groin areas, known as dhobie itch. Like the other ringworm fungi, this one thrives in

London Scientific Fotos

The microsporum fungus (above) causes ringworm of the scalp (above right). It grows outwards in a ring and gives the scalp a patchy appearance.

As a precaution against athlete's foot, swimmers often have to walk through a special foot-bath (below) before entering a public swimming pool.

damp, warm conditions, which explains why infection is most common in people who wear tight-fitting underwear and trousers. It is also a problem for the obese and is especially prevalent in men and women of all ages in hot weather when sweat becomes trapped in the groin area.

Treatment and prevention

The exact treatment of ringworm depends on the site of the infection and the infecting fungus. For athlete's foot there are various anti-fungal powders, creams and sprays available. For these to be effective, however, their application must be combined with rigorous attention to foot hygiene and thorough drying of the feet, particularly between the toes. Similar chemical remedies can be effective in treating ringworm of the nails, but in severe cases, the antibiotic griseofulvin will be prescribed.

Ringworm of the scalp is also treated with griseofulvin, although mild cases may respond effectively to anti-fungal creams. As with athlete's foot, ringworm of the scalp demands close attention to hygiene. The scalp must be washed and dried regularly, and all brushes, combs and towels sterilized. With dhobie itch, in addition to using anti-fungal preparations, cleanliness, thorough drying after washing and wearing sensible clothes are essential.

Although many of the anti-fungal ointments, powders and sprays for the local treatment of mild ringworm are available over the counter from pharmacies without a prescription, it is always wise to get medical advice if these prove ineffective. The doctor will be able to prescribe stronger treatments, including antibiotics if necessary, and give useful advice on how to clear the problem up and prevent its recurrence. It is a wise precaution to ensure that anyone suffering from a ringworm infection does not share towels, combs or similar items with other members of the family.

Phil Babb

Salmonella

Q **Is it true that you can always kill all the salmonellae in a piece of meat by cooking it?**

A Yes, as a general rule this is true. Most of the salmonellae are very sensitive to the effects of heat so that cooking for four minutes at a temperature above 60°C (165.6°F) will kill nearly all varieties.

However there are two snags to this. First there is the problem that apparently adequate cooking of foods like sausages or pieces of meat may leave the middle almost uncooked so that the sort of temperatures required to ensure killing of salmonellae bacteria are never reached.

The second point is that food may be cooked properly so that no salmonellae could survive, but it may then be handled with infected utensils which re-infect the food and allow the salmonellae organisms to multiply.

Q **Does salmonella also infect animals?**

A Yes. In fact salmonella infects most common domestic animals and this leads to their being such an important form of food poisoning. It is solely salmonella typhi, the organism responsible for causing typhoid fever, that only infects humans, and this is probably bound up with the fact that it causes such a different sort of illness. Poultry, followed by pigs, sheep and cattle are most commonly affected, and cross-infection of food can therefore occur very easily unless great care is taken about hygiene in all aspects of food preparation.

Q **Is it possible to get rid of salmonella which is in food by freezing it?**

A No. Salmonellae are not killed by ordinary domestic freezing, but they will stop growing while they are frozen. This means that if you put an infected piece of food in the freezer and then take it out to defrost, it will be just as badly poisoned as it was originally. For this reason it is essential to make sure that foods like chicken have been thoroughly cooked through after they have been frozen and then thawed out.

Food poisoning can have many different causes, but most frequently the culprit is one of the salmonellae bacilli. Good hygiene, and care in the storage and preparation of a wide variety of foods can prevent this condition.

Food poisoning is something that many of us experience at some time in our lives, and the bacteria responsible for causing it are often members of the salmonellae group. Although food poisoning can be quite a mild disease, it can occasionally be serious, particularly in babies. Typhoid, on the other hand, is nearly always serious, and this too is caused by one of the salmonellae bacteria.

Modern methods of hygiene and food preparation have considerably reduced the number of outbreaks of salmonella food poisoning, although the huge quantities of food that are now produced in factories and distributed to shops to be sold for eating unreheated have themselves created problems. Even tiny slips in hygiene can lead to big outbreaks of this common disease.

What are salmonellae?
The salmonellae are a group or family of small, rod-shaped bacteria – technically called bacilli. These are divided into two main groups. The first group are the typhoid organisms, salmonella typhi and the various types of salmonella paratyphi. These produce typhoid fever or, in the case of salmonella paratyphi, a disease very much like it called paratyphoid fever. The typhoid group of salmonellae only infect humans, and they are not caught from animals, except under very unusual circumstances.

The second group of salmonellae cause food poisoning. Nearly all infect more than one sort of animal, although they may be found in one species more commonly than in others. There are at least 1400 different types of these food poisoning salmonellae, but only a small number regularly cause any serious trouble in man. For typhoid organisms to spread there has to be some contamination of either food or water with in-

Don't be deceived by appearances: this chicken, which is raw inside, harbours salmonella. Only thorough cooking of a completely thawed bird will ensure that all the bacilli are completely destroyed.

Any salmonellae that survive the preparation of cooked meat will flourish and present a genuine health hazard.

Because cooked meat can be contaminated with bacilli from raw meat (inset), the two are kept separate in shops.

fected human faeces, but the situation is much more complicated in the case of the other sorts of infection, and food may become infected at almost any point along its journey from the farm to the table.

Spread of salmonella infection

Salmonellae always enter the body through the mouth. In the case of food poisoning, they then pass down through the stomach and into the intestines where they cause diarrhoea. Typhoid salmonellae also get into the bloodstream and the lymphatic system where they multi-

ply rapidly to give rise to the serious general illness that characterizes typhoid fever. This has an incubation period of between ten days and three weeks while food poisoning comes on within 48 hours of eating contaminated food.

Salmonellae live naturally in the intestines of a wide range of animals, including chickens, rats, cattle, frogs, birds – even elephants and camels. They may exist in one animal without causing any problems, and then infect another, eventually causing severe diarrhoea in humans. The fact that salmonella are so

common among domestic animals also leads to the high risk of food becoming contaminated.

Salmonellae are killed by being heated, so that freshly cooked food should be quite safe provided that it has been heated right through: cooking for four minutes at a temperature above 60°C (165.6°F) should be sufficient to kill nearly all varieties. Conversely, freezing does not kill these organisms; rather, it only inhibits their ability to grow. When food is re-cooked, the salmonellae then return to normal. This is why it is essential to take precautions with frozen food: make sure that you do not re-freeze meat without having cooked it right through, and do not allow any sort of contamination between the time you cook it and put it into the freezer.

Certain foods can be a serious risk. The first of these is chicken, although poultry in general seem to be particularly likely to harbour the disease. The poultry industry depends upon freezing for the storing and transport of the food, and in turn this has led to a great increase in the number of attacks of food poisoning due to salmonella. If the chicken meat becomes contaminated with intestinal contents during the process of preparation of the carcass for freezing, then the salmonella will have the chance to multiply while the meat is thawing. The salmonellae will be killed if the meat is thoroughly cooked, but this doesn't always happen, particularly if the chicken is cooked on a rotisserie. Also, if the chicken is not thawed fully, cooking will be insufficient to kill the salmonellae that are residing in the partially warmed inside.

Eggs, especially duck eggs, can also be infected, although this is probably quite rare in chicken eggs since they are nearly always cooked before eating. However, when eggs are made up into bulk food, problems can arise since one bad egg can infect the rest; all bulk eggs, particularly

Causes and symptoms of salmonella food poisoning

Organism	Host	Source of human infection	Symptoms
Salmonella typhimurium	Many different kinds of species, particularly cattle	Food infection, often when cooked food is contaminated by contact with uncooked meat	Can produce severe diarrhoea, leading to septicaemia (blood-poisoning) in some cases
Salmonella hadar and salmonella agona	Usually poultry	Cross-contamination of cooked meat, or contamination before freezing with inadequate heating through	Usually diarrhoea.
Salmonella cholerasuis	Pigs	Same as for typhimurium	Common in the Far East. Causes diarrhoea and, like typhimurium, may give septicaemia
Salmonella dublin	Cattle	Food contamination	Usually diarrhoea. Tends to cause disease in cattle much more than in humans

351

Q I read somewhere that the acid in your stomach destroys salmonella. If this is true, then why do people manage to get infected with it?

A It is certainly true that stomach acid provides an important barrier to infection. Food tends to stay in the stomach longer than liquids, so that infected drink may be a greater hazard than infected food. It also appears that people with no stomach acid as a result of either illness or an operation are more at risk of being infected.

Q I've heard that duck eggs are very likely to give you salmonella. Is this correct?

A Yes. Of all foods, duck eggs are perhaps the most likely to be carrying salmonella. However, just because an egg is infected doesn't mean that you'll become ill since the salmonellae are destroyed by heat.

Q I thought that vegetables and salads were to blame for most food poisoning. Is this true?

A No, this is certainly not the case in developed countries like Great Britain. Elsewhere in the world, vegetables and salads may be a source of salmonella if they have become infected either as a result of an infected water supply or as a result of manuring with raw faeces – often human faeces. If you are abroad and catering for yourself, you should wash your vegetables only in water that you know to be clean and uncontaminated. Similarly, fruits that have been washed and peeled are also safe to eat.

Q Is it true that food poisoning is worse for children and babies than for adults?

A Yes. Any cause of diarrhoea in babies can be very serious: because they have so little extra fluid in their bodies, babies can collapse and die from dehydration that much earlier. In the world as a whole, food poisoning and other causes of diarrhoea are by far the commonest causes of death in previously healthy babies. It is extremely important to seek help if your baby gets diarrhoea, and keep up his or her fluid intake.

Idyllic – or potentially dangerous? Salmonellae live naturally in the intestines of animals, leading to cross-contamination. This may lead to infection in humans.

powdered eggs, should be heated.

Cooked and prepared meat are serious risks if strict hygiene is not observed. A pie or slice of cooked meat is an ideal place for the organism to grow if it has survived manufacture, and there is always the risk that it will be contaminated with a bit of infected raw meat while in the shop. The raw meat probably won't cause any trouble, since however heavily contaminated it is, the salmonellae in it are likely to be destroyed during cooking.

Carriers
Some people can become carriers of salmonella. Although this is actually more common with the typhoid and paratyphoid salmonellae, it can also happen with food poisoning organisms. If the salmonella carrier also happens to be a food handler, then there is a great risk of passing on the infection. When carriers pass on the disease, it is often through cakes and cream-containing products – ideal places for the organisms to grow.

Symptoms
The main symptom of salmonella food poisoning is diarrhoea, which is often accompanied by pain in the abdomen. There may be a little vomiting, but this is not often severe. In a few cases some of the organisms may spread through into the bloodstream and cause the sort of feverish illness that typhoid causes; however this is rare. Occasionally there may be an infection in odd places like the membranes of the brain (meningitis) or an infection in the bone (osteomyelitis).

Treatment and outlook
There is no really effective treatment for salmonella food poisoning. Medicines to

TAKE CARE
Preventing food poisoning

● Defrost chicken completely, then make sure to cook it through
● If reheating meat, be sure that it is cooked thoroughly
● Boil all eggs, especially duck eggs
● Ensure that manufactured foods such as sausages and pies are well cooked
● Keep all perishable foods refrigerated
● Never leave open tins of food in the refrigerator
● Never let raw meat come into contact with cooked meat
● Cover any food that is left out so that flies can't get at it
● Know the source of your fish, especially shellfish
● Wash your hands after going to the lavatory, before cooking and during cooking. Wash hands and utensils if you're handling raw and cooked meat
● If you get food poisoning, do not handle other people's food: this is especially important if you are in the catering trade

stop the diarrhoea such as kaolin mixture or codeine phosphate tablets are often given; though it is possible that damping down of the normal movements of the intestines (peristalsis) may lead to the infecting salmonella becoming established in the intestinal wall and so prolong the infection. Antibiotics are usually ineffective, and may even be dangerous as they suppress the growth of the normal bacteria that live in the intestine, which can in turn allow the salmonella to thrive, making the disease worse. Experiments have suggested that people are more likely to be carriers if the infection is treated with antibiotics.

The only useful treatment is probably bed rest and drinking plenty of fluids: recovery from food poisoning usually takes place in a day or two.

Salpingitis

Inflammation of the Fallopian tubes often responds well to antibiotics, but a severe case can cause infertility. Any infection in a woman's reproductive organs should therefore be treated immediately.

Q Is it possible to tell if the Fallopian tubes have been blocked by salpingitis?

A Yes, there are three main tests that can be done. However it is important that they are done after the infection has been cured, otherwise they may make the infection worse. One test is called a hysterosalpingogram; this involves X-ray screening to see if a dye that has been injected through the cervix will spill out of both Fallopian tubes into the abdominal cavity, or whether the tube is obstructed.

A test called a tubal insufflation may be done. This involves passing carbon dioxide through the cervix and noting any rise in gas pressure which will indicate blocked tubes. Finally, an instrument called a laparoscope may be used to look directly into the womb, ovaries and tubes. A blue dye can be injected through the cervix at the same time which will spill out of the Fallopian tubes if they are open.

Q Is salpingitis always caused by venereal disease?

A No, there are many causes; but two of the micro-organisms that cause venereal disease can cause salpingitis. The first is gonococcus, gonorrhoea; the second chlamydia trachomatis, cause of NSU (non-specific urethritis).

Q Why are women who have had an abortion slightly more likely to get salpingitis?

A During an abortion it is possible to introduce infection already present at the neck of the womb into the womb itself, and this may then spread to the Fallopian tubes. Most clinics now check for infection and treat any that is present before performing the abortion. Another problem is that the lining of the womb is raw and becomes more easily infected, especially if any tissue from the pregnancy is left behind to form a base on which infection can grow. Should a woman start to get pain or heavy bleeding after an abortion, she should see her doctor immediately as prompt treatment with antibiotics may be necessary to prevent salpingitis.

Salpingitis is a major gynaecological problem. It means inflammation of the Fallopian tubes (the oviducts), the tubes that the eggs normally pass through on their way to the womb and where fertilization of the egg occurs. It is thought that the inflammation is caused by bacteria, but doctors can usually only isolate bacteria from about half of the Fallopian tubes that they examine.

Chronic and acute conditions

Salpingitis is usually described as acute or chronic. During acute salpingitis the Fallopian tubes become congested with blood and so look deep red and swollen. Later they may return to normal or they may release a sticky secretion. This can either stick the walls of the tubes together and block them, or make the tubes stick to other structures in the abdominal cavity such as the bowel.

The Fallopian tubes can also swell into a bag of pus which occasionally will burst, causing severe inflammation to spread throughout the abdominal cavity. Fortunately this is very rare. It is more common for the pus in the tube to be replaced by a clear, watery fluid so that the Fallopian tube becomes a thin-walled, mis-shapen structure distended with fluid, rather than the normal tubular structure down which an egg can pass.

It is not uncommon for a woman to have an attack of salpingitis and completely recover, so that her ability to conceive and have a normal pregnancy is unaffected.

Zefa

Normal and infected Fallopian tubes

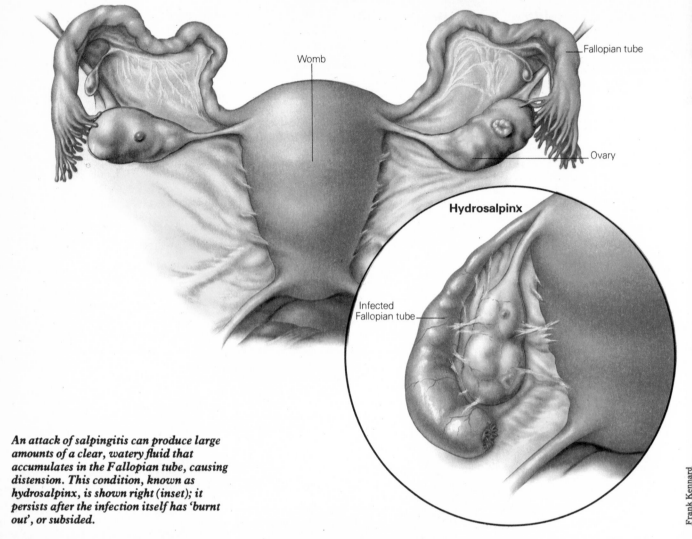

Womb

Fallopian tube

Ovary

Hydrosalpinx

Infected
Fallopian tube

Frank Kennard

An attack of salpingitis can produce large amounts of a clear, watery fluid that accumulates in the Fallopian tube, causing distension. This condition, known as hydrosalpinx, is shown right (inset); it persists after the infection itself has 'burnt out', or subsided.

Chronic salpingitis may follow acute salpingitis. In this case the inflammation decreases but never completely disappears. The chronic condition may also be a result of continuous mild inflammation which never becomes severe enough to damage the tubes seriously.

Because there is a rich supply of lymph channels between the Fallopian tubes, infection in one tube nearly always travels to the tube on the other side of the uterus.

Causes of infection

The Fallopian tubes may become infected by bacteria carried in the blood. This was commonly the case in the past when some women contracted tuberculosis in their tubes. Today it is more usual for the infection to spread directly from the vagina or the uterus. For example gonococci, the micro-organisms responsible for gonorrhoea, may be introduced into the vagina by a woman's partner during sexual intercourse and then spread up the genital tract to the Fallopian tubes. Infection may also enter the Fallopian tubes after childbirth, an abortion or a miscarriage, causing inflammation in both the vagina and the tubes.

Finally, there may also be a spread of infection from a nearby abdominal organ, for example from an infected appendix.

It is probable that the increase in sexual freedom, together with the large number of abortions performed today have increased the risk of women contracting salpingitis. It is also known that women who are fitted with an intra-uterine contraceptive (IUD) are at slightly greater risk of developing salpingitis. This may be because some of the threads attached to the earlier types of IUD were capable of acting as a wick along which bacteria from the vagina could travel further. Today, intra-uterine devices are fitted with monofilament nylon threads which do not act as a wick and therefore are much safer.

Symptoms

Women with acute salpingitis often have an unpleasant vaginal discharge and a slightly raised temperature. They develop pain in the lower part of the abdomen which gradually increases in severity. They feel generally unwell and may notice that coughing or laughing makes the pain worse. If they attempt sexual intercourse during this time they usually find it greatly increases the pain and may actually be impossible.

In cases of chronic salpingitis, women may previously have experienced the above symptoms, but these may have settled to a dull ache in the lower part of the stomach. This occasionally gets slightly worse, especially if the woman is constipated. The dull ache may also get worse when the woman has her periods.

Treatment

If possible, it is important to find which bacteria are causing the inflammation so

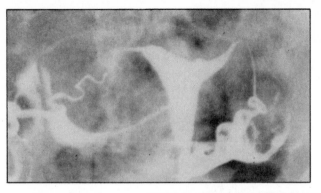

By doing a special test, a hysterosalpinogram, doctors can usually tell if the Fallopian tubes are open or blocked. The X-ray of the abdominal cavity (left) was taken after a dye had been injected into the cervix. The dye has spilled out of the tubes, indicating that they are open.

In this X-ray (right) there is no spilling of the dye into the tube on the left which is very enlarged and completely blocked. Only some of the dye has flowed through the tube on the right. These changes have taken place because of serious inflammation of the Fallopian tubes.

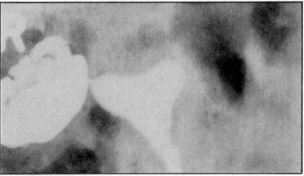

that the most effective antibiotic can be prescribed. In doing this it is assumed that the same bacteria are also present in the lower genital tract, and bacterial swabs are therefore taken from the urethra, vagina and cervix to try and culture them in the laboratory. In some hospitals, doctors also look at the Fallopian tubes through an instrument called a laparoscope and take bacterial swabs directly from the tubes. In cases of acute salpingitis a laproscopy is normally only done if there is genuine doubt about the exact diagnosis.

Women with acute salpingitis always require pain-killing tablets or injections as well as plenty of rest and a correctly prescribed course of the appropriate antibiotic drug.

Chronic salpingitis is usually treated with frequent courses of antibiotics. Deep heat treatment is also sometimes used in conjunction with the medication. This increases the blood supply to the area which helps the antibiotics to reach the infected tissue. Unfortunately, this condition can be very difficult to cure and women may suffer recurrent discomfort for years.

Dangers of salpingitis
Many women who have salpingitis make complete recoveries but there are many possible consequences of the condition. A woman may become infertile because the tubes are so severely damaged that the eggs are no longer able to meet and be fertilized by sperm.

When damage is less severe the egg may be fertilized in the tube but will not

travel on to implant in the womb; instead it implants in the damaged tube. This condition is called an ectopic pregnancy and both the embryo and the tube must be surgically removed.

The sticky secretion released from an infected tube can make the bowel become attached to the tubes. This can give a patient discomfort, especially if she is constipated. The ovaries, which normally float in the pelvis, can also become stuck down behind the womb. These are always tender when touched; usually during sexual intercourse they move and so avoid pressure, but after salpingitis this may no longer be the case. As the ovaries may be exceptionally tender, sex becomes uncomfortable. Finally, the woman may be left with small areas of infected tissue that can occasionally spread and cause further pain.

Outlook
The outlook for salpingitis depends on the severity of the attack and how promptly it is treated. Attempts have been made to treat some of the complications already mentioned but at present they are not always successful. For example, it is sometimes possible to operate to unblock Fallopian tubes. It is also possible to re-mobilize ovaries which are stuck behind the uterus and cause pain on intercourse.

The best chance of managing salpingitis in the future may be to prevent it occurring by early treatment of vaginal infections and the careful screening of women for infection before they are given abortions.

Sarcoma

Q Does sarcoma mean the same thing as a tumour?

A A sarcoma is just a particular type of tumour, of which there are many. It is a malignant tumour, that is, it can spread to other parts of the body. Unlike the more common type of malignant tumour – a carcinoma – a sarcoma arises in the connective body tissue.

Q I have often heard of cancer referred to as a 'carcinoma', but never as a 'sarcoma'. Are sarcomas very common?

A No. Compared with other malignant tumours, such as a carcinoma of the breast or lung, sarcomas are very uncommon indeed. Sometimes they appear to be just like a carcinoma when they are first discovered, and it is only when the tumour has been removed and examined under a microscope that it can be diagnosed as a sarcoma.

Q What sort of person develops sarcomas, and are there any factors, such as smoking, which may cause them?

A Sarcomas occur in a much younger age group than do other types of malignant tumour. They can, therefore, occur in children, and in early adulthood. Unlike a carcinoma of the lung, for example, there is no evidence that smoking increases the incidence of sarcomas, and no other risk factors have been implicated.

Q Is surgery the only treatment which is used for sarcomas?

A No, surgery is not the only type of treatment available, although, wherever possible, it is the preferred course of action. Because these tumours appear to spread into the bloodstream early on in their course, there is a high proportion of cases where patients already have secondary tumours in other parts of the body when they first go to see a doctor, and surgery may not be recommended. There have been many cases of successful treatment of these secondary tumours using cytotoxic drugs, and occasionally using X-ray treatment.

A sarcoma is a form of cancer affecting the body's connective tissue. It has the ability to spread rapidly, but fortunately this type of tumour is not very common.

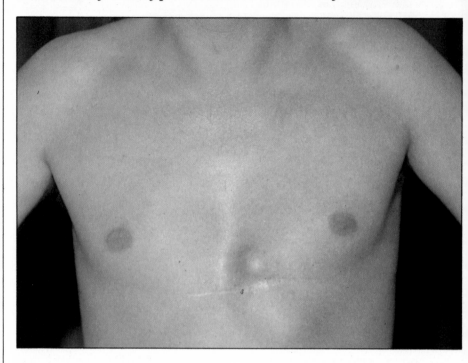

The fleshy malignant tumour, known as a sarcoma, appears here as a lump on the chest. Treatment will involve surgery or the use of special anti-cancer drugs.

A sarcoma is a certain type of malignant tumour. Its name comes from the Greek word meaning 'flesh', because many of these tumours are fleshy in nature.

The body tissues are divided broadly into epithelium, which is the tissue that forms lining membranes, and connective tissue, which is the tissue that makes up the main substance of the body, and includes muscles, bone, fibrous tissue and fat. Malignant tumours which arise from the epithelium are known as carcinomas, and malignant tumours which arise from the connective tissue are known as sarcomas. All these tumours have the potential for spreading to other parts of the body, and as such can be called cancers (see pp 74-79).

Types of sarcoma

As a group of tumours, sarcomas are far less common than carcinomas, and tend to affect a much younger age group. Different sarcomas present different problems depending on their exact anatomical location; they can occur anywhere there is muscle, bone, fibrous tissue, fat or lymph tissue.

A typical sarcoma is in the bone – an osteosarcoma – and commonly occurs at the lower end of the femur, or thigh bone. The patient, who may well be in his or her late teens or early twenties, will first notice a dull pain in the bone. Eventually the pain becomes more severe, and a lump becomes apparent.

Treatment

The main treatment of a sarcoma is surgical removal wherever possible. In the treatment of an osteosarcoma, however, at the lower end of the femur, it may be necessary to amputate the leg. Of course, other sarcomas in more superficial parts of the limb may be removable without a radical operation.

If a sarcoma spreads, it usually does so via the bloodstream, so that secondary growths may occur in the lungs or the liver. When this happens, it is obviously not possible to perform further surgery. In this case, the patient would nowadays be treated with special drugs known as cytotoxic drugs. These drugs work by killing cells which are rapidly dividing, such as tumour cells. Some of them are given as a course of injections, and some are given as tablets. There are now many cases of patients who had widespread sarcomas and have been successfully treated with these cytotoxic drugs.

Scabies

An infection of the skin caused by mites, scabies produces a highly irritating rash. Fortunately it can be easily cured.

Q I had scabies and treated myself with the prescribed lotion following my doctor's instructions. I still have an itchy rash What should I do?

A The irritation from scabies may take a week or two to subside. Some of the allergic symptoms may linger even after the mites have been killed. Occasionally a new treatment may be necessary either because you have caught a fresh infection or the original was inadequately treated. On the whole a new treatment is only advised if evidence of fresh scabies mites can be seen.

Q Do animals have anything to do with spreading scabies?

A Only human mites cause scabies in humans. The mites can live on animal skin, but survive only a short time, so that animals are not an important factor in the spread of scabies. Animal mites cause mange in animals and can occasionally produce a scabies-like rash in humans. In Britain, dog mites sometimes infect children so a dog with mange could perhaps cause scabies in certain cases.

Q My son has scabies and the doctor says the whole family has to be treated. No one else has any symptoms, so why is this necessary?

A The itchy rash of scabies may take a week or so to develop after the original mite infection. It is therefore more sensible to treat all the family and any other close contacts on the suspicion that they may have caught the infection, rather than leave them to develop scabies. If they are not treated, such close contacts may even re-infect the person who has just been cured. Therefore your whole family should be treated together.

Q Is it true that there is currently a scabies epidemic in Britain?

A Yes. These epidemics seem to recur globally about every 15 years. Thus there was an outbreak in the late 1940s and again in the 1960s, recurring now in the '80s.

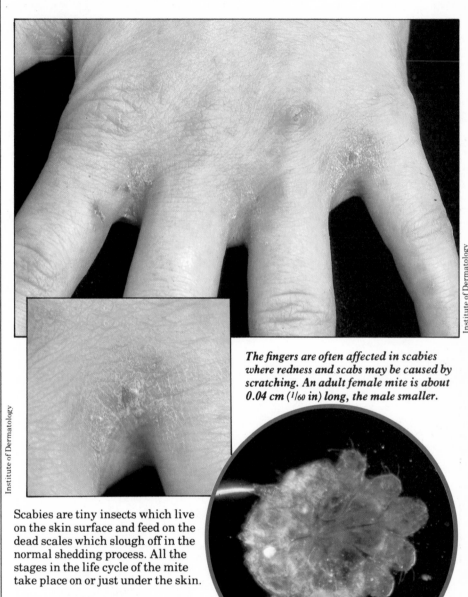

Institute of Dermatology

The fingers are often affected in scabies where redness and scabs may be caused by scratching. An adult female mite is about 0.04 cm (1/60 in) long, the male smaller.

C. James Webb

Scabies are tiny insects which live on the skin surface and feed on the dead scales which slough off in the normal shedding process. All the stages in the life cycle of the mite take place on or just under the skin.

How scabies is caused
When breeding, the fertilized female mite digs a burrow in the surface layers of the skin and lays her eggs along the tunnel. The female then dies but the eggs subsequently hatch into larvae. These eat their way out of the burrow to the surface again, where they mature into new adult mites after several days.

In the course of this maturation they often transfer to other humans, or even animals, who come into close enough contact for migration to occur. In practice, they do not live long on animals or clothing, so this means of transmission is relatively uncommon. They are most commonly spread by close personal contact, such as when sharing a bed.

When the mites have matured, they mate, and though the male soon dies, the female goes through the breeding cycle, thus perpetuating the infection. The whole cycle, from the time that eggs are laid to the maturation of fresh mites, takes about two weeks.

Symptoms

There are no symptoms until the females start their reproductive burrows, which are dug most frequently on the hands and wrists. They usually appear as a thin red line between the fingers, and this virtually clinches a diagnosis. The elbows, feet, ankles, penis, scrotum and nipples are also common sites for burrows. They are rarely found on the chest and back, and mites seem to avoid the head altogether. The burrows may itch, or may pass unnoticed even after the larvae have hatched into new mites.

After a few weeks the body develops an allergic response to the insects' repeated burrowing, and this shows itself in a generalized skin rash consisting of red itchy spots and blotches. The itching is the worst problem and leads to intense scratching, particularly at night and when the skin is warm. The skin may even bleed from being scratched so much and bacterial infection may then create a further complication. It is therefore sensible to seek treatment before the skin has been damaged too much.

The burrows continue to appear wherever a female is laying eggs. They are usually 0.5 – 1.5 cm (¹/₅-³/₅ in) in length and may be curved or S-shaped. The average female moves under the skin very slowly so that a new burrow can take up to a week to form. A clear little blister may appear at the end of the burrow where the female dies.

Diagnosis and treatment

Anyone suffering from scabies soon seeks medical help because of the irritation. By this stage the rash is a confusing picture of allergic patches of inflammation,

Life cycle of the mite

Adult male   Adult female

Adult female   Egg

Immature adult   Larva

The female mite lays her eggs under the skin. Each egg hatches into a larva which develops into an immature adult feeding on or just under the skin. After a few days it is fully mature and able to reproduce.

scratch marks and burrows. The diagnosis is confirmed by extracting a female mite from her burrow by means of a needle, and examining her appearance under magnification.

Once the diagnosis is certain, treatment is simple and effective. A lotion of benzyl benzoate or of gamma benzene hexachloride is used to kill the mites on the skin surface; provided re-infection is avoided all the symptoms will subside. The mites are quite resilient so the lotion must be left on the skin for some time. After a course of treatment has been correctly followed, the scabies should be cured although the allergic response of a red itchy rash may take several days to clear up completely.

Anyone who has been in close personal contact with an infected person should also be treated since the mites spread easily in this way. In the latent period between infection and the development of symptoms fresh mites may be released before the newly-infected contact has sought treatment. Therefore everyone in the family or household should be treated to prevent an outbreak.

Complications and outlook

Complications from scabies are rare and not serious. Secondary bacterial infection of the skin may occur where it has been damaged by scratching.

In people whose natural resistance to infection is low there may be very heavy infestations of mites, causing large outbreaks of scabies, for example in army camps. But even in these cases the treatment is effective and complications are an unusual development.

Provided that a correct diagnosis is made, the treatment is safe and works well so that the skin will soon return to normal. Fresh infections may be avoided by ensuring that all possible contacts are treated at the same time.

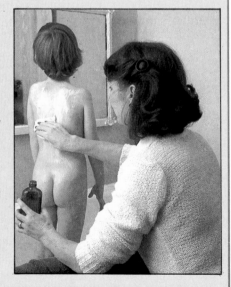

Treatment for scabies

- Take a hot bath and scrub the skin thoroughly
- Apply the lotion to all the skin except the head – mites do not attack the head and so will not survive there
- Take particular care to treat the areas most likely to be affected, including between the fingers, the elbows, genitals, feet and ankles
- Treat the areas which do not seem to be affected – mites may be present but no symptoms may yet have appeared
- Let the lotion dry and do not bathe for 24 hours. Repeat the treatment on three successive days
- Make fresh applications to the hands and feet if the original is washed off
- Take care that all clothes and bed linen that may have been contaminated are thoroughly laundered

Steve Bielschowsky

Scarlet fever

Once one of the most dreaded diseases of childhood, scarlet fever is now far less prevalent and its symptoms less severe. Prompt treatment with penicillin minimizes complications and leads to a complete cure.

Q In my grandfather's time, scarlet fever used to be a common cause of death among children, but nowadays you rarely hear about it. Is this because of the effect of antibiotics?

A No, although the disease is less of a problem than it used to be. It seems as though the streptococcus – the organism that causes the disease – is a lot less virulent: that is, it causes less serious symptoms. This change in the pattern of behaviour of the streptococcus began at the end of the last century, well before antibiotics were invented. Nobody knows why this change happened.

Q Is scarlatina the same as scarlet fever?

A Yes, it is. Some doctors used to use the word to describe mild cases of the disease, as this lessened the fear that many people had of the illness. However, scarlatina isn't a very useful term.

Q My grandmother used to say that you could always tell that a person had scarlet fever because there was a white line around the mouth. Is this really true?

A It is certainly true that there is often a pale area around the mouth in an otherwise red face: doctors call this circum-oral pallor. Although it is a sign that often occurs in scarlet fever, it is by no means specific to that disease, and you can often see it in measles, for example.

Q If I get scarlet fever, will I have to be isolated?

A No. In the old days you would have been rushed off to a fever hospital, but now 24 hours of penicillin will probably stop the streptococcus from causing an infection in anyone else.

Q Can you be vaccinated against scarlet fever?

A No. There are many different strains of streptococcus, and therefore a vaccine wouldn't necessarily protect you against the disease.

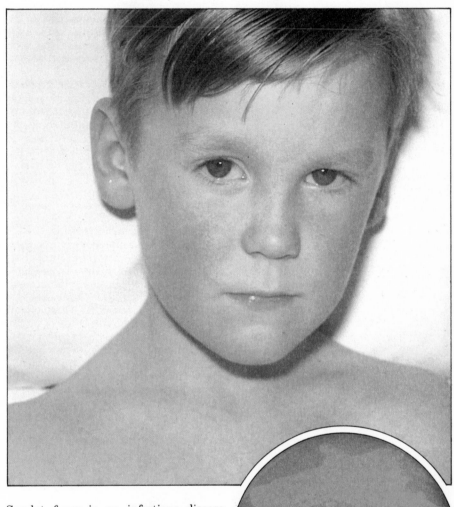

C. James Webb

Scarlet fever is an infectious disease which is caused by a bacterium. It is characterized by a sore throat and a red – if not actually scarlet – rash. Treatment with penicillin will prevent complications and effect a complete cure.

Causes

Scarlet fever is caused by the streptococcus pyogenes bacterium. To differentiate one type of bacterium from another, they are grown separately on bacteriological plates that contain blood.

Some types break down the blood, leaving a clear ring around the little colonies of bacteria. This is called haemolysis ('blood breaking'). The streptococcus pyogenes bacterium is a beta-haemolytic: this means it breaks down blood totally, leaving a clear halo around each colony.

The streptococcus pyogenes bacterium that causes scarlet fever is beta-haemolytic: it breaks down blood to leave a clear halo around its colonies (inset). The bacterium infects the throat, but its toxins produce symptoms throughout the body.

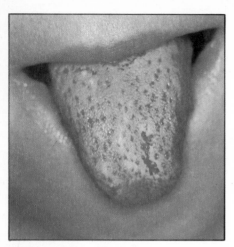

White 'strawberry' tongue is one of the early symptoms; later the tongue turns red.

berry tongue. As the exudate peels off, the tongue is left rather red and raw with its papillae still showing prominently to make it look like a strawberry. This is called red strawberry tongue.

One of the most typical and striking effects of the disease then occurs as the rash begins to fade. The skin starts to peel off and, in more serious cases, it may peel off in great sheets (desquamation). In the past it was not uncommon to see an entire cast of a hand in the form of dead skin, although nowadays such occurrences are extremely rare.

Although the disease is nearly always caught from a sore throat, there are other ways it can be communicated. It may enter the skin through a wound of some sort and in the past it was not uncommon to catch it as a result of infection entering through the womb or the vagina during childbirth.

Dangers

Infection can spread to the ears causing otitis media (middle ear infection) and to the lymph glands, producing a serious abscess-forming illness. Infection may also lodge in the nose: this is a trivial complication with little or no symptoms, but it can lead to the spread of the disease as a result of 'droplet infection' when one of the carriers sneezes.

Other problems are a result of the body's immune (defence) system having

Prompt treatment with penicillin has meant that the disease is no longer infectious after 24 hours. Isolation is not necessary; patients can be nursed at home.

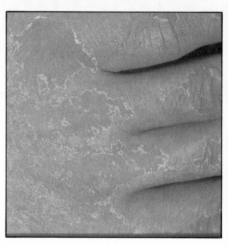

Once the rash fades, the skin on the hands will begin to peel off.

an abnormal response to the streptococcus and producing one of the two types of sensitivity reaction. The first is nephritis or Brights disease, where the kidneys become inflamed and the second is acute rheumatic fever, where a rash, joint pains and even heart damage may occur as a result of the body's sensitivity to the streptococcal toxins.

Treatment and outlook

Scarlet fever is treated with penicillin: this drug kills the bacteria in the throat and stops it producing the toxin that gives rise to the disease. Even minor cases are treated this way for, after 24 hours of penicillin, the organism is no longer infectious.

In doing so, it indicates that the streptococcus must be producing and excreting a toxic substance, since the bacterium is having an effect beyond the bounds of the colony itself. In fact it is the organism's ability to produce toxins that leads to scarlet fever, since the organism itself only infects the throat, but the effects of its toxins show up all over the body.

Symptoms

Scarlet fever usually starts within two to four days of incubation, but the limits of the incubation period are between one and seven days.

One of the most characteristic aspects of the disease is that it starts in a dramatic manner, with a sudden temperature accompanied by vomiting and a sore throat. At this stage the tonsils are infected, and have a whitish crust or exudate on them. Less serious infections don't cause vomiting, and nowadays the disease can be so mild that children don't even have a sore throat.

The day after the disease starts, the rash which gives it its name breaks out. This is a diffuse reddening of the skin caused by all the little blood vessels opening up. If you press down over an area of affected skin, the skin will whiten with the pressure. The rash starts on the face and then spreads down to affect the rest of the body. The farther away from the face it gets, the likelier it is to form actual spots rather than a uniform redness: these spots tend to be found on the legs and to a lesser extent on the hands. The rash usually lasts for about two or three days.

While the rash is appearing and then fading away, there are a series of changes that affect the tongue. First there is a creamy white exudate all over it with the tongue's little papillae pointing up through it. This is known as white straw-

Steve Bielschowsky

Sciatica

Sharp stabbing pains down the leg and difficulties in moving can be signs of sciatica. Fortunately, there are various forms of treatment for this common condition – but bed-rest is usually all that is required.

Q I get a lot of backache while doing my housework. Could I be suffering from sciatica?

A Sciatica is the name given to the type of back pain which radiates down the back of the leg. However, slipped discs may start with a pain only in the back before the disc starts pressing on the nerves to the leg – which causes sciatica. Most people with 'bad backs' do not have slipped discs but the ligaments and muscles in the back are strained.

Q A friend of mine had repeated attacks of sciatica and had an operation which seems to have relieved the problem. Would such treatment help my recently developed sciatica?

A If this is your first attack of sciatica, your doctor will probably not recommend an operation so long as he is quite confident that a slipped disc is the cause (which it usually is). Most people with sciatica find that it improves if they can rest their backs properly and for long enough.

Q My doctor has ordered a myelogram X-ray of my back because of my bad pain. Does this mean that he is worried that there might be some serious cause behind it?

A Probably not. If your doctor has ordered this test, he is probably doing so in order to locate the disc that is causing the pain. He then may seek advice as to whether an operation would help, or whether he ought to continue with the medical treatment.

Q How can I prevent another attack of sciatica now that I have at last recovered?

A There are quite a lot of simple things that you can bear in mind in order to protect your back from undue strain which might cause another disc to rupture. The most important thing is to avoid putting your back under any strain whatsoever when you lift objects or even bend down. Remember – always flex your knees when bending over.

Sciatica occurs most often as the result of 'slipped discs'. Although this condition may affect nerves in the arms and the legs, it is the particular pressure on certain nerves on their way to the back of the leg which causes the sharp, stabbing pain that is characteristic of sciatica. The pain may come on suddenly or more gradually, and may be recurrent if the discs between the vertebrae do not heal up.

The sciatic nerve

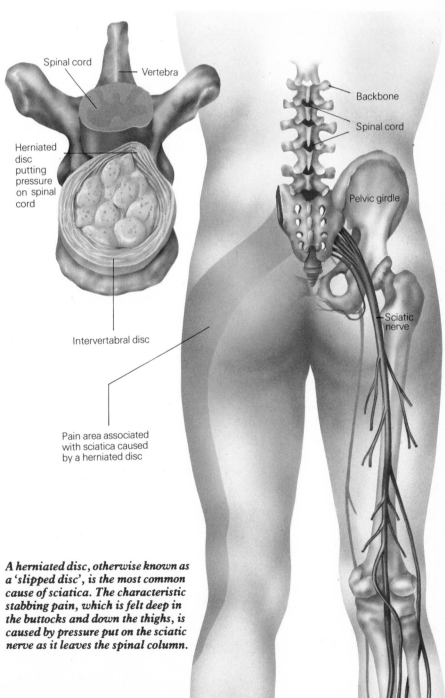

Spinal cord

Vertebra

Herniated disc putting pressure on spinal cord

Intervertabral disc

Pain area associated with sciatica caused by a herniated disc

Backbone

Spinal cord

Pelvic girdle

Sciatic nerve

A herniated disc, otherwise known as a 'slipped disc', is the most common cause of sciatica. The characteristic stabbing pain, which is felt deep in the buttocks and down the thighs, is caused by pressure put on the sciatic nerve as it leaves the spinal column.

Mick Saunders

To ascertain the cause of the sciatica and whether surgery will be necessary, a special X-ray, which uses radio-opaque dye, is performed. This X-ray, known as a myelogram (right), revealed a defect due to a protruding disc (extension) and a less noticeable blunting of the nerve roots (flexion). During the laminectomy, a large degenerate disc was removed (far right).

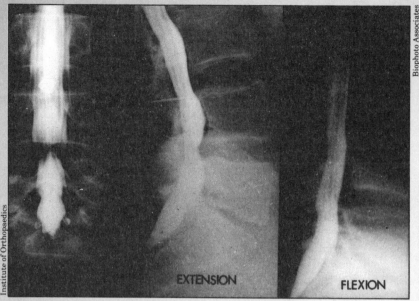

EXTENSION

FLEXION

Causes

Most people who suffer from sciatica do so because the discs in the backbone become weakened, either through age or as a result of excessive strain.

The discs are pads of tissue which separate the vertebrae – the cylinder-shaped bones which make up the spine. Together, the discs and vertebrae give the spine the necessary flexibility for us to stretch and bend. Each disc consists of a soft centre, which acts as a shock absorber, and a tough fibrous outer layer. With age, or sometimes as a result of excessive strain being applied to the back, this outer layer weakens in parts, allowing the soft centre to bulge out – a condition rather inaccurately known as a 'slipped disc'. It is this protrusion that puts pressure on the nerve to the leg and causes the pain of sciatica.

The same sort of pain can be caused by other diseases in the region of the nerve roots as they leave the spinal canal. These other diseases are very uncommon but have to be considered by the doctor when he or she is treating someone suffering from sciatica. For example, the nerve roots can be irritated by pressure from a tumour in the spine or from a collection of inflamed tissue, which may occur after injuries to the spine or following surgery. These other causes can be identified through examination and X-ray tests.

The effects

Pain low in the middle of the back is often the first thing that is noticed when the discs start to bulge out or 'slip'. This may happen suddenly during a bending or stretching action, or may come on more gradually during days of hard work such as doing housework, washing or lifting heavy objects. As the bulging disc presses on the nerves in the spinal canal, a sharper pain is felt going down the back of the leg into the foot. This is because the nerves most often pressed upon are those which form the major component of the sciatic nerve which supplies this part of the leg and foot. Most of the pain is usually felt deep in the buttock and the back of the thigh.

If the trouble gets worse, the slightest movement – even coughing or sneezing – will bring on or intensify these pains. Sitting for any length of time, particularly in a car, will be painful, as in this position the nerves being pressed upon are quite stretched and this makes the irritation worse. A doctor can test for this effect by lifting a patient's leg straight up while he or she is lying down. How far the doctor can lift the patient's leg, before pain occurs, indicates the severity of the irritation to the nerves.

As any movement may cause the pain to reappear, all a person with bad sciatica will want to do is to lie on his back with his knees bent to relieve the tension on the nerves to the leg. Walking may be especially difficult with tiredness and pulling pains developing often after quite a short distance.

Pressure on the nerve roots which causes the pain felt in sciatica can also produce other changes, some of which may be noticed by the sufferer, others may only be picked up by the doctor.

Often one or other of the reflexes in the leg becomes diminished as the nerve conducts its messages less well. This does not cause the patient any problem in its own right; it is, in fact, a useful symptom as it enables a doctor to know exactly which nerve is being affected. If the pressure is severe then some weakness may occur,

but this is uncommon with slipped discs. More often the sensation over the outer side of the foot may be diminished so that the skin feels slightly numb or some pins and needles may be felt in this area. This is because the nerve root involved in sciatica supplies this part of the leg.

Treatment

Sciatica due to a slipped disc, while very unpleasant on occasions, and often disabling when it occurs, will usually improve on its own if the proper measures are taken. The initial problem is to relieve the pain and this is most easily done by resting in bed in the position which is most comfortable. It may be helpful to have the shoulders raised a little with pillows to ease the curve on the lower back, since the muscles there will have gone into some spasm in response to the pain. All unnecessary movement must be avoided. If the spine is rested in this way for some time – and it can take several weeks – the disc will heal up and the protrusion which has caused the sciatic pain will be reabsorbed.

During the time that the pain is bad a doctor may prescribe painkillers, but so long as adequate rest can be provided for the back, ordinary analgesic drugs such

as aspirin or paracetamol are usually adequate. The crucial thing is to stay in bed and to resist the temptation to get up and about when the disc is only half healed or the whole process will return to square one. Often the harder the bed on which one rests the better, since soft beds encourage the spine to sag and therefore put more pressure on the discs between the vertebrae in the back. Once the sciatica has improved it is equally important to avoid putting undue strain on the back – and, of course *not* to lift heavy objects.

Surgical treatment of sciatica is reserved as a last resort. This measure is usually for those who have had repeated episodes of sciatica which have not improved with the ordinary treatment of bed-rest, and those who stand to lose a lot of ill-afforded time off work. However surgery can only be successfully performed on certain types of disc problem, so special X-rays of the spinal canal may need to be performed before a decision to operate can be made. The test, called a myelogram, consists of some special dye which shows on an X-ray being injected (via a lumbar puncture) into the fluid-filled space around the nerve roots. The X-rays taken then show up the shadow of the spinal cord and its nerve roots, and reveal the disc or whatever is causing the symptoms. From these pictures the doctor can see whether an operation is possible and how extensive it should be to solve the problem.

If the sciatica is being caused by a single disc bulging out, the protrusion can be removed. If there are a lot of discs producing pressure on the nerves, then a part of the back of the spine can be taken off to relieve the pressure.

If you are prone to bouts of backache – not only sciatica – try this simple exercise for at least 15 minutes a day. Lie on the floor with your head resting on a small pile of books. Keep your back straight, your knees bent and your feet firmly on the ground (left).

Shingles

Q My grandmother had shingles, and the rash seemed to wrap itself around her like a belt. Is this usual?

A Yes, it is common. The main characteristic of the disease is that it is an infection which nearly always spreads out from the spinal cord through the nerves of sensation. Each nerve supplies an area of skin called a dermatome, and these dermatomes are arranged down the surface of the body like a series of belts or horizontal stripes. Normally shingles will affect one nerve's dermatome on one side of the body only, although it is possible for more than one nerve to be affected.

Q When my father had shingles it was so painful that he couldn't move for a week. Is this normal?

A Unfortunately it is normal for the condition to be painful in the early stages, although the pain will often diminish as soon as the rash has broken out. Usually the surface tenderness is not too bad after the rash has settled down, although very occasionally you will get a persistent pain over the affected area, which is called post-herpetic neuralgia.

Q Is it true that if you have shingles down both sides you will die if the two areas meet up?

A No, this is definitely an old wives' tale. There is no truth in it at all. No one dies of shingles, although the disease can occur in people who are ill with other diseases and may add to their deterioration.

Q Is it true that elderly people should avoid children with chickenpox because of the risk of catching shingles?

A Both diseases are caught from the same virus, but there is very little evidence that shingles can be caught from people with chickenpox. However, it does seem possible for infection to work the other way around, and for people to get chickenpox from someone who suffers from shingles.

This painful disease is caused by the same virus as chickenpox, and affects mainly adults. It can be debilitating, but will not cause long-term damage.

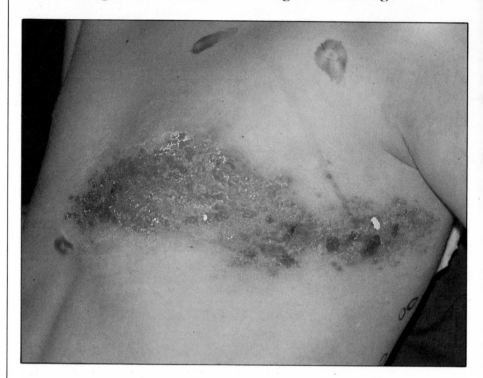

Shingles, which is caused by a virus, consists of a rash made up of vesicles (fluid-filled clear spots). The rash creeps around the body, forming a kind of band.

Shingles is a very painful disease that tends to affect the elderly and the ill. It is not dangerous and complete recovery nearly always occurs. The medical name for the condition is Herpes zoster – which is Greek for a creeping girdle – and the disease shows up as a belt-like rash around the body.

Causes

Shingles and chickenpox are both caused by the same virus, although the two diseases are quite different. Their only similarity is that they both produce a rash with vesicles (fluid-filled clear spots) on the skin.

Chickenpox and shingles tend to occur in very different age groups. Chickenpox primarily affects children, while shingles is very rare in childhood. Most cases crop up after the age of 40. Many doctors think that everyone who gets shingles must have had chickenpox in the past, but it is difficult to prove. It is also contended that chickenpox may be caught from shingles, but the reverse does not seem to happen.

Symptoms

Shingles starts with pain felt on the surface of the skin where the disease is going to strike. This pain may get worse over the next few days, and the skin will redden. At this point the rash starts to break out, with little vesicles forming on the skin. The pain tends to diminish as the rash advances, but it may still be quite severe. The rash will often creep around one side of the body, causing the clear belt- or band-like condition that characterizes the disease. The areas most commonly affected are the chest and upper part of the abdomen; the lower abdomen, limbs, neck and face are involved less often.

The disease has this band-like appearance because the virus spreads down sensory nerves from the spinal cord. These nerves emerge in pairs from between each of the vertebrae in the backbone, and each one supplies a band of skin – known as a dermatome – on one half of the body.

Once the rash has appeared it will persist for several days, and the vesicles may even run together to form a mat of affected skin with a crust over it. Eventually, though, the rash will clear, leaving normal skin behind. Sometimes there will be minor scarring or depigmentation. The pain usually disappears with the rash or soon after.

Aside from affecting mainly older people, shingles is also typically found in patients suffering from other diseases which tends to suppress the activity of the immune system. Examples of such diseases are leukaemia or a lymphoma.

Unusual forms of the disease

There may be variations in the disease. It is thought that shingles can actually occur without the tell-tale rash. This is very difficult to prove, but it is a likely explanation for the occasional patient who has a nasty pain in the area where

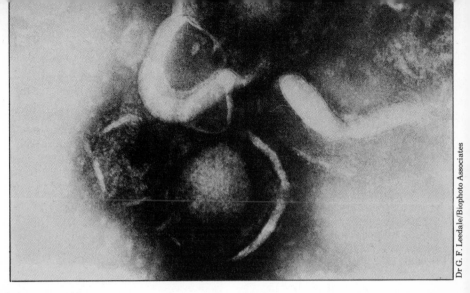

Distribution of dermatomes

The area of skin supplied by one spinal nerve is called a dermatome. Dermatomes extend around the body from front to back, never crossing the midline. The different

colours represent dermatomes associated with different segments of the spinal cord. Shingles spreads along the dermatomes, hence its characteristic appearance.

This electron micrograph shows one particle of the shingles virus, Herpes zoster (centre) – magnified 200,000 times.

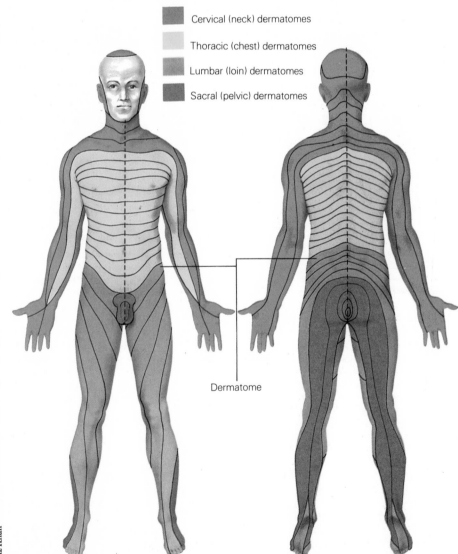

Cervical (neck) dermatomes

Thoracic (chest) dermatomes

Lumbar (loin) dermatomes

Sacral (pelvic) dermatomes

Dermatome

you would expect a patch of shingles to develop.

Sometimes the disease is not confined to the sensory part of the nervous system, and muscle weakness may occur with an attack of shingles. This suggests that the motor nerve as well as the nerves of sensation are involved.

Shingles can also affect areas supplied by the nerves of the head which do not in fact arise from the spinal cord, but from the brain. Although any area of the face can be involved it usually affects the opthalmic branch of the trigeminal nerve – the main nerve of sensation in the face. Generally the skin around the eye is affected, but occasionally the eye itself is involved. Another area that may be affected is the ear, when it is called the Ramsay Hunt syndrome (after the neurologist who first described it).

Dangers

The main danger of the disease is the development of post-herpetic neuralgia. This means that the pain associated with the condition does not abate as the rash disappears. This is more likely to happen when the trigeminal nerve of the face is involved. This form of the disease may also be dangerous, since the eye may become involved, leading to inflammation and in rare cases even blindness.

Treatment

No truly effective treatment for shingles has been developed as yet. However, it has been suggested that post-herpetic neuralgia is less likely to happen if the area is treated with idoxuridine at an early stage, and many doctors use this as a matter of routine, particularly if the face is involved.

Although this disease is both common and painful, it will not usually cause any long-term or permanent damage.

Sickle-cell anaemia

Q I have been told that I have a sickle-cell trait. Does this mean I could suddenly become anaemic?

A No, this is not a serious problem. The sickle-cell trait means that you have inherited a gene that gives rise to sickle-cell disease from one parent, but it is paired with a normal gene from your other parent. Although the abnormality can be seen in blood tests it does not cause any serious complications. Doctors may just take extra care when you have an anaesthetic.

Q Do you need to have blood transfusions if you have sickle-cell disease?

A Possibly. One of the problems with the disease is that the red blood cells are very unstable and tend to break down easily causing anaemia. It may be necessary to treat this anaemia with blood transfusions, particularly in pregnancy. Exchange transfusions are given more often however. A proportion of the patient's blood is removed and replaced with normal blood. This kind of treatment is used for sickle-cell crises where blood vessels are blocked off by abnormal blood cells.

Q I have heard that there are many kinds of sickle-cell disease. Is this correct?

A There is only one true kind of sickle cell disease, where the red blood cells carry the abnormal haemoglobin S. What you have heard does have some truth in it however, in that there are many other kinds of abnormal haemoglobin which can all give rise to problems. It is quite possible to inherit the genes for two different types of abnormal haemoglobin from your parents. This leads to diseases where both abnormalities are found. In fact the combination of haemoglobin S and another abnormal haemoglobin C is quite common, and is called SC disease. There are over 300 kinds of abnormal haemoglobin but by no means all of them give rise to any problems.

Sickle-cell anaemia results from an abnormality in the haemoglobin – the oxygen-carrying pigment in the blood. It is a serious condition but can be controlled.

The blood cells in sickle-cell anaemia twist into a characteristic 'sickle' shape (inset), unlike the normal round cells of healthy blood.

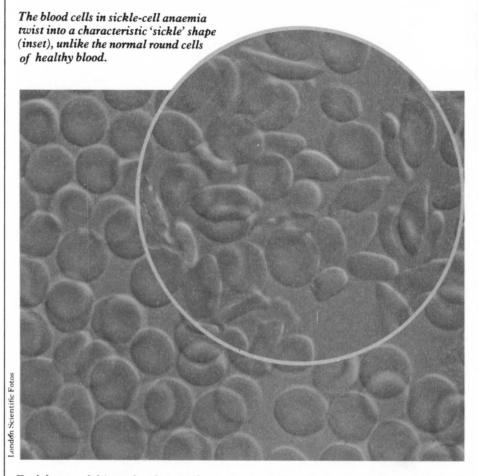

London Scientific Fotos

Each haemoglobin molecule is made up of a central haem portion – an iron compound responsible for carrying oxygen around the body – attached to which are four chains of globin molecules. The structure of the globin molecules determines that the haemoglobin will take up oxygen from the lungs and release it into the tissues where it is needed. Sickle-cell anaemia results from abnormalities in the globin structure.

This particular type of abnormal haemoglobin is called haemoglobin S, as distinct from normal haemoglobin A which is found in the blood in quantities after birth.

Causes

This abnormality is genetic, which means that it is passed from parent to child at conception. Every characteristic in the body is controlled by a pair of genes, found in every body cell, one of which is inherited from the mother and one from the father. In the case of haemoglobin if you inherit one normal gene, the bone marrow will make a mixture of normal haemoglobin A and abnormal haemoglobin S. This is known as the sickle-cell trait. When both the controlling genes are abnormal the full-blown disease will result, with the red blood cells containing a very high proportion of abnormal haemoglobin. People affected in this way are called homozygotes, while those with only one abnormal gene are referred to as heterozygote people.

Sickle-cell disease is found in all parts of the world where malaria is, or has been, prevalent. Thus it is common in Africa, and in people of African origin who live in the West Indies and North and South America. It is also a problem in Britain among West Indians who originally came from Africa; and it is found in the Mediterranean, India and Western Asia generally.

The inherited abnormality is thought

to be so common because it may also give protection against malaria. Thus the process of evolution has not tended to act against people carrying the sickle gene, unless they are seriously affected. In other words, people with the sickle-cell trait, which produces no symptoms, will have a greater chance of surviving because of their greater resistance to malaria, at the expense of the relatively few individuals who have the full-blown disease which will cause serious problems in most cases.

level of the blood falls too low. The haemoglobin molecules in the red cells then 'sickle' or become twisted into an abnormal shape, making the cells themselves twisted. These are known as sickle cells and give the disease its name.

The deformed cells tend to block off small blood vessels making the blood clot and thus stopping the tissues from receiving oxygen. Painful infarctions (areas of tissues which have died because of blocked circulation) then occur. The bones are often affected in this way.

Treatment
Treatment consists chiefly in treating the crises as they arise by rehydrating the patient with plenty of fluids and giving oxygen when necessary. It is also possible to give exchange transfusions so that abnormal sickle cells are replaced by normal blood.

Sickle-cell anaemia occurs wherever malaria is prevalent. Thus it is found both in countries of Africa, and among African families who have emigrated elsewhere.

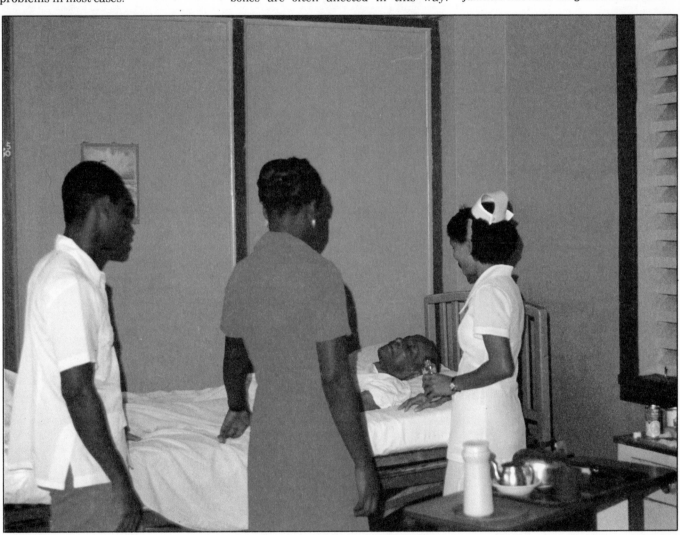

Symptoms
With homozygous sickle-cell disease – the disease resulting from two abnormal genes – the effects are very variable. In Africa probably about 10 per cent of children with the problem reach adult life. At the same time it is possible for the disease to produce no symptoms, and only be discovered on a routine blood test.

Chronic anaemia can result from the continuous breakdown of red blood cells, but the greatest problem is the incidence of 'crises' which occur when the oxygen-

People with the sickle-cell trait may also be liable to crises under certain circumstances, such as during an anaesthetic.

The spleen can become enlarged as it separates abnormal cells from the blood. As time goes on, however, infarction of the spleen will result so that it can no longer be felt in the abdomen. People with sickle-cell anaemia are also more prone to infection, arising particularly from pneumococcus bacteria which cause lobar pneumonia. The disease also leads to ulcers on the legs.

Outlook
Advances have been made in the prevention of the disease through genetic counselling, and by testing the blood of potential parents for the abnormal sickle cell trait. Another preventive measure is to use the technique of ammiocentesis to obtain and examine samples of foetal blood in early pregnancy. In this way it is possible to locate an abnormality of the haemoglobin including that of sickle-cell disease. If it is found, a termination of the pregnancy may be advised by the doctor.

Silicosis

Of all the occupational lung diseases caused by dust, silicosis is the most common and serious. There is no cure, so prevention of this condition is essential.

Q I have worked with sand-blasting machinery for two years. Am I likely to get silicosis?

A No. The term sand-blasting should not be taken too literally these days. The use of sand or other materials containing free silica is prohibited by law, and relatively harmless substitutes are used.

Q Is there a connection between silicosis and tuberculosis?

A In the 1930s silicosis was common and so was TB among ordinary workers, and it was not unusual for both diseases to occur together. Also, there did seem to be an extra predisposition to TB in silicosis sufferers. These days, TB still occurs under certain circumstances, but is less likely to occur in the sort of people who risk contracting silicosis.

Q My son is training to become a stonemason. I am worried that he might get silicosis. Is this very likely?

A No. Silicosis is not a serious problem among stonemasons these days. However, stringent precautions need to be taken when dealing with such stones as granite and sandstone which have a high silica content. Precautions include using water when cutting the stones, in order to dampen the dust, and wearing breathing protection.

Q Is it true that some people are more likely to get silicosis than others?

A Yes. There have been cases where miners have developed silicosis after being employed for only a few months drilling rock which had a high silica content, while others have carried out similar work for up to 30 years with no apparent ill effects. No definite explanations have been given for the different susceptibilities. Those people who use more energy in their work will breathe particles more deeply into their lungs and could face greater risks; and those with previous lung disease are also said to be more susceptible to silicosis.

This quarry worker in Okinawa, Japan wears a protective mask which prevents him from inhaling particles of dust that could otherwise damage his lungs.

Silicosis is a serious lung disease caused by inhaling dust particles of free silica – a substance found in stones such as quartz, granite, sandstone and flint.

Occupational risks

The nicknames given to silicosis over the years are an indication of the types of job in which this disease commonly occurred – names such as grinders' rot, masons' disease, miners' phthisis, potters' rot and stonemasons' disease.

Today, however, with improved protection and the increased use of safe substitute materials, silicosis is a far rarer disease then it once was – although mining is still a common cause of exposure to silica.

In sand-blasting, for instance – an occupation traditionally linked with silicosis – the use of sand is now prohibited. Comparatively safe substitutes have been found in corundum or silicon carbide. Also, silicosis is no longer a problem for stonemasons. When dealing with siliceous stones, they take the precautions of using water to dampen the dust and wearing breathing protection.

Despite stringent dust controls, the danger of silicosis still lurks in the pottery industry. The main hazard, here, is with the ground flint used to improve the clay. Substitutes such as a mixture of quartz and cristobalite are now used but, unfortunately, these materials also contain silica and so pose a risk. A safer alternative, allumina, is considered too expensive for general use. Because of this, protective masks are worn.

Symptoms and outlook

The symptoms of silicosis are divided into three main stages. Firstly, the victim gets breathless and may have an unproductive cough. In the second stage, breathlessness becomes worse and physical exertion is difficult. In the third stage, the victim is completely incapacitated and suffers fatigue, loss of weight, productive cough and chest pain.

However, before these symptoms appear and serious damage has been done to the lungs, silicosis can and should be diagnosed by X-ray tests. Provided this is done early enough, and the cause of the disease removed – this may mean a change of occupation – the silicosis need not be progressive. But, if it is allowed to progress, the lungs will fail to absorb enough oxygen for the blood and heart failure may even occur.

There is no cure for silicosis. Therefore it is vital to prevent people from being exposed to silica. This is done by finding safe substitutes, by controlling the dust through effective exhaust ventilation or by the use of protective clothing – in some cases this may mean a suit with its own air supply.

Sinusitis

Q I suffer from catarrh every winter and can't seem to shake it off. My doctor says I have sinusitis. What can be done to help me with this condition?

A Catarrh is a very common problem, and sinusitis is only one of a number of causes. If you have a blocked nose or if the discharge from your nose is persistently thick, yellow or green, and you have pain in your face or behind the eyes, then antibiotics may be helpful. It may even be necessary for you to have an operation to release the fluid and reduce the pressure inside the bone. If you smoke, you should stop.

Q My two-year-old daughter has a constantly runny nose and is very irritable. Could she have sinusitis?

A Sinusitis is very rare in young children because the sinuses are poorly developed. It is much more likely that she has had a cold or throat infection. If yellow or green discharge from both nostrils persists for weeks it is possible that her adenoids are enlarged. If the discharge is from only one nostril, she may have pushed a small foreign body, such as a bead, up her nose.

Q My teenage son recently had an attack of sinusitis. He is a keen swimmer. When can he swim again?

A The increased pressure underwater promotes sinusitis by forcing any infected material from the nose up into the sinuses. When your son is over the acute attack he can safely swim as long as he does not dive or swim underwater until all signs of infection have disappeared.

Q I developed sinusitis a few days after I had an upper tooth removed. Could this have been the cause of the infection?

A Yes. About 10 per cent of cases of maxillary sinusitis are caused by a tooth abscess or dental extraction since the maxillary sinuses lie close to the upper teeth.

Sinusitis – infection of the air cavities in the front of the skull – is a common problem. It often causes considerable discomfort, but can usually be treated successfully.

Tom Belshaw

The sinuses – small cavities in the bones of the face – contain air, thus contributing to the skull's lightness. The sinus cavities are linked with the nose and upper throat, and so are vulnerable to the spread of infection from these areas. There are two kinds of sinusitis – acute and chronic – with differing symptoms.

In an attack of sinusitis, pain may be felt in the forehead; behind the eyes and nose; at the back of the head or neck; or beneath the eyes and up to the forehead.

Causes
The nose and sinuses are lined with special cells which produce mucus to combat an initial infection, for example from a cold or influenza virus. When the virus enters the body, this mucus production increases – which makes the lining of the nose and sinuses swell and block up the communicating channels between them. The mucus can no longer escape, pressure builds up and the infection in the sinuses is trapped. Bacteria which normally live in the nose and sinuses now multiply and the sinuses become filled with yellow or green pus. It is this pus which, being under pressure, creates the symptoms of sinusitis.

Dental infections, fractures of the facial bones or gunshot wounds may also bring about sinusitis. Poor drainage of the nose, and enlarged, infected adenoids and tonsils are likewise contributory factors of this condition.

Symptoms and dangers
Acute sinusitis gives rise to pain, and sometimes redness and swelling over the sinus. The patient may have a severe localized headache, depending on which sinus is affected. Frontal sinusitis, for example, produces pain above the eyes. With maxillary sinusitis there is pain in the cheeks, which is often throbbing and made worse by stooping or moving the head. The nose is blocked on the affected side but there may be very little discharge. The senses of smell and taste are usually reduced.

Chronic sinusitis produces nasal discharge, low-grade pain, a blocked nose, cough and in children a tendency to ear infections. The infection continues for weeks or months, and often follows an acute initial infection.

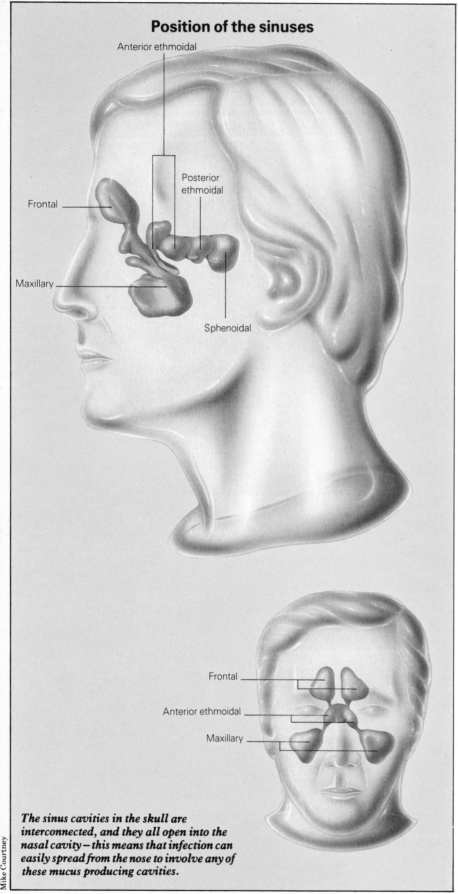

Position of the sinuses

Anterior ethmoidal

Posterior ethmoidal

Frontal

Maxillary

Sphenoidal

Frontal

Anterior ethmoidal

Maxillary

The sinus cavities in the skull are interconnected, and they all open into the nasal cavity – this means that infection can easily spread from the nose to involve any of these mucus producing cavities.

Mike Courtney

Sometimes infection of one of the frontal sinuses spreads around the eye, causing double vision, swelling of the eyelids or even an abscess behind the eyeball pushing it outwards. Meningitis or a brain abscess may also develop. Middle ear infections often occur with maxillary sinusitis and can result in deafness in the case of children. The infection may also spread downwards causing laryngitis or pneumonia.

Treatment
It is important to treat sinusitis and all related infections very thoroughly to prevent the development of possible serious complications.

An X-ray may be taken to locate trapped fluid. Polyps – overgrowths of the mucus membrane lining the nose – may be present. Acute sinusitis is treated with antibiotics, decongestant nose-drops perhaps containing ephedrine, menthol inhalations and painkillers.

In some cases it may be necessary to drain out the pus from the sinus through a small hole made on the inside of the nose. An operation may also be of use in chronic sinusitis or where there are polyps. In children with sinusitis it is often best to remove the adenoids and tonsils. Washing out the sinuses with a salt water solution can also be helpful after pus has been drained off.

Outlook
Sinusitis can be quite difficult to treat once a chronic condition has become established, and each ensuring infection can cause a more stubborn chronic infection than the last.

Efficient nose-blowing, closing one nostril at a time, can help. Nose-drops and sprays should not be used for more than a week on end as they can create further problems – they are only of value in short courses. Antibiotics help to cure infection, but since these are absorbed into the bloodstream it is difficult for them to work in the middle of a sinus where there is no blood supply.

Acute sinusitis often clears up with antibiotics and nose-drops. Chronic sinusitis, however, may be tediously prolonged, especially if the sufferer is a heavy smoker. Sinusitis is commoner in the winter, partly because damp weather seems to aggravate the condition, and partly because there are more germs around at that time of the year which cause upper respiratory infections. A sufferer may be quite free from symptoms in the summer but spend every winter having to contend with a blocked nose and low-grade pain. Fortunately, however, serious complications from sinusitis are rare nowadays.

Skin and skin diseases

Q Why are skin conditions always made worse by emotional upsets?

A Most ill health is made worse by emotional upsets and the skin is no exception, but because it is visible patients with skin disease are more disturbed by their complaint than patients with other disorders. Emotion can alter the state of the skin's irritability and sweating mechanisms. Conditions where these factors are particularly important, such as eczema, will be aggravated by unhappiness, anxiety or depression.

Q I have developed an allergy to nickel through wearing cheap jewellery. Will I always be allergic?

A Allergy to nickel is fairly common in those who either wear or handle it. There is always an interval between first contact with nickel and the development of the allergy. Traces of nickel are absorbed through the skin and the body reacts by forming antibodies so that any further contact results in an itchy skin rash. If no further contact occurs there will be a gradual lessening of the allergy, but usually it remains to a degree throughout life.

Q I have bald patches on my scalp and beard area. Will they re-grow in time?

A The commonest cause of bald patches is a condition called alopecia areata, which frequently starts in childhood and may run in families. Hair is lost over clear-cut round areas often a few weeks after stress or shock. It usually settles down, and in most cases the hair has re-grown in three to six months so that treatment is not necessary.

Q My husband is only 20 and is already going bald. Is this normal?

A Yes. Loss of hair in men may begin any time after puberty, and is a result of higher male hormone levels. Often there is a strong hereditary factor as well. Treatment is best avoided since there is at present no certain method of stimulating hair growth.

We never think of it as such, but the skin is an organ – in fact the largest we possess. It not only protects us from injury and infection, it keeps the body's temperature and moisture content stable at all times.

The skin is much more than a simple wrapping around our bodies. It is an active and versatile organ which is waterproof so that we do not dry up in the heat or melt in the rain, and it protects us from the damaging radiation of sunlight. It is tough enough to act as a shield against injury, yet supple enough to permit movement. It conserves heat or cools the body as required, thus keeping our internal temperature constant.

Skin diseases may be a nuisance and an embarrassment, but they are seldom dangerous and are very rarely fatal. They cause a vast amount of ill health, however, by their frequency and persistence.

Structure of the skin

The skin is made up of two main parts. The outermost part – the epidermis – consists of several layers of cells, the lowest of which are called the 'mother' cells. Here the cells are constantly dividing and moving up to the surface, where they flatten, die and are transformed into a material called keratin which is finally shed as tiny, barely visible scales. It takes three to four weeks for a cell in the lowest layer to reach the skin surface.

This outer protective layer is firmly attached to an underlying layer called the dermis. Tiny, finger-like bulges from the dermis fit into sockets in the epidermis, and this waviness at the junction of the two layers of skin gives rise to ridges, which are most obvious at the fingertips and give us our fingerprints. The dermis is made up of bundles of protein fibres – called collagen – and elastic fibres. Embedded in the dermis are sweat, sebaceous and apocrine glands, hair follicles, blood vessels and nerves. The nerves penetrate the epidermis but the blood vessels are confined to the dermis. The hairs and ducts from the glands pass through the epidermis to the surface.

Your skin type as well as your colouring are determined by heredity. Hair and nails are formed from skin cells and these too are determined by genetic factors.

Steve Bielschowsky

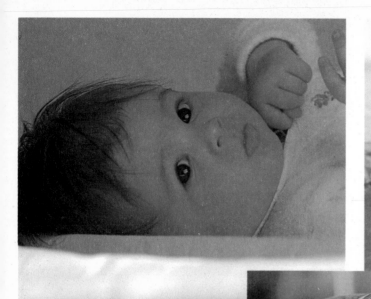

Glands and nerves

Each sweat gland is formed of a coiled tube of epidermal cells which leads into the sweat duct to open out on the skin surface. The sweat glands are controlled by the nervous system and are stimulated to secrete either by emotion or by the body's need to lose heat.

The sebaceous glands open into the hair follicles and are made up of specialized epidermal cells which produce grease or sebum. They are most numerous on the head, face, chest and back. Their function is to lubricate the hair shaft and surrounding skin and they are controlled by sex hormones.

The apocrine glands develop at puberty and are found in the armpits, breasts and near the genitals. They are odour-producing and are a sexual characteristic. When they begin to function they secrete a thick milky substance.

There is a fine network of nerve endings in both layers of skin, and they are particularly numerous at the fingertips. They transmit pleasurable sensations of warmth and touch, as well as cold, pressure, itching and pain which may evoke protective reflexes.

Hair and nails

Hair and nails are both specialized forms of keratin. Although nails are produced by living skin cells the nail itself is dead and will not hurt or bleed if it is damaged. The visible part of the nail is called the nail body and its shape is partly determined by genetic factors. The bottom part of the nail – the root – is implanted in a groove in the skin. The cuticle overlaps the root, which is the site of active growth. As the cells divide and move

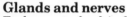

How does the smooth, firm skin of a baby become the wrinkled skin of an old person? It is a gradual process dependent on two changes – with time the lubricating glands produce less moisture, and the skin's supporting fibres lose their natural elasticity. As cell growth slows down, an old skin cannot heal as quickly as a young one, and hair colour and skin bloom fade.

upwards they become thickened and toughened with keratin, and when they die they become part of the nail itself.

Hair is formed by cells in the hair follicles and there are two types: fine, downy hair which is found over most of the body except the palms of the hands and soles of the feet, and thick, pigmented hair which is present on the scalp, eyebrows, beard and genital areas.

Hair grows in cycles, a long growing phase being followed by a short resting period. Hairs in the resting phase constitute up to 15 per cent of the total 100,000 hairs on the scalp. The normal daily hair loss is between 20 and 100 hairs. Scalp hair grows about 0.8 cm (⅓ in) per month and continues to grow for up to three years. The rapid growth of scalp hair makes it more susceptible to damage from disease, toxic drugs and hormones.

The shape of our hair follicles is inherited and this determines whether hair is straight or curly, together with the angle of the hair bulb in the shaft. If it lies straight, the hair will be straight, if bent, the hair will curl.

Skin colour

Skin colour is due to the black pigment melanin which is produced by pigment cells in the lowest layer of the epidermis. There is the same number of pigment-producing cells in the skin of all races but the amount of melanin produced varies. In dark-skinned people there is more melanin than in light-skinned people.

Other factors contributing to skin colour are the blood in the blood vessels of the skin and the natural yellowish tinge of the skin tissue. The state of the blood within the blood vessels can greatly change skin colour. Thus we become 'white' with fear when small vessels close off, 'red' with anger due to an increased blood flow, and 'blue' with cold when most of the oxygen in the blood moves out to the tissues as the blood flow slows down.

Wound healing

All wounds heal by scar formation unless they are very superficial, such as a graze. Children heal faster then adults but they also produce a larger quantity of scar

Structure of the skin

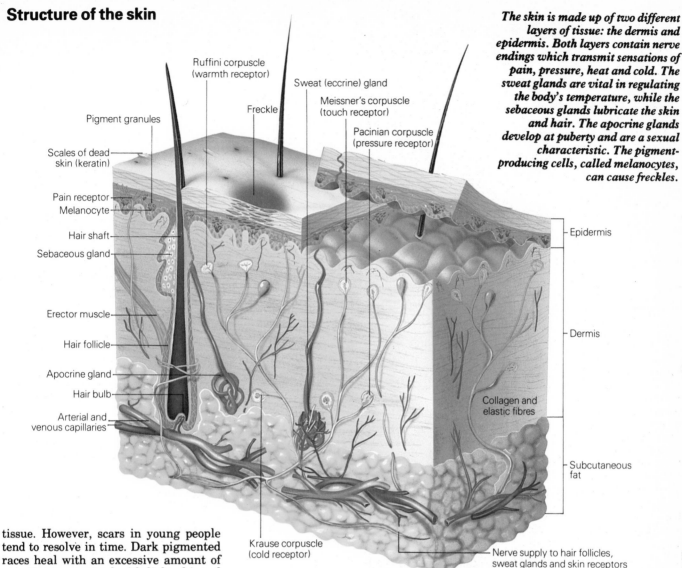

Pigment granules

Scales of dead skin (keratin)

Pain receptor
Melanocyte

Hair shaft

Sebaceous gland

Erector muscle

Hair follicle

Apocrine gland

Hair bulb

Arterial and venous capillaries

Ruffini corpuscle (warmth receptor)

Freckle

Sweat (eccrine) gland

Meissner's corpuscle (touch receptor)

Pacinian corpuscle (pressure receptor)

Epidermis

Dermis

Collagen and elastic fibres

Subcutaneous fat

Krause corpuscle (cold receptor)

Nerve supply to hair follicles, sweat glands and skin receptors

Aziz Khan

The skin is made up of two different layers of tissue: the dermis and epidermis. Both layers contain nerve endings which transmit sensations of pain, pressure, heat and cold. The sweat glands are vital in regulating the body's temperature, while the sebaceous glands lubricate the skin and hair. The apocrine glands develop at puberty and are a sexual characteristic. The pigment-producing cells, called melanocytes, can cause freckles.

tissue. However, scars in young people tend to resolve in time. Dark pigmented races heal with an excessive amount of scar tissue compared with light-skinned people as a general rule.

The healing process involves many changes. First the wound bleeds and becomes filled with a blood clot which dries to form a scab. Blood vessels and fibrous tissue grow in from the cut surfaces of the wound, and the end result is a scar which gradually becomes paler in colour with time.

Skin conditions in children

Birthmarks are darker coloured areas which are present on a baby's skin at birth or appear soon afterwards. They include strawberry marks, moles and port wine stains. Many birthmarks do not require treatment and disappear of their own accord. Strawberry marks, for instance, appear a few weeks after birth and grow rapidly for a while, but the majority disappear completely by the time the child goes to school.

Moles are not usually present at birth but develop in childhood, gradually in-

creasing in size during adult life and possibly disappearing in old age. They are formed from collections of the pigment-producing cells in the skin and their significance is that they may very occasionally become malignant.

Babies and children have their own particular complaints – these include infant cradle cap, nappy rash and chilblains. Cradle cap is a normal collection of scales and grease which stick together and adhere to the scalp. It can be removed by gentle shampooing after the scales have been softened with olive oil the night before.

Nappy rash is a red rash in the crotch and nappy area which can spread to involve the thighs and lower abdomen. It results from irritation produced by the bacterial decomposition of urine and faeces. Since it is caused by the friction of a wet or soiled nappy, it is essential to change nappies frequently, leaving them

off whenever possible and avoiding the use of plastic pants. The skin should be washed with emulsifying lotions rather than soap, and water-repellent ointments which act as a barrier should be applied. Sometimes mild steroids with anti-infective agents are necessary.

Chilblains are common in children who live in countries like Britain where the winters are cold. They occur on the toes, especially if tight-fitting shoes are worn, and on the fingers and ears. Sudden extreme changes in temperature should be avoided – although it is tempting to warm cold feet in front of the fire this only aggravates the condition. The affected area should be kept warm at all times.

Infection of the skin frequently occurs in childhood since the skin's natural defences have not yet been built up against bacteria, viruses and fungi. Impetigo is a bacterial infection of the superficial layers of skin which is parti-

The amount of melanin pigment in the skin is the major factor determining skin colour. It produces black and brown shades, while yellow tones are imparted by another pigment, carotene. The pigment-producing cells are larger in dark-skinned than fair-skinned races, but the number is constant. Dark-skinned people produce more melanin than fair people.

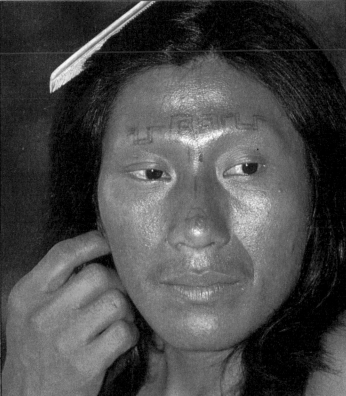

Sally and Richard Greenhill

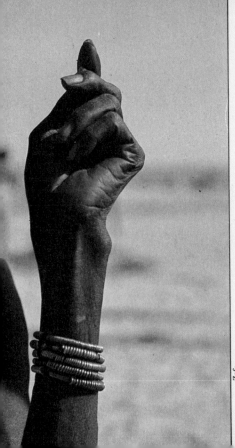

Zefa

V vision International

cularly likely to happen where skin is already damaged. It starts as a little red spot that enlarges and blisters to form a honey-coloured crust. It is easily treated with antibiotics.

Ringworm (see pp 348-49) is caused by several kinds of fungi and gets its name from the ringed appearance of the rash. Sites most commonly affected are the scalp, groin and feet. It is rare in adults because of their greater immunity and it is thought that the grease glands on the scalp may have some protective effect. Treatment is with anti-fungal preparations.

Warts are the commonest virus infection of the skin, which most children catch as easily as they catch chickenpox. They tend to be found on the hands, knees and soles of the feet, since the virus enters wherever the skin is broken. It lives in the outer layers of skin and causes very little damage so a wart may pass unnoticed for months or even years. When the body becomes aware of its presence it mobilizes its defences and the wart may disappear as if by magic – hence the success of many wart charms and cures.

Often warts increase rapidly in number before they disappear.

Since they heal without leaving a scar no treatment destructive enough to cause scarring should be used. Simple wart paints only should be applied, and the dead skin regularly pared away or frozen off. Treatment is usually successful but may take two to three months before having an effect.

Skin conditions in adolescence

The hormonal changes which occur at puberty affect the skin chiefly by activating the grease-producing glands.

Sweating and blushing can be annoying problems for teenagers. Excessive sweating of the armpits and hands which is caused by emotion and heat can be treated with aluminium chloride preparations applied locally. Blushing is not usually treated but tends to diminish as confidence increases.

Most teenagers develop a few acne spots which sometimes require medical attention. Acne (see pp 18-19) occurs earlier in girls than in boys because of the earlier onset of puberty. It usually resolves in the late teens and early twenties but some people continue to need treatment up to the age of 30 or even 40. Acne is due to the excessive production of sebum or grease which blocks the hair

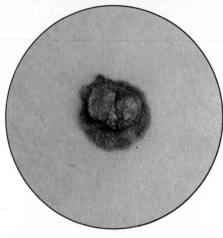

Q Why does some people's skin age faster than others?

A Inheritance is probably the single most important factor in the skin's tendency to age. Other influences involved are the environment, such as the amount of sun damage, and hormonal changes throughout life. The loss of elasticity which causes the wrinkles of old age is due to changes in the fibres in the supporting layer of skin. The skin also becomes drier and the hair thinner with age.

Q Do sun-tanning preparations really help a sun-tan?

A There are indeed sun-tanning preparations which claim to prevent sunburn and enhance tanning. This can only happen with an efficient sunscreen which prevents burning, thereby enabling the person to sunbathe for longer periods, and build up the protective pigmentation so that a gradual tan is produced. If you are very fair-skinned, you will find it virtually impossible to go brown however much you sunbathe, since your skin produces little pigment. And of course you are especially vulnerable to sunburn. Many sun-tanning preparations contain dyes which artificially colour the skin. Others contain a colourless substance which turns the outer skin layer brown. This is not a true tan as the pigment-producing cells have not been activated to produce melanin.

Q My father gets a cold sore when he sunbathes. What causes this?

A Cold sores are a very common virus infection of the skin. Most people are first infected in childhood and the infection may then pass unnoticed, but the virus remains latent in the cells of the skin. Later they may be re-activated by some stimulus such as sunlight, to give rise to a cold sore. They therefore recur in the same place.

Q Why do I get spots before my periods each month?

A This is very common in young women and is probably due to the fall in the hormone oestrogen before a period.

A malignant mole (left) is characterized by itching, bleeding or changes in colour or size. They usually develop in adulthood but if diagnosed early a cure is possible. Many babies are born with birthmarks, such as stork marks (below). These do not need treatment and will disappear in time. An allergic reaction is a common cause of dermatitis. For example, a housewife may find that detergent irritates her hands (bottom left). Treatment would be to avoid contact by wearing rubber gloves. Warts (bottom right) are common in childhood but simple treatments are usually effective.

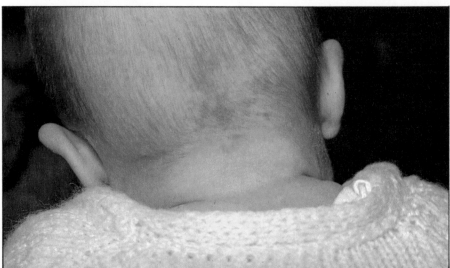

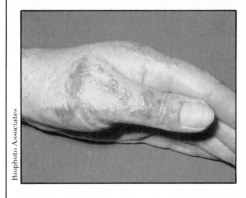

Biophoto Associates

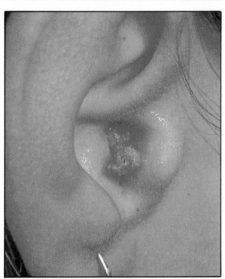

follicles. These then become infected with bacteria so that blackheads, pimples and pustules form.

Acne can and should be a successfully treated disease. Patients with mild acne require degreasing agents or keratolytics. Moderate or severe cases need oral antibiotics in addition to local treatment. Sunlight is usually beneficial as it dries up grease on the skin and helps to peel off the top layer.

Skin conditions in adults

As the skin ages there is a falling-off in the production of natural emollients and it becomes dry. This drying process results in cracks in the skin leaving it open to irritants at work or at home. Industrial dermatitis is a commoner cause of absence from work than any other industrial disease.

Dermatitis is the term used for eczema which is thought to be due to an external cause. Thus housewives may find that detergents irritate their hands, while industrial dermatitis may be caused by any one of a number of substances.

Contact dermatitis is the result of an allergy to a substance, such as the nickel in jewellery. The cure is always avoidance of the cause.

Eczema (see pp 130-31) is also common, giving rise to discomfort and disability at all ages. It presents different appearances at different stages and may last from a few days to a lifetime. Initially there is reddening of the affected skin with itching followed by pinhead swelling. Blisters then form and there is weeping and scaling.

Eczema is often inherited and is associated with asthma and hay fever. When all three occur in the same individual it is known as the atopic syndrome. Eczema cannot be cured but it can be controlled; it is not catching and does not leave scars. The skin of an eczema sufferer is more sensitive than normal, is usually itchy and has a tendency to dryness. Steroids are the mainstay of treatment and the weakest effective one is used. Irritants such as soap should always be avoided as they exacerbate the condition.

Skin allergies are often manifested in the development of urticaria or hives. The rash consists of white weals surrounded by reddened skin which itches but it does not last longer than a few hours. New weals may appear, however, so that the condition persists for days or weeks. The cause is often something that has been eaten – fruit or shellfish, for instance – while some people are allergic to preservatives and synthetic dyes.

The commonest fungus infection of the skin is athelete's foot (see page 46). The first signs are itching and peeling of the skin between the toes which are often worse on one foot. Relapses are common in the summer but the condition usually settles in cool weather and remedies are simple and effective.

Very occasionally a mole becomes malignant or cancerous. It can occur in a mole that has been present for years but if it is diagnosed early it can be removed and a cure is possible. It is always wise to remove a dubious-looking mole. A malignant mole can arise at any age but is very unusual in childhood.

Hot flushes tend to happen to women during the menopause because of the hormonal changes at this time. Sometimes the flushing over-stimulates the grease-producing glands to cause a condition called acne rosacea on the forehead, nose, cheeks and chin. The sebaceous glands may enlarge to such an extent on the nose that it becomes bulbous and lumpy in appearance. The treatment of acne rosacea is avoidance of those things which aggravate flushing, particularly hot drinks, and oral antibiotics can be very effective.

Skin conditions in old age

As the skin ages it not only dries out but it also loses its elasticity and does not heal so easily. Wounds leave only slight scars which may be barely visible in a few months. Many people also develop skin tags, sun-induced keratoses – greyish patches of skin – and seborrhoeic warts. These are brownish-black warty lesions which commonly appear on the covered parts of the body after the age of 50. They are easily treated by freezing or scraping off with a special instrument.

The commonest type of skin cancer is the rodent ulcer. These do occur in the UK, but are even more commonly found among fair-skinned people who live in sunny climates, such as Australia. They usually occur on the face and neck and are slow-growing. Usually the patient notices that a small crusty lesion has been present for some months and forms a new scab when the crust is removed. As it enlarges a depression forms in the centre and a rolled edge becomes visible. They are easily treated by local excision if small enough or by radiotherapy and are the least dangerous of cancers.

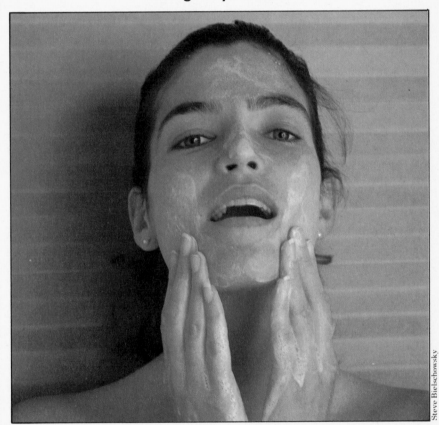

Caring for your skin

Steve Bielschowsky

● Skin care mainly consists in cleansing and moisturizing
● Cleansing creams are pure oil and cleansing milks are oil in water – both dissolve out dirt and make-up without drying the skin too much. Cleansers which can be rinsed off are suited to all skin types
● Skin tonics are mild lotions for all skin types which refresh and stimulate the skin and should be applied after cleansing and before moisturizing. The simplest are distilled water and rose-water. Astringent lotions are more suited to oily skins and help remove excess grease
● Moisturizers are creams with a low oil content which slow down the rate of moisture evaporation from the skin
● Skin foods are heavy moisturizers with a high oil content suitable for dry skins and night-time use
● Cleanse an oily skin with soap or a suitable cleanser, and protect with a non-oily moisturizer
● Cleanse normal skin with mild soap or a liquid or cream cleanser. Use a moisturizer under make-up and at night
● Cleanse a dry skin with a cleansing cream or a mild cleanser which can be rinsed away. Always use a moisturizer and night cream

Slipped disc

A slipped – or prolapsed – disc can cause a great deal of pain and temporarily restrict normal movement. However, in a large majority of cases letting nature take its course results in the patient's full recovery.

Q Does sleeping with a board under the mattress help to prevent a slipped disc?

A No, it won't prevent a slipped disc from occurring. However people with any back problem including a slipped disc, often find that a firm mattress helps their backs because it is more comfortable. This is because a soft mattress tends to sag in the middle so that lying on the bed actually bends the back. This is an uncomfortable position; you certainly would not like to walk about all day with a bent back. If you have a soft mattress, putting a hard board under it is a cheap and effective way of stopping it from sagging and making your sleep more comfortable.

Q Are women more prone to slipped discs than men?

A No. Two or three times as many men as women suffer from a slipped disc. The reasons for this are not clear, and contrary to a popular belief, heavy physical work is not associated with a greater likelihood of slipped disc. However a slipped disc is obviously more troublesome to a labourer than to someone who has a sedentary style of life.

Pregnant women can be much more likely to develop a slipped disc because of increasing weight, which puts an additional strain on the back, and the fact that hormones secreted during pregnancy cause a general softening of the ligaments and the muscles.

Q I read somewhere that a slipped disc can actually rupture. What causes this and what precisely happens when it does?

A In a sense all 'slipped' discs are ruptured discs. The disc is made of a tough outer layer and a soft inner core. A slipped disc occurs when the tough outer layer weakens, allowing the soft inner material to bulge out and press on the nerves around the spinal cord. If the outer layer cracks open, the inner material can escape completely into the area of the spinal cord. Perhaps this is the type of disc rupture that you read about.

Back problems are an extremely common cause of pain and suffering. It is estimated that more days of work are lost in the UK through backache than through strikes. There are many causes of backache, of which slipped disc is only one of the range of possibilities (see Back and backache pp 47-51). Although many cases of backache get better on their own. medical treatment should be sought if the pain is persistent, or is particularly severe.

What is a slipped disc?

The discs are pads of tissue situated between each of the vertebrae which make up the spine. Each disc consists of a tough, fibrous outer layer and a softer, jelly-like inner layer called the nucleus. The function of the disc is both to act as a strong connection between the vertebrae and as a cushion to absorb loads on the spinal column.

A slipped disc doesn't really slip; the tough outer layer cracks open and the softer inner layer protrudes, or prolapses out through the crack, like toothpaste coming out through the crack in a toothpaste tube. For this reason doctors prefer to speak of a disc protrusion or prolapse rather than a 'slipped' disc.

The soft inner layer of a disc is softest and most like jelly during childhood. Over the years this material gradually dries out so that by middle age it is like crab meat. As age increases it becomes even firmer. In the elderly the disc is really just a section of scar tissue. Disc protrusion therefore becomes more uncommon as age increases and it is really a disorder affecting young and early middle-aged adults.

The disc protrusion occurs where the outer layer of the disc is weakest, that is just in front of the nerve roots which emerge from the spinal cord at each vertebrae level. If a person has a slightly narrow spinal canal, the protruding disc material presses on the nerve root at that level and causes the symptoms of a slipped disc.

By far the commonest level of the spine to be affected is the lowermost part of the back. Here the greatest strains occur so it is not surprising that most discs which fail are at this level. It is possible, however, for discs to protrude at any level along the length of the spinal column – in the back or neck.

The classic slipped disc

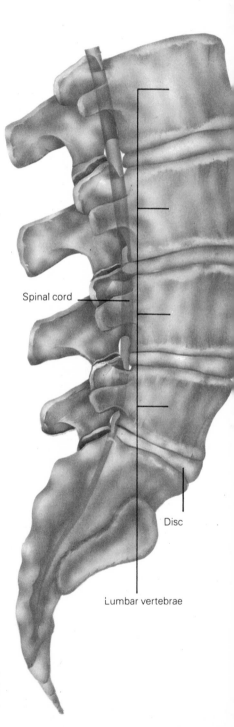

Spinal cord

Disc

Lumbar vertebrae

Mick Saunders

A slipped disc most frequently occurs in the lower part of the spine (lumbar and sacral region) (below left). The tough outer layer of the disc weakens, allowing the soft inner core to bulge out (below), causing pain and muscle weakness. When the bulge presses on a nearby spinal nerve, feeling may be lost in the lower part of the body. A special X-ray, called a radiculogram (right) is used in the diagnosis of this condition.

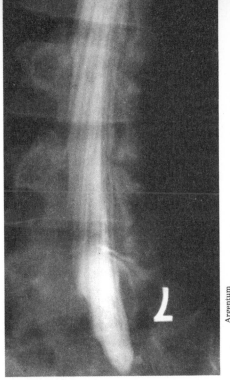

Argentum

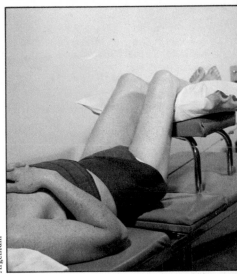

Over 90 per cent of those with a slipped disc will recover by resting in bed – from three days to three weeks – and letting nature take its course. If the symptoms are not alleviated, patients may have to spend time resting in hospital with their legs supported in such a way that pressure on the nerves can be relieved.

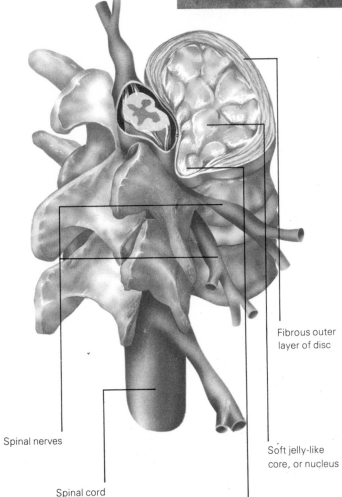

Fibrous outer layer of disc

Spinal nerves

Spinal cord

Prolapsed disc pressing on a spinal nerve

Soft jelly-like core, or nucleus

Causes

The disc begins to protrude when a crack develops in its tough outer layer. This is usually a result of wear and tear in the back as a result of normal ageing. One particularly heavy or awkward lift, a fall or even a sudden cough or sneeze may force some soft disc nucleus to protrude, giving rise to sudden symptoms.

Symptoms

When a protruding disc presses on a nerve root, symptoms occur both in the back and in the area which the nerve root supplies; in the lower back, this means the legs.

Symptoms in the back can include severe backacke which the sufferer will not be able to localize very accurately. He or she may also develop painful muscle spasms in the muscles that lie along each side of the spine, particularly in the early stages. The patient will feel more pain when moving about and some relief when lying flat. Coughing or sneezing can cause the protruding disc material to bulge out suddenly, causing a sharp pain in the back or legs. In addition there may be a curvature of the spine – the patient unconsciously 'leans away' from the side of the disc protrusion to try to take the pressure off the nerve root that is involved.

If the pressure on the nerve root is not too severe the nerve will continue to work but will be painful. The brain cannot tell that the painful pressure is coming from

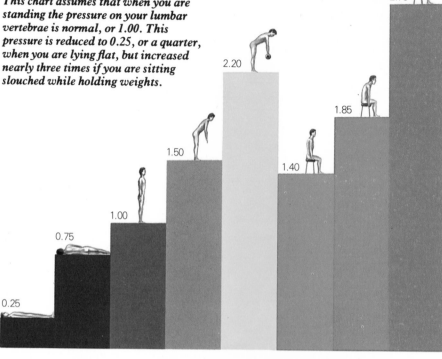

The vertebrae in the small of the back (lumbar vertebrae) take a great strain. This chart assumes that when you are standing the pressure on your lumbar vertebrae is normal, or 1.00. This pressure is reduced to 0.25, or a quarter, when you are lying flat, but increased nearly three times if you are sitting slouched while holding weights.

0.25   0.75   1.00   1.50   2.20   1.40   1.85   2.75

Aziz Khan

Q My friend put her back out when she was lifting a heavy chair. Does this mean that she had a slipped disc?

A The back consists of a series of bones, ligaments, discs and muscles. Injury to any one of these may occur while lifting heavy objects or lifting heavy objects incorrectly. This can give rise to acute pain in the back which may extend to the legs. Your friend would need to be examined by her doctor to establish whether the pain in her back was caused by a slipped disc, or whether it arose from some other cause.

Q Is it possible to cure a slipped disc by operating on the back?

A Yes, it is. Although over 90 per cent of people suffering from a slipped disc recover within two months, a small number of patients will need to have an operation. Such operations are used for patients whose slipped disc has shown up clearly on a special X-ray, and who have not responded to any other form of treatment. Occasionally a patient with a severe slipped disc which is pressing on the nerves to the bladder will need emergency treatment to relieve this pressure. Today, operations for slipped disc are successful in a large majority of cases – indeed 85 per cent of patients are completely relieved of back pain, or their condition is greatly improved.

Q My doctor thinks that I have a slipped disc and he is sending me to hospital to have my spine X-rayed. What will actually happen?

A The X-ray your doctor has recommended is called a radiculogram. A dye is injected into the membranes surrounding the nerves in the spinal cord. This dye is opaque to X-rays. If you have a slipped disc, the disc will protrude and this will show up as an indentation in the column of dye. Where an emerging nerve is not outlined by the dye, then this shows that the nerve is compressed. An operation, called a laminectomy, may then be performed to push aside the spinal cord and nerve roots in order to remove the disc material.

the area of the disc, but instead interprets the information as pain originating in the nerve end. In a lower back disc protrusion the sciatic nerve can therefore be irritated and the individual may feel pain in the thigh, calf, ankle or foot; this pain is called sciatica (see pp 361-63).

Most severe pressure on the nerve root may cause the nerve to stop functioning altogether. Areas of skin which this nerve supplies will become numb, so that a light touch or even a pinprick cannot be felt. Muscles supplied by the nerve will become weak or even completely paralyzed. The reflexes such as the knee jerk reflex may disappear. If only one nerve root is involved this is not too serious, since each nerve supplies only a small area of skin or a limited number of muscles. If the nerves to the bladder or genitals are affected, however, their function can be permanently lost and such cases need urgent medical attention to relieve the pressure on these nerves.

Treatment

Well over 90 per cent of people with acute disc protrusions get better simply by resting and waiting for nature to cure them. The soft inner disc material tends to dry up and shrink once it has undergone protrusion, thus relieving the pressure on the nerve root.

The main form of treatment therefore is rest. Once the doctor has examined the

Phil Babb

individual and confirmed that there is a straightforward disc prolapse he or she will advise the patient to rest by lying flat in bed. In the horizontal position the pressure within the disc which acts to force out the soft inner material is minimal. In the standing position this pressure is higher and when the back is bent, for example when sitting or bending over, the pressure is much higher. A saggy bed also bends the back so it is best to put boards under the mattress or even to put the mattress on the floor.

Pain-killing drugs are of help in dulling the pain in acute disc protrusion although they will probably not take it away altogether. Drugs which relax the muscles, such as diazepam (Valium) help to settle painful muscle spasm.

Most patients will get better if strict bed-rest is undertaken for a few days to three weeks. Great patience is required – there is no way that nature's healing processes can be speeded up. Getting up too soon will often result in a relapse.

You can't prevent a slipped disc but you can minimize its effects. By placing a board beneath your mattress – remembering to bend from the knees and to keep your back straight – you will be able to have a more comfortable night's sleep.

Patients who fail to make a recovery after a proper course of rest may need further treatment. This may entail a period of rest in hospital, perhaps with traction to the legs to help relieve the pain. If this fails a special X-ray may be necessary. Ordinary X-rays show only the bones of the spine – the disc itself shows only as a space between the bones and this space is not altered in an acute disc prolapse. The special X-ray is called a radiculogram or a myelogram. A dye which shows on X-rays is injected into the space just outside the spinal canal; if the disc is protruding, it shows as an indentation in the column of dye.

An operation to remove the protruding disc material may be necessary if an adequate course of rest fails to improve symptoms, if there are signs of rapidly worsening function of nerve roots or if the nerves to the bladder or the genitals are involved.

The operation (a laminectomy) involves making a small opening in the bones surrounding the spinal cord and gently pushing it aside along with the nerve roots in order to remove the disc material. Patients can usually get up within two weeks of this operation.

Operations for prolapsed disc have developed a bad reputation among the public, probably because in the past accurate diagnosis and careful selection of those patients most likely to benefit from surgery have not always been carried out. With modern methods the success rate of operations is high.

Many people suffering from disc prolapse receive other forms of treatment such as physiotherapy and manipulation. Physiotherapy may consist of heat treatment which temporarily lessens the pain, and traction exercises. Traction helps to relieve pain, probably by decreasing muscle spasm. Exercises help to strengthen the muscles of the back and stomach so that they can take some of the strain off the bones and joints in the spine. None of these treatments has been shown to speed up the healing process, but they make the individual more comfortable in the short term.

Manipulation is practised by many physiotherapists, some doctors and all osteopaths. The aim is to move the protruding disc material away from its point of contact on the nerve root and to free the nerve from any inflammation in the area. There is no evidence to show that the soft protruding disc material can actually be replaced into the firm outer casing of the disc – this would be like trying to suck toothpaste back into its tube – but enough movement to take some pressure off the nerve root may be achieved. Manipulation is probably more

useful in other types of back disorders, although some individuals receive excellent results from manipulation for prolapsed disc.

Another useful treatment is epidural injections. Here a quantity of local anaesthetic mixed with steroids is injected into the space just outside the spinal canal, so that it reaches the nerve roots where they emerge from the spinal cord. This is often combined with manipulation of the legs in order to move the sciatic nerve and to break down any small pieces of scar tissue that have formed around the nerve roots. This treatment is used where sciatica persists after the other signs of an acute disc prolapse have settled and often gives immediate relief from pain.

Back supports, corsets and plaster jackets are used by some doctors to prevent patients from bending their backs during the recovery period after a disc prolapse. Long-term use of a corset tends to weaken the back muscles so that the patient becomes uncomfortable when not wearing the support.

Prevention
People who have suffered from disc prolapse and those who are at risk because of their occupation need to learn to look after their backs. Proper lifting procedures such as keeping the back straight, bending at the knees rather than bending the back when picking things up from the floor, and avoiding lifting too much weight are all important. It is also vital not to become too over-weight – every pound of weight puts additional strain on the back. Regular exercise will increase the efficiency of the back muscles. Swimming is particularly beneficial since the effects of gravity are eliminated and the discs are not placed under undue strain. A firm mattress helps to prevent the back from sagging into a bent position; this is the principle of the 'orthopaedic' mattress.

Outlook
Some individuals fail to make a full recovery even following adequate treatment. It may be necessary for those in strenuous occupations to change to a less demanding job. The sufferer may have to adapt to a life which is not as active and recognize those things which particularly bother the back. The sympathetic understanding of employers, relatives and friends is important for such people.

The large majority of people who suffer from disc prolapse recover completely and are able to return to all their previous activities. The recovery process may take several months but patience is usually rewarded with a good result.

Sore throat

Q I always seem to get sore throats. What should I do about them?

A People have persistent or chronic sore throats for many quite different reasons. Smoking is one of the most common, and giving this up may be all that's necessary. However, it is often difficult to pinpoint the trouble, and it may be advisable for your doctor to send you to a throat specialist for investigation. It is important to have your complaint properly treated: so don't merely rely on gargling or sucking lozenges.

Q What is the best type of lozenge to suck?

A The most lozenges can do is to ease or soothe the soreness. They have no curative effect on the condition itself because most of the germs that are responsible for the sore throat are not on the surface of the throat but in the tissues below, where the chemicals in the lozenge – no matter how strong they are – simply cannot get at them. In fact, these strong antiseptic chemicals may actually make matters worse by causing a chemical inflammation on top of the inflammation from the infection that is already present. In addition, by killing off many of the normal organisms of the throat they may disturb the natural balance so drastically that other troubles – such as the growth of fungi – are actually encouraged. It is for these reasons that many doctors advise against using lozenges for sore throats. If you do want to suck them, however, opt for something very simple – such as fruit pastilles – rather than for the so-called 'antiseptic' lozenges. And if your sore throat is not better within a few days, see your doctor.

Q What is the difference between sore throat and tonsillitis?

A Sore throat is a *symptom*, that can have many causes and can result from inflammation in any of the tissues that surround the throat. The tonsils are part of these tissues; and tonsillitis is a medical term which refers specifically to inflammation of the tonsils. Thus tonsillitis is only one possible cause of sore throats.

This common symptom results from inflammation of the throat or the surrounding tissues. In most cases very simple treatment is all that is warranted.

The throat is one of the major passages of the body. Air constantly passes up and down from the nose and mouth to the lungs and back again; and food and drink periodically pass through the throat on their way from the mouth to the stomach. Obviously the throat is the only entry into the lungs or the stomach, so that all the air that we breathe and all the food and drink that we take have to pass through it. In addition the throat is exposed to any material coughed up from the lungs and bronchial passages or vomited up from the stomach.

The tissues that make up and surround the throat – the back of the tongue, the tonsils, the pharynx and the space at the back of the nose – are thus constantly exposed to the risk of infection, and it is hardly surprising that sore throat is one of the most common human ailments.

Three different views of the throat – inflammation of many of the tissues shown here may result in sore throat.

Causes

Sore throat is not a disease in itself: the basic feeling of soreness in the throat may be the result of inflammation of any of the tissues mentioned above. In addition, a sore throat is not necessarily caused by one particular germ, since there is a wide range of bacteria, viruses and other micro-organisms – such as fungi in the case of sore throat due to oral thrush – that can attack the throat.

In some cases the soreness is due not to infection, but to damage from other sources: swallowing food and drink that is too hot, discharge running down from the back of the nose, excessive smoking or sucking too many strong sweets. In some diseases – for example, influenza, scarlet fever, measles and diphtheria – a sore throat is only the first, and relatively unimportant, stage of a disease that develops into something much more widespread and serious. In most cases of sore throat, however, the trouble is confined to the throat.

The throat and surrounding tissue

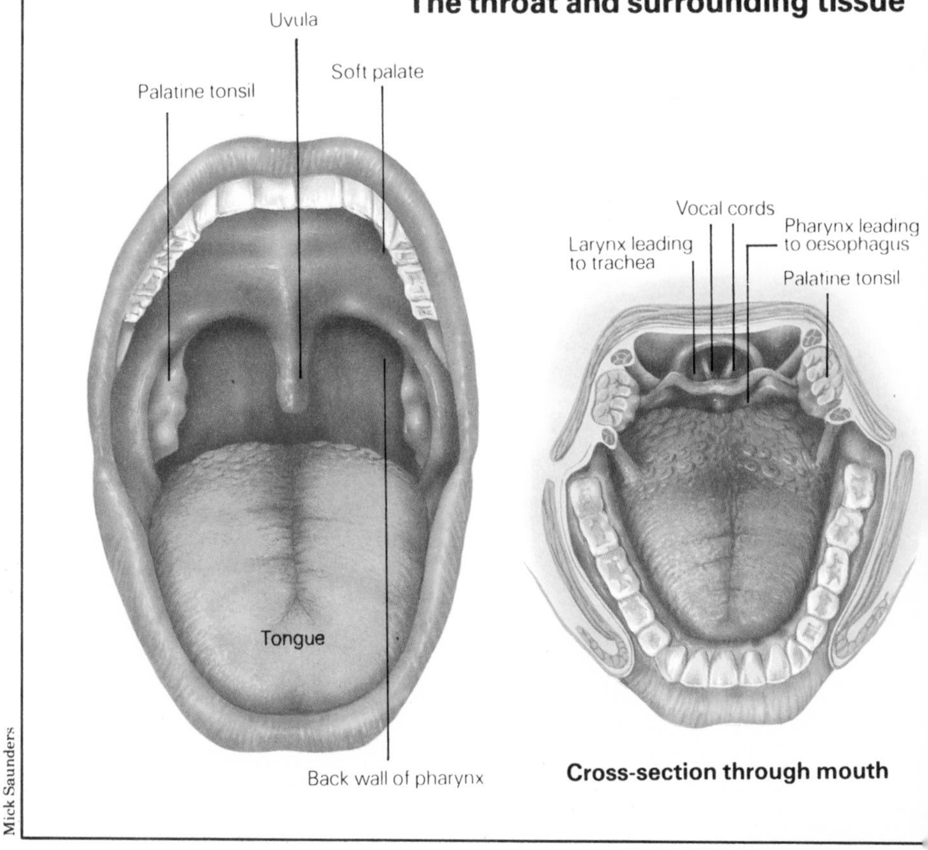

Uvula
Soft palate
Palatine tonsil
Tongue
Back wall of pharynx

Vocal cords
Larynx leading to trachea
Pharynx leading to oesophagus
Palatine tonsil

Cross-section through mouth

Mick Saunders

Gargling – even with something as mundane as ordinary salt and water or a mixture of aspirin and water – is an effective way of soothing the symptoms of a sore throat. In a Streptococcal throat (inset) the tissues of the throat and neighbouring organs such as the tonsils have been infected with streptococcus bacteria. This is what the infected area would look like to the doctor who examined the patient's throat.

The most common cause of sore throat is acute inflammation of the pharynx (leading to the oesophagus) called pharyngitis. Inflammation of the pharynx usually occurs suddenly, with a feeling of dryness and irritation as well as soreness. There is a constant desire to clear the throat, pain on swallowing, a persistent dry cough, and often headache and fever develop. Pharyngitis is usually due to infection by a virus rather than by bacteria, and taking antibiotics is not only useless, because viruses are unaffected by them, but may actually make things worse because of unwanted side-effects. Like most viral conditions, the infection clears up of its own accord in a few days and the only worthwhile treatment is to try to relieve the symptoms by means of hot drinks or the appropriate gargles.

Chronic pharyngitis may be the result of repeated attacks of acute pharyngitis, heavy smoking, working in dust or fumes, infected adenoids or tonsils, or discharge from the back of the nose or sinuses. It is important to find out exactly what is causing the chronic pharyngitis in order to make it permanently better.

Tonsillitis

Infections which start with a sore throat or pharyngitis often spread to nearby tissues and involve them too. The most commonly affected neighbouring organ is the tonsil. This is especially likely to be affected if the sore throat is due to infection with streptococcus bacteria – the septic or 'strep' throat. In sore throat associated with tonsillitis the pain becomes much more severe and swallowing is almost impossible. The affected tonsil is enlarged and red, the glands are swollen and tender and the patient will feel ill and have a high temperature. If the tonsillitis is not treated, quinsy – a peritonsillar abscess – may develop.

Another serious complication of an ordinary sore throat is when infection spreads from the pharynx to the Eustachian tube which leads to the inside of the ear. This causes otitis media, which is characterized by ear ache as well as a sore throat. Infection may also spread downwards from the pharynx into the voicebox or larynx, leading to laryngitis.

Diphtheria – thankfully much less common that it used to be – is yet another infection that involves a sore throat. This is characterized by the development of a membrane which is dirty grey in colour and a sweetish smell to the breath, as well as the sore throat.

Consulting your doctor

Most sore throats are more of a nuisance than an illness, clear up quickly on their own and require neither medical advice nor treatment. Nevertheless, some do not, and you should know when it is necessary to consult your doctor. If you have ever had rheumatic fever or nephritis, or you develop a rash or are running a fever of 38.9°C (102°F), or if your throat has a grey or yellow coating – then you are probably going to need medical help. You should also see your doctor if your sore throat shows no signs of improving by the third day.

Your doctor will probably look down your throat with a torch. He may wipe the back of your throat with a throat swab and send it to a laboratory for testing, so

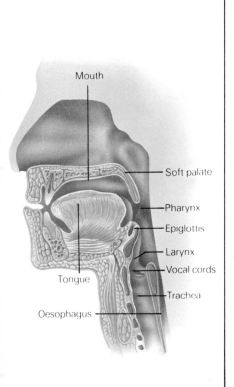

Mouth

Soft palate

Pharynx

Epiglottis

Larynx

Vocal cords

Tongue

Trachea

Oesophagus

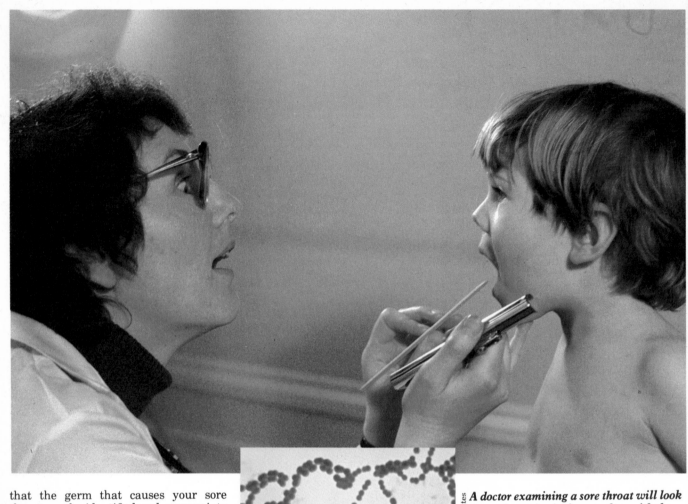

that the germ that causes your sore throat can be identified and appropriate treatment given. He may also feel your neck for enlarged glands, and examine your nose, ears and chest to see if they are involved too. If you have had a lot of sore throats your doctor may consider it necessary to refer you to a throat specialist for more conclusive diagnosis.

Self-help

Sore throat is one of those conditions for which you can do a great deal to help yourself. Hot drinks are soothing for a painful throat and it is worth putting yourself on a semi-solid food diet – so that swallowing is as free from pain as possible. Gargling is also helpful, though probably the relief is due more to the effect of the heat of the gargle than to what you choose to use as the gargle. Ordinary salt and water or a mixture of aspirin and water are effective; make up a salt gargle by putting two teaspoonsful of ordinary household salt in a teacup of hot – but not too hot – water and stirring until it is completely dissolved. Similarly, the aspirin gargle is made by dissolving two soluble aspirin in a teacup of hot water. It should be swallowed rather than spat out when you have

A doctor examining a sore throat will look down the patient's throat, often with the help of a torch to identify any inflammation that may be present. She may also take a throat swab to be sent to a laboratory for identification of the germ involved. The micrograph (left) shows streptococcus bacteria, which, by inflaming the tissues of the throat and surrounding organs, often causes sore throat. Corynebacterium diphtheriae (below) is the organism that causes diphtheria – a serious and potentially fatal infectious disease which is fortunately rare today.

finished gargling, so that the aspirin can do you good internally as well by its pain-killing and fever-reducing action.

In between gargling you may find it helpful to suck a soothing lozenge – fruit pastilles or formaldehyde lozenges are traditional and effective. If the soreness and irritation in your throat cause you to cough, old-fashioned lozenges, sucked as far back in your throat as you can manage, are safe and soothing. It should be pointed out, however, that the most lozenges will do is *soothe* your sore throat – not even the so-called 'antiseptic' lozenges have a specific medicinal property apart from their soothing effect.

Spina bifida

Q My sister had a spina bifida baby. Does this mean I am more likely to have one?

A Possibly, but the risks are quite small. Before you conceive, you should ask your doctor whether or not you need to take extra vitamins. It has been found in recent research that some mothers of spina bifida babies may have been lacking in certain vitamins. It is thus worthwhile consulting your doctor about this. Extra vitamins must anyway be obtained on prescription since they must be taken in regulated amounts. It is more dangerous to take too many than too few. As soon as you are pregnant, ask your hospital for a blood test to find out if the baby is normal. In addition, be sure to look after yourself properly during pregnancy. Eat a varied diet, get plenty of fresh air and suitable exercise, do not smoke or take drugs and drink very little alcohol. A healthy mother is far more likely to have a healthy baby.

Q Can a spina bifida baby grow into a perfectly normal adult and have normal children?

A Yes – it depends entirely on the type of spina bifida with which the baby is born. If the baby is only mildly affected, then the important nerves to the legs and bladder will be undamaged. In such a case the child will develop normally and be able to have perfectly normal children. However, adults with spina bifida do have a slightly increased risk of having a baby with spina bifida. On the other hand, if the baby is born with a severe form of the condition, he or she may have paralyzed legs and be unable to walk and will therefore be confined to a wheelchair. In addition, the majority of badly affected children have poor bladder control and need to wear a surgical appliance to collect their urine. Due to their numerous handicaps, severely affected adults tend not to get married, and those that do marry are likely to have sexual difficulties. Nevertheless, a few determined adults do marry despite being seriously handicapped, and it is possible for them to have quite normal children.

This serious congenital condition is often severely disabling and can be fatal. Many people do not realize, however, that some spina bifida babies may be nearly normal or may be successfully treated after birth.

Many people are confused about spina bifida because some affected children are normal whereas others are severely handicapped. This is because there are different types of spina bifida – the name simply means that some of the bones in the spine have not joined properly. Many people have such an abnormality without realizing it, because it can be a harmless condition which causes no disability.

Possible causes

Spina bifida occurs more commonly in some families than in others. The reasons for this are not fully understood. But once doctors know a spina bifida foetus has been conceived they may want to screen other members of the family – even cousins – who have become pregnant, as a risk has already been identified.

It has also been discovered recently that some mothers who have given birth to spina bifida babies may have been lacking in certain vitamins, and there is now some evidence to suggest that taking extra vitamins before conception may substantially reduce the chances of an affected baby being conceived. But these vitamins must only be prescribed by a doctor in the correct dosage.

Types of spina bifida

Sometimes a baby is born with a soft cyst on the back, which is called a 'meningocele'. It is usually on the neck or the bottom of the spine, but can occur at any point, and is an outward bulging of the fluid which surrounds the nerves and spinal cord. The danger is that the skin covering it may be very thin, and may

This little spina bifida boy can 'pedal' himself along on his tricycle just like any other child – he simply uses his hands, not his feet.

Q I am 40 and have just discovered that I am pregnant. Do I have a greater risk of having a baby with spina bifida?

A No, not unless you have already had a baby with an abnormal brain or spine, or unless you have had several miscarriages. Statistically, however, a baby with some congenital abnormality – such as Down's syndrome – is more likely to be born to a woman over 35. Both Down's syndrome and spina bifida can be detected by amniocentesis, the test where some of the amniotic fluid – the fluid surrounding the foetus – is extracted from the womb and examined. In the case of spina bifida, the amniotic fluid will contain certain chemicals in abnormal amounts.

Q I had an abortion after the baby was diagnosed as having spina bifida in an amniocentesis test. Does this mean that my future pregnancies will not be normal?

A Not necessarily, but you do run a greater than average risk of conceiving another baby with a deformity of the brain or spine. However, the risk is still fairly small. To be precise, if you were to have another 25 babies, it is likely that one would have spina bifida. The problem is that you have no way of telling whether it will be the next one or the 25th. The only way to be sure is to have an amniocentesis with each pregnancy. In addition, your obstetrician will probably recommend an ultrasound examination of the developing baby or even an examination of the foetus using a special little telescope inserted into the womb. This is called a fetoscope and enables the doctor to view the foetus directly. However, it would be pointless to have these tests unless you were prepared to have another termination if an abnormality were discovered. Before you get pregnant again, visit your doctor because you may be lacking in certain vitamins. He will then be able to give you the correct dose on prescription, since they must be taken in exactly the right amounts.

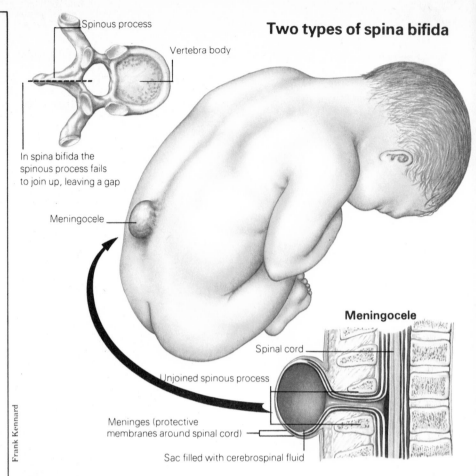

Frank Kennard

Two types of spina bifida

Spinous process

Vertebra body

In spina bifida the spinous process fails to join up, leaving a gap

Meningocele

Meningocele

Spinal cord

Unjoined spinous process

Meninges (protective membranes around spinal cord)

Sac filled with cerebrospinal fluid

become damaged and liable to infection. Early surgery is very successful in this type of spina bifida and the baby usually grows into a perfectly normal adult.

Unfortunately most cases of spina bifida are more serious. In these types of open spina bifida the baby is born with part of the backbone, some nerves and the spinal cord lying exposed at the bottom of the cyst which often bursts even before birth. Most of these babies will be handicapped, the severity of the handicap depending on the part of the back affected and the amount of damage to nerves.

Since the extent of nerve damage varies greatly the baby may have little or no disability or, at the other extreme, may be severely disabled. If the neck is affected, then the nerves used for breathing are usually damaged and nearly all these babies die soon after birth. If the very bottom of the spine is involved, only a few nerves going to the feet may be abnormal and the baby can be born with nothing more serious than club feet. This can be cured by physiotherapy which the mother can be taught so that she can treat the baby herself at home, or by orthopaedic surgery. Sometimes a few of the nerves which control the bladder are slightly damaged so that the child may be incontinent.

If the middle of the back is affected the results are far more serious. Generally, the higher the opening in the back, the worse is the outlook. All of these children will have at least some deformity or weakness of the legs – indeed some will never be able to walk and will be confined to a wheelchair. Others will be able to walk after many operations on their bones and tendons, provided they wear calipers for support.

Many of these children are incontinent of bowel and bladder and may need some form of incontinence control such as a catheter to drain the urine. A severely affected child may also develop curvature of the spine at puberty which can, however, be rectified by a major operation. Hydrocephalus – excessive water on the brain—often accompanies this kind of spina bifida. An operation has to be done, to drain this out into the chest or abdomen, through special tubes and valves. For various reasons, some of these children are also mentally retarded to differing degrees.

In another form of spina bifida the baby is born apparently normal except for a fatty lump at the bottom of the back. The danger of this is that it may be ignored because the baby can move his or her legs when newly born. However, many

Myelomeningocele

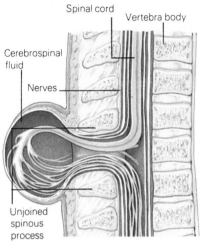

Spinal cord
Vertebra body
Cerebrospinal fluid
Nerves
Unjoined spinous process

In spina bifida, the two halves of the spinous process – which normally forms the vertebral arch – fail to join up. A baby may then be born with a meningocele, a cyst over the gap in the spine which contains spinal fluid. This can be treated by an operation on the newborn baby. A more serious form is the myelomeningocele, when some nerves and the spinal cord are exposed, and bones may even be missing. This always causes a degree of paralysis.

deteriorate as they get older, so it is very important that a specialist sees them for regular check-ups. An operation may be done to free the trapped nerves at the first sign of trouble, although this is not always completely successful.

asbah

Possible treatments

An expert should examine a baby born with spina bifida straightaway, even though this may mean that the baby has to be separated from his mother and sent to one of the big regional centres where he or she will be in the care of a paediatric surgeon.

A whole team of specialists can then decide whether or not the baby will benefit from surgery, often carried out before the baby is 24 hours old in order to achieve the best results and to reduce the risk of serious infection. Many surgeons will not recommend an operation if it is thought that the baby will grow up with severe deformities, lack of bladder control and hydrocephalus. However, some are willing to operate if this is what the parents wish.

If the baby cannot be helped by an urgent operation, then doctors differ in their advice to parents. Some doctors

Even if spina bifida means that you are confined to a wheelchair, this need not stop you taking part in normal activities.

recommend that the parents take the baby home as soon as they feel able to cope. Many of these babies die from meningitis within a few weeks. However, the others feed well and the spina bifida heals by itself in about six to eight weeks, although it frequently forms a big cyst which has to be removed several months later. Many of these babies develop fluid on the brain which has to be treated by an operation when they are three to six months old. Alternatively, some doctors think that they are best kept in hospital to be given regular painkillers. Sadly, severely affected babies do not feed well and most die within six months.

It rests with the parents to decide the kind of treatment they want their baby to have. In Britain, parents who keep their baby at home may find it helpful to contact any one of the spina bifida associations which can give support.

Prevention

If a pregnant woman comes from a family where spina bifida has already occurred, she should tell her obstetrician who will arrange for her to have a special blood test. If this is not absolutely normal, the woman is usually advised to have an amniocentesis test and an ultrasound examination of the foetus. The purpose of these tests is to find out if the baby is affected, and if so, to offer the mother a termination.

Since recent evidence suggests that taking extra vitamins will reduce the likelihood of a spina bifida baby being born, a woman should see her doctor before she conceives, in case she needs extra vitamins.

The fact that one of these children is handicapped does not inhibit either of them from playing naturally together.

387

Squint

Q What is meant by a 'lazy eye' and is this the same thing as a squint?

A A 'lazy' eye is an eye that has not reached its full visual potential. At birth the eyes are capable of seeing very little, and it is not until the age of five years that normal vision is fully acquired. Any disorder that interrupts this maturing process will, if untreated, result in a lazy eye with defective vision. Squint is the commonest condition that may result in a 'lazy eye'.

Q My five-year-old son wears glasses for his squint but I have noticed that he looks over the top of them or through the side. They can't be doing him much good if he isn't using them properly. Wouldn't he be better off wearing a patch over his eye to correct his squint?

A It sounds as though the prescription for his glasses is wrong. Certainly he obtains no benefit from wearing them unless he looks through the lenses. You should take him back to the eye specialist to have them checked. Patching one eye will not help as this is part of the treatment to correct a 'lazy eye'.

Q Does a person with a squint see 'double'?

A Yes. Initially, everyone with a squint sees double, but a child soon suppresses from his or her consciousness the image that is seen with the squinting eye, and so achieves comfortable single vision. An adult is less able to adapt to his predicament and may have to cover one eye to achieve single vision.

Q How many children are likely to get a squint and what happens if it isn't treated?

A Childhood squint is fairly common, occurring in about three per cent of children. It often occurs within families although it is not inherited directly. If a squint is not treated it can result in impaired vision in the affected eye and a weakening of the ability to see in the third dimension.

Squint is the inability to move both eyes in the same direction at the same time. The condition can affect adults, but occurs more commonly in children.

During the first six months of life a baby's eyes may move about randomly in any direction, but after this age they should move together. If the eyes are not parallel the child is said to have a squint, or strabismus. (This is also commonly called a 'turn' or a 'boss-eye'.) It has no connection with screwing up the eyes, an affectation of no consequence to which young children seem particularly prone.

Normally, a child is able to use both eyes together and blend the images seen with each eye into one unified perception with full three-dimensional vision. A child with a squint is unable to do this because the eyes are looking in different directions. He or she compensates for this by suppressing the image he sees with the deviating eye so that he is not troubled by double vision. Because the child's visual system is immature, this suppression results in permanent impairment of vision unless the condition is treated, and the squinting eye becomes 'lazy' (see Lazy eye page 214).

Most childhood squints are convergent with the squinting eye moving inwards. Divergent squint, when the eye moves outwards, is more common later in life, as is a vertical squint.

Silent film star Ben Turpin's rich comic talent was enhanced by his startling appearance. He capitalized on his squint to hilarious effect.

Kobal Collection

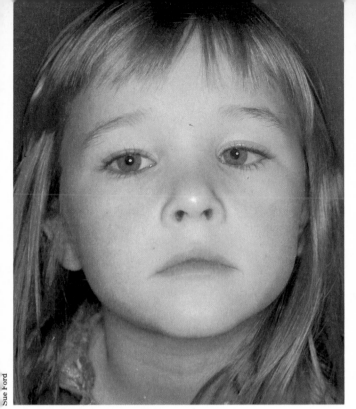
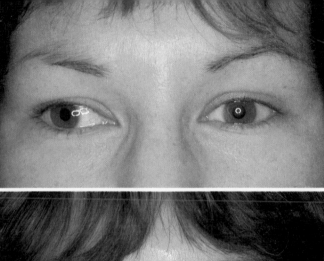
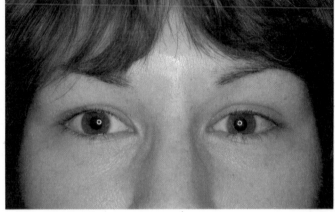

A squint is caused by an imbalance between the eye's muscles and focusing mechanism. Squints can be convergent – one eye moves inward (above), or divergent – one eye moves outward (far right). Surgery on the child with a divergent squint was very successful.

Causes and dangers of squint

Some squints are congenital, appearing at birth, but most infantile squints appear between the ages of two and four years, often after a childhood illness and initially only when the child is tired. Many factors are involved in its cause but it is usually associated with an imbalance between the focusing mechanism of the eye and the muscular control of the eye itself (see Eyes and eyesight pp 134-37).

Squint can also occur later in life, although this is less common. Because an adult's visual system is fully developed this type of squint is accompanied by troublesome double vision which the patient is often unable to suppress. Although there is no risk of the squinting eye becoming lazy, the disorientation caused by double vision – so that the world seems to swim around the sufferer – is severely incapacitating.

A squint in adult life is usually caused by damage to an ocular nerve or muscle and as such requires a thorough medical examination to identify the cause. Diabetes, high blood pressure and thyroid disorders are the common culprits.

Getting advice and treatment

If you think that your child may be developing a squint it is important that you seek medical advice immediately. Fortunately a lot of children only appear to be squinting because of the presence of vertical folds of skin on either side of the nasal bridge. By the time the child reaches school age the nasal bridge is more developed and the 'pseudo-squint' has disappeared. However, only a specialist can differentiate between a 'true' and an 'apparent' squint and the two may exist together. Do not let complacency jeopardize your child's vision, but always seek advice about the problem.

If glasses are necessary the child should be encouraged to wear them at all times and some squints are cured by glasses alone. It is important to realize that the glasses do not necessarily make the child's vision any clearer – their purpose is to reduce the amount of focusing that the eye muscles must exert. This relieves the excessive tendency towards in-

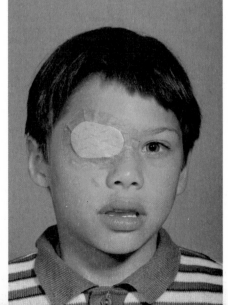

ward movement of the eye which is linked with focusing.

In many cases of squint, glasses only partly correct the condition and a full correction is only achieved with surgery on the muscles that move the eye. Essentially, this involves weakening the muscles that are overactive and strengthening the underactive muscles.

Squint operations are routine for the opthalmic surgeon and necessitate only a few days' stay in hospital for the child. After the operation there is surprisingly little discomfort and within three to four weeks the scars will have healed and become virtually invisible.

Squints that appear later in life are treated differently. Any underlying medical disorder must be dealt with and the initial aim of ocular treatment is to alleviate the troublesome double vision. This can be achieved either by occluding (covering) the deviating eye with a patch or by incorporating a prism into the patient's spectacle lens which artificially bends the light rays to compensate for the deviation. Adult squints which arise because of an impairment in control of eye movements sometimes improve with orthoptic exercises. These are designed to increase and strengthen the patient's ability to use the two eyes in unison.

If an ocular muscle is paralyzed surgery may be necessary. However it is essential that this is deferred for at least six months as spontaneous recovery is not unexceptional in these cases.

A lazy eye is usually the result of an untreated squint. Patching the normal eye will force the lazy eye to work.

Sterilization

Q How easy is it to reverse a sterilization operation?

A This depends on the method used. It is possible to attempt to reverse sterilization operations where only the Fallopian tubes have been obstructed. You must also convince your doctor of the importance to you of having another baby, since this is a major operation which is quite expensive to perform. There is often a long waiting list for it as it is not considered urgent. Even when performed by experts, the operation has only a 50 per cent chance of success. For this reason it is important to realize that if you are sterilized, it is very likely that you will never have another pregnancy even if you are prepared to undergo major surgery in an attempt to achieve it. Therefore you must be absolutely sure in your mind that you will never want to become pregnant again, so that you will have no regrets later on.

Q What are the dangers of having a sterilization operation reversed?

A Every operation involves a small risk as it puts extra strain on the heart and lungs, but probably the greatest risk of this kind of operation is the possibility that if you later conceive, the embryo will grow in one of the Fallopian tubes until it bursts through, causing severe internal haemorrhage. This is called an ectopic pregnancy.

Q When I recently had an abortion I asked to be sterilized at the same time as I do not want any more children. The doctor advised me against this. Can you explain why?

A There are two main reasons. Probably the most important is that you are marginally more likely to develop blood clots when sterilized at this time. These clots can travel to your heart or lungs which is obviously dangerous. The other reason that sterilization is not often done at the same time as an abortion is that doctors are worried in case a woman may be too distressed then to make the correct decision on such a radical matter.

This is obviously an effective, once-and-for-all method of contraception, and for some women it is suitable. But it is drastic – the woman must be prepared to rule out any possibility of ever having another child.

Anthea Sieveking/Vision International

The term sterilization is now used rather more loosely than it was when the procedure was first put into practice. This is because occasionally an operation is performed to attempt to reverse a sterilization operation.

Nevertheless, any woman choosing this method of contraception must be confident that she will want no more children even if her personal circumstances change, since it is potentially irreversible.

Methods of sterilization

For a woman to be fertile she must be able to release eggs from her ovaries; she must have intact Fallopian tubes along which the eggs can pass to the womb; and she must have a normal womb in which the fertilized egg can embed itself and develop into a foetus and eventually a baby. All methods of sterilization work by permanently blocking one or more of these stages.

Most sterilization operations consist in blocking the Fallopian tubes in one of a number of ways. This method is particularly popular as it involves a relatively minor operation, although it is still a slightly more risky procedure than sterilizing a man by vasectomy. Women sterilized in this way do not have sudden menopausal symptoms – as happens when the ovaries are involved – and their periods continue, although these may be slightly heavier.

The function of the Fallopian tubes may be permanently interrupted in a variety of ways. First, they may be completely removed, a method of sterili-

When a woman decides to be sterilized, the first step is for her to visit her general practitioner. He will then arrange an appointment for her with a gynaecologist at a hospital or clinic. Most gynaecologists prefer to interview the husband, too, to ensure that both partners are fully aware of the implications of this operation.

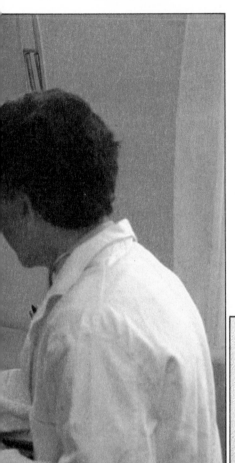

zation which is very unlikely to fail. Alternatively, a portion – about 1 cm (⅓ in) – may be cut away from the middle of each, or they may be cut through or burnt by the method of diathermy. The burn is made in only two places but the effect will travel along the tubes, thus damaging them. In some cases, clips are placed on both tubes, or a loop of each is pulled into a tight plastic ring. All these procedures, except for total removal of the Fallopian tubes, are potentially reversible, but any woman undergoing one of these operations should assume that it will make her permanently sterile. They are probably the methods most often used and there are seldom any complications with this type of operation.

Unfortunately, between one and four

Before performing a sterilization operation doctors have to be convinced that a woman has completed her family, and will want no more children, even if her personal situation should change. In the right circumstances, it can be an ideal form of contraception, and one which has no side-effects such as the Pill does. Sex, too, may be more enjoyable as the woman no longer has the ever-present fear of an unwanted pregnancy which can be inhibiting.

women in every thousand who have this type of operation subsequently become pregnant. This is probably because the tubes get unblocked. Another rare problem is that a fertilized egg can be trapped in one of the Fallopian tubes, where it grows until it ruptures the tube and passes into the abdominal cavity. This is called an ectopic pregnancy and is treated by surgically removing the affected tube. These problems are nevertheless uncommon and many women are very happy with this type of sterilization.

There are other methods which are not often used as they are less satisfactory. For example, it is possible to sterilize a woman by removing or damaging her ovaries, but she will then rapidly develop menopausal symptoms such as hot flushes. This method is usually contemplated only if the ovaries are already damaged or diseased.

Women and doctors seldom consider hysterectomy – the removal of the uterus – an ideal form of contraception because it involves a major operation. However, it may be a sensible choice if the woman has gynaecological problems such as large fibroids or very heavy periods, both of which may be effectively cured by hysterectomy.

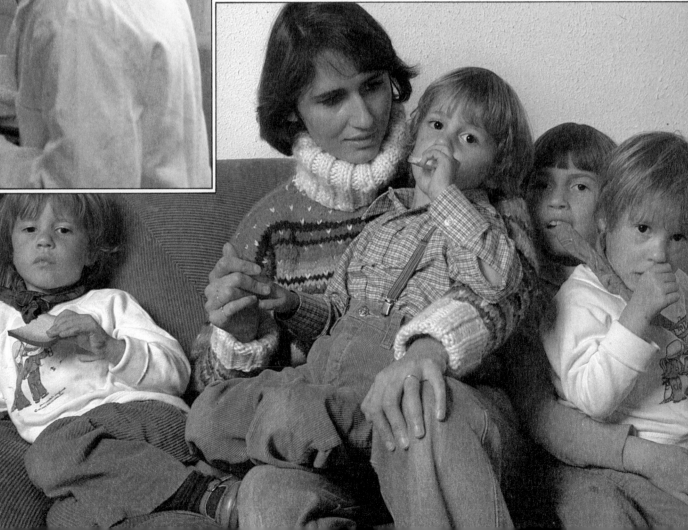

Sterilization by cutting the Fallopian tubes

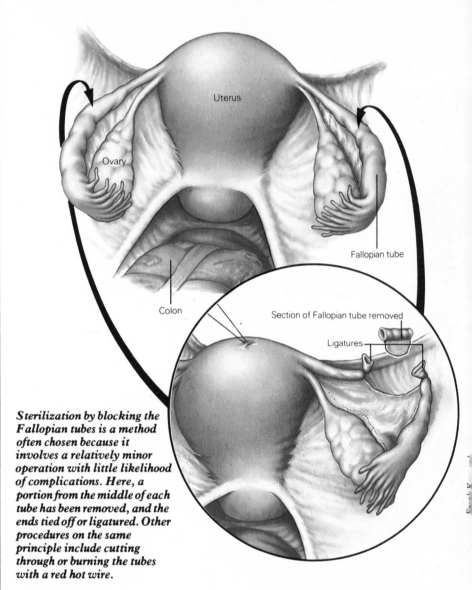

Sterilization by blocking the Fallopian tubes is a method often chosen because it involves a relatively minor operation with little likelihood of complications. Here, a portion from the middle of each tube has been removed, and the ends tied off or ligatured. Other procedures on the same principle include cutting through or burning the tubes with a red hot wire.

Advantages and disadvantages

When a woman decides to be sterilized she is making a major irreversible decision about her life which can yield many benefits. She will not have to make regular visits to the family planning clinic, and she will not have to worry in future about the side-effects which she might otherwise have suffered with another form of contraception. She may even find that she enjoys her sex life more when she is free from the fear of an unwanted pregnancy.

On the other hand, some women find that they enjoy sex more when they are running the risk of becoming pregnant. Moreover, there is always the possibility that a woman may at a later date want more children – for example if she were to form a new relationship or if any of her children should unfortunately die.

Doctors are also very worried about sterilizing women who are unmarried, have no children or are very young, especially as there are successful reversible forms of contraception on the market which may suit them better. Of course, in every case the decision to sterilize a woman will depend ultimately on the individual herself and her doctor.

For this reason it is extremely important for any woman contemplating sterilization to weigh up the pros and cons as rationally as possible. If she has any worries or questions, her doctor may set her mind at rest. Further, although the decision rests ultimately with her, she should also discuss her thoughts and feelings with her husband, whose agreement may be required.

Sterilization procedures

Site of sterilization	Procedure	Surgical method used	General remarks
Ovaries	Removal of both ovaries	Transverse incision in the abdominal wall just above the pubic hair line	Usually used only if the ovaries are diseased as this method precipitates the menopause
	Radiation of both ovaries	No operation required	Only used if a woman is very obese and requires sterilization – she will rapidly become menopausal
Fallopian tubes	Removal of both Fallopian tubes Removal of mid-portion of both tubes Cutting or burning of both tubes Placing clips on both tubes Pulling a loop of each tube through a tight plastic ring	Incision through vaginal or lower abdominal wall Incision through vaginal or lower abdominal wall or use of the laparoscope	Very unlikely to fail as a form of sterilization Probably the commonest methods used as they are all relatively minor operations with a low incidence of complications
Uterus	Removal of uterus (hysterectomy)	Incision in the lower abdomen	A method used if a woman has completed her family and has other gynaecological problems such as heavy periods or large fibroids
		Removal through the vagina	This method used if the woman has completed her family and has a vaginal prolapse

Why choose sterilization?

There seem to be three important times in a woman's life when she may consider sterilization as a form of contraception. The first may be when she is having an abortion. Although her decision is often completely rational, many doctors prefer not to sterilize a woman at the same time as performing an abortion. There are two main reasons for this. Firstly, she runs a greater risk of developing blood clots in her leg and pelvic veins during the operation, since she still has in her blood the altered levels of clotting factors which are associated with pregnancy. Secondly, many women may make the wrong decision at a time when they are undergoing much emotional turmoil.

Similar arguments apply against sterilizing a woman immediately after having a baby, as well as the further argument that it is sensible to be certain that the new baby will thrive. Often, however, women and doctors feel that the convenience of the mother being sterilized while still in hospital with the baby outweighs the disadvantages.

Women also choose sterilization as they approach middle age rather than continuing to take the Pill.

Arranging to be sterilized

Women can arrange to be sterilized by asking their family doctor to refer them to a hospital or private clinic to see a gynaecologist. Many gynaecologists prefer to interview the husband and wife together to be certain that they both understand what the operation entails and the disadvantages as well as the advantages of this form of contraception. If the gynaecologist is convinced that sterilization is appropriate, given all the circumstances of a case, he will arrange a convenient date for the operation to be performed. It is very important that the couple continue to take contraceptive precautions until the operation has been done, as it is possible for a pregnancy to continue normally if conception took place just before the operation.

After the operation

An instrument called a laparoscope is often used in performing a sterilization. This is a fine rod which allows a clear view of the Fallopian tubes, and along which the necessary instruments can be passed to perform the operation.

Laparoscopic sterilization is occasionally done while the woman is awake, but of course the area where the laparoscope is to be inserted is first made completely numb so that the operation is relatively painless. The majority of sterilizations are, however, performed under general anaesthetic and the woman is allowed home the next day. The scar will be tender for several days and most women prefer to rest as much as possible during this time, although this is difficult if a woman has a large family.

Unlike male sterilization, female sterilization is effective immediately so that a couple need not use any other form of contraception. Most women wait a week or so after being sterilized before having sexual intercourse so that their scars will have time to heal. If the woman has been sterilized by hysterectomy her scars will take even longer to heal, and she would be well advised to wait at least a month or even six weeks before attempting to have sexual intercourse.

Outlook

Stories abound about the disastrous consequences for a woman who has her Fallopian tubes blocked off. Most of these are completely untrue. The woman will not look different, become less feminine or lose interest in sex. Indeed, she will probably enjoy it more as she no longer has to worry about the possibility of an unwanted pregnancy. The operation will certainly not make her put on weight, she will still have periods and go through the menopause in exactly the same way as if she had not been sterilized.

Most surgeons performing the operation are well aware that a woman does not want an unsightly scar – and in most cases it will eventually be hidden at the umbilicus or by her pubic hair as it regrows.

It is very important for every woman to continue having routine smear tests after she has been sterilized, as she will still need to be screened against the possibility of developing cancer of the cervix.

Streptomycin

Q My father-in-law had his tuberculosis treated with streptomycin and now he finds he can't ride a bike. Why is this?

A One of the problems with streptomycin, and all the drugs that are related to it is that they can damage the ears, particularly the nerves that convey the messages concerning balance from the ears to the brain. Thus your father-in-law's ability to balance when riding his bike has been affected. These adverse effects are most likely to occur in people over the age of 40.

Q Is streptomycin only used in the treatment of tuberculosis?

A The main use has certainly been in the treatment of TB, although there certainly are other uses. For example, the drug is effective against the bacterium that causes plague—pasteurella pestis. Although streptomycin itself has a rather limited use these days, its related drugs, particularly one called gentamicin, are used frequently as they are widely effective.

Q Can you take streptomycin in the form of tablets, or can it only be injected?

A Unfortunately, it has to be given by injection. But there is an advantage to this as the antibiotic will not be absorbed by the intestines and will thus kill all the germs in the gut. In fact streptomycin is not much used for this purpose, but the closely related drug neomycin is used to prepare the large bowel for surgery.

Q If streptomycin is such a good drug for TB, why did they have to give me two other drugs as well?

A TB is an organism which is very liable to develop resistance to antibiotics. The problem can be avoided by giving three drugs at once. Any strain of the organism which is resistant to one drug does not have the chance to flourish since it is killed by one of the other two drugs given simultaneously.

This powerful antibiotic is one of the many available to doctors today. But use of streptomycin has to be carefully controlled because it can have side-effects.

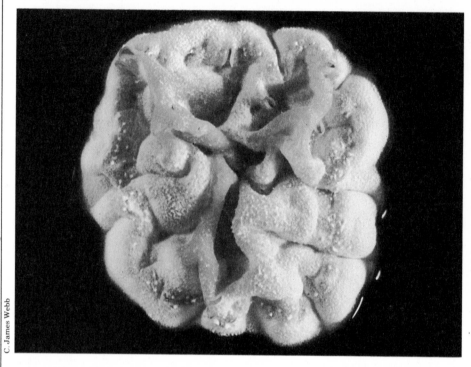

C. James Webb

Streptomycin, the second antibiotic ever to be discovered, has played a great role in medicine. It is effective against tuberculosis and it is the parent compound of a whole group of useful antibiotics. However, it has quite severe problems with toxicity and this limits its usefulness.

Streptomycin was discovered as the result of a search for compounds which had antibiotic activity. It is made from a mould called streptomyces griseus which was originally cultured from a heavily manured field, and also from a chicken's throat.

How it works

Streptomycin is one of the antibiotics that actually kills bacteria, rather than merely stopping their growth, like tetracycline for example. It works by poisoning the ribosomes in the bacteria, and it is the ribosomes that are responsible for protein production in the bacteria.

Streptomycin and all its related drugs called aminoglycosides, have to be given by injection, since they are not absorbed from the intestine after being taken by mouth. But one useful property of streptomycin and the other aminoglycosides is that they work well with penicillin. The drugs enhance each other's potency, a property called synergism.

Streptomycin is made from the soil fungus streptomyces griseus. This antibiotic is lethal to many different bacteria.

Side-effects

One of the things that has limited the use of streptomycin is the fact that it has quite severe side-effects.

The main side-effect is on the nerve to the ear, called the auditory nerve. In the case of streptomycin the effect is predominantly on the sense of balance, although the other aminoglycosides vary in their effects with some producing more effect on hearing than on balance. If someone does receive too much streptomycin, then he will notice ringing in the ears and giddiness. Although this is reduced as the drug is stopped, there may still be permanent effects, and the period of recovery can be very long.

The drug is excreted by the kidneys, so special caution has to be exercised with people who have kidney disease. In cases of kidney failure, where the related drug gentamicin is often used, it may only be necessary to give the drug once every two days since the excretion is delayed.

Despite this, streptomycin has saved many lives over the years, and it is still sometimes used in the treatment of tuberculosis.

Stress

Q **Is stress almost always destructive, or can people really thrive under pressure?**

A It really depends on how you define 'stress'. Doctors often refer to it in terms of some disease or disorder – something that develops once things have got out of hand, when 'coping' mechanisms have been inadequate and there has been some sort of breakdown in the person's physical or mental stability. Here, stress is seen as the result of failure to cope with a build-up of tension or strain, and is an indication that a destructive breakdown has developed.

In layman's terms, however, stress can be synonymous with strain and tension rather than a 'failure to cope'. In themselves strain and tension can certainly be constructive and creative; and we would, indeed, be dull, static and uninventive people without them. It is interesting to note the way in which a time of challenge that spells doom, disaster and breakdown to one person, is no less than the stimulus which turns out to be the absolute making of another.

Q **Is there any crunch point that is especially common in people who develop stress illnesses?**

A Yes. While there is a wide variety of quite different circumstances that cause different personalities to become the victims of stress, there is one particular set of circumstances that occurs much more commonly than others. It is when people cannot see that the goals that they have set themselves are beyond them, and that they need to readjust their sights. Ambition is a necessary and constructive force, but if serious stress disorders are to be avoided, it needs to be tempered with an ability to give up and change direction if it becomes clear that its achievement is either beyond one's capacity or is impossible to achieve for some other reason. The so-called 'mid-life crisis', when stress disorders reach epidemic proportions, is most commonly due to reasons of this nature.

The pace of life today takes its toll on us all. It causes varying degrees of stress which – unless certain preventive measures are taken – can mount up from simple tension to mental or physical breakdown.

Sally and Richard Greenhill

Conflict and stress between ourselves and both our environment and our fellow men is an inescapable fact of life. And the pressures that result from excessive stress are probably greater today than they have ever been before.

What stress does

Stress serves a useful purpose in stimulating effort, inventiveness and high standards. But when there is more then we can cope with, a stress disorder is likely to develop, and this illness may be either mental or physical in its main manifestations. Whether or not we get to a point of breakdown, and how this may affect us, depends on many factors such as the intensity of the stress to which we are subjected versus our capacity to contain and adapt to it. And this in turn will depend on the character features that we inherit at birth, the experience of our formative years and the effects of sub-

The hectic yet often monotonous life many of us are forced to lead makes a certain amount of stress unavoidable. What we can do, however, is take positive steps whenever possible to ensure that the pressures of life are kept to a minimum.

sequent successes and failures in coping with life's many ups and downs.

What is necessary for emotional health is a reasonably peaceful and yet fulfilling balance between ourselves and the circumstances in which we find ourselves and with which we have to live. It is important for us to bear in mind that a large number of factors are interacting together and that this creates a constantly changing picture which may hold still hardly long enough for us to grasp it in detail. It is not surprising, therefore, that most of us find ourselves, our state of mind at any particular time and our motives very confusing. Fortunately, the

Hong Kong's spectacularly beautiful harbour belies the fact that it is the world's most densely populated city: overcrowding and appalling living conditions are both prime causes of stress. Being stuck in a traffic jam (inset) can make the most calm person feel very tense.

Sally and Richard Greenhill

Tony Stone Associates

main features are usually clear and persistent enough for effective diagnosis and treatment to be possible, if necessary.

Mental and physical reactions

The ability to cope adequately with stress depends on a combination of constitutional or natural resources, character, training and experience.

Sudden intense stress, which is closely related to fear and represents a direct challenge to our basic instinct for survival, provokes a chemical and subsequently a physical response as well as the severe emotional feeling which we call panic. This consists of the production of greatly increased amounts of the hormone adrenalin from the adrenal glands, which are situated on top of each kidney. The adrenalin is released directly into the bloodstream and has an immediate effect in preparing the body to take immediate action in the direction of either fight or flight. This surge of adrenalin from the adrenal glands occurs in response to either physical or emotional stress and prepares a wide variety of body tissues and organs for a vigorous reaction to a crisis which may be severe enough to involve fear or panic.

When necessary, a variety of defence mechanisms may also be called upon, usually subconsciously. This may be done by discounting or refusing to recognize the reality that exists; denying the existence of unpleasant facts such as a major breakdown in a relationship, failure at work or in personal standards, or chronic illness. Aggression, hostility and virtual persecution towards others because of our own failings may occur. We may rationalize failure to achieve an objective by convincing ourselves that we did not really want it anyway. We may compensate for our failure in one direction by exceptional attainment in another. We may displace our distress by displaying friendliness and charm where we feel hostility and anxiety. It is usually only when these defence mechanisms are exhausted or prove inadequate that stress disorders result.

The signs of stress

Stress disorders are often preceded by feelings of excessive anxiety, fear, distress, guilt and shame. In physical terms, prolonged, repeated or severe stress can precipitate a wide variety of disturbances of bodily functions. These are often referred to as psychosomatic illnesses and include many cases of 'tension' headache, digestive disorders and skin disease. Stress may also play a part in causing high blood pressure, hardening of the arteries, heart attacks and strokes.

Stresses that are fundamentally emotional or social often carry the added problem that they may be almost self-perpetuating, because of the alterations that they bring about in the victim's scale of values and way of looking at things. Even though their reactions to it may vary, most people can agree that a rash is a rash and that a raised temperature constitutes a fever. But a depressed person is likely to see everything – both within himself and in the world outside – in substantially different tones from the rest of us, and his reactions may well be disturbed by this disorientation as well as by his depression.

Weighing up the cost of stress

As with all the other things that are likely to get in the way of us living as long as we would like to do, it is better to try to prevent the situation arising in the first

Q Does our threshold for stress change as we grow older?

A For most people it certainly does. Children and adolescents often suffer considerably from stress, particularly if they do not have secure home circumstances; they find the breadth of the biological and emotional changes that are taking place in them quite overwhelming, and more than they can cope with. Thereafter, if the gradual growth of experience of life's buffetings leads to the development of maturity and wisdom, the likelihood of stress disorders becomes progressively less. For most people, the least stressful period of their lives is likely to be in their fifties and sixties, when they are at the peak of their careers, any 'mid-life crisis' is past, and their families have grown up. Unfortunately, after this period may come a time of renewed stress associated with the tensions that can be brought about by retirement and the limitations imposed by ageing.

Q Is everybody equally likely to suffer from stress?

A No, there are substantial differences in how each of us reacts to stressful circumstances. As with many other things in life – such as discomfort, pain, disability and so on – some of us have a high threshold and can put up with a great amount of adversity without showing any signs of stress, while other people are distressed by quite minor levels of inconvenience.

Q Is it only people's personality that determines whether or not they suffer from stress disorders?

A No. Whether or not a stress disorder develops in a particular person depends on the balance between two different sets of factors. The first relates to the person's personality, experience and state of mental and physical health; the second to the intensity of the strain to which the person is being subjected: some will be 'heavy' enough to break anybody, while others will be 'light' enough to bother nobody. What happens in the majority of cases, between the two extremes, will depend on the personality factor.

place, than to rely on treatment after the event. With stress, however, this is often easier said than done, since the circumstances under which most of us have to live today make some degree of pressure almost inevitable. Nevertheless, sitting down and taking a long, hard look at ourselves in order to assess where we are most vulnerable to the impact of stress, and how we can either deflect it or deal with it, will pay great dividends. In doing this we need to see – as accurately and objectively as possible – precisely where we are in our lives and whether the cost of having got there and of staying there is really worthwhile.

We need next to review our ambitions and plans for the future, along the same critical lines. In doing so we may come to feel that in pursuit of achievement, the balance between the stress cost and the reward has slowly but steadily shifted to a point at which the price we are paying in risking our very lives far exceeds the

real rewards we are getting – or are ever likely to get. If this is the case, a substantial revision of our present way of life is called for – in the interests of sheer survival. This inevitably means a major change in future goals and plans – and probably in our attitudes about living and what life should contain as well. Perhaps what is required is no less than a virtual about-turn from the frantic, killing attempt to be first in the rat-race to an understanding that it is not really that important after all – and certainly not worth the price of a coronary or a stroke or a mental breakdown.

Coping with unavoidable stress
Sometimes the circumstances – or the personalities involved – are such that preventing or deflecting the stress may not be possible. In this case, attention should be concentrated on living with it and coping with it at the lowest possible health cost. This again involves objective,

J. Allen Cash

Homer Sykes

Different people have different ways of alleviating stress – but unfortunately some of the methods used can be extremely destructive (left). High rates of unemployment make job-hunting (above) a major cause of worry and tension for a great many people.
We do not have to wait until we are adult to experience the stresses and strains of life. Teenagers often spend several years of their lives under great pressure to pass exams (above right).

accurate assessment of the realities of the situation, and positive, practical planning for its treatment. Here, since the details of every personal predicament are quite different, nobody should dream of offering more than guidelines; a scaffolding on which an individual plan for not only surviving, but also for overcoming, conquering and even thriving on the inevitable stresses of life can be constructed.

The first principle is to avoid throwing up our hands in horror in the belief that nothing can be changed and that all is lost; when we seriously get down to the nitty-gritty of situations there is always far more in them that can be changed than we had imagined. Job, home circumstances, relationships – we may seem hopelessly trapped and without any room

At times even the most patient of mothers will find it hard to cope with the job of looking after young children.

for manoeuvre in any of them; but all can be shifted sufficiently to give survival space if the need is great enough. And action must be taken in this direction, as unselfishly and with as much care of other people's rights and needs as possible, before anything else is considered.

Once we have taken all possible steps to reduce our level of stress to the minimum, we should direct our efforts to ensuring that the impact of that burden is made as light as possible. Basically this means adopting – and living out – an attitude of bending as smoothly and gracefully as possible with what we

cannot stand up against. Both history and our own contemporaries rightly put a premium on endeavour, but it is far more folly than virtue to lose our life or our health tilting at unnecessary windmills. Wisdom here is to recognize what are essential confrontations in the preservation of mental and moral integrity; and what are really only exercises in personal vanity, based on an unrealistic – and usually disastrously fruitless – determination never to be beaten. Whenever possible, the blows of life should be either side-stepped or bowed to, rather than met in a head-on collision.

Anthea Sieveking/Vision International

Q Are there any worthwhile things that one can do to decrease the likelihood of suffering a stress breakdown?

A There are almost always things that we can do to improve matters substantially. As with every other field of health, the most reliable as well as the biggest dividends come from prevention. Regularly – at least once a year – stand back and take a long, hard look at your life. Assess the past and the present in terms of what you have achieved in various fields, and what it has cost you in terms of strain and tension; and the future in terms of what you would like and what you are realistically able to achieve. Is the race you have set yourself one that you can have any real hope of winning? And even if you do, is that particular prize going to be worth what you will have paid for it? Would it really be so bad if you finally gave up the rat-race, and ended up sane and healthy instead? Look too at the conflicts and contradictions in your life – and make positive plans to untangle them before they throttle you. Make sure, especially, that your life has plenty of variety, for example, between work, leisure time, hobbies and friends. People who keep all their eggs in one basket are very much more at risk than those whose lives contain many interests.

Q Are there are any particular factors that are likely to result in the development of stress problems?

A Yes, there are many of them – and strangely enough often representing opposite ends of the same pole! For instance, a job that is too undemanding or boring is just as likely to be stressful as one that involves overworking or too much responsibility. Gross conflict between what a job demands and what it is reasonably possible to achieve is a prime recipe for disaster. So also is too wide a gap between desires and expectations on the one hand and actual achievements and rewards on the other.

There are, of course, other factors that may aggravate the situation and make a stress disorder more likely: two or more stress factors acting together, such as losing a job at the same time as a marital crisis.

Releasing pent-up feelings

There will be some situations in which a considerable degree of stress is absolutely unavoidable. Most of these, since they are likely to seem either unreasonable, unprovoked or unjust, will lead to our feeling angry. This is the most destructive and harmful form of stress, and it is vitally important that steps are taken to deal with it. There are only two satisfactory ways of doing this – by releasing it or by sublimating it. The alternative, repressing stress, merely allows the development of stress-related illness.

Relax by getting away from it all. The choice is yours: a quiet family picnic; or perhaps a trip to the funfair – it may look hair-raising, but it will certainly take your mind off your problems!

Releasing anger means giving it open expression by making our feelings known to those concerned – even if this does mean losing our temper. So long as we take the precaution of making sure that we are right, and are not being unjust, this is by far the best course; much more is usually gained in a relationship by clearing the air than is ever lost by the outburst. Our society sets far too much store on preserving peace at all costs, where a forthright expression of feelings, even if accompanied by some heat, would do far more good.

If direct release of anger is not possible, some alternative action should be sought —preferably one that will provide a physical outlet for the powerful feelings of tension and frustration that are involved. Thumping a punchbag, chopping up wood, ripping up waste paper, tearing out weeds, jogging or cycling to exhaustion are all ways of doing this. More passive ways, involving sublimating and neutralizing the tension, rather than its active release, include such methods as massage, yoga and the various forms of meditation. Some alternative ways of escaping stress and tension may be actually harmful: over-eating, smoking, over-indulgence in alcohol, drug-taking, sulking, reckless driving and other forms of aggressive behaviour are all negative ways in which stress can be channelled.

When dealing with stress, it is important not to make things more difficult than they need be, and so add to the hazards of the situation. Refusing help when we are really badly in need of it or obstinately holding out too long on our own, feeling that it is an indication of weakness or inadequacy to seek or follow advice – these are all ways in which most of us have at some time or other added unnecessarily to our burdens.

If the mother looks after the children all day, every day, then there are many ways in which the father can help to ease the strain. He could look after the children when he is not working or he could take over the night-time feed of a bottle-fed baby.

A guide to stress

The way we feel mentally or emotionally can often affect the way our bodies function – and we can feel just as unwell from this as from physical causes. For example, we may faint because we are physically ill or because we have had a sudden shock or are extremely upset. Consultation and examination by a doctor is, therefore, usually necessary to decide if our feeling unwell is physical or emotional in origin.

What sort of people we are, in both body and personality, depends partly on what we inherited and were born with, and partly on what has happened to us since. Anxiety is a normal reaction to threatening situations, but if we have experienced a lot of anxiety and insecurity in early childhood, we are likely to become over-anxious in later life. All babies naturally become frustrated, angry and anxious at times; but it is the child who is persistently neglected, unloved and lonely who is likely to grow into a nervous, anxious, aggressive and disturbed adolescent. Growing up inevitably brings problems – especially in relation to parents and other sources of authority, levels of achievement at work and at play, and the hazards of puberty. It is how these situations are handled,

rather than the problems themselves, that is important to future mental health.

Worries and anxieties will occur from time to time throughout our adult lives – in relation to work and career, social and sexual relationships, illnesses and bereavements. The demands of 'civilized' behaviour also give rise to tension. They insist that we do many things that we do not really wish to do, and that we forgo many things that we want. The anxieties and tensions may become so great that work is no longer possible and the whole of life becomes a disintegrating muddle. Unless help is at hand, the strain tends to get worse and worse, and may increase to the breaking point that we call a 'nervous breakdown'.

If people are able to talk their problems out with someone they respect – partner, parent, teacher, friend, doctor – or share responsibility for decisions with others, the level of stress is often very greatly decreased. Continuing or repeated stress takes its toll not only on the mind, but on the body as well. Skin and digestive problems result, and continuing stress may even help to worsen blood pressure and arterial disease including heart attacks.

Depression is normally brought about by unhappy circumstances such as a broken love affair, persistent conflict with somebody close, a death in the family, a debilitating illness or loss of a job. Some people, however, have wide swings of mood – being either very much up or very much down – and tend to be depressive by nature, irrespective of circumstances.

Anybody who has repeated bouts of anxiety or depression should get help, rather than simply trying to cope on his own. And anyone who has been severely depressed for a prolonged period is likely to need help as a matter of urgency. In trying to go on for too long without assistance there is considerable risk of death from accident or suicide. This is particularly common in situations of loneliness or social insecurity. Lovers, friends and family are usually the source of greatest help at times of mental or emotional trouble, and they should be sought out first. Doctors may be able to help too, and the Church – even if you are a stranger to it – can often provide counsel and consolation. In real desperation or emergency do not hesitate to call on the Samaritans whose local number and address will be in the telephone book.

401

Stroke

Q My mother had a serious stroke when she was 53. Does this put me at risk of having one at that comparatively young age?

A Not necessarily. Your chances of having a stroke depend to some extent on what caused your mother's disease. If high blood pressure was behind it, then it may be advisable to have your blood pressure checked; if high blood pressure is found, suitable treatment can be given. If there is a long history of stroke in your family, then it is important that you do not add to the risk by smoking.

Q Does taking the contraceptive pill increase the risk of having a stroke?

A In a tiny number of women, strokes have occurred while they were on the Pill. For this reason doctors try to discourage women who are over 40 from taking the Pill. There is far less risk in women who are under 40, although doctors will dissuade women from continuing with the Pill if they have a history of migraine, as in this instance the Pill does increase slightly the chances of having a stroke at a younger age.

Q Are there any operations available to treat people who have had a stroke, and how successful are they?

A In the past, operations have been tried to unblock the artery whose obstruction has caused a stroke. These were not very successful, and often they made the situation worse. Occasionally one of the larger arteries in the neck may be narrowed or roughened inside and an operation on this may prevent further damaging strokes. In most people who have had a stroke, however, surgery has little to offer.

Q My father recently had a stroke and he seems to have lost his ability to speak. Will it return?

A To some extent it is very likely to come back. Sometimes people may not be able to speak at all in the first few days after a stroke and then recover nearly completely.

With little or no warning a stroke can cause sudden weakness, paralysis or even death. But however fearsome this common affliction may be, rehabilitation can help survivors overcome any resulting disability.

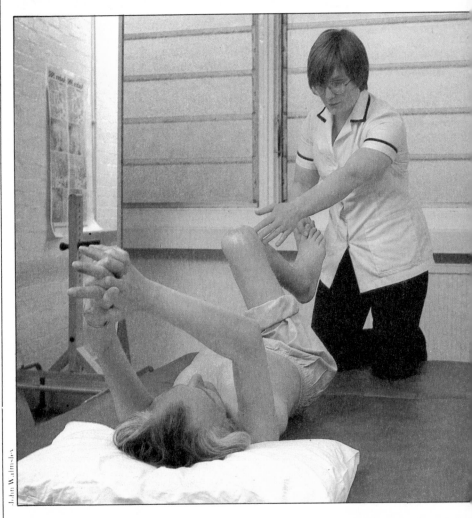

A stroke need not signal the end to a person's useful and active life. With physiotherapy, both in the early and later stages of a stroke, the function of affected limbs may be restored to varying degrees.

About a quarter of the people registered as physically handicapped in the United Kingdom have been disabled by strokes. Strokes often – though not exclusively – attack the elderly and are one of the most common causes of death in the Western world. Present advances in medical research, however, particularly in connection with the role of high blood pressure, have helped our understanding of this illness. Many strokes are now preventable through early identification and treatment of those at risk.

What is a stroke?

Most people have some idea of what a stroke is, which is a testament to how often the disease occurs. The common factor in all strokes is that due to disease of the blood vessel which supplies a particular part of the brain, a section of the brain suddenly stops working. This means that the person involved often has little or no warning that something is wrong before he or she is struck down with weakness or paralysis down one side of the body. This may be accompanied by aphasia – loss of the power of speech – or other problems in higher brain functions. Some strokes can occur away from the parts of the brain that control movement, so that this paralysis – also called hemiplegia – does not happen; but the first type of stroke is much more common.

What causes stroke?

Like the rest of the body, the brain must have a constant supply of blood reaching it through its arteries. If one of these arteries becomes blocked, the part of the brain that it feeds will die because of the lack of oxygen and food which would normally be carried in the blood. Fortunately in the brain there are many cross-connections between neighbouring blood vessels so that the area of damage is generally restricted. However, even that part of the brain which does not die may swell and damage the rest of the brain.

The other way in which strokes may be caused is when blood vessels in the brain burst. When this happens the blood rushes into the brain under pressure, severely damaging nerve fibres.

These two basic mechanisms, cerebral infarction (when the artery is blocked) and cerebral haemorrhage (when there is bleeding into the brain) can be brought about by a number of different disorders.

Diseases which cause strokes

Obstruction of an artery in the brain can result from a disease which produces a blockage in the artery itself – a cerebral thrombosis – or when a blood clot passes up the blood supply to the brain artery and gets stuck there. This is called a cerebral embolism.

Thrombosis – or blood-clotting – most usually occurs when an artery of the brain becomes furred-up: fatty material accumulates in the walls of the artery. This is typical of a disease called atherosclerosis, which also causes the heart's blood vessels to clot, resulting in heart attacks (see Heart attack pp 167-68. Occasionally other problems in the arteries can cause thrombosis. These include inflammation of the artery, which can occur on its own or as a result of some serious infections.

Embolisms can be caused by heart diseases or by disorders in the main arteries in the neck from which the blood enters the brain. Thus heart disease and strokes are linked, not only because the same disease of the arteries can cause trouble in both the heart and the brain, but also because in many diseases of the heart, blood clots form on the valves or on the damaged inside walls of the heart and these then fly off as emboli to cause strokes.

Cerebral haemorrhages – when the blood vessels in the brain burst – also have a number of causes. The most common is when there are weak places – called aneurysms – in the walls of the brain's arteries which then burst, often under the influence of a higher than normal blood pressure. In the larger brain arteries at the base of the skull, these aneurysms may be congenital (the patient is born with them), although they may not rupture until late in life if at all.

High blood pressure also has a tendency to produce weak places in the smaller arteries within the substance of the brain from which brain haemorrhage then occurs. Less common causes of

Strokes can be caused by haemorrhages or blockages (infarctions) in the brain. Many haemorrhages are caused by weakened arteries (aneurysms) rupturing. Infarctions are caused either when a blood clot forms in a diseased cerebral artery (thrombus), or when a clot travels from some other area of the body and lodges in the brain (embolus).

Major causes of strokes

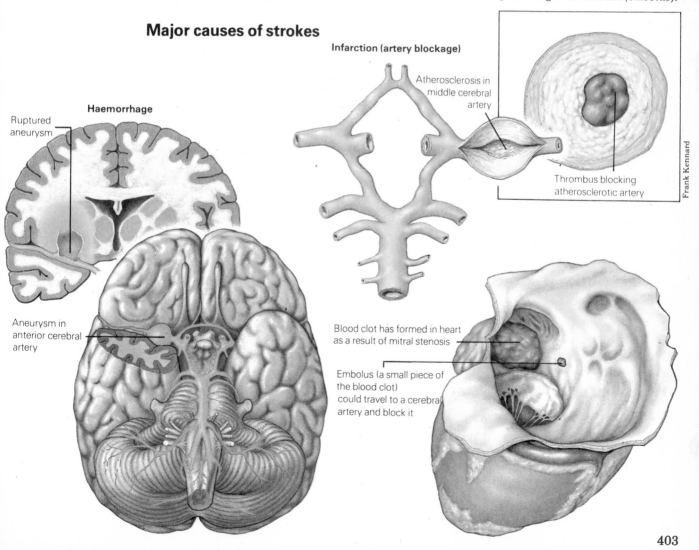

Infarction (artery blockage)

Atherosclerosis in middle cerebral artery

Thrombus blocking atherosclerotic artery

Haemorrhage

Ruptured aneurysm

Aneurysm in anterior cerebral artery

Blood clot has formed in heart as a result of mitral stenosis

Embolus (a small piece of the blood clot) could travel to a cerebral artery and block it

Frank Kennard

403

Q Does everyone who has had a stroke have to be admitted to hospital?

A This would depend upon the severity of the stroke, and the facilities available in the stroke patient's home which would enable him to be properly looked after. In some areas, special teams of physiotherapists are available to treat people in their own home. However, often people with strokes do need to come into hospital while they are very disabled so that their stroke can be properly assessed both in terms of treatment and of prevention of further strokes, if possible.

Q Is there any point in having someone's blood pressure treated after they have had a stroke, or is it like shutting the stable door after the horse has bolted?

A Immediately after a stroke, the blood pressure is usually left alone for a few days, since a sudden drop may impair the flow of blood to the damaged areas in the brain. However, careful studies have shown that later on it is important to treat the blood pressure vigorously to prevent further strokes, which might cause further disability.

Q My uncle had a bad heart attack and then a few weeks later he suddenly became paralyzed down his left side. Was this connected with his heart attack, and why did this happen at all?

A After a heart attack, blood clots form on the inside wall of the chamber of the heart that has been affected. On occasions, part of this clot can become dislodged and fly upwards to block off one of the brain's blood vessels, thus producing a stroke. This can be prevented to some degree by giving those patients who have had very serious heart attacks anticoagulant drugs.

Q Is it possible to prevent people having strokes?

A Yes. If patients with high blood pressure are identified and treated early, this can greatly reduce the risk of a stroke.

cerebral haemorrhage can occur as a result of the presence of small, abnormally formed blood vessels in the brain, rather like the strawberry marks that are a similar abnormality of the blood vessels in the skin. This is called arterio-venous anomaly and is again congenital.

Who is at risk?
Certain people have a higher risk of having strokes than others. The main conditions which predispose to stroke are diabetes, high blood pressure, having a high serum cholesterol and smoking cigarettes. In addition, stroke seems to run in some families, though because it is such a common condition this is difficult to prove. Finally, there are people with heart diseases that can cause stroke by embolism. Thus people with a high risk

A stroke can be caused by a blockage in any of the four pairs of cerebral arteries. Each type has different results, depending on the area of the brain that is affected. A blockage in an anterior artery is very common and one in the basilar is usually fatal.

Damage caused by a stroke

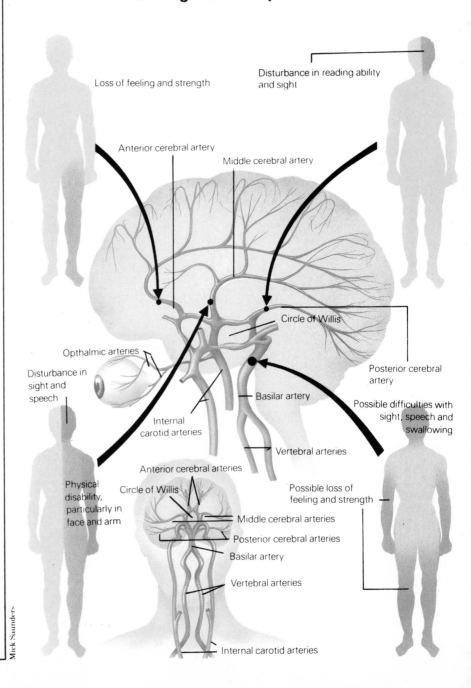

Loss of feeling and strength

Disturbance in reading ability and sight

Anterior cerebral artery

Middle cerebral artery

Circle of Willis

Opthalmic arteries

Disturbance in sight and speech

Posterior cerebral artery

Possible difficulties with sight, speech and swallowing

Internal carotid arteries

Basilar artery

Vertebral arteries

Physical disability, particularly in face and arm

Anterior cerebral arteries

Circle of Willis

Possible loss of feeling and strength

Middle cerebral arteries

Posterior cerebral arteries

Basilar artery

Vertebral arteries

Internal carotid arteries

Mick Saunders

can often be identified and preventive measures taken to reduce the chances of a stroke occurring.

Symptoms

Some stroke patients have a warning attack in the weeks or months before a major stroke. These warning attacks can take the form of short-lived episodes of weakness down one side or transient blacking out of vision in one eye – a sign of blockage in one of the blood vessels to the retina. Most stroke patients, however, do not get any warning: what really typifies a stroke is the suddenness with which it happens. In most cases, disabilities such as loss of function of one side of the body or loss of speech reaches

its maximum within minutes, though occasionally it may take hours. In the following days and weeks, there will be an improvement as some of the brain cells recover, and after six months the disabilities will be considerably less than at the onset of the stroke.

Other symptoms may include loss of vision in the right or left hand half of each eye (visual field defect), difficulty in dressing or finding the way around familiar surroundings, and a host of other subtle difficulties in brain function. If a large area of the brain was damaged at the start of the stroke, the patient may not have a clear awareness of what has happened, or may ignore everything that happens on one side of his body. As the damaged brain swells, he may become drowsy or lose consciousness. This may happen much more quickly in brain haemorrhages, since the surge of blood into the brain causes much early damage to the mechanisms that maintain alertness.

Treatment

Initial treatment consists of limiting the amount of damage that may be caused by swelling spreading to the unaffected parts of the brain. This is done by paying close attention to the blood pressure and administering certain drugs, particularly steroids. Very seldom can

Many stroke patients recover sufficiently to be able to drive a car. However before they actually do so, they must take special examinations to test their reflexes. The physiotherapist sits beside the patient and notes their reaction to various manoeuvres in a simulated car. The architect below, who had a stroke, is re-learning to use the tools of his trade, this time with his non-affected hand.

surgeons remove blood clots which are causing pressure as they are often situated in inaccessible parts of the brain.

However, the main care of patients who have had strokes lies in the hands of nursing staff, physiotherapists, speech therapists and occupational therapists. Careful nursing is very important to prevent the emergence of bedsores and chest troubles which can seriously impair

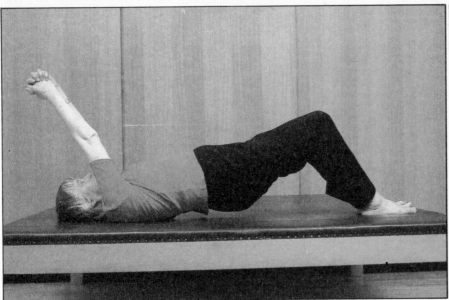

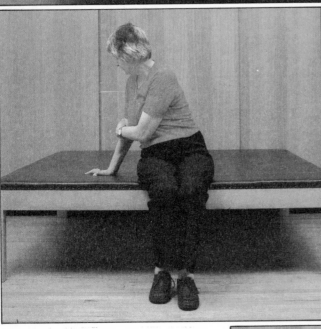

Stroke patients can do various exercises in their own home. These include using their strong arm to support their weak arm (above left) or paralyzed side (above) by pulling it up. Additional strengthening can be achieved by doing swivelling exercises (far left) or pressing exercises (left) which require propping up the weak arm. Better balance can be gained by raising the body to a half-seated position (below)

the recovery from a stroke. During this vulnerable period when the stroke patient is often unable to care for himself, good nursing can literally save his life.

Physiotherapists maximize the effect of movement as it returns to affected limbs. Later they will become even more vital because the therapy they suggest may make all the difference between a patient's becoming seriously handicapped or able to fend for himself despite residual disabilities.

Treatment takes two forms. In the early stages, physiotherapists ensure that the unused limbs remain supple and unnecessary stiffness does not set in. Later, when the patient is up and about (and this happens as early as possible since prolonged periods in bed can be dangerous) the physiotherapist concentrates on overcoming the abnormal reflex movements that interfere with the return of more useful muscle power.

Speech therapy plays an important role when the stroke has affected the power of speech. Speech therapists will be able to identify the difficulties the patient has and will work to encourage the return of speech, which often does come back to a greater or lesser extent. Further treatment by speech therapists consists of retraining patients with aphasia to make the best of the speech faculties that are left to them.

Occupational therapists try to prepare the patient for a return to as normal a life as possible. The patient's disabilities are assessed and the therapist works out ways of overcoming problems that resist physiotherapy.

The stroke patient at home

Many stroke patients have a spell in hospital while they are physically dependent (often in special stroke units) and then further recovery will proceed apace when they go home. This means that the patient's family will need a lot of support and guidance to make sure that they are not so overprotective that they slow his recovery. Thus, the work of the physiotherapists and occupational therapists often extends to the home where they can continue to supervise his recovery. Many special aids are available for use in the home for facilitating such ordinary tasks as bathing, cooking or eating which often present difficulties.

Preventing a stroke

The recent major advances in stroke research have been concerned with prevention. The fact that in the last 15 years in the USA the number of strokes has declined is indicative of the effectiveness of the research. This is due mainly to the successful identification and treatment of high blood pressure – in fact it has been shown that careful treatment of high blood pressure can significantly reduce the risk of developing a stroke. Often the difficulty is that most people with high blood pressure feel perfectly well and may need some convincing to take their tablets religiously to keep it down. Generally your doctor will take your blood pressure as a matter of routine when you consult him so that he can detect high blood pressure before it leads to trouble.

After minor strokes from which the patient may have recovered completely, it is an important part of treatment to try to prevent another more serious episode occurring in the future. Sometimes surgery can be performed on the large blood vessels in the neck: this may be done if the blood vessels have roughened parts in their lining from which clots fly off as emboli. Small doses of aspirin are also being tried for stroke prevention, since it has been found that relatively small amounts of the drug affect the clotting ability of the blood – not much, but enough to prevent the brain's blood vessels from clotting.

Other drugs called anticoagulants reduce the blood's liability to clot, and these are used to prevent a stroke when one of the predisposing heart conditions is identified. Many other drugs which can prevent stroke in those at risk are now undergoing trials.

Outlook

Although stroke can be a fatal illness, the majority of its victims recover to some degree. At least half of those who have a stroke progress to a point where they can look after themselves while the remainder may have to depend on people to look after them at home. So although stroke is a serious illness, patients should avail themselves of the hospital and therapeutic treatment available to help them overcome their disability.

Speech therapy is essential for many stroke patients. Where speech has been lost, the patient practises lip movements in front of a mirror (left) or points to cards to test recognition of everyday objects (above). Where a patient's selected language response has become confused, he will try to fill in the missing letters in words that refer to the pictures on a set of cards.

Stye

Q Is it true that styes are caused by dandruff?

A Styes do seem to occur more commonly in people suffering from seborrhoeic dermatitis. This condition affects the scalp and produces dandruff and also causes a scaly inflammation of the eyebrows and eyelids. When the dandruff is treated the styes often clear up too.

Q I have heard that styes are very infectious. Is it true?

A The bacteria causing styes are infectious and certain virulent types seem to be responsible for recurrent infections. It is therefore best for anyone with a stye to avoid rubbing the eyes as this can spread the infection into other sebaceous glands. A separate towel and face flannel should be used to stop the infection spreading to other members of the household. An antibiotic ointment may prevent the discharging pus from infecting other glands, although they cannot do much to a stye once it has formed.

Q Is it safe to pull out the eyelash over a stye?

A Yes, it will help the pus to drain out. It is best to soften the eyelid with a hot compress first – this will also help to ease the pain. The eyelash can then be pulled out easily with a pair of tweezers and the stye should discharge spontaneously. If the relevant eyelash is not obvious, the eyelids should be left alone. Either the stye is not yet 'ripe' or it may be an internal stye, in which case there is no related eyelash.

Q I have a small painless nodule under my eyelid. Is this a stye?

A What you describe could be a Meibomian cyst, which is the end result of an internal stye. The infection has been conquered by white cells but a pocket of sterile pus is left behind and is felt as a persistent hard lump like a small hailstone. There is no need to do anything about it, but it can be removed surgically for cosmetic reasons.

Children and adolescents often suffer from styes – painful and unsightly swellings in the eyelid. While minor surgery may be required in some cases, antibiotic ointment and first aid are usually all that is needed.

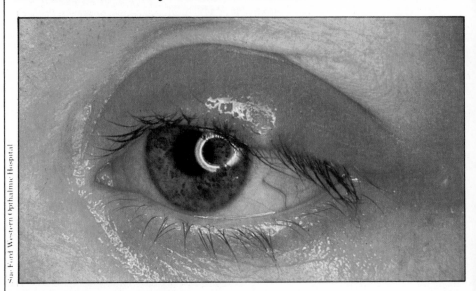

Infection of one of the sebaceous glands in the eyelid can produce an external stye – an obvious red, angry pustule which causes pain and a feeling of grittiness (above).

There are two types of stye, depending on which of the eyelid glands is affected. On the outside are sebaceous glands in hair follicles, associated with the eyelashes, which secrete greasy sebum to protect the surface of the eye. Unfortunately, this sebum may block the gland and trap bacteria and an 'external' stye will then result. On the inside the eye has a further special line of glands called the Meibomian glands. These are also sebaceous glands, but have no associated hair follicles. They open through the conjunctiva to the back of the eyelid and the secretion they produce may also block the gland: trapped infection then leads to an 'internal' stye.

Causes
Styes are associated with a general tendency to dry skin and eczema, as in seborrhoeic dermatitis. Dandruff, flaking skin around the eyelashes and eyebrows are all related to this condition, and styes may be a complication of it. However, many children get styes with no underlying skin disease and in these cases the cause is unknown. But if styes persist in recurring, an underlying condition must be suspected. As in all infections, general ill health and lack of physical fitness will make styes more common.

Symptoms
The eye may be troublesome for a day or two before the stye appears. During this time itchiness and a sensation of 'some-

thing in the eye' may be felt. The actual stye comes up over the course of one to two days, starting as a local painful spot and then swelling to an obvious, red, angry pustule. An external stye is easily recognized on the eyelid but to see an internal stye the eyelid must be turned out to expose the back. Internal styes are usually more painful than external, as the distending Meibomian gland will stretch the whole eyelid.

As the stye forms, the pain in the lid and the feeling of grittiness get worse. Bright light aggravates the pain (photophobia) and the eye seems to be continually weeping. A fretful child with photophobia, a snuffly nose from all the crying and eye problems may be diagnosed as having a more serious illness such as measles; but recognition of the actual stye and the absence of symptoms in the other eye should clarify the problem.

Treatment
If recognized early enough, antibiotic eye ointment or drops can prevent a stye forming. Usually, however, by the time the diagnosis has been made the pustule is already formed and antibiotics are then ineffective. The only treatment at this stage is to encourage the pus to discharge.

If styes keep recurring, antibiotic eye drops may help to prevent any discharging pus from infecting other sebaceous glands in the eyelid and aggravating the condition.

Local warmth from a hot compress will increase the blood flow and soften the eyelid, relieving pain and encouraging the infection to clear. A simple hot compress can be made from a pad of lint or cotton wool wound over a wooden spoon and held under the hot tap. It should be as warm as can be tolerated and held in contact with the closed eye for 10 minutes at a time. For an external stye the offending hair follicle can easily be identified. If the eyelash is pulled out with tweezers the stye will often discharge spontaneously, relieving the pain and the swelling.

Unfortunately, internal styes are more difficult to deal with. The infected Meibomian gland tries in vain to discharge to the surface, but the tough eyelid prevents this. The result is that the white cells eventually overcome the infection – so the symptoms go away – but they remain in situ as a cyst of sterile pus. This Meibomian cyst can be felt as a little painless nodule under the eyelid and a small surgical operation is required to remove it. Under local anaesthetic the eyelid is turned back and the cyst incised; the pus discharges and the conjunctival surface swiftly heals.

In cases of recurrent styes antibiotic ointments may be helpful in preventing any discharging pus from infecting other sebaceous glands on the eyelid. Rubbing the eye can transfer the infection and controlling dandruff is important since

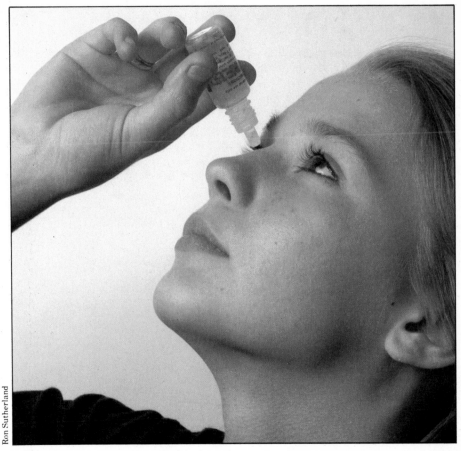

Ron Sutherland

this condition seems to cause styes. Where inflammation of the eyelids (blepharitis) is the cause, prolonged courses of antibiotics and mild steroid drops may be helpful.

Some children suffer from recurrent styes in crops. These do not harm the eye but they are painful and unpleasant. Unfortunately, the cause is still unknown in most cases, but you should discuss the problem with your doctor as there may be an underlying associated problem, such as seborrhoeic dermatitis, which will respond to treatment.

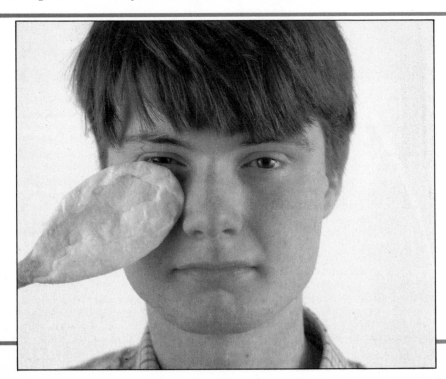

Ron Sutherland

FIRST AID

If you have a stye

Do . . .
● take steps to control dandruff. Washing your hair regularly with an anti-dandruff shampoo will help to prevent a recurrence
● apply a hot compress – a wooden spoon wrapped in lint or cotton wool and held under the hot tap will suffice. Hold it to your eye for 10 minutes at a time and it will help to relieve the pain and inflammation
● remove the offending eyelash if the stye is external; it will then discharge spontaneously

Do Not . . .
● rub your eyes, however tempted you may be: you risk spreading the infection to other sebaceous glands
● share your towel or face flannel with other members of the household or you will place them at risk too

Teeth and Teething

Q Why do some people have crooked teeth and not others?

A The development of the teeth and jaws is mainly controlled by the genetic factors inherited from the parents. Each individual, however, has a unique assortment of genes and it is possible, for example, for a child to inherit large teeth from one parent and small jaws from the other, leading to overcrowding. Teeth in irregular positions can, however, usually be aligned and made to bite together by the use of orthodontic appliances.

Q Does an impacted wisdom tooth always have to be removed?

A An impacted wisdom tooth is one which is unable to grow properly because its path of eruption is blocked, usually by the tooth in front. Some impacted wisdom teeth are highly prone to infection, especially those which are only partially through the gum. Such teeth are best removed to avoid recurrent bouts of infection. On the other hand, very deeply placed wisdom teeth may be best left alone if their removal requires the loss of an excessive amount of bone. Some impacted wisdom teeth, during their development, may contribute to overcrowding of the lower incisors and should therefore be removed. A dentist will decide which is the appropriate course of action.

Q My sister's baby was born with a tooth that had to be removed. Does this mean that there will be one missing when the teeth finally erupt?

A About one in 5000 babies are born with one or two teeth already present in the mouth – Julius Caesar and Napoleon, for example, are both reputed to have had this distinction. It sometimes runs in families. These teeth are not fully formed and will fall out; occasionally, however, they present a danger of choking the baby, and so it is better to have them removed. The teeth will develop normally later on.

The day that a baby sprouts a tiny tooth is a memorable moment, but it is also the prelude to the development of teeth, whose function it is to tear and grind food so that it can be easily swallowed and digested.

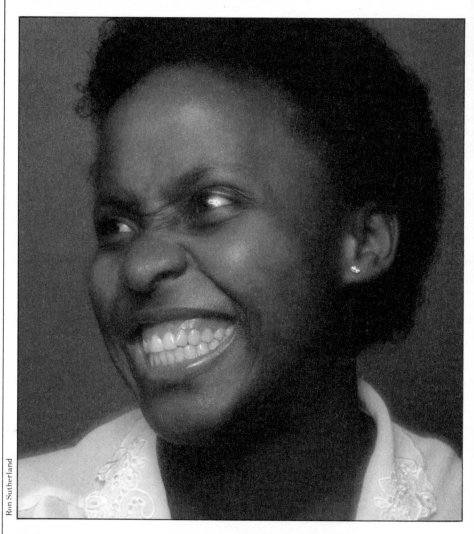

Ron Sutherland

The teeth are hard bone-like structures implanted in the sockets of the jaws. Two successive sets occur in a lifetime.

Anatomy

Each tooth consists of two parts: the 'crown', which is the portion visible within the mouth, and the 'root', which is the part embedded within the jaw-bone. The roots of the teeth are usually longer than the crowns. Front teeth have only one root, while those placed further back generally have two or three roots.

The major structural element of a tooth is composed of a calcified tissue known as 'dentine'. Dentine is a hard bone-like material which contains living cells. It is a sensitive tissue and gives the sensation of pain when stimulated either thermally

Would that we all had such a perfect set of teeth! Heredity is crucial, but we can all take care of what we've got.

or by chemical means. The dentine of the crown is covered by a protective layer of enamel, an extremely hard cell-free and insensitive tissue. The root is covered with a layer of 'cementum', a substance that is somewhat similar to dentine and which helps anchor the tooth in its socket.

The centre of the tooth is in the form of a hollow chamber filled with a sensitive connective tissue known as the dental pulp. This extends from within the crown right down to the end of the root, which is open at its deepest part. Through this opening, minute blood vessels and nerves run into the pulp chamber.

Support of teeth

Each tooth is attached by its root to the jaw-bone; the part of the jaw which supports the teeth is known as the alveolar process. The mode of attachment is, however, complex and teeth are attached to the jaw by fibres known as the periodontal ligament. This consists of a series of tough collagen fibres which run from the cementum covering the root to the adjacent alveolar bone. These fibres are interspersed with connective tissue which also contains blood vessels and nerve fibres.

The mode of attachment of the teeth results in a very small degree of natural mobility. This serves as a kind of buffer which may protect the teeth and bone from damage when biting.

A zone of crucial importance in this system is at the neck of the tooth where the crown and root merge. In this region a cuff of gum is tightly joined to the tooth and serves to protect the underlying supporting tissues from infection and other harmful influences.

Types of teeth

There are two series of human teeth. Deciduous teeth are those present during childhood and are all usually shed. Deciduous teeth can be divided into three categories: incisors, canines and molars. The permanent teeth are those which replace and also extend the initial series. These teeth can be divided into the same types as the deciduous teeth, and in addition there is a further category known as the premolars, which are intermediate

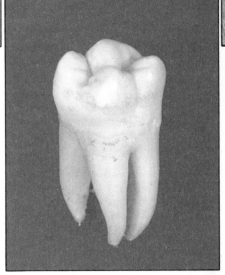

Each tooth consists of several layers: a stout shell of dentine (coloured blue and yellow); cement covering the root (blue); and the crown's protective layer of enamel (yellow). The brown is plaque.

both in form and position between canines (eye teeth) and molars.

Incisors are characterized by a narrow blade-like 'incised edge', and the incisors in opposite jaws work by shearing past each other like the blades of a pair of scissors. Canines and pointed teeth are well adapted for a tearing action, while molars and premolars are effective at grinding food rather than cutting it.

Teeth form an even, oval-shaped arch with the incisors at the front and the canines, premolars and molars progressively placed further back. The dental arches normally fit together in such a way that on biting the teeth opposite interlock each other.

Dental decay can occur in all parts of a tooth and a mouthful of fillings will be the result. So be sure you take care of your teeth and attend a dentist regularly.

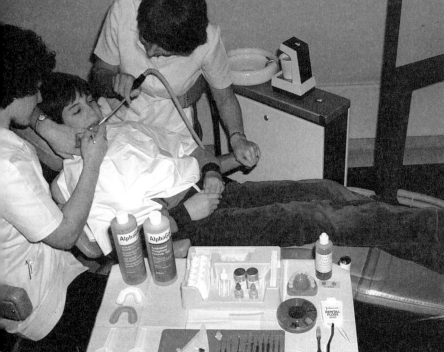

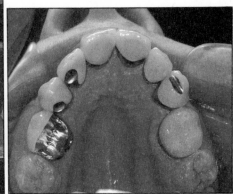

Deciduous (baby) and permanent teeth

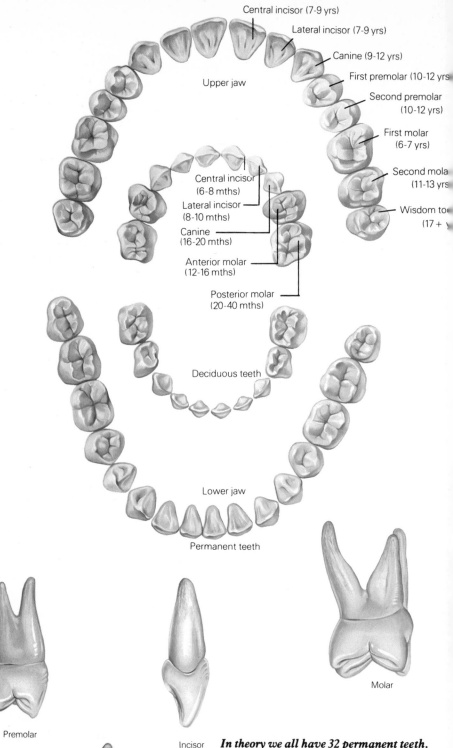

Upper jaw

Central incisor (7-9 yrs)
Lateral incisor (7-9 yrs)
Canine (9-12 yrs)
First premolar (10-12 yrs)
Second premolar (10-12 yrs)
First molar (6-7 yrs)
Second molar (11-13 yrs)
Wisdom tooth (17 + yrs)

Central incisor (6-8 mths)
Lateral incisor (8-10 mths)
Canine (16-20 mths)
Anterior molar (12-16 mths)
Posterior molar (20-40 mths)

Deciduous teeth

Lower jaw

Permanent teeth

Premolar

Incisor

Canine

Molar

In theory we all have 32 permanent teeth. The arrangement of these is exactly the same in the upper and lower jaw. In each jaw there are 4 incisors, 2 canines, 4 premolars and 8 molars – 16 in total. Babies and young children have only 20 deciduous teeth: again, in each jaw there are 4 incisors, 2 canines, and 4 molars – 10 in all. Incisors cut food; canines tear it; and molars and premolars grind it. As man has evolved, teeth have changed: canines have become far less pointed, and many people never develop any wisdom teeth.

Elaine Keenan

Q I broke my front teeth in a car accident. Can they be repaired?

A If only a small piece of enamel is broken off, then the sharp edges can be smoothed. Where much of the tooth is missing, the tooth can be repaired by using a filling material bonded to the rest of the tooth, or a crown can be fitted. Where the root of the tooth has been fractured, usually the only treatment is to extract the tooth and replace it.

Q When milk teeth decay, why are they filled if they are going to fall out anyway?

A If teeth do decay, it is usually preferable to fill them rather than take them out since the early loss of milk teeth may result in the permanent teeth drifting into incorrect positions. Also, removal of teeth at the first signs of dental disease may make a child think that tooth loss is inevitable, and hence he won't take good care of his teeth.

Q My son had a convulsion and started running a high temperature. I thought this was because he was teething – but my doctor sent him to the hospital. Was this necessary?

A Teething does not cause high temperatures or any serious illnesses, although a child may be teething at the same time as he or she develops an illness. Your doctor was aware of this; he knew how important it was to make sure that there was no other cause for your son's temperature and convulsion.

Q Should I give my baby fluoride tablets – which I've heard prevent tooth decay?

A There is substantial evidence that the addition of fluoride to toothpaste and to water which contains a low level of natural fluoride helps prevent tooth decay, particularly in children. It will be a good idea to give your baby tablets if you live in an area where there is no extra fluoride in the water supply – but talk to your dentist about this before going ahead.

The deciduous teeth begin to erupt about half-way through the first year of life — a painful process for many babies (left). These are the central incisors. The first permanent teeth to erupt are molars, around the age of 6. By the early twenties, everyone normally has a full set.

Camilla Zessel

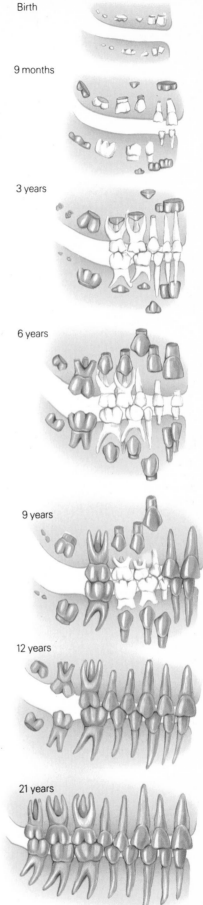

Birth

9 months

3 years

6 years

9 years

12 years

21 years

Elaine Keenan

Development of teeth

The first sign of the development of the teeth occurs when the foetus is only six weeks old. At this stage the epithelial (lining) cells of the primitive mouth increase in number and form a thick band which has the shape of the dental arch. At a series of points corresponding to individual teeth, this band produces bud-like in-growths into the tissue which the epithelium covers. These buds then become bell-shaped and gradually grow in such a way as to map out the shape of the eventual junction between enamel and dentine. Certain cells then go on to form the dentine, while others give rise to enamel.

The edges of the 'bell' continue to grow deeper and eventually map out the entire roots of the teeth, although this process is not complete until about one year after the deciduous teeth have emerged. At birth the only sign of the occlusion is provided by the 'gum pads', which are thickened bands of gum tissue. Around the age of six months, the first of the lower incisors begins to come through the gum, a process known as dental eruption. The age at which this occurs is variable: a very few babies have teeth at birth, while in others they may not emerge until the age of one.

After the lower incisors have emerged, the upper incisors begin to erupt, and these are followed by canines and molars, although the precise sequence may vary. Teething problems may be associated with any of the deciduous teeth.

By the age of two-and-a-half to three, the child will usually have a complete set of 20 milk teeth. Ideally they should be spaced in such a way that provides room for the larger permanent teeth.

Subsequently, after the age of six, lower then upper deciduous incisors become loose and are replaced by the permanent teeth. The permanent molars develop not in the place of the deciduous molars but behind them. The first permanent molars come through at the age of 6, the second molars at the age of 12, and the third molars, or wisdom teeth, around the age of 18. There is, however, considerable variation in the timing of the emergence of all the teeth. About 25 per cent of people never develop one or more wisdom teeth. The reason for this may be an evolutionary one: as the jaw has got smaller, the number of teeth has lessened. Some wisdom teeth may never erupt through the gum and if they become impacted (wedged closely together under the gum) they may need to be removed. This happens in 50 per cent of people.

Cross-section of a molar

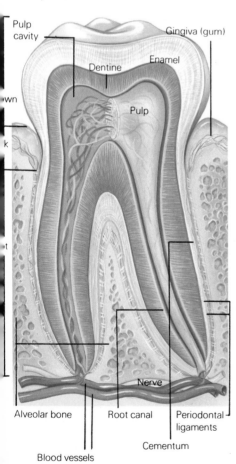

Pulp cavity

Gingiva (gum)

Dentine

Enamel

wn

Pulp

k

t

Alveolar bone

Root canal

Periodontal ligaments

Nerve

Cementum

Blood vessels

Changes in teeth arrangement

The part of the jaw that supports the milk teeth increases very little in size from the age when all the milk teeth have erupted. Milk teeth tend to be smaller than their permanent replacements and only when the large permanent incisors have erupted does the final form of the dental arches become apparent. The upper permanent incisors often appear out of proportion to the child's face when they first come through, but this naturally becomes less apparent as the face grows while the teeth remain the same size. Any tendency for the upper incisor teeth to protrude usually only becomes obvious when the milk teeth are replaced: the larger permanent teeth will exaggerate any discrepancy in their position. Similarly, crowding often only becomes clear when the permanent teeth erupt.

During the six years or so that it takes for the milk teeth to be entirely replaced by their 32 permanent successors, it is very common for a gap to appear between the upper incisors. This gap usually tends to close when the permanent canines erupt as they push the incisors together. Discrepancies either in the alignment or in the bite of the teeth may require orthodontic treatment to bring the teeth into the correct position (see Orthodontics pp 268-72).

Tooth eruption and teething

Tooth eruption is a normal developmental process, and can be quite painless, but many babies appear to suffer from a lot of discomfort, particularly as each new tooth breaks through. Sometimes a baby whose new tooth is hurting develops a red, inflamed patch on his cheek, and the gum may also become red. There is often excessive dribbling, rubbing of the mouth and crying; the cheeks may appear pinker than usual. Symptoms such as fever or diarrhoea are unlikely to be due to teething as is commonly supposed, and if they persist, medical advice should be sought immediately.

Where teething causes the baby some distress, a number of measures can be taken. Because the teething baby will occasionally suck or bite frantically on anything he or she can reach, you can give him a teething ring or hard dummy or, alternatively, a piece of raw carrot or a hard rusk. Never give a baby sweets to suck: they will not do much to relieve discomfort and will almost certainly be detrimental to the developing teeth. In some cases it may be advisable to apply creams which have the effect of a local anaesthetic on the child's sore gum, but bear in mind that they wear off rather quickly because the teething baby tends to salivate and dribble so much.

Anthea Sieveking/Vision International

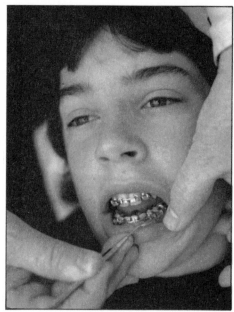

The lessons of good dental care last a lifetime. Teething babies should be given carrots to relieve discomfort – not tooth-decaying sweets. The proper way to brush teeth should be taught early. And if teeth are crooked, spaced or protruding, orthodontic appliances can be fitted to correct them.

Other problems

Not all teeth develop perfectly, and in some babies there may be problems.

Sometimes a tense bluish swelling – called an eruption cyst – appears over a molar tooth before it erupts. This will disappear once the tooth has emerged and will not require treatment.

Anodontia or absent teeth is extremely rare, although the absence of individual teeth is a phenomenon that occurs in 5 per cent of people.

Occasionally there will be a delayed development of teeth. This can occur in a number of diseases affecting growth, for example rickets (insufficient calcium in the bones and teeth). Children with Down's syndrome may also have delayed development of their teeth. It should be stressed, however, that this is extremely rare. It is not uncommon for teeth to erupt in many babies as late as 18 months.

There is a wide variation in the colour of teeth that appear in a baby's mouth, ranging from glistening brown to deep cream. If a pregnant woman or a baby is given tetracycline antibiotics, the drug may combine with the calcium to cause a brown discoloration.

'Twinning' occurs when two of the baby's teeth become joined together. This usually happens with the incisor milk teeth. The second incisors often develop quite normally.

Termination

Q Is it dangerous to have a number of terminations? I have heard that it is.

A Yes, it can be, because there is a real risk of sterility from having *repeated* terminations. The cervix (neck of the womb) can become stretched, making it easier for germs to enter the womb. As a result, the fallopian tubes may become blocked due to infection, so the eggs released by the ovaries cannot reach the womb to be fertilized. Stretching of the cervix can also lead to miscarriage, though a stitch across the opening of the cervix can usually—but not always— retain the foetus to its full term.

Q I had a termination as a teenager. Now I am about to have a medical which involves an internal examination. Will the doctor be able to tell that I have had an abortion?

A This is not very likely—especially if it was an early termination carried out by vacuum suction. In any case, there is no need to worry even if he does find evidence. A doctor is bound to keep all medical information about you confidential.

Q What should I do if I have excessive bleeding after a termination

A See your doctor immediately.

Q I have heard that having a termination can make you infertile. Is there any truth in this?

A No, only if the operation goes wrong, and that rarely happens these days. In fact, current medical thinking suggests that, in some cases, the woman can be *more* fertile afterwards. This is because the lining of the womb may be scraped away during the D and C type of abortion, and a fertilized egg is more likely to attach itself to a new lining than an old one. A woman having trouble conceiving is sometimes advised to have a 'scrape'. With the vacuum method of abortion, however, a woman is only as likely to become pregnant as she would be normally, since it is the contents of the womb that are removed, not the lining.

Nobody likes the idea of termination. But the woman who thinks she needs one should understand what is involved and how to get sympathetic counselling and help.

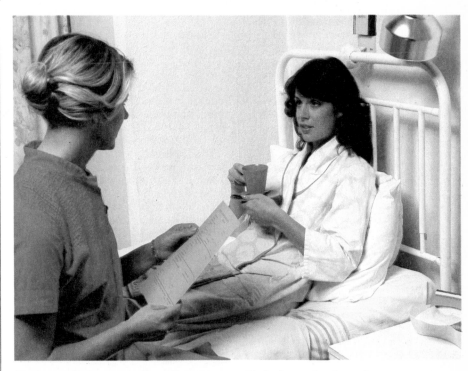

Doctors refer to any ending of pregnancy before the 28th week even if it is due to natural causes, as abortion, but to most people abortion means the artificial termination of an unwanted pregnancy. Once, abortion meant a sordid and risky backstreet procedure, but today women who need a termination can usually have one safely in a hospital or clinic.

However, there are laws against indiscriminate terminations and it should never be regarded as a substitute for contraception. Generally, each case has to be judged on its merits and two independent medical opinions are usually required before a termination can be performed.

Reasons for a termination

These can be roughly divided into the social and the medical. The most common non-medical reason is that the pregnancy was unplanned and unwanted. It may have resulted from contraceptive failure (or no contraception at all), from a casual affair, or even from rape. Other reasons include unfavourable circumstances, such as inadequate housing, a low income, or an unstable relationship between the couple.

In some cases, the pregnant woman may already have all the children she can cope with, or she may be in her forties and

Today's terminations of pregnancy, performed early, are practically risk-free and the after-effects are minimal.

view a late baby with alarm. On the other hand, a pregnant teenager may not be willing or able to bring up a child.

The main medical reasons for termination concern the risk of mental or physical abnormality in the baby or the possibility of harm to the mother if the pregnancy continues. Termination is generally recommended if German measles (rubella) has been contracted in the first three months.

Termination may also be suggested where spina bifida (a serious defect of the spinal cord) or chromosome disorders, such as mongolism (which causes a child to be born mentally defective), are detected.

Counselling

Any woman who feels she should have a termination will need to discuss the matter with someone. Counselling before any decision on a termination is taken is essential. Many women have very confused feelings about termination and require professional guidance.

Sometimes the solution may be to have the baby adopted. This decision can be the right one for a woman who may feel that

415

termination is morally wrong. And sometimes the troubles and fears that a woman gives as her reasons for wanting a termination can be alleviated by counselling. However, a woman who really wants and needs a termination will always receive help.

How terminations are carried out

Early terminations when the pregnancy is in its initial stages of development, are quicker, easier and much preferred by patients, doctors and nursing staff. After four to five months the foetus begins to move, and termination at this stage may be followed by lactation (milk flow) which can be extremely distressing.

Two methods are currently used to carry out an early termination. The first, D and E (dilation and evacuation), which is more commonly known as either vacuum suction or vacuum curettage, is carried out when the foetus is between seven and 12 weeks old.

The second termination technique is a D and C (dilation and curettage). This is generally used for pregnancies of

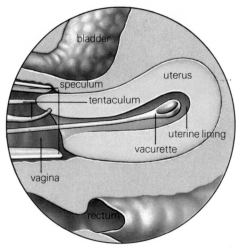

between eight and 12 weeks, but this can be extended to 15 weeks in some cases.

After the first three months of pregnancy, other methods have to be used. But whereas in the early stages the methods used are relatively safe, late termination does have an element of risk.

Such late termination (sometimes called a prostaglanin are carried out at about 16 to 28 weeks. Because the foetus is no longer small enough to be extracted by suction or curettage, a termination inducing solution is injected, usually vaginally but sometimes via a drip, into the amniotic sac, known as the 'bag-of-waters', surrounding the foetus. This causes the patient to go into labour so that the termination occurs through the natural process of delivery.

Before 16 weeks, the sac is not large enough to be located accurately, so this process of inducing labour by injections into the amniotic sac (bag of waters) cannot be used safely before this time. A more recent method introduces a solution—usually in the form of prostaglandin pessaries—into the top of the vagina close to the womb, rather than the sac. This have proved to be effective in bringing on labour and has few side-effects.

There is a last method of carrying out a late termination, (16 to 28 weeks). Called a hysterotomy (not be confused with hysterectomy), it is only used when in-

Early terminations can be carried out by D&E (right), which takes ten minutes under general anaesthetic. The vagina is opened with a speculum and the exact depth of the womb (uterus) measured. The neck of the womb (cervix) is then gently opened. A tentaculum holds it open and the tip of a vacurette (a rigid tube) is inserted. This is attached to a suction pump which frees and draws out the foetal material along with the early afterbirth. D&C (above) is done in the same way except that a curette (a metal loop with a handle) loosens the foetal material, which is removed from the uterus with forceps. The scale diagram (far right) shows the size of the female reproductive organs in relation to the whole body.

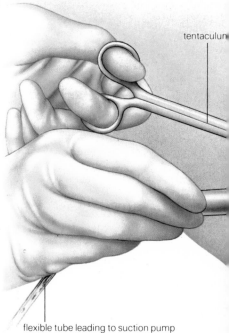

flexible tube leading to suction pump

duction methods have proved unsuccessful. As in a caesarean section, the foetus is removed through a small incision in the abdomen, usually just below the pubic hairline. However, this technique has the highest risk of complications and it can sometimes limit a woman to caesarean births in the future.

After-effects

There is very little danger attached to having a termination in a hospital or clinic. The real danger is to the woman who goes to the back-street abortionist—where she could run the risk of infection, a punctured womb and even death.

But there are a few minor side-effects which can occur after even the most well-conducted termination. A woman who is too energetic during the 48 hours following the operation may find she experiences heavy bleeding, and this will require bedrest. Blood loss following termination varies from woman to woman: it may finish after a few days, like a period, or it may go on for two or three weeks. Some women get intermittent cramp pains for a few days.

Sudden pain, excessive bleeding, or a rise in temperature should always be reported to your doctor immediately.

Because the cervix will remain open for a while after most types of termination, there is a slight risk of infection. If an infection spreads to the fallopian tubes it could result in infertility. To reduce this risk, tampons or any other internal protection must not be used to staunch bleeding until after the first period has passed. Instead use sanitary towels.

Some doctors also recommend not sitting or lying in a bath after the operation, though kneeling upright is all right.

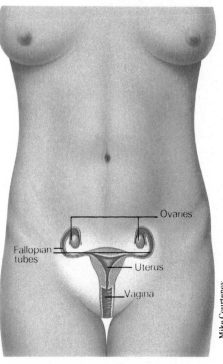

Ovaries

Fallopian tubes

Uterus

Vagina

Mike Courtency

Reassurance

After all terminations, final counselling should include contraceptive advice. For the older woman who has completed her family, counselling should include discussion of sterilization for her or a vasectomy for her husband.

Occasionally, psychological effects are felt after termination, and these may be more likely after late termination. Such emotional upsets may involve a sense of guilt and can lead to depression and a sense of loss or bereavement. This is not abnormal, and no woman should feel that, because terminations are relatively simple, she should just be able to breeze through it without any emotion. A great deal will depend on the circumstances that dictated the termination, on the attitude of the partner, family and friends, and on the quality of the counselling before the decision was taken. Emotional support is a vital part of the care a woman who is having a termination needs.

If you are pregnant and think you need a termination

DO

● see your doctor as soon as your period is two weeks overdue. There can be many reasons for a missed period, and only a pregnancy test or an internal examination can tell you if you're expecting a baby.

● take a positive attitude. Abortion is not a shameful matter today and the people who are there to help you will not try to make you feel guilty.

● consider alternatives, such as adoption, before making a decision. Your doctor or a professional counsellor can give guidance.

DON'T

● try old-fashioned 'remedies'—throwing yourself downstairs, for example, or gin and hot baths. You could injure yourself severely—and still be pregnant.

● under any circumstances go to a back-street abortionist. You could suffer irreparable damage and still be pregnant.

● listen to myths, such as 'If you have a termination, you'll never feel much pleasure in love-making again', or, 'You'll always have difficult pregnancies once you've had a termination. They are nonsense.

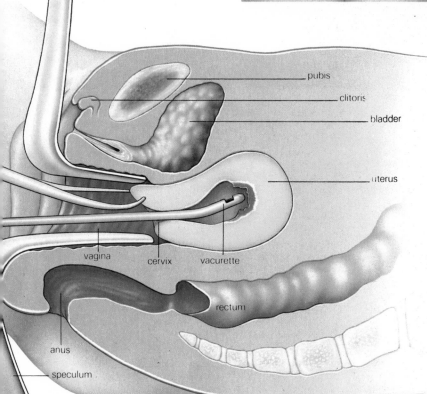

pubis

clitoris

bladder

uterus

vagina

cervix

vacurette

rectum

anus

speculum

Frank Kennard

417

Tetanus

Q Can you be immunized against tetanus?

A Not only can you be immunized, you most definitely should be. Children are given a vaccine against this serious disease with their first series of injections and then are given a booster dose as they start school. Older people may have escaped vaccination and should ask their doctor to give them one, since they will otherwise be at a much greater risk of infection.

If you have been vaccinated you should have a booster dose about every 5 years. When people go to a casualty department with wounds of various sorts they are often given a booster. The vaccination is actually against the toxin, or poison, rather than the bacteria that make it, since it is the toxin that causes all the trouble.

Q Can you only get tetanus in a wound made by a rusty, rather than a clean, object?

A No, the spores of tetanus are very common in our environment and it is certainly possible to infect yourself, even with an object that is apparently clean. However, the highest concentration of spores is certainly to be found in the soil and in manure, and something like a rusty nail is perhaps more likely to have been in contact with spores; therefore you might be a bit more likely to get an infection from such an object.

Q Is it true that tetanus paralyzes you so that you can hear everything around you but you can't move or speak?

A No. Tetanus is caused by a toxin that acts directly on the nervous system. The effects of the toxin are to produce both a generalized rigidity of muscle – leading to 'lockjaw', a name sometimes given to the disease – and to produce generalized spasms. These spasms can be exhausting and even fatal if they occur frequently. In order to prevent them, sedation is used. If this fails then the patient may be deliberately paralyzed with drugs and have his or her breathing taken over by a ventilator.

A rusty nail, a clumsy step – and the resulting wound could be the ideal breeding ground for the virulent bacterium that causes tetanus. The disease can be fatal, so adequate immunization is of the utmost importance.

Sally and Richard Greenhill

Tetanus is a frightening and dangerous disease that can often be fatal, even with the best of medical care. However, all the techniques of intensive care can be brought to bear on sufferers in developed countries and there is no doubt that modern treatment does significantly reduce the number of deaths from this disease.

Cause
Tetanus is caused by a bacterium called Clostridium tetani. This organism is found freely in the soil, and is more likely to be encountered in manured and cultivated soil since it is very common in animal dung. However it is not confined to the soil; street dust from the centre of a town certainly contains the spores of the bacteria and they can even be found inside buildings in quite large amounts.

The bacterium has one very important characteristic that controls the way the disease behaves: it is killed off by oxygen and only grows in oxygen-free surroundings. This is why the bacteria have to be introduced into the body via a wound of some sort, since the blood supply and therefore the oxygen supply are cut off as a result of the tissue damage. The deeper and more contaminated a wound is, the worse the risk of tetanus.

The toxin that the bacterium makes is a deadly substance, exceeded in potency only by the toxin responsible for botulism. A tenth of a milligram is the fatal dose for an adult. From its site of production in the wound contaminated by the bacteria, the toxin passes into the spinal cord and the brain. It is thought that it travels through the nerves, although spread via the blood could also be important. Once in the nervous system the toxin cannot be neutralized by antibodies either produced by the body after immunization or given as antitoxin.

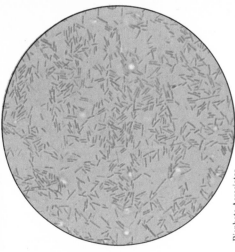

Biophoto Associates

Once in the body, the bacterium may grow in an area with no blood supply – making it difficult for antibiotics to reach.

Symptoms

The incubation period is six to ten days as a rule, although in rare cases it may be several months. At the other extreme, symptoms can occur within a day. There is a short vague illness with headache, general illness and fever, but the important first signs are due to the generalized muscle rigidity that is one of the two classical symptoms of the disease. This especially affects the jaw muscles – giving rise to 'lock jaw' by which name the disease is sometimes known – the muscles of the abdomen, which are found to be firm on examination, and the muscles of the back. Eventually the back may be arched right over and the neck bent right back.

Spasms develop later and can be brought on by any stimulus. Minor spasms may simply affect the face, with contraction of the facial muscles into a ghastly grin – known by the chilling Latin title risus sardonicus, meaning sardonic smile. Breathing can be affected by these spasms and when they become more generalized they lead to even more exaggerated arching of the back and neck.

The difficulty in looking after tetanus patients really becomes marked when the disease interferes with the way that the brain controls vital functions. The heart may be affected, leading to abnormalities of rhythm and either very low, or very high blood pressure. Sometimes the temperature may shoot up rapidly.

Treatment

The aim of treatment is to tide the patient over the period of illness without any of the possible fatal problems occurring. These problems include exhaustion due to spasm, asphyxia during spasm, pneumonia due to stomach contents entering the lungs, and death due to disorders of control of vital functions such as the heartbeat and blood pressure.

In milder cases, simple sedation and the avoidance of all types of disturbance will prevent spasms, but in the more severe cases a tracheotomy (see page 212) is performed, and the patient is treated by total paralysis using curare (a paralyzing drug), while breathing is taken over by a ventilator.

The disease is likely to be most severe when the incubation period has been short, and when there has been less than 48 hours between the first symptom and the first spasm.

Prevention

Immunization with what is known as tetanus toxoid is given with a baby's first immunization, and boosters are given when starting school and again on leaving. After that, a booster should be given every 5 years – or more often if you are at special risk, for example if you work on the land. In people who have not been immunized it is necessary to give an antitoxin after any serious wound.

It is possible to cut down the risks of the disease by very careful cleaning of wounds and the use of large doses of penicillin. However, adequate immunization can abolish the risk completely. This disease is often fatal and it is up to all of us to make sure that we are immunized.

Brian Harris/Colorific!

People who work on land – such as gardeners and farmers – are most likely to catch tetanus. The bacterium is commonly found in animal dung, a normal component of fertilized and cultivated soil.

Throat

The air we breathe has to pass through the throat on its way to the lungs, as does our food before reaching the digestive tract. Any obstruction to this vital passage, then, can represent a serious threat to life.

'Throat' is a term popularly used to describe the area that leads into the respiratory and digestive tracts. It extends from the oral and nasal cavities to the oesophagus and trachea, and is composed of two main parts: the pharynx and the larynx.

Anatomy of the throat

The main component of the throat is the pharynx, a muscular tube about 12 cm long stretching from the base of the skull into the oesophagus. It is the passage through which

Structures of the throat

The pharynx is a muscular tube lined by mucous membrane. For practical purposes it is divided into three areas. The part behind the nasal cavity is termed the nasopharynx; the area behind the mouth the oropharynx; and that behind the

everything we eat, drink and breathe has to pass, the junction point of all nasal and oral passages. The pharynx is also connected to the ears by drainage channels — the Eustachian tubes — which help to equalize air pressure on each side of the ear-drums.

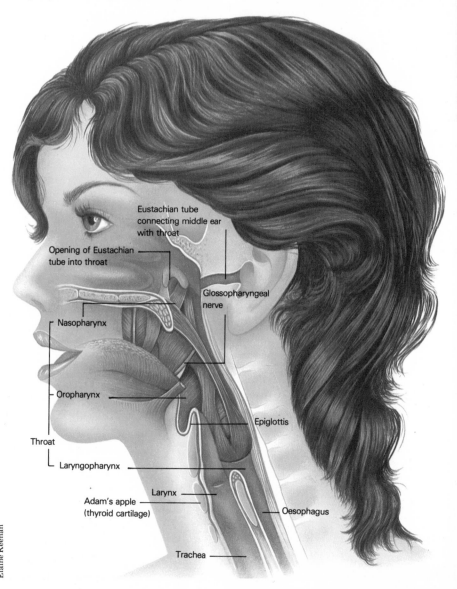

Eustachian tube connecting middle ear with throat

Opening of Eustachian tube into throat

Glossopharyngeal nerve

Nasopharynx

Oropharynx

Epiglottis

Throat

Laryngopharynx

Larynx

Adam's apple (thyroid cartilage)

Oesophagus

Trachea

Elaine Keenan

larynx, the laryngopharynx. Clumps of lymphoid tissue lie in the lining of the pharynx; these are the adenoids in the nasopharynx and the tonsils in the oropharynx. They protect the entrance to the food and air passages.

The larynx is the other major part of the throat. It is situated in front of the laryngopharynx and is made up of a framework of cartilage which is swathed in muscles both internally and externally, and is lined by a respiratory membrane.

The larynx is a specialized section of the windpipe, with a flap-valve – the epiglottis – hovering over the inlet to the airway. The epiglottis acts as a type of umbrella against a shower of food and drink when we eat or drink.

The vocal cords are located in the larynx and are held in place by special cartilages. They are suspended across the airway and produce sound when vibrated by controlled air movement.

Functions of the throat

Because the throat is an assembly of different components, it has a variety of functions. The most obvious of these are to channel food and liquid into the digestive tract, and air into the lungs; this essential task is carried out by the pharynx.

The movements of the pharynx must be co-ordinated to ensure that the respiratory gases end up in the lungs and food ends up in the oesophagus. This co-ordination is achieved by a plexus, or network, of nerves – the pharyngeal plexus. Its activity is controlled in the lower brain stem which brings together information from both the respiratory and swallowing centres higher in the brain.

Therefore, when food is thrown into the oropharynx by the tongue it is swiftly sent into the oesphagus by a wave of muscle contractions that travel down the pharynx. At the same time mechanisms are triggered off to prevent the food entering the larynx.

No less important are the functions of the larynx; to produce sound and protect the airway. Like the pharynx, the larynx achieves this through a complex co-ordinated nerve supply to its muscles. The nerves that supply the larynx are under the same central influence in the brain as those that supply the pharynx.

Throat disorders

The pharynx and larynx are prone to a number of infections caused by viruses or bacteria, and also to damage by physical agents such as excessive smoking or drinking. Either of these factors can lead, for example, to chronic laryngitis (see pp 210-13) and pharyngitis (see page 293).

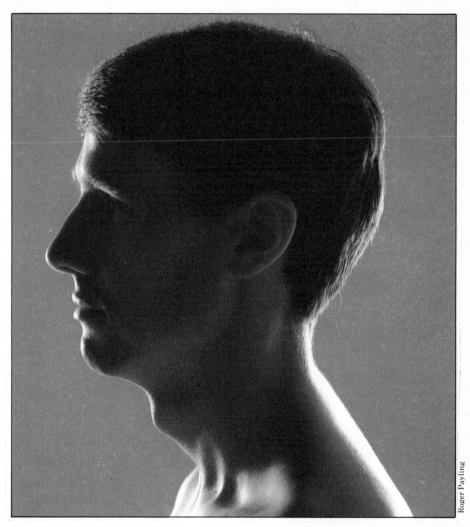

Roger Pavling

Other throat infections include nasopharyngitis, a viral infection of the mucous membranes lining the nasopharynx. It begins with a burning feeling in the throat that builds up in intensity and is aggravated by speaking and swallowing. The discomfort is accompanied by a general feeling of being unwell which lasts from one to two days.

This condition is often confused with tonsillitis; as the tonsils and the nasopharynx are adjacent to each other an infection in either area gives rise to similar symptoms. However, in tonsillitis the symptoms are much more severe.

The nasopharynx is also the site of the adenoids, and repeated infections in this area of the throat can cause them to enlarge. Patients with excessively large adenoids are unable to breathe through their nose and consequently have persistently gaping mouths. An increase in adenoid tissue may block the natural drainage channel – the Eustachian tube – from the middle ear and cause an accumulation of fluid in this cavity. In severe cases, deafness may result and the condition also predisposes to recurrent

The thyroid cartilage surrounding the larynx creates the projection called the Adam's apple. It is more prominent in men because they have larger vocal cords.

attacks of otitis media (infection of the middle ear). Children are most affected, and are frequently admitted to hospital for drainage of the middle ear fluid and removal of their adenoids.

Papillomatosis is caused by a virus that affects the larynx; it occurs both in children and in adults. The virus is very similar to that which produces warts on the skin. As the papillomata increase in size they restrict the air passage and may even choke the patient. Like warts on the skin the growths will disappear spontaneously, but in severe cases surgery is required to remove them.

Throat cancers

Cancer of the pharynx is an unusual condition that occurs in middle and old age. Patients complain of a progressively painful difficulty in swallowing. The pain is not only experienced at the site of the disease but also radiates to the ear. In a

421

Q My husband has just been told that he has cancer of the larynx. What are his chances of being cured?

A Most forms of cancer in the larynx respond well to treatment. With modern radiotherapy techniques a cure rate of about 90 per cent is quite common. However, the doctors will want to keep a close eye on your husband for the rest of his life, in order to treat any recurrent problems as they arise.

Q What is the correct action to take when someone is choking on something – such as a bone or a peanut – that they have swallowed?

A First take hold of the person firmly from behind and give a very strong and very sharp 'bear hug'. If the patient is a child, turn him or her upside down to do this. In most patients this will dislodge the object explosively.

Q Why are disorders of the throat accompanied by pain in the ear?

A Throat infections may cause pain in the ear because of the phenomenon of pain referral. This occurs when the same nerve supplies the two different, but close-lying structures. The patient is unable to discern from which site the pain arises.

Q My son is always getting ear infections and we have been told that he should have an adenoidectomy. Will this definitely cure him?

A It is never possible for a doctor to guarantee that any treatment will be totally successful. However, very enlarged adenoids are frequently implicated in recurrent otitis media (an infection in the middle ear) and it is only right to remove them in the hope that this is the cause of the problem. It is very important to try to minimize infectious attacks in the ear and prevent the deafness which can be associated with them, so if your ear surgeon recommends an adenoidectomy you should seriously consider it.

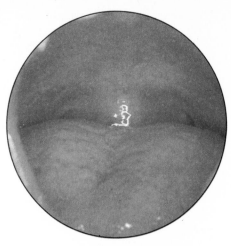

Caused by the streptococcus bacterium, 'strep' throat is a common throat infection which can be very painful.

large number of patients a lump will appear on one side of the neck. While this is a very serious condition, a considerable proportion of patients can be greatly helped by radiotherapy or surgery.

Laryngeal cancer is more common but it is one form of cancer that can be cured if the disease is diagnosed and treated early. Cancer of the larynx occurs most frequently in late middle age and is much more common in men than in women. Most patients are, or have been, heavy smokers for much of their life.

While progressive hoarseness is the commonest symptom, patients may also complain of an odd feeling in the throat, slight difficulty in breathing, pain in their ear, or pain radiating from the throat to the ear. Occasionally they may cough up a small amount of blood.

The majority of cases are cured by a course of radiotherapy. However in a few cases the disease recurs or fails to respond to radiation treatment and surgery is necessary.

Foreign objects in the throat

A wide variety of foreign objects have been found in the pharynx, ranging from fishbones to coins and bottle tops. All are potentially dangerous as they can perforate the pharyngeal wall and set up serious infection in the surrounding tissues.

Patients who have swallowed a foreign object are rarely in any doubt about its presence; every attempt to swallow even their own saliva is excrutiatingly painful. If the object is lodged high in the pharynx it is frequently possible to remove it in the casualty department of a hospital. However if it has lodged lower down, for example in the laryngo-pharynx, it must be removed under a general anaesthetic.

Foreign bodies that are inhaled into the larynx can threaten a patient's life and little time should be lost in getting treatment. The younger the patient the more serious the condition, as the diameter of a child's airway is so narrow that even a small object is likely to obstruct it totally.

Removal of any object from the larynx is a matter of surgical urgency, and may require a temporary tracheostomy to protect the lower airway and maintain adequate breathing. Recovery from this surgery is very swift.

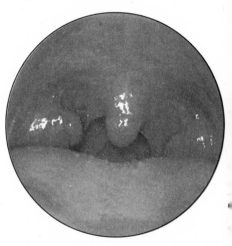

Infection can spread rapidly throughout the throat; in this case tonsillitis, usually caused by a streptococcus, has developed.

Home help for a sore throat

A sore throat that accompanies the common cold or other minor infections can be treated at home. Here are some proven remedies you might try.

Make up a gargling solution by dissolving two teaspoonfuls of household salt in a teacupful of hot, but not boiling, water. Stir until the salt has dissolved, then use to gargle. Make sure you spit the solution out of your mouth when you have finished.

Alternatively, you can use an aspirin gargle by dissolving two soluble aspirin tablets in a teacupful of hot water. If you swallow this when you have gargled, the aspirin will relieve some of the pain and reduce any fever you might have.

Drink plenty of hot liquids and try to eat only soft or liquid foods such as soups, so that you do not take anything into your throat that might cause further damage or inflammation.

Lozenges, particularly those that contain formaldehyde, can soothe the throat and prevent it from becoming dry. As you suck the lozenge, keep it as far back on your tongue as you can.

Thrombosis

Q Will giving up smoking really lessen my chances of suffering from a coronary thrombosis?

A There is no doubt that a cigarette smoker stands a considerably greater chance of having a heart attack as well as chronic bronchitis and cancer. Doctors are now quite convinced that as soon as a person stops smoking, the chances of contracting these life-threatening conditions decrease. Five years after stopping smoking a reformed smoker is at no greater risk from a heart attack than someone who has never smoked.

Q Is it true that doctors prescribe rat poison for thrombosis?

A It is true that the anticoagulant drug warfarin is also used to kill rats and mice. The group of anticoagulants were discovered when cattle feeding on sweet clover were found to be suffering from bruising and haemorrhages. A powerful anticoagulant was discovered in the plants on which the cattle were grazing.
  Warfarin is commonly used to prevent thrombosis and is prescribed only in very small doses. Blood clotting is carefully controlled by the doctor who usually orders a blood test every few weeks.

Q Can the contraceptive pill cause thrombosis? I read that this could happen and it has made me very wary as I am thinking of going on the Pill.

A There tends to be a higher incidence of thrombosis in women who take a high-dosage oral contraceptive, particularly if they are over 35, overweight and smoke.
  The modern low-dosage oestrogen pill, on the other hand, has only a very small risk of causing thrombosis – indeed a smaller chance than in pregnancy itself. Of those who develop thrombotic side-effects, the majority suffer from thrombophlebitis of the legs, and should immediately arrange with their doctor to start some alternative form of birth control.

Heart attacks, strokes and even varicose veins all have a single cause – a thrombosis, which is a blood clot in an artery or a vein that blocks circulation. Can anything be done to minimize the risk of this occurring?

Although the smoker, the obese and the diabetic are more prone to thrombotic diseases, they can occur even among the healthy. But risks can be minimized and appropriate measures taken.

Thrombus formation

The blood forms a clot (or thrombus) as a normal, healthy protective process, by which bleeding from a damaged blood vessel is stopped and the repair process begins. There are three stages in the process of stopping bleeding from a small blood vessel: constriction, formation of a platelet plug and clotting.
  As soon as bleeding begins, the damaged vessel constricts, slowing blood flow and attracting platelets to the site of the damage. Platelets are tiny blood cells which suddenly become sticky and adhere to each other and to the lining of the vessel, temporarily plugging the hole. Finally a clot will form. Thromboplastin,

an extract from the blood vessel wall, oozes from the torn edges of the vessel. This starts a chain reaction in which fibrinogen, a soluble blood protein, is changed into long strands of fibrin forming a meshwork to trap passing red blood cells and platelets. In the last stage of clot formation, the fibrin mesh tightens, fluid is squeezed out of the clot and the torn vessel walls pull together.

How a thrombosis occurs

When blood circulation through the heart, limbs or brain is sluggish; or the blood contains an excess of clotting factors; or the blood vessels are affected by atheroma, a clot may block a major artery or vein. The thrombosis may occur in different parts of the body.

Doctors encourage patients to become mobile as soon as possible after surgery to prevent the chance of a thrombosis.

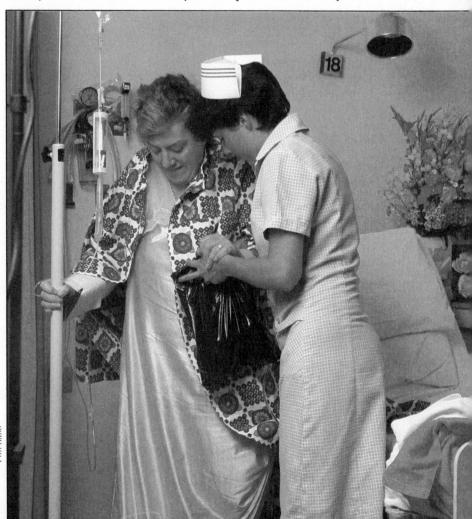

Phil Babb

Q A friend told me that you can get gangrene from a blood clot. Is she correct?

A Gangrene occurs when living muscle and skin is deprived of its blood supply and begins to die. Gas gangrene is a complication of massive penetrating wounds contaminated by Clostridium welchii, a bacterium normally growing in the bowel. Gas gangrene of the arm or leg was commonly seen following bullet or shrapnel wounds, which were left unattended until only amputation of part of the limb could prevent the infection from affecting the whole body.

Dry gangrene is less dramatic but much commoner. It often occurs when a blood clot blocks the blood flow in an artery supplying blood to an arm or leg. Fingers or toes are usually affected first by discoloration, cold and sometimes pain. Eventually the digits may turn black and the gangrene spreads up the limb to a level that is determined by the site of the blockage.

Q I had rheumatic fever as a child and have been told by my doctor that I have a damaged heart valve. He has now prescribed an anticoagulant drug for me. Why is this necessary?

A Rheumatic fever was once a very common childhood disease. It is less common now, but many of the sufferers have narrowed or stiffened heart valves, which produce murmurs or abnormal sounds which are detected during a medical examination. Damaged valves often interfere with the pumping action of the heart and can lead to irregularities of heart rhythm.

Both of these complications can result in blood clotting in the chambers of the heart. To make the blood clot more slowly, and prevent clots from forming, anticoagulant drugs such as warfarin are prescribed for patients. Often the only way to improve the performance of the heart and prevent further damage is to replace the damaged valve with a metal or plastic valve. These replacement valves still need anticoagulant protection, and most doctors advise their patients to remain on warfarin or similar drugs.

When thrombosis occurs in one of the coronary arteries of the heart, a patient has a heart attack or myocardial infarction. Thrombosis in the brain results in a stroke. Thrombosis in a leg vein causes phlebitis; thrombosis in the artery supplying a limb may result in gangrene.

An embolism occurs when a thrombus forming in a major blood vessel or on the lining of the heart breaks loose and is swept away by the bloodstream to become lodged in a narrow vessel, completely cutting off the blood supply to part of the lung or brain or to an arm or leg. Because of the anatomy of the circulatory system, thrombosis in a leg vein may break loose to form a pulmonary embolism in the lung. But if the clot originates from one of the neck arteries, it may be carried into the brain to produce a cerebral embolism.

Why does a thrombosis occur?

Thrombosis nearly always results from one or a combination of the following: cardiovascular disease; prolonged immobilization; the aftermath of major surgery; pregnancy; or the Pill.

Apparently some individuals are more susceptible to thrombosis than others. In these there is usually both an abnormality of blood vessels and a hypercoagulable state in which blood has a tendency to clot more easily than normal. Any attempt to reduce the risk of thrombosis must either entail preventing or correcting the disease in the heart or blood vessels, or reducing the ease with which clotting occurs in the blood.

Disorders of the blood vessels

It is said that we are only as old as our arteries. Certainly as we grow older signs of degenerative disease become more marked in the major arteries. Patholo-gists describe this degenerative process as atheroma and the effect on the blood vessels as arteriosclerosis, or hardening of the arteries. Arteriosclerosis is most likely to occur first in the heart and the major arteries where the arteries are subjected to the most stress. Not surprisingly, when the blood pressure is abnormally raised, then arteriosclerosis develops early in the blood vessels supplying the heart, brain and limbs. The arteries become narrower and more rigid, which has the effect of significantly reducing the flow of blood.

Atheroma in its earliest form can be detected in childhood. Tiny yellowish flecks develop in the linings of the major arteries, particularly where they branch or split into smaller tributaries. By middle age the flecks have become distinct streaks, rich in cholesterol. The lining of the vessel may then become roughened and cracked. Platelets are attracted to the cracked surface and eventually a small clot may grow into the cavity of the artery. This may create a turbulence in blood flow, which may finally tear the clot loose, resulting in a dangerous embolism of the brain or the limbs.

The chambers of the heart are a common place for clots to form, particularly in the heart valves. This is especially likely to happen if the valves are already damaged or narrowed. Rheumatic fever in childhood is still the commonest cause of valvular disease, although it is a relative rarity in today's children. Some people in the middle or older age group are still coming to their doctors with illness brought about by a long forgotten attack of rheumatic fever in childhood.

A thrombus may form in the heart's atria if they are beating irregularly or

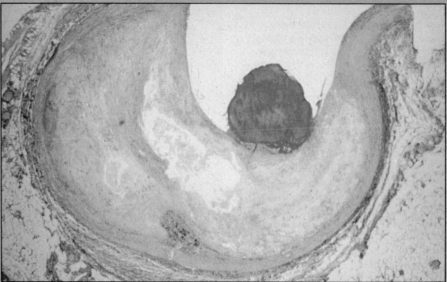

One of the commonest places for a clot to form is in the heart. This cross-section of a coronary artery clearly shows a small clot that has grown within it.

CNRI/Vision International

fibrillating. Occasionally after a severe coronary thrombosis a whole area of the left ventricle, the main pumping chamber of the heart, becomes thin, wasted and fails to contract effectively. This is a likely site for a thrombus which all too often leads to a serious embolism.

Coronary thrombosis

Coronary thrombosis is the common cause of what the general public calls a heart attack and doctors usually refer to as myocardial infarction (see Heart attack pp 167-68). One person in three will be affected by coronary artery disease, and it is still the commonest single cause of death in Great Britain. Until the age of 70, about four times as many men as women suffer a coronary thrombosis. Over 70, women are just as likely to be affected as men.

Those most at risk of a heart attack are male, overweight, have a diet rich in fats and lead a stressful life with minimal exercise. In addition, diabetics and people whose families have a history of heart attacks are prone to it. However the biggest group of risk-takers are smokers: a cigarette smoker is five times more likely to suffer a heart attack than a non-smoker – all other factors being equal.

A thrombosis is far less likely to occur in those who are fit and active – so take up a sport or embark on a keep-fit programme.

Causes, symptoms, treatment

The two coronary arteries, embedded in the muscular walls of the heart, divert oxygen-rich blood, fresh from the lungs, to small vessels feeding all parts of the heart muscle. It is vital that these arteries remain open; even a slight narrowing of the coronary arteries may cause symptoms during times of exertion.

Persons at risk from coronary disease have a tendency to form fatty deposits which roughen the lining of the arteries and narrow the central channel. If the blockage occurs gradually, the person may experience pain only on exertion.

To prevent thrombotic diseases

- stop smoking
- if you are overweight, start to rid yourself of those extra pounds
- diabetics should stick religiously to their diet and take their medication
- attend your antenatal clinic regularly for check-ups if you are pregnant
- after an operation, follow your doctor's orders and get mobile as soon as possible
- don't cut down on your medication if you feel well but suffer from high blood pressure
- embark on a programme of regular exercise: a thrombosis is much less common in individuals who are fit and active, regardless of age

Q Six months ago I had deep vein thrombosis which was a complication of my hysterectomy, but my leg still swells from time to time. Is this usual?

A The veins in the legs contain valves which allow blood to flow against gravity towards the heart, but prevent back-flow stagnation of blood in the lower legs and feet. When a blood clot forms in these veins, the valves are often damaged. The clot is eventually digested and removed by enzymes in the blood and blood flow is restored. For many weeks after the thrombosis, increased pressure may force fluid into the tissues causing the legs to swell, particularly after a person stands for a long time.

Anyone who has deep vein thrombosis should avoid long periods standing, try to do some exercise such as walking, and wear support stockings. These will usually help to relieve the symptoms.

Q Can varicose veins be dangerous or are they just ugly?

A Varicose veins are rarely more than an unsightly nuisance. Some people can develop painful, and red hard swollen areas known as superficial thrombophlebitis. Varicose veins increase the danger of a deep-vein thrombosis after an operation or pregnancy. It is not unknown for a cut or a fall to cause serious bleeding from a prominent varicose vein.

Varicose vein sufferers should avoid prolonged standing and wear special support stockings or tights, but in serious cases an operation on the veins may be required to deal with the condition.

Q A girl at work suffers from something called phlebitis. What is it?

A Phlebitis is an inflammation of a vein, usually in the leg, caused by a blood clot forming in the vein. It is fairly painful, and the area may be red, swollen and tender to the touch. Fortunately, phlebitis usually disappears in a week or two without any serious consequences, but there may be recurrent attacks throughout a person's life.

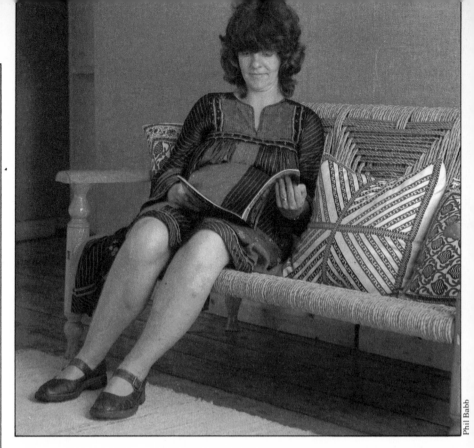

Phil Babb

This is typical of the pain of angina, and usually is severe enough to make the sufferer stop what he is doing. The angina pain then subsides. Although frightening, it serves as a warning, making the sufferer rest long enough for blood flow to be restored to the oxygen-starved muscle before serious damage can be done, and allowing time for new circulatory channels to open up over the following weeks.

When a coronary thrombosis develops at a site of narrowing it completely blocks the blood supply to part of the heart muscle. That part will be so severely damaged that it will cease to contract normally; the symptoms, then, will be sudden and severe. Patients experience crushing chest pain which is sometimes also felt in the arm and jaw; they may feel breathless and sweat profusely. These symptoms do not necessarily begin when the person is exerting himself and do not usually improve even when he rests.

Coronary thrombosis almost always requires treatment in hospital, though patients will be allowed out of bed for short periods within the first fortnight and will embark on a programme of graduated exercise. It is believed that once a firm scar has replaced the damaged heart muscle, exercise will encourage the formation of new channels to replace the thrombosed artery.

Cerebral thrombosis

Strokes are one of the most common causes of death and disablement. Those most at risk are people who suffer from

One of the most common causes of thrombosis is varicose veins – the bane of some pregnant women's lives. The veins can often cause itching, sometimes pain and, rarely, skin ulceration. The symptoms can be alleviated by taking frequent rests, and by wearing support stockings or tights.

high blood pressure, or who are diabetics, have a high serum cholesterol, and who smoke. Strokes may run in families. Some people with heart disease are predisposed to strokes.

Causes, symptoms, treatment

A stroke can be caused by bleeding from a weakened artery into the brain (cerebral haemorrhage); a sudden blockage of an artery by a flake of material that has come adrift from a diseased artery or from the heart (embolism); or a more gradual blockage by clot formation within a diseased artery of the brain (thrombosis). The arterial disease that predisposes to all three types is arteriosclerosis.

The effect of a stroke depends entirely on the size and situation of the affected area of the brain. If the right side of the brain is damaged, there is usually weakness, paralysis of the facial muscles, with loss of sensation in the left arm and leg. If the left side of the brain is affected, the patient may lose total or partial control of speech and be paralyzed on the right side of the body.

Cerebral thrombosis produces sudden paralysis or weakness which begins to improve within hours of the stroke occurring. Recovery is helped by early encouragement of the patient, and physiotherapy and/or speech therapy. A high proportion of stroke victims make a full recovery, but in the rest the degree of recovery will depend on the severity of the initial damage to the brain.

Thrombophlebitis

Phlebitis is an inflammation of a vein; it is usually associated with a blockage of the vein by a blood clot. The clot forms in a limb – frequently in the leg and rarely in the arm.

Causes, symptoms, treatment

Thrombophlebitis can either be superficial or deep vein. The commonest cause of superficial thrombophlebitis is varicose veins. The veins lie directly under the skin and at points connect with the deeper veins. If the blood flow is sluggish, with the blood's component parts settling out, clotting may occur and the veins will become inflamed. In most cases varicose veins, which are more common in women, are no more than an unsightly nuisance. They are made worse by standing and pregnancy, and frequently cause itching, sometimes pain and rarely ulceration of the skin. At times they can cause more serious problems, especially during pregnancy or when a patient is confined to bed by some immobilizing illness or after an operation. The veins may then become painful and hard. The inflammation usually disappears on its own, but a hot water bottle will give relief.

Deep vein thrombophlebitis is more serious and is likely to occur in varicose veins sufferers. When varicose veins are so large that most of the blood being pumped back from the legs to the heart is carried in dilated veins beneath the skin, the blood flow through the main leg veins can be so slow as to encourage formation of an extensive clot. The thrombus, in addition to causing a painful hot swollen limb, can permanently damage the valves which ensure that the blood flows towards the heart and against the force of gravity. In the majority of patients the thrombosis resolves completely and normal blood circulation is restored, but in a few the aching and swelling of the limb may recur on prolonged standing.

Biophoto Associates

A thrombosis can sometimes be fatal: here a clot has completely enveloped the internal carotid artery of the neck.

Thrombotic diseases

Disease	Causes	Symptoms	Dangers	Treatment	Prevention
Coronary thrombosis	Stress. High blood pressure. Diabetes. Arteriosclerosis (hardening of the arteries)	Faintness. Breathlessness. Increasing crushing chest pain	Irregular heartbeat. Low blood pressure. Congestion of the lungs. Other thromboses	Bed-rest. Pain relief. Oxygen. Drugs to stabilize heart rhythm and blood pressure	Stop smoking. Lose weight. Take regular exercise. Avoid stress
Cerebral thrombosis and embolism	Heart disease. High blood pressure. Also arteriosclerosis	One-sided weakness of the face, arm and/or leg. Loss of feeling. Drowsiness. Difficulty with speech. Unsteadiness	Chest infection. Pressure sores. Stiffening of joints. Depression	Retraining exercises. Speech therapy. Anticoagulant drugs	Stop smoking. Have your blood pressure checked yearly
Venous thrombosis (phlebitis)	Immobilization. Major surgical operations. Varicose veins. Pregnancy and occasionally the contraceptive pill	Pain and swelling. Also tenderness. Discoloration of the lower leg	Pleurisy. Massive embolism of the lung. Post-phlebitic limb	Rest and elevation of the limb. Support stockings. Exercise. Anticoagulant drugs	Patients with varicose veins: wear support tights and stockings. Phlebitis sufferers: seek specialist advice during pregnancy, or before starting the Pill or undergoing surgery
Arterial thrombosis and embolism	Heart disease. Diabetes. Smoking. Also arteriosclerosis	Limb pain. Numbness and cold. Blackening of fingers or toes	Gangrene	Bed-rest. Surgical removal of clot. By-pass operation. Anticoagulant drugs	Stop smoking. Diabetes sufferers: keep closely to diet

Thyroid

Q I am very nervous and anxious all the time and I seem to be very irritable with the children. Is it possible that I have an over-active thyroid?

A Yes, although there may be some initial difficulty in differentiating between symptoms of the disease and those of pure anxiety. This thyroid disorder is often associated with weight loss, and there may be the characteristic protruding eyes of Grave's disease – the main form of thyrotoxicosis, or over-active thyroid. If you find that you are shaky and have a lot of difficulty tolerating heat, then these might suggest that your thyroid is at fault. In any case, the tests for thyrotoxicosis are very straightforward to do and if your doctor has any suspicion that this might be the trouble, he or she will arrange for you to have a blood test so that a firm diagnosis can be made.

Q I have an over-active thyroid and my doctor is sending me to the hospital to see a specialist. I am terrified that I will need an operation; do you think this will be necessary? Are there other forms of treatment I can try?

A It is possible that you will be advised to have an operation although your worries about having it done might lead the doctor to suggest alternative treatment. First, you could be given tablets to take for about 18 months, to suppress the activity of the gland. This has the disadvantage that the condition might recur in the future. Second, you could be given treatment with radio-iodine (radioactive iodine which is all taken up by the thyroid) which then reduces the level of thyroid activity. This has the advantage of being simple and the condition is unlikely to recur. However this type of treatment is not given to very young people or to women who might become pregnant, since there is a theoretical risk of causing malignancy (cancer) in the patient or in subsequent children. There is also a definite risk of under-activity of the thyroid occurring after treatment, but this in turn is very easy to control.

Problems associated with the thyroid and the hormone that it produces are fairly common. However, many of the disorders respond extremely well to treatment and in fact can be completely cured once they have been identified.

The thyroid gland

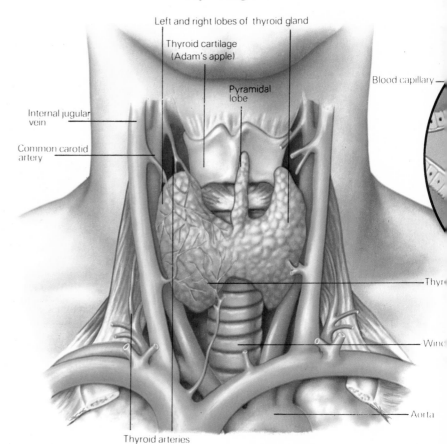

Left and right lobes of thyroid gland
Thyroid cartilage (Adam's apple)
Pyramidal lobe
Blood capillary
Internal jugular vein
Common carotid artery
Thyr
Wind
Aorta
Thyroid arteries

Problems associated with the thyroid gland cause the commonest type of hormonal disorders, affecting large numbers of people. However many of these problems can be completely cured, mainly because the hormone produced by the gland can be easily prepared and administered by mouth.

Of the wide range of thyroid disorders, by far the most important are those of over-activity – thyrotoxicosis or hyperthyroidism – and of under-activity – myxoedema or hypothyroidism. Both of these problems are a lot more common in women than in men and up to 2 per cent of the adult female population may have difficulty from an over-active thyroid at some stage, with under-activity being only slightly less common. One other disorder is worth noting here: thyroiditis, which is an inflammation of the thyroid as a result of a virus infection.

Where is the thyroid gland?
The thyroid gland is found in the neck, just below the level of the larynx, which can be seen or felt as the Adam's apple. There are two lobes to the gland, and these lie just in front and at either side of, the windpipe, or trachea, as it passes down the front of the neck. The two lobes are connected by a small bridge of tissue, and there may be a smaller central lobe called the pyramidal lobe. In an adult, the gland will weigh about 20 gm (²/₃ oz).

What does it do?
The function of the gland is to make the thyroid hormone, thyroxine. When the gland is looked at under a microscope, many small 'follicles' can be seen; these are islands of tissue containing collections of colloid, a protein substance to which thyroid hormone is bound and from which it can be released by enzymes.

The anatomical drawing (below left) shows the position of the thyroid gland in relation to the surrounding structures in the throat, which include the Adam's apple and the trachea. The inset is a section of the thyroid, which shows clearly the cells that produce and store the essential hormone thyroxine.

ection through thyroid

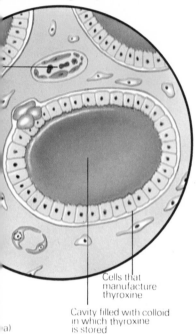

Cells that
manufacture
thyroxine

Cavity filled with colloid
in which thyroxine
is stored

Alan Hutchinson Library

It is not possible to tie the activity of thyroxine down to one specific thing. It is released from the gland and is then probably taken up from the blood into all the cells of the body. There appears to be a receptor on the surface of the cell nucleus that responds to the hormone. The overall effect of the hormone is to increase the amount of energy that the cell uses; it also increases the amount of protein that the cell manufactures. Although the exact role of the hormone in the cell is not known, it is essential for life.

The thyroid gland contains iodine that is vital for its activity and functioning. This is the only part of the body that requires iodine and the thyroid is very efficient at trapping all the available iodine from the blood. An absence of iodine in the diet results in malfunction of the thyroid and the growth of the gland, a condition called endemic goitre.

Control of thyroid activity

The thyroid is one of the endocrine (hormone-producing) glands, and like so many of them it is under the control of the pituitary. The pituitary produces a hormone called Thyroid Stimulating Hormone, or TSH, which increases the amount of thyroid hormone that is released from the gland. The amount of TSH that the pituitary produces increases if the amount of thyroxine circulating in the system falls, and decreases if it rises – a system called 'negative feedback' – which will result in a relatively constant level of thyroid hormone in the blood.

The pituitary is itself under the influence of the hypothalamus and the amount of TSH that is produced will be increased if there is a release of a substance called TRH (TSH Releasing Hormone) from the hypothalamus.

In some areas of the world – such as the Matto Grosso in Brazil – the normal diet lacks iodine. This deficiency causes the thyroid to malfunction and swell, leading to endemic goitre – the disfiguring condition this woman is suffering from.

This situation is further complicated by the fact that thyroid hormone comes in two versions, according to the number of iodine atoms that it contains. Most of the hormone released from the gland is in the form of tetraiodothyronine, which contains four iodine atoms and is known as T4. However, the active hormone at the cell level is triiodothyronine, which contains three atoms and is known as T3. Although the gland releases some T3 into the blood, most of its output is T4, and this is converted into T3 in the tissues. Sometimes the tissues switch the way that they convert T4 to produce an ineffective com-

429

Q I know a lot of people who have had thyroid problems, and most of them are women. Is it really so much commoner in women than in men?

A Yes. Under-activity of the gland happens in about 14 in every thousand women and only about one in every thousand men. An over-active thyroid occurs in at least 20 in every thousand women, but again in only about one or two in every thousand men. Generally, though, thyroid disorders are quite common, with over 3 per cent of women likely to have some type of thyroid difficulty. Most thyroid disorders can be treated effectively and easily.

Q I had an over-active thyroid and they treated me in the clinic with tablets. Although I have been better for the past two years they still insist on seeing me. Why is this necessary?

A Thyrotoxicosis is a disease which responds well to treatment with tablets. However the disease has a very great tendency to recur and there may be several years between any two attacks. The importance of this is that it is a very good idea to diagnose the disease in the early stages, since it is not only easier to treat, but irreversible changes in processes such as the heart rhythm may occur if the disease progresses too far. For these reasons the clinical doctors will want to keep an eye on you.

Q Is it true that your hair falls out if you have myxoedema?

A Myxoedema is under-activity of the thyroid gland, and it leads to dry, coarse hair that is very difficult to manage. The disease is also associated with alopecia, where the hair roots die and the hair falls out. However this is not a direct result of the low thyroid levels.

Q Is it possible for thyroid disorders to run in families?

A Yes, and this is quite common. It is also interesting to note that one family member might have an over-active thyroid while another has an under-active thyroid.

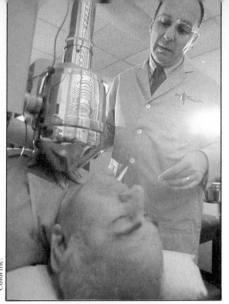

One of the tools used for diagnosing a malfunctioning thyroid and for detecting and identifying nodules in the tissue of the gland is an isotope scan (above).

This bulbous red mass (above right) is a grossly enlarged thyroid gland which was removed. It measures over 25 cm (10 in).

A thyroidectomy – surgery to remove over-active tissue – may be necessary to combat hyperthyroidism. The scar left by the operation is insignificant (right).

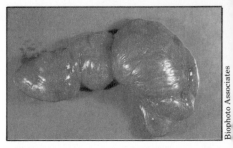

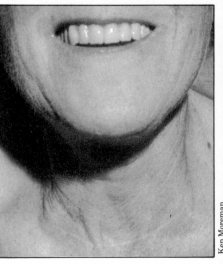

pound called reverse T3. This means that there will be less thyroid hormone activity in the tissues even though the hormone level in the blood is adequate.

Goitre

Any enlargement of the thyroid gland is called goitre. Small but still visible goitres are found in about 15 per cent of the population, with about four times as many in women as in men. Usually these are of no significance.

In the past, iodine deficiency would have been the main cause of goitre but now most are caused by over-activity of the thyroid or are simple goitres that are not related to any abnormality of the thyroid's function. In a few cases, goitres are isolated lumps (nodules) in the substance of the thyroid, and these should be investigated using an isotope scan to see whether the lump is composed of functioning tissue. If it is not, and if an ultrasound scan shows that it is solid, then it could be malignant and may need a surgical exploration.

Over-active thyroid glands

Most cases of thyroid over-activity are caused by Grave's disease. A goitre is usually present and the eyes become protruding and staring – a sign that many people associate with thyroid problems. It is the basic disease process that causes the symptoms and not the over-activity.

Grave's disease is caused by the presence of antibodies in the blood. Although these antibodies do not destroy thyroid tissue they stimulate the gland to produce thyroid hormone. It is not known why some people are more prone to making these antibodies than others, although there is certainly genetic susceptibility. This can be demonstrated by the fact that many sufferers have a specific type of tissue group.

The effects of an over-active thyroid are weight loss, and increased appetite, anxiety and nervousness (sometimes with a tremor), palpitations of the heart, sweating with intolerance to heat and irritability. In addition to eye problems there may be weakness of the muscles, particularly at the shoulders and hips.

Once Grave's disease is suspected then the majority of cases can be diagnosed very simply by measuring the level of the thyroid hormone in the blood. Often the T3 level is measured as well as, or instead of, the T4 level, since T3 is always raised in Grave's disease, while it is possible to have the disease with a normal T4 level.

Treatment is given to suppress thyroid activity. This can be done with tablets for a year or more. If the gland is very large then it may be appropriate to operate to remove some of it. The alternative is to give a dose of radioactive iodine. This is of course taken up by the thyroid so it presents no danger to other tissues. It will reduce the level of thyroid activity over the course of approximately six weeks.

Thyroid problems

Problem	Cause	Effects	Treatment
Simple goitre	Unknown	Swelling of the thyroid, producing a swelling of the neck	Often unnecessary but in many cases the problem responds to low doses of thyroid hormone tablets
Endemic goitre	Lack of iodine in the diet	May lead to deficiency of thyroid hormone	Replacement of iodine in the diet
Myxoedema or hypo-thyroidism	Inadequate levels of thyroid hormone in the blood. May be caused by Hashimoto's disease or auto-immune thyroid failure	Problem develops slowly, leading to dry, rough skin, tiredness, intolerance to cold, increase in weight, constipation, hoarse voice and deafness	Replacement of thyroid hormone in tablet form
Thyrotoxicosis or hyperthyroidism	Most commonly, Grave's disease; others include nodules in the thyroid, either single or multiple	Increase in appetite (often with weight loss), sensitivity to heat, disorders of heart rhythm, nervousness, tiredness and sweating. In some cases there is muscular weakness	Various treatments including use of tablets, surgery to remove over-active thyroid tissue, use of radioactive iodine administered by mouth
Grave's disease	Presence of antibodies in the blood which stimulate the thyroid	Causes thyrotoxicosis; also affects the eyes, causing the 'pop eyes' associated with over-active thyroid	Troublesome eye problems can necessitate surgery, either to tack down the lids to protect the eyes or to try to reduce the amount of eye protrusion
Thyroiditis	Inflammation of the thyroid gland resulting from a virus infection	Painful swollen gland that may come on suddenly. Mild thyrotoxicosis may result	Usually unnecessary; pain killers may be given. In severe cases steroid drugs are sometimes used to damp down the inflammation
Dyshormonogenesis	Inherited abnormality in the way the gland makes hormones. Of six different types the most common is Pendred's syndrome which is associated with deafness	A low level of hormone in the blood may cause the same effects as myxoedema. There is often a large goitre	Thyroid hormone
Congenital hypo-thyroidism (cretinism)	Failure of the foetal thyroid to develop	Mental and physical retardation is the major effect; it occurs in about one in every 4000 births	Early diagnosis is vital, since with prompt thyroid treatment there will be normal development; retardism will otherwise occur

Problem	Incidence		Treatment
Cancer:			
(1) Papillary	The commonest type; occurs in young children, including children		By surgery, followed by radioactive iodine treatment if necessary. Outlook is good
(2) Follicular	Slightly less common; also occurs in young people		As for papillary carcinoma. Outlook is good
(3) Anaplastic	Uncommon; occurs in the elderly		Surgery is often impossible. X-ray treatment may be used
(4) Medullary	Very uncommon		Surgery. Outlook is good in most cases

While the hormone levels are being brought under control the symptoms can be decreased by drugs which block the effects of adrenalin, since high levels of thyroid seem to produce an increased response to adrenalin.

Under-active thyroid glands

This condition of the thyroid gland (myxoedma) is also caused by antibodies in the gland which seem to destroy it. Hashimoto's disease is very similar, except that the antibodies set up a long-term inflammation of the gland, causing goitre but leading to thyroid failure.

In many cases weight gain results, together with a lack of energy, dry thick skin, intolerance to cold, a slow heartbeat, hoarseness and deafness, and a typical puffy face. The presence of hypothyroidism makes elderly people much more susceptible to hypothermia.

Under-activity of the thyroid is readily picked up by blood tests. The level of T4 is reduced, but this can occur on its own in severe illness, for example. Much more important is the high level of TSH that is found in the blood, as the pituitary gland tries to drive the thyroid on to produce enough hormones.

Once a diagnosis is made, the thyroid hormone T4 can be given by mouth. The dose is built up fairly gradually since there is a risk of making patients with heart disease worse; myxoedema predisposes to coronary artery disease since it causes a very high level of cholesterol.

Patients with myxoedema must continue to take medication for the rest of their lives. Although Grave's disease is not quite as easy to treat as myxoedema, the results of treatment in both conditions is really very satisfactory, and the outlook is very good in both once the early difficulties have passed.

Tonsils

Q How soon after an attack of tonsillitis is it safe to have an operation to remove the tonsils?

A Two to three weeks is the accepted period, after which the risk of abnormal post-operative bleeding returns to normal. If a child has attacks of tonsillitis every 10 days and is due for a tonsillectomy, the doctor will no doubt put him or her on a course of antibiotics for three weeks before the operation. This eliminates the possibility of the child being sent home when he is taken to the hospital for surgery.

Q Should I suck aspirin rather than swallow them when I have a sore throat?

A No. You would not hold an aspirin on your forehead if you had a headache, which would be equivalent to sucking an aspirin for a sore throat. In fact, sucking aspirin can be dangerous, as it can cause a chemical burn on the mucous membranes lining the mouth and the throat.

Q Will I be more prone to infections after I have had my tonsils out?

A No. Your tonsils probably only have a significant function during the first few years of life, which is one of the reasons doctors prefer not to remove them from a child who is very young.

Q My three-year-old son has very frequent attacks of tonsillitis, but the surgeon is really reluctant to take them out. Why is this?

A At three years of age your son will probably weigh between 12 and 18 kg (26 to 40 lb) and therefore his total blood volume will be between 950 and 1400 ml (1⅔ and 2½ pt). A loss of 120 ml (⅕ pt), which is the average loss for the operation, would deprive him of between 8 and 12 per cent of his blood and cause a dangerous condition. Should he bleed heavily after the operation his condition would become very serious indeed.

The tonsils have a role to perform in the body and should be allowed to carry it out. But throughout life they are subject to a variety of diseases for which removal is sometimes the only appropriate remedy.

Position of tonsils

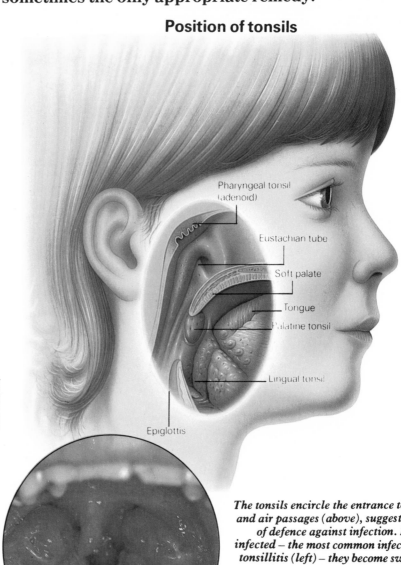

Mike Courtney

Pharyngeal tonsil (adenoid)

Eustachian tube

Soft palate

Tongue

Palatine tonsil

Lingual tonsil

Epiglottis

The tonsils encircle the entrance to the food and air passages (above), suggesting a role of defence against infection. But when infected – the most common infection being tonsillitis (left) – they become swollen and inflamed, making swallowing, and even breathing, difficult and painful.

The tonsils are part of a ring of lymphoid tissue (Waldeyer's ring) which encircles the entrance to the food and air passages in the throat. Although they are present at birth they are relatively small, but grow rapidly during the first few years of life, only to regress after puberty. However they do not disappear completely.

The tonsils' exact function is not known

but it has been suggested that they play a significant role in maintaining the body's immune system. They are ideally situated to scrutinize ingested material and to react to those which pose a threat to the body. This immunity is given by lymphocytes produced by the tonsils. In addition the tonsils produce antibodies which deal with infections locally.

Tonsillitis
Almost everyone will have suffered an attack of tonsillitis at some time in life. The organism producing the infection is

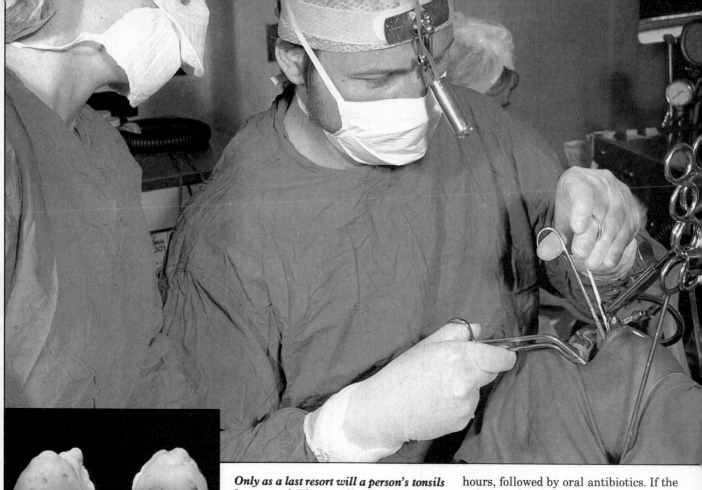

Only as a last resort will a person's tonsils be removed. They are dissected from the pharyngeal wall while the patient is under general anaesthetic (above). These removed tonsils (left) show patches of scar tissue from repeated bouts of tonsillitis.

usually a streptococcus (a certain type of bacterium).

It is often easy to tell tonsillitis from a simple sore throat as the duration of the illness is considerably longer – approximately a week. Symptoms vary with the severity of the infection but they always include marked discomfort in the pharynx (see page 420) making swallowing painful. Pain from the throat may also be felt in the ear. Some patients even experience discomfort on turning their heads due to swelling of the glands in this region. A raised temperature almost always accompanies the infection, but it varies in degree. Children, for example, tend to develop higher temperatures and consequently more symptoms – such as malaise and vomiting – than adults. And some children may have no symptoms in the throat but complain of abdominal pain instead.

When the tonsils are infected they become enlarged and inflamed with specks of pus exuding from their surfaces. Fortunately the infection responds well

to common antibiotics and improvement can be expected within 36 to 48 hours. Symptoms can be alleviated by eating soft foods and lots of liquids, and painkillers such as aspirin both relieve the pain and reduce the temperature.

Tonsillitis tends to occur most frequently between the ages of four and six years and then again around puberty. The more often the tonsils are infected the more prone they are to persistent and recurrent infection. A stage is therefore reached when removal of the tonsils is the only sensible way of controlling the disease.

In some cases an infection is so severe that an abscess forms in the tissue around the tonsils. This is known as peritonsillar abscess, or quinsy. Quinsy usually affects one side of the tonsils and is very rare in children. The affected tonsil swells to a considerable extent and may prevent swallowing altogether. Local inflammation contributes to this disability by limiting the opening of the jaw. Oral antibiotics are not only difficult to swallow but also are rarely effective. Higher doses of antibiotics are given by intramuscular injections for 24 to 36

hours, followed by oral antibiotics. If the quinsy is 'ripe' – that is the abscess is pointing – recovery may be accelerated by lancing the abscess and allowing the pus to drain.

In exceptional cases an infection is not limited to the tonsils but spreads both down the neck to the chest and up towards the base of the skull – a parapharyngeal abscess. This is a life-threatening condition and requires urgent admission to hospital, where drainage and the administration of massive doses of powerful antibiotics can be undertaken. Patients who have had quinsy are thought to be more susceptible to this complication and are therefore advised to have their tonsils out even if they have not been troubled previously by recurrent tonsillitis.

Viral infections of the tonsils
Tonsillar tissue can be affected by viral infections which commonly lead to a sore throat. Symptoms are similar to those of tonsillitis, but are milder and last for only 24 to 48 hours.

The tonsils are also affected in glandular fever when a sore throat is accompanied by severe lassitude, joint pains and generalized swelling of all the lymph glands. In this condition the tonsils are covered by a white membrane and the adjacent palate is dotted with splinter-like haemorrhages. Neither of these conditions is an indication that a tonsillectomy is necessary, as both occur

Q My husband will shortly be going into hospital to have his tonsils out. How long should he expect to be off work and how should I look after him at home?

A Most adult patients take about two weeks to recover completely. This includes one week in the hospital and at least one week resting at home. It is very important that you encourage your husband to eat as abrasive a diet as he can tolerate so that the site of the operation is kept clean. If it was your child who was having the operation, the recommendation would be the same, with the additional precaution that he or she should not come into contact with other children for at least a week.

Q If a person's tonsils are larger than normal, should they be removed?

A The size of the tonsils alone rarely necessitates their surgical removal. However, in a few cases a person's tonsils are so enlarged that they obstruct the air passage and a tonsillectomy must be performed. The obstruction occurs mainly at night; while the person is asleep he or she stops breathing intermittently, which makes him wake up. There can be far-reaching consequences of this condition which is known as sleep apnoea. Subjects may become lethargic, undergo personality changes and may even become incontinent. Very rarely, the chronic deprivation of oxygen can lead to heart failure and irregularities of the heart rate.

Q Is it true that some children have to have their tonsils removed to stop them from going deaf?

A Yes. In children, attacks of tonsillitis may precipitate attacks of otitis media (an infection of the middle ear) or it may prevent a complete recovery from secretory otitis media, a condition known more commonly as 'glue ears'. In these cases the surgeon may advise tonsillectomy in order to prevent possible damage to the middle ear and avoid the deafness, which although temporary, is associated with these conditions.

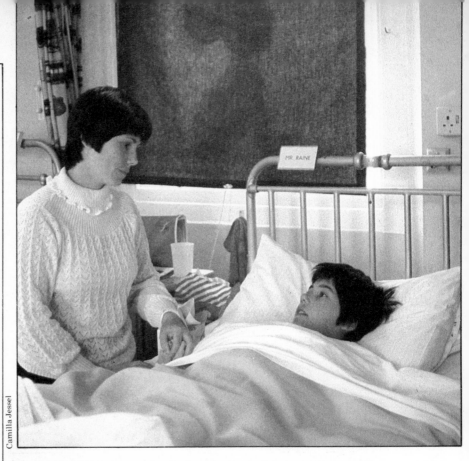

Camilla Jessel

just as frequently in people who have had operations to remove their tonsils for a variety of other reasons.

Tonsillectomy
A tonsillectomy is performed under general anaesthetic. The tonsils are dissected away from the pharyngeal wall and the resulting bleeding is controlled by ligatures. On average about 120 ml (1/5 pt) of blood is lost during the operation, irrespective of the age of the patient. Surgeons are therefore very reluctant to operate on children who are very small or below the age of four; such an amount of blood loss is a significant proportion of their total blood volume. However if an operation is necessary, the child will be given an intravenous drip for about 12 hours after the tonsillectomy.

The only serious complication that may arise after the operation is further haemorrhage. When this occurs it is usually within the first few hours and requires a return to the theatre for further ligation.

Bleeding may also occur six to ten days after the operation if the tonsil bed becomes infected. Patients mostly affected are those who eat poorly post-operatively or have had an attack of tonsillitis immediately before admission to hospital. This late bleeding is treated with antibiotics but if the patient has lost a lot of blood a transfusion or a course of iron tablets may be necessary to stimulate rapid replacement of the lost blood.

Children tend to recover from the

Although children recover very quickly from a tonsillectomy, being in hospital can be a lonely experience. The reassuring presence of a parent, especially just before and after surgery, helps speed recovery.

operation more quickly than adults and only require one to two days in hospital. Adults however may need four to five days' hospitalization before they are fit enough to be discharged.

Tumours of the tonsils
Tumours of the tonsils are uncommon but may occur at any age. Lymphomas may cause a sudden tonsillar enlargement and are usually associated with swollen glands in other parts of the body – for example, under the arms and in the groin. In general, they respond well to treatment and a large proportion of patients are cured.

Another type of tumour is known as squamous cell carcinoma. It tends to occur in the older age group and men are more frequently affected than women. The condition results in a unilaterally enlarged and painful tonsil which may be ulcerated. Variable degrees of difficulty and pain on swallowing are experienced and in advanced cases it may be impossible for the patient to swallow his or her own saliva. Similarly, as the disease progresses the tumour spreads to the glands in the neck. With patients who receive early treatment a recovery rate of at least 50 per cent can be expected.

Toxic shock syndrome

First described in America in 1978, toxic shock syndrome now appears to be a world-wide phenomenon. It nearly always affects young women – almost invariably tampon users – who develop the condition during periods.

Q **Does toxic shock syndrome only affect women?**

A No. However the problem seems to be largely confined to women, and in the vast majority of cases, it has occurred during the course of a period. Oddly though, the syndrome was first recognized in children and teenagers, and only four of these original cases had started their periods, although three of these four actually got the disease during the course of a period.

Toxic shock syndrome has been reported in a number of men, all of whom had a skin infection with a staphylococcus. One of these men was a plumber who had cleared a lavatory blocked with tampons.

Q **Is toxic shock syndrome really a new disease, or did doctors never realize that it existed?**

A This really does seem to be a new disease. It may have occurred from time to time in the past, but it seemed to start in earnest in the late 1970s. The first report was in 1978, and this was followed by many other reports in 1980, so that during the first nine months of 1980 over 300 cases were recognized in America. The disease appears to be caused by toxins (poisons) produced by the staphylococcus – a common bacterium that infects the skin – and it may be that there has been some change in this organism to make it responsible for this new disease.

Q **If you have had the syndrome once, can you get it again?**

A Yes. Some women have even had three, four or five attacks. One of the things that seems to prevent repeated attacks is treatment with an antibiotic that will kill the staphylococcus, so that it is no longer in the vagina during periods.

Q **Will using tampons put you at risk of getting the disease?**

A The chances are slim. The disease seems to be much more common during the course of a menstrual period, and sufferers almost invariably were tampon users, but millions of women use tampons with no ill-effect at all.

Toxic shock syndrome is a potentially fatal illness that almost exclusively affects women during the course of their periods. There is very good evidence to suggest that its occurrence is related to the use of tampons during periods, particularly the new super-absorbent sorts which are based on a rayon and cellulose compound. However this evidence is not conclusive, and it is very important to remember that millions of women use tampons while, as a recent American study has shown, the syndrome only happens in about 6 out of every 100,000 women.

Causes

The important ingredients in causing the syndrome seem to be the occurrence of a period, probably the use of a tampon and the presence of staphylococci in the vagina. Although staphylococci are not invariably found in the vagina, they are present in many more cases with the

How toxic shock syndrome occurs

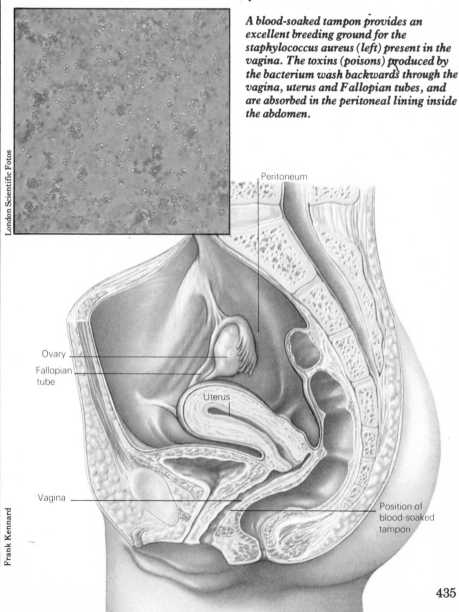

A blood-soaked tampon provides an excellent breeding ground for the staphylococcus aureus (left) present in the vagina. The toxins (poisons) produced by the bacterium wash backwards through the vagina, uterus and Fallopian tubes, and are absorbed in the peritoneal lining inside the abdomen.

Peritoneum

Ovary

Fallopian tube

Uterus

Vagina

Position of blood-soaked tampon

London Scientific Fotos

Frank Kennard

Headaches and disorientation

High fever

Photophobia (discomfort on looking at light)

Kidney failure

Abdominal pain

Low blood pressure

Diarrhoea

Rash on palms, soles and fingers

Aching pains in muscles and skin

Ron Sutherland

syndrome than not. It has been suggested that when the staphylococcus is present in the vagina, and a period starts, then the presence of a blood-soaked tampon will provide an excellent culture medium for the organisms to grow on. It is thought that the symptoms result from the production of a toxin (poison) by the staphylococcus, which may then wash backwards up through the vagina, uterus and Fallopian tubes, to be absorbed from the peritoneal lining inside of the abdomen.

About 95 per cent of reported cases have happened in women who are having periods. The syndrome tends to occur in very young women, with the average age of 23, and 30 per cent of cases happen in girls aged between 15 and 21. No particular type of tampon has been associated with the disease, although it is possible that the new super-absorbent types, which have become widely used since the 1970s, may have some part to play. This led, in America, to the withdrawal from the market of a tampon made by a particular manufacturer.

Curiously, the disease seems to be less common in women who are using the Pill. This could perhaps be explained by the fact that the amount of menstrual flow is reduced, but this can't be the only explanation.

Symptoms and dangers
Toxic shock syndrome is characterized by a high fever of over 39°C (102.2°F), a low blood pressure (shock, in the emergency doctor's language); a flattish skin rash that leads on to the loss of skin from the hands and feet after a week or two; and often a quite marked eye infection.

Additionally, there will be involvement of at least four of the body's main systems. Failure of the kidneys is very common, as is diarrhoea. There is nearly always myalgia – aching pains in the muscles – of the sort people get with 'flu. Headaches and disorientation occur, and there may be evidence of disturbance of the function of the liver.

Typically the illness develops suddenly on the fourth day of a menstrual period. The fever occurs first, and there may be abdominal pain. Watery diarrhoea develops during the first 24 hours in most cases. Then myalgia occurs: it is extremely painful in the muscles and the skin. The rash appears during the first 24 hours, but it may not be noticed and may be mistaken for the first flush of fever. Later it becomes more marked, usually affecting the fingers, and sometimes the palms and the soles.

As the disease progresses, other problems such as pain in the joints and discomfort on looking towards a light

(photophobia) may occur. The kidneys often fail, and stop passing enough urine so that the level of waste products in the blood starts to rise. The kidney failure is probably related to the drop in blood pressure, as the kidneys are very sensitive to any changes in the amount of blood flowing to them.

Most patients recover after 10 days, but at a rather late stage, the skin is lost from the palms and soles, and often from the face and even the tongue. The death rate from the disease is not easy to assess, but it is probably around 2 or 3 per cent.

Treatment and outlook
The most important aspect of the treatment is replacing fluid intravenously in order to correct the working of the circulation. The other problems that can happen have to be faced as they occur: a patient running into breathing difficulty might have to be put on a respirator, for

example. There is no evidence that the infection with staphylococci involves the blood, but it is very worth while treating the patient with antibiotics to eradicate the organisms from the vagina. Not only may this hasten recovery from the illness, but it may also prevent repeated attacks.

Prevention
The best way to avoid the syndrome is to change tampons regularly and frequently during a period. Although there is no direct evidence that this helps, it seems reasonable on the basis of what we know of the disease. If possible, it may be wise to try external protection in the form of sanitary pads during the later stages of the period. Although there seems little doubt that the disease is directly related to the use of tampons, few women would be prepared to forgo their use completely to avoid such an uncommon condition.

Trichinosis

One the commonest worm infections in man, trichinosis can be a serious illness. Prevention is simple, however, and consists mainly in ensuring that pork – which contains the parasite – is always properly cooked.

Q Are you only likely to get trichinosis in the tropics, or could you catch it in this country?

A You certainly could get it in this country – in fact, it is wrong to think of it as a tropical disease, since it is rare in the tropics but quite common in Europe and America. Infection occurs through eating pork which is infected, so it is most common in those countries where a lot of pork is eaten.

Q I was told that there was evidence of trichinosis on my chest X-ray, but I don't ever remember being ill. Can you have the disease without knowing it?

A Yes. It is not only possible but also common to have the disease without being aware of it. The reason why abnormalities are seen on X-ray is that the larvae form cysts in the muscles which protect them for up to two years; eventually, however, the cysts become calcified (impregnated with chalk), and this calcification shows up on the X-ray. In the USA studies have been done on muscle samples taken at post mortem and these have shown some evidence of infection in 20 per cent of cases. The figure for the UK is nearer one per cent.

Q Can trichinosis be prevented in any effective way?

A Yes. One of the most effective ways of preventing it is not to eat pork. This is a method that has been practised for centuries according to religious custom by Jews, Muslims and Hindus. In societies where pork is eaten, people can be protected by freezing meat before cooking, or by cooking it thoroughly. Irradiation of pork using radioactive cobalt or caesium has even been used. Another important area is to take care with the raising of pigs. Uncooked pig swill may contain infected raw pig scraps, or possibly even faeces from an infected animal so this can lead to the spread of infection. The disease is fairly widespread in the animal kingdom, and rats may certainly be infected. This is another source of infection, since pigs sometimes kill rats.

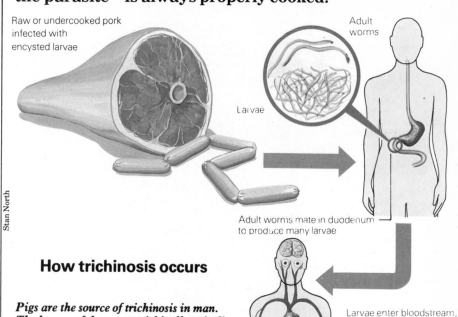

Raw or undercooked pork infected with encysted larvae

Adult worms

Larvae

Stan North

Adult worms mate in duodenum to produce many larvae

Larvae enter bloodstream, usually via hepatic portal vein, and commonly settle in the heart, brain and eyes.

How trichinosis occurs

Pigs are the source of trichinosis in man. The larvae of the worm trichinella spiralis form protective cysts in the muscles of the pig, and if infected pork is eaten, the larvae are released, mature and breed. The new larvae circulate around the body until they reach muscles in which to lodge. Infected pig swill perpetuates the cycle.

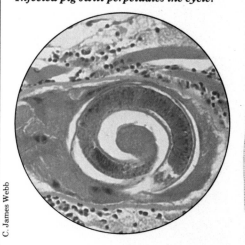

C. James Webb

Larvae in skeletal muscle develop viable cysts

Trichinosis is widespread throughout the world. It is commonest in Europe and in North America and is fairly uncommon in tropical countries. It does not occur in Australia or in the islands of the Pacific.

Cause

The illness is caused by a small worm called trichinella spiralis, which may infest all meat-eating creatures. It lives in the intestine in its adult form and male and female worms mate to produce huge numbers of larvae. These then spread through the bloodstream to the muscles, where they form protective cysts in which they can survive for a long period. In the meantime the adult worms in the intestines die. Each female probably lives about four to eight weeks and during this time will produce about 1500 larvae.

Tony Stone Associates

Trichinosis can be prevented by the proper care of pigs, particularly by ensuring that their food is free from contamination.

The infection of the next host will occur if the original animal is caught and eaten by a predator. If this happens the muscles are of course eaten, the cysts around the larvae dissolve and new adults develop in the new host.

When the infecting larvae enter the duodenum of the new host, they work their way through the wall of the intestine and pass through four developmental stages before becoming an adult male or female. These then return to the lumen (central space) of the intestine. As adult worms they are just visible, the male being about 1.6mm long and the female 4mm. The male has a testis and the female an ovary and a coiled tubular womb. Mating takes place as soon as two adult worms are present in the lumen of the bowel, and the female then starts to produce the larvae.

Once a larva is produced it passes into the bloodstream and can come to rest anywhere in the body. The commoner places include the heart, brain and eye as well as the ordinary muscles that the parasite is in fact seeking. It is only these larvae that form a protective cyst – the ones that find themselves in other organs soon disintegrate.

The main strain of the parasite is found in man – and in pigs, dogs, rats and cats. The main source of infection is therefore pork, as far as man is concerned. The habit of eating uncooked pork sausages is particularly dangerous and infection runs quite high in Germany and in countries such as the United States which have a strong German influence.

A second important biological strain is found in Arctic regions, and here the typical hosts are whales, walruses, seals, squirrels, foxes and dogs. Bears, particularly polar bears, are very likely to become infected, being the most powerful predators in the Arctic.

Symptoms

Most cases of trichinosis occur without giving any signs of infection, and they are only discovered by examining muscle samples under the microscope, which have been taken at post mortem. There is thus evidence to suggest that up to 20 per cent of the people in the USA, and one per cent of the UK population, have a degree of infection. Cysts in the muscles can also be made out on X-ray film as a result of calcification after about two years.

Symptoms occur with a very heavy infection. Diarrhoea and vomiting may result when the larvae invade the walls of the intestine, and this may also provoke an allergic rash on the trunk and extremities. The major symptoms – of which there are four – appear when the larvae leave the intestine and start to circulate around the body. There will be fever, swelling of the eyelids and tissue around the eyes, pain in the muscles – which can be very severe – and a high level of eosinophils (a type of white blood cell) in the blood. Heart failure may develop if large numbers of larvae invade the heart.

By the third stage of the disease, when the larvae are forming cysts in the muscles, the patient may be very weak and death may occur simply through exhaustion and poor nutrition. The brain can also become severely affected and there may be various neurological problems. In serious infections, the fever will recover first, with the muscular pains persisting for some time. However there may also be some secondary problem that proves fatal.

Treatment and prevention

If the full-blown disease develops, steroid drugs are given to damp down the effects of the inflammation caused by the larvae. A drug called thiabendazole will kill the adult worms and this is done to prevent the production of new larvae, although the larvae themselves cannot be killed.

Prevention consists in the proper preparation of pork, particularly with adequate cooking, and in reducing the risks of pigs becoming infected.

The dietary practice of not eating pork has long been part of the Jewish religion – it is the surest way of preventing infection.

Trichomoniasis

Q I have developed an unpleasant vaginal discharge which has the characteristics of a trichomonas infection. Is there something I can do, such as douching, to get rid of it myself?

A No – certain cure can only follow taking the particular drug needed for the specific germ causing your vaginitis. This depends on accurate identification of this organism from examination of a specimen of the discharge. There is no short-cut which would enable you to deal with the matter on your own. You would be very unwise to try to treat yourself by douching since, if you did happen to have something more serious than trichomonas, the risk of flushing infected material up into your womb or tubes could have tragic results in spreading the infection.

Q My girlfriend has just been told that she has a trichomonas infection in her vagina. She says she hasn't been with anyone else, but as I have no symptoms myself and know that I have been only with her, surely she must be deceiving me?

A This is a situation that worries and upsets a lot of couples. But, the truth of the matter is that although it seems difficult to understand how a vaginal infection can be caught other than through intercourse with an infected man, a substantial proportion of cases are not acquired in this way but by using a lavatory that was contaminated by an infected person a short time previously, or borrowing an unwittingly infected friend's towel or flannel.

Q When I had trichomoniasis, my boyfriend was given tablets even though there was nothing wrong with him. Why?

A Even though your boyfriend may not have had trichomoniasis – it is not always sexually transmitted – there is a possibility that he had a mild infection without any symptoms. If this was the case you might well have become infected again when you started having intercourse after your treatment.

Trichomoniasis or 'Trich' is a common and highly infectious condition affecting the genitals. The symptoms are both irritating and unpleasant, but fortunately this condition responds well to treatment.

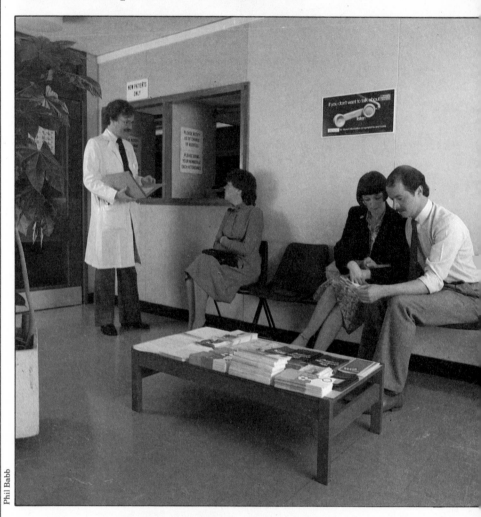

Phil Babb

Trichomoniasis is a common condition, with at least one in five women likely to have it at some time during their lives. It can affect men, being responsible for about 4 per cent of cases of Non Specific Urethritis, but more often gives rise to disease in women, for whom it is among the common causes of vaginal discharge.

Causes

The trichomonas organism (trichomonas vaginalis) responsible for the infection is rather unusual. It is neither a bacterium nor a virus, but a one-celled, pear-shaped protozoon or parasite. Its five whip-like tentacles enable it both to swim about in the vaginal secretion and to attract particles of material on which it lives.

Although trichomoniasis can often be caught as a result of having intercourse

A case of suspected trichomoniasis can be fully investigated at a Special Clinic – under expert but informal medical care.

with somebody who already has the infection, it can be contracted in other ways. Indeed, the fact that the trichomonas infection occurs in a very much greater number of women than men, that it does not usually survive for long in males, and that the infection can develop in women who are not having intercourse confirm this. The answer to this apparent mystery lies in the ability of the trichomonas organism – unlike other sexually transmitted organisms such as the gonococcus – to survive outside the human body for at least 30 minutes on objects with which the genital parts of an infected person have come in contact. It

439

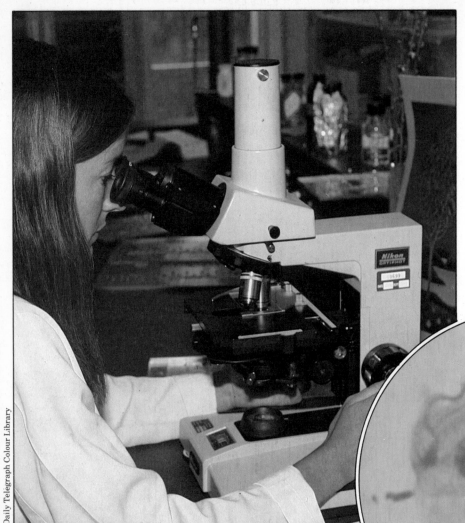

Daily Telegraph Colour Library

are particularly advisable if the infection is likely to have been caught through sexual intercourse with a casual partner, since it is possible to have acquired other infections, such as gonorrhoea or thrush, at the same time. It is wise, therefore, to confirm or eliminate the presence of other infections so that appropriate additional treatment can be given if necessary. A full investigation can be carried out at a Special Clinic – that is, a clinic which specializes in venereal diseases.

Treatment

The treatment of trichomonas infection usually consists of taking oral doses of metronidazole (Flagyl) or another closely related drug. It is important that the effectiveness of the cure is checked after treatment, by the examination of vaginal secretion to make sure that no organism has survived. Until this has been done,

is, therefore, one of the few basically sexually transmitted diseases that can actually be caught from a lavatory seat as well as from contaminated towels, flannels or clothing.

Symptoms

Fortunately, almost all cases of trichomoniasis can be easily and completely cured. Usually, its only manifestation is vaginitis (inflammation of the vagina), the main symptom of which is a profuse vaginal discharge – this is generally quite runny, yellow to green in colour and has a strong odour. The discharge is often accompanied by soreness and irritation of the genital area. It is very unusual for any organ other than the vagina – either in the pelvis or elsewhere in the body – to be involved, and the infection has virtually no complications.

Diagnosis

The diagnosis of trichomoniasis can only be made by seeing the actual trichomonas organism under a microscope in a specimen of the vaginal discharge: there

When diagnosing trichomoniasis, a specimen of vaginal discharge is examined under a microscope. The presence of the organism trichomonas vaginalis (inset) will clinch the diagnosis.

are no blood or other tests which will reveal it. There are, however, a large number of diseases that can give rise to vaginal discharge of one sort or another. And, even though the nature of the discharge may strongly suggest that it is trichomonas infection, this can only be proved and other possible causes ruled out by an internal examination and by looking at the discharge under the microscope.

Since trichomoniasis can only be cured completely by one particular type of drug (and there is no single treatment that is effective for all types of vaginal discharge), it is important that a positive identification is made of the trichomonas organism. Vaginal examination and tests

the patient should refrain from intercourse to avoid both the possibility of reinfection and of contaminating anybody else. Since a considerable proportion of cases are sexually transmitted, and to avoid a situation in which a couple will continually re-infect each other, the patient's partner is usually advised either to undergo the tests as well, or to take a course of metronidazole as a precautionary measure.

It should be noted, however, that medical research in the USA has shown some evidence of serious side-effects in certain animals following the use of metronidazole, some doctors may therefore prefer to prescribe vaginal pessaries and gels when possible.

Tunnel vision

Q I know somebody who has a guide-dog but who can read books and newspapers with ease. Can you explain this?

A Many people who have tunnel vision caused by retinitis pigmentosa are regarded as being technically blind, although they can often read print. This is because the central part of the retina, the macula, is still in good condition; it is on the macula that fine focus is concentrated in reading. Often the amount that is seen is so little that only a line or word at a time can actually be seen. The classic retinitis pigmentosa sufferer with tunnel vision can read the print in a book without being able to see the whole page at one glance.

Q Tunnel vision runs in my family. I am now 30 and think I am beginning to be affected by it, but don't want to say too much about it because I drive for a living. I find driving quite easy, except at night; if I'm careful can I continue without endangering anyone?

A You should definitely not be driving without consulting your doctor. In tunnel vision the central part of the retina is in good condition, allowing a limited but clear picture of objects directly ahead and in the distance and, in the case of driving, an ability to see traffic lights, other cars' licence plates and so on. The vision that is missing is the important part that completes the entire picture or field of vision. People with tunnel vision have a restricted field; and if it is severely restricted then, when driving a car, they are unlikely to see traffic approaching from either side although they can see clearly directly ahead.

Q I have had tunnel vision, caused by glaucoma, for the past 10 years. Will I eventually go blind?

A If your condition has been kept in balance for 10 years then it may well remain as it is; early diagnosis and treatment can reduce the damage done to the retina. But don't hesitate to talk to your doctor about it if you are very worried.

As the name suggests, having tunnel vision is rather like looking down a long dark tunnel. Everything around the patient is unseen, except for what lies directly ahead.

Tunnel vision is sometimes known as tube vision, which is a very accurate description of how someone with this condition sees the world. It almost always affects both eyes and all that can be seen is what is being looked at directly.

Causes
Tunnel vision is a symptom of two eye disorders: retinitis pigmentosa and glaucoma (see page 158), both of which cause damage to the retina (the light sensitive area at the back of the eye).

Light enters the eye through the pupil, the black hole visible at the front of the eye, passes through the aqueous humour, a clear liquid, and so to the lens. The lens projects the light through another liquid, the vitreous humour, and then on to the retina at the back of the eye.

The highly sensitive nerve cells that form the retina are, in fact, the ends of the optic nerve; once an image is projected on to the retina it passes along the optic nerve into the brain.

In normal vision the entire image projected on the retina is received and transmitted. The centre of the retina gives detailed vision, the outer part, peripheral vision, giving an overall field of vision.

In tunnel vision the peripheral vision is missing, producing some loss of the total field because the outer parts of the retina are damaged. Someone with tunnel vision therefore has little problem with distant objects or reading, but cannot see things to either left or right, up or down, without moving his or her head.

Outlook and treatment
Damage to the cells of the retina cannot be reversed. However, those patients whose tunnel vision is caused by glaucoma have a good chance of retaining some sight with correct treatment.

Unfortunately there is no known treatment for tunnel vision caused by retinitis pigmentosa. Some patients' fields of vision become little more than a pinpoint; and with other patients, total blindness can follow. However, it should be emphasized that the majority of sufferers do not go totally blind.

Mrs Drummond-Walker presents a bewildering picture – a person with a guide dog and a book. She has tunnel vision and her peripheral vision is thereby so reduced that she needs a dog, although she can still see a few words at a time when reading

Phil Babb

Ulcers

Q Why do my mouth ulcers sting when I eat some fruit, or even some salty crisps?

A Many fruits – especially citrus fruits like lemons or oranges – contain some acidic substances, such as ascorbic acid. Where the lining of the mucous membrane in the mouth is broken, the acids can stimulate the nerve endings beneath the membrane, producing the sensation of pain. Normally, of course, the membrane provides protection against such acid 'attack'.

Q My teenage daughter keeps on getting ulcers on her forearm, but the doctor says that he cannot do anything about it as she is inflicting the injuries on herself. How can this be?

A The doctor probably suspects that your daughter is suffering from a psychological disturbance called hysteria. This condition is rather uncommon nowadays, but one of the symptoms may be self-inflicted injury, performed perhaps to gain attention or avoid some anxiety producing situation at home, school or work. The person concerned may be totally unaware that he is injuring himself. Perhaps you could discuss with your doctor the possibility of psychiatric counselling.

Q I have a rather embarrassing ulcer in my groin region. What could this be due to?

A There are a number of possible causes of an ulcer in the groin, ranging from mild irritation or even injury, to more serious sexually transmitted diseases. You should see your doctor as soon as possible to have the cause of the ulcer diagnosed.

Q My father is bed-ridden and suffers from bedsores. How can these be prevented?

A A special air mattress will help considerably. This has sections which can be alternately inflated and deflated to change the pressure-bearing areas while the patient lies still. Rubbing a barrier cream into the likely spots will also help to reduce the chance of bedsores.

Although commonly associated with gastric problems, ulcers do occur elsewhere on the body. Caused by a variety of factors – from disease to injury – they range from a mild irritation to a serious condition.

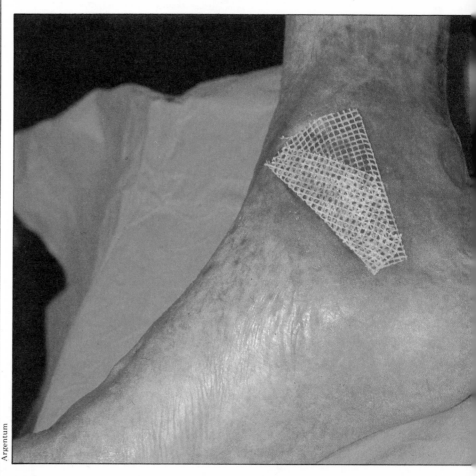

Argentum

Where an area of tissue loss occurs or erosion on the surface of the skin or internal membrane takes place, an ulcer is formed. It is often circular or oval in shape and sometimes irregular in outline. Ulcers on the surface of the body vary considerably in their depth, some involving skin loss only, but others extending deep into the muscle or bone beneath the skin.

The causes of ulcers are also numerous and range from a mild irritation or injury to a serious disease.

Perhaps the most serious and familiar type of ulcers occur within the digestive tract (see Gastric and duodenal ulcers pp 148-49 and Peptic ulcer pp 286-87). Here we are concerned with those ulcers that occur on the surface of the body. The most common sites for these are inside the mouth, on the lips and face, in the groin region, on the legs and around the hips and lower back.

Mouth and lip ulcers

Mouth ulcers are a very common problem and can occur as a 'one-off' condition, or as a recurrent disease where the ulcers appear and disappear in periodic cycles.

Almost everyone has at some time or other suffered the discomfort of the non-recurrent type of mouth ulcer. They are brought on by a variety of factors, but are usually due to some identifiable physical, chemical or biological cause, or are a symptom of some underlying condition.

Physical causes of mouth ulceration include irritation from jagged teeth, compulsive cheek-chewing, too vigorous use of a toothbrush or burning from hot food or drink.

Chemical causes include caustic drugs, tablets or sweets dissolved in the mouth, strong antiseptics and mouthwashes and chemicals used in dental treatment.

These two types of ulcers tend to clear up quickly on their own accord, but are

A leg ulcer is first cleaned, covered with a sterile gauze pad cut to fit, padded for protection and then bandaged so that even pressure is applied to the wound.
The aphthous ulcer (seen here on the tongue) is the most common of all single mouth ulcers and can be caused by broken teeth or sharp, spicy food (right).

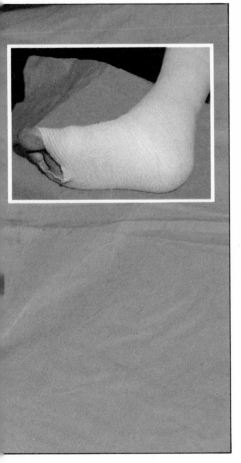

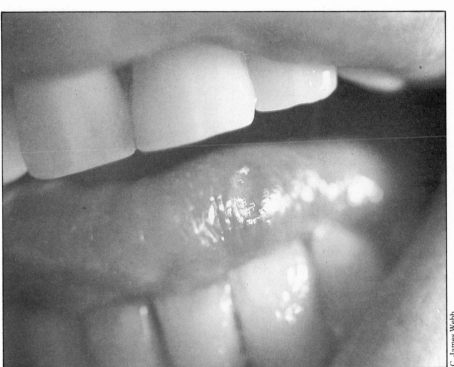

C. James Webb

Recurrent mouth ulcers affect about one person in three. They usually consist of numerous small, painful ulcers on or inside the lips, on the tongue, throat or roof of the mouth and may persist for a week or two, disappear and then appear again some weeks or months later.

The causes of recurrent mouth ulcers are not so well understood, but it is known that those confined to the lips are nearly always due to the herpes simplex virus. Those inside the mouth may also be caused by herpes, but in some cases they are probably due to an allergy to something in the mouth, a nutritional deficiency or to anaemia or coeliac disease.

The treatment of mouth ulcers depends greatly on the cause; for instance, dental therapy for jagged or decayed teeth, surgery for lip cancer, and a gluten-free diet for coeliac disease. In many cases of recurrent ulceration, where the exact cause cannot be found, mouthwashes, tablets and analgesic creams and jellies are often prescribed by the doctor to help soothe the pain. Herpetic ulcers are usually treated by frequent applications of a substance called idoxuridine, though this is not normally used in the mouth.

It is extremely important that when an ulcer becomes persistent, or when you suffer occasional bouts of ulcers, you visit

extremely sensitive to salty and sour tastes like crisps or lemons.

Biological causes include the syphilis bacterium, various fungi and the herpes simplex virus. A syphilitic chancre in the mouth is rare, but very serious. It is sexually acquired, consisting of a single round, button-sized and painless ulcer on the lips or tongue. On the other hand, an acute herpes infection in the mouth consists of numerous, much smaller, painful ulcers on the gums, tongue and membranes which line the inside of the cheeks or the inside of the lips.

Non-recurrent, but persistent mouth ulcers may also be a symptom of diabetes, various blood diseases and tuberculosis. Cancer of the lip, though uncommon, often first appears as an ulcer.

Habitual cheek-biting can become so self-destructive as to cause a line of tissue breakdown that soon leads to an ulcer.

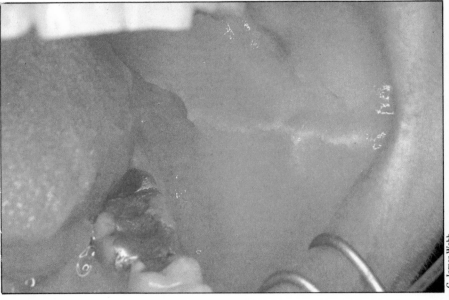

C. James Webb

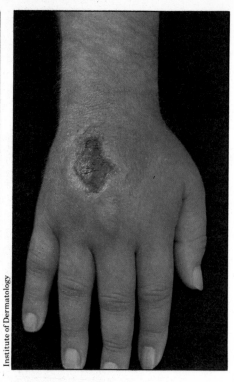

A faulty drip attached to the hand caused this ulcer; the anti-cancer drug used accidently leaked out onto the skin.

your doctor to have the cause diagnosed. A strong mouthwash or gargle may sound the most likely method of treating a mouth ulcer, but the solution of the mouthwash may be strong enough to worsen the condition. In addition, the underlying cause will remain untreated. So it is essential that you seek medical advice immediately.

Leg ulcers

Like mouth ulcers, leg ulcers are quite common and have a number of different causes: injury, infection, blood disease – like sickle-cell anaemia – and cancer, are frequent causes. The most common cause, however, is disease of the blood vessels in the legs.

Blocked or narrow arteries diminish the blood supply to the tissues, causing the tissues to die and break down and so produce an ulcer. Ulcers of this type tend to occur on the lower leg or foot and have a quite regular 'punched out' appearance. They may be several centimetres wide, quite deep and are very painful indeed.

Defective valves in the veins not only cause varicose veins but can also bring about ulcers in the legs through the slow circulation of blood. In this case, the tissues break down to form large, shallow ulcers over the inside of the lower leg and ankle. The ulcers are not particularly painful, but may ache considerably.

The immediate treatment for leg ulcers is aimed at keeping the area as free from infection as possible. This includes frequent cleaning, the use of antiseptic ointments or soaks, the application of a sterile foam pad, and bandaging. Pain-killing drugs may also be prescribed.

Long-term treatment is also necessary to tackle the underlying cause. This may range from antibiotic therapy – if there is an underlying infectious disease – to surgery to remove or to seal off the defective veins.

Other ulcers

Pressure sores – which are known medically as decubitus ulcers – commonly affect elderly, bed-ridden and long-term

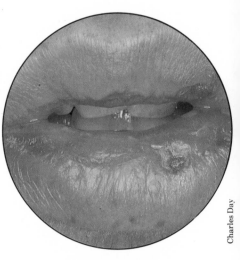

Herpes is often the cause of clusters of small ulcers on the lips, a condition which is also known as gingivo-stomatitis.

patients. These are caused by constant pressure impairing the blood circulation through an area of skin and underlying tissue, and commonly occur on the hips, heels and the base of the spine.

The rodent ulcer is a particularly nasty ulcer that occurs on the face. This is actually a type of skin cancer, starting as a red lump which grows and breaks down to form a circular ulcer. Without treatment this continues to grow and spread, but surgical removal or radiation therapy can result in a complete cure.

Ulcers in the groin region can occur for a variety of reasons including sexually acquired herpes or syphilis. Any ulcer in the groin area should be investigated immediately by your doctor as there is a chance that it may be due to syphilis – a very serious disease if left untreated.

Any persistent, suspicious or spreading ulcer should obviously be brought to the attention of your doctor as soon as possible.

Urethritis

Q Is urethritis always caused by venereal disease?

A No, not always; but a sexually transmitted infection is by far the commonest cause. This is not really surprising as the penis in men, and the area around the vagina that includes the opening of the urethra in women, are the parts of the body that are usually in closest contact during intercourse.

Women may also get urethritis as a result of contamination from the anus. To avoid this hazard women should always wipe themselves after going to the lavatory, or dry themselves after having a bath, from the front towards the back and never the other way round.

Q Can urethritis always be completely cured?

A Yes, virtually always, though this does depend on doing tests to identify the precise cause so that appropriate treatment – usually an antibiotic can be given. But just taking the antibiotic may not be sufficient to produce a cure since, like any other infected area of the body, the urethra needs a period of rest for full recovery. New lining tissue has to become established and replace that which has been destroyed by the inflammation. Thus it is usually necessary to refrain from intercourse for about two weeks until this has happened. Otherwise, the mechanical stress and friction on the urethra will damage the new lining tissue before it has had a chance to settle down. A further attack of urethritis is then likely.

Q Somebody told me the other day that her little boy had hypospadias. What on earth does that mean?

A Hypospadias is an uncommon abnormality in the development of the penis occurring before birth which results in the opening, or meatus, being on the underside of the penis rather than at the tip. In most cases there is no particular difficulty in passing urine, having intercourse, or having children, and no treatment is necessary. In the few cases where there is a problem it can be put right by a small operation.

The channel along which urine passes from the body – the urethra – is a common site of infection, which can be very painful and always needs medical attention.

The urethra is the duct which extends from the bladder to an opening on the outside of the body. In both sexes its function is to discharge urine. In men, the urethra is also the channel through which semen is ejaculated.

The male urethra
The mature male urethra averages 20 cm (about 8 in) in length and consists of three sections. The first or prostatic section is about 2.5 cm (1 in) long and passes from the sphincter, or valve, at the outlet of the bladder through the middle of the prostate gland.

The middle part of the urethra in the male is only about 12 mm (½ in) long and is often called the membranous urethra.

The final – and, at over 15 cm (6 in), the longest – section is called the spongy or cavernous urethra. This section is within the penis and opens at the urethral meatus (the slit in the tip).

The female urethra
In women the urethra is very much shorter and its only function is to be a channel for the disposal of urine. It is about 1 cm (⅓ in) in diameter and is also surrounded with mucous glands. The fact that it is so short and opens into a relatively exposed, contaminated area explains why women frequently get urinary infections.

Urethritis
Inflammation of the urethra, called urethritis, is the commonest urethral disorder and it can have many causes. The commonest are infections acquired as a result of sexual intercourse with an infected partner.

The symptoms in the male are development of a discharge which 'leaks' out from the urethral meatus and increasing pain on urinating. In addition, there is a desire to urinate frequently. In women it is usually only the pain (dysuria) and the frequency of urination that are present. These symptoms are often put down to cystitis or inflammation of the bladder, but it is more commonly the urethra that is involved.

It is most important that all cases of urethritis are fully investigated and treated, as otherwise permanent damage can be done both to the urethra itself and to the reproductive organs.

Cross-section of the urethra

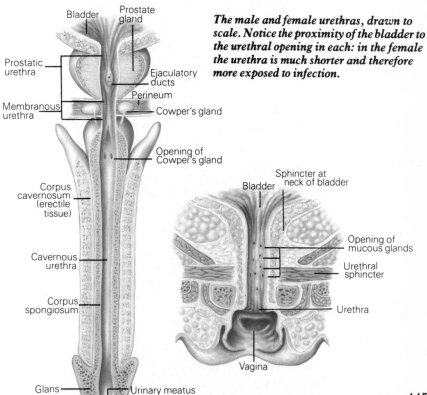

The male and female urethras, drawn to scale. Notice the proximity of the bladder to the urethral opening in each: in the female the urethra is much shorter and therefore more exposed to infection.

Bladder — Prostate gland — Prostatic urethra — Ejaculatory ducts — Perineum — Membranous urethra — Cowper's gland — Opening of Cowper's gland — Corpus cavernosum (erectile tissue) — Cavernous urethra — Corpus spongiosum — Glans — Urinary meatus

Bladder — Sphincter at neck of bladder — Opening of mucous glands — Urethral sphincter — Urethra — Vagina

Frank Kennard

Vaccinations

Q My son got a rash and a mild cold a week after he was given his measles shot. My mother said that this was what happened in measles itself. Was she right?

A Yes. The measles vaccine, like many of the really successful vaccines, consists of an attenuated (weakened) strain of the virus itself, which is given as an injection of live virus. This is likely to produce the minor reaction that your son had – a 'mini-attack' of the disease. Anyone who has seen the misery of a young child with full-blown measles would be the first to agree that the mild reaction to a measles shot is preferable to suffering the disease itself.

Q When my daughter became due for her TB jab, the hospital ran a test on her and said that she didn't need the vaccine at all. Why was this?

A Tuberculosis is an unusual type of infection. It is quite common for people to be exposed to the illness in the latter years of childhood. When this happens a child may suffer no symptoms at all, and build up an immunity that keeps the disease in check. Thus a child in this situation will not need the immunizing injection – since he or she already has immunity. The original test injection is an extract of the cell wall of the bacteria, and it is 'read' two days later. A red weal on the site of the injection is evidence of a previous tuberculosis infection.

Q How is a vaccine weakened so that the germs build up immunity and yet do not cause the disease?

A It is really the anti-virus vaccines that are used in the 'live' form. This means that living viruses are injected into the patient – so they must belong to a strain that is going to introduce immunity without causing serious disease.

These strains are produced by growing repeated cultures of the original virus on a suitable medium or by infecting and reinfecting a series of animals such as mice. This continues until the virus has lost its virulence.

Like so many medical advances, vaccination developed almost by accident – when doctors discovered that inoculation with cowpox virus prevented smallpox. Now vaccines offer complete protection against many diseases.

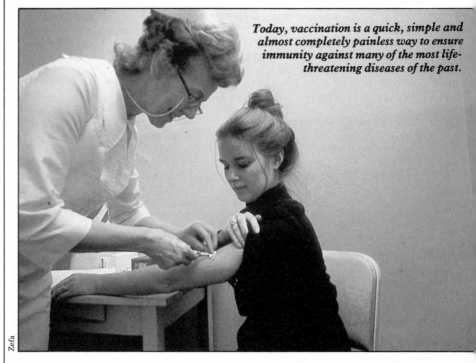

Today, vaccination is a quick, simple and almost completely painless way to ensure immunity against many of the most life-threatening diseases of the past.

The development and use of vaccines has revolutionized treatment of many serious diseases. For example, with the help of an effective vaccine, one killer disease – smallpox – has been eradicated from the face of the earth, while another, diphtheria, has all but disappeared from developed areas of the world.

The body's defence system

The body's first line of defence is obviously the skin, which cannot be crossed unless it is broken. The lining membrane of the gut and the lungs are also constantly assaulted by organisms, and their main protection lies in the mucus-secreting glands. The final line of defence is the complex, blood-based immune system, which comes into action if the skin or a mucous membrane is breached by a foreign organism.

One of the main features of the immune system is the activity of the antibodies, which are protein molecules that are carried in a dissolved form in the blood. Their function is to help to control and 'bind' infecting organisms, which can then be attacked by phagocytes. Lymphocytes also play a starring role: these white blood cells are involved in making antibodies and include cells which attack organisms directly – giving rise to what is called cellular immunity. Cellular immunity is a very important process for dealing with organisms that are capable of infiltrating the cells themselves – one example of such an organism is the tuberculosis bacillus.

Vaccines work by introducing the immune system to an infecting organism in such a way that the body's defences are prepared for an actual attack by the disease. As a general rule vaccines are better at building up antibodies than at establishing cellular immunity.

The origin of vaccination

Like many of the great advances of medicine, vaccination was an accepted technique before its theoretical basis was understood. In the late eighteenth century an English surgeon, Edward Jenner, heard that milkmaids who had cowpox seemed to have a degree of immunity against smallpox, and he reasoned correctly that this might point to a way of preventing the dreaded disease. He proceeded to inject the fluid from the pustules of cowpox into people at risk from smallpox, with good results. (Cowpox is called vaccinia – hence 'vaccination'.) The reason the cowpox fluid worked was because the vaccinia virus is so similar to the smallpox virus that it creates effective antibodies to smallpox without giving rise to serious disease. This all happened long before anyone knew what an antibody was.

Live vaccines

The vaccinia virus is alive and in certain conditions it may cause serious disease. For example, people with eczema may actually contract a fatal infection from vaccinia if they have been vaccinated. In most cases, however, vaccinia is a virus which is actually 'attenuated' for the average individual – this means that it does not normally cause serious disease. In order to provide adequate protection in other diseases such as polio, German measles, yellow fever and the like, the original virulent (disease-producing) virus has to be treated in the laboratory so that its virulence is reduced while its capacity to create immunity is preserved. This is done by growing generations of viruses until they eventually lose their capacity to cause serious disease.

'Killed' vaccines

In some cases, particularly with bacterial infections, it is not possible to produce

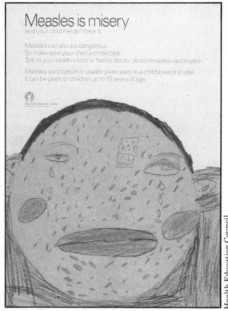

Variations on the theme of public health: the poster (above) is part of a campaign to persuade parents to have their children inoculated against measles. A medical team vaccinates villagers in Zaire (below) in an attempt to control diseases endemic in that part of the world.

live vaccines and dead bacteria extracts are used instead. The vaccines against whooping cough or cholera are examples.

Generally, however, live vaccines are often superior to using extracts of killed organisms. In addition, a vaccine like the polio vaccine can be administered by mouth, so that it goes straight to the normal port of entry of the disease – the gut. This means that local defences with antibodies can be built up in the gut wall.

Vaccines in common use

In most developed countries pre-school children are offered protection against tetanus, diphtheria and whooping cough in the form of a combined vaccine called a triple vaccine. Oral polio vaccine is also given at this time. Measles vaccine may also be given in the second year of life, and rubella vaccine (German measles vaccine) is given to teenage girls to guard against the disease in future pregnancy (see Immunization pp 185–7

Travellers may be offered a variety of other vaccines to prevent yellow fever, typhoid and cholera – in fact some countries require certificates of immunization against these diseases: check with the relevant consulate or a travel agent before you travel.

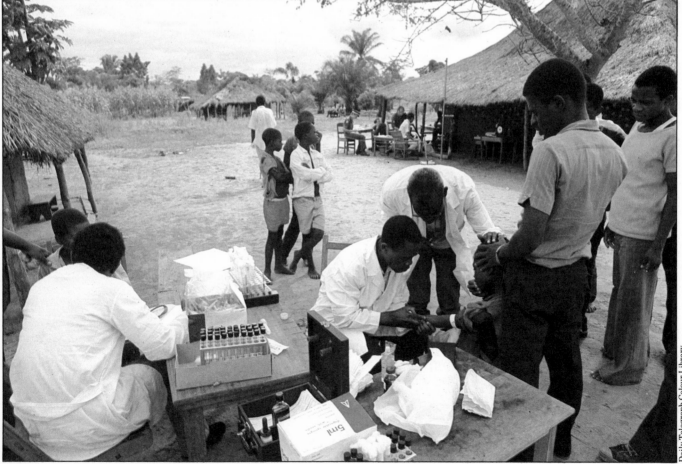

Varicose veins

Our upright stance, with all its many advantages, has not come without a price. For many, this price may include varicose veins – those twisted knots of vein that snake embarrassingly across the lower legs.

Q Do varicose veins run in families? Both my mother and my father have had trouble with them, and I am wondering whether I will be affected?

A Yes, they do run in families, but no definite inherited link has been identified. All that can be said is that you are more likely to develop varicose veins. However, there is not a lot you can do to avoid developing them apart from refraining from standing still for long periods.

Q I have a few varicose veins, and I would like to have them treated, but my husband and I would like to have some more children. Is it better to wait until after I have had all my children before having them treated?

A In general, it would be better, unless, of course, they are causing a lot of trouble at the moment. There is no doubt that pregnancy makes varicose veins worse, and it would be more sensible to have them treated after having all your children.

Q I have a friend who has a very nasty ulcer on her ankle, and also has varicose veins. Are the two connected?

A They may be. Sometimes, particular sorts of varicose veins can lead to breakdown of the skin in the lower leg with the formation of an ulcer. However, the majority of patients with varicose veins do not have an ulcer, and so the two do not invariably go together.

Q I have heard that varicose veins can be treated with injections, thus making an operation unnecessary. Is this true, and if so, does having injections make it difficult to have an operation later on?

A Some varicose veins can be treated by injections. The ones that are suitable are small ones, confined to the area below the knee. Having injections does not affect subsequent surgery, should it prove necessary.

Ron Sutherland

Veins are said to be varicose when they become tortuous, thin-walled and widened and easily visible below the skin. The veins in the superficial tissues of the legs are most commonly affected.

There is no known cause for varicose veins of the legs, but there are many factors which may lead to a worsening of varicose veins which are already present. Varicose veins do run in families, but there is no clear-cut reason for this. They are also much more common in women than they are in men.

One might think that a doorman's job is a cushy number, straining only his capacity for politeness. In fact, standing immobile for long periods puts him much at risk of getting varicose veins.

The veins

Normally, the blood which supplies the tissues of the lower limb flows down the arteries to the feet and then back up the veins, and so to the heart. In the lower limb, there are two systems of veins: the deep system, and the superficial system.

Removing varicose veins

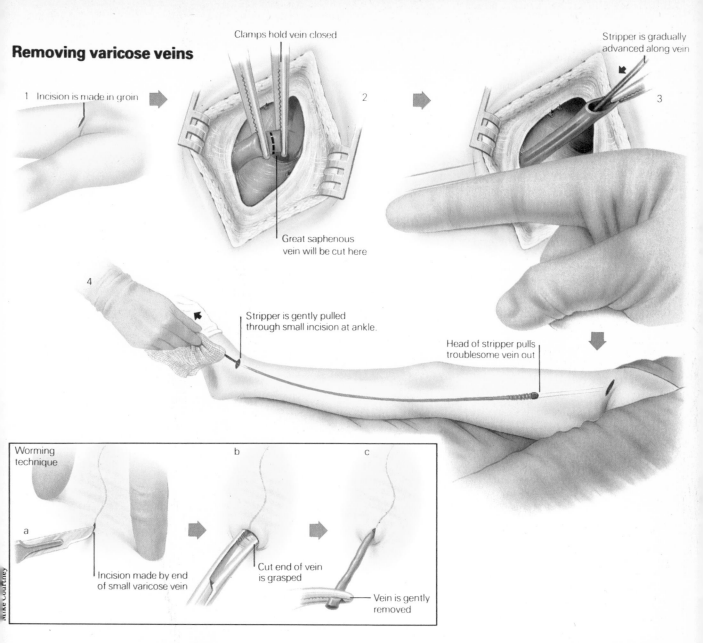

1 Incision is made in groin

Clamps hold vein closed

Great saphenous vein will be cut here

2

Stripper is gradually advanced along vein

3

4

Stripper is gently pulled through small incision at ankle.

Head of stripper pulls troublesome vein out

Worming technique

a

b

c

Incision made by end of small varicose vein

Cut end of vein is grasped

Vein is gently removed

It is the superficial system that is affected as it consists of veins in the tissues between the muscle and the skin, veins which can easily be seen and are called varicose when they become enlarged.

Both the superficial and deep veins contain valves every few centimetres. These valves consist of tiny folds of the lining of the vein, and they allow blood to flow up the limb, but not the other way.

In patients with varicose veins, these valves are found to be defective. It is not clear whether the defective valves cause the varicose veins, or whether it is the other way round. However, the final effect of having defective valves is that the blood in the vein can flow *down* the vein, leading to stretching of its wall.

The superficial veins of the lower limb are divided into two main veins, the long saphenous and the short saphenous veins. The long saphenous vein carries

blood from the front of the foot, up the inner side of the leg and goes deeply into the thigh just below the groin. The short saphenous vein carries blood from the outer side of the foot up to the back of the knee, where it also goes deeply to join the deep system of veins. The long saphenous vein and its many branches are the commonest site of varicose veins.

Aggravating factors

Although there are no obvious causes of varicose veins there are a number of factors that increase their possibility.

Pregnancy: many women notice varicose veins after pregnancy. It is probable that the veins were abnormal before pregnancy, but that pregnancy made them worse. There are two theoretical reasons why this should happen. First, the presence of an enlarged uterus leads to pressure on the veins in

(1) The patient lies on a tilted table with the feet raised. The troublesome veins have already been marked on the skin. An incision is made in the groin area and the fascias are divided until the great saphenous vein is revealed. (2) The vein is lifted, clamped and divided; all the branches are tied off. (3) The stripper – a thin tube – is then introduced into the groin end; it is advanced down the vein with the surgeon's finger tracing the vein's path to ensure that the stripper's way is clear. (4) A small transverse incision is made on the inside of the ankle and the stripper is withdrawn through it. Again, the surgeon traces the path of the vein. The leg is raised to reduce bleeding. (5) Tortuous tributaries are removed. Small incisions are made at sites of uncomfortable veins. Sections are removed using artery forceps. All incisions are stitched, and finally, bandages are applied to the leg.

Q Is there anything that can be done to treat the patches of tiny purple veins that I seem to have developed on my legs? They do not cause me any bother, apart from the fact that they are unsightly.

A Unfortunately, these groups of tiny veins, or venular flares, as they are called, are impossible to treat. They are, however, associated with varicose veins and it may be that if you have treatment for the varicose veins they will cease to get any worse. Don't forget that minor blemishes on the legs may be a lot less unsightly than scars from operations, or brown skin stains from injection treatment.

Q Is it true that certain types of job can cause varicose veins?

A Probably. Standing still for long periods of time increases the amount of blood in the veins of the legs and may worsen varicose veins. However, it is probably a combination of the tendency to develop varicose veins and the prolonged standing which leads to the final outcome. There are many people who have varicose veins who do not stand for long periods, and conversely there are many people whose job entails standing, who do not have varicose veins. For those people who do have to spend long periods of time standing up, some form of exercise during your break is advisable. Also, as you stand working, make a point of squeezing and relaxing your leg muscles; this helps pump blood up the veins.

Q There seems to be a lot of argument about whether or not varicose veins cause pain in the legs. Can they cause pain, and if so, what sort of pain do they cause?

A Varicose veins can cause pain in the legs, but usually only if the veins are severely affected. The pain is usually worse at the end of the day and may be felt at night as a sort of night-cramp. It is very important that pain in the legs is not automatically attributed to varicose veins, as there may be another abnormality in the leg, such as arthritis or arterial disease, causing the pain.

One type of treatment involves injecting different parts of the vein with a special substance, causing inflammation (right). The leg will then be bandaged very tightly, so that the varicose vein is compressed.

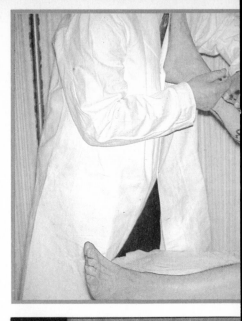

the pelvis, causing increased pressure in the veins of the leg. This pressure may cause the veins to become swollen. Second, hormones which are produced during pregnancy lead to a general softening-up of supporting tissues to allow the baby's head to pass through the birth canal, and the supporting tissues of the veins may also be similarly affected.

Obesity: varicose veins can be brought on through obesity because of increased pressure inside the abdomen, together with general weakening of fibrous tissue in the wall of the vein.

Prolonged standing: jobs which require prolonged standing may put an undue strain on the veins of the legs, especially if they have to be kept still.

Injury: sometimes, a large varicose vein develops at the site of an injury, such as where a cricket ball hits the leg. This may be the only varicose vein in an otherwise normal leg.

Deep vein thrombosis: occasionally, patients who have had a deep vein thrombosis may develop varicose veins in the lower leg, but these are usually of a different pattern compared with the more common varicose veins which start in the superficial veins.

Effects of varicose veins
Varicose veins do not look pleasant, and by far the commonest reason for people to seek medical help for their varicose veins is because the veins are unsightly. But varicose veins can cause complications and these may necessitate surgical or other treatment.

Because they are thin-walled and near the surface, they are more susceptible to injury. This, coupled with the fact that the blood flow is much more sluggish in varicose veins, can lead to a thrombosis in the vein. The resulting inflammation around the thrombosis – known as phlebitis – causes pain and redness in the affected area.

For unknown reasons, some patients with varicose veins develop quite bad eczema on the lower leg. This eczema can be treated with skin preparations, but if the varicose veins are treated, then the eczema usually disappears.

Varicose veins in all their unsightliness . . . They are more common in women than men, but it's comforting to realize that there are many types of treatment available, including surgery, injections and bandages, and that they can be controlled.

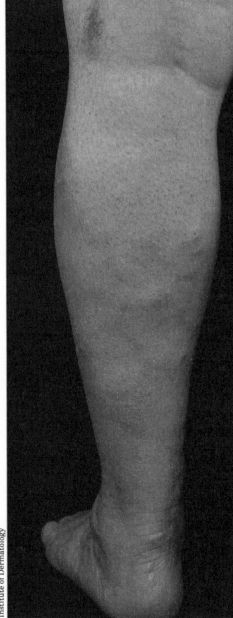

Institute of Dermatology

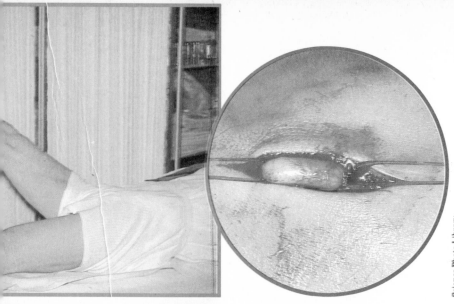

The modern approach to operating on varicose veins involves making an incision in the groin area and pushing a tube down the vein (above and below). As the tube works its way down, any obstructions in the vein are cleared. The tube is then removed and the incision stitched up.

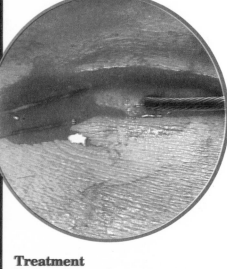

Treatment

Various forms of treatment have been tried, but nowadays the treatment is divided into surgery, injections and other forms, such as the wearing of bandages and support stockings.

Surgery: the aim of surgery in varicose veins is twofold. First, an attempt is made to remove the unsightly veins. Second, an operation is done to prevent the veins coming back again.

The first part of the treatment involves making several tiny little cuts in the skin over the veins, and removing them a segment at a time. The distance between the cuts will vary, but may be 5 cm (2 in).

The second part of the operation – treating the root cause of these particular varicose veins – may be more difficult,

and it is here that careful examination of the pattern of the individual patient's veins is of vital importance. By examining the patient first lying down and then standing up, the surgeon determines whether the long or the short saphenous vein is at fault, and at which point along the vein the trouble arises.

It is usually found that the valves in the upper part of the long saphenous vein (in the groin) are causing the problem, allowing blood to leak back down the vein. If the long saphenous vein is therefore tied off in the groin, then the pressure is taken off this vein at points lower down. The blood which would normally flow through the long saphenous vein finds its way back to the heart via a different vein, of which there are dozens in the leg.

This sort of surgery, although it may seem quite elaborate, is relatively minor for the patient. Usually he or she is in hospital for one or two days and can get up and walk the day after the operation.

Injections: in this form of treatment a special substance is injected into different parts of the vein, causing the lining of the vein to become inflamed. The leg is then tightly bandaged – and remains so for about a month – so that the vein is compressed. The object of the treatment is to get the opposite walls of the vein to stick together permanently, thus effectively closing it.

The main disadvantage of this form of treatment is that it is only effective on small varicose veins, and only if they are situated below the knee (it is virtually impossible to get a bandage to stay on the thigh for more than a few hours).

Bandages: there are no other forms of treatment which are capable of actually removing varicose veins once they are present, but the wearing of support stockings or tights can help to prevent varicose veins from getting any worse. These stockings are specially designed to give firm, even pressure all the way up the leg, and are usually quite comfortable.

Taking care

If you have varicose veins, the chances are that you will always have a few prominent veins for the rest of your life, even if you have the existing ones treated. There is no guarantee that they will not appear elsewhere after treatment. However, there are some things you can do to try and prevent them reappearing!

Try not to do too much standing, if at all possible. Walking is fine, but do not stand still for long periods.

When you sit down, always try to put your feet up on a stool or chair, so that the blood in the legs can flow more easily back up the body to the heart.

Vasectomy

Q I am thinking of having a vasectomy but am worried that it will affect my virility. Does this ever happen?

A Generally, there is no medical reason why a vasectomy should have any effect on virility, or any aspect of your sex life except fertility. A few men do find a temporary slackening of sexual desire after the operation but this is usually caused by psychological factors. For example, it may be due to anxiety about the operation having some effect on sexual performance or sexual desire.

Q How soon after a vasectomy is it safe to have intercourse without using some kind of birth control?

A Sperm capable of fertilization have been known to survive in the seminal vesicles for as long as six months after vasectomy, but it is usually more like four to six weeks. However, it is important not to rely on these figures; and specimens of semen should be examined under a microscope to make quite certain that there are no sperm remaining in the seminal fluid before you have intercourse without using some method of birth control.

Q My wife died soon after I had a vasectomy. I am now planning to remarry and both my future wife and I want to have children. Is this wholly impossible or is there any way in which the vasectomy can be reversed?

A Vasectomies have been successfully reversed, but this is a difficult procedure with no guarantee of success in the end. The operation involves finding the cut ends of the vas deferens and meticulously sewing the various layers together again. Even if this is done the internal tube may not remain open; and if it is open, sperm antibodies can prevent the development of satisfactory sperm. At present, the pregnancy rate in the partners of men who have had vasectomies reversed is no more than 60 per cent.

Male sterilization is one of the most reliable forms of birth control. It requiries only minor surgery – but should never be undertaken lightly because there is no guarantee that the effect can ever be reversed.

The decision to have a vasectomy has to be a rational one: it should only be made after a great deal of thought and discussion – with both your partner and your doctor.

Vasectomy is a permanent form of sterilization or birth control for males. It is equivalent to the operation in a woman in which the Fallopian tubes, along which eggs pass from the ovary to the womb, are either cut, tied, clipped or sealed, so that she cannot become pregnant. Both operations are intended to result in a permanent inability to have children; therefore no couple should consider sterilization unless they are certain that there is absolutely no possibility of either of them wanting children in the future.

How it works

Sterilization in males consists of removing a section of the vas deferens – the duct which sperm pass along when released from the testis. Sperm are manufactured from cells that make up the walls of small tubes (seminiferous tubules) which form each testis. When sperm have matured they collect in larger tubes, the vasa efferentia. These join together and pass out of the testis as the epididymis, a long coiled tube almost wrapped around the outside of the testis. When the epididymis leaves the area of the testis it becomes a long thin channel – the vas deferens. This is grouped together with the arteries, veins and lymphatics that supply the testis. Together they form a thick cord called the spermatic cord.

From the scrotum or bag in which the

testes lie, the two spermatic cords pass up into the lower part of the abdomen and loop over the lower end of each ureter (the tube carrying urine from the kidney to the bladder), before joining the urethra (the tube that takes urine away from the bladder) where it runs through the prostate gland. At this junction, the newly made sperm are stored in pouch-like structures, called seminal vesicles, until they are required. Then during ejaculation, the sperm, now in a fluid called semen, are pushed forcefully down the urethra and out at the tip of the penis – and during sexual intercourse, deep into the vagina.

There are many ways in which contraception can be achieved: some, such as using the sheath and the cap, depend on creating a physical barrier; others, such as the IUD, or coil, interfere with the fertilized ovum establishing itself in the womb; and another, the Pill, interferes with the production of the monthly egg. Sterilization in a male consists of removing a section of the vas deferens, which gives this method the name, vasectomy. It works on the basis that if a piece of the vas deferens is missing it will be quite impossible for sperm to pass along it from the testes to be released and bring about fertilization.

Pros and cons of vasectomy

All methods of birth control have their own particular advantages and disadvantages, and it is very important that individuals choose the one that is best suited to their personal needs and circumstances. Vasectomy, because it is basically permanent and irreversible, is not something to be undertaken lightly.

Men who consider vasectomy are usually in their late forties or fifties, already have children, feel that their families are complete and prefer this method of birth control to any other.

Vasectomy has the great advantage of being absolutely reliable and permanent. However its permanency is also, under certain circumstances, a disadvantage – a reversal of the surgical procedure is at the very least difficult and expensive, and, in many cases, impossible.

The decision to have or not have a vasectomy is not one that men have to make entirely on their own, although it is in the end their decision and one for

The vasectomy operation is simple. Local anaesthetic is given; an incision is made in the skin of the scrotum (1). Part of the vas deferens is pulled out (2). It is cut in two places 2.5cm (1 in) apart and the intervening section removed (3). The ends are folded back (4). The site is closed and the operation repeated on the other side (5).

which they must take full responsibility. Doctors insist that patients fully understand what is involved and may want a signed statement to this effect before they will undertake the operation.

It is also important that a decision to have a vasectomy is taken jointly by husband and wife. Although it is the husband who will have the vasectomy, it will inevitably have some effect on his marriage. Therefore, before planning the operation a man should discuss the pros and cons with his wife and family doctor.

The operation

The operation is quite straightforward and minor. It does not require hospitalization but can be done in the doctor's surgery, a family planning clinic or the out-patient department of a hospital.

The vasectomy is done under local anaesthetic; two or three small injections are given into the site of the operation to deaden the area. The section of the vas deferens chosen for removal is that part which is most easily accessible and lies at the neck of the scrotum, just below where

How a vasectomy is performed

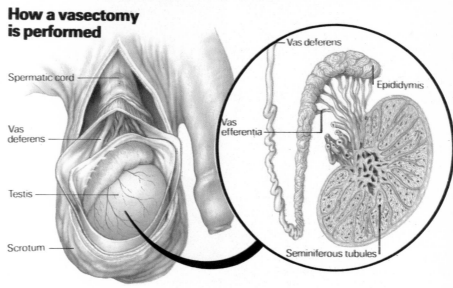

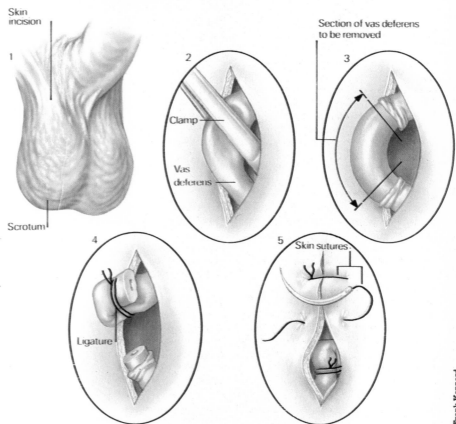

Q Is there a noticeable scar after a vasectomy?

A Usually the skin heals so well that you would have to look very carefully to find the scar. It is definitely nothing to worry about.

Q A friend of mine had a vasectomy and he told me that the whole area became swollen and turned blue. Is this usual?

A Fortunately, not. It would appear that your friend developed a scrotal haematoma. This occurs when a severed blood vessel oozes into the sack, or scrotum, and it happens only rarely.

Q What should a man thinking about having a vasectomy bear in mind before going ahead with the operation?

A The most important thing for him to understand fully is that although reversal may sometimes be impossible, the operation should be regarded as a permanent measure. It is vital that he doesn't enter into it with the expectation that he may be able to change his mind at a later date and have it all reversed.

Apart from that, he and his partner need to be quite sure that they will not want more children in the future. They also need to be sure that their relationship is stable, and likely to last. So there is no question of the man wanting to reserve the possibility of having children with some other partner in the future if the present relationship comes to an end. In general, this is a method of contraception for the older man.

Q Have the major western religions made any pronouncement on vasectomy?

A The Church of England feels that vasectomy is a voluntary business, but stresses that young and unmarried men should not consider having the operation. The Catholic Church is opposed to any form of birth control except the rhythm method. The Orthodox Jewish view is as firmly against the procedure as the Catholic one; and there has been no statement of opinion from Muslim religious authorities.

In India vasectomy has been a controversial issue, not least because of suggestions of coercion. It's crucial to reassure the population and allay fears (right).

Rex Features

The evergreen entertainer and bon vivant Dean Martin is one celebrity known to have had a vasectomy, and talked freely about his operation (above).

it joins the rest of the body. A small vertical cut is made through the anaesthetized skin and the vas deferens identified. It is then cut in two places 2.5 cm (1 inch) apart and the intervening section is removed. The ends are usually folded back on themselves before being securely tied with a material, such as silk, which will not dissolve or disintegrate. The wound is closed with a few stitches and the procedure is repeated on the other side. The whole operation takes only half an hour or less.

After surgery
The wound usually heals in a few days, after which the stitches are removed. There may be some soreness when the anaesthetic wears off, but this is normal. In a few patients there may be some bleeding into the wound, and this can cause pain, swelling and discolouration for a few days. Intercourse is likely to be painful for a day or two and most men avoid it until the stitches are removed.

The main thing to understand about a vasectomy is that there is a time lag between the operation and the time when the patient is in fact infertile. This is because a certain number of sperm are stored in two little pouches called the seminal vesicles. They have already passed up the vas deferens and 'escaped' before the vasectomy has been done. These sperm can remain capable of fertilization for several months after the operation. Usually, it is reckoned that by the time three months have elapsed they should all have been used up, but there are cases where pregnancy has occurred six months later. The exact time cannot be predicted, but is related to the number of times that the man ejaculates after the operation. If he has frequent sexual intercourse, then he will 'use up' the remaining sperm more quickly. To guard against unwanted pregnancy during this time other forms of contraception, such as a sheath, should be used. It is customary to examine two specimens of semen at eight and 12 weeks after the operation, and if these contain no sperm, then it is considered safe to carry on with unprotected intercourse.

If seminal analysis after six months still shows the presence of sperm, then

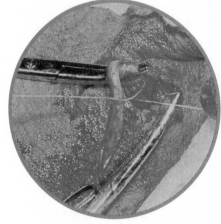

In the later stages of the operation to remove a section of the vas deferens (below), the cut ends are folded back on themselves and ligatures are made – they are securely tied with material that will not dissolve or disintegrate. A reversal of the process – called reanastomosis – aims at the reconstruction of a tube between the epididymis and the seminal vesicle, and is commonly performed on only one side. The ease with which the operation can be done depends on how much of the vas deferens was removed.

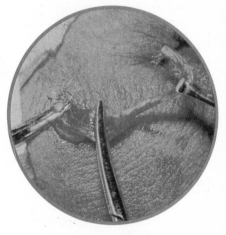

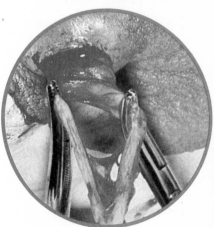

the patient should be investigated for the possibility of having two vasa deferentia on one side, one of which has been missed.

Effects of vasectomy

It is important to realize that the operation of vasectomy is simply an interruption to the flow of *sperm* into the part where the *semen* is collected. Even though millions of sperm are released during normal intercourse, they are so small that their total volume will not make any appreciable difference to the volume of the semen. The other function of the testes, that of producing male hormones which are released directly into the bloodstream, is not affected in any way by a vasectomy, nor is a man's sexual drive or ability.

There is some evidence that tying off the vas deferens on each side can lead to the formation of antibodies against the patient's own sperm. This occurs in very few patients, and is of no relevance unless the patient wishes to have a reversal of his vasectomy. However, in this case the main obstacle to a successful reversal is the sheer mechanics of joining up two tiny

tubes in the midst of a large amount of scar tissue.

Apart from the occasional case of antibodies to sperm, there are no known other effects. The possibility that vasectomy might cause an increase in the incidence of atheroma (hardening of the arteries) has not been borne out by any scientific evidence.

Outlook

Vasectomy is virtually always completely and permanently successful. It is also singularly free of complications. Very rarely the two ends of the severed vas deferens manage to join up again – resulting in an unexpected and apparently miraculous pregnancy of the man's partner – but this is extremely unlikely.

Attempts have been made – with a view to making the procedure less permanent and thus more acceptable to a large number of men – to design an operation which, while still being completely reliable, could be easily reversed if the man subsequently wished it. However, nothing along these lines is generally available at the moment.

Venereal diseases

Q Is it possible to have VD without knowing about it?

A It most certainly is. People can carry the germs causing these diseases without being ill, and are unaware that they are infected. In particular, about 80 per cent of women who turn out to have gonorrhoea have no idea that anything is wrong with them.

Q Is it possible to 'catch' VD from a dirty lavatory seat?

A This is simply wishful thinking and virtually never happens – except, strangely enough, in the case of trichomoniasis. As the name implies, sexually transmitted diseases are caught by having sexual intercourse with somebody who already has the disease.

Q I have heard a lot about a new venereal disease called AIDS. What does this stand for?

A AIDS stands for 'Acquired Immune Deficiency Syndrome', and it is not strictly a venereal disease. It was noticed that a small number of young homosexuals were developing unusual fungus and parasitic infections and also that others developed rare tumours. The common factor between these things was a deficiency in the immune system—the body's own defense system. It seems that something in the homosexual life-style, perhaps the greatly increased risk of VD of all sorts and the resulting strain on the immune system, was causing this immune deficiency.

AIDS has also been found in a few non-homosexuals, including drug addicts and Haitian men.

Q Is there any way of telling it somebody has VD?

A Not really, other than from medical tests. If a person sleeps around or has a reputation for changing partners frequently, then he or she is likely to get infected at some time. With a new partner the wisest thing is to take sensible precautions – such as insisting that a sheath is used – until you know the person well enough to be sure of him or her.

Sexual freedom such as we have today ironically carries with it at least one inhibiting factor – the very real risk of catching VD. A cure may not always be easy so it is essential to know how best it can be avoided.

Bavaria Verlag

Veneral disease, often referred to as sexually transmitted disease, is in fact not a single disease but a collection of twelve or so quite different conditions that are grouped together because they are all acquired as a result of sexual intercourse with a person who has already contracted the infection.

There are four that are particularly troublesome: syphilis, gonorrhoea, non-specific urethritis and genital herpes. Less serious veneral diseases include trichomoniasis, thrush or monilia, pubic lice and genital warts.

In many parts of the world, such as in Mexico (above), prostitutes are regularly checked for VD as theirs is obviously a very high risk profession.

VD and casual sex

In spite of modern and effective treatment, more people in Europe and America today have venereal disease than at any time in the past twenty to thirty years. The reason for this increase, especially among young people, is that the development of new contraceptives has led to an alteration in views and habits in sexual behaviour, and, consequently, greater sexual freedom at an earlier age. However, we have still to learn that the modern, freer approach to sex brings with it a need for more awareness and thoughtfulness towards one's partner, not less.

Syphilis

Syphilis is the most serious of the contagious venereal infections since it is the only one likely to result, if untreated, in permanent disability or even death. The bacteria are spread from one person to another during intercourse. They can also be passed from an infected mother to her child during pregnancy, so that a baby may be born with congenital syphilis. Routine blood testing of all expectant mothers and the treatment of those found to be infected has made congenital syphilis a rare condition.

The incubation period of syphilis varies widely as do the symptoms of the first or primary stage of the disease. This makes for great difficulty in the early recognition of the disease which is essential if total and permanent cure is to be achieved.

The usual indication is a single painless ulcer appearing where the germ has entered the body – in or around the genitals, anus or mouth. The ulcer heals by itself, unfortunately leading many people to think that it could not have been very important and to neglect to do anything about it. An added complication is that sometimes an ulcer does not appear at all. For this reason it is essential that anyone who thinks that he or she may have been in contact with venereal disease goes to a Special Clinic to make sure, since it is only if treatment is given in the early stages that a cure can be guaranteed.

Gonorrhoea

Gonorrhoea is another infectious bacterial disease, contracted by sexual intercourse with an infected person, and is now nearly as common as measles. About 80 per cent of infected women have no symptoms and are generally unaware that they have it. Some have pain passing urine (dysuria) or cystitis and some develop lower abdominal pain from involvement of the Fallopian tubes (salpingitis) which can well lead to subsequent sterility. Diagnosis, which is not easy and is best carried out at a Special Clinic, consists of finding the bacteria in specimens obtained during a vaginal

If there is the slightest possibility that you may have contracted VD, you should go to a Special Clinic where routine diagnostic tests will be carried out.

examination. In men the situation is quite different. In less than a week after being infected, pain on passing urine develops followed by a profuse discharge of pus from the hole at the end of the penis, the urinary meatus. The diagnosis of gonorrhoea is confirmed by finding the bacteria in the discharge.

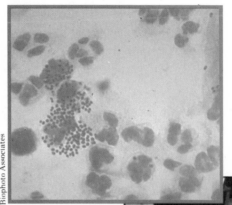

Diagnosis of gonorrhoea is made by microscopic examination, which reveals the presence of the bacteria neisseria gonorrhoeae (above) in the specimen. This is taken from the vagina, or in men, from urinary discharge.

Treatment in both sexes is usually by a single dose of penicillin given either as an injection or as capsules; abstention from alcohol and sexual intercourse for several weeks is also important. The relief of symptoms after treatment is dramatic, but it is vital that supervision is maintained to make sure that the cure is permanent and complete. An attack of gonorrhoea confers no immunity for the future. Patients have a clear responsibility to ensure that all those with whom they have recently had sexual contact are made aware of the facts and go for examination. The use of a sheath during intercourse gives considerable protection to both partners. Gonorrhoea is not hereditary but a gonococcal infection can be passed on to babies and young girls either during birth or by close contact with an infected mother.

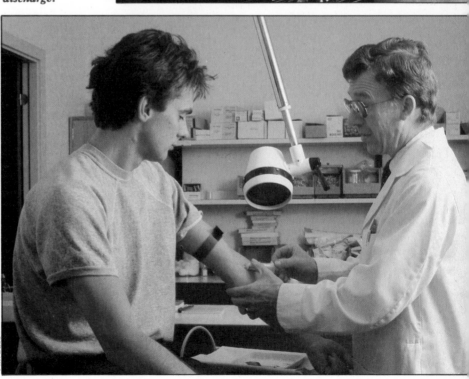

457

Q Can VD make it more difficult to get pregnant?

A Yes. Sexually transmitted diseases are more likely to cause permanent damage in women than in men. One of the most important ways they can affect women is make them sterile and unable to have babies because the tube down which the monthly egg or ovum passes becomes blocked as a result of disease.

Q Does either urinating or washing immediately after sexual intercourse have any effect in reducing the risk of getting VD?

A Washing the sexual parts thoroughly with soap and water and passing urine after sex certainly reduce the risk of catching a sexually transmitted disease, especially in men, but they do not eliminate the risk completely. Using a sheath, or condom, offers a much greater degree of protection.

Q Can one become immune to venereal disease?

A Unlike diseases such as measles, an attack of one of the venereal diseases does not protect against future attacks. Sexually transmitted diseases can then be caught many times and people do not as a rule become immune to them.

Q Can veneral disease affect an unborn baby?

A Unfortunately, yes, and this is one of the great tragedies of VD. Syphilis may cause miscarriage, stillbirth, serious deformities or even death of the baby. This is why all expectant mothers have blood tests for syphilis during their pregnancy; should they turn out to be positive it is possible to give treatment to protect the baby. Genital herpes can also be fatal if passed by a woman to her baby during childbirth. And if there are open vesicles at the time of birth, the baby will be delivered by Caesarean. In addition it is possible for gonorrhoea and chlamydia to affect the baby's eyes if the bacteria are active when it is born.

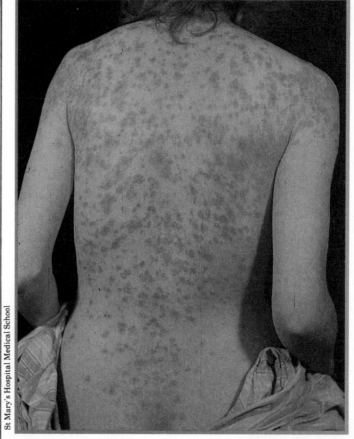

St Mary's Hospital Medical School

Unless treated immediately, syphilis will move into its secondary stage with the development of a skin rash which can vary greatly in type and intensity. A roseolar rash (left) affects the trunk and limbs. Left untreated, the rash eventually fades and the disease enters the dormant stage. In addition, the skin may be affected by a papular rash which can also occur on the palms of the hands and on the soles of the feet (below). A microscopic view (right) of the genital herpes virus, which causes the formation of painful blisters in and around the genitals. As yet there is no cure.

NSU

NonSpecific Urethritis or NSU is a condition which is one of the most extraordinary challenges facing medicine today. The number of cases continues to increase at an amazing rate, making it now more common than all the other venereal diseases put together. Yet, in spite of a vast amount of research and the discovery that many – but by no means all – cases are associated with the chlamydia germ, the real cause is still not clear, and we do not really know why some men get it and others do not. Some cases get better quite quickly and present no problem; however, in some men recurrences are common.

As its name implies, NSU is a urethritis – an inflammation of the urethra – that has no specific cause. This distinguises it from the other main cause of urethritis which is gonorrhoea. And, since the treatment, management and implications of gonorrhoea and NSU are quite different, one of the specialist's first tasks in dealing with a case of what appears to be NSU is to make sure, by means of microscopic examination and laboratory tests of the discharge, that it is not a mild case of gonorrhoea in disguise.

The main symptom is a discharge from the tip of the penis. The discharge is usually clear white to grey in colour, as

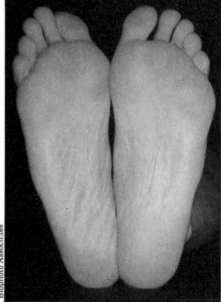

Biophoto Associates

Syphilis is a severe, sexually-transmitted infection caused by the treponema pallidum bacterium. Right: thread-like spiral cells of the bacteria.

Biophoto Associates

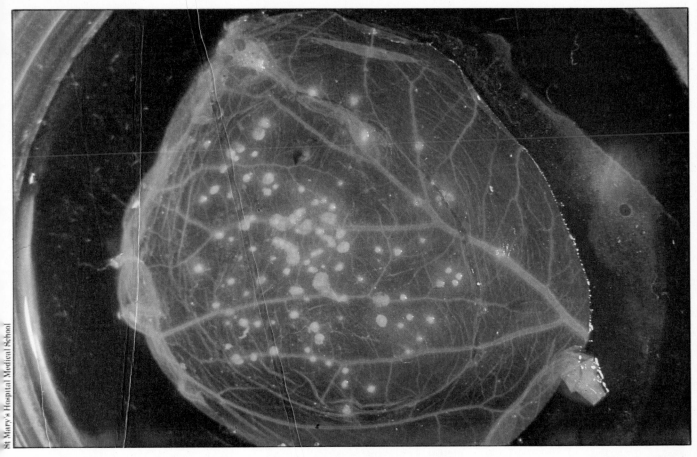

opposed to the creamy yellow matter that is characteristic of gonorrhoea – and is therefore quite similar to semen in appearance. The quantity varies a great deal but is usually not very much, and may amount to no more that moistness at the tip of the penis. The second common symptom is pain on passing urine. Again the severity of this is very variable, often not occurring at all or being no more than a feeling of irritation.

Genital herpes

Genital herpes is a sexually transmitted disease which has reached epidemic proportions in America. The main problem is

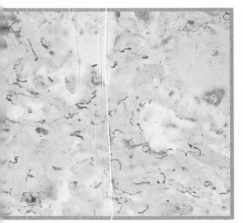

that being a virus, herpes cannot be cured and so each new sufferer adds to the pool of carriers.

There are two types of herpes simplex virus, both of which cause painful blisters (vesicles), localized swelling and sometimes fever. HSV 1 is usually found around the mouth (cold sores). HSV 2 is spread by sexual contact and the blisters can be found in and around the genitals, around the anus, on the bladder, buttocks, thighs and legs of both sexes.

This condition exists in two states – latent and active. After the first attack the virus travels up a local sensory nerve and then lies dormant in the body. It waits until something triggers off an attack, and then emerges again, usually in the same spot time and time again, as a painful blister. During latent periods when no blisters are open, sexual partners will not catch herpes from the carrier, but when blisters are open the carrier is extremely contagious. If the vesicles are inside the vagina, on the cervix or in the urethra, it is possible that the carrier will be unaware of their existence. Attacks appear to be linked to physical and emotional low points – such as during times of depression or stress, illness, just before a period or during bad weather, or to local stimulation of affected areas.

Although painful and depressing to an adult, genital herpes is often fatal if it is passed by a pregnant sufferer to her baby as it passes down the birth canal. A pregnant woman who has suffered genital herpes – even if she has not had an attack for some time – should always tell the medical team looking after her, of her affliction. They will monitor her during the pregnancy and then if there are open vesicles at the time of birth, the baby can be saved if delivered by Caesarean section.

Since a virus inextricably entwines itself with the cells of the host, and anything that harms the virus invariably harms the host, genital herpes cannot yet be cured: but there are ways of speeding up the recovery time of attacks and making them less unpleasant. Keeping the affected areas clean and dry will stop secondary infection. Salt baths and cold compresses will ease pain. Keeping stress-free and healthy will help your body erect defences against attacks. In most cases, attacks will come most months for the first year, and gradually tail-off, becoming less frequent as the years go by.

Idoxuridine can be used in a solution to paint the vesicles, and in some cases will help – as can an enzyme called cytarabine. In serious cases Vidarabine is

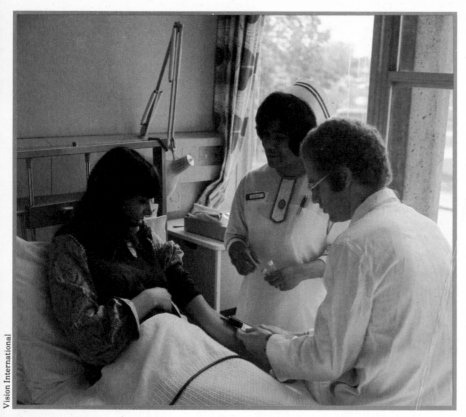

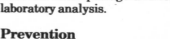

used – but it can only be given intravenously, so is only used for hospital cases. A virus research unit in the UK has produced a vaccine, but this obviously must be used before the virus is contracted, and cannot help after.

Since genital herpes has been linked to cancer of the cervix, women sufferers should have regular smear checks – at least once a year.

Identifying discharge

Women often worry that vaginal discharge or a change in what is normal for them, may mean that they have caught VD. Fortunately, however, although a vaginal discharge needs to be thought about carefully, and may well need tests and treatment, a great many turn out to be normal and only a few are caused by anything serious. First, the quantity or amount of discharge, which is often what gives rise to alarm, can vary widely from one woman to another and is particularly likely to increase in certain situations. What is important, in relation to the possibility of infection or other disease, is not the quantity but quality or type of discharge.

Clear mucous discharges are unlikely to be caused by disease; but a discharge that is discoloured, causes soreness or irritation of the vagina or vulva, or is smelly, is much more likely to be related to infection somewhere in the female genital organs. A thin, yellow discharge

Venereal disease can have tragic consequences for a baby born to an infected mother. The routine blood-testing of all pregnant women for syphilis (above) has helped to ensure that far fewer babies are afflicted with this terrible disease than was the case in the past.

is particularly suggestive of trichomonas infection; a thick, white one of thrush (monilia); and brown discharges are really decomposed blood, and this an indication of internal bleeding. This is most likely to be due to erosion or ulceration of the neck of the womb or cervix, but it can also be caused by cancer of the womb, and must therefore always be investigated.

Do not let an unpleasant discharge continue for more than a week before consulting your doctor or going to a Special Clinic about it. You should in any case do so without delay if it is accompanied by fever or abdominal pain, if there is a possibility of venereal disease, if it is blood-stained or brown and you are not close to an expected period, or it is accompanied by pain on passing urine, soreness, irritation or is smelly. The doctor will need to know about the character of the discharge and recent sexual relationships. He will probably examine the vagina with a gloved hand and with a plastic or metal instrument (vaginal speculum), shining a light up it so that he or she can see inside clearly. He

may take specimens from the vagina and the neck of the womb, and possibly also from the water passage and rectum, for laboratory analysis.

Prevention

What, if anything, can you do that will improve your chances of not getting venereal disease? Ideally, of course, VD is best avoided by being faithful to one lover. Certainly you should think about the risk before you have sexual intercourse with somebody you do not know very well, and take certain precautions. Remember that the use of a sheath or condom will give both of you a considerable degree of protection against all forms of venereal disease.

Nevertheless, there are things that are worth doing afterwards if you have neglected to take precautions. For both the man and the woman thorough washing of the genital area with soap and water after intercourse will kill a large proportion of the bacteria with which they may have been contaminated. For men, passing urine has the additional benefit that it is quite likely to flush out of

Vision International

Colorific

the water passage (urethra) any microbes that may have got in there during intercourse. Urinating will have the same effect in women of course, but they have the disadvantage that in them sexually transmitted diseases usually develop in the vagina and neck of the womb rather than in the urethra.

Women often wonder about the value and advisability of douching either to prevent or treat discharges. Although a time-honoured practice, its disadvantages outweigh its advantages; since there is nothing positively in its favour and there is a risk that any infected material is as likely to be flushed upwards into the uterus as to be washed out – a definitely undesirable result. The most useful thing that women can achieve in this direction is to soak themselves in a hot bath, allowing the water to flow freely into the vagina. Unless advised by a doctor do not apply any antiseptic lotions or ointments either inside or outside the genitals – and *never, never* pour strong antiseptic into the urethra or vagina. This is a dangerous thing to do and could well lead to serious and permanent internal damage.

Where to go for help

If you think that there is the *slightest* chance that you might have VD, go to a Special Clinic to find out for sure. Special Clinics – sometimes called VD clinics or Genito-urinary departments – exist in most towns, and you can find out the time they are open either by telephoning your local hospital or from public notices.

In most clinics you will be seen without an appointment or a letter from your own doctor. Everything that takes place at the clinic is strictly confidential and you will usually be referred to by a number, so that your anonymity is completely preserved. No information will be given about you in response to queries from your spouse or partner, friends, parents, school, employer, or anybody else. The clinic notes are kept quite separately from any medical records that may exist about you in some other part of the hospital, so that there is no possibility of cross-reference between them. The clinic staff are there to help you, not to judge you, and the atmosphere in most clinics is very friendly and helpful.

Despite modern medical know-how, VD is still a major problem today. The graph shows that although syphilis is being somewhat controlled, there is an overall rise in the cases of NSU and gonorrohoea.

Incidence of venereal disease

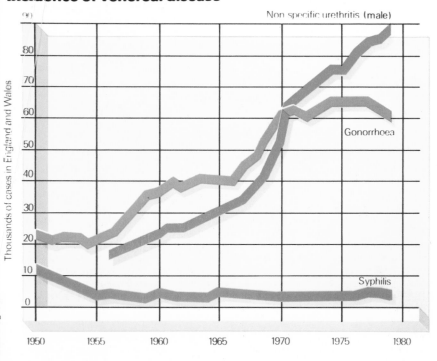

Non specific urethritis (male)

Thousands of cases in England and Wales

90

80

70

60

50

40

30

20

10

0

Gonorrhoea

Syphilis

1950   1955   1960   1965   1970   1975   1980

Verruca

Q Can you catch verrucae at the local swimming pool?

A Yes. This is the most likely place to catch the infection because after swimming the soles of the feet are softened and the skin's defences are therefore weaker. The infection is caught from the changing room floor and the surrounding area, not from the water itself. To reduce the risk, local authorities used to forbid verruca sufferers to use their pools, but nowadays thin rubber shoes can usually be bought at the entrance, and if these are put on immediately there is no danger of spreading the infection.

Q My 13-year-old daughter has a verruca. Is her younger brother likely to catch it?

A Yes. At his age he probably has no immunity to the virus and so is at risk of being infected. There are two ways of preventing this. First, if you treat your daughter's verruca every day with one of the proprietary wart paints and then cover it with a waterproof plaster, she will not shed the virus around the house. Secondly, if both she and her brother use their own towels, bath mats and footwear, and dry their feet immediately after bathing, he will be unlikely to pick up the infection.

Q Do preparations bought over the counter really help in treating verrucae?

A Yes, they certainly do, and in two ways. First, daily painting with a wart paint and rubbing down the horny cap with a pumice stone or emery board rapidly relieve the pain of walking on a verruca. Secondly, treatment kills the surface virus, lessening the danger of spreading it to others. About 50 per cent of verrucae respond to such simple measures. The problem is that the treatment must be continued until the verruca has gone, which usually takes about three months. Too often the sufferer gets bored or discouraged and so doesn't persist with the treatment for long enough. It is easy to tell if a verruca is cured, because it ceases to hurt, tiny black spots may be seen in it and the skin then returns entirely to normal.

Many of us know how painful a verruca can be – and how persistent. But, fortunately, even the most stubborn ones can usually be cured, and very often are by the sufferer's sheer perseverance with a simple treatment.

Verruca is simply the Latin word for a wart, and has been adopted into the English language to refer to a wart on the sole of the foot. Doctors are consulted more often about verrucae than other warts because they are more painful and annoying than warts elsewhere. Sometimes they are also referred to as plantar warts by doctors.

Cause

Warts are caused by a virus that enters the skin through tiny injuries, especially if it is wet and soggy. Most verrucae arise on the weight-bearing parts of the sole, that is the heel and ball, not the instep.

A virus is a particle of living matter that can only reproduce itself inside a living cell, borrowing some of the cell's contents for this purpose. After the virus enters the epidermal cell there is an incubation period of several months, while the virus is multiplying and spreading, before enough skin cells are infected and deformed to produce a visible wart.

The epidermal cells deformed by the virus cause a hard, horny swelling – the wart – which on the sole of the foot is pressed inwards by standing and walking, irritating the sensitive nerve endings under the skin.

There are several strains of human wart virus. Verrucae are due to one strain, although the patient often has warts elsewhere. Another strain that affects only the soles of the feet causes a mosaic wart. This looks like a honeycomb and is actually a mass of closely-packed polygonal warts, often at least 2.5 cm (1 in). across. Mosiac warts are extremely resistant to treatment and often last for several years, but fortunately they are not nearly as painful as verrucae.

Verrucae, like other common virus diseases, are unusual in infancy but begin to occur during the school years, reaching a peak at about the age of nine. They then decline in frequency becoming rarer after the middle twenties. Curiously, the sex incidence is equal up to the age of six but then they become commoner in girls.

Appearance

Like verrucae, corns and callosities are also painful and horny, and it may be very difficult to tell them apart. But if the horny cap of a verruca is carefully pared away, four distinguishing features will be clearly seen.

First, the verruca becomes wider the more skin is pared away. It is shaped like a pyramid with the point at the surface, and there is more hidden in the skin than is visible above it. It also has a horny collar which pushes aside the tiny lines on the skin of the sole. These never run

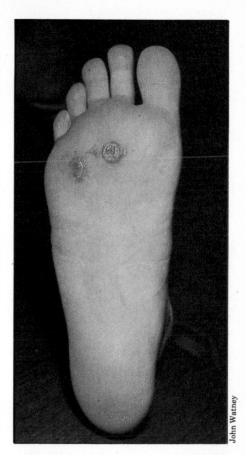

Verrucae are particularly painful because they are pressed into the sole of the foot by standing and walking. The horny skin of each verruca should be rubbed down daily and a proprietary wart paint applied.

across the verruca but encircle it and its horny collar. Finally, when the skin can no longer be pared without causing pain, pin-point bleeding spots appear. However, if the verruca has already been killed, the tiny blood vessels are clotted showing as a few speckled black spots on the surface. This is therefore a sign that the verruca is healing.

In contrast, a corn is widest at the top and narrows to a point within the skin. On paring, it shows a white, smooth appearance like ground glass, and it has no collar. A callosity is simply thick skin with a greatly increased horny layer. The fine skin lines run through it and are often more obvious in the thick skin of a callosity.

Verrucae occur where the sole touches the ground but rarely at an exact point of pressure as is the case with corns and callosities. Therefore if the bit of hard painful skin has been present less than two years in a child or young adult, and is not exactly over a bony knot, it is probably a verruca. If it has been present more than two years over a bony knob in an older person, it is probably a corn or a

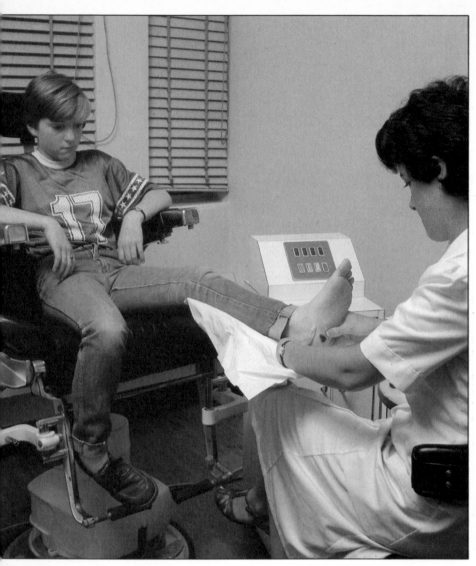

The key to curing a verruca is persistence, since some can take months to disappear. The progress of the verruca should be checked every month by your doctor or nurse at the local clinic. They will be able to tell when it has healed completely.

callosity. Occasionally, a verruca may arise in a callosity, and will be revealed by careful paring.

Progress
The verruca wart virus which is relatively harmless, and only affects a tiny area of the outer layer of skin, is often overlooked by the body's defences for many months. This is why warts last so long. Other viruses – like the chicken pox virus – spread throughout the body and rapidly stimulate its chemical and cellular defences, so that the illness clears in a week or two. Warts, on the other hand, last for months or years.

When the body finally notices the verrucae and mounts an offensive, they

shrivel up and disappear leaving no scar – as if by magic. This accounts for the 'success' of many wart charms. About 20 per cent clear in six months and the majority within two years. Once this immunity is learnt it is readily available to prevent re-infection. Sometimes, as a result of illness or the use of immuno-suppressive drugs, this immunity fades and warts recur, so that further treatment will be needed.

Treatment
There are no medicines or injections to kill the verruca virus in the way that antibiotics kill bacteria. The aims of local treatment are to destroy the skin cells containing the virus, and to stimulate the body's own defence mechanisms. It is thought that by killing the cells and the virus inside them, the body's defence mechanisms are more readily stimulated. Moreover, local treatment which kills the surface virus makes the verruca less infectious to others.

Local treatments that can be safely used in the home include paints, gels and soaks, which contain salicylic acid, formaldehyde or related drugs. Rubbing down the horny cap of a verruca relieves the pain of walking on it, and if this is not done a layer of dead, hard tissue builds up over the verruca, shielding it from the paint you have to put on.

If there are many small verrucae an alternative treatment is to soak the affected sole in a saucer of formalin in solution every night and morning for 10 minutes. Since formalin is drying and will cause normal skin to crack, the skin between the toes and around the verrucae should be protected with vaseline.

Salicylic acid can be used in the form of plasters, and stronger preparations like Chlorsal and Posalfilin are stronger preparations which can cause inflammation in normal skin, and should be used under medical supervision.

Any treatment may take up to three months. If the verruca persists, then treatment by freezing is indicated and this has to be given by a doctor or at a hospital. If this treatment is unavailable, the core of the verruca will have to be scooped out under anaesthetic, and the base and sides cauterized. The resulting hole is covered with a sterile dressing and kept dry until it heals. Verrucae are never cut out as this would leave a scar which might be persistently painful.

Prevention
Most verrucae are caught at swimming pools, since the skin barrier is weaker when it is wet. People with verrucae should therefore wear the thin rubber shoes that can be bought at swimming pools. In the home, a child can be prevented from spreading the virus by using his or her own towel and bath mat, and by covering the verruca with a waterproof plaster.

Treating a verruca

- Wash the foot in warm water, soaking it for at least five minutes
- Dry with your towel which no-one else must use
- Rub the hard skin away with an emery board or pumice stone
- Apply a drop of paint to the verruca with a pointed stick and let it dry
- Cover with a plaster
- Let your nurse or doctor check the verruca each month
- Continue treatment daily until they think it is cured
- See your doctor if the verruca becomes more painful

Vitiligo

**This condition causes pale patches to appear on the skin –
usually on the face and hands. Though these can be
unsightly, vitiligo is not a serious disease.**

Q **I have found white spots developing on my hands. Could this be vitiligo?**

A Yes, quite possibly. Vitiligo usually starts as small white spots on parts of the skin exposed to the sun, like the backs of the hands. If this is going to develop into vitiligo, the spots will enlarge and run into each other, perhaps over a few months. Vitiligo is not serious in itself, but it would be wise to consult your doctor about it.

Q **Can you inherit a tendency to vitiligo?**

A Yes. Though there is no definite pattern of inheritance, about 30 per cent of sufferers have a family history of the condition.

Q **Vitiligo appeared on my face and hands some years ago, and now I have been told my thyroid gland is failing. Could there be a connection?**

A Yes, vitiligo seems to be associated with all the auto-immune diseases of hormone glands. An auto-immune disease is where the body's immune system turns against its own tissue for some reason. Vitiligo can be associated with failure of the thyroid and of the adrenal glands, and it can also be associated with pernicious anaemia. More than one of these diseases can occur in the same patient, and the fact that all these problems tend to occur together as led to the suggestion that vitiligo too is an auto-immune disease. Most doctors believe this to be the case, though there is no definite proof.

Q **Does vitiligo get better of its own accord?**

A No. Unfortunately, this condition is unlikely to improve much, and once the pigment has been lost from the skin, there is little chance of it returning. On the credit side, though, the disease is no more than a slight cosmetic embarrassment, and the only problem is the increased risk of sunburn. Make-up can conceal any unsightly patches.

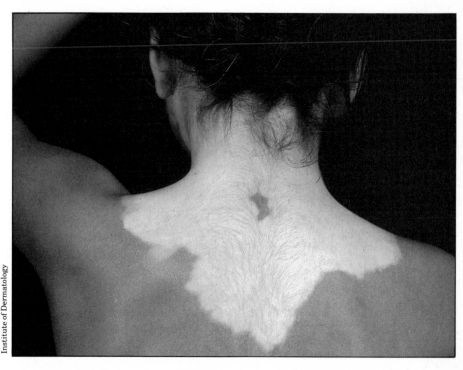

Institute of Dermatology

Vitiligo is a condition where areas of skin lose their pigment and show up as very pale patches. Fortunately, the disease has no serious consequences, although it can represent quite an important cosmetic problem.

Vitiligo is not uncommon – it may occur in as many as one per cent of the world's population. Although many people are affected, the extent of the problem is often very slight. It seems that women are more likely than men to seek advice about this essentially cosmetic disease, but in fact the overall incidence may be the same in both sexes.

Causes and symptoms
There are a number of suggestions as to the cause of vitiligo, but today most doctors favour the auto-immune theory. An auto-immune disease is one where the body's own immune system has turned against some part of the body; often the hormone-secreting glands are involved. As vitiligo is associated with auto-immune failure of hormone glands in many patients, it is thought that it too may be auto-immune, with antibodies being made to pigment-producing cells. However, there is no proof that such antibodies really occur.

The disease has only one symptom, the

Although not a serious threat to health, the patchy loss of pigment which is characteristic of vitiligo can cause a considerable amount of distress.

disorder of pigmentation that can be seen on the skin. Usually this is found in areas that are exposed to the sun, although eventually it may become more widespread. The depigmented areas start as little spots which then run together to produce enlarging areas of pale skin. Often the area bordering the depigmented skin is more heavily pigmented than usual.

About half the sufferers start losing pigment before the age of 20. The pale areas may develop quite quickly over the course of a few months, and then remain unchanged for years. Hair growing in pale areas may lose its colour in the course of time.

Treatment
There is no really satisfactory treatment. Drugs called psoralens have been tried, often combined with ultraviolet light, but although there may be some improvement, there is also a risk of toxicity. Steroid creams may be used on the affected patches, and this can produce a limited degree of improvement.

Vomiting

Q What is the best first aid treatment for vomiting?

A Avoid solid foods which are likely to make you vomit more. Take plenty of bland fluids – like water, diluted milk or squashes – but no fizzy or alcoholic drinks. If you find it impossible to keep the fluids down, suck ice cubes. A teaspoonful of bicarbonate of soda diluted in a teacup of water or milk can also be helpful. As you feel better, take soups and custards. Work back to your normal diet over three or four days.

Q I have often heard people say that they had almost vomited up their insides. Can this really happen?

A No. This is really just a figure of speech and rather colourfully describes a severe bout. Vomiting – especially if caused by food poisoning or severe gastro-enteritis – can be extremely unpleasant and distressing. But no matter how violently or persistently you vomit, there is no possibility at all that you will damage your internal organs.

Q Is it necessary always to see your doctor about vomiting?

A No. In the great majority of cases vomiting only lasts for a day or two and usually has a fairly obvious cause. However, if you get regular bouts of vomiting, or if it is accompanied by abdominal pain, or if you have recently had a knock on the head, or there is a possibility that you may be pregnant, then you should certainly arrange to see your doctor. Go to your doctor immediately if the vomit contains blood.

Q I have had repeated vomiting bouts for some time now, and have been persuaded to go and have tests. But I am rather worried; what is involved?

A After initial examination by your doctor, you may be sent for an X-ray examination of your stomach. A visit to a specialist may be required, and he may take a direct look in your stomach with an endoscope. The tests are quite simple and should cause you no pain.

Accompanied by nausea, giddiness and faintness, vomiting is an exhausting and unpleasant experience. But it is a mechanism of survival that warns us of danger.

Vomiting refers to the forceful ejection of the contents of the stomach through the mouth. Commonly known as 'being sick' or 'throwing up', it is an unpleasant and often exhausting experience, and can be caused by a number of conditions.

Mechanism
The actual mechanism behind the ejection of food is quite straightforward. At the onset of vomiting, the pylorus – a muscular valve through which food normally passes from the stomach into the intestines – closes. The waves of stomach contractions which normally push food downwards into the intestines go into reverse, causing pressure inside the stomach to build up until the contents burst out through the mouth.

There are three main areas of the body which, when stimulated, can bring about vomiting; although the mechanism is the same in each case, the causes are very different.

Stomach irritation
Irritation of the stomach lining is the most common cause of vomiting. This can be brought on by a surprising variety of conditions including gastritis, gastro-enteritis (see pp 150-51), peritonitis and appendicitis (see pp 31-33) and ulcers (see pp 150-51); tonsillitis can also cause vomiting in young children. These types of complaint are associated with viral infections and inflammation, and should be treated as soon as possible by your doctor.

The commonest cause of stomach irritation is eating or drinking to excess, or taking in contaminated or impure food. The body actually protects itself against potentially harmful substances and does its best to expel what it has recognized as dangerous. The bout of vomiting is usually short-lived, lasting a day or two, and is rarely serious.

Putting fingers down the back of the throat will also cause vomiting, and use is made of this reflex action in trying to make people empty their stomach of certain poisonous substances that have been swallowed. The function of this reflex is to protect the body from swallowing anything that is unsuitable.

The ears and motion sickness
Motion sickness is another common cause of vomiting. This results from contrasting information reaching the brain from the various different organs of balance. At the centre of this are the semicircular canals in the ear. If what we see conflicts with the information from these canals and the brain is not able to

For some, sea travel has always been a challenge! This 19th-century caricature of the wretched passengers on a packet ship illustrates a hazard still true today.

Mary Evans Picture Library

The mechanism of vomiting

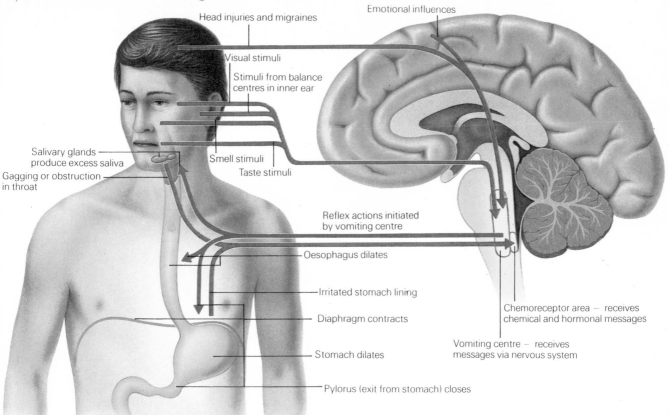

Head injuries and migraines

Emotional influences

Visual stimuli

Stimuli from balance centres in inner ear

Salivary glands produce excess saliva

Smell stimuli

Gagging or obstruction in throat

Taste stimuli

Reflex actions initiated by vomiting centre

Oesophagus dilates

Irritated stomach lining

Diaphragm contracts

Chemoreceptor area — receives chemical and hormonal messages

Stomach dilates

Vomiting centre — receives messages via nervous system

Pylorus (exit from stomach) closes

---

interpret the two, then it triggers off impulses to the vomiting centre in the brain. This apparent 'warning' action results in nausea and vomiting.

Poor travellers are well aware of this problem, but it can also afflict sufferers of Menière's (inner ear) disease, or syndrome, in which the organs of hearing and balance are affected.

The brain
A blow to the head – it doesn't even have to be a hard blow – can be the cause of vomiting, and this usually indicates the likelihood of serious bleeding inside the skull. The desire to vomit usually occurs some time after the blow – often when one has completely forgotten about the injury, even a couple of days later – and indicates a damaged blood vessel that has allowed pressure to accumulate on the brain and around the vomiting centre. This must be treated as soon as possible, as there is a very real danger that the person can slip into a coma.

Morning sickness
Vomiting also frequently occurs in pregnancy. Known as 'morning sickness', this form of vomiting is not fully understood, but it is believed that it is related to the changing level of hormones in the blood during early pregnancy. In a few women, the vomiting is persistent and severe and may even necessitate a spell in hospital.

Repeated vomiting
Repeated bouts of vomiting are often regarded as a symptom of a serious disorder and should be brought to your doctor's attention immediately.

What is brought up in the vomit is also important. It will usually consist of the

Vomiting is a reflex action. Nerve impulses from around the body carry messages – of danger, irritation or even confusion – to the vomiting centre in the brain-stem. Toxic agents or hormonal changes act upon the chemoreceptor area nearby, and this also stimulates the vomiting centre. At the same time, impulses passing to the cortex produce feelings of nausea. When the vomiting threshold is passed, the vomiting centre initiates a number of physical changes that result in the ejection of the stomach's contents through the mouth.

last meal you have had or may be almost entirely yellow-green, bitter bile. However, if it contains any sign of blood, then the implications are very serious and you should get medical advice straight away. The blood may look like dark coffee beans, as it will have congealed in the stomach well before the vomiting started.

Treatment
Where vomiting has taken on a repetitive nature, or if it is accompanied by fever and general malaise, then the condition must be diagnosed by the doctor, and the root cause treated.

When someone has been sick, avoid giving solid foods; diluted milk, and plenty of water is fine until the person feels able to return to a normal diet.

467

Wax in the ear

Q I've always used cotton buds to clean my ears, but my doctor told me this could be harmful. Why is this?

A Cleaning the internal parts of the ear is completely unnecessary because the ear has its own self-cleaning mechanism. Cotton wool buds can cause minute abrasions of the skin and expose the deeper layers of bacteria.

By using a bud, you also interfere with the natural cleaning process by pushing wax deeper into the ear canal, causing blockage and deafness. Should it be necessary for a doctor to examine your ears, the impacted wax will block the view of the ear-drum and delay diagnosis.

Q Is it possible to become deaf from ear-wax?

A Yes. Ear-wax can cause temporary deafness. A small amount of wax in the ear canal does no harm. However if the canal is blocked completely over a period of time, or if the wax swells suddenly due to water entering the ear canal, a moderate degree of hearing loss, discomfort and pain may result.

Q Do some people have more wax in their ears than others?

A Yes. Some people, especially those who work in a very dusty environment, or who have eczema of the ear skin, profuse hair growth in the ears or infections of the canal skin, are more likely to have a build-up of excess ear-wax.

Q Does having your ears syringed hurt at all?

A Ear syringeing carried out by skilled medical personnel should be free from pain and discomfort – but no-one would say that it was an enjoyable experience.

Q Is it safe to attempt to syringe your own ears?

A No. If you find that your ears are blocked or you have some other complaint, consult your doctor. Hearing is very precious and any attempt to remove wax by yourself could be dangerous.

Although unsightly to look at, ear-wax does have a useful function: to provide a barrier against infection. The only time it needs to be dealt with is when it accumulates – and then medical help will be needed.

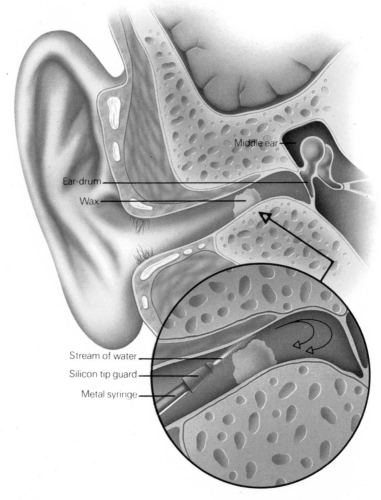

Middle ear

Ear-drum

Wax

Stream of water

Silicon tip guard

Metal syringe

Richard Barry

Ear-wax or cerumen consists of a mixture of the oil secretions of the modified sweat glands situated in the outer third of the ear canal, scales from the skin and dust particles. It is sticky, water-resistant and forms a natural barrier against infection.

Although ear-wax is harmless, and is usually removed by the ear's self-cleaning mechanism, it may occasionally accumulate, causing temporary deafness. Medical treatment should be sought when this occurs.

Problems

In normal circumstances, wax does not accumulate in the ears, as it is continually being moved outwards by the movement of the jaw-bones and the natural shedding of the skin.

To remove wax that has become lodged in the ear, a syringe is carefully inserted into the ear canal and a jet of warm water is sprayed in, softening the wax. Then the ear is thoroughly cleaned and dried.

However some people do produce more ear-wax than others. An accumulation is more likely to occur in people employed in dusty occupations, or those who have excess hair in their ears, or those who have an inflammation of the skin or scalp.

Accumulated wax may cause a variety of symptoms, the chief one being temporary deafness. The wax may become impacted at the narrowest part of the ear canal by unskilled attempts to remove it with matches, hairpins, cotton wool buds or other implements. Accumulated wax

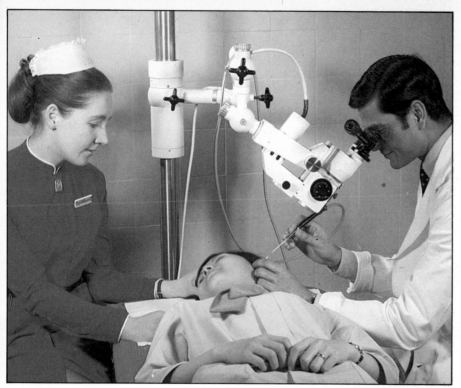

his head turned to one side. Using a metal or plastic speculum, the specialist examines the ear with a microscope. Wax, any foreign body or debris can then be removed with fine forceps. But if there is a discharge of soft wax, then this can be aspirated (drawn out) using a suction tube which is attached to a vacuum pump.

Like most procedures, suction clearance is very safe in experienced hands, and is a most satisfactory way of clearing accumulated wax from the ears.

The warning against trying to clear the wax out of your ears yourself should, however, be reiterated. Far too much damage is done by people poking about with little sticks or hairpins and the like. In particular, never use them on babies. If you cannot remove what you can see at the opening of the ear, and wipe it easily, leave it alone.

may cause irritation and noises in the ear, but rarely pain.

Sudden deafness together with a feeling of pressure may occur after taking a swim or shower: this is due to water entering the ear and causing the wax to swell. Attempts to clear the ears will only push the wax deeper into the ear canal, and this will cause pain, noises in the ear or, more rarely, dizziness.

Treatment
Impacted wax is one of the commonest conditions seen in a doctor's surgery. A doctor can remove the wax safely by picking it out with very fine forceps or by a blunt hook under direct vision.

Alternatively, the wax can be removed by syringeing the ears. This is a safe procedure in experienced hands. Before syringeing, the doctor may advise the patient to put drops such as bicarbonate of soda in solution, warm olive oil or a wax solvent in the ears to soften the wax and make it easier to syringe.

Syringeing is a painless procedure. A jet of warm water is forced into the ear canal without touching the skin with the syringe's metal tip. The ear is then carefully cleaned and dried. Relief from deafness is immediate and dramatic. Special care and gentleness is required when syringeing a child's ears. If the child is reluctant or unco-operative, it may be better to have the wax removed under anaesthesia.

If the patient has a previous history of ear trouble or has had an operation on his or her ears, there may be perforation of the ear-drum. The normal drum is not easily ruptured, but where there has been

With the suction clearance method, the ear is examined under a magnifying microscope with the aid of a plastic or metal speculum. Wax, a foreign body or debris may either be removed with a fine forceps, or aspirated by a suction tube attached to a vacuum pump.

a perforation which has healed, the scar tissue is vulnerable to injury and great care must be taken during syringeing.

Where wax has accumulated in large amounts and has become solid, it should be removed by a specialist in hospital. The procedure is carried out by a suction machine, together with an operating microscope that provides high magnification and powerful illumination. The patient lies on his back on a couch, with

---

General points
● Never insert 'hard objects like safety pins, matches or paper-clips into your ears as a means of cleaning them; you could cause injury
● If you have inflamed ears or sensitive skin, do not allow water to enter your ears. When bathing or washing your hair, protect your ears by placing a plug of cotton wool covered with vaseline in the opening of the ear canal
● If you have dry skin that is causing itching in your ears, regular use of a few drops of warm olive oil once a week helps to keep the skin soft and moist and will ease the itching
● Always seek medical attention when you have an ear complaint: never try to treat it yourself

---

Care of the ears

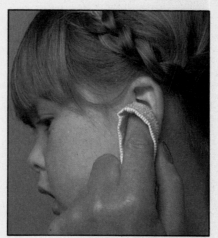

Daily care
● Wash the outer part of your ears with soap and water, and dry them gently with a soft towel. Do not rub the skin
● Should water enter your ears, hold the ear lobe and shake it gently after turning your head sideways. Usually the water will run out
● If water is trapped in your ears and the wax expands and causes discomfort, do not try to remove it yourself. Consult your doctor
● If removal of wax is necessary, your doctor is the expert, not you. Remember that one famous specialist warned patients 'never to put anything smaller than your elbow in your ears'.

Whooping cough

Q Do most doctors now advise immunization against whooping cough?

A Yes, providing there is no history of convulsions or brain damage in you or your children, it has been shown that the risks of severe illness from whooping cough are greater than from the vaccine.

Q Why is whooping cough such a dangerous illness in babies and small children?

A Children who have whooping cough produce very thick, sticky mucus in the air passages to the lungs, which can prevent air getting to the lungs unless it is coughed away. Small children are sometimes too weak to cough up this sticky plug and their lungs get blocked; the babies can suffer lack of oxygen, which causes brain damage. They are also likely to get pneumonia on top of whooping cough.

Q Does a baby get natural immunity to whooping cough from its mother?

A No. Pertussis antibodies, or the cells in the blood that fight the whooping cough infection do not seem to pass across the placenta, so that babies are born without any protection against whooping cough. They can get some immunity, if they are breast fed, from the colostrum (the breast 'milk' in the first days after birth). But it is such a dangerous illness in small babies that if they come into contact with it they must immediately be given antibiotics.

Q My three-year-old son has just recovered from whooping cough, but he still has the whoop. How long will this last?

A It varies, but it can be as long as three or four months before it disappears. Also, every time he has a cold the whoop may get worse – but don't worry, it's not another attack of whooping cough. Incidentally, the Chinese call it 'the hundred day cough' because it can drag on for so long. But, of course, some of the whoops may be habit.

Highly infectious and very distressing for its sufferers, whooping cough can be one of childhood's most dangerous illnesses. However, it can be effectively prevented by immunization in infancy.

Whooping cough, or pertussis as it is medically known, is a highly infectious bacterial disease caused by Bordetella pertussis. Anybody who has neither had, nor been immunized against whooping cough, can catch it. The disease is spread by droplets of bacteria in the air. The bacteria settle in the mucous lining of the respiratory tract (lungs and throat), causing inflammation and production of a thick sticky mucus.

Incidence of whooping cough

Children between one and four years old are most susceptible, although since immunization, more adolescents and adults are the source of the disease. The death rate is highest in babies less than one year old, and particularly under four months. Epidemics tend to occur in three-year cycles, starting in January and peaking in the spring, like many other respiratory infections.

An attack of whooping cough confers life-long protection. Unlike many other infectious diseases, protection does not seem to be transferred to babies from the mother, so they are susceptible from birth. Some immunity is transferred to a breast-fed baby in the colostrum (the fluid secreted from the mother's breasts for the first few days after giving birth).

Since the introduction of immunization against whooping cough there has been a fall in both incidence and deaths, but immunization is neither complete nor permanent, and some adults who were immunized as children do still catch whooping cough, although it is usually a mild attack with few complications.

Whooping cough immunization carries a minimal risk of complications – so a parent is asked to sign a standard form consenting to the vaccination and exonerating the doctor who gives it from responsibility.

Mike Abrahams/Network

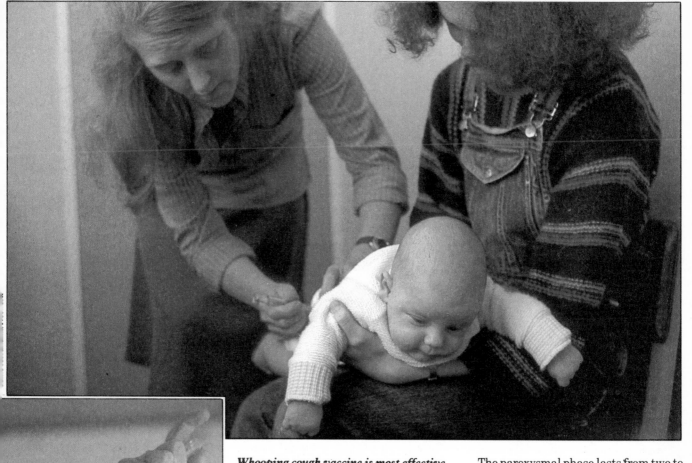

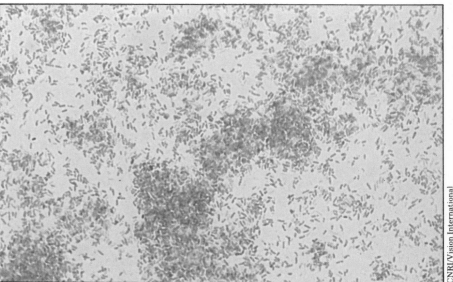

Whooping cough vaccine is most effective when given as part of a triple vaccine (left), the other two being diphtheria and tetanus. This three-month-old baby is receiving the first of three doses. In the 48 hours following a vaccination a baby may suffer a slight reaction and become feverish or irritable. Redness or swelling often occurs at the site of the injection, but will soon settle down, leaving a small lump which disappears in a month or two.

Course of the illness

The incubation period lasts 6–20 days from contact, with 7 days as an average. The patient is infectious from the catarrhal phase for about four weeks, and should be isolated for a month or until the cough has stopped. In particular, children under one year should be kept away from those with the condition.

The illness can be divided into three distinct stages: the catarrhal phase, the paroxysmal phase and the convalescent phase. The catarrhal phase lasts one or two weeks. Initially the symptoms are rather like a cold: runny nose; red, runny eyes; a slight cough and temperature.

The organism Bordetella pertussis causes whooping cough and is used to make the vaccine. This works by stimulating the body to produce antibodies to resist the infection.

The paroxysmal phase lasts from two to four or more weeks, and in this stage there are episodes of coughing, becoming increasingly worse and more frequent – up to around 40 bouts a day. The bouts consist of 5-10 repetitive coughs while breathing out, followed by a sudden effort to breathe in, which in older children produces the characteristic 'whoop'. The face goes red or blue, the eyes bulge, the tongue sticks out, both eyes and nose run

CNRI/Vision International

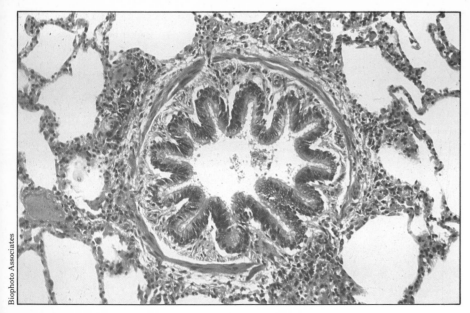

Biophoto Associates

Complications.

Most of the deaths from whooping cough are caused by complications, such as pneumonia. Usually pneumonia is not due to pertussis bacteria, but to other invading bacteria, which enter the affected lungs. Plugs of mucus may block off the bronchi (the tubes leading the air from the throat to the lungs) and cause the lung to collapse; then it may become infected by bacteria. Sometimes the lung collapse is permanent.

Ear infections frequently occur at the same time. The lack of oxygen to the brain during a severe coughing spell can cause convulsions or loss of consciousness. The pertussis bacteria can also affect the brain tissues, causing inflammation. Haemorrhage or bleeding can occur into the brain, or from the nose. Sometimes the pressure of coughing can cause part of the intestines (the rectum) to come out of the patient's anus. Often babies cannot keep down enough fluid and food and become dehydrated. About 10 per cent of children require hospital admission.

and the veins in the neck become more obvious. Episodes of this coughing occur until the patient manages to dislodge the plug of mucus. During this time, in severe attacks, young children may lack oxygen and stop breathing or have a convulsion. At the end of the coughing bout the child will vomit. The vomiting is really more characteristic of whooping cough than the whoop. These episodes are extremely exhausting and infants become tired and lose weight.

Attacks can be triggered by movement, yawning, sneezing, eating, drinking or even by thinking about them. In between attacks, the patient appears relatively well.

During convalescence the paroxysmal cough, whoop and vomit gradually subside although the cough and whoop may last for many weeks or months – and often recur if the child catches a cold or throat infection.

Whooping cough particularly affects the bronchioles – the tubes that carry air to the lungs (seen here in cross section).

Diagnosis

The diagnosis is usually made on the clinical symptoms, but in older children and adults with a milder attack this can be difficult. The best method is to take a swab from the back of the nose and do a culture (inoculate the material into a special substance on which the bacteria can grow so that a diagnosis can be made). Blood tests are not very helpful, though the number of lymphocytes (a type of defensive blood cell) may be very high, which aids diagnosis. Otherwise, two samples of blood are needed, at the beginning and end of the illness, to show a rise in pertussis antibodies during that time; if the sample is not taken early enough, it won't show a large enough rise to make the diagnosis.

A child with whooping cough should be kept warm at all times. Your doctor may prescribe antibiotics which will make the child less infectious to others. The most trying period is the paroxysmal phase when coughing is most severe and persistent. This can last up to four weeks, and subsides over the following months until recovery is complete.

Treatment

Antibiotics are not helpful once the illness has begun, but if the antibiotic erythromycin is given to a child who has been in contact with the disease, *before* any symptoms appear, the severity of the illness may be reduced. The drug is given to children who have whooping cough as it makes these children less infectious to others. Other treatment is symptomatic: avoiding stimuli which cause coughing; a warm room, especially at night; small frequent drinks and meals, and no rushing about. Children who go blue during coughing bouts or cannot keep down fluid need hospital admission for oxygen, therapy, suction to remove mucous plugs, and replacement of fluids either by a tube through the nose into the stomach, or by injection into a vein. Some doctors give mild sedatives to reduce coughing spells.

Prevention

Lifelong prevention only occurs after an attack of whooping cough, so that pertussis can only be prevented by active immunization with the pertussis vaccine.

The vaccine consists of a suspension of killed organisms of Bordetella pertussis. They stimulate the body to produce antibodies without actually giving rise to an attack of whooping cough.

The vaccine has to be given in three doses to give about 95 per cent protection against the disease. The vaccine is more effective if given at the same time as diphtheria and tetanus vaccine – hence the triple vaccine of diphtheria, tetanus

Daily Telegraph Colour Library

Q My daughter had whooping cough last winter and since then has had a series of coughs and colds. Does this mean that the illness has weakened her resistance to infection?

A No. It's probably just bad luck. However, you should ask your doctor to check her over as sometimes part of the lung collapses after whooping cough and this may be her problem. I'm sure she'll start to pick up again in the summer.

Q Is croup the same as whooping cough?

A No – croup arises from a viral infection which causes swelling of the larynx (voice box) so that when a child breathes in there is rather a harsh bark. It's not usually associated with a paroxysmal cough or vomiting and gets better in a few days.

Q My granddaughter has a bad cough which sounds very much like a whoop and she sometimes retches at the end of a coughing fit. Could this be whooping cough?

A Yes, it might be. Although sometimes the phlegm in a bad cough can cause vomiting it rarely causes a whoop. Take her to your doctor and keep her away from other children, particularly babies, until you know for sure.

Q Is it possible to get whooping cough even after immunization?

A Yes, it is, though it's a much milder disease with few complications. It's more likely to occur in teenagers and adults who were immunized as babies than in children.

Q My child has had fits and the doctor won't give her whooping cough vaccine. Should she also not have had the tetanus and diphtheria jab?

A No, there is no evidence at all that the tetanus and diphtheria vaccine causes any neurological problems and it is very important that she should have these and the polio vaccine which is usually given at the same time.

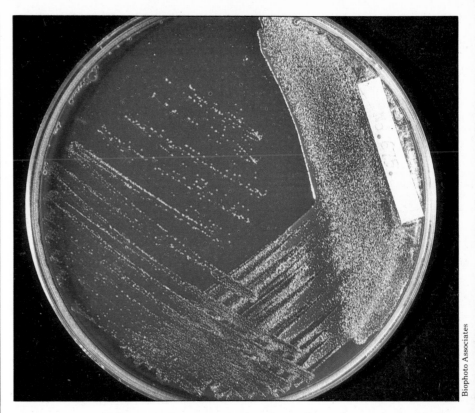

Biophoto Associates

Whooping cough is diagnosed by taking a swab from the patient's nose, and using it to prepare a bacterial culture. The organism can thus be accurately identified.

and pertussis given to most infants. The vaccine is usually first given at three months old, then two months later and six months after that.

When not to vaccinate
Because of the risk of complications, pertussis vaccine should not be given to any child who has a temperature or feverish illness; has had convulsions or whose parents or brothers and/or sisters have had convulsions; has late development; or has a known disorder of the central nervous system. If there is any severe local or general reaction such as a very high temperature, confusion, odd behaviour or a convulsion after the first immunization, pertussis vaccine should be left out of subsequent vaccinations.

Contrary to former beliefs, hay fever and eczema in the family are not contra-indications to having the vaccine.

Side-effects of vaccination
Following vaccination either with pertussis alone or with the triple vaccine, there may be a mild feverish illness over the next 48 hours, or your baby may just be a bit miserable; older children may complain of a headache. There is often redness and swelling at the site of the injection which usually settles after a few

days, a small firm lump may be felt for a couple of months afterwards.

Serious complications generally occur in the first week, usually in the first 72 hours; these may be convulsions, often associated with a high temperature, or, extremely rarely, encephalitis which may lead to permanent brain damage. Complications can be kept to a minimum by strictly keeping to the rules concerning which children should and should not have the vaccine.

Either your own doctor or the children's clinic doctor or nurse may give pertussis vaccine. They will know your medical history, but in addition, will ask you about any family history of convulsions or brain damage. They know the risks, both of catching whooping cough and of the complications of the vaccine, and will discuss any worries with you.

The immunization controversy
Before 1957, when whooping cough vaccine was recommended for most children, there were about 100,000 cases per year, and about one child in each thousand died. The number of cases and the number of deaths fell rapidly until in 1967 the annual rate had fallen to only about 10,000 cases. At this stage about 80 per cent of children were being vaccinated. Then in 1974 some doctors produced a report which showed that following whooping cough vaccine, some children had convulsions or encephalitis and developed permanent brain damage.

473

The doctors could not, however, prove whether this occurred because of the vaccine, or whether the children might have developed this illness anyhow. The media became interested and following the publicity there was a vaccine scare, when doctors and parents alike turned against pertussis vaccine. As a result, in 1978 and 1979 there occurred the largest epidemic of whooping cough in 20 years, with 66,000 cases in 1978. The main peaks of the disease occurred in areas where fewer vaccinations were given.

The risk of brain damage

Two committees were set up to make an investigation into whether pertussis immunization could cause convulsion and brain damage, or whether these things occurred by chance.

The committees examined children who were and were not immunized from 1976 to 1979. What they found was that childen were between two and five times more likely to have an acute neurological disorder (convulsions or encephalitis) in the few days after the pertussis vaccination than at any other time. This was not so if they had only the diphtheria and tetanus injections. The risk of a serious neurological disorder after pertussis vaccination is one in 110,000 and permanent brain damage one in 310,000. If every child has a full course of three injections this gives a risk of one in 100,000 for each child.

The committees also showed that the children most at risk of developing serious neurological disorders are those who have any of the contra-indications given above. They showed that pertussis

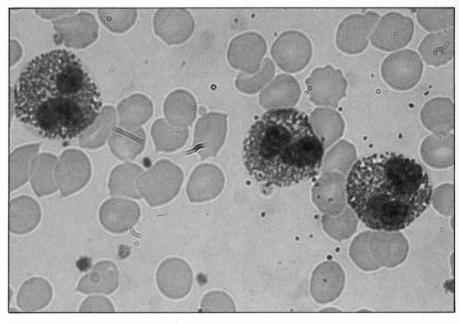

vaccine does prevent whooping cough in children, and will do so in a community, providing that about 80 per cent of children are immunized.

Finally, the committees also showed that whooping cough is an extremely unpleasant disease, and that during the 1976–79 period, for the two deaths from pertussis immunization, there were 28 deaths from whooping cough, with 5,000 hospital admissions, 200 cases of pneumonia and 83 cases of convulsions, caused by the illness.

In Britain we are still in the throes of a whooping cough epidemic, with the number of cases regularly increasing. The only effective way of combating the

A mild attack of whooping cough may be difficult to diagnose. In this case, raised level of lymphocytes (the large stained cells) in a blood sample, may be a useful aid in identifying the illness.

illness is by ensuring that children are vaccinated against it. Thus it is important to remember that a child runs a far greater risk from catching the illness itself than from being immunized and that doctors take great care to identify children who are at risk from the vaccine.

It is hoped that in the future safer vaccines will be developed which will also confer an even greater immunity.

Incidence of whooping cough in England and Wales

After the introduction of vaccination, the number of cases of whooping cough dropped dramatically. But there has recently been an epidemic due to the vaccine controversy, although, compared to the disease the vaccine is relatively safe.

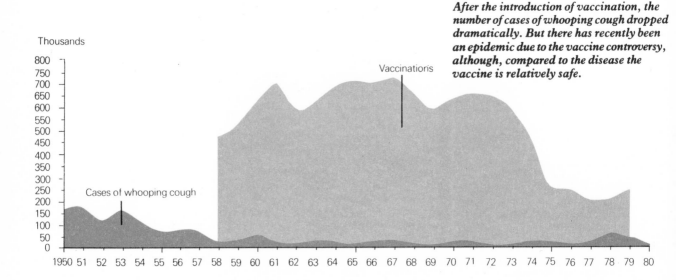

First Aid Handbook

Accidents will happen. And when they do – whether it is in the home, at work or on the road – a good first aider is invaluable. He or she can minimize the effects, ease pain and in severe cases even save lives.

This section will give you all the basic information that you need to deal with the more common emergencies. It gives a quick and easy step-by-step guide to emergency first aid. You will, of course, be able to find very detailed background information in the previous pages of *First Aid and Family Health* by looking up relevant headings in the index.

The aims of all first aid are to keep the patient alive, protect him or her from further damage and to be as reassuring as possible. In short, the first aider's task is to safeguard the victim until the doctor or nurse arrives to take over.

First, you should ensure that the patient is still breathing and treat if necessary. Then you should staunch any bleeding and treat for unconsciousness. Next you need to protect the patient by immobilizing fractures, treating burns, dressing wounds and, finally, minimizing shock. Throughout this process you need to be comforting.

Always make sure that you have an accessible record of your doctor's telephone number, but never hesitate to call the emergency services – it is always better to ring for an ambulance than drive a patient yourself.

Artificial respiration

- **Establish that breathing has stopped**
- **Clear mouth and hold head back**
- **Pinch patient's nose and take a deep breath**
- **Place mouth over patient's and breathe into patient**
- **Repeat this procedure, regulating your puffs by the rise and fall of the patient's chest**

Take note

● In the case of a young child or baby, cover both the mouth and nose when giving artificial respiration. Be careful not to blow too hard – just enough to raise the child's chest. You will need to give about 20 puffs a minute

● If the mouth is injured and you cannot give mouth-to-mouth resuscitation, hold the mouth firmly shut by applying pressure underneath the chin. Give artificial respiration through the patient's nose

● If the treatment is interrupted, for example if the patient vomits, restart by giving four quick breaths. This gives an immediate supply of oxygen

● As an alternative to opening the patient's mouth by pulling the chin down, you may prefer to place a hand under the neck and raise it slightly. This usually makes the mouth fall open of its own accord

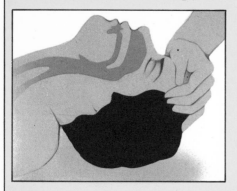

1 To ensure the tongue does not block the throat, place hand on forehead and tip patient's head right back

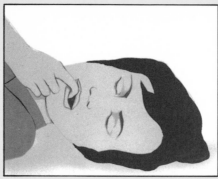

2 Turn head to one side. Using your forefinger, sweep around mouth and scoop out any blockages. Tip head back again

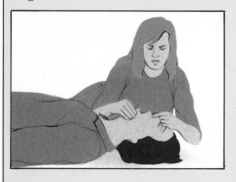

3 If the mouth is closed, grasp chin and pull open gently. Pinch the nose firmly shut and take a deep breath

4 Place your mouth over patient's, ensuring a firm seal. Give four quick breaths in rapid succession

Always check if the victim is still breathing before giving artificial respiration. One way to establish this is by holding a pair of spectacles in front of his mouth – if the glass mists over, then breathing continues. Cover the patient as quickly as possible with a blanket or an overcoat, to prevent heat loss. The covering should be loose though, with the chest clearly visible, so that you can see whether or not the patient is breathing.

5 Remove mouth, but keep head close. You should feel and hear air leaving patient's mouth and the chest will sink. Now give a single breath, just hard enough to raise chest. Continue, giving breaths at normal breathing speed until breathing resumes

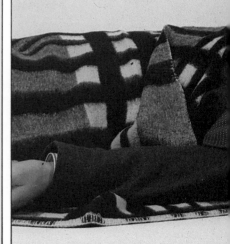

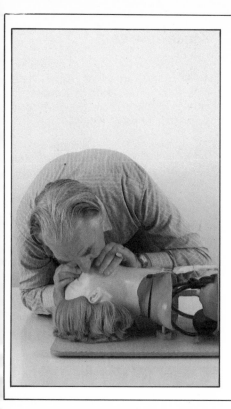

Make sure you . . .

DO keep fingers and hands clear of the patient's lips and neck at all times; they could obstruct breathing

DON'T blow too hard: just raise patient's chest visibly; otherwise you may damage lung tissue

DON'T try to drain water or fluid from the lungs of a person who is feared drowned. The victim's first need is for oxygen and air will bubble through liquid in the windpipe

DON'T practise on a person who is breathing normally. If you enrol in a first aid class, there will be life-like manikins provided

DON'T worry if the person vomits as this is quite common. Stop your breathing for long enough to turn his head and clear the mouth

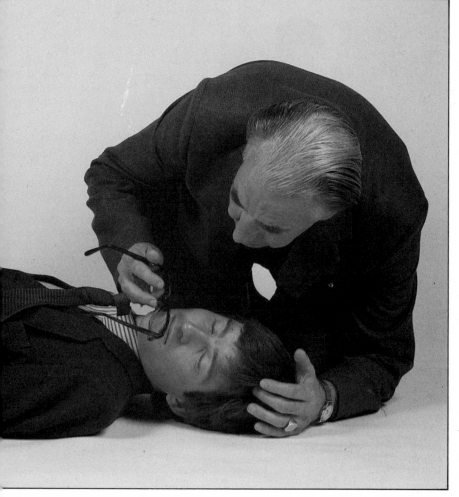

What next?

1. Send any onlookers for medical aid. Do not allow anyone to crowd around and interfere with first aid treatment being given

2. Ease any tight clothing. If possible, the patient should be lightly and loosely covered to prevent heat loss, but the contour of the chest should still be clearly visible

3. Sometimes it is enough to tilt the head back. The patient may have stopped breathing because of a simple blockage and holding the head back may free the airway. If this is the case, the patient will probably start to gasp for breath. He should be placed in the recovery position and precautions should be taken to minimize shock

4. Throughout first aid treatment, keep checking that the head is tilted right back and the nose firmly pinched. It is easy to overlook these things if you are concentrating on giving artificial respiration

5. Every three minutes or so, you may interrupt the treatment to see if the patient has started to breathe naturally. This also has the advantage of giving you a short break. If breathing has not resumed begin giving artificial respiration again, starting with four quick breaths and then resuming single puffs. If breathing has started, keep the head well back and watch carefully in case breathing stops again. Once respiration is steady treat as for unconsciousness (see page 498).

6. Continue giving artificial respiration until breathing starts spontaneously or medical help arrives and can take over. People have been known to survive up to eight hours after treatment began, so don't give up

7. If the patient's heartbeat has stopped, heart compression will have to be used to get it going again. The only acceptable indication of a stopped heart is the complete lack of a pulse. Heart compression is a difficult technique to learn and apply, so try to attend a first aid course to supplement the information given in this issue

Bites and stings

- **All bites and stings need different treatment**
- **Animal bites need to be washed thoroughly**
- **Adder bites must be bandaged tightly**
- **Bee stings have to be removed**
- **Jellyfish stings need to have tentacles removed**

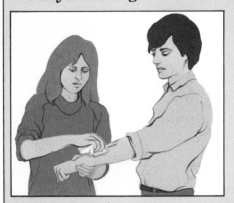

1 Animal bites should be treated like ordinary wounds (see page 500) except that the wound itself should be washed. Consult a doctor to check for infection

2 In a case of adder bite, wipe venom from wound; bandage pad on tightly so area is under firm pressure. Keep patient absolutely still, preferably lying down

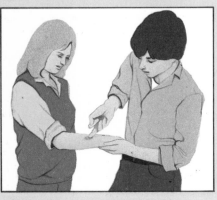

3 Bee stings are usually left in the wound and continue to pump in venom after the insect has gone. Scrape the sting out sideways with a fingernail or knife

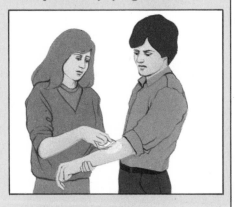

4 Sometimes jellyfish tentacles stick to the skin. Wash with sea water, remove tentacles left with a covered hand. Smooth on calamine lotion. Seek medical aid

Make sure you . . .

DO remember to clean any bite or sting with clean, warm water and, if possible, soap that does not contain perfume or detergent. You can then apply a mild antiseptic

DO reassure the victim of an adder bite. People are often unnecessarily frightened by the idea of snake venom; it may help to remind them that many people have been bitten by far more venomous snakes and they lived to tell the tale. If you have been bitten by a snake in a foreign country, try and remember what it looked like: a good description will save a great deal of medical time

DO apply calamine lotion or cream to insect bites or stings, including those from gnats and fleas. Antihistamine cream is no longer recommended for home use

DO get medical help quickly in the following instances:
1. Stings inside the mouth
2. Patients known to be allergic
3. Signs of shock – pallor, sweating, collapse and breathing difficulties
4. Stinging by swarms of insects

DON'T apply vinegar to wasp stings or ammonia to bee stings, these are no longer considered useful remedies

DON'T use tweezers to try and remove a bee sting, you will put pressure on the sting itself and cause it to release more venom into the wound. Use fingernail or knife blade

DON'T treat adder bites by cutting the area, trying to suck out the venom or by applying a tourniquet. These treatments are now considered dangerous

Prickly plants

- Stings from plants like hogweed and nettle should be washed with cool water. Calamine cream or lotion may help to relieve the discomfort

- Plants with prickles and thorns do not strictly sting, but they do break the skin surface and this can lead to infection, such as tetanus. Visible thorns should be pulled out with fine tweezers. But if they are deeply embedded, apply a small dressing and see a doctor or nurse who will remove the thorns for you

- Cacti can leave hundreds of fine needles' embedded in the skin. These are very difficult to pull out and most uncomfortable to leave in. Take a sticky plaster or piece of sellotape and press it on to the prickled area. As you remove the sticky surface it will take the prickles with it

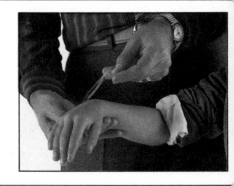

Take note

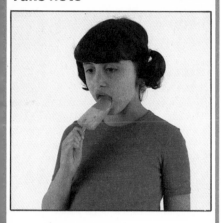

● In the case of a sting inside the mouth, medical aid should be sought immediately. The mouth may swell and breathing can be seriously impaired as a result. While you are waiting for help, swelling can be minimized by using cold mouthwashes, sucking ice cubes or even eating ice lollies

● The risk of infection is high with any animal bite so it is always wise to consult a doctor. This is obviously particularly important if there is even the slightest risk of rabies. If the attacking animal was thought to be rabid or you are not in Great Britain, scrub the wound to bleeding point and report to the nearest hospital immediately

● If jellyfish tentacles adhere to a sting, cover with vinegar or flour, if available; otherwise wet sand will be a reasonable alternative. Using the flat of a knife blade, scrape the sand off the area and wash with salt water

● If you cannot get a bee sting out using your fingernail or knife blade edge you can use a sterilized needle or pin. Hold the pointed end in the blue part of the flame from a lighter or match; this will sterilize the point

● Most poisonous fish live in quite warm seas, but there are two small stinging fish that bury themselves in the sand around the European coast. They are called the Greater and Lesser Weever and they have poison glands at the base of their fins. The poison has a similar effect to snake venom, causing quite severe pain and inflammation. If you think that you have stood on one of these fish or handled one when you were fishing you should consult a doctor. The fish are a yellow-brown colour with dark streaks

What next?

1. Make sure that the patient does not scratch the affected area. The irritation and itchiness can be very annoying, but scratching or rubbing often only makes it more intolerable. It also helps to spread the venom and it certainly increases the chances of developing an infection. Calamine lotion or cream can help to reduce any irritation

2. Any pain resulting from bites and stings usually resolves itself quite quickly and naturally within the following hour or two. If you do want to take some sort of painkiller, aspirin or paracetamol may speed up the relief of pain. The pain caused by adder bites tends to get progressively worse for some time after the incident, so it is sensible to give the patient some pain-killing tablets immediately

3. The risk of infection is always high, particularly with bites. If the injured area becomes red, swollen or more painful over the next couple of days, the doctor should be consulted.

It is always sensible to visit a doctor in the case of animal and snake bites, when infections or other complications are particularly likely

4. Shock can be caused by any form of bite or sting, no matter how minor. It is especially likely if the victim is elderly or very young, but any patient may suffer an allergic reaction to the venom, or just be very frightened. Always treat as for shock (see page 496). Send for medical help as quickly as possible, but do not leave the patient alone. Keep the affected area absolutely still, as if it were fractured

5. All plant and animal poisons are very different, but they all contain a substance called histamine, which can produce symptoms that vary from rashes to serious breathing difficulties. In the more severe instances, doctors may administer an antihistamine either by tablet or injection. This helps to counteract the effects of the poison

A party in a lush garden is one of the delights of childhood. But it is as well for parents to be aware that the undergrowth may contain creatures that bite or sting.

Bleeding

- **Apply pressure to the wound with your hand to stop the bleeding**
- **Raise the injured part to diminish the force of the blood flow at the injury**
- **Maintain pressure even after a clot has formed**
- **Move the limb as little as possible as there may be further injuries**
- **Improvise a pad and hold it securely over the wound with a bandage**

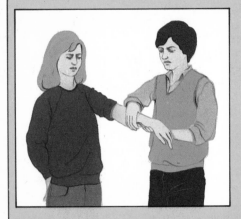

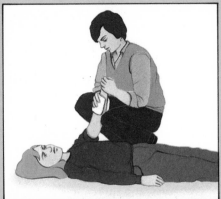

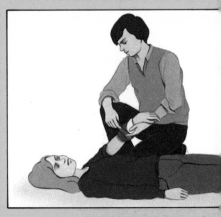

1 Staunch the bleeding by placing your hand immediately over the wound and applying firm pressure; or, if this is easier and equally effective, pinch the edges of the wound firmly together

2 Lay the patient down and raise his arm. Maintaining pressure all the time, use your free hand to make any available material (such as a handkerchief) into a pad. Hold firmly over the wound

3 Still maintaining pressure, find other material (such as a belt, scarf or tie) which will act as a bandage. Wrap this tightly around the pad, and secure it with a very firm knot

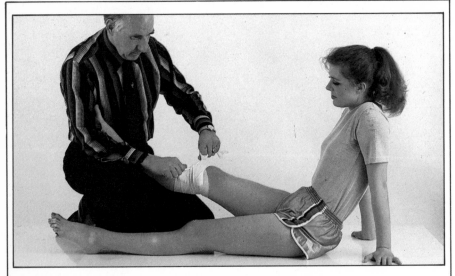

Make sure you . . .

DO tie the bandage very firmly, much more so than you would to secure an ordinary dressing. But never apply a tourniquet

DO get your patient lying down, or at least sitting down, as soon as possible, and thereafter make sure he is not disturbed

DON'T waste time washing your hands or looking for orthodox sterile dressings. Priority goes to speed – the risk of haemorrhage is far greater than the risk of infection

DON'T ask the patient to use his own hand to exert pressure – he may be too weak

Take note

- Keep checking on a bleeding patient for signs of shock. In an extreme case, he will be faint, pale, cold, sweating, thirsty and have a rapid, shallow pulse and breathing rate. At its worst, breathing is laboured and gasping

- If any of the above signs appear in a patient without visible injury, suspect internal bleeding

- Be suspicious of an external blow which has left no significant mark on the skin, but has had the force to imprint a pattern of bruising from overlying objects, such as a buckle or pocket contents. In such a case there may be internal damage with bleeding

- Stomach bleeding becomes obvious if the patient vomits blood. The colour of the blood depends on how long it has lain in the stomach. Sometimes it is brown or black and resembles coffee grounds – this means there has been time for stomach acids to work on it. Equally it may be red in colour – this is also an indication of an internal haemorrhage, but of a more severe type

What to do in an emergency

Coughing up blood
Place patient in recovery position (see page 499), but if breathing is difficult, get him half propped up, leaning on pillows. If you know from which side the blood is coming, let him lie towards that side. Clean away any blood from his mouth. Get medical aid quickly. The smallest amount of blood coughed up must be reported to a doctor.

Vomiting blood
Place the patient in the recovery position. Clear away any vomit from his mouth. Get medical aid or an ambulance urgently. Keep the vomit for the doctor to examine.

Blood which collects for some time in the stomach before being vomited will be acted on by digestive juices, which will alter its colour to brown or black. If red blood is vomited, the bleeding is probably severe and fast.

Slight but sustained bleeding in the stomach will give rise not to vomiting, but to black, tarry-looking stools. This also requires medical attention.

Internal bleeding
Pain or discomfort can be deceptively slight. If the patient shows signs of shock (faintness, pallor, coldness, sweating, thirst, fast and weak pulse and breathing), lay him down, preferably in the recovery position or with his head low and legs raised. Loosen tight clothing and cover him with a blanket or coat. Give no additional heat, and nothing by mouth. Send for urgent medical help or an ambulance.

What next?

1. The risk of shock is high when the patient has lost a lot of blood, so keep him warmly but loosely covered; stay with him

2. In severe cases of bleeding call an ambulance immediately, and give details of the accident

3. Let the patient lie quietly and avoid any movement of the injured part; keep limb elevated

4. Keep a close watch on the bandage. If there are signs of renewed bleeding, do not remove it, but apply more pressure, make another pad and bandage and apply these on top

Different types of bleeding

Bleeding from a palm
Keep the patient's arm raised. Make a thick pad from material available, and get the patient to clench his fist round this. Make an improvised bandage, wrap it firmly around the pad and knot it securely at the back of the hand.

Nosebleed
Make the patient sit up, bend forward and pinch the lower half of his nose between finger and thumb for at least 10 minutes without letting go. If necessary, he can spit out any blood from his mouth into a bowl. Do not let him blow his nose or sniff. A nosebleed after a blow on the head could be due to a skull injury, so get immediate medical advice from your doctor.

Bleeding from a tooth socket
This might happen following a tooth extraction. Make the patient bite hard for at least 10 minutes on a thick pad placed over, but not into, the socket. If he cups his hand under his chin, with his elbow resting on a table, this will help to maintain pressure and be less tiring. He should not use a mouthwash as this could displace any clots that are forming.

Bleeding from a tongue
Sit the patient up and make him bend forward. Grip the tongue firmly between finger and thumb with a clean handkerchief. Keep up the pressure for 10 minutes, letting the patient take the grip himself.

Burns

- **If there are flames, smother with cloth or water; get medical aid**
In the event of ordinary household burns:
- **Immerse affected area in cold water for at least 10 minutes**
- **Cover burnt area with clean, dry dressing and guard against shock**
- **Lay patient down and phone for ambulance or doctor**

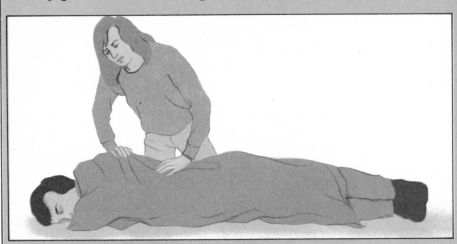

If the patient's clothes are on fire, lay him down and smother the flames by pressing down with any thick cloth – towel, curtain, rug or jacket that comes to hand. Protect the patient's face by bringing the cloth down to fan the fire away from the head and towards the feet. Wrap the cloth firmly around the patient – but don't roll him around on the floor: this would expose other parts of his body to the flames. Once the fire is out, pull away charred or smouldering cloth. Leave anything sticking to the skin alone to avoid further injury

1 Plunge the burnt limb into cold water; keep the cold tap running. Leave it immersed for at least 10 minutes. Alternatively, cover the area with a thick cloth soaked in water. Keep it damp

2 Cover the burnt area with a clean, dry dressing (see page 501), which you bandage or strap on lightly – once the area has been well cooled, and not before. Do not apply lotions or ointments

3 In severe cases, keep the patient lying down. Elevate the burnt limb to reduce swelling. A leg, for instance, can be kept high on pillows; an arm can be propped up on anything handy

Take note

- Scalds are due to moist heat as from steam or boiling water. Clothes saturated in steam, boiling water or hot fat will continue to burn the skin unless they are taken off quickly. For a scalded throat, cool fast with mouthfuls of cold water or by sucking ice

- Dry heat burns come from flames or from contact with hot objects. Friction can cause burns, as when sliding down a rope with firmly closed hands. Electricity can also cause deep burns

- Corrosive chemicals like strong acids can burn severely. For chemical burns dilute and wash away the substance with lots of water until you are confident that it has all gone. Remove any contaminated clothing. For chemicals in the eye, turn the patient, lying down, on the affected side. Gently pull open the eyelids. Pour streams of water into and over the eye to wash out the chemical. Cover with a clean, dry pad. Seek medical help. It is important to act as quickly as possible

- The significant damage in burns is beneath the skin where the heat is retained. Apart from tissue destruction the major effect is dilation of the blood vessels which allows plasma to ooze from them forming blisters. If the skin surface has been destroyed there will be no cover to hold in the fluid, and the plasma loss can be considerable. The risk of shock is high and must be guarded against (see page 496). Fluid loss can be offset by giving the patient small amounts of sweetened water.

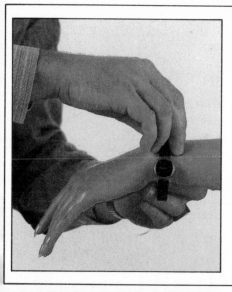

Make sure you . . .

DO remove anything which might constrict if the burnt part swells

DO keep the burnt limb elevated to reduce swelling

DON'T roll the patient around on the floor to extinguish the flames of burning clothes; just apply firm pressure to the area

DON'T attempt to pull away anything that is stuck to the area which has been burnt

DON'T apply any creams or ointments to the burn

1. With any large burn there is a real risk of shock, and you should follow the advice given on page 496 In such cases the depth of the burn is not as significant as the surface area affected: the greater the amount of skin involved, the greater the volume of plasma oozing from the damaged vessels, and the higher the risk of shock becomes

2. Burns offer an exception to the general first aid rule of not giving anything by mouth to the injured person. Here you may give the patient about half a glassful of tepid water every 15 or 20 minutes. The water may be sweetened slightly, but remember that fluids can cause nausea and vomiting when the patient is suffering from shock. The liquid helps to replace body fluids that have been lost as a result of plasma loss caused by the burn

3. If there is a possibility that medical help will be delayed, give the patient half a glass of salt and soda solution (½ teaspoon table salt and ½ teaspoon baking soda per litre/2 pints of water). Give a child about two fluid ounces and an infant about one fluid once. Discontinue fluids if vomiting occurs or if the patient indicates that he does not feel well. If in any doubt, stop giving fluids

4. Get anyone who has been badly burnt or scalded to hospital as soon as possible. In young children, especially infants, even small burns should be regarded as very serious and hospital treatment sought. Call an ambulance: it is speedier and allows the patient to remain lying down. If he continues in severe pain during transit to hospital, keep a cold wet cloth on the burnt area. Reassure him at all times during the journey

This child is about to suffer a most serious but common injury – a bad scald. Make sure that kettles, teapots, saucepans and the like are kept well out of the reach of inquisitive hands: that means away from the edge of a table or work surface. Do not place hot containers on table mats, table cloths or towels – where they can be pulled off easily – and never leave biscuits or sweets near to teapots or kettles. A child will simply be blind to the dangers and, in his haste to reach the biscuits, may knock the boiling tea over himself.

Choking

- **As long as the patient can cough vigorously, do not interfere**
- **If he cannot cough, alternate back blows with abdominal thrusts**
- **Should the patient collapse, give artificial respiration**
- **When airways are completely blocked, try to remove the obstruction**
- **Have a doctor examine the patient if blows or thrusts have been used**

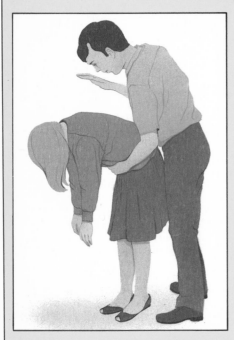

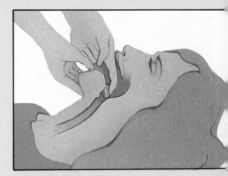

1 If the patient is not able to dislodge the object by vigorous coughing, bend her over and slap hard with the heel of your hand between the shoulder blades

2 If four backslaps fail to loosen the object, give abdominal thrusts. Should the obstruction remain, try alternating backslaps with thrusts

3 If the patient's airways are completely obstructed and you cannot get air into the patient's lungs by artificial respiration, you must try to find and remove the object. Place a curved finger into the mouth and probe the area gently. Be careful not to ram the finger straight in so you don't push the object deeper into the throat. Start at the side of the cheek, moving the finger to the back of the mouth; then hook the finger forward to dislodge the object. Pull it out of the mouth quickly, in case the patient sucks it back into the throat again

Make sure you . . .

DO stay with the patient, even if he is able to speak and cough

DO try to keep the patient calm; if the irritating object is in the throat, the windpipe – which is encircled by muscles – will react by going into spasm. Any anxiety on the part of the patient could increase the tension of the muscles. Thus the problem will worsen as the object causing the obstruction is held more tightly

DO give very hard blows to the back, if this is necessary. Most people who administer blows high on the back do not appreciate how hard these should be to dislodge the object

DO Make very certain that small children are provided with safe toys. Avoid those that have small parts which can be easily removed

DO keep all small objects out of a baby's or toddler's reach. At these stages, children are particularly likely to put anything into their mouth

DO make sure that the patient is checked by a doctor if you have had to administer hard blows to the back, or abdominal thrusts. Either of these can cause internal damage. In addition, have a doctor examine the patient if you have given artificial respiration

DON'T resort to backslaps and abdominal thrusts before allowing the patient to try and dislodge the object by coughing

Take note

● If the patient can still cough vigorously and speak to you, stand by. Encourage but do not interfere. Advise him to try separate heavy coughs

● Should this technique fail, bend the patient forward. Give him a hard blow between the shoulder blades with the heel of your hand. If one blow fails, try further ones, until four blows have been given. This can be done when the patient is standing or sitting. If he is on the ground, turn him on to his side

● Bend a child over your lap or lay him along a flexed thigh. A baby can be held upside down, firmly by the legs

● If the object is still in place, and the patient is weakening, give abdominal thrusts. Encircle patient's waist from behind. Place one fist, thumb-side first, halfway between the navel and the lower end of the breastbone. Cup your other hand over the fist

● Give a hard thrust (inwards and a little upwards). This may shoot the obstruction into or out of the mouth

● If one thrust fails, try further ones until a total of four have been given

● If the patient is on the ground, turn him on to his back and kneel astride his thighs. Straighten his head. Place the heel of one hand halfway between the navel and the lower end of the breastbone. Place the heel of the other hand over the first. Continue as above

● In the case of a small child, hold him head down, lying on your partly bent thigh. Use two or three fingers only

● If these actions fail, continue a series of four back blows, alternating with four abdominal thrusts

● If the patient stops breathing begin artificial respiration

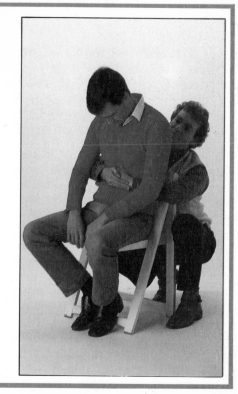

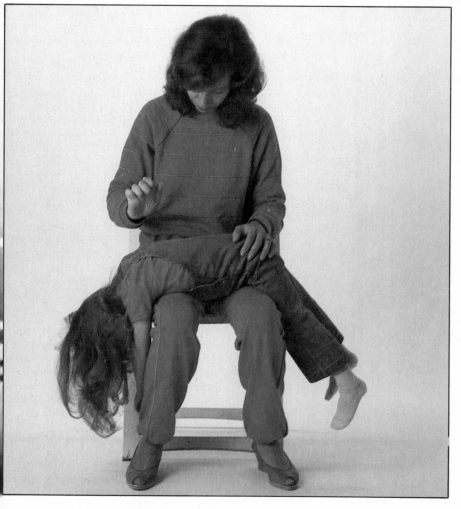

What next?

1. When something 'goes down the wrong way', it can either obstruct the back of the throat or it could have moved a little further down and be blocking the windpipe

2. If the obstructing object comes free and moves into the patient's mouth, seize it and pull it out quickly, in case the patient's next sudden breath sucks it back again

3. If the patient feels faint or vomits, put him in the recovery position (see page 499).

4. In every case where you have used the abdominal thrust, you must watch your patient carefully, even if he seems fit again

5. The patient should be seen by a doctor or sent to hospital for observation as soon as possible. In rare cases the thrust damages an internal organ and medical treatment is necessarry. This is a calculated risk you must take – the alternative might be death

If a child is choking, bend her over your knee and, using the heal of your hand, give hard blows between the shoulder blades.

485

Electric shock

- **Turn the electricity supply off at mains**
- **Do not touch the victim until you have done this**
- **Check that the victim is breathing**
- **Use artificial respiration if necessary**
- **Check for bleeding and bone fractures**
- **Treat any burns by cooling**
- **Send for medical help urgently**

General points

- The vast majority of electrical injuries occur in the home; so make sure that your electrical appliances and home wiring are in good working order

- Do not touch a shock victim until he has been separated from the current, or the mains supply has been turned off. If you do touch him, you too may receive a shock

- If you cannot turn the current off use a dry implement made of non-conductive material – like a broom or chair – to separate him from the 'live' apparatus. Act quickly

- When the victim is free, check that he is breathing. He may need artificial respiration at once

- Try to ascertain the extent of injury. A severe shock will cause burns and even cuts and fractures if the victim has fallen or been thrown. Use dry dressing to protect cuts and burns. If burns are minor, cool them (see page 482)

- Immediately call for an ambulance. Stay with the victim. Watch for signs of collapse (whiteness and sweating), until ambulance arrives. Place victim in recovery position

Make sure you . . .

DO turn off the mains electricity supply before starting any work on the house wiring circuit and disconnect any appliance that you are about to mend

DON'T handle any switches, plugs or appliances in the kitchen with wet hands

DON'T overload sockets with adaptors. Try to have only one appliance per socket and remember to turn off sockets when not in use

DON'T attempt to rescue the victim of a very high voltage shock, unless he has been thrown at least 20 metres from the source. This type of hazard exists in some factories and roadside pylons

What next?

1. After sending for an ambulance, keep a close eye on the patient. Do not allow crowds to gather round him, make sure he is warm and comfortable and watch for signs of deterioration

2. If the victim stops breathing at any time then give him artificial respiration until he either starts breathing again, or the ambulance arrives

3. If the victim's heart stops beating then give him heart massage. This must be learnt at first aid class

4. If the victim's breathing and heartbeat recover, then lay him on his stomach, turn his head to one side and draw up the arm and leg of that side; i.e. place the victim in the recovery position

If you discover the victim of an electric shock do not touch him until he is separated from the current, as you may receive an equally forceful shock yourself. Turn off the mains supply immediately. If this is not possible, separate him from the live apparatus by means of a dry implement made of non-conductive material – the wooden handle of a broom is ideal. Once free, check whether or not the victim is breathing – he may require urgent artificial respiration.

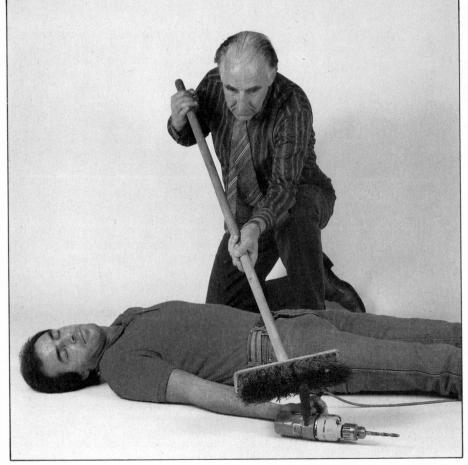

Exposure and cold

- Exposure to cold can cause lasting damage to the body's tissues
- Complications associated with exposure include frostbite and hypothermia
- The extremeties – nose, fingers and toes – are most affected
- Any attempt at rapid re-warming can cause further tissue damage

Exposure

Symptoms of exposure include physical and mental slowing down, decrease in reasoning power, change in mood, slurred speech, shivering and cramp followed by possible collapse. Once these symptoms are detected, stop the patient moving and get him to shelter. Remove any wet clothing and replace with blankets, sleeping bag or fresh clothing. Cover the patient's head and face, but leave mouth, nose and eyes free. If the patient is conscious, give warm, sweet drinks. Under no circumstances give alcohol.

Frostbite

If subjected to intense cold, the tissues under the skin may freeze. This is caused by the formation of minute ice particles and disruption of the blood supply brought on by clumps of red blood cells which then block the vessels. Where frostbite – numb, white tissue – is suspected, remove wet clothing and constricting objects (such as a ring) from the affected part. Apply a dry, protective cover after gently dabbing away any moisture. Let the frostbitten area warm up gradually. Do not heat it in any way, and do not rub it.

Hypothermia

A patient with hypothermia is extremely cold all over with a puffy skin which is white or blue, except for a child, who looks pink. The heartbeat will be slow and weak. When this occurs, keep the patient in bed in the recovery position. Cover the patient with blankets, but keep them loose. Do not use hot water bottles or an electric blanket as excessive heat may damage the patient. Make sure that all open windows are shut and then warm the room with any available heater. If conscious give warm sweet drinks.

Make sure you . . .

DO cover the head in extreme cold to protect against excessive loss of body heat

DO ensure that both the young and the elderly sleep in warm conditions as they are particularly vulnerable to low temperatures

DO use suitable protective clothing when outside in extremely cold conditions. On long trips, take high energy foods – such as chocolate and glucose – and flasks of hot, sweet drinks

DON'T give a patient any alcohol as this encourages the body to lose heat rather than retain it

When children set off on hiking or camping expeditions where they risk exposure to cold or damp weather, make sure they are supplied with thermal blankets which are excellent at retaining the body's heat. They are light to carry and take up very little space. The commonsense reaction of warming a cold child in front of a fire is correct in cases of chill and slight exposure – after a bad soaking, for example. However, victims of severe exposure and frostbite should never be placed in front of a roaring fire, as rapid re-heating may cause further tissue damage.

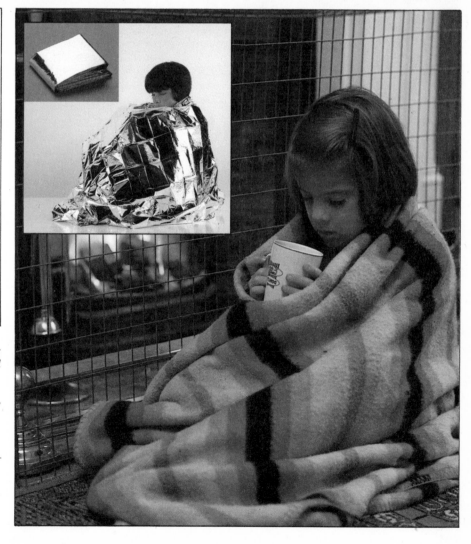

Falls

- **Do not try to pick the patient up immediately, but check for injuries**
- **If a fracture is suspected, do not move him**
- **If just a fall, help the patient on to all fours placing a stool in front of him**
- **Get him to bend one knee and lean forward**
- **Move to one side, help him to push himself up**

1 Clear the area of any extraneous objects. If the patient has use of arms and legs, turn her face down. Stand over her legs. By holding on to her hip regions, help her on to all fours

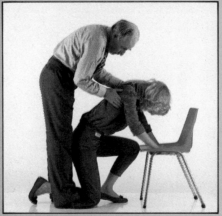

2 Place a stool or chair in front of her. Help her put her hands on the seat. Get her to bend one knee and lean forward carefully. At this point you will still be straddling the patient's legs

3 Move to one side of her. Put one hand in the armpit of that side and the other on the elbow. Now help her to push herself up, using the chair as additional support. Lift as gently as possible

Take note

● Has the patient injured himself? Do not try to pick him up at once. Establish that he is conscious. Ask if there is any pain. Check for bleeding (page 480), for wounds (see page 500) and for fractures

● Is it safe to move him? This will not be advisable if there is any chance of a fracture. In particular, a fall from a height, a blow to the back or pain in the back or neck might mean a fractured spine. If this is suspected, do not move him. Make the patient comfortable; immediately call for medical help

● Most patients will be able to get up by themselves. The elderly and the weak may need help

● If the patient cannot use arms and legs properly, spread a blanket and, with someone's aid, roll him onto the centre. Rolling each edge towards him, grasp the blanket firmly, one person at the top and the other at the bottom, and carry the patient to a couch or bed

Make sure you . . .

DO examine the patient carefully for injuries; give treatment where appropriate. When lifting him, have regard for your own back: lift correctly — and as gently as possible

DON'T attempt to move the patient if there is the slightest chance that he may have sustained a fracture. Let him lie where he is until expert help arrives

DON'T try to pick him up at once. Advise him to lie still

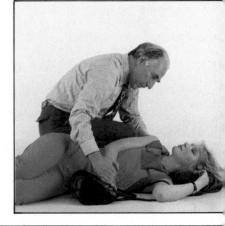

Watchpoint

1. Get a doctor if the patient's condition is uncertain, especially if he has developed a new weakness or a mental change, if he has hurt his head or if he has completely lost consciousness

2. If the patient's legs are weak, get him sitting on the floor and place a low stool behind him. Help him to put his hands on the seat and bend forward; he can then use his arms to push up and sit on the stool. Put a higher stool or chair behind the first one; repeat the manoeuvre to get him sitting on this one

3. Can a recurrence be avoided? Ask yourself why the patient fell. If general weakness was the cause, discuss medication with the doctor or the need for a walking frame

Fits

- **When patient collapses, rigid, tip head well back, loosen clothes**
- **Don't try to control thrashing limbs, surround patient with cushions**
- **When jerking stops, keep head tipped well back**
- **If uninjured and safe to move, place the patient in recovery position**

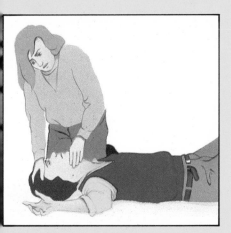

1 The patient lies rigid. To ensure a clear airway, the head should be tipped well back. Any tight clothing should already have been eased. Remember that the patient may have injured himself in falling

2 When convulsions start, do not attempt to control the thrashing limbs; instead surround the patient with soft buffers to protect him from self-inflicted injuries and move dangerous objects out of the way

3 The patient stops jerking and relaxes, but remains unconscious. Keep the head tilted back; look for injuries. If it is safe to move him, put him on his side in the recovery position as illustrated immediately above

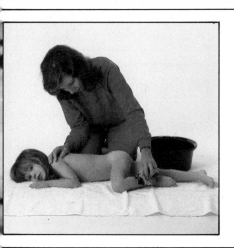

Fever Fits

A small child developing a high fever may react with a brief convulsion.

- Stay by his side; tip head back; put him in the recovery position. Take off his clothes and cool him with a cold, wet sponge. Check temperature with a thermometer in the armpit: aim to reduce it by only one or two degrees

- Send for the doctor

- After recovery keep the child lightly covered

Take note

- An epileptic attack or a child's feverish convulsion may be alarming, but generally such seizures are short-lived

- Attacks vary from patient to patient. Most often, they come without warning. The patient falls unconscious; he may cry out and not be aware he has done so

- The patient begins jerking his limbs and face or thrashing about; this can last 30 seconds. He may froth at the mouth; he may hold his breath; he may bite his tongue; he may be incontinent

- When the patient stops jerking, he will remain unconscious for some minutes. Then he will come to, perhaps drowsily. If he is accustomed to his attacks, he may want to take care of himself and wave helping hands away

- Unless there are familiar people to look after him, you should get him to hospital – by ambulance, if this is at all possible

Make sure you . . .

DO ease any tight clothing when the fit starts. Tip the patient's head well back to ensure that he does not choke during the fit

DO mop away any froth that has come from the patient's mouth during the course of the convulsion

DON'T try to control jerking or thrashing limbs; just try to prevent self-inflicted injuries

DON'T attempt to push anything between the teeth – except a soft pad, which will not slip back and block the throat

Fractures

- **Keep the patient still and cover with a blanket**
- **Attend to such injuries as an open wound or bleeding before dealing with the fracture**
- **If necessary, protect the broken bone**
- **Stay with the patient, and make him comfortable until professional help arrives**

1 Simple arm sling: support elbow, keeping hand raised. Pass bandage between chest and arm

2 Bring bandage up over forearm and around back of neck. Tie points together over hollow above collar-bone. Pin loose end at elbow

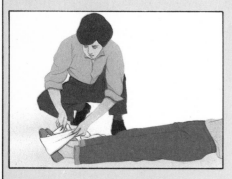

3 Figure-of-eight bandage: carefully place patient's feet together. Lay middle of broad bandage across the soles of the feet

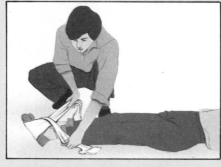

4 Bring ends of bandage to front of feet; cross over the insteps. Continue 'wrapping' bandage by carrying ends to back of ankles

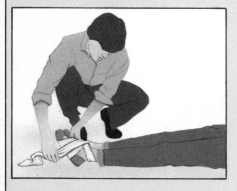

5 Cross ends, bring them back to front of ankles and cross again. Take ends back under soles. Secure in place by tying

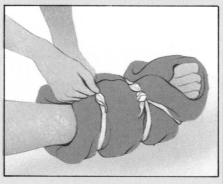

6 Foot and ankle bandage: Use flat cushion or folded cloth around ankle and foot. Secure by tying with narrow bandages

Immobilizing fractures

Jaw:
gently clear mouth of any blood or dentures. Put thick pad under and around jaw. (Patient's cupped hand can support it temporarily.) Secure by placing bandage over pad; bring ends up over ears and tie on top of the patient's head.

Collar-bone:
keep point of elbow supported until sling can hold it; support arm on side of fracture with a sling (left, figures 1 and 2). Place soft pad under armpit. Secure upper arm against chest—place wide bandage over arm, across back and chest and tie under armpit on unaffected side.

Leg:
keep patient lying down. Place padding between legs from groin to just above ankles. Put bandage around knees and tie on side. Make figure-of-eight bandage (left, figures 3, 4 and 5) around feet and ankles.

Arm:
if elbow can be bent without pain, place pad in armpit and support forearm with sling (left, figures 1 and 2). Make certain that the forearm slopes slightly upwards.
  If elbow is straight and painful to bend, keep patient lying down. Place

Take note

● Unless the patient is in a dangerous situation, warn him not to move

● Look for and control any bleeding (see page 480). Dress any wounds (see page 500). If possible, do this without moving the patient.

● If expert help is likely to come quickly, let the patient wait, lying quietly, and make him comfortable

● If help is delayed or the patient has to be transported to a doctor, immobilize the fractured part. Make sure that you immobilize not only the whole length of the bone but also the joint

● Protect the patient from shock (see page 496)

● Protect the patient from further injury

padding between arm and body. Secure arm to body with three wide bandages (as collar-bone, above).

Foot and ankle:
see left, figure 6.

To immobilize a fractured arm or collar-bone, place a pad between the patient's arm and his body. Secure the arm in place with three wide bandages: around the upper arm and chest; around the lower arm and chest; and around the wrist and thighs.

Make sure you . . .

DO use a sound part of the patient's body as a splint (for example leg to leg, arm to chest) if you have to immobilize a fracture. Whenever possible, move uninjured part to the injured part

DO place thick padding (use cotton wool, folded towels, scarves, socks and so one) to fill spaces between two parts of the body

DO tie the parts together with firm bandages (if bandages are not handy, use scarves, neckties, handkerchiefs and so on)

DO tie any knots over the uninjured part

DO avoid having a bandage directly over a fracture of the limb

DO check that any bandages or slings are not so tight that they cut off the circulation

DON'T give any food, liquid or tablets to the patient before professional help arrives

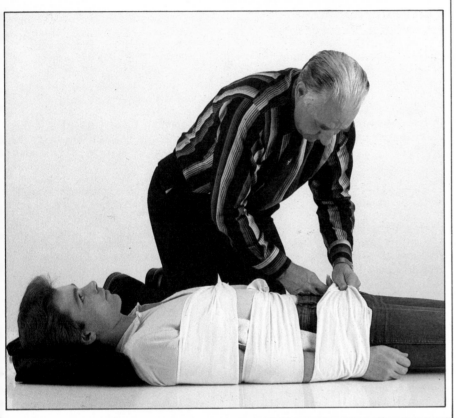

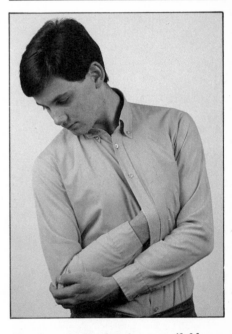

If a triangular bandage is not available, an adequate emergency sling can be rapidly improvised from clothing. The patient's arm can be placed inside his shirt, supported by the fastened buttons. A necktie can be used, or the hem of the patient's jacket can be taken up over the fractured arm and pinned to the lapel.

Watch point

• In the case of a broken backbone, the fracture of a vertebra might create loose pieces of bone that could enter the spinal cord, causing permanent paralysis and loss of feeling

• If there is any possibility of such a fracture, **do not move the patient**. Let him lie as you found him and wait for the doctor or ambulancemen

• Meanwhile, make certain he cannot move. Place cushions or other soft articles between the patient's body and any pieces of furniture

• Deciding whether someone has broken a bone can be difficult – many of the 'classic' features are relevant to other injuries such as a sprain. For example, an initial symptom that is quite common is pain. Yet a severe contusion, without a break, can be extremely painful and sometimes a major fracture only hurts a little

• Restricted movement of the injured part and swelling of tissues in the area can be symptomatic of both sprains and fractures. Also, many fractures retain the broken bone ends in good anatomical position so that another classical feature, deformity, is not always present

• In diagnosing a fracture, the history of the injury should be taken into account. The likelihood of bone damage is high if there was considerable force, such as a hard blow or a fall. Yet this can be deceptive as well, since diseased bones or, in the elderly, brittle ones, can break relatively easily.

However, anyone who administers first aid will do no harm by suspecting a fracture, where circumstances suggest it, and taking the appropriate action

Heart attack

- **Place the patient in a resting position**
- **Keep the upper part of the body raised**
- **Call or send for an ambulance immediately**
- **Loosen any tight clothing at neck and waist**
- **If breathing stops, give artificial respiration**
- **Keep patient warm by covering with a blanket**

When a person suffers a heart attack, prompt action is of crucial importance. Make sure you perform the following in the correct order.

1 Place the patient in a resting position at once – in bed, on a sofa or in an armchair

2 Loosen clothes at the neck and the waist

3 If the patient appears very breathless let him sit up against a bed-rest banked with pillows. The bed-rest can be improvised with a light chair set upside-down against the wall

4 If there is nothing suitable against which the patient can rest, use your body as a prop

5 Keep him well, but loosely, covered. Open the window so that the room is well ventilated

6 Call, or send a bystander, for an ambulance immediately. Specify the nature of the problem

7 Alleviate the patient's fears by maintaining a calm attitude of sympathy but confidence about recovery

8 Reassure the patient that medical help has been sent for and is on its way

9 Remain with the patient to comfort him but avoid fussing and prevent others from crowding around him

10 If the patient loses consciousness and ceases breathing, begin artificial respiration at once (see page 476)

11 If the heart stops beating the patient will also need heart compression; however, this must be learned at a first aid class

Take note

- The heart muscle depends on small arteries for the blood supply that keeps it going. If these vessels have become so narrow that they cannot provide the extra blood needed when a person exerts himself or feels a strong emotion, the result is a pain in the chest. The condition is known as angina; the pain is vice-like and sometimes spreads to the neck, shoulders and arms

- During a severe heart attack a clot blocking one of the arteries cuts off the blood from part of the heart muscle. Known as coronary thrombosis, the attack results in intense pain. The patient collapses, is pale, sweats and has a fast, weak and sometimes irregular pulse

- In some cases symptoms are mild and similar to those of indigestion. When in doubt, treat as a heart attack

- Acute heart failure is different from the above conditions. Here, a weakened heart muscle suddenly ceases the normal pumping action. Blood flowing into the heart from the lungs is not fully propelled forward and the lungs become congested. There is no pain but the patient's breathing is very wet and bubbly and he may cough up watery, blood-tinged sputum

What next?

1. Following treatment and recovery the patient may or may not be at risk of having further attacks, either soon after or in the years after the initial occurrence. It is difficult to make an accurate prediction

2. What is certain, is that the patient will increase his chances of being spared a repetition of the attack and of living out the remainder of a normal lifespan if he closely follows the doctor's advice

3. Particular care should be taken with diet and, if applicable, the patient should give up smoking

4. The patient should follow his doctor's instructions about starting on a positive and healthy exercise programme

Poisoning

- **Call, or send for an ambulance immediately**
- **A conscious patient should be given fluids**
- **If unconscious, put in the recovery position**
- **If he is not breathing, give artificial respiration**

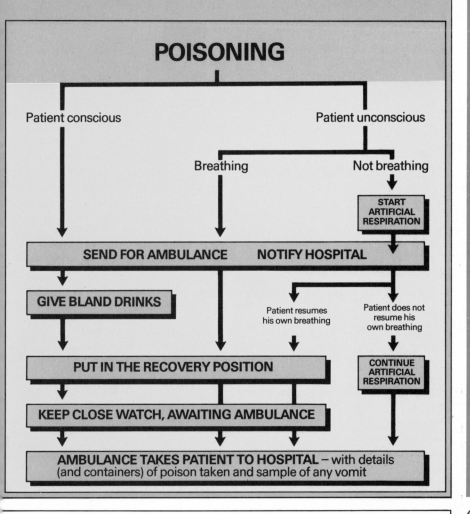

POISONING

Patient conscious → SEND FOR AMBULANCE → GIVE BLAND DRINKS → PUT IN THE RECOVERY POSITION → KEEP CLOSE WATCH, AWAITING AMBULANCE

Patient unconscious →
- Breathing → NOTIFY HOSPITAL → PUT IN THE RECOVERY POSITION
- Not breathing → START ARTIFICIAL RESPIRATION → NOTIFY HOSPITAL
  - Patient resumes his own breathing → PUT IN THE RECOVERY POSITION
  - Patient does not resume his own breathing → CONTINUE ARTIFICIAL RESPIRATION

AMBULANCE TAKES PATIENT TO HOSPITAL – with details (and containers) of poison taken and sample of any vomit

Take note

- If possible, notify the hospital that the patient is coming and which poison has been taken

- If the patient is alert enough to swallow, give him at least two tumblerfuls of bland fluid: milk, milk and water, barley water or plain water. These should be drunk slowly. Do not give salt drinks

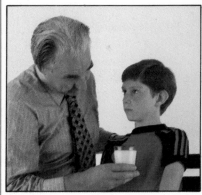

- Do not try to make the patient vomit. If he vomits spontaneously, clear the throat and mouth to protect his breathing. Send a small sample of the vomit to the hospital (in a bottle labelled with your estimate of the total amount vomited)

- Send any containers (even if empty) of the substance taken by the patient

- Closely watch the patient in case he vomits, loses consciousness or stops breathing. The attempted suicide must be guarded from making another attempt

Fumes and smoke
- Make sure that you do not rush into the danger area unprepared. Have a safety line tied round you, with its end in the hands of someone outside
- If possible, put a moist towel or handkerchief over your mouth and nose. Take a couple of deep breaths in and out before you go in. Then hold your breath
- If the smoke is from a fire, travel along the floor
- Support the patient and lead him out. If he cannot walk, drag him out with your hands under his armpits
- If no fire burns or smoulders, open doors and windows. In case of fire, keep them shut

Pesticides
- These are very variable in their action. The more dangerous, if used as sprays, can harm if swallowed, breathed in or absorbed through skin
- The effects of pesticide poisoning can be cumulative, causing headaches, lassitude, muscle ache, weakness, sweating, vomiting, difficulty in or even cessation of breathing
- Get the patient out of the spray area and put him to rest. Wearing gloves, remove any contaminated clothing (put them into closed plastic bags); thoroughly wash his skin. Check the pesticide container label for advice
- If necessary, give artificial respiration
- Summon medical help immediately

What next?

1. If the accident took place in your home, you must take steps to ensure that it cannot occur again

2. Note why the poison was accessible. Remember that all potentially poisonous substances should be kept in locked cupboards, or at least out of a child's reach

3. Make sure that poisons are clearly labelled, and if possible, kept in their original containers. Apart from being a safety measure, the containers usually give instructions on what to do in an emergency

Road accidents

- Search the area for any people thrown clear of the vehicles
- Establish an order for treatment priority among the victims
- Treat patients for breathing, bleeding and unconsciousness
- Set up red warning triangle and delegate traffic control to an onlooker
- Send for emergency services giving thorough details of accident

1 Stop your car a short distance away and park well into the side of road. Turn on hazard and headlights to help you see exactly what has happened

2 Extinguish any smoke coming from vehicles, but leave victims in position unless fire is a risk. Prevent further damage by immobilizing vehicles

3 Look for victims who have been thrown clear of vehicles, e.g. into ditches or over hedges, Establish an order for priority treatment

4 Treat victims in order of priority. Deal with breathing, bleeding and unconsciousness in that order. Move victims as little as possible

5 Set up a red warning triangle about 65 m (200 yds) from the site of accident. Employ any onlookers as traffic controllers during the emergency

6 Send first available person for emergency services, giving information about location, number of cars and injured and types of injury

Always be prepared

You should always carry a first aid kit in your car. Many of the accident victims who die before reaching hospital could have been saved if simple first aid measures had been taken promptly, so being prepared could be really vital. If you carry your own kit you will not only be able to give thorough first aid to the victims of an accident that you come across, but it will also be available should you unfortunately be involved in an accident yourself.

The first aid kit should be kept in a clearly marked waterproof case, preferably in the glove compartment. The kit should include the following:
    packs of gauze and cotton wool
    5 and 7.5cm (2 and 3in) bandages
    medium and large sterile dressings
    a large torch
    a large pair of scissors
    pencil and paper for messages
You should also carry a red warning triangle and a small fire extinguisher.

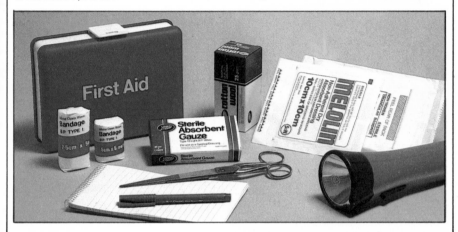

What next?

1. While you are waiting for the emergency services, try to discourage other motorists and passers-by from hanging around unless they can offer expert help

2. Keep area between your car and the crash clear at all times so that the emergency services will have somewhere safe to stop near the accident

3. Stay with the accident victims until the ambulances arrive. Watch them carefully to ensure that breathing does not stop, bleeding does not resume and no one loses consciousness. Try to be reassuring

4. Take advantage of any spare time to gather information to help the emergency services. Collect a list of names and addresses from the least injured victims and take a note of the vehicle number plates. Give all this to the police or ambulancemen when they arrive. You should also give a thorough account of any first aid measures that you have taken and make any general observations

Make sure you . . .

DO ensure that there are no more accident victims. Park your car a short distance away and well off the road. Make sure that the passing traffic is aware that an accident has occurred by putting red warning triangles up and asking a passer-by to control the traffic

DO check that the vehicles are safe – switch off the ignition, apply brakes and, if possible, put in gear

DO use any available material, such as car rugs or coats, to keep the victims as warm as possible

DON'T move accident victims from vehicles unless there is a danger of fire. It is a natural human tendency, but you may waste valuable time and even exacerbate existing injuries. The rescue services have special tools to cut people out of damaged vehicles and this difficult task is best left for them to deal with

DON'T smoke anywhere near the location of the car crash – leaking petrol may catch fire

Shock

- **Shock is caused by many types of severe injury; it is due to failure of the circulation**
- **Always tend to major injuries first**
- **Minimize shock by laying the patient down at site of accident, keeping his head low and legs raised**
- **Loosen tight clothing and keep lightly covered**

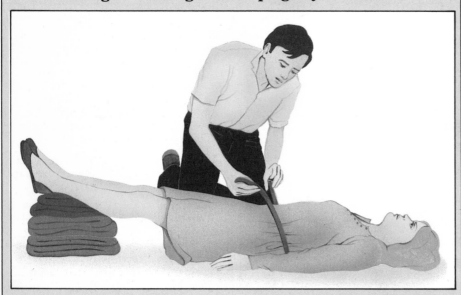

1 Stop bleeding (see page 480). If possible, treat patient on the spot. Lay him down with head low and legs raised about 0.5m (18in). Reduce movement to a minimum

2 Loosen tight clothing such as belts and collars. Dress wounds with clean, dry material (see page 500). If injuries allow, put patient in recovery position

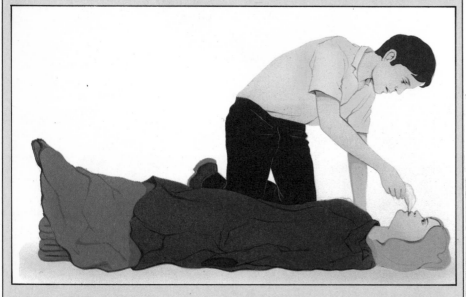

3 Loosely cover patient with coats or blankets to keep warm. As you give first aid, explain what you are doing, the patient may be frightened and need reassurance

4 If the patient is thirsty, soak a piece of cloth, such as a handkerchief, in water and let him suck this. Stay with the patient until medical aid arrives

Take note

- Shock is caused by a marked loss of body fluid. This may be in the form of internal or external bleeding, or it may be blood plasma loss as a result of damage done by a serious burn

- Body fluid loss causes the heart to beat faster and weaker, and the blood pressure falls. As a consequence, the entire body receives inadequate supplies of oxygen.

- First aid should be given to prevent shock even if the accident victim looks and feels fairly fit. But always treat for breathing, bleeding, burns and fractures first

- A badly shocked victim will look pale, bluish, cold and sweaty and will also be mentally slow. Breathing will be shallow and the pulse will be fast and feeble

What next?

1. Keep a careful watch on the patient to make sure that he is breathing properly, that he does not start, or resume, bleeding and does not vomit. Cover with blankets but do not heat the patient with hot water bottles or electric blankets – these will draw blood away from vital organs where it is needed

2. Do not give the victim any food, drink or tablets. Stimulants, such as alcohol and cigarettes should be totally avoided

3. Even if the patient seems to be unconscious, do not talk or whisper to bystanders. He may well hear you and understand what is being said – at this time he needs reassurance not more anxiety

Sprains and strains

- Let the patient rest the injured part in the most comfortable position, slightly raised if possible
- Cover the affected area with a cold compress, keeping in position for approximately 30 minutes
- Protect the area with a pad of wool or cotton cloth
- Bandage from well below hurt area to well above

What next?

1 Spraining means damaging the ligaments around a joint. Apply a cold compress, then remove it and cover with a pad

2 Starting well below the damaged joint, firmly wrap a bandage around it, leaving strips of padding visible

3 A strain involves a muscle in any part of the body. Cover with a cold compress, then remove it and make a thick pad

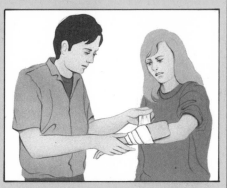

4 Wrap a crêpe or elasticized bandage around the injured area. Do this firmly but not tightly, and cover the padding

1. The strain or sprain needs rest and support in the form of a firm bandage. An elastic bandage is best, but it is easy to put it on so tight that it damages the underlying nerves and blood vessels. A thick wool or cotton pad helps to protect the area from this sort of constriction. But you must warn the patient that if any part of the affected limb becomes cold, numb or puffy the bandage is probably too tight

2. If pain is severe, but there is clearly no other injury, the patient may have aspirin or paracetamol. But never take a chance, if the pain seems too severe and you have the slightest doubt about a possible fracture, get medical aid urgently

3. Sprains and strains are often more of a problem than people realize. Bandaging supports the limb and reduces pain, but movement is still very limited. Several days may elapse before normal activity can be resumed. Check with your doctor before you do anything strenuous

Take note

- In both strains and sprains the muscle or ligament has been overstretched by a powerful movement. Sometimes small blood vessels will also be torn and a bruise forms. The area will be painful, bruised and swollen

- Swelling can be minimized by cooling the area with a cold compress. This is only effective if applied within half an hour of the accident. After this the injury will be swollen and no amount of cooling will help to reduce it

- To make a cold compress: use thick cloth, such as a folded towel; soak it in cold water; wring it out so it is just moist; place on the sore area; keep in place for about half an hour; moisten if it begins to dry out too much

- If you think there is the slightest chance that the patient has fractured a bone, treat as for fractures (see page 490). You will be in good company: many doctors have to do exactly this until they have the results of an X-ray

Unconsciousness

- If the patient is not breathing, begin artificial respiration immediately
- Clear the patient's mouth of any vomit, blood or displaced dentures
- Control any bleeding, check for other wounds and for possible fractures
- If it is safe to move patient, turn gently into recovery position
- If possible, stay with patient and send someone for medical help

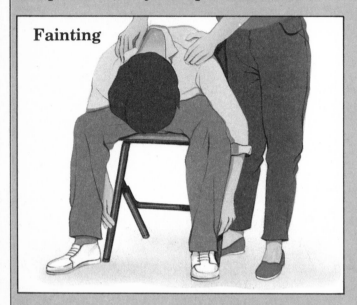

Fainting

1 When a person who is sitting feels faint and it is impossible to lay him down (for example, in a concert hall), tell him to bend all the way forward, with his head low between his legs. He should try to relax completely. Do not leave him, but stay next to him to support him in case he loses consciousness

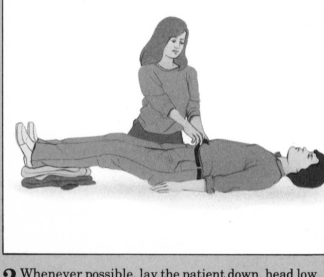

2 Whenever possible, lay the patient down, head low and legs raised. Loosen tight clothing at neck. If he is conscious tell him to take deep, slow breaths. As he recovers give him cold water to drink. Advise him to remain where he is for five minutes before trying to sit up slowly

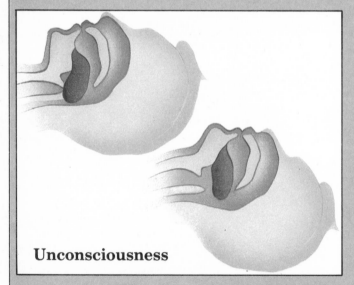

Unconsciousness

1 In an unconscious person, the tongue is likely to flop backwards and obstruct the opening of the windpipe. Bend the head right back; the tongue will then be carried up with the jaw and the airway will open. Do this without twisting the neck. If necessary give artificial respiration

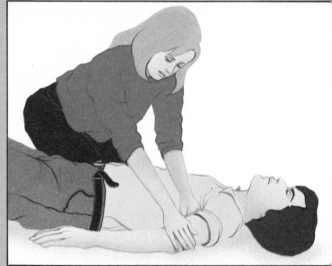

2 Stop bleeding (see page 480) and dress wounds (see page 500). Check for fractures. Feel firmly but gently with hands flat, from one end of the body to the other, taking note of any swellings. If you suspect a fracture, leave the patient lying as he is, otherwise lay him in recovery position and cover with blankets

Make sure you . . .

DO remember to check the patient's breathing before you do anything else. If he is lying on his back, his tongue may be obstructing the airways. This must be treated as an emergency

DO remove anything, such as a pillow, from under the patient's head if he is breathing with difficulty

DO follow the routine to safeguard breathing, stop bleeding and protect against further harm before considering moving the patient into the recovery position

DON'T twist or turn the neck when moving the head, in case there has been some injury to the upper part of the spinal column

DON'T try to make the unconscious person drink. The fluid would run in to the windpipe. Even if he responds vaguely to touch and speech, his ability to swallow may be impaired

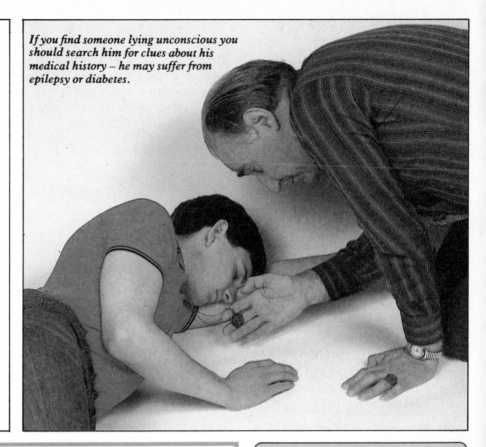

If you find someone lying unconscious you should search him for clues about his medical history – he may suffer from epilepsy or diabetes.

Take note

● Examine the patient to see if he is breathing. If not, then begin artificial respiration immediately

● If the patient is breathing noisily and with difficulty, quickly (using a curved finger) scoop the mouth clear of any airway obstruction such as vomit, blood, or displaced dentures. Bend the head back and keep it in this position

● Look for any severe bleeding. Control it at once (see page 480)

● Check for any other wounds. Cover them at once with a dressing (you may have to improvise one; see page 500)

● Search for any possible fractures. If you suspect a fracture which would be made worse by moving the patient, leave him as he is. Note that a fractured spine is almost impossible to discern in an unconscious patient, but the circumstances (for example, a fall from a height or a blow to the back) may suggest it. *If so the patient must definitely not be moved!*

● If it is safe to move the patient, turn him gently into the recovery position (illustrated below)

● Send for medical help or call an ambulance

What next?

1. The cause of the patient's unconsciousness may be unknown. This is for the doctor to diagnose and to treat. Your responsibility is to call for medical aid and administer first aid, if necessary

2. Even if there is no sign of emergency at first, keep watching the patient carefully in case his breathing stops and he needs artificial respiration, or he vomits. If he does vomit, clear his mouth using a curved finger

3. If the patient is unknown to you and you will not harm him with your movements, search his person for any cards, bracelets, badges or other medical tags. These will tell you if the patient suffers from a condition such as diabetes or epilepsy and they should be handed to the doctor or ambulance attendants

4. If you suspect that the patient has a fracture, and medical help will be delayed or you have to transport the patient to hospital, immobilize the part which has been fractured (see page 490)

Recovery position

Wounds

- **Wash the skin around the wound, moving outwards from the edge**
- **Put gauze over the wound, then a thick pad, and bandage firmly**
- **Keep the patient, and especially the injured part, at rest**
- **Protect the patient against shock and seek medical attention**

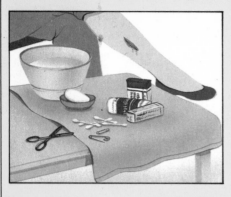

1 For dressing a wound you need several articles from a first aid box: cotton wool, gauze, bandages. You will also need soap and water

2 Wash only the skin around the area, not the wound. Use cotton wool moistened with warm water; clean from edge outwards

3 Put gauze over the wound, covering beyond the wound area. Place thick pad over gauze and bandage dressing firmly

Making a ring pad

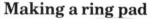

1 Use a long thin fold of material such as a large handkerchief. Form one end into a circle

2 Hold the circle and slip the end through the loop. Keep looping the long, free end around the circle

3 When the bandage has been totally used up, you will have a firm, thick ring to protect a wound

Objects in wounds

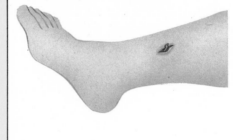

1 If an object is lying on the surface of a wound, brush it away with a clean piece of gauze. However, if an object has become embedded, you must leave it undisturbed; it will be removed when medical assistance is available

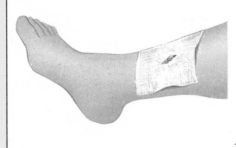

2 Carefully cover the wound with a piece of sterile gauze; it should be sufficiently large so that it extends well beyond the area of the wound itself. If the piece of gauze is too small, it may slip and a little part of the wound may become exposed

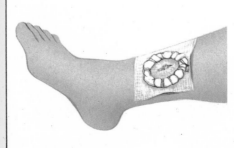

3 Make a ring pad from a large handkerchief or a small towel and place this round the object in the wound. This will prevent the object being pressed on by the thick pad and bandage you will place over it. Once the wound is bandaged, expert medical advice should be sought

- Sit or lay the patient down

- Temporarily protect the wound with the cleanest cover you can find. Wash your hands and collect the material needed: soap, water, cotton wool, gauze, bandage (or their improvised substitutes). Place them on a clean surface close to hand

- Wash the skin around the wound (not the wound itself). Use wool moistened with water and soap. Use a clean piece of cotton wool for each separate stroke. Move the cotton wool outwards from the wound edge

- Put gauze over the wound; make sure it is large enough to extend well beyond the wounded area and over the cleaned skin

- On top of the gauze, set a thick pad of cotton wool

- Bandage firmly (but not tightly). Each bandage turn should overlap the previous one by two-thirds of its width

- Keep the wounded part at rest

- Protect the patient against shock (see page 496)

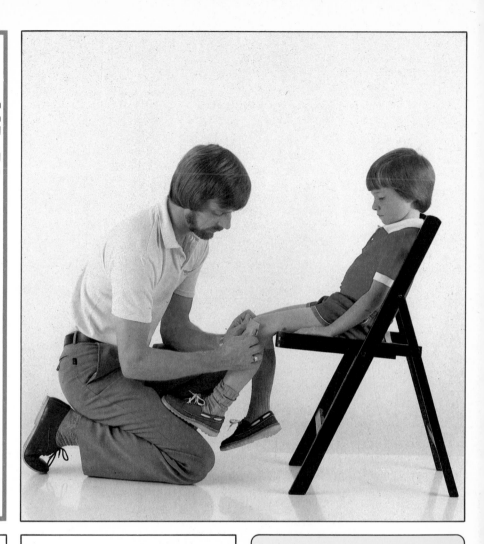

Dressings

- Convenient, ready-made, all-in-one dressings come with the gauze and the pad attached to the bandage

- Adhesive dressings are either in continuous strips to be cut to size or in different sizes of single dressings. They are useful for dressing small, superficial wounds. After partly peeling off the protective cover, apply the gauze pad that is now exposed on to the wound, and pull away the cover

- Tubular gauze is fitted over toes and fingers by means of a metal or plastic applicator

- An improvised gauze dressing can be made from most smooth, clean materials such as a handkerchief, towel or pillowcase. One or two folded handkerchiefs will serve as a pad. Cloths folded lengthwise (a handkerchief, scarf, sock, stocking and so on) will serve as bandages

Dressing an eye wound

For an eye wound, bandage or tape a large soft clean pad over the whole eye, without putting any pressure on it. If it hurts the patient to move his eye, cover both eyes, as the two automatically move together. Seek medical help – trying to remove foreign bodies may do more damage.

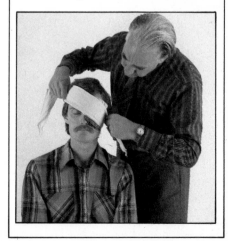

What next?

1. The slight bleeding of most wounds is soon brought under control by the pressure of ordinary dressings and bandaging. (If bleeding is severe, see page 480)

2. In the case of wounds, the aim of first aid is to protect the part from becoming further infected and damaged. The person administering first aid should limit his help to cleaning around the wound – if circumstances permit – and to covering it.

3. In giving first aid, do not use antiseptic or antibiotic lotions and creams. They may interfere with healing

4. With any wound there is the risk of tetanus, and the deeper the cut, the higher the risk. Even if the patient has been immunized against tetanus, he should see a doctor

Sterile
triangular bandages

Calamine lotion or cream

Cotton wool

Crêpe or
elasticated bandages

Strong plastic
or metal box

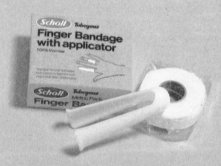
Perforated film absorbent dressing (2 of each size)

Adhesive
dressing strip

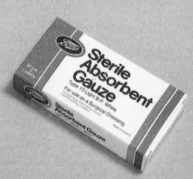
Finger-size tubular gauze with applicator

Paper
handkerchiefs

Plain bandages

Paracetamol or
soluble aspirin

Scissors

Fine-pointed tweezers

6 safety pins

White gauze

THE HOME FIRST AID KIT

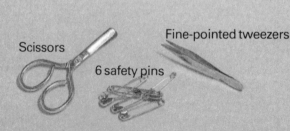

A first aid kit should be stored in a strong, clearly marked box with a well-fitting lid. It should only contain those things required in an emergency – general remedies can be kept in the bathroom medicine chest. The kit must be kept handy, but completely out of a child's reach. The contents should be replenished regularly – dressing packs must be replaced once opened.

Index

A

507